State Rankings 2014

Other titles in the State Fact Finder series

Crime State Rankings *(now part of State Stats)*
Education State Rankings *(now part of State Stats)*
Health Care State Rankings *(now part of State Stats)*
City Crime Rankings

State Stats online database

What is **State Stats**? Drawing together the statistics from the *State Rankings* series of books by CQ Press and Morgan Quitno Press, **State Stats** is a regularly updated database from CQ Press that delivers a dynamic and engaging user experience that is unmatched in other resources. Featuring data from more than 80 different government and nongovernment sources and backed by a rich collection of more than 2,000 current and historical data series on popular topics of research interest, **State Stats** uniquely allows users to discover, view, and export key information measures for the 50 states and the District of Columbia.

Check it out online at http://library.cqpress.com/statestats.

State Stats makes research easy by providing in one place annual measures dating back more than 15 years. Data series are displayed in a clear and consistent format with detailed source information. Numerous topics are covered in categories including Agriculture; Crime and Law Enforcement; Defense; Demographics; Economics; Education; Employment and Labor; Geography, Energy, and the Environment; Health and Medicine; Social Welfare; Taxes and Government Finance; Transportation.

The benefit of **State Stats** is in its ease of use and clean and concise presentation of data and trends. An intuitive interface lets users easily browse by state or by topic, and then compare across states or across time. Users can then share, save, and export data. **State Stats** also features CQ Press's CiteNow!® function for generating source citations in APA, MLA, Chicago, or Bluebook styles.

Users can:

- Analyze data patterns by comparing across states, data series, and time

- Create and export custom visuals including line charts, scatter plots, and maps

- Generate tables and download data for statistical research

- Toggle user display between interactive visual and tabular data view

- Engage a moveable timeline to discover trends

- Explore interactive maps featuring zoom and hover functions

State Stats is cross-searchable with other CQ Press online products including *CQ Researcher* and the *CQ Press U.S. Political Stats.* Ongoing updates to **State Stats** throughout the year ensure that users have the most current data available.

Working on an advanced data research project? The optional advanced State Stats Data Cart allows for bulk data export across single-click download of complete data series and multiple series.

State Rankings 2014

A Statistical View of America

Editors

Kathleen O'Leary Morgan
and
Scott Morgan

Los Angeles | London | New Delhi
Singapore | Washington DC

Los Angeles | London | New Delhi
Singapore | Washington DC

FOR INFORMATION:

CQ Press
An Imprint of SAGE Publications, Inc.
2455 Teller Road
Thousand Oaks, California 91320
E-mail: order@sagepub.com

SAGE Publications Ltd.
1 Oliver's Yard
55 City Road
London, EC1Y 1SP
United Kingdom

SAGE Publications India Pvt. Ltd.
B 1/I 1 Mohan Cooperative Industrial Area
Mathura Road, New Delhi 110 044
India

SAGE Publications Asia-Pacific Pte. Ltd.
3 Church Street
#10-04 Samsung Hub
Singapore 049483

Printed in the United States of America

SFI® Certified Sourcing
www.sfiprogram.org
SFI-00453

ISBN 978-1-4833-4784-4 (cloth)
ISBN 978-1-4833-4783-7 (paper)
ISSN 1057-3623

Developmental Editor: John Martino
Production Editor: Tracy Buyan
Cover Designer: Michael Dubowe
Marketing Manager: Carmel Schrire

14 15 16 17 18 10 9 8 7 6 5 4 3 2 1

Contents

Detailed Table of Contents

XIV. SOCIAL WELFARE

XV. TRANSPORTATION

Introduction and Methodology

State Rankings 2014 provides an easily accessible collection of data in a broad range of quality of life factors in the United States. In this latest 2014 edition, *State Ranking* compares data from the 50 states and the District of Columbia in 567 tables in the following 15 different livability categories: agriculture, crime and law enforcement, defense, economy, education, employment and labor, energy and environment, geography, federal government finances, state and local government finances, health, households and housing, population, social welfare, and transportation.

Purpose of This Book

State Rankings 2014 translates complicated and often convoluted statistics into meaningful, easy-to-understand information. Too often there is an abundance of data but far too little information putting that data into context. This book allows researchers, legislators, policy analysts, journalists, and the general public to access information in a manner that not only provides basic facts about a state's quality of life, but also gives a meaningful framework by comparing individual states against the rest of the country.

These data and rankings can be used in a variety of ways, by a variety of audiences, including the following examples:

- Policy makers can use the data to help identify areas warranting further study.
- Journalists can easily find impartial state information that puts stories into context.
- The general public can see how a particular state is faring compared to other states.
- Librarians can use the data as a quick reference to assist patrons in research and offer the sources and Web sites included as a starting point for finding other related data.

The comparison rankings in *State Rankings 2014* provide an annual snapshot of how the states are doing in the 15 livability categories mentioned above. There are two principle approaches to using these rankings. The first is to examine how a state is doing compared to all other states via the comparison rankings in this book. The second approach is to compare a state to itself over a given period of time. Both approaches are important to achieving a good understanding of how and whether a state is making progress. It is important to keep in mind that the rankings are not a definitive determination of which state is the "best." However, since so many issues are surrounded by emotions, tracking them by the numbers can help bring the discussion back to a more balanced, unbiased review that in the end leads to better decisions.

Data and Limitations

The data featured in *State Rankings 2014* were chosen specifically by the editors from a variety of government and private sector sources. The statistics presented are intended to cover a broad array of quality-of-life subject areas, giving users of the book a solid collection of state information. Nonetheless, the statistics are not inclusive of all the possible data that might be available. The statistics in the book are the latest available from the sources. In a few cases, we have retained tables that have not been updated for several years because we believe our readers will find the data relevant, even if updates are not available. In other cases, we replaced obsolete data with new tables. Longtime users should note in particular that we have updated Government Finances: Federal with new government spending data from the OMB's USASpending.gov, but differences in methodology make that data difficult to compare with past editions.

Previous editions of the book have used the term "most livable" when describing states with the highest livability ranking. This term is no longer being used, because it is purely descriptive—at no time do we attempt to explain *why* a particular state is ranking higher or lower in livability factors than others or against the national average. This explanation—currently sought by social science researchers—is beyond the scope of this book. While our selection of factors clearly affects the rankings, we believe the rankings provide a solid measurement of how the fifty states and Washington, DC are faring with regard to quality of life in the United States. Researchers, practitioners, and others can confidently use the data to understand livability issues and guide policy decisions.

Methodology

The comparison rankings for *State Rankings 2014* are determined using the same methodology as we have used for the past twenty-plus years. The editors used the previously mentioned 15 livability categories to select 44 quality of life factors from a broad range of economic, educational, health-oriented, public safety, and environmental statistics. Overall comparison rankings were determined by averaging each state's ranking for each category. The scale is one to fifty, the higher the number, the higher the state is in the rankings (i.e., 50 is the best score to receive). Data used are for the most recent year for which comparable numbers are available from most states. All factors are given equal weight.

The 567 tables provided in *State Rankings 2014* then are ranked highest to lowest without any subjective determination as to whether a subject is "positive" or "negative." For the state comparison rankings, the editors do make a subjective determination as to whether something is "positive" or "negative." Twenty-five of the 44 factors were determined to be negative and the remaining nineteen were viewed as positive.

The reason for this division between positive and negative is that if a state ranks first in crime rate (i.e., it has the highest crime rate), its comparison ranking is reduced. Whereas if a state ranks first in per capita personal income (i.e., it has the highest income), its comparison ranking is increased. To account for this, we subtract the rankings for the positive factors from 51 so that a state with the highest ranking in a positive factor ends up with a 50 for that factor (remember, high numbers are best.)

Once we have chosen the factors and divided them into positive and negative groupings, we simply average the ranking for each state in all 44 factors. If a state is missing data for a given factor, its standing is based on the average ranking for the remaining factors. The book uses the latest available data for each livability factor.

As an example, Maine ranks 37th in crime rate (negative factor), 41st in personal bankruptcy rate (negative factor), and ranks 8th in percent of eligible population reported voting in 2010 (positive factor). The 37th and 41st rankings go straight into the comparison formula whereas the number eight ranking in percent of eligible population reported voting is first subtracted from 51 with the resulting 43 going into the ranking. For these three factors for Maine, we would average 37, 41, and 43 with the result being 40.33. If these three factors were the only ones we used, then the resulting average of 40.33 would be the figure we would use to compare Maine to the other 49 states. However, for the *State Rankings* comparison rankings, an additional 41 factors are added into the calculations before the final results are determined.

Designed with the researcher in mind, the numbers shown in *State Rankings* require no additional calculations to convert them from millions, thousands, etc. All states are ranked on a high-to-low basis, with any ties among the states listed alphabetically for a given ranking. Negative numbers are shown in parentheses. For tables displaying national totals (as opposed to rates, per capita, etc.), a separate column is included that shows what percent of the national total each individual state's total represents. This column is headed by "% of USA." This percentage figure is particularly interesting when compared with a state's population in a given year. Rates may be per 10,000 persons, per 100,000 persons, or per some other denominator; these are clearly explained by the text following the national rate and, if necessary, the footnotes.

To further assist readers, source information and footnotes clearly are shown at the bottom of each page, while national totals, rates, and percentages are prominently displayed at the top of each table. Every other line is shaded in gray for easier reading. Numerous information-finding tools are provided: a thorough table of contents, table listings at the beginning of each chapter and a detailed index. In addition, a roster of sources, with addresses, phone numbers and Web sites is found in the back of the book.

About the Editors

Kathleen O'Leary Morgan holds a master's degree in public administration and has served in a number of media and legislative liaison positions within the U.S. Department of Transportation, where she also served as deputy director of congressional affairs.

Scott Morgan is an attorney who served as chief counsel to Robert Dole's 1988 presidential campaign.

The 2014 State Rankings

ALPHA ORDER

RANK	STATE	AVG	13 RANK	CHANGE
48	Alabama	18.95	48	0
24	Alaska	25.36	13	-11
43	Arizona	20.18	39	-4
47	Arkansas	18.98	46	-1
36	California	22.55	31	-5
13	Colorado	28.43	11	-2
14	Connecticut	28.11	15	1
30	Delaware	24.43	28	-2
37	Florida	22.39	42	5
39	Georgia	21.07	40	1
22	Hawaii	25.73	23	1
17	Idaho	27.61	22	5
27	Illinois	24.88	27	0
29	Indiana	24.48	35	6
5	Iowa	32.55	6	1
18	Kansas	27.18	16	-2
49	Kentucky	18.61	47	-2
40	Louisiana	20.61	38	-2
10	Maine	30.25	12	2
15	Maryland	28.07	19	4
8	Massachusetts	31.20	10	2
32	Michigan	23.61	34	2
2	Minnesota	34.16	1	-1
50	Mississippi	18.48	50	0
31	Missouri	23.98	30	-1
20	Montana	26.66	16	-4
4	Nebraska	32.70	5	1
42	Nevada	20.30	37	-5
1	New Hampshire	34.70	7	6
16	New Jersey	27.66	18	2
46	New Mexico	19.09	45	-1
26	New York	24.95	26	0
34	North Carolina	22.82	41	7
3	North Dakota	33.16	2	-1
35	Ohio	22.61	36	1
38	Oklahoma	21.68	32	-6
23	Oregon	25.48	24	1
33	Pennsylvania	23.07	33	0
28	Rhode Island	24.61	29	1
45	South Carolina	19.34	48	3
11	South Dakota	29.36	9	-2
41	Tennessee	20.32	44	3
25	Texas	24.98	25	0
7	Utah	31.77	7	0
6	Vermont	32.05	3	-3
12	Virginia	29.30	14	2
19	Washington	26.70	20	1
44	West Virginia	20.00	43	-1
21	Wisconsin	26.48	21	0
9	Wyoming	31.18	4	-5

RANK ORDER

RANK	STATE	AVG	13 RANK	CHANGE
1	New Hampshire	34.70	7	6
2	Minnesota	34.16	1	-1
3	North Dakota	33.16	2	-1
4	Nebraska	32.70	5	1
5	Iowa	32.55	6	1
6	Vermont	32.05	3	-3
7	Utah	31.77	7	0
8	Massachusetts	31.20	10	2
9	Wyoming	31.18	4	-5
10	Maine	30.25	12	2
11	South Dakota	29.36	9	-2
12	Virginia	29.30	14	2
13	Colorado	28.43	11	-2
14	Connecticut	28.11	15	1
15	Maryland	28.07	19	4
16	New Jersey	27.66	18	2
17	Idaho	27.61	22	5
18	Kansas	27.18	16	-2
19	Washington	26.70	20	1
20	Montana	26.66	16	-4
21	Wisconsin	26.48	21	0
22	Hawaii	25.73	23	1
23	Oregon	25.48	24	1
24	Alaska	25.36	13	-11
25	Texas	24.98	25	0
26	New York	24.95	26	0
27	Illinois	24.88	27	0
28	Rhode Island	24.61	29	1
29	Indiana	24.48	35	6
30	Delaware	24.43	28	-2
31	Missouri	23.98	30	-1
32	Michigan	23.61	34	2
33	Pennsylvania	23.07	33	0
34	North Carolina	22.82	41	7
35	Ohio	22.61	36	1
36	California	22.55	31	-5
37	Florida	22.39	42	5
38	Oklahoma	21.68	32	-6
39	Georgia	21.07	40	1
40	Louisiana	20.61	38	-2
41	Tennessee	20.32	44	3
42	Nevada	20.30	37	-5
43	Arizona	20.18	39	-4
44	West Virginia	20.00	43	-1
45	South Carolina	19.34	48	3
46	New Mexico	19.09	45	-1
47	Arkansas	18.98	46	-1
48	Alabama	18.95	48	0
49	Kentucky	18.61	47	-2
50	Mississippi	18.48	50	0

Date Each State Admitted to Statehood*

ALPHA ORDER

RANK	STATE	DATE OF ADMISSION
22	Alabama	December 14, 1819
49	Alaska	January 3, 1959
48	Arizona	February 14, 1912
25	Arkansas	June 15, 1836
31	California	September 9, 1850
38	Colorado	August 1, 1876
5	Connecticut	January 9, 1788
1	Delaware	December 7, 1787
27	Florida	March 3, 1845
4	Georgia	January 2, 1788
50	Hawaii	August 21, 1959
43	Idaho	July 3, 1890
21	Illinois	December 3, 1818
19	Indiana	December 11, 1816
29	Iowa	December 28, 1846
34	Kansas	January 29, 1861
15	Kentucky	June 1, 1792
18	Louisiana	April 30, 1812
23	Maine	March 15, 1820
7	Maryland	April 28, 1788
6	Massachusetts	February 6, 1788
26	Michigan	January 26, 1837
32	Minnesota	May 11, 1858
20	Mississippi	December 10, 1817
24	Missouri	August 10, 1821
41	Montana	November 8, 1889
37	Nebraska	March 1, 1867
36	Nevada	October 31, 1864
9	New Hampshire	June 21, 1788
3	New Jersey	December 18, 1787
47	New Mexico	January 6, 1912
11	New York	July 26, 1788
12	North Carolina	November 21, 1789
39	North Dakota	November 2, 1889
17	Ohio	March 1, 1803
46	Oklahoma	November 16, 1907
33	Oregon	February 14, 1859
2	Pennsylvania	December 12, 1787
13	Rhode Island	May 29, 1790
8	South Carolina	May 23, 1788
39	South Dakota	November 2, 1889
16	Tennessee	June 1, 1796
28	Texas	December 29, 1845
45	Utah	January 4, 1896
14	Vermont	March 4, 1791
10	Virginia	June 26, 1788
42	Washington	November 11, 1889
35	West Virginia	June 20, 1863
30	Wisconsin	May 29, 1848
44	Wyoming	July 10, 1890

RANK ORDER

RANK	STATE	DATE OF ADMISSION
1	Delaware	December 7, 1787
2	Pennsylvania	December 12, 1787
3	New Jersey	December 18, 1787
4	Georgia	January 2, 1788
5	Connecticut	January 9, 1788
6	Massachusetts	February 6, 1788
7	Maryland	April 28, 1788
8	South Carolina	May 23, 1788
9	New Hampshire	June 21, 1788
10	Virginia	June 26, 1788
11	New York	July 26, 1788
12	North Carolina	November 21, 1789
13	Rhode Island	May 29, 1790
14	Vermont	March 4, 1791
15	Kentucky	June 1, 1792
16	Tennessee	June 1, 1796
17	Ohio	March 1, 1803
18	Louisiana	April 30, 1812
19	Indiana	December 11, 1816
20	Mississippi	December 10, 1817
21	Illinois	December 3, 1818
22	Alabama	December 14, 1819
23	Maine	March 15, 1820
24	Missouri	August 10, 1821
25	Arkansas	June 15, 1836
26	Michigan	January 26, 1837
27	Florida	March 3, 1845
28	Texas	December 29, 1845
29	Iowa	December 28, 1846
30	Wisconsin	May 29, 1848
31	California	September 9, 1850
32	Minnesota	May 11, 1858
33	Oregon	February 14, 1859
34	Kansas	January 29, 1861
35	West Virginia	June 20, 1863
36	Nevada	October 31, 1864
37	Nebraska	March 1, 1867
38	Colorado	August 1, 1876
39	North Dakota	November 2, 1889
39	South Dakota	November 2, 1889
41	Montana	November 8, 1889
42	Washington	November 11, 1889
43	Idaho	July 3, 1890
44	Wyoming	July 10, 1890
45	Utah	January 4, 1896
46	Oklahoma	November 16, 1907
47	New Mexico	January 6, 1912
48	Arizona	February 14, 1912
49	Alaska	January 3, 1959
50	Hawaii	August 21, 1959

Source: U.S. Bureau of the Census
"1980 Census of Population" (vol. 1, part A, PC80-1-A)
*First thirteen states show date of ratification of Constitution.

STATE FAST FACTS

STATE	NICKNAME	CAPITAL	POPULATION*	AREA**
Alabama	Heart of Dixie	Montgomery	4,833,722	52,420
Alaska	The Last Frontier	Juneau	735,132	665,384
Arizona	Grand Canyon State	Phoenix	6,626,624	113,990
Arkansas	The Natural State	Little Rock	2,959,373	53,179
California	Golden State	Sacramento	38,332,521	163,695
Colorado	Centennial State	Denver	5,268,367	104,094
Connecticut	Constitution State	Hartford	3,596,080	5,543
Delaware	First State	Dover	925,749	2,489
Florida	Sunshine State	Tallahassee	19,552,860	65,758
Georgia	Peach State	Atlanta	9,992,167	59,425
Hawaii	Aloha State	Honolulu	1,404,054	10,932
Idaho	Gem State	Boise	1,612,136	83,569
Illinois	Land of Lincoln	Springfield	12,882,135	57,914
Indiana	Hoosier State	Indianapolis	6,570,902	36,420
Iowa	Hawkeye State	Des Moines	3,090,416	56,273
Kansas	Sunflower State	Topeka	2,893,957	82,278
Kentucky	Bluegrass State	Frankfort	4,395,295	40,408
Louisiana	Pelican State	Baton Rouge	4,625,470	52,378
Maine	Pine Tree State	Augusta	1,328,302	35,380
Maryland	Free State	Annapolis	5,928,814	12,406
Massachusetts	Bay State	Boston	6,692,824	10,554
Michigan	Great Lake State	Lansing	9,895,622	96,714
Minnesota	North Star State	St. Paul	5,420,380	86,936
Mississippi	Magnolia State	Jackson	2,991,207	48,432
Missouri	Show Me State	Jefferson City	6,044,171	69,707
Montana	Treasure State	Helena	1,015,165	147,040
Nebraska	Cornhusker State	Lincoln	1,868,516	77,348
Nevada	Silver State	Carson City	2,790,136	110,572
New Hampshire	Granite State	Concord	1,323,459	9,349
New Jersey	Garden State	Trenton	8,899,339	8,723
New Mexico	Land of Enchantment	Santa Fe	2,085,287	121,590
New York	Empire State	Albany	19,651,127	54,555
North Carolina	Tar Heel State	Raleigh	9,848,060	53,819
North Dakota	Peace Garden State	Bismarck	723,393	70,698
Ohio	Buckeye State	Columbus	11,570,808	44,826
Oklahoma	Sooner State	Oklahoma City	3,850,568	69,899
Oregon	Beaver State	Salem	3,930,065	98,379
Pennsylvania	Keystone State	Harrisburg	12,773,801	46,054
Rhode Island	Ocean State	Providence	1,051,511	1,545
South Carolina	Palmetto State	Columbia	4,774,839	32,020
South Dakota	Mount Rushmore State	Pierre	844,877	77,116
Tennessee	Volunteer State	Nashville	6,495,978	42,144
Texas	Lone Star State	Austin	26,448,193	268,596
Utah	Beehive State	Salt Lake City	2,900,872	84,897
Vermont	Green Mountain State	Montpelier	626,630	9,616
Virginia	Old Dominion	Richmond	8,260,405	42,775
Washington	Evergreen State	Olympia	6,971,406	71,298
West Virginia	Mountain State	Charleston	1,854,304	24,230
Wisconsin	Badger State	Madison	5,742,713	65,496
Wyoming	Equality State	Cheyenne	582,658	97,813

U.S. Bureau of the Census, "Population Estimates" (December 2013, http://www.census.gov/popest/data/index.html)

**Total of land and water area in square miles.

STATE SONG	STATE FLOWER	STATE TREE	STATE BIRD
Alabama	Camellia	Southern Pine	Yellowhammer
Alaska's Flag	Forget-Me-Not	Sitka Spruce	Willow Ptarmigan
Arizona	Saguaro Cactus Blossom	Palo Verde	Cactus Wren
Arkansas	Apple Blossom	Pine	Mockingbird
I Love You, California	Golden Poppy	California Redwood	California Valley Quail
Where the Columbines Grow	Rocky Mountain Columbine	Colorado Blue Spruce	Lark Bunting
Yankee Doodle Dandy	Mountain Laurel	White Oak	American Robin
Our Delaware	Peach Blossom	American Holly	Blue Hen Chicken
Swanee River	Orange Blossom	Sabal Palmetto Palm	Mockingbird
Georgia On My Mind	Cherokee Rose	Live Oak	Brown Thrasher
Hawaii Ponoi	Yellow Hibiscus	Candlenut	Nene
Here We Have Idaho	Syringa	White Pine	Mountain Bluebird
Illinois	Purple Violet	White Oak	Cardinal
On the Banks of the Wabash, Far Away	Peony	Tulip Poplar	Cardinal
The Song of Iowa	Wild Rose	Oak	Eastern Goldfinch
Home on the Range	Sunflower	Cottonwood	Western Meadowlark
My Old Kentucky Home	Goldenrod	Tulip Tree	Cardinal
Give Me Louisiana	Magnolia	Cypress	Eastern Brown Pelican
State of Maine Song	White Pine Cone and Tassel	Eastern White Pine	Chickadee
Maryland, My Maryland	Black-eyed Susan	White Oak	Baltimore Oriole
All Hail to Massachusetts	Mayflower	American Elm	Chickadee
Michigan, My Michigan	Apple Blossom	White Pine	Robin
Hail! Minnesota	Pink and White Lady's Slipper	Red Pine	Common Loon
Go, Mississippi!	Magnolia	Magnolia	Mockingbird
Missouri Waltz	Hawthorn	Dogwood	Bluebird
Montana	Bitterroot	Ponderosa Pine	Western Meadowlark
Beautiful Nebraska	Goldenrod	Cottonwood	Western Meadowlark
Home Means Nevada	Sagebrush	Single-Leaf Pinon	Mountain Bluebird
Old New Hampshire	Purple Lilac	White Birch	Purple Finch
Ode to New Jersey	Purple Violet	Red Oak	Eastern Goldfinch
O Fair New Mexico	Yucca	Pinon	Roadrunner
I Love New York	Rose	Sugar Maple	Bluebird
The Old North State	Dogwood	Pine	Cardinal
North Dakota Hymn	Wild Prairie Rose	American Elm	Western Meadowlark
Beautiful Ohio	Scarlet Carnation	Buckeye	Cardinal
Oklahoma!	Mistletoe	Redbud	Scissortailed Flycatcher
Oregon, My Oregon	Oregon Grape	Douglas Fir	Western Meadowlark
Hail! Pennsylvania	Mountain Laurel	Hemlock	Ruffed Grouse
Rhode Island	Violet	Red Maple	Rhode Island Red
Carolina	Yellow Jessamine	Palmetto	Carolina Wren
Hail, South Dakota	Pasque Flower	Black Hills Spruce	Ringnecked Pheasant
The Tennessee Waltz	Iris	Tulip Poplar	Mockingbird
Texas, Our Texas	Bluebonnet	Pecan	Mockingbird
Utah, We Love Thee	Sego Lily	Blue Spruce	Seagull
Hail, Vermont	Red Clover	Sugar Maple	Hermit Thrush
Carry Me Back to Old Virginia	Dogwood	Dogwood	Cardinal
Washington, My Home	Western Rhododendron	Western Hemlock	Willow Goldfinch
The West Virginia Hills; This Is My West Virginia; and West Virginia, My Home, Sweet Home	Big Rhododendron	Sugar Maple	Cardinal
On Wisconsin!	Wood Violet	Sugar Maple	Robin
Wyoming	Indian Paintbrush	Cottonwood	Meadowlark

I. Agriculture

Number of Farms in 2012

National Total = 2,170,000 Farms*

RANK	STATE	FARMS	% of USA	RANK	STATE	FARMS	% of USA
21	Alabama	46,500	2.1%	1	Texas	244,700	11.3%
50	Alaska	680	0.0%	2	Missouri	106,000	4.9%
37	Arizona	15,500	0.7%	3	Iowa	92,200	4.2%
17	Arkansas	47,800	2.2%	4	Kentucky	85,500	3.9%
6	California	80,500	3.7%	4	Oklahoma	85,500	3.9%
26	Colorado	36,300	1.7%	6	California	80,500	3.7%
45	Connecticut	4,900	0.2%	7	Minnesota	79,400	3.7%
48	Delaware	2,500	0.1%	8	Wisconsin	76,800	3.5%
18	Florida	47,500	2.2%	9	Tennessee	76,000	3.5%
19	Georgia	47,000	2.2%	10	Illinois	74,300	3.4%
43	Hawaii	7,500	0.3%	11	Ohio	73,400	3.4%
33	Idaho	24,500	1.1%	12	Kansas	65,500	3.0%
10	Illinois	74,300	3.4%	13	Pennsylvania	62,100	2.9%
14	Indiana	60,000	2.8%	14	Indiana	60,000	2.8%
3	Iowa	92,200	4.2%	15	Michigan	54,700	2.5%
12	Kansas	65,500	3.0%	16	North Carolina	50,000	2.3%
4	Kentucky	85,500	3.9%	17	Arkansas	47,800	2.2%
30	Louisiana	29,000	1.3%	18	Florida	47,500	2.2%
41	Maine	8,100	0.4%	19	Georgia	47,000	2.2%
38	Maryland	12,800	0.6%	20	Nebraska	46,700	2.2%
42	Massachusetts	7,700	0.4%	21	Alabama	46,500	2.1%
15	Michigan	54,700	2.5%	22	Virginia	46,200	2.1%
7	Minnesota	79,400	3.7%	23	Mississippi	42,300	1.9%
23	Mississippi	42,300	1.9%	24	Washington	39,300	1.8%
2	Missouri	106,000	4.9%	25	Oregon	38,100	1.8%
31	Montana	28,600	1.3%	26	Colorado	36,300	1.7%
20	Nebraska	46,700	2.2%	27	New York	36,000	1.7%
47	Nevada	2,950	0.1%	28	North Dakota	31,600	1.5%
46	New Hampshire	4,150	0.2%	29	South Dakota	31,000	1.4%
40	New Jersey	10,200	0.5%	30	Louisiana	29,000	1.3%
34	New Mexico	23,800	1.1%	31	Montana	28,600	1.3%
27	New York	36,000	1.7%	32	South Carolina	26,700	1.2%
16	North Carolina	50,000	2.3%	33	Idaho	24,500	1.1%
28	North Dakota	31,600	1.5%	34	New Mexico	23,800	1.1%
11	Ohio	73,400	3.4%	35	West Virginia	22,100	1.0%
4	Oklahoma	85,500	3.9%	36	Utah	16,400	0.8%
25	Oregon	38,100	1.8%	37	Arizona	15,500	0.7%
13	Pennsylvania	62,100	2.9%	38	Maryland	12,800	0.6%
49	Rhode Island	1,220	0.1%	39	Wyoming	10,800	0.5%
32	South Carolina	26,700	1.2%	40	New Jersey	10,200	0.5%
29	South Dakota	31,000	1.4%	41	Maine	8,100	0.4%
9	Tennessee	76,000	3.5%	42	Massachusetts	7,700	0.4%
1	Texas	244,700	11.3%	43	Hawaii	7,500	0.3%
36	Utah	16,400	0.8%	44	Vermont	7,000	0.3%
44	Vermont	7,000	0.3%	45	Connecticut	4,900	0.2%
22	Virginia	46,200	2.1%	46	New Hampshire	4,150	0.2%
24	Washington	39,300	1.8%	47	Nevada	2,950	0.1%
35	West Virginia	22,100	1.0%	48	Delaware	2,500	0.1%
8	Wisconsin	76,800	3.5%	49	Rhode Island	1,220	0.1%
39	Wyoming	10,800	0.5%	50	Alaska	680	0.0%
					District of Columbia	0	0.0%

Source: U.S. Department of Agriculture, National Agricultural Statistics Service
   "Farms and Land in Farms" (http://usda.mannlib.cornell.edu/MannUsda/viewDocumentInfo.do?documentID=1259)
*A farm is any establishment from which $1,000 or more of agricultural products were sold or would normally be sold during the year. This includes places with five or more horses, except horses in boarding stables or racetracks.

Land in Farms in 2012

National Total = 914,000,000 Acres*

ALPHA ORDER

RANK	STATE	ACRES	% of USA
31	Alabama	8,850,000	1.0%
44	Alaska	880,000	0.1%
15	Arizona	26,100,000	2.9%
23	Arkansas	13,500,000	1.5%
16	California	25,400,000	2.8%
9	Colorado	31,300,000	3.4%
49	Connecticut	400,000	0.0%
47	Delaware	490,000	0.1%
30	Florida	9,250,000	1.0%
28	Georgia	10,400,000	1.1%
43	Hawaii	1,110,000	0.1%
24	Idaho	11,400,000	1.2%
14	Illinois	26,600,000	2.9%
20	Indiana	14,700,000	1.6%
10	Iowa	30,700,000	3.4%
3	Kansas	46,000,000	5.0%
21	Kentucky	14,000,000	1.5%
34	Louisiana	7,950,000	0.9%
41	Maine	1,350,000	0.1%
40	Maryland	2,050,000	0.2%
46	Massachusetts	520,000	0.1%
29	Michigan	9,900,000	1.1%
13	Minnesota	26,800,000	2.9%
25	Mississippi	11,150,000	1.2%
12	Missouri	29,000,000	3.2%
2	Montana	58,800,000	6.4%
4	Nebraska	45,500,000	5.0%
37	Nevada	5,840,000	0.6%
48	New Hampshire	470,000	0.1%
45	New Jersey	730,000	0.1%
5	New Mexico	43,900,000	4.8%
36	New York	7,000,000	0.8%
32	North Carolina	8,500,000	0.9%
7	North Dakota	39,600,000	4.3%
22	Ohio	13,550,000	1.5%
8	Oklahoma	34,800,000	3.8%
17	Oregon	16,500,000	1.8%
35	Pennsylvania	7,700,000	0.8%
50	Rhode Island	70,000	0.0%
38	South Carolina	4,800,000	0.5%
6	South Dakota	43,650,000	4.8%
27	Tennessee	10,800,000	1.2%
1	Texas	128,000,000	14.0%
26	Utah	11,100,000	1.2%
42	Vermont	1,220,000	0.1%
33	Virginia	8,050,000	0.9%
19	Washington	14,800,000	1.6%
39	West Virginia	3,620,000	0.4%
18	Wisconsin	15,000,000	1.6%
11	Wyoming	30,200,000	3.3%

RANK ORDER

RANK	STATE	ACRES	% of USA
1	Texas	128,000,000	14.0%
2	Montana	58,800,000	6.4%
3	Kansas	46,000,000	5.0%
4	Nebraska	45,500,000	5.0%
5	New Mexico	43,900,000	4.8%
6	South Dakota	43,650,000	4.8%
7	North Dakota	39,600,000	4.3%
8	Oklahoma	34,800,000	3.8%
9	Colorado	31,300,000	3.4%
10	Iowa	30,700,000	3.4%
11	Wyoming	30,200,000	3.3%
12	Missouri	29,000,000	3.2%
13	Minnesota	26,800,000	2.9%
14	Illinois	26,600,000	2.9%
15	Arizona	26,100,000	2.9%
16	California	25,400,000	2.8%
17	Oregon	16,500,000	1.8%
18	Wisconsin	15,000,000	1.6%
19	Washington	14,800,000	1.6%
20	Indiana	14,700,000	1.6%
21	Kentucky	14,000,000	1.5%
22	Ohio	13,550,000	1.5%
23	Arkansas	13,500,000	1.5%
24	Idaho	11,400,000	1.2%
25	Mississippi	11,150,000	1.2%
26	Utah	11,100,000	1.2%
27	Tennessee	10,800,000	1.2%
28	Georgia	10,400,000	1.1%
29	Michigan	9,900,000	1.1%
30	Florida	9,250,000	1.0%
31	Alabama	8,850,000	1.0%
32	North Carolina	8,500,000	0.9%
33	Virginia	8,050,000	0.9%
34	Louisiana	7,950,000	0.9%
35	Pennsylvania	7,700,000	0.8%
36	New York	7,000,000	0.8%
37	Nevada	5,840,000	0.6%
38	South Carolina	4,800,000	0.5%
39	West Virginia	3,620,000	0.4%
40	Maryland	2,050,000	0.2%
41	Maine	1,350,000	0.1%
42	Vermont	1,220,000	0.1%
43	Hawaii	1,110,000	0.1%
44	Alaska	880,000	0.1%
45	New Jersey	730,000	0.1%
46	Massachusetts	520,000	0.1%
47	Delaware	490,000	0.1%
48	New Hampshire	470,000	0.1%
49	Connecticut	400,000	0.0%
50	Rhode Island	70,000	0.0%
	District of Columbia	0	0.0%

Source: U.S. Department of Agriculture, National Agricultural Statistics Service
    "Farms and Land in Farms" (http://usda.mannlib.cornell.edu/MannUsda/viewDocumentInfo.do?documentID=1259)
*A farm is any establishment from which $1,000 or more of agricultural products were sold or would normally be sold during the year. This includes places with five or more horses, except horses in boarding stables or racetracks.

Average Number of Acres per Farm in 2012

National Average = 421 Acres*

ALPHA ORDER			RANK ORDER		
RANK	STATE	ACRES	RANK	STATE	ACRES
32	Alabama	190	1	Wyoming	2,796
7	Alaska	1,294	2	Montana	2,056
5	Arizona	1,684	3	Nevada	1,980
22	Arkansas	282	4	New Mexico	1,845
21	California	316	5	Arizona	1,684
10	Colorado	862	6	South Dakota	1,408
47	Connecticut	82	7	Alaska	1,294
28	Delaware	196	8	North Dakota	1,253
29	Florida	195	9	Nebraska	974
27	Georgia	221	10	Colorado	862
43	Hawaii	148	11	Kansas	702
14	Idaho	465	12	Utah	677
18	Illinois	358	13	Texas	523
26	Indiana	245	14	Idaho	465
20	Iowa	333	15	Oregon	433
11	Kansas	702	16	Oklahoma	407
40	Kentucky	164	17	Washington	377
23	Louisiana	274	18	Illinois	358
39	Maine	167	19	Minnesota	338
42	Maryland	160	20	Iowa	333
49	Massachusetts	68	21	California	316
34	Michigan	181	22	Arkansas	282
19	Minnesota	338	23	Louisiana	274
25	Mississippi	264	23	Missouri	274
23	Missouri	274	25	Mississippi	264
2	Montana	2,056	26	Indiana	245
9	Nebraska	974	27	Georgia	221
3	Nevada	1,980	28	Delaware	196
46	New Hampshire	113	29	Florida	195
48	New Jersey	72	29	Wisconsin	195
4	New Mexico	1,845	31	New York	194
31	New York	194	32	Alabama	190
38	North Carolina	170	33	Ohio	185
8	North Dakota	1,253	34	Michigan	181
33	Ohio	185	35	South Carolina	180
16	Oklahoma	407	36	Vermont	174
15	Oregon	433	36	Virginia	174
45	Pennsylvania	124	38	North Carolina	170
50	Rhode Island	57	39	Maine	167
35	South Carolina	180	40	Kentucky	164
6	South Dakota	1,408	40	West Virginia	164
44	Tennessee	142	42	Maryland	160
13	Texas	523	43	Hawaii	148
12	Utah	677	44	Tennessee	142
36	Vermont	174	45	Pennsylvania	124
36	Virginia	174	46	New Hampshire	113
17	Washington	377	47	Connecticut	82
40	West Virginia	164	48	New Jersey	72
29	Wisconsin	195	49	Massachusetts	68
1	Wyoming	2,796	50	Rhode Island	57
				District of Columbia**	NA

Source: U.S. Department of Agriculture, National Agricultural Statistics Service
   "Farms and Land in Farms" (http://usda.mannlib.cornell.edu/MannUsda/viewDocumentInfo.do?documentID=1259)
*A farm is any establishment from which $1,000 or more of agricultural products were sold or would normally be sold during the year. This includes places with five or more horses, except horses in boarding stables or racetracks.
**Not applicable.

Average per-Acre Value of Farmland in 2013

National Average = $2,900 per Acre*

ALPHA ORDER				RANK ORDER		
RANK	STATE	PER-ACRE VALUE		RANK	STATE	PER-ACRE VALUE
36	Alabama	$2,000		1	New Jersey	$12,700
NA	Alaska**	NA		2	Rhode Island	11,800
20	Arizona	3,800		3	Connecticut	11,000
26	Arkansas	3,000		4	Massachusetts	10,600
9	California	7,300		5	Iowa	8,400
44	Colorado	1,280		6	Delaware	8,100
3	Connecticut	11,000		7	Illinois	7,800
6	Delaware	8,100		8	Maryland	7,500
17	Florida	4,500		9	California	7,300
22	Georgia	3,600		10	Indiana	6,900
NA	Hawaii**	NA		11	Ohio	5,600
33	Idaho	2,200		12	Pennsylvania	5,300
7	Illinois	7,800		13	Michigan	4,800
10	Indiana	6,900		14	Minnesota	4,750
5	Iowa	8,400		15	North Carolina	4,550
38	Kansas	1,900		15	Virginia	4,550
23	Kentucky	3,300		17	Florida	4,500
31	Louisiana	2,550		18	New Hampshire	4,450
37	Maine	1,970		19	Wisconsin	4,400
8	Maryland	7,500		20	Arizona	3,800
4	Massachusetts	10,600		20	Tennessee	3,800
13	Michigan	4,800		22	Georgia	3,600
14	Minnesota	4,750		23	Kentucky	3,300
35	Mississippi	2,140		24	Missouri	3,100
24	Missouri	3,100		25	Nebraska	3,050
46	Montana	790		26	Arkansas	3,000
25	Nebraska	3,050		27	South Carolina	2,850
45	Nevada	1,050		28	Vermont	2,800
18	New Hampshire	4,450		29	West Virginia	2,750
1	New Jersey	12,700		30	New York	2,600
48	New Mexico	550		31	Louisiana	2,550
30	New York	2,600		32	Washington	2,350
15	North Carolina	4,550		33	Idaho	2,200
42	North Dakota	1,690		34	Oregon	2,150
11	Ohio	5,600		35	Mississippi	2,140
43	Oklahoma	1,590		36	Alabama	2,000
34	Oregon	2,150		37	Maine	1,970
12	Pennsylvania	5,300		38	Kansas	1,900
2	Rhode Island	11,800		38	Utah	1,900
27	South Carolina	2,850		40	Texas	1,810
41	South Dakota	1,800		41	South Dakota	1,800
20	Tennessee	3,800		42	North Dakota	1,690
40	Texas	1,810		43	Oklahoma	1,590
38	Utah	1,900		44	Colorado	1,280
28	Vermont	2,800		45	Nevada	1,050
15	Virginia	4,550		46	Montana	790
32	Washington	2,350		47	Wyoming	560
29	West Virginia	2,750		48	New Mexico	550
19	Wisconsin	4,400		NA	Alaska**	NA
47	Wyoming	560		NA	Hawaii**	NA
					District of Columbia**	NA

Source: U.S. Department of Agriculture, National Agricultural Statistics Service
"Land Values and Cash Rents" (http://usda.mannlib.cornell.edu/MannUsda/viewDocumentInfo.do?documentID=1446)
*Value of farmland and buildings in nominal dollars.
**Not applicable or available.

Percent Change in Average per-Acre Value of Farmland: 2012 to 2013

National Percent Change = 9.4% Increase*

RANK	STATE	PERCENT CHANGE
36	Alabama	0.0
NA	Alaska**	NA
16	Arizona	5.6
18	Arkansas	5.3
31	California	1.4
11	Colorado	9.4
42	Connecticut	(0.9)
36	Delaware	0.0
47	Florida	(2.2)
23	Georgia	2.9
NA	Hawaii**	NA
22	Idaho	3.8
7	Illinois	16.4
10	Indiana	11.3
3	Iowa	20.0
4	Kansas	18.0
12	Kentucky	8.2
15	Louisiana	6.3
36	Maine	0.0
19	Maryland	4.2
34	Massachusetts	1.0
8	Michigan	12.9
6	Minnesota	17.3
36	Mississippi	0.0
14	Missouri	6.9
21	Montana	3.9
5	Nebraska	17.8
36	Nevada	0.0
47	New Hampshire	(2.2)
20	New Jersey	4.1
45	New Mexico	(1.8)
46	New York	(1.9)
32	North Carolina	1.1
1	North Dakota	36.3
9	Ohio	12.0
13	Oklahoma	7.4
25	Oregon	2.4
28	Pennsylvania	1.9
43	Rhode Island	(1.7)
43	South Carolina	(1.7)
2	South Dakota	28.6
24	Tennessee	2.7
35	Texas	0.6
16	Utah	5.6
30	Vermont	1.8
26	Virginia	2.2
26	Washington	2.2
28	West Virginia	1.9
32	Wisconsin	1.1
36	Wyoming	0.0

RANK	STATE	PERCENT CHANGE
1	North Dakota	36.3
2	South Dakota	28.6
3	Iowa	20.0
4	Kansas	18.0
5	Nebraska	17.8
6	Minnesota	17.3
7	Illinois	16.4
8	Michigan	12.9
9	Ohio	12.0
10	Indiana	11.3
11	Colorado	9.4
12	Kentucky	8.2
13	Oklahoma	7.4
14	Missouri	6.9
15	Louisiana	6.3
16	Arizona	5.6
16	Utah	5.6
18	Arkansas	5.3
19	Maryland	4.2
20	New Jersey	4.1
21	Montana	3.9
22	Idaho	3.8
23	Georgia	2.9
24	Tennessee	2.7
25	Oregon	2.4
26	Virginia	2.2
26	Washington	2.2
28	Pennsylvania	1.9
28	West Virginia	1.9
30	Vermont	1.8
31	California	1.4
32	North Carolina	1.1
32	Wisconsin	1.1
34	Massachusetts	1.0
35	Texas	0.6
36	Alabama	0.0
36	Delaware	0.0
36	Maine	0.0
36	Mississippi	0.0
36	Nevada	0.0
36	Wyoming	0.0
42	Connecticut	(0.9)
43	Rhode Island	(1.7)
43	South Carolina	(1.7)
45	New Mexico	(1.8)
46	New York	(1.9)
47	Florida	(2.2)
47	New Hampshire	(2.2)
NA	Alaska**	NA
NA	Hawaii**	NA
	District of Columbia**	NA

Source: U.S. Department of Agriculture, National Agricultural Statistics Service
"Land Values and Cash Rents" (http://usda.mannlib.cornell.edu/MannUsda/viewDocumentInfo.do?documentID=1446)
*Value of farmland and buildings in nominal dollars.
**Not applicable or available.

Net Farm Income in 2012

National Total = $113,813,381,512*

ALPHA ORDER

RANK	STATE	FARM INCOME	% of USA
27	Alabama	$1,384,611,636	1.2%
48	Alaska	11,107,512	0.0%
33	Arizona	902,974,790	0.8%
19	Arkansas	1,979,479,416	1.7%
1	California	16,001,126,129	14.1%
24	Colorado	1,753,342,146	1.5%
46	Connecticut	75,477,032	0.1%
41	Delaware	272,204,070	0.2%
16	Florida	2,522,210,614	2.2%
8	Georgia	4,214,043,478	3.7%
40	Hawaii	329,963,992	0.3%
14	Idaho	2,745,404,023	2.4%
9	Illinois	4,173,945,737	3.7%
11	Indiana	3,290,744,166	2.9%
2	Iowa	9,254,749,955	8.1%
13	Kansas	3,014,912,796	2.6%
25	Kentucky	1,540,664,355	1.4%
23	Louisiana	1,779,420,277	1.6%
43	Maine	191,601,387	0.2%
36	Maryland	727,340,301	0.6%
45	Massachusetts	99,134,587	0.1%
17	Michigan	2,236,865,568	2.0%
3	Minnesota	8,172,164,294	7.2%
20	Mississippi	1,939,511,946	1.7%
22	Missouri	1,794,697,793	1.6%
30	Montana	1,294,909,562	1.1%
4	Nebraska	5,952,229,500	5.2%
42	Nevada	222,574,672	0.2%
50	New Hampshire	568,420	0.0%
39	New Jersey	339,611,038	0.3%
28	New Mexico	1,358,390,736	1.2%
29	New York	1,296,263,793	1.1%
6	North Carolina	4,319,945,655	3.8%
7	North Dakota	4,279,095,530	3.8%
15	Ohio	2,567,694,845	2.3%
26	Oklahoma	1,403,608,323	1.2%
31	Oregon	959,935,956	0.8%
21	Pennsylvania	1,833,490,493	1.6%
49	Rhode Island	4,547,995	0.0%
35	South Carolina	734,915,397	0.6%
10	South Dakota	3,643,004,647	3.2%
34	Tennessee	812,614,316	0.7%
5	Texas	5,145,163,729	4.5%
37	Utah	363,640,694	0.3%
44	Vermont	159,652,106	0.1%
32	Virginia	932,203,409	0.8%
18	Washington	2,160,404,109	1.9%
47	West Virginia	64,224,486	0.1%
12	Wisconsin	3,200,564,410	2.8%
38	Wyoming	356,381,692	0.3%

RANK ORDER

RANK	STATE	FARM INCOME	% of USA
1	California	$16,001,126,129	14.1%
2	Iowa	9,254,749,955	8.1%
3	Minnesota	8,172,164,294	7.2%
4	Nebraska	5,952,229,500	5.2%
5	Texas	5,145,163,729	4.5%
6	North Carolina	4,319,945,655	3.8%
7	North Dakota	4,279,095,530	3.8%
8	Georgia	4,214,043,478	3.7%
9	Illinois	4,173,945,737	3.7%
10	South Dakota	3,643,004,647	3.2%
11	Indiana	3,290,744,166	2.9%
12	Wisconsin	3,200,564,410	2.8%
13	Kansas	3,014,912,796	2.6%
14	Idaho	2,745,404,023	2.4%
15	Ohio	2,567,694,845	2.3%
16	Florida	2,522,210,614	2.2%
17	Michigan	2,236,865,568	2.0%
18	Washington	2,160,404,109	1.9%
19	Arkansas	1,979,479,416	1.7%
20	Mississippi	1,939,511,946	1.7%
21	Pennsylvania	1,833,490,493	1.6%
22	Missouri	1,794,697,793	1.6%
23	Louisiana	1,779,420,277	1.6%
24	Colorado	1,753,342,146	1.5%
25	Kentucky	1,540,664,355	1.4%
26	Oklahoma	1,403,608,323	1.2%
27	Alabama	1,384,611,636	1.2%
28	New Mexico	1,358,390,736	1.2%
29	New York	1,296,263,793	1.1%
30	Montana	1,294,909,562	1.1%
31	Oregon	959,935,956	0.8%
32	Virginia	932,203,409	0.8%
33	Arizona	902,974,790	0.8%
34	Tennessee	812,614,316	0.7%
35	South Carolina	734,915,397	0.6%
36	Maryland	727,340,301	0.6%
37	Utah	363,640,694	0.3%
38	Wyoming	356,381,692	0.3%
39	New Jersey	339,611,038	0.3%
40	Hawaii	329,963,992	0.3%
41	Delaware	272,204,070	0.2%
42	Nevada	222,574,672	0.2%
43	Maine	191,601,387	0.2%
44	Vermont	159,652,106	0.1%
45	Massachusetts	99,134,587	0.1%
46	Connecticut	75,477,032	0.1%
47	West Virginia	64,224,486	0.1%
48	Alaska	11,107,512	0.0%
49	Rhode Island	4,547,995	0.0%
50	New Hampshire	568,420	0.0%
	District of Columbia	0	0.0%

Source: U.S. Department of Agriculture, Economic Research Service
"Net Farm Income and Value of Production per Acre for States, 2012
(http://www.ers.usda.gov/data/FarmIncome/FinfidmuXls.htm)
*Net farm income is a measure of the net value of production in a given year. It is determined by subtracting total production expenses from gross farm income.

Net Farm Income per Operation in 2012

National Average = $52,625 per Operation*

ALPHA ORDER

RANK	STATE	PER OPERATION
32	Alabama	$29,640
43	Alaska	16,822
13	Arizona	58,940
26	Arkansas	41,454
1	California	199,080
20	Colorado	48,272
45	Connecticut	15,498
6	Delaware	108,976
19	Florida	53,235
9	Georgia	89,505
24	Hawaii	43,956
5	Idaho	112,065
16	Illinois	56,206
18	Indiana	54,880
8	Iowa	100,233
21	Kansas	46,332
41	Kentucky	18,040
12	Louisiana	61,376
36	Maine	23,714
15	Maryland	56,800
46	Massachusetts	12,988
27	Michigan	40,906
7	Minnesota	103,090
22	Mississippi	45,936
42	Missouri	16,988
23	Montana	45,232
3	Nebraska	127,594
11	Nevada	75,240
50	New Hampshire	113
31	New Jersey	33,480
14	New Mexico	57,195
28	New York	35,890
10	North Carolina	86,360
2	North Dakota	135,324
29	Ohio	34,965
44	Oklahoma	16,280
35	Oregon	25,114
33	Pennsylvania	29,512
48	Rhode Island	3,705
34	South Carolina	27,540
4	South Dakota	116,864
47	Tennessee	10,650
39	Texas	20,920
38	Utah	22,341
37	Vermont	22,794
40	Virginia	20,184
17	Washington	55,042
49	West Virginia	2,952
25	Wisconsin	41,535
30	Wyoming	33,552

RANK ORDER

RANK	STATE	PER OPERATION
1	California	$199,080
2	North Dakota	135,324
3	Nebraska	127,594
4	South Dakota	116,864
5	Idaho	112,065
6	Delaware	108,976
7	Minnesota	103,090
8	Iowa	100,233
9	Georgia	89,505
10	North Carolina	86,360
11	Nevada	75,240
12	Louisiana	61,376
13	Arizona	58,940
14	New Mexico	57,195
15	Maryland	56,800
16	Illinois	56,206
17	Washington	55,042
18	Indiana	54,880
19	Florida	53,235
20	Colorado	48,272
21	Kansas	46,332
22	Mississippi	45,936
23	Montana	45,232
24	Hawaii	43,956
25	Wisconsin	41,535
26	Arkansas	41,454
27	Michigan	40,906
28	New York	35,890
29	Ohio	34,965
30	Wyoming	33,552
31	New Jersey	33,480
32	Alabama	29,640
33	Pennsylvania	29,512
34	South Carolina	27,540
35	Oregon	25,114
36	Maine	23,714
37	Vermont	22,794
38	Utah	22,341
39	Texas	20,920
40	Virginia	20,184
41	Kentucky	18,040
42	Missouri	16,988
43	Alaska	16,822
44	Oklahoma	16,280
45	Connecticut	15,498
46	Massachusetts	12,988
47	Tennessee	10,650
48	Rhode Island	3,705
49	West Virginia	2,952
50	New Hampshire	113

District of Columbia**	NA

Source: CQ Press using data from U.S. Department of Agriculture, Economic Research Service
"Net Farm Income and Value of Production per Acre for States, 2012
(http://www.ers.usda.gov/data-products/farm-income-and-wealth-statistics.aspx)
*Calculated by multiplying average acres per farm by average net farm income per acre.
**Not applicable.

Net Farm Income per Acre in 2012

National Average = $125 per Acre*

<table>
<tr><td colspan="3">ALPHA ORDER</td><td colspan="3">RANK ORDER</td></tr>
<tr><td>RANK</td><td>STATE</td><td>PER ACRE</td><td>RANK</td><td>STATE</td><td>PER ACRE</td></tr>
<tr><td>23</td><td>Alabama</td><td>$156</td><td>1</td><td>California</td><td>$630</td></tr>
<tr><td>48</td><td>Alaska</td><td>13</td><td>2</td><td>Delaware</td><td>556</td></tr>
<tr><td>43</td><td>Arizona</td><td>35</td><td>3</td><td>North Carolina</td><td>508</td></tr>
<tr><td>25</td><td>Arkansas</td><td>147</td><td>4</td><td>New Jersey</td><td>465</td></tr>
<tr><td>1</td><td>California</td><td>630</td><td>5</td><td>Georgia</td><td>405</td></tr>
<tr><td>39</td><td>Colorado</td><td>56</td><td>6</td><td>Maryland</td><td>355</td></tr>
<tr><td>18</td><td>Connecticut</td><td>189</td><td>7</td><td>Minnesota</td><td>305</td></tr>
<tr><td>2</td><td>Delaware</td><td>556</td><td>8</td><td>Iowa</td><td>301</td></tr>
<tr><td>10</td><td>Florida</td><td>273</td><td>9</td><td>Hawaii</td><td>297</td></tr>
<tr><td>5</td><td>Georgia</td><td>405</td><td>10</td><td>Florida</td><td>273</td></tr>
<tr><td>9</td><td>Hawaii</td><td>297</td><td>11</td><td>Idaho</td><td>241</td></tr>
<tr><td>11</td><td>Idaho</td><td>241</td><td>12</td><td>Pennsylvania</td><td>238</td></tr>
<tr><td>22</td><td>Illinois</td><td>157</td><td>13</td><td>Michigan</td><td>226</td></tr>
<tr><td>14</td><td>Indiana</td><td>224</td><td>14</td><td>Indiana</td><td>224</td></tr>
<tr><td>8</td><td>Iowa</td><td>301</td><td>14</td><td>Louisiana</td><td>224</td></tr>
<tr><td>35</td><td>Kansas</td><td>66</td><td>16</td><td>Wisconsin</td><td>213</td></tr>
<tr><td>31</td><td>Kentucky</td><td>110</td><td>17</td><td>Massachusetts</td><td>191</td></tr>
<tr><td>14</td><td>Louisiana</td><td>224</td><td>18</td><td>Connecticut</td><td>189</td></tr>
<tr><td>27</td><td>Maine</td><td>142</td><td>18</td><td>Ohio</td><td>189</td></tr>
<tr><td>6</td><td>Maryland</td><td>355</td><td>20</td><td>New York</td><td>185</td></tr>
<tr><td>17</td><td>Massachusetts</td><td>191</td><td>21</td><td>Mississippi</td><td>174</td></tr>
<tr><td>13</td><td>Michigan</td><td>226</td><td>22</td><td>Illinois</td><td>157</td></tr>
<tr><td>7</td><td>Minnesota</td><td>305</td><td>23</td><td>Alabama</td><td>156</td></tr>
<tr><td>21</td><td>Mississippi</td><td>174</td><td>24</td><td>South Carolina</td><td>153</td></tr>
<tr><td>37</td><td>Missouri</td><td>62</td><td>25</td><td>Arkansas</td><td>147</td></tr>
<tr><td>46</td><td>Montana</td><td>22</td><td>26</td><td>Washington</td><td>146</td></tr>
<tr><td>28</td><td>Nebraska</td><td>131</td><td>27</td><td>Maine</td><td>142</td></tr>
<tr><td>42</td><td>Nevada</td><td>38</td><td>28</td><td>Nebraska</td><td>131</td></tr>
<tr><td>50</td><td>New Hampshire</td><td>1</td><td>28</td><td>Vermont</td><td>131</td></tr>
<tr><td>4</td><td>New Jersey</td><td>465</td><td>30</td><td>Virginia</td><td>116</td></tr>
<tr><td>45</td><td>New Mexico</td><td>31</td><td>31</td><td>Kentucky</td><td>110</td></tr>
<tr><td>20</td><td>New York</td><td>185</td><td>32</td><td>North Dakota</td><td>108</td></tr>
<tr><td>3</td><td>North Carolina</td><td>508</td><td>33</td><td>South Dakota</td><td>83</td></tr>
<tr><td>32</td><td>North Dakota</td><td>108</td><td>34</td><td>Tennessee</td><td>75</td></tr>
<tr><td>18</td><td>Ohio</td><td>189</td><td>35</td><td>Kansas</td><td>66</td></tr>
<tr><td>40</td><td>Oklahoma</td><td>40</td><td>36</td><td>Rhode Island</td><td>65</td></tr>
<tr><td>38</td><td>Oregon</td><td>58</td><td>37</td><td>Missouri</td><td>62</td></tr>
<tr><td>12</td><td>Pennsylvania</td><td>238</td><td>38</td><td>Oregon</td><td>58</td></tr>
<tr><td>36</td><td>Rhode Island</td><td>65</td><td>39</td><td>Colorado</td><td>56</td></tr>
<tr><td>24</td><td>South Carolina</td><td>153</td><td>40</td><td>Oklahoma</td><td>40</td></tr>
<tr><td>33</td><td>South Dakota</td><td>83</td><td>40</td><td>Texas</td><td>40</td></tr>
<tr><td>34</td><td>Tennessee</td><td>75</td><td>42</td><td>Nevada</td><td>38</td></tr>
<tr><td>40</td><td>Texas</td><td>40</td><td>43</td><td>Arizona</td><td>35</td></tr>
<tr><td>44</td><td>Utah</td><td>33</td><td>44</td><td>Utah</td><td>33</td></tr>
<tr><td>28</td><td>Vermont</td><td>131</td><td>45</td><td>New Mexico</td><td>31</td></tr>
<tr><td>30</td><td>Virginia</td><td>116</td><td>46</td><td>Montana</td><td>22</td></tr>
<tr><td>26</td><td>Washington</td><td>146</td><td>47</td><td>West Virginia</td><td>18</td></tr>
<tr><td>47</td><td>West Virginia</td><td>18</td><td>48</td><td>Alaska</td><td>13</td></tr>
<tr><td>16</td><td>Wisconsin</td><td>213</td><td>49</td><td>Wyoming</td><td>12</td></tr>
<tr><td>49</td><td>Wyoming</td><td>12</td><td>50</td><td>New Hampshire</td><td>1</td></tr>
<tr><td></td><td></td><td></td><td></td><td>District of Columbia**</td><td>NA</td></tr>
</table>

Source: CQ Press using data from U.S. Department of Agriculture, Economic Research Service
"Net Farm Income and Value of Production per Acre for States, 2012
(http://www.ers.usda.gov/data-products/farm-income-and-wealth-statistics.aspx)
*Net farm income is a measure of the net value of production in a given year. It is determined by subtracting total production expenses from gross farm income.
**Not applicable.

Farm Income: Cash Receipts from Commodities in 2012

National Total = $395,068,677,000*

ALPHA ORDER

RANK	STATE	FARM INCOME	% of USA
25	Alabama	$5,349,114,000	1.4%
50	Alaska	30,954,000	0.0%
31	Arizona	3,909,695,000	1.0%
15	Arkansas	9,421,594,000	2.4%
1	California	44,738,132,000	11.3%
20	Colorado	7,638,232,000	1.9%
46	Connecticut	543,829,000	0.1%
39	Delaware	1,180,546,000	0.3%
19	Florida	8,252,525,000	2.1%
14	Georgia	9,779,096,000	2.5%
41	Hawaii	729,321,000	0.2%
21	Idaho	7,586,979,000	1.9%
6	Illinois	19,649,939,000	5.0%
9	Indiana	12,052,964,000	3.1%
2	Iowa	31,985,370,000	8.1%
7	Kansas	16,223,254,000	4.1%
27	Kentucky	5,284,095,000	1.3%
29	Louisiana	4,127,882,000	1.0%
43	Maine	702,945,000	0.2%
36	Maryland	2,329,861,000	0.6%
47	Massachusetts	510,006,000	0.1%
18	Michigan	8,293,622,000	2.1%
5	Minnesota	20,580,696,000	5.2%
24	Mississippi	6,235,891,000	1.6%
13	Missouri	9,940,400,000	2.5%
33	Montana	3,745,101,000	0.9%
3	Nebraska	24,465,882,000	6.2%
42	Nevada	717,590,000	0.2%
48	New Hampshire	183,921,000	0.0%
40	New Jersey	1,139,186,000	0.3%
30	New Mexico	4,019,802,000	1.0%
26	New York	5,287,766,000	1.3%
10	North Carolina	11,706,602,000	3.0%
17	North Dakota	8,684,221,000	2.2%
11	Ohio	10,066,756,000	2.5%
22	Oklahoma	7,038,174,000	1.8%
28	Oregon	4,817,294,000	1.2%
23	Pennsylvania	6,868,357,000	1.7%
49	Rhode Island	62,082,000	0.0%
35	South Carolina	2,928,327,000	0.7%
12	South Dakota	10,013,470,000	2.5%
32	Tennessee	3,849,846,000	1.0%
4	Texas	22,726,067,000	5.8%
37	Utah	1,688,836,000	0.4%
44	Vermont	699,313,000	0.2%
34	Virginia	3,576,417,000	0.9%
16	Washington	9,293,914,000	2.4%
45	West Virginia	652,069,000	0.2%
8	Wisconsin	12,110,055,000	3.1%
38	Wyoming	1,650,684,000	0.4%

RANK ORDER

RANK	STATE	FARM INCOME	% of USA
1	California	$44,738,132,000	11.3%
2	Iowa	31,985,370,000	8.1%
3	Nebraska	24,465,882,000	6.2%
4	Texas	22,726,067,000	5.8%
5	Minnesota	20,580,696,000	5.2%
6	Illinois	19,649,939,000	5.0%
7	Kansas	16,223,254,000	4.1%
8	Wisconsin	12,110,055,000	3.1%
9	Indiana	12,052,964,000	3.1%
10	North Carolina	11,706,602,000	3.0%
11	Ohio	10,066,756,000	2.5%
12	South Dakota	10,013,470,000	2.5%
13	Missouri	9,940,400,000	2.5%
14	Georgia	9,779,096,000	2.5%
15	Arkansas	9,421,594,000	2.4%
16	Washington	9,293,914,000	2.4%
17	North Dakota	8,684,221,000	2.2%
18	Michigan	8,293,622,000	2.1%
19	Florida	8,252,525,000	2.1%
20	Colorado	7,638,232,000	1.9%
21	Idaho	7,586,979,000	1.9%
22	Oklahoma	7,038,174,000	1.8%
23	Pennsylvania	6,868,357,000	1.7%
24	Mississippi	6,235,891,000	1.6%
25	Alabama	5,349,114,000	1.4%
26	New York	5,287,766,000	1.3%
27	Kentucky	5,284,095,000	1.3%
28	Oregon	4,817,294,000	1.2%
29	Louisiana	4,127,882,000	1.0%
30	New Mexico	4,019,802,000	1.0%
31	Arizona	3,909,695,000	1.0%
32	Tennessee	3,849,846,000	1.0%
33	Montana	3,745,101,000	0.9%
34	Virginia	3,576,417,000	0.9%
35	South Carolina	2,928,327,000	0.7%
36	Maryland	2,329,861,000	0.6%
37	Utah	1,688,836,000	0.4%
38	Wyoming	1,650,684,000	0.4%
39	Delaware	1,180,546,000	0.3%
40	New Jersey	1,139,186,000	0.3%
41	Hawaii	729,321,000	0.2%
42	Nevada	717,590,000	0.2%
43	Maine	702,945,000	0.2%
44	Vermont	699,313,000	0.2%
45	West Virginia	652,069,000	0.2%
46	Connecticut	543,829,000	0.1%
47	Massachusetts	510,006,000	0.1%
48	New Hampshire	183,921,000	0.0%
49	Rhode Island	62,082,000	0.0%
50	Alaska	30,954,000	0.0%
	District of Columbia	0	0.0%

Source: U.S. Department of Agriculture, Economic Research Service
   "Farm Marketings" (http://www.ers.usda.gov/data-products/farm-income-and-wealth-statistics.aspx)
*Commodities include crops and livestock.

Farm Income: Crops in 2012

National Total = $223,484,520,000

ALPHA ORDER

RANK	STATE	FARM INCOME	% of USA
33	Alabama	$1,419,722,000	0.6%
50	Alaska	24,945,000	0.0%
30	Arizona	2,137,479,000	1.0%
16	Arkansas	4,774,403,000	2.1%
1	California	32,583,470,000	14.6%
24	Colorado	2,898,399,000	1.3%
44	Connecticut	362,403,000	0.2%
42	Delaware	377,429,000	0.2%
12	Florida	6,591,512,000	2.9%
18	Georgia	4,473,959,000	2.0%
38	Hawaii	631,244,000	0.3%
20	Idaho	3,590,281,000	1.6%
3	Illinois	17,033,617,000	7.6%
6	Indiana	8,574,545,000	3.8%
2	Iowa	18,861,660,000	8.4%
9	Kansas	7,097,141,000	3.2%
26	Kentucky	2,421,984,000	1.1%
23	Louisiana	2,962,500,000	1.3%
43	Maine	363,193,000	0.2%
35	Maryland	1,142,914,000	0.5%
41	Massachusetts	398,388,000	0.2%
15	Michigan	5,329,559,000	2.4%
4	Minnesota	13,161,060,000	5.9%
22	Mississippi	3,176,356,000	1.4%
14	Missouri	5,517,318,000	2.5%
28	Montana	2,260,720,000	1.0%
5	Nebraska	12,694,629,000	5.7%
45	Nevada	287,042,000	0.1%
48	New Hampshire	89,808,000	0.0%
36	New Jersey	1,036,048,000	0.5%
37	New Mexico	828,276,000	0.4%
29	New York	2,195,210,000	1.0%
19	North Carolina	4,356,417,000	1.9%
8	North Dakota	7,555,628,000	3.4%
11	Ohio	6,794,025,000	3.0%
31	Oklahoma	1,528,490,000	0.7%
21	Oregon	3,397,585,000	1.5%
25	Pennsylvania	2,558,522,000	1.1%
49	Rhode Island	51,502,000	0.0%
34	South Carolina	1,370,073,000	0.6%
13	South Dakota	6,438,535,000	2.9%
27	Tennessee	2,300,095,000	1.0%
7	Texas	7,659,939,000	3.4%
39	Utah	525,456,000	0.2%
47	Vermont	106,865,000	0.0%
32	Virginia	1,447,782,000	0.6%
10	Washington	6,981,651,000	3.1%
46	West Virginia	126,451,000	0.1%
17	Wisconsin	4,559,974,000	2.0%
40	Wyoming	428,313,000	0.2%

RANK ORDER

RANK	STATE	FARM INCOME	% of USA
1	California	$32,583,470,000	14.6%
2	Iowa	18,861,660,000	8.4%
3	Illinois	17,033,617,000	7.6%
4	Minnesota	13,161,060,000	5.9%
5	Nebraska	12,694,629,000	5.7%
6	Indiana	8,574,545,000	3.8%
7	Texas	7,659,939,000	3.4%
8	North Dakota	7,555,628,000	3.4%
9	Kansas	7,097,141,000	3.2%
10	Washington	6,981,651,000	3.1%
11	Ohio	6,794,025,000	3.0%
12	Florida	6,591,512,000	2.9%
13	South Dakota	6,438,535,000	2.9%
14	Missouri	5,517,318,000	2.5%
15	Michigan	5,329,559,000	2.4%
16	Arkansas	4,774,403,000	2.1%
17	Wisconsin	4,559,974,000	2.0%
18	Georgia	4,473,959,000	2.0%
19	North Carolina	4,356,417,000	1.9%
20	Idaho	3,590,281,000	1.6%
21	Oregon	3,397,585,000	1.5%
22	Mississippi	3,176,356,000	1.4%
23	Louisiana	2,962,500,000	1.3%
24	Colorado	2,898,399,000	1.3%
25	Pennsylvania	2,558,522,000	1.1%
26	Kentucky	2,421,984,000	1.1%
27	Tennessee	2,300,095,000	1.0%
28	Montana	2,260,720,000	1.0%
29	New York	2,195,210,000	1.0%
30	Arizona	2,137,479,000	1.0%
31	Oklahoma	1,528,490,000	0.7%
32	Virginia	1,447,782,000	0.6%
33	Alabama	1,419,722,000	0.6%
34	South Carolina	1,370,073,000	0.6%
35	Maryland	1,142,914,000	0.5%
36	New Jersey	1,036,048,000	0.5%
37	New Mexico	828,276,000	0.4%
38	Hawaii	631,244,000	0.3%
39	Utah	525,456,000	0.2%
40	Wyoming	428,313,000	0.2%
41	Massachusetts	398,388,000	0.2%
42	Delaware	377,429,000	0.2%
43	Maine	363,193,000	0.2%
44	Connecticut	362,403,000	0.2%
45	Nevada	287,042,000	0.1%
46	West Virginia	126,451,000	0.1%
47	Vermont	106,865,000	0.0%
48	New Hampshire	89,808,000	0.0%
49	Rhode Island	51,502,000	0.0%
50	Alaska	24,945,000	0.0%
	District of Columbia	0	0.0%

Source: U.S. Department of Agriculture, Economic Research Service
"Farm Marketings" (http://www.ers.usda.gov/data-products/farm-income-and-wealth-statistics.aspx)

Farm Income: Livestock in 2012

National Total = $171,584,157,000*

ALPHA ORDER

RANK	STATE	FARM INCOME	% of USA
16	Alabama	$3,929,392,000	2.3%
50	Alaska	6,009,000	0.0%
28	Arizona	1,772,216,000	1.0%
12	Arkansas	4,647,191,000	2.7%
3	California	12,154,662,000	7.1%
11	Colorado	4,739,833,000	2.8%
44	Connecticut	181,426,000	0.1%
39	Delaware	803,117,000	0.5%
29	Florida	1,661,013,000	1.0%
10	Georgia	5,305,137,000	3.1%
47	Hawaii	98,077,000	0.1%
15	Idaho	3,996,698,000	2.3%
25	Illinois	2,616,322,000	1.5%
18	Indiana	3,478,419,000	2.0%
2	Iowa	13,123,710,000	7.6%
5	Kansas	9,126,113,000	5.3%
24	Kentucky	2,862,111,000	1.7%
36	Louisiana	1,165,382,000	0.7%
43	Maine	339,752,000	0.2%
35	Maryland	1,186,947,000	0.7%
45	Massachusetts	111,618,000	0.1%
23	Michigan	2,964,063,000	1.7%
7	Minnesota	7,419,636,000	4.3%
22	Mississippi	3,059,535,000	1.8%
13	Missouri	4,423,082,000	2.6%
32	Montana	1,484,381,000	0.9%
4	Nebraska	11,771,253,000	6.9%
42	Nevada	430,548,000	0.3%
48	New Hampshire	94,113,000	0.1%
46	New Jersey	103,138,000	0.1%
20	New Mexico	3,191,526,000	1.9%
21	New York	3,092,556,000	1.8%
8	North Carolina	7,350,185,000	4.3%
38	North Dakota	1,128,593,000	0.7%
19	Ohio	3,272,731,000	1.9%
9	Oklahoma	5,509,684,000	3.2%
33	Oregon	1,419,709,000	0.8%
14	Pennsylvania	4,309,835,000	2.5%
49	Rhode Island	10,580,000	0.0%
30	South Carolina	1,558,254,000	0.9%
17	South Dakota	3,574,935,000	2.1%
31	Tennessee	1,549,751,000	0.9%
1	Texas	15,066,128,000	8.8%
37	Utah	1,163,380,000	0.7%
40	Vermont	592,448,000	0.3%
27	Virginia	2,128,635,000	1.2%
26	Washington	2,312,263,000	1.3%
41	West Virginia	525,618,000	0.3%
6	Wisconsin	7,550,081,000	4.4%
34	Wyoming	1,222,371,000	0.7%

RANK ORDER

RANK	STATE	FARM INCOME	% of USA
1	Texas	$15,066,128,000	8.8%
2	Iowa	13,123,710,000	7.6%
3	California	12,154,662,000	7.1%
4	Nebraska	11,771,253,000	6.9%
5	Kansas	9,126,113,000	5.3%
6	Wisconsin	7,550,081,000	4.4%
7	Minnesota	7,419,636,000	4.3%
8	North Carolina	7,350,185,000	4.3%
9	Oklahoma	5,509,684,000	3.2%
10	Georgia	5,305,137,000	3.1%
11	Colorado	4,739,833,000	2.8%
12	Arkansas	4,647,191,000	2.7%
13	Missouri	4,423,082,000	2.6%
14	Pennsylvania	4,309,835,000	2.5%
15	Idaho	3,996,698,000	2.3%
16	Alabama	3,929,392,000	2.3%
17	South Dakota	3,574,935,000	2.1%
18	Indiana	3,478,419,000	2.0%
19	Ohio	3,272,731,000	1.9%
20	New Mexico	3,191,526,000	1.9%
21	New York	3,092,556,000	1.8%
22	Mississippi	3,059,535,000	1.8%
23	Michigan	2,964,063,000	1.7%
24	Kentucky	2,862,111,000	1.7%
25	Illinois	2,616,322,000	1.5%
26	Washington	2,312,263,000	1.3%
27	Virginia	2,128,635,000	1.2%
28	Arizona	1,772,216,000	1.0%
29	Florida	1,661,013,000	1.0%
30	South Carolina	1,558,254,000	0.9%
31	Tennessee	1,549,751,000	0.9%
32	Montana	1,484,381,000	0.9%
33	Oregon	1,419,709,000	0.8%
34	Wyoming	1,222,371,000	0.7%
35	Maryland	1,186,947,000	0.7%
36	Louisiana	1,165,382,000	0.7%
37	Utah	1,163,380,000	0.7%
38	North Dakota	1,128,593,000	0.7%
39	Delaware	803,117,000	0.5%
40	Vermont	592,448,000	0.3%
41	West Virginia	525,618,000	0.3%
42	Nevada	430,548,000	0.3%
43	Maine	339,752,000	0.2%
44	Connecticut	181,426,000	0.1%
45	Massachusetts	111,618,000	0.1%
46	New Jersey	103,138,000	0.1%
47	Hawaii	98,077,000	0.1%
48	New Hampshire	94,113,000	0.1%
49	Rhode Island	10,580,000	0.0%
50	Alaska	6,009,000	0.0%
	District of Columbia	0	0.0%

Source: U.S. Department of Agriculture, Economic Research Service
  "Farm Marketings" (http://www.ers.usda.gov/data-products/farm-income-and-wealth-statistics.aspx)
*Includes livestock products.

Farm Income: Government Payments in 2012

National Total = $10,635,118,000*

ALPHA ORDER					RANK ORDER			
RANK	STATE	FARM INCOME	% of USA		RANK	STATE	FARM INCOME	% of USA
30	Alabama	$117,995,000	1.1%		1	Iowa	$855,352,000	8.0%
46	Alaska	12,358,000	0.1%		2	Texas	838,063,000	7.9%
36	Arizona	50,218,000	0.5%		3	Illinois	630,770,000	5.9%
10	Arkansas	365,119,000	3.4%		4	Minnesota	534,668,000	5.0%
15	California	287,532,000	2.7%		5	Kansas	518,589,000	4.9%
22	Colorado	215,677,000	2.0%		6	Nebraska	480,334,000	4.5%
49	Connecticut	8,892,000	0.1%		7	North Carolina	430,403,000	4.0%
43	Delaware	15,404,000	0.1%		8	North Dakota	409,094,000	3.8%
34	Florida	69,139,000	0.7%		9	Missouri	395,991,000	3.7%
18	Georgia	256,716,000	2.4%		10	Arkansas	365,119,000	3.4%
48	Hawaii	11,448,000	0.1%		11	South Dakota	330,831,000	3.1%
27	Idaho	126,650,000	1.2%		12	Indiana	322,962,000	3.0%
3	Illinois	630,770,000	5.9%		13	Kentucky	303,414,000	2.9%
12	Indiana	322,962,000	3.0%		14	Oklahoma	295,627,000	2.8%
1	Iowa	855,352,000	8.0%		15	California	287,532,000	2.7%
5	Kansas	518,589,000	4.9%		16	Wisconsin	281,827,000	2.6%
13	Kentucky	303,414,000	2.9%		17	Ohio	279,818,000	2.6%
21	Louisiana	219,135,000	2.1%		18	Georgia	256,716,000	2.4%
41	Maine	21,876,000	0.2%		19	Montana	239,263,000	2.2%
35	Maryland	56,199,000	0.5%		20	Mississippi	219,148,000	2.1%
42	Massachusetts	16,975,000	0.2%		21	Louisiana	219,135,000	2.1%
25	Michigan	175,384,000	1.6%		22	Colorado	215,677,000	2.0%
4	Minnesota	534,668,000	5.0%		23	Washington	203,661,000	1.9%
20	Mississippi	219,148,000	2.1%		24	Tennessee	176,238,000	1.7%
9	Missouri	395,991,000	3.7%		25	Michigan	175,384,000	1.6%
19	Montana	239,263,000	2.2%		26	Virginia	139,942,000	1.3%
6	Nebraska	480,334,000	4.5%		27	Idaho	126,650,000	1.2%
45	Nevada	12,877,000	0.1%		28	Pennsylvania	119,283,000	1.1%
44	New Hampshire	14,874,000	0.1%		29	Oregon	118,040,000	1.1%
47	New Jersey	11,927,000	0.1%		30	Alabama	117,995,000	1.1%
33	New Mexico	97,672,000	0.9%		31	South Carolina	110,159,000	1.0%
32	New York	104,277,000	1.0%		32	New York	104,277,000	1.0%
7	North Carolina	430,403,000	4.0%		33	New Mexico	97,672,000	0.9%
8	North Dakota	409,094,000	3.8%		34	Florida	69,139,000	0.7%
17	Ohio	279,818,000	2.6%		35	Maryland	56,199,000	0.5%
14	Oklahoma	295,627,000	2.8%		36	Arizona	50,218,000	0.5%
29	Oregon	118,040,000	1.1%		37	Wyoming	42,573,000	0.4%
28	Pennsylvania	119,283,000	1.1%		38	Utah	39,467,000	0.4%
50	Rhode Island	3,858,000	0.0%		39	West Virginia	25,165,000	0.2%
31	South Carolina	110,159,000	1.0%		40	Vermont	22,231,000	0.2%
11	South Dakota	330,831,000	3.1%		41	Maine	21,876,000	0.2%
24	Tennessee	176,238,000	1.7%		42	Massachusetts	16,975,000	0.2%
2	Texas	838,063,000	7.9%		43	Delaware	15,404,000	0.1%
38	Utah	39,467,000	0.4%		44	New Hampshire	14,874,000	0.1%
40	Vermont	22,231,000	0.2%		45	Nevada	12,877,000	0.1%
26	Virginia	139,942,000	1.3%		46	Alaska	12,358,000	0.1%
23	Washington	203,661,000	1.9%		47	New Jersey	11,927,000	0.1%
39	West Virginia	25,165,000	0.2%		48	Hawaii	11,448,000	0.1%
16	Wisconsin	281,827,000	2.6%		49	Connecticut	8,892,000	0.1%
37	Wyoming	42,573,000	0.4%		50	Rhode Island	3,858,000	0.0%
						District of Columbia	0	0.0%

Source: U.S. Department of Agriculture, Economic Research Service
   "Farm Income" (http://www.ers.usda.gov/Data/FarmIncome/FinfidmuXls.htm)
*Government payments made directly to farmers in cash.

Acres Planted in 2013

National Total = 324,795,000 Acres*

ALPHA ORDER

RANK	STATE	ACRES	% of USA
30	Alabama	2,410,000	0.7%
NA	Alaska**	NA	NA
38	Arizona	745,000	0.2%
15	Arkansas	7,682,000	2.4%
23	California	4,009,000	1.2%
18	Colorado	5,916,000	1.8%
46	Connecticut	74,000	0.0%
40	Delaware	492,000	0.2%
35	Florida	1,187,000	0.4%
24	Georgia	3,848,000	1.2%
48	Hawaii	18,000	0.0%
22	Idaho	4,502,000	1.4%
4	Illinois	23,055,000	7.1%
10	Indiana	12,330,000	3.8%
1	Iowa	24,320,000	7.5%
3	Kansas	23,474,000	7.2%
16	Kentucky	6,567,000	2.0%
27	Louisiana	3,563,000	1.1%
44	Maine	269,000	0.1%
32	Maryland	1,607,000	0.5%
45	Massachusetts	104,000	0.0%
17	Michigan	6,504,000	2.0%
7	Minnesota	19,454,000	6.0%
21	Mississippi	4,504,000	1.4%
9	Missouri	14,624,000	4.5%
13	Montana	9,566,000	2.9%
6	Nebraska	19,553,000	6.0%
41	Nevada	380,000	0.1%
47	New Hampshire	64,000	0.0%
42	New Jersey	312,000	0.1%
37	New Mexico	975,000	0.3%
28	New York	3,148,000	1.0%
20	North Carolina	5,035,000	1.6%
5	North Dakota	20,387,000	6.3%
12	Ohio	10,164,000	3.1%
11	Oklahoma	10,497,000	3.2%
31	Oregon	2,144,000	0.7%
26	Pennsylvania	3,651,000	1.1%
49	Rhode Island	11,000	0.0%
33	South Carolina	1,604,000	0.5%
8	South Dakota	17,855,000	5.5%
19	Tennessee	5,246,000	1.6%
2	Texas	24,019,000	7.4%
36	Utah	1,026,000	0.3%
43	Vermont	272,000	0.1%
29	Virginia	2,869,000	0.9%
25	Washington	3,667,000	1.1%
39	West Virginia	674,000	0.2%
14	Wisconsin	7,951,000	2.4%
34	Wyoming	1,420,000	0.4%

RANK ORDER

RANK	STATE	ACRES	% of USA
1	Iowa	24,320,000	7.5%
2	Texas	24,019,000	7.4%
3	Kansas	23,474,000	7.2%
4	Illinois	23,055,000	7.1%
5	North Dakota	20,387,000	6.3%
6	Nebraska	19,553,000	6.0%
7	Minnesota	19,454,000	6.0%
8	South Dakota	17,855,000	5.5%
9	Missouri	14,624,000	4.5%
10	Indiana	12,330,000	3.8%
11	Oklahoma	10,497,000	3.2%
12	Ohio	10,164,000	3.1%
13	Montana	9,566,000	2.9%
14	Wisconsin	7,951,000	2.4%
15	Arkansas	7,682,000	2.4%
16	Kentucky	6,567,000	2.0%
17	Michigan	6,504,000	2.0%
18	Colorado	5,916,000	1.8%
19	Tennessee	5,246,000	1.6%
20	North Carolina	5,035,000	1.6%
21	Mississippi	4,504,000	1.4%
22	Idaho	4,502,000	1.4%
23	California	4,009,000	1.2%
24	Georgia	3,848,000	1.2%
25	Washington	3,667,000	1.1%
26	Pennsylvania	3,651,000	1.1%
27	Louisiana	3,563,000	1.1%
28	New York	3,148,000	1.0%
29	Virginia	2,869,000	0.9%
30	Alabama	2,410,000	0.7%
31	Oregon	2,144,000	0.7%
32	Maryland	1,607,000	0.5%
33	South Carolina	1,604,000	0.5%
34	Wyoming	1,420,000	0.4%
35	Florida	1,187,000	0.4%
36	Utah	1,026,000	0.3%
37	New Mexico	975,000	0.3%
38	Arizona	745,000	0.2%
39	West Virginia	674,000	0.2%
40	Delaware	492,000	0.2%
41	Nevada	380,000	0.1%
42	New Jersey	312,000	0.1%
43	Vermont	272,000	0.1%
44	Maine	269,000	0.1%
45	Massachusetts	104,000	0.0%
46	Connecticut	74,000	0.0%
47	New Hampshire	64,000	0.0%
48	Hawaii	18,000	0.0%
49	Rhode Island	11,000	0.0%
NA	Alaska**	NA	NA
	District of Columbia**	NA	NA

Source: U.S. Department of Agriculture, National Agricultural Statistics Service
   "Crop Production: 2013 Summary" (January 2014)
   (http://usda.mannlib.cornell.edu/MannUsda/viewDocumentInfo.do?documentID=1047)
*Estimated totals.
**No acreage or not available.

Acres Harvested in 2013

National Total = 303,755,000 Acres*

ALPHA ORDER

RANK ORDER

RANK	STATE	ACRES	% of USA		RANK	STATE	ACRES	% of USA
30	Alabama	2,309,000	0.8%		1	Iowa	23,981,000	7.9%
NA	Alaska**	NA	NA		2	Illinois	22,854,000	7.5%
37	Arizona	733,000	0.2%		3	Kansas	21,881,000	7.2%
15	Arkansas	7,560,000	2.5%		4	North Dakota	19,995,000	6.6%
27	California	3,508,000	1.2%		5	Minnesota	19,066,000	6.3%
19	Colorado	4,890,000	1.6%		6	Nebraska	18,756,000	6.2%
46	Connecticut	70,000	0.0%		7	South Dakota	16,874,000	5.6%
40	Delaware	472,000	0.2%		8	Texas	16,292,000	5.4%
35	Florida	1,163,000	0.4%		9	Missouri	14,373,000	4.7%
24	Georgia	3,557,000	1.2%		10	Indiana	12,270,000	4.0%
48	Hawaii	18,000	0.0%		11	Ohio	10,083,000	3.3%
22	Idaho	4,338,000	1.4%		12	Montana	9,135,000	3.0%
2	Illinois	22,854,000	7.5%		13	Oklahoma	7,874,000	2.6%
10	Indiana	12,270,000	4.0%		14	Wisconsin	7,633,000	2.5%
1	Iowa	23,981,000	7.9%		15	Arkansas	7,560,000	2.5%
3	Kansas	21,881,000	7.2%		16	Kentucky	6,447,000	2.1%
16	Kentucky	6,447,000	2.1%		17	Michigan	6,433,000	2.1%
26	Louisiana	3,525,000	1.2%		18	Tennessee	5,099,000	1.7%
44	Maine	260,000	0.1%		19	Colorado	4,890,000	1.6%
33	Maryland	1,489,000	0.5%		20	North Carolina	4,876,000	1.6%
45	Massachusetts	101,000	0.0%		21	Mississippi	4,441,000	1.5%
17	Michigan	6,433,000	2.1%		22	Idaho	4,338,000	1.4%
5	Minnesota	19,066,000	6.3%		23	Washington	3,605,000	1.2%
21	Mississippi	4,441,000	1.5%		24	Georgia	3,557,000	1.2%
9	Missouri	14,373,000	4.7%		25	Pennsylvania	3,551,000	1.2%
12	Montana	9,135,000	3.0%		26	Louisiana	3,525,000	1.2%
6	Nebraska	18,756,000	6.2%		27	California	3,508,000	1.2%
41	Nevada	365,000	0.1%		28	New York	3,093,000	1.0%
47	New Hampshire	63,000	0.0%		29	Virginia	2,754,000	0.9%
42	New Jersey	304,000	0.1%		30	Alabama	2,309,000	0.8%
39	New Mexico	555,000	0.2%		31	Oregon	2,099,000	0.7%
28	New York	3,093,000	1.0%		32	South Carolina	1,556,000	0.5%
20	North Carolina	4,876,000	1.6%		33	Maryland	1,489,000	0.5%
4	North Dakota	19,995,000	6.6%		34	Wyoming	1,350,000	0.4%
11	Ohio	10,083,000	3.3%		35	Florida	1,163,000	0.4%
13	Oklahoma	7,874,000	2.6%		36	Utah	964,000	0.3%
31	Oregon	2,099,000	0.7%		37	Arizona	733,000	0.2%
25	Pennsylvania	3,551,000	1.2%		38	West Virginia	670,000	0.2%
49	Rhode Island	11,000	0.0%		39	New Mexico	555,000	0.2%
32	South Carolina	1,556,000	0.5%		40	Delaware	472,000	0.2%
7	South Dakota	16,874,000	5.6%		41	Nevada	365,000	0.1%
18	Tennessee	5,099,000	1.7%		42	New Jersey	304,000	0.1%
8	Texas	16,292,000	5.4%		43	Vermont	265,000	0.1%
36	Utah	964,000	0.3%		44	Maine	260,000	0.1%
43	Vermont	265,000	0.1%		45	Massachusetts	101,000	0.0%
29	Virginia	2,754,000	0.9%		46	Connecticut	70,000	0.0%
23	Washington	3,605,000	1.2%		47	New Hampshire	63,000	0.0%
38	West Virginia	670,000	0.2%		48	Hawaii	18,000	0.0%
14	Wisconsin	7,633,000	2.5%		49	Rhode Island	11,000	0.0%
34	Wyoming	1,350,000	0.4%		NA	Alaska**	NA	NA
						District of Columbia**	NA	NA

Source: U.S. Department of Agriculture, National Agricultural Statistics Service
"Crop Production: 2013 Summary" (January 2014)
(http://usda.mannlib.cornell.edu/MannUsda/viewDocumentInfo.do?documentID=1047)
*Estimated totals.
**No acreage or not available.

Acres Harvested: Corn in 2013

National Total = 87,668,000 Acres*

ALPHA ORDER

RANK	STATE	ACRES	% of USA
28	Alabama	295,000	0.3%
NA	Alaska**	NA	NA
37	Arizona	51,000	0.1%
17	Arkansas	870,000	1.0%
29	California	180,000	0.2%
16	Colorado	990,000	1.1%
NA	Connecticut**	NA	NA
30	Delaware	174,000	0.2%
34	Florida	78,000	0.1%
23	Georgia	465,000	0.5%
NA	Hawaii**	NA	NA
31	Idaho	120,000	0.1%
2	Illinois	11,800,000	13.5%
6	Indiana	5,850,000	6.7%
1	Iowa	13,100,000	14.9%
7	Kansas	4,000,000	4.6%
14	Kentucky	1,430,000	1.6%
22	Louisiana	670,000	0.8%
NA	Maine**	NA	NA
24	Maryland	420,000	0.5%
NA	Massachusetts**	NA	NA
12	Michigan	2,250,000	2.6%
4	Minnesota	8,150,000	9.3%
19	Mississippi	830,000	0.9%
10	Missouri	3,200,000	3.7%
35	Montana	75,000	0.1%
3	Nebraska	9,550,000	10.9%
NA	Nevada**	NA	NA
NA	New Hampshire**	NA	NA
33	New Jersey	80,000	0.1%
38	New Mexico	39,000	0.0%
21	New York	690,000	0.8%
17	North Carolina	870,000	1.0%
9	North Dakota	3,600,000	4.1%
8	Ohio	3,740,000	4.3%
27	Oklahoma	310,000	0.4%
39	Oregon	36,000	0.0%
15	Pennsylvania	1,090,000	1.2%
NA	Rhode Island**	NA	NA
26	South Carolina	335,000	0.4%
5	South Dakota	5,860,000	6.7%
20	Tennessee	820,000	0.9%
13	Texas	2,000,000	2.3%
41	Utah	31,000	0.0%
NA	Vermont**	NA	NA
25	Virginia	360,000	0.4%
32	Washington	105,000	0.1%
39	West Virginia	36,000	0.0%
11	Wisconsin	3,050,000	3.5%
36	Wyoming	68,000	0.1%

RANK ORDER

RANK	STATE	ACRES	% of USA
1	Iowa	13,100,000	14.9%
2	Illinois	11,800,000	13.5%
3	Nebraska	9,550,000	10.9%
4	Minnesota	8,150,000	9.3%
5	South Dakota	5,860,000	6.7%
6	Indiana	5,850,000	6.7%
7	Kansas	4,000,000	4.6%
8	Ohio	3,740,000	4.3%
9	North Dakota	3,600,000	4.1%
10	Missouri	3,200,000	3.7%
11	Wisconsin	3,050,000	3.5%
12	Michigan	2,250,000	2.6%
13	Texas	2,000,000	2.3%
14	Kentucky	1,430,000	1.6%
15	Pennsylvania	1,090,000	1.2%
16	Colorado	990,000	1.1%
17	Arkansas	870,000	1.0%
17	North Carolina	870,000	1.0%
19	Mississippi	830,000	0.9%
20	Tennessee	820,000	0.9%
21	New York	690,000	0.8%
22	Louisiana	670,000	0.8%
23	Georgia	465,000	0.5%
24	Maryland	420,000	0.5%
25	Virginia	360,000	0.4%
26	South Carolina	335,000	0.4%
27	Oklahoma	310,000	0.4%
28	Alabama	295,000	0.3%
29	California	180,000	0.2%
30	Delaware	174,000	0.2%
31	Idaho	120,000	0.1%
32	Washington	105,000	0.1%
33	New Jersey	80,000	0.1%
34	Florida	78,000	0.1%
35	Montana	75,000	0.1%
36	Wyoming	68,000	0.1%
37	Arizona	51,000	0.1%
38	New Mexico	39,000	0.0%
39	Oregon	36,000	0.0%
39	West Virginia	36,000	0.0%
41	Utah	31,000	0.0%
NA	Alaska**	NA	NA
NA	Connecticut**	NA	NA
NA	Hawaii**	NA	NA
NA	Maine**	NA	NA
NA	Massachusetts**	NA	NA
NA	Nevada**	NA	NA
NA	New Hampshire**	NA	NA
NA	Rhode Island**	NA	NA
NA	Vermont**	NA	NA
	District of Columbia**	NA	NA

Source: U.S. Department of Agriculture, National Agricultural Statistics Service
"Crop Production: 2013 Summary" (January 2014)
(http://usda.mannlib.cornell.edu/MannUsda/viewDocumentInfo.do?documentID=1047)
*Estimated totals. Acres harvested for grain.
**No acreage or not available.

Acres Harvested: Soybeans in 2013

National Total = 75,869,000 Acres*

ALPHA ORDER					RANK ORDER			
RANK	STATE	ACRES	% of USA		RANK	STATE	ACRES	% of USA
22	Alabama	425,000	0.6%		1	Illinois	9,420,000	12.4%
NA	Alaska**	NA	NA		2	Iowa	9,240,000	12.2%
NA	Arizona**	NA	NA		3	Minnesota	6,620,000	8.7%
11	Arkansas	3,230,000	4.3%		4	Missouri	5,550,000	7.3%
NA	California**	NA	NA		5	Indiana	5,190,000	6.8%
NA	Colorado**	NA	NA		6	Nebraska	4,760,000	6.3%
NA	Connecticut**	NA	NA		7	North Dakota	4,620,000	6.1%
27	Delaware	163,000	0.2%		8	South Dakota	4,580,000	6.0%
30	Florida	30,000	0.0%		9	Ohio	4,430,000	5.8%
26	Georgia	225,000	0.3%		10	Kansas	3,540,000	4.7%
NA	Hawaii**	NA	NA		11	Arkansas	3,230,000	4.3%
NA	Idaho**	NA	NA		12	Mississippi	1,990,000	2.6%
1	Illinois	9,420,000	12.4%		13	Michigan	1,890,000	2.5%
5	Indiana	5,190,000	6.8%		14	Kentucky	1,640,000	2.2%
2	Iowa	9,240,000	12.2%		15	Wisconsin	1,550,000	2.0%
10	Kansas	3,540,000	4.7%		16	Tennessee	1,520,000	2.0%
14	Kentucky	1,640,000	2.2%		17	North Carolina	1,420,000	1.9%
18	Louisiana	1,110,000	1.5%		18	Louisiana	1,110,000	1.5%
NA	Maine**	NA	NA		19	Virginia	590,000	0.8%
21	Maryland	475,000	0.6%		20	Pennsylvania	535,000	0.7%
NA	Massachusetts**	NA	NA		21	Maryland	475,000	0.6%
13	Michigan	1,890,000	2.5%		22	Alabama	425,000	0.6%
3	Minnesota	6,620,000	8.7%		23	Oklahoma	335,000	0.4%
12	Mississippi	1,990,000	2.6%		24	South Carolina	310,000	0.4%
4	Missouri	5,550,000	7.3%		25	New York	278,000	0.4%
NA	Montana**	NA	NA		26	Georgia	225,000	0.3%
6	Nebraska	4,760,000	6.3%		27	Delaware	163,000	0.2%
NA	Nevada**	NA	NA		28	Texas	95,000	0.1%
NA	New Hampshire**	NA	NA		29	New Jersey	87,000	0.1%
29	New Jersey	87,000	0.1%		30	Florida	30,000	0.0%
NA	New Mexico**	NA	NA		31	West Virginia	21,000	0.0%
25	New York	278,000	0.4%		NA	Alaska**	NA	NA
17	North Carolina	1,420,000	1.9%		NA	Arizona**	NA	NA
7	North Dakota	4,620,000	6.1%		NA	California**	NA	NA
9	Ohio	4,430,000	5.8%		NA	Colorado**	NA	NA
23	Oklahoma	335,000	0.4%		NA	Connecticut**	NA	NA
NA	Oregon**	NA	NA		NA	Hawaii**	NA	NA
20	Pennsylvania	535,000	0.7%		NA	Idaho**	NA	NA
NA	Rhode Island**	NA	NA		NA	Maine**	NA	NA
24	South Carolina	310,000	0.4%		NA	Massachusetts**	NA	NA
8	South Dakota	4,580,000	6.0%		NA	Montana**	NA	NA
16	Tennessee	1,520,000	2.0%		NA	Nevada**	NA	NA
28	Texas	95,000	0.1%		NA	New Hampshire**	NA	NA
NA	Utah**	NA	NA		NA	New Mexico**	NA	NA
NA	Vermont**	NA	NA		NA	Oregon**	NA	NA
19	Virginia	590,000	0.8%		NA	Rhode Island**	NA	NA
NA	Washington**	NA	NA		NA	Utah**	NA	NA
31	West Virginia	21,000	0.0%		NA	Vermont**	NA	NA
15	Wisconsin	1,550,000	2.0%		NA	Washington**	NA	NA
NA	Wyoming**	NA	NA		NA	Wyoming**	NA	NA
					NA	District of Columbia**	NA	NA

Source: U.S. Department of Agriculture, National Agricultural Statistics Service
"Crop Production: 2013 Summary" (January 2014)
(http://usda.mannlib.cornell.edu/MannUsda/viewDocumentInfo.do?documentID=1047)
*Estimated totals.
**No acreage or not available.

Acres Harvested: Wheat in 2013

National Total = 45,157,000 Acres*

ALPHA ORDER						RANK ORDER				
RANK	STATE	ACRES	% of USA			RANK	STATE	ACRES	% of USA	

RANK	STATE	ACRES	% of USA	RANK	STATE	ACRES	% of USA
26	Alabama	270,000	0.6%	1	Kansas	8,400,000	18.6%
NA	Alaska**	NA	NA	2	North Dakota	6,035,000	13.4%
35	Arizona	89,000	0.2%	3	Montana	5,220,000	11.6%
17	Arkansas	615,000	1.4%	4	Oklahoma	3,400,000	7.5%
22	California	407,000	0.9%	5	Texas	2,250,000	5.0%
8	Colorado	1,649,000	3.7%	6	Washington	2,155,000	4.8%
NA	Connecticut**	NA	NA	7	South Dakota	1,839,000	4.1%
36	Delaware	78,000	0.2%	8	Colorado	1,649,000	3.7%
40	Florida	19,000	0.0%	9	Idaho	1,241,000	2.7%
24	Georgia	350,000	0.8%	10	Minnesota	1,187,000	2.6%
NA	Hawaii**	NA	NA	11	Nebraska	1,130,000	2.5%
9	Idaho	1,241,000	2.7%	12	Missouri	1,000,000	2.2%
15	Illinois	830,000	1.8%	13	North Carolina	920,000	2.0%
21	Indiana	440,000	1.0%	14	Oregon	868,000	1.9%
39	Iowa	21,000	0.0%	15	Illinois	830,000	1.8%
1	Kansas	8,400,000	18.6%	16	Ohio	665,000	1.5%
18	Kentucky	610,000	1.4%	17	Arkansas	615,000	1.4%
30	Louisiana	250,000	0.6%	18	Kentucky	610,000	1.4%
NA	Maine**	NA	NA	19	Michigan	600,000	1.3%
28	Maryland	260,000	0.6%	20	Tennessee	540,000	1.2%
NA	Massachusetts**	NA	NA	21	Indiana	440,000	1.0%
19	Michigan	600,000	1.3%	22	California	407,000	0.9%
10	Minnesota	1,187,000	2.6%	23	Mississippi	385,000	0.9%
23	Mississippi	385,000	0.9%	24	Georgia	350,000	0.8%
12	Missouri	1,000,000	2.2%	25	Virginia	275,000	0.6%
3	Montana	5,220,000	11.6%	26	Alabama	270,000	0.6%
11	Nebraska	1,130,000	2.5%	27	Wisconsin	265,000	0.6%
41	Nevada	14,000	0.0%	28	Maryland	260,000	0.6%
NA	New Hampshire**	NA	NA	29	South Carolina	255,000	0.6%
38	New Jersey	29,000	0.1%	30	Louisiana	250,000	0.6%
37	New Mexico	70,000	0.2%	31	Pennsylvania	160,000	0.4%
34	New York	115,000	0.3%	32	Utah	124,000	0.3%
13	North Carolina	920,000	2.0%	33	Wyoming	120,000	0.3%
2	North Dakota	6,035,000	13.4%	34	New York	115,000	0.3%
16	Ohio	665,000	1.5%	35	Arizona	89,000	0.2%
4	Oklahoma	3,400,000	7.5%	36	Delaware	78,000	0.2%
14	Oregon	868,000	1.9%	37	New Mexico	70,000	0.2%
31	Pennsylvania	160,000	0.4%	38	New Jersey	29,000	0.1%
NA	Rhode Island**	NA	NA	39	Iowa	21,000	0.0%
29	South Carolina	255,000	0.6%	40	Florida	19,000	0.0%
7	South Dakota	1,839,000	4.1%	41	Nevada	14,000	0.0%
20	Tennessee	540,000	1.2%	42	West Virginia	7,000	0.0%
5	Texas	2,250,000	5.0%	NA	Alaska**	NA	NA
32	Utah	124,000	0.3%	NA	Connecticut**	NA	NA
NA	Vermont**	NA	NA	NA	Hawaii**	NA	NA
25	Virginia	275,000	0.6%	NA	Maine**	NA	NA
6	Washington	2,155,000	4.8%	NA	Massachusetts**	NA	NA
42	West Virginia	7,000	0.0%	NA	New Hampshire**	NA	NA
27	Wisconsin	265,000	0.6%	NA	Rhode Island**	NA	NA
33	Wyoming	120,000	0.3%	NA	Vermont**	NA	NA
					District of Columbia**	NA	NA

Source: U.S. Department of Agriculture, National Agricultural Statistics Service
"Crop Production: 2013 Summary" (January 2014)
(http://usda.mannlib.cornell.edu/MannUsda/viewDocumentInfo.do?documentID=1047)
*Estimated totals.
**No acreage or not available.

Cattle on Farms in 2014

National Total = 87,730,000 Cattle*

RANK	STATE	CATTLE	% of USA
26	Alabama	1,240,000	1.4%
49	Alaska	10,000	0.0%
32	Arizona	920,000	1.0%
17	Arkansas	1,660,000	1.9%
4	California	5,250,000	6.0%
11	Colorado	2,480,000	2.8%
44	Connecticut	47,000	0.1%
48	Delaware	16,000	0.0%
18	Florida	1,620,000	1.8%
30	Georgia	1,000,000	1.1%
42	Hawaii	130,000	0.1%
13	Idaho	2,190,000	2.5%
27	Illinois	1,130,000	1.3%
33	Indiana	870,000	1.0%
7	Iowa	3,700,000	4.2%
3	Kansas	5,800,000	6.6%
14	Kentucky	2,090,000	2.4%
36	Louisiana	790,000	0.9%
43	Maine	85,000	0.1%
41	Maryland	182,000	0.2%
45	Massachusetts	39,000	0.0%
28	Michigan	1,120,000	1.3%
12	Minnesota	2,280,000	2.6%
31	Mississippi	930,000	1.1%
6	Missouri	3,800,000	4.3%
10	Montana	2,550,000	2.9%
2	Nebraska	6,150,000	7.0%
37	Nevada	455,000	0.5%
46	New Hampshire	32,000	0.0%
47	New Jersey	29,000	0.0%
22	New Mexico	1,290,000	1.5%
21	New York	1,450,000	1.7%
34	North Carolina	810,000	0.9%
15	North Dakota	1,770,000	2.0%
25	Ohio	1,250,000	1.4%
5	Oklahoma	4,300,000	4.9%
23	Oregon	1,280,000	1.5%
18	Pennsylvania	1,620,000	1.8%
50	Rhode Island	5,000	0.0%
39	South Carolina	360,000	0.4%
8	South Dakota	3,650,000	4.2%
16	Tennessee	1,760,000	2.0%
1	Texas	10,900,000	12.4%
35	Utah	800,000	0.9%
40	Vermont	260,000	0.3%
20	Virginia	1,530,000	1.7%
29	Washington	1,100,000	1.3%
38	West Virginia	380,000	0.4%
9	Wisconsin	3,350,000	3.8%
24	Wyoming	1,270,000	1.4%

RANK	STATE	CATTLE	% of USA
1	Texas	10,900,000	12.4%
2	Nebraska	6,150,000	7.0%
3	Kansas	5,800,000	6.6%
4	California	5,250,000	6.0%
5	Oklahoma	4,300,000	4.9%
6	Missouri	3,800,000	4.3%
7	Iowa	3,700,000	4.2%
8	South Dakota	3,650,000	4.2%
9	Wisconsin	3,350,000	3.8%
10	Montana	2,550,000	2.9%
11	Colorado	2,480,000	2.8%
12	Minnesota	2,280,000	2.6%
13	Idaho	2,190,000	2.5%
14	Kentucky	2,090,000	2.4%
15	North Dakota	1,770,000	2.0%
16	Tennessee	1,760,000	2.0%
17	Arkansas	1,660,000	1.9%
18	Florida	1,620,000	1.8%
18	Pennsylvania	1,620,000	1.8%
20	Virginia	1,530,000	1.7%
21	New York	1,450,000	1.7%
22	New Mexico	1,290,000	1.5%
23	Oregon	1,280,000	1.5%
24	Wyoming	1,270,000	1.4%
25	Ohio	1,250,000	1.4%
26	Alabama	1,240,000	1.4%
27	Illinois	1,130,000	1.3%
28	Michigan	1,120,000	1.3%
29	Washington	1,100,000	1.3%
30	Georgia	1,000,000	1.1%
31	Mississippi	930,000	1.1%
32	Arizona	920,000	1.0%
33	Indiana	870,000	1.0%
34	North Carolina	810,000	0.9%
35	Utah	800,000	0.9%
36	Louisiana	790,000	0.9%
37	Nevada	455,000	0.5%
38	West Virginia	380,000	0.4%
39	South Carolina	360,000	0.4%
40	Vermont	260,000	0.3%
41	Maryland	182,000	0.2%
42	Hawaii	130,000	0.1%
43	Maine	85,000	0.1%
44	Connecticut	47,000	0.1%
45	Massachusetts	39,000	0.0%
46	New Hampshire	32,000	0.0%
47	New Jersey	29,000	0.0%
48	Delaware	16,000	0.0%
49	Alaska	10,000	0.0%
50	Rhode Island	5,000	0.0%
	District of Columbia	0	0.0%

Source: U.S. Department of Agriculture, National Agricultural Statistics Service
  "Cattle" (http://usda.mannlib.cornell.edu/MannUsda/viewDocumentInfo.do?documentID=1017)
*As of January 1, 2014.

Milk Cows on Farms in 2012

National Total = 9,233,000 Milk Cows*

ALPHA ORDER

RANK	STATE	MILK COWS	% of USA
42	Alabama	10,000	0.1%
50	Alaska	400	0.0%
13	Arizona	188,000	2.0%
42	Arkansas	10,000	0.1%
1	California	1,782,000	19.3%
15	Colorado	134,000	1.5%
34	Connecticut	18,000	0.2%
47	Delaware	4,900	0.1%
18	Florida	123,000	1.3%
25	Georgia	80,000	0.9%
48	Hawaii	2,000	0.0%
4	Idaho	580,000	6.3%
20	Illinois	100,000	1.1%
14	Indiana	175,000	1.9%
12	Iowa	204,000	2.2%
17	Kansas	126,000	1.4%
26	Kentucky	74,000	0.8%
36	Louisiana	17,000	0.2%
32	Maine	33,000	0.4%
28	Maryland	51,000	0.6%
41	Massachusetts	12,000	0.1%
8	Michigan	375,000	4.1%
6	Minnesota	465,000	5.0%
38	Mississippi	14,000	0.2%
22	Missouri	94,000	1.0%
38	Montana	14,000	0.2%
27	Nebraska	56,000	0.6%
33	Nevada	29,000	0.3%
38	New Hampshire	14,000	0.2%
45	New Jersey	7,000	0.1%
9	New Mexico	330,000	3.6%
3	New York	610,000	6.6%
31	North Carolina	46,000	0.5%
34	North Dakota	18,000	0.2%
10	Ohio	270,000	2.9%
30	Oklahoma	48,000	0.5%
18	Oregon	123,000	1.3%
5	Pennsylvania	536,000	5.8%
49	Rhode Island	1,000	0.0%
37	South Carolina	16,000	0.2%
23	South Dakota	92,000	1.0%
29	Tennessee	50,000	0.5%
7	Texas	436,000	4.7%
24	Utah	90,000	1.0%
16	Vermont	133,000	1.4%
21	Virginia	96,000	1.0%
11	Washington	262,000	2.8%
42	West Virginia	10,000	0.1%
2	Wisconsin	1,270,000	13.8%
46	Wyoming	6,000	0.1%

RANK ORDER

RANK	STATE	MILK COWS	% of USA
1	California	1,782,000	19.3%
2	Wisconsin	1,270,000	13.8%
3	New York	610,000	6.6%
4	Idaho	580,000	6.3%
5	Pennsylvania	536,000	5.8%
6	Minnesota	465,000	5.0%
7	Texas	436,000	4.7%
8	Michigan	375,000	4.1%
9	New Mexico	330,000	3.6%
10	Ohio	270,000	2.9%
11	Washington	262,000	2.8%
12	Iowa	204,000	2.2%
13	Arizona	188,000	2.0%
14	Indiana	175,000	1.9%
15	Colorado	134,000	1.5%
16	Vermont	133,000	1.4%
17	Kansas	126,000	1.4%
18	Florida	123,000	1.3%
18	Oregon	123,000	1.3%
20	Illinois	100,000	1.1%
21	Virginia	96,000	1.0%
22	Missouri	94,000	1.0%
23	South Dakota	92,000	1.0%
24	Utah	90,000	1.0%
25	Georgia	80,000	0.9%
26	Kentucky	74,000	0.8%
27	Nebraska	56,000	0.6%
28	Maryland	51,000	0.6%
29	Tennessee	50,000	0.5%
30	Oklahoma	48,000	0.5%
31	North Carolina	46,000	0.5%
32	Maine	33,000	0.4%
33	Nevada	29,000	0.3%
34	Connecticut	18,000	0.2%
34	North Dakota	18,000	0.2%
36	Louisiana	17,000	0.2%
37	South Carolina	16,000	0.2%
38	Mississippi	14,000	0.2%
38	Montana	14,000	0.2%
38	New Hampshire	14,000	0.2%
41	Massachusetts	12,000	0.1%
42	Alabama	10,000	0.1%
42	Arkansas	10,000	0.1%
42	West Virginia	10,000	0.1%
45	New Jersey	7,000	0.1%
46	Wyoming	6,000	0.1%
47	Delaware	4,900	0.1%
48	Hawaii	2,000	0.0%
49	Rhode Island	1,000	0.0%
50	Alaska	400	0.0%
	District of Columbia	0	0.0%

Source: U.S. Department of Agriculture, National Agricultural Statistics Service
    "Milk Production, Disposition and Income: 2012 Summary" (April 2013)
    (http://usda.mannlib.cornell.edu/MannUsda/viewDocumentInfo.do?documentID=1105)
*Average number during year. Excludes heifers not yet fresh.

Milk Production in 2012

National Total = 200,324,000,000 Pounds of Milk*

ALPHA ORDER

RANK	STATE	POUNDS	% of USA
44	Alabama	132,000,000	0.1%
50	Alaska	5,700,000	0.0%
12	Arizona	4,508,000,000	2.3%
43	Arkansas	133,000,000	0.1%
1	California	41,801,000,000	20.9%
15	Colorado	3,213,000,000	1.6%
34	Connecticut	358,000,000	0.2%
47	Delaware	93,800,000	0.0%
19	Florida	2,338,000,000	1.2%
24	Georgia	1,530,000,000	0.8%
48	Hawaii	28,400,000	0.0%
3	Idaho	13,558,000,000	6.8%
21	Illinois	1,951,000,000	1.0%
14	Indiana	3,739,000,000	1.9%
13	Iowa	4,433,000,000	2.2%
16	Kansas	2,731,000,000	1.4%
27	Kentucky	1,120,000,000	0.6%
39	Louisiana	224,000,000	0.1%
33	Maine	613,000,000	0.3%
28	Maryland	979,000,000	0.5%
40	Massachusetts	219,000,000	0.1%
8	Michigan	8,889,000,000	4.4%
7	Minnesota	9,071,000,000	4.5%
41	Mississippi	201,000,000	0.1%
25	Missouri	1,404,000,000	0.7%
36	Montana	299,000,000	0.1%
26	Nebraska	1,186,000,000	0.6%
32	Nevada	666,000,000	0.3%
38	New Hampshire	275,000,000	0.1%
45	New Jersey	130,000,000	0.1%
9	New Mexico	8,149,000,000	4.1%
4	New York	13,196,000,000	6.6%
29	North Carolina	940,000,000	0.5%
35	North Dakota	347,000,000	0.2%
11	Ohio	5,355,000,000	2.7%
30	Oklahoma	849,000,000	0.4%
18	Oregon	2,513,000,000	1.3%
5	Pennsylvania	10,493,000,000	5.2%
49	Rhode Island	18,300,000	0.0%
37	South Carolina	277,000,000	0.1%
20	South Dakota	1,968,000,000	1.0%
31	Tennessee	805,000,000	0.4%
6	Texas	9,596,000,000	4.8%
21	Utah	1,951,000,000	1.0%
17	Vermont	2,569,000,000	1.3%
23	Virginia	1,727,000,000	0.9%
10	Washington	6,234,000,000	3.1%
42	West Virginia	158,000,000	0.1%
2	Wisconsin	27,224,000,000	13.6%
46	Wyoming	124,900,000	0.1%

RANK ORDER

RANK	STATE	POUNDS	% of USA
1	California	41,801,000,000	20.9%
2	Wisconsin	27,224,000,000	13.6%
3	Idaho	13,558,000,000	6.8%
4	New York	13,196,000,000	6.6%
5	Pennsylvania	10,493,000,000	5.2%
6	Texas	9,596,000,000	4.8%
7	Minnesota	9,071,000,000	4.5%
8	Michigan	8,889,000,000	4.4%
9	New Mexico	8,149,000,000	4.1%
10	Washington	6,234,000,000	3.1%
11	Ohio	5,355,000,000	2.7%
12	Arizona	4,508,000,000	2.3%
13	Iowa	4,433,000,000	2.2%
14	Indiana	3,739,000,000	1.9%
15	Colorado	3,213,000,000	1.6%
16	Kansas	2,731,000,000	1.4%
17	Vermont	2,569,000,000	1.3%
18	Oregon	2,513,000,000	1.3%
19	Florida	2,338,000,000	1.2%
20	South Dakota	1,968,000,000	1.0%
21	Illinois	1,951,000,000	1.0%
21	Utah	1,951,000,000	1.0%
23	Virginia	1,727,000,000	0.9%
24	Georgia	1,530,000,000	0.8%
25	Missouri	1,404,000,000	0.7%
26	Nebraska	1,186,000,000	0.6%
27	Kentucky	1,120,000,000	0.6%
28	Maryland	979,000,000	0.5%
29	North Carolina	940,000,000	0.5%
30	Oklahoma	849,000,000	0.4%
31	Tennessee	805,000,000	0.4%
32	Nevada	666,000,000	0.3%
33	Maine	613,000,000	0.3%
34	Connecticut	358,000,000	0.2%
35	North Dakota	347,000,000	0.2%
36	Montana	299,000,000	0.1%
37	South Carolina	277,000,000	0.1%
38	New Hampshire	275,000,000	0.1%
39	Louisiana	224,000,000	0.1%
40	Massachusetts	219,000,000	0.1%
41	Mississippi	201,000,000	0.1%
42	West Virginia	158,000,000	0.1%
43	Arkansas	133,000,000	0.1%
44	Alabama	132,000,000	0.1%
45	New Jersey	130,000,000	0.1%
46	Wyoming	124,900,000	0.1%
47	Delaware	93,800,000	0.0%
48	Hawaii	28,400,000	0.0%
49	Rhode Island	18,300,000	0.0%
50	Alaska	5,700,000	0.0%
	District of Columbia	0	0.0%

Source: U.S. Department of Agriculture, National Agricultural Statistics Service
"Milk Production, Disposition and Income: 2012 Summary" (April 2013)
(http://usda.mannlib.cornell.edu/MannUsda/viewDocumentInfo.do?documentID=1105)
*Excludes milk suckled by calves.

Milk Production per Milk Cow in 2012

National Average = 21,697 Pounds of Milk per Cow*

RANK	STATE	POUNDS
49	Alabama	13,200
46	Alaska	14,250
2	Arizona	23,979
48	Arkansas	13,300
6	California	23,457
3	Colorado	23,978
22	Connecticut	19,889
31	Delaware	19,143
33	Florida	19,008
32	Georgia	19,125
47	Hawaii	14,200
7	Idaho	23,376
26	Illinois	19,510
16	Indiana	21,366
10	Iowa	21,730
12	Kansas	21,675
43	Kentucky	15,135
50	Louisiana	13,176
34	Maine	18,576
30	Maryland	19,196
37	Massachusetts	18,250
5	Michigan	23,704
27	Minnesota	19,508
45	Mississippi	14,357
44	Missouri	14,936
17	Montana	21,357
18	Nebraska	21,179
8	Nevada	22,966
24	New Hampshire	19,643
35	New Jersey	18,571
1	New Mexico	24,694
13	New York	21,633
20	North Carolina	20,435
29	North Dakota	19,278
23	Ohio	19,833
39	Oklahoma	17,688
21	Oregon	20,431
25	Pennsylvania	19,576
36	Rhode Island	18,300
40	South Carolina	17,313
15	South Dakota	21,391
41	Tennessee	16,100
9	Texas	22,009
11	Utah	21,678
28	Vermont	19,316
38	Virginia	17,990
4	Washington	23,794
42	West Virginia	15,800
14	Wisconsin	21,436
19	Wyoming	20,817

RANK	STATE	POUNDS
1	New Mexico	24,694
2	Arizona	23,979
3	Colorado	23,978
4	Washington	23,794
5	Michigan	23,704
6	California	23,457
7	Idaho	23,376
8	Nevada	22,966
9	Texas	22,009
10	Iowa	21,730
11	Utah	21,678
12	Kansas	21,675
13	New York	21,633
14	Wisconsin	21,436
15	South Dakota	21,391
16	Indiana	21,366
17	Montana	21,357
18	Nebraska	21,179
19	Wyoming	20,817
20	North Carolina	20,435
21	Oregon	20,431
22	Connecticut	19,889
23	Ohio	19,833
24	New Hampshire	19,643
25	Pennsylvania	19,576
26	Illinois	19,510
27	Minnesota	19,508
28	Vermont	19,316
29	North Dakota	19,278
30	Maryland	19,196
31	Delaware	19,143
32	Georgia	19,125
33	Florida	19,008
34	Maine	18,576
35	New Jersey	18,571
36	Rhode Island	18,300
37	Massachusetts	18,250
38	Virginia	17,990
39	Oklahoma	17,688
40	South Carolina	17,313
41	Tennessee	16,100
42	West Virginia	15,800
43	Kentucky	15,135
44	Missouri	14,936
45	Mississippi	14,357
46	Alaska	14,250
47	Hawaii	14,200
48	Arkansas	13,300
49	Alabama	13,200
50	Louisiana	13,176

District of Columbia**   NA

Source: U.S. Department of Agriculture, National Agricultural Statistics Service
    "Milk Production, Disposition and Income: 2012 Summary" (April 2013)
      (http://usda.mannlib.cornell.edu/MannUsda/viewDocumentInfo.do?documentID=1105)
*Excludes milk suckled by calves.
**Not applicable.

Hogs and Pigs on Farms in 2013

National Total = 65,940,000 Hogs and Pigs*

ALPHA ORDER

RANK	STATE	HOGS AND PIGS	% of USA
30	Alabama	85,000	0.1%
48	Alaska	1,000	0.0%
22	Arizona	175,000	0.3%
27	Arkansas	115,000	0.2%
28	California	95,000	0.1%
15	Colorado	690,000	1.0%
43	Connecticut	3,500	0.0%
39	Delaware	6,000	0.0%
33	Florida	15,000	0.0%
25	Georgia	141,000	0.2%
34	Hawaii	11,500	0.0%
NA	Idaho**	NA	NA
4	Illinois	4,650,000	7.1%
5	Indiana	3,750,000	5.7%
1	Iowa	20,500,000	31.1%
10	Kansas	1,760,000	2.7%
18	Kentucky	315,000	0.5%
38	Louisiana	8,000	0.0%
41	Maine	4,500	0.0%
32	Maryland	22,000	0.0%
36	Massachusetts	8,500	0.0%
13	Michigan	1,060,000	1.6%
3	Minnesota	8,000,000	12.1%
17	Mississippi	500,000	0.8%
7	Missouri	2,850,000	4.3%
24	Montana	166,000	0.3%
6	Nebraska	3,100,000	4.7%
45	Nevada	2,000	0.0%
42	New Hampshire	3,800	0.0%
35	New Jersey	9,000	0.0%
47	New Mexico	1,200	0.0%
31	New York	66,000	0.1%
2	North Carolina	8,700,000	13.2%
26	North Dakota	135,000	0.2%
8	Ohio	2,220,000	3.4%
9	Oklahoma	1,990,000	3.0%
36	Oregon	8,500	0.0%
12	Pennsylvania	1,110,000	1.7%
46	Rhode Island	1,900	0.0%
21	South Carolina	245,000	0.4%
11	South Dakota	1,210,000	1.8%
22	Tennessee	175,000	0.3%
16	Texas	600,000	0.9%
14	Utah	710,000	1.1%
44	Vermont	3,200	0.0%
20	Virginia	255,000	0.4%
NA	Washington**	NA	NA
40	West Virginia	5,000	0.0%
19	Wisconsin	305,000	0.5%
29	Wyoming	90,000	0.1%

RANK ORDER

RANK	STATE	HOGS AND PIGS	% of USA
1	Iowa	20,500,000	31.1%
2	North Carolina	8,700,000	13.2%
3	Minnesota	8,000,000	12.1%
4	Illinois	4,650,000	7.1%
5	Indiana	3,750,000	5.7%
6	Nebraska	3,100,000	4.7%
7	Missouri	2,850,000	4.3%
8	Ohio	2,220,000	3.4%
9	Oklahoma	1,990,000	3.0%
10	Kansas	1,760,000	2.7%
11	South Dakota	1,210,000	1.8%
12	Pennsylvania	1,110,000	1.7%
13	Michigan	1,060,000	1.6%
14	Utah	710,000	1.1%
15	Colorado	690,000	1.0%
16	Texas	600,000	0.9%
17	Mississippi	500,000	0.8%
18	Kentucky	315,000	0.5%
19	Wisconsin	305,000	0.5%
20	Virginia	255,000	0.4%
21	South Carolina	245,000	0.4%
22	Arizona	175,000	0.3%
22	Tennessee	175,000	0.3%
24	Montana	166,000	0.3%
25	Georgia	141,000	0.2%
26	North Dakota	135,000	0.2%
27	Arkansas	115,000	0.2%
28	California	95,000	0.1%
29	Wyoming	90,000	0.1%
30	Alabama	85,000	0.1%
31	New York	66,000	0.1%
32	Maryland	22,000	0.0%
33	Florida	15,000	0.0%
34	Hawaii	11,500	0.0%
35	New Jersey	9,000	0.0%
36	Massachusetts	8,500	0.0%
36	Oregon	8,500	0.0%
38	Louisiana	8,000	0.0%
39	Delaware	6,000	0.0%
40	West Virginia	5,000	0.0%
41	Maine	4,500	0.0%
42	New Hampshire	3,800	0.0%
43	Connecticut	3,500	0.0%
44	Vermont	3,200	0.0%
45	Nevada	2,000	0.0%
46	Rhode Island	1,900	0.0%
47	New Mexico	1,200	0.0%
48	Alaska	1,000	0.0%
NA	Idaho**	NA	NA
NA	Washington**	NA	NA
	District of Columbia	0	0.0%

Source: U.S. Department of Agriculture, National Agricultural Statistics Service
   "Quarterly Hogs and Pigs" (http://usda.mannlib.cornell.edu/MannUsda/viewDocumentInfo.do?documentID=1086)
*As of December 1, 2013.
**Not available. Figures for Idaho and Washington withheld to avoid disclosing data for individual operations. The two states combined had 62,000 hogs and pigs.

Chickens in 2012

National Total = 8,437,900,000 Chickens*

ALPHA ORDER

RANK	STATE	CHICKENS	% of USA
2	Alabama	1,003,600,000	11.9%
NA	Alaska***	NA	NA
NA	Arizona***	NA	NA
3	Arkansas	977,100,000	11.6%
NA	California**	NA	NA
NA	Colorado***	NA	NA
NA	Connecticut***	NA	NA
12	Delaware	212,000,000	2.5%
18	Florida	59,500,000	0.7%
1	Georgia	1,361,700,000	16.1%
NA	Hawaii***	NA	NA
NA	Idaho***	NA	NA
NA	Illinois**	NA	NA
NA	Indiana**	NA	NA
NA	Iowa**	NA	NA
NA	Kansas***	NA	NA
7	Kentucky	309,500,000	3.7%
NA	Louisiana**	NA	NA
NA	Maine***	NA	NA
8	Maryland	304,000,000	3.6%
NA	Massachusetts***	NA	NA
NA	Michigan**	NA	NA
20	Minnesota	45,500,000	0.5%
5	Mississippi	751,300,000	8.9%
9	Missouri	271,600,000	3.2%
NA	Montana***	NA	NA
NA	Nebraska**	NA	NA
NA	Nevada***	NA	NA
NA	New Hampshire***	NA	NA
NA	New Jersey***	NA	NA
NA	New Mexico***	NA	NA
NA	New York**	NA	NA
4	North Carolina	799,700,000	9.5%
NA	North Dakota***	NA	NA
17	Ohio	63,200,000	0.7%
13	Oklahoma	211,800,000	2.5%
NA	Oregon**	NA	NA
15	Pennsylvania	154,500,000	1.8%
NA	Rhode Island***	NA	NA
11	South Carolina	222,800,000	2.6%
NA	South Dakota***	NA	NA
14	Tennessee	167,600,000	2.0%
6	Texas	602,500,000	7.1%
NA	Utah***	NA	NA
NA	Vermont***	NA	NA
10	Virginia	240,500,000	2.9%
NA	Washington**	NA	NA
16	West Virginia	94,000,000	1.1%
19	Wisconsin	51,700,000	0.6%
NA	Wyoming***	NA	NA

RANK ORDER

RANK	STATE	CHICKENS	% of USA
1	Georgia	1,361,700,000	16.1%
2	Alabama	1,003,600,000	11.9%
3	Arkansas	977,100,000	11.6%
4	North Carolina	799,700,000	9.5%
5	Mississippi	751,300,000	8.9%
6	Texas	602,500,000	7.1%
7	Kentucky	309,500,000	3.7%
8	Maryland	304,000,000	3.6%
9	Missouri	271,600,000	3.2%
10	Virginia	240,500,000	2.9%
11	South Carolina	222,800,000	2.6%
12	Delaware	212,000,000	2.5%
13	Oklahoma	211,800,000	2.5%
14	Tennessee	167,600,000	2.0%
15	Pennsylvania	154,500,000	1.8%
16	West Virginia	94,000,000	1.1%
17	Ohio	63,200,000	0.7%
18	Florida	59,500,000	0.7%
19	Wisconsin	51,700,000	0.6%
20	Minnesota	45,500,000	0.5%
NA	Alaska***	NA	NA
NA	Arizona***	NA	NA
NA	California**	NA	NA
NA	Colorado***	NA	NA
NA	Connecticut***	NA	NA
NA	Hawaii***	NA	NA
NA	Idaho***	NA	NA
NA	Illinois**	NA	NA
NA	Indiana**	NA	NA
NA	Iowa**	NA	NA
NA	Kansas***	NA	NA
NA	Louisiana**	NA	NA
NA	Maine***	NA	NA
NA	Massachusetts***	NA	NA
NA	Michigan**	NA	NA
NA	Montana***	NA	NA
NA	Nebraska**	NA	NA
NA	Nevada***	NA	NA
NA	New Hampshire***	NA	NA
NA	New Jersey***	NA	NA
NA	New Mexico***	NA	NA
NA	New York**	NA	NA
NA	North Dakota***	NA	NA
NA	Oregon**	NA	NA
NA	Rhode Island***	NA	NA
NA	South Dakota***	NA	NA
NA	Utah***	NA	NA
NA	Vermont***	NA	NA
NA	Washington**	NA	NA
NA	Wyoming***	NA	NA
	District of Columbia***	NA	NA

Source: U.S. Department of Agriculture, National Agricultural Statistics Service
   "Poultry - Production and Value: 2012 Summary" (April 2013)
   (http://usda.mannlib.cornell.edu/MannUsda/viewDocumentInfo.do?documentID=1130)
*Broilers. Total includes numbers for states not shown separately but excludes states producing less than 500,000 birds. **These states produced a combined total of 535,800,000 chickens. They are combined to avoid disclosing individual operations. National total does not include chickens used for egg production. ***Produces fewer than 500,000 chickens or are not available.

Eggs Produced in 2012

National Total = 92,894,000,000 Eggs*

ALPHA ORDER

RANK	STATE	EGGS	% of USA
14	Alabama	2,139,000,000	2.3%
NA	Alaska**	NA	NA
NA	Arizona**	NA	NA
10	Arkansas	3,011,000,000	3.2%
5	California	5,451,000,000	5.9%
20	Colorado	1,297,000,000	1.4%
30	Connecticut	651,000,000	0.7%
NA	Delaware**	NA	NA
13	Florida	2,514,000,000	2.7%
7	Georgia	4,303,000,000	4.6%
NA	Hawaii**	NA	NA
NA	Idaho**	NA	NA
21	Illinois	1,217,000,000	1.3%
4	Indiana	6,804,000,000	7.3%
1	Iowa	14,499,000,000	15.6%
NA	Kansas**	NA	NA
23	Kentucky	1,037,000,000	1.1%
32	Louisiana	533,000,000	0.6%
25	Maine	998,000,000	1.1%
31	Maryland	647,000,000	0.7%
37	Massachusetts	36,000,000	0.0%
8	Michigan	3,460,000,000	3.7%
11	Minnesota	2,830,000,000	3.0%
17	Mississippi	1,381,000,000	1.5%
15	Missouri	1,968,000,000	2.1%
35	Montana	119,000,000	0.1%
12	Nebraska	2,723,000,000	2.9%
NA	Nevada**	NA	NA
NA	New Hampshire**	NA	NA
NA	New Jersey**	NA	NA
NA	New Mexico**	NA	NA
19	New York	1,312,000,000	1.4%
9	North Carolina	3,086,000,000	3.3%
NA	North Dakota**	NA	NA
2	Ohio	7,685,000,000	8.3%
26	Oklahoma	741,000,000	0.8%
28	Oregon	694,000,000	0.7%
3	Pennsylvania	7,139,000,000	7.7%
NA	Rhode Island**	NA	NA
22	South Carolina	1,129,000,000	1.2%
29	South Dakota	666,000,000	0.7%
33	Tennessee	311,000,000	0.3%
6	Texas	5,098,000,000	5.5%
24	Utah	1,005,000,000	1.1%
36	Vermont	60,000,000	0.1%
27	Virginia	696,000,000	0.7%
16	Washington	1,905,000,000	2.1%
34	West Virginia	224,000,000	0.2%
18	Wisconsin	1,372,000,000	1.5%
38	Wyoming	2,400,000	0.0%

RANK ORDER

RANK	STATE	EGGS	% of USA
1	Iowa	14,499,000,000	15.6%
2	Ohio	7,685,000,000	8.3%
3	Pennsylvania	7,139,000,000	7.7%
4	Indiana	6,804,000,000	7.3%
5	California	5,451,000,000	5.9%
6	Texas	5,098,000,000	5.5%
7	Georgia	4,303,000,000	4.6%
8	Michigan	3,460,000,000	3.7%
9	North Carolina	3,086,000,000	3.3%
10	Arkansas	3,011,000,000	3.2%
11	Minnesota	2,830,000,000	3.0%
12	Nebraska	2,723,000,000	2.9%
13	Florida	2,514,000,000	2.7%
14	Alabama	2,139,000,000	2.3%
15	Missouri	1,968,000,000	2.1%
16	Washington	1,905,000,000	2.1%
17	Mississippi	1,381,000,000	1.5%
18	Wisconsin	1,372,000,000	1.5%
19	New York	1,312,000,000	1.4%
20	Colorado	1,297,000,000	1.4%
21	Illinois	1,217,000,000	1.3%
22	South Carolina	1,129,000,000	1.2%
23	Kentucky	1,037,000,000	1.1%
24	Utah	1,005,000,000	1.1%
25	Maine	998,000,000	1.1%
26	Oklahoma	741,000,000	0.8%
27	Virginia	696,000,000	0.7%
28	Oregon	694,000,000	0.7%
29	South Dakota	666,000,000	0.7%
30	Connecticut	651,000,000	0.7%
31	Maryland	647,000,000	0.7%
32	Louisiana	533,000,000	0.6%
33	Tennessee	311,000,000	0.3%
34	West Virginia	224,000,000	0.2%
35	Montana	119,000,000	0.1%
36	Vermont	60,000,000	0.1%
37	Massachusetts	36,000,000	0.0%
38	Wyoming	2,400,000	0.0%
NA	Alaska**	NA	NA
NA	Arizona**	NA	NA
NA	Delaware**	NA	NA
NA	Hawaii**	NA	NA
NA	Idaho**	NA	NA
NA	Kansas**	NA	NA
NA	Nevada**	NA	NA
NA	New Hampshire**	NA	NA
NA	New Jersey**	NA	NA
NA	New Mexico**	NA	NA
NA	North Dakota**	NA	NA
NA	Rhode Island**	NA	NA
	District of Columbia	0	0.0%

Source: U.S. Department of Agriculture, National Agricultural Statistics Service
  "Poultry - Production and Value: 2012 Summary" (April 2013)
    (http://usda.mannlib.cornell.edu/MannUsda/viewDocumentInfo.do?documentID=1130)
*Includes hatching and market (table) eggs. **These states produced a combined 2,153,000,000 eggs. They are combined to avoid disclosing individual operations.

II. Crime and Law Enforcement

I. Arrests:

Important Note Regarding Arrest Numbers

The state arrest numbers reported by the FBI and shown on page 55 are only from those law enforcement agencies that submitted complete arrests reports for 12 months in 2012. The arrest rates were calculated by the editors using population totals provided by the FBI for those jurisdictions reporting. Reports from law enforcement agencies in Alabama, Hawaii, and the District of Columbia were insufficient to calculate rates. Reports from Illinois, Louisiana, Mississippi, New York, Utah, and Washington represented less than 60 percent of their state population. Rates for these states should be interpreted with caution.

V. Juveniles:

Important Note Regarding Juvenile Arrest Rates

The juvenile arrest rates shown on page 56 were calculated by the editors as follows:

The state arrest numbers reported by the FBI are only from those law enforcement agencies that submitted complete arrests reports for 12 months in 2012. Included in the FBI report are population totals of these reporting jurisdictions by state. Using these FBI population figures, we first determined what percentage the FBI numbers represented of each state's total resident population. Next, using 2012 Census state estimates for 10- to 17-year-olds, we multiplied the percentages derived from the FBI population figures into the Census Bureau's total juvenile population counts. The resulting juvenile population is the base that was used to determine juvenile arrests per 100,000 juvenile population. The national rate was calculated in the same manner.

Reports from law enforcement agencies in Alabama, Hawaii, and the District of Columbia were insufficient to calculate rates. Reports from Illinois, Louisiana, Mississippi, New York, Utah, and Washington represented less than 60 percent of their state population. Rates for these states should be interpreted with caution.

Crimes in 2012

National Total = 10,189,902 Crimes*

ALPHA ORDER

RANK	STATE	CRIMES	% of USA
19	Alabama	190,571	1.9%
46	Alaska	24,449	0.2%
12	Arizona	260,038	2.6%
28	Arkansas	121,776	1.2%
1	California	1,210,409	11.9%
24	Colorado	155,293	1.5%
34	Connecticut	86,994	0.9%
40	Delaware	35,659	0.3%
3	Florida	727,075	7.1%
7	Georgia	375,920	3.7%
39	Hawaii	46,147	0.5%
42	Idaho	34,969	0.3%
6	Illinois	385,416	3.8%
15	Indiana	220,634	2.2%
36	Iowa	77,951	0.8%
30	Kansas	100,942	1.0%
29	Kentucky	121,578	1.2%
21	Louisiana	185,804	1.8%
41	Maine	34,992	0.3%
20	Maryland	190,086	1.9%
22	Massachusetts	170,042	1.7%
10	Michigan	295,023	2.9%
25	Minnesota	150,571	1.5%
32	Mississippi	91,692	0.9%
14	Missouri	226,745	2.2%
45	Montana	28,706	0.3%
37	Nebraska	55,932	0.5%
31	Nevada	94,273	0.9%
43	New Hampshire	33,174	0.3%
16	New Jersey	207,208	2.0%
35	New Mexico	86,754	0.9%
4	New York	455,750	4.5%
8	North Carolina	363,058	3.6%
49	North Dakota	15,775	0.2%
5	Ohio	394,478	3.9%
26	Oklahoma	147,645	1.4%
27	Oregon	135,376	1.3%
9	Pennsylvania	320,999	3.2%
44	Rhode Island	29,668	0.3%
17	South Carolina	206,947	2.0%
47	South Dakota	19,850	0.2%
13	Tennessee	259,214	2.5%
2	Texas	982,535	9.6%
33	Utah	91,300	0.9%
48	Vermont	15,909	0.2%
18	Virginia	192,549	1.9%
11	Washington	272,719	2.7%
38	West Virginia	49,747	0.5%
23	Wisconsin	156,577	1.5%
50	Wyoming	14,383	0.1%

RANK ORDER

RANK	STATE	CRIMES	% of USA
1	California	1,210,409	11.9%
2	Texas	982,535	9.6%
3	Florida	727,075	7.1%
4	New York	455,750	4.5%
5	Ohio	394,478	3.9%
6	Illinois	385,416	3.8%
7	Georgia	375,920	3.7%
8	North Carolina	363,058	3.6%
9	Pennsylvania	320,999	3.2%
10	Michigan	295,023	2.9%
11	Washington	272,719	2.7%
12	Arizona	260,038	2.6%
13	Tennessee	259,214	2.5%
14	Missouri	226,745	2.2%
15	Indiana	220,634	2.2%
16	New Jersey	207,208	2.0%
17	South Carolina	206,947	2.0%
18	Virginia	192,549	1.9%
19	Alabama	190,571	1.9%
20	Maryland	190,086	1.9%
21	Louisiana	185,804	1.8%
22	Massachusetts	170,042	1.7%
23	Wisconsin	156,577	1.5%
24	Colorado	155,293	1.5%
25	Minnesota	150,571	1.5%
26	Oklahoma	147,645	1.4%
27	Oregon	135,376	1.3%
28	Arkansas	121,776	1.2%
29	Kentucky	121,578	1.2%
30	Kansas	100,942	1.0%
31	Nevada	94,273	0.9%
32	Mississippi	91,692	0.9%
33	Utah	91,300	0.9%
34	Connecticut	86,994	0.9%
35	New Mexico	86,754	0.9%
36	Iowa	77,951	0.8%
37	Nebraska	55,932	0.5%
38	West Virginia	49,747	0.5%
39	Hawaii	46,147	0.5%
40	Delaware	35,659	0.3%
41	Maine	34,992	0.3%
42	Idaho	34,969	0.3%
43	New Hampshire	33,174	0.3%
44	Rhode Island	29,668	0.3%
45	Montana	28,706	0.3%
46	Alaska	24,449	0.2%
47	South Dakota	19,850	0.2%
48	Vermont	15,909	0.2%
49	North Dakota	15,775	0.2%
50	Wyoming	14,383	0.1%
	District of Columbia	38,600	0.4%

Source: CQ Press using reported data from the Federal Bureau of Investigation
"Crime in the United States 2012" (Uniform Crime Reports, September 16, 2013, http://www.fbi.gov/about-us/cjis/ucr/)
*Includes murder, rape, robbery, aggravated assault, burglary, larceny-theft, and motor vehicle theft.

Crime Rate in 2012

National Rate = 3,246.1 Crimes per 100,000 Population*

ALPHA ORDER				RANK ORDER		
RANK	STATE	RATE		RANK	STATE	RATE
8	Alabama	3,952.1		1	South Carolina	4,381.0
21	Alaska	3,342.6		2	New Mexico	4,159.8
6	Arizona	3,968.1		3	Arkansas	4,129.2
3	Arkansas	4,129.2		4	Louisiana	4,037.5
25	California	3,181.8		5	Tennessee	4,015.0
28	Colorado	2,993.6		6	Arizona	3,968.1
44	Connecticut	2,423.0		7	Washington	3,954.2
9	Delaware	3,888.3		8	Alabama	3,952.1
14	Florida	3,763.8		9	Delaware	3,888.3
11	Georgia	3,789.5		10	Oklahoma	3,870.3
22	Hawaii	3,314.4		11	Georgia	3,789.5
50	Idaho	2,191.4		12	Texas	3,770.4
29	Illinois	2,993.5		13	Missouri	3,765.3
20	Indiana	3,374.9		14	Florida	3,763.8
40	Iowa	2,535.7		15	North Carolina	3,722.9
16	Kansas	3,497.8		16	Kansas	3,497.8
34	Kentucky	2,775.5		17	Oregon	3,471.8
4	Louisiana	4,037.5		18	Ohio	3,417.1
37	Maine	2,632.6		19	Nevada	3,417.0
23	Maryland	3,230.3		20	Indiana	3,374.9
38	Massachusetts	2,558.5		21	Alaska	3,342.6
30	Michigan	2,985.0		22	Hawaii	3,314.4
33	Minnesota	2,799.2		23	Maryland	3,230.3
26	Mississippi	3,071.8		24	Utah	3,197.6
13	Missouri	3,765.3		25	California	3,181.8
31	Montana	2,855.9		26	Mississippi	3,071.8
27	Nebraska	3,014.3		27	Nebraska	3,014.3
19	Nevada	3,417.0		28	Colorado	2,993.6
42	New Hampshire	2,511.9		29	Illinois	2,993.5
47	New Jersey	2,337.5		30	Michigan	2,985.0
2	New Mexico	4,159.8		31	Montana	2,855.9
48	New York	2,328.8		32	Rhode Island	2,824.7
15	North Carolina	3,722.9		33	Minnesota	2,799.2
49	North Dakota	2,254.8		34	Kentucky	2,775.5
18	Ohio	3,417.1		35	Wisconsin	2,734.3
10	Oklahoma	3,870.3		36	West Virginia	2,681.2
17	Oregon	3,471.8		37	Maine	2,632.6
41	Pennsylvania	2,515.0		38	Massachusetts	2,558.5
32	Rhode Island	2,824.7		39	Vermont	2,541.3
1	South Carolina	4,381.0		40	Iowa	2,535.7
45	South Dakota	2,381.9		41	Pennsylvania	2,515.0
5	Tennessee	4,015.0		42	New Hampshire	2,511.9
12	Texas	3,770.4		43	Wyoming	2,495.2
24	Utah	3,197.6		44	Connecticut	2,423.0
39	Vermont	2,541.3		45	South Dakota	2,381.9
46	Virginia	2,352.2		46	Virginia	2,352.2
7	Washington	3,954.2		47	New Jersey	2,337.5
36	West Virginia	2,681.2		48	New York	2,328.8
35	Wisconsin	2,734.3		49	North Dakota	2,254.8
43	Wyoming	2,495.2		50	Idaho	2,191.4
					District of Columbia	6,104.5

Source: CQ Press using reported data from the Federal Bureau of Investigation
    "Crime in the United States 2012" (Uniform Crime Reports, September 16, 2013, http://www.fbi.gov/about-us/cjis/ucr/)
*Includes murder, rape, robbery, aggravated assault, burglary, larceny-theft, and motor vehicle theft.

Percent Change in Crime Rate: 2011 to 2012

National Percent Change = 1.4% Decrease*

ALPHA ORDER			RANK ORDER		
RANK	STATE	PERCENT CHANGE	RANK	STATE	PERCENT CHANGE
26	Alabama	(1.8)	1	South Dakota	12.7
6	Alaska	2.9	2	West Virginia	11.7
20	Arizona	0.0	3	Nevada	8.7
27	Arkansas	(2.6)	4	Montana	7.0
5	California	6.2	5	California	6.2
6	Colorado	2.9	6	Alaska	2.9
23	Connecticut	(0.2)	6	Colorado	2.9
28	Delaware	(2.7)	8	North Dakota	2.7
49	Florida	(6.7)	9	Oregon	2.1
46	Georgia	(5.6)	9	Washington	2.1
36	Hawaii	(3.5)	11	Kansas	1.6
39	Idaho	(3.8)	12	Wisconsin	1.3
36	Illinois	(3.5)	13	New Mexico	1.2
35	Indiana	(3.4)	14	New York	1.1
29	Iowa	(2.8)	14	Oklahoma	1.1
11	Kansas	1.6	16	Minnesota	0.8
47	Kentucky	(6.4)	17	Utah	0.4
42	Louisiana	(4.7)	18	Wyoming	0.2
25	Maine	(1.4)	19	Missouri	0.1
38	Maryland	(3.6)	20	Arizona	0.0
41	Massachusetts	(4.5)	21	Michigan	(0.1)
21	Michigan	(0.1)	21	Nebraska	(0.1)
16	Minnesota	0.8	23	Connecticut	(0.2)
48	Mississippi	(6.5)	24	Vermont	(0.5)
19	Missouri	0.1	25	Maine	(1.4)
4	Montana	7.0	26	Alabama	(1.8)
21	Nebraska	(0.1)	27	Arkansas	(2.6)
3	Nevada	8.7	28	Delaware	(2.7)
50	New Hampshire	(7.1)	29	Iowa	(2.8)
43	New Jersey	(4.8)	29	Pennsylvania	(2.8)
13	New Mexico	1.2	31	Rhode Island	(2.9)
14	New York	1.1	32	South Carolina	(3.0)
34	North Carolina	(3.2)	33	Texas	(3.1)
8	North Dakota	2.7	34	North Carolina	(3.2)
45	Ohio	(5.2)	35	Indiana	(3.4)
14	Oklahoma	1.1	36	Hawaii	(3.5)
9	Oregon	2.1	36	Illinois	(3.5)
29	Pennsylvania	(2.8)	38	Maryland	(3.6)
31	Rhode Island	(2.9)	39	Idaho	(3.8)
32	South Carolina	(3.0)	40	Virginia	(4.2)
1	South Dakota	12.7	41	Massachusetts	(4.5)
43	Tennessee	(4.8)	42	Louisiana	(4.7)
33	Texas	(3.1)	43	New Jersey	(4.8)
17	Utah	0.4	43	Tennessee	(4.8)
24	Vermont	(0.5)	45	Ohio	(5.2)
40	Virginia	(4.2)	46	Georgia	(5.6)
9	Washington	2.1	47	Kentucky	(6.4)
2	West Virginia	11.7	48	Mississippi	(6.5)
12	Wisconsin	1.3	49	Florida	(6.7)
18	Wyoming	0.2	50	New Hampshire	(7.1)
				District of Columbia	1.9

Source: CQ Press using reported data from the Federal Bureau of Investigation

"Crime in the United States 2012" (Uniform Crime Reports, September 16, 2013, http://www.fbi.gov/about-us/cjis/ucr/)

*Includes murder, rape, robbery, aggravated assault, burglary, larceny-theft, and motor vehicle theft.

Violent Crimes in 2012

National Total = 1,214,464 Violent Crimes*

RANK	STATE	CRIMES	% of USA
20	Alabama	21,693	1.8%
40	Alaska	4,412	0.4%
12	Arizona	28,108	2.3%
27	Arkansas	13,835	1.1%
1	California	160,944	13.3%
25	Colorado	16,023	1.3%
31	Connecticut	10,160	0.8%
38	Delaware	5,020	0.4%
3	Florida	94,087	7.7%
9	Georgia	37,591	3.1%
41	Hawaii	3,330	0.3%
42	Idaho	3,318	0.3%
5	Illinois	53,403	4.4%
19	Indiana	22,602	1.9%
34	Iowa	8,112	0.7%
30	Kansas	10,232	0.8%
32	Kentucky	9,752	0.8%
18	Louisiana	22,868	1.9%
48	Maine	1,631	0.1%
13	Maryland	28,055	2.3%
15	Massachusetts	26,953	2.2%
6	Michigan	44,922	3.7%
28	Minnesota	12,419	1.0%
35	Mississippi	7,786	0.6%
14	Missouri	27,155	2.2%
43	Montana	2,736	0.2%
39	Nebraska	4,814	0.4%
23	Nevada	16,763	1.4%
46	New Hampshire	2,481	0.2%
17	New Jersey	25,727	2.1%
29	New Mexico	11,660	1.0%
4	New York	79,610	6.6%
11	North Carolina	34,464	2.8%
47	North Dakota	1,712	0.1%
10	Ohio	34,595	2.8%
22	Oklahoma	17,902	1.5%
33	Oregon	9,653	0.8%
7	Pennsylvania	44,503	3.7%
45	Rhode Island	2,651	0.2%
16	South Carolina	26,397	2.2%
44	South Dakota	2,682	0.2%
8	Tennessee	41,550	3.4%
2	Texas	106,476	8.8%
36	Utah	5,876	0.5%
50	Vermont	893	0.1%
26	Virginia	15,564	1.3%
21	Washington	20,386	1.7%
37	West Virginia	5,869	0.5%
24	Wisconsin	16,064	1.3%
49	Wyoming	1,161	0.1%

RANK	STATE	CRIMES	% of USA
1	California	160,944	13.3%
2	Texas	106,476	8.8%
3	Florida	94,087	7.7%
4	New York	79,610	6.6%
5	Illinois	53,403	4.4%
6	Michigan	44,922	3.7%
7	Pennsylvania	44,503	3.7%
8	Tennessee	41,550	3.4%
9	Georgia	37,591	3.1%
10	Ohio	34,595	2.8%
11	North Carolina	34,464	2.8%
12	Arizona	28,108	2.3%
13	Maryland	28,055	2.3%
14	Missouri	27,155	2.2%
15	Massachusetts	26,953	2.2%
16	South Carolina	26,397	2.2%
17	New Jersey	25,727	2.1%
18	Louisiana	22,868	1.9%
19	Indiana	22,602	1.9%
20	Alabama	21,693	1.8%
21	Washington	20,386	1.7%
22	Oklahoma	17,902	1.5%
23	Nevada	16,763	1.4%
24	Wisconsin	16,064	1.3%
25	Colorado	16,023	1.3%
26	Virginia	15,564	1.3%
27	Arkansas	13,835	1.1%
28	Minnesota	12,419	1.0%
29	New Mexico	11,660	1.0%
30	Kansas	10,232	0.8%
31	Connecticut	10,160	0.8%
32	Kentucky	9,752	0.8%
33	Oregon	9,653	0.8%
34	Iowa	8,112	0.7%
35	Mississippi	7,786	0.6%
36	Utah	5,876	0.5%
37	West Virginia	5,869	0.5%
38	Delaware	5,020	0.4%
39	Nebraska	4,814	0.4%
40	Alaska	4,412	0.4%
41	Hawaii	3,330	0.3%
42	Idaho	3,318	0.3%
43	Montana	2,736	0.2%
44	South Dakota	2,682	0.2%
45	Rhode Island	2,651	0.2%
46	New Hampshire	2,481	0.2%
47	North Dakota	1,712	0.1%
48	Maine	1,631	0.1%
49	Wyoming	1,161	0.1%
50	Vermont	893	0.1%
	District of Columbia	7,864	0.6%

Source: Reported data from the Federal Bureau of Investigation
   "Crime in the United States 2012" (Uniform Crime Reports, September 16, 2013, http://www.fbi.gov/about-us/cjis/ucr/)
*Violent crimes are offenses of murder, forcible rape, robbery, and aggravated assault.

Violent Crime Rate in 2012

National Rate = 386.9 Violent Crimes per 100,000 Population*

ALPHA ORDER				RANK ORDER		
RANK	STATE	RATE		RANK	STATE	RATE
14	Alabama	449.9		1	Tennessee	643.6
3	Alaska	603.2		2	Nevada	607.6
15	Arizona	428.9		3	Alaska	603.2
11	Arkansas	469.1		4	New Mexico	559.1
16	California	423.1		5	South Carolina	558.8
28	Colorado	308.9		6	Delaware	547.4
32	Connecticut	283.0		7	Louisiana	496.9
6	Delaware	547.4		8	Florida	487.1
8	Florida	487.1		9	Maryland	476.8
21	Georgia	378.9		10	Oklahoma	469.3
41	Hawaii	239.2		11	Arkansas	469.1
44	Idaho	207.9		12	Michigan	454.5
17	Illinois	414.8		13	Missouri	450.9
25	Indiana	345.7		14	Alabama	449.9
35	Iowa	263.9		15	Arizona	428.9
22	Kansas	354.6		16	California	423.1
43	Kentucky	222.6		17	Illinois	414.8
7	Louisiana	496.9		18	Texas	408.6
50	Maine	122.7		19	New York	406.8
9	Maryland	476.8		20	Massachusetts	405.5
20	Massachusetts	405.5		21	Georgia	378.9
12	Michigan	454.5		22	Kansas	354.6
42	Minnesota	230.9		23	North Carolina	353.4
36	Mississippi	260.8		24	Pennsylvania	348.7
13	Missouri	450.9		25	Indiana	345.7
34	Montana	272.2		26	South Dakota	321.8
37	Nebraska	259.4		27	West Virginia	316.3
2	Nevada	607.6		28	Colorado	308.9
48	New Hampshire	187.9		29	Ohio	299.7
31	New Jersey	290.2		30	Washington	295.6
4	New Mexico	559.1		31	New Jersey	290.2
19	New York	406.8		32	Connecticut	283.0
23	North Carolina	353.4		33	Wisconsin	280.5
40	North Dakota	244.7		34	Montana	272.2
29	Ohio	299.7		35	Iowa	263.9
10	Oklahoma	469.3		36	Mississippi	260.8
39	Oregon	247.6		37	Nebraska	259.4
24	Pennsylvania	348.7		38	Rhode Island	252.4
38	Rhode Island	252.4		39	Oregon	247.6
5	South Carolina	558.8		40	North Dakota	244.7
26	South Dakota	321.8		41	Hawaii	239.2
1	Tennessee	643.6		42	Minnesota	230.9
18	Texas	408.6		43	Kentucky	222.6
45	Utah	205.8		44	Idaho	207.9
49	Vermont	142.6		45	Utah	205.8
47	Virginia	190.1		46	Wyoming	201.4
30	Washington	295.6		47	Virginia	190.1
27	West Virginia	316.3		48	New Hampshire	187.9
33	Wisconsin	280.5		49	Vermont	142.6
46	Wyoming	201.4		50	Maine	122.7
					District of Columbia	1,243.7

Source: Reported data from the Federal Bureau of Investigation
   "Crime in the United States 2012" (Uniform Crime Reports, September 16, 2013, http://www.fbi.gov/about-us/cjis/ucr/)
*Violent crimes are offenses of murder, forcible rape, robbery, and aggravated assault.

Percent Change in Violent Crime Rate: 2011 to 2012

National Percent Change = 0.0% Change*

<table>
<tr><td colspan="3">ALPHA ORDER</td><td colspan="3">RANK ORDER</td></tr>
<tr><td>RANK</td><td>STATE</td><td>PERCENT CHANGE</td><td>RANK</td><td>STATE</td><td>PERCENT CHANGE</td></tr>
<tr><td>3</td><td>Alabama</td><td>7.2</td><td>1</td><td>South Dakota</td><td>25.9</td></tr>
<tr><td>28</td><td>Alaska</td><td>(1.1)</td><td>2</td><td>Wisconsin</td><td>12.3</td></tr>
<tr><td>9</td><td>Arizona</td><td>3.5</td><td>3</td><td>Alabama</td><td>7.2</td></tr>
<tr><td>35</td><td>Arkansas</td><td>(2.7)</td><td>4</td><td>Nevada</td><td>7.0</td></tr>
<tr><td>10</td><td>California</td><td>2.9</td><td>5</td><td>West Virginia</td><td>6.7</td></tr>
<tr><td>31</td><td>Colorado</td><td>(1.8)</td><td>6</td><td>Tennessee</td><td>5.9</td></tr>
<tr><td>13</td><td>Connecticut</td><td>2.6</td><td>7</td><td>Utah</td><td>4.4</td></tr>
<tr><td>37</td><td>Delaware</td><td>(3.4)</td><td>8</td><td>Indiana</td><td>4.2</td></tr>
<tr><td>44</td><td>Florida</td><td>(5.4)</td><td>9</td><td>Arizona</td><td>3.5</td></tr>
<tr><td>20</td><td>Georgia</td><td>1.1</td><td>10</td><td>California</td><td>2.9</td></tr>
<tr><td>42</td><td>Hawaii</td><td>(4.9)</td><td>11</td><td>Idaho</td><td>2.8</td></tr>
<tr><td>11</td><td>Idaho</td><td>2.8</td><td>12</td><td>Michigan</td><td>2.7</td></tr>
<tr><td>33</td><td>Illinois</td><td>(2.2)</td><td>13</td><td>Connecticut</td><td>2.6</td></tr>
<tr><td>8</td><td>Indiana</td><td>4.2</td><td>13</td><td>Iowa</td><td>2.6</td></tr>
<tr><td>13</td><td>Iowa</td><td>2.6</td><td>13</td><td>Oklahoma</td><td>2.6</td></tr>
<tr><td>25</td><td>Kansas</td><td>(0.3)</td><td>16</td><td>Rhode Island</td><td>2.5</td></tr>
<tr><td>47</td><td>Kentucky</td><td>(7.1)</td><td>17</td><td>New York</td><td>2.4</td></tr>
<tr><td>49</td><td>Louisiana</td><td>(10.4)</td><td>18</td><td>Nebraska</td><td>2.3</td></tr>
<tr><td>26</td><td>Maine</td><td>(0.5)</td><td>19</td><td>North Carolina</td><td>2.1</td></tr>
<tr><td>37</td><td>Maryland</td><td>(3.4)</td><td>20</td><td>Georgia</td><td>1.1</td></tr>
<tr><td>43</td><td>Massachusetts</td><td>(5.1)</td><td>21</td><td>Missouri</td><td>0.8</td></tr>
<tr><td>12</td><td>Michigan</td><td>2.7</td><td>22</td><td>Minnesota</td><td>0.2</td></tr>
<tr><td>22</td><td>Minnesota</td><td>0.2</td><td>23</td><td>Washington</td><td>0.1</td></tr>
<tr><td>36</td><td>Mississippi</td><td>(3.0)</td><td>24</td><td>Texas</td><td>0.0</td></tr>
<tr><td>21</td><td>Missouri</td><td>0.8</td><td>25</td><td>Kansas</td><td>(0.3)</td></tr>
<tr><td>29</td><td>Montana</td><td>(1.4)</td><td>26</td><td>Maine</td><td>(0.5)</td></tr>
<tr><td>18</td><td>Nebraska</td><td>2.3</td><td>27</td><td>Oregon</td><td>(0.7)</td></tr>
<tr><td>4</td><td>Nevada</td><td>7.0</td><td>28</td><td>Alaska</td><td>(1.1)</td></tr>
<tr><td>50</td><td>New Hampshire</td><td>(13.6)</td><td>29</td><td>Montana</td><td>(1.4)</td></tr>
<tr><td>45</td><td>New Jersey</td><td>(5.7)</td><td>29</td><td>North Dakota</td><td>(1.4)</td></tr>
<tr><td>34</td><td>New Mexico</td><td>(2.4)</td><td>31</td><td>Colorado</td><td>(1.8)</td></tr>
<tr><td>17</td><td>New York</td><td>2.4</td><td>31</td><td>Ohio</td><td>(1.8)</td></tr>
<tr><td>19</td><td>North Carolina</td><td>2.1</td><td>33</td><td>Illinois</td><td>(2.2)</td></tr>
<tr><td>29</td><td>North Dakota</td><td>(1.4)</td><td>34</td><td>New Mexico</td><td>(2.4)</td></tr>
<tr><td>31</td><td>Ohio</td><td>(1.8)</td><td>35</td><td>Arkansas</td><td>(2.7)</td></tr>
<tr><td>13</td><td>Oklahoma</td><td>2.6</td><td>36</td><td>Mississippi</td><td>(3.0)</td></tr>
<tr><td>27</td><td>Oregon</td><td>(0.7)</td><td>37</td><td>Delaware</td><td>(3.4)</td></tr>
<tr><td>40</td><td>Pennsylvania</td><td>(3.8)</td><td>37</td><td>Maryland</td><td>(3.4)</td></tr>
<tr><td>16</td><td>Rhode Island</td><td>2.5</td><td>37</td><td>Vermont</td><td>(3.4)</td></tr>
<tr><td>46</td><td>South Carolina</td><td>(6.4)</td><td>40</td><td>Pennsylvania</td><td>(3.8)</td></tr>
<tr><td>1</td><td>South Dakota</td><td>25.9</td><td>40</td><td>Virginia</td><td>(3.8)</td></tr>
<tr><td>6</td><td>Tennessee</td><td>5.9</td><td>42</td><td>Hawaii</td><td>(4.9)</td></tr>
<tr><td>24</td><td>Texas</td><td>0.0</td><td>43</td><td>Massachusetts</td><td>(5.1)</td></tr>
<tr><td>7</td><td>Utah</td><td>4.4</td><td>44</td><td>Florida</td><td>(5.4)</td></tr>
<tr><td>37</td><td>Vermont</td><td>(3.4)</td><td>45</td><td>New Jersey</td><td>(5.7)</td></tr>
<tr><td>40</td><td>Virginia</td><td>(3.8)</td><td>46</td><td>South Carolina</td><td>(6.4)</td></tr>
<tr><td>23</td><td>Washington</td><td>0.1</td><td>47</td><td>Kentucky</td><td>(7.1)</td></tr>
<tr><td>5</td><td>West Virginia</td><td>6.7</td><td>48</td><td>Wyoming</td><td>(8.2)</td></tr>
<tr><td>2</td><td>Wisconsin</td><td>12.3</td><td>49</td><td>Louisiana</td><td>(10.4)</td></tr>
<tr><td>48</td><td>Wyoming</td><td>(8.2)</td><td>50</td><td>New Hampshire</td><td>(13.6)</td></tr>
<tr><td></td><td></td><td></td><td></td><td>District of Columbia</td><td>3.6</td></tr>
</table>

Source: Reported data from the Federal Bureau of Investigation
  "Crime in the United States 2012" (Uniform Crime Reports, September 16, 2013, http://www.fbi.gov/about-us/cjis/ucr/)
*Violent crimes are offenses of murder, forcible rape, robbery, and aggravated assault.

Murders in 2012

National Total = 14,827 Murders*

ALPHA ORDER

RANK	STATE	MURDERS	% of USA
17	Alabama	342	2.3%
41	Alaska	30	0.2%
16	Arizona	358	2.4%
25	Arkansas	173	1.2%
1	California	1,884	12.7%
27	Colorado	162	1.1%
28	Connecticut	146	1.0%
36	Delaware	57	0.4%
3	Florida	1,009	6.8%
8	Georgia	581	3.9%
42	Hawaii	29	0.2%
42	Idaho	29	0.2%
4	Illinois	744	5.0%
20	Indiana	310	2.1%
39	Iowa	45	0.3%
34	Kansas	84	0.6%
24	Kentucky	195	1.3%
9	Louisiana	495	3.3%
46	Maine	25	0.2%
15	Maryland	369	2.5%
30	Massachusetts	121	0.8%
5	Michigan	689	4.6%
32	Minnesota	99	0.7%
21	Mississippi	220	1.5%
12	Missouri	389	2.6%
45	Montana	27	0.2%
37	Nebraska	53	0.4%
29	Nevada	124	0.8%
48	New Hampshire	15	0.1%
13	New Jersey	388	2.6%
31	New Mexico	116	0.8%
7	New York	684	4.6%
11	North Carolina	479	3.2%
44	North Dakota	28	0.2%
9	Ohio	495	3.3%
22	Oklahoma	216	1.5%
33	Oregon	92	0.6%
6	Pennsylvania	685	4.6%
40	Rhode Island	34	0.2%
18	South Carolina	324	2.2%
46	South Dakota	25	0.2%
13	Tennessee	388	2.6%
2	Texas	1,144	7.7%
38	Utah	50	0.3%
50	Vermont	8	0.1%
19	Virginia	314	2.1%
23	Washington	206	1.4%
35	West Virginia	72	0.5%
25	Wisconsin	173	1.2%
49	Wyoming	14	0.1%

RANK ORDER

RANK	STATE	MURDERS	% of USA
1	California	1,884	12.7%
2	Texas	1,144	7.7%
3	Florida	1,009	6.8%
4	Illinois	744	5.0%
5	Michigan	689	4.6%
6	Pennsylvania	685	4.6%
7	New York	684	4.6%
8	Georgia	581	3.9%
9	Louisiana	495	3.3%
9	Ohio	495	3.3%
11	North Carolina	479	3.2%
12	Missouri	389	2.6%
13	New Jersey	388	2.6%
13	Tennessee	388	2.6%
15	Maryland	369	2.5%
16	Arizona	358	2.4%
17	Alabama	342	2.3%
18	South Carolina	324	2.2%
19	Virginia	314	2.1%
20	Indiana	310	2.1%
21	Mississippi	220	1.5%
22	Oklahoma	216	1.5%
23	Washington	206	1.4%
24	Kentucky	195	1.3%
25	Arkansas	173	1.2%
25	Wisconsin	173	1.2%
27	Colorado	162	1.1%
28	Connecticut	146	1.0%
29	Nevada	124	0.8%
30	Massachusetts	121	0.8%
31	New Mexico	116	0.8%
32	Minnesota	99	0.7%
33	Oregon	92	0.6%
34	Kansas	84	0.6%
35	West Virginia	72	0.5%
36	Delaware	57	0.4%
37	Nebraska	53	0.4%
38	Utah	50	0.3%
39	Iowa	45	0.3%
40	Rhode Island	34	0.2%
41	Alaska	30	0.2%
42	Hawaii	29	0.2%
42	Idaho	29	0.2%
44	North Dakota	28	0.2%
45	Montana	27	0.2%
46	Maine	25	0.2%
46	South Dakota	25	0.2%
48	New Hampshire	15	0.1%
49	Wyoming	14	0.1%
50	Vermont	8	0.1%
	District of Columbia	88	0.6%

Source: Reported data from the Federal Bureau of Investigation
"Crime in the United States 2012" (Uniform Crime Reports, September 16, 2013, http://www.fbi.gov/about-us/cjis/ucr/)
*Includes nonnegligent manslaughter.

Murder Rate in 2012

National Rate = 4.7 Murders per 100,000 Population*

ALPHA ORDER				RANK ORDER		
RANK	STATE	RATE		RANK	STATE	RATE
3	Alabama	7.1		1	Louisiana	10.8
26	Alaska	4.1		2	Mississippi	7.4
15	Arizona	5.5		3	Alabama	7.1
10	Arkansas	5.9		4	Michigan	7.0
18	California	5.0		5	South Carolina	6.9
33	Colorado	3.1		6	Missouri	6.5
26	Connecticut	4.1		7	Maryland	6.3
8	Delaware	6.2		8	Delaware	6.2
17	Florida	5.2		9	Tennessee	6.0
10	Georgia	5.9		10	Arkansas	5.9
42	Hawaii	2.1		10	Georgia	5.9
44	Idaho	1.8		12	Illinois	5.8
12	Illinois	5.8		13	Oklahoma	5.7
20	Indiana	4.7		14	New Mexico	5.6
48	Iowa	1.5		15	Arizona	5.5
37	Kansas	2.9		16	Pennsylvania	5.4
21	Kentucky	4.5		17	Florida	5.2
1	Louisiana	10.8		18	California	5.0
43	Maine	1.9		19	North Carolina	4.9
7	Maryland	6.3		20	Indiana	4.7
44	Massachusetts	1.8		21	Kentucky	4.5
4	Michigan	7.0		21	Nevada	4.5
44	Minnesota	1.8		23	New Jersey	4.4
2	Mississippi	7.4		23	Texas	4.4
6	Missouri	6.5		25	Ohio	4.3
39	Montana	2.7		26	Alaska	4.1
37	Nebraska	2.9		26	Connecticut	4.1
21	Nevada	4.5		28	North Dakota	4.0
50	New Hampshire	1.1		29	West Virginia	3.9
23	New Jersey	4.4		30	Virginia	3.8
14	New Mexico	5.6		31	New York	3.5
31	New York	3.5		32	Rhode Island	3.2
19	North Carolina	4.9		33	Colorado	3.1
28	North Dakota	4.0		34	South Dakota	3.0
25	Ohio	4.3		34	Washington	3.0
13	Oklahoma	5.7		34	Wisconsin	3.0
40	Oregon	2.4		37	Kansas	2.9
16	Pennsylvania	5.4		37	Nebraska	2.9
32	Rhode Island	3.2		39	Montana	2.7
5	South Carolina	6.9		40	Oregon	2.4
34	South Dakota	3.0		40	Wyoming	2.4
9	Tennessee	6.0		42	Hawaii	2.1
23	Texas	4.4		43	Maine	1.9
44	Utah	1.8		44	Idaho	1.8
49	Vermont	1.3		44	Massachusetts	1.8
30	Virginia	3.8		44	Minnesota	1.8
34	Washington	3.0		44	Utah	1.8
29	West Virginia	3.9		48	Iowa	1.5
34	Wisconsin	3.0		49	Vermont	1.3
40	Wyoming	2.4		50	New Hampshire	1.1
					District of Columbia	13.9

Source: Reported data from the Federal Bureau of Investigation
   "Crime in the United States 2012" (Uniform Crime Reports, September 16, 2013, http://www.fbi.gov/about-us/cjis/ucr/)
*Includes nonnegligent manslaughter.

Percent of Murders Involving Firearms in 2012

National Percent = 69.3% of Murders*

<table>
<tr><td colspan="3">ALPHA ORDER</td><td colspan="3">RANK ORDER</td></tr>
<tr><td>RANK</td><td>STATE</td><td>PERCENT</td><td>RANK</td><td>STATE</td><td>PERCENT</td></tr>
<tr><td>NA</td><td>Alabama**</td><td>NA</td><td>1</td><td>Illinois*</td><td>86.2</td></tr>
<tr><td>43</td><td>Alaska</td><td>37.9</td><td>2</td><td>Louisiana</td><td>81.3</td></tr>
<tr><td>20</td><td>Arizona</td><td>65.7</td><td>3</td><td>Nebraska</td><td>80.8</td></tr>
<tr><td>25</td><td>Arkansas</td><td>65.1</td><td>4</td><td>Michigan</td><td>78.6</td></tr>
<tr><td>18</td><td>California</td><td>69.4</td><td>5</td><td>Connecticut</td><td>76.7</td></tr>
<tr><td>35</td><td>Colorado</td><td>57.5</td><td>6</td><td>Pennsylvania</td><td>76.3</td></tr>
<tr><td>5</td><td>Connecticut</td><td>76.7</td><td>7</td><td>Maryland</td><td>75.9</td></tr>
<tr><td>13</td><td>Delaware</td><td>71.9</td><td>7</td><td>Mississippi</td><td>75.9</td></tr>
<tr><td>NA</td><td>Florida**</td><td>NA</td><td>9</td><td>Indiana</td><td>74.5</td></tr>
<tr><td>12</td><td>Georgia</td><td>72.1</td><td>10</td><td>South Carolina</td><td>73.1</td></tr>
<tr><td>NA</td><td>Hawaii**</td><td>NA</td><td>11</td><td>Missouri</td><td>72.8</td></tr>
<tr><td>23</td><td>Idaho</td><td>65.4</td><td>12</td><td>Georgia</td><td>72.1</td></tr>
<tr><td>1</td><td>Illinois*</td><td>86.2</td><td>13</td><td>Delaware</td><td>71.9</td></tr>
<tr><td>9</td><td>Indiana</td><td>74.5</td><td>14</td><td>West Virginia</td><td>71.2</td></tr>
<tr><td>36</td><td>Iowa</td><td>56.8</td><td>15</td><td>New Jersey</td><td>70.9</td></tr>
<tr><td>32</td><td>Kansas</td><td>59.5</td><td>16</td><td>Oklahoma</td><td>70.3</td></tr>
<tr><td>28</td><td>Kentucky</td><td>63.5</td><td>17</td><td>Virginia</td><td>70.1</td></tr>
<tr><td>2</td><td>Louisiana</td><td>81.3</td><td>18</td><td>California</td><td>69.4</td></tr>
<tr><td>37</td><td>Maine</td><td>56.0</td><td>19</td><td>Ohio</td><td>67.8</td></tr>
<tr><td>7</td><td>Maryland</td><td>75.9</td><td>20</td><td>Arizona</td><td>65.7</td></tr>
<tr><td>34</td><td>Massachusetts</td><td>57.9</td><td>20</td><td>North Carolina</td><td>65.7</td></tr>
<tr><td>4</td><td>Michigan</td><td>78.6</td><td>22</td><td>Tennessee</td><td>65.6</td></tr>
<tr><td>42</td><td>Minnesota</td><td>46.1</td><td>23</td><td>Idaho</td><td>65.4</td></tr>
<tr><td>7</td><td>Mississippi</td><td>75.9</td><td>24</td><td>Texas</td><td>65.3</td></tr>
<tr><td>11</td><td>Missouri</td><td>72.8</td><td>25</td><td>Arkansas</td><td>65.1</td></tr>
<tr><td>41</td><td>Montana</td><td>50.0</td><td>26</td><td>New Hampshire</td><td>64.3</td></tr>
<tr><td>3</td><td>Nebraska</td><td>80.8</td><td>27</td><td>Wisconsin</td><td>63.9</td></tr>
<tr><td>30</td><td>Nevada</td><td>60.3</td><td>28</td><td>Kentucky</td><td>63.5</td></tr>
<tr><td>26</td><td>New Hampshire</td><td>64.3</td><td>29</td><td>New Mexico</td><td>61.5</td></tr>
<tr><td>15</td><td>New Jersey</td><td>70.9</td><td>30</td><td>Nevada</td><td>60.3</td></tr>
<tr><td>29</td><td>New Mexico</td><td>61.5</td><td>31</td><td>New York</td><td>59.7</td></tr>
<tr><td>31</td><td>New York</td><td>59.7</td><td>32</td><td>Kansas</td><td>59.5</td></tr>
<tr><td>20</td><td>North Carolina</td><td>65.7</td><td>33</td><td>Utah</td><td>59.2</td></tr>
<tr><td>46</td><td>North Dakota</td><td>25.0</td><td>34</td><td>Massachusetts</td><td>57.9</td></tr>
<tr><td>19</td><td>Ohio</td><td>67.8</td><td>35</td><td>Colorado</td><td>57.5</td></tr>
<tr><td>16</td><td>Oklahoma</td><td>70.3</td><td>36</td><td>Iowa</td><td>56.8</td></tr>
<tr><td>40</td><td>Oregon</td><td>51.9</td><td>37</td><td>Maine</td><td>56.0</td></tr>
<tr><td>6</td><td>Pennsylvania</td><td>76.3</td><td>38</td><td>Rhode Island</td><td>55.9</td></tr>
<tr><td>38</td><td>Rhode Island</td><td>55.9</td><td>39</td><td>Washington</td><td>54.6</td></tr>
<tr><td>10</td><td>South Carolina</td><td>73.1</td><td>40</td><td>Oregon</td><td>51.9</td></tr>
<tr><td>45</td><td>South Dakota</td><td>28.6</td><td>41</td><td>Montana</td><td>50.0</td></tr>
<tr><td>22</td><td>Tennessee</td><td>65.6</td><td>42</td><td>Minnesota</td><td>46.1</td></tr>
<tr><td>24</td><td>Texas</td><td>65.3</td><td>43</td><td>Alaska</td><td>37.9</td></tr>
<tr><td>33</td><td>Utah</td><td>59.2</td><td>44</td><td>Wyoming</td><td>35.7</td></tr>
<tr><td>46</td><td>Vermont</td><td>25.0</td><td>45</td><td>South Dakota</td><td>28.6</td></tr>
<tr><td>17</td><td>Virginia</td><td>70.1</td><td>46</td><td>North Dakota</td><td>25.0</td></tr>
<tr><td>39</td><td>Washington</td><td>54.6</td><td>46</td><td>Vermont</td><td>25.0</td></tr>
<tr><td>14</td><td>West Virginia</td><td>71.2</td><td>NA</td><td>Alabama**</td><td>NA</td></tr>
<tr><td>27</td><td>Wisconsin</td><td>63.9</td><td>NA</td><td>Florida**</td><td>NA</td></tr>
<tr><td>44</td><td>Wyoming</td><td>35.7</td><td>NA</td><td>Hawaii**</td><td>NA</td></tr>
<tr><td></td><td></td><td></td><td></td><td>District of Columbia**</td><td>NA</td></tr>
</table>

Source: CQ Press using reported data from the Federal Bureau of Investigation
   "Crime in the United States 2012" (Uniform Crime Reports, September 16, 2013, http://www.fbi.gov/about-us/cjis/ucr/)
*Of the 12,711 murders in 2012 for which supplemental data were received by the F.B.I. There were an additional 2,116 murders
for which the type of murder weapon was not reported to the F.B.I. Includes nonnegligent manslaughter. National and state
percents based on reporting jurisdictions only. Illinois's percent is for Chicago and Rockford only.
**Not available.

Rapes in 2012

National Total = 84,376 Rapes*

RANK	STATE	RAPES	% of USA
22	Alabama	1,296	1.5%
39	Alaska	583	0.7%
9	Arizona	2,277	2.7%
24	Arkansas	1,247	1.5%
1	California	7,837	9.3%
12	Colorado	2,113	2.5%
34	Connecticut	919	1.1%
48	Delaware	243	0.3%
3	Florida	5,260	6.2%
11	Georgia	2,124	2.5%
46	Hawaii	285	0.3%
40	Idaho	479	0.6%
6	Illinois	3,570	4.2%
16	Indiana	1,667	2.0%
35	Iowa	871	1.0%
29	Kansas	1,053	1.2%
23	Kentucky	1,272	1.5%
27	Louisiana	1,158	1.4%
44	Maine	372	0.4%
25	Maryland	1,235	1.5%
17	Massachusetts	1,642	1.9%
4	Michigan	4,589	5.4%
18	Minnesota	1,638	1.9%
36	Mississippi	822	1.0%
20	Missouri	1,511	1.8%
43	Montana	379	0.4%
37	Nebraska	711	0.8%
33	Nevada	931	1.1%
41	New Hampshire	449	0.5%
30	New Jersey	1,035	1.2%
31	New Mexico	957	1.1%
8	New York	2,848	3.4%
14	North Carolina	1,984	2.4%
47	North Dakota	272	0.3%
5	Ohio	3,658	4.3%
19	Oklahoma	1,588	1.9%
28	Oregon	1,140	1.4%
7	Pennsylvania	3,327	3.9%
45	Rhode Island	288	0.3%
15	South Carolina	1,679	2.0%
38	South Dakota	585	0.7%
13	Tennessee	2,032	2.4%
2	Texas	7,711	9.1%
32	Utah	943	1.1%
50	Vermont	121	0.1%
21	Virginia	1,452	1.7%
10	Washington	2,193	2.6%
42	West Virginia	421	0.5%
26	Wisconsin	1,219	1.4%
49	Wyoming	154	0.2%

RANK	STATE	RAPES	% of USA
1	California	7,837	9.3%
2	Texas	7,711	9.1%
3	Florida	5,260	6.2%
4	Michigan	4,589	5.4%
5	Ohio	3,658	4.3%
6	Illinois	3,570	4.2%
7	Pennsylvania	3,327	3.9%
8	New York	2,848	3.4%
9	Arizona	2,277	2.7%
10	Washington	2,193	2.6%
11	Georgia	2,124	2.5%
12	Colorado	2,113	2.5%
13	Tennessee	2,032	2.4%
14	North Carolina	1,984	2.4%
15	South Carolina	1,679	2.0%
16	Indiana	1,667	2.0%
17	Massachusetts	1,642	1.9%
18	Minnesota	1,638	1.9%
19	Oklahoma	1,588	1.9%
20	Missouri	1,511	1.8%
21	Virginia	1,452	1.7%
22	Alabama	1,296	1.5%
23	Kentucky	1,272	1.5%
24	Arkansas	1,247	1.5%
25	Maryland	1,235	1.5%
26	Wisconsin	1,219	1.4%
27	Louisiana	1,158	1.4%
28	Oregon	1,140	1.4%
29	Kansas	1,053	1.2%
30	New Jersey	1,035	1.2%
31	New Mexico	957	1.1%
32	Utah	943	1.1%
33	Nevada	931	1.1%
34	Connecticut	919	1.1%
35	Iowa	871	1.0%
36	Mississippi	822	1.0%
37	Nebraska	711	0.8%
38	South Dakota	585	0.7%
39	Alaska	583	0.7%
40	Idaho	479	0.6%
41	New Hampshire	449	0.5%
42	West Virginia	421	0.5%
43	Montana	379	0.4%
44	Maine	372	0.4%
45	Rhode Island	288	0.3%
46	Hawaii	285	0.3%
47	North Dakota	272	0.3%
48	Delaware	243	0.3%
49	Wyoming	154	0.2%
50	Vermont	121	0.1%
	District of Columbia	236	0.3%

Source: Reported data from the Federal Bureau of Investigation
   "Crime in the United States 2012" (Uniform Crime Reports, September 16, 2013, http://www.fbi.gov/about-us/cjis/ucr/)
*Forcible rape is the carnal knowledge of a female forcibly and against her will. Assaults or attempts to commit rape by force or threat of force are included. However, statutory rape without force and other sex offenses are excluded.

Rape Rate in 2012

National Rate = 26.9 Rapes per 100,000 Population*

ALPHA ORDER

RANK	STATE	RATE
31	Alabama	26.9
1	Alaska	79.7
13	Arizona	34.7
5	Arkansas	42.3
44	California	20.6
7	Colorado	40.7
35	Connecticut	25.6
33	Delaware	26.5
30	Florida	27.2
41	Georgia	21.4
45	Hawaii	20.5
21	Idaho	30.0
27	Illinois	27.7
36	Indiana	25.5
25	Iowa	28.3
11	Kansas	36.5
24	Kentucky	29.0
37	Louisiana	25.2
26	Maine	28.0
43	Maryland	21.0
39	Massachusetts	24.7
3	Michigan	46.4
20	Minnesota	30.5
28	Mississippi	27.5
38	Missouri	25.1
10	Montana	37.7
9	Nebraska	38.3
15	Nevada	33.7
14	New Hampshire	34.0
50	New Jersey	11.7
4	New Mexico	45.9
49	New York	14.6
46	North Carolina	20.3
8	North Dakota	38.9
18	Ohio	31.7
6	Oklahoma	41.6
23	Oregon	29.2
34	Pennsylvania	26.1
29	Rhode Island	27.4
12	South Carolina	35.5
2	South Dakota	70.2
19	Tennessee	31.5
22	Texas	29.6
16	Utah	33.0
47	Vermont	19.3
48	Virginia	17.7
17	Washington	31.8
40	West Virginia	22.7
42	Wisconsin	21.3
32	Wyoming	26.7

RANK ORDER

RANK	STATE	RATE
1	Alaska	79.7
2	South Dakota	70.2
3	Michigan	46.4
4	New Mexico	45.9
5	Arkansas	42.3
6	Oklahoma	41.6
7	Colorado	40.7
8	North Dakota	38.9
9	Nebraska	38.3
10	Montana	37.7
11	Kansas	36.5
12	South Carolina	35.5
13	Arizona	34.7
14	New Hampshire	34.0
15	Nevada	33.7
16	Utah	33.0
17	Washington	31.8
18	Ohio	31.7
19	Tennessee	31.5
20	Minnesota	30.5
21	Idaho	30.0
22	Texas	29.6
23	Oregon	29.2
24	Kentucky	29.0
25	Iowa	28.3
26	Maine	28.0
27	Illinois	27.7
28	Mississippi	27.5
29	Rhode Island	27.4
30	Florida	27.2
31	Alabama	26.9
32	Wyoming	26.7
33	Delaware	26.5
34	Pennsylvania	26.1
35	Connecticut	25.6
36	Indiana	25.5
37	Louisiana	25.2
38	Missouri	25.1
39	Massachusetts	24.7
40	West Virginia	22.7
41	Georgia	21.4
42	Wisconsin	21.3
43	Maryland	21.0
44	California	20.6
45	Hawaii	20.5
46	North Carolina	20.3
47	Vermont	19.3
48	Virginia	17.7
49	New York	14.6
50	New Jersey	11.7

	District of Columbia	37.3

Source: Reported data from the Federal Bureau of Investigation
"Crime in the United States 2012" (Uniform Crime Reports, September 16, 2013, http://www.fbi.gov/about-us/cjis/ucr/)
*Forcible rape is the carnal knowledge of a female forcibly and against her will. Assaults or attempts to commit rape by force or threat of force are included. However, statutory rape without force and other sex offenses are excluded.

Robberies in 2012

National Total = 354,522 Robberies*

ALPHA ORDER					RANK ORDER			
RANK	STATE	ROBBERIES	% of USA		RANK	STATE	ROBBERIES	% of USA
20	Alabama	5,020	1.4%		1	California	56,521	15.9%
42	Alaska	630	0.2%		2	Texas	30,382	8.6%
14	Arizona	7,386	2.1%		3	New York	28,655	8.1%
31	Arkansas	2,320	0.7%		4	Florida	23,889	6.7%
1	California	56,521	15.9%		5	Illinois	19,471	5.5%
28	Colorado	3,395	1.0%		6	Pennsylvania	15,673	4.4%
25	Connecticut	3,687	1.0%		7	Ohio	15,235	4.3%
35	Delaware	1,492	0.4%		8	Georgia	12,463	3.5%
4	Florida	23,889	6.7%		9	New Jersey	11,385	3.2%
8	Georgia	12,463	3.5%		10	Michigan	10,434	2.9%
38	Hawaii	1,040	0.3%		11	Maryland	10,141	2.9%
45	Idaho	243	0.1%		12	North Carolina	9,392	2.6%
5	Illinois	19,471	5.5%		13	Tennessee	8,169	2.3%
15	Indiana	6,598	1.9%		14	Arizona	7,386	2.1%
39	Iowa	962	0.3%		15	Indiana	6,598	1.9%
34	Kansas	1,500	0.4%		16	Massachusetts	6,552	1.8%
26	Kentucky	3,535	1.0%		17	Missouri	5,782	1.6%
19	Louisiana	5,475	1.5%		18	Washington	5,745	1.6%
44	Maine	423	0.1%		19	Louisiana	5,475	1.5%
11	Maryland	10,141	2.9%		20	Alabama	5,020	1.4%
16	Massachusetts	6,552	1.8%		21	Nevada	4,918	1.4%
10	Michigan	10,434	2.9%		22	Virginia	4,706	1.3%
27	Minnesota	3,475	1.0%		23	Wisconsin	4,622	1.3%
32	Mississippi	2,284	0.6%		24	South Carolina	4,489	1.3%
17	Missouri	5,782	1.6%		25	Connecticut	3,687	1.0%
46	Montana	191	0.1%		26	Kentucky	3,535	1.0%
36	Nebraska	1,130	0.3%		27	Minnesota	3,475	1.0%
21	Nevada	4,918	1.4%		28	Colorado	3,395	1.0%
43	New Hampshire	472	0.1%		29	Oklahoma	3,231	0.9%
9	New Jersey	11,385	3.2%		30	Oregon	2,413	0.7%
33	New Mexico	1,847	0.5%		31	Arkansas	2,320	0.7%
3	New York	28,655	8.1%		32	Mississippi	2,284	0.6%
12	North Carolina	9,392	2.6%		33	New Mexico	1,847	0.5%
48	North Dakota	131	0.0%		34	Kansas	1,500	0.4%
7	Ohio	15,235	4.3%		35	Delaware	1,492	0.4%
29	Oklahoma	3,231	0.9%		36	Nebraska	1,130	0.3%
30	Oregon	2,413	0.7%		37	Utah	1,100	0.3%
6	Pennsylvania	15,673	4.4%		38	Hawaii	1,040	0.3%
41	Rhode Island	713	0.2%		39	Iowa	962	0.3%
24	South Carolina	4,489	1.3%		40	West Virginia	838	0.2%
47	South Dakota	158	0.0%		41	Rhode Island	713	0.2%
13	Tennessee	8,169	2.3%		42	Alaska	630	0.2%
2	Texas	30,382	8.6%		43	New Hampshire	472	0.1%
37	Utah	1,100	0.3%		44	Maine	423	0.1%
49	Vermont	112	0.0%		45	Idaho	243	0.1%
22	Virginia	4,706	1.3%		46	Montana	191	0.1%
18	Washington	5,745	1.6%		47	South Dakota	158	0.0%
40	West Virginia	838	0.2%		48	North Dakota	131	0.0%
23	Wisconsin	4,622	1.3%		49	Vermont	112	0.0%
50	Wyoming	61	0.0%		50	Wyoming	61	0.0%
						District of Columbia	4,036	1.1%

Source: Reported data from the Federal Bureau of Investigation
"Crime in the United States 2012" (Uniform Crime Reports, September 16, 2013, http://www.fbi.gov/about-us/cjis/ucr/)
*Robbery is the taking or attempting to take anything of value by force or threat of force.

Robbery Rate in 2012

National Rate = 112.9 Robberies per 100,000 Population*

ALPHA ORDER

RANK	STATE	RATE
17	Alabama	104.1
25	Alaska	86.1
15	Arizona	112.7
30	Arkansas	78.7
5	California	148.6
34	Colorado	65.4
18	Connecticut	102.7
3	Delaware	162.7
11	Florida	123.7
10	Georgia	125.6
32	Hawaii	74.7
49	Idaho	15.2
4	Illinois	151.2
19	Indiana	100.9
44	Iowa	31.3
39	Kansas	52.0
28	Kentucky	80.7
13	Louisiana	119.0
43	Maine	31.8
2	Maryland	172.3
20	Massachusetts	98.6
16	Michigan	105.6
35	Minnesota	64.6
31	Mississippi	76.5
22	Missouri	96.0
45	Montana	19.0
37	Nebraska	60.9
1	Nevada	178.3
42	New Hampshire	35.7
8	New Jersey	128.4
24	New Mexico	88.6
6	New York	146.4
21	North Carolina	96.3
47	North Dakota	18.7
7	Ohio	132.0
26	Oklahoma	84.7
36	Oregon	61.9
12	Pennsylvania	122.8
33	Rhode Island	67.9
23	South Carolina	95.0
45	South Dakota	19.0
9	Tennessee	126.5
14	Texas	116.6
41	Utah	38.5
48	Vermont	17.9
38	Virginia	57.5
27	Washington	83.3
40	West Virginia	45.2
28	Wisconsin	80.7
50	Wyoming	10.6

RANK ORDER

RANK	STATE	RATE
1	Nevada	178.3
2	Maryland	172.3
3	Delaware	162.7
4	Illinois	151.2
5	California	148.6
6	New York	146.4
7	Ohio	132.0
8	New Jersey	128.4
9	Tennessee	126.5
10	Georgia	125.6
11	Florida	123.7
12	Pennsylvania	122.8
13	Louisiana	119.0
14	Texas	116.6
15	Arizona	112.7
16	Michigan	105.6
17	Alabama	104.1
18	Connecticut	102.7
19	Indiana	100.9
20	Massachusetts	98.6
21	North Carolina	96.3
22	Missouri	96.0
23	South Carolina	95.0
24	New Mexico	88.6
25	Alaska	86.1
26	Oklahoma	84.7
27	Washington	83.3
28	Kentucky	80.7
28	Wisconsin	80.7
30	Arkansas	78.7
31	Mississippi	76.5
32	Hawaii	74.7
33	Rhode Island	67.9
34	Colorado	65.4
35	Minnesota	64.6
36	Oregon	61.9
37	Nebraska	60.9
38	Virginia	57.5
39	Kansas	52.0
40	West Virginia	45.2
41	Utah	38.5
42	New Hampshire	35.7
43	Maine	31.8
44	Iowa	31.3
45	Montana	19.0
45	South Dakota	19.0
47	North Dakota	18.7
48	Vermont	17.9
49	Idaho	15.2
50	Wyoming	10.6
	District of Columbia	638.3

Source: Reported data from the Federal Bureau of Investigation
"Crime in the United States 2012" (Uniform Crime Reports, September 16, 2013, http://www.fbi.gov/about-us/cjis/ucr/)
*Robbery is the taking or attempting to take anything of value by force or threat of force.

Aggravated Assaults in 2012

National Total = 760,739 Aggravated Assaults*

ALPHA ORDER

RANK	STATE	ASSAULTS	% of USA
18	Alabama	15,035	2.0%
39	Alaska	3,169	0.4%
14	Arizona	18,087	2.4%
25	Arkansas	10,095	1.3%
1	California	94,702	12.4%
24	Colorado	10,353	1.4%
33	Connecticut	5,408	0.7%
38	Delaware	3,228	0.4%
3	Florida	63,929	8.4%
10	Georgia	22,423	2.9%
43	Hawaii	1,976	0.3%
41	Idaho	2,567	0.3%
6	Illinois	29,618	3.9%
19	Indiana	14,027	1.8%
31	Iowa	6,234	0.8%
29	Kansas	7,595	1.0%
34	Kentucky	4,750	0.6%
16	Louisiana	15,740	2.1%
49	Maine	811	0.1%
15	Maryland	16,310	2.1%
13	Massachusetts	18,638	2.4%
7	Michigan	29,210	3.8%
30	Minnesota	7,207	0.9%
36	Mississippi	4,460	0.6%
12	Missouri	19,473	2.6%
42	Montana	2,139	0.3%
40	Nebraska	2,920	0.4%
23	Nevada	10,790	1.4%
46	New Hampshire	1,545	0.2%
20	New Jersey	12,919	1.7%
28	New Mexico	8,740	1.1%
4	New York	47,423	6.2%
9	North Carolina	22,609	3.0%
47	North Dakota	1,281	0.2%
17	Ohio	15,207	2.0%
21	Oklahoma	12,867	1.7%
32	Oregon	6,008	0.8%
8	Pennsylvania	24,818	3.3%
45	Rhode Island	1,616	0.2%
11	South Carolina	19,905	2.6%
44	South Dakota	1,914	0.3%
5	Tennessee	30,961	4.1%
2	Texas	67,239	8.8%
37	Utah	3,783	0.5%
50	Vermont	652	0.1%
27	Virginia	9,092	1.2%
22	Washington	12,242	1.6%
35	West Virginia	4,538	0.6%
26	Wisconsin	10,050	1.3%
48	Wyoming	932	0.1%

RANK ORDER

RANK	STATE	ASSAULTS	% of USA
1	California	94,702	12.4%
2	Texas	67,239	8.8%
3	Florida	63,929	8.4%
4	New York	47,423	6.2%
5	Tennessee	30,961	4.1%
6	Illinois	29,618	3.9%
7	Michigan	29,210	3.8%
8	Pennsylvania	24,818	3.3%
9	North Carolina	22,609	3.0%
10	Georgia	22,423	2.9%
11	South Carolina	19,905	2.6%
12	Missouri	19,473	2.6%
13	Massachusetts	18,638	2.4%
14	Arizona	18,087	2.4%
15	Maryland	16,310	2.1%
16	Louisiana	15,740	2.1%
17	Ohio	15,207	2.0%
18	Alabama	15,035	2.0%
19	Indiana	14,027	1.8%
20	New Jersey	12,919	1.7%
21	Oklahoma	12,867	1.7%
22	Washington	12,242	1.6%
23	Nevada	10,790	1.4%
24	Colorado	10,353	1.4%
25	Arkansas	10,095	1.3%
26	Wisconsin	10,050	1.3%
27	Virginia	9,092	1.2%
28	New Mexico	8,740	1.1%
29	Kansas	7,595	1.0%
30	Minnesota	7,207	0.9%
31	Iowa	6,234	0.8%
32	Oregon	6,008	0.8%
33	Connecticut	5,408	0.7%
34	Kentucky	4,750	0.6%
35	West Virginia	4,538	0.6%
36	Mississippi	4,460	0.6%
37	Utah	3,783	0.5%
38	Delaware	3,228	0.4%
39	Alaska	3,169	0.4%
40	Nebraska	2,920	0.4%
41	Idaho	2,567	0.3%
42	Montana	2,139	0.3%
43	Hawaii	1,976	0.3%
44	South Dakota	1,914	0.3%
45	Rhode Island	1,616	0.2%
46	New Hampshire	1,545	0.2%
47	North Dakota	1,281	0.2%
48	Wyoming	932	0.1%
49	Maine	811	0.1%
50	Vermont	652	0.1%
	District of Columbia	3,504	0.5%

Source: Reported data from the Federal Bureau of Investigation
"Crime in the United States 2012" (Uniform Crime Reports, September 16, 2013, http://www.fbi.gov/about-us/cjis/ucr/)
*Aggravated assault is an attack for the purpose of inflicting severe bodily injury.

Aggravated Assault Rate in 2012

National Rate = 242.3 Aggravated Assaults per 100,000 Population*

ALPHA ORDER

RANK	STATE	RATE
12	Alabama	311.8
2	Alaska	433.2
16	Arizona	276.0
7	Arkansas	342.3
19	California	248.9
29	Colorado	199.6
39	Connecticut	150.6
6	Delaware	352.0
10	Florida	330.9
25	Georgia	226.0
42	Hawaii	141.9
35	Idaho	160.9
23	Illinois	230.0
26	Indiana	214.6
28	Iowa	202.8
17	Kansas	263.2
48	Kentucky	108.4
8	Louisiana	342.0
50	Maine	61.0
15	Maryland	277.2
14	Massachusetts	280.4
13	Michigan	295.5
43	Minnesota	134.0
40	Mississippi	149.4
11	Missouri	323.4
27	Montana	212.8
36	Nebraska	157.4
5	Nevada	391.1
46	New Hampshire	117.0
41	New Jersey	145.7
4	New Mexico	419.1
21	New York	242.3
22	North Carolina	231.8
31	North Dakota	183.1
45	Ohio	131.7
9	Oklahoma	337.3
37	Oregon	154.1
30	Pennsylvania	194.4
38	Rhode Island	153.9
3	South Carolina	421.4
24	South Dakota	229.7
1	Tennessee	479.6
18	Texas	258.0
44	Utah	132.5
49	Vermont	104.2
47	Virginia	111.1
32	Washington	177.5
20	West Virginia	244.6
33	Wisconsin	175.5
34	Wyoming	161.7

RANK ORDER

RANK	STATE	RATE
1	Tennessee	479.6
2	Alaska	433.2
3	South Carolina	421.4
4	New Mexico	419.1
5	Nevada	391.1
6	Delaware	352.0
7	Arkansas	342.3
8	Louisiana	342.0
9	Oklahoma	337.3
10	Florida	330.9
11	Missouri	323.4
12	Alabama	311.8
13	Michigan	295.5
14	Massachusetts	280.4
15	Maryland	277.2
16	Arizona	276.0
17	Kansas	263.2
18	Texas	258.0
19	California	248.9
20	West Virginia	244.6
21	New York	242.3
22	North Carolina	231.8
23	Illinois	230.0
24	South Dakota	229.7
25	Georgia	226.0
26	Indiana	214.6
27	Montana	212.8
28	Iowa	202.8
29	Colorado	199.6
30	Pennsylvania	194.4
31	North Dakota	183.1
32	Washington	177.5
33	Wisconsin	175.5
34	Wyoming	161.7
35	Idaho	160.9
36	Nebraska	157.4
37	Oregon	154.1
38	Rhode Island	153.9
39	Connecticut	150.6
40	Mississippi	149.4
41	New Jersey	145.7
42	Hawaii	141.9
43	Minnesota	134.0
44	Utah	132.5
45	Ohio	131.7
46	New Hampshire	117.0
47	Virginia	111.1
48	Kentucky	108.4
49	Vermont	104.2
50	Maine	61.0

	District of Columbia	554.1

Source: Reported data from the Federal Bureau of Investigation
"Crime in the United States 2012" (Uniform Crime Reports, September 16, 2013, http://www.fbi.gov/about-us/cjis/ucr/)
*Aggravated assault is an attack for the purpose of inflicting severe bodily injury.

Property Crimes in 2012

National Total = 8,975,438 Property Crimes*

RANK	STATE	CRIMES	% of USA
19	Alabama	168,878	1.9%
46	Alaska	20,037	0.2%
12	Arizona	231,930	2.6%
29	Arkansas	107,941	1.2%
1	California	1,049,465	11.7%
24	Colorado	139,270	1.6%
34	Connecticut	76,834	0.9%
43	Delaware	30,639	0.3%
3	Florida	632,988	7.1%
6	Georgia	338,329	3.8%
39	Hawaii	42,817	0.5%
41	Idaho	31,651	0.4%
7	Illinois	332,013	3.7%
15	Indiana	198,032	2.2%
36	Iowa	69,839	0.8%
30	Kansas	90,710	1.0%
28	Kentucky	111,826	1.2%
20	Louisiana	162,936	1.8%
40	Maine	33,361	0.4%
21	Maryland	162,031	1.8%
22	Massachusetts	143,089	1.6%
11	Michigan	250,101	2.8%
25	Minnesota	138,152	1.5%
32	Mississippi	83,906	0.9%
14	Missouri	199,590	2.2%
45	Montana	25,970	0.3%
37	Nebraska	51,118	0.6%
33	Nevada	77,510	0.9%
42	New Hampshire	30,693	0.3%
16	New Jersey	181,481	2.0%
35	New Mexico	75,094	0.8%
4	New York	376,140	4.2%
8	North Carolina	328,594	3.7%
49	North Dakota	14,063	0.2%
5	Ohio	359,883	4.0%
26	Oklahoma	129,743	1.4%
27	Oregon	125,723	1.4%
9	Pennsylvania	276,496	3.1%
44	Rhode Island	27,017	0.3%
17	South Carolina	180,550	2.0%
47	South Dakota	17,168	0.2%
13	Tennessee	217,664	2.4%
2	Texas	876,059	9.8%
31	Utah	85,424	1.0%
48	Vermont	15,016	0.2%
18	Virginia	176,985	2.0%
10	Washington	252,333	2.8%
38	West Virginia	43,878	0.5%
23	Wisconsin	140,513	1.6%
50	Wyoming	13,222	0.1%

RANK	STATE	CRIMES	% of USA
1	California	1,049,465	11.7%
2	Texas	876,059	9.8%
3	Florida	632,988	7.1%
4	New York	376,140	4.2%
5	Ohio	359,883	4.0%
6	Georgia	338,329	3.8%
7	Illinois	332,013	3.7%
8	North Carolina	328,594	3.7%
9	Pennsylvania	276,496	3.1%
10	Washington	252,333	2.8%
11	Michigan	250,101	2.8%
12	Arizona	231,930	2.6%
13	Tennessee	217,664	2.4%
14	Missouri	199,590	2.2%
15	Indiana	198,032	2.2%
16	New Jersey	181,481	2.0%
17	South Carolina	180,550	2.0%
18	Virginia	176,985	2.0%
19	Alabama	168,878	1.9%
20	Louisiana	162,936	1.8%
21	Maryland	162,031	1.8%
22	Massachusetts	143,089	1.6%
23	Wisconsin	140,513	1.6%
24	Colorado	139,270	1.6%
25	Minnesota	138,152	1.5%
26	Oklahoma	129,743	1.4%
27	Oregon	125,723	1.4%
28	Kentucky	111,826	1.2%
29	Arkansas	107,941	1.2%
30	Kansas	90,710	1.0%
31	Utah	85,424	1.0%
32	Mississippi	83,906	0.9%
33	Nevada	77,510	0.9%
34	Connecticut	76,834	0.9%
35	New Mexico	75,094	0.8%
36	Iowa	69,839	0.8%
37	Nebraska	51,118	0.6%
38	West Virginia	43,878	0.5%
39	Hawaii	42,817	0.5%
40	Maine	33,361	0.4%
41	Idaho	31,651	0.4%
42	New Hampshire	30,693	0.3%
43	Delaware	30,639	0.3%
44	Rhode Island	27,017	0.3%
45	Montana	25,970	0.3%
46	Alaska	20,037	0.2%
47	South Dakota	17,168	0.2%
48	Vermont	15,016	0.2%
49	North Dakota	14,063	0.2%
50	Wyoming	13,222	0.1%
	District of Columbia	30,736	0.3%

Source: Reported data from the Federal Bureau of Investigation
"Crime in the United States 2012" (Uniform Crime Reports, September 16, 2013, http://www.fbi.gov/about-us/cjis/ucr/)
*Property crimes are offenses of burglary, larceny-theft, and motor vehicle theft.

Property Crime Rate in 2012

National Rate = 2,859.2 Property Crimes per 100,000 Population*

ALPHA ORDER

RANK	STATE	RATE
7	Alabama	3,502.2
27	Alaska	2,739.4
6	Arizona	3,539.2
2	Arkansas	3,660.1
24	California	2,758.7
28	Colorado	2,684.7
45	Connecticut	2,140.0
13	Delaware	3,340.9
15	Florida	3,276.7
8	Georgia	3,410.6
19	Hawaii	3,075.2
49	Idaho	1,983.5
30	Illinois	2,578.7
20	Indiana	3,029.2
41	Iowa	2,271.8
17	Kansas	3,143.2
33	Kentucky	2,552.9
5	Louisiana	3,540.6
35	Maine	2,509.9
26	Maryland	2,753.5
44	Massachusetts	2,153.0
34	Michigan	2,530.5
32	Minnesota	2,568.3
22	Mississippi	2,811.0
14	Missouri	3,314.4
29	Montana	2,583.7
25	Nebraska	2,754.9
23	Nevada	2,809.4
39	New Hampshire	2,324.0
47	New Jersey	2,047.3
4	New Mexico	3,600.7
50	New York	1,922.0
11	North Carolina	3,369.5
48	North Dakota	2,010.1
18	Ohio	3,117.4
9	Oklahoma	3,401.0
16	Oregon	3,224.2
42	Pennsylvania	2,166.3
31	Rhode Island	2,572.3
1	South Carolina	3,822.2
46	South Dakota	2,060.1
10	Tennessee	3,371.4
12	Texas	3,361.8
21	Utah	2,991.8
37	Vermont	2,398.7
43	Virginia	2,162.1
3	Washington	3,658.6
38	West Virginia	2,364.9
36	Wisconsin	2,453.8
40	Wyoming	2,293.8

RANK ORDER

RANK	STATE	RATE
1	South Carolina	3,822.2
2	Arkansas	3,660.1
3	Washington	3,658.6
4	New Mexico	3,600.7
5	Louisiana	3,540.6
6	Arizona	3,539.2
7	Alabama	3,502.2
8	Georgia	3,410.6
9	Oklahoma	3,401.0
10	Tennessee	3,371.4
11	North Carolina	3,369.5
12	Texas	3,361.8
13	Delaware	3,340.9
14	Missouri	3,314.4
15	Florida	3,276.7
16	Oregon	3,224.2
17	Kansas	3,143.2
18	Ohio	3,117.4
19	Hawaii	3,075.2
20	Indiana	3,029.2
21	Utah	2,991.8
22	Mississippi	2,811.0
23	Nevada	2,809.4
24	California	2,758.7
25	Nebraska	2,754.9
26	Maryland	2,753.5
27	Alaska	2,739.4
28	Colorado	2,684.7
29	Montana	2,583.7
30	Illinois	2,578.7
31	Rhode Island	2,572.3
32	Minnesota	2,568.3
33	Kentucky	2,552.9
34	Michigan	2,530.5
35	Maine	2,509.9
36	Wisconsin	2,453.8
37	Vermont	2,398.7
38	West Virginia	2,364.9
39	New Hampshire	2,324.0
40	Wyoming	2,293.8
41	Iowa	2,271.8
42	Pennsylvania	2,166.3
43	Virginia	2,162.1
44	Massachusetts	2,153.0
45	Connecticut	2,140.0
46	South Dakota	2,060.1
47	New Jersey	2,047.3
48	North Dakota	2,010.1
49	Idaho	1,983.5
50	New York	1,922.0

District of Columbia   4,860.8

Source: Reported data from the Federal Bureau of Investigation
"Crime in the United States 2012" (Uniform Crime Reports, September 16, 2013, http://www.fbi.gov/about-us/cjis/ucr/)
*Property crimes are offenses of burglary, larceny-theft, and motor vehicle theft.

Percent Change in Property Crime Rate: 2011 to 2012

National Percent Change = 1.6% Decrease*

ALPHA ORDER			RANK ORDER		
RANK	STATE	PERCENT CHANGE	RANK	STATE	PERCENT CHANGE
30	Alabama	(2.9)	1	West Virginia	12.5
6	Alaska	3.8	2	South Dakota	10.9
21	Arizona	(0.4)	3	Nevada	9.1
27	Arkansas	(2.6)	4	Montana	7.9
5	California	6.8	5	California	6.8
7	Colorado	3.4	6	Alaska	3.8
23	Connecticut	(0.6)	7	Colorado	3.4
27	Delaware	(2.6)	8	North Dakota	3.2
49	Florida	(6.8)	9	Oregon	2.3
45	Georgia	(6.3)	10	Washington	2.2
31	Hawaii	(3.4)	11	Kansas	1.8
41	Idaho	(4.4)	11	New Mexico	1.8
36	Illinois	(3.7)	13	Wyoming	1.1
39	Indiana	(4.2)	14	Minnesota	0.8
31	Iowa	(3.4)	14	New York	0.8
11	Kansas	1.8	14	Oklahoma	0.8
45	Kentucky	(6.3)	17	Utah	0.1
38	Louisiana	(3.9)	17	Wisconsin	0.1
25	Maine	(1.4)	19	Missouri	0.0
35	Maryland	(3.6)	20	Nebraska	(0.3)
41	Massachusetts	(4.4)	21	Arizona	(0.4)
23	Michigan	(0.6)	21	Vermont	(0.4)
14	Minnesota	0.8	23	Connecticut	(0.6)
49	Mississippi	(6.8)	23	Michigan	(0.6)
19	Missouri	0.0	25	Maine	(1.4)
4	Montana	7.9	26	South Carolina	(2.5)
20	Nebraska	(0.3)	27	Arkansas	(2.6)
3	Nevada	9.1	27	Delaware	(2.6)
47	New Hampshire	(6.5)	27	Pennsylvania	(2.6)
43	New Jersey	(4.7)	30	Alabama	(2.9)
11	New Mexico	1.8	31	Hawaii	(3.4)
14	New York	0.8	31	Iowa	(3.4)
36	North Carolina	(3.7)	31	Rhode Island	(3.4)
8	North Dakota	3.2	34	Texas	(3.5)
44	Ohio	(5.5)	35	Maryland	(3.6)
14	Oklahoma	0.8	36	Illinois	(3.7)
9	Oregon	2.3	36	North Carolina	(3.7)
27	Pennsylvania	(2.6)	38	Louisiana	(3.9)
31	Rhode Island	(3.4)	39	Indiana	(4.2)
26	South Carolina	(2.5)	39	Virginia	(4.2)
2	South Dakota	10.9	41	Idaho	(4.4)
48	Tennessee	(6.6)	41	Massachusetts	(4.4)
34	Texas	(3.5)	43	New Jersey	(4.7)
17	Utah	0.1	44	Ohio	(5.5)
21	Vermont	(0.4)	45	Georgia	(6.3)
39	Virginia	(4.2)	45	Kentucky	(6.3)
10	Washington	2.2	47	New Hampshire	(6.5)
1	West Virginia	12.5	48	Tennessee	(6.6)
17	Wisconsin	0.1	49	Florida	(6.8)
13	Wyoming	1.1	49	Mississippi	(6.8)
				District of Columbia	1.5

Source: Reported data from the Federal Bureau of Investigation
"Crime in the United States 2012" (Uniform Crime Reports, September 16, 2013, http://www.fbi.gov/about-us/cjis/ucr/)
*Property crimes are offenses of burglary, larceny-theft, and motor vehicle theft.

Burglaries in 2012

National Total = 2,103,787 Burglaries*

<table>
<tr><td colspan="4">ALPHA ORDER</td><td colspan="4">RANK ORDER</td></tr>
<tr><td>RANK</td><td>STATE</td><td>BURGLARIES</td><td>% of USA</td><td>RANK</td><td>STATE</td><td>BURGLARIES</td><td>% of USA</td></tr>
<tr><td>15</td><td>Alabama</td><td>47,481</td><td>2.3%</td><td>1</td><td>California</td><td>245,767</td><td>11.7%</td></tr>
<tr><td>48</td><td>Alaska</td><td>2,950</td><td>0.1%</td><td>2</td><td>Texas</td><td>204,810</td><td>9.7%</td></tr>
<tr><td>13</td><td>Arizona</td><td>52,934</td><td>2.5%</td><td>3</td><td>Florida</td><td>153,563</td><td>7.3%</td></tr>
<tr><td>23</td><td>Arkansas</td><td>31,890</td><td>1.5%</td><td>4</td><td>Ohio</td><td>103,421</td><td>4.9%</td></tr>
<tr><td>1</td><td>California</td><td>245,767</td><td>11.7%</td><td>5</td><td>North Carolina</td><td>99,323</td><td>4.7%</td></tr>
<tr><td>28</td><td>Colorado</td><td>26,157</td><td>1.2%</td><td>6</td><td>Georgia</td><td>86,789</td><td>4.1%</td></tr>
<tr><td>35</td><td>Connecticut</td><td>14,711</td><td>0.7%</td><td>7</td><td>Illinois</td><td>71,101</td><td>3.4%</td></tr>
<tr><td>41</td><td>Delaware</td><td>7,371</td><td>0.4%</td><td>8</td><td>Michigan</td><td>65,665</td><td>3.1%</td></tr>
<tr><td>3</td><td>Florida</td><td>153,563</td><td>7.3%</td><td>9</td><td>New York</td><td>64,553</td><td>3.1%</td></tr>
<tr><td>6</td><td>Georgia</td><td>86,789</td><td>4.1%</td><td>10</td><td>Washington</td><td>60,725</td><td>2.9%</td></tr>
<tr><td>39</td><td>Hawaii</td><td>7,979</td><td>0.4%</td><td>11</td><td>Pennsylvania</td><td>56,859</td><td>2.7%</td></tr>
<tr><td>42</td><td>Idaho</td><td>7,186</td><td>0.3%</td><td>12</td><td>Tennessee</td><td>56,181</td><td>2.7%</td></tr>
<tr><td>7</td><td>Illinois</td><td>71,101</td><td>3.4%</td><td>13</td><td>Arizona</td><td>52,934</td><td>2.5%</td></tr>
<tr><td>14</td><td>Indiana</td><td>47,612</td><td>2.3%</td><td>14</td><td>Indiana</td><td>47,612</td><td>2.3%</td></tr>
<tr><td>34</td><td>Iowa</td><td>17,096</td><td>0.8%</td><td>15</td><td>Alabama</td><td>47,481</td><td>2.3%</td></tr>
<tr><td>33</td><td>Kansas</td><td>18,767</td><td>0.9%</td><td>16</td><td>South Carolina</td><td>45,086</td><td>2.1%</td></tr>
<tr><td>24</td><td>Kentucky</td><td>29,587</td><td>1.4%</td><td>17</td><td>Missouri</td><td>42,466</td><td>2.0%</td></tr>
<tr><td>19</td><td>Louisiana</td><td>42,140</td><td>2.0%</td><td>18</td><td>New Jersey</td><td>42,338</td><td>2.0%</td></tr>
<tr><td>40</td><td>Maine</td><td>7,461</td><td>0.4%</td><td>19</td><td>Louisiana</td><td>42,140</td><td>2.0%</td></tr>
<tr><td>22</td><td>Maryland</td><td>33,732</td><td>1.6%</td><td>20</td><td>Oklahoma</td><td>35,731</td><td>1.7%</td></tr>
<tr><td>21</td><td>Massachusetts</td><td>34,540</td><td>1.6%</td><td>21</td><td>Massachusetts</td><td>34,540</td><td>1.6%</td></tr>
<tr><td>8</td><td>Michigan</td><td>65,665</td><td>3.1%</td><td>22</td><td>Maryland</td><td>33,732</td><td>1.6%</td></tr>
<tr><td>29</td><td>Minnesota</td><td>25,378</td><td>1.2%</td><td>23</td><td>Arkansas</td><td>31,890</td><td>1.5%</td></tr>
<tr><td>26</td><td>Mississippi</td><td>28,076</td><td>1.3%</td><td>24</td><td>Kentucky</td><td>29,587</td><td>1.4%</td></tr>
<tr><td>17</td><td>Missouri</td><td>42,466</td><td>2.0%</td><td>25</td><td>Virginia</td><td>29,511</td><td>1.4%</td></tr>
<tr><td>46</td><td>Montana</td><td>3,894</td><td>0.2%</td><td>26</td><td>Mississippi</td><td>28,076</td><td>1.3%</td></tr>
<tr><td>38</td><td>Nebraska</td><td>8,735</td><td>0.4%</td><td>27</td><td>Wisconsin</td><td>27,945</td><td>1.3%</td></tr>
<tr><td>30</td><td>Nevada</td><td>22,120</td><td>1.1%</td><td>28</td><td>Colorado</td><td>26,157</td><td>1.2%</td></tr>
<tr><td>44</td><td>New Hampshire</td><td>5,444</td><td>0.3%</td><td>29</td><td>Minnesota</td><td>25,378</td><td>1.2%</td></tr>
<tr><td>18</td><td>New Jersey</td><td>42,338</td><td>2.0%</td><td>30</td><td>Nevada</td><td>22,120</td><td>1.1%</td></tr>
<tr><td>32</td><td>New Mexico</td><td>21,384</td><td>1.0%</td><td>31</td><td>Oregon</td><td>21,901</td><td>1.0%</td></tr>
<tr><td>9</td><td>New York</td><td>64,553</td><td>3.1%</td><td>32</td><td>New Mexico</td><td>21,384</td><td>1.0%</td></tr>
<tr><td>5</td><td>North Carolina</td><td>99,323</td><td>4.7%</td><td>33</td><td>Kansas</td><td>18,767</td><td>0.9%</td></tr>
<tr><td>49</td><td>North Dakota</td><td>2,377</td><td>0.1%</td><td>34</td><td>Iowa</td><td>17,096</td><td>0.8%</td></tr>
<tr><td>4</td><td>Ohio</td><td>103,421</td><td>4.9%</td><td>35</td><td>Connecticut</td><td>14,711</td><td>0.7%</td></tr>
<tr><td>20</td><td>Oklahoma</td><td>35,731</td><td>1.7%</td><td>36</td><td>Utah</td><td>12,943</td><td>0.6%</td></tr>
<tr><td>31</td><td>Oregon</td><td>21,901</td><td>1.0%</td><td>37</td><td>West Virginia</td><td>11,291</td><td>0.5%</td></tr>
<tr><td>11</td><td>Pennsylvania</td><td>56,859</td><td>2.7%</td><td>38</td><td>Nebraska</td><td>8,735</td><td>0.4%</td></tr>
<tr><td>43</td><td>Rhode Island</td><td>5,949</td><td>0.3%</td><td>39</td><td>Hawaii</td><td>7,979</td><td>0.4%</td></tr>
<tr><td>16</td><td>South Carolina</td><td>45,086</td><td>2.1%</td><td>40</td><td>Maine</td><td>7,461</td><td>0.4%</td></tr>
<tr><td>47</td><td>South Dakota</td><td>3,258</td><td>0.2%</td><td>41</td><td>Delaware</td><td>7,371</td><td>0.4%</td></tr>
<tr><td>12</td><td>Tennessee</td><td>56,181</td><td>2.7%</td><td>42</td><td>Idaho</td><td>7,186</td><td>0.3%</td></tr>
<tr><td>2</td><td>Texas</td><td>204,810</td><td>9.7%</td><td>43</td><td>Rhode Island</td><td>5,949</td><td>0.3%</td></tr>
<tr><td>36</td><td>Utah</td><td>12,943</td><td>0.6%</td><td>44</td><td>New Hampshire</td><td>5,444</td><td>0.3%</td></tr>
<tr><td>45</td><td>Vermont</td><td>3,965</td><td>0.2%</td><td>45</td><td>Vermont</td><td>3,965</td><td>0.2%</td></tr>
<tr><td>25</td><td>Virginia</td><td>29,511</td><td>1.4%</td><td>46</td><td>Montana</td><td>3,894</td><td>0.2%</td></tr>
<tr><td>10</td><td>Washington</td><td>60,725</td><td>2.9%</td><td>47</td><td>South Dakota</td><td>3,258</td><td>0.2%</td></tr>
<tr><td>37</td><td>West Virginia</td><td>11,291</td><td>0.5%</td><td>48</td><td>Alaska</td><td>2,950</td><td>0.1%</td></tr>
<tr><td>27</td><td>Wisconsin</td><td>27,945</td><td>1.3%</td><td>49</td><td>North Dakota</td><td>2,377</td><td>0.1%</td></tr>
<tr><td>50</td><td>Wyoming</td><td>2,125</td><td>0.1%</td><td>50</td><td>Wyoming</td><td>2,125</td><td>0.1%</td></tr>
<tr><td></td><td></td><td></td><td></td><td></td><td>District of Columbia</td><td>3,519</td><td>0.2%</td></tr>
</table>

Source: Reported data from the Federal Bureau of Investigation
   "Crime in the United States 2012" (Uniform Crime Reports, September 16, 2013, http://www.fbi.gov/about-us/cjis/ucr/)
*Burglary is the unlawful entry of a structure to commit a felony or theft. Attempts are included.

Burglary Rate in 2012

National Rate = 670.2 Burglaries per 100,000 Population*

ALPHA ORDER			RANK ORDER		
RANK	STATE	RATE	RANK	STATE	RATE
4	Alabama	984.7	1	Arkansas	1,081.3
44	Alaska	403.3	2	New Mexico	1,025.3
13	Arizona	807.8	3	North Carolina	1,018.5
1	Arkansas	1,081.3	4	Alabama	984.7
23	California	646.1	5	South Carolina	954.5
34	Colorado	504.2	6	Mississippi	940.6
43	Connecticut	409.7	7	Oklahoma	936.6
14	Delaware	803.7	8	Louisiana	915.7
16	Florida	794.9	9	Ohio	895.9
11	Georgia	874.9	10	Washington	880.5
27	Hawaii	573.1	11	Georgia	874.9
40	Idaho	450.3	12	Tennessee	870.2
32	Illinois	552.2	13	Arizona	807.8
18	Indiana	728.3	14	Delaware	803.7
31	Iowa	556.1	15	Nevada	801.8
22	Kansas	650.3	16	Florida	794.9
20	Kentucky	675.4	17	Texas	785.9
8	Louisiana	915.7	18	Indiana	728.3
30	Maine	561.3	19	Missouri	705.2
26	Maryland	573.2	20	Kentucky	675.4
33	Massachusetts	519.7	21	Michigan	664.4
21	Michigan	664.4	22	Kansas	650.3
37	Minnesota	471.8	23	California	646.1
6	Mississippi	940.6	24	Vermont	633.4
19	Missouri	705.2	25	West Virginia	608.5
46	Montana	387.4	26	Maryland	573.2
38	Nebraska	470.8	27	Hawaii	573.1
15	Nevada	801.8	28	Rhode Island	566.4
42	New Hampshire	412.2	29	Oregon	561.7
36	New Jersey	477.6	30	Maine	561.3
2	New Mexico	1,025.3	31	Iowa	556.1
50	New York	329.9	32	Illinois	552.2
3	North Carolina	1,018.5	33	Massachusetts	519.7
49	North Dakota	339.8	34	Colorado	504.2
9	Ohio	895.9	35	Wisconsin	488.0
7	Oklahoma	936.6	36	New Jersey	477.6
29	Oregon	561.7	37	Minnesota	471.8
41	Pennsylvania	445.5	38	Nebraska	470.8
28	Rhode Island	566.4	39	Utah	453.3
5	South Carolina	954.5	40	Idaho	450.3
45	South Dakota	391.0	41	Pennsylvania	445.5
12	Tennessee	870.2	42	New Hampshire	412.2
17	Texas	785.9	43	Connecticut	409.7
39	Utah	453.3	44	Alaska	403.3
24	Vermont	633.4	45	South Dakota	391.0
48	Virginia	360.5	46	Montana	387.4
10	Washington	880.5	47	Wyoming	368.7
25	West Virginia	608.5	48	Virginia	360.5
35	Wisconsin	488.0	49	North Dakota	339.8
47	Wyoming	368.7	50	New York	329.9

District of Columbia   556.5

Source: Reported data from the Federal Bureau of Investigation
"Crime in the United States 2012" (Uniform Crime Reports, September 16, 2013, http://www.fbi.gov/about-us/cjis/ucr/)
*Burglary is the unlawful entry of a structure to commit a felony or theft. Attempts are included.

Larceny-Thefts in 2012

National Total = 6,150,598 Larceny-Thefts*

ALPHA ORDER					RANK ORDER			
RANK	STATE	THEFTS	% of USA		RANK	STATE	THEFTS	% of USA
21	Alabama	111,523	1.8%		1	California	635,090	10.3%
46	Alaska	15,565	0.3%		2	Texas	606,253	9.9%
11	Arizona	159,838	2.6%		3	Florida	442,095	7.2%
29	Arkansas	70,327	1.1%		4	New York	294,239	4.8%
1	California	635,090	10.3%		5	Ohio	236,950	3.9%
24	Colorado	101,021	1.6%		6	Illinois	235,222	3.8%
32	Connecticut	55,674	0.9%		7	Georgia	223,004	3.6%
43	Delaware	21,832	0.4%		8	North Carolina	213,151	3.5%
3	Florida	442,095	7.2%		9	Pennsylvania	204,609	3.3%
7	Georgia	223,004	3.6%		10	Washington	165,206	2.7%
38	Hawaii	31,233	0.5%		11	Arizona	159,838	2.6%
42	Idaho	23,101	0.4%		12	Michigan	159,321	2.6%
6	Illinois	235,222	3.8%		13	Tennessee	148,503	2.4%
16	Indiana	136,759	2.2%		14	Missouri	140,816	2.3%
34	Iowa	48,720	0.8%		15	Virginia	138,398	2.3%
31	Kansas	65,165	1.1%		16	Indiana	136,759	2.2%
28	Kentucky	75,571	1.2%		17	New Jersey	122,662	2.0%
20	Louisiana	112,915	1.8%		18	South Carolina	122,263	2.0%
40	Maine	24,905	0.4%		19	Maryland	113,274	1.8%
19	Maryland	113,274	1.8%		20	Louisiana	112,915	1.8%
25	Massachusetts	99,317	1.6%		21	Alabama	111,523	1.8%
12	Michigan	159,321	2.6%		22	Wisconsin	104,352	1.7%
23	Minnesota	104,316	1.7%		23	Minnesota	104,316	1.7%
33	Mississippi	51,508	0.8%		24	Colorado	101,021	1.6%
14	Missouri	140,816	2.3%		25	Massachusetts	99,317	1.6%
44	Montana	20,387	0.3%		26	Oregon	93,619	1.5%
37	Nebraska	38,236	0.6%		27	Oklahoma	82,448	1.3%
36	Nevada	45,372	0.7%		28	Kentucky	75,571	1.2%
41	New Hampshire	24,226	0.4%		29	Arkansas	70,327	1.1%
17	New Jersey	122,662	2.0%		30	Utah	66,482	1.1%
35	New Mexico	48,247	0.8%		31	Kansas	65,165	1.1%
4	New York	294,239	4.8%		32	Connecticut	55,674	0.9%
8	North Carolina	213,151	3.5%		33	Mississippi	51,508	0.8%
49	North Dakota	10,535	0.2%		34	Iowa	48,720	0.8%
5	Ohio	236,950	3.9%		35	New Mexico	48,247	0.8%
27	Oklahoma	82,448	1.3%		36	Nevada	45,372	0.7%
26	Oregon	93,619	1.5%		37	Nebraska	38,236	0.6%
9	Pennsylvania	204,609	3.3%		38	Hawaii	31,233	0.5%
45	Rhode Island	18,440	0.3%		39	West Virginia	30,378	0.5%
18	South Carolina	122,263	2.0%		40	Maine	24,905	0.4%
47	South Dakota	12,845	0.2%		41	New Hampshire	24,226	0.4%
13	Tennessee	148,503	2.4%		42	Idaho	23,101	0.4%
2	Texas	606,253	9.9%		43	Delaware	21,832	0.4%
30	Utah	66,482	1.1%		44	Montana	20,387	0.3%
48	Vermont	10,616	0.2%		45	Rhode Island	18,440	0.3%
15	Virginia	138,398	2.3%		46	Alaska	15,565	0.3%
10	Washington	165,206	2.7%		47	South Dakota	12,845	0.2%
39	West Virginia	30,378	0.5%		48	Vermont	10,616	0.2%
22	Wisconsin	104,352	1.7%		49	North Dakota	10,535	0.2%
50	Wyoming	10,513	0.2%		50	Wyoming	10,513	0.2%
						District of Columbia	23,556	0.4%

Source: Reported data from the Federal Bureau of Investigation
   "Crime in the United States 2012" (Uniform Crime Reports, September 16, 2013, http://www.fbi.gov/about-us/cjis/ucr/)
*Larceny-theft is the unlawful taking of property without use of force, violence, or fraud. Attempts are included. Motor vehicle thefts are excluded.

Larceny-Theft Rate in 2012

National Rate = 1,959.3 Larceny-Thefts per 100,000 Population*

<table>
<thead>
<tr><th colspan="3">ALPHA ORDER</th><th colspan="3">RANK ORDER</th></tr>
<tr><th>RANK</th><th>STATE</th><th>RATE</th><th>RANK</th><th>STATE</th><th>RATE</th></tr>
</thead>
<tbody>
<tr><td>12</td><td>Alabama</td><td>2,312.8</td><td>1</td><td>South Carolina</td><td>2,588.3</td></tr>
<tr><td>20</td><td>Alaska</td><td>2,128.0</td><td>2</td><td>Louisiana</td><td>2,453.7</td></tr>
<tr><td>3</td><td>Arizona</td><td>2,439.1</td><td>3</td><td>Arizona</td><td>2,439.1</td></tr>
<tr><td>6</td><td>Arkansas</td><td>2,384.7</td><td>4</td><td>Oregon</td><td>2,400.9</td></tr>
<tr><td>38</td><td>California</td><td>1,669.5</td><td>5</td><td>Washington</td><td>2,395.3</td></tr>
<tr><td>25</td><td>Colorado</td><td>1,947.4</td><td>6</td><td>Arkansas</td><td>2,384.7</td></tr>
<tr><td>44</td><td>Connecticut</td><td>1,550.7</td><td>7</td><td>Delaware</td><td>2,380.6</td></tr>
<tr><td>7</td><td>Delaware</td><td>2,380.6</td><td>8</td><td>Missouri</td><td>2,338.4</td></tr>
<tr><td>14</td><td>Florida</td><td>2,288.6</td><td>9</td><td>Utah</td><td>2,328.4</td></tr>
<tr><td>16</td><td>Georgia</td><td>2,248.0</td><td>10</td><td>Texas</td><td>2,326.4</td></tr>
<tr><td>17</td><td>Hawaii</td><td>2,243.2</td><td>11</td><td>New Mexico</td><td>2,313.4</td></tr>
<tr><td>49</td><td>Idaho</td><td>1,447.7</td><td>12</td><td>Alabama</td><td>2,312.8</td></tr>
<tr><td>30</td><td>Illinois</td><td>1,826.9</td><td>13</td><td>Tennessee</td><td>2,300.1</td></tr>
<tr><td>21</td><td>Indiana</td><td>2,092.0</td><td>14</td><td>Florida</td><td>2,288.6</td></tr>
<tr><td>43</td><td>Iowa</td><td>1,584.8</td><td>15</td><td>Kansas</td><td>2,258.0</td></tr>
<tr><td>15</td><td>Kansas</td><td>2,258.0</td><td>16</td><td>Georgia</td><td>2,248.0</td></tr>
<tr><td>35</td><td>Kentucky</td><td>1,725.2</td><td>17</td><td>Hawaii</td><td>2,243.2</td></tr>
<tr><td>2</td><td>Louisiana</td><td>2,453.7</td><td>18</td><td>North Carolina</td><td>2,185.7</td></tr>
<tr><td>28</td><td>Maine</td><td>1,873.7</td><td>19</td><td>Oklahoma</td><td>2,161.3</td></tr>
<tr><td>27</td><td>Maryland</td><td>1,924.9</td><td>20</td><td>Alaska</td><td>2,128.0</td></tr>
<tr><td>48</td><td>Massachusetts</td><td>1,494.4</td><td>21</td><td>Indiana</td><td>2,092.0</td></tr>
<tr><td>41</td><td>Michigan</td><td>1,612.0</td><td>22</td><td>Nebraska</td><td>2,060.7</td></tr>
<tr><td>26</td><td>Minnesota</td><td>1,939.3</td><td>23</td><td>Ohio</td><td>2,052.5</td></tr>
<tr><td>34</td><td>Mississippi</td><td>1,725.6</td><td>24</td><td>Montana</td><td>2,028.3</td></tr>
<tr><td>8</td><td>Missouri</td><td>2,338.4</td><td>25</td><td>Colorado</td><td>1,947.4</td></tr>
<tr><td>24</td><td>Montana</td><td>2,028.3</td><td>26</td><td>Minnesota</td><td>1,939.3</td></tr>
<tr><td>22</td><td>Nebraska</td><td>2,060.7</td><td>27</td><td>Maryland</td><td>1,924.9</td></tr>
<tr><td>39</td><td>Nevada</td><td>1,644.6</td><td>28</td><td>Maine</td><td>1,873.7</td></tr>
<tr><td>29</td><td>New Hampshire</td><td>1,834.3</td><td>29</td><td>New Hampshire</td><td>1,834.3</td></tr>
<tr><td>50</td><td>New Jersey</td><td>1,383.7</td><td>30</td><td>Illinois</td><td>1,826.9</td></tr>
<tr><td>11</td><td>New Mexico</td><td>2,313.4</td><td>31</td><td>Wyoming</td><td>1,823.9</td></tr>
<tr><td>47</td><td>New York</td><td>1,503.5</td><td>32</td><td>Wisconsin</td><td>1,822.3</td></tr>
<tr><td>18</td><td>North Carolina</td><td>2,185.7</td><td>33</td><td>Rhode Island</td><td>1,755.7</td></tr>
<tr><td>46</td><td>North Dakota</td><td>1,505.8</td><td>34</td><td>Mississippi</td><td>1,725.6</td></tr>
<tr><td>23</td><td>Ohio</td><td>2,052.5</td><td>35</td><td>Kentucky</td><td>1,725.2</td></tr>
<tr><td>19</td><td>Oklahoma</td><td>2,161.3</td><td>36</td><td>Vermont</td><td>1,695.8</td></tr>
<tr><td>4</td><td>Oregon</td><td>2,400.9</td><td>37</td><td>Virginia</td><td>1,690.7</td></tr>
<tr><td>42</td><td>Pennsylvania</td><td>1,603.1</td><td>38</td><td>California</td><td>1,669.5</td></tr>
<tr><td>33</td><td>Rhode Island</td><td>1,755.7</td><td>39</td><td>Nevada</td><td>1,644.6</td></tr>
<tr><td>1</td><td>South Carolina</td><td>2,588.3</td><td>40</td><td>West Virginia</td><td>1,637.3</td></tr>
<tr><td>45</td><td>South Dakota</td><td>1,541.4</td><td>41</td><td>Michigan</td><td>1,612.0</td></tr>
<tr><td>13</td><td>Tennessee</td><td>2,300.1</td><td>42</td><td>Pennsylvania</td><td>1,603.1</td></tr>
<tr><td>10</td><td>Texas</td><td>2,326.4</td><td>43</td><td>Iowa</td><td>1,584.8</td></tr>
<tr><td>9</td><td>Utah</td><td>2,328.4</td><td>44</td><td>Connecticut</td><td>1,550.7</td></tr>
<tr><td>36</td><td>Vermont</td><td>1,695.8</td><td>45</td><td>South Dakota</td><td>1,541.4</td></tr>
<tr><td>37</td><td>Virginia</td><td>1,690.7</td><td>46</td><td>North Dakota</td><td>1,505.8</td></tr>
<tr><td>5</td><td>Washington</td><td>2,395.3</td><td>47</td><td>New York</td><td>1,503.5</td></tr>
<tr><td>40</td><td>West Virginia</td><td>1,637.3</td><td>48</td><td>Massachusetts</td><td>1,494.4</td></tr>
<tr><td>32</td><td>Wisconsin</td><td>1,822.3</td><td>49</td><td>Idaho</td><td>1,447.7</td></tr>
<tr><td>31</td><td>Wyoming</td><td>1,823.9</td><td>50</td><td>New Jersey</td><td>1,383.7</td></tr>
<tr><td></td><td></td><td></td><td></td><td>District of Columbia</td><td>3,725.3</td></tr>
</tbody>
</table>

Source: Reported data from the Federal Bureau of Investigation
"Crime in the United States 2012" (Uniform Crime Reports, September 16, 2013, http://www.fbi.gov/about-us/cjis/ucr/)
*Larceny-theft is the unlawful taking of property without use of force, violence, or fraud. Attempts are included. Motor vehicle thefts are excluded.

Motor Vehicle Thefts in 2012

National Total = 721,053 Motor Vehicle Thefts*

<table>
<tr><td colspan="4">ALPHA ORDER</td><td colspan="4">RANK ORDER</td></tr>
<tr><td>RANK</td><td>STATE</td><td>THEFTS</td><td>% of USA</td><td>RANK</td><td>STATE</td><td>THEFTS</td><td>% of USA</td></tr>
<tr><td>23</td><td>Alabama</td><td>9,874</td><td>1.4%</td><td>1</td><td>California</td><td>168,608</td><td>23.4%</td></tr>
<tr><td>42</td><td>Alaska</td><td>1,522</td><td>0.2%</td><td>2</td><td>Texas</td><td>64,996</td><td>9.0%</td></tr>
<tr><td>9</td><td>Arizona</td><td>19,158</td><td>2.7%</td><td>3</td><td>Florida</td><td>37,330</td><td>5.2%</td></tr>
<tr><td>33</td><td>Arkansas</td><td>5,724</td><td>0.8%</td><td>4</td><td>Georgia</td><td>28,536</td><td>4.0%</td></tr>
<tr><td>1</td><td>California</td><td>168,608</td><td>23.4%</td><td>5</td><td>Washington</td><td>26,402</td><td>3.7%</td></tr>
<tr><td>19</td><td>Colorado</td><td>12,092</td><td>1.7%</td><td>6</td><td>Illinois</td><td>25,690</td><td>3.6%</td></tr>
<tr><td>31</td><td>Connecticut</td><td>6,449</td><td>0.9%</td><td>7</td><td>Michigan</td><td>25,115</td><td>3.5%</td></tr>
<tr><td>43</td><td>Delaware</td><td>1,436</td><td>0.2%</td><td>8</td><td>Ohio</td><td>19,512</td><td>2.7%</td></tr>
<tr><td>3</td><td>Florida</td><td>37,330</td><td>5.2%</td><td>9</td><td>Arizona</td><td>19,158</td><td>2.7%</td></tr>
<tr><td>4</td><td>Georgia</td><td>28,536</td><td>4.0%</td><td>10</td><td>New York</td><td>17,348</td><td>2.4%</td></tr>
<tr><td>38</td><td>Hawaii</td><td>3,605</td><td>0.5%</td><td>11</td><td>New Jersey</td><td>16,481</td><td>2.3%</td></tr>
<tr><td>44</td><td>Idaho</td><td>1,364</td><td>0.2%</td><td>12</td><td>Missouri</td><td>16,308</td><td>2.3%</td></tr>
<tr><td>6</td><td>Illinois</td><td>25,690</td><td>3.6%</td><td>13</td><td>North Carolina</td><td>16,120</td><td>2.2%</td></tr>
<tr><td>16</td><td>Indiana</td><td>13,661</td><td>1.9%</td><td>14</td><td>Pennsylvania</td><td>15,028</td><td>2.1%</td></tr>
<tr><td>37</td><td>Iowa</td><td>4,023</td><td>0.6%</td><td>15</td><td>Maryland</td><td>15,025</td><td>2.1%</td></tr>
<tr><td>29</td><td>Kansas</td><td>6,778</td><td>0.9%</td><td>16</td><td>Indiana</td><td>13,661</td><td>1.9%</td></tr>
<tr><td>30</td><td>Kentucky</td><td>6,668</td><td>0.9%</td><td>17</td><td>South Carolina</td><td>13,201</td><td>1.8%</td></tr>
<tr><td>28</td><td>Louisiana</td><td>7,881</td><td>1.1%</td><td>18</td><td>Tennessee</td><td>12,980</td><td>1.8%</td></tr>
<tr><td>48</td><td>Maine</td><td>995</td><td>0.1%</td><td>19</td><td>Colorado</td><td>12,092</td><td>1.7%</td></tr>
<tr><td>15</td><td>Maryland</td><td>15,025</td><td>2.1%</td><td>20</td><td>Oklahoma</td><td>11,564</td><td>1.6%</td></tr>
<tr><td>24</td><td>Massachusetts</td><td>9,232</td><td>1.3%</td><td>21</td><td>Oregon</td><td>10,203</td><td>1.4%</td></tr>
<tr><td>7</td><td>Michigan</td><td>25,115</td><td>3.5%</td><td>22</td><td>Nevada</td><td>10,018</td><td>1.4%</td></tr>
<tr><td>26</td><td>Minnesota</td><td>8,458</td><td>1.2%</td><td>23</td><td>Alabama</td><td>9,874</td><td>1.4%</td></tr>
<tr><td>35</td><td>Mississippi</td><td>4,322</td><td>0.6%</td><td>24</td><td>Massachusetts</td><td>9,232</td><td>1.3%</td></tr>
<tr><td>12</td><td>Missouri</td><td>16,308</td><td>2.3%</td><td>25</td><td>Virginia</td><td>9,076</td><td>1.3%</td></tr>
<tr><td>41</td><td>Montana</td><td>1,689</td><td>0.2%</td><td>26</td><td>Minnesota</td><td>8,458</td><td>1.2%</td></tr>
<tr><td>36</td><td>Nebraska</td><td>4,147</td><td>0.6%</td><td>27</td><td>Wisconsin</td><td>8,216</td><td>1.1%</td></tr>
<tr><td>22</td><td>Nevada</td><td>10,018</td><td>1.4%</td><td>28</td><td>Louisiana</td><td>7,881</td><td>1.1%</td></tr>
<tr><td>47</td><td>New Hampshire</td><td>1,023</td><td>0.1%</td><td>29</td><td>Kansas</td><td>6,778</td><td>0.9%</td></tr>
<tr><td>11</td><td>New Jersey</td><td>16,481</td><td>2.3%</td><td>30</td><td>Kentucky</td><td>6,668</td><td>0.9%</td></tr>
<tr><td>34</td><td>New Mexico</td><td>5,463</td><td>0.8%</td><td>31</td><td>Connecticut</td><td>6,449</td><td>0.9%</td></tr>
<tr><td>10</td><td>New York</td><td>17,348</td><td>2.4%</td><td>32</td><td>Utah</td><td>5,999</td><td>0.8%</td></tr>
<tr><td>13</td><td>North Carolina</td><td>16,120</td><td>2.2%</td><td>33</td><td>Arkansas</td><td>5,724</td><td>0.8%</td></tr>
<tr><td>45</td><td>North Dakota</td><td>1,151</td><td>0.2%</td><td>34</td><td>New Mexico</td><td>5,463</td><td>0.8%</td></tr>
<tr><td>8</td><td>Ohio</td><td>19,512</td><td>2.7%</td><td>35</td><td>Mississippi</td><td>4,322</td><td>0.6%</td></tr>
<tr><td>20</td><td>Oklahoma</td><td>11,564</td><td>1.6%</td><td>36</td><td>Nebraska</td><td>4,147</td><td>0.6%</td></tr>
<tr><td>21</td><td>Oregon</td><td>10,203</td><td>1.4%</td><td>37</td><td>Iowa</td><td>4,023</td><td>0.6%</td></tr>
<tr><td>14</td><td>Pennsylvania</td><td>15,028</td><td>2.1%</td><td>38</td><td>Hawaii</td><td>3,605</td><td>0.5%</td></tr>
<tr><td>39</td><td>Rhode Island</td><td>2,628</td><td>0.4%</td><td>39</td><td>Rhode Island</td><td>2,628</td><td>0.4%</td></tr>
<tr><td>17</td><td>South Carolina</td><td>13,201</td><td>1.8%</td><td>40</td><td>West Virginia</td><td>2,209</td><td>0.3%</td></tr>
<tr><td>46</td><td>South Dakota</td><td>1,065</td><td>0.1%</td><td>41</td><td>Montana</td><td>1,689</td><td>0.2%</td></tr>
<tr><td>18</td><td>Tennessee</td><td>12,980</td><td>1.8%</td><td>42</td><td>Alaska</td><td>1,522</td><td>0.2%</td></tr>
<tr><td>2</td><td>Texas</td><td>64,996</td><td>9.0%</td><td>43</td><td>Delaware</td><td>1,436</td><td>0.2%</td></tr>
<tr><td>32</td><td>Utah</td><td>5,999</td><td>0.8%</td><td>44</td><td>Idaho</td><td>1,364</td><td>0.2%</td></tr>
<tr><td>50</td><td>Vermont</td><td>435</td><td>0.1%</td><td>45</td><td>North Dakota</td><td>1,151</td><td>0.2%</td></tr>
<tr><td>25</td><td>Virginia</td><td>9,076</td><td>1.3%</td><td>46</td><td>South Dakota</td><td>1,065</td><td>0.1%</td></tr>
<tr><td>5</td><td>Washington</td><td>26,402</td><td>3.7%</td><td>47</td><td>New Hampshire</td><td>1,023</td><td>0.1%</td></tr>
<tr><td>40</td><td>West Virginia</td><td>2,209</td><td>0.3%</td><td>48</td><td>Maine</td><td>995</td><td>0.1%</td></tr>
<tr><td>27</td><td>Wisconsin</td><td>8,216</td><td>1.1%</td><td>49</td><td>Wyoming</td><td>584</td><td>0.1%</td></tr>
<tr><td>49</td><td>Wyoming</td><td>584</td><td>0.1%</td><td>50</td><td>Vermont</td><td>435</td><td>0.1%</td></tr>
<tr><td></td><td></td><td></td><td></td><td></td><td>District of Columbia</td><td>3,661</td><td>0.5%</td></tr>
</table>

Source: Reported data from the Federal Bureau of Investigation
"Crime in the United States 2012" (Uniform Crime Reports, September 16, 2013, http://www.fbi.gov/about-us/cjis/ucr/)
*Includes the theft or attempted theft of a self-propelled vehicle. Excludes motorboats, construction equipment, airplanes, and farming equipment.

Motor Vehicle Theft Rate in 2012

National Rate = 229.7 Motor Vehicle Thefts per 100,000 Population*

ALPHA ORDER				RANK ORDER		
RANK	STATE	RATE		RANK	STATE	RATE
22	Alabama	204.8		1	California	443.2
21	Alaska	208.1		2	Washington	382.8
5	Arizona	292.3		3	Nevada	363.1
25	Arkansas	194.1		4	Oklahoma	303.1
1	California	443.2		5	Arizona	292.3
17	Colorado	233.1		6	Georgia	287.7
28	Connecticut	179.6		7	South Carolina	279.5
35	Delaware	156.6		8	Missouri	270.8
26	Florida	193.2		9	New Mexico	261.9
6	Georgia	287.7		10	Oregon	261.7
11	Hawaii	258.9		11	Hawaii	258.9
47	Idaho	85.5		12	Maryland	255.3
24	Illinois	199.5		13	Michigan	254.1
20	Indiana	209.0		14	Rhode Island	250.2
40	Iowa	130.9		15	Texas	249.4
16	Kansas	234.9		16	Kansas	234.9
36	Kentucky	152.2		17	Colorado	233.1
29	Louisiana	171.3		18	Nebraska	223.5
49	Maine	74.9		19	Utah	210.1
12	Maryland	255.3		20	Indiana	209.0
39	Massachusetts	138.9		21	Alaska	208.1
13	Michigan	254.1		22	Alabama	204.8
34	Minnesota	157.2		23	Tennessee	201.0
37	Mississippi	144.8		24	Illinois	199.5
8	Missouri	270.8		25	Arkansas	194.1
31	Montana	168.0		26	Florida	193.2
18	Nebraska	223.5		27	New Jersey	185.9
3	Nevada	363.1		28	Connecticut	179.6
48	New Hampshire	77.5		29	Louisiana	171.3
27	New Jersey	185.9		30	Ohio	169.0
9	New Mexico	261.9		31	Montana	168.0
46	New York	88.6		32	North Carolina	165.3
32	North Carolina	165.3		33	North Dakota	164.5
33	North Dakota	164.5		34	Minnesota	157.2
30	Ohio	169.0		35	Delaware	156.6
4	Oklahoma	303.1		36	Kentucky	152.2
10	Oregon	261.7		37	Mississippi	144.8
43	Pennsylvania	117.7		38	Wisconsin	143.5
14	Rhode Island	250.2		39	Massachusetts	138.9
7	South Carolina	279.5		40	Iowa	130.9
41	South Dakota	127.8		41	South Dakota	127.8
23	Tennessee	201.0		42	West Virginia	119.1
15	Texas	249.4		43	Pennsylvania	117.7
19	Utah	210.1		44	Virginia	110.9
50	Vermont	69.5		45	Wyoming	101.3
44	Virginia	110.9		46	New York	88.6
2	Washington	382.8		47	Idaho	85.5
42	West Virginia	119.1		48	New Hampshire	77.5
38	Wisconsin	143.5		49	Maine	74.9
45	Wyoming	101.3		50	Vermont	69.5
					District of Columbia	579.0

Source: Reported data from the Federal Bureau of Investigation
"Crime in the United States 2012" (Uniform Crime Reports, September 16, 2013, http://www.fbi.gov/about-us/cjis/ucr/)
*Includes the theft or attempted theft of a self-propelled vehicle. Excludes motorboats, construction equipment, airplanes, and farming equipment.

Rate of Consumer Fraud Complaints in 2012

National Rate = 539.1 Complaints per 100,000 Population*

ALPHA ORDER			RANK ORDER		
RANK	STATE	RATE	RANK	STATE	RATE
30	Alabama	403.8	1	Florida	693.5
33	Alaska	393.5	2	Georgia	590.2
8	Arizona	510.2	3	Maryland	564.2
46	Arkansas	344.1	4	Delaware	563.2
11	California	492.3	5	Nevada	559.9
6	Colorado	545.2	6	Colorado	545.2
17	Connecticut	443.0	7	Virginia	517.4
4	Delaware	563.2	8	Arizona	510.2
1	Florida	693.5	9	Michigan	500.9
2	Georgia	590.2	10	New Hampshire	499.7
22	Hawaii	429.0	11	California	492.3
27	Idaho	419.4	12	Washington	488.9
32	Illinois	397.7	13	New Jersey	480.2
38	Indiana	374.6	14	Oregon	471.8
49	Iowa	296.3	15	Texas	458.6
40	Kansas	368.8	16	Massachusetts	443.4
43	Kentucky	360.0	17	Connecticut	443.0
31	Louisiana	399.9	18	Pennsylvania	441.9
34	Maine	393.0	19	Tennessee	435.1
3	Maryland	564.2	20	Ohio	434.2
16	Massachusetts	443.4	21	Rhode Island	433.1
9	Michigan	500.9	22	Hawaii	429.0
35	Minnesota	391.3	23	Missouri	427.2
48	Mississippi	319.1	24	North Carolina	422.6
23	Missouri	427.2	25	New York	420.5
39	Montana	371.0	26	South Carolina	420.2
36	Nebraska	380.9	27	Idaho	419.4
5	Nevada	559.9	28	New Mexico	416.0
10	New Hampshire	499.7	29	North Dakota	403.9
13	New Jersey	480.2	30	Alabama	403.8
28	New Mexico	416.0	31	Louisiana	399.9
25	New York	420.5	32	Illinois	397.7
24	North Carolina	422.6	33	Alaska	393.5
29	North Dakota	403.9	34	Maine	393.0
20	Ohio	434.2	35	Minnesota	391.3
45	Oklahoma	345.3	36	Nebraska	380.9
14	Oregon	471.8	37	Wisconsin	378.6
18	Pennsylvania	441.9	38	Indiana	374.6
21	Rhode Island	433.1	39	Montana	371.0
26	South Carolina	420.2	40	Kansas	368.8
50	South Dakota	291.2	41	Wyoming	365.5
19	Tennessee	435.1	42	Vermont	363.1
15	Texas	458.6	43	Kentucky	360.0
44	Utah	347.0	44	Utah	347.0
42	Vermont	363.1	45	Oklahoma	345.3
7	Virginia	517.4	46	Arkansas	344.1
12	Washington	488.9	47	West Virginia	334.4
47	West Virginia	334.4	48	Mississippi	319.1
37	Wisconsin	378.6	49	Iowa	296.3
41	Wyoming	365.5	50	South Dakota	291.2
				District of Columbia	752.1

Source: Federal Trade Commission, Consumer Sentinel
"Consumer Sentinel Network Data Book for January - December 2012" (February 2013, http://www.ftc.gov/sentinel/)
*National rate includes complaints not shown by state. Rates do not include identity theft or "Do Not Call" registry complaints.

Rate of Identity Theft Complaints in 2012

National Rate = 117.6 Complaints per 100,000 Population*

ALPHA ORDER			RANK ORDER		
RANK	STATE	RATE	RANK	STATE	RATE
10	Alabama	104.9	1	Florida	361.3
45	Alaska	51.7	2	Georgia	193.9
8	Arizona	107.3	3	California	122.7
28	Arkansas	74.4	4	Michigan	122.2
3	California	122.7	5	New York	110.1
15	Colorado	93.8	6	Nevada	109.9
22	Connecticut	81.2	7	Texas	108.6
13	Delaware	98.4	8	Arizona	107.3
1	Florida	361.3	9	Maryland	105.0
2	Georgia	193.9	10	Alabama	104.9
48	Hawaii	47.3	11	Illinois	100.9
38	Idaho	56.7	12	Mississippi	100.2
11	Illinois	100.9	13	Delaware	98.4
33	Indiana	67.5	14	New Jersey	95.1
43	Iowa	52.3	15	Colorado	93.8
30	Kansas	72.0	16	Rhode Island	91.7
39	Kentucky	56.2	17	South Carolina	90.6
21	Louisiana	87.6	18	New Mexico	89.1
46	Maine	50.1	19	Pennsylvania	88.7
9	Maryland	105.0	20	Tennessee	88.1
29	Massachusetts	73.4	21	Louisiana	87.6
4	Michigan	122.2	22	Connecticut	81.2
34	Minnesota	63.9	23	North Carolina	81.1
12	Mississippi	100.2	24	Virginia	80.8
27	Missouri	74.8	25	Washington	77.9
47	Montana	49.8	26	Ohio	77.0
37	Nebraska	57.6	27	Missouri	74.8
6	Nevada	109.9	28	Arkansas	74.4
36	New Hampshire	59.2	29	Massachusetts	73.4
14	New Jersey	95.1	30	Kansas	72.0
18	New Mexico	89.1	31	Wisconsin	70.8
5	New York	110.1	32	Oklahoma	67.8
23	North Carolina	81.1	33	Indiana	67.5
49	North Dakota	41.2	34	Minnesota	63.9
26	Ohio	77.0	35	Oregon	63.3
32	Oklahoma	67.8	36	New Hampshire	59.2
35	Oregon	63.3	37	Nebraska	57.6
19	Pennsylvania	88.7	38	Idaho	56.7
16	Rhode Island	91.7	39	Kentucky	56.2
17	South Carolina	90.6	40	Utah	55.5
50	South Dakota	39.6	41	Wyoming	55.2
20	Tennessee	88.1	42	West Virginia	54.0
7	Texas	108.6	43	Iowa	52.3
40	Utah	55.5	44	Vermont	52.1
44	Vermont	52.1	45	Alaska	51.7
24	Virginia	80.8	46	Maine	50.1
25	Washington	77.9	47	Montana	49.8
42	West Virginia	54.0	48	Hawaii	47.3
31	Wisconsin	70.8	49	North Dakota	41.2
41	Wyoming	55.2	50	South Dakota	39.6
				District of Columbia	169.1

Source: Federal Trade Commission, Consumer Sentinel
"Consumer Sentinel Network Data Book for January - December 2012" (February 2013, http://www.ftc.gov/sentinel/)
*National rate includes complaints not shown by state. Rates do not include consumer fraud or "Do Not Call" registry complaints.

Reported Arrest Rate in 2012

National Rate = 3,929.6 Reported Arrests per 100,000 Population*

RANK	STATE	RATE
NA	Alabama**	NA
1	Alaska	6,385.8
17	Arizona	4,322.2
7	Arkansas	5,496.4
39	California	3,282.4
15	Colorado	4,547.3
40	Connecticut	3,252.0
16	Delaware	4,328.0
11	Florida	4,976.9
31	Georgia	3,741.4
NA	Hawaii**	NA
23	Idaho	4,053.7
NA	Illinois**	NA
32	Indiana	3,638.2
29	Iowa	3,788.7
30	Kansas	3,782.6
18	Kentucky	4,279.9
8	Louisiana	5,335.4
27	Maine	3,852.4
24	Maryland	4,014.4
46	Massachusetts	2,245.9
44	Michigan	2,757.8
NA	Minnesota**	NA
2	Mississippi	6,147.5
10	Missouri	5,164.7
37	Montana	3,409.8
14	Nebraska	4,592.4
9	Nevada	5,182.0
26	New Hampshire	3,894.9
28	New Jersey	3,802.2
6	New Mexico	5,568.5
43	New York**	3,134.4
12	North Carolina	4,964.9
19	North Dakota	4,244.9
42	Ohio	3,159.5
33	Oklahoma	3,561.3
35	Oregon	3,538.6
34	Pennsylvania	3,541.3
41	Rhode Island	3,178.6
22	South Carolina	4,118.5
13	South Dakota	4,728.8
3	Tennessee	6,077.1
25	Texas	4,000.7
20	Utah	4,193.9
45	Vermont	2,342.9
21	Virginia	4,149.2
38	Washington	3,331.9
36	West Virginia	3,415.1
4	Wisconsin	6,033.1
5	Wyoming	5,843.0

RANK	STATE	RATE
1	Alaska	6,385.8
2	Mississippi	6,147.5
3	Tennessee	6,077.1
4	Wisconsin	6,033.1
5	Wyoming	5,843.0
6	New Mexico	5,568.5
7	Arkansas	5,496.4
8	Louisiana	5,335.4
9	Nevada	5,182.0
10	Missouri	5,164.7
11	Florida	4,976.9
12	North Carolina	4,964.9
13	South Dakota	4,728.8
14	Nebraska	4,592.4
15	Colorado	4,547.3
16	Delaware	4,328.0
17	Arizona	4,322.2
18	Kentucky	4,279.9
19	North Dakota	4,244.9
20	Utah	4,193.9
21	Virginia	4,149.2
22	South Carolina	4,118.5
23	Idaho	4,053.7
24	Maryland	4,014.4
25	Texas	4,000.7
26	New Hampshire	3,894.9
27	Maine	3,852.4
28	New Jersey	3,802.2
29	Iowa	3,788.7
30	Kansas	3,782.6
31	Georgia	3,741.4
32	Indiana	3,638.2
33	Oklahoma	3,561.3
34	Pennsylvania	3,541.3
35	Oregon	3,538.6
36	West Virginia	3,415.1
37	Montana	3,409.8
38	Washington	3,331.9
39	California	3,282.4
40	Connecticut	3,252.0
41	Rhode Island	3,178.6
42	Ohio	3,159.5
43	New York**	3,134.4
44	Michigan	2,757.8
45	Vermont	2,342.9
46	Massachusetts	2,245.9
NA	Alabama**	NA
NA	Hawaii**	NA
NA	Illinois**	NA
NA	Minnesota**	NA
	District of Columbia**	NA

Source: CQ Press using reported data from the Federal Bureau of Investigation
  "Crime in the United States 2012" (Uniform Crime Reports, September 16, 2013, http://www.fbi.gov/about-us/cjis/ucr/)
*By law enforcement agencies submitting complete reports to the F.B.I. for 12 months in 2012. These rates based on population estimates for areas under the jurisdiction of those agencies reporting. Arrest rate based on the F.B.I. estimate of total arrests is 3,885.4 reported and unreported arrests per 100,000 population.
**Not available. New York's figure does not include New York City.

Reported Juvenile Arrest Rate in 2012

National Rate = 3,939.8 Reported Arrests per 100,000 Juvenile Population*

ALPHA ORDER				RANK ORDER		
RANK	STATE	RATE		RANK	STATE	RATE
NA	Alabama**	NA		1	Wisconsin	11,215.2
13	Alaska	5,003.6		2	Wyoming	7,559.6
15	Arizona	4,958.6		3	North Dakota	7,423.2
28	Arkansas	3,700.6		4	South Dakota	7,305.4
41	California	2,836.4		5	Montana	7,214.8
9	Colorado	5,386.2		6	Nebraska	6,405.9
39	Connecticut	3,021.9		7	Louisiana	5,472.7
14	Delaware	4,975.8		8	Pennsylvania	5,455.1
23	Florida	4,266.8		9	Colorado	5,386.2
32	Georgia	3,483.7		10	Idaho	5,287.6
NA	Hawaii**	NA		11	Utah	5,245.2
10	Idaho	5,287.6		12	Iowa	5,090.8
NA	Illinois**	NA		13	Alaska	5,003.6
26	Indiana	4,099.9		14	Delaware	4,975.8
12	Iowa	5,090.8		15	Arizona	4,958.6
37	Kansas	3,126.2		16	Missouri	4,862.9
45	Kentucky	1,605.6		17	New Mexico	4,855.9
7	Louisiana	5,472.7		18	Oregon	4,602.4
24	Maine	4,250.4		19	Tennessee	4,592.2
25	Maryland	4,232.4		20	New Hampshire	4,521.8
44	Massachusetts	1,835.9		21	Nevada	4,515.7
42	Michigan	2,443.0		22	Mississippi	4,282.4
NA	Minnesota**	NA		23	Florida	4,266.8
22	Mississippi	4,282.4		24	Maine	4,250.4
16	Missouri	4,862.9		25	Maryland	4,232.4
5	Montana	7,214.8		26	Indiana	4,099.9
6	Nebraska	6,405.9		27	Texas	3,720.5
21	Nevada	4,515.7		28	Arkansas	3,700.6
20	New Hampshire	4,521.8		29	New York**	3,690.5
40	New Jersey	2,914.8		30	Rhode Island	3,658.0
17	New Mexico	4,855.9		31	North Carolina	3,565.1
29	New York**	3,690.5		32	Georgia	3,483.7
31	North Carolina	3,565.1		33	South Carolina	3,429.1
3	North Dakota	7,423.2		34	Washington	3,412.5
35	Ohio	3,255.2		35	Ohio	3,255.2
36	Oklahoma	3,254.0		36	Oklahoma	3,254.0
18	Oregon	4,602.4		37	Kansas	3,126.2
8	Pennsylvania	5,455.1		38	Virginia	3,066.3
30	Rhode Island	3,658.0		39	Connecticut	3,021.9
33	South Carolina	3,429.1		40	New Jersey	2,914.8
4	South Dakota	7,305.4		41	California	2,836.4
19	Tennessee	4,592.2		42	Michigan	2,443.0
27	Texas	3,720.5		43	Vermont	1,954.4
11	Utah	5,245.2		44	Massachusetts	1,835.9
43	Vermont	1,954.4		45	Kentucky	1,605.6
38	Virginia	3,066.3		46	West Virginia	1,314.9
34	Washington	3,412.5		NA	Alabama**	NA
46	West Virginia	1,314.9		NA	Hawaii**	NA
1	Wisconsin	11,215.2		NA	Illinois**	NA
2	Wyoming	7,559.6		NA	Minnesota**	NA
					District of Columbia**	NA

Source: CQ Press using reported data from the Federal Bureau of Investigation
"Crime in the United States 2012" (Uniform Crime Reports, September 16, 2013, http://www.fbi.gov/about-us/cjis/ucr/)
*By law enforcement agencies submitting complete reports to the F.B.I. for 12 months in 2012. Arrests of youths 17 years and younger divided into population of 10 to 17 year olds.
**Not available. New York's figure does not include New York City.

Prisoners in State Correctional Institutions: Year End 2012

National Total = 1,352,582 State Prisoners*

ALPHA ORDER

RANK	STATE	PRISONERS	% of USA
14	Alabama	32,431	2.4%
41	Alaska	5,633	0.4%
11	Arizona	40,080	3.0%
29	Arkansas	14,654	1.1%
2	California	134,534	9.9%
25	Colorado	20,462	1.5%
26	Connecticut	17,530	1.3%
38	Delaware	6,914	0.5%
3	Florida	101,930	7.5%
4	Georgia	55,457	4.1%
40	Hawaii	5,831	0.4%
35	Idaho	7,985	0.6%
8	Illinois	49,348	3.6%
16	Indiana	28,831	2.1%
34	Iowa	8,733	0.6%
33	Kansas	9,682	0.7%
23	Kentucky	22,110	1.6%
10	Louisiana	40,172	3.0%
48	Maine	2,108	0.2%
24	Maryland	21,522	1.6%
31	Massachusetts	11,308	0.8%
9	Michigan	43,636	3.2%
32	Minnesota	9,938	0.7%
22	Mississippi	22,319	1.7%
15	Missouri	31,247	2.3%
44	Montana	3,609	0.3%
42	Nebraska	4,705	0.3%
30	Nevada	12,883	1.0%
46	New Hampshire	2,790	0.2%
19	New Jersey	23,225	1.7%
39	New Mexico	6,727	0.5%
5	New York	54,210	4.0%
12	North Carolina	37,136	2.7%
50	North Dakota	1,512	0.1%
7	Ohio	50,876	3.8%
18	Oklahoma	25,225	1.9%
28	Oregon	14,840	1.1%
6	Pennsylvania	51,125	3.8%
45	Rhode Island	3,318	0.2%
21	South Carolina	22,388	1.7%
43	South Dakota	3,650	0.3%
17	Tennessee	28,411	2.1%
1	Texas	166,372	12.3%
37	Utah	6,962	0.5%
49	Vermont	2,034	0.2%
13	Virginia	37,044	2.7%
27	Washington	17,271	1.3%
36	West Virginia	7,070	0.5%
20	Wisconsin	22,600	1.7%
47	Wyoming	2,204	0.2%

RANK ORDER

RANK	STATE	PRISONERS	% of USA
1	Texas	166,372	12.3%
2	California	134,534	9.9%
3	Florida	101,930	7.5%
4	Georgia	55,457	4.1%
5	New York	54,210	4.0%
6	Pennsylvania	51,125	3.8%
7	Ohio	50,876	3.8%
8	Illinois	49,348	3.6%
9	Michigan	43,636	3.2%
10	Louisiana	40,172	3.0%
11	Arizona	40,080	3.0%
12	North Carolina	37,136	2.7%
13	Virginia	37,044	2.7%
14	Alabama	32,431	2.4%
15	Missouri	31,247	2.3%
16	Indiana	28,831	2.1%
17	Tennessee	28,411	2.1%
18	Oklahoma	25,225	1.9%
19	New Jersey	23,225	1.7%
20	Wisconsin	22,600	1.7%
21	South Carolina	22,388	1.7%
22	Mississippi	22,319	1.7%
23	Kentucky	22,110	1.6%
24	Maryland	21,522	1.6%
25	Colorado	20,462	1.5%
26	Connecticut	17,530	1.3%
27	Washington	17,271	1.3%
28	Oregon	14,840	1.1%
29	Arkansas	14,654	1.1%
30	Nevada	12,883	1.0%
31	Massachusetts	11,308	0.8%
32	Minnesota	9,938	0.7%
33	Kansas	9,682	0.7%
34	Iowa	8,733	0.6%
35	Idaho	7,985	0.6%
36	West Virginia	7,070	0.5%
37	Utah	6,962	0.5%
38	Delaware	6,914	0.5%
39	New Mexico	6,727	0.5%
40	Hawaii	5,831	0.4%
41	Alaska	5,633	0.4%
42	Nebraska	4,705	0.3%
43	South Dakota	3,650	0.3%
44	Montana	3,609	0.3%
45	Rhode Island	3,318	0.2%
46	New Hampshire	2,790	0.2%
47	Wyoming	2,204	0.2%
48	Maine	2,108	0.2%
49	Vermont	2,034	0.2%
50	North Dakota	1,512	0.1%
	District of Columbia**	NA	NA

Source: U.S. Department of Justice, Bureau of Justice Statistics
  "Prisoners in 2012" (December 2013, NCJ 243920, http://bjs.ojp.usdoj.gov/)
*As of December 31, 2012. Totals reflect all prisoners, including those sentenced to a year or less and those unsentenced.
National total does not include 217,815 prisoners under federal jurisdiction. State and federal prisoners combined total 1,570,397.
**Responsibility for sentenced felons in D.C. was transferred to the Federal Bureau of Prisons in 2001.

State Prisoner Imprisonment Rate in 2012

National Rate = 418 State Prisoners per 100,000 Population*

ALPHA ORDER

RANK	STATE	RATE
3	Alabama	650
21	Alaska	401
6	Arizona	583
11	Arkansas	494
31	California	351
23	Colorado	392
32	Connecticut	333
15	Delaware	448
8	Florida	524
7	Georgia	542
37	Hawaii	273
10	Idaho	499
NA	Illinois**	NA
17	Indiana	440
35	Iowa	282
33	Kansas	325
12	Kentucky	489
1	Louisiana	893
47	Maine	145
27	Maryland	360
44	Massachusetts	199
16	Michigan	441
46	Minnesota	184
2	Mississippi	717
9	Missouri	518
28	Montana	358
39	Nebraska	247
NA	Nevada**	NA
43	New Hampshire	211
38	New Jersey	261
34	New Mexico	315
36	New York	276
29	North Carolina	357
42	North Dakota	213
17	Ohio	440
4	Oklahoma	648
25	Oregon	378
22	Pennsylvania	398
45	Rhode Island	190
13	South Carolina	458
20	South Dakota	434
19	Tennessee	438
5	Texas	601
40	Utah	242
40	Vermont	242
14	Virginia	451
NA	Washington**	NA
25	West Virginia	378
29	Wisconsin	357
24	Wyoming	379

RANK ORDER

RANK	STATE	RATE
1	Louisiana	893
2	Mississippi	717
3	Alabama	650
4	Oklahoma	648
5	Texas	601
6	Arizona	583
7	Georgia	542
8	Florida	524
9	Missouri	518
10	Idaho	499
11	Arkansas	494
12	Kentucky	489
13	South Carolina	458
14	Virginia	451
15	Delaware	448
16	Michigan	441
17	Indiana	440
17	Ohio	440
19	Tennessee	438
20	South Dakota	434
21	Alaska	401
22	Pennsylvania	398
23	Colorado	392
24	Wyoming	379
25	Oregon	378
25	West Virginia	378
27	Maryland	360
28	Montana	358
29	North Carolina	357
29	Wisconsin	357
31	California	351
32	Connecticut	333
33	Kansas	325
34	New Mexico	315
35	Iowa	282
36	New York	276
37	Hawaii	273
38	New Jersey	261
39	Nebraska	247
40	Utah	242
40	Vermont	242
42	North Dakota	213
43	New Hampshire	211
44	Massachusetts	199
45	Rhode Island	190
46	Minnesota	184
47	Maine	145
NA	Illinois**	NA
NA	Nevada**	NA
NA	Washington**	NA
	District of Columbia***	NA

Source: U.S. Department of Justice, Bureau of Justice Statistics
    "Prisoners in 2012 - Advance Counts" (July 2013, NCJ 242467, http://bjs.ojp.usdoj.gov/)
*Advance figures as of December 31, 2012. Includes only inmates sentenced to more than one year. Does not include federal imprisonment rate of 62 prisoners per 100,000 population. State and federal combined imprisonment rate is 480 prisoners per 100,000 population. **Not available.
***Responsibility for sentenced felons in D.C. was transferred to the Federal Bureau of Prisons in 2001.

Percent Change in Number of State Prisoners: 2011 to 2012

National Percent Change = 2.2% Decrease*

ALPHA ORDER				RANK ORDER		
RANK	STATE	PERCENT CHANGE		RANK	STATE	PERCENT CHANGE
21	Alabama	0.5		1	New Hampshire	6.7
20	Alaska	0.6		2	North Dakota	6.3
22	Arizona	0.1		3	Mississippi	4.4
49	Arkansas	(9.0)		4	Kansas	3.8
50	California	(10.1)		5	West Virginia	3.6
48	Colorado	(6.9)		6	South Dakota	3.3
45	Connecticut	(4.3)		7	Idaho	3.2
8	Delaware	2.6		8	Delaware	2.6
31	Florida	(1.1)		8	Kentucky	2.6
28	Georgia	(0.9)		10	Oregon	2.3
41	Hawaii	(3.4)		11	Illinois	1.9
7	Idaho	3.2		11	Nebraska	1.9
11	Illinois	1.9		13	Michigan	1.6
25	Indiana	(0.3)		14	Minnesota	1.4
44	Iowa	(4.2)		15	Missouri	1.3
4	Kansas	3.8		16	Louisiana	1.2
8	Kentucky	2.6		16	Utah	1.2
16	Louisiana	1.2		18	Wyoming	1.0
32	Maine	(1.7)		19	Nevada	0.8
46	Maryland	(4.6)		20	Alaska	0.6
37	Massachusetts	(2.7)		21	Alabama	0.5
13	Michigan	1.6		22	Arizona	0.1
14	Minnesota	1.4		23	Ohio	(0.2)
3	Mississippi	4.4		23	Tennessee	(0.2)
15	Missouri	1.3		25	Indiana	(0.3)
33	Montana	(1.9)		25	Wisconsin	(0.3)
11	Nebraska	1.9		27	Rhode Island	(0.6)
19	Nevada	0.8		28	Georgia	(0.9)
1	New Hampshire	6.7		28	Pennsylvania	(0.9)
36	New Jersey	(2.6)		28	Vermont	(0.9)
43	New Mexico	(3.9)		31	Florida	(1.1)
34	New York	(2.2)		32	Maine	(1.7)
47	North Carolina	(5.8)		33	Montana	(1.9)
2	North Dakota	6.3		34	New York	(2.2)
23	Ohio	(0.2)		35	South Carolina	(2.3)
39	Oklahoma	(2.9)		36	New Jersey	(2.6)
10	Oregon	2.3		37	Massachusetts	(2.7)
28	Pennsylvania	(0.9)		38	Virginia	(2.8)
27	Rhode Island	(0.6)		39	Oklahoma	(2.9)
35	South Carolina	(2.3)		40	Washington	(3.2)
6	South Dakota	3.3		41	Hawaii	(3.4)
23	Tennessee	(0.2)		41	Texas	(3.4)
41	Texas	(3.4)		43	New Mexico	(3.9)
16	Utah	1.2		44	Iowa	(4.2)
28	Vermont	(0.9)		45	Connecticut	(4.3)
38	Virginia	(2.8)		46	Maryland	(4.6)
40	Washington	(3.2)		47	North Carolina	(5.8)
5	West Virginia	3.6		48	Colorado	(6.9)
25	Wisconsin	(0.3)		49	Arkansas	(9.0)
18	Wyoming	1.0		50	California	(10.1)
					District of Columbia**	NA

Source: U.S. Department of Justice, Bureau of Justice Statistics
   "Prisoners in 2012" (December 2013, NCJ 243920, http://bjs.ojp.usdoj.gov/)
*From December 31, 2011 to December 31, 2012. Includes inmates sentenced to more than one year and those sentenced to a year or less or with no sentence. The percent change in number of prisoners under federal jurisdiction during the same period was an 0.7% increase. The combined state and federal decrease was 1.8%.
**Responsibility for sentenced felons in D.C. was transferred to the Federal Bureau of Prisons in 2001.

Prisoners under Sentence of Death in 2011

National Total = 3,026 State Prisoners*

ALPHA ORDER

RANK	STATE	PRISONERS	% of USA
5	Alabama	196	6.5%
NA	Alaska**	NA	NA
8	Arizona	130	4.3%
17	Arkansas	39	1.3%
1	California	705	23.3%
31	Colorado	3	0.1%
24	Connecticut	10	0.3%
20	Delaware	18	0.6%
2	Florida	393	13.0%
9	Georgia	96	3.2%
NA	Hawaii**	NA	NA
21	Idaho	13	0.4%
NA	Illinois**	NA	NA
22	Indiana	12	0.4%
NA	Iowa**	NA	NA
25	Kansas	9	0.3%
19	Kentucky	34	1.1%
10	Louisiana	87	2.9%
NA	Maine**	NA	NA
29	Maryland	5	0.2%
NA	Massachusetts**	NA	NA
NA	Michigan**	NA	NA
NA	Minnesota**	NA	NA
14	Mississippi	57	1.9%
16	Missouri	46	1.5%
32	Montana	2	0.1%
23	Nebraska	11	0.4%
12	Nevada	81	2.7%
34	New Hampshire	1	0.0%
NA	New Jersey**	NA	NA
32	New Mexico	2	0.1%
36	New York	0	0.0%
6	North Carolina	158	5.2%
NA	North Dakota**	NA	NA
7	Ohio	142	4.7%
13	Oklahoma	63	2.1%
18	Oregon	36	1.2%
4	Pennsylvania	207	6.8%
NA	Rhode Island**	NA	NA
15	South Carolina	52	1.7%
30	South Dakota	4	0.1%
10	Tennessee	87	2.9%
3	Texas	301	9.9%
27	Utah	8	0.3%
NA	Vermont**	NA	NA
25	Virginia	9	0.3%
27	Washington	8	0.3%
NA	West Virginia**	NA	NA
NA	Wisconsin**	NA	NA
34	Wyoming	1	0.0%

RANK ORDER

RANK	STATE	PRISONERS	% of USA
1	California	705	23.3%
2	Florida	393	13.0%
3	Texas	301	9.9%
4	Pennsylvania	207	6.8%
5	Alabama	196	6.5%
6	North Carolina	158	5.2%
7	Ohio	142	4.7%
8	Arizona	130	4.3%
9	Georgia	96	3.2%
10	Louisiana	87	2.9%
10	Tennessee	87	2.9%
12	Nevada	81	2.7%
13	Oklahoma	63	2.1%
14	Mississippi	57	1.9%
15	South Carolina	52	1.7%
16	Missouri	46	1.5%
17	Arkansas	39	1.3%
18	Oregon	36	1.2%
19	Kentucky	34	1.1%
20	Delaware	18	0.6%
21	Idaho	13	0.4%
22	Indiana	12	0.4%
23	Nebraska	11	0.4%
24	Connecticut	10	0.3%
25	Kansas	9	0.3%
25	Virginia	9	0.3%
27	Utah	8	0.3%
27	Washington	8	0.3%
29	Maryland	5	0.2%
30	South Dakota	4	0.1%
31	Colorado	3	0.1%
32	Montana	2	0.1%
32	New Mexico	2	0.1%
34	New Hampshire	1	0.0%
34	Wyoming	1	0.0%
36	New York	0	0.0%
NA	Alaska**	NA	NA
NA	Hawaii**	NA	NA
NA	Illinois**	NA	NA
NA	Iowa**	NA	NA
NA	Maine**	NA	NA
NA	Massachusetts**	NA	NA
NA	Michigan**	NA	NA
NA	Minnesota**	NA	NA
NA	New Jersey**	NA	NA
NA	North Dakota**	NA	NA
NA	Rhode Island**	NA	NA
NA	Vermont**	NA	NA
NA	West Virginia**	NA	NA
NA	Wisconsin**	NA	NA
	District of Columbia**	NA	NA

Source: U.S. Department of Justice, Bureau of Justice Statistics
    "Capital Punishment 2011" (Bulletin, July 2013, NCJ 242185, http://bjs.ojp.usdoj.gov/)
*As of December 31, 2011. Does not include 57 federal prisoners under sentence of death. There were 43 executions in 2011.
**No death penalty as of December 31, 2011.

Rate of State and Local Police Officers in 2011

National Rate = 22.1 Officers per 10,000 Population*

RANK	STATE	RATE	RANK	STATE	RATE
19	Alabama	22.0	1	New York	37.4
48	Alaska	15.7	2	New Jersey	30.3
13	Arizona	22.4	3	Louisiana	29.5
9	Arkansas	24.1	3	Massachusetts	29.5
36	California	18.1	5	Illinois	27.5
28	Colorado	20.3	6	Wyoming	27.3
15	Connecticut	22.2	7	Rhode Island	24.5
32	Delaware	19.2	8	Maryland	24.2
22	Florida	21.6	9	Arkansas	24.1
20	Georgia	21.8	10	South Carolina	23.4
21	Hawaii	21.7	11	Mississippi	22.7
37	Idaho	17.9	12	North Carolina	22.5
5	Illinois	27.5	13	Arizona	22.4
38	Indiana	17.8	13	Missouri	22.4
40	Iowa	17.2	15	Connecticut	22.2
15	Kansas	22.2	15	Kansas	22.2
41	Kentucky	17.1	17	New Hampshire	22.1
3	Louisiana	29.5	17	Tennessee	22.1
46	Maine	15.9	19	Alabama	22.0
8	Maryland	24.2	20	Georgia	21.8
3	Massachusetts	29.5	21	Hawaii	21.7
42	Michigan	16.6	22	Florida	21.6
45	Minnesota	16.0	23	Texas	20.9
11	Mississippi	22.7	24	New Mexico	20.8
13	Missouri	22.4	25	Pennsylvania	20.7
39	Montana	17.7	25	Wisconsin	20.7
28	Nebraska	20.3	27	Virginia	20.4
33	Nevada	19.0	28	Colorado	20.3
17	New Hampshire	22.1	28	Nebraska	20.3
2	New Jersey	30.3	30	Oklahoma	20.2
24	New Mexico	20.8	31	Ohio	20.1
1	New York	37.4	32	Delaware	19.2
12	North Carolina	22.5	33	Nevada	19.0
34	North Dakota	18.3	34	North Dakota	18.3
31	Ohio	20.1	34	South Dakota	18.3
30	Oklahoma	20.2	36	California	18.1
44	Oregon	16.1	37	Idaho	17.9
25	Pennsylvania	20.7	38	Indiana	17.8
7	Rhode Island	24.5	39	Montana	17.7
10	South Carolina	23.4	40	Iowa	17.2
34	South Dakota	18.3	41	Kentucky	17.1
17	Tennessee	22.1	42	Michigan	16.6
23	Texas	20.9	43	West Virginia	16.4
49	Utah	15.6	44	Oregon	16.1
46	Vermont	15.9	45	Minnesota	16.0
27	Virginia	20.4	46	Maine	15.9
50	Washington	15.5	46	Vermont	15.9
43	West Virginia	16.4	48	Alaska	15.7
25	Wisconsin	20.7	49	Utah	15.6
6	Wyoming	27.3	50	Washington	15.5
				District of Columbia	62.6

Source: CQ Press using data from U.S. Bureau of the Census, Governments Division
"Government Employment and Payroll" (http://www.census.gov/govs/apes/index.html)
*Full-time equivalent as of March 2011. Does not include employees of police departments who are not officers.

Per Capita State and Local Government Expenditures for Police Protection in 2011
National Per Capita = $309*

ALPHA ORDER

RANK	STATE	PER CAPITA
35	Alabama	$237
2	Alaska	452
12	Arizona	325
49	Arkansas	185
4	California	400
13	Colorado	323
19	Connecticut	299
14	Delaware	320
5	Florida	385
38	Georgia	232
20	Hawaii	280
33	Idaho	241
9	Illinois	360
45	Indiana	199
44	Iowa	210
29	Kansas	255
50	Kentucky	161
11	Louisiana	329
45	Maine	199
8	Maryland	370
14	Massachusetts	320
33	Michigan	241
17	Minnesota	309
43	Mississippi	222
22	Missouri	278
27	Montana	258
41	Nebraska	223
3	Nevada	421
26	New Hampshire	267
6	New Jersey	378
18	New Mexico	306
1	New York	462
30	North Carolina	254
41	North Dakota	223
23	Ohio	277
35	Oklahoma	237
21	Oregon	279
32	Pennsylvania	246
10	Rhode Island	339
40	South Carolina	227
47	South Dakota	197
25	Tennessee	268
28	Texas	257
37	Utah	234
24	Vermont	276
31	Virginia	252
39	Washington	230
48	West Virginia	192
16	Wisconsin	310
7	Wyoming	377

RANK ORDER

RANK	STATE	PER CAPITA
1	New York	$462
2	Alaska	452
3	Nevada	421
4	California	400
5	Florida	385
6	New Jersey	378
7	Wyoming	377
8	Maryland	370
9	Illinois	360
10	Rhode Island	339
11	Louisiana	329
12	Arizona	325
13	Colorado	323
14	Delaware	320
14	Massachusetts	320
16	Wisconsin	310
17	Minnesota	309
18	New Mexico	306
19	Connecticut	299
20	Hawaii	280
21	Oregon	279
22	Missouri	278
23	Ohio	277
24	Vermont	276
25	Tennessee	268
26	New Hampshire	267
27	Montana	258
28	Texas	257
29	Kansas	255
30	North Carolina	254
31	Virginia	252
32	Pennsylvania	246
33	Idaho	241
33	Michigan	241
35	Alabama	237
35	Oklahoma	237
37	Utah	234
38	Georgia	232
39	Washington	230
40	South Carolina	227
41	Nebraska	223
41	North Dakota	223
43	Mississippi	222
44	Iowa	210
45	Indiana	199
45	Maine	199
47	South Dakota	197
48	West Virginia	192
49	Arkansas	185
50	Kentucky	161
	District of Columbia	955

Source: CQ Press using data from U.S. Bureau of the Census, Governments Division
"2011 State and Local Government Finances" (http://www.census.gov/govs/local/)
*Direct general expenditures.

Per Capita State and Local Government Expenditures for Corrections in 2011

National Per Capita = $235*

ALPHA ORDER

RANK	STATE	PER CAPITA
43	Alabama	$155
1	Alaska	397
21	Arizona	226
30	Arkansas	184
2	California	361
15	Colorado	237
27	Connecticut	192
7	Delaware	294
22	Florida	225
17	Georgia	230
50	Hawaii	139
30	Idaho	184
37	Illinois	172
44	Indiana	154
45	Iowa	153
33	Kansas	176
38	Kentucky	168
8	Louisiana	286
46	Maine	148
6	Maryland	295
41	Massachusetts	159
20	Michigan	227
40	Minnesota	163
29	Mississippi	186
47	Missouri	143
14	Montana	241
25	Nebraska	198
12	Nevada	255
48	New Hampshire	140
16	New Jersey	234
5	New Mexico	300
4	New York	302
24	North Carolina	199
32	North Dakota	177
39	Ohio	167
36	Oklahoma	173
10	Oregon	271
13	Pennsylvania	254
28	Rhode Island	188
48	South Carolina	140
26	South Dakota	194
41	Tennessee	159
19	Texas	228
34	Utah	175
23	Vermont	202
9	Virginia	273
17	Washington	230
34	West Virginia	175
11	Wisconsin	270
3	Wyoming	356

RANK ORDER

RANK	STATE	PER CAPITA
1	Alaska	$397
2	California	361
3	Wyoming	356
4	New York	302
5	New Mexico	300
6	Maryland	295
7	Delaware	294
8	Louisiana	286
9	Virginia	273
10	Oregon	271
11	Wisconsin	270
12	Nevada	255
13	Pennsylvania	254
14	Montana	241
15	Colorado	237
16	New Jersey	234
17	Georgia	230
17	Washington	230
19	Texas	228
20	Michigan	227
21	Arizona	226
22	Florida	225
23	Vermont	202
24	North Carolina	199
25	Nebraska	198
26	South Dakota	194
27	Connecticut	192
28	Rhode Island	188
29	Mississippi	186
30	Arkansas	184
30	Idaho	184
32	North Dakota	177
33	Kansas	176
34	Utah	175
34	West Virginia	175
36	Oklahoma	173
37	Illinois	172
38	Kentucky	168
39	Ohio	167
40	Minnesota	163
41	Massachusetts	159
41	Tennessee	159
43	Alabama	155
44	Indiana	154
45	Iowa	153
46	Maine	148
47	Missouri	143
48	New Hampshire	140
48	South Carolina	140
50	Hawaii	139

District of Columbia   415

Source: CQ Press using data from U.S. Bureau of the Census, Governments Division
   "2011 State and Local Government Finances" (http://www.census.gov/govs/local/)
*Direct general expenditures.

Per Capita State and Local Government Expenditures for Judicial and Legal Services in 2011
National Per Capita = $138*

ALPHA ORDER

RANK	STATE	PER CAPITA
43	Alabama	$86
1	Alaska	313
15	Arizona	144
50	Arkansas	70
2	California	236
17	Colorado	132
5	Connecticut	192
7	Delaware	170
26	Florida	115
36	Georgia	103
6	Hawaii	173
22	Idaho	120
27	Illinois	114
48	Indiana	74
31	Iowa	111
34	Kansas	105
24	Kentucky	116
10	Louisiana	159
49	Maine	73
16	Maryland	136
14	Massachusetts	145
28	Michigan	113
18	Minnesota	131
46	Mississippi	76
44	Missouri	79
11	Montana	154
38	Nebraska	97
9	Nevada	165
41	New Hampshire	87
8	New Jersey	167
12	New Mexico	153
3	New York	217
45	North Carolina	78
31	North Dakota	111
13	Ohio	152
41	Oklahoma	87
28	Oregon	113
18	Pennsylvania	131
24	Rhode Island	116
47	South Carolina	75
39	South Dakota	95
39	Tennessee	95
33	Texas	106
20	Utah	122
30	Vermont	112
37	Virginia	102
20	Washington	122
23	West Virginia	117
35	Wisconsin	104
4	Wyoming	204

RANK ORDER

RANK	STATE	PER CAPITA
1	Alaska	$313
2	California	236
3	New York	217
4	Wyoming	204
5	Connecticut	192
6	Hawaii	173
7	Delaware	170
8	New Jersey	167
9	Nevada	165
10	Louisiana	159
11	Montana	154
12	New Mexico	153
13	Ohio	152
14	Massachusetts	145
15	Arizona	144
16	Maryland	136
17	Colorado	132
18	Minnesota	131
18	Pennsylvania	131
20	Utah	122
20	Washington	122
22	Idaho	120
23	West Virginia	117
24	Kentucky	116
24	Rhode Island	116
26	Florida	115
27	Illinois	114
28	Michigan	113
28	Oregon	113
30	Vermont	112
31	Iowa	111
31	North Dakota	111
33	Texas	106
34	Kansas	105
35	Wisconsin	104
36	Georgia	103
37	Virginia	102
38	Nebraska	97
39	South Dakota	95
39	Tennessee	95
41	New Hampshire	87
41	Oklahoma	87
43	Alabama	86
44	Missouri	79
45	North Carolina	78
46	Mississippi	76
47	South Carolina	75
48	Indiana	74
49	Maine	73
50	Arkansas	70

District of Columbia	184

Source: CQ Press using data from U.S. Bureau of the Census, Governments Division
"2011 State and Local Government Finances" (http://www.census.gov/govs/local/)
*Direct general expenditures. Includes courts, prosecution and legal services, and public defense.

III. Defense

Homeland Security Grants in 2013

National Total = $913,389,689*

ALPHA ORDER					RANK ORDER			

RANK	STATE	GRANTS	% of USA		RANK	STATE	GRANTS	% of USA
20	Alabama	$3,459,364	0.4%		1	New York	$241,023,122	26.4%
20	Alaska	3,459,364	0.4%		2	California	168,238,685	18.4%
13	Arizona	9,472,417	1.0%		3	Illinois	81,950,798	9.0%
20	Arkansas	3,459,364	0.4%		4	Texas	57,209,688	6.3%
2	California	168,238,685	18.4%		5	Pennsylvania	29,285,656	3.2%
17	Colorado	6,459,364	0.7%		6	New Jersey	28,927,276	3.2%
20	Connecticut	3,459,364	0.4%		7	Massachusetts	22,453,349	2.5%
20	Delaware	3,459,364	0.4%		8	Florida	18,074,272	2.0%
8	Florida	18,074,272	2.0%		9	Georgia	11,418,784	1.3%
9	Georgia	11,418,784	1.3%		10	Michigan	11,289,215	1.2%
20	Hawaii	3,459,364	0.4%		11	Washington	11,146,176	1.2%
20	Idaho	3,459,364	0.4%		12	Maryland	10,825,727	1.2%
3	Illinois	81,950,798	9.0%		13	Arizona	9,472,417	1.0%
20	Indiana	3,459,364	0.4%		14	Minnesota	8,959,364	1.0%
20	Iowa	3,459,364	0.4%		15	North Carolina	7,773,429	0.9%
20	Kansas	3,459,364	0.4%		16	Ohio	6,693,676	0.7%
20	Kentucky	3,459,364	0.4%		17	Colorado	6,459,364	0.7%
20	Louisiana	3,459,364	0.4%		17	Missouri	6,459,364	0.7%
20	Maine	3,459,364	0.4%		19	Virginia	6,446,710	0.7%
12	Maryland	10,825,727	1.2%		20	Alabama	3,459,364	0.4%
7	Massachusetts	22,453,349	2.5%		20	Alaska	3,459,364	0.4%
10	Michigan	11,289,215	1.2%		20	Arkansas	3,459,364	0.4%
14	Minnesota	8,959,364	1.0%		20	Connecticut	3,459,364	0.4%
20	Mississippi	3,459,364	0.4%		20	Delaware	3,459,364	0.4%
17	Missouri	6,459,364	0.7%		20	Hawaii	3,459,364	0.4%
20	Montana	3,459,364	0.4%		20	Idaho	3,459,364	0.4%
20	Nebraska	3,459,364	0.4%		20	Indiana	3,459,364	0.4%
20	Nevada	3,459,364	0.4%		20	Iowa	3,459,364	0.4%
20	New Hampshire	3,459,364	0.4%		20	Kansas	3,459,364	0.4%
6	New Jersey	28,927,276	3.2%		20	Kentucky	3,459,364	0.4%
20	New Mexico	3,459,364	0.4%		20	Louisiana	3,459,364	0.4%
1	New York	241,023,122	26.4%		20	Maine	3,459,364	0.4%
15	North Carolina	7,773,429	0.9%		20	Mississippi	3,459,364	0.4%
20	North Dakota	3,459,364	0.4%		20	Montana	3,459,364	0.4%
16	Ohio	6,693,676	0.7%		20	Nebraska	3,459,364	0.4%
20	Oklahoma	3,459,364	0.4%		20	Nevada	3,459,364	0.4%
20	Oregon	3,459,364	0.4%		20	New Hampshire	3,459,364	0.4%
5	Pennsylvania	29,285,656	3.2%		20	New Mexico	3,459,364	0.4%
20	Rhode Island	3,459,364	0.4%		20	North Dakota	3,459,364	0.4%
20	South Carolina	3,459,364	0.4%		20	Oklahoma	3,459,364	0.4%
20	South Dakota	3,459,364	0.4%		20	Oregon	3,459,364	0.4%
20	Tennessee	3,459,364	0.4%		20	Rhode Island	3,459,364	0.4%
4	Texas	57,209,688	6.3%		20	South Carolina	3,459,364	0.4%
20	Utah	3,459,364	0.4%		20	South Dakota	3,459,364	0.4%
20	Vermont	3,459,364	0.4%		20	Tennessee	3,459,364	0.4%
19	Virginia	6,446,710	0.7%		20	Utah	3,459,364	0.4%
11	Washington	11,146,176	1.2%		20	Vermont	3,459,364	0.4%
20	West Virginia	3,459,364	0.4%		20	West Virginia	3,459,364	0.4%
20	Wisconsin	3,459,364	0.4%		20	Wisconsin	3,459,364	0.4%
20	Wyoming	3,459,364	0.4%		20	Wyoming	3,459,364	0.4%
						District of Columbia	55,420,121	6.1%

Source: CQ Press using data from U.S. Department of Homeland Security
   "FY 2013 Homeland Security Grant Program (HSGP)" (http://www.fema.gov/media-library/assets/documents/32611?id=7513)
*For fiscal year 2013. National total includes $6,622,212 in grants to U.S. territories. The Homeland Security Grant Program (HSGP) includes three sub-grant programs: State Homeland Security Program (SHSP), Urban Area Security Initiative (UASI), and Operation Stonegarden (OPSG). Law Enforcement Terrorism Prevention Activities (LETPA) allocations are a 25 percent subset of the SHSP and UASI allocations.

Per Capita Homeland Security Grants in 2013

National Per Capita = $2.87*

ALPHA ORDER				RANK ORDER		
RANK	STATE	PER CAPITA		RANK	STATE	PER CAPITA
45	Alabama	$0.72		1	New York	$12.27
6	Alaska	4.71		2	Illinois	6.36
26	Arizona	1.43		3	Wyoming	5.94
31	Arkansas	1.17		4	Vermont	5.52
7	California	4.39		5	North Dakota	4.78
28	Colorado	1.23		6	Alaska	4.71
37	Connecticut	0.96		7	California	4.39
9	Delaware	3.74		8	South Dakota	4.09
38	Florida	0.92		9	Delaware	3.74
33	Georgia	1.14		10	Montana	3.41
16	Hawaii	2.46		11	Massachusetts	3.35
19	Idaho	2.15		12	Rhode Island	3.29
2	Illinois	6.36		13	New Jersey	3.25
49	Indiana	0.53		14	New Hampshire	2.61
35	Iowa	1.12		15	Maine	2.60
29	Kansas	1.20		16	Hawaii	2.46
41	Kentucky	0.79		17	Pennsylvania	2.29
44	Louisiana	0.75		18	Texas	2.16
15	Maine	2.60		19	Idaho	2.15
22	Maryland	1.83		20	West Virginia	1.87
11	Massachusetts	3.35		21	Nebraska	1.85
33	Michigan	1.14		22	Maryland	1.83
24	Minnesota	1.65		23	New Mexico	1.66
32	Mississippi	1.16		24	Minnesota	1.65
36	Missouri	1.07		25	Washington	1.60
10	Montana	3.41		26	Arizona	1.43
21	Nebraska	1.85		27	Nevada	1.24
27	Nevada	1.24		28	Colorado	1.23
14	New Hampshire	2.61		29	Kansas	1.20
13	New Jersey	3.25		30	Utah	1.19
23	New Mexico	1.66		31	Arkansas	1.17
1	New York	12.27		32	Mississippi	1.16
41	North Carolina	0.79		33	Georgia	1.14
5	North Dakota	4.78		33	Michigan	1.14
48	Ohio	0.58		35	Iowa	1.12
39	Oklahoma	0.90		36	Missouri	1.07
40	Oregon	0.88		37	Connecticut	0.96
17	Pennsylvania	2.29		38	Florida	0.92
12	Rhode Island	3.29		39	Oklahoma	0.90
45	South Carolina	0.72		40	Oregon	0.88
8	South Dakota	4.09		41	Kentucky	0.79
49	Tennessee	0.53		41	North Carolina	0.79
18	Texas	2.16		43	Virginia	0.78
30	Utah	1.19		44	Louisiana	0.75
4	Vermont	5.52		45	Alabama	0.72
43	Virginia	0.78		45	South Carolina	0.72
25	Washington	1.60		47	Wisconsin	0.60
20	West Virginia	1.87		48	Ohio	0.58
47	Wisconsin	0.60		49	Indiana	0.53
3	Wyoming	5.94		49	Tennessee	0.53
					District of Columbia	85.73

Source: CQ Press using data from U.S. Department of Homeland Security
"FY 2013 Homeland Security Grant Program (HSGP)" (http://www.fema.gov/media-library/assets/documents/32611?id=7513)
*For fiscal year 2013. National total includes $6,622,212 in grants to U.S. territories. The Homeland Security Grant Program (HSGP) includes three sub-grant programs: State Homeland Security Program (SHSP), Urban Area Security Initiative (UASI), and Operation Stonegarden (OPSG). Law Enforcement Terrorism Prevention Activities (LETPA) allocations are a 25 percent subset of the SHSP and UASI allocations.

U.S. Department of Defense Domestic Expenditures in 2009

National Total = $527,824,146,000*

ALPHA ORDER

RANK	STATE	EXPENDITURES	% of USA
11	Alabama	$14,291,629,000	2.7%
31	Alaska	4,888,348,000	0.9%
8	Arizona	15,308,486,000	2.9%
37	Arkansas	2,673,622,000	0.5%
2	California	56,742,620,000	10.8%
18	Colorado	10,725,693,000	2.0%
15	Connecticut	12,638,248,000	2.4%
47	Delaware	876,158,000	0.2%
4	Florida	22,802,179,000	4.3%
6	Georgia	18,607,996,000	3.5%
25	Hawaii	8,800,669,000	1.7%
46	Idaho	934,634,000	0.2%
20	Illinois	9,237,211,000	1.8%
21	Indiana	9,188,013,000	1.7%
40	Iowa	2,089,452,000	0.4%
28	Kansas	6,867,835,000	1.3%
16	Kentucky	12,285,425,000	2.3%
22	Louisiana	9,149,589,000	1.7%
38	Maine	2,382,017,000	0.5%
5	Maryland	19,926,029,000	3.8%
9	Massachusetts	15,081,759,000	2.9%
26	Michigan	7,288,503,000	1.4%
35	Minnesota	2,806,926,000	0.5%
29	Mississippi	5,689,655,000	1.1%
12	Missouri	14,281,251,000	2.7%
48	Montana	853,639,000	0.2%
39	Nebraska	2,142,336,000	0.4%
34	Nevada	3,268,456,000	0.6%
41	New Hampshire	2,014,350,000	0.4%
17	New Jersey	11,019,807,000	2.1%
33	New Mexico	3,270,536,000	0.6%
13	New York	13,562,174,000	2.6%
10	North Carolina	14,677,953,000	2.8%
43	North Dakota	1,100,340,000	0.2%
19	Ohio	10,256,353,000	1.9%
27	Oklahoma	7,103,675,000	1.3%
36	Oregon	2,695,604,000	0.5%
7	Pennsylvania	16,789,144,000	3.2%
42	Rhode Island	1,431,162,000	0.3%
23	South Carolina	9,020,997,000	1.7%
45	South Dakota	1,026,194,000	0.2%
30	Tennessee	5,362,492,000	1.0%
3	Texas	42,082,905,000	8.0%
32	Utah	4,361,476,000	0.8%
49	Vermont	828,433,000	0.2%
1	Virginia	56,933,799,000	10.8%
14	Washington	13,524,233,000	2.6%
44	West Virginia	1,063,251,000	0.2%
24	Wisconsin	8,898,053,000	1.7%
50	Wyoming	566,662,000	0.1%

RANK ORDER

RANK	STATE	EXPENDITURES	% of USA
1	Virginia	$56,933,799,000	10.8%
2	California	56,742,620,000	10.8%
3	Texas	42,082,905,000	8.0%
4	Florida	22,802,179,000	4.3%
5	Maryland	19,926,029,000	3.8%
6	Georgia	18,607,996,000	3.5%
7	Pennsylvania	16,789,144,000	3.2%
8	Arizona	15,308,486,000	2.9%
9	Massachusetts	15,081,759,000	2.9%
10	North Carolina	14,677,953,000	2.8%
11	Alabama	14,291,629,000	2.7%
12	Missouri	14,281,251,000	2.7%
13	New York	13,562,174,000	2.6%
14	Washington	13,524,233,000	2.6%
15	Connecticut	12,638,248,000	2.4%
16	Kentucky	12,285,425,000	2.3%
17	New Jersey	11,019,807,000	2.1%
18	Colorado	10,725,693,000	2.0%
19	Ohio	10,256,353,000	1.9%
20	Illinois	9,237,211,000	1.8%
21	Indiana	9,188,013,000	1.7%
22	Louisiana	9,149,589,000	1.7%
23	South Carolina	9,020,997,000	1.7%
24	Wisconsin	8,898,053,000	1.7%
25	Hawaii	8,800,669,000	1.7%
26	Michigan	7,288,503,000	1.4%
27	Oklahoma	7,103,675,000	1.3%
28	Kansas	6,867,835,000	1.3%
29	Mississippi	5,689,655,000	1.1%
30	Tennessee	5,362,492,000	1.0%
31	Alaska	4,888,348,000	0.9%
32	Utah	4,361,476,000	0.8%
33	New Mexico	3,270,536,000	0.6%
34	Nevada	3,268,456,000	0.6%
35	Minnesota	2,806,926,000	0.5%
36	Oregon	2,695,604,000	0.5%
37	Arkansas	2,673,622,000	0.5%
38	Maine	2,382,017,000	0.5%
39	Nebraska	2,142,336,000	0.4%
40	Iowa	2,089,452,000	0.4%
41	New Hampshire	2,014,350,000	0.4%
42	Rhode Island	1,431,162,000	0.3%
43	North Dakota	1,100,340,000	0.2%
44	West Virginia	1,063,251,000	0.2%
45	South Dakota	1,026,194,000	0.2%
46	Idaho	934,634,000	0.2%
47	Delaware	876,158,000	0.2%
48	Montana	853,639,000	0.2%
49	Vermont	828,433,000	0.2%
50	Wyoming	566,662,000	0.1%
	District of Columbia	8,406,175,000	1.6%

Source: U.S. Department of Defense
"Atlas/Data Abstract for the United States" (http://siadapp.dmdc.osd.mil/personnel/L03/fy09/09top.htm)
*Expenditures for payroll, grants, and prime contracts ($25,000 or more) for civil and military functions. Does not include payroll, contracts, or grants to U.S. territories and other countries.

Per Capita U.S. Department of Defense Domestic Expenditures in 2009

National Per Capita = $1,719*

ALPHA ORDER				RANK ORDER		
RANK	**STATE**	**PER CAPITA**		**RANK**	**STATE**	**PER CAPITA**
6	Alabama	$3,035		1	Virginia	$7,223
2	Alaska	6,999		2	Alaska	6,999
10	Arizona	2,321		3	Hawaii	6,795
39	Arkansas	925		4	Connecticut	3,592
26	California	1,535		5	Maryland	3,496
12	Colorado	2,135		6	Alabama	3,035
4	Connecticut	3,592		7	Kentucky	2,848
38	Delaware	990		8	Kansas	2,436
35	Florida	1,230		9	Missouri	2,385
18	Georgia	1,893		10	Arizona	2,321
3	Hawaii	6,795		11	Massachusetts	2,287
48	Idaho	605		12	Colorado	2,135
44	Illinois	715		13	Louisiana	2,037
28	Indiana	1,430		14	Washington	2,029
46	Iowa	695		15	South Carolina	1,978
8	Kansas	2,436		16	Mississippi	1,927
7	Kentucky	2,848		16	Oklahoma	1,927
13	Louisiana	2,037		18	Georgia	1,893
19	Maine	1,807		19	Maine	1,807
5	Maryland	3,496		20	North Dakota	1,701
11	Massachusetts	2,287		21	Texas	1,698
43	Michigan	731		22	New Mexico	1,627
50	Minnesota	533		23	Wisconsin	1,574
16	Mississippi	1,927		24	Utah	1,566
9	Missouri	2,385		25	North Carolina	1,565
41	Montana	876		26	California	1,535
36	Nebraska	1,192		27	New Hampshire	1,521
34	Nevada	1,237		28	Indiana	1,430
27	New Hampshire	1,521		29	Rhode Island	1,359
32	New Jersey	1,266		30	Pennsylvania	1,332
22	New Mexico	1,627		30	Vermont	1,332
47	New York	694		32	New Jersey	1,266
25	North Carolina	1,565		33	South Dakota	1,263
20	North Dakota	1,701		34	Nevada	1,237
40	Ohio	889		35	Florida	1,230
16	Oklahoma	1,927		36	Nebraska	1,192
45	Oregon	705		37	Wyoming	1,041
30	Pennsylvania	1,332		38	Delaware	990
29	Rhode Island	1,359		39	Arkansas	925
15	South Carolina	1,978		40	Ohio	889
33	South Dakota	1,263		41	Montana	876
42	Tennessee	852		42	Tennessee	852
21	Texas	1,698		43	Michigan	731
24	Utah	1,566		44	Illinois	715
30	Vermont	1,332		45	Oregon	705
1	Virginia	7,223		46	Iowa	695
14	Washington	2,029		47	New York	694
49	West Virginia	584		48	Idaho	605
23	Wisconsin	1,574		49	West Virginia	584
37	Wyoming	1,041		50	Minnesota	533
					District of Columbia	14,018

Source: CQ Press using data from U.S. Department of Defense
"Atlas/Data Abstract for the United States" (http://siadapp.dmdc.osd.mil/personnel/L03/fy09/09top.htm)
*Expenditures for payroll, grants, and prime contracts ($25,000 or more) for civil and military functions. Does not include payroll, contracts, or grants to U.S. territories and other countries.

U.S. Department of Defense Total Contracts in 2009

National Total = $327,461,911,000*

<table>
<tr><td colspan="4">ALPHA ORDER</td><td colspan="4">RANK ORDER</td></tr>
<tr><th>RANK</th><th>STATE</th><th>CONTRACTS</th><th>% of USA</th><th>RANK</th><th>STATE</th><th>CONTRACTS</th><th>% of USA</th></tr>
<tr><td>11</td><td>Alabama</td><td>$9,501,617,000</td><td>2.9%</td><td>1</td><td>California</td><td>$41,697,621,000</td><td>12.7%</td></tr>
<tr><td>32</td><td>Alaska</td><td>2,180,004,000</td><td>0.7%</td><td>2</td><td>Virginia</td><td>38,731,568,000</td><td>11.8%</td></tr>
<tr><td>8</td><td>Arizona</td><td>12,064,904,000</td><td>3.7%</td><td>3</td><td>Texas</td><td>22,483,566,000</td><td>6.9%</td></tr>
<tr><td>40</td><td>Arkansas</td><td>985,545,000</td><td>0.3%</td><td>4</td><td>Massachusetts</td><td>13,347,134,000</td><td>4.1%</td></tr>
<tr><td>1</td><td>California</td><td>41,697,621,000</td><td>12.7%</td><td>5</td><td>Florida</td><td>13,188,889,000</td><td>4.0%</td></tr>
<tr><td>21</td><td>Colorado</td><td>5,544,160,000</td><td>1.7%</td><td>6</td><td>Maryland</td><td>12,911,613,000</td><td>3.9%</td></tr>
<tr><td>9</td><td>Connecticut</td><td>11,817,700,000</td><td>3.6%</td><td>7</td><td>Pennsylvania</td><td>12,362,728,000</td><td>3.8%</td></tr>
<tr><td>47</td><td>Delaware</td><td>315,358,000</td><td>0.1%</td><td>8</td><td>Arizona</td><td>12,064,904,000</td><td>3.7%</td></tr>
<tr><td>5</td><td>Florida</td><td>13,188,889,000</td><td>4.0%</td><td>9</td><td>Connecticut</td><td>11,817,700,000</td><td>3.6%</td></tr>
<tr><td>15</td><td>Georgia</td><td>7,039,405,000</td><td>2.1%</td><td>10</td><td>Missouri</td><td>10,453,949,000</td><td>3.2%</td></tr>
<tr><td>30</td><td>Hawaii</td><td>2,377,271,000</td><td>0.7%</td><td>11</td><td>Alabama</td><td>9,501,617,000</td><td>2.9%</td></tr>
<tr><td>49</td><td>Idaho</td><td>166,118,000</td><td>0.1%</td><td>12</td><td>New York</td><td>8,544,864,000</td><td>2.6%</td></tr>
<tr><td>20</td><td>Illinois</td><td>5,936,547,000</td><td>1.8%</td><td>13</td><td>New Jersey</td><td>8,226,697,000</td><td>2.5%</td></tr>
<tr><td>16</td><td>Indiana</td><td>6,795,168,000</td><td>2.1%</td><td>14</td><td>Wisconsin</td><td>7,673,970,000</td><td>2.3%</td></tr>
<tr><td>39</td><td>Iowa</td><td>1,285,344,000</td><td>0.4%</td><td>15</td><td>Georgia</td><td>7,039,405,000</td><td>2.1%</td></tr>
<tr><td>27</td><td>Kansas</td><td>3,158,303,000</td><td>1.0%</td><td>16</td><td>Indiana</td><td>6,795,168,000</td><td>2.1%</td></tr>
<tr><td>17</td><td>Kentucky</td><td>6,534,291,000</td><td>2.0%</td><td>17</td><td>Kentucky</td><td>6,534,291,000</td><td>2.0%</td></tr>
<tr><td>18</td><td>Louisiana</td><td>6,407,579,000</td><td>2.0%</td><td>18</td><td>Louisiana</td><td>6,407,579,000</td><td>2.0%</td></tr>
<tr><td>38</td><td>Maine</td><td>1,407,038,000</td><td>0.4%</td><td>19</td><td>Ohio</td><td>6,249,462,000</td><td>1.9%</td></tr>
<tr><td>6</td><td>Maryland</td><td>12,911,613,000</td><td>3.9%</td><td>20</td><td>Illinois</td><td>5,936,547,000</td><td>1.8%</td></tr>
<tr><td>4</td><td>Massachusetts</td><td>13,347,134,000</td><td>4.1%</td><td>21</td><td>Colorado</td><td>5,544,160,000</td><td>1.7%</td></tr>
<tr><td>22</td><td>Michigan</td><td>5,331,864,000</td><td>1.6%</td><td>22</td><td>Michigan</td><td>5,331,864,000</td><td>1.6%</td></tr>
<tr><td>37</td><td>Minnesota</td><td>1,529,964,000</td><td>0.5%</td><td>23</td><td>South Carolina</td><td>5,298,645,000</td><td>1.6%</td></tr>
<tr><td>26</td><td>Mississippi</td><td>3,447,072,000</td><td>1.1%</td><td>24</td><td>Washington</td><td>5,173,959,000</td><td>1.6%</td></tr>
<tr><td>10</td><td>Missouri</td><td>10,453,949,000</td><td>3.2%</td><td>25</td><td>North Carolina</td><td>3,994,861,000</td><td>1.2%</td></tr>
<tr><td>48</td><td>Montana</td><td>288,759,000</td><td>0.1%</td><td>26</td><td>Mississippi</td><td>3,447,072,000</td><td>1.1%</td></tr>
<tr><td>41</td><td>Nebraska</td><td>931,306,000</td><td>0.3%</td><td>27</td><td>Kansas</td><td>3,158,303,000</td><td>1.0%</td></tr>
<tr><td>33</td><td>Nevada</td><td>1,818,505,000</td><td>0.6%</td><td>28</td><td>Tennessee</td><td>3,083,056,000</td><td>0.9%</td></tr>
<tr><td>35</td><td>New Hampshire</td><td>1,567,821,000</td><td>0.5%</td><td>29</td><td>Oklahoma</td><td>2,880,203,000</td><td>0.9%</td></tr>
<tr><td>13</td><td>New Jersey</td><td>8,226,697,000</td><td>2.5%</td><td>30</td><td>Hawaii</td><td>2,377,271,000</td><td>0.7%</td></tr>
<tr><td>34</td><td>New Mexico</td><td>1,604,488,000</td><td>0.5%</td><td>31</td><td>Utah</td><td>2,206,025,000</td><td>0.7%</td></tr>
<tr><td>12</td><td>New York</td><td>8,544,864,000</td><td>2.6%</td><td>32</td><td>Alaska</td><td>2,180,004,000</td><td>0.7%</td></tr>
<tr><td>25</td><td>North Carolina</td><td>3,994,861,000</td><td>1.2%</td><td>33</td><td>Nevada</td><td>1,818,505,000</td><td>0.6%</td></tr>
<tr><td>45</td><td>North Dakota</td><td>437,227,000</td><td>0.1%</td><td>34</td><td>New Mexico</td><td>1,604,488,000</td><td>0.5%</td></tr>
<tr><td>19</td><td>Ohio</td><td>6,249,462,000</td><td>1.9%</td><td>35</td><td>New Hampshire</td><td>1,567,821,000</td><td>0.5%</td></tr>
<tr><td>29</td><td>Oklahoma</td><td>2,880,203,000</td><td>0.9%</td><td>36</td><td>Oregon</td><td>1,545,991,000</td><td>0.5%</td></tr>
<tr><td>36</td><td>Oregon</td><td>1,545,991,000</td><td>0.5%</td><td>37</td><td>Minnesota</td><td>1,529,964,000</td><td>0.5%</td></tr>
<tr><td>7</td><td>Pennsylvania</td><td>12,362,728,000</td><td>3.8%</td><td>38</td><td>Maine</td><td>1,407,038,000</td><td>0.4%</td></tr>
<tr><td>42</td><td>Rhode Island</td><td>661,794,000</td><td>0.2%</td><td>39</td><td>Iowa</td><td>1,285,344,000</td><td>0.4%</td></tr>
<tr><td>23</td><td>South Carolina</td><td>5,298,645,000</td><td>1.6%</td><td>40</td><td>Arkansas</td><td>985,545,000</td><td>0.3%</td></tr>
<tr><td>44</td><td>South Dakota</td><td>444,618,000</td><td>0.1%</td><td>41</td><td>Nebraska</td><td>931,306,000</td><td>0.3%</td></tr>
<tr><td>28</td><td>Tennessee</td><td>3,083,056,000</td><td>0.9%</td><td>42</td><td>Rhode Island</td><td>661,794,000</td><td>0.2%</td></tr>
<tr><td>3</td><td>Texas</td><td>22,483,566,000</td><td>6.9%</td><td>43</td><td>Vermont</td><td>549,931,000</td><td>0.2%</td></tr>
<tr><td>31</td><td>Utah</td><td>2,206,025,000</td><td>0.7%</td><td>44</td><td>South Dakota</td><td>444,618,000</td><td>0.1%</td></tr>
<tr><td>43</td><td>Vermont</td><td>549,931,000</td><td>0.2%</td><td>45</td><td>North Dakota</td><td>437,227,000</td><td>0.1%</td></tr>
<tr><td>2</td><td>Virginia</td><td>38,731,568,000</td><td>11.8%</td><td>46</td><td>West Virginia</td><td>396,440,000</td><td>0.1%</td></tr>
<tr><td>24</td><td>Washington</td><td>5,173,959,000</td><td>1.6%</td><td>47</td><td>Delaware</td><td>315,358,000</td><td>0.1%</td></tr>
<tr><td>46</td><td>West Virginia</td><td>396,440,000</td><td>0.1%</td><td>48</td><td>Montana</td><td>288,759,000</td><td>0.1%</td></tr>
<tr><td>14</td><td>Wisconsin</td><td>7,673,970,000</td><td>2.3%</td><td>49</td><td>Idaho</td><td>166,118,000</td><td>0.1%</td></tr>
<tr><td>50</td><td>Wyoming</td><td>140,406,000</td><td>0.0%</td><td>50</td><td>Wyoming</td><td>140,406,000</td><td>0.0%</td></tr>
<tr><td></td><td></td><td></td><td></td><td></td><td>District of Columbia</td><td>4,740,563,000</td><td>1.4%</td></tr>
</table>

Source: U.S. Department of Defense
"Atlas/Data Abstract for the United States" (http://siadapp.dmdc.osd.mil/personnel/L03/fy09/09top.htm)
*Includes prime contracts ($25,000 or more) for civil and military functions. Does not include contracts to U.S. territories and other countries.

Per Capita U.S. Department of Defense Total Contracts in 2009

National Per Capita = $1,067*

ALPHA ORDER				RANK ORDER		
RANK	STATE	PER CAPITA		RANK	STATE	PER CAPITA
6	Alabama	$2,018		1	Virginia	$4,914
3	Alaska	3,121		2	Connecticut	3,359
8	Arizona	1,829		3	Alaska	3,121
45	Arkansas	341		4	Maryland	2,265
16	California	1,128		5	Massachusetts	2,024
18	Colorado	1,103		6	Alabama	2,018
2	Connecticut	3,359		7	Hawaii	1,835
44	Delaware	356		8	Arizona	1,829
30	Florida	711		9	Missouri	1,746
29	Georgia	716		10	Kentucky	1,515
7	Hawaii	1,835		11	Louisiana	1,426
50	Idaho	107		12	Wisconsin	1,357
39	Illinois	460		13	New Hampshire	1,184
20	Indiana	1,058		14	Mississippi	1,168
41	Iowa	427		15	South Carolina	1,162
17	Kansas	1,120		16	California	1,128
10	Kentucky	1,515		17	Kansas	1,120
11	Louisiana	1,426		18	Colorado	1,103
19	Maine	1,067		19	Maine	1,067
4	Maryland	2,265		20	Indiana	1,058
5	Massachusetts	2,024		21	Pennsylvania	981
36	Michigan	535		22	New Jersey	945
47	Minnesota	291		23	Texas	907
14	Mississippi	1,168		24	Vermont	884
9	Missouri	1,746		25	New Mexico	798
46	Montana	296		26	Utah	792
37	Nebraska	518		27	Oklahoma	781
31	Nevada	688		28	Washington	776
13	New Hampshire	1,184		29	Georgia	716
22	New Jersey	945		30	Florida	711
25	New Mexico	798		31	Nevada	688
40	New York	437		32	North Dakota	676
42	North Carolina	426		33	Rhode Island	628
32	North Dakota	676		34	South Dakota	547
35	Ohio	541		35	Ohio	541
27	Oklahoma	781		36	Michigan	535
43	Oregon	404		37	Nebraska	518
21	Pennsylvania	981		38	Tennessee	490
33	Rhode Island	628		39	Illinois	460
15	South Carolina	1,162		40	New York	437
34	South Dakota	547		41	Iowa	427
38	Tennessee	490		42	North Carolina	426
23	Texas	907		43	Oregon	404
26	Utah	792		44	Delaware	356
24	Vermont	884		45	Arkansas	341
1	Virginia	4,914		46	Montana	296
28	Washington	776		47	Minnesota	291
49	West Virginia	218		48	Wyoming	258
12	Wisconsin	1,357		49	West Virginia	218
48	Wyoming	258		50	Idaho	107
					District of Columbia	7,905

Source: CQ Press using data from U.S. Department of Defense
"Atlas/Data Abstract for the United States" (http://siadapp.dmdc.osd.mil/personnel/L03/fy09/09top.htm)
*Includes prime contracts ($25,000 or more) for civil and military functions. Does not include contracts to U.S. territories and other countries.

U.S. Department of Defense Grants in 2009

National Total = $5,192,057,000*

ALPHA ORDER

RANK	STATE	GRANTS	% of USA
27	Alabama	$66,056,000	1.3%
35	Alaska	48,783,000	0.9%
17	Arizona	105,948,000	2.0%
26	Arkansas	66,370,000	1.3%
2	California	476,541,000	9.2%
31	Colorado	56,411,000	1.1%
18	Connecticut	100,249,000	1.9%
47	Delaware	24,042,000	0.5%
7	Florida	195,371,000	3.8%
21	Georgia	73,944,000	1.4%
20	Hawaii	78,931,000	1.5%
28	Idaho	59,296,000	1.1%
9	Illinois	172,126,000	3.3%
32	Indiana	54,724,000	1.1%
30	Iowa	56,852,000	1.1%
37	Kansas	41,857,000	0.8%
23	Kentucky	70,382,000	1.4%
33	Louisiana	53,861,000	1.0%
12	Maine	128,298,000	2.5%
1	Maryland	476,575,000	9.2%
4	Massachusetts	243,995,000	4.7%
11	Michigan	129,652,000	2.5%
24	Minnesota	68,900,000	1.3%
49	Mississippi	18,237,000	0.4%
38	Missouri	40,466,000	0.8%
46	Montana	24,236,000	0.5%
29	Nebraska	59,049,000	1.1%
43	Nevada	35,345,000	0.7%
42	New Hampshire	35,647,000	0.7%
16	New Jersey	121,890,000	2.3%
39	New Mexico	39,587,000	0.8%
6	New York	198,631,000	3.8%
14	North Carolina	124,942,000	2.4%
44	North Dakota	32,174,000	0.6%
8	Ohio	172,421,000	3.3%
15	Oklahoma	123,839,000	2.4%
19	Oregon	98,566,000	1.9%
5	Pennsylvania	216,030,000	4.2%
45	Rhode Island	26,333,000	0.5%
41	South Carolina	39,365,000	0.8%
25	South Dakota	67,933,000	1.3%
36	Tennessee	44,134,000	0.9%
3	Texas	300,450,000	5.8%
40	Utah	39,483,000	0.8%
50	Vermont	16,997,000	0.3%
10	Virginia	130,816,000	2.5%
13	Washington	126,539,000	2.4%
34	West Virginia	49,988,000	1.0%
22	Wisconsin	72,192,000	1.4%
48	Wyoming	21,236,000	0.4%

RANK ORDER

RANK	STATE	GRANTS	% of USA
1	Maryland	$476,575,000	9.2%
2	California	476,541,000	9.2%
3	Texas	300,450,000	5.8%
4	Massachusetts	243,995,000	4.7%
5	Pennsylvania	216,030,000	4.2%
6	New York	198,631,000	3.8%
7	Florida	195,371,000	3.8%
8	Ohio	172,421,000	3.3%
9	Illinois	172,126,000	3.3%
10	Virginia	130,816,000	2.5%
11	Michigan	129,652,000	2.5%
12	Maine	128,298,000	2.5%
13	Washington	126,539,000	2.4%
14	North Carolina	124,942,000	2.4%
15	Oklahoma	123,839,000	2.4%
16	New Jersey	121,890,000	2.3%
17	Arizona	105,948,000	2.0%
18	Connecticut	100,249,000	1.9%
19	Oregon	98,566,000	1.9%
20	Hawaii	78,931,000	1.5%
21	Georgia	73,944,000	1.4%
22	Wisconsin	72,192,000	1.4%
23	Kentucky	70,382,000	1.4%
24	Minnesota	68,900,000	1.3%
25	South Dakota	67,933,000	1.3%
26	Arkansas	66,370,000	1.3%
27	Alabama	66,056,000	1.3%
28	Idaho	59,296,000	1.1%
29	Nebraska	59,049,000	1.1%
30	Iowa	56,852,000	1.1%
31	Colorado	56,411,000	1.1%
32	Indiana	54,724,000	1.1%
33	Louisiana	53,861,000	1.0%
34	West Virginia	49,988,000	1.0%
35	Alaska	48,783,000	0.9%
36	Tennessee	44,134,000	0.9%
37	Kansas	41,857,000	0.8%
38	Missouri	40,466,000	0.8%
39	New Mexico	39,587,000	0.8%
40	Utah	39,483,000	0.8%
41	South Carolina	39,365,000	0.8%
42	New Hampshire	35,647,000	0.7%
43	Nevada	35,345,000	0.7%
44	North Dakota	32,174,000	0.6%
45	Rhode Island	26,333,000	0.5%
46	Montana	24,236,000	0.5%
47	Delaware	24,042,000	0.5%
48	Wyoming	21,236,000	0.4%
49	Mississippi	18,237,000	0.4%
50	Vermont	16,997,000	0.3%
	District of Columbia	66,367,000	1.3%

Source: U.S. Department of Defense
    "Atlas/Data Abstract for the United States" (http://siadapp.dmdc.osd.mil/personnel/L03/fy09/09top.htm)
*Includes grants for civil and military functions. Does not include contracts to U.S. territories and other countries.

Per Capita U.S. Department of Defense Grants in 2009

National Per Capita = $16.91*

ALPHA ORDER

RANK	STATE	PER CAPITA
31	Alabama	$14.03
4	Alaska	69.84
27	Arizona	16.06
20	Arkansas	22.97
38	California	12.89
42	Colorado	11.23
12	Connecticut	28.49
15	Delaware	27.16
43	Florida	10.54
47	Georgia	7.52
5	Hawaii	60.94
8	Idaho	38.36
34	Illinois	13.33
46	Indiana	8.52
23	Iowa	18.90
29	Kansas	14.85
26	Kentucky	16.31
41	Louisiana	11.99
1	Maine	97.32
2	Maryland	83.62
9	Massachusetts	37.00
37	Michigan	13.00
36	Minnesota	13.08
50	Mississippi	6.18
49	Missouri	6.76
19	Montana	24.86
11	Nebraska	32.87
33	Nevada	13.37
16	New Hampshire	26.91
32	New Jersey	14.00
21	New Mexico	19.70
44	New York	10.16
35	North Carolina	13.32
6	North Dakota	49.74
28	Ohio	14.94
10	Oklahoma	33.59
17	Oregon	25.76
24	Pennsylvania	17.14
18	Rhode Island	25.00
45	South Carolina	8.63
2	South Dakota	83.62
48	Tennessee	7.01
40	Texas	12.12
30	Utah	14.18
14	Vermont	27.34
25	Virginia	16.60
22	Washington	18.99
13	West Virginia	27.47
39	Wisconsin	12.77
7	Wyoming	39.02

RANK ORDER

RANK	STATE	PER CAPITA
1	Maine	$97.32
2	Maryland	83.62
2	South Dakota	83.62
4	Alaska	69.84
5	Hawaii	60.94
6	North Dakota	49.74
7	Wyoming	39.02
8	Idaho	38.36
9	Massachusetts	37.00
10	Oklahoma	33.59
11	Nebraska	32.87
12	Connecticut	28.49
13	West Virginia	27.47
14	Vermont	27.34
15	Delaware	27.16
16	New Hampshire	26.91
17	Oregon	25.76
18	Rhode Island	25.00
19	Montana	24.86
20	Arkansas	22.97
21	New Mexico	19.70
22	Washington	18.99
23	Iowa	18.90
24	Pennsylvania	17.14
25	Virginia	16.60
26	Kentucky	16.31
27	Arizona	16.06
28	Ohio	14.94
29	Kansas	14.85
30	Utah	14.18
31	Alabama	14.03
32	New Jersey	14.00
33	Nevada	13.37
34	Illinois	13.33
35	North Carolina	13.32
36	Minnesota	13.08
37	Michigan	13.00
38	California	12.89
39	Wisconsin	12.77
40	Texas	12.12
41	Louisiana	11.99
42	Colorado	11.23
43	Florida	10.54
44	New York	10.16
45	South Carolina	8.63
46	Indiana	8.52
47	Georgia	7.52
48	Tennessee	7.01
49	Missouri	6.76
50	Mississippi	6.18
	District of Columbia	110.67

Source: CQ Press using data from U.S. Department of Defense
"Atlas/Data Abstract for the United States" (http://siadapp.dmdc.osd.mil/personnel/L03/fy09/09top.htm)
*Includes grants for civil and military functions. Does not include contracts to U.S. territories and other countries.

U.S. Department of Defense Domestic Personnel in 2009

National Total = 2,617,048 Personnel*

ALPHA ORDER

RANK	STATE	PERSONNEL	% of USA
17	Alabama	58,789	2.2%
26	Alaska	33,281	1.3%
21	Arizona	44,662	1.7%
31	Arkansas	23,936	0.9%
1	California	236,963	9.1%
15	Colorado	59,480	2.3%
43	Connecticut	10,908	0.4%
44	Delaware	10,373	0.4%
6	Florida	105,724	4.0%
5	Georgia	140,358	5.4%
10	Hawaii	68,550	2.6%
41	Idaho	12,575	0.5%
19	Illinois	50,965	1.9%
25	Indiana	35,113	1.3%
38	Iowa	15,419	0.6%
20	Kansas	44,761	1.7%
11	Kentucky	65,226	2.5%
22	Louisiana	42,056	1.6%
42	Maine	11,829	0.5%
8	Maryland	80,126	3.1%
30	Massachusetts	25,458	1.0%
29	Michigan	29,448	1.1%
32	Minnesota	23,905	0.9%
24	Mississippi	36,351	1.4%
18	Missouri	51,676	2.0%
47	Montana	9,967	0.4%
36	Nebraska	18,128	0.7%
35	Nevada	18,440	0.7%
49	New Hampshire	5,973	0.2%
23	New Jersey	39,202	1.5%
33	New Mexico	23,266	0.9%
9	New York	72,233	2.8%
4	North Carolina	159,041	6.1%
39	North Dakota	13,788	0.5%
14	Ohio	61,785	2.4%
16	Oklahoma	59,428	2.3%
37	Oregon	15,646	0.6%
12	Pennsylvania	64,619	2.5%
45	Rhode Island	10,300	0.4%
13	South Carolina	62,026	2.4%
46	South Dakota	10,280	0.4%
28	Tennessee	32,084	1.2%
2	Texas	235,972	9.0%
27	Utah	33,054	1.3%
50	Vermont	5,246	0.2%
3	Virginia	177,982	6.8%
7	Washington	93,611	3.6%
40	West Virginia	12,648	0.5%
34	Wisconsin	20,689	0.8%
48	Wyoming	7,818	0.3%

RANK ORDER

RANK	STATE	PERSONNEL	% of USA
1	California	236,963	9.1%
2	Texas	235,972	9.0%
3	Virginia	177,982	6.8%
4	North Carolina	159,041	6.1%
5	Georgia	140,358	5.4%
6	Florida	105,724	4.0%
7	Washington	93,611	3.6%
8	Maryland	80,126	3.1%
9	New York	72,233	2.8%
10	Hawaii	68,550	2.6%
11	Kentucky	65,226	2.5%
12	Pennsylvania	64,619	2.5%
13	South Carolina	62,026	2.4%
14	Ohio	61,785	2.4%
15	Colorado	59,480	2.3%
16	Oklahoma	59,428	2.3%
17	Alabama	58,789	2.2%
18	Missouri	51,676	2.0%
19	Illinois	50,965	1.9%
20	Kansas	44,761	1.7%
21	Arizona	44,662	1.7%
22	Louisiana	42,056	1.6%
23	New Jersey	39,202	1.5%
24	Mississippi	36,351	1.4%
25	Indiana	35,113	1.3%
26	Alaska	33,281	1.3%
27	Utah	33,054	1.3%
28	Tennessee	32,084	1.2%
29	Michigan	29,448	1.1%
30	Massachusetts	25,458	1.0%
31	Arkansas	23,936	0.9%
32	Minnesota	23,905	0.9%
33	New Mexico	23,266	0.9%
34	Wisconsin	20,689	0.8%
35	Nevada	18,440	0.7%
36	Nebraska	18,128	0.7%
37	Oregon	15,646	0.6%
38	Iowa	15,419	0.6%
39	North Dakota	13,788	0.5%
40	West Virginia	12,648	0.5%
41	Idaho	12,575	0.5%
42	Maine	11,829	0.5%
43	Connecticut	10,908	0.4%
44	Delaware	10,373	0.4%
45	Rhode Island	10,300	0.4%
46	South Dakota	10,280	0.4%
47	Montana	9,967	0.4%
48	Wyoming	7,818	0.3%
49	New Hampshire	5,973	0.2%
50	Vermont	5,246	0.2%
	District of Columbia	35,890	1.4%

Source: U.S. Department of Defense
"Atlas/Data Abstract for the United States" (http://siadapp.dmdc.osd.mil/personnel/L03/fy09/09top.htm)
*Includes Active Duty Military, Civilian, Reserve, and National Guard personnel. Does not include personnel in U.S. territories or in other countries.

U.S. Department of Defense Active Duty Military Personnel in 2009

National Total = 1,088,465 Personnel*

ALPHA ORDER

RANK	STATE	PERSONNEL	% of USA
20	Alabama	11,896	1.1%
15	Alaska	23,178	2.1%
17	Arizona	21,343	2.0%
28	Arkansas	6,717	0.6%
2	California	117,806	10.8%
10	Colorado	35,404	3.3%
42	Connecticut	1,914	0.2%
34	Delaware	3,870	0.4%
8	Florida	42,642	3.9%
4	Georgia	73,988	6.8%
9	Hawaii	40,874	3.8%
32	Idaho	4,967	0.5%
22	Illinois	10,111	0.9%
39	Indiana	3,108	0.3%
46	Iowa	1,296	0.1%
14	Kansas	25,482	2.3%
7	Kentucky	43,138	4.0%
19	Louisiana	17,398	1.6%
48	Maine	730	0.1%
13	Maryland	29,160	2.7%
38	Massachusetts	3,205	0.3%
40	Michigan	2,858	0.3%
43	Minnesota	1,897	0.2%
24	Mississippi	9,895	0.9%
18	Missouri	17,925	1.6%
35	Montana	3,623	0.3%
27	Nebraska	6,845	0.6%
23	Nevada	10,034	0.9%
49	New Hampshire	675	0.1%
29	New Jersey	6,673	0.6%
21	New Mexico	11,038	1.0%
12	New York	29,553	2.7%
3	North Carolina	116,073	10.7%
26	North Dakota	7,209	0.7%
25	Ohio	8,261	0.8%
16	Oklahoma	21,673	2.0%
44	Oregon	1,615	0.1%
31	Pennsylvania	5,215	0.5%
45	Rhode Island	1,490	0.1%
11	South Carolina	32,518	3.0%
33	South Dakota	3,910	0.4%
36	Tennessee	3,511	0.3%
1	Texas	131,548	12.1%
30	Utah	6,237	0.6%
50	Vermont	565	0.1%
5	Virginia	63,160	5.8%
6	Washington	46,161	4.2%
47	West Virginia	1,199	0.1%
41	Wisconsin	2,046	0.2%
37	Wyoming	3,407	0.3%

RANK ORDER

RANK	STATE	PERSONNEL	% of USA
1	Texas	131,548	12.1%
2	California	117,806	10.8%
3	North Carolina	116,073	10.7%
4	Georgia	73,988	6.8%
5	Virginia	63,160	5.8%
6	Washington	46,161	4.2%
7	Kentucky	43,138	4.0%
8	Florida	42,642	3.9%
9	Hawaii	40,874	3.8%
10	Colorado	35,404	3.3%
11	South Carolina	32,518	3.0%
12	New York	29,553	2.7%
13	Maryland	29,160	2.7%
14	Kansas	25,482	2.3%
15	Alaska	23,178	2.1%
16	Oklahoma	21,673	2.0%
17	Arizona	21,343	2.0%
18	Missouri	17,925	1.6%
19	Louisiana	17,398	1.6%
20	Alabama	11,896	1.1%
21	New Mexico	11,038	1.0%
22	Illinois	10,111	0.9%
23	Nevada	10,034	0.9%
24	Mississippi	9,895	0.9%
25	Ohio	8,261	0.8%
26	North Dakota	7,209	0.7%
27	Nebraska	6,845	0.6%
28	Arkansas	6,717	0.6%
29	New Jersey	6,673	0.6%
30	Utah	6,237	0.6%
31	Pennsylvania	5,215	0.5%
32	Idaho	4,967	0.5%
33	South Dakota	3,910	0.4%
34	Delaware	3,870	0.4%
35	Montana	3,623	0.3%
36	Tennessee	3,511	0.3%
37	Wyoming	3,407	0.3%
38	Massachusetts	3,205	0.3%
39	Indiana	3,108	0.3%
40	Michigan	2,858	0.3%
41	Wisconsin	2,046	0.2%
42	Connecticut	1,914	0.2%
43	Minnesota	1,897	0.2%
44	Oregon	1,615	0.1%
45	Rhode Island	1,490	0.1%
46	Iowa	1,296	0.1%
47	West Virginia	1,199	0.1%
48	Maine	730	0.1%
49	New Hampshire	675	0.1%
50	Vermont	565	0.1%
	District of Columbia	13,424	1.2%

Source: U.S. Department of Defense
"Atlas/Data Abstract for the United States" (http://siadapp.dmdc.osd.mil/personnel/L03/fy09/09top.htm)
*Does not include active duty personnel in U.S. territories, in other countries or others undistributed.

U.S. Department of Defense Domestic Civilian Personnel in 2009

National Total = 709,265 Personnel*

ALPHA ORDER

RANK	STATE	PERSONNEL	% of USA
10	Alabama	24,794	3.5%
32	Alaska	5,356	0.8%
22	Arizona	9,591	1.4%
34	Arkansas	4,168	0.6%
2	California	61,365	8.7%
18	Colorado	11,585	1.6%
39	Connecticut	2,625	0.4%
45	Delaware	1,622	0.2%
6	Florida	28,429	4.0%
4	Georgia	37,012	5.2%
13	Hawaii	18,400	2.6%
44	Idaho	1,716	0.2%
14	Illinois	15,770	2.2%
19	Indiana	10,932	1.5%
43	Iowa	1,733	0.2%
27	Kansas	7,800	1.1%
25	Kentucky	8,962	1.3%
31	Louisiana	6,647	0.9%
29	Maine	6,946	1.0%
5	Maryland	34,966	4.9%
30	Massachusetts	6,918	1.0%
24	Michigan	8,972	1.3%
38	Minnesota	2,752	0.4%
23	Mississippi	9,124	1.3%
21	Missouri	9,982	1.4%
46	Montana	1,596	0.2%
35	Nebraska	3,785	0.5%
40	Nevada	2,319	0.3%
49	New Hampshire	1,047	0.1%
15	New Jersey	15,217	2.1%
28	New Mexico	7,029	1.0%
17	New York	12,318	1.7%
12	North Carolina	20,426	2.9%
42	North Dakota	1,910	0.3%
9	Ohio	25,001	3.5%
11	Oklahoma	22,115	3.1%
36	Oregon	3,561	0.5%
8	Pennsylvania	27,107	3.8%
33	Rhode Island	4,372	0.6%
20	South Carolina	10,406	1.5%
47	South Dakota	1,388	0.2%
26	Tennessee	7,967	1.1%
3	Texas	48,057	6.8%
16	Utah	14,818	2.1%
50	Vermont	729	0.1%
1	Virginia	89,713	12.6%
7	Washington	27,980	3.9%
41	West Virginia	2,146	0.3%
37	Wisconsin	2,810	0.4%
48	Wyoming	1,193	0.2%

RANK ORDER

RANK	STATE	PERSONNEL	% of USA
1	Virginia	89,713	12.6%
2	California	61,365	8.7%
3	Texas	48,057	6.8%
4	Georgia	37,012	5.2%
5	Maryland	34,966	4.9%
6	Florida	28,429	4.0%
7	Washington	27,980	3.9%
8	Pennsylvania	27,107	3.8%
9	Ohio	25,001	3.5%
10	Alabama	24,794	3.5%
11	Oklahoma	22,115	3.1%
12	North Carolina	20,426	2.9%
13	Hawaii	18,400	2.6%
14	Illinois	15,770	2.2%
15	New Jersey	15,217	2.1%
16	Utah	14,818	2.1%
17	New York	12,318	1.7%
18	Colorado	11,585	1.6%
19	Indiana	10,932	1.5%
20	South Carolina	10,406	1.5%
21	Missouri	9,982	1.4%
22	Arizona	9,591	1.4%
23	Mississippi	9,124	1.3%
24	Michigan	8,972	1.3%
25	Kentucky	8,962	1.3%
26	Tennessee	7,967	1.1%
27	Kansas	7,800	1.1%
28	New Mexico	7,029	1.0%
29	Maine	6,946	1.0%
30	Massachusetts	6,918	1.0%
31	Louisiana	6,647	0.9%
32	Alaska	5,356	0.8%
33	Rhode Island	4,372	0.6%
34	Arkansas	4,168	0.6%
35	Nebraska	3,785	0.5%
36	Oregon	3,561	0.5%
37	Wisconsin	2,810	0.4%
38	Minnesota	2,752	0.4%
39	Connecticut	2,625	0.4%
40	Nevada	2,319	0.3%
41	West Virginia	2,146	0.3%
42	North Dakota	1,910	0.3%
43	Iowa	1,733	0.2%
44	Idaho	1,716	0.2%
45	Delaware	1,622	0.2%
46	Montana	1,596	0.2%
47	South Dakota	1,388	0.2%
48	Wyoming	1,193	0.2%
49	New Hampshire	1,047	0.1%
50	Vermont	729	0.1%
	District of Columbia	16,088	2.3%

Source: U.S. Department of Defense
    "Atlas/Data Abstract for the United States" (http://siadapp.dmdc.osd.mil/personnel/L03/fy09/09top.htm)
*Does not include civilian personnel in U.S. territories or civilian personnel in other countries. Includes military and civil functions.

U.S. Department of Defense Reserve and National Guard Personnel in 2009

National Total = 819,318 Personnel*

ALPHA ORDER

RANK	STATE	PERSONNEL	% of USA
12	Alabama	22,099	2.7%
44	Alaska	4,747	0.6%
26	Arizona	13,728	1.7%
28	Arkansas	13,051	1.6%
1	California	57,792	7.1%
29	Colorado	12,491	1.5%
37	Connecticut	6,369	0.8%
42	Delaware	4,881	0.6%
3	Florida	34,653	4.2%
6	Georgia	29,358	3.6%
35	Hawaii	9,276	1.1%
39	Idaho	5,892	0.7%
9	Illinois	25,084	3.1%
13	Indiana	21,073	2.6%
30	Iowa	12,390	1.5%
32	Kansas	11,479	1.4%
27	Kentucky	13,126	1.6%
18	Louisiana	18,011	2.2%
48	Maine	4,153	0.5%
22	Maryland	16,000	2.0%
25	Massachusetts	15,335	1.9%
19	Michigan	17,618	2.2%
16	Minnesota	19,256	2.4%
20	Mississippi	17,332	2.1%
10	Missouri	23,769	2.9%
43	Montana	4,748	0.6%
36	Nebraska	7,498	0.9%
38	Nevada	6,087	0.7%
47	New Hampshire	4,251	0.5%
21	New Jersey	17,312	2.1%
40	New Mexico	5,199	0.6%
5	New York	30,362	3.7%
11	North Carolina	22,542	2.8%
45	North Dakota	4,669	0.6%
7	Ohio	28,523	3.5%
24	Oklahoma	15,640	1.9%
33	Oregon	10,470	1.3%
4	Pennsylvania	32,297	3.9%
46	Rhode Island	4,438	0.5%
17	South Carolina	19,102	2.3%
41	South Dakota	4,982	0.6%
14	Tennessee	20,606	2.5%
2	Texas	56,367	6.9%
31	Utah	11,999	1.5%
49	Vermont	3,952	0.5%
8	Virginia	25,109	3.1%
15	Washington	19,470	2.4%
34	West Virginia	9,303	1.1%
23	Wisconsin	15,833	1.9%
50	Wyoming	3,218	0.4%

RANK ORDER

RANK	STATE	PERSONNEL	% of USA
1	California	57,792	7.1%
2	Texas	56,367	6.9%
3	Florida	34,653	4.2%
4	Pennsylvania	32,297	3.9%
5	New York	30,362	3.7%
6	Georgia	29,358	3.6%
7	Ohio	28,523	3.5%
8	Virginia	25,109	3.1%
9	Illinois	25,084	3.1%
10	Missouri	23,769	2.9%
11	North Carolina	22,542	2.8%
12	Alabama	22,099	2.7%
13	Indiana	21,073	2.6%
14	Tennessee	20,606	2.5%
15	Washington	19,470	2.4%
16	Minnesota	19,256	2.4%
17	South Carolina	19,102	2.3%
18	Louisiana	18,011	2.2%
19	Michigan	17,618	2.2%
20	Mississippi	17,332	2.1%
21	New Jersey	17,312	2.1%
22	Maryland	16,000	2.0%
23	Wisconsin	15,833	1.9%
24	Oklahoma	15,640	1.9%
25	Massachusetts	15,335	1.9%
26	Arizona	13,728	1.7%
27	Kentucky	13,126	1.6%
28	Arkansas	13,051	1.6%
29	Colorado	12,491	1.5%
30	Iowa	12,390	1.5%
31	Utah	11,999	1.5%
32	Kansas	11,479	1.4%
33	Oregon	10,470	1.3%
34	West Virginia	9,303	1.1%
35	Hawaii	9,276	1.1%
36	Nebraska	7,498	0.9%
37	Connecticut	6,369	0.8%
38	Nevada	6,087	0.7%
39	Idaho	5,892	0.7%
40	New Mexico	5,199	0.6%
41	South Dakota	4,982	0.6%
42	Delaware	4,881	0.6%
43	Montana	4,748	0.6%
44	Alaska	4,747	0.6%
45	North Dakota	4,669	0.6%
46	Rhode Island	4,438	0.5%
47	New Hampshire	4,251	0.5%
48	Maine	4,153	0.5%
49	Vermont	3,952	0.5%
50	Wyoming	3,218	0.4%
	District of Columbia	6,378	0.8%

Source: U.S. Department of Defense
"Atlas/Data Abstract for the United States" (http://siadapp.dmdc.osd.mil/personnel/L03/fy09/09top.htm)
*Does not include reserve and national guard personnel in U.S. territories.

U.S. Department of Defense Total Compensation in 2009

National Total = $195,170,178,000*

ALPHA ORDER

RANK	STATE	COMPENSATION	% of USA
13	Alabama	$4,723,956,000	2.4%
24	Alaska	2,659,561,000	1.4%
20	Arizona	3,137,634,000	1.6%
31	Arkansas	1,621,707,000	0.8%
3	California	14,568,458,000	7.5%
11	Colorado	5,125,122,000	2.6%
41	Connecticut	720,299,000	0.4%
46	Delaware	536,758,000	0.3%
6	Florida	9,417,919,000	4.8%
4	Georgia	11,494,647,000	5.9%
9	Hawaii	6,344,467,000	3.3%
42	Idaho	709,220,000	0.4%
21	Illinois	3,128,538,000	1.6%
25	Indiana	2,338,121,000	1.2%
39	Iowa	747,256,000	0.4%
19	Kansas	3,667,675,000	1.9%
10	Kentucky	5,680,752,000	2.9%
22	Louisiana	2,688,149,000	1.4%
38	Maine	846,681,000	0.4%
8	Maryland	6,537,841,000	3.3%
32	Massachusetts	1,490,630,000	0.8%
29	Michigan	1,826,987,000	0.9%
34	Minnesota	1,208,062,000	0.6%
27	Mississippi	2,224,346,000	1.1%
17	Missouri	3,786,836,000	1.9%
45	Montana	540,644,000	0.3%
35	Nebraska	1,151,981,000	0.6%
33	Nevada	1,414,606,000	0.7%
48	New Hampshire	410,882,000	0.2%
23	New Jersey	2,671,220,000	1.4%
30	New Mexico	1,626,461,000	0.8%
12	New York	4,818,679,000	2.5%
5	North Carolina	10,558,150,000	5.4%
43	North Dakota	630,939,000	0.3%
16	Ohio	3,834,470,000	2.0%
15	Oklahoma	4,099,633,000	2.1%
37	Oregon	1,051,047,000	0.5%
14	Pennsylvania	4,210,386,000	2.2%
40	Rhode Island	743,035,000	0.4%
18	South Carolina	3,682,987,000	1.9%
47	South Dakota	513,643,000	0.3%
26	Tennessee	2,235,302,000	1.1%
1	Texas	19,298,889,000	9.9%
28	Utah	2,115,968,000	1.1%
50	Vermont	261,505,000	0.1%
2	Virginia	18,071,415,000	9.3%
7	Washington	8,223,735,000	4.2%
44	West Virginia	616,823,000	0.3%
36	Wisconsin	1,151,891,000	0.6%
49	Wyoming	405,020,000	0.2%

RANK ORDER

RANK	STATE	COMPENSATION	% of USA
1	Texas	$19,298,889,000	9.9%
2	Virginia	18,071,415,000	9.3%
3	California	14,568,458,000	7.5%
4	Georgia	11,494,647,000	5.9%
5	North Carolina	10,558,150,000	5.4%
6	Florida	9,417,919,000	4.8%
7	Washington	8,223,735,000	4.2%
8	Maryland	6,537,841,000	3.3%
9	Hawaii	6,344,467,000	3.3%
10	Kentucky	5,680,752,000	2.9%
11	Colorado	5,125,122,000	2.6%
12	New York	4,818,679,000	2.5%
13	Alabama	4,723,956,000	2.4%
14	Pennsylvania	4,210,386,000	2.2%
15	Oklahoma	4,099,633,000	2.1%
16	Ohio	3,834,470,000	2.0%
17	Missouri	3,786,836,000	1.9%
18	South Carolina	3,682,987,000	1.9%
19	Kansas	3,667,675,000	1.9%
20	Arizona	3,137,634,000	1.6%
21	Illinois	3,128,538,000	1.6%
22	Louisiana	2,688,149,000	1.4%
23	New Jersey	2,671,220,000	1.4%
24	Alaska	2,659,561,000	1.4%
25	Indiana	2,338,121,000	1.2%
26	Tennessee	2,235,302,000	1.1%
27	Mississippi	2,224,346,000	1.1%
28	Utah	2,115,968,000	1.1%
29	Michigan	1,826,987,000	0.9%
30	New Mexico	1,626,461,000	0.8%
31	Arkansas	1,621,707,000	0.8%
32	Massachusetts	1,490,630,000	0.8%
33	Nevada	1,414,606,000	0.7%
34	Minnesota	1,208,062,000	0.6%
35	Nebraska	1,151,981,000	0.6%
36	Wisconsin	1,151,891,000	0.6%
37	Oregon	1,051,047,000	0.5%
38	Maine	846,681,000	0.4%
39	Iowa	747,256,000	0.4%
40	Rhode Island	743,035,000	0.4%
41	Connecticut	720,299,000	0.4%
42	Idaho	709,220,000	0.4%
43	North Dakota	630,939,000	0.3%
44	West Virginia	616,823,000	0.3%
45	Montana	540,644,000	0.3%
46	Delaware	536,758,000	0.3%
47	South Dakota	513,643,000	0.3%
48	New Hampshire	410,882,000	0.2%
49	Wyoming	405,020,000	0.2%
50	Vermont	261,505,000	0.1%
	District of Columbia	3,599,245,000	1.8%

Source: U.S. Department of Defense
  "Atlas/Data Abstract for the United States" (http://siadapp.dmdc.osd.mil/personnel/L03/fy09/09top.htm)
*Includes Civilian Pay, Military Active Duty Pay, Reserve, National Guard Pay, and Retired Military Pay. Based on location
of recipient. Does not include recipients in U.S. territories and other countries.

U.S. Department of Defense Military Active Duty Pay in 2009

National Total = $84,459,939,000*

ALPHA ORDER

RANK	STATE	PAYROLL	% of USA
20	Alabama	$1,254,790,000	1.5%
13	Alaska	2,077,719,000	2.5%
19	Arizona	1,262,572,000	1.5%
28	Arkansas	435,036,000	0.5%
5	California	5,182,809,000	6.1%
9	Colorado	2,965,503,000	3.5%
41	Connecticut	198,163,000	0.2%
38	Delaware	216,219,000	0.3%
10	Florida	2,816,465,000	3.3%
3	Georgia	6,668,434,000	7.9%
6	Hawaii	4,529,364,000	5.4%
36	Idaho	261,607,000	0.3%
21	Illinois	738,269,000	0.9%
31	Indiana	350,647,000	0.4%
45	Iowa	140,071,000	0.2%
12	Kansas	2,465,253,000	2.9%
8	Kentucky	4,339,243,000	5.1%
17	Louisiana	1,417,143,000	1.7%
47	Maine	113,348,000	0.1%
14	Maryland	2,012,820,000	2.4%
33	Massachusetts	319,863,000	0.4%
35	Michigan	263,638,000	0.3%
39	Minnesota	206,036,000	0.2%
23	Mississippi	629,352,000	0.7%
18	Missouri	1,310,799,000	1.6%
42	Montana	187,506,000	0.2%
29	Nebraska	434,949,000	0.5%
24	Nevada	600,019,000	0.7%
49	New Hampshire	73,429,000	0.1%
27	New Jersey	543,053,000	0.6%
26	New Mexico	571,288,000	0.7%
11	New York	2,701,191,000	3.2%
2	North Carolina	7,012,462,000	8.3%
32	North Dakota	335,954,000	0.4%
22	Ohio	640,496,000	0.8%
15	Oklahoma	1,678,570,000	2.0%
44	Oregon	140,868,000	0.2%
25	Pennsylvania	574,034,000	0.7%
46	Rhode Island	120,400,000	0.1%
16	South Carolina	1,530,304,000	1.8%
40	South Dakota	198,438,000	0.2%
34	Tennessee	282,250,000	0.3%
1	Texas	11,128,462,000	13.2%
30	Utah	431,738,000	0.5%
50	Vermont	64,177,000	0.1%
4	Virginia	6,214,491,000	7.4%
7	Washington	4,407,343,000	5.2%
48	West Virginia	106,870,000	0.1%
37	Wisconsin	222,262,000	0.3%
43	Wyoming	177,223,000	0.2%

RANK ORDER

RANK	STATE	PAYROLL	% of USA
1	Texas	$11,128,462,000	13.2%
2	North Carolina	7,012,462,000	8.3%
3	Georgia	6,668,434,000	7.9%
4	Virginia	6,214,491,000	7.4%
5	California	5,182,809,000	6.1%
6	Hawaii	4,529,364,000	5.4%
7	Washington	4,407,343,000	5.2%
8	Kentucky	4,339,243,000	5.1%
9	Colorado	2,965,503,000	3.5%
10	Florida	2,816,465,000	3.3%
11	New York	2,701,191,000	3.2%
12	Kansas	2,465,253,000	2.9%
13	Alaska	2,077,719,000	2.5%
14	Maryland	2,012,820,000	2.4%
15	Oklahoma	1,678,570,000	2.0%
16	South Carolina	1,530,304,000	1.8%
17	Louisiana	1,417,143,000	1.7%
18	Missouri	1,310,799,000	1.6%
19	Arizona	1,262,572,000	1.5%
20	Alabama	1,254,790,000	1.5%
21	Illinois	738,269,000	0.9%
22	Ohio	640,496,000	0.8%
23	Mississippi	629,352,000	0.7%
24	Nevada	600,019,000	0.7%
25	Pennsylvania	574,034,000	0.7%
26	New Mexico	571,288,000	0.7%
27	New Jersey	543,053,000	0.6%
28	Arkansas	435,036,000	0.5%
29	Nebraska	434,949,000	0.5%
30	Utah	431,738,000	0.5%
31	Indiana	350,647,000	0.4%
32	North Dakota	335,954,000	0.4%
33	Massachusetts	319,863,000	0.4%
34	Tennessee	282,250,000	0.3%
35	Michigan	263,638,000	0.3%
36	Idaho	261,607,000	0.3%
37	Wisconsin	222,262,000	0.3%
38	Delaware	216,219,000	0.3%
39	Minnesota	206,036,000	0.2%
40	South Dakota	198,438,000	0.2%
41	Connecticut	198,163,000	0.2%
42	Montana	187,506,000	0.2%
43	Wyoming	177,223,000	0.2%
44	Oregon	140,868,000	0.2%
45	Iowa	140,071,000	0.2%
46	Rhode Island	120,400,000	0.1%
47	Maine	113,348,000	0.1%
48	West Virginia	106,870,000	0.1%
49	New Hampshire	73,429,000	0.1%
50	Vermont	64,177,000	0.1%
	District of Columbia	1,906,999,000	2.3%

Source: U.S. Department of Defense
"Atlas/Data Abstract for the United States" (http://siadapp.dmdc.osd.mil/personnel/L03/fy09/09top.htm)
*Based on location of recipient. Does not include recipients in U.S. territories and other countries.

U.S. Department of Defense Civilian Pay in 2009

National Total = $49,735,662,000*

ALPHA ORDER					RANK ORDER			
RANK	STATE	PAYROLL	% of USA		RANK	STATE	PAYROLL	% of USA
9	Alabama	$1,808,239,000	3.6%		1	Virginia	$7,447,686,000	15.0%
33	Alaska	321,206,000	0.6%		2	California	4,570,024,000	9.2%
22	Arizona	626,966,000	1.3%		3	Maryland	2,995,038,000	6.0%
35	Arkansas	235,881,000	0.5%		4	Texas	2,917,913,000	5.9%
2	California	4,570,024,000	9.2%		5	Georgia	2,288,362,000	4.6%
17	Colorado	786,177,000	1.6%		6	Florida	1,942,655,000	3.9%
37	Connecticut	184,190,000	0.4%		7	Washington	1,873,338,000	3.8%
45	Delaware	98,410,000	0.2%		8	Ohio	1,824,865,000	3.7%
6	Florida	1,942,655,000	3.9%		9	Alabama	1,808,239,000	3.6%
5	Georgia	2,288,362,000	4.6%		10	Pennsylvania	1,788,532,000	3.6%
14	Hawaii	1,163,627,000	2.3%		11	Oklahoma	1,339,260,000	2.7%
44	Idaho	100,861,000	0.2%		12	New Jersey	1,290,072,000	2.6%
15	Illinois	1,069,790,000	2.2%		13	North Carolina	1,210,521,000	2.4%
20	Indiana	705,646,000	1.4%		14	Hawaii	1,163,627,000	2.3%
43	Iowa	102,185,000	0.2%		15	Illinois	1,069,790,000	2.2%
29	Kansas	471,455,000	0.9%		16	Utah	954,215,000	1.9%
26	Kentucky	508,305,000	1.0%		17	Colorado	786,177,000	1.6%
31	Louisiana	414,120,000	0.8%		18	New York	784,658,000	1.6%
30	Maine	440,345,000	0.9%		19	Michigan	705,769,000	1.4%
3	Maryland	2,995,038,000	6.0%		20	Indiana	705,646,000	1.4%
25	Massachusetts	539,474,000	1.1%		21	South Carolina	638,047,000	1.3%
19	Michigan	705,769,000	1.4%		22	Arizona	626,966,000	1.3%
38	Minnesota	177,452,000	0.4%		23	Missouri	586,610,000	1.2%
24	Mississippi	585,976,000	1.2%		24	Mississippi	585,976,000	1.2%
23	Missouri	586,610,000	1.2%		25	Massachusetts	539,474,000	1.1%
46	Montana	91,395,000	0.2%		26	Kentucky	508,305,000	1.0%
34	Nebraska	250,642,000	0.5%		27	New Mexico	483,878,000	1.0%
40	Nevada	143,070,000	0.3%		28	Tennessee	476,959,000	1.0%
48	New Hampshire	74,277,000	0.1%		29	Kansas	471,455,000	0.9%
12	New Jersey	1,290,072,000	2.6%		30	Maine	440,345,000	0.9%
27	New Mexico	483,878,000	1.0%		31	Louisiana	414,120,000	0.8%
18	New York	784,658,000	1.6%		32	Rhode Island	391,187,000	0.8%
13	North Carolina	1,210,521,000	2.4%		33	Alaska	321,206,000	0.6%
42	North Dakota	108,116,000	0.2%		34	Nebraska	250,642,000	0.5%
8	Ohio	1,824,865,000	3.7%		35	Arkansas	235,881,000	0.5%
11	Oklahoma	1,339,260,000	2.7%		36	Oregon	231,630,000	0.5%
36	Oregon	231,630,000	0.5%		37	Connecticut	184,190,000	0.4%
10	Pennsylvania	1,788,532,000	3.6%		38	Minnesota	177,452,000	0.4%
32	Rhode Island	391,187,000	0.8%		39	Wisconsin	160,743,000	0.3%
21	South Carolina	638,047,000	1.3%		40	Nevada	143,070,000	0.3%
47	South Dakota	76,881,000	0.2%		41	West Virginia	126,119,000	0.3%
28	Tennessee	476,959,000	1.0%		42	North Dakota	108,116,000	0.2%
4	Texas	2,917,913,000	5.9%		43	Iowa	102,185,000	0.2%
16	Utah	954,215,000	1.9%		44	Idaho	100,861,000	0.2%
50	Vermont	44,921,000	0.1%		45	Delaware	98,410,000	0.2%
1	Virginia	7,447,686,000	15.0%		46	Montana	91,395,000	0.2%
7	Washington	1,873,338,000	3.8%		47	South Dakota	76,881,000	0.2%
41	West Virginia	126,119,000	0.3%		48	New Hampshire	74,277,000	0.1%
39	Wisconsin	160,743,000	0.3%		49	Wyoming	69,027,000	0.1%
49	Wyoming	69,027,000	0.1%		50	Vermont	44,921,000	0.1%
						District of Columbia	1,508,947,000	3.0%

Source: U.S. Department of Defense
   "Atlas/Data Abstract for the United States" (http://siadapp.dmdc.osd.mil/personnel/L03/fy09/09top.htm)
*Based on location of recipient. Does not include recipients in U.S. territories and other countries.

U.S. Department of Defense Reserve and National Guard Pay in 2009

National Total = $22,758,996,000*

ALPHA ORDER

ALPHA ORDER

RANK	STATE	PAYROLL	% of USA
11	Alabama	$617,055,000	2.7%
46	Alaska	90,592,000	0.4%
36	Arizona	180,724,000	0.8%
18	Arkansas	518,376,000	2.3%
2	California	1,391,094,000	6.1%
33	Colorado	285,229,000	1.3%
38	Connecticut	149,873,000	0.7%
49	Delaware	74,623,000	0.3%
7	Florida	826,134,000	3.6%
6	Georgia	868,244,000	3.8%
30	Hawaii	315,642,000	1.4%
41	Idaho	116,236,000	0.5%
10	Illinois	680,329,000	3.0%
5	Indiana	905,556,000	4.0%
29	Iowa	321,928,000	1.4%
28	Kansas	334,444,000	1.5%
27	Kentucky	391,231,000	1.7%
26	Louisiana	410,608,000	1.8%
47	Maine	87,175,000	0.4%
25	Maryland	421,636,000	1.9%
31	Massachusetts	312,302,000	1.4%
24	Michigan	437,538,000	1.9%
17	Minnesota	557,666,000	2.5%
16	Mississippi	558,821,000	2.5%
3	Missouri	1,268,807,000	5.6%
43	Montana	110,398,000	0.5%
35	Nebraska	198,307,000	0.9%
37	Nevada	151,343,000	0.7%
48	New Hampshire	78,753,000	0.3%
19	New Jersey	507,311,000	2.2%
39	New Mexico	148,491,000	0.7%
8	New York	782,279,000	3.4%
9	North Carolina	729,587,000	3.2%
44	North Dakota	110,138,000	0.5%
12	Ohio	609,867,000	2.7%
20	Oklahoma	496,151,000	2.2%
32	Oregon	300,719,000	1.3%
4	Pennsylvania	1,011,822,000	4.4%
40	Rhode Island	117,397,000	0.5%
21	South Carolina	485,464,000	2.1%
42	South Dakota	115,571,000	0.5%
14	Tennessee	572,830,000	2.5%
1	Texas	1,520,699,000	6.7%
23	Utah	448,935,000	2.0%
45	Vermont	92,561,000	0.4%
13	Virginia	603,453,000	2.7%
15	Washington	563,322,000	2.5%
34	West Virginia	216,627,000	1.0%
22	Wisconsin	470,144,000	2.1%
50	Wyoming	70,775,000	0.3%

RANK ORDER

RANK	STATE	PAYROLL	% of USA
1	Texas	$1,520,699,000	6.7%
2	California	1,391,094,000	6.1%
3	Missouri	1,268,807,000	5.6%
4	Pennsylvania	1,011,822,000	4.4%
5	Indiana	905,556,000	4.0%
6	Georgia	868,244,000	3.8%
7	Florida	826,134,000	3.6%
8	New York	782,279,000	3.4%
9	North Carolina	729,587,000	3.2%
10	Illinois	680,329,000	3.0%
11	Alabama	617,055,000	2.7%
12	Ohio	609,867,000	2.7%
13	Virginia	603,453,000	2.7%
14	Tennessee	572,830,000	2.5%
15	Washington	563,322,000	2.5%
16	Mississippi	558,821,000	2.5%
17	Minnesota	557,666,000	2.5%
18	Arkansas	518,376,000	2.3%
19	New Jersey	507,311,000	2.2%
20	Oklahoma	496,151,000	2.2%
21	South Carolina	485,464,000	2.1%
22	Wisconsin	470,144,000	2.1%
23	Utah	448,935,000	2.0%
24	Michigan	437,538,000	1.9%
25	Maryland	421,636,000	1.9%
26	Louisiana	410,608,000	1.8%
27	Kentucky	391,231,000	1.7%
28	Kansas	334,444,000	1.5%
29	Iowa	321,928,000	1.4%
30	Hawaii	315,642,000	1.4%
31	Massachusetts	312,302,000	1.4%
32	Oregon	300,719,000	1.3%
33	Colorado	285,229,000	1.3%
34	West Virginia	216,627,000	1.0%
35	Nebraska	198,307,000	0.9%
36	Arizona	180,724,000	0.8%
37	Nevada	151,343,000	0.7%
38	Connecticut	149,873,000	0.7%
39	New Mexico	148,491,000	0.7%
40	Rhode Island	117,397,000	0.5%
41	Idaho	116,236,000	0.5%
42	South Dakota	115,571,000	0.5%
43	Montana	110,398,000	0.5%
44	North Dakota	110,138,000	0.5%
45	Vermont	92,561,000	0.4%
46	Alaska	90,592,000	0.4%
47	Maine	87,175,000	0.4%
48	New Hampshire	78,753,000	0.3%
49	Delaware	74,623,000	0.3%
50	Wyoming	70,775,000	0.3%
	District of Columbia	124,189,000	0.5%

Source: U.S. Department of Defense
"Atlas/Data Abstract for the United States" (http://siadapp.dmdc.osd.mil/personnel/L03/fy09/09top.htm)
*Based on location of recipient. Does not include recipients in U.S. territories and other countries.

U.S. Department of Defense Retired Military Pay in 2009

National Total = $38,215,581,000*

ALPHA ORDER

RANK	STATE	PAYROLL	% of USA
11	Alabama	$1,043,872,000	2.7%
42	Alaska	170,044,000	0.4%
10	Arizona	1,067,372,000	2.8%
24	Arkansas	432,414,000	1.1%
4	California	3,424,531,000	9.0%
9	Colorado	1,088,213,000	2.8%
39	Connecticut	188,073,000	0.5%
45	Delaware	147,506,000	0.4%
1	Florida	3,832,665,000	10.0%
5	Georgia	1,669,607,000	4.4%
30	Hawaii	335,834,000	0.9%
37	Idaho	230,516,000	0.6%
16	Illinois	640,150,000	1.7%
29	Indiana	376,272,000	1.0%
41	Iowa	183,072,000	0.5%
27	Kansas	396,523,000	1.0%
23	Kentucky	441,973,000	1.2%
22	Louisiana	446,278,000	1.2%
38	Maine	205,813,000	0.5%
8	Maryland	1,108,347,000	2.9%
32	Massachusetts	318,991,000	0.8%
26	Michigan	420,042,000	1.1%
36	Minnesota	266,908,000	0.7%
21	Mississippi	450,197,000	1.2%
17	Missouri	620,620,000	1.6%
44	Montana	151,345,000	0.4%
35	Nebraska	268,083,000	0.7%
20	Nevada	520,174,000	1.4%
40	New Hampshire	184,423,000	0.5%
31	New Jersey	330,784,000	0.9%
25	New Mexico	422,804,000	1.1%
19	New York	550,551,000	1.4%
6	North Carolina	1,605,580,000	4.2%
49	North Dakota	76,731,000	0.2%
15	Ohio	759,242,000	2.0%
18	Oklahoma	585,652,000	1.5%
28	Oregon	377,830,000	1.0%
14	Pennsylvania	835,998,000	2.2%
47	Rhode Island	114,051,000	0.3%
12	South Carolina	1,029,172,000	2.7%
46	South Dakota	122,753,000	0.3%
13	Tennessee	903,263,000	2.4%
3	Texas	3,731,815,000	9.8%
34	Utah	281,080,000	0.7%
50	Vermont	59,846,000	0.2%
2	Virginia	3,805,785,000	10.0%
7	Washington	1,379,732,000	3.6%
43	West Virginia	167,207,000	0.4%
33	Wisconsin	298,742,000	0.8%
48	Wyoming	87,995,000	0.2%

RANK ORDER

RANK	STATE	PAYROLL	% of USA
1	Florida	$3,832,665,000	10.0%
2	Virginia	3,805,785,000	10.0%
3	Texas	3,731,815,000	9.8%
4	California	3,424,531,000	9.0%
5	Georgia	1,669,607,000	4.4%
6	North Carolina	1,605,580,000	4.2%
7	Washington	1,379,732,000	3.6%
8	Maryland	1,108,347,000	2.9%
9	Colorado	1,088,213,000	2.8%
10	Arizona	1,067,372,000	2.8%
11	Alabama	1,043,872,000	2.7%
12	South Carolina	1,029,172,000	2.7%
13	Tennessee	903,263,000	2.4%
14	Pennsylvania	835,998,000	2.2%
15	Ohio	759,242,000	2.0%
16	Illinois	640,150,000	1.7%
17	Missouri	620,620,000	1.6%
18	Oklahoma	585,652,000	1.5%
19	New York	550,551,000	1.4%
20	Nevada	520,174,000	1.4%
21	Mississippi	450,197,000	1.2%
22	Louisiana	446,278,000	1.2%
23	Kentucky	441,973,000	1.2%
24	Arkansas	432,414,000	1.1%
25	New Mexico	422,804,000	1.1%
26	Michigan	420,042,000	1.1%
27	Kansas	396,523,000	1.0%
28	Oregon	377,830,000	1.0%
29	Indiana	376,272,000	1.0%
30	Hawaii	335,834,000	0.9%
31	New Jersey	330,784,000	0.9%
32	Massachusetts	318,991,000	0.8%
33	Wisconsin	298,742,000	0.8%
34	Utah	281,080,000	0.7%
35	Nebraska	268,083,000	0.7%
36	Minnesota	266,908,000	0.7%
37	Idaho	230,516,000	0.6%
38	Maine	205,813,000	0.5%
39	Connecticut	188,073,000	0.5%
40	New Hampshire	184,423,000	0.5%
41	Iowa	183,072,000	0.5%
42	Alaska	170,044,000	0.4%
43	West Virginia	167,207,000	0.4%
44	Montana	151,345,000	0.4%
45	Delaware	147,506,000	0.4%
46	South Dakota	122,753,000	0.3%
47	Rhode Island	114,051,000	0.3%
48	Wyoming	87,995,000	0.2%
49	North Dakota	76,731,000	0.2%
50	Vermont	59,846,000	0.2%
	District of Columbia	59,110,000	0.2%

Source: U.S. Department of Defense
   "Atlas/Data Abstract for the United States" (http://siadapp.dmdc.osd.mil/personnel/L03/fy09/09top.htm)
*Based on location of recipient. Does not include recipients in U.S. territories and other countries.

Veterans in 2013

National Total = 21,972,964 Veterans*

ALPHA ORDER

RANK	STATE	VETERANS	% of USA
20	Alabama	414,963	1.9%
46	Alaska	74,671	0.3%
13	Arizona	527,400	2.4%
29	Arkansas	250,095	1.1%
1	California	1,795,455	8.2%
22	Colorado	390,824	1.8%
34	Connecticut	207,759	0.9%
44	Delaware	78,016	0.4%
3	Florida	1,520,563	6.9%
8	Georgia	774,464	3.5%
41	Hawaii	116,947	0.5%
39	Idaho	138,108	0.6%
10	Illinois	744,710	3.4%
16	Indiana	490,380	2.2%
30	Iowa	233,815	1.1%
33	Kansas	223,708	1.0%
26	Kentucky	339,334	1.5%
28	Louisiana	315,342	1.4%
40	Maine	127,694	0.6%
17	Maryland	443,076	2.0%
23	Massachusetts	374,809	1.7%
11	Michigan	660,773	3.0%
24	Minnesota	360,754	1.6%
32	Mississippi	225,469	1.0%
15	Missouri	497,874	2.3%
43	Montana	101,597	0.5%
38	Nebraska	138,773	0.6%
31	Nevada	225,933	1.0%
42	New Hampshire	110,778	0.5%
18	New Jersey	425,094	1.9%
36	New Mexico	170,699	0.8%
5	New York	885,796	4.0%
9	North Carolina	769,384	3.5%
49	North Dakota	56,213	0.3%
6	Ohio	877,894	4.0%
25	Oklahoma	340,395	1.5%
27	Oregon	322,355	1.5%
4	Pennsylvania	953,644	4.3%
47	Rhode Island	69,206	0.3%
19	South Carolina	420,968	1.9%
45	South Dakota	75,687	0.3%
14	Tennessee	521,267	2.4%
2	Texas	1,667,740	7.6%
37	Utah	150,771	0.7%
50	Vermont	48,812	0.2%
7	Virginia	840,398	3.8%
12	Washington	602,272	2.7%
35	West Virginia	173,389	0.8%
21	Wisconsin	409,419	1.9%
48	Wyoming	56,518	0.3%

RANK ORDER

RANK	STATE	VETERANS	% of USA
1	California	1,795,455	8.2%
2	Texas	1,667,740	7.6%
3	Florida	1,520,563	6.9%
4	Pennsylvania	953,644	4.3%
5	New York	885,796	4.0%
6	Ohio	877,894	4.0%
7	Virginia	840,398	3.8%
8	Georgia	774,464	3.5%
9	North Carolina	769,384	3.5%
10	Illinois	744,710	3.4%
11	Michigan	660,773	3.0%
12	Washington	602,272	2.7%
13	Arizona	527,400	2.4%
14	Tennessee	521,267	2.4%
15	Missouri	497,874	2.3%
16	Indiana	490,380	2.2%
17	Maryland	443,076	2.0%
18	New Jersey	425,094	1.9%
19	South Carolina	420,968	1.9%
20	Alabama	414,963	1.9%
21	Wisconsin	409,419	1.9%
22	Colorado	390,824	1.8%
23	Massachusetts	374,809	1.7%
24	Minnesota	360,754	1.6%
25	Oklahoma	340,395	1.5%
26	Kentucky	339,334	1.5%
27	Oregon	322,355	1.5%
28	Louisiana	315,342	1.4%
29	Arkansas	250,095	1.1%
30	Iowa	233,815	1.1%
31	Nevada	225,933	1.0%
32	Mississippi	225,469	1.0%
33	Kansas	223,708	1.0%
34	Connecticut	207,759	0.9%
35	West Virginia	173,389	0.8%
36	New Mexico	170,699	0.8%
37	Utah	150,771	0.7%
38	Nebraska	138,773	0.6%
39	Idaho	138,108	0.6%
40	Maine	127,694	0.6%
41	Hawaii	116,947	0.5%
42	New Hampshire	110,778	0.5%
43	Montana	101,597	0.5%
44	Delaware	78,016	0.4%
45	South Dakota	75,687	0.3%
46	Alaska	74,671	0.3%
47	Rhode Island	69,206	0.3%
48	Wyoming	56,518	0.3%
49	North Dakota	56,213	0.3%
50	Vermont	48,812	0.2%
	District of Columbia	31,166	0.1%

Source: U.S. Department of Veteran Affairs
  "Veteran Data and Information" (http://www.va.gov/vetdata/Veteran_Population.asp)
*Estimates based on 2010 data. Includes 199,794 veterans in U.S. territories or other countries.

Percent of Adult Population Who Are Veterans in 2013

National Percent = 9.1%*

ALPHA ORDER				RANK ORDER		
RANK	STATE	PERCENT		RANK	STATE	PERCENT
12	Alabama	11.2		1	Alaska	13.7
1	Alaska	13.7		2	Virginia	13.3
18	Arizona	10.7		3	Montana	13.0
12	Arkansas	11.2		4	Wyoming	12.8
48	California	6.2		5	Maine	12.0
30	Colorado	9.9		5	South Dakota	12.0
46	Connecticut	7.4		7	Idaho	11.8
14	Delaware	11.0		7	Oklahoma	11.8
30	Florida	9.9		7	West Virginia	11.8
23	Georgia	10.4		10	South Carolina	11.6
18	Hawaii	10.7		11	Washington	11.3
7	Idaho	11.8		12	Alabama	11.2
45	Illinois	7.6		12	Arkansas	11.2
30	Indiana	9.9		14	Delaware	11.0
30	Iowa	9.9		15	New Mexico	10.9
24	Kansas	10.3		16	Missouri	10.8
27	Kentucky	10.1		16	Nevada	10.8
39	Louisiana	9.1		18	Arizona	10.7
5	Maine	12.0		18	Hawaii	10.7
35	Maryland	9.8		20	New Hampshire	10.6
47	Massachusetts	7.1		20	Oregon	10.6
41	Michigan	8.7		22	Tennessee	10.5
40	Minnesota	8.8		23	Georgia	10.4
27	Mississippi	10.1		24	Kansas	10.3
16	Missouri	10.8		24	North Carolina	10.3
3	Montana	13.0		24	North Dakota	10.3
29	Nebraska	10.0		27	Kentucky	10.1
16	Nevada	10.8		27	Mississippi	10.1
20	New Hampshire	10.6		29	Nebraska	10.0
48	New Jersey	6.2		30	Colorado	9.9
15	New Mexico	10.9		30	Florida	9.9
50	New York	5.8		30	Indiana	9.9
24	North Carolina	10.3		30	Iowa	9.9
24	North Dakota	10.3		30	Ohio	9.9
30	Ohio	9.9		35	Maryland	9.8
7	Oklahoma	11.8		36	Vermont	9.7
20	Oregon	10.6		37	Pennsylvania	9.5
37	Pennsylvania	9.5		38	Wisconsin	9.3
43	Rhode Island	8.3		39	Louisiana	9.1
10	South Carolina	11.6		40	Minnesota	8.8
5	South Dakota	12.0		41	Michigan	8.7
22	Tennessee	10.5		41	Texas	8.7
41	Texas	8.7		43	Rhode Island	8.3
44	Utah	7.7		44	Utah	7.7
36	Vermont	9.7		45	Illinois	7.6
2	Virginia	13.3		46	Connecticut	7.4
11	Washington	11.3		47	Massachusetts	7.1
7	West Virginia	11.8		48	California	6.2
38	Wisconsin	9.3		48	New Jersey	6.2
4	Wyoming	12.8		50	New York	5.8
				District of Columbia		6.0

Source: CQ Press using data from U.S. Department of Veteran Affairs
"Veteran Data and Information" (http://www.va.gov/vetdata/Veteran_Population.asp)
*Estimates based on 2010 data. National figures does not include veterans in U.S. territories or other countries. Percent calculated with population 18 years old and older in 2012.

U.S. Military Fatalities in Iraq and Afghanistan as of January 28, 2014

National Total = 6,779 Fatalities*

RANK	STATE	FATALITIES	% of USA
25	Alabama	105	1.5%
46	Alaska	23	0.3%
13	Arizona	151	2.2%
29	Arkansas	89	1.3%
1	California	725	10.7%
26	Colorado	100	1.5%
38	Connecticut	47	0.7%
49	Delaware	19	0.3%
3	Florida	342	5.0%
9	Georgia	214	3.2%
43	Hawaii	36	0.5%
36	Idaho	50	0.7%
7	Illinois	249	3.7%
12	Indiana	154	2.3%
32	Iowa	72	1.1%
31	Kansas	73	1.1%
23	Kentucky	109	1.6%
20	Louisiana	123	1.8%
36	Maine	50	0.7%
22	Maryland	117	1.7%
18	Massachusetts	124	1.8%
8	Michigan	224	3.3%
27	Minnesota	96	1.4%
30	Mississippi	80	1.2%
15	Missouri	143	2.1%
40	Montana	40	0.6%
33	Nebraska	60	0.9%
35	Nevada	54	0.8%
42	New Hampshire	38	0.6%
20	New Jersey	123	1.8%
34	New Mexico	55	0.8%
4	New York	292	4.3%
11	North Carolina	186	2.7%
48	North Dakota	20	0.3%
6	Ohio	275	4.1%
17	Oklahoma	125	1.8%
24	Oregon	108	1.6%
5	Pennsylvania	290	4.3%
50	Rhode Island	16	0.2%
28	South Carolina	94	1.4%
45	South Dakota	24	0.4%
16	Tennessee	140	2.1%
2	Texas	600	8.9%
38	Utah	47	0.7%
44	Vermont	26	0.4%
10	Virginia	196	2.9%
14	Washington	147	2.2%
41	West Virginia	39	0.6%
18	Wisconsin	124	1.8%
47	Wyoming	22	0.3%

RANK	STATE	FATALITIES	% of USA
1	California	725	10.7%
2	Texas	600	8.9%
3	Florida	342	5.0%
4	New York	292	4.3%
5	Pennsylvania	290	4.3%
6	Ohio	275	4.1%
7	Illinois	249	3.7%
8	Michigan	224	3.3%
9	Georgia	214	3.2%
10	Virginia	196	2.9%
11	North Carolina	186	2.7%
12	Indiana	154	2.3%
13	Arizona	151	2.2%
14	Washington	147	2.2%
15	Missouri	143	2.1%
16	Tennessee	140	2.1%
17	Oklahoma	125	1.8%
18	Massachusetts	124	1.8%
18	Wisconsin	124	1.8%
20	Louisiana	123	1.8%
20	New Jersey	123	1.8%
22	Maryland	117	1.7%
23	Kentucky	109	1.6%
24	Oregon	108	1.6%
25	Alabama	105	1.5%
26	Colorado	100	1.5%
27	Minnesota	96	1.4%
28	South Carolina	94	1.4%
29	Arkansas	89	1.3%
30	Mississippi	80	1.2%
31	Kansas	73	1.1%
32	Iowa	72	1.1%
33	Nebraska	60	0.9%
34	New Mexico	55	0.8%
35	Nevada	54	0.8%
36	Idaho	50	0.7%
36	Maine	50	0.7%
38	Connecticut	47	0.7%
38	Utah	47	0.7%
40	Montana	40	0.6%
41	West Virginia	39	0.6%
42	New Hampshire	38	0.6%
43	Hawaii	36	0.5%
44	Vermont	26	0.4%
45	South Dakota	24	0.4%
46	Alaska	23	0.3%
47	Wyoming	22	0.3%
48	North Dakota	20	0.3%
49	Delaware	19	0.3%
50	Rhode Island	16	0.2%
	District of Columbia	10	0.1%

Source: U.S. Department of Defense, Defense Casualty Analysis System
"U.S. Military Casualties" (https://www.dmdc.osd.mil/dcas/pages/report_sum_all.xhtml)
*Total includes 113 deaths of soldiers from U.S. territories. Total does not include deaths of United Kingdom soldiers or other coalition nations. Includes 5,322 combat and 1,457 noncombat deaths. Includes 4,476 deaths in Iraq and 2,303 deaths in Afghanistan.

Rate of U.S. Military Fatalities in Iraq and Afghanistan as of January 28, 2014

National Rate = 2.1 Fatalities per 100,000 Population*

ALPHA ORDER

RANK	STATE	RATE
29	Alabama	2.2
7	Alaska	3.1
23	Arizona	2.3
9	Arkansas	3.0
38	California	1.9
38	Colorado	1.9
50	Connecticut	1.3
32	Delaware	2.1
45	Florida	1.7
32	Georgia	2.1
16	Hawaii	2.6
7	Idaho	3.1
38	Illinois	1.9
23	Indiana	2.3
23	Iowa	2.3
18	Kansas	2.5
18	Kentucky	2.5
13	Louisiana	2.7
3	Maine	3.8
36	Maryland	2.0
38	Massachusetts	1.9
23	Michigan	2.3
44	Minnesota	1.8
13	Mississippi	2.7
20	Missouri	2.4
2	Montana	3.9
5	Nebraska	3.2
38	Nevada	1.9
10	New Hampshire	2.9
49	New Jersey	1.4
16	New Mexico	2.6
47	New York	1.5
38	North Carolina	1.9
11	North Dakota	2.8
20	Ohio	2.4
5	Oklahoma	3.2
13	Oregon	2.7
23	Pennsylvania	2.3
47	Rhode Island	1.5
36	South Carolina	2.0
11	South Dakota	2.8
29	Tennessee	2.2
23	Texas	2.3
46	Utah	1.6
1	Vermont	4.1
20	Virginia	2.4
32	Washington	2.1
32	West Virginia	2.1
29	Wisconsin	2.2
3	Wyoming	3.8

RANK ORDER

RANK	STATE	RATE
1	Vermont	4.1
2	Montana	3.9
3	Maine	3.8
3	Wyoming	3.8
5	Nebraska	3.2
5	Oklahoma	3.2
7	Alaska	3.1
7	Idaho	3.1
9	Arkansas	3.0
10	New Hampshire	2.9
11	North Dakota	2.8
11	South Dakota	2.8
13	Louisiana	2.7
13	Mississippi	2.7
13	Oregon	2.7
16	Hawaii	2.6
16	New Mexico	2.6
18	Kansas	2.5
18	Kentucky	2.5
20	Missouri	2.4
20	Ohio	2.4
20	Virginia	2.4
23	Arizona	2.3
23	Indiana	2.3
23	Iowa	2.3
23	Michigan	2.3
23	Pennsylvania	2.3
23	Texas	2.3
29	Alabama	2.2
29	Tennessee	2.2
29	Wisconsin	2.2
32	Delaware	2.1
32	Georgia	2.1
32	Washington	2.1
32	West Virginia	2.1
36	Maryland	2.0
36	South Carolina	2.0
38	California	1.9
38	Colorado	1.9
38	Illinois	1.9
38	Massachusetts	1.9
38	Nevada	1.9
38	North Carolina	1.9
44	Minnesota	1.8
45	Florida	1.7
46	Utah	1.6
47	New York	1.5
47	Rhode Island	1.5
49	New Jersey	1.4
50	Connecticut	1.3

	District of Columbia	1.5

Source: CQ Press using data from U.S. Department of Defense, Defense Casualty Analysis System
"U.S. Military Casualties" (https://www.dmdc.osd.mil/dcas/pages/report_sum_all.xhtml)
*National rate does not include deaths of soldiers from U.S. territories. Includes combat and noncombat deaths. Calculated with 2013 population estimates.

U.S. Military Wounded in Iraq and Afghanistan as of January 28, 2014

National Total = 51,874 Wounded*

ALPHA ORDER

RANK	STATE	WOUNDED	% of USA
18	Alabama	851	1.6%
46	Alaska	156	0.3%
14	Arizona	1,138	2.2%
29	Arkansas	643	1.2%
1	California	4,790	9.2%
22	Colorado	805	1.6%
35	Connecticut	418	0.8%
50	Delaware	81	0.2%
3	Florida	2,451	4.7%
9	Georgia	1,463	2.8%
43	Hawaii	207	0.4%
36	Idaho	387	0.7%
7	Illinois	1,732	3.3%
15	Indiana	1,088	2.1%
31	Iowa	617	1.2%
30	Kansas	622	1.2%
27	Kentucky	742	1.4%
21	Louisiana	826	1.6%
41	Maine	316	0.6%
28	Maryland	667	1.3%
20	Massachusetts	831	1.6%
8	Michigan	1,619	3.1%
26	Minnesota	745	1.4%
33	Mississippi	437	0.8%
13	Missouri	1,175	2.3%
40	Montana	323	0.6%
39	Nebraska	334	0.6%
37	Nevada	369	0.7%
42	New Hampshire	293	0.6%
24	New Jersey	753	1.5%
34	New Mexico	420	0.8%
4	New York	2,291	4.4%
10	North Carolina	1,420	2.7%
49	North Dakota	116	0.2%
5	Ohio	2,021	3.9%
19	Oklahoma	847	1.6%
23	Oregon	780	1.5%
6	Pennsylvania	1,976	3.8%
45	Rhode Island	163	0.3%
25	South Carolina	747	1.4%
44	South Dakota	194	0.4%
16	Tennessee	1,000	1.9%
2	Texas	4,296	8.3%
32	Utah	449	0.9%
47	Vermont	151	0.3%
12	Virginia	1,181	2.3%
11	Washington	1,278	2.5%
38	West Virginia	357	0.7%
17	Wisconsin	908	1.8%
48	Wyoming	149	0.3%

RANK ORDER

RANK	STATE	WOUNDED	% of USA
1	California	4,790	9.2%
2	Texas	4,296	8.3%
3	Florida	2,451	4.7%
4	New York	2,291	4.4%
5	Ohio	2,021	3.9%
6	Pennsylvania	1,976	3.8%
7	Illinois	1,732	3.3%
8	Michigan	1,619	3.1%
9	Georgia	1,463	2.8%
10	North Carolina	1,420	2.7%
11	Washington	1,278	2.5%
12	Virginia	1,181	2.3%
13	Missouri	1,175	2.3%
14	Arizona	1,138	2.2%
15	Indiana	1,088	2.1%
16	Tennessee	1,000	1.9%
17	Wisconsin	908	1.8%
18	Alabama	851	1.6%
19	Oklahoma	847	1.6%
20	Massachusetts	831	1.6%
21	Louisiana	826	1.6%
22	Colorado	805	1.6%
23	Oregon	780	1.5%
24	New Jersey	753	1.5%
25	South Carolina	747	1.4%
26	Minnesota	745	1.4%
27	Kentucky	742	1.4%
28	Maryland	667	1.3%
29	Arkansas	643	1.2%
30	Kansas	622	1.2%
31	Iowa	617	1.2%
32	Utah	449	0.9%
33	Mississippi	437	0.8%
34	New Mexico	420	0.8%
35	Connecticut	418	0.8%
36	Idaho	387	0.7%
37	Nevada	369	0.7%
38	West Virginia	357	0.7%
39	Nebraska	334	0.6%
40	Montana	323	0.6%
41	Maine	316	0.6%
42	New Hampshire	293	0.6%
43	Hawaii	207	0.4%
44	South Dakota	194	0.4%
45	Rhode Island	163	0.3%
46	Alaska	156	0.3%
47	Vermont	151	0.3%
48	Wyoming	149	0.3%
49	North Dakota	116	0.2%
50	Delaware	81	0.2%
	District of Columbia	29	0.1%

Source: U.S. Department of Defense, Defense Casualty Analysis System
"U.S. Military Casualties" (https://www.dmdc.osd.mil/dcas/pages/report_sum_all.xhtml)
*Total includes 4,222 wounded soldiers from U.S. territories. Total does not include wounded soldiers of United Kingdom or other coalition nations. Only includes wounded in action. Includes 32,236 wounded in Iraq and 19,638 wounded in Afghanistan.

IV. Economy

Gross Domestic Product in 2012

National Total = $15,566,077,000,000*

ALPHA ORDER					RANK ORDER			

RANK	STATE	G.D.P.	% of USA		RANK	STATE	G.D.P.	% of USA
26	Alabama	$183,547,000,000	1.2%		1	California	$2,003,479,000,000	12.9%
44	Alaska	51,859,000,000	0.3%		2	Texas	1,397,369,000,000	9.0%
20	Arizona	266,891,000,000	1.7%		3	New York	1,205,930,000,000	7.7%
34	Arkansas	109,557,000,000	0.7%		4	Florida	777,164,000,000	5.0%
1	California	2,003,479,000,000	12.9%		5	Illinois	695,238,000,000	4.5%
19	Colorado	274,048,000,000	1.8%		6	Pennsylvania	600,897,000,000	3.9%
24	Connecticut	229,317,000,000	1.5%		7	Ohio	509,393,000,000	3.3%
40	Delaware	65,984,000,000	0.4%		8	New Jersey	508,003,000,000	3.3%
4	Florida	777,164,000,000	5.0%		9	North Carolina	455,973,000,000	2.9%
11	Georgia	433,569,000,000	2.8%		10	Virginia	445,876,000,000	2.9%
38	Hawaii	72,424,000,000	0.5%		11	Georgia	433,569,000,000	2.8%
42	Idaho	58,243,000,000	0.4%		12	Massachusetts	403,823,000,000	2.6%
5	Illinois	695,238,000,000	4.5%		13	Michigan	400,504,000,000	2.6%
16	Indiana	298,625,000,000	1.9%		14	Washington	375,730,000,000	2.4%
30	Iowa	152,436,000,000	1.0%		15	Maryland	317,678,000,000	2.0%
31	Kansas	138,953,000,000	0.9%		16	Indiana	298,625,000,000	1.9%
28	Kentucky	173,466,000,000	1.1%		17	Minnesota	294,729,000,000	1.9%
23	Louisiana	243,264,000,000	1.6%		18	Tennessee	277,036,000,000	1.8%
43	Maine	53,656,000,000	0.3%		19	Colorado	274,048,000,000	1.8%
15	Maryland	317,678,000,000	2.0%		20	Arizona	266,891,000,000	1.7%
12	Massachusetts	403,823,000,000	2.6%		21	Wisconsin	261,548,000,000	1.7%
13	Michigan	400,504,000,000	2.6%		22	Missouri	258,832,000,000	1.7%
17	Minnesota	294,729,000,000	1.9%		23	Louisiana	243,264,000,000	1.6%
35	Mississippi	101,490,000,000	0.7%		24	Connecticut	229,317,000,000	1.5%
22	Missouri	258,832,000,000	1.7%		25	Oregon	198,702,000,000	1.3%
48	Montana	40,422,000,000	0.3%		26	Alabama	183,547,000,000	1.2%
36	Nebraska	99,557,000,000	0.6%		27	South Carolina	176,217,000,000	1.1%
32	Nevada	133,584,000,000	0.9%		28	Kentucky	173,466,000,000	1.1%
41	New Hampshire	64,697,000,000	0.4%		29	Oklahoma	160,953,000,000	1.0%
8	New Jersey	508,003,000,000	3.3%		30	Iowa	152,436,000,000	1.0%
37	New Mexico	80,600,000,000	0.5%		31	Kansas	138,953,000,000	0.9%
3	New York	1,205,930,000,000	7.7%		32	Nevada	133,584,000,000	0.9%
9	North Carolina	455,973,000,000	2.9%		33	Utah	130,486,000,000	0.8%
46	North Dakota	46,016,000,000	0.3%		34	Arkansas	109,557,000,000	0.7%
7	Ohio	509,393,000,000	3.3%		35	Mississippi	101,490,000,000	0.7%
29	Oklahoma	160,953,000,000	1.0%		36	Nebraska	99,557,000,000	0.6%
25	Oregon	198,702,000,000	1.3%		37	New Mexico	80,600,000,000	0.5%
6	Pennsylvania	600,897,000,000	3.9%		38	Hawaii	72,424,000,000	0.5%
45	Rhode Island	50,956,000,000	0.3%		39	West Virginia	69,380,000,000	0.4%
27	South Carolina	176,217,000,000	1.1%		40	Delaware	65,984,000,000	0.4%
47	South Dakota	42,464,000,000	0.3%		41	New Hampshire	64,697,000,000	0.4%
18	Tennessee	277,036,000,000	1.8%		42	Idaho	58,243,000,000	0.4%
2	Texas	1,397,369,000,000	9.0%		43	Maine	53,656,000,000	0.3%
33	Utah	130,486,000,000	0.8%		44	Alaska	51,859,000,000	0.3%
50	Vermont	27,296,000,000	0.2%		45	Rhode Island	50,956,000,000	0.3%
10	Virginia	445,876,000,000	2.9%		46	North Dakota	46,016,000,000	0.3%
14	Washington	375,730,000,000	2.4%		47	South Dakota	42,464,000,000	0.3%
39	West Virginia	69,380,000,000	0.4%		48	Montana	40,422,000,000	0.3%
21	Wisconsin	261,548,000,000	1.7%		49	Wyoming	38,422,000,000	0.2%
49	Wyoming	38,422,000,000	0.2%		50	Vermont	27,296,000,000	0.2%
						District of Columbia	109,793,000,000	0.7%

Source: U.S. Department of Commerce, Bureau of Economic Analysis
    "Gross Domestic Product Data" (http://www.bea.gov/iTable/index_regional.cfm)
*G.D.P. is the market value of goods and services produced by the labor and property located in a state. It is the state counterpart to the nation's Gross Domestic Product. This was formerly known as Gross State Product (G.S.P.).

Percent Change in Gross Domestic Product: 2008 to 2012
(Adjusted to Constant 2005 Dollars)
National Percent Change = 3.2% Increase*

ALPHA ORDER

RANK ORDER

RANK	STATE	PERCENT CHANGE		RANK	STATE	PERCENT CHANGE
36	Alabama	0.9		1	North Dakota	35.0
5	Alaska	9.0		2	Texas	12.5
49	Arizona	(4.4)		3	Oregon	10.1
32	Arkansas	2.5		4	West Virginia	9.3
43	California	(0.3)		5	Alaska	9.0
25	Colorado	3.9		6	Louisiana	7.9
48	Connecticut	(2.6)		7	Utah	7.7
18	Delaware	4.5		8	Nebraska	7.3
47	Florida	(2.5)		9	Maryland	6.3
40	Georgia	0.0		10	Indiana	5.6
27	Hawaii	3.0		11	Washington	5.5
44	Idaho	(0.8)		12	Massachusetts	5.3
34	Illinois	2.3		12	Virginia	5.3
10	Indiana	5.6		14	New York	5.2
16	Iowa	4.9		15	Vermont	5.0
25	Kansas	3.9		16	Iowa	4.9
21	Kentucky	4.4		16	South Dakota	4.9
6	Louisiana	7.9		18	Delaware	4.5
36	Maine	0.9		18	Minnesota	4.5
9	Maryland	6.3		18	Montana	4.5
12	Massachusetts	5.3		21	Kentucky	4.4
36	Michigan	0.9		22	New Hampshire	4.2
18	Minnesota	4.5		22	Tennessee	4.2
44	Mississippi	(0.8)		24	North Carolina	4.0
41	Missouri	(0.2)		25	Colorado	3.9
18	Montana	4.5		25	Kansas	3.9
8	Nebraska	7.3		27	Hawaii	3.0
50	Nevada	(5.5)		27	South Carolina	3.0
22	New Hampshire	4.2		29	Oklahoma	2.9
46	New Jersey	(1.3)		29	Wisconsin	2.9
33	New Mexico	2.4		31	Pennsylvania	2.6
14	New York	5.2		32	Arkansas	2.5
24	North Carolina	4.0		33	New Mexico	2.4
1	North Dakota	35.0		34	Illinois	2.3
35	Ohio	1.2		35	Ohio	1.2
29	Oklahoma	2.9		36	Alabama	0.9
3	Oregon	10.1		36	Maine	0.9
31	Pennsylvania	2.6		36	Michigan	0.9
39	Rhode Island	0.8		39	Rhode Island	0.8
27	South Carolina	3.0		40	Georgia	0.0
16	South Dakota	4.9		41	Missouri	(0.2)
22	Tennessee	4.2		41	Wyoming	(0.2)
2	Texas	12.5		43	California	(0.3)
7	Utah	7.7		44	Idaho	(0.8)
15	Vermont	5.0		44	Mississippi	(0.8)
12	Virginia	5.3		46	New Jersey	(1.3)
11	Washington	5.5		47	Florida	(2.5)
4	West Virginia	9.3		48	Connecticut	(2.6)
29	Wisconsin	2.9		49	Arizona	(4.4)
41	Wyoming	(0.2)		50	Nevada	(5.5)
					District of Columbia	4.9

Source: CQ Press using data from U.S. Department of Commerce, Bureau of Economic Analysis
   "Gross Domestic Product Data" (http://www.bea.gov/iTable/index_regional.cfm)
*G.D.P. is the market value of goods and services produced by the labor and property located in a state. It is the state counterpart to the nation's Gross Domestic Product. This was formerly known as Gross State Product (G.S.P.). Adjusted for inflation using chained 2005 dollars.

Average Annual Change in Gross Domestic Product: 2008 to 2012
(Adjusted to Constant 2005 Dollars)
National Annual Percent Change = 0.6% Increase*

ALPHA ORDER

RANK	STATE	PERCENT CHANGE
35	Alabama	0.2
5	Alaska	1.7
49	Arizona	(0.9)
31	Arkansas	0.5
43	California	(0.1)
22	Colorado	0.8
47	Connecticut	(0.5)
18	Delaware	0.9
47	Florida	(0.5)
40	Georgia	0.0
27	Hawaii	0.6
44	Idaho	(0.2)
31	Illinois	0.5
10	Indiana	1.1
12	Iowa	1.0
22	Kansas	0.8
18	Kentucky	0.9
6	Louisiana	1.5
35	Maine	0.2
9	Maryland	1.2
12	Massachusetts	1.0
35	Michigan	0.2
18	Minnesota	0.9
44	Mississippi	(0.2)
40	Missouri	0.0
18	Montana	0.9
8	Nebraska	1.4
50	Nevada	(1.1)
22	New Hampshire	0.8
46	New Jersey	(0.3)
31	New Mexico	0.5
12	New York	1.0
22	North Carolina	0.8
1	North Dakota	6.2
35	Ohio	0.2
27	Oklahoma	0.6
3	Oregon	2.0
31	Pennsylvania	0.5
35	Rhode Island	0.2
27	South Carolina	0.6
12	South Dakota	1.0
22	Tennessee	0.8
2	Texas	2.4
6	Utah	1.5
12	Vermont	1.0
12	Virginia	1.0
10	Washington	1.1
4	West Virginia	1.8
27	Wisconsin	0.6
40	Wyoming	0.0

RANK ORDER

RANK	STATE	PERCENT CHANGE
1	North Dakota	6.2
2	Texas	2.4
3	Oregon	2.0
4	West Virginia	1.8
5	Alaska	1.7
6	Louisiana	1.5
6	Utah	1.5
8	Nebraska	1.4
9	Maryland	1.2
10	Indiana	1.1
10	Washington	1.1
12	Iowa	1.0
12	Massachusetts	1.0
12	New York	1.0
12	South Dakota	1.0
12	Vermont	1.0
12	Virginia	1.0
18	Delaware	0.9
18	Kentucky	0.9
18	Minnesota	0.9
18	Montana	0.9
22	Colorado	0.8
22	Kansas	0.8
22	New Hampshire	0.8
22	North Carolina	0.8
22	Tennessee	0.8
27	Hawaii	0.6
27	Oklahoma	0.6
27	South Carolina	0.6
27	Wisconsin	0.6
31	Arkansas	0.5
31	Illinois	0.5
31	New Mexico	0.5
31	Pennsylvania	0.5
35	Alabama	0.2
35	Maine	0.2
35	Michigan	0.2
35	Ohio	0.2
35	Rhode Island	0.2
40	Georgia	0.0
40	Missouri	0.0
40	Wyoming	0.0
43	California	(0.1)
44	Idaho	(0.2)
44	Mississippi	(0.2)
46	New Jersey	(0.3)
47	Connecticut	(0.5)
47	Florida	(0.5)
49	Arizona	(0.9)
50	Nevada	(1.1)

District of Columbia	1.0

Source: CQ Press using data from U.S. Department of Commerce, Bureau of Economic Analysis
   "Gross Domestic Product Data" (http://www.bea.gov/iTable/index_regional.cfm)
*G.D.P. is the market value of goods and services produced by the labor and property located in a state. It is the state counterpart to the nation's Gross Domestic Product. This was formerly known as Gross State Product (G.S.P.). Adjusted for inflation using chained 2005 dollars.

Per Capita Gross Domestic Product in 2012

National Per Capita = $49,587*

ALPHA ORDER

RANK ORDER

RANK	STATE	PER CAPITA		RANK	STATE	PER CAPITA
45	Alabama	$38,064		1	Delaware	$71,949
2	Alaska	70,899		2	Alaska	70,899
38	Arizona	40,726		3	Wyoming	66,657
48	Arkansas	37,149		4	North Dakota	65,772
18	California	52,666		5	Connecticut	63,870
17	Colorado	52,828		6	New York	61,621
5	Connecticut	63,870		7	Massachusetts	60,760
1	Delaware	71,949		8	New Jersey	57,307
41	Florida	40,231		9	Minnesota	54,791
33	Georgia	43,707		10	Washington	54,477
19	Hawaii	52,017		11	Virginia	54,469
49	Idaho	36,499		12	Illinois	53,998
12	Illinois	53,998		13	Maryland	53,985
30	Indiana	45,680		14	Nebraska	53,654
22	Iowa	49,586		15	Texas	53,623
26	Kansas	48,149		16	Louisiana	52,862
43	Kentucky	39,600		17	Colorado	52,828
16	Louisiana	52,862		18	California	52,666
40	Maine	40,367		19	Hawaii	52,017
13	Maryland	53,985		20	Oregon	50,958
7	Massachusetts	60,760		21	South Dakota	50,956
39	Michigan	40,523		22	Iowa	49,586
9	Minnesota	54,791		23	New Hampshire	48,986
50	Mississippi	34,001		24	Rhode Island	48,516
35	Missouri	42,981		25	Nevada	48,419
42	Montana	40,215		26	Kansas	48,149
14	Nebraska	53,654		27	Pennsylvania	47,079
25	Nevada	48,419		28	North Carolina	46,757
23	New Hampshire	48,986		29	Utah	45,700
8	New Jersey	57,307		30	Indiana	45,680
44	New Mexico	38,647		31	Wisconsin	45,674
6	New York	61,621		32	Ohio	44,125
28	North Carolina	46,757		33	Georgia	43,707
4	North Dakota	65,772		34	Vermont	43,603
32	Ohio	44,125		35	Missouri	42,981
37	Oklahoma	42,192		36	Tennessee	42,910
20	Oregon	50,958		37	Oklahoma	42,192
27	Pennsylvania	47,079		38	Arizona	40,726
24	Rhode Island	48,516		39	Michigan	40,523
47	South Carolina	37,305		40	Maine	40,367
21	South Dakota	50,956		41	Florida	40,231
36	Tennessee	42,910		42	Montana	40,215
15	Texas	53,623		43	Kentucky	39,600
29	Utah	45,700		44	New Mexico	38,647
34	Vermont	43,603		45	Alabama	38,064
11	Virginia	54,469		46	West Virginia	37,393
10	Washington	54,477		47	South Carolina	37,305
46	West Virginia	37,393		48	Arkansas	37,149
31	Wisconsin	45,674		49	Idaho	36,499
3	Wyoming	66,657		50	Mississippi	34,001

	District of Columbia	173,634

Source: CQ Press using data from U.S. Department of Commerce, Bureau of Economic Analysis
"Gross Domestic Product Data" (http://www.bea.gov/iTable/index_regional.cfm)
*G.D.P. is the market value of goods and services produced by the labor and property located in a state. It is the state counterpart to the nation's Gross Domestic Product. This was formerly known as Gross State Product (G.S.P.).

Percent Change in Per Capita Gross Domestic Product: 2008 to 2012
(Adjusted to Constant 2005 Dollars)
National Percent Change = 0.0% Change*

ALPHA ORDER

RANK	STATE	PERCENT CHANGE
36	Alabama	(1.3)
14	Alaska	2.4
49	Arizona	(8.3)
32	Arkansas	(0.1)
44	California	(4.1)
40	Colorado	(2.1)
43	Connecticut	(3.8)
27	Delaware	0.7
48	Florida	(6.5)
44	Georgia	(4.1)
38	Hawaii	(1.5)
46	Idaho	(4.6)
20	Illinois	1.3
8	Indiana	3.8
11	Iowa	3.0
23	Kansas	1.1
15	Kentucky	2.2
6	Louisiana	4.0
24	Maine	1.0
12	Maryland	2.7
13	Massachusetts	2.5
17	Michigan	1.6
16	Minnesota	1.9
40	Mississippi	(2.1)
39	Missouri	(1.8)
18	Montana	1.5
7	Nebraska	3.9
50	Nevada	(9.1)
8	New Hampshire	3.8
42	New Jersey	(3.0)
36	New Mexico	(1.3)
10	New York	3.3
33	North Carolina	(0.7)
1	North Dakota	26.9
25	Ohio	0.9
34	Oklahoma	(1.0)
3	Oregon	6.5
19	Pennsylvania	1.4
20	Rhode Island	1.3
35	South Carolina	(1.2)
29	South Dakota	0.6
26	Tennessee	0.8
4	Texas	4.9
30	Utah	0.4
5	Vermont	4.7
27	Virginia	0.7
30	Washington	0.4
2	West Virginia	8.4
20	Wisconsin	1.3
47	Wyoming	(5.5)

RANK ORDER

RANK	STATE	PERCENT CHANGE
1	North Dakota	26.9
2	West Virginia	8.4
3	Oregon	6.5
4	Texas	4.9
5	Vermont	4.7
6	Louisiana	4.0
7	Nebraska	3.9
8	Indiana	3.8
8	New Hampshire	3.8
10	New York	3.3
11	Iowa	3.0
12	Maryland	2.7
13	Massachusetts	2.5
14	Alaska	2.4
15	Kentucky	2.2
16	Minnesota	1.9
17	Michigan	1.6
18	Montana	1.5
19	Pennsylvania	1.4
20	Illinois	1.3
20	Rhode Island	1.3
20	Wisconsin	1.3
23	Kansas	1.1
24	Maine	1.0
25	Ohio	0.9
26	Tennessee	0.8
27	Delaware	0.7
27	Virginia	0.7
29	South Dakota	0.6
30	Utah	0.4
30	Washington	0.4
32	Arkansas	(0.1)
33	North Carolina	(0.7)
34	Oklahoma	(1.0)
35	South Carolina	(1.2)
36	Alabama	(1.3)
36	New Mexico	(1.3)
38	Hawaii	(1.5)
39	Missouri	(1.8)
40	Colorado	(2.1)
40	Mississippi	(2.1)
42	New Jersey	(3.0)
43	Connecticut	(3.8)
44	California	(4.1)
44	Georgia	(4.1)
46	Idaho	(4.6)
47	Wyoming	(5.5)
48	Florida	(6.5)
49	Arizona	(8.3)
50	Nevada	(9.1)

District of Columbia (3.7)

Source: CQ Press using data from U.S. Department of Commerce, Bureau of Economic Analysis
   "Gross Domestic Product Data" (http://www.bea.gov/iTable/index_regional.cfm)
*G.D.P. is the market value of goods and services produced by the labor and property located in a state. It is the state counterpart to the nation's Gross Domestic Product. This was formerly known as Gross State Product (G.S.P.). Adjusted for inflation using chained 2005 dollars.

Personal Income in 2012

National Total = $13,401,868,693,000*

ALPHA ORDER

RANK ORDER

RANK	STATE	INCOME	% of USA		RANK	STATE	INCOME	% of USA
25	Alabama	$171,782,909,000	1.3%		1	California	$1,711,110,319,000	12.8%
48	Alaska	34,215,563,000	0.3%		2	Texas	1,080,709,649,000	8.1%
19	Arizona	235,780,739,000	1.8%		3	New York	1,019,514,062,000	7.6%
33	Arkansas	102,402,574,000	0.8%		4	Florida	779,338,815,000	5.8%
1	California	1,711,110,319,000	12.8%		5	Illinois	577,008,488,000	4.3%
21	Colorado	234,142,330,000	1.7%		6	Pennsylvania	556,692,387,000	4.2%
23	Connecticut	211,499,831,000	1.6%		7	New Jersey	475,393,092,000	3.5%
44	Delaware	38,462,662,000	0.3%		8	Ohio	453,556,274,000	3.4%
4	Florida	779,338,815,000	5.8%		9	Virginia	385,403,843,000	2.9%
11	Georgia	365,740,189,000	2.7%		10	Michigan	370,598,555,000	2.8%
40	Hawaii	61,294,803,000	0.5%		11	Georgia	365,740,189,000	2.7%
41	Idaho	53,853,716,000	0.4%		12	Massachusetts	363,459,345,000	2.7%
5	Illinois	577,008,488,000	4.3%		13	North Carolina	361,301,305,000	2.7%
18	Indiana	241,242,521,000	1.8%		14	Washington	313,212,035,000	2.3%
30	Iowa	129,503,257,000	1.0%		15	Maryland	305,826,774,000	2.3%
31	Kansas	120,732,283,000	0.9%		16	Minnesota	248,663,407,000	1.9%
27	Kentucky	153,494,780,000	1.1%		17	Tennessee	243,256,486,000	1.8%
24	Louisiana	181,372,591,000	1.4%		18	Indiana	241,242,521,000	1.8%
42	Maine	52,477,565,000	0.4%		19	Arizona	235,780,739,000	1.8%
15	Maryland	305,826,774,000	2.3%		20	Missouri	235,153,679,000	1.8%
12	Massachusetts	363,459,345,000	2.7%		21	Colorado	234,142,330,000	1.7%
10	Michigan	370,598,555,000	2.8%		22	Wisconsin	232,129,105,000	1.7%
16	Minnesota	248,663,407,000	1.9%		23	Connecticut	211,499,831,000	1.6%
35	Mississippi	98,721,708,000	0.7%		24	Louisiana	181,372,591,000	1.4%
20	Missouri	235,153,679,000	1.8%		25	Alabama	171,782,909,000	1.3%
45	Montana	37,561,941,000	0.3%		26	South Carolina	161,863,730,000	1.2%
36	Nebraska	80,052,414,000	0.6%		27	Kentucky	153,494,780,000	1.1%
32	Nevada	103,076,310,000	0.8%		28	Oregon	151,241,129,000	1.1%
39	New Hampshire	62,150,236,000	0.5%		29	Oklahoma	148,798,993,000	1.1%
7	New Jersey	475,393,092,000	3.5%		30	Iowa	129,503,257,000	1.0%
37	New Mexico	73,159,160,000	0.5%		31	Kansas	120,732,283,000	0.9%
3	New York	1,019,514,062,000	7.6%		32	Nevada	103,076,310,000	0.8%
13	North Carolina	361,301,305,000	2.7%		33	Arkansas	102,402,574,000	0.8%
47	North Dakota	36,305,820,000	0.3%		34	Utah	98,797,168,000	0.7%
8	Ohio	453,556,274,000	3.4%		35	Mississippi	98,721,708,000	0.7%
29	Oklahoma	148,798,993,000	1.1%		36	Nebraska	80,052,414,000	0.6%
28	Oregon	151,241,129,000	1.1%		37	New Mexico	73,159,160,000	0.5%
6	Pennsylvania	556,692,387,000	4.2%		38	West Virginia	63,968,460,000	0.5%
43	Rhode Island	47,253,091,000	0.4%		39	New Hampshire	62,150,236,000	0.5%
26	South Carolina	161,863,730,000	1.2%		40	Hawaii	61,294,803,000	0.5%
46	South Dakota	36,383,703,000	0.3%		41	Idaho	53,853,716,000	0.4%
17	Tennessee	243,256,486,000	1.8%		42	Maine	52,477,565,000	0.4%
2	Texas	1,080,709,649,000	8.1%		43	Rhode Island	47,253,091,000	0.4%
34	Utah	98,797,168,000	0.7%		44	Delaware	38,462,662,000	0.3%
50	Vermont	26,914,633,000	0.2%		45	Montana	37,561,941,000	0.3%
9	Virginia	385,403,843,000	2.9%		46	South Dakota	36,383,703,000	0.3%
14	Washington	313,212,035,000	2.3%		47	North Dakota	36,305,820,000	0.3%
38	West Virginia	63,968,460,000	0.5%		48	Alaska	34,215,563,000	0.3%
22	Wisconsin	232,129,105,000	1.7%		49	Wyoming	28,053,707,000	0.2%
49	Wyoming	28,053,707,000	0.2%		50	Vermont	26,914,633,000	0.2%
						District of Columbia	47,240,557,000	0.4%

Source: U.S. Department of Commerce, Bureau of Economic Analysis
"Annual State Personal Income" (http://www.bea.gov/iTable/iTable.cfm?ReqID=70&step=1)
*The national total shown here is the sum of the state estimates. It differs from the national income and product accounts
(NIPA) estimate of personal income because it omits the earnings of federal civilian and military personnel stationed abroad and
of U.S. residents employed abroad temporarily by private U.S. firms.

Change in Personal Income: 2011 to 2012

National Percent Change = 3.5% Increase*

ALPHA ORDER

RANK	STATE	PERCENT CHANGE		RANK	STATE	PERCENT CHANGE
42	Alabama	2.6		1	North Dakota	12.4
15	Alaska	3.7		2	Texas	4.9
15	Arizona	3.7		3	Utah	4.7
25	Arkansas	3.3		4	Montana	4.5
9	California	4.0		4	Washington	4.5
10	Colorado	3.9		6	Minnesota	4.4
49	Connecticut	2.0		7	Oklahoma	4.2
47	Delaware	2.3		8	Oregon	4.1
28	Florida	3.2		9	California	4.0
18	Georgia	3.6		10	Colorado	3.9
10	Hawaii	3.9		10	Hawaii	3.9
25	Idaho	3.3		10	North Carolina	3.9
42	Illinois	2.6		10	Tennessee	3.9
15	Indiana	3.7		14	Ohio	3.8
37	Iowa	2.8		15	Alaska	3.7
35	Kansas	2.9		15	Arizona	3.7
23	Kentucky	3.4		15	Indiana	3.7
37	Louisiana	2.8		18	Georgia	3.6
28	Maine	3.2		18	Maryland	3.6
18	Maryland	3.6		18	Mississippi	3.6
28	Massachusetts	3.2		18	South Carolina	3.6
22	Michigan	3.5		22	Michigan	3.5
6	Minnesota	4.4		23	Kentucky	3.4
18	Mississippi	3.6		23	Vermont	3.4
34	Missouri	3.0		25	Arkansas	3.3
4	Montana	4.5		25	Idaho	3.3
47	Nebraska	2.3		25	Pennsylvania	3.3
44	Nevada	2.4		28	Florida	3.2
37	New Hampshire	2.8		28	Maine	3.2
37	New Jersey	2.8		28	Massachusetts	3.2
35	New Mexico	2.9		28	Virginia	3.2
44	New York	2.4		28	West Virginia	3.2
10	North Carolina	3.9		33	Wyoming	3.1
1	North Dakota	12.4		34	Missouri	3.0
14	Ohio	3.8		35	Kansas	2.9
7	Oklahoma	4.2		35	New Mexico	2.9
8	Oregon	4.1		37	Iowa	2.8
25	Pennsylvania	3.3		37	Louisiana	2.8
44	Rhode Island	2.4		37	New Hampshire	2.8
18	South Carolina	3.6		37	New Jersey	2.8
50	South Dakota	(0.2)		41	Wisconsin	2.7
10	Tennessee	3.9		42	Alabama	2.6
2	Texas	4.9		42	Illinois	2.6
3	Utah	4.7		44	Nevada	2.4
23	Vermont	3.4		44	New York	2.4
28	Virginia	3.2		44	Rhode Island	2.4
4	Washington	4.5		47	Delaware	2.3
28	West Virginia	3.2		47	Nebraska	2.3
41	Wisconsin	2.7		49	Connecticut	2.0
33	Wyoming	3.1		50	South Dakota	(0.2)
					District of Columbia	3.6

Source: U.S. Department of Commerce, Bureau of Economic Analysis
"Annual State Personal Income" (http://www.bea.gov/iTable/iTable.cfm?ReqID=70&step=1)
*Based on revised 2011 figures.

Per Capita Personal Income in 2012

National Per Capita = $42,693*

RANK	STATE	PER CAPITA		RANK	STATE	PER CAPITA
42	Alabama	$35,625		1	Connecticut	$58,908
10	Alaska	46,778		2	Massachusetts	54,687
41	Arizona	35,979		3	New Jersey	53,628
45	Arkansas	34,723		4	New York	52,095
15	California	44,980		5	Maryland	51,971
13	Colorado	45,135		6	North Dakota	51,893
1	Connecticut	58,908		7	Wyoming	48,670
23	Delaware	41,940		8	Virginia	47,082
27	Florida	40,344		9	New Hampshire	47,058
40	Georgia	36,869		10	Alaska	46,778
17	Hawaii	44,024		11	Minnesota	46,227
49	Idaho	33,749		12	Washington	45,413
16	Illinois	44,815		13	Colorado	45,135
39	Indiana	36,902		14	Rhode Island	44,990
22	Iowa	42,126		15	California	44,980
24	Kansas	41,835		16	Illinois	44,815
44	Kentucky	35,041		17	Hawaii	44,024
29	Louisiana	39,413		18	South Dakota	43,659
28	Maine	39,481		19	Pennsylvania	43,616
5	Maryland	51,971		20	Nebraska	43,143
2	Massachusetts	54,687		21	Vermont	42,994
35	Michigan	37,497		22	Iowa	42,126
11	Minnesota	46,227		23	Delaware	41,940
50	Mississippi	33,073		24	Kansas	41,835
31	Missouri	39,049		25	Texas	41,471
36	Montana	37,370		26	Wisconsin	40,537
20	Nebraska	43,143		27	Florida	40,344
37	Nevada	37,361		28	Maine	39,481
9	New Hampshire	47,058		29	Louisiana	39,413
3	New Jersey	53,628		30	Ohio	39,289
43	New Mexico	35,079		31	Missouri	39,049
4	New York	52,095		32	Oklahoma	39,006
38	North Carolina	37,049		33	Oregon	38,786
6	North Dakota	51,893		34	Tennessee	37,678
30	Ohio	39,289		35	Michigan	37,497
32	Oklahoma	39,006		36	Montana	37,370
33	Oregon	38,786		37	Nevada	37,361
19	Pennsylvania	43,616		38	North Carolina	37,049
14	Rhode Island	44,990		39	Indiana	36,902
48	South Carolina	34,266		40	Georgia	36,869
18	South Dakota	43,659		41	Arizona	35,979
34	Tennessee	37,678		42	Alabama	35,625
25	Texas	41,471		43	New Mexico	35,079
46	Utah	34,601		44	Kentucky	35,041
21	Vermont	42,994		45	Arkansas	34,723
8	Virginia	47,082		46	Utah	34,601
12	Washington	45,413		47	West Virginia	34,477
47	West Virginia	34,477		48	South Carolina	34,266
26	Wisconsin	40,537		49	Idaho	33,749
7	Wyoming	48,670		50	Mississippi	33,073

| | | | | | District of Columbia | 74,710 |

Source: U.S. Department of Commerce, Bureau of Economic Analysis
"Annual State Personal Income" (http://www.bea.gov/iTable/iTable.cfm?ReqID=70&step=1)
*The national figure is based on the sum of the state estimates. It differs from the national income and product accounts (NIPA) estimate of personal income because it omits the earnings of federal civilian and military personnel stationed abroad and of U.S. residents employed abroad temporarily by private U.S. firms.

Change in Per Capita Personal Income: 2011 to 2012

National Percent Change = 2.7% Increase*

ALPHA ORDER

RANK	STATE	PERCENT CHANGE
41	Alabama	2.1
34	Alaska	2.4
24	Arizona	2.6
20	Arkansas	2.9
15	California	3.1
30	Colorado	2.5
45	Connecticut	1.7
48	Delaware	1.2
44	Florida	1.8
30	Georgia	2.5
24	Hawaii	2.6
24	Idaho	2.6
30	Illinois	2.5
7	Indiana	3.4
34	Iowa	2.4
37	Kansas	2.3
15	Kentucky	3.1
40	Louisiana	2.2
15	Maine	3.1
24	Maryland	2.6
37	Massachusetts	2.3
7	Michigan	3.4
4	Minnesota	3.7
7	Mississippi	3.4
21	Missouri	2.8
2	Montana	3.8
46	Nebraska	1.6
49	Nevada	1.1
24	New Hampshire	2.6
37	New Jersey	2.3
21	New Mexico	2.8
43	New York	1.9
21	North Carolina	2.8
1	North Dakota	9.9
2	Ohio	3.8
5	Oklahoma	3.5
7	Oregon	3.4
15	Pennsylvania	3.1
30	Rhode Island	2.5
24	South Carolina	2.6
50	South Dakota	(1.3)
19	Tennessee	3.0
12	Texas	3.3
12	Utah	3.3
7	Vermont	3.4
41	Virginia	2.1
5	Washington	3.5
14	West Virginia	3.2
34	Wisconsin	2.4
46	Wyoming	1.6

RANK ORDER

RANK	STATE	PERCENT CHANGE
1	North Dakota	9.9
2	Montana	3.8
2	Ohio	3.8
4	Minnesota	3.7
5	Oklahoma	3.5
5	Washington	3.5
7	Indiana	3.4
7	Michigan	3.4
7	Mississippi	3.4
7	Oregon	3.4
7	Vermont	3.4
12	Texas	3.3
12	Utah	3.3
14	West Virginia	3.2
15	California	3.1
15	Kentucky	3.1
15	Maine	3.1
15	Pennsylvania	3.1
19	Tennessee	3.0
20	Arkansas	2.9
21	Missouri	2.8
21	New Mexico	2.8
21	North Carolina	2.8
24	Arizona	2.6
24	Hawaii	2.6
24	Idaho	2.6
24	Maryland	2.6
24	New Hampshire	2.6
24	South Carolina	2.6
30	Colorado	2.5
30	Georgia	2.5
30	Illinois	2.5
30	Rhode Island	2.5
34	Alaska	2.4
34	Iowa	2.4
34	Wisconsin	2.4
37	Kansas	2.3
37	Massachusetts	2.3
37	New Jersey	2.3
40	Louisiana	2.2
41	Alabama	2.1
41	Virginia	2.1
43	New York	1.9
44	Florida	1.8
45	Connecticut	1.7
46	Nebraska	1.6
46	Wyoming	1.6
48	Delaware	1.2
49	Nevada	1.1
50	South Dakota	(1.3)

| | District of Columbia | 1.3 |

Source: U.S. Department of Commerce, Bureau of Economic Analysis
   "Annual State Personal Income" (http://www.bea.gov/iTable/iTable.cfm?ReqID=70&step=1)
*Based on revised 2011 figures.

Per Capita Disposable Personal Income in 2012

National Per Capita = $38,000*

ALPHA ORDER

RANK	STATE	PER CAPITA
42	Alabama	$32,467
9	Alaska	42,306
41	Arizona	32,797
45	Arkansas	31,675
17	California	39,416
15	Colorado	40,069
1	Connecticut	49,562
25	Delaware	36,983
26	Florida	36,760
40	Georgia	33,168
16	Hawaii	39,956
49	Idaho	30,913
18	Illinois	39,242
39	Indiana	33,217
22	Iowa	38,257
24	Kansas	37,539
44	Kentucky	31,676
28	Louisiana	36,042
29	Maine	35,834
5	Maryland	45,324
2	Massachusetts	46,947
37	Michigan	33,672
12	Minnesota	40,670
50	Mississippi	30,449
31	Missouri	35,229
36	Montana	33,734
20	Nebraska	38,883
35	Nevada	33,866
8	New Hampshire	42,502
3	New Jersey	46,856
43	New Mexico	32,314
6	New York	44,355
38	North Carolina	33,333
4	North Dakota	46,460
32	Ohio	35,153
30	Oklahoma	35,461
34	Oregon	34,466
21	Pennsylvania	38,739
14	Rhode Island	40,361
46	South Carolina	31,346
13	South Dakota	40,427
33	Tennessee	34,898
23	Texas	37,723
47	Utah	31,329
19	Vermont	38,981
10	Virginia	41,369
11	Washington	41,259
48	West Virginia	31,270
27	Wisconsin	36,230
7	Wyoming	43,788

RANK ORDER

RANK	STATE	PER CAPITA
1	Connecticut	$49,562
2	Massachusetts	46,947
3	New Jersey	46,856
4	North Dakota	46,460
5	Maryland	45,324
6	New York	44,355
7	Wyoming	43,788
8	New Hampshire	42,502
9	Alaska	42,306
10	Virginia	41,369
11	Washington	41,259
12	Minnesota	40,670
13	South Dakota	40,427
14	Rhode Island	40,361
15	Colorado	40,069
16	Hawaii	39,956
17	California	39,416
18	Illinois	39,242
19	Vermont	38,981
20	Nebraska	38,883
21	Pennsylvania	38,739
22	Iowa	38,257
23	Texas	37,723
24	Kansas	37,539
25	Delaware	36,983
26	Florida	36,760
27	Wisconsin	36,230
28	Louisiana	36,042
29	Maine	35,834
30	Oklahoma	35,461
31	Missouri	35,229
32	Ohio	35,153
33	Tennessee	34,898
34	Oregon	34,466
35	Nevada	33,866
36	Montana	33,734
37	Michigan	33,672
38	North Carolina	33,333
39	Indiana	33,217
40	Georgia	33,168
41	Arizona	32,797
42	Alabama	32,467
43	New Mexico	32,314
44	Kentucky	31,676
45	Arkansas	31,675
46	South Carolina	31,346
47	Utah	31,329
48	West Virginia	31,270
49	Idaho	30,913
50	Mississippi	30,449

District of Columbia   65,677

Source: U.S. Department of Commerce, Bureau of Economic Analysis
    "Annual State Personal Income" (http://www.bea.gov/iTable/iTable.cfm?ReqID=70&step=1)
*Disposable personal income is personal income less personal tax and nontax payments. It is the income available to persons for spending or saving.

Median Household Income in 2012

National Median = $51,336*

ALPHA ORDER

ALPHA ORDER

RANK	STATE	INCOME	RANK	STATE	INCOME
43	Alabama	$43,350	1	Maryland	$69,920
7	Alaska	61,066	2	New Hampshire	68,415
30	Arizona	48,689	3	Connecticut	66,844
49	Arkansas	40,606	4	New Jersey	65,548
13	California	56,222	5	Massachusetts	64,153
8	Colorado	60,180	6	Virginia	64,043
3	Connecticut	66,844	7	Alaska	61,066
18	Delaware	54,307	8	Colorado	60,180
38	Florida	46,175	9	Washington	59,790
36	Georgia	47,171	10	Hawaii	59,748
10	Hawaii	59,748	11	Minnesota	58,641
31	Idaho	48,640	12	Utah	58,235
22	Illinois	52,284	13	California	56,222
37	Indiana	46,707	14	Wyoming	56,044
23	Iowa	52,110	15	Vermont	55,808
32	Kansas	48,538	16	North Dakota	55,673
47	Kentucky	41,687	17	Nebraska	54,755
48	Louisiana	40,660	18	Delaware	54,307
27	Maine	50,121	19	Rhode Island	53,495
1	Maryland	69,920	20	Wisconsin	53,083
5	Massachusetts	64,153	21	Oregon	52,555
29	Michigan	49,549	22	Illinois	52,284
11	Minnesota	58,641	23	Iowa	52,110
50	Mississippi	39,592	24	Pennsylvania	51,245
34	Missouri	48,248	25	New York	50,600
44	Montana	43,226	26	Texas	50,591
17	Nebraska	54,755	27	Maine	50,121
28	Nevada	49,759	28	Nevada	49,759
2	New Hampshire	68,415	29	Michigan	49,549
4	New Jersey	65,548	30	Arizona	48,689
41	New Mexico	44,605	31	Idaho	48,640
25	New York	50,600	32	Kansas	48,538
40	North Carolina	44,620	33	South Dakota	48,461
16	North Dakota	55,673	34	Missouri	48,248
39	Ohio	46,093	35	Oklahoma	47,755
35	Oklahoma	47,755	36	Georgia	47,171
21	Oregon	52,555	37	Indiana	46,707
24	Pennsylvania	51,245	38	Florida	46,175
19	Rhode Island	53,495	39	Ohio	46,093
45	South Carolina	43,078	40	North Carolina	44,620
33	South Dakota	48,461	41	New Mexico	44,605
46	Tennessee	42,266	42	West Virginia	43,765
26	Texas	50,591	43	Alabama	43,350
12	Utah	58,235	44	Montana	43,226
15	Vermont	55,808	45	South Carolina	43,078
6	Virginia	64,043	46	Tennessee	42,266
9	Washington	59,790	47	Kentucky	41,687
42	West Virginia	43,765	48	Louisiana	40,660
20	Wisconsin	53,083	49	Arkansas	40,606
14	Wyoming	56,044	50	Mississippi	39,592
				District of Columbia	60,534

Source: U.S. Bureau of the Census
  "Median Household Income by State" (http://www.census.gov/hhes/www/income/data/historical/household/index.html)
*This is a 3-year-average of inflation-adjusted single-year medians for the years 2010 through 2012.

Bankruptcy Filings in 2013

National Total = 1,072,807 Bankruptcies*

ALPHA ORDER

RANK	STATE	BANKRUPTCIES	% of USA
12	Alabama	27,678	2.5%
50	Alaska	638	0.1%
17	Arizona	24,046	2.2%
30	Arkansas	12,580	1.1%
1	California	149,203	13.5%
18	Colorado	23,976	2.2%
34	Connecticut	7,321	0.7%
40	Delaware	3,581	0.3%
2	Florida	77,923	7.0%
4	Georgia	60,305	5.4%
44	Hawaii	2,313	0.2%
36	Idaho	5,643	0.5%
3	Illinois	68,125	6.2%
10	Indiana	34,495	3.1%
35	Iowa	5,892	0.5%
32	Kansas	8,604	0.8%
22	Kentucky	18,672	1.7%
23	Louisiana	15,972	1.4%
43	Maine	2,575	0.2%
20	Maryland	23,193	2.1%
28	Massachusetts	13,201	1.2%
6	Michigan	44,032	4.0%
24	Minnesota	15,003	1.4%
29	Mississippi	12,938	1.2%
15	Missouri	25,951	2.3%
45	Montana	1,851	0.2%
37	Nebraska	5,362	0.5%
26	Nevada	14,483	1.3%
42	New Hampshire	3,376	0.3%
11	New Jersey	28,882	2.6%
38	New Mexico	4,502	0.4%
9	New York	37,192	3.4%
21	North Carolina	19,438	1.8%
49	North Dakota	872	0.1%
5	Ohio	48,695	4.4%
31	Oklahoma	10,981	1.0%
27	Oregon	13,677	1.2%
13	Pennsylvania	27,563	2.5%
41	Rhode Island	3,547	0.3%
33	South Carolina	7,618	0.7%
46	South Dakota	1,366	0.1%
7	Tennessee	42,910	3.9%
8	Texas	42,780	3.9%
25	Utah	14,939	1.3%
48	Vermont	933	0.1%
14	Virginia	26,578	2.4%
16	Washington	25,730	2.3%
39	West Virginia	3,765	0.3%
19	Wisconsin	23,473	2.1%
47	Wyoming	1,241	0.1%

RANK ORDER

RANK	STATE	BANKRUPTCIES	% of USA
1	California	149,203	13.5%
2	Florida	77,923	7.0%
3	Illinois	68,125	6.2%
4	Georgia	60,305	5.4%
5	Ohio	48,695	4.4%
6	Michigan	44,032	4.0%
7	Tennessee	42,910	3.9%
8	Texas	42,780	3.9%
9	New York	37,192	3.4%
10	Indiana	34,495	3.1%
11	New Jersey	28,882	2.6%
12	Alabama	27,678	2.5%
13	Pennsylvania	27,563	2.5%
14	Virginia	26,578	2.4%
15	Missouri	25,951	2.3%
16	Washington	25,730	2.3%
17	Arizona	24,046	2.2%
18	Colorado	23,976	2.2%
19	Wisconsin	23,473	2.1%
20	Maryland	23,193	2.1%
21	North Carolina	19,438	1.8%
22	Kentucky	18,672	1.7%
23	Louisiana	15,972	1.4%
24	Minnesota	15,003	1.4%
25	Utah	14,939	1.3%
26	Nevada	14,483	1.3%
27	Oregon	13,677	1.2%
28	Massachusetts	13,201	1.2%
29	Mississippi	12,938	1.2%
30	Arkansas	12,580	1.1%
31	Oklahoma	10,981	1.0%
32	Kansas	8,604	0.8%
33	South Carolina	7,618	0.7%
34	Connecticut	7,321	0.7%
35	Iowa	5,892	0.5%
36	Idaho	5,643	0.5%
37	Nebraska	5,362	0.5%
38	New Mexico	4,502	0.4%
39	West Virginia	3,765	0.3%
40	Delaware	3,581	0.3%
41	Rhode Island	3,547	0.3%
42	New Hampshire	3,376	0.3%
43	Maine	2,575	0.2%
44	Hawaii	2,313	0.2%
45	Montana	1,851	0.2%
46	South Dakota	1,366	0.1%
47	Wyoming	1,241	0.1%
48	Vermont	933	0.1%
49	North Dakota	872	0.1%
50	Alaska	638	0.1%
	District of Columbia	855	0.1%

Source: CQ Press using data from Administrative Office of the U.S. Courts
"Table F-2, U.S. Bankruptcy Courts" (http://www.uscourts.gov/Statistics/BankruptcyStatistics.aspx)
*For 12 months through September 2013. Includes business (34,892) and non-business (1,072,807) filings. Includes all chapters of bankruptcy. National total includes 10,794 bankruptcies in U.S. territories.

Personal Bankruptcy Rate in 2013

National Rate = 336 Personal Bankruptcies per 100,000 Population*

ALPHA ORDER

RANK	STATE	RATE
3	Alabama	563
50	Alaska	78
20	Arizona	349
13	Arkansas	415
18	California	376
8	Colorado	440
37	Connecticut	195
30	Delaware	270
16	Florida	383
2	Georgia	587
44	Hawaii	158
21	Idaho	339
4	Illinois	516
5	Indiana	515
40	Iowa	183
27	Kansas	291
12	Kentucky	416
23	Louisiana	337
41	Maine	182
17	Maryland	382
38	Massachusetts	191
9	Michigan	434
31	Minnesota	268
10	Mississippi	423
11	Missouri	419
43	Montana	175
28	Nebraska	278
7	Nevada	499
32	New Hampshire	235
25	New Jersey	314
33	New Mexico	208
42	New York	181
39	North Carolina	190
49	North Dakota	116
14	Ohio	413
29	Oklahoma	277
22	Oregon	338
33	Pennsylvania	208
24	Rhode Island	325
46	South Carolina	154
45	South Dakota	155
1	Tennessee	650
47	Texas	152
6	Utah	504
48	Vermont	143
25	Virginia	314
19	Washington	358
36	West Virginia	196
15	Wisconsin	399
35	Wyoming	200

RANK ORDER

RANK	STATE	RATE
1	Tennessee	650
2	Georgia	587
3	Alabama	563
4	Illinois	516
5	Indiana	515
6	Utah	504
7	Nevada	499
8	Colorado	440
9	Michigan	434
10	Mississippi	423
11	Missouri	419
12	Kentucky	416
13	Arkansas	415
14	Ohio	413
15	Wisconsin	399
16	Florida	383
17	Maryland	382
18	California	376
19	Washington	358
20	Arizona	349
21	Idaho	339
22	Oregon	338
23	Louisiana	337
24	Rhode Island	325
25	New Jersey	314
25	Virginia	314
27	Kansas	291
28	Nebraska	278
29	Oklahoma	277
30	Delaware	270
31	Minnesota	268
32	New Hampshire	235
33	New Mexico	208
33	Pennsylvania	208
35	Wyoming	200
36	West Virginia	196
37	Connecticut	195
38	Massachusetts	191
39	North Carolina	190
40	Iowa	183
41	Maine	182
42	New York	181
43	Montana	175
44	Hawaii	158
45	South Dakota	155
46	South Carolina	154
47	Texas	152
48	Vermont	143
49	North Dakota	116
50	Alaska	78
	District of Columbia	122

Source: CQ Press using data from Administrative Office of the U.S. Courts
"Table F-2, U.S. Bankruptcy Courts" (http://www.uscourts.gov/Statistics/BankruptcyStatistics.aspx)
*For 12 months through September 2013. National rate does not include bankruptcies or population in U.S. territories. Includes all nonbusiness bankruptcies.

Percent Change in Personal Bankruptcy Rate: 2012 to 2013

National Percent Change = 12.7% Decrease*

ALPHA ORDER				RANK ORDER		
RANK	STATE	PERCENT CHANGE		RANK	STATE	PERCENT CHANGE
4	Alabama	(3.4)		1	Mississippi	1.4
50	Alaska	(27.8)		2	Louisiana	(1.7)
44	Arizona	(20.9)		3	Illinois	(2.1)
5	Arkansas	(3.5)		4	Alabama	(3.4)
47	California	(25.5)		5	Arkansas	(3.5)
30	Colorado	(14.2)		6	Maryland	(4.0)
31	Connecticut	(14.5)		7	Tennessee	(4.3)
45	Delaware	(21.1)		8	Missouri	(5.0)
15	Florida	(8.4)		9	Indiana	(6.0)
22	Georgia	(10.5)		10	South Carolina	(6.1)
32	Hawaii	(14.6)		10	Wyoming	(6.1)
39	Idaho	(15.7)		12	Ohio	(6.6)
3	Illinois	(2.1)		13	Kansas	(7.3)
9	Indiana	(6.0)		14	West Virginia	(8.0)
27	Iowa	(12.4)		15	Florida	(8.4)
13	Kansas	(7.3)		16	New Mexico	(8.8)
18	Kentucky	(9.0)		16	Pennsylvania	(8.8)
2	Louisiana	(1.7)		18	Kentucky	(9.0)
42	Maine	(17.3)		19	Nebraska	(9.4)
6	Maryland	(4.0)		20	Vermont	(9.5)
49	Massachusetts	(26.8)		20	Wisconsin	(9.5)
32	Michigan	(14.6)		22	Georgia	(10.5)
37	Minnesota	(15.5)		23	Utah	(10.6)
1	Mississippi	1.4		24	Washington	(10.9)
8	Missouri	(5.0)		25	Oklahoma	(11.5)
32	Montana	(14.6)		26	North Carolina	(12.0)
19	Nebraska	(9.4)		27	Iowa	(12.4)
48	Nevada	(26.5)		28	New Jersey	(13.7)
43	New Hampshire	(20.1)		29	Virginia	(14.0)
28	New Jersey	(13.7)		30	Colorado	(14.2)
16	New Mexico	(8.8)		31	Connecticut	(14.5)
32	New York	(14.6)		32	Hawaii	(14.6)
26	North Carolina	(12.0)		32	Michigan	(14.6)
45	North Dakota	(21.1)		32	Montana	(14.6)
12	Ohio	(6.6)		32	New York	(14.6)
25	Oklahoma	(11.5)		32	Texas	(14.6)
37	Oregon	(15.5)		37	Minnesota	(15.5)
16	Pennsylvania	(8.8)		37	Oregon	(15.5)
40	Rhode Island	(16.2)		39	Idaho	(15.7)
10	South Carolina	(6.1)		40	Rhode Island	(16.2)
41	South Dakota	(16.7)		41	South Dakota	(16.7)
7	Tennessee	(4.3)		42	Maine	(17.3)
32	Texas	(14.6)		43	New Hampshire	(20.1)
23	Utah	(10.6)		44	Arizona	(20.9)
20	Vermont	(9.5)		45	Delaware	(21.1)
29	Virginia	(14.0)		45	North Dakota	(21.1)
24	Washington	(10.9)		47	California	(25.5)
14	West Virginia	(8.0)		48	Nevada	(26.5)
20	Wisconsin	(9.5)		49	Massachusetts	(26.8)
10	Wyoming	(6.1)		50	Alaska	(27.8)
					District of Columbia	(9.0)

Source: CQ Press using data from Administrative Office of the U.S. Courts
"Table F-2, U.S. Bankruptcy Courts" (http://www.uscourts.gov/Statistics/BankruptcyStatistics.aspx)
*Twelve months ending in September 2012 to 12 months ending in September 2013. National rate does not include bankruptcies or population in U.S. territories. Includes all nonbusiness bankruptcies.

Business Bankruptcy Rate in 2011

National Rate = 0.8% of Existing Firms*

ALPHA ORDER				RANK ORDER		
RANK	STATE	RATE		RANK	STATE	RATE
14	Alabama	0.8		1	Delaware	3.3
46	Alaska	0.4		2	Nevada	2.1
4	Arizona	1.3		3	New Hampshire	1.5
14	Arkansas	0.8		4	Arizona	1.3
6	California	1.1		4	Georgia	1.3
10	Colorado	0.9		6	California	1.1
37	Connecticut	0.5		7	Florida	1.0
1	Delaware	3.3		7	Tennessee	1.0
7	Florida	1.0		7	Utah	1.0
4	Georgia	1.3		10	Colorado	0.9
20	Hawaii	0.7		10	Michigan	0.9
14	Idaho	0.8		10	Mississippi	0.9
14	Illinois	0.8		10	Texas	0.9
20	Indiana	0.7		14	Alabama	0.8
28	Iowa	0.6		14	Arkansas	0.8
37	Kansas	0.5		14	Idaho	0.8
20	Kentucky	0.7		14	Illinois	0.8
14	Louisiana	0.8		14	Louisiana	0.8
20	Maine	0.7		14	Washington	0.8
28	Maryland	0.6		20	Hawaii	0.7
46	Massachusetts	0.4		20	Indiana	0.7
10	Michigan	0.9		20	Kentucky	0.7
28	Minnesota	0.6		20	Maine	0.7
10	Mississippi	0.9		20	North Carolina	0.7
37	Missouri	0.5		20	Ohio	0.7
46	Montana	0.4		20	West Virginia	0.7
37	Nebraska	0.5		20	Wisconsin	0.7
2	Nevada	2.1		28	Iowa	0.6
3	New Hampshire	1.5		28	Maryland	0.6
28	New Jersey	0.6		28	Minnesota	0.6
28	New Mexico	0.6		28	New Jersey	0.6
37	New York	0.5		28	New Mexico	0.6
20	North Carolina	0.7		28	Oklahoma	0.6
49	North Dakota	0.3		28	Oregon	0.6
20	Ohio	0.7		28	Rhode Island	0.6
28	Oklahoma	0.6		28	Virginia	0.6
28	Oregon	0.6		37	Connecticut	0.5
37	Pennsylvania	0.5		37	Kansas	0.5
28	Rhode Island	0.6		37	Missouri	0.5
37	South Carolina	0.5		37	Nebraska	0.5
37	South Dakota	0.5		37	New York	0.5
7	Tennessee	1.0		37	Pennsylvania	0.5
10	Texas	0.9		37	South Carolina	0.5
7	Utah	1.0		37	South Dakota	0.5
50	Vermont	0.2		37	Wyoming	0.5
28	Virginia	0.6		46	Alaska	0.4
14	Washington	0.8		46	Massachusetts	0.4
20	West Virginia	0.7		46	Montana	0.4
20	Wisconsin	0.7		49	North Dakota	0.3
37	Wyoming	0.5		50	Vermont	0.2
					District of Columbia	0.4

Source: CQ Press using data from U.S. Small Business Administration
"The Small Business Economy 2012" (http://www.sba.gov/advocacy/849/6282)
*Firms can be in more than one state. Firms filing for bankruptcy in 2011 as a percent of employer firms existing at the beginning of 2011 based on 2010 counts.

2014 State Business Tax Climate Index

National Average Score = 5.24*

ALPHA ORDER

RANK	STATE	SCORE
21	Alabama	5.21
4	Alaska	7.24
22	Arizona	5.20
34	Arkansas	4.89
48	California	3.76
19	Colorado	5.27
42	Connecticut	4.47
13	Delaware	5.75
5	Florida	6.91
32	Georgia	4.92
30	Hawaii	5.02
18	Idaho	5.31
31	Illinois	5.00
10	Indiana	5.99
40	Iowa	4.55
20	Kansas	5.22
27	Kentucky	5.08
33	Louisiana	4.90
29	Maine	5.04
41	Maryland	4.49
25	Massachusetts	5.09
14	Michigan	5.73
47	Minnesota	4.06
17	Mississippi	5.36
16	Missouri	5.47
7	Montana	6.24
34	Nebraska	4.89
3	Nevada	7.46
8	New Hampshire	6.08
49	New Jersey	3.45
38	New Mexico	4.72
50	New York	3.45
44	North Carolina	4.35
28	North Dakota	5.05
39	Ohio	4.58
36	Oklahoma	4.88
12	Oregon	5.75
24	Pennsylvania	5.11
46	Rhode Island	4.14
37	South Carolina	4.86
2	South Dakota	7.52
15	Tennessee	5.59
11	Texas	5.91
9	Utah	6.01
45	Vermont	4.14
26	Virginia	5.09
6	Washington	6.32
23	West Virginia	5.19
43	Wisconsin	4.43
1	Wyoming	7.58

RANK ORDER

RANK	STATE	SCORE
1	Wyoming	7.58
2	South Dakota	7.52
3	Nevada	7.46
4	Alaska	7.24
5	Florida	6.91
6	Washington	6.32
7	Montana	6.24
8	New Hampshire	6.08
9	Utah	6.01
10	Indiana	5.99
11	Texas	5.91
12	Oregon	5.75
13	Delaware	5.75
14	Michigan	5.73
15	Tennessee	5.59
16	Missouri	5.47
17	Mississippi	5.36
18	Idaho	5.31
19	Colorado	5.27
20	Kansas	5.22
21	Alabama	5.21
22	Arizona	5.20
23	West Virginia	5.19
24	Pennsylvania	5.11
25	Massachusetts	5.09
26	Virginia	5.09
27	Kentucky	5.08
28	North Dakota	5.05
29	Maine	5.04
30	Hawaii	5.02
31	Illinois	5.00
32	Georgia	4.92
33	Louisiana	4.90
34	Arkansas	4.89
34	Nebraska	4.89
36	Oklahoma	4.88
37	South Carolina	4.86
38	New Mexico	4.72
39	Ohio	4.58
40	Iowa	4.55
41	Maryland	4.49
42	Connecticut	4.47
43	Wisconsin	4.43
44	North Carolina	4.35
45	Vermont	4.14
46	Rhode Island	4.14
47	Minnesota	4.06
48	California	3.76
49	New Jersey	3.45
50	New York	3.45

District of Columbia   4.37

Source: The Tax Foundation
"State Business Tax Climate Index" (October 2013, http://taxfoundation.org/article/2014-state-business-tax-climate-index)
*This index looks at levels of taxation and complexity of compliance to compare the states on how "business friendly" each state is compared to the others. The scale for each factor considered is one to ten, with ten being the "best." Rankings are based on unrounded scores and reflect those of The Tax Foundation.

Fortune 500 Companies in 2013

National Total = 500 Companies*

ALPHA ORDER

RANK ORDER

RANK	STATE	COMPANIES	% of USA		RANK	STATE	COMPANIES	% of USA
35	Alabama	1	0.2%		1	California	54	10.8%
39	Alaska	0	0.0%		2	New York	52	10.4%
21	Arizona	6	1.2%		2	Texas	52	10.4%
21	Arkansas	6	1.2%		4	Illinois	32	6.4%
1	California	54	10.8%		5	Ohio	27	5.4%
16	Colorado	10	2.0%		6	Virginia	23	4.6%
11	Connecticut	16	3.2%		7	New Jersey	21	4.2%
32	Delaware	2	0.4%		7	Pennsylvania	21	4.2%
13	Florida	15	3.0%		9	Michigan	19	3.8%
11	Georgia	16	3.2%		9	Minnesota	19	3.8%
39	Hawaii	0	0.0%		11	Connecticut	16	3.2%
35	Idaho	1	0.2%		11	Georgia	16	3.2%
4	Illinois	32	6.4%		13	Florida	15	3.0%
21	Indiana	6	1.2%		14	Massachusetts	12	2.4%
32	Iowa	2	0.4%		14	North Carolina	12	2.4%
29	Kansas	3	0.6%		16	Colorado	10	2.0%
24	Kentucky	5	1.0%		16	Missouri	10	2.0%
29	Louisiana	3	0.6%		16	Wisconsin	10	2.0%
39	Maine	0	0.0%		19	Tennessee	9	1.8%
26	Maryland	4	0.8%		20	Washington	8	1.6%
14	Massachusetts	12	2.4%		21	Arizona	6	1.2%
9	Michigan	19	3.8%		21	Arkansas	6	1.2%
9	Minnesota	19	3.8%		21	Indiana	6	1.2%
39	Mississippi	0	0.0%		24	Kentucky	5	1.0%
16	Missouri	10	2.0%		24	Nebraska	5	1.0%
39	Montana	0	0.0%		26	Maryland	4	0.8%
24	Nebraska	5	1.0%		26	Nevada	4	0.8%
26	Nevada	4	0.8%		26	Oklahoma	4	0.8%
39	New Hampshire	0	0.0%		29	Kansas	3	0.6%
7	New Jersey	21	4.2%		29	Louisiana	3	0.6%
39	New Mexico	0	0.0%		29	Rhode Island	3	0.6%
2	New York	52	10.4%		32	Delaware	2	0.4%
14	North Carolina	12	2.4%		32	Iowa	2	0.4%
39	North Dakota	0	0.0%		32	Oregon	2	0.4%
5	Ohio	27	5.4%		35	Alabama	1	0.2%
26	Oklahoma	4	0.8%		35	Idaho	1	0.2%
32	Oregon	2	0.4%		35	South Carolina	1	0.2%
7	Pennsylvania	21	4.2%		35	Utah	1	0.2%
29	Rhode Island	3	0.6%		39	Alaska	0	0.0%
35	South Carolina	1	0.2%		39	Hawaii	0	0.0%
39	South Dakota	0	0.0%		39	Maine	0	0.0%
19	Tennessee	9	1.8%		39	Mississippi	0	0.0%
2	Texas	52	10.4%		39	Montana	0	0.0%
35	Utah	1	0.2%		39	New Hampshire	0	0.0%
39	Vermont	0	0.0%		39	New Mexico	0	0.0%
6	Virginia	23	4.6%		39	North Dakota	0	0.0%
20	Washington	8	1.6%		39	South Dakota	0	0.0%
39	West Virginia	0	0.0%		39	Vermont	0	0.0%
16	Wisconsin	10	2.0%		39	West Virginia	0	0.0%
39	Wyoming	0	0.0%		39	Wyoming	0	0.0%
						District of Columbia	3	0.6%

Source: Fortune magazine
  "Fortune 500" (April 8, 2013, Vol. 167, No. 5)
*By state where each company's headquarters is located.

Employer Firms in 2010

National Total = 5,734,538 Firms*

ALPHA ORDER

RANK	STATE	FIRMS	% of USA
26	Alabama	75,518	1.3%
50	Alaska	16,462	0.3%
21	Arizona	102,175	1.8%
33	Arkansas	51,072	0.9%
1	California	690,454	12.0%
15	Colorado	125,820	2.2%
27	Connecticut	72,747	1.3%
46	Delaware	19,679	0.3%
3	Florida	400,840	7.0%
10	Georgia	170,245	3.0%
43	Hawaii	25,383	0.4%
37	Idaho	36,660	0.6%
5	Illinois	253,612	4.4%
18	Indiana	110,961	1.9%
30	Iowa	63,402	1.1%
31	Kansas	59,170	1.0%
29	Kentucky	69,572	1.2%
24	Louisiana	81,299	1.4%
39	Maine	33,773	0.6%
20	Maryland	108,246	1.9%
14	Massachusetts	137,406	2.4%
9	Michigan	174,345	3.0%
17	Minnesota	117,687	2.1%
35	Mississippi	45,813	0.8%
16	Missouri	117,832	2.1%
40	Montana	31,358	0.5%
36	Nebraska	41,974	0.7%
34	Nevada	47,352	0.8%
41	New Hampshire	31,025	0.5%
7	New Jersey	193,722	3.4%
38	New Mexico	35,655	0.6%
2	New York	444,895	7.8%
11	North Carolina	168,938	2.9%
48	North Dakota	18,169	0.3%
8	Ohio	190,184	3.3%
28	Oklahoma	71,972	1.3%
23	Oregon	87,996	1.5%
6	Pennsylvania	231,192	4.0%
44	Rhode Island	24,556	0.4%
25	South Carolina	78,883	1.4%
45	South Dakota	21,637	0.4%
22	Tennessee	97,976	1.7%
4	Texas	394,392	6.9%
32	Utah	57,664	1.0%
47	Vermont	18,596	0.3%
12	Virginia	149,271	2.6%
13	Washington	144,377	2.5%
42	West Virginia	29,609	0.5%
19	Wisconsin	110,435	1.9%
49	Wyoming	17,585	0.3%

RANK ORDER

RANK	STATE	FIRMS	% of USA
1	California	690,454	12.0%
2	New York	444,895	7.8%
3	Florida	400,840	7.0%
4	Texas	394,392	6.9%
5	Illinois	253,612	4.4%
6	Pennsylvania	231,192	4.0%
7	New Jersey	193,722	3.4%
8	Ohio	190,184	3.3%
9	Michigan	174,345	3.0%
10	Georgia	170,245	3.0%
11	North Carolina	168,938	2.9%
12	Virginia	149,271	2.6%
13	Washington	144,377	2.5%
14	Massachusetts	137,406	2.4%
15	Colorado	125,820	2.2%
16	Missouri	117,832	2.1%
17	Minnesota	117,687	2.1%
18	Indiana	110,961	1.9%
19	Wisconsin	110,435	1.9%
20	Maryland	108,246	1.9%
21	Arizona	102,175	1.8%
22	Tennessee	97,976	1.7%
23	Oregon	87,996	1.5%
24	Louisiana	81,299	1.4%
25	South Carolina	78,883	1.4%
26	Alabama	75,518	1.3%
27	Connecticut	72,747	1.3%
28	Oklahoma	71,972	1.3%
29	Kentucky	69,572	1.2%
30	Iowa	63,402	1.1%
31	Kansas	59,170	1.0%
32	Utah	57,664	1.0%
33	Arkansas	51,072	0.9%
34	Nevada	47,352	0.8%
35	Mississippi	45,813	0.8%
36	Nebraska	41,974	0.7%
37	Idaho	36,660	0.6%
38	New Mexico	35,655	0.6%
39	Maine	33,773	0.6%
40	Montana	31,358	0.5%
41	New Hampshire	31,025	0.5%
42	West Virginia	29,609	0.5%
43	Hawaii	25,383	0.4%
44	Rhode Island	24,556	0.4%
45	South Dakota	21,637	0.4%
46	Delaware	19,679	0.3%
47	Vermont	18,596	0.3%
48	North Dakota	18,169	0.3%
49	Wyoming	17,585	0.3%
50	Alaska	16,462	0.3%
	District of Columbia	16,913	0.3%

Source: U.S. Small Business Administration
"The Small Business Economy 2012" (http://www.sba.gov/advocacy/849/6282)
*Updated figures. State totals do not add to the U.S. figure as firms can be in more than one state.

New Employer Firms in 2011

National Total = 1,433,703 New Firms*

RANK	STATE	FIRMS	% of USA
29	Alabama	14,335	1.0%
49	Alaska	4,466	0.3%
16	Arizona	30,030	2.1%
25	Arkansas	17,175	1.2%
1	California	165,536	11.5%
13	Colorado	36,375	2.5%
34	Connecticut	10,999	0.8%
46	Delaware	5,081	0.4%
2	Florida	129,059	9.0%
7	Georgia	52,788	3.7%
45	Hawaii	5,117	0.4%
35	Idaho	10,797	0.8%
5	Illinois	60,208	4.2%
19	Indiana	23,681	1.7%
33	Iowa	12,719	0.9%
32	Kansas	12,893	0.9%
27	Kentucky	16,230	1.1%
24	Louisiana	17,398	1.2%
36	Maine	9,228	0.6%
17	Maryland	28,586	2.0%
14	Massachusetts	33,323	2.3%
10	Michigan	40,946	2.9%
18	Minnesota	27,700	1.9%
37	Mississippi	8,987	0.6%
20	Missouri	22,058	1.5%
40	Montana	8,522	0.6%
38	Nebraska	8,732	0.6%
31	Nevada	13,597	0.9%
41	New Hampshire	8,287	0.6%
11	New Jersey	39,494	2.8%
39	New Mexico	8,675	0.6%
3	New York	108,231	7.5%
8	North Carolina	42,758	3.0%
44	North Dakota	5,289	0.4%
12	Ohio	38,296	2.7%
30	Oklahoma	14,244	1.0%
22	Oregon	21,487	1.5%
6	Pennsylvania	54,929	3.8%
42	Rhode Island	6,786	0.5%
26	South Carolina	17,168	1.2%
47	South Dakota	4,829	0.3%
28	Tennessee	15,954	1.1%
4	Texas	87,955	6.1%
23	Utah	18,411	1.3%
48	Vermont	4,604	0.3%
9	Virginia	41,879	2.9%
15	Washington	30,416	2.1%
43	West Virginia	6,463	0.5%
21	Wisconsin	21,713	1.5%
50	Wyoming	4,151	0.3%

RANK	STATE	FIRMS	% of USA
1	California	165,536	11.5%
2	Florida	129,059	9.0%
3	New York	108,231	7.5%
4	Texas	87,955	6.1%
5	Illinois	60,208	4.2%
6	Pennsylvania	54,929	3.8%
7	Georgia	52,788	3.7%
8	North Carolina	42,758	3.0%
9	Virginia	41,879	2.9%
10	Michigan	40,946	2.9%
11	New Jersey	39,494	2.8%
12	Ohio	38,296	2.7%
13	Colorado	36,375	2.5%
14	Massachusetts	33,323	2.3%
15	Washington	30,416	2.1%
16	Arizona	30,030	2.1%
17	Maryland	28,586	2.0%
18	Minnesota	27,700	1.9%
19	Indiana	23,681	1.7%
20	Missouri	22,058	1.5%
21	Wisconsin	21,713	1.5%
22	Oregon	21,487	1.5%
23	Utah	18,411	1.3%
24	Louisiana	17,398	1.2%
25	Arkansas	17,175	1.2%
26	South Carolina	17,168	1.2%
27	Kentucky	16,230	1.1%
28	Tennessee	15,954	1.1%
29	Alabama	14,335	1.0%
30	Oklahoma	14,244	1.0%
31	Nevada	13,597	0.9%
32	Kansas	12,893	0.9%
33	Iowa	12,719	0.9%
34	Connecticut	10,999	0.8%
35	Idaho	10,797	0.8%
36	Maine	9,228	0.6%
37	Mississippi	8,987	0.6%
38	Nebraska	8,732	0.6%
39	New Mexico	8,675	0.6%
40	Montana	8,522	0.6%
41	New Hampshire	8,287	0.6%
42	Rhode Island	6,786	0.5%
43	West Virginia	6,463	0.5%
44	North Dakota	5,289	0.4%
45	Hawaii	5,117	0.4%
46	Delaware	5,081	0.4%
47	South Dakota	4,829	0.3%
48	Vermont	4,604	0.3%
49	Alaska	4,466	0.3%
50	Wyoming	4,151	0.3%
	District of Columbia	5,118	0.4%

Source: U.S. Small Business Administration
"The Small Business Economy 2012" (http://www.sba.gov/advocacy/849/6282)
*Establishment openings and closings represent quarterly business turnover for new and existing establishments, which can belong to small or large firms (seasonally adjusted).

Rate of New Employer Firms in 2011

National Rate = 25.0% of Existing Firms*

ALPHA ORDER

RANK	STATE	RATE
47	Alabama	19.0
14	Alaska	27.1
6	Arizona	29.4
1	Arkansas	33.6
24	California	24.0
8	Colorado	28.9
50	Connecticut	15.1
17	Delaware	25.8
2	Florida	32.2
4	Georgia	31.0
41	Hawaii	20.2
5	Idaho	29.5
26	Illinois	23.7
37	Indiana	21.3
42	Iowa	20.1
33	Kansas	21.8
30	Kentucky	23.3
36	Louisiana	21.4
12	Maine	27.3
16	Maryland	26.4
21	Massachusetts	24.3
28	Michigan	23.5
28	Minnesota	23.5
46	Mississippi	19.6
48	Missouri	18.7
13	Montana	27.2
39	Nebraska	20.8
9	Nevada	28.7
15	New Hampshire	26.7
40	New Jersey	20.4
21	New Mexico	24.3
21	New York	24.3
18	North Carolina	25.3
7	North Dakota	29.1
42	Ohio	20.1
44	Oklahoma	19.8
20	Oregon	24.4
25	Pennsylvania	23.8
11	Rhode Island	27.6
33	South Carolina	21.8
31	South Dakota	22.3
49	Tennessee	16.3
31	Texas	22.3
3	Utah	31.9
19	Vermont	24.8
10	Virginia	28.1
38	Washington	21.1
33	West Virginia	21.8
45	Wisconsin	19.7
27	Wyoming	23.6

RANK ORDER

RANK	STATE	RATE
1	Arkansas	33.6
2	Florida	32.2
3	Utah	31.9
4	Georgia	31.0
5	Idaho	29.5
6	Arizona	29.4
7	North Dakota	29.1
8	Colorado	28.9
9	Nevada	28.7
10	Virginia	28.1
11	Rhode Island	27.6
12	Maine	27.3
13	Montana	27.2
14	Alaska	27.1
15	New Hampshire	26.7
16	Maryland	26.4
17	Delaware	25.8
18	North Carolina	25.3
19	Vermont	24.8
20	Oregon	24.4
21	Massachusetts	24.3
21	New Mexico	24.3
21	New York	24.3
24	California	24.0
25	Pennsylvania	23.8
26	Illinois	23.7
27	Wyoming	23.6
28	Michigan	23.5
28	Minnesota	23.5
30	Kentucky	23.3
31	South Dakota	22.3
31	Texas	22.3
33	Kansas	21.8
33	South Carolina	21.8
33	West Virginia	21.8
36	Louisiana	21.4
37	Indiana	21.3
38	Washington	21.1
39	Nebraska	20.8
40	New Jersey	20.4
41	Hawaii	20.2
42	Iowa	20.1
42	Ohio	20.1
44	Oklahoma	19.8
45	Wisconsin	19.7
46	Mississippi	19.6
47	Alabama	19.0
48	Missouri	18.7
49	Tennessee	16.3
50	Connecticut	15.1

District of Columbia — 30.3

Source: CQ Press using data from U.S. Small Business Administration
"The Small Business Economy 2012" (http://www.sba.gov/advocacy/849/6282)
*Establishment openings and closings represent quarterly business turnover for new and existing establishments, which can belong to small or large firms (seasonally adjusted). Firms can be in more than one state. Rate represents the number of employer firms started in 2011 as a percent of existing firms at the beginning of 2011 based on 2010 counts.

Employer Firm Terminations in 2011

National Total = 1,434,390 Terminations*

ALPHA ORDER

RANK	STATE	FIRMS	% of USA
30	Alabama	14,770	1.0%
48	Alaska	4,237	0.3%
16	Arizona	29,889	2.1%
24	Arkansas	17,085	1.2%
1	California	172,682	12.1%
13	Colorado	35,152	2.5%
35	Connecticut	11,196	0.8%
45	Delaware	5,392	0.4%
2	Florida	124,471	8.7%
7	Georgia	53,005	3.7%
44	Hawaii	6,384	0.4%
34	Idaho	11,674	0.8%
5	Illinois	59,944	4.2%
19	Indiana	24,147	1.7%
32	Iowa	12,842	0.9%
33	Kansas	12,706	0.9%
27	Kentucky	16,340	1.1%
25	Louisiana	16,659	1.2%
37	Maine	9,003	0.6%
17	Maryland	28,988	2.0%
14	Massachusetts	32,654	2.3%
8	Michigan	40,531	2.8%
18	Minnesota	25,370	1.8%
36	Mississippi	9,415	0.7%
21	Missouri	22,493	1.6%
41	Montana	8,136	0.6%
40	Nebraska	8,179	0.6%
31	Nevada	12,928	0.9%
39	New Hampshire	8,219	0.6%
12	New Jersey	38,268	2.7%
38	New Mexico	8,806	0.6%
3	New York	106,278	7.5%
10	North Carolina	39,453	2.8%
49	North Dakota	4,027	0.3%
9	Ohio	40,221	2.8%
28	Oklahoma	16,069	1.1%
22	Oregon	21,889	1.5%
6	Pennsylvania	57,766	4.1%
42	Rhode Island	6,740	0.5%
23	South Carolina	17,106	1.2%
47	South Dakota	4,684	0.3%
29	Tennessee	15,856	1.1%
4	Texas	83,154	5.8%
26	Utah	16,493	1.2%
46	Vermont	4,686	0.3%
11	Virginia	39,279	2.8%
15	Washington	31,557	2.2%
43	West Virginia	6,466	0.5%
20	Wisconsin	22,707	1.6%
50	Wyoming	4,010	0.3%

RANK ORDER

RANK	STATE	FIRMS	% of USA
1	California	172,682	12.1%
2	Florida	124,471	8.7%
3	New York	106,278	7.5%
4	Texas	83,154	5.8%
5	Illinois	59,944	4.2%
6	Pennsylvania	57,766	4.1%
7	Georgia	53,005	3.7%
8	Michigan	40,531	2.8%
9	Ohio	40,221	2.8%
10	North Carolina	39,453	2.8%
11	Virginia	39,279	2.8%
12	New Jersey	38,268	2.7%
13	Colorado	35,152	2.5%
14	Massachusetts	32,654	2.3%
15	Washington	31,557	2.2%
16	Arizona	29,889	2.1%
17	Maryland	28,988	2.0%
18	Minnesota	25,370	1.8%
19	Indiana	24,147	1.7%
20	Wisconsin	22,707	1.6%
21	Missouri	22,493	1.6%
22	Oregon	21,889	1.5%
23	South Carolina	17,106	1.2%
24	Arkansas	17,085	1.2%
25	Louisiana	16,659	1.2%
26	Utah	16,493	1.2%
27	Kentucky	16,340	1.1%
28	Oklahoma	16,069	1.1%
29	Tennessee	15,856	1.1%
30	Alabama	14,770	1.0%
31	Nevada	12,928	0.9%
32	Iowa	12,842	0.9%
33	Kansas	12,706	0.9%
34	Idaho	11,674	0.8%
35	Connecticut	11,196	0.8%
36	Mississippi	9,415	0.7%
37	Maine	9,003	0.6%
38	New Mexico	8,806	0.6%
39	New Hampshire	8,219	0.6%
40	Nebraska	8,179	0.6%
41	Montana	8,136	0.6%
42	Rhode Island	6,740	0.5%
43	West Virginia	6,466	0.5%
44	Hawaii	6,384	0.4%
45	Delaware	5,392	0.4%
46	Vermont	4,686	0.3%
47	South Dakota	4,684	0.3%
48	Alaska	4,237	0.3%
49	North Dakota	4,027	0.3%
50	Wyoming	4,010	0.3%
	District of Columbia	4,384	0.3%

Source: U.S. Small Business Administration
"The Small Business Economy 2012" (http://www.sba.gov/advocacy/849/6282)
*Establishment openings and closings represent quarterly business turnover for new and existing establishments, which can belong to small or large firms (seasonally adjusted).

Rate of Employer Firm Terminations in 2011

National Rate = 24.8% of Existing Firms*

ALPHA ORDER

RANK	STATE	RATE
46	Alabama	19.6
16	Alaska	25.7
5	Arizona	29.3
1	Arkansas	33.5
19	California	25.0
7	Colorado	27.9
50	Connecticut	15.4
8	Delaware	27.4
3	Florida	31.1
3	Georgia	31.1
17	Hawaii	25.2
2	Idaho	31.8
25	Illinois	23.6
33	Indiana	21.8
44	Iowa	20.3
38	Kansas	21.5
26	Kentucky	23.5
43	Louisiana	20.5
12	Maine	26.7
11	Maryland	26.8
24	Massachusetts	23.8
28	Michigan	23.2
36	Minnesota	21.6
41	Mississippi	20.6
48	Missouri	19.1
15	Montana	25.9
47	Nebraska	19.5
10	Nevada	27.3
13	New Hampshire	26.5
45	New Jersey	19.8
22	New Mexico	24.7
23	New York	23.9
27	North Carolina	23.4
31	North Dakota	22.2
39	Ohio	21.1
30	Oklahoma	22.3
21	Oregon	24.9
19	Pennsylvania	25.0
8	Rhode Island	27.4
35	South Carolina	21.7
36	South Dakota	21.6
49	Tennessee	16.2
39	Texas	21.1
6	Utah	28.6
17	Vermont	25.2
14	Virginia	26.3
32	Washington	21.9
33	West Virginia	21.8
41	Wisconsin	20.6
29	Wyoming	22.8

RANK ORDER

RANK	STATE	RATE
1	Arkansas	33.5
2	Idaho	31.8
3	Florida	31.1
3	Georgia	31.1
5	Arizona	29.3
6	Utah	28.6
7	Colorado	27.9
8	Delaware	27.4
8	Rhode Island	27.4
10	Nevada	27.3
11	Maryland	26.8
12	Maine	26.7
13	New Hampshire	26.5
14	Virginia	26.3
15	Montana	25.9
16	Alaska	25.7
17	Hawaii	25.2
17	Vermont	25.2
19	California	25.0
19	Pennsylvania	25.0
21	Oregon	24.9
22	New Mexico	24.7
23	New York	23.9
24	Massachusetts	23.8
25	Illinois	23.6
26	Kentucky	23.5
27	North Carolina	23.4
28	Michigan	23.2
29	Wyoming	22.8
30	Oklahoma	22.3
31	North Dakota	22.2
32	Washington	21.9
33	Indiana	21.8
33	West Virginia	21.8
35	South Carolina	21.7
36	Minnesota	21.6
36	South Dakota	21.6
38	Kansas	21.5
39	Ohio	21.1
39	Texas	21.1
41	Mississippi	20.6
41	Wisconsin	20.6
43	Louisiana	20.5
44	Iowa	20.3
45	New Jersey	19.8
46	Alabama	19.6
47	Nebraska	19.5
48	Missouri	19.1
49	Tennessee	16.2
50	Connecticut	15.4
	District of Columbia	25.9

Source: CQ Press using data from U.S. Small Business Administration
   "The Small Business Economy 2012" (http://www.sba.gov/advocacy/849/6282)
*Establishment openings and closings represent quarterly business turnover for new and existing establishments, which can belong to small or large firms (seasonally adjusted). Firms can be in more than one state. Rate represents the number of employer firms ceasing operations in 2011 as a percent of existing firms at the beginning of 2011 based on 2010 counts. Some state terminations result in successor firms which are not listed as new firms, thus making terminations higher than formations for most states.

V. Education

(Continued)

(Continued)

Estimated Percent of School-Age Population in Public Schools in 2011

National Percent = 92.0%*

ALPHA ORDER

ALPHA ORDER

RANK	STATE	PERCENT
22	Alabama	91.8
3	Alaska	98.7
26	Arizona	91.2
9	Arkansas	93.8
11	California	93.4
6	Colorado	95.0
19	Connecticut	92.5
47	Delaware	86.9
34	Florida	90.5
17	Georgia	92.8
50	Hawaii	83.1
40	Idaho	89.3
20	Illinois	92.1
38	Indiana	89.7
8	Iowa	94.4
16	Kansas	93.0
27	Kentucky	91.0
47	Louisiana	86.9
9	Maine	93.8
47	Maryland	86.9
21	Massachusetts	91.9
18	Michigan	92.7
33	Minnesota	90.6
32	Mississippi	90.7
39	Missouri	89.4
42	Montana	88.2
29	Nebraska	90.8
25	Nevada	91.6
23	New Hampshire	91.7
15	New Jersey	93.1
34	New Mexico	90.5
46	New York	87.6
36	North Carolina	89.9
29	North Dakota	90.8
41	Ohio	88.5
5	Oklahoma	98.5
27	Oregon	91.0
43	Pennsylvania	88.0
43	Rhode Island	88.0
12	South Carolina	93.3
45	South Dakota	87.9
29	Tennessee	90.8
3	Texas	98.7
7	Utah	94.7
1	Vermont	102.1
14	Virginia	93.2
23	Washington	91.7
2	West Virginia	100.5
37	Wisconsin	89.8
12	Wyoming	93.3

RANK ORDER

RANK	STATE	PERCENT
1	Vermont	102.1
2	West Virginia	100.5
3	Alaska	98.7
3	Texas	98.7
5	Oklahoma	98.5
6	Colorado	95.0
7	Utah	94.7
8	Iowa	94.4
9	Arkansas	93.8
9	Maine	93.8
11	California	93.4
12	South Carolina	93.3
12	Wyoming	93.3
14	Virginia	93.2
15	New Jersey	93.1
16	Kansas	93.0
17	Georgia	92.8
18	Michigan	92.7
19	Connecticut	92.5
20	Illinois	92.1
21	Massachusetts	91.9
22	Alabama	91.8
23	New Hampshire	91.7
23	Washington	91.7
25	Nevada	91.6
26	Arizona	91.2
27	Kentucky	91.0
27	Oregon	91.0
29	Nebraska	90.8
29	North Dakota	90.8
29	Tennessee	90.8
32	Mississippi	90.7
33	Minnesota	90.6
34	Florida	90.5
34	New Mexico	90.5
36	North Carolina	89.9
37	Wisconsin	89.8
38	Indiana	89.7
39	Missouri	89.4
40	Idaho	89.3
41	Ohio	88.5
42	Montana	88.2
43	Pennsylvania	88.0
43	Rhode Island	88.0
45	South Dakota	87.9
46	New York	87.6
47	Delaware	86.9
47	Louisiana	86.9
47	Maryland	86.9
50	Hawaii	83.1
	District of Columbia	103.1

Source: CQ Press using data from U.S. Department of Education, National Center for Education Statistics
   "Common Core of Data (CCD) Database" (http://nces.ed.gov/ccd/)
*Estimate based on 2011 Census population estimates for 5- to 17-year-olds compared to estimated 2010-2011 school year public school student membership. Student membership figures include counts for pre-kindergarten programs. Figures higher than 100 percent reflect using different sources for population and for student membership.

Regular Public Elementary and Secondary School Districts in 2011

National Total = 13,592 Districts*

ALPHA ORDER					RANK ORDER			
RANK	STATE	DISTRICTS	% of USA		RANK	STATE	DISTRICTS	% of USA
35	Alabama	133	1.0%		1	Texas	1,031	7.6%
43	Alaska	53	0.4%		2	California	955	7.0%
23	Arizona	224	1.6%		3	Illinois	868	6.4%
21	Arkansas	239	1.8%		4	New York	695	5.1%
2	California	955	7.0%		5	Ohio	615	4.5%
27	Colorado	178	1.3%		6	New Jersey	613	4.5%
30	Connecticut	169	1.2%		7	Michigan	551	4.1%
48	Delaware	19	0.1%		8	Oklahoma	526	3.9%
41	Florida	67	0.5%		9	Missouri	522	3.8%
26	Georgia	180	1.3%		10	Pennsylvania	500	3.7%
50	Hawaii	1	0.0%		11	Wisconsin	424	3.1%
36	Idaho	116	0.9%		12	Montana	417	3.1%
3	Illinois	868	6.4%		13	Iowa	359	2.6%
18	Indiana	293	2.2%		14	Minnesota	337	2.5%
13	Iowa	359	2.6%		15	Kansas	312	2.3%
15	Kansas	312	2.3%		16	Washington	295	2.2%
29	Kentucky	174	1.3%		17	Vermont	294	2.2%
40	Louisiana	70	0.5%		18	Indiana	293	2.2%
22	Maine	235	1.7%		19	Nebraska	251	1.8%
47	Maryland	24	0.2%		20	Massachusetts	244	1.8%
20	Massachusetts	244	1.8%		21	Arkansas	239	1.8%
7	Michigan	551	4.1%		22	Maine	235	1.7%
14	Minnesota	337	2.5%		23	Arizona	224	1.6%
31	Mississippi	152	1.1%		24	Oregon	186	1.4%
9	Missouri	522	3.8%		25	North Dakota	183	1.3%
12	Montana	417	3.1%		26	Georgia	180	1.3%
19	Nebraska	251	1.8%		27	Colorado	178	1.3%
49	Nevada	17	0.1%		27	New Hampshire	178	1.3%
27	New Hampshire	178	1.3%		29	Kentucky	174	1.3%
6	New Jersey	613	4.5%		30	Connecticut	169	1.2%
38	New Mexico	89	0.7%		31	Mississippi	152	1.1%
4	New York	695	5.1%		31	South Dakota	152	1.1%
37	North Carolina	115	0.8%		33	Tennessee	137	1.0%
25	North Dakota	183	1.3%		34	Virginia	134	1.0%
5	Ohio	615	4.5%		35	Alabama	133	1.0%
8	Oklahoma	526	3.9%		36	Idaho	116	0.9%
24	Oregon	186	1.4%		37	North Carolina	115	0.8%
10	Pennsylvania	500	3.7%		38	New Mexico	89	0.7%
46	Rhode Island	32	0.2%		39	South Carolina	86	0.6%
39	South Carolina	86	0.6%		40	Louisiana	70	0.5%
31	South Dakota	152	1.1%		41	Florida	67	0.5%
33	Tennessee	137	1.0%		42	West Virginia	55	0.4%
1	Texas	1,031	7.6%		43	Alaska	53	0.4%
45	Utah	41	0.3%		44	Wyoming	49	0.4%
17	Vermont	294	2.2%		45	Utah	41	0.3%
34	Virginia	134	1.0%		46	Rhode Island	32	0.2%
16	Washington	295	2.2%		47	Maryland	24	0.2%
42	West Virginia	55	0.4%		48	Delaware	19	0.1%
11	Wisconsin	424	3.1%		49	Nevada	17	0.1%
44	Wyoming	49	0.4%		50	Hawaii	1	0.0%
						District of Columbia	2	0.0%

Source: U.S. Department of Education, National Center for Education Statistics
"Numbers and Types of Public Elementary and Secondary Education Agencies" (http://nces.ed.gov/pubs2012/2012326.pdf)
*For school year 2010-2011. Regular school districts are agencies responsible for providing free public education for school-age children residing within their jurisdiction. Included in these figures are districts that reported having no students. This can occur when a small district has no pupils or contracts with another district to educate the students school its jurisdiction.

Public Elementary and Secondary Schools in 2012

National Total = 98,328 Schools*

ALPHA ORDER

RANK	STATE	SCHOOLS	% of USA
23	Alabama	1,618	1.6%
44	Alaska	511	0.5%
15	Arizona	2,252	2.3%
32	Arkansas	1,108	1.1%
1	California	10,170	10.3%
20	Colorado	1,813	1.8%
31	Connecticut	1,150	1.2%
50	Delaware	221	0.2%
5	Florida	4,212	4.3%
13	Georgia	2,388	2.4%
49	Hawaii	287	0.3%
38	Idaho	762	0.8%
4	Illinois	4,336	4.4%
18	Indiana	1,933	2.0%
27	Iowa	1,411	1.4%
28	Kansas	1,359	1.4%
24	Kentucky	1,565	1.6%
26	Louisiana	1,437	1.5%
42	Maine	621	0.6%
25	Maryland	1,451	1.5%
19	Massachusetts	1,835	1.9%
7	Michigan	3,550	3.6%
12	Minnesota	2,392	2.4%
34	Mississippi	1,069	1.1%
11	Missouri	2,408	2.4%
37	Montana	826	0.8%
33	Nebraska	1,090	1.1%
41	Nevada	649	0.7%
45	New Hampshire	477	0.5%
9	New Jersey	2,596	2.6%
36	New Mexico	866	0.9%
3	New York	4,752	4.8%
10	North Carolina	2,577	2.6%
43	North Dakota	513	0.5%
6	Ohio	3,714	3.8%
22	Oklahoma	1,774	1.8%
29	Oregon	1,261	1.3%
8	Pennsylvania	3,181	3.2%
48	Rhode Island	308	0.3%
30	South Carolina	1,223	1.2%
40	South Dakota	704	0.7%
21	Tennessee	1,802	1.8%
2	Texas	8,697	8.8%
35	Utah	1,020	1.0%
47	Vermont	320	0.3%
17	Virginia	2,170	2.2%
14	Washington	2,365	2.4%
39	West Virginia	759	0.8%
16	Wisconsin	2,243	2.3%
46	Wyoming	354	0.4%

RANK ORDER

RANK	STATE	SCHOOLS	% of USA
1	California	10,170	10.3%
2	Texas	8,697	8.8%
3	New York	4,752	4.8%
4	Illinois	4,336	4.4%
5	Florida	4,212	4.3%
6	Ohio	3,714	3.8%
7	Michigan	3,550	3.6%
8	Pennsylvania	3,181	3.2%
9	New Jersey	2,596	2.6%
10	North Carolina	2,577	2.6%
11	Missouri	2,408	2.4%
12	Minnesota	2,392	2.4%
13	Georgia	2,388	2.4%
14	Washington	2,365	2.4%
15	Arizona	2,252	2.3%
16	Wisconsin	2,243	2.3%
17	Virginia	2,170	2.2%
18	Indiana	1,933	2.0%
19	Massachusetts	1,835	1.9%
20	Colorado	1,813	1.8%
21	Tennessee	1,802	1.8%
22	Oklahoma	1,774	1.8%
23	Alabama	1,618	1.6%
24	Kentucky	1,565	1.6%
25	Maryland	1,451	1.5%
26	Louisiana	1,437	1.5%
27	Iowa	1,411	1.4%
28	Kansas	1,359	1.4%
29	Oregon	1,261	1.3%
30	South Carolina	1,223	1.2%
31	Connecticut	1,150	1.2%
32	Arkansas	1,108	1.1%
33	Nebraska	1,090	1.1%
34	Mississippi	1,069	1.1%
35	Utah	1,020	1.0%
36	New Mexico	866	0.9%
37	Montana	826	0.8%
38	Idaho	762	0.8%
39	West Virginia	759	0.8%
40	South Dakota	704	0.7%
41	Nevada	649	0.7%
42	Maine	621	0.6%
43	North Dakota	513	0.5%
44	Alaska	511	0.5%
45	New Hampshire	477	0.5%
46	Wyoming	354	0.4%
47	Vermont	320	0.3%
48	Rhode Island	308	0.3%
49	Hawaii	287	0.3%
50	Delaware	221	0.2%
	District of Columbia	228	0.2%

Source: U.S. Department of Education, National Center for Education Statistics
"Selected Statistics From the Common Core of Data: School Year 2011-12" (http://nces.ed.gov/pubs2013/2013441.pdf)
*For school year 2011-2012.

Private Elementary and Secondary Schools in 2012

National Total = 30,861 Schools*

ALPHA ORDER				RANK ORDER			
RANK	STATE	SCHOOLS	% of USA	RANK	STATE	SCHOOLS	% of USA
25	Alabama	402	1.3%	1	California	3,479	11.3%
48	Alaska	51	0.2%	2	Pennsylvania	2,325	7.5%
28	Arizona	341	1.1%	3	New York	1,931	6.3%
32	Arkansas	234	0.8%	4	Florida	1,880	6.1%
1	California	3,479	11.3%	5	Illinois	1,572	5.1%
22	Colorado	414	1.3%	6	Texas	1,502	4.9%
23	Connecticut	406	1.3%	7	New Jersey	1,289	4.2%
42	Delaware	124	0.4%	8	Missouri**	1,270	4.1%
4	Florida	1,880	6.1%	9	Indiana	969	3.1%
16	Georgia	710	2.3%	10	Ohio	968	3.1%
41	Hawaii	134	0.4%	11	Wisconsin	844	2.7%
42	Idaho	124	0.4%	12	Massachusetts	803	2.6%
5	Illinois	1,572	5.1%	13	Michigan	791	2.6%
9	Indiana	969	3.1%	14	Virginia	755	2.4%
30	Iowa	300	1.0%	15	Maryland	736	2.4%
24	Kansas**	404	1.3%	16	Georgia	710	2.3%
29	Kentucky	329	1.1%	17	North Carolina	642	2.1%
26	Louisiana	394	1.3%	18	Washington	633	2.1%
38	Maine	157	0.5%	19	Tennessee	512	1.7%
15	Maryland	736	2.4%	20	Minnesota	504	1.6%
12	Massachusetts	803	2.6%	21	Oregon	432	1.4%
13	Michigan	791	2.6%	22	Colorado	414	1.3%
20	Minnesota	504	1.6%	23	Connecticut	406	1.3%
34	Mississippi	221	0.7%	24	Kansas**	404	1.3%
8	Missouri**	1,270	4.1%	25	Alabama	402	1.3%
46	Montana	111	0.4%	26	Louisiana	394	1.3%
33	Nebraska	222	0.7%	27	South Carolina	378	1.2%
38	Nevada	157	0.5%	28	Arizona	341	1.1%
31	New Hampshire	278	0.9%	29	Kentucky	329	1.1%
7	New Jersey	1,289	4.2%	30	Iowa	300	1.0%
36	New Mexico	174	0.6%	31	New Hampshire	278	0.9%
3	New York	1,931	6.3%	32	Arkansas	234	0.8%
17	North Carolina	642	2.1%	33	Nebraska	222	0.7%
49	North Dakota	46	0.1%	34	Mississippi	221	0.7%
10	Ohio	968	3.1%	35	Oklahoma	181	0.6%
35	Oklahoma	181	0.6%	36	New Mexico	174	0.6%
21	Oregon	432	1.4%	37	Utah	160	0.5%
2	Pennsylvania	2,325	7.5%	38	Maine	157	0.5%
40	Rhode Island	144	0.5%	38	Nevada	157	0.5%
27	South Carolina	378	1.2%	40	Rhode Island	144	0.5%
47	South Dakota	74	0.2%	41	Hawaii	134	0.4%
19	Tennessee	512	1.7%	42	Delaware	124	0.4%
6	Texas	1,502	4.9%	42	Idaho	124	0.4%
37	Utah	160	0.5%	42	West Virginia	124	0.4%
45	Vermont	114	0.4%	45	Vermont	114	0.4%
14	Virginia	755	2.4%	46	Montana	111	0.4%
18	Washington	633	2.1%	47	South Dakota	74	0.2%
42	West Virginia	124	0.4%	48	Alaska	51	0.2%
11	Wisconsin	844	2.7%	49	North Dakota	46	0.1%
50	Wyoming	38	0.1%	50	Wyoming	38	0.1%
					District of Columbia	79	0.3%

Source: U.S. Department of Education, National Center for Education Statistics
   "Characteristics of Private Schools in the United States" (http://nces.ed.gov/pubsearch/pubsinfo.asp?pubid=2013316)
*For school year 2011-2012. Includes private schools that provide instruction for one or more grades kindergarten through 12 (or comparable ungraded levels).
**Interpret data for these states with caution.

Private Elementary and Secondary School Enrollment in 2012

National Total = 4,494,845 Students*

ALPHA ORDER

RANK	STATE	STUDENTS	% of USA
22	Alabama	67,479	1.5%
49	Alaska	4,087	0.1%
29	Arizona	43,134	1.0%
35	Arkansas	25,164	0.6%
1	California	523,088	11.6%
27	Colorado	45,697	1.0%
24	Connecticut	58,399	1.3%
37	Delaware	21,667	0.5%
3	Florida	284,238	6.3%
9	Georgia	120,488	2.7%
33	Hawaii	33,994	0.8%
44	Idaho	11,262	0.3%
5	Illinois	226,265	5.0%
16	Indiana	111,872	2.5%
25	Iowa	58,180	1.3%
31	Kansas	39,016	0.9%
23	Kentucky	60,590	1.3%
14	Louisiana	112,645	2.5%
41	Maine	17,011	0.4%
10	Maryland	117,657	2.6%
13	Massachusetts	112,684	2.5%
11	Michigan	116,461	2.6%
21	Minnesota	76,693	1.7%
28	Mississippi	45,419	1.0%
12	Missouri	115,553	2.6%
46	Montana	8,561	0.2%
32	Nebraska	36,163	0.8%
39	Nevada	20,396	0.5%
38	New Hampshire	21,264	0.5%
8	New Jersey	166,508	3.7%
40	New Mexico	19,360	0.4%
2	New York	430,293	9.6%
17	North Carolina	106,661	2.4%
48	North Dakota	6,535	0.1%
7	Ohio	190,810	4.2%
34	Oklahoma	30,063	0.7%
30	Oregon	42,694	0.9%
4	Pennsylvania	240,993	5.4%
36	Rhode Island	22,539	0.5%
26	South Carolina	47,259	1.1%
45	South Dakota	10,266	0.2%
19	Tennessee	81,499	1.8%
6	Texas	223,469	5.0%
42	Utah	15,498	0.3%
47	Vermont	8,323	0.2%
18	Virginia	98,439	2.2%
20	Washington	77,279	1.7%
43	West Virginia	11,890	0.3%
15	Wisconsin	112,025	2.5%
50	Wyoming	1,947	0.0%

RANK ORDER

RANK	STATE	STUDENTS	% of USA
1	California	523,088	11.6%
2	New York	430,293	9.6%
3	Florida	284,238	6.3%
4	Pennsylvania	240,993	5.4%
5	Illinois	226,265	5.0%
6	Texas	223,469	5.0%
7	Ohio	190,810	4.2%
8	New Jersey	166,508	3.7%
9	Georgia	120,488	2.7%
10	Maryland	117,657	2.6%
11	Michigan	116,461	2.6%
12	Missouri	115,553	2.6%
13	Massachusetts	112,684	2.5%
14	Louisiana	112,645	2.5%
15	Wisconsin	112,025	2.5%
16	Indiana	111,872	2.5%
17	North Carolina	106,661	2.4%
18	Virginia	98,439	2.2%
19	Tennessee	81,499	1.8%
20	Washington	77,279	1.7%
21	Minnesota	76,693	1.7%
22	Alabama	67,479	1.5%
23	Kentucky	60,590	1.3%
24	Connecticut	58,399	1.3%
25	Iowa	58,180	1.3%
26	South Carolina	47,259	1.1%
27	Colorado	45,697	1.0%
28	Mississippi	45,419	1.0%
29	Arizona	43,134	1.0%
30	Oregon	42,694	0.9%
31	Kansas	39,016	0.9%
32	Nebraska	36,163	0.8%
33	Hawaii	33,994	0.8%
34	Oklahoma	30,063	0.7%
35	Arkansas	25,164	0.6%
36	Rhode Island	22,539	0.5%
37	Delaware	21,667	0.5%
38	New Hampshire	21,264	0.5%
39	Nevada	20,396	0.5%
40	New Mexico	19,360	0.4%
41	Maine	17,011	0.4%
42	Utah	15,498	0.3%
43	West Virginia	11,890	0.3%
44	Idaho	11,262	0.3%
45	South Dakota	10,266	0.2%
46	Montana	8,561	0.2%
47	Vermont	8,323	0.2%
48	North Dakota	6,535	0.1%
49	Alaska	4,087	0.1%
50	Wyoming	1,947	0.0%
	District of Columbia	15,368	0.3%

Source: U.S. Department of Education, National Center for Education Statistics
  "Characteristics of Private Schools in the United States" (http://nces.ed.gov/pubsearch/pubsinfo.asp?pubid=2013316)
*For school year 2011-2012. Includes private schools that provide instruction for one or more grades kindergarten through 12 (or comparable ungraded levels).

Enrollment in Public Elementary and Secondary Schools in 2012

National Total = 49,521,669 Students*

ALPHA ORDER

RANK	STATE	STUDENTS	% of USA
23	Alabama	744,621	1.5%
45	Alaska	131,167	0.3%
13	Arizona	1,080,319	2.2%
34	Arkansas	483,114	1.0%
1	California	6,287,834	12.7%
20	Colorado	854,265	1.7%
30	Connecticut	554,437	1.1%
46	Delaware	128,946	0.3%
4	Florida	2,668,156	5.4%
8	Georgia	1,685,016	3.4%
42	Hawaii	182,706	0.4%
39	Idaho	279,873	0.6%
5	Illinois	2,083,097	4.2%
15	Indiana	1,040,765	2.1%
31	Iowa	495,870	1.0%
33	Kansas	486,108	1.0%
26	Kentucky	681,987	1.4%
25	Louisiana	703,390	1.4%
41	Maine	188,969	0.4%
21	Maryland	854,086	1.7%
17	Massachusetts	953,369	1.9%
9	Michigan	1,573,537	3.2%
22	Minnesota	839,738	1.7%
32	Mississippi	490,619	1.0%
18	Missouri	916,584	1.9%
44	Montana	142,349	0.3%
37	Nebraska	301,296	0.6%
35	Nevada	439,634	0.9%
40	New Hampshire	191,900	0.4%
11	New Jersey	1,356,431	2.7%
36	New Mexico	337,225	0.7%
3	New York	2,704,718	5.5%
10	North Carolina	1,507,864	3.0%
48	North Dakota	97,646	0.2%
7	Ohio	1,740,030	3.5%
27	Oklahoma	666,120	1.3%
29	Oregon	568,208	1.1%
6	Pennsylvania	1,771,395	3.6%
43	Rhode Island	142,854	0.3%
24	South Carolina	727,186	1.5%
47	South Dakota	128,016	0.3%
16	Tennessee	999,693	2.0%
2	Texas	5,000,470	10.1%
28	Utah	598,832	1.2%
50	Vermont	89,908	0.2%
12	Virginia	1,257,883	2.5%
14	Washington	1,045,453	2.1%
38	West Virginia	282,870	0.6%
19	Wisconsin	871,105	1.8%
49	Wyoming	90,099	0.2%

RANK ORDER

RANK	STATE	STUDENTS	% of USA
1	California	6,287,834	12.7%
2	Texas	5,000,470	10.1%
3	New York	2,704,718	5.5%
4	Florida	2,668,156	5.4%
5	Illinois	2,083,097	4.2%
6	Pennsylvania	1,771,395	3.6%
7	Ohio	1,740,030	3.5%
8	Georgia	1,685,016	3.4%
9	Michigan	1,573,537	3.2%
10	North Carolina	1,507,864	3.0%
11	New Jersey	1,356,431	2.7%
12	Virginia	1,257,883	2.5%
13	Arizona	1,080,319	2.2%
14	Washington	1,045,453	2.1%
15	Indiana	1,040,765	2.1%
16	Tennessee	999,693	2.0%
17	Massachusetts	953,369	1.9%
18	Missouri	916,584	1.9%
19	Wisconsin	871,105	1.8%
20	Colorado	854,265	1.7%
21	Maryland	854,086	1.7%
22	Minnesota	839,738	1.7%
23	Alabama	744,621	1.5%
24	South Carolina	727,186	1.5%
25	Louisiana	703,390	1.4%
26	Kentucky	681,987	1.4%
27	Oklahoma	666,120	1.3%
28	Utah	598,832	1.2%
29	Oregon	568,208	1.1%
30	Connecticut	554,437	1.1%
31	Iowa	495,870	1.0%
32	Mississippi	490,619	1.0%
33	Kansas	486,108	1.0%
34	Arkansas	483,114	1.0%
35	Nevada	439,634	0.9%
36	New Mexico	337,225	0.7%
37	Nebraska	301,296	0.6%
38	West Virginia	282,870	0.6%
39	Idaho	279,873	0.6%
40	New Hampshire	191,900	0.4%
41	Maine	188,969	0.4%
42	Hawaii	182,706	0.4%
43	Rhode Island	142,854	0.3%
44	Montana	142,349	0.3%
45	Alaska	131,167	0.3%
46	Delaware	128,946	0.3%
47	South Dakota	128,016	0.3%
48	North Dakota	97,646	0.2%
49	Wyoming	90,099	0.2%
50	Vermont	89,908	0.2%
	District of Columbia	73,911	0.1%

Source: U.S. Department of Education, National Center for Education Statistics
   "Selected Statistics From the Common Core of Data: School Year 2011-12" (http://nces.ed.gov/pubs2013/2013441.pdf)
*For school year 2011-2012.

Public Elementary and Secondary School Teachers in 2012

National Total = 3,103,263 Teachers*

ALPHA ORDER

RANK	STATE	TEACHERS	% of USA
24	Alabama	47,723	1.5%
49	Alaska	8,088	0.3%
21	Arizona	50,800	1.6%
31	Arkansas	33,983	1.1%
2	California	268,689	8.7%
23	Colorado	48,078	1.5%
26	Connecticut	43,805	1.4%
46	Delaware	8,587	0.3%
4	Florida	175,006	5.6%
7	Georgia	111,133	3.6%
42	Hawaii	11,458	0.4%
39	Idaho	15,990	0.5%
5	Illinois	131,777	4.2%
16	Indiana	62,339	2.0%
30	Iowa	34,658	1.1%
29	Kansas	37,407	1.2%
27	Kentucky	41,860	1.3%
22	Louisiana	48,657	1.6%
41	Maine	14,888	0.5%
17	Maryland	57,589	1.9%
13	Massachusetts	69,342	2.2%
12	Michigan	86,997	2.8%
20	Minnesota	52,832	1.7%
32	Mississippi	32,007	1.0%
15	Missouri	66,252	2.1%
44	Montana	10,153	0.3%
35	Nebraska	22,182	0.7%
37	Nevada	21,132	0.7%
40	New Hampshire	15,049	0.5%
8	New Jersey	109,719	3.5%
36	New Mexico	21,957	0.7%
3	New York	209,527	6.8%
10	North Carolina	97,308	3.1%
47	North Dakota	8,525	0.3%
9	Ohio	107,972	3.5%
28	Oklahoma	41,349	1.3%
33	Oregon	26,791	0.9%
6	Pennsylvania	124,646	4.0%
43	Rhode Island	11,414	0.4%
25	South Carolina	46,782	1.5%
45	South Dakota	9,247	0.3%
14	Tennessee	66,382	2.1%
1	Texas	324,282	10.4%
34	Utah	25,970	0.8%
48	Vermont	8,364	0.3%
11	Virginia	90,832	2.9%
19	Washington	53,119	1.7%
38	West Virginia	20,247	0.7%
18	Wisconsin	56,245	1.8%
50	Wyoming	7,847	0.3%

RANK ORDER

RANK	STATE	TEACHERS	% of USA
1	Texas	324,282	10.4%
2	California	268,689	8.7%
3	New York	209,527	6.8%
4	Florida	175,006	5.6%
5	Illinois	131,777	4.2%
6	Pennsylvania	124,646	4.0%
7	Georgia	111,133	3.6%
8	New Jersey	109,719	3.5%
9	Ohio	107,972	3.5%
10	North Carolina	97,308	3.1%
11	Virginia	90,832	2.9%
12	Michigan	86,997	2.8%
13	Massachusetts	69,342	2.2%
14	Tennessee	66,382	2.1%
15	Missouri	66,252	2.1%
16	Indiana	62,339	2.0%
17	Maryland	57,589	1.9%
18	Wisconsin	56,245	1.8%
19	Washington	53,119	1.7%
20	Minnesota	52,832	1.7%
21	Arizona	50,800	1.6%
22	Louisiana	48,657	1.6%
23	Colorado	48,078	1.5%
24	Alabama	47,723	1.5%
25	South Carolina	46,782	1.5%
26	Connecticut	43,805	1.4%
27	Kentucky	41,860	1.3%
28	Oklahoma	41,349	1.3%
29	Kansas	37,407	1.2%
30	Iowa	34,658	1.1%
31	Arkansas	33,983	1.1%
32	Mississippi	32,007	1.0%
33	Oregon	26,791	0.9%
34	Utah	25,970	0.8%
35	Nebraska	22,182	0.7%
36	New Mexico	21,957	0.7%
37	Nevada	21,132	0.7%
38	West Virginia	20,247	0.7%
39	Idaho	15,990	0.5%
40	New Hampshire	15,049	0.5%
41	Maine	14,888	0.5%
42	Hawaii	11,458	0.4%
43	Rhode Island	11,414	0.4%
44	Montana	10,153	0.3%
45	South Dakota	9,247	0.3%
46	Delaware	8,587	0.3%
47	North Dakota	8,525	0.3%
48	Vermont	8,364	0.3%
49	Alaska	8,088	0.3%
50	Wyoming	7,847	0.3%
	District of Columbia	6,278	0.2%

Source: U.S. Department of Education, National Center for Education Statistics
"Selected Statistics From the Common Core of Data: School Year 2011-12" (http://nces.ed.gov/pubs2013/2013441.pdf)
*For school year 2011-2012. Counts are full-time equivalent figures.

Pupil-Teacher Ratio in Public Elementary and Secondary Schools in 2012

National Ratio = 16.0 Pupils Per Teacher*

ALPHA ORDER

RANK	STATE	RATIO
18	Alabama	15.6
12	Alaska	16.2
3	Arizona	21.3
32	Arkansas	14.2
1	California	23.4
8	Colorado	17.8
44	Connecticut	12.7
28	Delaware	15.0
25	Florida	15.2
25	Georgia	15.2
15	Hawaii	15.9
9	Idaho	17.5
17	Illinois	15.8
10	Indiana	16.7
31	Iowa	14.3
41	Kansas	13.0
11	Kentucky	16.3
30	Louisiana	14.5
44	Maine	12.7
29	Maryland	14.8
39	Massachusetts	13.7
7	Michigan	18.1
15	Minnesota	15.9
24	Mississippi	15.3
36	Missouri	13.8
34	Montana	14.0
40	Nebraska	13.6
5	Nevada	20.8
43	New Hampshire	12.8
47	New Jersey	12.4
22	New Mexico	15.4
42	New York	12.9
19	North Carolina	15.5
48	North Dakota	11.5
13	Ohio	16.1
13	Oklahoma	16.1
4	Oregon	21.2
32	Pennsylvania	14.2
46	Rhode Island	12.5
19	South Carolina	15.5
36	South Dakota	13.8
27	Tennessee	15.1
22	Texas	15.4
2	Utah	23.1
50	Vermont	10.7
36	Virginia	13.8
6	Washington	19.7
34	West Virginia	14.0
19	Wisconsin	15.5
48	Wyoming	11.5

RANK ORDER

RANK	STATE	RATIO
1	California	23.4
2	Utah	23.1
3	Arizona	21.3
4	Oregon	21.2
5	Nevada	20.8
6	Washington	19.7
7	Michigan	18.1
8	Colorado	17.8
9	Idaho	17.5
10	Indiana	16.7
11	Kentucky	16.3
12	Alaska	16.2
13	Ohio	16.1
13	Oklahoma	16.1
15	Hawaii	15.9
15	Minnesota	15.9
17	Illinois	15.8
18	Alabama	15.6
19	North Carolina	15.5
19	South Carolina	15.5
19	Wisconsin	15.5
22	New Mexico	15.4
22	Texas	15.4
24	Mississippi	15.3
25	Florida	15.2
25	Georgia	15.2
27	Tennessee	15.1
28	Delaware	15.0
29	Maryland	14.8
30	Louisiana	14.5
31	Iowa	14.3
32	Arkansas	14.2
32	Pennsylvania	14.2
34	Montana	14.0
34	West Virginia	14.0
36	Missouri	13.8
36	South Dakota	13.8
36	Virginia	13.8
39	Massachusetts	13.7
40	Nebraska	13.6
41	Kansas	13.0
42	New York	12.9
43	New Hampshire	12.8
44	Connecticut	12.7
44	Maine	12.7
46	Rhode Island	12.5
47	New Jersey	12.4
48	North Dakota	11.5
48	Wyoming	11.5
50	Vermont	10.7
	District of Columbia	11.8

Source: U.S. Department of Education, National Center for Education Statistics
  "Selected Statistics From the Common Core of Data: School Year 2011-12" (http://nces.ed.gov/pubs2013/2013441.pdf)
*For school year 2011-2012. Based on full-time equivalency counts of teachers.

Estimated Average Salary of Public School Teachers in 2013
(National Education Association)
National Average = $56,383*

ALPHA ORDER

RANK	STATE	SALARY
38	Alabama	$47,949
6	Alaska	65,468
29	Arizona	49,885
44	Arkansas	46,632
4	California	69,324
31	Colorado	49,844
3	Connecticut	69,766
11	Delaware	59,679
43	Florida	46,944
22	Georgia	52,880
20	Hawaii	54,300
32	Idaho	49,734
12	Illinois	59,113
25	Indiana	51,456
24	Iowa	51,528
41	Kansas	47,464
27	Kentucky	50,326
26	Louisiana	51,381
36	Maine	48,119
7	Maryland	65,265
2	Massachusetts	73,129
10	Michigan	61,560
16	Minnesota	56,268
49	Mississippi	41,994
40	Missouri	47,517
28	Montana	49,999
34	Nebraska	48,931
17	Nevada	55,957
18	New Hampshire	55,599
5	New Jersey	68,797
45	New Mexico	46,573
1	New York	75,279
47	North Carolina	45,947
42	North Dakota	47,344
14	Ohio	58,092
48	Oklahoma	44,128
13	Oregon	58,758
8	Pennsylvania	63,521
9	Rhode Island	63,474
39	South Carolina	47,924
50	South Dakota	39,580
35	Tennessee	48,289
37	Texas	48,110
33	Utah	49,393
23	Vermont	52,526
30	Virginia	49,869
21	Washington	53,571
46	West Virginia	46,405
19	Wisconsin	55,171
15	Wyoming	57,920

RANK ORDER

RANK	STATE	SALARY
1	New York	$75,279
2	Massachusetts	73,129
3	Connecticut	69,766
4	California	69,324
5	New Jersey	68,797
6	Alaska	65,468
7	Maryland	65,265
8	Pennsylvania	63,521
9	Rhode Island	63,474
10	Michigan	61,560
11	Delaware	59,679
12	Illinois	59,113
13	Oregon	58,758
14	Ohio	58,092
15	Wyoming	57,920
16	Minnesota	56,268
17	Nevada	55,957
18	New Hampshire	55,599
19	Wisconsin	55,171
20	Hawaii	54,300
21	Washington	53,571
22	Georgia	52,880
23	Vermont	52,526
24	Iowa	51,528
25	Indiana	51,456
26	Louisiana	51,381
27	Kentucky	50,326
28	Montana	49,999
29	Arizona	49,885
30	Virginia	49,869
31	Colorado	49,844
32	Idaho	49,734
33	Utah	49,393
34	Nebraska	48,931
35	Tennessee	48,289
36	Maine	48,119
37	Texas	48,110
38	Alabama	47,949
39	South Carolina	47,924
40	Missouri	47,517
41	Kansas	47,464
42	North Dakota	47,344
43	Florida	46,944
44	Arkansas	46,632
45	New Mexico	46,573
46	West Virginia	46,405
47	North Carolina	45,947
48	Oklahoma	44,128
49	Mississippi	41,994
50	South Dakota	39,580

| | District of Columbia | 70,906 |

Source: National Education Association, Washington, D.C.
"Rankings and Estimates" (Copyright © 2012, NEA, used with permission, http://www.nea.org/home/54597.htm)
*Estimates for school year 2012-2013 for classroom teachers.

Average Teacher's Salary as a Percent of Average Annual Pay in 2012

National Average = 113.4% of Average Annual Pay*

ALPHA ORDER				RANK ORDER		
RANK	STATE	PERCENT		RANK	STATE	PERCENT
33	Alabama	114.3		1	Idaho	135.9
12	Alaska	126.3		2	Rhode Island	134.5
41	Arizona	108.1		3	Montana	132.8
19	Arkansas	121.6		4	Michigan	131.8
20	California	121.4		5	Oregon	131.2
48	Colorado	97.8		6	Wisconsin	129.8
37	Connecticut	112.1		7	Ohio	129.7
30	Delaware	114.5		8	Pennsylvania	129.6
41	Florida	108.1		9	Wyoming	129.1
32	Georgia	114.4		10	Vermont	126.7
14	Hawaii	124.9		11	Nevada	126.5
1	Idaho	135.9		12	Alaska	126.3
38	Illinois	111.8		13	Iowa	126.1
16	Indiana	123.6		14	Hawaii	124.9
13	Iowa	126.1		15	Kentucky	123.7
30	Kansas	114.5		16	Indiana	123.6
15	Kentucky	123.7		16	Maine	123.6
26	Louisiana	117.3		16	Nebraska	123.6
16	Maine	123.6		19	Arkansas	121.6
22	Maryland	119.3		20	California	121.4
23	Massachusetts	118.9		20	South Carolina	121.4
4	Michigan	131.8		22	Maryland	119.3
36	Minnesota	112.7		23	Massachusetts	118.9
27	Mississippi	116.6		24	New York	118.6
39	Missouri	110.0		25	Utah	118.1
3	Montana	132.8		26	Louisiana	117.3
16	Nebraska	123.6		27	Mississippi	116.6
11	Nevada	126.5		28	New Jersey	115.8
34	New Hampshire	113.7		29	West Virginia	115.4
28	New Jersey	115.8		30	Delaware	114.5
35	New Mexico	113.3		30	Kansas	114.5
24	New York	118.6		32	Georgia	114.4
44	North Carolina	106.6		33	Alabama	114.3
47	North Dakota	101.7		34	New Hampshire	113.7
7	Ohio	129.7		35	New Mexico	113.3
45	Oklahoma	106.3		36	Minnesota	112.7
5	Oregon	131.2		37	Connecticut	112.1
8	Pennsylvania	129.6		38	Illinois	111.8
2	Rhode Island	134.5		39	Missouri	110.0
20	South Carolina	121.4		40	Tennessee	108.5
43	South Dakota	107.3		41	Arizona	108.1
40	Tennessee	108.5		41	Florida	108.1
49	Texas	95.4		43	South Dakota	107.3
25	Utah	118.1		44	North Carolina	106.6
10	Vermont	126.7		45	Oklahoma	106.3
49	Virginia	95.4		46	Washington	101.8
46	Washington	101.8		47	North Dakota	101.7
29	West Virginia	115.4		48	Colorado	97.8
6	Wisconsin	129.8		49	Texas	95.4
9	Wyoming	129.1		49	Virginia	95.4
					District of Columbia	84.3

Source: CQ Press using data from National Education Association, Washington, D.C.
"Rankings and Estimates" (Copyright © 2012, NEA, used with permission, http://www.nea.org/home/54597.htm)
"Quarterly Census of Employment and Wages" (http://www.bls.gov/cew/home.htm)
*Average of public elementary and secondary teacher salary for school years 2011-2012 and 2012-2013 compared to each state's 2012 average annual pay for all workers covered by federal unemployment.

Percent of Public School Fourth Graders
Proficient or Better in Reading in 2013
National Percent = 34%*

RANK	STATE	PERCENT
37	Alabama	31
44	Alaska	27
41	Arizona	28
35	Arkansas	32
44	California	27
8	Colorado	41
4	Connecticut	43
13	Delaware	38
12	Florida	39
29	Georgia	34
39	Hawaii	30
33	Idaho	33
29	Illinois	34
13	Indiana	38
13	Iowa	38
13	Kansas	38
24	Kentucky	36
48	Louisiana	23
18	Maine	37
2	Maryland	45
1	Massachusetts	47
37	Michigan	31
8	Minnesota	41
49	Mississippi	21
25	Missouri	35
25	Montana	35
18	Nebraska	37
44	Nevada	27
2	New Hampshire	45
6	New Jersey	42
49	New Mexico	21
18	New York	37
25	North Carolina	35
29	North Dakota	34
18	Ohio	37
39	Oklahoma	30
33	Oregon	33
10	Pennsylvania	40
13	Rhode Island	38
41	South Carolina	28
35	South Dakota	32
29	Tennessee	34
41	Texas	28
18	Utah	37
6	Vermont	42
4	Virginia	43
10	Washington	40
44	West Virginia	27
25	Wisconsin	35
18	Wyoming	37

RANK	STATE	PERCENT
1	Massachusetts	47
2	Maryland	45
2	New Hampshire	45
4	Connecticut	43
4	Virginia	43
6	New Jersey	42
6	Vermont	42
8	Colorado	41
8	Minnesota	41
10	Pennsylvania	40
10	Washington	40
12	Florida	39
13	Delaware	38
13	Indiana	38
13	Iowa	38
13	Kansas	38
13	Rhode Island	38
18	Maine	37
18	Nebraska	37
18	New York	37
18	Ohio	37
18	Utah	37
18	Wyoming	37
24	Kentucky	36
25	Missouri	35
25	Montana	35
25	North Carolina	35
25	Wisconsin	35
29	Georgia	34
29	Illinois	34
29	North Dakota	34
29	Tennessee	34
33	Idaho	33
33	Oregon	33
35	Arkansas	32
35	South Dakota	32
37	Alabama	31
37	Michigan	31
39	Hawaii	30
39	Oklahoma	30
41	Arizona	28
41	South Carolina	28
41	Texas	28
44	Alaska	27
44	California	27
44	Nevada	27
44	West Virginia	27
48	Louisiana	23
49	Mississippi	21
49	New Mexico	21
	District of Columbia	23

Source: U.S. Department of Education, National Center for Education Statistics
  "The Nation's Report Card: Reading 2013" (http://nces.ed.gov/nationsreportcard/)
*There are four achievement levels: Below Basic, Basic, Proficient, and Advanced. Proficient represents solid academic mastery for 4th graders. Students reaching this level have demonstrated competency over challenging subject matter, including subject matter knowledge, application of such knowledge to real-world situations, and analytical skills appropriate to the subject matter.

Percent of Public School Eighth Graders
Proficient or Better in Reading in 2013
National Percent = 34%*

RANK	STATE	PERCENT
46	Alabama	25
37	Alaska	31
44	Arizona	28
39	Arkansas	30
41	California	29
10	Colorado	40
3	Connecticut	45
31	Delaware	33
31	Florida	33
36	Georgia	32
44	Hawaii	28
14	Idaho	38
21	Illinois	36
28	Indiana	35
18	Iowa	37
21	Kansas	36
14	Kentucky	38
48	Louisiana	24
14	Maine	38
6	Maryland	42
1	Massachusetts	48
31	Michigan	33
9	Minnesota	41
50	Mississippi	20
21	Missouri	36
10	Montana	40
18	Nebraska	37
39	Nevada	30
5	New Hampshire	44
2	New Jersey	46
49	New Mexico	22
28	New York	35
31	North Carolina	33
30	North Dakota	34
12	Ohio	39
41	Oklahoma	29
18	Oregon	37
6	Pennsylvania	42
21	Rhode Island	36
41	South Carolina	29
21	South Dakota	36
31	Tennessee	33
37	Texas	31
12	Utah	39
3	Vermont	45
21	Virginia	36
6	Washington	42
46	West Virginia	25
21	Wisconsin	36
14	Wyoming	38

RANK	STATE	PERCENT
1	Massachusetts	48
2	New Jersey	46
3	Connecticut	45
3	Vermont	45
5	New Hampshire	44
6	Maryland	42
6	Pennsylvania	42
6	Washington	42
9	Minnesota	41
10	Colorado	40
10	Montana	40
12	Ohio	39
12	Utah	39
14	Idaho	38
14	Kentucky	38
14	Maine	38
14	Wyoming	38
18	Iowa	37
18	Nebraska	37
18	Oregon	37
21	Illinois	36
21	Kansas	36
21	Missouri	36
21	Rhode Island	36
21	South Dakota	36
21	Virginia	36
21	Wisconsin	36
28	Indiana	35
28	New York	35
30	North Dakota	34
31	Delaware	33
31	Florida	33
31	Michigan	33
31	North Carolina	33
31	Tennessee	33
36	Georgia	32
37	Alaska	31
37	Texas	31
39	Arkansas	30
39	Nevada	30
41	California	29
41	Oklahoma	29
41	South Carolina	29
44	Arizona	28
44	Hawaii	28
46	Alabama	25
46	West Virginia	25
48	Louisiana	24
49	New Mexico	22
50	Mississippi	20
	District of Columbia	17

Source: U.S. Department of Education, National Center for Education Statistics
   "The Nation's Report Card: Reading 2013" (http://nces.ed.gov/nationsreportcard/)
*There are four achievement levels: Below Basic, Basic, Proficient, and Advanced. Proficient represents solid academic mastery for 8th graders. Students reaching this level have demonstrated competency over challenging subject matter, including subject matter knowledge, application of such knowledge to real-world situations, and analytical skills appropriate to the subject matter.

Percent of Public School Fourth Graders Proficient or Better in Mathematics in 2013
National Percent = 41%*

RANK	STATE	PERCENT
48	Alabama	30
40	Alaska	37
30	Arizona	40
36	Arkansas	39
46	California	33
6	Colorado	50
19	Connecticut	45
25	Delaware	42
27	Florida	41
36	Georgia	39
18	Hawaii	46
30	Idaho	40
36	Illinois	39
4	Indiana	52
8	Iowa	48
8	Kansas	48
27	Kentucky	41
49	Louisiana	26
14	Maine	47
14	Maryland	47
3	Massachusetts	58
40	Michigan	37
1	Minnesota	59
49	Mississippi	26
36	Missouri	39
19	Montana	45
19	Nebraska	45
45	Nevada	34
1	New Hampshire	59
7	New Jersey	49
47	New Mexico	31
30	New York	40
19	North Carolina	45
8	North Dakota	48
8	Ohio	48
42	Oklahoma	36
30	Oregon	40
23	Pennsylvania	44
25	Rhode Island	42
43	South Carolina	35
30	South Dakota	40
30	Tennessee	40
27	Texas	41
23	Utah	44
4	Vermont	52
14	Virginia	47
8	Washington	48
43	West Virginia	35
14	Wisconsin	47
8	Wyoming	48

RANK	STATE	PERCENT
1	Minnesota	59
1	New Hampshire	59
3	Massachusetts	58
4	Indiana	52
4	Vermont	52
6	Colorado	50
7	New Jersey	49
8	Iowa	48
8	Kansas	48
8	North Dakota	48
8	Ohio	48
8	Washington	48
8	Wyoming	48
14	Maine	47
14	Maryland	47
14	Virginia	47
14	Wisconsin	47
18	Hawaii	46
19	Connecticut	45
19	Montana	45
19	Nebraska	45
19	North Carolina	45
23	Pennsylvania	44
23	Utah	44
25	Delaware	42
25	Rhode Island	42
27	Florida	41
27	Kentucky	41
27	Texas	41
30	Arizona	40
30	Idaho	40
30	New York	40
30	Oregon	40
30	South Dakota	40
30	Tennessee	40
36	Arkansas	39
36	Georgia	39
36	Illinois	39
36	Missouri	39
40	Alaska	37
40	Michigan	37
42	Oklahoma	36
43	South Carolina	35
43	West Virginia	35
45	Nevada	34
46	California	33
47	New Mexico	31
48	Alabama	30
49	Louisiana	26
49	Mississippi	26
	District of Columbia	28

Source: U.S. Department of Education, National Center for Education Statistics
"The Nation's Report Card: Mathematics 2013" (http://nces.ed.gov/nationsreportcard/)
*There are four achievement levels: Below Basic, Basic, Proficient, and Advanced. Proficient represents solid academic mastery for 4th graders. Students reaching this level have demonstrated competency over challenging subject matter, including subject matter knowledge, application of such knowledge to real-world situations, and analytical skills appropriate to the subject matter.

Percent of Public School Eighth Graders Proficient or Better in Mathematics in 2013
National Percent = 34%*

ALPHA ORDER

RANK	STATE	PERCENT
50	Alabama	20
30	Alaska	33
35	Arizona	31
41	Arkansas	28
41	California	28
6	Colorado	42
20	Connecticut	37
30	Delaware	33
35	Florida	31
40	Georgia	29
33	Hawaii	32
22	Idaho	36
22	Illinois	36
15	Indiana	38
22	Iowa	36
10	Kansas	40
38	Kentucky	30
48	Louisiana	21
10	Maine	40
20	Maryland	37
1	Massachusetts	55
38	Michigan	30
3	Minnesota	47
48	Mississippi	21
30	Missouri	33
10	Montana	40
22	Nebraska	36
41	Nevada	28
3	New Hampshire	47
2	New Jersey	49
47	New Mexico	23
33	New York	32
22	North Carolina	36
9	North Dakota	41
10	Ohio	40
45	Oklahoma	25
29	Oregon	34
6	Pennsylvania	42
22	Rhode Island	36
35	South Carolina	31
15	South Dakota	38
41	Tennessee	28
15	Texas	38
22	Utah	36
3	Vermont	47
15	Virginia	38
6	Washington	42
46	West Virginia	24
10	Wisconsin	40
15	Wyoming	38

RANK ORDER

RANK	STATE	PERCENT
1	Massachusetts	55
2	New Jersey	49
3	Minnesota	47
3	New Hampshire	47
3	Vermont	47
6	Colorado	42
6	Pennsylvania	42
6	Washington	42
9	North Dakota	41
10	Kansas	40
10	Maine	40
10	Montana	40
10	Ohio	40
10	Wisconsin	40
15	Indiana	38
15	South Dakota	38
15	Texas	38
15	Virginia	38
15	Wyoming	38
20	Connecticut	37
20	Maryland	37
22	Idaho	36
22	Illinois	36
22	Iowa	36
22	Nebraska	36
22	North Carolina	36
22	Rhode Island	36
22	Utah	36
29	Oregon	34
30	Alaska	33
30	Delaware	33
30	Missouri	33
33	Hawaii	32
33	New York	32
35	Arizona	31
35	Florida	31
35	South Carolina	31
38	Kentucky	30
38	Michigan	30
40	Georgia	29
41	Arkansas	28
41	California	28
41	Nevada	28
41	Tennessee	28
45	Oklahoma	25
46	West Virginia	24
47	New Mexico	23
48	Louisiana	21
48	Mississippi	21
50	Alabama	20
	District of Columbia	19

Source: U.S. Department of Education, National Center for Education Statistics
"The Nation's Report Card: Mathematics 2013" (http://nces.ed.gov/nationsreportcard/)
*There are four achievement levels: Below Basic, Basic, Proficient, and Advanced. Proficient represents solid academic mastery for 8th graders. Students reaching this level have demonstrated competency over challenging subject matter, including subject matter knowledge, application of such knowledge to real-world situations, and analytical skills appropriate to the subject matter.

Percent of Population Graduated from High School in 2012

National Percent = 86.4%*

RANK	STATE	PERCENT
45	Alabama	84.0
3	Alaska	92.0
35	Arizona	85.7
42	Arkansas	84.8
49	California	81.5
12	Colorado	90.6
18	Connecticut	89.9
26	Delaware	88.5
33	Florida	86.5
39	Georgia	85.0
15	Hawaii	90.4
20	Idaho	89.8
30	Illinois	87.6
30	Indiana	87.6
8	Iowa	91.6
17	Kansas	90.2
46	Kentucky	83.8
47	Louisiana	83.0
8	Maine	91.6
23	Maryland	89.1
21	Massachusetts	89.7
22	Michigan	89.2
2	Minnesota	92.5
48	Mississippi	82.3
28	Missouri	88.0
1	Montana	92.8
13	Nebraska	90.5
40	Nevada	84.9
4	New Hampshire	91.8
27	New Jersey	88.3
44	New Mexico	84.4
36	New York	85.3
37	North Carolina	85.2
5	North Dakota	91.7
25	Ohio	88.8
32	Oklahoma	86.7
18	Oregon	89.9
24	Pennsylvania	88.9
34	Rhode Island	86.1
40	South Carolina	84.9
13	South Dakota	90.5
38	Tennessee	85.1
50	Texas	81.4
10	Utah	91.0
5	Vermont	91.7
29	Virginia	87.9
15	Washington	90.4
43	West Virginia	84.5
11	Wisconsin	90.7
5	Wyoming	91.7

RANK	STATE	PERCENT
1	Montana	92.8
2	Minnesota	92.5
3	Alaska	92.0
4	New Hampshire	91.8
5	North Dakota	91.7
5	Vermont	91.7
5	Wyoming	91.7
8	Iowa	91.6
8	Maine	91.6
10	Utah	91.0
11	Wisconsin	90.7
12	Colorado	90.6
13	Nebraska	90.5
13	South Dakota	90.5
15	Hawaii	90.4
15	Washington	90.4
17	Kansas	90.2
18	Connecticut	89.9
18	Oregon	89.9
20	Idaho	89.8
21	Massachusetts	89.7
22	Michigan	89.2
23	Maryland	89.1
24	Pennsylvania	88.9
25	Ohio	88.8
26	Delaware	88.5
27	New Jersey	88.3
28	Missouri	88.0
29	Virginia	87.9
30	Illinois	87.6
30	Indiana	87.6
32	Oklahoma	86.7
33	Florida	86.5
34	Rhode Island	86.1
35	Arizona	85.7
36	New York	85.3
37	North Carolina	85.2
38	Tennessee	85.1
39	Georgia	85.0
40	Nevada	84.9
40	South Carolina	84.9
42	Arkansas	84.8
43	West Virginia	84.5
44	New Mexico	84.4
45	Alabama	84.0
46	Kentucky	83.8
47	Louisiana	83.0
48	Mississippi	82.3
49	California	81.5
50	Texas	81.4
	District of Columbia	88.6

Source: U.S. Bureau of the Census
    "2012 American Community Survey-Table R1501" (http://www.census.gov/acs/www/index.html)
*Persons age 25 and older. Includes equivalency status.

Public High School Graduates in 2010

National Total = 3,128,022 Graduates*

RANK	STATE	GRADUATES	% of USA
23	Alabama	43,166	1.4%
45	Alaska	8,245	0.3%
19	Arizona	61,145	2.0%
33	Arkansas	28,276	0.9%
1	California	404,987	12.9%
22	Colorado	49,321	1.6%
29	Connecticut	34,495	1.1%
47	Delaware	8,133	0.3%
4	Florida	156,130	5.0%
10	Georgia	91,561	2.9%
42	Hawaii	10,998	0.4%
38	Idaho	17,793	0.6%
5	Illinois	139,035	4.4%
15	Indiana	64,551	2.1%
30	Iowa	34,462	1.1%
31	Kansas	31,642	1.0%
24	Kentucky	42,664	1.4%
27	Louisiana	36,573	1.2%
41	Maine	14,069	0.4%
21	Maryland	59,078	1.9%
16	Massachusetts	64,462	2.1%
8	Michigan	110,682	3.5%
20	Minnesota	59,667	1.9%
34	Mississippi	25,478	0.8%
17	Missouri	63,994	2.0%
43	Montana	10,075	0.3%
36	Nebraska	19,370	0.6%
35	Nevada	20,956	0.7%
40	New Hampshire	15,034	0.5%
9	New Jersey	96,225	3.1%
37	New Mexico	18,595	0.6%
3	New York	183,826	5.9%
11	North Carolina	88,704	2.8%
49	North Dakota	7,155	0.2%
7	Ohio	123,437	3.9%
26	Oklahoma	38,503	1.2%
28	Oregon	34,671	1.1%
6	Pennsylvania	131,182	4.2%
44	Rhode Island	9,908	0.3%
25	South Carolina	40,438	1.3%
46	South Dakota	8,162	0.3%
18	Tennessee	62,408	2.0%
2	Texas	280,894	9.0%
32	Utah	31,481	1.0%
48	Vermont	7,199	0.2%
12	Virginia	81,511	2.6%
13	Washington	66,046	2.1%
39	West Virginia	17,651	0.6%
14	Wisconsin	64,687	2.1%
50	Wyoming	5,695	0.2%

RANK	STATE	GRADUATES	% of USA
1	California	404,987	12.9%
2	Texas	280,894	9.0%
3	New York	183,826	5.9%
4	Florida	156,130	5.0%
5	Illinois	139,035	4.4%
6	Pennsylvania	131,182	4.2%
7	Ohio	123,437	3.9%
8	Michigan	110,682	3.5%
9	New Jersey	96,225	3.1%
10	Georgia	91,561	2.9%
11	North Carolina	88,704	2.8%
12	Virginia	81,511	2.6%
13	Washington	66,046	2.1%
14	Wisconsin	64,687	2.1%
15	Indiana	64,551	2.1%
16	Massachusetts	64,462	2.1%
17	Missouri	63,994	2.0%
18	Tennessee	62,408	2.0%
19	Arizona	61,145	2.0%
20	Minnesota	59,667	1.9%
21	Maryland	59,078	1.9%
22	Colorado	49,321	1.6%
23	Alabama	43,166	1.4%
24	Kentucky	42,664	1.4%
25	South Carolina	40,438	1.3%
26	Oklahoma	38,503	1.2%
27	Louisiana	36,573	1.2%
28	Oregon	34,671	1.1%
29	Connecticut	34,495	1.1%
30	Iowa	34,462	1.1%
31	Kansas	31,642	1.0%
32	Utah	31,481	1.0%
33	Arkansas	28,276	0.9%
34	Mississippi	25,478	0.8%
35	Nevada	20,956	0.7%
36	Nebraska	19,370	0.6%
37	New Mexico	18,595	0.6%
38	Idaho	17,793	0.6%
39	West Virginia	17,651	0.6%
40	New Hampshire	15,034	0.5%
41	Maine	14,069	0.4%
42	Hawaii	10,998	0.4%
43	Montana	10,075	0.3%
44	Rhode Island	9,908	0.3%
45	Alaska	8,245	0.3%
46	South Dakota	8,162	0.3%
47	Delaware	8,133	0.3%
48	Vermont	7,199	0.2%
49	North Dakota	7,155	0.2%
50	Wyoming	5,695	0.2%
	District of Columbia	3,602	0.1%

Source: U.S. Department of Education, National Center for Education Statistics
    "Public School Graduates and Dropouts from the Common Core of Data: School Year 2009-10" (NCES 2013309)
    (http://nces.ed.gov/pubsearch/pubsinfo.asp?pubid=2013309)
*Diploma recipients for school year 2009-2010. Excludes persons receiving high school equivalency certificates.

Averaged Freshman Graduation Rate for Public High Schools in 2010

National Average = 78.2%*

ALPHA ORDER

RANK	STATE	PERCENT
43	Alabama	71.8
37	Alaska	75.5
42	Arizona	74.7
41	Arkansas	75.0
29	California	78.2
24	Colorado	79.8
40	Connecticut	75.1
37	Delaware	75.5
44	Florida	70.8
45	Georgia	69.9
39	Hawaii	75.4
10	Idaho	84.0
16	Illinois	81.9
30	Indiana	77.2
5	Iowa	87.9
8	Kansas	84.5
23	Kentucky	79.9
46	Louisiana	68.8
13	Maine	82.8
15	Maryland	82.2
14	Massachusetts	82.6
36	Michigan	75.9
4	Minnesota	88.2
49	Mississippi	63.8
12	Missouri	83.7
16	Montana	81.9
11	Nebraska	83.8
50	Nevada	57.8
7	New Hampshire	86.3
6	New Jersey	87.2
48	New Mexico	67.3
35	New York	76.0
32	North Carolina	76.9
3	North Dakota	88.4
19	Ohio	81.4
27	Oklahoma	78.5
34	Oregon	76.3
9	Pennsylvania	84.1
33	Rhode Island	76.4
47	South Carolina	68.2
18	South Dakota	81.8
21	Tennessee	80.4
25	Texas	78.9
26	Utah	78.6
1	Vermont	91.4
20	Virginia	81.2
30	Washington	77.2
28	West Virginia	78.3
2	Wisconsin	91.1
22	Wyoming	80.3

RANK ORDER

RANK	STATE	PERCENT
1	Vermont	91.4
2	Wisconsin	91.1
3	North Dakota	88.4
4	Minnesota	88.2
5	Iowa	87.9
6	New Jersey	87.2
7	New Hampshire	86.3
8	Kansas	84.5
9	Pennsylvania	84.1
10	Idaho	84.0
11	Nebraska	83.8
12	Missouri	83.7
13	Maine	82.8
14	Massachusetts	82.6
15	Maryland	82.2
16	Illinois	81.9
16	Montana	81.9
18	South Dakota	81.8
19	Ohio	81.4
20	Virginia	81.2
21	Tennessee	80.4
22	Wyoming	80.3
23	Kentucky	79.9
24	Colorado	79.8
25	Texas	78.9
26	Utah	78.6
27	Oklahoma	78.5
28	West Virginia	78.3
29	California	78.2
30	Indiana	77.2
30	Washington	77.2
32	North Carolina	76.9
33	Rhode Island	76.4
34	Oregon	76.3
35	New York	76.0
36	Michigan	75.9
37	Alaska	75.5
37	Delaware	75.5
39	Hawaii	75.4
40	Connecticut	75.1
41	Arkansas	75.0
42	Arizona	74.7
43	Alabama	71.8
44	Florida	70.8
45	Georgia	69.9
46	Louisiana	68.8
47	South Carolina	68.2
48	New Mexico	67.3
49	Mississippi	63.8
50	Nevada	57.8

District of Columbia	59.9

Source: U.S. Department of Education, National Center for Education Statistics
"Public School Graduates and Dropouts from the Common Core of Data: School Year 2009-10" (NCES 2013309)
(http://nces.ed.gov/pubsearch/pubsinfo.asp?pubid=2013309)

*This rate is an estimate of the percentage of an entering freshman class graduating in 4 years. For 2009-10, it equals the total number of diploma recipients in 2009-10 divided by the average membership of the 8th-grade class in 2005-06, the 9th-grade class in 2006-07, and the 10th-grade class in 2007-08.

Public High School Dropout Rate in 2010

National Rate = 3.4%*

ALPHA ORDER

RANK	STATE	RATE
45	Alabama	1.8
3	Alaska	6.9
1	Arizona	7.8
21	Arkansas	3.6
10	California	4.6
6	Colorado	5.3
27	Connecticut	3.0
19	Delaware	3.9
38	Florida	2.3
20	Georgia	3.8
7	Hawaii	5.2
49	Idaho	1.4
29	Illinois	2.9
46	Indiana	1.6
24	Iowa	3.4
42	Kansas	2.1
26	Kentucky	3.2
8	Louisiana	4.8
15	Maine	4.2
31	Maryland	2.7
30	Massachusetts	2.8
13	Michigan	4.3
46	Minnesota	1.6
2	Mississippi	7.4
23	Missouri	3.5
13	Montana	4.3
39	Nebraska	2.2
12	Nevada	4.5
50	New Hampshire	1.2
46	New Jersey	1.6
3	New Mexico	6.9
21	New York	3.6
9	North Carolina	4.7
39	North Dakota	2.2
15	Ohio	4.2
36	Oklahoma	2.4
24	Oregon	3.4
42	Pennsylvania	2.1
10	Rhode Island	4.6
27	South Carolina	3.0
34	South Dakota	2.6
31	Tennessee	2.7
31	Texas	2.7
34	Utah	2.6
36	Vermont	2.4
42	Virginia	2.1
15	Washington	4.2
18	West Virginia	4.0
39	Wisconsin	2.2
5	Wyoming	6.0

RANK ORDER

RANK	STATE	RATE
1	Arizona	7.8
2	Mississippi	7.4
3	Alaska	6.9
3	New Mexico	6.9
5	Wyoming	6.0
6	Colorado	5.3
7	Hawaii	5.2
8	Louisiana	4.8
9	North Carolina	4.7
10	California	4.6
10	Rhode Island	4.6
12	Nevada	4.5
13	Michigan	4.3
13	Montana	4.3
15	Maine	4.2
15	Ohio	4.2
15	Washington	4.2
18	West Virginia	4.0
19	Delaware	3.9
20	Georgia	3.8
21	Arkansas	3.6
21	New York	3.6
23	Missouri	3.5
24	Iowa	3.4
24	Oregon	3.4
26	Kentucky	3.2
27	Connecticut	3.0
27	South Carolina	3.0
29	Illinois	2.9
30	Massachusetts	2.8
31	Maryland	2.7
31	Tennessee	2.7
31	Texas	2.7
34	South Dakota	2.6
34	Utah	2.6
36	Oklahoma	2.4
36	Vermont	2.4
38	Florida	2.3
39	Nebraska	2.2
39	North Dakota	2.2
39	Wisconsin	2.2
42	Kansas	2.1
42	Pennsylvania	2.1
42	Virginia	2.1
45	Alabama	1.8
46	Indiana	1.6
46	Minnesota	1.6
46	New Jersey	1.6
49	Idaho	1.4
50	New Hampshire	1.2

District of Columbia   7.0

Source: U.S. Department of Education, National Center for Education Statistics
"Public School Graduates and Dropouts from the Common Core of Data: School Year 2009-10" (NCES 2013309)
(http://nces.ed.gov/pubsearch/pubsinfo.asp?pubid=2013309)
*"Event" dropout rates showing the number of 9th-12th grade dropouts divided by the number of students enrolled at the beginning of the school year in those grades.

ACT Average Composite Score in 2013

National Average = 20.9*

ALPHA ORDER

RANK	STATE	AVERAGE SCORE
36	Alabama	20.4
28	Alaska	21.1
44	Arizona	19.6
39	Arkansas	20.2
15	California	22.2
36	Colorado	20.4
2	Connecticut	24.0
9	Delaware	22.9
44	Florida	19.6
31	Georgia	20.7
40	Hawaii	20.1
16	Idaho	22.1
33	Illinois	20.6
22	Indiana	21.7
16	Iowa	22.1
20	Kansas	21.8
44	Kentucky	19.6
47	Louisiana	19.5
4	Maine	23.5
14	Maryland	22.3
1	Massachusetts	24.1
41	Michigan	19.9
6	Minnesota	23.0
49	Mississippi	18.9
23	Missouri	21.6
26	Montana	21.3
24	Nebraska	21.5
26	Nevada	21.3
3	New Hampshire	23.8
6	New Jersey	23.0
41	New Mexico	19.9
5	New York	23.4
50	North Carolina	18.7
35	North Dakota	20.5
20	Ohio	21.8
30	Oklahoma	20.8
24	Oregon	21.5
11	Pennsylvania	22.7
11	Rhode Island	22.7
36	South Carolina	20.4
19	South Dakota	21.9
47	Tennessee	19.5
29	Texas	20.9
31	Utah	20.7
6	Vermont	23.0
13	Virginia	22.6
10	Washington	22.8
33	West Virginia	20.6
16	Wisconsin	22.1
43	Wyoming	19.8

RANK ORDER

RANK	STATE	AVERAGE SCORE
1	Massachusetts	24.1
2	Connecticut	24.0
3	New Hampshire	23.8
4	Maine	23.5
5	New York	23.4
6	Minnesota	23.0
6	New Jersey	23.0
6	Vermont	23.0
9	Delaware	22.9
10	Washington	22.8
11	Pennsylvania	22.7
11	Rhode Island	22.7
13	Virginia	22.6
14	Maryland	22.3
15	California	22.2
16	Idaho	22.1
16	Iowa	22.1
16	Wisconsin	22.1
19	South Dakota	21.9
20	Kansas	21.8
20	Ohio	21.8
22	Indiana	21.7
23	Missouri	21.6
24	Nebraska	21.5
24	Oregon	21.5
26	Montana	21.3
26	Nevada	21.3
28	Alaska	21.1
29	Texas	20.9
30	Oklahoma	20.8
31	Georgia	20.7
31	Utah	20.7
33	Illinois	20.6
33	West Virginia	20.6
35	North Dakota	20.5
36	Alabama	20.4
36	Colorado	20.4
36	South Carolina	20.4
39	Arkansas	20.2
40	Hawaii	20.1
41	Michigan	19.9
41	New Mexico	19.9
43	Wyoming	19.8
44	Arizona	19.6
44	Florida	19.6
44	Kentucky	19.6
47	Louisiana	19.5
47	Tennessee	19.5
49	Mississippi	18.9
50	North Carolina	18.7

District of Columbia	20.4

Source: The American College Testing Program (Copyright © 2013)
   "Average ACT Scores by State" (http://www.act.org/newsroom/)
*The ACT score range is 1 to 36. Approximately 1.8 million 2013 U.S. high school students took the test. Caution should be used in using ACT scores to compare states. The percentage of high school students taking the test varies greatly from one state to another. For example, all 11th grade students in Colorado, Illinois, Kentucky, Louisiana, Michigan, Tennessee, Utah, and Wyoming are required to take the test but, in Maine, only 8 percent of 11th grade students took the test.

Education Expenditures by State and Local Governments in 2011

National Total = $861,130,583,000*

ALPHA ORDER

RANK	STATE	EXPENDITURES	% of USA
21	Alabama	$13,370,655,000	1.6%
41	Alaska	3,376,705,000	0.4%
20	Arizona	13,385,017,000	1.6%
31	Arkansas	8,446,175,000	1.0%
1	California	102,228,064,000	11.9%
22	Colorado	13,203,613,000	1.5%
26	Connecticut	11,789,282,000	1.4%
43	Delaware	3,134,169,000	0.4%
4	Florida	38,691,438,000	4.5%
10	Georgia	24,832,351,000	2.9%
42	Hawaii	3,345,400,000	0.4%
44	Idaho	3,131,029,000	0.4%
6	Illinois	34,669,254,000	4.0%
17	Indiana	16,270,151,000	1.9%
29	Iowa	9,636,273,000	1.1%
32	Kansas	8,366,291,000	1.0%
27	Kentucky	11,466,117,000	1.3%
24	Louisiana	12,118,671,000	1.4%
40	Maine	3,458,596,000	0.4%
15	Maryland	18,258,312,000	2.1%
14	Massachusetts	18,761,469,000	2.2%
9	Michigan	28,697,437,000	3.3%
18	Minnesota	15,388,894,000	1.8%
34	Mississippi	7,250,853,000	0.8%
19	Missouri	13,746,802,000	1.6%
46	Montana	2,596,472,000	0.3%
36	Nebraska	5,700,817,000	0.7%
38	Nevada	5,576,914,000	0.6%
39	New Hampshire	3,772,584,000	0.4%
8	New Jersey	30,551,441,000	3.5%
35	New Mexico	6,778,349,000	0.8%
3	New York	71,545,006,000	8.3%
11	North Carolina	23,735,316,000	2.8%
49	North Dakota	2,231,853,000	0.3%
7	Ohio	33,310,313,000	3.9%
30	Oklahoma	9,393,181,000	1.1%
28	Oregon	10,513,873,000	1.2%
5	Pennsylvania	35,400,439,000	4.1%
45	Rhode Island	3,049,159,000	0.4%
25	South Carolina	12,066,922,000	1.4%
50	South Dakota	2,086,181,000	0.2%
23	Tennessee	12,759,853,000	1.5%
2	Texas	74,047,357,000	8.6%
33	Utah	7,773,247,000	0.9%
48	Vermont	2,377,847,000	0.3%
12	Virginia	22,270,393,000	2.6%
13	Washington	18,785,682,000	2.2%
37	West Virginia	5,595,864,000	0.6%
16	Wisconsin	17,350,331,000	2.0%
47	Wyoming	2,495,867,000	0.3%

RANK ORDER

RANK	STATE	EXPENDITURES	% of USA
1	California	$102,228,064,000	11.9%
2	Texas	74,047,357,000	8.6%
3	New York	71,545,006,000	8.3%
4	Florida	38,691,438,000	4.5%
5	Pennsylvania	35,400,439,000	4.1%
6	Illinois	34,669,254,000	4.0%
7	Ohio	33,310,313,000	3.9%
8	New Jersey	30,551,441,000	3.5%
9	Michigan	28,697,437,000	3.3%
10	Georgia	24,832,351,000	2.9%
11	North Carolina	23,735,316,000	2.8%
12	Virginia	22,270,393,000	2.6%
13	Washington	18,785,682,000	2.2%
14	Massachusetts	18,761,469,000	2.2%
15	Maryland	18,258,312,000	2.1%
16	Wisconsin	17,350,331,000	2.0%
17	Indiana	16,270,151,000	1.9%
18	Minnesota	15,388,894,000	1.8%
19	Missouri	13,746,802,000	1.6%
20	Arizona	13,385,017,000	1.6%
21	Alabama	13,370,655,000	1.6%
22	Colorado	13,203,613,000	1.5%
23	Tennessee	12,759,853,000	1.5%
24	Louisiana	12,118,671,000	1.4%
25	South Carolina	12,066,922,000	1.4%
26	Connecticut	11,789,282,000	1.4%
27	Kentucky	11,466,117,000	1.3%
28	Oregon	10,513,873,000	1.2%
29	Iowa	9,636,273,000	1.1%
30	Oklahoma	9,393,181,000	1.1%
31	Arkansas	8,446,175,000	1.0%
32	Kansas	8,366,291,000	1.0%
33	Utah	7,773,247,000	0.9%
34	Mississippi	7,250,853,000	0.8%
35	New Mexico	6,778,349,000	0.8%
36	Nebraska	5,700,817,000	0.7%
37	West Virginia	5,595,864,000	0.6%
38	Nevada	5,576,914,000	0.6%
39	New Hampshire	3,772,584,000	0.4%
40	Maine	3,458,596,000	0.4%
41	Alaska	3,376,705,000	0.4%
42	Hawaii	3,345,400,000	0.4%
43	Delaware	3,134,169,000	0.4%
44	Idaho	3,131,029,000	0.4%
45	Rhode Island	3,049,159,000	0.4%
46	Montana	2,596,472,000	0.3%
47	Wyoming	2,495,867,000	0.3%
48	Vermont	2,377,847,000	0.3%
49	North Dakota	2,231,853,000	0.3%
50	South Dakota	2,086,181,000	0.2%
	District of Columbia	2,342,304,000	0.3%

Source: U.S. Bureau of the Census, Governments Division
   "2011 State and Local Government Finances" (http://www.census.gov/govs/local/)
*Direct general expenditures for higher, secondary, elementary, and, "other" education. Includes capital outlays.

Per Capita State and Local Government Expenditures for Education in 2011

National Per Capita = $2,764*

ALPHA ORDER

RANK	STATE	PER CAPITA
24	Alabama	$2,783
1	Alaska	4,665
46	Arizona	2,070
21	Arkansas	2,874
30	California	2,713
37	Colorado	2,581
7	Connecticut	3,287
6	Delaware	3,451
48	Florida	2,028
39	Georgia	2,531
44	Hawaii	2,427
50	Idaho	1,977
31	Illinois	2,696
40	Indiana	2,497
10	Iowa	3,145
15	Kansas	2,915
33	Kentucky	2,626
32	Louisiana	2,649
34	Maine	2,603
11	Maryland	3,127
23	Massachusetts	2,840
16	Michigan	2,906
20	Minnesota	2,878
43	Mississippi	2,435
45	Missouri	2,288
34	Montana	2,603
12	Nebraska	3,095
47	Nevada	2,050
22	New Hampshire	2,863
5	New Jersey	3,458
8	New Mexico	3,261
4	New York	3,669
42	North Carolina	2,459
9	North Dakota	3,259
19	Ohio	2,886
41	Oklahoma	2,482
29	Oregon	2,718
25	Pennsylvania	2,778
17	Rhode Island	2,902
36	South Carolina	2,582
38	South Dakota	2,533
49	Tennessee	1,994
18	Texas	2,889
26	Utah	2,762
3	Vermont	3,795
28	Virginia	2,748
27	Washington	2,753
14	West Virginia	3,017
13	Wisconsin	3,039
2	Wyoming	4,399

RANK ORDER

RANK	STATE	PER CAPITA
1	Alaska	$4,665
2	Wyoming	4,399
3	Vermont	3,795
4	New York	3,669
5	New Jersey	3,458
6	Delaware	3,451
7	Connecticut	3,287
8	New Mexico	3,261
9	North Dakota	3,259
10	Iowa	3,145
11	Maryland	3,127
12	Nebraska	3,095
13	Wisconsin	3,039
14	West Virginia	3,017
15	Kansas	2,915
16	Michigan	2,906
17	Rhode Island	2,902
18	Texas	2,889
19	Ohio	2,886
20	Minnesota	2,878
21	Arkansas	2,874
22	New Hampshire	2,863
23	Massachusetts	2,840
24	Alabama	2,783
25	Pennsylvania	2,778
26	Utah	2,762
27	Washington	2,753
28	Virginia	2,748
29	Oregon	2,718
30	California	2,713
31	Illinois	2,696
32	Louisiana	2,649
33	Kentucky	2,626
34	Maine	2,603
34	Montana	2,603
36	South Carolina	2,582
37	Colorado	2,581
38	South Dakota	2,533
39	Georgia	2,531
40	Indiana	2,497
41	Oklahoma	2,482
42	North Carolina	2,459
43	Mississippi	2,435
44	Hawaii	2,427
45	Missouri	2,288
46	Arizona	2,070
47	Nevada	2,050
48	Florida	2,028
49	Tennessee	1,994
50	Idaho	1,977

District of Columbia 3,784

Source: CQ Press using data from U.S. Bureau of the Census, Governments Division
"2011 State and Local Government Finances" (http://www.census.gov/govs/local/)
*Direct general expenditures for higher, secondary, elementary, and, "other" education. Includes capital outlays.

Expenditures for Education as a Percent of All State and Local Government Expenditures in 2011
National Percent = 33.3%*

ALPHA ORDER

RANK	STATE	PERCENT
9	Alabama	37.8
50	Alaska	26.4
38	Arizona	31.4
1	Arkansas	40.6
46	California	28.9
36	Colorado	32.0
21	Connecticut	35.3
14	Delaware	36.5
48	Florida	28.0
5	Georgia	38.8
49	Hawaii	27.4
44	Idaho	29.9
28	Illinois	33.2
19	Indiana	35.5
16	Iowa	36.4
16	Kansas	36.4
19	Kentucky	35.5
47	Louisiana	28.3
39	Maine	30.5
12	Maryland	36.6
39	Massachusetts	30.5
4	Michigan	38.9
33	Minnesota	32.6
41	Mississippi	30.4
29	Missouri	33.1
36	Montana	32.0
3	Nebraska	39.3
45	Nevada	29.8
11	New Hampshire	36.9
10	New Jersey	37.5
24	New Mexico	34.9
41	New York	30.4
21	North Carolina	35.3
25	North Dakota	34.7
21	Ohio	35.3
14	Oklahoma	36.5
29	Oregon	33.1
33	Pennsylvania	32.6
31	Rhode Island	33.0
26	South Carolina	33.9
27	South Dakota	33.8
43	Tennessee	30.3
2	Texas	39.9
8	Utah	38.2
7	Vermont	38.5
12	Virginia	36.6
35	Washington	32.5
6	West Virginia	38.7
16	Wisconsin	36.4
31	Wyoming	33.0

RANK ORDER

RANK	STATE	PERCENT
1	Arkansas	40.6
2	Texas	39.9
3	Nebraska	39.3
4	Michigan	38.9
5	Georgia	38.8
6	West Virginia	38.7
7	Vermont	38.5
8	Utah	38.2
9	Alabama	37.8
10	New Jersey	37.5
11	New Hampshire	36.9
12	Maryland	36.6
12	Virginia	36.6
14	Delaware	36.5
14	Oklahoma	36.5
16	Iowa	36.4
16	Kansas	36.4
16	Wisconsin	36.4
19	Indiana	35.5
19	Kentucky	35.5
21	Connecticut	35.3
21	North Carolina	35.3
21	Ohio	35.3
24	New Mexico	34.9
25	North Dakota	34.7
26	South Carolina	33.9
27	South Dakota	33.8
28	Illinois	33.2
29	Missouri	33.1
29	Oregon	33.1
31	Rhode Island	33.0
31	Wyoming	33.0
33	Minnesota	32.6
33	Pennsylvania	32.6
35	Washington	32.5
36	Colorado	32.0
36	Montana	32.0
38	Arizona	31.4
39	Maine	30.5
39	Massachusetts	30.5
41	Mississippi	30.4
41	New York	30.4
43	Tennessee	30.3
44	Idaho	29.9
45	Nevada	29.8
46	California	28.9
47	Louisiana	28.3
48	Florida	28.0
49	Hawaii	27.4
50	Alaska	26.4

| | District of Columbia | 22.6 |

Source: CQ Press using data from U.S. Bureau of the Census, Governments Division
   "2011 State and Local Government Finances" (http://www.census.gov/govs/local/)
*Direct general expenditures for higher, secondary, elementary, and "other" education as a percent of all direct general expenditures. Includes capital outlays.

State and Local Government Expenditures for Elementary and Secondary Education in 2011
National Total = $564,862,357,000*

ALPHA ORDER

RANK	STATE	EXPENDITURES	% of USA
25	Alabama	$7,602,838,000	1.3%
40	Alaska	2,459,961,000	0.4%
24	Arizona	8,066,255,000	1.4%
31	Arkansas	5,361,913,000	0.9%
1	California	63,482,302,000	11.2%
22	Colorado	8,185,316,000	1.4%
21	Connecticut	8,535,528,000	1.5%
45	Delaware	1,733,515,000	0.3%
4	Florida	26,304,058,000	4.7%
10	Georgia	16,880,214,000	3.0%
43	Hawaii	1,938,691,000	0.3%
44	Idaho	1,898,594,000	0.3%
6	Illinois	24,526,656,000	4.3%
18	Indiana	9,737,968,000	1.7%
29	Iowa	5,749,910,000	1.0%
32	Kansas	5,258,252,000	0.9%
27	Kentucky	6,754,701,000	1.2%
23	Louisiana	8,173,663,000	1.4%
41	Maine	2,443,312,000	0.4%
14	Maryland	12,026,838,000	2.1%
13	Massachusetts	13,019,880,000	2.3%
9	Michigan	17,511,552,000	3.1%
17	Minnesota	9,984,789,000	1.8%
33	Mississippi	4,275,596,000	0.8%
19	Missouri	9,425,857,000	1.7%
47	Montana	1,621,407,000	0.3%
37	Nebraska	3,580,214,000	0.6%
36	Nevada	4,012,361,000	0.7%
39	New Hampshire	2,768,396,000	0.5%
7	New Jersey	23,429,839,000	4.1%
35	New Mexico	4,058,681,000	0.7%
2	New York	55,420,282,000	9.8%
12	North Carolina	13,133,835,000	2.3%
50	North Dakota	1,233,523,000	0.2%
8	Ohio	22,089,312,000	3.9%
30	Oklahoma	5,506,234,000	1.0%
28	Oregon	6,019,375,000	1.1%
5	Pennsylvania	24,682,167,000	4.4%
42	Rhode Island	2,201,660,000	0.4%
26	South Carolina	7,590,661,000	1.3%
49	South Dakota	1,304,302,000	0.2%
20	Tennessee	8,610,554,000	1.5%
3	Texas	47,014,113,000	8.3%
34	Utah	4,084,498,000	0.7%
48	Vermont	1,471,329,000	0.3%
11	Virginia	14,277,830,000	2.5%
15	Washington	11,421,314,000	2.0%
38	West Virginia	3,314,898,000	0.6%
16	Wisconsin	10,862,164,000	1.9%
46	Wyoming	1,640,623,000	0.3%

RANK ORDER

RANK	STATE	EXPENDITURES	% of USA
1	California	$63,482,302,000	11.2%
2	New York	55,420,282,000	9.8%
3	Texas	47,014,113,000	8.3%
4	Florida	26,304,058,000	4.7%
5	Pennsylvania	24,682,167,000	4.4%
6	Illinois	24,526,656,000	4.3%
7	New Jersey	23,429,839,000	4.1%
8	Ohio	22,089,312,000	3.9%
9	Michigan	17,511,552,000	3.1%
10	Georgia	16,880,214,000	3.0%
11	Virginia	14,277,830,000	2.5%
12	North Carolina	13,133,835,000	2.3%
13	Massachusetts	13,019,880,000	2.3%
14	Maryland	12,026,838,000	2.1%
15	Washington	11,421,314,000	2.0%
16	Wisconsin	10,862,164,000	1.9%
17	Minnesota	9,984,789,000	1.8%
18	Indiana	9,737,968,000	1.7%
19	Missouri	9,425,857,000	1.7%
20	Tennessee	8,610,554,000	1.5%
21	Connecticut	8,535,528,000	1.5%
22	Colorado	8,185,316,000	1.4%
23	Louisiana	8,173,663,000	1.4%
24	Arizona	8,066,255,000	1.4%
25	Alabama	7,602,838,000	1.3%
26	South Carolina	7,590,661,000	1.3%
27	Kentucky	6,754,701,000	1.2%
28	Oregon	6,019,375,000	1.1%
29	Iowa	5,749,910,000	1.0%
30	Oklahoma	5,506,234,000	1.0%
31	Arkansas	5,361,913,000	0.9%
32	Kansas	5,258,252,000	0.9%
33	Mississippi	4,275,596,000	0.8%
34	Utah	4,084,498,000	0.7%
35	New Mexico	4,058,681,000	0.7%
36	Nevada	4,012,361,000	0.7%
37	Nebraska	3,580,214,000	0.6%
38	West Virginia	3,314,898,000	0.6%
39	New Hampshire	2,768,396,000	0.5%
40	Alaska	2,459,961,000	0.4%
41	Maine	2,443,312,000	0.4%
42	Rhode Island	2,201,660,000	0.4%
43	Hawaii	1,938,691,000	0.3%
44	Idaho	1,898,594,000	0.3%
45	Delaware	1,733,515,000	0.3%
46	Wyoming	1,640,623,000	0.3%
47	Montana	1,621,407,000	0.3%
48	Vermont	1,471,329,000	0.3%
49	South Dakota	1,304,302,000	0.2%
50	North Dakota	1,233,523,000	0.2%
	District of Columbia	2,174,626,000	0.4%

Source: U.S. Bureau of the Census, Governments Division
"2011 State and Local Government Finances" (http://www.census.gov/govs/local/)
*Direct general expenditures. Includes capital outlays.

Per Capita State and Local Government Expenditures for Elementary and Secondary Education in 2011
National Per Capita = $1,813*

ALPHA ORDER

RANK	STATE	PER CAPITA
36	Alabama	$1,583
1	Alaska	3,398
49	Arizona	1,247
23	Arkansas	1,825
30	California	1,685
34	Colorado	1,600
5	Connecticut	2,380
15	Delaware	1,909
46	Florida	1,378
29	Georgia	1,720
45	Hawaii	1,407
50	Idaho	1,199
16	Illinois	1,907
40	Indiana	1,494
18	Iowa	1,877
22	Kansas	1,832
39	Kentucky	1,547
25	Louisiana	1,787
20	Maine	1,839
9	Maryland	2,060
10	Massachusetts	1,971
27	Michigan	1,773
19	Minnesota	1,867
44	Mississippi	1,436
37	Missouri	1,569
32	Montana	1,625
12	Nebraska	1,943
41	Nevada	1,475
7	New Hampshire	2,101
4	New Jersey	2,652
11	New Mexico	1,953
3	New York	2,842
47	North Carolina	1,361
24	North Dakota	1,801
14	Ohio	1,914
42	Oklahoma	1,455
38	Oregon	1,556
13	Pennsylvania	1,937
8	Rhode Island	2,096
33	South Carolina	1,624
35	South Dakota	1,584
48	Tennessee	1,345
21	Texas	1,834
43	Utah	1,451
6	Vermont	2,348
28	Virginia	1,762
31	Washington	1,674
25	West Virginia	1,787
17	Wisconsin	1,902
2	Wyoming	2,892

RANK ORDER

RANK	STATE	PER CAPITA
1	Alaska	$3,398
2	Wyoming	2,892
3	New York	2,842
4	New Jersey	2,652
5	Connecticut	2,380
6	Vermont	2,348
7	New Hampshire	2,101
8	Rhode Island	2,096
9	Maryland	2,060
10	Massachusetts	1,971
11	New Mexico	1,953
12	Nebraska	1,943
13	Pennsylvania	1,937
14	Ohio	1,914
15	Delaware	1,909
16	Illinois	1,907
17	Wisconsin	1,902
18	Iowa	1,877
19	Minnesota	1,867
20	Maine	1,839
21	Texas	1,834
22	Kansas	1,832
23	Arkansas	1,825
24	North Dakota	1,801
25	Louisiana	1,787
25	West Virginia	1,787
27	Michigan	1,773
28	Virginia	1,762
29	Georgia	1,720
30	California	1,685
31	Washington	1,674
32	Montana	1,625
33	South Carolina	1,624
34	Colorado	1,600
35	South Dakota	1,584
36	Alabama	1,583
37	Missouri	1,569
38	Oregon	1,556
39	Kentucky	1,547
40	Indiana	1,494
41	Nevada	1,475
42	Oklahoma	1,455
43	Utah	1,451
44	Mississippi	1,436
45	Hawaii	1,407
46	Florida	1,378
47	North Carolina	1,361
48	Tennessee	1,345
49	Arizona	1,247
50	Idaho	1,199

District of Columbia 3,513

Source: CQ Press using data from U.S. Bureau of the Census, Governments Division
"2011 State and Local Government Finances" (http://www.census.gov/govs/local/)
*Direct general expenditures. Includes capital outlays.

Expenditures for Elementary and Secondary Education as a Percent of All State and Local Government Expenditures in 2011
National Percent = 21.9%*

<table>
<tr><td colspan="3">ALPHA ORDER</td><td colspan="3">RANK ORDER</td></tr>
<tr><td>RANK</td><td>STATE</td><td>PERCENT</td><td>RANK</td><td>STATE</td><td>PERCENT</td></tr>
<tr><td>23</td><td>Alabama</td><td>21.5</td><td>1</td><td>New Jersey</td><td>28.7</td></tr>
<tr><td>41</td><td>Alaska</td><td>19.2</td><td>2</td><td>New Hampshire</td><td>27.0</td></tr>
<tr><td>45</td><td>Arizona</td><td>18.9</td><td>3</td><td>Georgia</td><td>26.4</td></tr>
<tr><td>4</td><td>Arkansas</td><td>25.8</td><td>4</td><td>Arkansas</td><td>25.8</td></tr>
<tr><td>48</td><td>California</td><td>17.9</td><td>5</td><td>Connecticut</td><td>25.6</td></tr>
<tr><td>38</td><td>Colorado</td><td>19.8</td><td>6</td><td>Texas</td><td>25.3</td></tr>
<tr><td>5</td><td>Connecticut</td><td>25.6</td><td>7</td><td>Nebraska</td><td>24.7</td></tr>
<tr><td>35</td><td>Delaware</td><td>20.2</td><td>8</td><td>Maryland</td><td>24.1</td></tr>
<tr><td>43</td><td>Florida</td><td>19.1</td><td>9</td><td>Rhode Island</td><td>23.9</td></tr>
<tr><td>3</td><td>Georgia</td><td>26.4</td><td>10</td><td>Michigan</td><td>23.8</td></tr>
<tr><td>50</td><td>Hawaii</td><td>15.9</td><td>10</td><td>Vermont</td><td>23.8</td></tr>
<tr><td>47</td><td>Idaho</td><td>18.1</td><td>12</td><td>New York</td><td>23.6</td></tr>
<tr><td>13</td><td>Illinois</td><td>23.5</td><td>13</td><td>Illinois</td><td>23.5</td></tr>
<tr><td>28</td><td>Indiana</td><td>21.2</td><td>14</td><td>Ohio</td><td>23.4</td></tr>
<tr><td>21</td><td>Iowa</td><td>21.7</td><td>14</td><td>Virginia</td><td>23.4</td></tr>
<tr><td>16</td><td>Kansas</td><td>22.9</td><td>16</td><td>Kansas</td><td>22.9</td></tr>
<tr><td>32</td><td>Kentucky</td><td>20.9</td><td>16</td><td>West Virginia</td><td>22.9</td></tr>
<tr><td>43</td><td>Louisiana</td><td>19.1</td><td>18</td><td>Wisconsin</td><td>22.8</td></tr>
<tr><td>23</td><td>Maine</td><td>21.5</td><td>19</td><td>Missouri</td><td>22.7</td></tr>
<tr><td>8</td><td>Maryland</td><td>24.1</td><td>19</td><td>Pennsylvania</td><td>22.7</td></tr>
<tr><td>28</td><td>Massachusetts</td><td>21.2</td><td>21</td><td>Iowa</td><td>21.7</td></tr>
<tr><td>10</td><td>Michigan</td><td>23.8</td><td>21</td><td>Wyoming</td><td>21.7</td></tr>
<tr><td>31</td><td>Minnesota</td><td>21.1</td><td>23</td><td>Alabama</td><td>21.5</td></tr>
<tr><td>48</td><td>Mississippi</td><td>17.9</td><td>23</td><td>Maine</td><td>21.5</td></tr>
<tr><td>19</td><td>Missouri</td><td>22.7</td><td>23</td><td>Nevada</td><td>21.5</td></tr>
<tr><td>37</td><td>Montana</td><td>20.0</td><td>26</td><td>Oklahoma</td><td>21.4</td></tr>
<tr><td>7</td><td>Nebraska</td><td>24.7</td><td>27</td><td>South Carolina</td><td>21.3</td></tr>
<tr><td>23</td><td>Nevada</td><td>21.5</td><td>28</td><td>Indiana</td><td>21.2</td></tr>
<tr><td>2</td><td>New Hampshire</td><td>27.0</td><td>28</td><td>Massachusetts</td><td>21.2</td></tr>
<tr><td>1</td><td>New Jersey</td><td>28.7</td><td>28</td><td>South Dakota</td><td>21.2</td></tr>
<tr><td>32</td><td>New Mexico</td><td>20.9</td><td>31</td><td>Minnesota</td><td>21.1</td></tr>
<tr><td>12</td><td>New York</td><td>23.6</td><td>32</td><td>Kentucky</td><td>20.9</td></tr>
<tr><td>40</td><td>North Carolina</td><td>19.5</td><td>32</td><td>New Mexico</td><td>20.9</td></tr>
<tr><td>41</td><td>North Dakota</td><td>19.2</td><td>34</td><td>Tennessee</td><td>20.5</td></tr>
<tr><td>14</td><td>Ohio</td><td>23.4</td><td>35</td><td>Delaware</td><td>20.2</td></tr>
<tr><td>26</td><td>Oklahoma</td><td>21.4</td><td>36</td><td>Utah</td><td>20.1</td></tr>
<tr><td>45</td><td>Oregon</td><td>18.9</td><td>37</td><td>Montana</td><td>20.0</td></tr>
<tr><td>19</td><td>Pennsylvania</td><td>22.7</td><td>38</td><td>Colorado</td><td>19.8</td></tr>
<tr><td>9</td><td>Rhode Island</td><td>23.9</td><td>38</td><td>Washington</td><td>19.8</td></tr>
<tr><td>27</td><td>South Carolina</td><td>21.3</td><td>40</td><td>North Carolina</td><td>19.5</td></tr>
<tr><td>28</td><td>South Dakota</td><td>21.2</td><td>41</td><td>Alaska</td><td>19.2</td></tr>
<tr><td>34</td><td>Tennessee</td><td>20.5</td><td>41</td><td>North Dakota</td><td>19.2</td></tr>
<tr><td>6</td><td>Texas</td><td>25.3</td><td>43</td><td>Florida</td><td>19.1</td></tr>
<tr><td>36</td><td>Utah</td><td>20.1</td><td>43</td><td>Louisiana</td><td>19.1</td></tr>
<tr><td>10</td><td>Vermont</td><td>23.8</td><td>45</td><td>Arizona</td><td>18.9</td></tr>
<tr><td>14</td><td>Virginia</td><td>23.4</td><td>45</td><td>Oregon</td><td>18.9</td></tr>
<tr><td>38</td><td>Washington</td><td>19.8</td><td>47</td><td>Idaho</td><td>18.1</td></tr>
<tr><td>16</td><td>West Virginia</td><td>22.9</td><td>48</td><td>California</td><td>17.9</td></tr>
<tr><td>18</td><td>Wisconsin</td><td>22.8</td><td>48</td><td>Mississippi</td><td>17.9</td></tr>
<tr><td>21</td><td>Wyoming</td><td>21.7</td><td>50</td><td>Hawaii</td><td>15.9</td></tr>
<tr><td></td><td></td><td></td><td></td><td>District of Columbia</td><td>20.9</td></tr>
</table>

Source: CQ Press using data from U.S. Bureau of the Census, Governments Division
"2011 State and Local Government Finances" (http://www.census.gov/govs/local/)
*Direct general expenditures as a percent of all direct general expenditures. Includes capital outlays.

Estimated Per Pupil Public Elementary and Secondary School Current Expenditures in 2013
National Per Pupil = $11,068*

ALPHA ORDER

RANK	STATE	PER PUPIL
41	Alabama	$8,779
4	Alaska	18,192
50	Arizona	6,949
14	Arkansas	13,215
38	California	9,202
28	Colorado	10,199
7	Connecticut	16,272
11	Delaware	14,890
43	Florida	8,637
33	Georgia	9,654
19	Hawaii	11,569
44	Idaho	8,528
15	Illinois	12,927
22	Indiana	11,129
36	Iowa	9,411
32	Kansas	9,689
31	Kentucky	9,891
27	Louisiana	10,310
24	Maine	10,414
9	Maryland	15,287
10	Massachusetts	15,211
13	Michigan	13,686
18	Minnesota	11,632
35	Mississippi	9,427
29	Missouri	10,093
23	Montana	10,645
34	Nebraska	9,621
45	Nevada	8,501
8	New Hampshire	15,394
3	New Jersey	19,291
25	New Mexico	10,397
2	New York	19,523
47	North Carolina	8,433
40	North Dakota	8,849
30	Ohio	9,941
46	Oklahoma	8,481
21	Oregon	11,254
12	Pennsylvania	14,467
5	Rhode Island	17,666
39	South Carolina	8,898
37	South Dakota	9,347
42	Tennessee	8,695
48	Texas	7,886
49	Utah	7,129
1	Vermont	19,752
20	Virginia	11,457
26	Washington	10,313
17	West Virginia	12,116
16	Wisconsin	12,555
6	Wyoming	16,577

RANK ORDER

RANK	STATE	PER PUPIL
1	Vermont	$19,752
2	New York	19,523
3	New Jersey	19,291
4	Alaska	18,192
5	Rhode Island	17,666
6	Wyoming	16,577
7	Connecticut	16,272
8	New Hampshire	15,394
9	Maryland	15,287
10	Massachusetts	15,211
11	Delaware	14,890
12	Pennsylvania	14,467
13	Michigan	13,686
14	Arkansas	13,215
15	Illinois	12,927
16	Wisconsin	12,555
17	West Virginia	12,116
18	Minnesota	11,632
19	Hawaii	11,569
20	Virginia	11,457
21	Oregon	11,254
22	Indiana	11,129
23	Montana	10,645
24	Maine	10,414
25	New Mexico	10,397
26	Washington	10,313
27	Louisiana	10,310
28	Colorado	10,199
29	Missouri	10,093
30	Ohio	9,941
31	Kentucky	9,891
32	Kansas	9,689
33	Georgia	9,654
34	Nebraska	9,621
35	Mississippi	9,427
36	Iowa	9,411
37	South Dakota	9,347
38	California	9,202
39	South Carolina	8,898
40	North Dakota	8,849
41	Alabama	8,779
42	Tennessee	8,695
43	Florida	8,637
44	Idaho	8,528
45	Nevada	8,501
46	Oklahoma	8,481
47	North Carolina	8,433
48	Texas	7,886
49	Utah	7,129
50	Arizona	6,949
	District of Columbia	14,406

Source: National Education Association, Washington, D.C.
"Rankings and Estimates" (Copyright © 2012, NEA, used with permission, http://www.nea.org/home/54597.htm)
*Estimates for school year 2012-2013. Based on student membership.

Higher Education Expenditures by State and Local Governments in 2011

National Total = $252,270,144,000*

ALPHA ORDER

RANK	STATE	EXPENDITURES	% of USA
17	Alabama	$4,965,533,000	2.0%
44	Alaska	804,687,000	0.3%
19	Arizona	4,581,965,000	1.8%
34	Arkansas	2,415,979,000	1.0%
1	California	33,924,657,000	13.4%
20	Colorado	4,524,651,000	1.8%
32	Connecticut	2,634,179,000	1.0%
41	Delaware	1,069,356,000	0.4%
5	Florida	9,561,941,000	3.8%
13	Georgia	5,760,641,000	2.3%
38	Hawaii	1,311,756,000	0.5%
40	Idaho	1,081,700,000	0.4%
8	Illinois	8,688,799,000	3.4%
16	Indiana	5,522,656,000	2.2%
25	Iowa	3,473,156,000	1.4%
31	Kansas	2,844,866,000	1.1%
23	Kentucky	3,774,528,000	1.5%
30	Louisiana	3,138,128,000	1.2%
46	Maine	794,851,000	0.3%
15	Maryland	5,554,128,000	2.2%
18	Massachusetts	4,666,758,000	1.8%
4	Michigan	10,219,623,000	4.1%
21	Minnesota	4,405,616,000	1.7%
33	Mississippi	2,587,705,000	1.0%
24	Missouri	3,616,927,000	1.4%
45	Montana	797,111,000	0.3%
36	Nebraska	1,859,131,000	0.7%
39	Nevada	1,283,450,000	0.5%
43	New Hampshire	842,663,000	0.3%
14	New Jersey	5,702,285,000	2.3%
35	New Mexico	2,392,724,000	0.9%
3	New York	14,190,472,000	5.6%
6	North Carolina	9,289,635,000	3.7%
42	North Dakota	884,248,000	0.4%
9	Ohio	8,590,415,000	3.4%
26	Oklahoma	3,358,720,000	1.3%
22	Oregon	4,146,073,000	1.6%
7	Pennsylvania	8,860,132,000	3.5%
50	Rhode Island	615,842,000	0.2%
27	South Carolina	3,358,072,000	1.3%
49	South Dakota	672,371,000	0.3%
28	Tennessee	3,324,173,000	1.3%
2	Texas	24,833,195,000	9.8%
29	Utah	3,308,138,000	1.3%
47	Vermont	734,522,000	0.3%
10	Virginia	7,067,344,000	2.8%
11	Washington	5,926,165,000	2.3%
37	West Virginia	1,586,126,000	0.6%
12	Wisconsin	5,869,385,000	2.3%
48	Wyoming	685,288,000	0.3%

RANK ORDER

RANK	STATE	EXPENDITURES	% of USA
1	California	$33,924,657,000	13.4%
2	Texas	24,833,195,000	9.8%
3	New York	14,190,472,000	5.6%
4	Michigan	10,219,623,000	4.1%
5	Florida	9,561,941,000	3.8%
6	North Carolina	9,289,635,000	3.7%
7	Pennsylvania	8,860,132,000	3.5%
8	Illinois	8,688,799,000	3.4%
9	Ohio	8,590,415,000	3.4%
10	Virginia	7,067,344,000	2.8%
11	Washington	5,926,165,000	2.3%
12	Wisconsin	5,869,385,000	2.3%
13	Georgia	5,760,641,000	2.3%
14	New Jersey	5,702,285,000	2.3%
15	Maryland	5,554,128,000	2.2%
16	Indiana	5,522,656,000	2.2%
17	Alabama	4,965,533,000	2.0%
18	Massachusetts	4,666,758,000	1.8%
19	Arizona	4,581,965,000	1.8%
20	Colorado	4,524,651,000	1.8%
21	Minnesota	4,405,616,000	1.7%
22	Oregon	4,146,073,000	1.6%
23	Kentucky	3,774,528,000	1.5%
24	Missouri	3,616,927,000	1.4%
25	Iowa	3,473,156,000	1.4%
26	Oklahoma	3,358,720,000	1.3%
27	South Carolina	3,358,072,000	1.3%
28	Tennessee	3,324,173,000	1.3%
29	Utah	3,308,138,000	1.3%
30	Louisiana	3,138,128,000	1.2%
31	Kansas	2,844,866,000	1.1%
32	Connecticut	2,634,179,000	1.0%
33	Mississippi	2,587,705,000	1.0%
34	Arkansas	2,415,979,000	1.0%
35	New Mexico	2,392,724,000	0.9%
36	Nebraska	1,859,131,000	0.7%
37	West Virginia	1,586,126,000	0.6%
38	Hawaii	1,311,756,000	0.5%
39	Nevada	1,283,450,000	0.5%
40	Idaho	1,081,700,000	0.4%
41	Delaware	1,069,356,000	0.4%
42	North Dakota	884,248,000	0.4%
43	New Hampshire	842,663,000	0.3%
44	Alaska	804,687,000	0.3%
45	Montana	797,111,000	0.3%
46	Maine	794,851,000	0.3%
47	Vermont	734,522,000	0.3%
48	Wyoming	685,288,000	0.3%
49	South Dakota	672,371,000	0.3%
50	Rhode Island	615,842,000	0.2%
	District of Columbia	167,678,000	0.1%

Source: U.S. Bureau of the Census, Governments Division
"2011 State and Local Government Finances" (http://www.census.gov/govs/local/)
*Direct general expenditures. Includes capital outlays.

Per Capita State and Local Government Expenditures for Higher Education in 2011
National Per Capita = $810*

ALPHA ORDER

RANK	STATE	PER CAPITA
11	Alabama	$1,034
8	Alaska	1,112
36	Arizona	708
29	Arkansas	822
19	California	900
21	Colorado	884
33	Connecticut	734
3	Delaware	1,178
49	Florida	501
46	Georgia	587
17	Hawaii	952
40	Idaho	683
41	Illinois	676
27	Indiana	848
7	Iowa	1,134
14	Kansas	991
25	Kentucky	864
39	Louisiana	686
45	Maine	598
18	Maryland	951
37	Massachusetts	706
10	Michigan	1,035
28	Minnesota	824
23	Mississippi	869
44	Missouri	602
31	Montana	799
13	Nebraska	1,009
50	Nevada	472
43	New Hampshire	639
42	New Jersey	645
6	New Mexico	1,151
34	New York	728
16	North Carolina	963
1	North Dakota	1,291
32	Ohio	744
20	Oklahoma	888
9	Oregon	1,072
38	Pennsylvania	695
47	Rhode Island	586
35	South Carolina	719
30	South Dakota	816
48	Tennessee	519
15	Texas	969
4	Utah	1,175
5	Vermont	1,172
22	Virginia	872
23	Washington	869
26	West Virginia	855
12	Wisconsin	1,028
2	Wyoming	1,208

RANK ORDER

RANK	STATE	PER CAPITA
1	North Dakota	$1,291
2	Wyoming	1,208
3	Delaware	1,178
4	Utah	1,175
5	Vermont	1,172
6	New Mexico	1,151
7	Iowa	1,134
8	Alaska	1,112
9	Oregon	1,072
10	Michigan	1,035
11	Alabama	1,034
12	Wisconsin	1,028
13	Nebraska	1,009
14	Kansas	991
15	Texas	969
16	North Carolina	963
17	Hawaii	952
18	Maryland	951
19	California	900
20	Oklahoma	888
21	Colorado	884
22	Virginia	872
23	Mississippi	869
23	Washington	869
25	Kentucky	864
26	West Virginia	855
27	Indiana	848
28	Minnesota	824
29	Arkansas	822
30	South Dakota	816
31	Montana	799
32	Ohio	744
33	Connecticut	734
34	New York	728
35	South Carolina	719
36	Arizona	708
37	Massachusetts	706
38	Pennsylvania	695
39	Louisiana	686
40	Idaho	683
41	Illinois	676
42	New Jersey	645
43	New Hampshire	639
44	Missouri	602
45	Maine	598
46	Georgia	587
47	Rhode Island	586
48	Tennessee	519
49	Florida	501
50	Nevada	472

District of Columbia	271

Source: CQ Press using data from U.S. Bureau of the Census, Governments Division
"2011 State and Local Government Finances" (http://www.census.gov/govs/local/)
*Direct general expenditures. Includes capital outlays.

Expenditures for Higher Education as a Percent of All State and Local Government Expenditures in 2011
National Percent = 9.8%*

ALPHA ORDER

RANK	STATE	PERCENT
2	Alabama	14.0
49	Alaska	6.3
25	Arizona	10.7
18	Arkansas	11.6
30	California	9.6
21	Colorado	11.0
40	Connecticut	7.9
11	Delaware	12.5
46	Florida	6.9
35	Georgia	9.0
25	Hawaii	10.7
27	Idaho	10.3
37	Illinois	8.3
15	Indiana	12.0
7	Iowa	13.1
12	Kansas	12.4
17	Kentucky	11.7
43	Louisiana	7.3
44	Maine	7.0
20	Maryland	11.1
42	Massachusetts	7.6
3	Michigan	13.9
32	Minnesota	9.3
23	Mississippi	10.9
36	Missouri	8.7
29	Montana	9.8
10	Nebraska	12.8
46	Nevada	6.9
38	New Hampshire	8.2
44	New Jersey	7.0
13	New Mexico	12.3
50	New York	6.0
4	North Carolina	13.8
4	North Dakota	13.8
33	Ohio	9.1
8	Oklahoma	13.0
8	Oregon	13.0
38	Pennsylvania	8.2
48	Rhode Island	6.7
31	South Carolina	9.4
23	South Dakota	10.9
40	Tennessee	7.9
6	Texas	13.4
1	Utah	16.2
16	Vermont	11.9
18	Virginia	11.6
27	Washington	10.3
21	West Virginia	11.0
13	Wisconsin	12.3
33	Wyoming	9.1

RANK ORDER

RANK	STATE	PERCENT
1	Utah	16.2
2	Alabama	14.0
3	Michigan	13.9
4	North Carolina	13.8
4	North Dakota	13.8
6	Texas	13.4
7	Iowa	13.1
8	Oklahoma	13.0
8	Oregon	13.0
10	Nebraska	12.8
11	Delaware	12.5
12	Kansas	12.4
13	New Mexico	12.3
13	Wisconsin	12.3
15	Indiana	12.0
16	Vermont	11.9
17	Kentucky	11.7
18	Arkansas	11.6
18	Virginia	11.6
20	Maryland	11.1
21	Colorado	11.0
21	West Virginia	11.0
23	Mississippi	10.9
23	South Dakota	10.9
25	Arizona	10.7
25	Hawaii	10.7
27	Idaho	10.3
27	Washington	10.3
29	Montana	9.8
30	California	9.6
31	South Carolina	9.4
32	Minnesota	9.3
33	Ohio	9.1
33	Wyoming	9.1
35	Georgia	9.0
36	Missouri	8.7
37	Illinois	8.3
38	New Hampshire	8.2
38	Pennsylvania	8.2
40	Connecticut	7.9
40	Tennessee	7.9
42	Massachusetts	7.6
43	Louisiana	7.3
44	Maine	7.0
44	New Jersey	7.0
46	Florida	6.9
46	Nevada	6.9
48	Rhode Island	6.7
49	Alaska	6.3
50	New York	6.0

	District of Columbia	1.6

Source: CQ Press using data from U.S. Bureau of the Census, Governments Division
  "2011 State and Local Government Finances" (http://www.census.gov/govs/local/)
*Direct general expenditures for higher education as a percent of all direct general expenditures. Includes capital outlays.

Average Faculty Salary at Institutions of Higher Education in 2012

National Average = $76,570*

ALPHA ORDER

RANK	STATE	AVERAGE SALARY
36	Alabama	$65,998
18	Alaska	73,864
14	Arizona	77,222
50	Arkansas	56,191
4	California	92,320
26	Colorado	70,383
3	Connecticut	93,210
5	Delaware	92,312
22	Florida	71,329
33	Georgia	68,530
13	Hawaii	78,370
46	Idaho	58,903
11	Illinois	80,111
19	Indiana	73,459
29	Iowa	69,902
39	Kansas	63,848
43	Kentucky	61,554
38	Louisiana	64,453
21	Maine	71,775
15	Maryland	75,721
1	Massachusetts	96,523
9	Michigan	81,359
23	Minnesota	71,060
49	Mississippi	56,368
32	Missouri	68,547
47	Montana	57,198
35	Nebraska	67,684
12	Nevada	79,496
10	New Hampshire	80,698
2	New Jersey	95,945
41	New Mexico	62,196
6	New York	88,638
34	North Carolina	68,153
42	North Dakota	62,134
20	Ohio	72,355
40	Oklahoma	62,687
31	Oregon	68,890
8	Pennsylvania	81,942
7	Rhode Island	86,931
44	South Carolina	61,027
48	South Dakota	56,633
37	Tennessee	65,592
25	Texas	70,637
16	Utah	74,816
17	Vermont	73,991
24	Virginia	71,030
30	Washington	69,146
45	West Virginia	60,041
27	Wisconsin	70,265
28	Wyoming	70,155

RANK ORDER

RANK	STATE	AVERAGE SALARY
1	Massachusetts	$96,523
2	New Jersey	95,945
3	Connecticut	93,210
4	California	92,320
5	Delaware	92,312
6	New York	88,638
7	Rhode Island	86,931
8	Pennsylvania	81,942
9	Michigan	81,359
10	New Hampshire	80,698
11	Illinois	80,111
12	Nevada	79,496
13	Hawaii	78,370
14	Arizona	77,222
15	Maryland	75,721
16	Utah	74,816
17	Vermont	73,991
18	Alaska	73,864
19	Indiana	73,459
20	Ohio	72,355
21	Maine	71,775
22	Florida	71,329
23	Minnesota	71,060
24	Virginia	71,030
25	Texas	70,637
26	Colorado	70,383
27	Wisconsin	70,265
28	Wyoming	70,155
29	Iowa	69,902
30	Washington	69,146
31	Oregon	68,890
32	Missouri	68,547
33	Georgia	68,530
34	North Carolina	68,153
35	Nebraska	67,684
36	Alabama	65,998
37	Tennessee	65,592
38	Louisiana	64,453
39	Kansas	63,848
40	Oklahoma	62,687
41	New Mexico	62,196
42	North Dakota	62,134
43	Kentucky	61,554
44	South Carolina	61,027
45	West Virginia	60,041
46	Idaho	58,903
47	Montana	57,198
48	South Dakota	56,633
49	Mississippi	56,368
50	Arkansas	56,191
	District of Columbia	99,141

Source: U.S. Department of Education, National Center for Education Statistics
   "Digest of Education Statistics 2012" (http://nces.ed.gov/programs/digest/index.asp)
*For 2011-2012 school year. For full-time instructional faculty on 9-month contracts at four-year and two-year public and private degree-granting institutions.

Average Student Costs at Public Institutions of Higher Education in 2012

National Average = $16,789*

ALPHA ORDER

RANK	STATE	AVERAGE COSTS
28	Alabama	$15,499
35	Alaska	14,528
12	Arizona	19,227
42	Arkansas	13,044
7	California	20,780
22	Colorado	17,169
10	Connecticut	19,815
5	Delaware	20,980
37	Florida	13,590
31	Georgia	14,799
24	Hawaii	16,356
48	Idaho	12,340
4	Illinois	21,142
23	Indiana	17,043
26	Iowa	15,653
38	Kansas	13,457
25	Kentucky	15,913
46	Louisiana	12,602
14	Maine	18,618
20	Maryland	17,446
9	Massachusetts	20,339
11	Michigan	19,230
21	Minnesota	17,286
44	Mississippi	12,814
27	Missouri	15,634
41	Montana	13,103
34	Nebraska	14,584
30	Nevada	15,033
1	New Hampshire	23,315
2	New Jersey	23,165
43	New Mexico	12,874
19	New York	17,558
36	North Carolina	13,687
45	North Dakota	12,801
13	Ohio	18,668
47	Oklahoma	12,585
17	Oregon	17,591
5	Pennsylvania	20,980
8	Rhode Island	20,634
15	South Carolina	18,076
40	South Dakota	13,321
33	Tennessee	14,622
29	Texas	15,355
50	Utah	11,319
3	Vermont	22,496
16	Virginia	17,967
18	Washington	17,588
39	West Virginia	13,444
32	Wisconsin	14,710
49	Wyoming	12,022

RANK ORDER

RANK	STATE	AVERAGE COSTS
1	New Hampshire	$23,315
2	New Jersey	23,165
3	Vermont	22,496
4	Illinois	21,142
5	Delaware	20,980
5	Pennsylvania	20,980
7	California	20,780
8	Rhode Island	20,634
9	Massachusetts	20,339
10	Connecticut	19,815
11	Michigan	19,230
12	Arizona	19,227
13	Ohio	18,668
14	Maine	18,618
15	South Carolina	18,076
16	Virginia	17,967
17	Oregon	17,591
18	Washington	17,588
19	New York	17,558
20	Maryland	17,446
21	Minnesota	17,286
22	Colorado	17,169
23	Indiana	17,043
24	Hawaii	16,356
25	Kentucky	15,913
26	Iowa	15,653
27	Missouri	15,634
28	Alabama	15,499
29	Texas	15,355
30	Nevada	15,033
31	Georgia	14,799
32	Wisconsin	14,710
33	Tennessee	14,622
34	Nebraska	14,584
35	Alaska	14,528
36	North Carolina	13,687
37	Florida	13,590
38	Kansas	13,457
39	West Virginia	13,444
40	South Dakota	13,321
41	Montana	13,103
42	Arkansas	13,044
43	New Mexico	12,874
44	Mississippi	12,814
45	North Dakota	12,801
46	Louisiana	12,602
47	Oklahoma	12,585
48	Idaho	12,340
49	Wyoming	12,022
50	Utah	11,319

District of Columbia**   NA

Source: U.S. Department of Education, National Center for Education Statistics
    "Digest of Education Statistics 2012" (http://nces.ed.gov/programs/digest/index.asp)
*Data for 2011-2012 school year. Based on average in-state tuition, room and board, and fees for full-time students in public four-year institutions for an entire academic year.
**Not available.

Average Student Costs at Private Institutions of Higher Education in 2012

National Average = $33,716*

ALPHA ORDER				RANK ORDER		
RANK	STATE	AVERAGE COSTS		RANK	STATE	AVERAGE COSTS
43	Alabama	$22,021		1	Massachusetts	$48,343
24	Alaska	29,695		2	Connecticut	46,854
45	Arizona	20,466		3	Rhode Island	44,448
38	Arkansas	24,032		4	Vermont	43,606
11	California	39,039		5	New York	43,559
28	Colorado	29,021		6	Maryland	43,109
2	Connecticut	46,854		7	Pennsylvania	42,168
40	Delaware	23,800		8	Maine	41,201
25	Florida	29,594		9	New Jersey	41,053
22	Georgia	31,956		10	New Hampshire	40,574
36	Hawaii	24,875		11	California	39,039
49	Idaho	14,095		12	Oregon	38,723
15	Illinois	35,219		13	Washington	38,295
18	Indiana	34,094		14	Louisiana	36,354
41	Iowa	23,052		15	Illinois	35,219
31	Kansas	27,484		16	Ohio	34,771
33	Kentucky	26,326		17	North Carolina	34,695
14	Louisiana	36,354		18	Indiana	34,094
8	Maine	41,201		19	Minnesota	33,461
6	Maryland	43,109		20	Texas	33,215
1	Massachusetts	48,343		21	Wisconsin	32,599
37	Michigan	24,740		22	Georgia	31,956
19	Minnesota	33,461		23	Tennessee	30,052
44	Mississippi	20,741		24	Alaska	29,695
32	Missouri	26,810		25	Florida	29,594
35	Montana	25,388		26	Nevada	29,164
34	Nebraska	25,846		27	Virginia	29,098
26	Nevada	29,164		28	Colorado	29,021
10	New Hampshire	40,574		29	Oklahoma	28,285
9	New Jersey	41,053		30	South Carolina	27,685
39	New Mexico	23,808		31	Kansas	27,484
5	New York	43,559		32	Missouri	26,810
17	North Carolina	34,695		33	Kentucky	26,326
47	North Dakota	16,386		34	Nebraska	25,846
16	Ohio	34,771		35	Montana	25,388
29	Oklahoma	28,285		36	Hawaii	24,875
12	Oregon	38,723		37	Michigan	24,740
7	Pennsylvania	42,168		38	Arkansas	24,032
3	Rhode Island	44,448		39	New Mexico	23,808
30	South Carolina	27,685		40	Delaware	23,800
42	South Dakota	22,802		41	Iowa	23,052
23	Tennessee	30,052		42	South Dakota	22,802
20	Texas	33,215		43	Alabama	22,021
48	Utah	14,859		44	Mississippi	20,741
4	Vermont	43,606		45	Arizona	20,466
27	Virginia	29,098		46	West Virginia	18,828
13	Washington	38,295		47	North Dakota	16,386
46	West Virginia	18,828		48	Utah	14,859
21	Wisconsin	32,599		49	Idaho	14,095
NA	Wyoming**	NA		NA	Wyoming**	NA
					District of Columbia	47,122

Source: U.S. Department of Education, National Center for Education Statistics
    "Digest of Education Statistics 2012" (http://nces.ed.gov/programs/digest/index.asp)
*Data for 2011-2012 school year. Based on average in-state tuition, room and board, and fees for full-time students in private four-year institutions for an entire academic year.
**Not available.

Institutions of Higher Education in 2012

National Total = 4,706 Institutions*

ALPHA ORDER

RANK	STATE	INSTITUTIONS	% of USA
23	Alabama	76	1.6%
50	Alaska	9	0.2%
20	Arizona	87	1.8%
31	Arkansas	51	1.1%
1	California	460	9.8%
17	Colorado	91	1.9%
32	Connecticut	47	1.0%
48	Delaware	12	0.3%
5	Florida	240	5.1%
9	Georgia	139	3.0%
44	Hawaii	21	0.4%
46	Idaho	18	0.4%
7	Illinois	182	3.9%
16	Indiana	107	2.3%
26	Iowa	67	1.4%
26	Kansas	67	1.4%
21	Kentucky	79	1.7%
24	Louisiana	73	1.6%
38	Maine	32	0.7%
29	Maryland	62	1.3%
12	Massachusetts	124	2.6%
14	Michigan	111	2.4%
13	Minnesota	116	2.5%
35	Mississippi	42	0.9%
10	Missouri	137	2.9%
43	Montana	22	0.5%
35	Nebraska	42	0.9%
40	Nevada	26	0.6%
39	New Hampshire	29	0.6%
25	New Jersey	68	1.4%
34	New Mexico	44	0.9%
2	New York	303	6.4%
8	North Carolina	148	3.1%
44	North Dakota	21	0.4%
6	Ohio	222	4.7%
28	Oklahoma	63	1.3%
29	Oregon	62	1.3%
3	Pennsylvania	265	5.6%
47	Rhode Island	13	0.3%
22	South Carolina	77	1.6%
41	South Dakota	25	0.5%
14	Tennessee	111	2.4%
4	Texas	260	5.5%
35	Utah	42	0.9%
42	Vermont	24	0.5%
11	Virginia	131	2.8%
18	Washington	88	1.9%
33	West Virginia	46	1.0%
18	Wisconsin	88	1.9%
49	Wyoming	11	0.2%

RANK ORDER

RANK	STATE	INSTITUTIONS	% of USA
1	California	460	9.8%
2	New York	303	6.4%
3	Pennsylvania	265	5.6%
4	Texas	260	5.5%
5	Florida	240	5.1%
6	Ohio	222	4.7%
7	Illinois	182	3.9%
8	North Carolina	148	3.1%
9	Georgia	139	3.0%
10	Missouri	137	2.9%
11	Virginia	131	2.8%
12	Massachusetts	124	2.6%
13	Minnesota	116	2.5%
14	Michigan	111	2.4%
14	Tennessee	111	2.4%
16	Indiana	107	2.3%
17	Colorado	91	1.9%
18	Washington	88	1.9%
18	Wisconsin	88	1.9%
20	Arizona	87	1.8%
21	Kentucky	79	1.7%
22	South Carolina	77	1.6%
23	Alabama	76	1.6%
24	Louisiana	73	1.6%
25	New Jersey	68	1.4%
26	Iowa	67	1.4%
26	Kansas	67	1.4%
28	Oklahoma	63	1.3%
29	Maryland	62	1.3%
29	Oregon	62	1.3%
31	Arkansas	51	1.1%
32	Connecticut	47	1.0%
33	West Virginia	46	1.0%
34	New Mexico	44	0.9%
35	Mississippi	42	0.9%
35	Nebraska	42	0.9%
35	Utah	42	0.9%
38	Maine	32	0.7%
39	New Hampshire	29	0.6%
40	Nevada	26	0.6%
41	South Dakota	25	0.5%
42	Vermont	24	0.5%
43	Montana	22	0.5%
44	Hawaii	21	0.4%
44	North Dakota	21	0.4%
46	Idaho	18	0.4%
47	Rhode Island	13	0.3%
48	Delaware	12	0.3%
49	Wyoming	11	0.2%
50	Alaska	9	0.2%
	District of Columbia	20	0.4%

Source: U.S. Department of Education, National Center for Education Statistics
   "Digest of Education Statistics 2012" (http://nces.ed.gov/programs/digest/index.asp)
*For 2011-2012 school year. Consists of 2,968 four-year and 1,738 two-year public and private (profit and not-for-profit)
degree-granting institutions. Includes five U.S. Service Schools not shown by state.

Enrollment in Institutions of Higher Education in 2011

National Total = 20,994,113 Students*

ALPHA ORDER					RANK ORDER			
RANK	STATE	STUDENTS	% of USA		RANK	STATE	STUDENTS	% of USA
24	Alabama	318,686	1.5%		1	California	2,685,893	12.8%
50	Alaska	34,932	0.2%		2	Texas	1,564,387	7.5%
6	Arizona	796,986	3.8%		3	New York	1,318,142	6.3%
33	Arkansas	179,281	0.9%		4	Florida	1,143,698	5.4%
1	California	2,685,893	12.8%		5	Illinois	892,881	4.3%
22	Colorado	365,820	1.7%		6	Arizona	796,986	3.8%
32	Connecticut	201,638	1.0%		7	Pennsylvania	787,789	3.8%
44	Delaware	56,516	0.3%		8	Ohio	735,026	3.5%
4	Florida	1,143,698	5.4%		9	Michigan	685,526	3.3%
12	Georgia	565,459	2.7%		10	Virginia	588,465	2.8%
41	Hawaii	79,018	0.4%		11	North Carolina	585,013	2.8%
39	Idaho	90,142	0.4%		12	Georgia	565,459	2.7%
5	Illinois	892,881	4.3%		13	Massachusetts	508,554	2.4%
14	Indiana	457,824	2.2%		14	Indiana	457,824	2.2%
21	Iowa	372,146	1.8%		15	Minnesota	457,752	2.2%
31	Kansas	216,662	1.0%		16	Missouri	456,997	2.2%
25	Kentucky	293,766	1.4%		17	New Jersey	443,750	2.1%
26	Louisiana	265,856	1.3%		18	Maryland	380,097	1.8%
43	Maine	72,297	0.3%		19	Wisconsin	376,603	1.8%
18	Maryland	380,097	1.8%		20	Washington	372,841	1.8%
13	Massachusetts	508,554	2.4%		21	Iowa	372,146	1.8%
9	Michigan	685,526	3.3%		22	Colorado	365,820	1.7%
15	Minnesota	457,752	2.2%		23	Tennessee	350,275	1.7%
34	Mississippi	179,090	0.9%		24	Alabama	318,686	1.5%
16	Missouri	456,997	2.2%		25	Kentucky	293,766	1.4%
47	Montana	54,042	0.3%		26	Louisiana	265,856	1.3%
37	Nebraska	142,875	0.7%		27	Utah	264,396	1.3%
38	Nevada	121,013	0.6%		28	South Carolina	260,002	1.2%
42	New Hampshire	77,444	0.4%		29	Oregon	259,061	1.2%
17	New Jersey	443,750	2.1%		30	Oklahoma	230,154	1.1%
36	New Mexico	157,555	0.8%		31	Kansas	216,662	1.0%
3	New York	1,318,142	6.3%		32	Connecticut	201,638	1.0%
11	North Carolina	585,013	2.8%		33	Arkansas	179,281	0.9%
46	North Dakota	55,772	0.3%		34	Mississippi	179,090	0.9%
8	Ohio	735,026	3.5%		35	West Virginia	162,308	0.8%
30	Oklahoma	230,154	1.1%		36	New Mexico	157,555	0.8%
29	Oregon	259,061	1.2%		37	Nebraska	142,875	0.7%
7	Pennsylvania	787,789	3.8%		38	Nevada	121,013	0.6%
40	Rhode Island	84,644	0.4%		39	Idaho	90,142	0.4%
28	South Carolina	260,002	1.2%		40	Rhode Island	84,644	0.4%
45	South Dakota	55,899	0.3%		41	Hawaii	79,018	0.4%
23	Tennessee	350,275	1.7%		42	New Hampshire	77,444	0.4%
2	Texas	1,564,387	7.5%		43	Maine	72,297	0.3%
27	Utah	264,396	1.3%		44	Delaware	56,516	0.3%
48	Vermont	45,143	0.2%		45	South Dakota	55,899	0.3%
10	Virginia	588,465	2.8%		46	North Dakota	55,772	0.3%
20	Washington	372,841	1.8%		47	Montana	54,042	0.3%
35	West Virginia	162,308	0.8%		48	Vermont	45,143	0.2%
19	Wisconsin	376,603	1.8%		49	Wyoming	38,092	0.2%
49	Wyoming	38,092	0.2%		50	Alaska	34,932	0.2%
						District of Columbia	90,213	0.4%

Source: U.S. Department of Education, National Center for Education Statistics
   "Digest of Education Statistics 2012" (http://nces.ed.gov/programs/digest/index.asp)
*Fall 2011 enrollment. Includes full-time and part-time students at Title IV eligible, degree-granting four-year and two-year institutions. National total includes 15,692 students at U.S. Service Schools not shown by state.

Enrollment Rate in Institutions of Higher Education in 2011

National Rate = 676 Students per 1,000 Population 18 to 24 Years Old*

ALPHA ORDER

RANK	STATE	RATE
28	Alabama	657
50	Alaska	455
1	Arizona	1,237
30	Arkansas	628
22	California	676
11	Colorado	731
36	Connecticut	609
34	Delaware	617
29	Florida	646
44	Georgia	568
37	Hawaii	598
41	Idaho	575
13	Illinois	714
17	Indiana	696
2	Iowa	1,198
10	Kansas	739
15	Kentucky	701
46	Louisiana	558
31	Maine	624
21	Maryland	677
9	Massachusetts	748
18	Michigan	690
4	Minnesota	908
40	Mississippi	579
6	Missouri	772
47	Montana	555
6	Nebraska	772
49	Nevada	483
33	New Hampshire	621
42	New Jersey	573
8	New Mexico	761
26	New York	664
35	North Carolina	613
26	North Dakota	664
24	Ohio	666
39	Oklahoma	593
14	Oregon	711
32	Pennsylvania	622
16	Rhode Island	699
48	South Carolina	541
23	South Dakota	673
43	Tennessee	571
38	Texas	595
5	Utah	808
19	Vermont	682
12	Virginia	723
45	Washington	560
3	West Virginia	946
20	Wisconsin	678
24	Wyoming	666

RANK ORDER

RANK	STATE	RATE
1	Arizona	1,237
2	Iowa	1,198
3	West Virginia	946
4	Minnesota	908
5	Utah	808
6	Missouri	772
6	Nebraska	772
8	New Mexico	761
9	Massachusetts	748
10	Kansas	739
11	Colorado	731
12	Virginia	723
13	Illinois	714
14	Oregon	711
15	Kentucky	701
16	Rhode Island	699
17	Indiana	696
18	Michigan	690
19	Vermont	682
20	Wisconsin	678
21	Maryland	677
22	California	676
23	South Dakota	673
24	Ohio	666
24	Wyoming	666
26	New York	664
26	North Dakota	664
28	Alabama	657
29	Florida	646
30	Arkansas	628
31	Maine	624
32	Pennsylvania	622
33	New Hampshire	621
34	Delaware	617
35	North Carolina	613
36	Connecticut	609
37	Hawaii	598
38	Texas	595
39	Oklahoma	593
40	Mississippi	579
41	Idaho	575
42	New Jersey	573
43	Tennessee	571
44	Georgia	568
45	Washington	560
46	Louisiana	558
47	Montana	555
48	South Carolina	541
49	Nevada	483
50	Alaska	455

District of Columbia	1,071

Source: CQ Press using data from U.S. Department of Education, National Center for Education Statistics
   "Digest of Education Statistics 2012" (http://nces.ed.gov/programs/digest/index.asp)
*Based on fall 2011 enrollment and population. National rate includes U.S. Service Schools. Includes students at four-year and two-year public and private degree-granting institutions. Enrollment based on location of institution. Population based on residence.

Enrollment in Public Institutions of Higher Education in 2011

National Total = 15,110,196 Students*

ALPHA ORDER

RANK	STATE	STUDENTS	% of USA
21	Alabama	260,523	1.7%
49	Alaska	32,158	0.2%
12	Arizona	366,116	2.4%
33	Arkansas	158,760	1.1%
1	California	2,178,629	14.4%
19	Colorado	269,298	1.8%
35	Connecticut	126,487	0.8%
47	Delaware	40,698	0.3%
3	Florida	803,200	5.3%
9	Georgia	428,708	2.8%
40	Hawaii	60,330	0.4%
39	Idaho	65,753	0.4%
5	Illinois	577,043	3.8%
14	Indiana	340,264	2.3%
31	Iowa	178,491	1.2%
29	Kansas	186,475	1.2%
23	Kentucky	233,427	1.5%
25	Louisiana	225,210	1.5%
41	Maine	50,253	0.3%
16	Maryland	314,383	2.1%
24	Massachusetts	227,005	1.5%
6	Michigan	554,741	3.7%
18	Minnesota	274,192	1.8%
32	Mississippi	160,611	1.1%
20	Missouri	260,585	1.7%
42	Montana	48,912	0.3%
36	Nebraska	106,794	0.7%
37	Nevada	105,048	0.7%
45	New Hampshire	43,333	0.3%
13	New Jersey	359,458	2.4%
34	New Mexico	146,515	1.0%
4	New York	731,914	4.8%
8	North Carolina	470,989	3.1%
43	North Dakota	48,868	0.3%
7	Ohio	542,774	3.6%
28	Oklahoma	197,373	1.3%
26	Oregon	215,466	1.4%
10	Pennsylvania	428,269	2.8%
46	Rhode Island	43,254	0.3%
27	South Carolina	208,302	1.4%
44	South Dakota	43,729	0.3%
22	Tennessee	241,917	1.6%
2	Texas	1,367,005	9.0%
30	Utah	179,208	1.2%
50	Vermont	27,132	0.2%
11	Virginia	413,761	2.7%
15	Washington	317,066	2.1%
38	West Virginia	95,634	0.6%
17	Wisconsin	296,795	2.0%
48	Wyoming	36,368	0.2%

RANK ORDER

RANK	STATE	STUDENTS	% of USA
1	California	2,178,629	14.4%
2	Texas	1,367,005	9.0%
3	Florida	803,200	5.3%
4	New York	731,914	4.8%
5	Illinois	577,043	3.8%
6	Michigan	554,741	3.7%
7	Ohio	542,774	3.6%
8	North Carolina	470,989	3.1%
9	Georgia	428,708	2.8%
10	Pennsylvania	428,269	2.8%
11	Virginia	413,761	2.7%
12	Arizona	366,116	2.4%
13	New Jersey	359,458	2.4%
14	Indiana	340,264	2.3%
15	Washington	317,066	2.1%
16	Maryland	314,383	2.1%
17	Wisconsin	296,795	2.0%
18	Minnesota	274,192	1.8%
19	Colorado	269,298	1.8%
20	Missouri	260,585	1.7%
21	Alabama	260,523	1.7%
22	Tennessee	241,917	1.6%
23	Kentucky	233,427	1.5%
24	Massachusetts	227,005	1.5%
25	Louisiana	225,210	1.5%
26	Oregon	215,466	1.4%
27	South Carolina	208,302	1.4%
28	Oklahoma	197,373	1.3%
29	Kansas	186,475	1.2%
30	Utah	179,208	1.2%
31	Iowa	178,491	1.2%
32	Mississippi	160,611	1.1%
33	Arkansas	158,760	1.1%
34	New Mexico	146,515	1.0%
35	Connecticut	126,487	0.8%
36	Nebraska	106,794	0.7%
37	Nevada	105,048	0.7%
38	West Virginia	95,634	0.6%
39	Idaho	65,753	0.4%
40	Hawaii	60,330	0.4%
41	Maine	50,253	0.3%
42	Montana	48,912	0.3%
43	North Dakota	48,868	0.3%
44	South Dakota	43,729	0.3%
45	New Hampshire	43,333	0.3%
46	Rhode Island	43,254	0.3%
47	Delaware	40,698	0.3%
48	Wyoming	36,368	0.2%
49	Alaska	32,158	0.2%
50	Vermont	27,132	0.2%
	District of Columbia	5,280	0.0%

Source: U.S. Department of Education, National Center for Education Statistics
"Digest of Education Statistics 2012" (http://nces.ed.gov/programs/digest/index.asp)
*Fall 2011 enrollment. Includes full-time and part-time students at Title IV eligible, degree-granting four-year and two-year institutions. National total includes 15,692 students at U.S. Service Schools not shown by state.

Enrollment in Private Institutions of Higher Education in 2011

National Total = 5,883,917 Students*

ALPHA ORDER

RANK	STATE	STUDENTS	% of USA
27	Alabama	58,163	1.0%
49	Alaska	2,774	0.0%
3	Arizona	430,870	7.3%
39	Arkansas	20,521	0.3%
2	California	507,264	8.6%
19	Colorado	96,522	1.6%
23	Connecticut	75,151	1.3%
44	Delaware	15,818	0.3%
5	Florida	340,498	5.8%
14	Georgia	136,751	2.3%
40	Hawaii	18,688	0.3%
37	Idaho	24,389	0.4%
6	Illinois	315,838	5.4%
16	Indiana	117,560	2.0%
10	Iowa	193,655	3.3%
36	Kansas	30,187	0.5%
26	Kentucky	60,339	1.0%
32	Louisiana	40,646	0.7%
38	Maine	22,044	0.4%
25	Maryland	65,714	1.1%
7	Massachusetts	281,549	4.8%
15	Michigan	130,785	2.2%
12	Minnesota	183,560	3.1%
41	Mississippi	18,479	0.3%
9	Missouri	196,412	3.3%
48	Montana	5,130	0.1%
33	Nebraska	36,081	0.6%
43	Nevada	15,965	0.3%
34	New Hampshire	34,111	0.6%
21	New Jersey	84,292	1.4%
46	New Mexico	11,040	0.2%
1	New York	586,228	10.0%
17	North Carolina	114,024	1.9%
47	North Dakota	6,904	0.1%
11	Ohio	192,252	3.3%
35	Oklahoma	32,781	0.6%
30	Oregon	43,595	0.7%
4	Pennsylvania	359,520	6.1%
31	Rhode Island	41,390	0.7%
29	South Carolina	51,700	0.9%
45	South Dakota	12,170	0.2%
18	Tennessee	108,358	1.8%
8	Texas	197,382	3.4%
20	Utah	85,188	1.4%
42	Vermont	18,011	0.3%
13	Virginia	174,704	3.0%
28	Washington	55,775	0.9%
24	West Virginia	66,674	1.1%
22	Wisconsin	79,808	1.4%
50	Wyoming	1,724	0.0%

RANK ORDER

RANK	STATE	STUDENTS	% of USA
1	New York	586,228	10.0%
2	California	507,264	8.6%
3	Arizona	430,870	7.3%
4	Pennsylvania	359,520	6.1%
5	Florida	340,498	5.8%
6	Illinois	315,838	5.4%
7	Massachusetts	281,549	4.8%
8	Texas	197,382	3.4%
9	Missouri	196,412	3.3%
10	Iowa	193,655	3.3%
11	Ohio	192,252	3.3%
12	Minnesota	183,560	3.1%
13	Virginia	174,704	3.0%
14	Georgia	136,751	2.3%
15	Michigan	130,785	2.2%
16	Indiana	117,560	2.0%
17	North Carolina	114,024	1.9%
18	Tennessee	108,358	1.8%
19	Colorado	96,522	1.6%
20	Utah	85,188	1.4%
21	New Jersey	84,292	1.4%
22	Wisconsin	79,808	1.4%
23	Connecticut	75,151	1.3%
24	West Virginia	66,674	1.1%
25	Maryland	65,714	1.1%
26	Kentucky	60,339	1.0%
27	Alabama	58,163	1.0%
28	Washington	55,775	0.9%
29	South Carolina	51,700	0.9%
30	Oregon	43,595	0.7%
31	Rhode Island	41,390	0.7%
32	Louisiana	40,646	0.7%
33	Nebraska	36,081	0.6%
34	New Hampshire	34,111	0.6%
35	Oklahoma	32,781	0.6%
36	Kansas	30,187	0.5%
37	Idaho	24,389	0.4%
38	Maine	22,044	0.4%
39	Arkansas	20,521	0.3%
40	Hawaii	18,688	0.3%
41	Mississippi	18,479	0.3%
42	Vermont	18,011	0.3%
43	Nevada	15,965	0.3%
44	Delaware	15,818	0.3%
45	South Dakota	12,170	0.2%
46	New Mexico	11,040	0.2%
47	North Dakota	6,904	0.1%
48	Montana	5,130	0.1%
49	Alaska	2,774	0.0%
50	Wyoming	1,724	0.0%
	District of Columbia	84,933	1.4%

Source: U.S. Department of Education, National Center for Education Statistics
   "Digest of Education Statistics 2012" (http://nces.ed.gov/programs/digest/index.asp)
*Fall 2011 enrollment. Includes full-time and part-time students at Title IV eligible, degree-granting four-year and two-year institutions.

Percent of Population with a Bachelor's Degree or More in 2012

National Percent = 29.1%*

ALPHA ORDER				RANK ORDER		
RANK	STATE	PERCENT		RANK	STATE	PERCENT
44	Alabama	23.3		1	Massachusetts	39.3
23	Alaska	28.0		2	Colorado	37.5
28	Arizona	27.3		3	Connecticut	37.1
48	Arkansas	21.0		4	Maryland	36.9
14	California	30.9		5	New Jersey	36.2
2	Colorado	37.5		6	Vermont	35.8
3	Connecticut	37.1		7	Virginia	35.5
19	Delaware	29.5		8	New Hampshire	34.6
30	Florida	26.8		9	New York	33.4
22	Georgia	28.2		10	Minnesota	33.2
17	Hawaii	30.1		11	Washington	31.7
37	Idaho	25.5		12	Illinois	31.6
12	Illinois	31.6		13	Rhode Island	31.4
43	Indiana	23.4		14	California	30.9
33	Iowa	26.3		15	Utah	30.7
16	Kansas	30.4		16	Kansas	30.4
47	Kentucky	21.8		17	Hawaii	30.1
46	Louisiana	22.0		18	Oregon	29.9
23	Maine	28.0		19	Delaware	29.5
4	Maryland	36.9		20	Montana	29.4
1	Massachusetts	39.3		21	Nebraska	29.0
36	Michigan	26.0		22	Georgia	28.2
10	Minnesota	33.2		23	Alaska	28.0
49	Mississippi	20.7		23	Maine	28.0
32	Missouri	26.4		25	North Dakota	27.9
20	Montana	29.4		26	Pennsylvania	27.8
21	Nebraska	29.0		27	North Carolina	27.4
45	Nevada	22.4		28	Arizona	27.3
8	New Hampshire	34.6		29	Wisconsin	27.1
5	New Jersey	36.2		30	Florida	26.8
35	New Mexico	26.1		31	Texas	26.7
9	New York	33.4		32	Missouri	26.4
27	North Carolina	27.4		33	Iowa	26.3
25	North Dakota	27.9		33	South Dakota	26.3
38	Ohio	25.2		35	New Mexico	26.1
42	Oklahoma	23.8		36	Michigan	26.0
18	Oregon	29.9		37	Idaho	25.5
26	Pennsylvania	27.8		38	Ohio	25.2
13	Rhode Island	31.4		39	South Carolina	25.1
39	South Carolina	25.1		40	Wyoming	24.7
33	South Dakota	26.3		41	Tennessee	24.3
41	Tennessee	24.3		42	Oklahoma	23.8
31	Texas	26.7		43	Indiana	23.4
15	Utah	30.7		44	Alabama	23.3
6	Vermont	35.8		45	Nevada	22.4
7	Virginia	35.5		46	Louisiana	22.0
11	Washington	31.7		47	Kentucky	21.8
50	West Virginia	18.6		48	Arkansas	21.0
29	Wisconsin	27.1		49	Mississippi	20.7
40	Wyoming	24.7		50	West Virginia	18.6
					District of Columbia	53.0

Source: U.S. Bureau of the Census
   "2012 American Community Survey-Table R1502" (http://www.census.gov/acs/www/index.html)
*Persons age 25 and older.

Percent of Population Who Have Completed an Advanced Degree in 2012

National Percent = 10.9%*

ALPHA ORDER

RANK	STATE	PERCENT
37	Alabama	8.6
17	Alaska	10.9
24	Arizona	10.2
50	Arkansas	7.2
13	California	11.3
8	Colorado	13.7
3	Connecticut	16.6
12	Delaware	11.4
29	Florida	9.6
22	Georgia	10.4
21	Hawaii	10.5
41	Idaho	8.2
11	Illinois	12.0
39	Indiana	8.4
41	Iowa	8.2
17	Kansas	10.9
36	Kentucky	8.9
47	Louisiana	7.5
26	Maine	9.8
2	Maryland	16.9
1	Massachusetts	17.1
25	Michigan	10.0
20	Minnesota	10.8
46	Mississippi	7.6
27	Missouri	9.7
33	Montana	9.2
27	Nebraska	9.7
47	Nevada	7.5
10	New Hampshire	12.6
7	New Jersey	13.8
16	New Mexico	11.2
5	New York	14.4
30	North Carolina	9.3
39	North Dakota	8.4
30	Ohio	9.3
44	Oklahoma	7.9
13	Oregon	11.3
17	Pennsylvania	10.9
9	Rhode Island	12.8
34	South Carolina	9.1
43	South Dakota	8.1
37	Tennessee	8.6
35	Texas	9.0
22	Utah	10.4
6	Vermont	13.9
4	Virginia	14.9
13	Washington	11.3
49	West Virginia	7.3
30	Wisconsin	9.3
45	Wyoming	7.8

RANK ORDER

RANK	STATE	PERCENT
1	Massachusetts	17.1
2	Maryland	16.9
3	Connecticut	16.6
4	Virginia	14.9
5	New York	14.4
6	Vermont	13.9
7	New Jersey	13.8
8	Colorado	13.7
9	Rhode Island	12.8
10	New Hampshire	12.6
11	Illinois	12.0
12	Delaware	11.4
13	California	11.3
13	Oregon	11.3
13	Washington	11.3
16	New Mexico	11.2
17	Alaska	10.9
17	Kansas	10.9
17	Pennsylvania	10.9
20	Minnesota	10.8
21	Hawaii	10.5
22	Georgia	10.4
22	Utah	10.4
24	Arizona	10.2
25	Michigan	10.0
26	Maine	9.8
27	Missouri	9.7
27	Nebraska	9.7
29	Florida	9.6
30	North Carolina	9.3
30	Ohio	9.3
30	Wisconsin	9.3
33	Montana	9.2
34	South Carolina	9.1
35	Texas	9.0
36	Kentucky	8.9
37	Alabama	8.6
37	Tennessee	8.6
39	Indiana	8.4
39	North Dakota	8.4
41	Idaho	8.2
41	Iowa	8.2
43	South Dakota	8.1
44	Oklahoma	7.9
45	Wyoming	7.8
46	Mississippi	7.6
47	Louisiana	7.5
47	Nevada	7.5
49	West Virginia	7.3
50	Arkansas	7.2

District of Columbia   30.0

Source: U.S. Bureau of the Census
    "2012 American Community Survey-Table R1503" (http://www.census.gov/acs/www/index.html)
*Persons age 25 and older who have earned a master's degree or higher.

Public Libraries and Branches in 2010

National Total = 16,417 Libraries and Branches*

ALPHA ORDER

RANK	STATE	LIBRARIES	% of USA
22	Alabama	289	1.8%
44	Alaska	91	0.6%
31	Arizona	216	1.3%
30	Arkansas	219	1.3%
1	California	1,107	6.7%
24	Colorado	250	1.5%
27	Connecticut	230	1.4%
50	Delaware	32	0.2%
9	Florida	525	3.2%
14	Georgia	392	2.4%
49	Hawaii	51	0.3%
39	Idaho	139	0.8%
4	Illinois	783	4.8%
12	Indiana	434	2.6%
8	Iowa	553	3.4%
16	Kansas	358	2.2%
34	Kentucky	200	1.2%
20	Louisiana	336	2.0%
29	Maine	221	1.3%
36	Maryland	184	1.1%
11	Massachusetts	455	2.8%
6	Michigan	653	4.0%
18	Minnesota	357	2.2%
25	Mississippi	235	1.4%
16	Missouri	358	2.2%
42	Montana	110	0.7%
26	Nebraska	234	1.4%
45	Nevada	86	0.5%
28	New Hampshire	226	1.4%
13	New Jersey	432	2.6%
43	New Mexico	108	0.7%
2	New York	1,066	6.5%
15	North Carolina	387	2.4%
46	North Dakota	82	0.5%
5	Ohio	720	4.4%
33	Oklahoma	207	1.3%
32	Oregon	215	1.3%
7	Pennsylvania	634	3.9%
48	Rhode Island	73	0.4%
35	South Carolina	193	1.2%
41	South Dakota	125	0.8%
22	Tennessee	289	1.8%
3	Texas	852	5.2%
40	Utah	126	0.8%
38	Vermont	161	1.0%
19	Virginia	354	2.2%
21	Washington	334	2.0%
37	West Virginia	174	1.1%
10	Wisconsin	460	2.8%
47	Wyoming	76	0.5%

RANK ORDER

RANK	STATE	LIBRARIES	% of USA
1	California	1,107	6.7%
2	New York	1,066	6.5%
3	Texas	852	5.2%
4	Illinois	783	4.8%
5	Ohio	720	4.4%
6	Michigan	653	4.0%
7	Pennsylvania	634	3.9%
8	Iowa	553	3.4%
9	Florida	525	3.2%
10	Wisconsin	460	2.8%
11	Massachusetts	455	2.8%
12	Indiana	434	2.6%
13	New Jersey	432	2.6%
14	Georgia	392	2.4%
15	North Carolina	387	2.4%
16	Kansas	358	2.2%
16	Missouri	358	2.2%
18	Minnesota	357	2.2%
19	Virginia	354	2.2%
20	Louisiana	336	2.0%
21	Washington	334	2.0%
22	Alabama	289	1.8%
22	Tennessee	289	1.8%
24	Colorado	250	1.5%
25	Mississippi	235	1.4%
26	Nebraska	234	1.4%
27	Connecticut	230	1.4%
28	New Hampshire	226	1.4%
29	Maine	221	1.3%
30	Arkansas	219	1.3%
31	Arizona	216	1.3%
32	Oregon	215	1.3%
33	Oklahoma	207	1.3%
34	Kentucky	200	1.2%
35	South Carolina	193	1.2%
36	Maryland	184	1.1%
37	West Virginia	174	1.1%
38	Vermont	161	1.0%
39	Idaho	139	0.8%
40	Utah	126	0.8%
41	South Dakota	125	0.8%
42	Montana	110	0.7%
43	New Mexico	108	0.7%
44	Alaska	91	0.6%
45	Nevada	86	0.5%
46	North Dakota	82	0.5%
47	Wyoming	76	0.5%
48	Rhode Island	73	0.4%
49	Hawaii	51	0.3%
50	Delaware	32	0.2%
	District of Columbia	25	0.2%

Source: Institute of Museum and Library Services
  "Public Library Survey Fiscal Year 2010" (January 2013, http://www.imls.gov/research/default.aspx)
*For fiscal year 2010. Total of central and branch outlets. Does not include bookmobiles. There are 8,951 public libraries.

Rate of Public Libraries and Branches in 2010

National Average = 18,842 Population per Library*

ALPHA ORDER

RANK	STATE	RATE
25	Alabama	16,556
43	Alaska	7,847
5	Arizona	29,680
35	Arkansas	13,346
2	California	33,726
17	Colorado	20,194
28	Connecticut	15,551
7	Delaware	28,120
1	Florida	35,897
9	Georgia	24,783
8	Hawaii	26,750
38	Idaho	11,301
26	Illinois	16,399
30	Indiana	14,954
49	Iowa	5,516
42	Kansas	7,986
15	Kentucky	21,733
34	Louisiana	13,524
47	Maine	6,007
3	Maryland	31,457
32	Massachusetts	14,425
29	Michigan	15,127
31	Minnesota	14,876
36	Mississippi	12,635
24	Missouri	16,749
40	Montana	9,007
44	Nebraska	7,819
4	Nevada	31,439
48	New Hampshire	5,827
16	New Jersey	20,378
20	New Mexico	19,118
21	New York	18,198
10	North Carolina	24,700
41	North Dakota	8,224
27	Ohio	16,025
22	Oklahoma	18,162
23	Oregon	17,852
19	Pennsylvania	20,049
33	Rhode Island	14,421
11	South Carolina	24,020
46	South Dakota	6,530
14	Tennessee	21,995
6	Texas	29,628
13	Utah	22,025
50	Vermont	3,888
12	Virginia	22,670
18	Washington	20,191
39	West Virginia	10,655
37	Wisconsin	12,369
45	Wyoming	7,426

RANK ORDER

RANK	STATE	RATE
1	Florida	35,897
2	California	33,726
3	Maryland	31,457
4	Nevada	31,439
5	Arizona	29,680
6	Texas	29,628
7	Delaware	28,120
8	Hawaii	26,750
9	Georgia	24,783
10	North Carolina	24,700
11	South Carolina	24,020
12	Virginia	22,670
13	Utah	22,025
14	Tennessee	21,995
15	Kentucky	21,733
16	New Jersey	20,378
17	Colorado	20,194
18	Washington	20,191
19	Pennsylvania	20,049
20	New Mexico	19,118
21	New York	18,198
22	Oklahoma	18,162
23	Oregon	17,852
24	Missouri	16,749
25	Alabama	16,556
26	Illinois	16,399
27	Ohio	16,025
28	Connecticut	15,551
29	Michigan	15,127
30	Indiana	14,954
31	Minnesota	14,876
32	Massachusetts	14,425
33	Rhode Island	14,421
34	Louisiana	13,524
35	Arkansas	13,346
36	Mississippi	12,635
37	Wisconsin	12,369
38	Idaho	11,301
39	West Virginia	10,655
40	Montana	9,007
41	North Dakota	8,224
42	Kansas	7,986
43	Alaska	7,847
44	Nebraska	7,819
45	Wyoming	7,426
46	South Dakota	6,530
47	Maine	6,007
48	New Hampshire	5,827
49	Iowa	5,516
50	Vermont	3,888
	District of Columbia	24,200

Source: CQ Press using data from Institute of Museum and Library Services
"Public Library Survey Fiscal Year 2010" (January 2013, http://www.imls.gov/research/default.aspx)
*For fiscal year 2010. Based on total of central and branch outlets. Does not include bookmobiles.

Rate of Books in Public Libraries in 2010

National Rate = 2,613 Books per 1,000 Population*

ALPHA ORDER			RANK ORDER		
RANK	STATE	RATE	RANK	STATE	RATE
40	Alabama	2,017	1	Massachusetts	4,996
19	Alaska	3,314	2	Vermont	4,646
50	Arizona	1,395	3	New Hampshire	4,532
33	Arkansas	2,248	4	Maine	4,527
41	California	2,002	5	Wyoming	4,426
32	Colorado	2,328	6	Rhode Island	4,404
7	Connecticut	4,104	7	Connecticut	4,104
38	Delaware	2,065	8	Iowa	3,972
45	Florida	1,754	9	Indiana	3,949
47	Georgia	1,726	10	Ohio	3,919
28	Hawaii	2,541	11	New York	3,767
25	Idaho	2,748	12	South Dakota	3,585
14	Illinois	3,522	13	Michigan	3,576
9	Indiana	3,949	14	Illinois	3,522
8	Iowa	3,972	15	North Dakota	3,520
16	Kansas	3,519	16	Kansas	3,519
37	Kentucky	2,077	17	Wisconsin	3,479
26	Louisiana	2,622	18	New Jersey	3,366
4	Maine	4,527	19	Alaska	3,314
30	Maryland	2,411	20	Nebraska	3,201
1	Massachusetts	4,996	21	Minnesota	2,936
13	Michigan	3,576	22	Missouri	2,890
21	Minnesota	2,936	23	West Virginia	2,839
43	Mississippi	1,876	24	Montana	2,820
22	Missouri	2,890	25	Idaho	2,748
24	Montana	2,820	26	Louisiana	2,622
20	Nebraska	3,201	27	Oregon	2,618
48	Nevada	1,681	28	Hawaii	2,541
3	New Hampshire	4,532	29	Utah	2,477
18	New Jersey	3,366	30	Maryland	2,411
36	New Mexico	2,144	31	Virginia	2,358
11	New York	3,767	32	Colorado	2,328
46	North Carolina	1,753	33	Arkansas	2,248
15	North Dakota	3,520	34	Washington	2,206
10	Ohio	3,919	35	Pennsylvania	2,186
42	Oklahoma	1,956	36	New Mexico	2,144
27	Oregon	2,618	37	Kentucky	2,077
35	Pennsylvania	2,186	38	Delaware	2,065
6	Rhode Island	4,404	38	South Carolina	2,065
38	South Carolina	2,065	40	Alabama	2,017
12	South Dakota	3,585	41	California	2,002
44	Tennessee	1,862	42	Oklahoma	1,956
49	Texas	1,657	43	Mississippi	1,876
29	Utah	2,477	44	Tennessee	1,862
2	Vermont	4,646	45	Florida	1,754
31	Virginia	2,358	46	North Carolina	1,753
34	Washington	2,206	47	Georgia	1,726
23	West Virginia	2,839	48	Nevada	1,681
17	Wisconsin	3,479	49	Texas	1,657
5	Wyoming	4,426	50	Arizona	1,395
				District of Columbia	3,147

Source: CQ Press using data from Institute of Museum and Library Services
   "Public Library Survey Fiscal Year 2010" (January 2013, http://www.imls.gov/research/default.aspx)
*For fiscal year 2010. Includes serial back files in print.

Rate of Electronic Books in Public Libraries in 2010

National Rate = 60 Electronic Books per 1,000 Population*

RANK	STATE	RATE
11	Alabama	88
8	Alaska	139
20	Arizona	43
39	Arkansas	9
30	California	20
19	Colorado	48
40	Connecticut	8
46	Delaware	4
16	Florida	54
47	Georgia	3
37	Hawaii	10
35	Idaho	13
17	Illinois	51
31	Indiana	18
41	Iowa	7
47	Kansas	3
23	Kentucky	34
34	Louisiana	14
9	Maine	110
32	Maryland	16
23	Massachusetts	34
21	Michigan	35
2	Minnesota	405
43	Mississippi	6
23	Missouri	34
3	Montana	307
5	Nebraska	219
28	Nevada	29
6	New Hampshire	167
26	New Jersey	32
43	New Mexico	6
15	New York	56
21	North Carolina	35
12	North Dakota	82
4	Ohio	249
47	Oklahoma	3
7	Oregon	166
17	Pennsylvania	51
13	Rhode Island	78
33	South Carolina	15
14	South Dakota	70
45	Tennessee	5
37	Texas	10
27	Utah	30
41	Vermont	7
9	Virginia	110
29	Washington	26
35	West Virginia	13
1	Wisconsin	483
50	Wyoming	1

RANK	STATE	RATE
1	Wisconsin	483
2	Minnesota	405
3	Montana	307
4	Ohio	249
5	Nebraska	219
6	New Hampshire	167
7	Oregon	166
8	Alaska	139
9	Maine	110
9	Virginia	110
11	Alabama	88
12	North Dakota	82
13	Rhode Island	78
14	South Dakota	70
15	New York	56
16	Florida	54
17	Illinois	51
17	Pennsylvania	51
19	Colorado	48
20	Arizona	43
21	Michigan	35
21	North Carolina	35
23	Kentucky	34
23	Massachusetts	34
23	Missouri	34
26	New Jersey	32
27	Utah	30
28	Nevada	29
29	Washington	26
30	California	20
31	Indiana	18
32	Maryland	16
33	South Carolina	15
34	Louisiana	14
35	Idaho	13
35	West Virginia	13
37	Hawaii	10
37	Texas	10
39	Arkansas	9
40	Connecticut	8
41	Iowa	7
41	Vermont	7
43	Mississippi	6
43	New Mexico	6
45	Tennessee	5
46	Delaware	4
47	Georgia	3
47	Kansas	3
47	Oklahoma	3
50	Wyoming	1
	District of Columbia	21

Source: CQ Press using data from Institute of Museum and Library Services
"Public Library Survey Fiscal Year 2010" (January 2013, http://www.imls.gov/research/default.aspx)
*For fiscal year 2010.

Internet Terminals in Public Libraries in 2010

National Total = 244,842 Terminals*

ALPHA ORDER

RANK	STATE	TERMINALS	% of USA
18	Alabama	4,773	1.9%
47	Alaska	610	0.2%
22	Arizona	4,403	1.8%
33	Arkansas	2,144	0.9%
1	California	18,846	7.7%
21	Colorado	4,470	1.8%
27	Connecticut	3,783	1.5%
49	Delaware	543	0.2%
4	Florida	15,564	6.4%
9	Georgia	7,599	3.1%
50	Hawaii	274	0.1%
37	Idaho	1,455	0.6%
5	Illinois	11,841	4.8%
8	Indiana	8,114	3.3%
25	Iowa	4,090	1.7%
29	Kansas	3,441	1.4%
26	Kentucky	3,876	1.6%
19	Louisiana	4,557	1.9%
36	Maine	1,470	0.6%
23	Maryland	4,239	1.7%
14	Massachusetts	5,597	2.3%
7	Michigan	10,484	4.3%
17	Minnesota	5,201	2.1%
32	Mississippi	2,409	1.0%
20	Missouri	4,472	1.8%
43	Montana	958	0.4%
34	Nebraska	1,903	0.8%
41	Nevada	1,264	0.5%
39	New Hampshire	1,343	0.5%
11	New Jersey	7,110	2.9%
38	New Mexico	1,373	0.6%
2	New York	16,681	6.8%
12	North Carolina	6,764	2.8%
48	North Dakota	567	0.2%
6	Ohio	11,388	4.7%
31	Oklahoma	2,414	1.0%
30	Oregon	2,781	1.1%
10	Pennsylvania	7,440	3.0%
42	Rhode Island	1,216	0.5%
28	South Carolina	3,493	1.4%
45	South Dakota	906	0.4%
24	Tennessee	4,234	1.7%
3	Texas	16,347	6.7%
35	Utah	1,756	0.7%
44	Vermont	937	0.4%
13	Virginia	6,104	2.5%
15	Washington	5,555	2.3%
40	West Virginia	1,324	0.5%
16	Wisconsin	5,274	2.2%
46	Wyoming	776	0.3%

RANK ORDER

RANK	STATE	TERMINALS	% of USA
1	California	18,846	7.7%
2	New York	16,681	6.8%
3	Texas	16,347	6.7%
4	Florida	15,564	6.4%
5	Illinois	11,841	4.8%
6	Ohio	11,388	4.7%
7	Michigan	10,484	4.3%
8	Indiana	8,114	3.3%
9	Georgia	7,599	3.1%
10	Pennsylvania	7,440	3.0%
11	New Jersey	7,110	2.9%
12	North Carolina	6,764	2.8%
13	Virginia	6,104	2.5%
14	Massachusetts	5,597	2.3%
15	Washington	5,555	2.3%
16	Wisconsin	5,274	2.2%
17	Minnesota	5,201	2.1%
18	Alabama	4,773	1.9%
19	Louisiana	4,557	1.9%
20	Missouri	4,472	1.8%
21	Colorado	4,470	1.8%
22	Arizona	4,403	1.8%
23	Maryland	4,239	1.7%
24	Tennessee	4,234	1.7%
25	Iowa	4,090	1.7%
26	Kentucky	3,876	1.6%
27	Connecticut	3,783	1.5%
28	South Carolina	3,493	1.4%
29	Kansas	3,441	1.4%
30	Oregon	2,781	1.1%
31	Oklahoma	2,414	1.0%
32	Mississippi	2,409	1.0%
33	Arkansas	2,144	0.9%
34	Nebraska	1,903	0.8%
35	Utah	1,756	0.7%
36	Maine	1,470	0.6%
37	Idaho	1,455	0.6%
38	New Mexico	1,373	0.6%
39	New Hampshire	1,343	0.5%
40	West Virginia	1,324	0.5%
41	Nevada	1,264	0.5%
42	Rhode Island	1,216	0.5%
43	Montana	958	0.4%
44	Vermont	937	0.4%
45	South Dakota	906	0.4%
46	Wyoming	776	0.3%
47	Alaska	610	0.2%
48	North Dakota	567	0.2%
49	Delaware	543	0.2%
50	Hawaii	274	0.1%
	District of Columbia	679	0.3%

Source: Institute of Museum and Library Services
"Public Library Survey Fiscal Year 2010" (January 2013, http://www.imls.gov/research/default.aspx)
*For fiscal year 2010. Total of public-use Internet terminals in central and branch outlets.

Rate of Internet Terminals in Public Libraries in 2010

National Rate = 14.9 Terminals per Library*

ALPHA ORDER			RANK ORDER		
RANK	STATE	RATE	RANK	STATE	RATE
16	Alabama	16.5	1	Florida	29.6
46	Alaska	6.7	2	Maryland	23.0
3	Arizona	20.4	3	Arizona	20.4
38	Arkansas	9.8	4	Georgia	19.4
12	California	17.0	4	Kentucky	19.4
9	Colorado	17.9	6	Texas	19.2
18	Connecticut	16.4	7	Indiana	18.7
12	Delaware	17.0	8	South Carolina	18.1
1	Florida	29.6	9	Colorado	17.9
4	Georgia	19.4	10	North Carolina	17.5
50	Hawaii	5.4	11	Virginia	17.2
35	Idaho	10.5	12	California	17.0
22	Illinois	15.1	12	Delaware	17.0
7	Indiana	18.7	14	Rhode Island	16.7
43	Iowa	7.4	15	Washington	16.6
39	Kansas	9.6	16	Alabama	16.5
4	Kentucky	19.4	16	New Jersey	16.5
27	Louisiana	13.6	18	Connecticut	16.4
46	Maine	6.7	19	Michigan	16.1
2	Maryland	23.0	20	Ohio	15.8
31	Massachusetts	12.3	21	New York	15.6
19	Michigan	16.1	22	Illinois	15.1
25	Minnesota	14.6	23	Nevada	14.7
36	Mississippi	10.3	23	Tennessee	14.7
30	Missouri	12.5	25	Minnesota	14.6
40	Montana	8.7	26	Utah	13.9
41	Nebraska	8.1	27	Louisiana	13.6
23	Nevada	14.7	28	Oregon	12.9
48	New Hampshire	5.9	29	New Mexico	12.7
16	New Jersey	16.5	30	Missouri	12.5
29	New Mexico	12.7	31	Massachusetts	12.3
21	New York	15.6	32	Oklahoma	11.7
10	North Carolina	17.5	32	Pennsylvania	11.7
45	North Dakota	6.9	34	Wisconsin	11.5
20	Ohio	15.8	35	Idaho	10.5
32	Oklahoma	11.7	36	Mississippi	10.3
28	Oregon	12.9	37	Wyoming	10.2
32	Pennsylvania	11.7	38	Arkansas	9.8
14	Rhode Island	16.7	39	Kansas	9.6
8	South Carolina	18.1	40	Montana	8.7
44	South Dakota	7.2	41	Nebraska	8.1
23	Tennessee	14.7	42	West Virginia	7.6
6	Texas	19.2	43	Iowa	7.4
26	Utah	13.9	44	South Dakota	7.2
49	Vermont	5.8	45	North Dakota	6.9
11	Virginia	17.2	46	Alaska	6.7
15	Washington	16.6	46	Maine	6.7
42	West Virginia	7.6	48	New Hampshire	5.9
34	Wisconsin	11.5	49	Vermont	5.8
37	Wyoming	10.2	50	Hawaii	5.4
				District of Columbia	27.2

Source: CQ Press using data from Institute of Museum and Library Services
"Public Library Survey Fiscal Year 2010" (January 2013, http://www.imls.gov/research/default.aspx)
*For fiscal year 2010. Total of public-use Internet terminals in central and branch outlets divided by the number of outlets.

Per Capita State Art Agencies' Legislative Appropriations in 2014

National Per Capita = $0.89*

ALPHA ORDER				RANK ORDER		
RANK	STATE	PER CAPITA		RANK	STATE	PER CAPITA
23	Alabama	$0.74		1	Minnesota	$6.31
12	Alaska	1.09		2	Hawaii	3.65
47	Arizona	0.15		3	Delaware	3.57
28	Arkansas	0.69		4	Maryland	2.57
46	California	0.15		5	New York	2.03
42	Colorado	0.38		6	Wyoming	2.01
11	Connecticut	1.54		7	Rhode Island	1.87
3	Delaware	3.57		8	New Jersey	1.84
19	Florida	0.82		9	Massachusetts	1.66
50	Georgia	0.06		10	Utah	1.56
2	Hawaii	3.65		11	Connecticut	1.54
41	Idaho	0.43		12	Alaska	1.09
21	Illinois	0.78		13	Tennessee	1.07
39	Indiana	0.45		14	Oklahoma	1.04
40	Iowa	0.43		15	North Dakota	1.04
49	Kansas	0.07		16	Vermont	1.02
29	Kentucky	0.64		17	Ohio	0.98
36	Louisiana	0.50		18	South Dakota	0.87
34	Maine	0.57		19	Florida	0.82
4	Maryland	2.57		20	Missouri	0.79
9	Massachusetts	1.66		21	Illinois	0.78
26	Michigan	0.71		22	Nebraska	0.78
1	Minnesota	6.31		23	Alabama	0.74
31	Mississippi	0.60		24	North Carolina	0.72
20	Missouri	0.79		25	Pennsylvania	0.71
33	Montana	0.57		26	Michigan	0.71
22	Nebraska	0.78		27	New Mexico	0.69
38	Nevada	0.46		28	Arkansas	0.69
43	New Hampshire	0.29		29	Kentucky	0.64
8	New Jersey	1.84		30	South Carolina	0.63
27	New Mexico	0.69		31	Mississippi	0.60
5	New York	2.03		32	Oregon	0.57
24	North Carolina	0.72		33	Montana	0.57
15	North Dakota	1.04		34	Maine	0.57
17	Ohio	0.98		35	West Virginia	0.55
14	Oklahoma	1.04		36	Louisiana	0.50
32	Oregon	0.57		37	Virginia	0.47
25	Pennsylvania	0.71		38	Nevada	0.46
7	Rhode Island	1.87		39	Indiana	0.45
30	South Carolina	0.63		40	Iowa	0.43
18	South Dakota	0.87		41	Idaho	0.43
13	Tennessee	1.07		42	Colorado	0.38
44	Texas	0.21		43	New Hampshire	0.29
10	Utah	1.56		44	Texas	0.21
16	Vermont	1.02		45	Washington	0.16
37	Virginia	0.47		46	California	0.15
45	Washington	0.16		47	Arizona	0.15
35	West Virginia	0.55		48	Wisconsin	0.13
48	Wisconsin	0.13		49	Kansas	0.07
6	Wyoming	2.01		50	Georgia	0.06
					District of Columbia	18.69

Source: CQ Press using data from National Assembly of State Arts Agencies
"Current State Arts Agency Budgets" (http://www.nasaa-arts.org/Research/Funding/)
*Projected figures for fiscal year 2014. Includes line item appropriations. Line items are legislative appropriations that are not controlled by the state art agencies but are passed through their budgets directly to another entity. Calculated using 2013 census population estimates. National per capita does not include appropriations or population in U.S. territories.

Federal Allocations for Head Start Program in 2012

National Total = $7,682,420,000*

ALPHA ORDER

RANK	STATE	EXPENDITURES	% of USA
16	Alabama	$125,717,736	1.6%
49	Alaska	14,373,541	0.2%
19	Arizona	121,746,967	1.6%
29	Arkansas	75,176,442	1.0%
1	California	957,971,585	12.5%
28	Colorado	80,798,717	1.1%
34	Connecticut	58,755,649	0.8%
47	Delaware	15,341,871	0.2%
5	Florida	313,310,850	4.1%
9	Georgia	198,596,452	2.6%
41	Hawaii	25,594,284	0.3%
40	Idaho	27,252,585	0.4%
4	Illinois	314,325,492	4.1%
22	Indiana	115,222,711	1.5%
33	Iowa	59,267,964	0.8%
32	Kansas	59,800,770	0.8%
17	Kentucky	125,505,972	1.6%
12	Louisiana	167,980,835	2.2%
38	Maine	31,534,389	0.4%
26	Maryland	89,394,017	1.2%
18	Massachusetts	122,724,674	1.6%
7	Michigan	267,668,992	3.5%
27	Minnesota	83,787,316	1.1%
10	Mississippi	180,315,944	2.3%
14	Missouri	138,965,174	1.8%
43	Montana	23,985,541	0.3%
37	Nebraska	42,187,836	0.5%
39	Nevada	29,960,223	0.4%
46	New Hampshire	15,540,919	0.2%
13	New Jersey	149,580,131	1.9%
31	New Mexico	62,550,656	0.8%
3	New York	493,984,026	6.4%
11	North Carolina	171,736,149	2.2%
45	North Dakota	20,059,789	0.3%
6	Ohio	286,668,880	3.7%
25	Oklahoma	97,666,553	1.3%
30	Oregon	70,304,700	0.9%
8	Pennsylvania	261,801,900	3.4%
42	Rhode Island	25,043,856	0.3%
24	South Carolina	99,208,187	1.3%
44	South Dakota	21,605,345	0.3%
15	Tennessee	137,123,145	1.8%
2	Texas	559,620,987	7.3%
36	Utah	45,113,078	0.6%
48	Vermont	15,143,423	0.2%
21	Virginia	115,286,747	1.5%
20	Washington	117,458,766	1.5%
35	West Virginia	58,201,030	0.8%
23	Wisconsin	105,184,250	1.4%
50	Wyoming	13,438,273	0.2%

RANK ORDER

RANK	STATE	EXPENDITURES	% of USA
1	California	$957,971,585	12.5%
2	Texas	559,620,987	7.3%
3	New York	493,984,026	6.4%
4	Illinois	314,325,492	4.1%
5	Florida	313,310,850	4.1%
6	Ohio	286,668,880	3.7%
7	Michigan	267,668,992	3.5%
8	Pennsylvania	261,801,900	3.4%
9	Georgia	198,596,452	2.6%
10	Mississippi	180,315,944	2.3%
11	North Carolina	171,736,149	2.2%
12	Louisiana	167,980,835	2.2%
13	New Jersey	149,580,131	1.9%
14	Missouri	138,965,174	1.8%
15	Tennessee	137,123,145	1.8%
16	Alabama	125,717,736	1.6%
17	Kentucky	125,505,972	1.6%
18	Massachusetts	122,724,674	1.6%
19	Arizona	121,746,967	1.6%
20	Washington	117,458,766	1.5%
21	Virginia	115,286,747	1.5%
22	Indiana	115,222,711	1.5%
23	Wisconsin	105,184,250	1.4%
24	South Carolina	99,208,187	1.3%
25	Oklahoma	97,666,553	1.3%
26	Maryland	89,394,017	1.2%
27	Minnesota	83,787,316	1.1%
28	Colorado	80,798,717	1.1%
29	Arkansas	75,176,442	1.0%
30	Oregon	70,304,700	0.9%
31	New Mexico	62,550,656	0.8%
32	Kansas	59,800,770	0.8%
33	Iowa	59,267,964	0.8%
34	Connecticut	58,755,649	0.8%
35	West Virginia	58,201,030	0.8%
36	Utah	45,113,078	0.6%
37	Nebraska	42,187,836	0.5%
38	Maine	31,534,389	0.4%
39	Nevada	29,960,223	0.4%
40	Idaho	27,252,585	0.4%
41	Hawaii	25,594,284	0.3%
42	Rhode Island	25,043,856	0.3%
43	Montana	23,985,541	0.3%
44	South Dakota	21,605,345	0.3%
45	North Dakota	20,059,789	0.3%
46	New Hampshire	15,540,919	0.2%
47	Delaware	15,341,871	0.2%
48	Vermont	15,143,423	0.2%
49	Alaska	14,373,541	0.2%
50	Wyoming	13,438,273	0.2%
	District of Columbia	27,867,030	0.4%

Source: U.S. Department of Health and Human Services, Administration for Children and Families
"Head Start Fact Sheet Fiscal Year 2012" (http://eclkc.ohs.acf.hhs.gov/hslc/mr/factsheets)
*For fiscal year 2012. National total includes $550,266,135 to Migrant and Native American programs and $295,379,244 to U.S. territories. Does not include $286,124,000 in "support activities" expenditures.

Head Start Program Enrollment in 2012

National Total = 956,497 Children*

ALPHA ORDER

RANK	STATE	ENROLLMENT	% of USA	RANK	STATE	ENROLLMENT	% of USA
15	Alabama	17,301	1.8%	1	California	104,950	10.9%
49	Alaska	1,761	0.2%	2	Texas	71,963	7.5%
21	Arizona	14,137	1.5%	3	New York	51,696	5.4%
29	Arkansas	10,814	1.1%	4	Illinois	41,644	4.3%
1	California	104,950	10.9%	5	Ohio	39,106	4.1%
30	Colorado	10,624	1.1%	6	Florida	38,304	4.0%
35	Connecticut	7,357	0.8%	7	Pennsylvania	36,955	3.8%
46	Delaware	2,209	0.2%	8	Michigan	35,961	3.7%
6	Florida	38,304	4.0%	9	Mississippi	27,323	2.8%
10	Georgia	25,112	2.6%	10	Georgia	25,112	2.6%
39	Hawaii	3,187	0.3%	11	Louisiana	22,054	2.3%
40	Idaho	3,135	0.3%	12	North Carolina	20,484	2.1%
4	Illinois	41,644	4.3%	13	Missouri	18,186	1.9%
18	Indiana	15,515	1.6%	14	Tennessee	17,323	1.8%
32	Iowa	8,133	0.8%	15	Alabama	17,301	1.8%
31	Kansas	8,751	0.9%	16	Kentucky	16,938	1.8%
16	Kentucky	16,938	1.8%	17	New Jersey	15,661	1.6%
11	Louisiana	22,054	2.3%	18	Indiana	15,515	1.6%
38	Maine	3,536	0.4%	19	Virginia	14,462	1.5%
28	Maryland	10,885	1.1%	20	Wisconsin	14,407	1.5%
23	Massachusetts	13,295	1.4%	21	Arizona	14,137	1.5%
8	Michigan	35,961	3.7%	22	Oklahoma	13,925	1.4%
27	Minnesota	11,410	1.2%	23	Massachusetts	13,295	1.4%
9	Mississippi	27,323	2.8%	24	South Carolina	13,225	1.4%
13	Missouri	18,186	1.9%	25	Oregon	12,502	1.3%
42	Montana	3,071	0.3%	26	Washington	12,404	1.3%
37	Nebraska	5,452	0.6%	27	Minnesota	11,410	1.2%
41	Nevada	3,100	0.3%	28	Maryland	10,885	1.1%
48	New Hampshire	1,764	0.2%	29	Arkansas	10,814	1.1%
17	New Jersey	15,661	1.6%	30	Colorado	10,624	1.1%
34	New Mexico	7,839	0.8%	31	Kansas	8,751	0.9%
3	New York	51,696	5.4%	32	Iowa	8,133	0.8%
12	North Carolina	20,484	2.1%	33	West Virginia	8,075	0.8%
45	North Dakota	2,498	0.3%	34	New Mexico	7,839	0.8%
5	Ohio	39,106	4.1%	35	Connecticut	7,357	0.8%
22	Oklahoma	13,925	1.4%	36	Utah	6,117	0.6%
25	Oregon	12,502	1.3%	37	Nebraska	5,452	0.6%
7	Pennsylvania	36,955	3.8%	38	Maine	3,536	0.4%
44	Rhode Island	2,966	0.3%	39	Hawaii	3,187	0.3%
24	South Carolina	13,225	1.4%	40	Idaho	3,135	0.3%
43	South Dakota	2,987	0.3%	41	Nevada	3,100	0.3%
14	Tennessee	17,323	1.8%	42	Montana	3,071	0.3%
2	Texas	71,963	7.5%	43	South Dakota	2,987	0.3%
36	Utah	6,117	0.6%	44	Rhode Island	2,966	0.3%
50	Vermont	1,562	0.2%	45	North Dakota	2,498	0.3%
19	Virginia	14,462	1.5%	46	Delaware	2,209	0.2%
26	Washington	12,404	1.3%	47	Wyoming	1,824	0.2%
33	West Virginia	8,075	0.8%	48	New Hampshire	1,764	0.2%
20	Wisconsin	14,407	1.5%	49	Alaska	1,761	0.2%
47	Wyoming	1,824	0.2%	50	Vermont	1,562	0.2%
					District of Columbia	3,328	0.3%

Source: U.S. Department of Health and Human Services, Administration for Children and Families
"Head Start Fact Sheet Fiscal Year 2012" (http://eclkc.ohs.acf.hhs.gov/hslc/mr/factsheets)
*For fiscal year 2012. National total includes 58,661 enrollees in Migrant and Native American programs and 40,618 enrollees in U.S. territories.

VI. Employment and Labor

Average Annual Pay in 2012

National Average = $49,289*

ALPHA ORDER			RANK ORDER		
RANK	STATE	ANNUAL PAY	RANK	STATE	ANNUAL PAY
32	Alabama	$41,990	1	New York	$62,669
11	Alaska	50,614	2	Connecticut	62,085
21	Arizona	45,593	3	Massachusetts	60,898
46	Arkansas	38,226	4	New Jersey	58,644
5	California	56,784	5	California	56,784
13	Colorado	50,563	6	Maryland	54,035
2	Connecticut	62,085	7	Illinois	52,194
9	Delaware	51,734	8	Washington	51,962
29	Florida	43,211	9	Delaware	51,734
19	Georgia	46,267	10	Virginia	51,646
27	Hawaii	43,385	11	Alaska	50,614
49	Idaho	36,152	12	Texas	50,579
7	Illinois	52,194	13	Colorado	50,563
36	Indiana	41,240	14	Minnesota	49,349
41	Iowa	40,343	15	Pennsylvania	48,397
37	Kansas	41,118	16	New Hampshire	48,272
40	Kentucky	40,451	17	Michigan	46,720
28	Louisiana	43,300	18	Rhode Island	46,716
45	Maine	38,606	19	Georgia	46,267
6	Maryland	54,035	20	North Dakota	45,909
3	Massachusetts	60,898	21	Arizona	45,593
17	Michigan	46,720	22	Wyoming	44,580
14	Minnesota	49,349	23	Oregon	44,258
50	Mississippi	35,875	24	Ohio	44,244
31	Missouri	42,695	25	Tennessee	43,961
47	Montana	37,096	26	Nevada	43,667
44	Nebraska	39,268	27	Hawaii	43,385
26	Nevada	43,667	28	Louisiana	43,300
16	New Hampshire	48,272	29	Florida	43,211
4	New Jersey	58,644	30	North Carolina	43,110
39	New Mexico	40,698	31	Missouri	42,695
1	New York	62,669	32	Alabama	41,990
30	North Carolina	43,110	33	Wisconsin	41,966
20	North Dakota	45,909	34	Oklahoma	41,633
24	Ohio	44,244	35	Utah	41,301
34	Oklahoma	41,633	36	Indiana	41,240
23	Oregon	44,258	37	Kansas	41,118
15	Pennsylvania	48,397	38	Vermont	40,967
18	Rhode Island	46,716	39	New Mexico	40,698
43	South Carolina	39,286	40	Kentucky	40,451
48	South Dakota	36,534	41	Iowa	40,343
25	Tennessee	43,961	42	West Virginia	39,727
12	Texas	50,579	43	South Carolina	39,286
35	Utah	41,301	44	Nebraska	39,268
38	Vermont	40,967	45	Maine	38,606
10	Virginia	51,646	46	Arkansas	38,226
8	Washington	51,962	47	Montana	37,096
42	West Virginia	39,727	48	South Dakota	36,534
33	Wisconsin	41,966	49	Idaho	36,152
22	Wyoming	44,580	50	Mississippi	35,875
				District of Columbia	82,783

Source: U.S. Department of Labor, Bureau of Labor Statistics
   "Quarterly Census of Employment and Wages" (http://www.bls.gov/cew/home.htm)
*Computed by dividing total annual wages of employees covered by unemployment insurance programs by the average monthly number of these employees. Includes bonuses, cash value of meals and lodging, tips and, in many states, employer contributions to certain deferred compensation plans such as 401(k) plans.

Percent Change in Average Annual Pay: 2011 to 2012

National Percent Change = 2.6% Change*

ALPHA ORDER

RANK	STATE	PERCENT CHANGE
37	Alabama	2.0
22	Alaska	2.5
27	Arizona	2.3
22	Arkansas	2.5
7	California	3.2
10	Colorado	3.0
46	Connecticut	1.5
26	Delaware	2.4
33	Florida	2.1
19	Georgia	2.6
33	Hawaii	2.1
46	Idaho	1.5
16	Illinois	2.7
22	Indiana	2.5
13	Iowa	2.9
15	Kansas	2.8
37	Kentucky	2.0
30	Louisiana	2.2
46	Maine	1.5
40	Maryland	1.9
33	Massachusetts	2.1
40	Michigan	1.9
9	Minnesota	3.1
19	Mississippi	2.6
10	Missouri	3.0
4	Montana	3.6
19	Nebraska	2.6
50	Nevada	1.3
33	New Hampshire	2.1
40	New Jersey	1.9
43	New Mexico	1.7
49	New York	1.4
27	North Carolina	2.3
1	North Dakota	9.9
10	Ohio	3.0
2	Oklahoma	3.8
16	Oregon	2.7
13	Pennsylvania	2.9
30	Rhode Island	2.2
30	South Carolina	2.2
7	South Dakota	3.2
5	Tennessee	3.5
2	Texas	3.8
22	Utah	2.5
43	Vermont	1.7
37	Virginia	2.0
6	Washington	3.4
45	West Virginia	1.6
27	Wisconsin	2.3
16	Wyoming	2.7

RANK ORDER

RANK	STATE	PERCENT CHANGE
1	North Dakota	9.9
2	Oklahoma	3.8
2	Texas	3.8
4	Montana	3.6
5	Tennessee	3.5
6	Washington	3.4
7	California	3.2
7	South Dakota	3.2
9	Minnesota	3.1
10	Colorado	3.0
10	Missouri	3.0
10	Ohio	3.0
13	Iowa	2.9
13	Pennsylvania	2.9
15	Kansas	2.8
16	Illinois	2.7
16	Oregon	2.7
16	Wyoming	2.7
19	Georgia	2.6
19	Mississippi	2.6
19	Nebraska	2.6
22	Alaska	2.5
22	Arkansas	2.5
22	Indiana	2.5
22	Utah	2.5
26	Delaware	2.4
27	Arizona	2.3
27	North Carolina	2.3
27	Wisconsin	2.3
30	Louisiana	2.2
30	Rhode Island	2.2
30	South Carolina	2.2
33	Florida	2.1
33	Hawaii	2.1
33	Massachusetts	2.1
33	New Hampshire	2.1
37	Alabama	2.0
37	Kentucky	2.0
37	Virginia	2.0
40	Maryland	1.9
40	Michigan	1.9
40	New Jersey	1.9
43	New Mexico	1.7
43	Vermont	1.7
45	West Virginia	1.6
46	Connecticut	1.5
46	Idaho	1.5
46	Maine	1.5
49	New York	1.4
50	Nevada	1.3

| | District of Columbia | 1.5 |

Source: CQ Press using data from U.S. Department of Labor, Bureau of Labor Statistics
  "Quarterly Census of Employment and Wages" (http://www.bls.gov/cew/home.htm)
*Includes bonuses, cash value of meals and lodging, tips and, in many states, employer contributions to certain deferred compensation plans such as 401(k) plans.

Median Earnings of Male Full-Time Workers in 2012

National Median = $47,473

RANK	STATE	EARNINGS
31	Alabama	$44,567
5	Alaska	57,068
34	Arizona	43,618
49	Arkansas	40,153
16	California	50,139
15	Colorado	50,509
1	Connecticut	61,097
14	Delaware	50,689
47	Florida	40,889
33	Georgia	43,707
25	Hawaii	45,748
43	Idaho	41,664
11	Illinois	51,262
26	Indiana	45,620
27	Iowa	45,305
30	Kansas	44,765
37	Kentucky	42,321
21	Louisiana	47,249
38	Maine	42,280
4	Maryland	57,447
3	Massachusetts	60,243
17	Michigan	49,897
13	Minnesota	50,885
50	Mississippi	40,081
35	Missouri	42,974
44	Montana	41,656
36	Nebraska	42,878
39	Nevada	42,137
6	New Hampshire	54,136
2	New Jersey	60,878
46	New Mexico	41,211
10	New York	51,274
40	North Carolina	41,859
24	North Dakota	45,888
23	Ohio	46,789
45	Oklahoma	41,415
20	Oregon	47,402
18	Pennsylvania	49,330
12	Rhode Island	50,975
42	South Carolina	41,740
48	South Dakota	40,721
41	Tennessee	41,828
28	Texas	44,802
19	Utah	48,540
29	Vermont	44,776
8	Virginia	52,125
7	Washington	52,529
32	West Virginia	44,159
22	Wisconsin	46,898
9	Wyoming	51,932

RANK	STATE	EARNINGS
1	Connecticut	$61,097
2	New Jersey	60,878
3	Massachusetts	60,243
4	Maryland	57,447
5	Alaska	57,068
6	New Hampshire	54,136
7	Washington	52,529
8	Virginia	52,125
9	Wyoming	51,932
10	New York	51,274
11	Illinois	51,262
12	Rhode Island	50,975
13	Minnesota	50,885
14	Delaware	50,689
15	Colorado	50,509
16	California	50,139
17	Michigan	49,897
18	Pennsylvania	49,330
19	Utah	48,540
20	Oregon	47,402
21	Louisiana	47,249
22	Wisconsin	46,898
23	Ohio	46,789
24	North Dakota	45,888
25	Hawaii	45,748
26	Indiana	45,620
27	Iowa	45,305
28	Texas	44,802
29	Vermont	44,776
30	Kansas	44,765
31	Alabama	44,567
32	West Virginia	44,159
33	Georgia	43,707
34	Arizona	43,618
35	Missouri	42,974
36	Nebraska	42,878
37	Kentucky	42,321
38	Maine	42,280
39	Nevada	42,137
40	North Carolina	41,859
41	Tennessee	41,828
42	South Carolina	41,740
43	Idaho	41,664
44	Montana	41,656
45	Oklahoma	41,415
46	New Mexico	41,211
47	Florida	40,889
48	South Dakota	40,721
49	Arkansas	40,153
50	Mississippi	40,081
	District of Columbia	66,754

Source: U.S. Bureau of the Census
"2012 American Community Survey-Table R2001" (http://www.census.gov/acs/www/index.html)

Median Earnings of Female Full-Time Workers in 2012

National Median = $37,412

<table>
<tr><td colspan="3">ALPHA ORDER</td><td colspan="3">RANK ORDER</td></tr>
<tr><td>RANK</td><td>STATE</td><td>EARNINGS</td><td>RANK</td><td>STATE</td><td>EARNINGS</td></tr>
<tr><td>44</td><td>Alabama</td><td>$31,674</td><td>1</td><td>Maryland</td><td>$49,000</td></tr>
<tr><td>6</td><td>Alaska</td><td>42,345</td><td>2</td><td>Connecticut</td><td>47,900</td></tr>
<tr><td>23</td><td>Arizona</td><td>35,974</td><td>3</td><td>New Jersey</td><td>47,878</td></tr>
<tr><td>49</td><td>Arkansas</td><td>30,843</td><td>4</td><td>Massachusetts</td><td>47,651</td></tr>
<tr><td>7</td><td>California</td><td>41,956</td><td>5</td><td>New York</td><td>43,000</td></tr>
<tr><td>14</td><td>Colorado</td><td>40,402</td><td>6</td><td>Alaska</td><td>42,345</td></tr>
<tr><td>2</td><td>Connecticut</td><td>47,900</td><td>7</td><td>California</td><td>41,956</td></tr>
<tr><td>9</td><td>Delaware</td><td>41,120</td><td>8</td><td>New Hampshire</td><td>41,774</td></tr>
<tr><td>30</td><td>Florida</td><td>34,202</td><td>9</td><td>Delaware</td><td>41,120</td></tr>
<tr><td>25</td><td>Georgia</td><td>35,479</td><td>10</td><td>Virginia</td><td>41,104</td></tr>
<tr><td>16</td><td>Hawaii</td><td>38,040</td><td>11</td><td>Rhode Island</td><td>41,074</td></tr>
<tr><td>47</td><td>Idaho</td><td>31,296</td><td>12</td><td>Washington</td><td>41,062</td></tr>
<tr><td>15</td><td>Illinois</td><td>40,309</td><td>13</td><td>Minnesota</td><td>40,595</td></tr>
<tr><td>34</td><td>Indiana</td><td>33,419</td><td>14</td><td>Colorado</td><td>40,402</td></tr>
<tr><td>27</td><td>Iowa</td><td>35,106</td><td>15</td><td>Illinois</td><td>40,309</td></tr>
<tr><td>31</td><td>Kansas</td><td>34,131</td><td>16</td><td>Hawaii</td><td>38,040</td></tr>
<tr><td>41</td><td>Kentucky</td><td>32,157</td><td>17</td><td>Vermont</td><td>38,017</td></tr>
<tr><td>45</td><td>Louisiana</td><td>31,586</td><td>18</td><td>Pennsylvania</td><td>37,414</td></tr>
<tr><td>28</td><td>Maine</td><td>35,057</td><td>19</td><td>Oregon</td><td>37,381</td></tr>
<tr><td>1</td><td>Maryland</td><td>49,000</td><td>20</td><td>Michigan</td><td>36,772</td></tr>
<tr><td>4</td><td>Massachusetts</td><td>47,651</td><td>21</td><td>Wisconsin</td><td>36,535</td></tr>
<tr><td>20</td><td>Michigan</td><td>36,772</td><td>22</td><td>Ohio</td><td>35,984</td></tr>
<tr><td>13</td><td>Minnesota</td><td>40,595</td><td>23</td><td>Arizona</td><td>35,974</td></tr>
<tr><td>50</td><td>Mississippi</td><td>30,287</td><td>24</td><td>Nevada</td><td>35,941</td></tr>
<tr><td>38</td><td>Missouri</td><td>32,868</td><td>25</td><td>Georgia</td><td>35,479</td></tr>
<tr><td>43</td><td>Montana</td><td>31,775</td><td>26</td><td>Texas</td><td>35,453</td></tr>
<tr><td>35</td><td>Nebraska</td><td>33,218</td><td>27</td><td>Iowa</td><td>35,106</td></tr>
<tr><td>24</td><td>Nevada</td><td>35,941</td><td>28</td><td>Maine</td><td>35,057</td></tr>
<tr><td>8</td><td>New Hampshire</td><td>41,774</td><td>29</td><td>North Carolina</td><td>34,421</td></tr>
<tr><td>3</td><td>New Jersey</td><td>47,878</td><td>30</td><td>Florida</td><td>34,202</td></tr>
<tr><td>37</td><td>New Mexico</td><td>33,074</td><td>31</td><td>Kansas</td><td>34,131</td></tr>
<tr><td>5</td><td>New York</td><td>43,000</td><td>32</td><td>Utah</td><td>34,062</td></tr>
<tr><td>29</td><td>North Carolina</td><td>34,421</td><td>33</td><td>North Dakota</td><td>33,877</td></tr>
<tr><td>33</td><td>North Dakota</td><td>33,877</td><td>34</td><td>Indiana</td><td>33,419</td></tr>
<tr><td>22</td><td>Ohio</td><td>35,984</td><td>35</td><td>Nebraska</td><td>33,218</td></tr>
<tr><td>46</td><td>Oklahoma</td><td>31,543</td><td>36</td><td>Wyoming</td><td>33,152</td></tr>
<tr><td>19</td><td>Oregon</td><td>37,381</td><td>37</td><td>New Mexico</td><td>33,074</td></tr>
<tr><td>18</td><td>Pennsylvania</td><td>37,414</td><td>38</td><td>Missouri</td><td>32,868</td></tr>
<tr><td>11</td><td>Rhode Island</td><td>41,074</td><td>39</td><td>South Carolina</td><td>32,402</td></tr>
<tr><td>39</td><td>South Carolina</td><td>32,402</td><td>40</td><td>Tennessee</td><td>32,398</td></tr>
<tr><td>42</td><td>South Dakota</td><td>31,792</td><td>41</td><td>Kentucky</td><td>32,157</td></tr>
<tr><td>40</td><td>Tennessee</td><td>32,398</td><td>42</td><td>South Dakota</td><td>31,792</td></tr>
<tr><td>26</td><td>Texas</td><td>35,453</td><td>43</td><td>Montana</td><td>31,775</td></tr>
<tr><td>32</td><td>Utah</td><td>34,062</td><td>44</td><td>Alabama</td><td>31,674</td></tr>
<tr><td>17</td><td>Vermont</td><td>38,017</td><td>45</td><td>Louisiana</td><td>31,586</td></tr>
<tr><td>10</td><td>Virginia</td><td>41,104</td><td>46</td><td>Oklahoma</td><td>31,543</td></tr>
<tr><td>12</td><td>Washington</td><td>41,062</td><td>47</td><td>Idaho</td><td>31,296</td></tr>
<tr><td>48</td><td>West Virginia</td><td>30,885</td><td>48</td><td>West Virginia</td><td>30,885</td></tr>
<tr><td>21</td><td>Wisconsin</td><td>36,535</td><td>49</td><td>Arkansas</td><td>30,843</td></tr>
<tr><td>36</td><td>Wyoming</td><td>33,152</td><td>50</td><td>Mississippi</td><td>30,287</td></tr>
<tr><td></td><td></td><td></td><td></td><td>District of Columbia</td><td>60,116</td></tr>
</table>

Source: U.S. Bureau of the Census
"2012 American Community Survey-Table R2002" (http://www.census.gov/acs/www/index.html)

State Minimum Wage Rates in 2014

National Rate = $7.25 per Hour*

ALPHA ORDER

RANK	STATE	MINIMUM WAGE
NA	Alabama**	NA
17	Alaska	7.75
15	Arizona	7.90
42	Arkansas	6.25
8	California	8.00
8	Colorado	8.00
4	Connecticut	8.70
22	Delaware	7.25
14	Florida	7.93
44	Georgia	5.15
22	Hawaii	7.25
22	Idaho	7.25
5	Illinois	8.25
22	Indiana	7.25
22	Iowa	7.25
22	Kansas	7.25
22	Kentucky	7.25
NA	Louisiana**	NA
18	Maine	7.50
22	Maryland	7.25
8	Massachusetts	8.00
21	Michigan	7.40
43	Minnesota	6.15
NA	Mississippi**	NA
18	Missouri	7.50
15	Montana	7.90
22	Nebraska	7.25
5	Nevada	8.25
22	New Hampshire	7.25
5	New Jersey	8.25
18	New Mexico	7.50
8	New York	8.00
22	North Carolina	7.25
22	North Dakota	7.25
13	Ohio	7.95
22	Oklahoma	7.25
2	Oregon	9.10
22	Pennsylvania	7.25
8	Rhode Island	8.00
NA	South Carolina**	NA
22	South Dakota	7.25
NA	Tennessee**	NA
22	Texas	7.25
22	Utah	7.25
3	Vermont	8.73
22	Virginia	7.25
1	Washington	9.32
22	West Virginia	7.25
22	Wisconsin	7.25
44	Wyoming	5.15

RANK ORDER

RANK	STATE	MINIMUM WAGE
1	Washington	$9.32
2	Oregon	9.10
3	Vermont	8.73
4	Connecticut	8.70
5	Illinois	8.25
5	Nevada	8.25
5	New Jersey	8.25
8	California	8.00
8	Colorado	8.00
8	Massachusetts	8.00
8	New York	8.00
8	Rhode Island	8.00
13	Ohio	7.95
14	Florida	7.93
15	Arizona	7.90
15	Montana	7.90
17	Alaska	7.75
18	Maine	7.50
18	Missouri	7.50
18	New Mexico	7.50
21	Michigan	7.40
22	Delaware	7.25
22	Hawaii	7.25
22	Idaho	7.25
22	Indiana	7.25
22	Iowa	7.25
22	Kansas	7.25
22	Kentucky	7.25
22	Maryland	7.25
22	Nebraska	7.25
22	New Hampshire	7.25
22	North Carolina	7.25
22	North Dakota	7.25
22	Oklahoma	7.25
22	Pennsylvania	7.25
22	South Dakota	7.25
22	Texas	7.25
22	Utah	7.25
22	Virginia	7.25
22	West Virginia	7.25
22	Wisconsin	7.25
42	Arkansas	6.25
43	Minnesota	6.15
44	Georgia	5.15
44	Wyoming	5.15
NA	Alabama**	NA
NA	Louisiana**	NA
NA	Mississippi**	NA
NA	South Carolina**	NA
NA	Tennessee**	NA

District of Columbia   8.25

Source: U.S. Department of Labor, Employment Standards Administration
    "Minimum Wage Laws in the States" (http://www.dol.gov/esa/minwage/america.htm)
*As of January 1, 2014. State minimum wage rates are for those employers and jobs not covered by the federal program.
**No separate state program.

Average Hourly Earnings of Production Workers on Manufacturing Payrolls in 2013
National Average = $24.64*

ALPHA ORDER

RANK	STATE	HOURLY EARNINGS
36	Alabama	$18.31
3	Alaska	22.27
27	Arizona	18.96
49	Arkansas	15.33
8	California	21.12
2	Colorado	24.60
7	Connecticut	21.53
47	Delaware	16.65
9	Florida	20.78
39	Georgia	18.25
23	Hawaii	19.11
6	Idaho	21.59
17	Illinois	19.42
31	Indiana	18.60
30	Iowa	18.70
33	Kansas	18.55
19	Kentucky	19.38
3	Louisiana	22.27
10	Maine	20.70
14	Maryland	19.91
5	Massachusetts	21.92
13	Michigan	20.09
12	Minnesota	20.15
38	Mississippi	18.29
25	Missouri	19.07
44	Montana	17.12
46	Nebraska	16.92
48	Nevada	16.44
31	New Hampshire	18.60
21	New Jersey	19.19
42	New Mexico	17.35
16	New York	19.45
45	North Carolina	16.97
28	North Dakota	18.89
15	Ohio	19.84
40	Oklahoma	18.07
23	Oregon	19.11
20	Pennsylvania	19.31
22	Rhode Island	19.18
26	South Carolina	19.04
43	South Dakota	17.20
41	Tennessee	17.60
11	Texas	20.50
36	Utah	18.31
35	Vermont	18.44
18	Virginia	19.40
1	Washington	25.48
34	West Virginia	18.45
29	Wisconsin	18.88
NA	Wyoming**	NA

RANK ORDER

RANK	STATE	HOURLY EARNINGS
1	Washington	$25.48
2	Colorado	24.60
3	Alaska	22.27
3	Louisiana	22.27
5	Massachusetts	21.92
6	Idaho	21.59
7	Connecticut	21.53
8	California	21.12
9	Florida	20.78
10	Maine	20.70
11	Texas	20.50
12	Minnesota	20.15
13	Michigan	20.09
14	Maryland	19.91
15	Ohio	19.84
16	New York	19.45
17	Illinois	19.42
18	Virginia	19.40
19	Kentucky	19.38
20	Pennsylvania	19.31
21	New Jersey	19.19
22	Rhode Island	19.18
23	Hawaii	19.11
23	Oregon	19.11
25	Missouri	19.07
26	South Carolina	19.04
27	Arizona	18.96
28	North Dakota	18.89
29	Wisconsin	18.88
30	Iowa	18.70
31	Indiana	18.60
31	New Hampshire	18.60
33	Kansas	18.55
34	West Virginia	18.45
35	Vermont	18.44
36	Alabama	18.31
36	Utah	18.31
38	Mississippi	18.29
39	Georgia	18.25
40	Oklahoma	18.07
41	Tennessee	17.60
42	New Mexico	17.35
43	South Dakota	17.20
44	Montana	17.12
45	North Carolina	16.97
46	Nebraska	16.92
47	Delaware	16.65
48	Nevada	16.44
49	Arkansas	15.33
NA	Wyoming**	NA
	District of Columbia**	NA

Source: U.S. Department of Labor, Bureau of Labor Statistics
  "State and Metro Area Employment, Hours and Earnings" (http://www.bls.gov/sae/home.htm)
*Preliminary data for December 2013. Not seasonally adjusted except for national figure.
**Not available.

Average Weekly Earnings of Production Workers
on Manufacturing Payrolls in 2013
National Average = $1,010.24*

ALPHA ORDER

RANK	STATE	WEEKLY EARNINGS
25	Alabama	$783.67
38	Alaska	730.46
30	Arizona	777.36
48	Arkansas	625.46
10	California	884.93
3	Colorado	974.16
7	Connecticut	902.11
47	Delaware	672.66
9	Florida	885.23
29	Georgia	779.28
34	Hawaii	756.76
11	Idaho	876.55
15	Illinois	833.12
32	Indiana	775.62
26	Iowa	783.53
16	Kansas	825.48
13	Kentucky	848.84
2	Louisiana	1,019.97
8	Maine	892.17
20	Maryland	802.37
4	Massachusetts	920.64
5	Michigan	906.06
14	Minnesota	848.32
27	Mississippi	780.98
23	Missouri	795.22
49	Montana	618.03
39	Nebraska	729.25
46	Nevada	690.48
24	New Hampshire	786.78
19	New Jersey	807.90
45	New Mexico	699.21
21	New York	801.34
40	North Carolina	726.32
44	North Dakota	714.04
12	Ohio	853.12
37	Oklahoma	739.06
31	Oregon	775.87
28	Pennsylvania	780.12
22	Rhode Island	795.97
18	South Carolina	811.10
41	South Dakota	725.84
42	Tennessee	723.36
6	Texas	904.05
36	Utah	741.56
43	Vermont	719.16
17	Virginia	818.68
1	Washington	1,067.61
35	West Virginia	741.69
33	Wisconsin	770.30
NA	Wyoming**	NA

RANK ORDER

RANK	STATE	WEEKLY EARNINGS
1	Washington	$1,067.61
2	Louisiana	1,019.97
3	Colorado	974.16
4	Massachusetts	920.64
5	Michigan	906.06
6	Texas	904.05
7	Connecticut	902.11
8	Maine	892.17
9	Florida	885.23
10	California	884.93
11	Idaho	876.55
12	Ohio	853.12
13	Kentucky	848.84
14	Minnesota	848.32
15	Illinois	833.12
16	Kansas	825.48
17	Virginia	818.68
18	South Carolina	811.10
19	New Jersey	807.90
20	Maryland	802.37
21	New York	801.34
22	Rhode Island	795.97
23	Missouri	795.22
24	New Hampshire	786.78
25	Alabama	783.67
26	Iowa	783.53
27	Mississippi	780.98
28	Pennsylvania	780.12
29	Georgia	779.28
30	Arizona	777.36
31	Oregon	775.87
32	Indiana	775.62
33	Wisconsin	770.30
34	Hawaii	756.76
35	West Virginia	741.69
36	Utah	741.56
37	Oklahoma	739.06
38	Alaska	730.46
39	Nebraska	729.25
40	North Carolina	726.32
41	South Dakota	725.84
42	Tennessee	723.36
43	Vermont	719.16
44	North Dakota	714.04
45	New Mexico	699.21
46	Nevada	690.48
47	Delaware	672.66
48	Arkansas	625.46
49	Montana	618.03
NA	Wyoming**	NA
	District of Columbia**	NA

Source: U.S. Department of Labor, Bureau of Labor Statistics
   "State and Metro Area Employment, Hours and Earnings" (http://www.bls.gov/sae/home.htm)
*Preliminary data for December 2013. Not seasonally adjusted except for national figure.
**Not available.

Average Work Week of Production Workers
on Manufacturing Payrolls in 2013
National Average = 41.0 Hours per Week*

ALPHA ORDER

RANK	STATE	WEEKLY HOURS
10	Alabama	42.8
49	Alaska	32.8
32	Arizona	41.0
34	Arkansas	40.8
23	California	41.9
44	Colorado	39.6
23	Connecticut	41.9
39	Delaware	40.4
14	Florida	42.6
12	Georgia	42.7
44	Hawaii	39.6
36	Idaho	40.6
9	Illinois	42.9
27	Indiana	41.7
23	Iowa	41.9
3	Kansas	44.5
5	Kentucky	43.8
1	Louisiana	45.8
6	Maine	43.1
41	Maryland	40.3
21	Massachusetts	42.0
2	Michigan	45.1
19	Minnesota	42.1
12	Mississippi	42.7
27	Missouri	41.7
48	Montana	36.1
6	Nebraska	43.1
21	Nevada	42.0
16	New Hampshire	42.3
19	New Jersey	42.1
41	New Mexico	40.3
30	New York	41.2
10	North Carolina	42.8
47	North Dakota	37.8
8	Ohio	43.0
33	Oklahoma	40.9
36	Oregon	40.6
39	Pennsylvania	40.4
29	Rhode Island	41.5
14	South Carolina	42.6
17	South Dakota	42.2
31	Tennessee	41.1
4	Texas	44.1
38	Utah	40.5
46	Vermont	39.0
17	Virginia	42.2
23	Washington	41.9
43	West Virginia	40.2
34	Wisconsin	40.8
NA	Wyoming**	NA

RANK ORDER

RANK	STATE	WEEKLY HOURS
1	Louisiana	45.8
2	Michigan	45.1
3	Kansas	44.5
4	Texas	44.1
5	Kentucky	43.8
6	Maine	43.1
6	Nebraska	43.1
8	Ohio	43.0
9	Illinois	42.9
10	Alabama	42.8
10	North Carolina	42.8
12	Georgia	42.7
12	Mississippi	42.7
14	Florida	42.6
14	South Carolina	42.6
16	New Hampshire	42.3
17	South Dakota	42.2
17	Virginia	42.2
19	Minnesota	42.1
19	New Jersey	42.1
21	Massachusetts	42.0
21	Nevada	42.0
23	California	41.9
23	Connecticut	41.9
23	Iowa	41.9
23	Washington	41.9
27	Indiana	41.7
27	Missouri	41.7
29	Rhode Island	41.5
30	New York	41.2
31	Tennessee	41.1
32	Arizona	41.0
33	Oklahoma	40.9
34	Arkansas	40.8
34	Wisconsin	40.8
36	Idaho	40.6
36	Oregon	40.6
38	Utah	40.5
39	Delaware	40.4
39	Pennsylvania	40.4
41	Maryland	40.3
41	New Mexico	40.3
43	West Virginia	40.2
44	Colorado	39.6
44	Hawaii	39.6
46	Vermont	39.0
47	North Dakota	37.8
48	Montana	36.1
49	Alaska	32.8
NA	Wyoming**	NA
	District of Columbia**	NA

Source: U.S. Department of Labor, Bureau of Labor Statistics
    "State and Metro Area Employment, Hours and Earnings" (http://www.bls.gov/sae/home.htm)
*Preliminary data for December 2013. Not seasonally adjusted except for national figure.
**Not available.

Average Weekly Unemployment Benefit in 2013

National Average = $309.21 a Week

ALPHA ORDER

RANK	STATE	BENEFIT
49	Alabama	$207.13
40	Alaska	249.56
47	Arizona	220.67
29	Arkansas	289.12
23	California	300.94
9	Colorado	356.94
12	Connecticut	344.80
42	Delaware	245.01
46	Florida	231.84
38	Georgia	266.72
2	Hawaii	423.81
39	Idaho	264.15
17	Illinois	322.87
43	Indiana	242.40
15	Iowa	335.72
14	Kansas	340.50
28	Kentucky	291.78
48	Louisiana	207.46
33	Maine	285.54
16	Maryland	329.35
1	Massachusetts	426.70
27	Michigan	292.51
6	Minnesota	376.70
50	Mississippi	194.27
44	Missouri	241.26
30	Montana	288.83
34	Nebraska	275.91
22	Nevada	302.93
31	New Hampshire	287.55
3	New Jersey	397.83
25	New Mexico	294.78
21	New York	308.32
32	North Carolina	287.51
4	North Dakota	396.80
18	Ohio	317.33
26	Oklahoma	292.93
19	Oregon	316.42
8	Pennsylvania	359.58
10	Rhode Island	350.61
41	South Carolina	248.13
37	South Dakota	272.50
45	Tennessee	236.88
13	Texas	341.35
11	Utah	345.43
20	Vermont	310.87
24	Virginia	295.81
5	Washington	388.58
36	West Virginia	274.52
35	Wisconsin	274.97
7	Wyoming	360.35

RANK ORDER

RANK	STATE	BENEFIT
1	Massachusetts	$426.70
2	Hawaii	423.81
3	New Jersey	397.83
4	North Dakota	396.80
5	Washington	388.58
6	Minnesota	376.70
7	Wyoming	360.35
8	Pennsylvania	359.58
9	Colorado	356.94
10	Rhode Island	350.61
11	Utah	345.43
12	Connecticut	344.80
13	Texas	341.35
14	Kansas	340.50
15	Iowa	335.72
16	Maryland	329.35
17	Illinois	322.87
18	Ohio	317.33
19	Oregon	316.42
20	Vermont	310.87
21	New York	308.32
22	Nevada	302.93
23	California	300.94
24	Virginia	295.81
25	New Mexico	294.78
26	Oklahoma	292.93
27	Michigan	292.51
28	Kentucky	291.78
29	Arkansas	289.12
30	Montana	288.83
31	New Hampshire	287.55
32	North Carolina	287.51
33	Maine	285.54
34	Nebraska	275.91
35	Wisconsin	274.97
36	West Virginia	274.52
37	South Dakota	272.50
38	Georgia	266.72
39	Idaho	264.15
40	Alaska	249.56
41	South Carolina	248.13
42	Delaware	245.01
43	Indiana	242.40
44	Missouri	241.26
45	Tennessee	236.88
46	Florida	231.84
47	Arizona	220.67
48	Louisiana	207.46
49	Alabama	207.13
50	Mississippi	194.27
	District of Columbia	299.46

Source: CQ Press using data from U.S. Department of Labor, Bureau of Labor Statistics
"Unemployment Insurance Data Summary" (http://workforcesecurity.doleta.gov/unemploy/finance.asp)

Workers' Compensation Benefit Payments in 2011

National Total = $60,210,113,000*

ALPHA ORDER

RANK	STATE	PAYMENTS	% of USA
29	Alabama	$616,022,000	1.0%
42	Alaska	238,789,000	0.4%
25	Arizona	711,801,000	1.2%
45	Arkansas	189,123,000	0.3%
1	California	10,477,086,000	17.4%
24	Colorado	760,599,000	1.3%
20	Connecticut	865,920,000	1.4%
44	Delaware	219,971,000	0.4%
5	Florida	2,711,148,000	4.5%
11	Georgia	1,389,746,000	2.3%
40	Hawaii	246,780,000	0.4%
41	Idaho	245,429,000	0.4%
3	Illinois	3,074,406,000	5.1%
28	Indiana	625,111,000	1.0%
27	Iowa	626,720,000	1.0%
32	Kansas	435,641,000	0.7%
26	Kentucky	656,441,000	1.1%
19	Louisiana	869,762,000	1.4%
39	Maine	252,017,000	0.4%
15	Maryland	1,006,998,000	1.7%
16	Massachusetts	962,596,000	1.6%
12	Michigan	1,301,061,000	2.2%
14	Minnesota	1,011,017,000	1.7%
34	Mississippi	334,430,000	0.6%
22	Missouri	813,686,000	1.4%
38	Montana	252,550,000	0.4%
35	Nebraska	321,306,000	0.5%
33	Nevada	381,176,000	0.6%
43	New Hampshire	227,488,000	0.4%
8	New Jersey	2,168,517,000	3.6%
36	New Mexico	275,783,000	0.5%
2	New York	5,097,055,000	8.5%
10	North Carolina	1,420,429,000	2.4%
49	North Dakota	125,960,000	0.2%
7	Ohio	2,232,596,000	3.7%
21	Oklahoma	839,308,000	1.4%
30	Oregon	568,516,000	0.9%
4	Pennsylvania	2,894,165,000	4.8%
46	Rhode Island	168,291,000	0.3%
18	South Carolina	874,227,000	1.5%
50	South Dakota	90,844,000	0.2%
23	Tennessee	783,729,000	1.3%
9	Texas	1,604,137,000	2.7%
37	Utah	256,742,000	0.4%
48	Vermont	136,795,000	0.2%
17	Virginia	875,090,000	1.5%
6	Washington	2,316,713,000	3.8%
31	West Virginia	505,924,000	0.8%
13	Wisconsin	1,099,950,000	1.8%
47	Wyoming	162,388,000	0.3%

RANK ORDER

RANK	STATE	PAYMENTS	% of USA
1	California	$10,477,086,000	17.4%
2	New York	5,097,055,000	8.5%
3	Illinois	3,074,406,000	5.1%
4	Pennsylvania	2,894,165,000	4.8%
5	Florida	2,711,148,000	4.5%
6	Washington	2,316,713,000	3.8%
7	Ohio	2,232,596,000	3.7%
8	New Jersey	2,168,517,000	3.6%
9	Texas	1,604,137,000	2.7%
10	North Carolina	1,420,429,000	2.4%
11	Georgia	1,389,746,000	2.3%
12	Michigan	1,301,061,000	2.2%
13	Wisconsin	1,099,950,000	1.8%
14	Minnesota	1,011,017,000	1.7%
15	Maryland	1,006,998,000	1.7%
16	Massachusetts	962,596,000	1.6%
17	Virginia	875,090,000	1.5%
18	South Carolina	874,227,000	1.5%
19	Louisiana	869,762,000	1.4%
20	Connecticut	865,920,000	1.4%
21	Oklahoma	839,308,000	1.4%
22	Missouri	813,686,000	1.4%
23	Tennessee	783,729,000	1.3%
24	Colorado	760,599,000	1.3%
25	Arizona	711,801,000	1.2%
26	Kentucky	656,441,000	1.1%
27	Iowa	626,720,000	1.0%
28	Indiana	625,111,000	1.0%
29	Alabama	616,022,000	1.0%
30	Oregon	568,516,000	0.9%
31	West Virginia	505,924,000	0.8%
32	Kansas	435,641,000	0.7%
33	Nevada	381,176,000	0.6%
34	Mississippi	334,430,000	0.6%
35	Nebraska	321,306,000	0.5%
36	New Mexico	275,783,000	0.5%
37	Utah	256,742,000	0.4%
38	Montana	252,550,000	0.4%
39	Maine	252,017,000	0.4%
40	Hawaii	246,780,000	0.4%
41	Idaho	245,429,000	0.4%
42	Alaska	238,789,000	0.4%
43	New Hampshire	227,488,000	0.4%
44	Delaware	219,971,000	0.4%
45	Arkansas	189,123,000	0.3%
46	Rhode Island	168,291,000	0.3%
47	Wyoming	162,388,000	0.3%
48	Vermont	136,795,000	0.2%
49	North Dakota	125,960,000	0.2%
50	South Dakota	90,844,000	0.2%
	District of Columbia	111,141,000	0.2%

Source: National Academy of Social Insurance (Washington, DC)
    "Workers' Compensation: Benefits, Coverage, and Costs, 2011" (http://www.nasi.org)
*Estimated payments from private insurance, state and federal funds, and self insurance. National total includes payments for federal civilian employee program, Black Lung Program, and other federal programs.

Workers' Compensation Benefit Payment per Covered Worker in 2011

National Average = $478*

ALPHA ORDER

RANK	STATE	AVERAGE
33	Alabama	$367
2	Alaska	783
44	Arizona	306
50	Arkansas	175
4	California	732
35	Colorado	354
12	Connecticut	543
11	Delaware	555
24	Florida	405
28	Georgia	388
19	Hawaii	442
23	Idaho	412
10	Illinois	562
47	Indiana	231
19	Iowa	442
38	Kansas	344
26	Kentucky	389
15	Louisiana	480
18	Maine	448
21	Maryland	432
43	Massachusetts	307
35	Michigan	354
25	Minnesota	396
41	Mississippi	335
40	Missouri	338
5	Montana	622
32	Nebraska	368
37	Nevada	348
31	New Hampshire	380
9	New Jersey	588
30	New Mexico	383
6	New York	614
26	North Carolina	389
38	North Dakota	344
17	Ohio	457
7	Oklahoma	610
34	Oregon	358
13	Pennsylvania	535
29	Rhode Island	385
14	South Carolina	520
46	South Dakota	240
42	Tennessee	319
49	Texas	192
48	Utah	226
16	Vermont	477
45	Virginia	264
1	Washington	856
3	West Virginia	767
22	Wisconsin	430
8	Wyoming	608

RANK ORDER

RANK	STATE	AVERAGE
1	Washington	$856
2	Alaska	783
3	West Virginia	767
4	California	732
5	Montana	622
6	New York	614
7	Oklahoma	610
8	Wyoming	608
9	New Jersey	588
10	Illinois	562
11	Delaware	555
12	Connecticut	543
13	Pennsylvania	535
14	South Carolina	520
15	Louisiana	480
16	Vermont	477
17	Ohio	457
18	Maine	448
19	Hawaii	442
19	Iowa	442
21	Maryland	432
22	Wisconsin	430
23	Idaho	412
24	Florida	405
25	Minnesota	396
26	Kentucky	389
26	North Carolina	389
28	Georgia	388
29	Rhode Island	385
30	New Mexico	383
31	New Hampshire	380
32	Nebraska	368
33	Alabama	367
34	Oregon	358
35	Colorado	354
35	Michigan	354
37	Nevada	348
38	Kansas	344
38	North Dakota	344
40	Missouri	338
41	Mississippi	335
42	Tennessee	319
43	Massachusetts	307
44	Arizona	306
45	Virginia	264
46	South Dakota	240
47	Indiana	231
48	Utah	226
49	Texas	192
50	Arkansas	175
	District of Columbia	225

Source: CQ Press using data from National Academy of Social Insurance (Washington, DC)
"Workers' Compensation: Benefits, Coverage, and Costs, 2011" (http://www.nasi.org)
*Estimated payments from private insurance, state and federal funds, and self insurance. National rate includes payments for federal civilian employee program, Black Lung Program, and other federal programs. Total divided by number of workers covered by workers' compensation.

Percent Change in Workers' Compensation Benefit Payments: 2010 to 2011

National Percent Change = 3.5% Increase*

ALPHA ORDER

RANK	STATE	PERCENT CHANGE
40	Alabama	(2.1)
7	Alaska	7.9
25	Arizona	1.4
46	Arkansas	(6.9)
6	California	8.4
44	Colorado	(5.3)
5	Connecticut	8.9
18	Delaware	3.8
10	Florida	6.5
42	Georgia	(4.3)
24	Hawaii	1.8
19	Idaho	3.6
20	Illinois	2.8
17	Indiana	4.4
2	Iowa	12.2
8	Kansas	7.5
36	Kentucky	(0.8)
16	Louisiana	4.5
28	Maine	0.2
11	Maryland	5.6
43	Massachusetts	(5.0)
22	Michigan	2.3
41	Minnesota	(2.3)
37	Mississippi	(0.9)
26	Missouri	1.0
44	Montana	(5.3)
22	Nebraska	2.3
50	Nevada	(11.3)
48	New Hampshire	(9.6)
13	New Jersey	5.4
29	New Mexico	(0.1)
3	New York	10.7
15	North Carolina	5.1
4	North Dakota	9.5
38	Ohio	(1.6)
34	Oklahoma	(0.6)
49	Oregon	(10.1)
32	Pennsylvania	(0.5)
14	Rhode Island	5.2
39	South Carolina	(1.9)
47	South Dakota	(9.5)
29	Tennessee	(0.1)
9	Texas	6.9
12	Utah	5.5
31	Vermont	(0.2)
1	Virginia	12.5
27	Washington	0.3
32	West Virginia	(0.5)
21	Wisconsin	2.6
35	Wyoming	(0.7)

RANK ORDER

RANK	STATE	PERCENT CHANGE
1	Virginia	12.5
2	Iowa	12.2
3	New York	10.7
4	North Dakota	9.5
5	Connecticut	8.9
6	California	8.4
7	Alaska	7.9
8	Kansas	7.5
9	Texas	6.9
10	Florida	6.5
11	Maryland	5.6
12	Utah	5.5
13	New Jersey	5.4
14	Rhode Island	5.2
15	North Carolina	5.1
16	Louisiana	4.5
17	Indiana	4.4
18	Delaware	3.8
19	Idaho	3.6
20	Illinois	2.8
21	Wisconsin	2.6
22	Michigan	2.3
22	Nebraska	2.3
24	Hawaii	1.8
25	Arizona	1.4
26	Missouri	1.0
27	Washington	0.3
28	Maine	0.2
29	New Mexico	(0.1)
29	Tennessee	(0.1)
31	Vermont	(0.2)
32	Pennsylvania	(0.5)
32	West Virginia	(0.5)
34	Oklahoma	(0.6)
35	Wyoming	(0.7)
36	Kentucky	(0.8)
37	Mississippi	(0.9)
38	Ohio	(1.6)
39	South Carolina	(1.9)
40	Alabama	(2.1)
41	Minnesota	(2.3)
42	Georgia	(4.3)
43	Massachusetts	(5.0)
44	Colorado	(5.3)
44	Montana	(5.3)
46	Arkansas	(6.9)
47	South Dakota	(9.5)
48	New Hampshire	(9.6)
49	Oregon	(10.1)
50	Nevada	(11.3)

| | District of Columbia | 5.4 |

Source: National Academy of Social Insurance (Washington, DC)
   "Workers' Compensation: Benefits, Coverage, and Costs, 2011" (http://www.nasi.org)
*Estimated payments from private insurance, state and federal funds, and self insurance. National rate includes payments for federal civilian employee program, Black Lung Program, and other federal programs.

Civilian Labor Force in 2013

National Total = 154,937,000 Workers*

ALPHA ORDER

ALPHA ORDER

RANK	STATE	LABOR FORCE	% of USA
24	Alabama	2,117,600	1.4%
48	Alaska	366,000	0.2%
20	Arizona	2,988,300	1.9%
34	Arkansas	1,327,900	0.9%
1	California	18,568,200	12.0%
22	Colorado	2,736,100	1.8%
28	Connecticut	1,848,500	1.2%
46	Delaware	439,500	0.3%
4	Florida	9,405,300	6.1%
8	Georgia	4,728,100	3.1%
42	Hawaii	655,600	0.4%
39	Idaho	772,600	0.5%
5	Illinois	6,538,700	4.2%
15	Indiana	3,180,000	2.1%
30	Iowa	1,672,500	1.1%
31	Kansas	1,487,400	1.0%
26	Kentucky	2,047,200	1.3%
25	Louisiana	2,090,500	1.3%
41	Maine	709,000	0.5%
16	Maryland	3,109,400	2.0%
13	Massachusetts	3,481,300	2.2%
9	Michigan	4,694,300	3.0%
21	Minnesota	2,971,600	1.9%
35	Mississippi	1,272,900	0.8%
19	Missouri	3,016,800	1.9%
44	Montana	510,400	0.3%
36	Nebraska	1,021,600	0.7%
33	Nevada	1,362,400	0.9%
40	New Hampshire	740,700	0.5%
11	New Jersey	4,506,000	2.9%
37	New Mexico	920,100	0.6%
3	New York	9,631,500	6.2%
10	North Carolina	4,656,300	3.0%
47	North Dakota	403,600	0.3%
7	Ohio	5,737,800	3.7%
29	Oklahoma	1,821,600	1.2%
27	Oregon	1,915,300	1.2%
6	Pennsylvania	6,443,500	4.2%
43	Rhode Island	550,500	0.4%
23	South Carolina	2,153,600	1.4%
45	South Dakota	450,400	0.3%
18	Tennessee	3,042,600	2.0%
2	Texas	12,852,600	8.3%
32	Utah	1,427,900	0.9%
49	Vermont	349,900	0.2%
12	Virginia	4,225,200	2.7%
14	Washington	3,455,700	2.2%
38	West Virginia	794,600	0.5%
17	Wisconsin	3,071,700	2.0%
50	Wyoming	308,500	0.2%

RANK ORDER

RANK	STATE	LABOR FORCE	% of USA
1	California	18,568,200	12.0%
2	Texas	12,852,600	8.3%
3	New York	9,631,500	6.2%
4	Florida	9,405,300	6.1%
5	Illinois	6,538,700	4.2%
6	Pennsylvania	6,443,500	4.2%
7	Ohio	5,737,800	3.7%
8	Georgia	4,728,100	3.1%
9	Michigan	4,694,300	3.0%
10	North Carolina	4,656,300	3.0%
11	New Jersey	4,506,000	2.9%
12	Virginia	4,225,200	2.7%
13	Massachusetts	3,481,300	2.2%
14	Washington	3,455,700	2.2%
15	Indiana	3,180,000	2.1%
16	Maryland	3,109,400	2.0%
17	Wisconsin	3,071,700	2.0%
18	Tennessee	3,042,600	2.0%
19	Missouri	3,016,800	1.9%
20	Arizona	2,988,300	1.9%
21	Minnesota	2,971,600	1.9%
22	Colorado	2,736,100	1.8%
23	South Carolina	2,153,600	1.4%
24	Alabama	2,117,600	1.4%
25	Louisiana	2,090,500	1.3%
26	Kentucky	2,047,200	1.3%
27	Oregon	1,915,300	1.2%
28	Connecticut	1,848,500	1.2%
29	Oklahoma	1,821,600	1.2%
30	Iowa	1,672,500	1.1%
31	Kansas	1,487,400	1.0%
32	Utah	1,427,900	0.9%
33	Nevada	1,362,400	0.9%
34	Arkansas	1,327,900	0.9%
35	Mississippi	1,272,900	0.8%
36	Nebraska	1,021,600	0.7%
37	New Mexico	920,100	0.6%
38	West Virginia	794,600	0.5%
39	Idaho	772,600	0.5%
40	New Hampshire	740,700	0.5%
41	Maine	709,000	0.5%
42	Hawaii	655,600	0.4%
43	Rhode Island	550,500	0.4%
44	Montana	510,400	0.3%
45	South Dakota	450,400	0.3%
46	Delaware	439,500	0.3%
47	North Dakota	403,600	0.3%
48	Alaska	366,000	0.2%
49	Vermont	349,900	0.2%
50	Wyoming	308,500	0.2%
	District of Columbia	366,300	0.2%

Source: U.S. Department of Labor, Bureau of Labor Statistics
   "Regional and State Employment and Unemployment" (press release, January 28, 2014, www.bls.gov/bls/newsrels.htm)
*Seasonally adjusted preliminary data as of December 2013. National total calculated through a different formula.

Employed Civilian Labor Force in 2013

National Total = 144,586,000 Employed Workers*

ALPHA ORDER

RANK	STATE	EMPLOYED	% of USA
24	Alabama	1,987,900	1.4%
48	Alaska	342,700	0.2%
21	Arizona	2,761,800	1.9%
34	Arkansas	1,229,400	0.9%
1	California	17,036,100	11.8%
22	Colorado	2,567,100	1.8%
29	Connecticut	1,712,000	1.2%
46	Delaware	412,100	0.3%
4	Florida	8,821,400	6.1%
8	Georgia	4,378,200	3.0%
42	Hawaii	625,800	0.4%
39	Idaho	728,600	0.5%
6	Illinois	5,973,400	4.1%
15	Indiana	2,961,900	2.0%
30	Iowa	1,602,300	1.1%
31	Kansas	1,414,800	1.0%
26	Kentucky	1,883,500	1.3%
25	Louisiana	1,971,300	1.4%
41	Maine	664,700	0.5%
16	Maryland	2,919,100	2.0%
13	Massachusetts	3,237,500	2.2%
10	Michigan	4,300,100	3.0%
19	Minnesota	2,834,300	2.0%
35	Mississippi	1,171,300	0.8%
18	Missouri	2,840,200	2.0%
44	Montana	483,800	0.3%
36	Nebraska	985,200	0.7%
33	Nevada	1,242,100	0.9%
40	New Hampshire	703,000	0.5%
11	New Jersey	4,177,400	2.9%
37	New Mexico	861,300	0.6%
3	New York	8,950,400	6.2%
9	North Carolina	4,333,600	3.0%
47	North Dakota	393,100	0.3%
7	Ohio	5,322,300	3.7%
28	Oklahoma	1,723,800	1.2%
27	Oregon	1,780,500	1.2%
5	Pennsylvania	6,000,200	4.1%
43	Rhode Island	500,600	0.3%
23	South Carolina	2,011,200	1.4%
45	South Dakota	434,400	0.3%
20	Tennessee	2,804,900	1.9%
2	Texas	12,087,900	8.4%
32	Utah	1,370,100	0.9%
49	Vermont	335,200	0.2%
12	Virginia	4,006,400	2.8%
14	Washington	3,227,800	2.2%
38	West Virginia	747,900	0.5%
17	Wisconsin	2,880,300	2.0%
50	Wyoming	295,000	0.2%

RANK ORDER

RANK	STATE	EMPLOYED	% of USA
1	California	17,036,100	11.8%
2	Texas	12,087,900	8.4%
3	New York	8,950,400	6.2%
4	Florida	8,821,400	6.1%
5	Pennsylvania	6,000,200	4.1%
6	Illinois	5,973,400	4.1%
7	Ohio	5,322,300	3.7%
8	Georgia	4,378,200	3.0%
9	North Carolina	4,333,600	3.0%
10	Michigan	4,300,100	3.0%
11	New Jersey	4,177,400	2.9%
12	Virginia	4,006,400	2.8%
13	Massachusetts	3,237,500	2.2%
14	Washington	3,227,800	2.2%
15	Indiana	2,961,900	2.0%
16	Maryland	2,919,100	2.0%
17	Wisconsin	2,880,300	2.0%
18	Missouri	2,840,200	2.0%
19	Minnesota	2,834,300	2.0%
20	Tennessee	2,804,900	1.9%
21	Arizona	2,761,800	1.9%
22	Colorado	2,567,100	1.8%
23	South Carolina	2,011,200	1.4%
24	Alabama	1,987,900	1.4%
25	Louisiana	1,971,300	1.4%
26	Kentucky	1,883,500	1.3%
27	Oregon	1,780,500	1.2%
28	Oklahoma	1,723,800	1.2%
29	Connecticut	1,712,000	1.2%
30	Iowa	1,602,300	1.1%
31	Kansas	1,414,800	1.0%
32	Utah	1,370,100	0.9%
33	Nevada	1,242,100	0.9%
34	Arkansas	1,229,400	0.9%
35	Mississippi	1,171,300	0.8%
36	Nebraska	985,200	0.7%
37	New Mexico	861,300	0.6%
38	West Virginia	747,900	0.5%
39	Idaho	728,600	0.5%
40	New Hampshire	703,000	0.5%
41	Maine	664,700	0.5%
42	Hawaii	625,800	0.4%
43	Rhode Island	500,600	0.3%
44	Montana	483,800	0.3%
45	South Dakota	434,400	0.3%
46	Delaware	412,100	0.3%
47	North Dakota	393,100	0.3%
48	Alaska	342,700	0.2%
49	Vermont	335,200	0.2%
50	Wyoming	295,000	0.2%
	District of Columbia	336,800	0.2%

Source: CQ Press using data from U.S. Department of Labor, Bureau of Labor Statistics
"Regional and State Employment and Unemployment" (press release, January 28, 2014, www.bls.gov/bls/newsrels.htm)
*Seasonally adjusted preliminary data as of December 2013. National total calculated through a different formula.

Employment to Population Ratio in 2013

National Percent = 58.2% of Population 16 Years and Older Employed*

ALPHA ORDER

RANK	STATE	PERCENT
48	Alabama	52.0
16	Alaska	60.7
44	Arizona	54.0
46	Arkansas	53.1
32	California	57.0
12	Colorado	62.8
22	Connecticut	59.1
37	Delaware	56.0
38	Florida	55.9
33	Georgia	56.8
39	Hawaii	55.8
18	Idaho	60.0
25	Illinois	58.7
30	Indiana	57.8
6	Iowa	65.9
11	Kansas	63.1
43	Kentucky	54.2
40	Louisiana	54.7
17	Maine	60.6
13	Maryland	62.1
19	Massachusetts	59.8
42	Michigan	54.5
3	Minnesota	66.7
49	Mississippi	50.4
21	Missouri	59.4
19	Montana	59.8
2	Nebraska	68.3
31	Nevada	57.2
7	New Hampshire	65.0
23	New Jersey	59.0
47	New Mexico	52.9
35	New York	56.6
36	North Carolina	56.2
1	North Dakota	70.0
27	Ohio	57.9
27	Oklahoma	57.9
33	Oregon	56.8
27	Pennsylvania	57.9
26	Rhode Island	58.2
45	South Carolina	53.4
3	South Dakota	66.7
40	Tennessee	54.7
15	Texas	61.0
3	Utah	66.7
9	Vermont	64.7
14	Virginia	61.3
24	Washington	58.8
50	West Virginia	49.3
10	Wisconsin	63.2
8	Wyoming	64.8

RANK ORDER

RANK	STATE	PERCENT
1	North Dakota	70.0
2	Nebraska	68.3
3	Minnesota	66.7
3	South Dakota	66.7
3	Utah	66.7
6	Iowa	65.9
7	New Hampshire	65.0
8	Wyoming	64.8
9	Vermont	64.7
10	Wisconsin	63.2
11	Kansas	63.1
12	Colorado	62.8
13	Maryland	62.1
14	Virginia	61.3
15	Texas	61.0
16	Alaska	60.7
17	Maine	60.6
18	Idaho	60.0
19	Massachusetts	59.8
19	Montana	59.8
21	Missouri	59.4
22	Connecticut	59.1
23	New Jersey	59.0
24	Washington	58.8
25	Illinois	58.7
26	Rhode Island	58.2
27	Ohio	57.9
27	Oklahoma	57.9
27	Pennsylvania	57.9
30	Indiana	57.8
31	Nevada	57.2
32	California	57.0
33	Georgia	56.8
33	Oregon	56.8
35	New York	56.6
36	North Carolina	56.2
37	Delaware	56.0
38	Florida	55.9
39	Hawaii	55.8
40	Louisiana	54.7
40	Tennessee	54.7
42	Michigan	54.5
43	Kentucky	54.2
44	Arizona	54.0
45	South Carolina	53.4
46	Arkansas	53.1
47	New Mexico	52.9
48	Alabama	52.0
49	Mississippi	50.4
50	West Virginia	49.3
	District of Columbia	63.1

Source: CQ Press using data from U.S. Department of Labor, Bureau of Labor Statistics
"Regional and State Employment and Unemployment" (press release, January 28, 2014, www.bls.gov/bls/newsrels.htm)
*Seasonally adjusted preliminary data as of December 2013. Calculated with 2012 population data.

Unemployed Civilian Labor Force in 2013

National Total = 10,351,000 Unemployed Workers*

ALPHA ORDER

RANK	STATE	UNEMPLOYED	% of USA
27	Alabama	129,700	1.3%
46	Alaska	23,300	0.2%
15	Arizona	226,500	2.2%
31	Arkansas	98,500	1.0%
1	California	1,532,100	14.8%
21	Colorado	169,000	1.6%
25	Connecticut	136,500	1.3%
44	Delaware	27,400	0.3%
4	Florida	583,900	5.6%
9	Georgia	349,900	3.4%
43	Hawaii	29,800	0.3%
40	Idaho	44,000	0.4%
5	Illinois	565,300	5.5%
17	Indiana	218,100	2.1%
34	Iowa	70,200	0.7%
33	Kansas	72,600	0.7%
22	Kentucky	163,700	1.6%
29	Louisiana	119,200	1.2%
39	Maine	44,300	0.4%
19	Maryland	190,300	1.8%
12	Massachusetts	243,800	2.4%
8	Michigan	394,200	3.8%
24	Minnesota	137,300	1.3%
30	Mississippi	101,600	1.0%
20	Missouri	176,600	1.7%
45	Montana	26,600	0.3%
42	Nebraska	36,400	0.4%
28	Nevada	120,300	1.2%
41	New Hampshire	37,700	0.4%
10	New Jersey	328,600	3.2%
35	New Mexico	58,800	0.6%
3	New York	681,100	6.6%
11	North Carolina	322,700	3.1%
50	North Dakota	10,500	0.1%
7	Ohio	415,500	4.0%
32	Oklahoma	97,800	0.9%
26	Oregon	134,800	1.3%
6	Pennsylvania	443,300	4.3%
37	Rhode Island	49,900	0.5%
23	South Carolina	142,400	1.4%
47	South Dakota	16,000	0.2%
13	Tennessee	237,700	2.3%
2	Texas	764,700	7.4%
36	Utah	57,800	0.6%
48	Vermont	14,700	0.1%
16	Virginia	218,800	2.1%
14	Washington	227,900	2.2%
38	West Virginia	46,700	0.5%
18	Wisconsin	191,400	1.8%
49	Wyoming	13,500	0.1%

RANK ORDER

RANK	STATE	UNEMPLOYED	% of USA
1	California	1,532,100	14.8%
2	Texas	764,700	7.4%
3	New York	681,100	6.6%
4	Florida	583,900	5.6%
5	Illinois	565,300	5.5%
6	Pennsylvania	443,300	4.3%
7	Ohio	415,500	4.0%
8	Michigan	394,200	3.8%
9	Georgia	349,900	3.4%
10	New Jersey	328,600	3.2%
11	North Carolina	322,700	3.1%
12	Massachusetts	243,800	2.4%
13	Tennessee	237,700	2.3%
14	Washington	227,900	2.2%
15	Arizona	226,500	2.2%
16	Virginia	218,800	2.1%
17	Indiana	218,100	2.1%
18	Wisconsin	191,400	1.8%
19	Maryland	190,300	1.8%
20	Missouri	176,600	1.7%
21	Colorado	169,000	1.6%
22	Kentucky	163,700	1.6%
23	South Carolina	142,400	1.4%
24	Minnesota	137,300	1.3%
25	Connecticut	136,500	1.3%
26	Oregon	134,800	1.3%
27	Alabama	129,700	1.3%
28	Nevada	120,300	1.2%
29	Louisiana	119,200	1.2%
30	Mississippi	101,600	1.0%
31	Arkansas	98,500	1.0%
32	Oklahoma	97,800	0.9%
33	Kansas	72,600	0.7%
34	Iowa	70,200	0.7%
35	New Mexico	58,800	0.6%
36	Utah	57,800	0.6%
37	Rhode Island	49,900	0.5%
38	West Virginia	46,700	0.5%
39	Maine	44,300	0.4%
40	Idaho	44,000	0.4%
41	New Hampshire	37,700	0.4%
42	Nebraska	36,400	0.4%
43	Hawaii	29,800	0.3%
44	Delaware	27,400	0.3%
45	Montana	26,600	0.3%
46	Alaska	23,300	0.2%
47	South Dakota	16,000	0.2%
48	Vermont	14,700	0.1%
49	Wyoming	13,500	0.1%
50	North Dakota	10,500	0.1%
	District of Columbia	29,500	0.3%

Source: U.S. Department of Labor, Bureau of Labor Statistics
    "Regional and State Employment and Unemployment" (press release, January 28, 2014, www.bls.gov/bls/newsrels.htm)
*Seasonally adjusted preliminary data as of December 2013. National total calculated through a different formula.

Unemployment Rate in 2013

National Rate = 6.7% of Labor Force Unemployed*

<table>
<tr><td colspan="3">ALPHA ORDER</td><td colspan="3">RANK ORDER</td></tr>
<tr><td>RANK</td><td>STATE</td><td>PERCENT</td><td>RANK</td><td>STATE</td><td>PERCENT</td></tr>
<tr><td>30</td><td>Alabama</td><td>6.1</td><td>1</td><td>Rhode Island</td><td>9.1</td></tr>
<tr><td>23</td><td>Alaska</td><td>6.4</td><td>2</td><td>Nevada</td><td>8.8</td></tr>
<tr><td>9</td><td>Arizona</td><td>7.6</td><td>3</td><td>Illinois</td><td>8.6</td></tr>
<tr><td>10</td><td>Arkansas</td><td>7.4</td><td>4</td><td>Michigan</td><td>8.4</td></tr>
<tr><td>5</td><td>California</td><td>8.3</td><td>5</td><td>California</td><td>8.3</td></tr>
<tr><td>25</td><td>Colorado</td><td>6.2</td><td>6</td><td>Kentucky</td><td>8.0</td></tr>
<tr><td>10</td><td>Connecticut</td><td>7.4</td><td>6</td><td>Mississippi</td><td>8.0</td></tr>
<tr><td>25</td><td>Delaware</td><td>6.2</td><td>8</td><td>Tennessee</td><td>7.8</td></tr>
<tr><td>25</td><td>Florida</td><td>6.2</td><td>9</td><td>Arizona</td><td>7.6</td></tr>
<tr><td>10</td><td>Georgia</td><td>7.4</td><td>10</td><td>Arkansas</td><td>7.4</td></tr>
<tr><td>43</td><td>Hawaii</td><td>4.5</td><td>10</td><td>Connecticut</td><td>7.4</td></tr>
<tr><td>35</td><td>Idaho</td><td>5.7</td><td>10</td><td>Georgia</td><td>7.4</td></tr>
<tr><td>3</td><td>Illinois</td><td>8.6</td><td>13</td><td>New Jersey</td><td>7.3</td></tr>
<tr><td>18</td><td>Indiana</td><td>6.9</td><td>14</td><td>Ohio</td><td>7.2</td></tr>
<tr><td>45</td><td>Iowa</td><td>4.2</td><td>15</td><td>New York</td><td>7.1</td></tr>
<tr><td>41</td><td>Kansas</td><td>4.9</td><td>16</td><td>Massachusetts</td><td>7.0</td></tr>
<tr><td>6</td><td>Kentucky</td><td>8.0</td><td>16</td><td>Oregon</td><td>7.0</td></tr>
<tr><td>35</td><td>Louisiana</td><td>5.7</td><td>18</td><td>Indiana</td><td>6.9</td></tr>
<tr><td>25</td><td>Maine</td><td>6.2</td><td>18</td><td>North Carolina</td><td>6.9</td></tr>
<tr><td>30</td><td>Maryland</td><td>6.1</td><td>18</td><td>Pennsylvania</td><td>6.9</td></tr>
<tr><td>16</td><td>Massachusetts</td><td>7.0</td><td>21</td><td>South Carolina</td><td>6.6</td></tr>
<tr><td>4</td><td>Michigan</td><td>8.4</td><td>21</td><td>Washington</td><td>6.6</td></tr>
<tr><td>42</td><td>Minnesota</td><td>4.6</td><td>23</td><td>Alaska</td><td>6.4</td></tr>
<tr><td>6</td><td>Mississippi</td><td>8.0</td><td>23</td><td>New Mexico</td><td>6.4</td></tr>
<tr><td>33</td><td>Missouri</td><td>5.9</td><td>25</td><td>Colorado</td><td>6.2</td></tr>
<tr><td>38</td><td>Montana</td><td>5.2</td><td>25</td><td>Delaware</td><td>6.2</td></tr>
<tr><td>48</td><td>Nebraska</td><td>3.6</td><td>25</td><td>Florida</td><td>6.2</td></tr>
<tr><td>2</td><td>Nevada</td><td>8.8</td><td>25</td><td>Maine</td><td>6.2</td></tr>
<tr><td>40</td><td>New Hampshire</td><td>5.1</td><td>25</td><td>Wisconsin</td><td>6.2</td></tr>
<tr><td>13</td><td>New Jersey</td><td>7.3</td><td>30</td><td>Alabama</td><td>6.1</td></tr>
<tr><td>23</td><td>New Mexico</td><td>6.4</td><td>30</td><td>Maryland</td><td>6.1</td></tr>
<tr><td>15</td><td>New York</td><td>7.1</td><td>32</td><td>Texas</td><td>6.0</td></tr>
<tr><td>18</td><td>North Carolina</td><td>6.9</td><td>33</td><td>Missouri</td><td>5.9</td></tr>
<tr><td>50</td><td>North Dakota</td><td>2.6</td><td>33</td><td>West Virginia</td><td>5.9</td></tr>
<tr><td>14</td><td>Ohio</td><td>7.2</td><td>35</td><td>Idaho</td><td>5.7</td></tr>
<tr><td>37</td><td>Oklahoma</td><td>5.4</td><td>35</td><td>Louisiana</td><td>5.7</td></tr>
<tr><td>16</td><td>Oregon</td><td>7.0</td><td>37</td><td>Oklahoma</td><td>5.4</td></tr>
<tr><td>18</td><td>Pennsylvania</td><td>6.9</td><td>38</td><td>Montana</td><td>5.2</td></tr>
<tr><td>1</td><td>Rhode Island</td><td>9.1</td><td>38</td><td>Virginia</td><td>5.2</td></tr>
<tr><td>21</td><td>South Carolina</td><td>6.6</td><td>40</td><td>New Hampshire</td><td>5.1</td></tr>
<tr><td>48</td><td>South Dakota</td><td>3.6</td><td>41</td><td>Kansas</td><td>4.9</td></tr>
<tr><td>8</td><td>Tennessee</td><td>7.8</td><td>42</td><td>Minnesota</td><td>4.6</td></tr>
<tr><td>32</td><td>Texas</td><td>6.0</td><td>43</td><td>Hawaii</td><td>4.5</td></tr>
<tr><td>47</td><td>Utah</td><td>4.1</td><td>44</td><td>Wyoming</td><td>4.4</td></tr>
<tr><td>45</td><td>Vermont</td><td>4.2</td><td>45</td><td>Iowa</td><td>4.2</td></tr>
<tr><td>38</td><td>Virginia</td><td>5.2</td><td>45</td><td>Vermont</td><td>4.2</td></tr>
<tr><td>21</td><td>Washington</td><td>6.6</td><td>47</td><td>Utah</td><td>4.1</td></tr>
<tr><td>33</td><td>West Virginia</td><td>5.9</td><td>48</td><td>Nebraska</td><td>3.6</td></tr>
<tr><td>25</td><td>Wisconsin</td><td>6.2</td><td>48</td><td>South Dakota</td><td>3.6</td></tr>
<tr><td>44</td><td>Wyoming</td><td>4.4</td><td>50</td><td>North Dakota</td><td>2.6</td></tr>
</table>

District of Columbia   8.1

Source: U.S. Department of Labor, Bureau of Labor Statistics
"Regional and State Employment and Unemployment" (press release, January 28, 2014, www.bls.gov/bls/newsrels.htm)
*Seasonally adjusted preliminary data as of December 2013. National figure calculated through a different formula.

Women in Civilian Labor Force in 2012

National Total = 72,684,000 Women*

ALPHA ORDER

RANK	STATE	WOMEN	% of USA
24	Alabama	1,026,000	1.4%
49	Alaska	168,000	0.2%
20	Arizona	1,385,000	1.9%
33	Arkansas	634,000	0.9%
1	California	8,358,000	11.5%
22	Colorado	1,256,000	1.7%
28	Connecticut	898,000	1.2%
45	Delaware	221,000	0.3%
4	Florida	4,467,000	6.1%
8	Georgia	2,291,000	3.2%
42	Hawaii	303,000	0.4%
40	Idaho	342,000	0.5%
5	Illinois	3,117,000	4.3%
17	Indiana	1,478,000	2.0%
30	Iowa	784,000	1.1%
31	Kansas	699,000	1.0%
25	Kentucky	979,000	1.3%
26	Louisiana	972,000	1.3%
41	Maine	338,000	0.5%
15	Maryland	1,546,000	2.1%
13	Massachusetts	1,720,000	2.4%
10	Michigan	2,199,000	3.0%
21	Minnesota	1,383,000	1.9%
32	Mississippi	637,000	0.9%
19	Missouri	1,437,000	2.0%
44	Montana	241,000	0.3%
36	Nebraska	487,000	0.7%
34	Nevada	626,000	0.9%
39	New Hampshire	353,000	0.5%
11	New Jersey	2,164,000	3.0%
37	New Mexico	450,000	0.6%
3	New York	4,540,000	6.2%
9	North Carolina	2,221,000	3.1%
47	North Dakota	184,000	0.3%
7	Ohio	2,710,000	3.7%
29	Oklahoma	824,000	1.1%
27	Oregon	926,000	1.3%
6	Pennsylvania	3,060,000	4.2%
43	Rhode Island	273,000	0.4%
23	South Carolina	1,060,000	1.5%
46	South Dakota	206,000	0.3%
18	Tennessee	1,438,000	2.0%
2	Texas	5,731,000	7.9%
35	Utah	597,000	0.8%
48	Vermont	173,000	0.2%
12	Virginia	1,989,000	2.7%
14	Washington	1,620,000	2.2%
38	West Virginia	373,000	0.5%
16	Wisconsin	1,479,000	2.0%
50	Wyoming	137,000	0.2%

RANK ORDER

RANK	STATE	WOMEN	% of USA
1	California	8,358,000	11.5%
2	Texas	5,731,000	7.9%
3	New York	4,540,000	6.2%
4	Florida	4,467,000	6.1%
5	Illinois	3,117,000	4.3%
6	Pennsylvania	3,060,000	4.2%
7	Ohio	2,710,000	3.7%
8	Georgia	2,291,000	3.2%
9	North Carolina	2,221,000	3.1%
10	Michigan	2,199,000	3.0%
11	New Jersey	2,164,000	3.0%
12	Virginia	1,989,000	2.7%
13	Massachusetts	1,720,000	2.4%
14	Washington	1,620,000	2.2%
15	Maryland	1,546,000	2.1%
16	Wisconsin	1,479,000	2.0%
17	Indiana	1,478,000	2.0%
18	Tennessee	1,438,000	2.0%
19	Missouri	1,437,000	2.0%
20	Arizona	1,385,000	1.9%
21	Minnesota	1,383,000	1.9%
22	Colorado	1,256,000	1.7%
23	South Carolina	1,060,000	1.5%
24	Alabama	1,026,000	1.4%
25	Kentucky	979,000	1.3%
26	Louisiana	972,000	1.3%
27	Oregon	926,000	1.3%
28	Connecticut	898,000	1.2%
29	Oklahoma	824,000	1.1%
30	Iowa	784,000	1.1%
31	Kansas	699,000	1.0%
32	Mississippi	637,000	0.9%
33	Arkansas	634,000	0.9%
34	Nevada	626,000	0.9%
35	Utah	597,000	0.8%
36	Nebraska	487,000	0.7%
37	New Mexico	450,000	0.6%
38	West Virginia	373,000	0.5%
39	New Hampshire	353,000	0.5%
40	Idaho	342,000	0.5%
41	Maine	338,000	0.5%
42	Hawaii	303,000	0.4%
43	Rhode Island	273,000	0.4%
44	Montana	241,000	0.3%
45	Delaware	221,000	0.3%
46	South Dakota	206,000	0.3%
47	North Dakota	184,000	0.3%
48	Vermont	173,000	0.2%
49	Alaska	168,000	0.2%
50	Wyoming	137,000	0.2%
	District of Columbia	184,000	0.3%

Source: U.S. Department of Labor, Bureau of Labor Statistics
   "Geographic Profiles of Employment and Unemployment, 2012" (http://www.bls.gov/gps/)
*Annual averages.

Percent of Women in the Civilian Labor Force in 2012

National Percent = 57.7% of Women*

ALPHA ORDER				RANK ORDER		
RANK	STATE	PERCENT		RANK	STATE	PERCENT
49	Alabama	52.0		1	Nebraska	67.7
10	Alaska	63.6		2	North Dakota	67.6
46	Arizona	54.0		3	Vermont	66.1
45	Arkansas	54.1		4	Minnesota	65.0
36	California	55.7		5	New Hampshire	64.7
13	Colorado	62.0		5	Wisconsin	64.7
16	Connecticut	60.7		7	Iowa	64.5
26	Delaware	58.3		8	South Dakota	64.2
38	Florida	55.5		9	Maryland	63.7
26	Georgia	58.3		10	Alaska	63.6
39	Hawaii	55.2		11	Kansas	62.5
33	Idaho	56.5		12	Wyoming	62.3
18	Illinois	60.3		13	Colorado	62.0
32	Indiana	57.0		14	Massachusetts	61.7
7	Iowa	64.5		15	Rhode Island	61.6
11	Kansas	62.5		16	Connecticut	60.7
35	Kentucky	55.8		17	Maine	60.5
48	Louisiana	52.9		18	Illinois	60.3
17	Maine	60.5		18	Montana	60.3
9	Maryland	63.7		20	Virginia	60.2
14	Massachusetts	61.7		21	New Jersey	59.7
44	Michigan	54.5		22	Missouri	59.3
4	Minnesota	65.0		23	Washington	59.1
47	Mississippi	53.3		24	Oregon	58.5
22	Missouri	59.3		25	Nevada	58.4
18	Montana	60.3		26	Delaware	58.3
1	Nebraska	67.7		26	Georgia	58.3
25	Nevada	58.4		26	Utah	58.3
5	New Hampshire	64.7		29	Pennsylvania	57.9
21	New Jersey	59.7		30	Ohio	57.8
41	New Mexico	54.9		31	Texas	57.7
36	New York	55.7		32	Indiana	57.0
34	North Carolina	56.1		33	Idaho	56.5
2	North Dakota	67.6		34	North Carolina	56.1
30	Ohio	57.8		35	Kentucky	55.8
40	Oklahoma	55.1		36	California	55.7
24	Oregon	58.5		36	New York	55.7
29	Pennsylvania	57.9		38	Florida	55.5
15	Rhode Island	61.6		39	Hawaii	55.2
41	South Carolina	54.9		40	Oklahoma	55.1
8	South Dakota	64.2		41	New Mexico	54.9
43	Tennessee	54.7		41	South Carolina	54.9
31	Texas	57.7		43	Tennessee	54.7
26	Utah	58.3		44	Michigan	54.5
3	Vermont	66.1		45	Arkansas	54.1
20	Virginia	60.2		46	Arizona	54.0
23	Washington	59.1		47	Mississippi	53.3
50	West Virginia	48.9		48	Louisiana	52.9
5	Wisconsin	64.7		49	Alabama	52.0
12	Wyoming	62.3		50	West Virginia	48.9
					District of Columbia	65.3

Source: U.S. Department of Labor, Bureau of Labor Statistics
"Geographic Profiles of Employment and Unemployment, 2012" (http://www.bls.gov/gps/)
*Annual averages.

Percent of Civilian Labor Force Comprised of Women in 2012

National Percent = 46.9% of Civilian Labor Force*

ALPHA ORDER				RANK ORDER		
RANK	STATE	PERCENT		RANK	STATE	PERCENT
26	Alabama	47.2		1	Maryland	49.6
41	Alaska	45.9		2	Delaware	49.3
41	Arizona	45.9		2	Massachusetts	49.3
31	Arkansas	47.0		4	Rhode Island	49.0
47	California	45.2		5	South Carolina	48.9
41	Colorado	45.9		6	Vermont	48.6
10	Connecticut	47.7		7	Maine	48.1
2	Delaware	49.3		7	Wisconsin	48.1
10	Florida	47.7		9	Mississippi	48.0
17	Georgia	47.5		10	Connecticut	47.7
33	Hawaii	46.9		10	Florida	47.7
49	Idaho	44.3		10	Iowa	47.7
26	Illinois	47.2		10	Missouri	47.7
33	Indiana	46.9		10	New Hampshire	47.7
10	Iowa	47.7		15	Montana	47.6
23	Kansas	47.3		15	Nebraska	47.6
19	Kentucky	47.4		17	Georgia	47.5
35	Louisiana	46.8		17	New York	47.5
7	Maine	48.1		19	Kentucky	47.4
1	Maryland	49.6		19	New Mexico	47.4
2	Massachusetts	49.3		19	Ohio	47.4
28	Michigan	47.1		19	Virginia	47.4
31	Minnesota	47.0		23	Kansas	47.3
9	Mississippi	48.0		23	North Carolina	47.3
10	Missouri	47.7		23	Oregon	47.3
15	Montana	47.6		26	Alabama	47.2
15	Nebraska	47.6		26	Illinois	47.2
44	Nevada	45.4		28	Michigan	47.1
10	New Hampshire	47.7		28	New Jersey	47.1
28	New Jersey	47.1		28	Pennsylvania	47.1
19	New Mexico	47.4		31	Arkansas	47.0
17	New York	47.5		31	Minnesota	47.0
23	North Carolina	47.3		33	Hawaii	46.9
38	North Dakota	46.5		33	Indiana	46.9
19	Ohio	47.4		35	Louisiana	46.8
44	Oklahoma	45.4		35	South Dakota	46.8
23	Oregon	47.3		37	Washington	46.7
28	Pennsylvania	47.1		38	North Dakota	46.5
4	Rhode Island	49.0		39	Tennessee	46.4
5	South Carolina	48.9		40	West Virginia	46.2
35	South Dakota	46.8		41	Alaska	45.9
39	Tennessee	46.4		41	Arizona	45.9
46	Texas	45.3		41	Colorado	45.9
50	Utah	43.7		44	Nevada	45.4
6	Vermont	48.6		44	Oklahoma	45.4
19	Virginia	47.4		46	Texas	45.3
37	Washington	46.7		47	California	45.2
40	West Virginia	46.2		48	Wyoming	44.5
7	Wisconsin	48.1		49	Idaho	44.3
48	Wyoming	44.5		50	Utah	43.7
					District of Columbia	50.7

Source: CQ Press using data from U.S. Department of Labor, Bureau of Labor Statistics
   "Geographic Profiles of Employment and Unemployment, 2012" (http://www.bls.gov/gps/)
*Annual averages.

Percent of Children under 6 Years Old with All Parents Working in 2012

National Percent = 64.9%

ALPHA ORDER

RANK	STATE	PERCENT
39	Alabama	63.2
44	Alaska	61.2
42	Arizona	61.4
32	Arkansas	64.6
45	California	60.8
41	Colorado	62.5
11	Connecticut	70.5
14	Delaware	68.4
20	Florida	67.3
37	Georgia	63.7
36	Hawaii	64.4
46	Idaho	60.2
16	Illinois	68.0
23	Indiana	67.0
2	Iowa	74.4
22	Kansas	67.1
27	Kentucky	65.2
10	Louisiana	70.7
29	Maine	65.1
8	Maryland	71.7
12	Massachusetts	69.9
24	Michigan	66.7
1	Minnesota	74.8
17	Mississippi	67.9
19	Missouri	67.6
31	Montana	64.8
6	Nebraska	72.6
30	Nevada	65.0
18	New Hampshire	67.8
25	New Jersey	66.4
40	New Mexico	62.6
32	New York	64.6
27	North Carolina	65.2
4	North Dakota	73.8
15	Ohio	68.1
34	Oklahoma	64.5
43	Oregon	61.3
20	Pennsylvania	67.3
5	Rhode Island	73.1
13	South Carolina	68.7
3	South Dakota	74.0
38	Tennessee	63.4
47	Texas	59.8
50	Utah	51.8
7	Vermont	72.4
26	Virginia	66.2
48	Washington	58.2
49	West Virginia	56.3
9	Wisconsin	71.4
34	Wyoming	64.5

RANK ORDER

RANK	STATE	PERCENT
1	Minnesota	74.8
2	Iowa	74.4
3	South Dakota	74.0
4	North Dakota	73.8
5	Rhode Island	73.1
6	Nebraska	72.6
7	Vermont	72.4
8	Maryland	71.7
9	Wisconsin	71.4
10	Louisiana	70.7
11	Connecticut	70.5
12	Massachusetts	69.9
13	South Carolina	68.7
14	Delaware	68.4
15	Ohio	68.1
16	Illinois	68.0
17	Mississippi	67.9
18	New Hampshire	67.8
19	Missouri	67.6
20	Florida	67.3
20	Pennsylvania	67.3
22	Kansas	67.1
23	Indiana	67.0
24	Michigan	66.7
25	New Jersey	66.4
26	Virginia	66.2
27	Kentucky	65.2
27	North Carolina	65.2
29	Maine	65.1
30	Nevada	65.0
31	Montana	64.8
32	Arkansas	64.6
32	New York	64.6
34	Oklahoma	64.5
34	Wyoming	64.5
36	Hawaii	64.4
37	Georgia	63.7
38	Tennessee	63.4
39	Alabama	63.2
40	New Mexico	62.6
41	Colorado	62.5
42	Arizona	61.4
43	Oregon	61.3
44	Alaska	61.2
45	California	60.8
46	Idaho	60.2
47	Texas	59.8
48	Washington	58.2
49	West Virginia	56.3
50	Utah	51.8

| | District of Columbia | 75.8 |

Source: U.S. Bureau of the Census
   "2012 American Community Survey-Table R2302" (http://www.census.gov/acs/www/index.html)

Job Growth: 2012 to 2013

National Percent Change = 1.6% Increase*

<table>
<tr><td colspan="3">ALPHA ORDER</td><td colspan="3">RANK ORDER</td></tr>
<tr><td>RANK</td><td>STATE</td><td>PERCENT CHANGE</td><td>RANK</td><td>STATE</td><td>PERCENT CHANGE</td></tr>
<tr><td>44</td><td>Alabama</td><td>0.6</td><td>1</td><td>North Dakota</td><td>4.0</td></tr>
<tr><td>50</td><td>Alaska</td><td>(0.7)</td><td>2</td><td>Florida</td><td>2.6</td></tr>
<tr><td>7</td><td>Arizona</td><td>2.0</td><td>3</td><td>Oregon</td><td>2.4</td></tr>
<tr><td>28</td><td>Arkansas</td><td>1.1</td><td>4</td><td>Texas</td><td>2.3</td></tr>
<tr><td>17</td><td>California</td><td>1.6</td><td>5</td><td>Delaware</td><td>2.2</td></tr>
<tr><td>9</td><td>Colorado</td><td>1.9</td><td>5</td><td>Georgia</td><td>2.2</td></tr>
<tr><td>41</td><td>Connecticut</td><td>0.7</td><td>7</td><td>Arizona</td><td>2.0</td></tr>
<tr><td>5</td><td>Delaware</td><td>2.2</td><td>7</td><td>South Carolina</td><td>2.0</td></tr>
<tr><td>2</td><td>Florida</td><td>2.6</td><td>9</td><td>Colorado</td><td>1.9</td></tr>
<tr><td>5</td><td>Georgia</td><td>2.2</td><td>9</td><td>Washington</td><td>1.9</td></tr>
<tr><td>17</td><td>Hawaii</td><td>1.6</td><td>11</td><td>Indiana</td><td>1.8</td></tr>
<tr><td>24</td><td>Idaho</td><td>1.3</td><td>11</td><td>Nevada</td><td>1.8</td></tr>
<tr><td>28</td><td>Illinois</td><td>1.1</td><td>13</td><td>Massachusetts</td><td>1.7</td></tr>
<tr><td>11</td><td>Indiana</td><td>1.8</td><td>13</td><td>Minnesota</td><td>1.7</td></tr>
<tr><td>37</td><td>Iowa</td><td>0.8</td><td>13</td><td>Mississippi</td><td>1.7</td></tr>
<tr><td>41</td><td>Kansas</td><td>0.7</td><td>13</td><td>Utah</td><td>1.7</td></tr>
<tr><td>47</td><td>Kentucky</td><td>0.3</td><td>17</td><td>California</td><td>1.6</td></tr>
<tr><td>34</td><td>Louisiana</td><td>1.0</td><td>17</td><td>Hawaii</td><td>1.6</td></tr>
<tr><td>28</td><td>Maine</td><td>1.1</td><td>17</td><td>Michigan</td><td>1.6</td></tr>
<tr><td>22</td><td>Maryland</td><td>1.4</td><td>17</td><td>North Carolina</td><td>1.6</td></tr>
<tr><td>13</td><td>Massachusetts</td><td>1.7</td><td>17</td><td>Wisconsin</td><td>1.6</td></tr>
<tr><td>17</td><td>Michigan</td><td>1.6</td><td>22</td><td>Maryland</td><td>1.4</td></tr>
<tr><td>13</td><td>Minnesota</td><td>1.7</td><td>22</td><td>South Dakota</td><td>1.4</td></tr>
<tr><td>13</td><td>Mississippi</td><td>1.7</td><td>24</td><td>Idaho</td><td>1.3</td></tr>
<tr><td>24</td><td>Missouri</td><td>1.3</td><td>24</td><td>Missouri</td><td>1.3</td></tr>
<tr><td>41</td><td>Montana</td><td>0.7</td><td>24</td><td>Wyoming</td><td>1.3</td></tr>
<tr><td>28</td><td>Nebraska</td><td>1.1</td><td>27</td><td>Oklahoma</td><td>1.2</td></tr>
<tr><td>11</td><td>Nevada</td><td>1.8</td><td>28</td><td>Arkansas</td><td>1.1</td></tr>
<tr><td>37</td><td>New Hampshire</td><td>0.8</td><td>28</td><td>Illinois</td><td>1.1</td></tr>
<tr><td>47</td><td>New Jersey</td><td>0.3</td><td>28</td><td>Maine</td><td>1.1</td></tr>
<tr><td>46</td><td>New Mexico</td><td>0.4</td><td>28</td><td>Nebraska</td><td>1.1</td></tr>
<tr><td>28</td><td>New York</td><td>1.1</td><td>28</td><td>New York</td><td>1.1</td></tr>
<tr><td>17</td><td>North Carolina</td><td>1.6</td><td>28</td><td>Tennessee</td><td>1.1</td></tr>
<tr><td>1</td><td>North Dakota</td><td>4.0</td><td>34</td><td>Louisiana</td><td>1.0</td></tr>
<tr><td>45</td><td>Ohio</td><td>0.5</td><td>34</td><td>Vermont</td><td>1.0</td></tr>
<tr><td>27</td><td>Oklahoma</td><td>1.2</td><td>34</td><td>West Virginia</td><td>1.0</td></tr>
<tr><td>3</td><td>Oregon</td><td>2.4</td><td>37</td><td>Iowa</td><td>0.8</td></tr>
<tr><td>47</td><td>Pennsylvania</td><td>0.3</td><td>37</td><td>New Hampshire</td><td>0.8</td></tr>
<tr><td>37</td><td>Rhode Island</td><td>0.8</td><td>37</td><td>Rhode Island</td><td>0.8</td></tr>
<tr><td>7</td><td>South Carolina</td><td>2.0</td><td>37</td><td>Virginia</td><td>0.8</td></tr>
<tr><td>22</td><td>South Dakota</td><td>1.4</td><td>41</td><td>Connecticut</td><td>0.7</td></tr>
<tr><td>28</td><td>Tennessee</td><td>1.1</td><td>41</td><td>Kansas</td><td>0.7</td></tr>
<tr><td>4</td><td>Texas</td><td>2.3</td><td>41</td><td>Montana</td><td>0.7</td></tr>
<tr><td>13</td><td>Utah</td><td>1.7</td><td>44</td><td>Alabama</td><td>0.6</td></tr>
<tr><td>34</td><td>Vermont</td><td>1.0</td><td>45</td><td>Ohio</td><td>0.5</td></tr>
<tr><td>37</td><td>Virginia</td><td>0.8</td><td>46</td><td>New Mexico</td><td>0.4</td></tr>
<tr><td>9</td><td>Washington</td><td>1.9</td><td>47</td><td>Kentucky</td><td>0.3</td></tr>
<tr><td>34</td><td>West Virginia</td><td>1.0</td><td>47</td><td>New Jersey</td><td>0.3</td></tr>
<tr><td>17</td><td>Wisconsin</td><td>1.6</td><td>47</td><td>Pennsylvania</td><td>0.3</td></tr>
<tr><td>24</td><td>Wyoming</td><td>1.3</td><td>50</td><td>Alaska</td><td>(0.7)</td></tr>
<tr><td></td><td></td><td></td><td></td><td>District of Columbia</td><td>(0.1)</td></tr>
</table>

Source: CQ Press using data from U.S. Department of Labor, Bureau of Labor Statistics
"Regional and State Employment and Unemployment" (press release, January 28, 2014, www.bls.gov/bls/newsrels.htm)
*Nonfarm jobs. December 2012 to December 2013, seasonally adjusted. National figure based on nonfarm employment from a different survey.

Employees on Nonfarm Payrolls in 2013

National Total = 136,877,000 Employees*

RANK	STATE	EMPLOYEES	% of USA
25	Alabama	1,894,900	1.4%
48	Alaska	333,100	0.2%
21	Arizona	2,537,600	1.9%
33	Arkansas	1,193,500	0.9%
1	California	14,767,800	10.8%
22	Colorado	2,379,700	1.7%
28	Connecticut	1,651,200	1.2%
46	Delaware	430,600	0.3%
4	Florida	7,645,000	5.6%
10	Georgia	4,078,300	3.0%
41	Hawaii	621,100	0.5%
40	Idaho	637,400	0.5%
5	Illinois	5,835,100	4.3%
14	Indiana	2,975,500	2.2%
30	Iowa	1,528,500	1.1%
31	Kansas	1,375,900	1.0%
26	Kentucky	1,842,800	1.3%
23	Louisiana	1,964,000	1.4%
42	Maine	600,500	0.4%
20	Maryland	2,625,200	1.9%
13	Massachusetts	3,354,600	2.5%
9	Michigan	4,092,700	3.0%
17	Minnesota	2,797,700	2.0%
35	Mississippi	1,127,100	0.8%
19	Missouri	2,721,800	2.0%
45	Montana	448,500	0.3%
36	Nebraska	971,800	0.7%
34	Nevada	1,180,100	0.9%
39	New Hampshire	640,300	0.5%
11	New Jersey	3,942,300	2.9%
37	New Mexico	810,400	0.6%
3	New York	8,943,800	6.5%
8	North Carolina	4,096,800	3.0%
44	North Dakota	456,100	0.3%
7	Ohio	5,200,600	3.8%
29	Oklahoma	1,636,800	1.2%
27	Oregon	1,682,700	1.2%
6	Pennsylvania	5,761,600	4.2%
43	Rhode Island	469,200	0.3%
24	South Carolina	1,913,300	1.4%
47	South Dakota	421,900	0.3%
18	Tennessee	2,771,100	2.0%
2	Texas	11,277,100	8.2%
32	Utah	1,288,000	0.9%
49	Vermont	309,100	0.2%
12	Virginia	3,777,300	2.8%
15	Washington	2,940,200	2.1%
38	West Virginia	773,900	0.6%
16	Wisconsin	2,840,500	2.1%
50	Wyoming	292,600	0.2%

RANK	STATE	EMPLOYEES	% of USA
1	California	14,767,800	10.8%
2	Texas	11,277,100	8.2%
3	New York	8,943,800	6.5%
4	Florida	7,645,000	5.6%
5	Illinois	5,835,100	4.3%
6	Pennsylvania	5,761,600	4.2%
7	Ohio	5,200,600	3.8%
8	North Carolina	4,096,800	3.0%
9	Michigan	4,092,700	3.0%
10	Georgia	4,078,300	3.0%
11	New Jersey	3,942,300	2.9%
12	Virginia	3,777,300	2.8%
13	Massachusetts	3,354,600	2.5%
14	Indiana	2,975,500	2.2%
15	Washington	2,940,200	2.1%
16	Wisconsin	2,840,500	2.1%
17	Minnesota	2,797,700	2.0%
18	Tennessee	2,771,100	2.0%
19	Missouri	2,721,800	2.0%
20	Maryland	2,625,200	1.9%
21	Arizona	2,537,600	1.9%
22	Colorado	2,379,700	1.7%
23	Louisiana	1,964,000	1.4%
24	South Carolina	1,913,300	1.4%
25	Alabama	1,894,900	1.4%
26	Kentucky	1,842,800	1.3%
27	Oregon	1,682,700	1.2%
28	Connecticut	1,651,200	1.2%
29	Oklahoma	1,636,800	1.2%
30	Iowa	1,528,500	1.1%
31	Kansas	1,375,900	1.0%
32	Utah	1,288,000	0.9%
33	Arkansas	1,193,500	0.9%
34	Nevada	1,180,100	0.9%
35	Mississippi	1,127,100	0.8%
36	Nebraska	971,800	0.7%
37	New Mexico	810,400	0.6%
38	West Virginia	773,900	0.6%
39	New Hampshire	640,300	0.5%
40	Idaho	637,400	0.5%
41	Hawaii	621,100	0.5%
42	Maine	600,500	0.4%
43	Rhode Island	469,200	0.3%
44	North Dakota	456,100	0.3%
45	Montana	448,500	0.3%
46	Delaware	430,600	0.3%
47	South Dakota	421,900	0.3%
48	Alaska	333,100	0.2%
49	Vermont	309,100	0.2%
50	Wyoming	292,600	0.2%
	District of Columbia	732,400	0.5%

Source: U.S. Department of Labor, Bureau of Labor Statistics
   "Regional and State Employment and Unemployment" (press release, January 28, 2014, www.bls.gov/bls/newsrels.htm)
*Seasonally adjusted preliminary data as of December 2013. National total calculated through a different formula.

Employees in Construction in 2013

National Total = 5,833,000 Employees*

RANK	STATE	EMPLOYEES	% of USA
25	Alabama	78,400	1.3%
47	Alaska	18,600	0.3%
16	Arizona	123,300	2.1%
35	Arkansas	47,400	0.8%
1	California	632,100	10.8%
17	Colorado	122,800	2.1%
32	Connecticut	56,000	1.0%
48	Delaware**	18,200	0.3%
3	Florida	373,600	6.4%
11	Georgia	149,400	2.6%
39	Hawaii**	32,100	0.6%
41	Idaho	31,100	0.5%
6	Illinois	183,100	3.1%
19	Indiana	115,900	2.0%
29	Iowa	66,400	1.1%
33	Kansas	55,900	1.0%
30	Kentucky	64,700	1.1%
13	Louisiana	133,700	2.3%
42	Maine	25,600	0.4%
10	Maryland**	150,600	2.6%
18	Massachusetts	119,100	2.0%
15	Michigan	126,600	2.2%
22	Minnesota	99,100	1.7%
31	Mississippi	56,400	1.0%
20	Missouri	108,900	1.9%
45	Montana	21,400	0.4%
36	Nebraska**	43,200	0.7%
34	Nevada	54,600	0.9%
44	New Hampshire	22,500	0.4%
14	New Jersey	127,500	2.2%
37	New Mexico	40,900	0.7%
4	New York	316,600	5.4%
9	North Carolina	166,400	2.9%
40	North Dakota	31,700	0.5%
7	Ohio	176,700	3.0%
28	Oklahoma	68,100	1.2%
26	Oregon	72,500	1.2%
5	Pennsylvania	220,500	3.8%
49	Rhode Island	15,400	0.3%
24	South Carolina	83,100	1.4%
45	South Dakota**	21,400	0.4%
21	Tennessee**	108,000	1.9%
2	Texas	611,100	10.5%
27	Utah	69,600	1.2%
50	Vermont	14,700	0.3%
8	Virginia	176,200	3.0%
12	Washington	142,400	2.4%
38	West Virginia	34,500	0.6%
23	Wisconsin	94,300	1.6%
43	Wyoming	23,600	0.4%

RANK	STATE	EMPLOYEES	% of USA
1	California	632,100	10.8%
2	Texas	611,100	10.5%
3	Florida	373,600	6.4%
4	New York	316,600	5.4%
5	Pennsylvania	220,500	3.8%
6	Illinois	183,100	3.1%
7	Ohio	176,700	3.0%
8	Virginia	176,200	3.0%
9	North Carolina	166,400	2.9%
10	Maryland**	150,600	2.6%
11	Georgia	149,400	2.6%
12	Washington	142,400	2.4%
13	Louisiana	133,700	2.3%
14	New Jersey	127,500	2.2%
15	Michigan	126,600	2.2%
16	Arizona	123,300	2.1%
17	Colorado	122,800	2.1%
18	Massachusetts	119,100	2.0%
19	Indiana	115,900	2.0%
20	Missouri	108,900	1.9%
21	Tennessee**	108,000	1.9%
22	Minnesota	99,100	1.7%
23	Wisconsin	94,300	1.6%
24	South Carolina	83,100	1.4%
25	Alabama	78,400	1.3%
26	Oregon	72,500	1.2%
27	Utah	69,600	1.2%
28	Oklahoma	68,100	1.2%
29	Iowa	66,400	1.1%
30	Kentucky	64,700	1.1%
31	Mississippi	56,400	1.0%
32	Connecticut	56,000	1.0%
33	Kansas	55,900	1.0%
34	Nevada	54,600	0.9%
35	Arkansas	47,400	0.8%
36	Nebraska**	43,200	0.7%
37	New Mexico	40,900	0.7%
38	West Virginia	34,500	0.6%
39	Hawaii**	32,100	0.6%
40	North Dakota	31,700	0.5%
41	Idaho	31,100	0.5%
42	Maine	25,600	0.4%
43	Wyoming	23,600	0.4%
44	New Hampshire	22,500	0.4%
45	Montana	21,400	0.4%
45	South Dakota**	21,400	0.4%
47	Alaska	18,600	0.3%
48	Delaware**	18,200	0.3%
49	Rhode Island	15,400	0.3%
50	Vermont	14,700	0.3%
	District of Columbia**	13,000	0.2%

Source: U.S. Department of Labor, Bureau of Labor Statistics

"Regional and State Employment and Unemployment" (press release, January 28, 2014, www.bls.gov/bls/newsrels.htm)

*Seasonally adjusted preliminary data as of December 2013. National total calculated through a different formula.

**Figures for states include employees in mining and logging.

Percent of Nonfarm Employees in Construction in 2013

National Percent = 4.3% of Employees*

ALPHA ORDER				RANK ORDER		
RANK	STATE	PERCENT		RANK	STATE	PERCENT
30	Alabama	4.1		1	Wyoming	8.1
5	Alaska	5.6		2	North Dakota	7.0
13	Arizona	4.9		3	Louisiana	6.8
33	Arkansas	4.0		4	Maryland**	5.7
23	California	4.3		5	Alaska	5.6
8	Colorado	5.2		6	Texas	5.4
44	Connecticut	3.4		6	Utah	5.4
28	Delaware**	4.2		8	Colorado	5.2
13	Florida	4.9		8	Hawaii**	5.2
38	Georgia	3.7		10	South Dakota**	5.1
8	Hawaii**	5.2		11	Mississippi	5.0
13	Idaho	4.9		11	New Mexico	5.0
49	Illinois	3.1		13	Arizona	4.9
35	Indiana	3.9		13	Florida	4.9
23	Iowa	4.3		13	Idaho	4.9
30	Kansas	4.1		16	Montana	4.8
40	Kentucky	3.5		16	Vermont	4.8
3	Louisiana	6.8		16	Washington	4.8
23	Maine	4.3		19	Virginia	4.7
4	Maryland**	5.7		20	Nevada	4.6
39	Massachusetts	3.6		21	West Virginia	4.5
49	Michigan	3.1		22	Nebraska**	4.4
40	Minnesota	3.5		23	California	4.3
11	Mississippi	5.0		23	Iowa	4.3
33	Missouri	4.0		23	Maine	4.3
16	Montana	4.8		23	Oregon	4.3
22	Nebraska**	4.4		23	South Carolina	4.3
20	Nevada	4.6		28	Delaware**	4.2
40	New Hampshire	3.5		28	Oklahoma	4.2
48	New Jersey	3.2		30	Alabama	4.1
11	New Mexico	5.0		30	Kansas	4.1
40	New York	3.5		30	North Carolina	4.1
30	North Carolina	4.1		33	Arkansas	4.0
2	North Dakota	7.0		33	Missouri	4.0
44	Ohio	3.4		35	Indiana	3.9
28	Oklahoma	4.2		35	Tennessee**	3.9
23	Oregon	4.3		37	Pennsylvania	3.8
37	Pennsylvania	3.8		38	Georgia	3.7
46	Rhode Island	3.3		39	Massachusetts	3.6
23	South Carolina	4.3		40	Kentucky	3.5
10	South Dakota**	5.1		40	Minnesota	3.5
35	Tennessee**	3.9		40	New Hampshire	3.5
6	Texas	5.4		40	New York	3.5
6	Utah	5.4		44	Connecticut	3.4
16	Vermont	4.8		44	Ohio	3.4
19	Virginia	4.7		46	Rhode Island	3.3
16	Washington	4.8		46	Wisconsin	3.3
21	West Virginia	4.5		48	New Jersey	3.2
46	Wisconsin	3.3		49	Illinois	3.1
1	Wyoming	8.1		49	Michigan	3.1
					District of Columbia**	1.8

Source: CQ Press using data from U.S. Department of Labor, Bureau of Labor Statistics
   "Regional and State Employment and Unemployment" (press release, January 28, 2014, www.bls.gov/bls/newsrels.htm)
*Seasonally adjusted preliminary data as of December 2013. National figure calculated through a different formula.
**Figures for states include employees in mining and logging.

Employees in Education and Health Services in 2013

National Total = 20,823,000 Employees*

ALPHA ORDER

RANK	STATE	EMPLOYEES	% of USA
29	Alabama	219,500	1.1%
49	Alaska	47,500	0.2%
21	Arizona	381,300	1.8%
32	Arkansas	176,500	0.8%
1	California	1,934,500	9.3%
23	Colorado	295,300	1.4%
22	Connecticut	328,300	1.6%
44	Delaware	70,700	0.3%
5	Florida	1,136,400	5.5%
12	Georgia	518,100	2.5%
43	Hawaii	77,600	0.4%
42	Idaho	92,800	0.4%
6	Illinois	880,700	4.2%
15	Indiana	443,200	2.1%
28	Iowa	225,600	1.1%
31	Kansas	188,600	0.9%
25	Kentucky	259,900	1.2%
24	Louisiana	284,300	1.4%
38	Maine	121,100	0.6%
16	Maryland	428,500	2.1%
8	Massachusetts	709,900	3.4%
10	Michigan	639,000	3.1%
14	Minnesota	497,500	2.4%
35	Mississippi	134,000	0.6%
17	Missouri	425,400	2.0%
45	Montana	69,500	0.3%
34	Nebraska	142,000	0.7%
40	Nevada	112,500	0.5%
39	New Hampshire	117,700	0.6%
9	New Jersey	645,300	3.1%
37	New Mexico	121,600	0.6%
2	New York	1,835,400	8.8%
11	North Carolina	565,600	2.7%
48	North Dakota	59,500	0.3%
6	Ohio	880,700	4.2%
27	Oklahoma	226,700	1.1%
26	Oregon	244,300	1.2%
4	Pennsylvania	1,175,300	5.6%
41	Rhode Island	103,600	0.5%
30	South Carolina	213,800	1.0%
46	South Dakota	68,200	0.3%
19	Tennessee	404,900	1.9%
3	Texas	1,512,200	7.3%
33	Utah	171,500	0.8%
47	Vermont	62,000	0.3%
13	Virginia	499,700	2.4%
20	Washington	397,100	1.9%
36	West Virginia	128,900	0.6%
18	Wisconsin	421,200	2.0%
50	Wyoming	26,800	0.1%

RANK ORDER

RANK	STATE	EMPLOYEES	% of USA
1	California	1,934,500	9.3%
2	New York	1,835,400	8.8%
3	Texas	1,512,200	7.3%
4	Pennsylvania	1,175,300	5.6%
5	Florida	1,136,400	5.5%
6	Illinois	880,700	4.2%
6	Ohio	880,700	4.2%
8	Massachusetts	709,900	3.4%
9	New Jersey	645,300	3.1%
10	Michigan	639,000	3.1%
11	North Carolina	565,600	2.7%
12	Georgia	518,100	2.5%
13	Virginia	499,700	2.4%
14	Minnesota	497,500	2.4%
15	Indiana	443,200	2.1%
16	Maryland	428,500	2.1%
17	Missouri	425,400	2.0%
18	Wisconsin	421,200	2.0%
19	Tennessee	404,900	1.9%
20	Washington	397,100	1.9%
21	Arizona	381,300	1.8%
22	Connecticut	328,300	1.6%
23	Colorado	295,300	1.4%
24	Louisiana	284,300	1.4%
25	Kentucky	259,900	1.2%
26	Oregon	244,300	1.2%
27	Oklahoma	226,700	1.1%
28	Iowa	225,600	1.1%
29	Alabama	219,500	1.1%
30	South Carolina	213,800	1.0%
31	Kansas	188,600	0.9%
32	Arkansas	176,500	0.8%
33	Utah	171,500	0.8%
34	Nebraska	142,000	0.7%
35	Mississippi	134,000	0.6%
36	West Virginia	128,900	0.6%
37	New Mexico	121,600	0.6%
38	Maine	121,100	0.6%
39	New Hampshire	117,700	0.6%
40	Nevada	112,500	0.5%
41	Rhode Island	103,600	0.5%
42	Idaho	92,800	0.4%
43	Hawaii	77,600	0.4%
44	Delaware	70,700	0.3%
45	Montana	69,500	0.3%
46	South Dakota	68,200	0.3%
47	Vermont	62,000	0.3%
48	North Dakota	59,500	0.3%
49	Alaska	47,500	0.2%
50	Wyoming	26,800	0.1%
	District of Columbia	116,900	0.6%

Source: U.S. Department of Labor, Bureau of Labor Statistics
"Regional and State Employment and Unemployment" (press release, January 28, 2014, www.bls.gov/bls/newsrels.htm)
*Seasonally adjusted preliminary data as of December 2013. National total calculated through a different formula.

Percent of Nonfarm Employees in Education and Health Services in 2013

National Percent = 15.2% of Employees*

ALPHA ORDER

RANK	STATE	PERCENT
47	Alabama	11.6
32	Alaska	14.3
20	Arizona	15.0
24	Arkansas	14.8
41	California	13.1
45	Colorado	12.4
7	Connecticut	19.9
12	Delaware	16.4
22	Florida	14.9
43	Georgia	12.7
44	Hawaii	12.5
27	Idaho	14.6
19	Illinois	15.1
22	Indiana	14.9
24	Iowa	14.8
36	Kansas	13.7
33	Kentucky	14.1
30	Louisiana	14.5
5	Maine	20.2
14	Maryland	16.3
2	Massachusetts	21.2
16	Michigan	15.6
9	Minnesota	17.8
46	Mississippi	11.9
16	Missouri	15.6
18	Montana	15.5
27	Nebraska	14.6
49	Nevada	9.5
8	New Hampshire	18.4
12	New Jersey	16.4
20	New Mexico	15.0
3	New York	20.5
35	North Carolina	13.8
42	North Dakota	13.0
10	Ohio	16.9
34	Oklahoma	13.9
30	Oregon	14.5
4	Pennsylvania	20.4
1	Rhode Island	22.1
48	South Carolina	11.2
15	South Dakota	16.2
27	Tennessee	14.6
38	Texas	13.4
39	Utah	13.3
6	Vermont	20.1
40	Virginia	13.2
37	Washington	13.5
11	West Virginia	16.7
24	Wisconsin	14.8
50	Wyoming	9.2

RANK ORDER

RANK	STATE	PERCENT
1	Rhode Island	22.1
2	Massachusetts	21.2
3	New York	20.5
4	Pennsylvania	20.4
5	Maine	20.2
6	Vermont	20.1
7	Connecticut	19.9
8	New Hampshire	18.4
9	Minnesota	17.8
10	Ohio	16.9
11	West Virginia	16.7
12	Delaware	16.4
12	New Jersey	16.4
14	Maryland	16.3
15	South Dakota	16.2
16	Michigan	15.6
16	Missouri	15.6
18	Montana	15.5
19	Illinois	15.1
20	Arizona	15.0
20	New Mexico	15.0
22	Florida	14.9
22	Indiana	14.9
24	Arkansas	14.8
24	Iowa	14.8
24	Wisconsin	14.8
27	Idaho	14.6
27	Nebraska	14.6
27	Tennessee	14.6
30	Louisiana	14.5
30	Oregon	14.5
32	Alaska	14.3
33	Kentucky	14.1
34	Oklahoma	13.9
35	North Carolina	13.8
36	Kansas	13.7
37	Washington	13.5
38	Texas	13.4
39	Utah	13.3
40	Virginia	13.2
41	California	13.1
42	North Dakota	13.0
43	Georgia	12.7
44	Hawaii	12.5
45	Colorado	12.4
46	Mississippi	11.9
47	Alabama	11.6
48	South Carolina	11.2
49	Nevada	9.5
50	Wyoming	9.2
	District of Columbia	16.0

Source: CQ Press using data from U.S. Department of Labor, Bureau of Labor Statistics
"Regional and State Employment and Unemployment" (press release, January 28, 2014, www.bls.gov/bls/newsrels.htm)
*Seasonally adjusted preliminary data as of December 2013. National figure calculated through a different formula.

Employees in Financial Activities in 2013

National Total = 7,915,000 Employees*

RANK	STATE	EMPLOYEES	% of USA
27	Alabama	93,300	1.2%
48	Alaska	13,200	0.2%
14	Arizona	189,000	2.4%
35	Arkansas	51,100	0.6%
1	California	783,200	9.9%
19	Colorado	143,900	1.8%
23	Connecticut	129,500	1.6%
37	Delaware	44,500	0.6%
4	Florida	509,000	6.4%
9	Georgia	233,800	3.0%
45	Hawaii	27,400	0.3%
42	Idaho	30,900	0.4%
5	Illinois	370,300	4.7%
22	Indiana	134,000	1.7%
24	Iowa	102,900	1.3%
31	Kansas	77,500	1.0%
29	Kentucky	88,200	1.1%
26	Louisiana	94,800	1.2%
41	Maine	31,600	0.4%
18	Maryland	144,200	1.8%
10	Massachusetts	207,400	2.6%
13	Michigan	195,000	2.5%
15	Minnesota	179,400	2.3%
36	Mississippi	44,900	0.6%
16	Missouri	170,800	2.2%
47	Montana	21,900	0.3%
33	Nebraska	71,400	0.9%
34	Nevada	54,200	0.7%
39	New Hampshire	35,200	0.4%
8	New Jersey	248,400	3.1%
38	New Mexico	37,000	0.5%
2	New York	680,400	8.6%
11	North Carolina	206,700	2.6%
46	North Dakota	23,500	0.3%
7	Ohio	278,600	3.5%
30	Oklahoma	80,300	1.0%
28	Oregon	88,900	1.1%
6	Pennsylvania	312,300	3.9%
40	Rhode Island	32,100	0.4%
25	South Carolina	101,800	1.3%
43	South Dakota	29,700	0.4%
21	Tennessee	139,700	1.8%
3	Texas	672,100	8.5%
32	Utah	73,000	0.9%
49	Vermont	12,300	0.2%
12	Virginia	199,300	2.5%
20	Washington	143,300	1.8%
44	West Virginia	28,500	0.4%
17	Wisconsin	159,600	2.0%
50	Wyoming	10,500	0.1%

RANK	STATE	EMPLOYEES	% of USA
1	California	783,200	9.9%
2	New York	680,400	8.6%
3	Texas	672,100	8.5%
4	Florida	509,000	6.4%
5	Illinois	370,300	4.7%
6	Pennsylvania	312,300	3.9%
7	Ohio	278,600	3.5%
8	New Jersey	248,400	3.1%
9	Georgia	233,800	3.0%
10	Massachusetts	207,400	2.6%
11	North Carolina	206,700	2.6%
12	Virginia	199,300	2.5%
13	Michigan	195,000	2.5%
14	Arizona	189,000	2.4%
15	Minnesota	179,400	2.3%
16	Missouri	170,800	2.2%
17	Wisconsin	159,600	2.0%
18	Maryland	144,200	1.8%
19	Colorado	143,900	1.8%
20	Washington	143,300	1.8%
21	Tennessee	139,700	1.8%
22	Indiana	134,000	1.7%
23	Connecticut	129,500	1.6%
24	Iowa	102,900	1.3%
25	South Carolina	101,800	1.3%
26	Louisiana	94,800	1.2%
27	Alabama	93,300	1.2%
28	Oregon	88,900	1.1%
29	Kentucky	88,200	1.1%
30	Oklahoma	80,300	1.0%
31	Kansas	77,500	1.0%
32	Utah	73,000	0.9%
33	Nebraska	71,400	0.9%
34	Nevada	54,200	0.7%
35	Arkansas	51,100	0.6%
36	Mississippi	44,900	0.6%
37	Delaware	44,500	0.6%
38	New Mexico	37,000	0.5%
39	New Hampshire	35,200	0.4%
40	Rhode Island	32,100	0.4%
41	Maine	31,600	0.4%
42	Idaho	30,900	0.4%
43	South Dakota	29,700	0.4%
44	West Virginia	28,500	0.4%
45	Hawaii	27,400	0.3%
46	North Dakota	23,500	0.3%
47	Montana	21,900	0.3%
48	Alaska	13,200	0.2%
49	Vermont	12,300	0.2%
50	Wyoming	10,500	0.1%
	District of Columbia	28,900	0.4%

Source: U.S. Department of Labor, Bureau of Labor Statistics
"Regional and State Employment and Unemployment" (press release, January 28, 2014, www.bls.gov/bls/newsrels.htm)
*Seasonally adjusted preliminary data as of December 2013. National total calculated through a different formula. Financial activities include insurance and real estate.

Percent of Nonfarm Employees in Financial Activities in 2013

National Percent = 5.8% of Employees*

ALPHA ORDER				RANK ORDER		
RANK	STATE	PERCENT		RANK	STATE	PERCENT
33	Alabama	4.9		1	Delaware	10.3
46	Alaska	4.0		2	Connecticut	7.8
4	Arizona	7.4		3	New York	7.6
45	Arkansas	4.3		4	Arizona	7.4
25	California	5.3		5	Nebraska	7.3
15	Colorado	6.0		6	South Dakota	7.0
2	Connecticut	7.8		7	Rhode Island	6.8
1	Delaware	10.3		8	Florida	6.7
8	Florida	6.7		8	Iowa	6.7
17	Georgia	5.7		10	Minnesota	6.4
44	Hawaii	4.4		11	Illinois	6.3
37	Idaho	4.8		11	Missouri	6.3
11	Illinois	6.3		11	New Jersey	6.3
43	Indiana	4.5		14	Massachusetts	6.2
8	Iowa	6.7		15	Colorado	6.0
19	Kansas	5.6		15	Texas	6.0
37	Kentucky	4.8		17	Georgia	5.7
37	Louisiana	4.8		17	Utah	5.7
25	Maine	5.3		19	Kansas	5.6
21	Maryland	5.5		19	Wisconsin	5.6
14	Massachusetts	6.2		21	Maryland	5.5
37	Michigan	4.8		21	New Hampshire	5.5
10	Minnesota	6.4		23	Ohio	5.4
46	Mississippi	4.0		23	Pennsylvania	5.4
11	Missouri	6.3		25	California	5.3
33	Montana	4.9		25	Maine	5.3
5	Nebraska	7.3		25	Oregon	5.3
41	Nevada	4.6		25	South Carolina	5.3
21	New Hampshire	5.5		25	Virginia	5.3
11	New Jersey	6.3		30	North Dakota	5.2
41	New Mexico	4.6		31	North Carolina	5.0
3	New York	7.6		31	Tennessee	5.0
31	North Carolina	5.0		33	Alabama	4.9
30	North Dakota	5.2		33	Montana	4.9
23	Ohio	5.4		33	Oklahoma	4.9
33	Oklahoma	4.9		33	Washington	4.9
25	Oregon	5.3		37	Idaho	4.8
23	Pennsylvania	5.4		37	Kentucky	4.8
7	Rhode Island	6.8		37	Louisiana	4.8
25	South Carolina	5.3		37	Michigan	4.8
6	South Dakota	7.0		41	Nevada	4.6
31	Tennessee	5.0		41	New Mexico	4.6
15	Texas	6.0		43	Indiana	4.5
17	Utah	5.7		44	Hawaii	4.4
46	Vermont	4.0		45	Arkansas	4.3
25	Virginia	5.3		46	Alaska	4.0
33	Washington	4.9		46	Mississippi	4.0
49	West Virginia	3.7		46	Vermont	4.0
19	Wisconsin	5.6		49	West Virginia	3.7
50	Wyoming	3.6		50	Wyoming	3.6
					District of Columbia	3.9

Source: CQ Press using data from U.S. Department of Labor, Bureau of Labor Statistics
 "Regional and State Employment and Unemployment" (press release, January 28, 2014, www.bls.gov/bls/newsrels.htm)
*Seasonally adjusted preliminary data as of December 2013. National figure calculated through a different formula. Financial activities include insurance and real estate.

Employees in Government in 2013

National Total = 21,849,000 Employees*

ALPHA ORDER

RANK	STATE	EMPLOYEES	% of USA
23	Alabama	369,300	1.7%
44	Alaska	82,500	0.4%
21	Arizona	411,300	1.9%
34	Arkansas	215,100	1.0%
1	California	2,353,100	10.8%
22	Colorado	404,600	1.9%
32	Connecticut	237,200	1.1%
48	Delaware	63,400	0.3%
4	Florida	1,071,800	4.9%
10	Georgia	671,100	3.1%
39	Hawaii	125,300	0.6%
40	Idaho	118,600	0.5%
5	Illinois	827,100	3.8%
16	Indiana	435,800	2.0%
30	Iowa	252,100	1.2%
29	Kansas	258,100	1.2%
27	Kentucky	334,400	1.5%
26	Louisiana	343,000	1.6%
41	Maine	97,800	0.4%
14	Maryland	506,400	2.3%
15	Massachusetts	442,000	2.0%
12	Michigan	603,900	2.8%
19	Minnesota	417,100	1.9%
31	Mississippi	244,200	1.1%
17	Missouri	431,800	2.0%
43	Montana	89,300	0.4%
36	Nebraska	168,600	0.8%
38	Nevada	152,700	0.7%
42	New Hampshire	89,800	0.4%
11	New Jersey	628,400	2.9%
35	New Mexico	191,600	0.9%
3	New York	1,440,100	6.6%
7	North Carolina	714,300	3.3%
45	North Dakota	79,700	0.4%
6	Ohio	740,000	3.4%
25	Oklahoma	351,700	1.6%
28	Oregon	292,100	1.3%
9	Pennsylvania	711,600	3.3%
49	Rhode Island	59,500	0.3%
24	South Carolina	354,200	1.6%
46	South Dakota	78,200	0.4%
18	Tennessee	418,100	1.9%
2	Texas	1,809,200	8.3%
33	Utah	217,800	1.0%
50	Vermont	54,300	0.2%
8	Virginia	713,800	3.3%
13	Washington	539,400	2.5%
37	West Virginia	155,500	0.7%
20	Wisconsin	414,600	1.9%
47	Wyoming	74,100	0.3%

RANK ORDER

RANK	STATE	EMPLOYEES	% of USA
1	California	2,353,100	10.8%
2	Texas	1,809,200	8.3%
3	New York	1,440,100	6.6%
4	Florida	1,071,800	4.9%
5	Illinois	827,100	3.8%
6	Ohio	740,000	3.4%
7	North Carolina	714,300	3.3%
8	Virginia	713,800	3.3%
9	Pennsylvania	711,600	3.3%
10	Georgia	671,100	3.1%
11	New Jersey	628,400	2.9%
12	Michigan	603,900	2.8%
13	Washington	539,400	2.5%
14	Maryland	506,400	2.3%
15	Massachusetts	442,000	2.0%
16	Indiana	435,800	2.0%
17	Missouri	431,800	2.0%
18	Tennessee	418,100	1.9%
19	Minnesota	417,100	1.9%
20	Wisconsin	414,600	1.9%
21	Arizona	411,300	1.9%
22	Colorado	404,600	1.9%
23	Alabama	369,300	1.7%
24	South Carolina	354,200	1.6%
25	Oklahoma	351,700	1.6%
26	Louisiana	343,000	1.6%
27	Kentucky	334,400	1.5%
28	Oregon	292,100	1.3%
29	Kansas	258,100	1.2%
30	Iowa	252,100	1.2%
31	Mississippi	244,200	1.1%
32	Connecticut	237,200	1.1%
33	Utah	217,800	1.0%
34	Arkansas	215,100	1.0%
35	New Mexico	191,600	0.9%
36	Nebraska	168,600	0.8%
37	West Virginia	155,500	0.7%
38	Nevada	152,700	0.7%
39	Hawaii	125,300	0.6%
40	Idaho	118,600	0.5%
41	Maine	97,800	0.4%
42	New Hampshire	89,800	0.4%
43	Montana	89,300	0.4%
44	Alaska	82,500	0.4%
45	North Dakota	79,700	0.4%
46	South Dakota	78,200	0.4%
47	Wyoming	74,100	0.3%
48	Delaware	63,400	0.3%
49	Rhode Island	59,500	0.3%
50	Vermont	54,300	0.2%
	District of Columbia	235,700	1.1%

Source: U.S. Department of Labor, Bureau of Labor Statistics
"Regional and State Employment and Unemployment" (press release, January 28, 2014, www.bls.gov/bls/newsrels.htm)
*Seasonally adjusted preliminary data as of December 2013. National total calculated through a different formula.

Percent of Nonfarm Employees in Government in 2013

National Percent = 16.0% of Employees*

RANK	STATE	PERCENT		RANK	STATE	PERCENT
9	Alabama	19.5		1	Wyoming	25.3
2	Alaska	24.8		2	Alaska	24.8
30	Arizona	16.2		3	New Mexico	23.6
18	Arkansas	18.0		4	Mississippi	21.7
33	California	15.9		5	Oklahoma	21.5
25	Colorado	17.0		6	Hawaii	20.2
42	Connecticut	14.4		7	West Virginia	20.1
39	Delaware	14.7		8	Montana	19.9
45	Florida	14.0		9	Alabama	19.5
27	Georgia	16.5		10	Maryland	19.3
6	Hawaii	20.2		11	Virginia	18.9
13	Idaho	18.6		12	Kansas	18.8
43	Illinois	14.2		13	Idaho	18.6
40	Indiana	14.6		14	South Carolina	18.5
27	Iowa	16.5		14	South Dakota	18.5
12	Kansas	18.8		16	Washington	18.3
17	Kentucky	18.1		17	Kentucky	18.1
20	Louisiana	17.5		18	Arkansas	18.0
29	Maine	16.3		19	Vermont	17.6
10	Maryland	19.3		20	Louisiana	17.5
47	Massachusetts	13.2		20	North Dakota	17.5
38	Michigan	14.8		22	North Carolina	17.4
37	Minnesota	14.9		22	Oregon	17.4
4	Mississippi	21.7		24	Nebraska	17.3
33	Missouri	15.9		25	Colorado	17.0
8	Montana	19.9		26	Utah	16.9
24	Nebraska	17.3		27	Georgia	16.5
48	Nevada	12.9		27	Iowa	16.5
45	New Hampshire	14.0		29	Maine	16.3
33	New Jersey	15.9		30	Arizona	16.2
3	New Mexico	23.6		31	New York	16.1
31	New York	16.1		32	Texas	16.0
22	North Carolina	17.4		33	California	15.9
20	North Dakota	17.5		33	Missouri	15.9
43	Ohio	14.2		33	New Jersey	15.9
5	Oklahoma	21.5		36	Tennessee	15.1
22	Oregon	17.4		37	Minnesota	14.9
50	Pennsylvania	12.4		38	Michigan	14.8
49	Rhode Island	12.7		39	Delaware	14.7
14	South Carolina	18.5		40	Indiana	14.6
14	South Dakota	18.5		40	Wisconsin	14.6
36	Tennessee	15.1		42	Connecticut	14.4
32	Texas	16.0		43	Illinois	14.2
26	Utah	16.9		43	Ohio	14.2
19	Vermont	17.6		45	Florida	14.0
11	Virginia	18.9		45	New Hampshire	14.0
16	Washington	18.3		47	Massachusetts	13.2
7	West Virginia	20.1		48	Nevada	12.9
40	Wisconsin	14.6		49	Rhode Island	12.7
1	Wyoming	25.3		50	Pennsylvania	12.4
					District of Columbia	32.2

ALPHA ORDER

RANK ORDER

Source: CQ Press using data from U.S. Department of Labor, Bureau of Labor Statistics
"Regional and State Employment and Unemployment" (press release, January 28, 2014, www.bls.gov/bls/newsrels.htm)
*Seasonally adjusted preliminary data as of December 2013. National figure calculated through a different formula.

Employees in Leisure and Hospitality in 2013

National Total = 14,291,000 Employees*

ALPHA ORDER

RANK	STATE	EMPLOYEES	% of USA
26	Alabama	181,200	1.3%
50	Alaska	32,200	0.2%
20	Arizona	278,500	1.9%
36	Arkansas	103,400	0.7%
1	California	1,696,300	11.9%
17	Colorado	291,800	2.0%
30	Connecticut	145,600	1.0%
46	Delaware	45,200	0.3%
3	Florida	1,039,700	7.3%
9	Georgia	422,900	3.0%
35	Hawaii	113,000	0.8%
42	Idaho	62,000	0.4%
5	Illinois	545,100	3.8%
15	Indiana	299,700	2.1%
31	Iowa	134,600	0.9%
34	Kansas	120,800	0.8%
27	Kentucky	180,400	1.3%
25	Louisiana	219,800	1.5%
41	Maine	64,800	0.5%
23	Maryland	252,700	1.8%
13	Massachusetts	334,400	2.3%
10	Michigan	394,600	2.8%
22	Minnesota	253,800	1.8%
33	Mississippi	124,300	0.9%
19	Missouri	283,300	2.0%
43	Montana	59,800	0.4%
38	Nebraska	83,300	0.6%
14	Nevada	324,800	2.3%
40	New Hampshire	65,400	0.5%
12	New Jersey	352,800	2.5%
37	New Mexico	89,100	0.6%
4	New York	827,400	5.8%
8	North Carolina	435,500	3.0%
47	North Dakota	38,400	0.3%
7	Ohio	506,800	3.5%
29	Oklahoma	156,400	1.1%
28	Oregon	179,600	1.3%
6	Pennsylvania	533,900	3.7%
44	Rhode Island	53,300	0.4%
24	South Carolina	230,700	1.6%
45	South Dakota	45,400	0.3%
16	Tennessee	292,700	2.0%
2	Texas	1,144,900	8.0%
32	Utah	126,500	0.9%
48	Vermont	35,400	0.2%
11	Virginia	367,900	2.6%
18	Washington	288,400	2.0%
39	West Virginia	74,500	0.5%
21	Wisconsin	276,200	1.9%
49	Wyoming	34,200	0.2%

RANK ORDER

RANK	STATE	EMPLOYEES	% of USA
1	California	1,696,300	11.9%
2	Texas	1,144,900	8.0%
3	Florida	1,039,700	7.3%
4	New York	827,400	5.8%
5	Illinois	545,100	3.8%
6	Pennsylvania	533,900	3.7%
7	Ohio	506,800	3.5%
8	North Carolina	435,500	3.0%
9	Georgia	422,900	3.0%
10	Michigan	394,600	2.8%
11	Virginia	367,900	2.6%
12	New Jersey	352,800	2.5%
13	Massachusetts	334,400	2.3%
14	Nevada	324,800	2.3%
15	Indiana	299,700	2.1%
16	Tennessee	292,700	2.0%
17	Colorado	291,800	2.0%
18	Washington	288,400	2.0%
19	Missouri	283,300	2.0%
20	Arizona	278,500	1.9%
21	Wisconsin	276,200	1.9%
22	Minnesota	253,800	1.8%
23	Maryland	252,700	1.8%
24	South Carolina	230,700	1.6%
25	Louisiana	219,800	1.5%
26	Alabama	181,200	1.3%
27	Kentucky	180,400	1.3%
28	Oregon	179,600	1.3%
29	Oklahoma	156,400	1.1%
30	Connecticut	145,600	1.0%
31	Iowa	134,600	0.9%
32	Utah	126,500	0.9%
33	Mississippi	124,300	0.9%
34	Kansas	120,800	0.8%
35	Hawaii	113,000	0.8%
36	Arkansas	103,400	0.7%
37	New Mexico	89,100	0.6%
38	Nebraska	83,300	0.6%
39	West Virginia	74,500	0.5%
40	New Hampshire	65,400	0.5%
41	Maine	64,800	0.5%
42	Idaho	62,000	0.4%
43	Montana	59,800	0.4%
44	Rhode Island	53,300	0.4%
45	South Dakota	45,400	0.3%
46	Delaware	45,200	0.3%
47	North Dakota	38,400	0.3%
48	Vermont	35,400	0.2%
49	Wyoming	34,200	0.2%
50	Alaska	32,200	0.2%
	District of Columbia	68,800	0.5%

Source: U.S. Department of Labor, Bureau of Labor Statistics
    "Regional and State Employment and Unemployment" (press release, January 28, 2014, www.bls.gov/bls/newsrels.htm)
*Seasonally adjusted preliminary data as of December 2013. National total calculated through a different formula.

Percent of Nonfarm Employees in Leisure and Hospitality in 2013

National Percent = 10.4% of Employees*

ALPHA ORDER			RANK ORDER		
RANK	STATE	PERCENT	RANK	STATE	PERCENT
35	Alabama	9.6	1	Nevada	27.5
30	Alaska	9.7	2	Hawaii	18.2
12	Arizona	11.0	3	Florida	13.6
48	Arkansas	8.7	4	Montana	13.3
8	California	11.5	5	Colorado	12.3
5	Colorado	12.3	6	South Carolina	12.1
45	Connecticut	8.8	7	Wyoming	11.7
20	Delaware	10.5	8	California	11.5
3	Florida	13.6	8	Vermont	11.5
21	Georgia	10.4	10	Rhode Island	11.4
2	Hawaii	18.2	11	Louisiana	11.2
30	Idaho	9.7	12	Arizona	11.0
40	Illinois	9.3	12	Mississippi	11.0
25	Indiana	10.1	12	New Mexico	11.0
45	Iowa	8.8	15	Maine	10.8
45	Kansas	8.8	15	South Dakota	10.8
27	Kentucky	9.8	17	Oregon	10.7
11	Louisiana	11.2	18	North Carolina	10.6
15	Maine	10.8	18	Tennessee	10.6
35	Maryland	9.6	20	Delaware	10.5
26	Massachusetts	10.0	21	Georgia	10.4
35	Michigan	9.6	21	Missouri	10.4
43	Minnesota	9.1	23	New Hampshire	10.2
12	Mississippi	11.0	23	Texas	10.2
21	Missouri	10.4	25	Indiana	10.1
4	Montana	13.3	26	Massachusetts	10.0
49	Nebraska	8.6	27	Kentucky	9.8
1	Nevada	27.5	27	Utah	9.8
23	New Hampshire	10.2	27	Washington	9.8
44	New Jersey	8.9	30	Alaska	9.7
12	New Mexico	11.0	30	Idaho	9.7
40	New York	9.3	30	Ohio	9.7
18	North Carolina	10.6	30	Virginia	9.7
50	North Dakota	8.4	30	Wisconsin	9.7
30	Ohio	9.7	35	Alabama	9.6
35	Oklahoma	9.6	35	Maryland	9.6
17	Oregon	10.7	35	Michigan	9.6
40	Pennsylvania	9.3	35	Oklahoma	9.6
10	Rhode Island	11.4	35	West Virginia	9.6
6	South Carolina	12.1	40	Illinois	9.3
15	South Dakota	10.8	40	New York	9.3
18	Tennessee	10.6	40	Pennsylvania	9.3
23	Texas	10.2	43	Minnesota	9.1
27	Utah	9.8	44	New Jersey	8.9
8	Vermont	11.5	45	Connecticut	8.8
30	Virginia	9.7	45	Iowa	8.8
27	Washington	9.8	45	Kansas	8.8
35	West Virginia	9.6	48	Arkansas	8.7
30	Wisconsin	9.7	49	Nebraska	8.6
7	Wyoming	11.7	50	North Dakota	8.4
				District of Columbia	9.4

Source: CQ Press using data from U.S. Department of Labor, Bureau of Labor Statistics
"Regional and State Employment and Unemployment" (press release, January 28, 2014, www.bls.gov/bls/newsrels.htm)
*Seasonally adjusted preliminary data as of December 2013. National figure calculated through a different formula.

Employees in Manufacturing in 2013

National Total = 12,028,000 Employees*

ALPHA ORDER

RANK	STATE	EMPLOYEES	% of USA
NA	Alabama**	NA	NA
47	Alaska	10,400	0.1%
27	Arizona	154,000	1.3%
26	Arkansas	154,700	1.3%
1	California	1,251,500	10.4%
30	Colorado	134,900	1.1%
25	Connecticut	159,200	1.3%
44	Delaware	25,500	0.2%
13	Florida	322,400	2.7%
11	Georgia	357,600	3.0%
46	Hawaii	13,900	0.1%
35	Idaho	58,100	0.5%
4	Illinois	577,600	4.8%
7	Indiana	491,200	4.1%
22	Iowa	215,600	1.8%
24	Kansas	164,900	1.4%
21	Kentucky	222,500	1.8%
28	Louisiana	145,700	1.2%
36	Maine	50,100	0.4%
32	Maryland	102,500	0.9%
17	Massachusetts	248,500	2.1%
6	Michigan	563,200	4.7%
14	Minnesota	306,800	2.6%
29	Mississippi	138,000	1.1%
16	Missouri	250,300	2.1%
45	Montana	18,200	0.2%
33	Nebraska	96,600	0.8%
40	Nevada	40,000	0.3%
34	New Hampshire	65,900	0.5%
18	New Jersey	247,600	2.1%
42	New Mexico	28,300	0.2%
9	New York	444,900	3.7%
10	North Carolina	444,200	3.7%
43	North Dakota	25,700	0.2%
3	Ohio	663,000	5.5%
NA	Oklahoma**	NA	NA
23	Oregon	176,200	1.5%
5	Pennsylvania	564,700	4.7%
39	Rhode Island	40,500	0.3%
20	South Carolina	224,700	1.9%
38	South Dakota	42,600	0.4%
12	Tennessee	325,300	2.7%
2	Texas	878,000	7.3%
31	Utah	121,500	1.0%
41	Vermont	32,200	0.3%
19	Virginia	232,900	1.9%
15	Washington	281,800	2.3%
37	West Virginia	48,600	0.4%
8	Wisconsin	468,200	3.9%
48	Wyoming	9,800	0.1%

RANK ORDER

RANK	STATE	EMPLOYEES	% of USA
1	California	1,251,500	10.4%
2	Texas	878,000	7.3%
3	Ohio	663,000	5.5%
4	Illinois	577,600	4.8%
5	Pennsylvania	564,700	4.7%
6	Michigan	563,200	4.7%
7	Indiana	491,200	4.1%
8	Wisconsin	468,200	3.9%
9	New York	444,900	3.7%
10	North Carolina	444,200	3.7%
11	Georgia	357,600	3.0%
12	Tennessee	325,300	2.7%
13	Florida	322,400	2.7%
14	Minnesota	306,800	2.6%
15	Washington	281,800	2.3%
16	Missouri	250,300	2.1%
17	Massachusetts	248,500	2.1%
18	New Jersey	247,600	2.1%
19	Virginia	232,900	1.9%
20	South Carolina	224,700	1.9%
21	Kentucky	222,500	1.8%
22	Iowa	215,600	1.8%
23	Oregon	176,200	1.5%
24	Kansas	164,900	1.4%
25	Connecticut	159,200	1.3%
26	Arkansas	154,700	1.3%
27	Arizona	154,000	1.3%
28	Louisiana	145,700	1.2%
29	Mississippi	138,000	1.1%
30	Colorado	134,900	1.1%
31	Utah	121,500	1.0%
32	Maryland	102,500	0.9%
33	Nebraska	96,600	0.8%
34	New Hampshire	65,900	0.5%
35	Idaho	58,100	0.5%
36	Maine	50,100	0.4%
37	West Virginia	48,600	0.4%
38	South Dakota	42,600	0.4%
39	Rhode Island	40,500	0.3%
40	Nevada	40,000	0.3%
41	Vermont	32,200	0.3%
42	New Mexico	28,300	0.2%
43	North Dakota	25,700	0.2%
44	Delaware	25,500	0.2%
45	Montana	18,200	0.2%
46	Hawaii	13,900	0.1%
47	Alaska	10,400	0.1%
48	Wyoming	9,800	0.1%
NA	Alabama**	NA	NA
NA	Oklahoma**	NA	NA
	District of Columbia**	NA	NA

Source: U.S. Department of Labor, Bureau of Labor Statistics

"Regional and State Employment and Unemployment" (press release, January 28, 2014, www.bls.gov/bls/newsrels.htm)

*Seasonally adjusted preliminary data as of December 2013. National total calculated through a different formula.

**The Bureau of Labor Statistics does not publish seasonally adjusted figures in this category for these states.

Percent of Nonfarm Employees in Manufacturing in 2013

National Percent = 8.8% of Employees*

ALPHA ORDER				RANK ORDER		
RANK	STATE	PERCENT		RANK	STATE	PERCENT
NA	Alabama**	NA		1	Indiana	16.5
47	Alaska	3.1		1	Wisconsin	16.5
36	Arizona	6.1		3	Iowa	14.1
5	Arkansas	13.0		4	Michigan	13.8
28	California	8.5		5	Arkansas	13.0
38	Colorado	5.7		6	Ohio	12.7
21	Connecticut	9.6		7	Mississippi	12.2
37	Delaware	5.9		8	Kentucky	12.1
41	Florida	4.2		9	Kansas	12.0
26	Georgia	8.8		10	South Carolina	11.7
48	Hawaii	2.2		10	Tennessee	11.7
25	Idaho	9.1		12	Minnesota	11.0
18	Illinois	9.9		13	North Carolina	10.8
1	Indiana	16.5		14	Oregon	10.5
3	Iowa	14.1		15	Vermont	10.4
9	Kansas	12.0		16	New Hampshire	10.3
8	Kentucky	12.1		17	South Dakota	10.1
31	Louisiana	7.4		18	Illinois	9.9
29	Maine	8.3		18	Nebraska	9.9
43	Maryland	3.9		20	Pennsylvania	9.8
31	Massachusetts	7.4		21	Connecticut	9.6
4	Michigan	13.8		21	Washington	9.6
12	Minnesota	11.0		23	Utah	9.4
7	Mississippi	12.2		24	Missouri	9.2
24	Missouri	9.2		25	Idaho	9.1
42	Montana	4.1		26	Georgia	8.8
18	Nebraska	9.9		27	Rhode Island	8.6
45	Nevada	3.4		28	California	8.5
16	New Hampshire	10.3		29	Maine	8.3
33	New Jersey	6.3		30	Texas	7.8
44	New Mexico	3.5		31	Louisiana	7.4
40	New York	5.0		31	Massachusetts	7.4
13	North Carolina	10.8		33	New Jersey	6.3
39	North Dakota	5.6		33	West Virginia	6.3
6	Ohio	12.7		35	Virginia	6.2
NA	Oklahoma**	NA		36	Arizona	6.1
14	Oregon	10.5		37	Delaware	5.9
20	Pennsylvania	9.8		38	Colorado	5.7
27	Rhode Island	8.6		39	North Dakota	5.6
10	South Carolina	11.7		40	New York	5.0
17	South Dakota	10.1		41	Florida	4.2
10	Tennessee	11.7		42	Montana	4.1
30	Texas	7.8		43	Maryland	3.9
23	Utah	9.4		44	New Mexico	3.5
15	Vermont	10.4		45	Nevada	3.4
35	Virginia	6.2		46	Wyoming	3.3
21	Washington	9.6		47	Alaska	3.1
33	West Virginia	6.3		48	Hawaii	2.2
1	Wisconsin	16.5		NA	Alabama**	NA
46	Wyoming	3.3		NA	Oklahoma**	NA
					District of Columbia**	NA

Source: CQ Press using data from U.S. Department of Labor, Bureau of Labor Statistics
"Regional and State Employment and Unemployment" (press release, January 28, 2014, www.bls.gov/bls/newsrels.htm)
*Seasonally adjusted preliminary data as of December 2013. National figure calculated through a different formula.
**The Bureau of Labor Statistics does not publish seasonally adjusted figures in this category for these states.

Employees in Mining and Logging in 2013

National Total = 886,000 Employees*

ALPHA ORDER

RANK	STATE	EMPLOYEES	% of USA
17	Alabama	12,400	1.4%
12	Alaska	18,200	2.1%
15	Arizona	12,900	1.5%
21	Arkansas	10,300	1.2%
8	California	29,900	3.4%
7	Colorado	30,400	3.4%
43	Connecticut	500	0.1%
NA	Delaware**	NA	NA
30	Florida	5,700	0.6%
24	Georgia	8,600	1.0%
NA	Hawaii**	NA	NA
33	Idaho	4,100	0.5%
20	Illinois	10,400	1.2%
27	Indiana	7,200	0.8%
38	Iowa	2,200	0.2%
19	Kansas	10,600	1.2%
11	Kentucky	18,300	2.1%
3	Louisiana	54,500	6.2%
37	Maine	2,700	0.3%
NA	Maryland**	NA	NA
40	Massachusetts	900	0.1%
25	Michigan	7,900	0.9%
26	Minnesota	7,300	0.8%
23	Mississippi	9,400	1.1%
34	Missouri	3,900	0.4%
22	Montana	9,600	1.1%
NA	Nebraska**	NA	NA
13	Nevada	16,900	1.9%
40	New Hampshire	900	0.1%
39	New Jersey	1,200	0.1%
10	New Mexico	25,200	2.8%
32	New York	5,000	0.6%
31	North Carolina	5,400	0.6%
6	North Dakota	35,300	4.0%
16	Ohio	12,800	1.4%
2	Oklahoma	54,600	6.2%
28	Oregon	6,800	0.8%
5	Pennsylvania	36,500	4.1%
44	Rhode Island	200	0.0%
35	South Carolina	3,700	0.4%
NA	South Dakota**	NA	NA
NA	Tennessee**	NA	NA
1	Texas	288,900	32.6%
14	Utah	13,300	1.5%
42	Vermont	800	0.1%
18	Virginia	10,800	1.2%
29	Washington	5,900	0.7%
4	West Virginia	36,900	4.2%
36	Wisconsin	3,500	0.4%
9	Wyoming	25,900	2.9%

RANK ORDER

RANK	STATE	EMPLOYEES	% of USA
1	Texas	288,900	32.6%
2	Oklahoma	54,600	6.2%
3	Louisiana	54,500	6.2%
4	West Virginia	36,900	4.2%
5	Pennsylvania	36,500	4.1%
6	North Dakota	35,300	4.0%
7	Colorado	30,400	3.4%
8	California	29,900	3.4%
9	Wyoming	25,900	2.9%
10	New Mexico	25,200	2.8%
11	Kentucky	18,300	2.1%
12	Alaska	18,200	2.1%
13	Nevada	16,900	1.9%
14	Utah	13,300	1.5%
15	Arizona	12,900	1.5%
16	Ohio	12,800	1.4%
17	Alabama	12,400	1.4%
18	Virginia	10,800	1.2%
19	Kansas	10,600	1.2%
20	Illinois	10,400	1.2%
21	Arkansas	10,300	1.2%
22	Montana	9,600	1.1%
23	Mississippi	9,400	1.1%
24	Georgia	8,600	1.0%
25	Michigan	7,900	0.9%
26	Minnesota	7,300	0.8%
27	Indiana	7,200	0.8%
28	Oregon	6,800	0.8%
29	Washington	5,900	0.7%
30	Florida	5,700	0.6%
31	North Carolina	5,400	0.6%
32	New York	5,000	0.6%
33	Idaho	4,100	0.5%
34	Missouri	3,900	0.4%
35	South Carolina	3,700	0.4%
36	Wisconsin	3,500	0.4%
37	Maine	2,700	0.3%
38	Iowa	2,200	0.2%
39	New Jersey	1,200	0.1%
40	Massachusetts	900	0.1%
40	New Hampshire	900	0.1%
42	Vermont	800	0.1%
43	Connecticut	500	0.1%
44	Rhode Island	200	0.0%
NA	Delaware**	NA	NA
NA	Hawaii**	NA	NA
NA	Maryland**	NA	NA
NA	Nebraska**	NA	NA
NA	South Dakota**	NA	NA
NA	Tennessee**	NA	NA
	District of Columbia**	NA	NA

Source: U.S. Department of Labor, Bureau of Labor Statistics

"Regional and State Employment and Unemployment" (press release, January 28, 2014, www.bls.gov/bls/newsrels.htm)

*Not seasonally adjusted preliminary data as of December 2013. National total calculated through a different formula.

**The Bureau of Labor Statistics does not publish figures in this category for these states.

Percent of Nonfarm Employees in Mining and Logging in 2013

National Percent = 0.6% of Employees*

ALPHA ORDER		
RANK	STATE	PERCENT
17	Alabama	0.7
3	Alaska	5.7
20	Arizona	0.5
14	Arkansas	0.9
26	California	0.2
11	Colorado	1.3
41	Connecticut	0.0
NA	Delaware**	NA
34	Florida	0.1
26	Georgia	0.2
NA	Hawaii**	NA
18	Idaho	0.6
26	Illinois	0.2
26	Indiana	0.2
34	Iowa	0.1
15	Kansas	0.8
12	Kentucky	1.0
7	Louisiana	2.8
21	Maine	0.4
NA	Maryland**	NA
41	Massachusetts	0.0
26	Michigan	0.2
23	Minnesota	0.3
15	Mississippi	0.8
34	Missouri	0.1
9	Montana	2.2
NA	Nebraska**	NA
10	Nevada	1.4
34	New Hampshire	0.1
41	New Jersey	0.0
6	New Mexico	3.1
34	New York	0.1
34	North Carolina	0.1
2	North Dakota	7.7
26	Ohio	0.2
5	Oklahoma	3.3
21	Oregon	0.4
18	Pennsylvania	0.6
41	Rhode Island	0.0
26	South Carolina	0.2
NA	South Dakota**	NA
NA	Tennessee**	NA
8	Texas	2.5
12	Utah	1.0
23	Vermont	0.3
23	Virginia	0.3
26	Washington	0.2
4	West Virginia	4.7
34	Wisconsin	0.1
1	Wyoming	8.9

RANK ORDER		
RANK	STATE	PERCENT
1	Wyoming	8.9
2	North Dakota	7.7
3	Alaska	5.7
4	West Virginia	4.7
5	Oklahoma	3.3
6	New Mexico	3.1
7	Louisiana	2.8
8	Texas	2.5
9	Montana	2.2
10	Nevada	1.4
11	Colorado	1.3
12	Kentucky	1.0
12	Utah	1.0
14	Arkansas	0.9
15	Kansas	0.8
15	Mississippi	0.8
17	Alabama	0.7
18	Idaho	0.6
18	Pennsylvania	0.6
20	Arizona	0.5
21	Maine	0.4
21	Oregon	0.4
23	Minnesota	0.3
23	Vermont	0.3
23	Virginia	0.3
26	California	0.2
26	Georgia	0.2
26	Illinois	0.2
26	Indiana	0.2
26	Michigan	0.2
26	Ohio	0.2
26	South Carolina	0.2
26	Washington	0.2
34	Florida	0.1
34	Iowa	0.1
34	Missouri	0.1
34	New Hampshire	0.1
34	New York	0.1
34	North Carolina	0.1
34	Wisconsin	0.1
41	Connecticut	0.0
41	Massachusetts	0.0
41	New Jersey	0.0
41	Rhode Island	0.0
NA	Delaware**	NA
NA	Hawaii**	NA
NA	Maryland**	NA
NA	Nebraska**	NA
NA	South Dakota**	NA
NA	Tennessee**	NA
	District of Columbia**	NA

Source: CQ Press using data from U.S. Department of Labor, Bureau of Labor Statistics
"Regional and State Employment and Unemployment" (press release, January 28, 2014, www.bls.gov/bls/newsrels.htm)
*Not seasonally adjusted preliminary data as of December 2013. National figure calculated through a different formula.
**The Bureau of Labor Statistics does not publish seasonally adjusted figures in this category for these states.

Employees in Professional and Business Services in 2013

National Total = 18,789,000 Employees*

ALPHA ORDER

RANK	STATE	EMPLOYEES	% of USA
24	Alabama	220,500	1.2%
48	Alaska	28,400	0.2%
16	Arizona	363,800	1.9%
34	Arkansas	126,100	0.7%
1	California	2,326,600	12.4%
15	Colorado	377,800	2.0%
28	Connecticut	202,900	1.1%
42	Delaware	61,100	0.3%
4	Florida	1,109,300	5.9%
10	Georgia	598,000	3.2%
39	Hawaii	77,400	0.4%
38	Idaho	78,600	0.4%
5	Illinois	898,300	4.8%
21	Indiana	311,800	1.7%
33	Iowa	134,000	0.7%
31	Kansas	161,300	0.9%
25	Kentucky	208,100	1.1%
26	Louisiana	205,500	1.1%
43	Maine	59,900	0.3%
14	Maryland	430,800	2.3%
13	Massachusetts	509,700	2.7%
11	Michigan	596,900	3.2%
20	Minnesota	341,800	1.8%
36	Mississippi	106,400	0.6%
18	Missouri	350,100	1.9%
45	Montana	42,900	0.2%
35	Nebraska	108,400	0.6%
32	Nevada	145,300	0.8%
40	New Hampshire	70,400	0.4%
9	New Jersey	618,100	3.3%
37	New Mexico	97,500	0.5%
3	New York	1,200,400	6.4%
12	North Carolina	565,000	3.0%
46	North Dakota	34,400	0.2%
7	Ohio	681,100	3.6%
29	Oklahoma	186,300	1.0%
27	Oregon	204,500	1.1%
6	Pennsylvania	745,600	4.0%
44	Rhode Island	59,000	0.3%
23	South Carolina	240,000	1.3%
47	South Dakota	29,300	0.2%
19	Tennessee	347,600	1.9%
2	Texas	1,492,100	7.9%
30	Utah	170,500	0.9%
49	Vermont	27,000	0.1%
8	Virginia	675,600	3.6%
17	Washington	357,600	1.9%
41	West Virginia	66,800	0.4%
22	Wisconsin	304,200	1.6%
50	Wyoming	18,300	0.1%

RANK ORDER

RANK	STATE	EMPLOYEES	% of USA
1	California	2,326,600	12.4%
2	Texas	1,492,100	7.9%
3	New York	1,200,400	6.4%
4	Florida	1,109,300	5.9%
5	Illinois	898,300	4.8%
6	Pennsylvania	745,600	4.0%
7	Ohio	681,100	3.6%
8	Virginia	675,600	3.6%
9	New Jersey	618,100	3.3%
10	Georgia	598,000	3.2%
11	Michigan	596,900	3.2%
12	North Carolina	565,000	3.0%
13	Massachusetts	509,700	2.7%
14	Maryland	430,800	2.3%
15	Colorado	377,800	2.0%
16	Arizona	363,800	1.9%
17	Washington	357,600	1.9%
18	Missouri	350,100	1.9%
19	Tennessee	347,600	1.9%
20	Minnesota	341,800	1.8%
21	Indiana	311,800	1.7%
22	Wisconsin	304,200	1.6%
23	South Carolina	240,000	1.3%
24	Alabama	220,500	1.2%
25	Kentucky	208,100	1.1%
26	Louisiana	205,500	1.1%
27	Oregon	204,500	1.1%
28	Connecticut	202,900	1.1%
29	Oklahoma	186,300	1.0%
30	Utah	170,500	0.9%
31	Kansas	161,300	0.9%
32	Nevada	145,300	0.8%
33	Iowa	134,000	0.7%
34	Arkansas	126,100	0.7%
35	Nebraska	108,400	0.6%
36	Mississippi	106,400	0.6%
37	New Mexico	97,500	0.5%
38	Idaho	78,600	0.4%
39	Hawaii	77,400	0.4%
40	New Hampshire	70,400	0.4%
41	West Virginia	66,800	0.4%
42	Delaware	61,100	0.3%
43	Maine	59,900	0.3%
44	Rhode Island	59,000	0.3%
45	Montana	42,900	0.2%
46	North Dakota	34,400	0.2%
47	South Dakota	29,300	0.2%
48	Alaska	28,400	0.2%
49	Vermont	27,000	0.1%
50	Wyoming	18,300	0.1%
	District of Columbia	156,300	0.8%

Source: U.S. Department of Labor, Bureau of Labor Statistics
"Regional and State Employment and Unemployment" (press release, January 28, 2014, www.bls.gov/bls/newsrels.htm)
*Seasonally adjusted preliminary data as of December 2013. National total calculated through a different formula.

Percent of Nonfarm Employees in Professional and Business Services in 2013

National Percent = 13.7% of Employees*

ALPHA ORDER

RANK	STATE	PERCENT
32	Alabama	11.6
47	Alaska	8.5
11	Arizona	14.3
38	Arkansas	10.6
4	California	15.8
3	Colorado	15.9
24	Connecticut	12.3
12	Delaware	14.2
10	Florida	14.5
8	Georgia	14.7
21	Hawaii	12.5
24	Idaho	12.3
6	Illinois	15.4
39	Indiana	10.5
44	Iowa	8.8
31	Kansas	11.7
34	Kentucky	11.3
39	Louisiana	10.5
41	Maine	10.0
2	Maryland	16.4
7	Massachusetts	15.2
9	Michigan	14.6
27	Minnesota	12.2
43	Mississippi	9.4
18	Missouri	12.9
42	Montana	9.6
35	Nebraska	11.2
24	Nevada	12.3
36	New Hampshire	11.0
5	New Jersey	15.7
30	New Mexico	12.0
14	New York	13.4
13	North Carolina	13.8
48	North Dakota	7.5
17	Ohio	13.1
33	Oklahoma	11.4
27	Oregon	12.2
18	Pennsylvania	12.9
20	Rhode Island	12.6
21	South Carolina	12.5
49	South Dakota	6.9
21	Tennessee	12.5
15	Texas	13.2
15	Utah	13.2
45	Vermont	8.7
1	Virginia	17.9
27	Washington	12.2
46	West Virginia	8.6
37	Wisconsin	10.7
50	Wyoming	6.3

RANK ORDER

RANK	STATE	PERCENT
1	Virginia	17.9
2	Maryland	16.4
3	Colorado	15.9
4	California	15.8
5	New Jersey	15.7
6	Illinois	15.4
7	Massachusetts	15.2
8	Georgia	14.7
9	Michigan	14.6
10	Florida	14.5
11	Arizona	14.3
12	Delaware	14.2
13	North Carolina	13.8
14	New York	13.4
15	Texas	13.2
15	Utah	13.2
17	Ohio	13.1
18	Missouri	12.9
18	Pennsylvania	12.9
20	Rhode Island	12.6
21	Hawaii	12.5
21	South Carolina	12.5
21	Tennessee	12.5
24	Connecticut	12.3
24	Idaho	12.3
24	Nevada	12.3
27	Minnesota	12.2
27	Oregon	12.2
27	Washington	12.2
30	New Mexico	12.0
31	Kansas	11.7
32	Alabama	11.6
33	Oklahoma	11.4
34	Kentucky	11.3
35	Nebraska	11.2
36	New Hampshire	11.0
37	Wisconsin	10.7
38	Arkansas	10.6
39	Indiana	10.5
39	Louisiana	10.5
41	Maine	10.0
42	Montana	9.6
43	Mississippi	9.4
44	Iowa	8.8
45	Vermont	8.7
46	West Virginia	8.6
47	Alaska	8.5
48	North Dakota	7.5
49	South Dakota	6.9
50	Wyoming	6.3

District of Columbia — 21.3

Source: CQ Press using data from U.S. Department of Labor, Bureau of Labor Statistics
"Regional and State Employment and Unemployment" (press release, January 28, 2014, www.bls.gov/bls/newsrels.htm)
*Seasonally adjusted preliminary data as of December 2013. National figure calculated through a different formula.

Employees in Trade, Transportation, and Public Utilities in 2013

National Total = 26,286,000 Employees*

ALPHA ORDER

RANK	STATE	EMPLOYEES	% of USA
25	Alabama	368,200	1.4%
48	Alaska	63,900	0.2%
20	Arizona	497,900	1.9%
33	Arkansas	253,100	1.0%
1	California	2,805,700	10.7%
22	Colorado	413,400	1.6%
29	Connecticut	300,700	1.1%
46	Delaware	76,200	0.3%
3	Florida	1,620,900	6.2%
8	Georgia	864,200	3.3%
42	Hawaii	116,900	0.4%
40	Idaho	130,500	0.5%
5	Illinois	1,185,000	4.5%
13	Indiana	589,800	2.2%
28	Iowa	312,400	1.2%
31	Kansas	257,200	1.0%
24	Kentucky	376,000	1.4%
23	Louisiana	394,300	1.5%
41	Maine	119,200	0.5%
21	Maryland	459,700	1.7%
15	Massachusetts	563,100	2.1%
11	Michigan	745,600	2.8%
18	Minnesota	521,800	2.0%
35	Mississippi	219,800	0.8%
17	Missouri	524,700	2.0%
44	Montana	90,500	0.3%
36	Nebraska	204,800	0.8%
34	Nevada	232,900	0.9%
37	New Hampshire	138,400	0.5%
9	New Jersey	835,300	3.2%
38	New Mexico	137,300	0.5%
4	New York	1,550,400	5.9%
10	North Carolina	774,400	2.9%
43	North Dakota	104,800	0.4%
7	Ohio	986,300	3.8%
30	Oklahoma	295,200	1.1%
27	Oregon	323,300	1.2%
6	Pennsylvania	1,113,500	4.2%
47	Rhode Island	74,700	0.3%
26	South Carolina	366,500	1.4%
45	South Dakota	84,900	0.3%
14	Tennessee	589,100	2.2%
2	Texas	2,274,000	8.7%
32	Utah	253,600	1.0%
49	Vermont	55,700	0.2%
12	Virginia	640,400	2.4%
16	Washington	562,900	2.1%
39	West Virginia	136,700	0.5%
19	Wisconsin	513,300	2.0%
50	Wyoming	55,100	0.2%

RANK ORDER

RANK	STATE	EMPLOYEES	% of USA
1	California	2,805,700	10.7%
2	Texas	2,274,000	8.7%
3	Florida	1,620,900	6.2%
4	New York	1,550,400	5.9%
5	Illinois	1,185,000	4.5%
6	Pennsylvania	1,113,500	4.2%
7	Ohio	986,300	3.8%
8	Georgia	864,200	3.3%
9	New Jersey	835,300	3.2%
10	North Carolina	774,400	2.9%
11	Michigan	745,600	2.8%
12	Virginia	640,400	2.4%
13	Indiana	589,800	2.2%
14	Tennessee	589,100	2.2%
15	Massachusetts	563,100	2.1%
16	Washington	562,900	2.1%
17	Missouri	524,700	2.0%
18	Minnesota	521,800	2.0%
19	Wisconsin	513,300	2.0%
20	Arizona	497,900	1.9%
21	Maryland	459,700	1.7%
22	Colorado	413,400	1.6%
23	Louisiana	394,300	1.5%
24	Kentucky	376,000	1.4%
25	Alabama	368,200	1.4%
26	South Carolina	366,500	1.4%
27	Oregon	323,300	1.2%
28	Iowa	312,400	1.2%
29	Connecticut	300,700	1.1%
30	Oklahoma	295,200	1.1%
31	Kansas	257,200	1.0%
32	Utah	253,600	1.0%
33	Arkansas	253,100	1.0%
34	Nevada	232,900	0.9%
35	Mississippi	219,800	0.8%
36	Nebraska	204,800	0.8%
37	New Hampshire	138,400	0.5%
38	New Mexico	137,300	0.5%
39	West Virginia	136,700	0.5%
40	Idaho	130,500	0.5%
41	Maine	119,200	0.5%
42	Hawaii	116,900	0.4%
43	North Dakota	104,800	0.4%
44	Montana	90,500	0.3%
45	South Dakota	84,900	0.3%
46	Delaware	76,200	0.3%
47	Rhode Island	74,700	0.3%
48	Alaska	63,900	0.2%
49	Vermont	55,700	0.2%
50	Wyoming	55,100	0.2%
	District of Columbia	27,600	0.1%

Source: U.S. Department of Labor, Bureau of Labor Statistics
"Regional and State Employment and Unemployment" (press release, January 28, 2014, www.bls.gov/bls/newsrels.htm)
*Seasonally adjusted preliminary data as of December 2013. National total calculated through a different formula.

Percent of Nonfarm Employees in
Trade, Transportation, and Public Utilities in 2013
National Percent = 19.2% of Employees*

ALPHA ORDER

RANK	STATE	PERCENT
23	Alabama	19.4
26	Alaska	19.2
21	Arizona	19.6
4	Arkansas	21.2
30	California	19.0
45	Colorado	17.4
37	Connecticut	18.2
42	Delaware	17.7
4	Florida	21.2
4	Georgia	21.2
33	Hawaii	18.8
9	Idaho	20.5
12	Illinois	20.3
18	Indiana	19.8
10	Iowa	20.4
35	Kansas	18.7
10	Kentucky	20.4
15	Louisiana	20.1
17	Maine	19.9
44	Maryland	17.5
49	Massachusetts	16.8
37	Michigan	18.2
35	Minnesota	18.7
22	Mississippi	19.5
24	Missouri	19.3
13	Montana	20.2
8	Nebraska	21.1
19	Nevada	19.7
2	New Hampshire	21.6
4	New Jersey	21.2
48	New Mexico	16.9
46	New York	17.3
32	North Carolina	18.9
1	North Dakota	23.0
30	Ohio	19.0
40	Oklahoma	18.0
26	Oregon	19.2
24	Pennsylvania	19.3
50	Rhode Island	15.9
26	South Carolina	19.2
15	South Dakota	20.1
3	Tennessee	21.3
13	Texas	20.2
19	Utah	19.7
40	Vermont	18.0
47	Virginia	17.0
29	Washington	19.1
42	West Virginia	17.7
39	Wisconsin	18.1
33	Wyoming	18.8

RANK ORDER

RANK	STATE	PERCENT
1	North Dakota	23.0
2	New Hampshire	21.6
3	Tennessee	21.3
4	Arkansas	21.2
4	Florida	21.2
4	Georgia	21.2
4	New Jersey	21.2
8	Nebraska	21.1
9	Idaho	20.5
10	Iowa	20.4
10	Kentucky	20.4
12	Illinois	20.3
13	Montana	20.2
13	Texas	20.2
15	Louisiana	20.1
15	South Dakota	20.1
17	Maine	19.9
18	Indiana	19.8
19	Nevada	19.7
19	Utah	19.7
21	Arizona	19.6
22	Mississippi	19.5
23	Alabama	19.4
24	Missouri	19.3
24	Pennsylvania	19.3
26	Alaska	19.2
26	Oregon	19.2
26	South Carolina	19.2
29	Washington	19.1
30	California	19.0
30	Ohio	19.0
32	North Carolina	18.9
33	Hawaii	18.8
33	Wyoming	18.8
35	Kansas	18.7
35	Minnesota	18.7
37	Connecticut	18.2
37	Michigan	18.2
39	Wisconsin	18.1
40	Oklahoma	18.0
40	Vermont	18.0
42	Delaware	17.7
42	West Virginia	17.7
44	Maryland	17.5
45	Colorado	17.4
46	New York	17.3
47	Virginia	17.0
48	New Mexico	16.9
49	Massachusetts	16.8
50	Rhode Island	15.9

District of Columbia   3.8

Source: CQ Press using data from U.S. Department of Labor, Bureau of Labor Statistics
   "Regional and State Employment and Unemployment" (press release, January 28, 2014, www.bls.gov/bls/newsrels.htm)
*Seasonally adjusted preliminary data as of December 2013. National figure calculated through a different formula.

VII. Energy and Environment

Energy Consumption in 2011

National Total = 97,387,300,000,000,000 BTUs*

ALPHA ORDER

RANK	STATE	BTUs	% of USA
17	Alabama	1,931,300,000,000,000	2.0%
38	Alaska	637,900,000,000,000	0.7%
26	Arizona	1,431,500,000,000,000	1.5%
31	Arkansas	1,117,100,000,000,000	1.1%
2	California	7,858,400,000,000,000	8.1%
25	Colorado	1,480,800,000,000,000	1.5%
35	Connecticut	741,600,000,000,000	0.8%
48	Delaware	271,600,000,000,000	0.3%
3	Florida	4,217,100,000,000,000	4.3%
9	Georgia	3,002,100,000,000,000	3.1%
47	Hawaii	286,000,000,000,000	0.3%
42	Idaho	525,600,000,000,000	0.5%
5	Illinois	3,977,800,000,000,000	4.1%
10	Indiana	2,869,200,000,000,000	2.9%
24	Iowa	1,512,600,000,000,000	1.6%
30	Kansas	1,162,500,000,000,000	1.2%
18	Kentucky	1,911,400,000,000,000	2.0%
4	Louisiana	4,055,300,000,000,000	4.2%
43	Maine	412,500,000,000,000	0.4%
27	Maryland	1,426,400,000,000,000	1.5%
28	Massachusetts	1,395,100,000,000,000	1.4%
11	Michigan	2,802,700,000,000,000	2.9%
20	Minnesota	1,866,600,000,000,000	1.9%
29	Mississippi	1,163,400,000,000,000	1.2%
19	Missouri	1,878,100,000,000,000	1.9%
44	Montana	397,500,000,000,000	0.4%
33	Nebraska	871,400,000,000,000	0.9%
39	Nevada	632,500,000,000,000	0.6%
46	New Hampshire	292,100,000,000,000	0.3%
13	New Jersey	2,438,500,000,000,000	2.5%
37	New Mexico	688,000,000,000,000	0.7%
8	New York	3,614,800,000,000,000	3.7%
12	North Carolina	2,572,700,000,000,000	2.6%
41	North Dakota	526,200,000,000,000	0.5%
6	Ohio	3,827,600,000,000,000	3.9%
23	Oklahoma	1,594,600,000,000,000	1.6%
32	Oregon	1,014,200,000,000,000	1.0%
7	Pennsylvania	3,725,300,000,000,000	3.8%
49	Rhode Island	183,900,000,000,000	0.2%
22	South Carolina	1,610,300,000,000,000	1.7%
45	South Dakota	382,400,000,000,000	0.4%
15	Tennessee	2,201,100,000,000,000	2.3%
1	Texas	12,206,600,000,000,000	12.5%
34	Utah	797,200,000,000,000	0.8%
50	Vermont	149,300,000,000,000	0.2%
14	Virginia	2,388,500,000,000,000	2.5%
16	Washington	2,080,200,000,000,000	2.1%
36	West Virginia	724,300,000,000,000	0.7%
21	Wisconsin	1,789,200,000,000,000	1.8%
40	Wyoming	553,000,000,000,000	0.6%

RANK ORDER

RANK	STATE	BTUs	% of USA
1	Texas	12,206,600,000,000,000	12.5%
2	California	7,858,400,000,000,000	8.1%
3	Florida	4,217,100,000,000,000	4.3%
4	Louisiana	4,055,300,000,000,000	4.2%
5	Illinois	3,977,800,000,000,000	4.1%
6	Ohio	3,827,600,000,000,000	3.9%
7	Pennsylvania	3,725,300,000,000,000	3.8%
8	New York	3,614,800,000,000,000	3.7%
9	Georgia	3,002,100,000,000,000	3.1%
10	Indiana	2,869,200,000,000,000	2.9%
11	Michigan	2,802,700,000,000,000	2.9%
12	North Carolina	2,572,700,000,000,000	2.6%
13	New Jersey	2,438,500,000,000,000	2.5%
14	Virginia	2,388,500,000,000,000	2.5%
15	Tennessee	2,201,100,000,000,000	2.3%
16	Washington	2,080,200,000,000,000	2.1%
17	Alabama	1,931,300,000,000,000	2.0%
18	Kentucky	1,911,400,000,000,000	2.0%
19	Missouri	1,878,100,000,000,000	1.9%
20	Minnesota	1,866,600,000,000,000	1.9%
21	Wisconsin	1,789,200,000,000,000	1.8%
22	South Carolina	1,610,300,000,000,000	1.7%
23	Oklahoma	1,594,600,000,000,000	1.6%
24	Iowa	1,512,600,000,000,000	1.6%
25	Colorado	1,480,800,000,000,000	1.5%
26	Arizona	1,431,500,000,000,000	1.5%
27	Maryland	1,426,400,000,000,000	1.5%
28	Massachusetts	1,395,100,000,000,000	1.4%
29	Mississippi	1,163,400,000,000,000	1.2%
30	Kansas	1,162,500,000,000,000	1.2%
31	Arkansas	1,117,100,000,000,000	1.1%
32	Oregon	1,014,200,000,000,000	1.0%
33	Nebraska	871,400,000,000,000	0.9%
34	Utah	797,200,000,000,000	0.8%
35	Connecticut	741,600,000,000,000	0.8%
36	West Virginia	724,300,000,000,000	0.7%
37	New Mexico	688,000,000,000,000	0.7%
38	Alaska	637,900,000,000,000	0.7%
39	Nevada	632,500,000,000,000	0.6%
40	Wyoming	553,000,000,000,000	0.6%
41	North Dakota	526,200,000,000,000	0.5%
42	Idaho	525,600,000,000,000	0.5%
43	Maine	412,500,000,000,000	0.4%
44	Montana	397,500,000,000,000	0.4%
45	South Dakota	382,400,000,000,000	0.4%
46	New Hampshire	292,100,000,000,000	0.3%
47	Hawaii	286,000,000,000,000	0.3%
48	Delaware	271,600,000,000,000	0.3%
49	Rhode Island	183,900,000,000,000	0.2%
50	Vermont	149,300,000,000,000	0.2%
	District of Columbia	180,300,000,000,000	0.2%

Source: U.S. Department of Energy, Energy Information Administration
   "State Energy Data 2011: Consumption" (http://www.eia.gov/state/seds/)
*British Thermal Units: The amount of heat required to raise the temperature of one pound of water one degree. National total includes 11.1 trillion Btu of net imports of coal coke that are not allocated to the states.

Per Capita Energy Consumption in 2011

National Per Capita = 312,551,695 BTUs*

ALPHA ORDER

RANK	STATE	PER CAPITA
13	Alabama	402,045,178
3	Alaska	881,247,755
43	Arizona	221,343,788
17	Arkansas	380,149,337
46	California	208,534,497
33	Colorado	289,427,794
48	Connecticut	206,762,898
30	Delaware	299,073,818
44	Florida	220,995,813
28	Georgia	305,947,744
47	Hawaii	207,527,742
21	Idaho	331,871,818
27	Illinois	309,321,673
9	Indiana	440,307,638
5	Iowa	493,652,779
12	Kansas	404,997,795
10	Kentucky	437,710,422
2	Louisiana	886,449,711
26	Maine	310,490,281
39	Maryland	244,264,477
45	Massachusetts	211,154,740
34	Michigan	283,765,968
18	Minnesota	349,073,429
15	Mississippi	390,736,121
25	Missouri	312,548,677
14	Montana	398,429,536
7	Nebraska	473,012,657
41	Nevada	232,534,371
42	New Hampshire	221,656,130
36	New Jersey	276,011,619
23	New Mexico	330,980,231
49	New York	185,358,998
37	North Carolina	266,570,567
4	North Dakota	768,466,863
22	Ohio	331,652,169
11	Oklahoma	421,387,768
38	Oregon	262,187,166
32	Pennsylvania	292,319,146
50	Rhode Island	175,035,169
19	South Carolina	344,570,959
8	South Dakota	464,307,006
20	Tennessee	343,933,322
6	Texas	476,229,156
35	Utah	283,262,867
40	Vermont	238,273,071
31	Virginia	294,717,032
29	Washington	304,868,621
16	West Virginia	390,477,587
24	Wisconsin	313,353,625
1	Wyoming	974,696,663

RANK ORDER

RANK	STATE	PER CAPITA
1	Wyoming	974,696,663
2	Louisiana	886,449,711
3	Alaska	881,247,755
4	North Dakota	768,466,863
5	Iowa	493,652,779
6	Texas	476,229,156
7	Nebraska	473,012,657
8	South Dakota	464,307,006
9	Indiana	440,307,638
10	Kentucky	437,710,422
11	Oklahoma	421,387,768
12	Kansas	404,997,795
13	Alabama	402,045,178
14	Montana	398,429,536
15	Mississippi	390,736,121
16	West Virginia	390,477,587
17	Arkansas	380,149,337
18	Minnesota	349,073,429
19	South Carolina	344,570,959
20	Tennessee	343,933,322
21	Idaho	331,871,818
22	Ohio	331,652,169
23	New Mexico	330,980,231
24	Wisconsin	313,353,625
25	Missouri	312,548,677
26	Maine	310,490,281
27	Illinois	309,321,673
28	Georgia	305,947,744
29	Washington	304,868,621
30	Delaware	299,073,818
31	Virginia	294,717,032
32	Pennsylvania	292,319,146
33	Colorado	289,427,794
34	Michigan	283,765,968
35	Utah	283,262,867
36	New Jersey	276,011,619
37	North Carolina	266,570,567
38	Oregon	262,187,166
39	Maryland	244,264,477
40	Vermont	238,273,071
41	Nevada	232,534,371
42	New Hampshire	221,656,130
43	Arizona	221,343,788
44	Florida	220,995,813
45	Massachusetts	211,154,740
46	California	208,534,497
47	Hawaii	207,527,742
48	Connecticut	206,762,898
49	New York	185,358,998
50	Rhode Island	175,035,169

District of Columbia   291,266,841

Source: CQ Press using data from U.S. Department of Energy, Energy Information Administration
   "State Energy Data 2011: Consumption" (http://www.eia.gov/state/seds/)
*British Thermal Units: The amount of heat required to raise the temperature of one pound of water one degree. National total
includes 11.1 trillion Btu of net imports of coal coke that are not allocated to the states.

Energy Prices in 2011

National Rate = $21.71 per Million BTUs*

<u>ALPHA ORDER</u>

RANK	STATE	RATE
38	Alabama	$19.85
10	Alaska	25.17
7	Arizona	25.23
41	Arkansas	19.63
13	California	24.14
28	Colorado	21.07
2	Connecticut	27.81
10	Delaware	25.17
9	Florida	25.18
25	Georgia	21.30
1	Hawaii	38.41
44	Idaho	19.22
43	Illinois	19.29
49	Indiana	17.52
47	Iowa	17.86
29	Kansas	20.81
35	Kentucky	20.35
48	Louisiana	17.69
24	Maine	21.67
8	Maryland	25.22
5	Massachusetts	25.90
31	Michigan	20.65
42	Minnesota	19.61
32	Mississippi	20.56
20	Missouri	22.26
23	Montana	21.72
45	Nebraska	19.08
15	Nevada	23.16
4	New Hampshire	27.36
14	New Jersey	24.00
17	New Mexico	22.69
10	New York	25.17
16	North Carolina	22.93
50	North Dakota	17.25
34	Ohio	20.43
40	Oklahoma	19.71
21	Oregon	22.02
18	Pennsylvania	22.58
6	Rhode Island	25.88
27	South Carolina	21.24
37	South Dakota	19.91
22	Tennessee	21.92
33	Texas	20.53
39	Utah	19.81
3	Vermont	27.77
19	Virginia	22.50
26	Washington	21.25
36	West Virginia	20.04
30	Wisconsin	20.70
46	Wyoming	17.90

<u>RANK ORDER</u>

RANK	STATE	RATE
1	Hawaii	$38.41
2	Connecticut	27.81
3	Vermont	27.77
4	New Hampshire	27.36
5	Massachusetts	25.90
6	Rhode Island	25.88
7	Arizona	25.23
8	Maryland	25.22
9	Florida	25.18
10	Alaska	25.17
10	Delaware	25.17
10	New York	25.17
13	California	24.14
14	New Jersey	24.00
15	Nevada	23.16
16	North Carolina	22.93
17	New Mexico	22.69
18	Pennsylvania	22.58
19	Virginia	22.50
20	Missouri	22.26
21	Oregon	22.02
22	Tennessee	21.92
23	Montana	21.72
24	Maine	21.67
25	Georgia	21.30
26	Washington	21.25
27	South Carolina	21.24
28	Colorado	21.07
29	Kansas	20.81
30	Wisconsin	20.70
31	Michigan	20.65
32	Mississippi	20.56
33	Texas	20.53
34	Ohio	20.43
35	Kentucky	20.35
36	West Virginia	20.04
37	South Dakota	19.91
38	Alabama	19.85
39	Utah	19.81
40	Oklahoma	19.71
41	Arkansas	19.63
42	Minnesota	19.61
43	Illinois	19.29
44	Idaho	19.22
45	Nebraska	19.08
46	Wyoming	17.90
47	Iowa	17.86
48	Louisiana	17.69
49	Indiana	17.52
50	North Dakota	17.25
	District of Columbia	27.04

Source: U.S. Department of Energy, Energy Information Administration
   "State Energy Data 2011: Prices and Expenditures" (http://www.eia.gov/state/seds/)
*British Thermal Units: The amount of heat required to raise the temperature of one pound of water one degree.

Energy Expenditures in 2011

National Total = $1,394,088,400,000*

ALPHA ORDER

RANK	STATE	EXPENDITURES	% of USA
19	Alabama	$24,479,300,000	1.8%
39	Alaska	7,739,300,000	0.6%
24	Arizona	22,464,700,000	1.6%
33	Arkansas	14,046,700,000	1.0%
2	California	136,096,400,000	9.8%
27	Colorado	19,332,700,000	1.4%
29	Connecticut	15,365,100,000	1.1%
48	Delaware	3,956,500,000	0.3%
3	Florida	68,013,200,000	4.9%
10	Georgia	42,404,700,000	3.0%
40	Hawaii	7,608,300,000	0.5%
42	Idaho	6,585,600,000	0.5%
7	Illinois	50,925,200,000	3.7%
14	Indiana	32,518,500,000	2.3%
28	Iowa	17,164,100,000	1.2%
32	Kansas	14,866,800,000	1.1%
23	Kentucky	23,149,200,000	1.7%
8	Louisiana	46,833,100,000	3.4%
41	Maine	7,317,300,000	0.5%
22	Maryland	23,203,900,000	1.7%
16	Massachusetts	27,248,300,000	2.0%
11	Michigan	39,498,900,000	2.8%
21	Minnesota	24,316,200,000	1.7%
30	Mississippi	15,169,000,000	1.1%
18	Missouri	26,750,300,000	1.9%
45	Montana	5,576,300,000	0.4%
35	Nebraska	9,971,200,000	0.7%
36	Nevada	9,670,800,000	0.7%
44	New Hampshire	5,964,600,000	0.4%
9	New Jersey	43,214,000,000	3.1%
38	New Mexico	8,845,800,000	0.6%
4	New York	65,876,900,000	4.7%
12	North Carolina	36,102,400,000	2.6%
43	North Dakota	6,409,300,000	0.5%
6	Ohio	50,995,500,000	3.7%
26	Oklahoma	19,765,500,000	1.4%
31	Oregon	14,941,000,000	1.1%
5	Pennsylvania	55,163,800,000	4.0%
49	Rhode Island	3,818,300,000	0.3%
25	South Carolina	21,174,900,000	1.5%
47	South Dakota	4,546,700,000	0.3%
15	Tennessee	29,699,400,000	2.1%
1	Texas	169,290,000,000	12.1%
34	Utah	10,430,700,000	0.7%
50	Vermont	3,151,000,000	0.2%
13	Virginia	33,914,700,000	2.4%
17	Washington	27,124,400,000	1.9%
37	West Virginia	8,887,900,000	0.6%
20	Wisconsin	24,356,400,000	1.7%
46	Wyoming	5,406,100,000	0.4%

RANK ORDER

RANK	STATE	EXPENDITURES	% of USA
1	Texas	$169,290,000,000	12.1%
2	California	136,096,400,000	9.8%
3	Florida	68,013,200,000	4.9%
4	New York	65,876,900,000	4.7%
5	Pennsylvania	55,163,800,000	4.0%
6	Ohio	50,995,500,000	3.7%
7	Illinois	50,925,200,000	3.7%
8	Louisiana	46,833,100,000	3.4%
9	New Jersey	43,214,000,000	3.1%
10	Georgia	42,404,700,000	3.0%
11	Michigan	39,498,900,000	2.8%
12	North Carolina	36,102,400,000	2.6%
13	Virginia	33,914,700,000	2.4%
14	Indiana	32,518,500,000	2.3%
15	Tennessee	29,699,400,000	2.1%
16	Massachusetts	27,248,300,000	2.0%
17	Washington	27,124,400,000	1.9%
18	Missouri	26,750,300,000	1.9%
19	Alabama	24,479,300,000	1.8%
20	Wisconsin	24,356,400,000	1.7%
21	Minnesota	24,316,200,000	1.7%
22	Maryland	23,203,900,000	1.7%
23	Kentucky	23,149,200,000	1.7%
24	Arizona	22,464,700,000	1.6%
25	South Carolina	21,174,900,000	1.5%
26	Oklahoma	19,765,500,000	1.4%
27	Colorado	19,332,700,000	1.4%
28	Iowa	17,164,100,000	1.2%
29	Connecticut	15,365,100,000	1.1%
30	Mississippi	15,169,000,000	1.1%
31	Oregon	14,941,000,000	1.1%
32	Kansas	14,866,800,000	1.1%
33	Arkansas	14,046,700,000	1.0%
34	Utah	10,430,700,000	0.7%
35	Nebraska	9,971,200,000	0.7%
36	Nevada	9,670,800,000	0.7%
37	West Virginia	8,887,900,000	0.6%
38	New Mexico	8,845,800,000	0.6%
39	Alaska	7,739,300,000	0.6%
40	Hawaii	7,608,300,000	0.5%
41	Maine	7,317,300,000	0.5%
42	Idaho	6,585,600,000	0.5%
43	North Dakota	6,409,300,000	0.5%
44	New Hampshire	5,964,600,000	0.4%
45	Montana	5,576,300,000	0.4%
46	Wyoming	5,406,100,000	0.4%
47	South Dakota	4,546,700,000	0.3%
48	Delaware	3,956,500,000	0.3%
49	Rhode Island	3,818,300,000	0.3%
50	Vermont	3,151,000,000	0.2%
	District of Columbia	2,396,000,000	0.2%

Source: U.S. Department of Energy, Energy Information Administration
 "State Energy Data 2011: Prices and Expenditures" (http://www.eia.gov/state/seds/)
*The national total includes $342 million for coal coke net imports, which are not allocated to the states.

Per Capita Energy Expenditures in 2011

National Per Capita = $4,474

<table>
<tr><td colspan="3">ALPHA ORDER</td><td colspan="3">RANK ORDER</td></tr>
<tr><td>RANK</td><td>STATE</td><td>PER CAPITA</td><td>RANK</td><td>STATE</td><td>PER CAPITA</td></tr>
<tr><td>15</td><td>Alabama</td><td>$5,096</td><td>1</td><td>Alaska</td><td>$10,692</td></tr>
<tr><td>1</td><td>Alaska</td><td>10,692</td><td>2</td><td>Louisiana</td><td>10,237</td></tr>
<tr><td>49</td><td>Arizona</td><td>3,474</td><td>3</td><td>Wyoming</td><td>9,529</td></tr>
<tr><td>21</td><td>Arkansas</td><td>4,780</td><td>4</td><td>North Dakota</td><td>9,360</td></tr>
<tr><td>46</td><td>California</td><td>3,612</td><td>5</td><td>Texas</td><td>6,605</td></tr>
<tr><td>42</td><td>Colorado</td><td>3,779</td><td>6</td><td>Iowa</td><td>5,602</td></tr>
<tr><td>31</td><td>Connecticut</td><td>4,284</td><td>7</td><td>Montana</td><td>5,589</td></tr>
<tr><td>28</td><td>Delaware</td><td>4,357</td><td>8</td><td>Hawaii</td><td>5,521</td></tr>
<tr><td>47</td><td>Florida</td><td>3,564</td><td>8</td><td>South Dakota</td><td>5,521</td></tr>
<tr><td>30</td><td>Georgia</td><td>4,322</td><td>10</td><td>Maine</td><td>5,508</td></tr>
<tr><td>8</td><td>Hawaii</td><td>5,521</td><td>11</td><td>Nebraska</td><td>5,413</td></tr>
<tr><td>35</td><td>Idaho</td><td>4,158</td><td>12</td><td>Kentucky</td><td>5,301</td></tr>
<tr><td>40</td><td>Illinois</td><td>3,960</td><td>13</td><td>Oklahoma</td><td>5,223</td></tr>
<tr><td>18</td><td>Indiana</td><td>4,990</td><td>14</td><td>Kansas</td><td>5,179</td></tr>
<tr><td>6</td><td>Iowa</td><td>5,602</td><td>15</td><td>Alabama</td><td>5,096</td></tr>
<tr><td>14</td><td>Kansas</td><td>5,179</td><td>16</td><td>Mississippi</td><td>5,095</td></tr>
<tr><td>12</td><td>Kentucky</td><td>5,301</td><td>17</td><td>Vermont</td><td>5,029</td></tr>
<tr><td>2</td><td>Louisiana</td><td>10,237</td><td>18</td><td>Indiana</td><td>4,990</td></tr>
<tr><td>10</td><td>Maine</td><td>5,508</td><td>19</td><td>New Jersey</td><td>4,891</td></tr>
<tr><td>39</td><td>Maryland</td><td>3,974</td><td>20</td><td>West Virginia</td><td>4,792</td></tr>
<tr><td>36</td><td>Massachusetts</td><td>4,124</td><td>21</td><td>Arkansas</td><td>4,780</td></tr>
<tr><td>37</td><td>Michigan</td><td>3,999</td><td>22</td><td>Tennessee</td><td>4,641</td></tr>
<tr><td>23</td><td>Minnesota</td><td>4,547</td><td>23</td><td>Minnesota</td><td>4,547</td></tr>
<tr><td>16</td><td>Mississippi</td><td>5,095</td><td>24</td><td>South Carolina</td><td>4,531</td></tr>
<tr><td>26</td><td>Missouri</td><td>4,452</td><td>25</td><td>New Hampshire</td><td>4,526</td></tr>
<tr><td>7</td><td>Montana</td><td>5,589</td><td>26</td><td>Missouri</td><td>4,452</td></tr>
<tr><td>11</td><td>Nebraska</td><td>5,413</td><td>27</td><td>Ohio</td><td>4,419</td></tr>
<tr><td>48</td><td>Nevada</td><td>3,555</td><td>28</td><td>Delaware</td><td>4,357</td></tr>
<tr><td>25</td><td>New Hampshire</td><td>4,526</td><td>29</td><td>Pennsylvania</td><td>4,329</td></tr>
<tr><td>19</td><td>New Jersey</td><td>4,891</td><td>30</td><td>Georgia</td><td>4,322</td></tr>
<tr><td>33</td><td>New Mexico</td><td>4,256</td><td>31</td><td>Connecticut</td><td>4,284</td></tr>
<tr><td>50</td><td>New York</td><td>3,378</td><td>32</td><td>Wisconsin</td><td>4,266</td></tr>
<tr><td>43</td><td>North Carolina</td><td>3,741</td><td>33</td><td>New Mexico</td><td>4,256</td></tr>
<tr><td>4</td><td>North Dakota</td><td>9,360</td><td>34</td><td>Virginia</td><td>4,185</td></tr>
<tr><td>27</td><td>Ohio</td><td>4,419</td><td>35</td><td>Idaho</td><td>4,158</td></tr>
<tr><td>13</td><td>Oklahoma</td><td>5,223</td><td>36</td><td>Massachusetts</td><td>4,124</td></tr>
<tr><td>41</td><td>Oregon</td><td>3,862</td><td>37</td><td>Michigan</td><td>3,999</td></tr>
<tr><td>29</td><td>Pennsylvania</td><td>4,329</td><td>38</td><td>Washington</td><td>3,975</td></tr>
<tr><td>45</td><td>Rhode Island</td><td>3,634</td><td>39</td><td>Maryland</td><td>3,974</td></tr>
<tr><td>24</td><td>South Carolina</td><td>4,531</td><td>40</td><td>Illinois</td><td>3,960</td></tr>
<tr><td>8</td><td>South Dakota</td><td>5,521</td><td>41</td><td>Oregon</td><td>3,862</td></tr>
<tr><td>22</td><td>Tennessee</td><td>4,641</td><td>42</td><td>Colorado</td><td>3,779</td></tr>
<tr><td>5</td><td>Texas</td><td>6,605</td><td>43</td><td>North Carolina</td><td>3,741</td></tr>
<tr><td>44</td><td>Utah</td><td>3,706</td><td>44</td><td>Utah</td><td>3,706</td></tr>
<tr><td>17</td><td>Vermont</td><td>5,029</td><td>45</td><td>Rhode Island</td><td>3,634</td></tr>
<tr><td>34</td><td>Virginia</td><td>4,185</td><td>46</td><td>California</td><td>3,612</td></tr>
<tr><td>38</td><td>Washington</td><td>3,975</td><td>47</td><td>Florida</td><td>3,564</td></tr>
<tr><td>20</td><td>West Virginia</td><td>4,792</td><td>48</td><td>Nevada</td><td>3,555</td></tr>
<tr><td>32</td><td>Wisconsin</td><td>4,266</td><td>49</td><td>Arizona</td><td>3,474</td></tr>
<tr><td>3</td><td>Wyoming</td><td>9,529</td><td>50</td><td>New York</td><td>3,378</td></tr>
<tr><td></td><td></td><td></td><td></td><td>District of Columbia</td><td>3,871</td></tr>
</table>

Source: CQ Press using data from U.S. Department of Energy, Energy Information Administration
"State Energy Data 2011: Prices and Expenditures" (http://www.eia.gov/state/seds/)

Average Monthly Electric Bill for Industrial Customers in 2012

National Average = $7,483 per Month

ALPHA ORDER

RANK	STATE	MONTHLY BILL
8	Alabama	$24,425
13	Alaska	15,329
24	Arizona	8,754
48	Arkansas	2,386
33	California	5,561
32	Colorado	5,571
26	Connecticut	8,104
10	Delaware	22,464
29	Florida	6,316
23	Georgia	8,972
1	Hawaii	133,212
49	Idaho	1,648
4	Illinois	36,206
16	Indiana	13,734
18	Iowa	11,868
45	Kansas	2,607
7	Kentucky	27,621
28	Louisiana	6,655
27	Maine	7,243
44	Maryland	3,393
25	Massachusetts	8,383
12	Michigan	15,471
20	Minnesota	11,585
17	Mississippi	12,267
21	Missouri	9,707
46	Montana	2,439
50	Nebraska	1,285
11	Nevada	19,800
31	New Hampshire	5,590
35	New Jersey	5,344
40	New Mexico	4,276
22	New York	9,390
15	North Carolina	13,843
30	North Dakota	6,079
14	Ohio	14,150
42	Oklahoma	3,850
47	Oregon	2,399
19	Pennsylvania	11,591
41	Rhode Island	4,264
5	South Carolina	32,173
36	South Dakota	5,159
2	Tennessee	85,815
39	Texas	4,750
38	Utah	4,822
3	Vermont	53,495
9	Virginia	24,389
43	Washington	3,427
37	West Virginia	5,013
6	Wisconsin	31,542
34	Wyoming	5,487

RANK ORDER

RANK	STATE	MONTHLY BILL
1	Hawaii	$133,212
2	Tennessee	85,815
3	Vermont	53,495
4	Illinois	36,206
5	South Carolina	32,173
6	Wisconsin	31,542
7	Kentucky	27,621
8	Alabama	24,425
9	Virginia	24,389
10	Delaware	22,464
11	Nevada	19,800
12	Michigan	15,471
13	Alaska	15,329
14	Ohio	14,150
15	North Carolina	13,843
16	Indiana	13,734
17	Mississippi	12,267
18	Iowa	11,868
19	Pennsylvania	11,591
20	Minnesota	11,585
21	Missouri	9,707
22	New York	9,390
23	Georgia	8,972
24	Arizona	8,754
25	Massachusetts	8,383
26	Connecticut	8,104
27	Maine	7,243
28	Louisiana	6,655
29	Florida	6,316
30	North Dakota	6,079
31	New Hampshire	5,590
32	Colorado	5,571
33	California	5,561
34	Wyoming	5,487
35	New Jersey	5,344
36	South Dakota	5,159
37	West Virginia	5,013
38	Utah	4,822
39	Texas	4,750
40	New Mexico	4,276
41	Rhode Island	4,264
42	Oklahoma	3,850
43	Washington	3,427
44	Maryland	3,393
45	Kansas	2,607
46	Montana	2,439
47	Oregon	2,399
48	Arkansas	2,386
49	Idaho	1,648
50	Nebraska	1,285
	District of Columbia	993,225

Source: U.S. Department of Energy, Energy Information Administration
"Electric Sales, Revenue and Average Price 2012" (http://www.eia.gov/electricity/sales_revenue_price/index.cfm)

Average Monthly Electric Bill for Commercial Customers in 2012

National Average = $629 per Month

<table>
<tr><td colspan="3">ALPHA ORDER</td><td colspan="3">RANK ORDER</td></tr>
<tr><td>RANK</td><td>STATE</td><td>MONTHLY BILL</td><td>RANK</td><td>STATE</td><td>MONTHLY BILL</td></tr>
<tr><td>23</td><td>Alabama</td><td>$541</td><td>1</td><td>Hawaii</td><td>$1,566</td></tr>
<tr><td>9</td><td>Alaska</td><td>733</td><td>2</td><td>Maryland</td><td>1,060</td></tr>
<tr><td>6</td><td>Arizona</td><td>772</td><td>3</td><td>Connecticut</td><td>1,053</td></tr>
<tr><td>46</td><td>Arkansas</td><td>428</td><td>4</td><td>New York</td><td>919</td></tr>
<tr><td>8</td><td>California</td><td>742</td><td>5</td><td>New Jersey</td><td>833</td></tr>
<tr><td>41</td><td>Colorado</td><td>449</td><td>6</td><td>Arizona</td><td>772</td></tr>
<tr><td>3</td><td>Connecticut</td><td>1,053</td><td>7</td><td>Virginia</td><td>751</td></tr>
<tr><td>10</td><td>Delaware</td><td>702</td><td>8</td><td>California</td><td>742</td></tr>
<tr><td>14</td><td>Florida</td><td>639</td><td>9</td><td>Alaska</td><td>733</td></tr>
<tr><td>12</td><td>Georgia</td><td>670</td><td>10</td><td>Delaware</td><td>702</td></tr>
<tr><td>1</td><td>Hawaii</td><td>1,566</td><td>11</td><td>Michigan</td><td>673</td></tr>
<tr><td>50</td><td>Idaho</td><td>334</td><td>12</td><td>Georgia</td><td>670</td></tr>
<tr><td>20</td><td>Illinois</td><td>573</td><td>13</td><td>Texas</td><td>668</td></tr>
<tr><td>25</td><td>Indiana</td><td>531</td><td>14</td><td>Florida</td><td>639</td></tr>
<tr><td>48</td><td>Iowa</td><td>368</td><td>15</td><td>Utah</td><td>626</td></tr>
<tr><td>25</td><td>Kansas</td><td>531</td><td>16</td><td>Rhode Island</td><td>623</td></tr>
<tr><td>39</td><td>Kentucky</td><td>458</td><td>17</td><td>Ohio</td><td>602</td></tr>
<tr><td>21</td><td>Louisiana</td><td>560</td><td>18</td><td>Minnesota</td><td>595</td></tr>
<tr><td>44</td><td>Maine</td><td>437</td><td>18</td><td>Wisconsin</td><td>595</td></tr>
<tr><td>2</td><td>Maryland</td><td>1,060</td><td>20</td><td>Illinois</td><td>573</td></tr>
<tr><td>27</td><td>Massachusetts</td><td>525</td><td>21</td><td>Louisiana</td><td>560</td></tr>
<tr><td>11</td><td>Michigan</td><td>673</td><td>22</td><td>Missouri</td><td>558</td></tr>
<tr><td>18</td><td>Minnesota</td><td>595</td><td>23</td><td>Alabama</td><td>541</td></tr>
<tr><td>36</td><td>Mississippi</td><td>464</td><td>23</td><td>North Dakota</td><td>541</td></tr>
<tr><td>22</td><td>Missouri</td><td>558</td><td>25</td><td>Indiana</td><td>531</td></tr>
<tr><td>48</td><td>Montana</td><td>368</td><td>25</td><td>Kansas</td><td>531</td></tr>
<tr><td>44</td><td>Nebraska</td><td>437</td><td>27</td><td>Massachusetts</td><td>525</td></tr>
<tr><td>43</td><td>Nevada</td><td>440</td><td>27</td><td>Washington</td><td>525</td></tr>
<tr><td>35</td><td>New Hampshire</td><td>475</td><td>29</td><td>New Mexico</td><td>518</td></tr>
<tr><td>5</td><td>New Jersey</td><td>833</td><td>29</td><td>Tennessee</td><td>518</td></tr>
<tr><td>29</td><td>New Mexico</td><td>518</td><td>31</td><td>North Carolina</td><td>515</td></tr>
<tr><td>4</td><td>New York</td><td>919</td><td>32</td><td>South Carolina</td><td>497</td></tr>
<tr><td>31</td><td>North Carolina</td><td>515</td><td>33</td><td>Wyoming</td><td>492</td></tr>
<tr><td>23</td><td>North Dakota</td><td>541</td><td>34</td><td>Pennsylvania</td><td>491</td></tr>
<tr><td>17</td><td>Ohio</td><td>602</td><td>35</td><td>New Hampshire</td><td>475</td></tr>
<tr><td>40</td><td>Oklahoma</td><td>454</td><td>36</td><td>Mississippi</td><td>464</td></tr>
<tr><td>38</td><td>Oregon</td><td>460</td><td>36</td><td>Vermont</td><td>464</td></tr>
<tr><td>34</td><td>Pennsylvania</td><td>491</td><td>38</td><td>Oregon</td><td>460</td></tr>
<tr><td>16</td><td>Rhode Island</td><td>623</td><td>39</td><td>Kentucky</td><td>458</td></tr>
<tr><td>32</td><td>South Carolina</td><td>497</td><td>40</td><td>Oklahoma</td><td>454</td></tr>
<tr><td>42</td><td>South Dakota</td><td>446</td><td>41</td><td>Colorado</td><td>449</td></tr>
<tr><td>29</td><td>Tennessee</td><td>518</td><td>42</td><td>South Dakota</td><td>446</td></tr>
<tr><td>13</td><td>Texas</td><td>668</td><td>43</td><td>Nevada</td><td>440</td></tr>
<tr><td>15</td><td>Utah</td><td>626</td><td>44</td><td>Maine</td><td>437</td></tr>
<tr><td>36</td><td>Vermont</td><td>464</td><td>44</td><td>Nebraska</td><td>437</td></tr>
<tr><td>7</td><td>Virginia</td><td>751</td><td>46</td><td>Arkansas</td><td>428</td></tr>
<tr><td>27</td><td>Washington</td><td>525</td><td>47</td><td>West Virginia</td><td>393</td></tr>
<tr><td>47</td><td>West Virginia</td><td>393</td><td>48</td><td>Iowa</td><td>368</td></tr>
<tr><td>18</td><td>Wisconsin</td><td>595</td><td>48</td><td>Montana</td><td>368</td></tr>
<tr><td>33</td><td>Wyoming</td><td>492</td><td>50</td><td>Idaho</td><td>334</td></tr>
<tr><td></td><td></td><td></td><td></td><td>District of Columbia</td><td>3,288</td></tr>
</table>

Source: U.S. Department of Energy, Energy Information Administration
"Electric Sales, Revenue and Average Price 2012" (http://www.eia.gov/electricity/sales_revenue_price/index.cfm)

Average Monthly Electric Bill for Residential Customers in 2012

National Average = $107 per Month

RANK	STATE	MONTHLY BILL
2	Alabama	$135
14	Alaska	117
13	Arizona	120
28	Arkansas	104
40	California	88
47	Colorado	81
7	Connecticut	127
5	Delaware	128
9	Florida	123
9	Georgia	123
1	Hawaii	203
40	Idaho	88
43	Illinois	87
25	Indiana	105
35	Iowa	94
22	Kansas	106
20	Kentucky	107
25	Louisiana	105
49	Maine	78
4	Maryland	129
35	Massachusetts	94
34	Michigan	95
39	Minnesota	90
12	Mississippi	122
18	Missouri	108
45	Montana	85
29	Nebraska	100
16	Nevada	111
30	New Hampshire	99
17	New Jersey	109
50	New Mexico	75
22	New York	106
14	North Carolina	117
30	North Dakota	99
25	Ohio	105
18	Oklahoma	108
35	Oregon	94
20	Pennsylvania	107
44	Rhode Island	86
3	South Carolina	132
30	South Dakota	99
9	Tennessee	123
5	Texas	128
48	Utah	79
33	Vermont	96
8	Virginia	124
40	Washington	88
22	West Virginia	106
38	Wisconsin	93
45	Wyoming	85

RANK	STATE	MONTHLY BILL
1	Hawaii	$203
2	Alabama	135
3	South Carolina	132
4	Maryland	129
5	Delaware	128
5	Texas	128
7	Connecticut	127
8	Virginia	124
9	Florida	123
9	Georgia	123
9	Tennessee	123
12	Mississippi	122
13	Arizona	120
14	Alaska	117
14	North Carolina	117
16	Nevada	111
17	New Jersey	109
18	Missouri	108
18	Oklahoma	108
20	Kentucky	107
20	Pennsylvania	107
22	Kansas	106
22	New York	106
22	West Virginia	106
25	Indiana	105
25	Louisiana	105
25	Ohio	105
28	Arkansas	104
29	Nebraska	100
30	New Hampshire	99
30	North Dakota	99
30	South Dakota	99
33	Vermont	96
34	Michigan	95
35	Iowa	94
35	Massachusetts	94
35	Oregon	94
38	Wisconsin	93
39	Minnesota	90
40	California	88
40	Idaho	88
40	Washington	88
43	Illinois	87
44	Rhode Island	86
45	Montana	85
45	Wyoming	85
47	Colorado	81
48	Utah	79
49	Maine	78
50	New Mexico	75
	District of Columbia	89

Source: U.S. Department of Energy, Energy Information Administration
"Electric Sales, Revenue and Average Price 2012" (http://www.eia.gov/electricity/sales_revenue_price/index.cfm)

Electricity Generated through Renewable Sources in 2010

National Total = 427,376,076,000 Kilowatthours*

ALPHA ORDER					RANK ORDER			

RANK	STATE	KWH	% of USA		RANK	STATE	KWH	% of USA
6	Alabama	11,081,240,000	2.6%		1	Washington	74,905,346,000	17.5%
44	Alaska	1,452,053,000	0.3%		2	California	58,880,591,000	13.8%
14	Arizona	6,941,067,000	1.6%		3	Oregon	35,299,140,000	8.3%
20	Arkansas	5,282,905,000	1.2%		4	New York	30,286,245,000	7.1%
2	California	58,880,591,000	13.8%		5	Texas	28,966,660,000	6.8%
22	Colorado	5,132,796,000	1.2%		6	Alabama	11,081,240,000	2.6%
45	Connecticut	1,130,327,000	0.3%		7	Montana	10,441,819,000	2.4%
50	Delaware	138,197,000	0.0%		8	Iowa	10,308,651,000	2.4%
23	Florida	4,664,197,000	1.1%		9	Idaho	10,168,254,000	2.4%
18	Georgia	6,502,265,000	1.5%		10	Tennessee	9,125,345,000	2.1%
48	Hawaii	817,391,000	0.2%		11	Maine	7,962,664,000	1.9%
9	Idaho	10,168,254,000	2.4%		12	Minnesota	7,480,043,000	1.8%
21	Illinois	5,256,702,000	1.2%		13	Oklahoma	6,968,744,000	1.6%
30	Indiana	3,699,378,000	0.9%		14	Arizona	6,941,067,000	1.6%
8	Iowa	10,308,651,000	2.4%		15	North Carolina	6,839,691,000	1.6%
32	Kansas	3,472,565,000	0.8%		16	South Dakota	6,610,551,000	1.5%
33	Kentucky	3,020,121,000	0.7%		17	Pennsylvania	6,577,376,000	1.5%
31	Louisiana	3,576,570,000	0.8%		18	Georgia	6,502,265,000	1.5%
11	Maine	7,962,664,000	1.9%		19	North Dakota	6,150,146,000	1.4%
38	Maryland	2,241,061,000	0.5%		20	Arkansas	5,282,905,000	1.2%
37	Massachusetts	2,270,073,000	0.5%		21	Illinois	5,256,702,000	1.2%
28	Michigan	4,083,005,000	1.0%		22	Colorado	5,132,796,000	1.2%
12	Minnesota	7,480,043,000	1.8%		23	Florida	4,664,197,000	1.1%
42	Mississippi	1,504,270,000	0.4%		24	Wisconsin	4,585,808,000	1.1%
35	Missouri	2,526,944,000	0.6%		25	Nevada	4,443,943,000	1.0%
7	Montana	10,441,819,000	2.4%		26	Wyoming	4,270,680,000	1.0%
41	Nebraska	1,807,009,000	0.4%		27	South Carolina	4,249,508,000	1.0%
25	Nevada	4,443,943,000	1.0%		28	Michigan	4,083,005,000	1.0%
34	New Hampshire	2,709,801,000	0.6%		29	Virginia	3,719,831,000	0.9%
47	New Jersey	868,173,000	0.2%		30	Indiana	3,699,378,000	0.9%
39	New Mexico	2,071,802,000	0.5%		31	Louisiana	3,576,570,000	0.8%
4	New York	30,286,245,000	7.1%		32	Kansas	3,472,565,000	0.8%
15	North Carolina	6,839,691,000	1.6%		33	Kentucky	3,020,121,000	0.7%
19	North Dakota	6,150,146,000	1.4%		34	New Hampshire	2,709,801,000	0.6%
46	Ohio	1,129,113,000	0.3%		35	Missouri	2,526,944,000	0.6%
13	Oklahoma	6,968,744,000	1.6%		36	West Virginia	2,306,533,000	0.5%
3	Oregon	35,299,140,000	8.3%		37	Massachusetts	2,270,073,000	0.5%
17	Pennsylvania	6,577,376,000	1.5%		38	Maryland	2,241,061,000	0.5%
49	Rhode Island	143,779,000	0.0%		39	New Mexico	2,071,802,000	0.5%
27	South Carolina	4,249,508,000	1.0%		40	Vermont	1,829,226,000	0.4%
16	South Dakota	6,610,551,000	1.5%		41	Nebraska	1,807,009,000	0.4%
10	Tennessee	9,125,345,000	2.1%		42	Mississippi	1,504,270,000	0.4%
5	Texas	28,966,660,000	6.8%		43	Utah	1,476,479,000	0.3%
43	Utah	1,476,479,000	0.3%		44	Alaska	1,452,053,000	0.3%
40	Vermont	1,829,226,000	0.4%		45	Connecticut	1,130,327,000	0.3%
29	Virginia	3,719,831,000	0.9%		46	Ohio	1,129,113,000	0.3%
1	Washington	74,905,346,000	17.5%		47	New Jersey	868,173,000	0.2%
36	West Virginia	2,306,533,000	0.5%		48	Hawaii	817,391,000	0.2%
24	Wisconsin	4,585,808,000	1.1%		49	Rhode Island	143,779,000	0.0%
26	Wyoming	4,270,680,000	1.0%		50	Delaware	138,197,000	0.0%
						District of Columbia**	NA	NA

Source: U.S. Department of Energy, Energy Information Administration
   "Renewable Energy Trends, 2010" (http://www.eia.gov/renewable/annual/trends/)
*Includes hydroelectric, geothermal, solar, wind, MSW/landfill gas, wood/wood waste and other biomass.
**Not reported.

Percent of Electricity Generated through Renewable Sources in 2010

National Percent = 10.4%*

ALPHA ORDER

RANK	STATE	PERCENT
22	Alabama	7.3
10	Alaska	21.5
26	Arizona	6.2
20	Arkansas	8.7
7	California	28.8
17	Colorado	10.1
38	Connecticut	3.4
46	Delaware	2.5
47	Florida	2.0
33	Georgia	4.7
21	Hawaii	7.5
1	Idaho	84.6
45	Illinois	2.6
40	Indiana	3.0
11	Iowa	17.9
23	Kansas	7.2
39	Kentucky	3.1
36	Louisiana	3.5
5	Maine	46.8
30	Maryland	5.1
28	Massachusetts	5.3
35	Michigan	3.7
13	Minnesota	13.9
43	Mississippi	2.8
44	Missouri	2.7
6	Montana	35.1
32	Nebraska	4.9
14	Nevada	12.6
15	New Hampshire	12.2
49	New Jersey	1.3
27	New Mexico	5.7
9	New York	22.1
28	North Carolina	5.3
12	North Dakota	17.7
50	Ohio	0.8
18	Oklahoma	9.6
4	Oregon	64.0
41	Pennsylvania	2.9
48	Rhode Island	1.9
34	South Carolina	4.1
3	South Dakota	65.8
16	Tennessee	11.1
25	Texas	7.0
36	Utah	3.5
8	Vermont	27.6
30	Virginia	5.1
2	Washington	72.4
41	West Virginia	2.9
24	Wisconsin	7.1
19	Wyoming	8.9

RANK ORDER

RANK	STATE	PERCENT
1	Idaho	84.6
2	Washington	72.4
3	South Dakota	65.8
4	Oregon	64.0
5	Maine	46.8
6	Montana	35.1
7	California	28.8
8	Vermont	27.6
9	New York	22.1
10	Alaska	21.5
11	Iowa	17.9
12	North Dakota	17.7
13	Minnesota	13.9
14	Nevada	12.6
15	New Hampshire	12.2
16	Tennessee	11.1
17	Colorado	10.1
18	Oklahoma	9.6
19	Wyoming	8.9
20	Arkansas	8.7
21	Hawaii	7.5
22	Alabama	7.3
23	Kansas	7.2
24	Wisconsin	7.1
25	Texas	7.0
26	Arizona	6.2
27	New Mexico	5.7
28	Massachusetts	5.3
28	North Carolina	5.3
30	Maryland	5.1
30	Virginia	5.1
32	Nebraska	4.9
33	Georgia	4.7
34	South Carolina	4.1
35	Michigan	3.7
36	Louisiana	3.5
36	Utah	3.5
38	Connecticut	3.4
39	Kentucky	3.1
40	Indiana	3.0
41	Pennsylvania	2.9
41	West Virginia	2.9
43	Mississippi	2.8
44	Missouri	2.7
45	Illinois	2.6
46	Delaware	2.5
47	Florida	2.0
48	Rhode Island	1.9
49	New Jersey	1.3
50	Ohio	0.8
	District of Columbia**	NA

Source: U.S. Department of Energy, Energy Information Administration
    "Renewable Energy Trends, 2010" (http://www.eia.gov/renewable/annual/trends/)
*Includes hydroelectric, geothermal, solar, wind, MSW/landfill gas, wood/wood waste and other biomass.
**Not reported.

Average Price of Natural Gas Delivered to Industrial Customers in 2012

National Average = $3.89 per Thousand Cubic Feet

ALPHA ORDER

RANK	STATE	RATE
43	Alabama	$4.35
32	Alaska	5.11
25	Arizona	5.78
19	Arkansas	6.38
26	California	5.77
24	Colorado	5.79
8	Connecticut	8.83
2	Delaware	11.61
17	Florida	6.96
40	Georgia	4.60
1	Hawaii	30.89
27	Idaho	5.73
28	Illinois	5.64
21	Indiana	6.19
38	Iowa	4.70
47	Kansas	3.95
46	Kentucky	3.96
50	Louisiana	2.96
4	Maine	10.35
10	Maryland	8.01
5	Massachusetts	9.82
15	Michigan	7.38
41	Minnesota	4.48
37	Mississippi	4.86
11	Missouri	7.93
14	Montana	7.54
44	Nebraska	4.34
16	Nevada	7.34
3	New Hampshire	10.48
12	New Jersey	7.87
35	New Mexico	4.87
18	New York	6.92
20	North Carolina	6.37
41	North Dakota	4.48
29	Ohio	5.48
13	Oklahoma	7.65
22	Oregon	5.87
7	Pennsylvania	9.58
6	Rhode Island	9.78
45	South Carolina	4.30
30	South Dakota	5.37
33	Tennessee	4.94
49	Texas	3.02
39	Utah	4.69
34	Vermont	4.89
31	Virginia	5.29
9	Washington	8.77
48	West Virginia	3.56
23	Wisconsin	5.81
35	Wyoming	4.87

RANK ORDER

RANK	STATE	RATE
1	Hawaii	$30.89
2	Delaware	11.61
3	New Hampshire	10.48
4	Maine	10.35
5	Massachusetts	9.82
6	Rhode Island	9.78
7	Pennsylvania	9.58
8	Connecticut	8.83
9	Washington	8.77
10	Maryland	8.01
11	Missouri	7.93
12	New Jersey	7.87
13	Oklahoma	7.65
14	Montana	7.54
15	Michigan	7.38
16	Nevada	7.34
17	Florida	6.96
18	New York	6.92
19	Arkansas	6.38
20	North Carolina	6.37
21	Indiana	6.19
22	Oregon	5.87
23	Wisconsin	5.81
24	Colorado	5.79
25	Arizona	5.78
26	California	5.77
27	Idaho	5.73
28	Illinois	5.64
29	Ohio	5.48
30	South Dakota	5.37
31	Virginia	5.29
32	Alaska	5.11
33	Tennessee	4.94
34	Vermont	4.89
35	New Mexico	4.87
35	Wyoming	4.87
37	Mississippi	4.86
38	Iowa	4.70
39	Utah	4.69
40	Georgia	4.60
41	Minnesota	4.48
41	North Dakota	4.48
43	Alabama	4.35
44	Nebraska	4.34
45	South Carolina	4.30
46	Kentucky	3.96
47	Kansas	3.95
48	West Virginia	3.56
49	Texas	3.02
50	Louisiana	2.96

District of Columbia*   NA

Source: U.S. Department of Energy, Energy Information Administration
"Natural Gas" (http://www.eia.gov/naturalgas/)
*Not available.

Average Price of Natural Gas Delivered to Commercial Customers in 2012

National Average = $8.10 per Thousand Cubic Feet

<table>
<tr><td colspan="3">ALPHA ORDER</td><td colspan="3">RANK ORDER</td></tr>
<tr><th>RANK</th><th>STATE</th><th>RATE</th><th>RANK</th><th>STATE</th><th>RATE</th></tr>
<tr><td>3</td><td>Alabama</td><td>$12.55</td><td>1</td><td>Hawaii</td><td>$47.03</td></tr>
<tr><td>29</td><td>Alaska</td><td>8.09</td><td>2</td><td>Delaware</td><td>13.31</td></tr>
<tr><td>16</td><td>Arizona</td><td>9.35</td><td>3</td><td>Alabama</td><td>12.55</td></tr>
<tr><td>30</td><td>Arkansas</td><td>7.99</td><td>4</td><td>Rhode Island</td><td>12.31</td></tr>
<tr><td>42</td><td>California</td><td>7.05</td><td>5</td><td>Maine</td><td>12.22</td></tr>
<tr><td>35</td><td>Colorado</td><td>7.58</td><td>6</td><td>Vermont</td><td>12.09</td></tr>
<tr><td>25</td><td>Connecticut</td><td>8.40</td><td>7</td><td>New Hampshire</td><td>11.95</td></tr>
<tr><td>2</td><td>Delaware</td><td>13.31</td><td>8</td><td>Massachusetts</td><td>10.68</td></tr>
<tr><td>9</td><td>Florida</td><td>10.41</td><td>9</td><td>Florida</td><td>10.41</td></tr>
<tr><td>13</td><td>Georgia</td><td>9.74</td><td>10</td><td>Pennsylvania</td><td>10.24</td></tr>
<tr><td>1</td><td>Hawaii</td><td>47.03</td><td>11</td><td>Maryland</td><td>10.00</td></tr>
<tr><td>38</td><td>Idaho</td><td>7.35</td><td>12</td><td>Washington</td><td>9.82</td></tr>
<tr><td>33</td><td>Illinois</td><td>7.77</td><td>13</td><td>Georgia</td><td>9.74</td></tr>
<tr><td>34</td><td>Indiana</td><td>7.68</td><td>14</td><td>Missouri</td><td>9.54</td></tr>
<tr><td>40</td><td>Iowa</td><td>7.13</td><td>15</td><td>West Virginia</td><td>9.39</td></tr>
<tr><td>19</td><td>Kansas</td><td>8.82</td><td>16</td><td>Arizona</td><td>9.35</td></tr>
<tr><td>28</td><td>Kentucky</td><td>8.28</td><td>17</td><td>Oklahoma</td><td>8.95</td></tr>
<tr><td>24</td><td>Louisiana</td><td>8.44</td><td>18</td><td>Oregon</td><td>8.91</td></tr>
<tr><td>5</td><td>Maine</td><td>12.22</td><td>19</td><td>Kansas</td><td>8.82</td></tr>
<tr><td>11</td><td>Maryland</td><td>10.00</td><td>20</td><td>Virginia</td><td>8.77</td></tr>
<tr><td>8</td><td>Massachusetts</td><td>10.68</td><td>21</td><td>South Carolina</td><td>8.67</td></tr>
<tr><td>27</td><td>Michigan</td><td>8.35</td><td>22</td><td>North Carolina</td><td>8.62</td></tr>
<tr><td>47</td><td>Minnesota</td><td>6.38</td><td>23</td><td>New Jersey</td><td>8.50</td></tr>
<tr><td>37</td><td>Mississippi</td><td>7.38</td><td>24</td><td>Louisiana</td><td>8.44</td></tr>
<tr><td>14</td><td>Missouri</td><td>9.54</td><td>25</td><td>Connecticut</td><td>8.40</td></tr>
<tr><td>31</td><td>Montana</td><td>7.98</td><td>26</td><td>Tennessee</td><td>8.36</td></tr>
<tr><td>49</td><td>Nebraska</td><td>6.19</td><td>27</td><td>Michigan</td><td>8.35</td></tr>
<tr><td>36</td><td>Nevada</td><td>7.43</td><td>28</td><td>Kentucky</td><td>8.28</td></tr>
<tr><td>7</td><td>New Hampshire</td><td>11.95</td><td>29</td><td>Alaska</td><td>8.09</td></tr>
<tr><td>23</td><td>New Jersey</td><td>8.50</td><td>30</td><td>Arkansas</td><td>7.99</td></tr>
<tr><td>48</td><td>New Mexico</td><td>6.31</td><td>31</td><td>Montana</td><td>7.98</td></tr>
<tr><td>32</td><td>New York</td><td>7.84</td><td>32</td><td>New York</td><td>7.84</td></tr>
<tr><td>22</td><td>North Carolina</td><td>8.62</td><td>33</td><td>Illinois</td><td>7.77</td></tr>
<tr><td>50</td><td>North Dakota</td><td>6.04</td><td>34</td><td>Indiana</td><td>7.68</td></tr>
<tr><td>41</td><td>Ohio</td><td>7.11</td><td>35</td><td>Colorado</td><td>7.58</td></tr>
<tr><td>17</td><td>Oklahoma</td><td>8.95</td><td>36</td><td>Nevada</td><td>7.43</td></tr>
<tr><td>18</td><td>Oregon</td><td>8.91</td><td>37</td><td>Mississippi</td><td>7.38</td></tr>
<tr><td>10</td><td>Pennsylvania</td><td>10.24</td><td>38</td><td>Idaho</td><td>7.35</td></tr>
<tr><td>4</td><td>Rhode Island</td><td>12.31</td><td>39</td><td>Wisconsin</td><td>7.34</td></tr>
<tr><td>21</td><td>South Carolina</td><td>8.67</td><td>40</td><td>Iowa</td><td>7.13</td></tr>
<tr><td>46</td><td>South Dakota</td><td>6.45</td><td>41</td><td>Ohio</td><td>7.11</td></tr>
<tr><td>26</td><td>Tennessee</td><td>8.36</td><td>42</td><td>California</td><td>7.05</td></tr>
<tr><td>45</td><td>Texas</td><td>6.63</td><td>43</td><td>Utah</td><td>7.00</td></tr>
<tr><td>43</td><td>Utah</td><td>7.00</td><td>44</td><td>Wyoming</td><td>6.72</td></tr>
<tr><td>6</td><td>Vermont</td><td>12.09</td><td>45</td><td>Texas</td><td>6.63</td></tr>
<tr><td>20</td><td>Virginia</td><td>8.77</td><td>46</td><td>South Dakota</td><td>6.45</td></tr>
<tr><td>12</td><td>Washington</td><td>9.82</td><td>47</td><td>Minnesota</td><td>6.38</td></tr>
<tr><td>15</td><td>West Virginia</td><td>9.39</td><td>48</td><td>New Mexico</td><td>6.31</td></tr>
<tr><td>39</td><td>Wisconsin</td><td>7.34</td><td>49</td><td>Nebraska</td><td>6.19</td></tr>
<tr><td>44</td><td>Wyoming</td><td>6.72</td><td>50</td><td>North Dakota</td><td>6.04</td></tr>
<tr><td></td><td></td><td></td><td></td><td>District of Columbia</td><td>11.19</td></tr>
</table>

Source: U.S. Department of Energy, Energy Information Administration
"Natural Gas" (http://www.eia.gov/naturalgas/)

Average Price of Natural Gas Delivered to Residential Customers in 2012

National Average = $10.71 per Thousand Cubic Feet

RANK	STATE	RATE
5	Alabama	$16.20
42	Alaska	8.47
7	Arizona	15.75
21	Arkansas	11.82
37	California	9.14
45	Colorado	8.31
10	Connecticut	14.17
8	Delaware	15.24
2	Florida	18.31
4	Georgia	16.23
1	Hawaii	52.86
46	Idaho	8.26
46	Illinois	8.26
38	Indiana	8.94
35	Iowa	9.46
31	Kansas	10.13
29	Kentucky	10.19
22	Louisiana	11.54
6	Maine	15.94
18	Maryland	12.17
13	Massachusetts	13.22
26	Michigan	10.86
49	Minnesota	8.00
34	Mississippi	9.59
16	Missouri	12.25
48	Montana	8.06
41	Nebraska	8.68
30	Nevada	10.14
11	New Hampshire	13.74
25	New Jersey	11.09
40	New Mexico	8.69
14	New York	12.97
17	North Carolina	12.19
50	North Dakota	7.43
33	Ohio	9.91
24	Oklahoma	11.10
23	Oregon	11.22
19	Pennsylvania	11.99
9	Rhode Island	14.29
12	South Carolina	13.25
44	South Dakota	8.39
32	Tennessee	9.95
28	Texas	10.55
39	Utah	8.70
3	Vermont	16.73
15	Virginia	12.42
20	Washington	11.87
27	West Virginia	10.83
36	Wisconsin	9.27
43	Wyoming	8.42

RANK ORDER

RANK	STATE	RATE
1	Hawaii	$52.86
2	Florida	18.31
3	Vermont	16.73
4	Georgia	16.23
5	Alabama	16.20
6	Maine	15.94
7	Arizona	15.75
8	Delaware	15.24
9	Rhode Island	14.29
10	Connecticut	14.17
11	New Hampshire	13.74
12	South Carolina	13.25
13	Massachusetts	13.22
14	New York	12.97
15	Virginia	12.42
16	Missouri	12.25
17	North Carolina	12.19
18	Maryland	12.17
19	Pennsylvania	11.99
20	Washington	11.87
21	Arkansas	11.82
22	Louisiana	11.54
23	Oregon	11.22
24	Oklahoma	11.10
25	New Jersey	11.09
26	Michigan	10.86
27	West Virginia	10.83
28	Texas	10.55
29	Kentucky	10.19
30	Nevada	10.14
31	Kansas	10.13
32	Tennessee	9.95
33	Ohio	9.91
34	Mississippi	9.59
35	Iowa	9.46
36	Wisconsin	9.27
37	California	9.14
38	Indiana	8.94
39	Utah	8.70
40	New Mexico	8.69
41	Nebraska	8.68
42	Alaska	8.47
43	Wyoming	8.42
44	South Dakota	8.39
45	Colorado	8.31
46	Idaho	8.26
46	Illinois	8.26
48	Montana	8.06
49	Minnesota	8.00
50	North Dakota	7.43

District of Columbia	12.10

Source: U.S. Department of Energy, Energy Information Administration
"Natural Gas" (http://www.eia.gov/naturalgas/)

Natural Gas Consumption in 2012

National Total = 25,533,448,000,000 Cubic Feet*

ALPHA ORDER

RANK	STATE	CUBIC FEET	% of USA
11	Alabama	666,738,000,000	2.6%
22	Alaska	343,110,000,000	1.3%
23	Arizona	332,079,000,000	1.3%
24	Arkansas	295,811,000,000	1.2%
2	California	2,403,385,000,000	9.4%
16	Colorado	443,367,000,000	1.7%
33	Connecticut	229,159,000,000	0.9%
41	Delaware	101,676,000,000	0.4%
4	Florida	1,328,469,000,000	5.2%
14	Georgia	615,768,000,000	2.4%
50	Hawaii	2,689,000,000	0.0%
43	Idaho	89,004,000,000	0.3%
7	Illinois	938,145,000,000	3.7%
13	Indiana	650,180,000,000	2.5%
25	Iowa	295,183,000,000	1.2%
29	Kansas	262,170,000,000	1.0%
34	Kentucky	224,591,000,000	0.9%
3	Louisiana	1,482,299,000,000	5.8%
48	Maine	68,266,000,000	0.3%
37	Maryland	208,948,000,000	0.8%
18	Massachusetts	416,351,000,000	1.6%
9	Michigan	790,149,000,000	3.1%
17	Minnesota	419,529,000,000	1.6%
15	Mississippi	474,189,000,000	1.9%
30	Missouri	255,875,000,000	1.0%
44	Montana	73,399,000,000	0.3%
38	Nebraska	158,758,000,000	0.6%
27	Nevada	273,505,000,000	1.1%
46	New Hampshire	72,069,000,000	0.3%
12	New Jersey	652,060,000,000	2.6%
32	New Mexico	244,584,000,000	1.0%
5	New York	1,223,059,000,000	4.8%
21	North Carolina	363,945,000,000	1.4%
45	North Dakota	72,740,000,000	0.3%
8	Ohio	842,959,000,000	3.3%
10	Oklahoma	691,992,000,000	2.7%
36	Oregon	215,830,000,000	0.8%
6	Pennsylvania	1,037,979,000,000	4.1%
42	Rhode Island	95,477,000,000	0.4%
31	South Carolina	244,850,000,000	1.0%
47	South Dakota	70,238,000,000	0.3%
26	Tennessee	277,289,000,000	1.1%
1	Texas	3,871,786,000,000	15.2%
35	Utah	223,040,000,000	0.9%
49	Vermont	8,191,000,000	0.0%
19	Virginia	410,108,000,000	1.6%
28	Washington	264,252,000,000	1.0%
40	West Virginia	129,612,000,000	0.5%
20	Wisconsin	402,657,000,000	1.6%
39	Wyoming	153,383,000,000	0.6%

RANK ORDER

RANK	STATE	CUBIC FEET	% of USA
1	Texas	3,871,786,000,000	15.2%
2	California	2,403,385,000,000	9.4%
3	Louisiana	1,482,299,000,000	5.8%
4	Florida	1,328,469,000,000	5.2%
5	New York	1,223,059,000,000	4.8%
6	Pennsylvania	1,037,979,000,000	4.1%
7	Illinois	938,145,000,000	3.7%
8	Ohio	842,959,000,000	3.3%
9	Michigan	790,149,000,000	3.1%
10	Oklahoma	691,992,000,000	2.7%
11	Alabama	666,738,000,000	2.6%
12	New Jersey	652,060,000,000	2.6%
13	Indiana	650,180,000,000	2.5%
14	Georgia	615,768,000,000	2.4%
15	Mississippi	474,189,000,000	1.9%
16	Colorado	443,367,000,000	1.7%
17	Minnesota	419,529,000,000	1.6%
18	Massachusetts	416,351,000,000	1.6%
19	Virginia	410,108,000,000	1.6%
20	Wisconsin	402,657,000,000	1.6%
21	North Carolina	363,945,000,000	1.4%
22	Alaska	343,110,000,000	1.3%
23	Arizona	332,079,000,000	1.3%
24	Arkansas	295,811,000,000	1.2%
25	Iowa	295,183,000,000	1.2%
26	Tennessee	277,289,000,000	1.1%
27	Nevada	273,505,000,000	1.1%
28	Washington	264,252,000,000	1.0%
29	Kansas	262,170,000,000	1.0%
30	Missouri	255,875,000,000	1.0%
31	South Carolina	244,850,000,000	1.0%
32	New Mexico	244,584,000,000	1.0%
33	Connecticut	229,159,000,000	0.9%
34	Kentucky	224,591,000,000	0.9%
35	Utah	223,040,000,000	0.9%
36	Oregon	215,830,000,000	0.8%
37	Maryland	208,948,000,000	0.8%
38	Nebraska	158,758,000,000	0.6%
39	Wyoming	153,383,000,000	0.6%
40	West Virginia	129,612,000,000	0.5%
41	Delaware	101,676,000,000	0.4%
42	Rhode Island	95,477,000,000	0.4%
43	Idaho	89,004,000,000	0.3%
44	Montana	73,399,000,000	0.3%
45	North Dakota	72,740,000,000	0.3%
46	New Hampshire	72,069,000,000	0.3%
47	South Dakota	70,238,000,000	0.3%
48	Maine	68,266,000,000	0.3%
49	Vermont	8,191,000,000	0.0%
50	Hawaii	2,689,000,000	0.0%
	District of Columbia	28,572,000,000	0.1%

Source: U.S. Department of Energy, Energy Information Administration
"Natural Gas Annual 2012" (http://www.eia.gov/naturalgas/annual/)
*National total includes 93,985,000,000 cubic feet of consumption in the Gulf of Mexico not shown by state.

Coal Mines in 2012

National Total = 1,229 Mines*

<table>
<tr><td colspan="4">ALPHA ORDER</td><td colspan="4">RANK ORDER</td></tr>
<tr><td>RANK</td><td>STATE</td><td>MINES</td><td>% of USA</td><td>RANK</td><td>STATE</td><td>MINES</td><td>% of USA</td></tr>
<tr><td>5</td><td>Alabama</td><td>46</td><td>3.7%</td><td>1</td><td>Kentucky</td><td>357</td><td>29.0%</td></tr>
<tr><td>22</td><td>Alaska</td><td>1</td><td>0.1%</td><td>2</td><td>West Virginia</td><td>264</td><td>21.5%</td></tr>
<tr><td>22</td><td>Arizona</td><td>1</td><td>0.1%</td><td>3</td><td>Pennsylvania</td><td>235</td><td>19.1%</td></tr>
<tr><td>19</td><td>Arkansas</td><td>2</td><td>0.2%</td><td>4</td><td>Virginia</td><td>96</td><td>7.8%</td></tr>
<tr><td>NA</td><td>California**</td><td>NA</td><td>NA</td><td>5</td><td>Alabama</td><td>46</td><td>3.7%</td></tr>
<tr><td>12</td><td>Colorado</td><td>12</td><td>1.0%</td><td>6</td><td>Ohio</td><td>39</td><td>3.2%</td></tr>
<tr><td>NA</td><td>Connecticut**</td><td>NA</td><td>NA</td><td>7</td><td>Indiana</td><td>29</td><td>2.4%</td></tr>
<tr><td>NA</td><td>Delaware**</td><td>NA</td><td>NA</td><td>8</td><td>Illinois</td><td>24</td><td>2.0%</td></tr>
<tr><td>NA</td><td>Florida**</td><td>NA</td><td>NA</td><td>9</td><td>Maryland</td><td>21</td><td>1.7%</td></tr>
<tr><td>NA</td><td>Georgia**</td><td>NA</td><td>NA</td><td>10</td><td>Wyoming</td><td>18</td><td>1.5%</td></tr>
<tr><td>NA</td><td>Hawaii**</td><td>NA</td><td>NA</td><td>11</td><td>Tennessee</td><td>14</td><td>1.1%</td></tr>
<tr><td>NA</td><td>Idaho**</td><td>NA</td><td>NA</td><td>12</td><td>Colorado</td><td>12</td><td>1.0%</td></tr>
<tr><td>8</td><td>Illinois</td><td>24</td><td>2.0%</td><td>12</td><td>Texas</td><td>12</td><td>1.0%</td></tr>
<tr><td>7</td><td>Indiana</td><td>29</td><td>2.4%</td><td>14</td><td>Utah</td><td>9</td><td>0.7%</td></tr>
<tr><td>NA</td><td>Iowa**</td><td>NA</td><td>NA</td><td>15</td><td>Oklahoma</td><td>7</td><td>0.6%</td></tr>
<tr><td>22</td><td>Kansas</td><td>1</td><td>0.1%</td><td>16</td><td>Montana</td><td>6</td><td>0.5%</td></tr>
<tr><td>1</td><td>Kentucky</td><td>357</td><td>29.0%</td><td>17</td><td>New Mexico</td><td>4</td><td>0.3%</td></tr>
<tr><td>19</td><td>Louisiana</td><td>2</td><td>0.2%</td><td>17</td><td>North Dakota</td><td>4</td><td>0.3%</td></tr>
<tr><td>NA</td><td>Maine**</td><td>NA</td><td>NA</td><td>19</td><td>Arkansas</td><td>2</td><td>0.2%</td></tr>
<tr><td>9</td><td>Maryland</td><td>21</td><td>1.7%</td><td>19</td><td>Louisiana</td><td>2</td><td>0.2%</td></tr>
<tr><td>NA</td><td>Massachusetts**</td><td>NA</td><td>NA</td><td>19</td><td>Missouri</td><td>2</td><td>0.2%</td></tr>
<tr><td>NA</td><td>Michigan**</td><td>NA</td><td>NA</td><td>22</td><td>Alaska</td><td>1</td><td>0.1%</td></tr>
<tr><td>NA</td><td>Minnesota**</td><td>NA</td><td>NA</td><td>22</td><td>Arizona</td><td>1</td><td>0.1%</td></tr>
<tr><td>22</td><td>Mississippi</td><td>1</td><td>0.1%</td><td>22</td><td>Kansas</td><td>1</td><td>0.1%</td></tr>
<tr><td>19</td><td>Missouri</td><td>2</td><td>0.2%</td><td>22</td><td>Mississippi</td><td>1</td><td>0.1%</td></tr>
<tr><td>16</td><td>Montana</td><td>6</td><td>0.5%</td><td>NA</td><td>California**</td><td>NA</td><td>NA</td></tr>
<tr><td>NA</td><td>Nebraska**</td><td>NA</td><td>NA</td><td>NA</td><td>Connecticut**</td><td>NA</td><td>NA</td></tr>
<tr><td>NA</td><td>Nevada**</td><td>NA</td><td>NA</td><td>NA</td><td>Delaware**</td><td>NA</td><td>NA</td></tr>
<tr><td>NA</td><td>New Hampshire**</td><td>NA</td><td>NA</td><td>NA</td><td>Florida**</td><td>NA</td><td>NA</td></tr>
<tr><td>NA</td><td>New Jersey**</td><td>NA</td><td>NA</td><td>NA</td><td>Georgia**</td><td>NA</td><td>NA</td></tr>
<tr><td>17</td><td>New Mexico</td><td>4</td><td>0.3%</td><td>NA</td><td>Hawaii**</td><td>NA</td><td>NA</td></tr>
<tr><td>NA</td><td>New York**</td><td>NA</td><td>NA</td><td>NA</td><td>Idaho**</td><td>NA</td><td>NA</td></tr>
<tr><td>NA</td><td>North Carolina**</td><td>NA</td><td>NA</td><td>NA</td><td>Iowa**</td><td>NA</td><td>NA</td></tr>
<tr><td>17</td><td>North Dakota</td><td>4</td><td>0.3%</td><td>NA</td><td>Maine**</td><td>NA</td><td>NA</td></tr>
<tr><td>6</td><td>Ohio</td><td>39</td><td>3.2%</td><td>NA</td><td>Massachusetts**</td><td>NA</td><td>NA</td></tr>
<tr><td>15</td><td>Oklahoma</td><td>7</td><td>0.6%</td><td>NA</td><td>Michigan**</td><td>NA</td><td>NA</td></tr>
<tr><td>NA</td><td>Oregon**</td><td>NA</td><td>NA</td><td>NA</td><td>Minnesota**</td><td>NA</td><td>NA</td></tr>
<tr><td>3</td><td>Pennsylvania</td><td>235</td><td>19.1%</td><td>NA</td><td>Nebraska**</td><td>NA</td><td>NA</td></tr>
<tr><td>NA</td><td>Rhode Island**</td><td>NA</td><td>NA</td><td>NA</td><td>Nevada**</td><td>NA</td><td>NA</td></tr>
<tr><td>NA</td><td>South Carolina**</td><td>NA</td><td>NA</td><td>NA</td><td>New Hampshire**</td><td>NA</td><td>NA</td></tr>
<tr><td>NA</td><td>South Dakota**</td><td>NA</td><td>NA</td><td>NA</td><td>New Jersey**</td><td>NA</td><td>NA</td></tr>
<tr><td>11</td><td>Tennessee</td><td>14</td><td>1.1%</td><td>NA</td><td>New York**</td><td>NA</td><td>NA</td></tr>
<tr><td>12</td><td>Texas</td><td>12</td><td>1.0%</td><td>NA</td><td>North Carolina**</td><td>NA</td><td>NA</td></tr>
<tr><td>14</td><td>Utah</td><td>9</td><td>0.7%</td><td>NA</td><td>Oregon**</td><td>NA</td><td>NA</td></tr>
<tr><td>NA</td><td>Vermont**</td><td>NA</td><td>NA</td><td>NA</td><td>Rhode Island**</td><td>NA</td><td>NA</td></tr>
<tr><td>4</td><td>Virginia</td><td>96</td><td>7.8%</td><td>NA</td><td>South Carolina**</td><td>NA</td><td>NA</td></tr>
<tr><td>NA</td><td>Washington**</td><td>NA</td><td>NA</td><td>NA</td><td>South Dakota**</td><td>NA</td><td>NA</td></tr>
<tr><td>2</td><td>West Virginia</td><td>264</td><td>21.5%</td><td>NA</td><td>Vermont**</td><td>NA</td><td>NA</td></tr>
<tr><td>NA</td><td>Wisconsin**</td><td>NA</td><td>NA</td><td>NA</td><td>Washington**</td><td>NA</td><td>NA</td></tr>
<tr><td>10</td><td>Wyoming</td><td>18</td><td>1.5%</td><td>NA</td><td>Wisconsin**</td><td>NA</td><td>NA</td></tr>
<tr><td></td><td></td><td></td><td></td><td></td><td>District of Columbia**</td><td>NA</td><td>NA</td></tr>
</table>

Source: U.S. Department of Energy, Energy Information Administration
   "Annual Coal Report" (released December 12, 2013, http://www.eia.gov/coal/annual/)
*National total includes 22 coal mines in refuse recovery not shown by state.
**Not available or no mines.

Coal Production in 2012

National Total = 1,016,458,000 Short Tons*

ALPHA ORDER

RANK	STATE	SHORT TONS	% of USA
13	Alabama	19,321,000	1.9%
20	Alaska	2,052,000	0.2%
16	Arizona	7,493,000	0.7%
24	Arkansas	98,000	0.0%
NA	California**	NA	NA
9	Colorado	28,566,000	2.8%
NA	Connecticut**	NA	NA
NA	Delaware**	NA	NA
NA	Florida**	NA	NA
NA	Georgia**	NA	NA
NA	Hawaii**	NA	NA
NA	Idaho**	NA	NA
5	Illinois	48,486,000	4.8%
7	Indiana	36,720,000	3.6%
NA	Iowa**	NA	NA
25	Kansas	16,000	0.0%
3	Kentucky	90,862,000	8.9%
17	Louisiana	3,971,000	0.4%
NA	Maine**	NA	NA
19	Maryland	2,283,000	0.2%
NA	Massachusetts**	NA	NA
NA	Michigan**	NA	NA
NA	Minnesota**	NA	NA
18	Mississippi	2,953,000	0.3%
23	Missouri	422,000	0.0%
8	Montana	36,694,000	3.6%
NA	Nebraska**	NA	NA
NA	Nevada**	NA	NA
NA	New Hampshire**	NA	NA
NA	New Jersey**	NA	NA
12	New Mexico	22,452,000	2.2%
NA	New York**	NA	NA
NA	North Carolina**	NA	NA
10	North Dakota	27,529,000	2.7%
11	Ohio	26,328,000	2.6%
22	Oklahoma	1,054,000	0.1%
NA	Oregon**	NA	NA
4	Pennsylvania	54,719,000	5.4%
NA	Rhode Island**	NA	NA
NA	South Carolina**	NA	NA
NA	South Dakota**	NA	NA
21	Tennessee	1,090,000	0.1%
6	Texas	44,178,000	4.3%
15	Utah	17,016,000	1.7%
NA	Vermont**	NA	NA
14	Virginia	18,965,000	1.9%
NA	Washington**	NA	NA
2	West Virginia	120,425,000	11.8%
NA	Wisconsin**	NA	NA
1	Wyoming	401,442,000	39.5%

RANK ORDER

RANK	STATE	SHORT TONS	% of USA
1	Wyoming	401,442,000	39.5%
2	West Virginia	120,425,000	11.8%
3	Kentucky	90,862,000	8.9%
4	Pennsylvania	54,719,000	5.4%
5	Illinois	48,486,000	4.8%
6	Texas	44,178,000	4.3%
7	Indiana	36,720,000	3.6%
8	Montana	36,694,000	3.6%
9	Colorado	28,566,000	2.8%
10	North Dakota	27,529,000	2.7%
11	Ohio	26,328,000	2.6%
12	New Mexico	22,452,000	2.2%
13	Alabama	19,321,000	1.9%
14	Virginia	18,965,000	1.9%
15	Utah	17,016,000	1.7%
16	Arizona	7,493,000	0.7%
17	Louisiana	3,971,000	0.4%
18	Mississippi	2,953,000	0.3%
19	Maryland	2,283,000	0.2%
20	Alaska	2,052,000	0.2%
21	Tennessee	1,090,000	0.1%
22	Oklahoma	1,054,000	0.1%
23	Missouri	422,000	0.0%
24	Arkansas	98,000	0.0%
25	Kansas	16,000	0.0%
NA	California**	NA	NA
NA	Connecticut**	NA	NA
NA	Delaware**	NA	NA
NA	Florida**	NA	NA
NA	Georgia**	NA	NA
NA	Hawaii**	NA	NA
NA	Idaho**	NA	NA
NA	Iowa**	NA	NA
NA	Maine**	NA	NA
NA	Massachusetts**	NA	NA
NA	Michigan**	NA	NA
NA	Minnesota**	NA	NA
NA	Nebraska**	NA	NA
NA	Nevada**	NA	NA
NA	New Hampshire**	NA	NA
NA	New Jersey**	NA	NA
NA	New York**	NA	NA
NA	North Carolina**	NA	NA
NA	Oregon**	NA	NA
NA	Rhode Island**	NA	NA
NA	South Carolina**	NA	NA
NA	South Dakota**	NA	NA
NA	Vermont**	NA	NA
NA	Washington**	NA	NA
NA	Wisconsin**	NA	NA
	District of Columbia**	NA	NA

Source: U.S. Department of Energy, Energy Information Administration
   "Annual Coal Report" (released December 12, 2013, http://www.eia.gov/coal/annual/)
*National total includes 1,324,000 short tons from refuse recovery not shown by state.
**Not available or no production.

Gasoline Used in 2012

National Total = 134,998,800,000 Gallons*

ALPHA ORDER

RANK	STATE	GALLONS	% of USA
22	Alabama	2,577,035,000	1.9%
50	Alaska	288,738,000	0.2%
20	Arizona	2,616,978,000	1.9%
32	Arkansas	1,434,181,000	1.1%
1	California	14,525,691,000	10.8%
26	Colorado	2,137,244,000	1.6%
31	Connecticut	1,449,384,000	1.1%
46	Delaware	436,706,000	0.3%
3	Florida	8,150,577,000	6.0%
7	Georgia	4,691,478,000	3.5%
44	Hawaii	450,286,000	0.3%
39	Idaho	704,611,000	0.5%
8	Illinois	4,649,208,000	3.4%
15	Indiana	3,017,750,000	2.2%
29	Iowa	1,636,231,000	1.2%
33	Kansas	1,260,688,000	0.9%
25	Kentucky	2,147,737,000	1.6%
24	Louisiana	2,247,906,000	1.7%
41	Maine	658,213,000	0.5%
17	Maryland	2,721,780,000	2.0%
16	Massachusetts	2,779,752,000	2.1%
9	Michigan	4,460,239,000	3.3%
21	Minnesota	2,579,198,000	1.9%
28	Mississippi	1,657,284,000	1.2%
14	Missouri	3,109,356,000	2.3%
42	Montana	506,158,000	0.4%
37	Nebraska	844,237,000	0.6%
34	Nevada	1,083,614,000	0.8%
40	New Hampshire	699,964,000	0.5%
11	New Jersey	4,058,680,000	3.0%
36	New Mexico	961,686,000	0.7%
4	New York	5,424,144,000	4.0%
10	North Carolina	4,311,886,000	3.2%
45	North Dakota	438,732,000	0.3%
6	Ohio	4,979,306,000	3.7%
27	Oklahoma	1,924,486,000	1.4%
30	Oregon	1,468,762,000	1.1%
5	Pennsylvania	5,036,098,000	3.7%
48	Rhode Island	365,350,000	0.3%
19	South Carolina	2,639,209,000	2.0%
43	South Dakota	464,982,000	0.3%
13	Tennessee	3,167,178,000	2.3%
2	Texas	12,444,478,000	9.2%
35	Utah	1,072,492,000	0.8%
49	Vermont	316,725,000	0.2%
12	Virginia	3,933,092,000	2.9%
18	Washington	2,685,167,000	2.0%
38	West Virginia	809,016,000	0.6%
23	Wisconsin	2,506,856,000	1.9%
47	Wyoming	371,512,000	0.3%

RANK ORDER

RANK	STATE	GALLONS	% of USA
1	California	14,525,691,000	10.8%
2	Texas	12,444,478,000	9.2%
3	Florida	8,150,577,000	6.0%
4	New York	5,424,144,000	4.0%
5	Pennsylvania	5,036,098,000	3.7%
6	Ohio	4,979,306,000	3.7%
7	Georgia	4,691,478,000	3.5%
8	Illinois	4,649,208,000	3.4%
9	Michigan	4,460,239,000	3.3%
10	North Carolina	4,311,886,000	3.2%
11	New Jersey	4,058,680,000	3.0%
12	Virginia	3,933,092,000	2.9%
13	Tennessee	3,167,178,000	2.3%
14	Missouri	3,109,356,000	2.3%
15	Indiana	3,017,750,000	2.2%
16	Massachusetts	2,779,752,000	2.1%
17	Maryland	2,721,780,000	2.0%
18	Washington	2,685,167,000	2.0%
19	South Carolina	2,639,209,000	2.0%
20	Arizona	2,616,978,000	1.9%
21	Minnesota	2,579,198,000	1.9%
22	Alabama	2,577,035,000	1.9%
23	Wisconsin	2,506,856,000	1.9%
24	Louisiana	2,247,906,000	1.7%
25	Kentucky	2,147,737,000	1.6%
26	Colorado	2,137,244,000	1.6%
27	Oklahoma	1,924,486,000	1.4%
28	Mississippi	1,657,284,000	1.2%
29	Iowa	1,636,231,000	1.2%
30	Oregon	1,468,762,000	1.1%
31	Connecticut	1,449,384,000	1.1%
32	Arkansas	1,434,181,000	1.1%
33	Kansas	1,260,688,000	0.9%
34	Nevada	1,083,614,000	0.8%
35	Utah	1,072,492,000	0.8%
36	New Mexico	961,686,000	0.7%
37	Nebraska	844,237,000	0.6%
38	West Virginia	809,016,000	0.6%
39	Idaho	704,611,000	0.5%
40	New Hampshire	699,964,000	0.5%
41	Maine	658,213,000	0.5%
42	Montana	506,158,000	0.4%
43	South Dakota	464,982,000	0.3%
44	Hawaii	450,286,000	0.3%
45	North Dakota	438,732,000	0.3%
46	Delaware	436,706,000	0.3%
47	Wyoming	371,512,000	0.3%
48	Rhode Island	365,350,000	0.3%
49	Vermont	316,725,000	0.2%
50	Alaska	288,738,000	0.2%
	District of Columbia	96,739,000	0.1%

Source: U.S. Department of Transportation, Federal Highway Administration
   "Highway Statistics 2012" (Table MF-21, http://www.fhwa.dot.gov/policyinformation/statistics/2012/)
*Includes gasoline for highway and nonhighway uses as well as for losses allowed for evaporation and handling. "Gasoline" includes gasohol but excludes "special fuels" such as diesel.

Per Capita Gasoline Used in 2012

National Per Capita = 431 Gallons*

ALPHA ORDER

RANK	STATE	PER CAPITA
5	Alabama	539
41	Alaska	397
39	Arizona	401
16	Arkansas	483
44	California	385
37	Colorado	410
38	Connecticut	409
17	Delaware	478
35	Florida	422
19	Georgia	476
49	Hawaii	340
34	Idaho	426
47	Illinois	367
23	Indiana	465
3	Iowa	559
28	Kansas	450
13	Kentucky	495
12	Louisiana	501
11	Maine	510
27	Maryland	453
36	Massachusetts	420
26	Michigan	454
24	Minnesota	463
7	Mississippi	535
9	Missouri	518
15	Montana	492
29	Nebraska	449
42	Nevada	394
8	New Hampshire	534
21	New Jersey	468
25	New Mexico	457
50	New York	283
29	North Carolina	449
2	North Dakota	587
33	Ohio	431
17	Oklahoma	478
45	Oregon	382
40	Pennsylvania	399
48	Rhode Island	358
4	South Carolina	549
6	South Dakota	538
13	Tennessee	495
20	Texas	470
46	Utah	379
10	Vermont	516
22	Virginia	467
43	Washington	391
31	West Virginia	444
32	Wisconsin	439
1	Wyoming	594

RANK ORDER

RANK	STATE	PER CAPITA
1	Wyoming	594
2	North Dakota	587
3	Iowa	559
4	South Carolina	549
5	Alabama	539
6	South Dakota	538
7	Mississippi	535
8	New Hampshire	534
9	Missouri	518
10	Vermont	516
11	Maine	510
12	Louisiana	501
13	Kentucky	495
13	Tennessee	495
15	Montana	492
16	Arkansas	483
17	Delaware	478
17	Oklahoma	478
19	Georgia	476
20	Texas	470
21	New Jersey	468
22	Virginia	467
23	Indiana	465
24	Minnesota	463
25	New Mexico	457
26	Michigan	454
27	Maryland	453
28	Kansas	450
29	Nebraska	449
29	North Carolina	449
31	West Virginia	444
32	Wisconsin	439
33	Ohio	431
34	Idaho	426
35	Florida	422
36	Massachusetts	420
37	Colorado	410
38	Connecticut	409
39	Arizona	401
40	Pennsylvania	399
41	Alaska	397
42	Nevada	394
43	Washington	391
44	California	385
45	Oregon	382
46	Utah	379
47	Illinois	367
48	Rhode Island	358
49	Hawaii	340
50	New York	283
	District of Columbia	170

Source: CQ Press using data from U.S. Department of Transportation, Federal Highway Administration
   "Highway Statistics 2012" (Table MF-21, http://www.fhwa.dot.gov/policyinformation/statistics/2012/)
*Includes gasoline for highway and nonhighway uses as well as for losses allowed for evaporation and handling. "Gasoline" includes gasohol but excludes "special fuels" such as diesel.

Daily Production of Crude Oil in 2012

National Total = 6,482,309 Barrels a Day*

<table>
<tr><td colspan="4">ALPHA ORDER</td><td colspan="4">RANK ORDER</td></tr>
<tr><td>RANK</td><td>STATE</td><td>BARRELS</td><td>% of USA</td><td>RANK</td><td>STATE</td><td>BARRELS</td><td>% of USA</td></tr>
<tr><td>15</td><td>Alabama</td><td>26,025</td><td>0.4%</td><td>1</td><td>Texas</td><td>1,986,336</td><td>30.6%</td></tr>
<tr><td>4</td><td>Alaska</td><td>525,596</td><td>8.1%</td><td>2</td><td>North Dakota</td><td>662,530</td><td>10.2%</td></tr>
<tr><td>30</td><td>Arizona</td><td>142</td><td>0.0%</td><td>3</td><td>California</td><td>536,404</td><td>8.3%</td></tr>
<tr><td>17</td><td>Arkansas</td><td>17,858</td><td>0.3%</td><td>4</td><td>Alaska</td><td>525,596</td><td>8.1%</td></tr>
<tr><td>3</td><td>California</td><td>536,404</td><td>8.3%</td><td>5</td><td>Oklahoma</td><td>238,134</td><td>3.7%</td></tr>
<tr><td>9</td><td>Colorado</td><td>134,888</td><td>2.1%</td><td>6</td><td>New Mexico</td><td>232,798</td><td>3.6%</td></tr>
<tr><td>NA</td><td>Connecticut**</td><td>NA</td><td>NA</td><td>7</td><td>Louisiana</td><td>192,954</td><td>3.0%</td></tr>
<tr><td>NA</td><td>Delaware**</td><td>NA</td><td>NA</td><td>8</td><td>Wyoming</td><td>157,716</td><td>2.4%</td></tr>
<tr><td>24</td><td>Florida</td><td>5,833</td><td>0.1%</td><td>9</td><td>Colorado</td><td>134,888</td><td>2.1%</td></tr>
<tr><td>NA</td><td>Georgia**</td><td>NA</td><td>NA</td><td>10</td><td>Kansas</td><td>119,347</td><td>1.8%</td></tr>
<tr><td>NA</td><td>Hawaii**</td><td>NA</td><td>NA</td><td>11</td><td>Utah</td><td>82,686</td><td>1.3%</td></tr>
<tr><td>NA</td><td>Idaho**</td><td>NA</td><td>NA</td><td>12</td><td>Montana</td><td>72,391</td><td>1.1%</td></tr>
<tr><td>14</td><td>Illinois</td><td>26,765</td><td>0.4%</td><td>13</td><td>Mississippi</td><td>65,995</td><td>1.0%</td></tr>
<tr><td>23</td><td>Indiana</td><td>6,421</td><td>0.1%</td><td>14</td><td>Illinois</td><td>26,765</td><td>0.4%</td></tr>
<tr><td>NA</td><td>Iowa**</td><td>NA</td><td>NA</td><td>15</td><td>Alabama</td><td>26,025</td><td>0.4%</td></tr>
<tr><td>10</td><td>Kansas</td><td>119,347</td><td>1.8%</td><td>16</td><td>Michigan</td><td>20,194</td><td>0.3%</td></tr>
<tr><td>20</td><td>Kentucky</td><td>8,738</td><td>0.1%</td><td>17</td><td>Arkansas</td><td>17,858</td><td>0.3%</td></tr>
<tr><td>7</td><td>Louisiana</td><td>192,954</td><td>3.0%</td><td>18</td><td>Ohio</td><td>13,325</td><td>0.2%</td></tr>
<tr><td>NA</td><td>Maine**</td><td>NA</td><td>NA</td><td>19</td><td>Pennsylvania</td><td>11,880</td><td>0.2%</td></tr>
<tr><td>NA</td><td>Maryland**</td><td>NA</td><td>NA</td><td>20</td><td>Kentucky</td><td>8,738</td><td>0.1%</td></tr>
<tr><td>NA</td><td>Massachusetts**</td><td>NA</td><td>NA</td><td>21</td><td>Nebraska</td><td>8,260</td><td>0.1%</td></tr>
<tr><td>16</td><td>Michigan</td><td>20,194</td><td>0.3%</td><td>22</td><td>West Virginia</td><td>7,030</td><td>0.1%</td></tr>
<tr><td>NA</td><td>Minnesota**</td><td>NA</td><td>NA</td><td>23</td><td>Indiana</td><td>6,421</td><td>0.1%</td></tr>
<tr><td>13</td><td>Mississippi</td><td>65,995</td><td>1.0%</td><td>24</td><td>Florida</td><td>5,833</td><td>0.1%</td></tr>
<tr><td>29</td><td>Missouri</td><td>473</td><td>0.0%</td><td>25</td><td>South Dakota</td><td>4,792</td><td>0.1%</td></tr>
<tr><td>12</td><td>Montana</td><td>72,391</td><td>1.1%</td><td>26</td><td>Nevada</td><td>1,005</td><td>0.0%</td></tr>
<tr><td>21</td><td>Nebraska</td><td>8,260</td><td>0.1%</td><td>27</td><td>New York</td><td>964</td><td>0.0%</td></tr>
<tr><td>26</td><td>Nevada</td><td>1,005</td><td>0.0%</td><td>28</td><td>Tennessee</td><td>787</td><td>0.0%</td></tr>
<tr><td>NA</td><td>New Hampshire**</td><td>NA</td><td>NA</td><td>29</td><td>Missouri</td><td>473</td><td>0.0%</td></tr>
<tr><td>NA</td><td>New Jersey**</td><td>NA</td><td>NA</td><td>30</td><td>Arizona</td><td>142</td><td>0.0%</td></tr>
<tr><td>6</td><td>New Mexico</td><td>232,798</td><td>3.6%</td><td>31</td><td>Virginia</td><td>25</td><td>0.0%</td></tr>
<tr><td>27</td><td>New York</td><td>964</td><td>0.0%</td><td>NA</td><td>Connecticut**</td><td>NA</td><td>NA</td></tr>
<tr><td>NA</td><td>North Carolina**</td><td>NA</td><td>NA</td><td>NA</td><td>Delaware**</td><td>NA</td><td>NA</td></tr>
<tr><td>2</td><td>North Dakota</td><td>662,530</td><td>10.2%</td><td>NA</td><td>Georgia**</td><td>NA</td><td>NA</td></tr>
<tr><td>18</td><td>Ohio</td><td>13,325</td><td>0.2%</td><td>NA</td><td>Hawaii**</td><td>NA</td><td>NA</td></tr>
<tr><td>5</td><td>Oklahoma</td><td>238,134</td><td>3.7%</td><td>NA</td><td>Idaho**</td><td>NA</td><td>NA</td></tr>
<tr><td>NA</td><td>Oregon**</td><td>NA</td><td>NA</td><td>NA</td><td>Iowa**</td><td>NA</td><td>NA</td></tr>
<tr><td>19</td><td>Pennsylvania</td><td>11,880</td><td>0.2%</td><td>NA</td><td>Maine**</td><td>NA</td><td>NA</td></tr>
<tr><td>NA</td><td>Rhode Island**</td><td>NA</td><td>NA</td><td>NA</td><td>Maryland**</td><td>NA</td><td>NA</td></tr>
<tr><td>NA</td><td>South Carolina**</td><td>NA</td><td>NA</td><td>NA</td><td>Massachusetts**</td><td>NA</td><td>NA</td></tr>
<tr><td>25</td><td>South Dakota</td><td>4,792</td><td>0.1%</td><td>NA</td><td>Minnesota**</td><td>NA</td><td>NA</td></tr>
<tr><td>28</td><td>Tennessee</td><td>787</td><td>0.0%</td><td>NA</td><td>New Hampshire**</td><td>NA</td><td>NA</td></tr>
<tr><td>1</td><td>Texas</td><td>1,986,336</td><td>30.6%</td><td>NA</td><td>New Jersey**</td><td>NA</td><td>NA</td></tr>
<tr><td>11</td><td>Utah</td><td>82,686</td><td>1.3%</td><td>NA</td><td>North Carolina**</td><td>NA</td><td>NA</td></tr>
<tr><td>NA</td><td>Vermont**</td><td>NA</td><td>NA</td><td>NA</td><td>Oregon**</td><td>NA</td><td>NA</td></tr>
<tr><td>31</td><td>Virginia</td><td>25</td><td>0.0%</td><td>NA</td><td>Rhode Island**</td><td>NA</td><td>NA</td></tr>
<tr><td>NA</td><td>Washington**</td><td>NA</td><td>NA</td><td>NA</td><td>South Carolina**</td><td>NA</td><td>NA</td></tr>
<tr><td>22</td><td>West Virginia</td><td>7,030</td><td>0.1%</td><td>NA</td><td>Vermont**</td><td>NA</td><td>NA</td></tr>
<tr><td>NA</td><td>Wisconsin**</td><td>NA</td><td>NA</td><td>NA</td><td>Washington**</td><td>NA</td><td>NA</td></tr>
<tr><td>8</td><td>Wyoming</td><td>157,716</td><td>2.4%</td><td>NA</td><td>Wisconsin**</td><td>NA</td><td>NA</td></tr>
<tr><td></td><td></td><td></td><td></td><td></td><td>District of Columbia**</td><td>NA</td><td>NA</td></tr>
</table>

Source: CQ Press using data from U.S. Department of Energy, Energy Information Administration
"Petroleum Supply Annual 2012, Volume 1" (http://tonto.eia.doe.gov/dnav/pet/pet_crd_crpdn_adc_mbbl_m.htm)
*National total includes 1,314,019 barrels a day in federal offshore production. Figures for Alaska, California, Louisiana, and Texas include state offshore production.
**No reported production.

Fossil Fuel Emissions in 2011

National Total = 5,407,900,000 Metric Tons of Carbon Dioxide (CO2)*

ALPHA ORDER

RANK	STATE	TONS OF CO2	% of USA
14	Alabama	129,620,000	2.4%
38	Alaska	38,160,000	0.7%
22	Arizona	93,280,000	1.7%
30	Arkansas	67,560,000	1.2%
2	California	360,000,000	6.7%
24	Colorado	91,980,000	1.7%
40	Connecticut	35,300,000	0.7%
48	Delaware	13,110,000	0.2%
5	Florida	230,980,000	4.3%
11	Georgia	156,430,000	2.9%
43	Hawaii	19,310,000	0.4%
46	Idaho	16,030,000	0.3%
6	Illinois	230,580,000	4.3%
8	Indiana	208,260,000	3.9%
25	Iowa	87,420,000	1.6%
27	Kansas	72,360,000	1.3%
12	Kentucky	148,360,000	2.7%
7	Louisiana	215,400,000	4.0%
44	Maine	17,630,000	0.3%
31	Maryland	65,800,000	1.2%
29	Massachusetts	68,890,000	1.3%
10	Michigan	160,260,000	3.0%
23	Minnesota	92,690,000	1.7%
34	Mississippi	61,210,000	1.1%
13	Missouri	135,540,000	2.5%
42	Montana	31,900,000	0.6%
36	Nebraska	52,260,000	1.0%
41	Nevada	33,850,000	0.6%
45	New Hampshire	16,410,000	0.3%
16	New Jersey	117,560,000	2.2%
35	New Mexico	56,600,000	1.0%
9	New York	166,320,000	3.1%
15	North Carolina	127,920,000	2.4%
37	North Dakota	50,340,000	0.9%
4	Ohio	236,630,000	4.4%
17	Oklahoma	107,920,000	2.0%
39	Oregon	37,250,000	0.7%
3	Pennsylvania	246,790,000	4.6%
49	Rhode Island	11,050,000	0.2%
26	South Carolina	80,210,000	1.5%
47	South Dakota	14,760,000	0.3%
18	Tennessee	105,730,000	2.0%
1	Texas	679,720,000	12.6%
32	Utah	63,970,000	1.2%
50	Vermont	5,900,000	0.1%
19	Virginia	99,860,000	1.8%
28	Washington	70,810,000	1.3%
21	West Virginia	95,970,000	1.8%
20	Wisconsin	98,050,000	1.8%
33	Wyoming	63,890,000	1.2%

RANK ORDER

RANK	STATE	TONS OF CO2	% of USA
1	Texas	679,720,000	12.6%
2	California	360,000,000	6.7%
3	Pennsylvania	246,790,000	4.6%
4	Ohio	236,630,000	4.4%
5	Florida	230,980,000	4.3%
6	Illinois	230,580,000	4.3%
7	Louisiana	215,400,000	4.0%
8	Indiana	208,260,000	3.9%
9	New York	166,320,000	3.1%
10	Michigan	160,260,000	3.0%
11	Georgia	156,430,000	2.9%
12	Kentucky	148,360,000	2.7%
13	Missouri	135,540,000	2.5%
14	Alabama	129,620,000	2.4%
15	North Carolina	127,920,000	2.4%
16	New Jersey	117,560,000	2.2%
17	Oklahoma	107,920,000	2.0%
18	Tennessee	105,730,000	2.0%
19	Virginia	99,860,000	1.8%
20	Wisconsin	98,050,000	1.8%
21	West Virginia	95,970,000	1.8%
22	Arizona	93,280,000	1.7%
23	Minnesota	92,690,000	1.7%
24	Colorado	91,980,000	1.7%
25	Iowa	87,420,000	1.6%
26	South Carolina	80,210,000	1.5%
27	Kansas	72,360,000	1.3%
28	Washington	70,810,000	1.3%
29	Massachusetts	68,890,000	1.3%
30	Arkansas	67,560,000	1.2%
31	Maryland	65,800,000	1.2%
32	Utah	63,970,000	1.2%
33	Wyoming	63,890,000	1.2%
34	Mississippi	61,210,000	1.1%
35	New Mexico	56,600,000	1.0%
36	Nebraska	52,260,000	1.0%
37	North Dakota	50,340,000	0.9%
38	Alaska	38,160,000	0.7%
39	Oregon	37,250,000	0.7%
40	Connecticut	35,300,000	0.7%
41	Nevada	33,850,000	0.6%
42	Montana	31,900,000	0.6%
43	Hawaii	19,310,000	0.4%
44	Maine	17,630,000	0.3%
45	New Hampshire	16,410,000	0.3%
46	Idaho	16,030,000	0.3%
47	South Dakota	14,760,000	0.3%
48	Delaware	13,110,000	0.2%
49	Rhode Island	11,050,000	0.2%
50	Vermont	5,900,000	0.1%
	District of Columbia	3,170,000	0.1%

Source: U.S. Environmental Protection Agency
   "Energy CO2 Emissions by State" (http://www.epa.gov/statelocalclimate/resources/state_energyco2inv.html)
*Carbon dioxide (CO2) emissions from fossil fuel combustion. This represents the largest source (92%) of total CO2 emissions from all emission sources. Emissions are based on the location where fossil fuels are used. Fuels can be used in one state to generate electricity consumed in another.

Per Capita Fossil Fuel Emissions in 2011

National Per Capita = 17.4 Metric Tons of Carbon Dioxide (CO2)*

ALPHA ORDER

RANK ORDER

RANK	STATE	PER CAPITA	RANK	STATE	PER CAPITA
13	Alabama	27.0	1	Wyoming	112.6
3	Alaska	52.8	2	North Dakota	73.5
31	Arizona	14.4	3	Alaska	52.8
16	Arkansas	23.0	4	West Virginia	51.7
47	California	9.6	5	Louisiana	47.1
22	Colorado	18.0	6	Kentucky	34.0
46	Connecticut	9.8	7	Indiana	32.0
31	Delaware	14.4	7	Montana	32.0
40	Florida	12.1	9	Iowa	28.5
30	Georgia	15.9	9	Oklahoma	28.5
33	Hawaii	14.0	11	Nebraska	28.4
45	Idaho	10.1	12	New Mexico	27.2
23	Illinois	17.9	13	Alabama	27.0
7	Indiana	32.0	14	Texas	26.5
9	Iowa	28.5	15	Kansas	25.2
15	Kansas	25.2	16	Arkansas	23.0
6	Kentucky	34.0	17	Utah	22.7
5	Louisiana	47.1	18	Missouri	22.6
34	Maine	13.3	19	Mississippi	20.6
41	Maryland	11.3	20	Ohio	20.5
43	Massachusetts	10.4	21	Pennsylvania	19.4
29	Michigan	16.2	22	Colorado	18.0
25	Minnesota	17.3	23	Illinois	17.9
19	Mississippi	20.6	23	South Dakota	17.9
18	Missouri	22.6	25	Minnesota	17.3
7	Montana	32.0	26	South Carolina	17.2
11	Nebraska	28.4	26	Wisconsin	17.2
37	Nevada	12.5	28	Tennessee	16.5
38	New Hampshire	12.4	29	Michigan	16.2
34	New Jersey	13.3	30	Georgia	15.9
12	New Mexico	27.2	31	Arizona	14.4
50	New York	8.5	31	Delaware	14.4
34	North Carolina	13.3	33	Hawaii	14.0
2	North Dakota	73.5	34	Maine	13.3
20	Ohio	20.5	34	New Jersey	13.3
9	Oklahoma	28.5	34	North Carolina	13.3
47	Oregon	9.6	37	Nevada	12.5
21	Pennsylvania	19.4	38	New Hampshire	12.4
42	Rhode Island	10.5	39	Virginia	12.3
26	South Carolina	17.2	40	Florida	12.1
23	South Dakota	17.9	41	Maryland	11.3
28	Tennessee	16.5	42	Rhode Island	10.5
14	Texas	26.5	43	Massachusetts	10.4
17	Utah	22.7	43	Washington	10.4
49	Vermont	9.4	45	Idaho	10.1
39	Virginia	12.3	46	Connecticut	9.8
43	Washington	10.4	47	California	9.6
4	West Virginia	51.7	47	Oregon	9.6
26	Wisconsin	17.2	49	Vermont	9.4
1	Wyoming	112.6	50	New York	8.5

District of Columbia 5.1

Source: CQ Press using data from U.S. Environmental Protection Agency
   "Energy CO2 Emissions by State" (http://www.epa.gov/statelocalclimate/resources/state_energyco2inv.html)
*Carbon dioxide (CO2) emissions from fossil fuel combustion. This represents the largest source (92%) of total CO2 emissions from all emission sources. Emissions are based on the location where fossil fuels are used. Fuels can be used in one state to generate electricity consumed in another.

Percent Change in Fossil Fuel Emissions: 2007 to 2011

National Percent Change = 8.4% Decrease*

ALPHA ORDER

RANK	STATE	PERCENT CHANGE
28	Alabama	(10.8)
34	Alaska	(13.1)
21	Arizona	(8.5)
2	Arkansas	6.7
30	California	(11.4)
17	Colorado	(6.5)
33	Connecticut	(12.5)
50	Delaware	(23.2)
23	Florida	(9.8)
38	Georgia	(14.9)
48	Hawaii	(19.7)
10	Idaho	(2.5)
14	Illinois	(5.0)
24	Indiana	(9.9)
6	Iowa	0.6
18	Kansas	(7.6)
15	Kentucky	(5.2)
5	Louisiana	0.8
42	Maine	(16.1)
40	Maryland	(15.8)
35	Massachusetts	(14.0)
31	Michigan	(11.5)
19	Minnesota	(7.8)
26	Mississippi	(10.2)
12	Missouri	(3.6)
41	Montana	(16.0)
1	Nebraska	17.6
47	Nevada	(19.1)
36	New Hampshire	(14.3)
29	New Jersey	(10.9)
12	New Mexico	(3.6)
45	New York	(17.1)
43	North Carolina	(16.4)
4	North Dakota	2.4
32	Ohio	(11.8)
9	Oklahoma	(1.3)
39	Oregon	(15.2)
26	Pennsylvania	(10.2)
8	Rhode Island	(0.8)
22	South Carolina	(9.7)
3	South Dakota	6.3
46	Tennessee	(17.9)
7	Texas	(0.3)
20	Utah	(8.0)
25	Vermont	(10.1)
49	Virginia	(21.7)
37	Washington	(14.6)
44	West Virginia	(16.6)
16	Wisconsin	(6.2)
11	Wyoming	(3.4)

RANK ORDER

RANK	STATE	PERCENT CHANGE
1	Nebraska	17.6
2	Arkansas	6.7
3	South Dakota	6.3
4	North Dakota	2.4
5	Louisiana	0.8
6	Iowa	0.6
7	Texas	(0.3)
8	Rhode Island	(0.8)
9	Oklahoma	(1.3)
10	Idaho	(2.5)
11	Wyoming	(3.4)
12	Missouri	(3.6)
12	New Mexico	(3.6)
14	Illinois	(5.0)
15	Kentucky	(5.2)
16	Wisconsin	(6.2)
17	Colorado	(6.5)
18	Kansas	(7.6)
19	Minnesota	(7.8)
20	Utah	(8.0)
21	Arizona	(8.5)
22	South Carolina	(9.7)
23	Florida	(9.8)
24	Indiana	(9.9)
25	Vermont	(10.1)
26	Mississippi	(10.2)
26	Pennsylvania	(10.2)
28	Alabama	(10.8)
29	New Jersey	(10.9)
30	California	(11.4)
31	Michigan	(11.5)
32	Ohio	(11.8)
33	Connecticut	(12.5)
34	Alaska	(13.1)
35	Massachusetts	(14.0)
36	New Hampshire	(14.3)
37	Washington	(14.6)
38	Georgia	(14.9)
39	Oregon	(15.2)
40	Maryland	(15.8)
41	Montana	(16.0)
42	Maine	(16.1)
43	North Carolina	(16.4)
44	West Virginia	(16.6)
45	New York	(17.1)
46	Tennessee	(17.9)
47	Nevada	(19.1)
48	Hawaii	(19.7)
49	Virginia	(21.7)
50	Delaware	(23.2)
	District of Columbia	(7.0)

Source: CQ Press using data from U.S. Environmental Protection Agency
"Energy CO2 Emissions by State" (http://www.epa.gov/statelocalclimate/resources/state_energyco2inv.html)
*Based on metric tons of carbon dioxide (CO2).

Toxic Releases: Total Pollution Released in 2012

National Total = 3,626,883,669 Pounds of Toxins*

RANK	STATE	POUNDS	% of USA
11	Alabama	81,590,091	2.2%
1	Alaska	876,721,634	24.2%
10	Arizona	85,509,846	2.4%
27	Arkansas	35,290,419	1.0%
30	California	31,707,203	0.9%
31	Colorado	28,606,663	0.8%
47	Connecticut	2,141,978	0.1%
43	Delaware	7,568,205	0.2%
18	Florida	62,918,425	1.7%
16	Georgia	65,392,625	1.8%
46	Hawaii	2,693,617	0.1%
26	Idaho	38,675,265	1.1%
7	Illinois	120,290,946	3.3%
6	Indiana	139,647,681	3.9%
25	Iowa	39,655,624	1.1%
36	Kansas	19,416,528	0.5%
13	Kentucky	77,986,319	2.2%
5	Louisiana	143,289,289	4.0%
41	Maine	12,046,792	0.3%
42	Maryland	8,262,420	0.2%
45	Massachusetts	3,567,275	0.1%
14	Michigan	70,038,763	1.9%
32	Minnesota	27,350,939	0.8%
20	Mississippi	55,622,343	1.5%
15	Missouri	69,735,412	1.9%
19	Montana	59,210,084	1.6%
34	Nebraska	23,590,024	0.7%
2	Nevada	285,874,773	7.9%
48	New Hampshire	822,371	0.0%
40	New Jersey	12,768,089	0.4%
33	New Mexico	24,763,210	0.7%
38	New York	17,257,529	0.5%
21	North Carolina	54,214,451	1.5%
28	North Dakota	34,480,922	1.0%
8	Ohio	116,871,981	3.2%
17	Oklahoma	65,389,776	1.8%
35	Oregon	23,198,111	0.6%
9	Pennsylvania	97,878,672	2.7%
50	Rhode Island	268,558	0.0%
22	South Carolina	49,310,415	1.4%
44	South Dakota	5,176,520	0.1%
12	Tennessee	78,787,463	2.2%
3	Texas	226,457,216	6.2%
4	Utah	191,961,034	5.3%
49	Vermont	310,901	0.0%
23	Virginia	42,361,499	1.2%
37	Washington	19,238,953	0.5%
24	West Virginia	39,743,554	1.1%
29	Wisconsin	34,040,973	0.9%
39	Wyoming	17,153,005	0.5%

RANK	STATE	POUNDS	% of USA
1	Alaska	876,721,634	24.2%
2	Nevada	285,874,773	7.9%
3	Texas	226,457,216	6.2%
4	Utah	191,961,034	5.3%
5	Louisiana	143,289,289	4.0%
6	Indiana	139,647,681	3.9%
7	Illinois	120,290,946	3.3%
8	Ohio	116,871,981	3.2%
9	Pennsylvania	97,878,672	2.7%
10	Arizona	85,509,846	2.4%
11	Alabama	81,590,091	2.2%
12	Tennessee	78,787,463	2.2%
13	Kentucky	77,986,319	2.2%
14	Michigan	70,038,763	1.9%
15	Missouri	69,735,412	1.9%
16	Georgia	65,392,625	1.8%
17	Oklahoma	65,389,776	1.8%
18	Florida	62,918,425	1.7%
19	Montana	59,210,084	1.6%
20	Mississippi	55,622,343	1.5%
21	North Carolina	54,214,451	1.5%
22	South Carolina	49,310,415	1.4%
23	Virginia	42,361,499	1.2%
24	West Virginia	39,743,554	1.1%
25	Iowa	39,655,624	1.1%
26	Idaho	38,675,265	1.1%
27	Arkansas	35,290,419	1.0%
28	North Dakota	34,480,922	1.0%
29	Wisconsin	34,040,973	0.9%
30	California	31,707,203	0.9%
31	Colorado	28,606,663	0.8%
32	Minnesota	27,350,939	0.8%
33	New Mexico	24,763,210	0.7%
34	Nebraska	23,590,024	0.7%
35	Oregon	23,198,111	0.6%
36	Kansas	19,416,528	0.5%
37	Washington	19,238,953	0.5%
38	New York	17,257,529	0.5%
39	Wyoming	17,153,005	0.5%
40	New Jersey	12,768,089	0.4%
41	Maine	12,046,792	0.3%
42	Maryland	8,262,420	0.2%
43	Delaware	7,568,205	0.2%
44	South Dakota	5,176,520	0.1%
45	Massachusetts	3,567,275	0.1%
46	Hawaii	2,693,617	0.1%
47	Connecticut	2,141,978	0.1%
48	New Hampshire	822,371	0.0%
49	Vermont	310,901	0.0%
50	Rhode Island	268,558	0.0%
	District of Columbia	27,283	0.0%

Source: U.S. Environmental Protection Agency, Office of Pollution Prevention and Toxics Information Management
"2012 Toxics Release Inventory" (http://www.epa.gov/triexplorer/)
*National total does not include 5,259,081 pounds of toxins in U.S. territories. Includes discharges to air, surface water, underground injection, and surface land. Includes both original (or manufacturing) industries and those added by EPA since it began tracking releases.

Toxic Releases: Total Air Emissions in 2012

National Total = 753,223,676 Pounds*

ALPHA ORDER

RANK	STATE	POUNDS	% of USA
7	Alabama	33,168,902	4.4%
48	Alaska	446,348	0.1%
37	Arizona	2,194,736	0.3%
20	Arkansas	16,395,622	2.2%
28	California	7,520,124	1.0%
35	Colorado	2,780,261	0.4%
46	Connecticut	855,661	0.1%
44	Delaware	1,109,209	0.1%
13	Florida	25,072,828	3.3%
4	Georgia	41,361,693	5.5%
39	Hawaii	1,876,897	0.2%
33	Idaho	4,572,651	0.6%
8	Illinois	29,029,593	3.9%
6	Indiana	38,892,127	5.2%
18	Iowa	19,570,214	2.6%
24	Kansas	9,996,714	1.3%
5	Kentucky	41,171,493	5.5%
2	Louisiana	51,628,735	6.9%
34	Maine	4,447,162	0.6%
31	Maryland	5,209,145	0.7%
41	Massachusetts	1,543,846	0.2%
14	Michigan	24,182,233	3.2%
26	Minnesota	9,177,885	1.2%
15	Mississippi	20,965,865	2.8%
23	Missouri	11,561,486	1.5%
40	Montana	1,761,481	0.2%
32	Nebraska	4,627,598	0.6%
42	Nevada	1,265,370	0.2%
47	New Hampshire	616,504	0.1%
38	New Jersey	2,142,968	0.3%
45	New Mexico	1,043,897	0.1%
29	New York	6,758,936	0.9%
12	North Carolina	26,641,726	3.5%
21	North Dakota	14,749,715	2.0%
3	Ohio	44,312,754	5.9%
17	Oklahoma	19,726,926	2.6%
30	Oregon	6,622,188	0.9%
11	Pennsylvania	27,765,131	3.7%
49	Rhode Island	107,255	0.0%
10	South Carolina	28,217,707	3.7%
43	South Dakota	1,219,388	0.2%
9	Tennessee	28,327,560	3.8%
1	Texas	60,486,694	8.0%
27	Utah	8,070,094	1.1%
50	Vermont	37,001	0.0%
16	Virginia	20,763,540	2.8%
25	Washington	9,898,022	1.3%
19	West Virginia	18,146,053	2.4%
22	Wisconsin	12,786,089	1.7%
36	Wyoming	2,386,422	0.3%

RANK ORDER

RANK	STATE	POUNDS	% of USA
1	Texas	60,486,694	8.0%
2	Louisiana	51,628,735	6.9%
3	Ohio	44,312,754	5.9%
4	Georgia	41,361,693	5.5%
5	Kentucky	41,171,493	5.5%
6	Indiana	38,892,127	5.2%
7	Alabama	33,168,902	4.4%
8	Illinois	29,029,593	3.9%
9	Tennessee	28,327,560	3.8%
10	South Carolina	28,217,707	3.7%
11	Pennsylvania	27,765,131	3.7%
12	North Carolina	26,641,726	3.5%
13	Florida	25,072,828	3.3%
14	Michigan	24,182,233	3.2%
15	Mississippi	20,965,865	2.8%
16	Virginia	20,763,540	2.8%
17	Oklahoma	19,726,926	2.6%
18	Iowa	19,570,214	2.6%
19	West Virginia	18,146,053	2.4%
20	Arkansas	16,395,622	2.2%
21	North Dakota	14,749,715	2.0%
22	Wisconsin	12,786,089	1.7%
23	Missouri	11,561,486	1.5%
24	Kansas	9,996,714	1.3%
25	Washington	9,898,022	1.3%
26	Minnesota	9,177,885	1.2%
27	Utah	8,070,094	1.1%
28	California	7,520,124	1.0%
29	New York	6,758,936	0.9%
30	Oregon	6,622,188	0.9%
31	Maryland	5,209,145	0.7%
32	Nebraska	4,627,598	0.6%
33	Idaho	4,572,651	0.6%
34	Maine	4,447,162	0.6%
35	Colorado	2,780,261	0.4%
36	Wyoming	2,386,422	0.3%
37	Arizona	2,194,736	0.3%
38	New Jersey	2,142,968	0.3%
39	Hawaii	1,876,897	0.2%
40	Montana	1,761,481	0.2%
41	Massachusetts	1,543,846	0.2%
42	Nevada	1,265,370	0.2%
43	South Dakota	1,219,388	0.2%
44	Delaware	1,109,209	0.1%
45	New Mexico	1,043,897	0.1%
46	Connecticut	855,661	0.1%
47	New Hampshire	616,504	0.1%
48	Alaska	446,348	0.1%
49	Rhode Island	107,255	0.0%
50	Vermont	37,001	0.0%
	District of Columbia	11,227	0.0%

Source: U.S. Environmental Protection Agency, Office of Pollution Prevention and Toxics Information Management
   "2012 Toxics Release Inventory" (http://www.epa.gov/triexplorer/)
*Includes fugitive and point source air emissions. National total does not include 4,251,939 pounds of emissions in U.S.
territories. Includes both original (or manufacturing) industries and those added by EPA since it began tracking releases.

Toxic Releases: Total Surface Water Discharges in 2012

National Total = 206,992,950 Pounds*

ALPHA ORDER

RANK	STATE	POUNDS	% of USA
4	Alabama	12,290,924	5.9%
37	Alaska	570,475	0.3%
48	Arizona	1,177	0.0%
17	Arkansas	4,250,380	2.1%
26	California	2,358,874	1.1%
36	Colorado	849,619	0.4%
40	Connecticut	223,997	0.1%
20	Delaware	3,777,904	1.8%
32	Florida	1,332,673	0.6%
8	Georgia	10,132,249	4.9%
38	Hawaii	435,662	0.2%
25	Idaho	2,470,923	1.2%
14	Illinois	6,130,604	3.0%
1	Indiana	18,311,874	8.8%
12	Iowa	6,829,092	3.3%
39	Kansas	302,239	0.1%
11	Kentucky	7,417,795	3.6%
3	Louisiana	12,644,689	6.1%
22	Maine	3,105,291	1.5%
35	Maryland	1,084,344	0.5%
47	Massachusetts	5,551	0.0%
31	Michigan	1,779,947	0.9%
30	Minnesota	1,861,487	0.9%
16	Mississippi	4,957,679	2.4%
27	Missouri	2,176,282	1.1%
41	Montana	195,669	0.1%
6	Nebraska	10,522,803	5.1%
34	Nevada	1,169,685	0.6%
49	New Hampshire	797	0.0%
13	New Jersey	6,191,385	3.0%
45	New Mexico	39,784	0.0%
15	New York	5,307,015	2.6%
9	North Carolina	8,899,571	4.3%
42	North Dakota	151,308	0.1%
10	Ohio	7,569,944	3.7%
18	Oklahoma	4,219,626	2.0%
33	Oregon	1,288,342	0.6%
7	Pennsylvania	10,475,081	5.1%
50	Rhode Island	600	0.0%
21	South Carolina	3,347,493	1.6%
29	South Dakota	1,895,777	0.9%
19	Tennessee	4,114,915	2.0%
2	Texas	16,572,655	8.0%
43	Utah	104,515	0.1%
44	Vermont	98,218	0.0%
5	Virginia	11,822,567	5.7%
24	Washington	2,728,520	1.3%
28	West Virginia	2,161,592	1.0%
23	Wisconsin	2,797,260	1.4%
46	Wyoming	15,149	0.0%

RANK ORDER

RANK	STATE	POUNDS	% of USA
1	Indiana	18,311,874	8.8%
2	Texas	16,572,655	8.0%
3	Louisiana	12,644,689	6.1%
4	Alabama	12,290,924	5.9%
5	Virginia	11,822,567	5.7%
6	Nebraska	10,522,803	5.1%
7	Pennsylvania	10,475,081	5.1%
8	Georgia	10,132,249	4.9%
9	North Carolina	8,899,571	4.3%
10	Ohio	7,569,944	3.7%
11	Kentucky	7,417,795	3.6%
12	Iowa	6,829,092	3.3%
13	New Jersey	6,191,385	3.0%
14	Illinois	6,130,604	3.0%
15	New York	5,307,015	2.6%
16	Mississippi	4,957,679	2.4%
17	Arkansas	4,250,380	2.1%
18	Oklahoma	4,219,626	2.0%
19	Tennessee	4,114,915	2.0%
20	Delaware	3,777,904	1.8%
21	South Carolina	3,347,493	1.6%
22	Maine	3,105,291	1.5%
23	Wisconsin	2,797,260	1.4%
24	Washington	2,728,520	1.3%
25	Idaho	2,470,923	1.2%
26	California	2,358,874	1.1%
27	Missouri	2,176,282	1.1%
28	West Virginia	2,161,592	1.0%
29	South Dakota	1,895,777	0.9%
30	Minnesota	1,861,487	0.9%
31	Michigan	1,779,947	0.9%
32	Florida	1,332,673	0.6%
33	Oregon	1,288,342	0.6%
34	Nevada	1,169,685	0.6%
35	Maryland	1,084,344	0.5%
36	Colorado	849,619	0.4%
37	Alaska	570,475	0.3%
38	Hawaii	435,662	0.2%
39	Kansas	302,239	0.1%
40	Connecticut	223,997	0.1%
41	Montana	195,669	0.1%
42	North Dakota	151,308	0.1%
43	Utah	104,515	0.1%
44	Vermont	98,218	0.0%
45	New Mexico	39,784	0.0%
46	Wyoming	15,149	0.0%
47	Massachusetts	5,551	0.0%
48	Arizona	1,177	0.0%
49	New Hampshire	797	0.0%
50	Rhode Island	600	0.0%
	District of Columbia	948	0.0%

Source: U.S. Environmental Protection Agency, Office of Pollution Prevention and Toxics Information Management
"2012 Toxics Release Inventory" (http://www.epa.gov/triexplorer/)
*National total does not include 276,939 pounds of discharges in U.S. territories. Includes both original (or manufacturing) industries and those added by EPA since it began tracking releases.

Hazardous Waste Sites on the National Priority List in 2014

National Total = 1,373 Sites*

ALPHA ORDER

RANK	STATE	SITES	% of USA
26	Alabama	15	1.1%
45	Alaska	6	0.4%
40	Arizona	9	0.7%
39	Arkansas	10	0.7%
2	California	98	7.1%
21	Colorado	20	1.5%
26	Connecticut	15	1.1%
31	Delaware	14	1.0%
6	Florida	56	4.1%
24	Georgia	17	1.2%
46	Hawaii	3	0.2%
40	Idaho	9	0.7%
9	Illinois	48	3.5%
13	Indiana	37	2.7%
35	Iowa	12	0.9%
34	Kansas	13	0.9%
31	Kentucky	14	1.0%
35	Louisiana	12	0.9%
31	Maine	14	1.0%
20	Maryland	21	1.5%
15	Massachusetts	32	2.3%
5	Michigan	67	4.9%
17	Minnesota	25	1.8%
40	Mississippi	9	0.7%
14	Missouri	33	2.4%
23	Montana	18	1.3%
26	Nebraska	15	1.1%
49	Nevada	1	0.1%
19	New Hampshire	22	1.6%
1	New Jersey	116	8.4%
26	New Mexico	15	1.1%
4	New York	87	6.3%
11	North Carolina	39	2.8%
50	North Dakota	0	0.0%
10	Ohio	43	3.1%
44	Oklahoma	8	0.6%
26	Oregon	15	1.1%
3	Pennsylvania	97	7.1%
35	Rhode Island	12	0.9%
17	South Carolina	25	1.8%
47	South Dakota	2	0.1%
24	Tennessee	17	1.2%
7	Texas	51	3.7%
22	Utah	19	1.4%
38	Vermont	11	0.8%
16	Virginia	31	2.3%
8	Washington	50	3.6%
40	West Virginia	9	0.7%
11	Wisconsin	39	2.8%
47	Wyoming	2	0.1%

RANK ORDER

RANK	STATE	SITES	% of USA
1	New Jersey	116	8.4%
2	California	98	7.1%
3	Pennsylvania	97	7.1%
4	New York	87	6.3%
5	Michigan	67	4.9%
6	Florida	56	4.1%
7	Texas	51	3.7%
8	Washington	50	3.6%
9	Illinois	48	3.5%
10	Ohio	43	3.1%
11	North Carolina	39	2.8%
11	Wisconsin	39	2.8%
13	Indiana	37	2.7%
14	Missouri	33	2.4%
15	Massachusetts	32	2.3%
16	Virginia	31	2.3%
17	Minnesota	25	1.8%
17	South Carolina	25	1.8%
19	New Hampshire	22	1.6%
20	Maryland	21	1.5%
21	Colorado	20	1.5%
22	Utah	19	1.4%
23	Montana	18	1.3%
24	Georgia	17	1.2%
24	Tennessee	17	1.2%
26	Alabama	15	1.1%
26	Connecticut	15	1.1%
26	Nebraska	15	1.1%
26	New Mexico	15	1.1%
26	Oregon	15	1.1%
31	Delaware	14	1.0%
31	Kentucky	14	1.0%
31	Maine	14	1.0%
34	Kansas	13	0.9%
35	Iowa	12	0.9%
35	Louisiana	12	0.9%
35	Rhode Island	12	0.9%
38	Vermont	11	0.8%
39	Arkansas	10	0.7%
40	Arizona	9	0.7%
40	Idaho	9	0.7%
40	Mississippi	9	0.7%
40	West Virginia	9	0.7%
44	Oklahoma	8	0.6%
45	Alaska	6	0.4%
46	Hawaii	3	0.2%
47	South Dakota	2	0.1%
47	Wyoming	2	0.1%
49	Nevada	1	0.1%
50	North Dakota	0	0.0%
	District of Columbia	1	0.1%

Source: U.S. Environmental Protection Agency
"National Priorities List (NPL) Sites in the United States" (http://www.epa.gov/superfund/sites/npl/)
*As of January 7, 2014. Includes final and proposed General Superfund and Federal Facilities Sites. National total includes 16 sites in Puerto Rico, two in Guam, and one in the U.S. Virgin Islands.

Hazardous Waste Sites on the National Priority List
per 10,000 Square Miles in 2014
National Rate = 3.6 Sites per 10,000 Square Miles*

ALPHA ORDER

RANK	STATE	RATE
27	Alabama	2.9
48	Alaska	0.1
45	Arizona	0.8
34	Arkansas	1.9
20	California	6.0
34	Colorado	1.9
5	Connecticut	27.1
3	Delaware	56.3
13	Florida	8.5
27	Georgia	2.9
30	Hawaii	2.7
43	Idaho	1.1
14	Illinois	8.3
11	Indiana	10.2
33	Iowa	2.1
39	Kansas	1.6
26	Kentucky	3.5
31	Louisiana	2.3
23	Maine	4.0
8	Maryland	16.9
4	Massachusetts	30.3
19	Michigan	6.9
27	Minnesota	2.9
34	Mississippi	1.9
22	Missouri	4.7
41	Montana	1.2
34	Nebraska	1.9
48	Nevada	0.1
6	New Hampshire	23.5
1	New Jersey	133.0
41	New Mexico	1.2
9	New York	15.9
16	North Carolina	7.2
50	North Dakota	0.0
12	Ohio	9.6
43	Oklahoma	1.1
40	Oregon	1.5
7	Pennsylvania	21.1
2	Rhode Island	77.7
15	South Carolina	7.8
46	South Dakota	0.3
23	Tennessee	4.0
34	Texas	1.9
32	Utah	2.2
10	Vermont	11.4
16	Virginia	7.2
18	Washington	7.0
25	West Virginia	3.7
20	Wisconsin	6.0
47	Wyoming	0.2

RANK ORDER

RANK	STATE	RATE
1	New Jersey	133.0
2	Rhode Island	77.7
3	Delaware	56.3
4	Massachusetts	30.3
5	Connecticut	27.1
6	New Hampshire	23.5
7	Pennsylvania	21.1
8	Maryland	16.9
9	New York	15.9
10	Vermont	11.4
11	Indiana	10.2
12	Ohio	9.6
13	Florida	8.5
14	Illinois	8.3
15	South Carolina	7.8
16	North Carolina	7.2
16	Virginia	7.2
18	Washington	7.0
19	Michigan	6.9
20	California	6.0
20	Wisconsin	6.0
22	Missouri	4.7
23	Maine	4.0
23	Tennessee	4.0
25	West Virginia	3.7
26	Kentucky	3.5
27	Alabama	2.9
27	Georgia	2.9
27	Minnesota	2.9
30	Hawaii	2.7
31	Louisiana	2.3
32	Utah	2.2
33	Iowa	2.1
34	Arkansas	1.9
34	Colorado	1.9
34	Mississippi	1.9
34	Nebraska	1.9
34	Texas	1.9
39	Kansas	1.6
40	Oregon	1.5
41	Montana	1.2
41	New Mexico	1.2
43	Idaho	1.1
43	Oklahoma	1.1
45	Arizona	0.8
46	South Dakota	0.3
47	Wyoming	0.2
48	Alaska	0.1
48	Nevada	0.1
50	North Dakota	0.0

District of Columbia**   NA

Source: CQ Press using data from U.S. Environmental Protection Agency
   "National Priorities List (NPL) Sites in the United States" (http://www.epa.gov/superfund/sites/npl/)
*As of January 7, 2014. Includes final and proposed General Superfund and Federal Facilities Sites. National rate excludes
sites and square miles in Puerto Rico, Guam and the Virgin Islands. Based on land and water area of states.
**The District of Columbia has one site in its 68 square miles.

Hazardous Waste Sites Deleted from the National Priorities List as of 2014

National Total = 374 Sites*

ALPHA ORDER

RANK	STATE	SITES	% of USA
43	Alabama	1	0.3%
31	Alaska	3	0.8%
31	Arizona	3	0.8%
13	Arkansas	7	1.9%
8	California	13	3.5%
31	Colorado	3	0.8%
31	Connecticut	3	0.8%
13	Delaware	7	1.9%
4	Florida	24	6.4%
22	Georgia	5	1.3%
43	Hawaii	1	0.3%
31	Idaho	3	0.8%
22	Illinois	5	1.3%
12	Indiana	9	2.4%
11	Iowa	10	2.7%
22	Kansas	5	1.3%
17	Kentucky	6	1.6%
9	Louisiana	12	3.2%
38	Maine	2	0.5%
27	Maryland	4	1.1%
17	Massachusetts	6	1.6%
6	Michigan	19	5.1%
5	Minnesota	21	5.6%
31	Mississippi	3	0.8%
22	Missouri	5	1.3%
48	Montana	0	0.0%
43	Nebraska	1	0.3%
48	Nevada	0	0.0%
48	New Hampshire	0	0.0%
1	New Jersey	33	8.8%
27	New Mexico	4	1.1%
2	New York	30	8.0%
31	North Carolina	3	0.8%
38	North Dakota	2	0.5%
13	Ohio	7	1.9%
13	Oklahoma	7	1.9%
27	Oregon	4	1.1%
3	Pennsylvania	29	7.8%
43	Rhode Island	1	0.3%
17	South Carolina	6	1.6%
38	South Dakota	2	0.5%
17	Tennessee	6	1.6%
9	Texas	12	3.2%
22	Utah	5	1.3%
38	Vermont	2	0.5%
27	Virginia	4	1.1%
7	Washington	17	4.5%
38	West Virginia	2	0.5%
17	Wisconsin	6	1.6%
43	Wyoming	1	0.3%

RANK ORDER

RANK	STATE	SITES	% of USA
1	New Jersey	33	8.8%
2	New York	30	8.0%
3	Pennsylvania	29	7.8%
4	Florida	24	6.4%
5	Minnesota	21	5.6%
6	Michigan	19	5.1%
7	Washington	17	4.5%
8	California	13	3.5%
9	Louisiana	12	3.2%
9	Texas	12	3.2%
11	Iowa	10	2.7%
12	Indiana	9	2.4%
13	Arkansas	7	1.9%
13	Delaware	7	1.9%
13	Ohio	7	1.9%
13	Oklahoma	7	1.9%
17	Kentucky	6	1.6%
17	Massachusetts	6	1.6%
17	South Carolina	6	1.6%
17	Tennessee	6	1.6%
17	Wisconsin	6	1.6%
22	Georgia	5	1.3%
22	Illinois	5	1.3%
22	Kansas	5	1.3%
22	Missouri	5	1.3%
22	Utah	5	1.3%
27	Maryland	4	1.1%
27	New Mexico	4	1.1%
27	Oregon	4	1.1%
27	Virginia	4	1.1%
31	Alaska	3	0.8%
31	Arizona	3	0.8%
31	Colorado	3	0.8%
31	Connecticut	3	0.8%
31	Idaho	3	0.8%
31	Mississippi	3	0.8%
31	North Carolina	3	0.8%
38	Maine	2	0.5%
38	North Dakota	2	0.5%
38	South Dakota	2	0.5%
38	Vermont	2	0.5%
38	West Virginia	2	0.5%
43	Alabama	1	0.3%
43	Hawaii	1	0.3%
43	Nebraska	1	0.3%
43	Rhode Island	1	0.3%
43	Wyoming	1	0.3%
48	Montana	0	0.0%
48	Nevada	0	0.0%
48	New Hampshire	0	0.0%
	District of Columbia	0	0.0%

Source: U.S. Environmental Protection Agency
"National Priorities List (NPL) Sites in the United States" (http://www.epa.gov/superfund/sites/npl/)
*Cumulative total as of January 7, 2014. National total includes six sites in Puerto Rico and four in other U.S. territories.

VIII. Geography

Total Area of States in Square Miles in 2010

National Total = 3,796,742 Square Miles*

RANK	STATE	MILES	% of USA
30	Alabama	52,420	1.4%
1	Alaska	665,384	17.5%
6	Arizona	113,990	3.0%
29	Arkansas	53,179	1.4%
3	California	163,695	4.3%
8	Colorado	104,094	2.7%
48	Connecticut	5,543	0.1%
49	Delaware	2,489	0.1%
22	Florida	65,758	1.7%
24	Georgia	59,425	1.6%
43	Hawaii	10,932	0.3%
14	Idaho	83,569	2.2%
25	Illinois	57,914	1.5%
38	Indiana	36,420	1.0%
26	Iowa	56,273	1.5%
15	Kansas	82,278	2.2%
37	Kentucky	40,408	1.1%
31	Louisiana	52,378	1.4%
39	Maine	35,380	0.9%
42	Maryland	12,406	0.3%
44	Massachusetts	10,554	0.3%
11	Michigan	96,714	2.5%
12	Minnesota	86,936	2.3%
32	Mississippi	48,432	1.3%
21	Missouri	69,707	1.8%
4	Montana	147,040	3.9%
16	Nebraska	77,348	2.0%
7	Nevada	110,572	2.9%
46	New Hampshire	9,349	0.2%
47	New Jersey	8,723	0.2%
5	New Mexico	121,590	3.2%
27	New York	54,555	1.4%
28	North Carolina	53,819	1.4%
19	North Dakota	70,698	1.9%
34	Ohio	44,826	1.2%
20	Oklahoma	69,899	1.8%
9	Oregon	98,379	2.6%
33	Pennsylvania	46,054	1.2%
50	Rhode Island	1,545	0.0%
40	South Carolina	32,020	0.8%
17	South Dakota	77,116	2.0%
36	Tennessee	42,144	1.1%
2	Texas	268,596	7.1%
13	Utah	84,897	2.2%
45	Vermont	9,616	0.3%
35	Virginia	42,775	1.1%
18	Washington	71,298	1.9%
41	West Virginia	24,230	0.6%
23	Wisconsin	65,496	1.7%
10	Wyoming	97,813	2.6%

RANK	STATE	MILES	% of USA
1	Alaska	665,384	17.5%
2	Texas	268,596	7.1%
3	California	163,695	4.3%
4	Montana	147,040	3.9%
5	New Mexico	121,590	3.2%
6	Arizona	113,990	3.0%
7	Nevada	110,572	2.9%
8	Colorado	104,094	2.7%
9	Oregon	98,379	2.6%
10	Wyoming	97,813	2.6%
11	Michigan	96,714	2.5%
12	Minnesota	86,936	2.3%
13	Utah	84,897	2.2%
14	Idaho	83,569	2.2%
15	Kansas	82,278	2.2%
16	Nebraska	77,348	2.0%
17	South Dakota	77,116	2.0%
18	Washington	71,298	1.9%
19	North Dakota	70,698	1.9%
20	Oklahoma	69,899	1.8%
21	Missouri	69,707	1.8%
22	Florida	65,758	1.7%
23	Wisconsin	65,496	1.7%
24	Georgia	59,425	1.6%
25	Illinois	57,914	1.5%
26	Iowa	56,273	1.5%
27	New York	54,555	1.4%
28	North Carolina	53,819	1.4%
29	Arkansas	53,179	1.4%
30	Alabama	52,420	1.4%
31	Louisiana	52,378	1.4%
32	Mississippi	48,432	1.3%
33	Pennsylvania	46,054	1.2%
34	Ohio	44,826	1.2%
35	Virginia	42,775	1.1%
36	Tennessee	42,144	1.1%
37	Kentucky	40,408	1.1%
38	Indiana	36,420	1.0%
39	Maine	35,380	0.9%
40	South Carolina	32,020	0.8%
41	West Virginia	24,230	0.6%
42	Maryland	12,406	0.3%
43	Hawaii	10,932	0.3%
44	Massachusetts	10,554	0.3%
45	Vermont	9,616	0.3%
46	New Hampshire	9,349	0.2%
47	New Jersey	8,723	0.2%
48	Connecticut	5,543	0.1%
49	Delaware	2,489	0.1%
50	Rhode Island	1,545	0.0%
	District of Columbia	68	0.0%

Source: U.S. Bureau of the Census
   "State Area Measurements" (http://www.census.gov/geo/reference/state-area.html)
*Total of land and water area. Revised figures as of January 1, 2010

Land Area of States in Square Miles in 2010

National Total = 3,531,905 Square Miles of Land Area*

ALPHA ORDER

RANK	STATE	MILES	% of USA
28	Alabama	50,645	1.4%
1	Alaska	570,641	16.2%
6	Arizona	113,594	3.2%
27	Arkansas	52,035	1.5%
3	California	155,779	4.4%
8	Colorado	103,642	2.9%
48	Connecticut	4,842	0.1%
49	Delaware	1,949	0.1%
26	Florida	53,625	1.5%
21	Georgia	57,513	1.6%
47	Hawaii	6,423	0.2%
11	Idaho	82,643	2.3%
24	Illinois	55,519	1.6%
38	Indiana	35,826	1.0%
23	Iowa	55,857	1.6%
13	Kansas	81,759	2.3%
37	Kentucky	39,486	1.1%
33	Louisiana	43,204	1.2%
39	Maine	30,843	0.9%
42	Maryland	9,707	0.3%
45	Massachusetts	7,800	0.2%
22	Michigan	56,539	1.6%
14	Minnesota	79,627	2.3%
31	Mississippi	46,923	1.3%
18	Missouri	68,742	1.9%
4	Montana	145,546	4.1%
15	Nebraska	76,824	2.2%
7	Nevada	109,781	3.1%
44	New Hampshire	8,953	0.3%
46	New Jersey	7,354	0.2%
5	New Mexico	121,298	3.4%
30	New York	47,126	1.3%
29	North Carolina	48,618	1.4%
17	North Dakota	69,001	2.0%
35	Ohio	40,861	1.2%
19	Oklahoma	68,595	1.9%
10	Oregon	95,988	2.7%
32	Pennsylvania	44,743	1.3%
50	Rhode Island	1,034	0.0%
40	South Carolina	30,061	0.9%
16	South Dakota	75,811	2.1%
34	Tennessee	41,235	1.2%
2	Texas	261,232	7.4%
12	Utah	82,170	2.3%
43	Vermont	9,217	0.3%
36	Virginia	39,490	1.1%
20	Washington	66,456	1.9%
41	West Virginia	24,038	0.7%
25	Wisconsin	54,158	1.5%
9	Wyoming	97,093	2.7%

RANK ORDER

RANK	STATE	MILES	% of USA
1	Alaska	570,641	16.2%
2	Texas	261,232	7.4%
3	California	155,779	4.4%
4	Montana	145,546	4.1%
5	New Mexico	121,298	3.4%
6	Arizona	113,594	3.2%
7	Nevada	109,781	3.1%
8	Colorado	103,642	2.9%
9	Wyoming	97,093	2.7%
10	Oregon	95,988	2.7%
11	Idaho	82,643	2.3%
12	Utah	82,170	2.3%
13	Kansas	81,759	2.3%
14	Minnesota	79,627	2.3%
15	Nebraska	76,824	2.2%
16	South Dakota	75,811	2.1%
17	North Dakota	69,001	2.0%
18	Missouri	68,742	1.9%
19	Oklahoma	68,595	1.9%
20	Washington	66,456	1.9%
21	Georgia	57,513	1.6%
22	Michigan	56,539	1.6%
23	Iowa	55,857	1.6%
24	Illinois	55,519	1.6%
25	Wisconsin	54,158	1.5%
26	Florida	53,625	1.5%
27	Arkansas	52,035	1.5%
28	Alabama	50,645	1.4%
29	North Carolina	48,618	1.4%
30	New York	47,126	1.3%
31	Mississippi	46,923	1.3%
32	Pennsylvania	44,743	1.3%
33	Louisiana	43,204	1.2%
34	Tennessee	41,235	1.2%
35	Ohio	40,861	1.2%
36	Virginia	39,490	1.1%
37	Kentucky	39,486	1.1%
38	Indiana	35,826	1.0%
39	Maine	30,843	0.9%
40	South Carolina	30,061	0.9%
41	West Virginia	24,038	0.7%
42	Maryland	9,707	0.3%
43	Vermont	9,217	0.3%
44	New Hampshire	8,953	0.3%
45	Massachusetts	7,800	0.2%
46	New Jersey	7,354	0.2%
47	Hawaii	6,423	0.2%
48	Connecticut	4,842	0.1%
49	Delaware	1,949	0.1%
50	Rhode Island	1,034	0.0%
	District of Columbia	61	0.0%

Source: U.S. Bureau of the Census
   "State Area Measurements" (http://www.census.gov/geo/reference/state-area.html)
*Includes dry land temporarily or partially covered by water, such as marshland, swamps, etc.; streams and canals under one-eighth mile wide; and lakes, reservoirs, and ponds under 40 acres. Revised figures as of August 2010.

Water Area of States in Square Miles in 2010

National Total = 264,837 Square Miles of Water*

RANK	STATE	MILES	% of USA
23	Alabama	1,775	0.7%
1	Alaska	94,743	35.8%
48	Arizona	396	0.1%
31	Arkansas	1,143	0.4%
6	California	7,916	3.0%
44	Colorado	452	0.2%
38	Connecticut	701	0.3%
40	Delaware	540	0.2%
3	Florida	12,133	4.6%
22	Georgia	1,912	0.7%
13	Hawaii	4,509	1.7%
33	Idaho	926	0.3%
19	Illinois	2,395	0.9%
39	Indiana	593	0.2%
45	Iowa	416	0.2%
42	Kansas	520	0.2%
34	Kentucky	921	0.3%
5	Louisiana	9,174	3.5%
12	Maine	4,537	1.7%
18	Maryland	2,699	1.0%
16	Massachusetts	2,754	1.0%
2	Michigan	40,175	15.2%
9	Minnesota	7,309	2.8%
25	Mississippi	1,509	0.6%
32	Missouri	965	0.4%
26	Montana	1,494	0.6%
41	Nebraska	524	0.2%
36	Nevada	791	0.3%
47	New Hampshire	397	0.1%
27	New Jersey	1,368	0.5%
49	New Mexico	292	0.1%
7	New York	7,429	2.8%
10	North Carolina	5,201	2.0%
24	North Dakota	1,698	0.6%
14	Ohio	3,965	1.5%
30	Oklahoma	1,304	0.5%
20	Oregon	2,391	0.9%
28	Pennsylvania	1,312	0.5%
43	Rhode Island	511	0.2%
21	South Carolina	1,960	0.7%
29	South Dakota	1,305	0.5%
35	Tennessee	909	0.3%
8	Texas	7,365	2.8%
17	Utah	2,727	1.0%
46	Vermont	400	0.2%
15	Virginia	3,285	1.2%
11	Washington	4,842	1.8%
50	West Virginia	192	0.1%
4	Wisconsin	11,339	4.3%
37	Wyoming	720	0.3%

RANK	STATE	MILES	% of USA
1	Alaska	94,743	35.8%
2	Michigan	40,175	15.2%
3	Florida	12,133	4.6%
4	Wisconsin	11,339	4.3%
5	Louisiana	9,174	3.5%
6	California	7,916	3.0%
7	New York	7,429	2.8%
8	Texas	7,365	2.8%
9	Minnesota	7,309	2.8%
10	North Carolina	5,201	2.0%
11	Washington	4,842	1.8%
12	Maine	4,537	1.7%
13	Hawaii	4,509	1.7%
14	Ohio	3,965	1.5%
15	Virginia	3,285	1.2%
16	Massachusetts	2,754	1.0%
17	Utah	2,727	1.0%
18	Maryland	2,699	1.0%
19	Illinois	2,395	0.9%
20	Oregon	2,391	0.9%
21	South Carolina	1,960	0.7%
22	Georgia	1,912	0.7%
23	Alabama	1,775	0.7%
24	North Dakota	1,698	0.6%
25	Mississippi	1,509	0.6%
26	Montana	1,494	0.6%
27	New Jersey	1,368	0.5%
28	Pennsylvania	1,312	0.5%
29	South Dakota	1,305	0.5%
30	Oklahoma	1,304	0.5%
31	Arkansas	1,143	0.4%
32	Missouri	965	0.4%
33	Idaho	926	0.3%
34	Kentucky	921	0.3%
35	Tennessee	909	0.3%
36	Nevada	791	0.3%
37	Wyoming	720	0.3%
38	Connecticut	701	0.3%
39	Indiana	593	0.2%
40	Delaware	540	0.2%
41	Nebraska	524	0.2%
42	Kansas	520	0.2%
43	Rhode Island	511	0.2%
44	Colorado	452	0.2%
45	Iowa	416	0.2%
46	Vermont	400	0.2%
47	New Hampshire	397	0.1%
48	Arizona	396	0.1%
49	New Mexico	292	0.1%
50	West Virginia	192	0.1%
	District of Columbia	7	0.0%

Source: U.S. Bureau of the Census
    "State Area Measurements" (http://www.census.gov/geo/reference/state-area.html)
*Includes permanent inland water surface, such as lakes, reservoirs, and ponds having an area of 40 acres or more, canals one-eighth mile or more in width; coastal waters behind or sheltered by headlands or islands separated by less than 1 nautical mile of water, and islands under 40 acres in area. Excludes areas of oceans, bays, etc., lying within U.S. jurisdiction but not defined as inland water. Revised figures as of August 2010.

Highest Point of Elevation in Feet

National High Point = 20,320 Feet Above Sea Level (Mt. McKinley, Alaska)

ALPHA ORDER

RANK	STATE	HIGHEST POINT
35	Alabama	2,407
1	Alaska	20,320
12	Arizona	12,633
34	Arkansas	2,753
2	California	14,494
3	Colorado	14,433
36	Connecticut	2,380
49	Delaware	448
50	Florida	345
25	Georgia	4,784
6	Hawaii	13,796
11	Idaho	12,662
45	Illinois	1,235
44	Indiana	1,257
42	Iowa	1,670
28	Kansas	4,039
27	Kentucky	4,145
48	Louisiana	535
22	Maine	5,268
32	Maryland	3,360
31	Massachusetts	3,491
38	Michigan	1,979
37	Minnesota	2,301
47	Mississippi	806
41	Missouri	1,772
10	Montana	12,799
20	Nebraska	5,424
9	Nevada	13,140
18	New Hampshire	6,288
40	New Jersey	1,803
8	New Mexico	13,161
21	New York	5,344
16	North Carolina	6,684
30	North Dakota	3,506
43	Ohio	1,550
23	Oklahoma	4,973
13	Oregon	11,239
33	Pennsylvania	3,213
46	Rhode Island	812
29	South Carolina	3,560
15	South Dakota	7,242
17	Tennessee	6,643
14	Texas	8,749
7	Utah	13,528
26	Vermont	4,393
19	Virginia	5,729
4	Washington	14,411
24	West Virginia	4,863
39	Wisconsin	1,951
5	Wyoming	13,804

RANK ORDER

RANK	STATE	HIGHEST POINT
1	Alaska	20,320
2	California	14,494
3	Colorado	14,433
4	Washington	14,411
5	Wyoming	13,804
6	Hawaii	13,796
7	Utah	13,528
8	New Mexico	13,161
9	Nevada	13,140
10	Montana	12,799
11	Idaho	12,662
12	Arizona	12,633
13	Oregon	11,239
14	Texas	8,749
15	South Dakota	7,242
16	North Carolina	6,684
17	Tennessee	6,643
18	New Hampshire	6,288
19	Virginia	5,729
20	Nebraska	5,424
21	New York	5,344
22	Maine	5,268
23	Oklahoma	4,973
24	West Virginia	4,863
25	Georgia	4,784
26	Vermont	4,393
27	Kentucky	4,145
28	Kansas	4,039
29	South Carolina	3,560
30	North Dakota	3,506
31	Massachusetts	3,491
32	Maryland	3,360
33	Pennsylvania	3,213
34	Arkansas	2,753
35	Alabama	2,407
36	Connecticut	2,380
37	Minnesota	2,301
38	Michigan	1,979
39	Wisconsin	1,951
40	New Jersey	1,803
41	Missouri	1,772
42	Iowa	1,670
43	Ohio	1,550
44	Indiana	1,257
45	Illinois	1,235
46	Rhode Island	812
47	Mississippi	806
48	Louisiana	535
49	Delaware	448
50	Florida	345
	District of Columbia	410

Source: U.S. Department of Interior, U.S. Geological Survey
"Elevations and Distances in the United States" (http://erg.usgs.gov/isb/pubs/booklets/elvadist/elvadist.html)

Lowest Point of Elevation in Feet

National Low Point = 282 Feet Below Sea Level (Death Valley, California)*

RANK	STATE	LOWEST POINT
3	Alabama	0
3	Alaska	0
26	Arizona	70
25	Arkansas	55
1	California	(282)
50	Colorado	3,315
3	Connecticut	0
3	Delaware	0
3	Florida	0
3	Georgia	0
3	Hawaii	0
42	Idaho	710
32	Illinois	279
34	Indiana	320
37	Iowa	480
41	Kansas	679
31	Kentucky	257
2	Louisiana	(8)
3	Maine	0
3	Maryland	0
3	Massachusetts	0
38	Michigan	571
40	Minnesota	601
3	Mississippi	0
29	Missouri	230
46	Montana	1,800
44	Nebraska	840
36	Nevada	479
3	New Hampshire	0
3	New Jersey	0
48	New Mexico	2,842
3	New York	0
3	North Carolina	0
43	North Dakota	750
35	Ohio	455
33	Oklahoma	289
3	Oregon	0
3	Pennsylvania	0
3	Rhode Island	0
3	South Carolina	0
45	South Dakota	966
28	Tennessee	178
3	Texas	0
47	Utah	2,000
27	Vermont	95
3	Virginia	0
3	Washington	0
30	West Virginia	240
39	Wisconsin	579
49	Wyoming	3,099

RANK	STATE	LOWEST POINT
1	California	(282)
2	Louisiana	(8)
3	Alabama*	0
3	Alaska	0
3	Connecticut	0
3	Delaware	0
3	Florida	0
3	Georgia	0
3	Hawaii	0
3	Maine	0
3	Maryland	0
3	Massachusetts	0
3	Mississippi	0
3	New Hampshire	0
3	New Jersey	0
3	New York	0
3	North Carolina	0
3	Oregon	0
3	Pennsylvania	0
3	Rhode Island	0
3	South Carolina	0
3	Texas	0
3	Virginia	0
3	Washington	0
25	Arkansas	55
26	Arizona	70
27	Vermont	95
28	Tennessee	178
29	Missouri	230
30	West Virginia	240
31	Kentucky	257
32	Illinois	279
33	Oklahoma	289
34	Indiana	320
35	Ohio	455
36	Nevada	479
37	Iowa	480
38	Michigan	571
39	Wisconsin	579
40	Minnesota	601
41	Kansas	679
42	Idaho	710
43	North Dakota	750
44	Nebraska	840
45	South Dakota	966
46	Montana	1,800
47	Utah	2,000
48	New Mexico	2,842
49	Wyoming	3,099
50	Colorado	3,315
	District of Columbia	1

Source: U.S. Department of Interior, U.S. Geological Survey
"Elevations and Distances in the United States" (http://erg.usgs.gov/isb/pubs/booklets/elvadist/elvadist.html)
*States with "0" have sea level as lowest point.

Approximate Mean Elevation in Feet

Approximate National Mean Elevation = 2,500 Feet Above Sea Level

<table>
<thead>
<tr><th colspan="3">ALPHA ORDER</th><th colspan="3">RANK ORDER</th></tr>
<tr><th>RANK</th><th>STATE</th><th>MEAN ELEVATION</th><th>RANK</th><th>STATE</th><th>MEAN ELEVATION</th></tr>
</thead>
<tbody>
<tr><td>40</td><td>Alabama</td><td>500</td><td>1</td><td>Colorado</td><td>6,800</td></tr>
<tr><td>15</td><td>Alaska</td><td>1,900</td><td>2</td><td>Wyoming</td><td>6,700</td></tr>
<tr><td>7</td><td>Arizona</td><td>4,100</td><td>3</td><td>Utah</td><td>6,100</td></tr>
<tr><td>36</td><td>Arkansas</td><td>650</td><td>4</td><td>New Mexico</td><td>5,700</td></tr>
<tr><td>11</td><td>California</td><td>2,900</td><td>5</td><td>Nevada</td><td>5,500</td></tr>
<tr><td>1</td><td>Colorado</td><td>6,800</td><td>6</td><td>Idaho</td><td>5,000</td></tr>
<tr><td>40</td><td>Connecticut</td><td>500</td><td>7</td><td>Arizona</td><td>4,100</td></tr>
<tr><td>50</td><td>Delaware</td><td>60</td><td>8</td><td>Montana</td><td>3,400</td></tr>
<tr><td>48</td><td>Florida</td><td>100</td><td>9</td><td>Oregon</td><td>3,300</td></tr>
<tr><td>37</td><td>Georgia</td><td>600</td><td>10</td><td>Hawaii</td><td>3,030</td></tr>
<tr><td>10</td><td>Hawaii</td><td>3,030</td><td>11</td><td>California</td><td>2,900</td></tr>
<tr><td>6</td><td>Idaho</td><td>5,000</td><td>12</td><td>Nebraska</td><td>2,600</td></tr>
<tr><td>37</td><td>Illinois</td><td>600</td><td>13</td><td>South Dakota</td><td>2,200</td></tr>
<tr><td>34</td><td>Indiana</td><td>700</td><td>14</td><td>Kansas</td><td>2,000</td></tr>
<tr><td>22</td><td>Iowa</td><td>1,100</td><td>15</td><td>Alaska</td><td>1,900</td></tr>
<tr><td>14</td><td>Kansas</td><td>2,000</td><td>15</td><td>North Dakota</td><td>1,900</td></tr>
<tr><td>33</td><td>Kentucky</td><td>750</td><td>17</td><td>Texas</td><td>1,700</td></tr>
<tr><td>48</td><td>Louisiana</td><td>100</td><td>17</td><td>Washington</td><td>1,700</td></tr>
<tr><td>37</td><td>Maine</td><td>600</td><td>19</td><td>West Virginia</td><td>1,500</td></tr>
<tr><td>43</td><td>Maryland</td><td>350</td><td>20</td><td>Oklahoma</td><td>1,300</td></tr>
<tr><td>40</td><td>Massachusetts</td><td>500</td><td>21</td><td>Minnesota</td><td>1,200</td></tr>
<tr><td>29</td><td>Michigan</td><td>900</td><td>22</td><td>Iowa</td><td>1,100</td></tr>
<tr><td>21</td><td>Minnesota</td><td>1,200</td><td>22</td><td>Pennsylvania</td><td>1,100</td></tr>
<tr><td>45</td><td>Mississippi</td><td>300</td><td>24</td><td>Wisconsin</td><td>1,050</td></tr>
<tr><td>32</td><td>Missouri</td><td>800</td><td>25</td><td>New Hampshire</td><td>1,000</td></tr>
<tr><td>8</td><td>Montana</td><td>3,400</td><td>25</td><td>New York</td><td>1,000</td></tr>
<tr><td>12</td><td>Nebraska</td><td>2,600</td><td>25</td><td>Vermont</td><td>1,000</td></tr>
<tr><td>5</td><td>Nevada</td><td>5,500</td><td>28</td><td>Virginia</td><td>950</td></tr>
<tr><td>25</td><td>New Hampshire</td><td>1,000</td><td>29</td><td>Michigan</td><td>900</td></tr>
<tr><td>46</td><td>New Jersey</td><td>250</td><td>29</td><td>Tennessee</td><td>900</td></tr>
<tr><td>4</td><td>New Mexico</td><td>5,700</td><td>31</td><td>Ohio</td><td>850</td></tr>
<tr><td>25</td><td>New York</td><td>1,000</td><td>32</td><td>Missouri</td><td>800</td></tr>
<tr><td>34</td><td>North Carolina</td><td>700</td><td>33</td><td>Kentucky</td><td>750</td></tr>
<tr><td>15</td><td>North Dakota</td><td>1,900</td><td>34</td><td>Indiana</td><td>700</td></tr>
<tr><td>31</td><td>Ohio</td><td>850</td><td>34</td><td>North Carolina</td><td>700</td></tr>
<tr><td>20</td><td>Oklahoma</td><td>1,300</td><td>36</td><td>Arkansas</td><td>650</td></tr>
<tr><td>9</td><td>Oregon</td><td>3,300</td><td>37</td><td>Georgia</td><td>600</td></tr>
<tr><td>22</td><td>Pennsylvania</td><td>1,100</td><td>37</td><td>Illinois</td><td>600</td></tr>
<tr><td>47</td><td>Rhode Island</td><td>200</td><td>37</td><td>Maine</td><td>600</td></tr>
<tr><td>43</td><td>South Carolina</td><td>350</td><td>40</td><td>Alabama</td><td>500</td></tr>
<tr><td>13</td><td>South Dakota</td><td>2,200</td><td>40</td><td>Connecticut</td><td>500</td></tr>
<tr><td>29</td><td>Tennessee</td><td>900</td><td>40</td><td>Massachusetts</td><td>500</td></tr>
<tr><td>17</td><td>Texas</td><td>1,700</td><td>43</td><td>Maryland</td><td>350</td></tr>
<tr><td>3</td><td>Utah</td><td>6,100</td><td>43</td><td>South Carolina</td><td>350</td></tr>
<tr><td>25</td><td>Vermont</td><td>1,000</td><td>45</td><td>Mississippi</td><td>300</td></tr>
<tr><td>28</td><td>Virginia</td><td>950</td><td>46</td><td>New Jersey</td><td>250</td></tr>
<tr><td>17</td><td>Washington</td><td>1,700</td><td>47</td><td>Rhode Island</td><td>200</td></tr>
<tr><td>19</td><td>West Virginia</td><td>1,500</td><td>48</td><td>Florida</td><td>100</td></tr>
<tr><td>24</td><td>Wisconsin</td><td>1,050</td><td>48</td><td>Louisiana</td><td>100</td></tr>
<tr><td>2</td><td>Wyoming</td><td>6,700</td><td>50</td><td>Delaware</td><td>60</td></tr>
<tr><td></td><td></td><td></td><td></td><td>District of Columbia</td><td>150</td></tr>
</tbody>
</table>

Source: U.S. Department of Interior, U.S. Geological Survey
"Elevations and Distances in the United States" (http://erg.usgs.gov/isb/pubs/booklets/elvadist/elvadist.html)

Normal Daily Mean Temperature*

ALPHA ORDER

RANK	STATE	MEAN TEMPERATURE
7	Alabama	63.7
50	Alaska	31.9
6	Arizona	63.9
10	Arkansas	62.0
12	California	60.3
38	Colorado	48.4
27	Connecticut	51.2
20	Delaware**	54.4
2	Florida	72.0
8	Georgia	63.6
1	Hawaii	75.7
31	Idaho	50.3
33	Illinois	50.1
24	Indiana	52.0
39	Iowa	48.1
22	Kansas	54.0
17	Kentucky	55.8
3	Louisiana	67.4
47	Maine	42.5
19	Maryland**	54.6
37	Massachusetts	49.3
45	Michigan	44.7
48	Minnesota	41.4
9	Mississippi	63.4
18	Missouri	55.2
46	Montana	44.0
36	Nebraska	49.4
24	Nevada	52.0
41	New Hampshire**	45.9
20	New Jersey	54.4
16	New Mexico	57.0
32	New York	50.2
13	North Carolina	60.1
49	North Dakota	41.3
34	Ohio	50.0
11	Oklahoma	60.5
28	Oregon	51.1
26	Pennsylvania	51.6
28	Rhode Island**	51.1
5	South Carolina	64.0
42	South Dakota	45.2
14	Tennessee	58.7
4	Texas	66.8
28	Utah	51.1
42	Vermont**	45.2
15	Virginia	57.2
34	Washington	50.0
23	West Virginia	52.7
40	Wisconsin	46.3
44	Wyoming	44.8

RANK ORDER

RANK	STATE	MEAN TEMPERATURE
1	Hawaii	75.7
2	Florida	72.0
3	Louisiana	67.4
4	Texas	66.8
5	South Carolina	64.0
6	Arizona	63.9
7	Alabama	63.7
8	Georgia	63.6
9	Mississippi	63.4
10	Arkansas	62.0
11	Oklahoma	60.5
12	California	60.3
13	North Carolina	60.1
14	Tennessee	58.7
15	Virginia	57.2
16	New Mexico	57.0
17	Kentucky	55.8
18	Missouri	55.2
19	Maryland**	54.6
20	Delaware**	54.4
20	New Jersey	54.4
22	Kansas	54.0
23	West Virginia	52.7
24	Indiana	52.0
24	Nevada	52.0
26	Pennsylvania	51.6
27	Connecticut	51.2
28	Oregon	51.1
28	Rhode Island**	51.1
28	Utah	51.1
31	Idaho	50.3
32	New York	50.2
33	Illinois	50.1
34	Ohio	50.0
34	Washington	50.0
36	Nebraska	49.4
37	Massachusetts	49.3
38	Colorado	48.4
39	Iowa	48.1
40	Wisconsin	46.3
41	New Hampshire**	45.9
42	South Dakota	45.2
42	Vermont**	45.2
44	Wyoming	44.8
45	Michigan	44.7
46	Montana	44.0
47	Maine	42.5
48	Minnesota	41.4
49	North Dakota	41.3
50	Alaska	31.9

District of Columbia 55.9

Source: CQ Press using data from U.S. Department of Commerce, National Oceanic and Atmospheric Administration
"Comparative Climatic Data Through 2012" (ftp://ftp.ncdc.noaa.gov/pub/data/ccd-data/CCD-2012.pdf)
*Based on 30-year averages, 1971-2000.
**Percentages from these states are from a single location. All other states are from two or more reporting cities within each state, which were averaged to determine each state's average.

Percent of Days That Are Sunny*

ALPHA ORDER				RANK ORDER		
RANK	STATE	PERCENT OF DAYS SUNNY		RANK	STATE	PERCENT OF DAYS SUNNY
26	Alabama	58		1	Arizona	85
50	Alaska	38		2	Nevada	76
1	Arizona	85		3	New Mexico	75
8	Arkansas	66		4	California	72
4	California	72		4	Colorado	72
4	Colorado	72		6	Utah	68
34	Connecticut**	56		7	Florida	67
36	Delaware**	55		8	Arkansas	66
7	Florida	67		8	Hawaii	66
16	Georgia	63		8	Kansas	66
8	Hawaii	66		8	Wyoming	66
14	Idaho	64		12	Oklahoma	65
31	Illinois	57		12	Texas	65
26	Indiana	58		14	Idaho	64
22	Iowa	60		14	Louisiana	64
8	Kansas	66		16	Georgia	63
36	Kentucky	55		16	Mississippi	63
14	Louisiana	64		16	Nebraska	63
31	Maine**	57		16	South Dakota	63
31	Maryland**	57		20	South Carolina	62
36	Massachusetts	55		21	Virginia	61
44	Michigan	49		22	Iowa	60
36	Minnesota	55		22	North Carolina	60
16	Mississippi	63		24	Montana	59
26	Missouri	58		24	North Dakota	59
24	Montana	59		26	Alabama	58
16	Nebraska	63		26	Indiana	58
2	Nevada	76		26	Missouri	58
48	New Hampshire	44		26	Rhode Island**	58
34	New Jersey**	56		26	Tennessee	58
3	New Mexico	75		31	Illinois	57
42	New York	51		31	Maine**	57
22	North Carolina	60		31	Maryland**	57
24	North Dakota	59		34	Connecticut**	56
42	Ohio	51		34	New Jersey**	56
12	Oklahoma	65		36	Delaware**	55
46	Oregon**	48		36	Kentucky	55
41	Pennsylvania	53		36	Massachusetts	55
26	Rhode Island**	58		36	Minnesota	55
20	South Carolina	62		40	Wisconsin	54
16	South Dakota	63		41	Pennsylvania	53
26	Tennessee	58		42	New York	51
12	Texas	65		42	Ohio	51
6	Utah	68		44	Michigan	49
44	Vermont**	49		44	Vermont**	49
21	Virginia	61		46	Oregon**	48
47	Washington	45		47	Washington	45
49	West Virginia**	40		48	New Hampshire	44
40	Wisconsin	54		49	West Virginia**	40
8	Wyoming	66		50	Alaska	38
					District of Columbia**	56

Source: CQ Press using data from U.S. Department of Commerce, National Oceanic and Atmospheric Administration
"Comparative Climatic Data Through 2012" (ftp://ftp.ncdc.noaa.gov/pub/data/ccd-data/CCD-2012.pdf)
*As a percent of possible sunshine updated through 2012.
**Percentages from these states are from a single location. All other states are from two or more reporting cities within each state, which were averaged to determine each state's average.

Average Wind Speed (MPH)*

RANK	STATE	MILES PER HOUR
41	Alabama	7.6
24	Alaska	9.3
42	Arizona	7.5
40	Arkansas	7.7
46	California	6.9
32	Colorado	8.5
19	Connecticut	9.6
26	Delaware**	9.0
33	Florida	8.3
45	Georgia	7.4
5	Hawaii	10.9
22	Idaho	9.4
18	Illinois	9.8
22	Indiana	9.4
6	Iowa	10.7
2	Kansas	12.0
39	Kentucky	7.8
36	Louisiana	8.1
27	Maine	8.9
30	Maryland**	8.6
1	Massachusetts	12.5
21	Michigan	9.5
11	Minnesota	10.2
48	Mississippi	6.5
13	Missouri	10.1
25	Montana	9.2
9	Nebraska	10.3
37	Nevada	8.0
47	New Hampshire**	6.7
15	New Jersey	10.0
16	New Mexico	9.9
11	New York	10.2
34	North Carolina	8.2
7	North Dakota	10.6
19	Ohio	9.6
3	Oklahoma	11.2
38	Oregon	7.9
30	Pennsylvania	8.6
8	Rhode Island	10.5
42	South Carolina	7.5
4	South Dakota	11.1
48	Tennessee	6.5
9	Texas	10.3
29	Utah**	8.8
27	Vermont**	8.9
34	Virginia	8.2
42	Washington	7.5
48	West Virginia	6.5
16	Wisconsin	9.9
13	Wyoming	10.1

RANK	STATE	MILES PER HOUR
1	Massachusetts	12.5
2	Kansas	12.0
3	Oklahoma	11.2
4	South Dakota	11.1
5	Hawaii	10.9
6	Iowa	10.7
7	North Dakota	10.6
8	Rhode Island	10.5
9	Nebraska	10.3
9	Texas	10.3
11	Minnesota	10.2
11	New York	10.2
13	Missouri	10.1
13	Wyoming	10.1
15	New Jersey	10.0
16	New Mexico	9.9
16	Wisconsin	9.9
18	Illinois	9.8
19	Connecticut	9.6
19	Ohio	9.6
21	Michigan	9.5
22	Idaho	9.4
22	Indiana	9.4
24	Alaska	9.3
25	Montana	9.2
26	Delaware**	9.0
27	Maine	8.9
27	Vermont**	8.9
29	Utah**	8.8
30	Maryland**	8.6
30	Pennsylvania	8.6
32	Colorado	8.5
33	Florida	8.3
34	North Carolina	8.2
34	Virginia	8.2
36	Louisiana	8.1
37	Nevada	8.0
38	Oregon	7.9
39	Kentucky	7.8
40	Arkansas	7.7
41	Alabama	7.6
42	Arizona	7.5
42	South Carolina	7.5
42	Washington	7.5
45	Georgia	7.4
46	California	6.9
47	New Hampshire**	6.7
48	Mississippi	6.5
48	Tennessee	6.5
48	West Virginia	6.5
	District of Columbia	8.4

Source: CQ Press using data from U.S. Department of Commerce, National Oceanic and Atmospheric Administration
"Comparative Climatic Data Through 2012" (ftp://ftp.ncdc.noaa.gov/pub/data/ccd-data/CCD-2012.pdf)
*Updated through 2012.
**Averages from these states are from a single location. All other states are from two or more reporting cities within each state,
which were averaged to determine each state's average.

Tornadoes in 2013

National Total = 942 Tornadoes*

ALPHA ORDER

RANK	STATE	TORNADOES	% of USA
15	Alabama	27	2.9%
43	Alaska	0	0.0%
38	Arizona	1	0.1%
13	Arkansas	30	3.2%
31	California	6	0.6%
15	Colorado	27	2.9%
33	Connecticut	3	0.3%
38	Delaware	1	0.1%
10	Florida	37	3.9%
15	Georgia	27	2.9%
43	Hawaii	0	0.0%
32	Idaho	5	0.5%
1	Illinois	69	7.3%
9	Indiana	41	4.4%
13	Iowa	30	3.2%
4	Kansas	58	6.2%
7	Kentucky	50	5.3%
12	Louisiana	34	3.6%
38	Maine	1	0.1%
25	Maryland	10	1.1%
38	Massachusetts	1	0.1%
22	Michigan	13	1.4%
24	Minnesota	11	1.2%
11	Mississippi	36	3.8%
6	Missouri	54	5.7%
25	Montana	10	1.1%
2	Nebraska	65	6.9%
43	Nevada	0	0.0%
43	New Hampshire	0	0.0%
33	New Jersey	3	0.3%
43	New Mexico	0	0.0%
27	New York	9	1.0%
23	North Carolina	12	1.3%
19	North Dakota	17	1.8%
18	Ohio	26	2.8%
5	Oklahoma	56	5.9%
33	Oregon	3	0.3%
27	Pennsylvania	9	1.0%
43	Rhode Island	0	0.0%
29	South Carolina	8	0.8%
20	South Dakota	15	1.6%
8	Tennessee	43	4.6%
2	Texas	65	6.9%
38	Utah	1	0.1%
43	Vermont	0	0.0%
33	Virginia	3	0.3%
37	Washington	2	0.2%
43	West Virginia	0	0.0%
20	Wisconsin	15	1.6%
29	Wyoming	8	0.8%

RANK ORDER

RANK	STATE	TORNADOES	% of USA
1	Illinois	69	7.3%
2	Nebraska	65	6.9%
2	Texas	65	6.9%
4	Kansas	58	6.2%
5	Oklahoma	56	5.9%
6	Missouri	54	5.7%
7	Kentucky	50	5.3%
8	Tennessee	43	4.6%
9	Indiana	41	4.4%
10	Florida	37	3.9%
11	Mississippi	36	3.8%
12	Louisiana	34	3.6%
13	Arkansas	30	3.2%
13	Iowa	30	3.2%
15	Alabama	27	2.9%
15	Colorado	27	2.9%
15	Georgia	27	2.9%
18	Ohio	26	2.8%
19	North Dakota	17	1.8%
20	South Dakota	15	1.6%
20	Wisconsin	15	1.6%
22	Michigan	13	1.4%
23	North Carolina	12	1.3%
24	Minnesota	11	1.2%
25	Maryland	10	1.1%
25	Montana	10	1.1%
27	New York	9	1.0%
27	Pennsylvania	9	1.0%
29	South Carolina	8	0.8%
29	Wyoming	8	0.8%
31	California	6	0.6%
32	Idaho	5	0.5%
33	Connecticut	3	0.3%
33	New Jersey	3	0.3%
33	Oregon	3	0.3%
33	Virginia	3	0.3%
37	Washington	2	0.2%
38	Arizona	1	0.1%
38	Delaware	1	0.1%
38	Maine	1	0.1%
38	Massachusetts	1	0.1%
38	Utah	1	0.1%
43	Alaska	0	0.0%
43	Hawaii	0	0.0%
43	Nevada	0	0.0%
43	New Hampshire	0	0.0%
43	New Mexico	0	0.0%
43	Rhode Island	0	0.0%
43	Vermont	0	0.0%
43	West Virginia	0	0.0%
	District of Columbia	0	0.0%

Source: National Weather Service, Storm Prediction Center
"Annual Severe Weather Report Summary - 2013" (www.spc.ncep.noaa.gov/climo/online/monthly/2013_annual_summary.html)
*Preliminary figures. Tornadoes striking more than one state are counted in each state.

Hazardous Weather Fatalities in 2012

National Total = 519 Fatalities*

RANK	STATE	FATALITIES	% of USA
11	Alabama	17	3.3%
37	Alaska	1	0.2%
19	Arizona	9	1.7%
21	Arkansas	8	1.5%
9	California	20	3.9%
23	Colorado	7	1.3%
30	Connecticut	3	0.6%
46	Delaware	0	0.0%
4	Florida	29	5.6%
37	Georgia	1	0.2%
37	Hawaii	1	0.2%
37	Idaho	1	0.2%
2	Illinois	47	9.1%
10	Indiana	19	3.7%
30	Iowa	3	0.6%
30	Kansas	3	0.6%
5	Kentucky	27	5.2%
15	Louisiana	12	2.3%
46	Maine	0	0.0%
27	Maryland	5	1.0%
46	Massachusetts	0	0.0%
19	Michigan	9	1.7%
23	Minnesota	7	1.3%
28	Mississippi	4	0.8%
3	Missouri	42	8.1%
28	Montana	4	0.8%
37	Nebraska	1	0.2%
15	Nevada	12	2.3%
37	New Hampshire	1	0.2%
6	New Jersey	24	4.6%
37	New Mexico	1	0.2%
1	New York	57	11.0%
15	North Carolina	12	2.3%
46	North Dakota	0	0.0%
18	Ohio	11	2.1%
12	Oklahoma	14	2.7%
30	Oregon	3	0.6%
8	Pennsylvania	23	4.4%
46	Rhode Island	0	0.0%
36	South Carolina	2	0.4%
37	South Dakota	1	0.2%
14	Tennessee	13	2.5%
6	Texas	24	4.6%
25	Utah	6	1.2%
30	Vermont	3	0.6%
21	Virginia	8	1.5%
25	Washington	6	1.2%
37	West Virginia	1	0.2%
12	Wisconsin	14	2.7%
30	Wyoming	3	0.6%

RANK	STATE	FATALITIES	% of USA
1	New York	57	11.0%
2	Illinois	47	9.1%
3	Missouri	42	8.1%
4	Florida	29	5.6%
5	Kentucky	27	5.2%
6	New Jersey	24	4.6%
6	Texas	24	4.6%
8	Pennsylvania	23	4.4%
9	California	20	3.9%
10	Indiana	19	3.7%
11	Alabama	17	3.3%
12	Oklahoma	14	2.7%
12	Wisconsin	14	2.7%
14	Tennessee	13	2.5%
15	Louisiana	12	2.3%
15	Nevada	12	2.3%
15	North Carolina	12	2.3%
18	Ohio	11	2.1%
19	Arizona	9	1.7%
19	Michigan	9	1.7%
21	Arkansas	8	1.5%
21	Virginia	8	1.5%
23	Colorado	7	1.3%
23	Minnesota	7	1.3%
25	Utah	6	1.2%
25	Washington	6	1.2%
27	Maryland	5	1.0%
28	Mississippi	4	0.8%
28	Montana	4	0.8%
30	Connecticut	3	0.6%
30	Iowa	3	0.6%
30	Kansas	3	0.6%
30	Oregon	3	0.6%
30	Vermont	3	0.6%
30	Wyoming	3	0.6%
36	South Carolina	2	0.4%
37	Alaska	1	0.2%
37	Georgia	1	0.2%
37	Hawaii	1	0.2%
37	Idaho	1	0.2%
37	Nebraska	1	0.2%
37	New Hampshire	1	0.2%
37	New Mexico	1	0.2%
37	South Dakota	1	0.2%
37	West Virginia	1	0.2%
46	Delaware	0	0.0%
46	Maine	0	0.0%
46	Massachusetts	0	0.0%
46	North Dakota	0	0.0%
46	Rhode Island	0	0.0%
	District of Columbia	0	0.0%

Source: National Weather Service, Water and Weather Services
"2012 Summary of Hazardous Weather Fatalities" (http://www.nws.noaa.gov/om/hazstats/state12.pdf)
*Includes lightning, tornado, thunderstorm, extreme temperature, flood, coastal storm, rip current, hurricane, winter storm, fog, avalanche, and other weather events. National total does not include 12 fatalities in U.S. waters or territories.

Cost of Damage from Hazardous Weather in 2012

National Total = $38,677,580,000*

ALPHA ORDER

RANK	STATE	DAMAGE	% of USA
42	Alabama	$7,450,000	0.0%
36	Alaska	24,150,000	0.1%
37	Arizona	21,700,000	0.1%
12	Arkansas	180,590,000	0.5%
30	California	37,020,000	0.1%
5	Colorado	1,162,830,000	3.0%
45	Connecticut	7,020,000	0.0%
43	Delaware	7,430,000	0.0%
15	Florida	129,230,000	0.3%
21	Georgia	61,390,000	0.2%
50	Hawaii	200,000	0.0%
10	Idaho	479,600,000	1.2%
4	Illinois	1,179,750,000	3.1%
19	Indiana	73,060,000	0.2%
3	Iowa	2,796,300,000	7.2%
9	Kansas	540,780,000	1.4%
13	Kentucky	165,080,000	0.4%
6	Louisiana	810,650,000	2.1%
49	Maine	1,100,000	0.0%
25	Maryland	47,900,000	0.1%
35	Massachusetts	26,190,000	0.1%
11	Michigan	197,070,000	0.5%
22	Minnesota	60,840,000	0.2%
29	Mississippi	39,130,000	0.1%
20	Missouri	72,410,000	0.2%
41	Montana	8,580,000	0.0%
8	Nebraska	550,880,000	1.4%
17	Nevada	82,150,000	0.2%
47	New Hampshire	5,280,000	0.0%
1	New Jersey	24,996,860,000	64.6%
28	New Mexico	39,330,000	0.1%
27	New York	39,940,000	0.1%
24	North Carolina	57,060,000	0.1%
46	North Dakota	6,000,000	0.0%
14	Ohio	135,990,000	0.4%
7	Oklahoma	656,180,000	1.7%
32	Oregon	30,760,000	0.1%
26	Pennsylvania	42,770,000	0.1%
39	Rhode Island	11,860,000	0.0%
40	South Carolina	9,380,000	0.0%
44	South Dakota	7,260,000	0.0%
18	Tennessee	81,770,000	0.2%
2	Texas	3,518,070,000	9.1%
34	Utah	27,230,000	0.1%
38	Vermont	14,630,000	0.0%
23	Virginia	57,580,000	0.1%
33	Washington	28,450,000	0.1%
16	West Virginia	102,560,000	0.3%
31	Wisconsin	32,930,000	0.1%
48	Wyoming	5,110,000	0.0%

RANK ORDER

RANK	STATE	DAMAGE	% of USA
1	New Jersey	$24,996,860,000	64.6%
2	Texas	3,518,070,000	9.1%
3	Iowa	2,796,300,000	7.2%
4	Illinois	1,179,750,000	3.1%
5	Colorado	1,162,830,000	3.0%
6	Louisiana	810,650,000	2.1%
7	Oklahoma	656,180,000	1.7%
8	Nebraska	550,880,000	1.4%
9	Kansas	540,780,000	1.4%
10	Idaho	479,600,000	1.2%
11	Michigan	197,070,000	0.5%
12	Arkansas	180,590,000	0.5%
13	Kentucky	165,080,000	0.4%
14	Ohio	135,990,000	0.4%
15	Florida	129,230,000	0.3%
16	West Virginia	102,560,000	0.3%
17	Nevada	82,150,000	0.2%
18	Tennessee	81,770,000	0.2%
19	Indiana	73,060,000	0.2%
20	Missouri	72,410,000	0.2%
21	Georgia	61,390,000	0.2%
22	Minnesota	60,840,000	0.2%
23	Virginia	57,580,000	0.1%
24	North Carolina	57,060,000	0.1%
25	Maryland	47,900,000	0.1%
26	Pennsylvania	42,770,000	0.1%
27	New York	39,940,000	0.1%
28	New Mexico	39,330,000	0.1%
29	Mississippi	39,130,000	0.1%
30	California	37,020,000	0.1%
31	Wisconsin	32,930,000	0.1%
32	Oregon	30,760,000	0.1%
33	Washington	28,450,000	0.1%
34	Utah	27,230,000	0.1%
35	Massachusetts	26,190,000	0.1%
36	Alaska	24,150,000	0.1%
37	Arizona	21,700,000	0.1%
38	Vermont	14,630,000	0.0%
39	Rhode Island	11,860,000	0.0%
40	South Carolina	9,380,000	0.0%
41	Montana	8,580,000	0.0%
42	Alabama	7,450,000	0.0%
43	Delaware	7,430,000	0.0%
44	South Dakota	7,260,000	0.0%
45	Connecticut	7,020,000	0.0%
46	North Dakota	6,000,000	0.0%
47	New Hampshire	5,280,000	0.0%
48	Wyoming	5,110,000	0.0%
49	Maine	1,100,000	0.0%
50	Hawaii	200,000	0.0%
	District of Columbia	100,000	0.0%

Source: National Weather Service, Water and Weather Services
"2012 Summary of Hazardous Weather Fatalities" (http://www.nws.noaa.gov/om/hazstats/state12.pdf)
*Includes property and crop damage from lightning, tornado, thunderstorm, extreme temperature, flood, coastal storm, rip current, hurricane, winter storm, fog, avalanche, and other weather events. National total does not include damage costs in U.S. territories.

National Park Service Land in 2013

National Total = 84,479,316 Acres*

ALPHA ORDER

RANK	STATE	ACRES	% of USA
41	Alabama	22,737	0.0%
1	Alaska	54,654,067	64.7%
3	Arizona	2,962,815	3.5%
25	Arkansas	104,977	0.1%
2	California	8,142,048	9.6%
11	Colorado	725,198	0.9%
46	Connecticut	7,782	0.0%
48	Delaware	900	0.0%
4	Florida	2,638,210	3.1%
34	Georgia	63,326	0.1%
17	Hawaii	369,166	0.4%
13	Idaho	518,224	0.6%
49	Illinois	115	0.0%
43	Indiana	15,540	0.0%
47	Iowa	2,713	0.0%
44	Kansas	11,636	0.0%
27	Kentucky	95,699	0.1%
39	Louisiana	23,545	0.0%
29	Maine	91,706	0.1%
31	Maryland	73,893	0.1%
35	Massachusetts	57,962	0.1%
12	Michigan	718,151	0.9%
20	Minnesota	301,330	0.4%
24	Mississippi	118,739	0.1%
30	Missouri	83,477	0.1%
8	Montana	1,274,364	1.5%
36	Nebraska	45,675	0.1%
10	Nevada	778,512	0.9%
42	New Hampshire	21,932	0.0%
26	New Jersey	99,243	0.1%
15	New Mexico	391,078	0.5%
32	New York	73,000	0.1%
14	North Carolina	407,045	0.5%
33	North Dakota	72,568	0.1%
37	Ohio	34,804	0.0%
45	Oklahoma	10,241	0.0%
21	Oregon	199,319	0.2%
22	Pennsylvania	138,015	0.2%
50	Rhode Island	5	0.0%
38	South Carolina	32,348	0.0%
19	South Dakota	302,998	0.4%
16	Tennessee	386,458	0.5%
9	Texas	1,247,913	1.5%
6	Utah	2,117,683	2.5%
40	Vermont	23,265	0.0%
18	Virginia	363,307	0.4%
7	Washington	1,967,532	2.3%
28	West Virginia	92,697	0.1%
23	Wisconsin	133,755	0.2%
5	Wyoming	2,396,424	2.8%

RANK ORDER

RANK	STATE	ACRES	% of USA
1	Alaska	54,654,067	64.7%
2	California	8,142,048	9.6%
3	Arizona	2,962,815	3.5%
4	Florida	2,638,210	3.1%
5	Wyoming	2,396,424	2.8%
6	Utah	2,117,683	2.5%
7	Washington	1,967,532	2.3%
8	Montana	1,274,364	1.5%
9	Texas	1,247,913	1.5%
10	Nevada	778,512	0.9%
11	Colorado	725,198	0.9%
12	Michigan	718,151	0.9%
13	Idaho	518,224	0.6%
14	North Carolina	407,045	0.5%
15	New Mexico	391,078	0.5%
16	Tennessee	386,458	0.5%
17	Hawaii	369,166	0.4%
18	Virginia	363,307	0.4%
19	South Dakota	302,998	0.4%
20	Minnesota	301,330	0.4%
21	Oregon	199,319	0.2%
22	Pennsylvania	138,015	0.2%
23	Wisconsin	133,755	0.2%
24	Mississippi	118,739	0.1%
25	Arkansas	104,977	0.1%
26	New Jersey	99,243	0.1%
27	Kentucky	95,699	0.1%
28	West Virginia	92,697	0.1%
29	Maine	91,706	0.1%
30	Missouri	83,477	0.1%
31	Maryland	73,893	0.1%
32	New York	73,000	0.1%
33	North Dakota	72,568	0.1%
34	Georgia	63,326	0.1%
35	Massachusetts	57,962	0.1%
36	Nebraska	45,675	0.1%
37	Ohio	34,804	0.0%
38	South Carolina	32,348	0.0%
39	Louisiana	23,545	0.0%
40	Vermont	23,265	0.0%
41	Alabama	22,737	0.0%
42	New Hampshire	21,932	0.0%
43	Indiana	15,540	0.0%
44	Kansas	11,636	0.0%
45	Oklahoma	10,241	0.0%
46	Connecticut	7,782	0.0%
47	Iowa	2,713	0.0%
48	Delaware	900	0.0%
49	Illinois	115	0.0%
50	Rhode Island	5	0.0%
	District of Columbia	7,131	0.0%

Source: National Park Service
   "Listing of Acreage by State" (unpublished data)
*As of December 31, 2013. Includes federal and nonfederal land in national parks, monuments, historic sites, recreation areas, preserves, battlefields, grasslands, seashores, parkways, trails, and rivers. Does not include land in national forest or wildlife areas. Includes 58,050 acres in U.S. territories.

Recreation Visits to National Park Service Areas in 2012

National Total = 282,765,682 Visits*

RANK	STATE	VISITS	% of USA
36	Alabama	717,724	0.3%
27	Alaska	2,412,524	0.9%
7	Arizona	9,979,972	3.5%
24	Arkansas	2,727,454	1.0%
1	California	35,991,200	12.7%
16	Colorado	5,811,546	2.1%
49	Connecticut	21,465	0.0%
50	Delaware	0	0.0%
6	Florida	10,366,613	3.7%
12	Georgia	7,350,309	2.6%
17	Hawaii	5,119,035	1.8%
40	Idaho	553,554	0.2%
42	Illinois	295,464	0.1%
29	Indiana	2,148,903	0.8%
44	Iowa	207,352	0.1%
45	Kansas	101,752	0.0%
30	Kentucky	1,717,853	0.6%
38	Louisiana	625,913	0.2%
26	Maine	2,431,052	0.9%
13	Maryland	6,658,643	2.4%
5	Massachusetts	10,487,447	3.7%
28	Michigan	2,192,477	0.8%
39	Minnesota	601,274	0.2%
14	Mississippi	6,449,713	2.3%
21	Missouri	4,171,826	1.5%
20	Montana	4,451,755	1.6%
41	Nebraska	304,046	0.1%
19	Nevada	4,808,929	1.7%
47	New Hampshire	33,663	0.0%
18	New Jersey	4,885,202	1.7%
33	New Mexico	1,502,808	0.5%
4	New York	12,633,278	4.5%
3	North Carolina	17,706,032	6.3%
37	North Dakota	669,242	0.2%
25	Ohio	2,611,158	0.9%
34	Oklahoma	1,497,654	0.5%
35	Oregon	875,271	0.3%
9	Pennsylvania	8,768,869	3.1%
46	Rhode Island	51,944	0.0%
31	South Carolina	1,566,756	0.6%
22	South Dakota	3,950,666	1.4%
10	Tennessee	8,414,094	3.0%
23	Texas	3,939,160	1.4%
8	Utah	9,503,304	3.4%
48	Vermont	32,403	0.0%
2	Virginia	23,398,517	8.3%
11	Washington	7,529,549	2.7%
32	West Virginia	1,543,425	0.5%
43	Wisconsin	273,933	0.1%
15	Wyoming	6,194,752	2.2%

RANK	STATE	VISITS	% of USA
1	California	35,991,200	12.7%
2	Virginia	23,398,517	8.3%
3	North Carolina	17,706,032	6.3%
4	New York	12,633,278	4.5%
5	Massachusetts	10,487,447	3.7%
6	Florida	10,366,613	3.7%
7	Arizona	9,979,972	3.5%
8	Utah	9,503,304	3.4%
9	Pennsylvania	8,768,869	3.1%
10	Tennessee	8,414,094	3.0%
11	Washington	7,529,549	2.7%
12	Georgia	7,350,309	2.6%
13	Maryland	6,658,643	2.4%
14	Mississippi	6,449,713	2.3%
15	Wyoming	6,194,752	2.2%
16	Colorado	5,811,546	2.1%
17	Hawaii	5,119,035	1.8%
18	New Jersey	4,885,202	1.7%
19	Nevada	4,808,929	1.7%
20	Montana	4,451,755	1.6%
21	Missouri	4,171,826	1.5%
22	South Dakota	3,950,666	1.4%
23	Texas	3,939,160	1.4%
24	Arkansas	2,727,454	1.0%
25	Ohio	2,611,158	0.9%
26	Maine	2,431,052	0.9%
27	Alaska	2,412,524	0.9%
28	Michigan	2,192,477	0.8%
29	Indiana	2,148,903	0.8%
30	Kentucky	1,717,853	0.6%
31	South Carolina	1,566,756	0.6%
32	West Virginia	1,543,425	0.5%
33	New Mexico	1,502,808	0.5%
34	Oklahoma	1,497,654	0.5%
35	Oregon	875,271	0.3%
36	Alabama	717,724	0.3%
37	North Dakota	669,242	0.2%
38	Louisiana	625,913	0.2%
39	Minnesota	601,274	0.2%
40	Idaho	553,554	0.2%
41	Nebraska	304,046	0.1%
42	Illinois	295,464	0.1%
43	Wisconsin	273,933	0.1%
44	Iowa	207,352	0.1%
45	Kansas	101,752	0.0%
46	Rhode Island	51,944	0.0%
47	New Hampshire	33,663	0.0%
48	Vermont	32,403	0.0%
49	Connecticut	21,465	0.0%
50	Delaware	0	0.0%
	District of Columbia	34,286,073	12.1%

Source: National Park Service, Public Use Statistics Office
"National Park Service Statistical Abstract 2012" (https://irma.nps.gov/Stats/Reports/AbstractsandForecasts)
*National total includes 2,192,133 visits in U.S. territories.

Percent Change in National Park Service Recreation Visits: 2011 to 2012

National Percent Change = 1.4% Increase*

ALPHA ORDER				RANK ORDER		
RANK	STATE	PERCENT CHANGE		RANK	STATE	PERCENT CHANGE
42	Alabama	(5.0)		1	Oklahoma	22.4
19	Alaska	3.4		2	North Dakota	13.1
37	Arizona	(1.5)		3	Kansas	12.6
43	Arkansas	(5.3)		4	Michigan	11.8
30	California	1.5		5	Vermont	11.5
33	Colorado	(0.1)		6	Nebraska	10.1
40	Connecticut	(4.2)		7	Maryland	9.8
NA	Delaware**	NA		8	Montana	9.6
39	Florida	(2.0)		9	Louisiana	8.3
25	Georgia	2.5		9	Tennessee	8.3
12	Hawaii	7.0		11	Ohio	8.0
46	Idaho	(8.0)		12	Hawaii	7.0
34	Illinois	(0.3)		13	Missouri	6.6
24	Indiana	2.6		14	Minnesota	5.0
41	Iowa	(4.4)		15	West Virginia	4.4
3	Kansas	12.6		16	Oregon	4.2
20	Kentucky	3.1		17	Wyoming	4.0
9	Louisiana	8.3		18	South Dakota	3.8
27	Maine	2.4		19	Alaska	3.4
7	Maryland	9.8		20	Kentucky	3.1
25	Massachusetts	2.5		21	New Hampshire	3.0
4	Michigan	11.8		21	North Carolina	3.0
14	Minnesota	5.0		23	Pennsylvania	2.8
45	Mississippi	(7.7)		24	Indiana	2.6
13	Missouri	6.6		25	Georgia	2.5
8	Montana	9.6		25	Massachusetts	2.5
6	Nebraska	10.1		27	Maine	2.4
38	Nevada	(1.6)		27	Utah	2.4
21	New Hampshire	3.0		29	Rhode Island	2.0
47	New Jersey	(8.8)		30	California	1.5
32	New Mexico	0.8		30	Washington	1.5
49	New York	(22.0)		32	New Mexico	0.8
21	North Carolina	3.0		33	Colorado	(0.1)
2	North Dakota	13.1		34	Illinois	(0.3)
11	Ohio	8.0		34	Virginia	(0.3)
1	Oklahoma	22.4		36	South Carolina	(1.4)
16	Oregon	4.2		37	Arizona	(1.5)
23	Pennsylvania	2.8		38	Nevada	(1.6)
29	Rhode Island	2.0		39	Florida	(2.0)
36	South Carolina	(1.4)		40	Connecticut	(4.2)
18	South Dakota	3.8		41	Iowa	(4.4)
9	Tennessee	8.3		42	Alabama	(5.0)
44	Texas	(6.5)		43	Arkansas	(5.3)
27	Utah	2.4		44	Texas	(6.5)
5	Vermont	11.5		45	Mississippi	(7.7)
34	Virginia	(0.3)		46	Idaho	(8.0)
30	Washington	1.5		47	New Jersey	(8.8)
15	West Virginia	4.4		48	Wisconsin	(12.5)
48	Wisconsin	(12.5)		49	New York	(22.0)
17	Wyoming	4.0		NA	Delaware**	NA
					District of Columbia	12.1

Source: National Park Service, Public Use Statistics Office
"National Park Service Statistical Abstract 2012" (https://irma.nps.gov/Stats/Reports/AbstractsandForecasts)
*National percent change includes visits in U.S. territories.
**Not applicable.

State Parks, Recreation Areas, and Natural Areas in 2010

National Total = 7,810 Areas*

ALPHA ORDER

RANK	STATE	AREAS	% of USA
50	Alabama	22	0.3%
11	Alaska	139	1.8%
45	Arizona	32	0.4%
34	Arkansas	52	0.7%
5	California	278	3.6%
9	Colorado	168	2.2%
12	Connecticut	137	1.8%
43	Delaware	34	0.4%
10	Florida	160	2.0%
26	Georgia	73	0.9%
28	Hawaii	68	0.9%
43	Idaho	34	0.4%
4	Illinois	319	4.1%
42	Indiana	37	0.5%
8	Iowa	179	2.3%
47	Kansas	25	0.3%
35	Kentucky	51	0.7%
31	Louisiana	60	0.8%
13	Maine	136	1.7%
30	Maryland	65	0.8%
3	Massachusetts	339	4.3%
18	Michigan	98	1.3%
1	Minnesota	1,783	22.8%
47	Mississippi	25	0.3%
21	Missouri	85	1.1%
28	Montana	68	0.9%
21	Nebraska	85	1.1%
47	Nevada	25	0.3%
19	New Hampshire	91	1.2%
16	New Jersey	117	1.5%
41	New Mexico	38	0.5%
2	New York	1,418	18.2%
27	North Carolina	70	0.9%
46	North Dakota	31	0.4%
25	Ohio	75	1.0%
39	Oklahoma	42	0.5%
6	Oregon	257	3.3%
15	Pennsylvania	121	1.5%
24	Rhode Island	77	1.0%
32	South Carolina	56	0.7%
14	South Dakota	131	1.7%
33	Tennessee	53	0.7%
20	Texas	90	1.2%
36	Utah	50	0.6%
17	Vermont	103	1.3%
38	Virginia	43	0.6%
7	Washington	201	2.6%
37	West Virginia	47	0.6%
23	Wisconsin	82	1.0%
40	Wyoming	40	0.5%

RANK ORDER

RANK	STATE	AREAS	% of USA
1	Minnesota	1,783	22.8%
2	New York	1,418	18.2%
3	Massachusetts	339	4.3%
4	Illinois	319	4.1%
5	California	278	3.6%
6	Oregon	257	3.3%
7	Washington	201	2.6%
8	Iowa	179	2.3%
9	Colorado	168	2.2%
10	Florida	160	2.0%
11	Alaska	139	1.8%
12	Connecticut	137	1.8%
13	Maine	136	1.7%
14	South Dakota	131	1.7%
15	Pennsylvania	121	1.5%
16	New Jersey	117	1.5%
17	Vermont	103	1.3%
18	Michigan	98	1.3%
19	New Hampshire	91	1.2%
20	Texas	90	1.2%
21	Missouri	85	1.1%
21	Nebraska	85	1.1%
23	Wisconsin	82	1.0%
24	Rhode Island	77	1.0%
25	Ohio	75	1.0%
26	Georgia	73	0.9%
27	North Carolina	70	0.9%
28	Hawaii	68	0.9%
28	Montana	68	0.9%
30	Maryland	65	0.8%
31	Louisiana	60	0.8%
32	South Carolina	56	0.7%
33	Tennessee	53	0.7%
34	Arkansas	52	0.7%
35	Kentucky	51	0.7%
36	Utah	50	0.6%
37	West Virginia	47	0.6%
38	Virginia	43	0.6%
39	Oklahoma	42	0.5%
40	Wyoming	40	0.5%
41	New Mexico	38	0.5%
42	Indiana	37	0.5%
43	Delaware	34	0.4%
43	Idaho	34	0.4%
45	Arizona	32	0.4%
46	North Dakota	31	0.4%
47	Kansas	25	0.3%
47	Mississippi	25	0.3%
47	Nevada	25	0.3%
50	Alabama	22	0.3%
	District of Columbia**	NA	NA

Source: The National Association of State Parks Directors
   "Annual Information Exchange" (http://www.naspd.org/)
*For the period July 1, 2009 through June 30, 2010. Includes operating and nonoperating state parks, recreation areas, natural areas, and other areas.
**Not applicable.

Visitors to State Parks and Recreation Areas in 2010

National Total = 740,733,016 Visitors*

RANK	STATE	VISITORS	% of USA
40	Alabama	3,838,568	0.5%
35	Alaska	5,405,238	0.7%
44	Arizona	2,267,407	0.3%
25	Arkansas	8,830,816	1.2%
1	California	65,036,234	8.8%
18	Colorado	12,285,251	1.7%
26	Connecticut	8,208,751	1.1%
36	Delaware	4,947,148	0.7%
11	Florida	20,110,021	2.7%
23	Georgia	9,722,243	1.3%
21	Hawaii	10,425,185	1.4%
39	Idaho	4,649,326	0.6%
6	Illinois	42,293,523	5.7%
14	Indiana	15,846,351	2.1%
17	Iowa	14,373,901	1.9%
28	Kansas	7,800,100	1.1%
33	Kentucky	7,013,120	0.9%
45	Louisiana	2,068,794	0.3%
43	Maine	2,602,097	0.4%
22	Maryland	10,131,635	1.4%
8	Massachusetts	35,270,780	4.8%
10	Michigan	21,167,130	2.9%
24	Minnesota	8,922,135	1.2%
48	Mississippi	1,217,409	0.2%
13	Missouri	16,214,980	2.2%
46	Montana	1,896,183	0.3%
19	Nebraska	11,143,763	1.5%
42	Nevada	3,045,556	0.4%
47	New Hampshire	1,585,665	0.2%
12	New Jersey	17,163,594	2.3%
37	New Mexico	4,768,710	0.6%
2	New York	56,322,000	7.6%
15	North Carolina	14,899,149	2.0%
49	North Dakota	1,086,058	0.1%
3	Ohio	53,813,556	7.3%
20	Oklahoma	11,087,826	1.5%
5	Oregon	43,755,240	5.9%
7	Pennsylvania	38,523,251	5.2%
34	Rhode Island	5,871,944	0.8%
27	South Carolina	8,197,483	1.1%
29	South Dakota	7,785,502	1.1%
9	Tennessee	29,918,632	4.0%
30	Texas	7,473,693	1.0%
38	Utah	4,682,959	0.6%
50	Vermont	758,282	0.1%
31	Virginia	7,463,460	1.0%
4	Washington	44,134,793	6.0%
32	West Virginia	7,171,461	1.0%
16	Wisconsin	14,469,998	2.0%
41	Wyoming	3,066,115	0.4%

RANK	STATE	VISITORS	% of USA
1	California	65,036,234	8.8%
2	New York	56,322,000	7.6%
3	Ohio	53,813,556	7.3%
4	Washington	44,134,793	6.0%
5	Oregon	43,755,240	5.9%
6	Illinois	42,293,523	5.7%
7	Pennsylvania	38,523,251	5.2%
8	Massachusetts	35,270,780	4.8%
9	Tennessee	29,918,632	4.0%
10	Michigan	21,167,130	2.9%
11	Florida	20,110,021	2.7%
12	New Jersey	17,163,594	2.3%
13	Missouri	16,214,980	2.2%
14	Indiana	15,846,351	2.1%
15	North Carolina	14,899,149	2.0%
16	Wisconsin	14,469,998	2.0%
17	Iowa	14,373,901	1.9%
18	Colorado	12,285,251	1.7%
19	Nebraska	11,143,763	1.5%
20	Oklahoma	11,087,826	1.5%
21	Hawaii	10,425,185	1.4%
22	Maryland	10,131,635	1.4%
23	Georgia	9,722,243	1.3%
24	Minnesota	8,922,135	1.2%
25	Arkansas	8,830,816	1.2%
26	Connecticut	8,208,751	1.1%
27	South Carolina	8,197,483	1.1%
28	Kansas	7,800,100	1.1%
29	South Dakota	7,785,502	1.1%
30	Texas	7,473,693	1.0%
31	Virginia	7,463,460	1.0%
32	West Virginia	7,171,461	1.0%
33	Kentucky	7,013,120	0.9%
34	Rhode Island	5,871,944	0.8%
35	Alaska	5,405,238	0.7%
36	Delaware	4,947,148	0.7%
37	New Mexico	4,768,710	0.6%
38	Utah	4,682,959	0.6%
39	Idaho	4,649,326	0.6%
40	Alabama	3,838,568	0.5%
41	Wyoming	3,066,115	0.4%
42	Nevada	3,045,556	0.4%
43	Maine	2,602,097	0.4%
44	Arizona	2,267,407	0.3%
45	Louisiana	2,068,794	0.3%
46	Montana	1,896,183	0.3%
47	New Hampshire	1,585,665	0.2%
48	Mississippi	1,217,409	0.2%
49	North Dakota	1,086,058	0.1%
50	Vermont	758,282	0.1%
	District of Columbia**	NA	NA

Source: The National Association of State Parks Directors
   "Annual Information Exchange" (http://www.naspd.org/)
*For the period July 1, 2009 through June 30, 2010. Includes operating and nonoperating state parks, recreation areas, natural areas, and other areas. Includes day and overnight visitors.
**Not applicable.

IX. Government Finances: Federal

Internal Revenue Service Gross Collections in 2012

National Total = $2,524,320,134,000*

ALPHA ORDER					RANK ORDER			
RANK	STATE	COLLECTIONS	% of USA		RANK	STATE	COLLECTIONS	% of USA
31	Alabama	$20,882,949,000	0.8%		1	California	$292,563,574,000	11.6%
47	Alaska	4,898,780,000	0.2%		2	Texas	219,459,878,000	8.7%
23	Arizona	34,850,436,000	1.4%		3	New York	201,167,954,000	8.0%
26	Arkansas	25,299,832,000	1.0%		4	Illinois	124,431,227,000	4.9%
1	California	292,563,574,000	11.6%		5	Florida	122,249,635,000	4.8%
22	Colorado	41,252,701,000	1.6%		6	New Jersey	111,377,490,000	4.4%
19	Connecticut	47,262,702,000	1.9%		7	Ohio	111,094,276,000	4.4%
30	Delaware	21,835,412,000	0.9%		8	Pennsylvania	108,961,515,000	4.3%
5	Florida	122,249,635,000	4.8%		9	Massachusetts	79,826,976,000	3.2%
11	Georgia	65,498,308,000	2.6%		10	Minnesota	78,685,402,000	3.1%
42	Hawaii	6,511,578,000	0.3%		11	Georgia	65,498,308,000	2.6%
41	Idaho	7,622,490,000	0.3%		12	Virginia	64,297,400,000	2.5%
4	Illinois	124,431,227,000	4.9%		13	North Carolina	61,600,064,000	2.4%
16	Indiana	51,238,512,000	2.0%		14	Michigan	59,210,158,000	2.3%
33	Iowa	18,753,596,000	0.7%		15	Washington	52,443,862,000	2.1%
29	Kansas	21,904,615,000	0.9%		16	Indiana	51,238,512,000	2.0%
27	Kentucky	25,085,813,000	1.0%		17	Missouri	48,413,247,000	1.9%
24	Louisiana	34,811,072,000	1.4%		18	Maryland	48,107,002,000	1.9%
44	Maine	6,229,189,000	0.2%		19	Connecticut	47,262,702,000	1.9%
18	Maryland	48,107,002,000	1.9%		20	Tennessee	47,010,303,000	1.9%
9	Massachusetts	79,826,976,000	3.2%		21	Wisconsin	41,498,033,000	1.6%
14	Michigan	59,210,158,000	2.3%		22	Colorado	41,252,701,000	1.6%
10	Minnesota	78,685,402,000	3.1%		23	Arizona	34,850,436,000	1.4%
38	Mississippi	10,458,549,000	0.4%		24	Louisiana	34,811,072,000	1.4%
17	Missouri	48,413,247,000	1.9%		25	Oklahoma	27,087,264,000	1.1%
48	Montana	4,383,727,000	0.2%		26	Arkansas	25,299,832,000	1.0%
32	Nebraska	19,795,254,000	0.8%		27	Kentucky	25,085,813,000	1.0%
36	Nevada	13,727,425,000	0.5%		28	Oregon	22,716,602,000	0.9%
39	New Hampshire	8,807,691,000	0.3%		29	Kansas	21,904,615,000	0.9%
6	New Jersey	111,377,490,000	4.4%		30	Delaware	21,835,412,000	0.9%
40	New Mexico	7,866,206,000	0.3%		31	Alabama	20,882,949,000	0.8%
3	New York	201,167,954,000	8.0%		32	Nebraska	19,795,254,000	0.8%
13	North Carolina	61,600,064,000	2.4%		33	Iowa	18,753,596,000	0.7%
45	North Dakota	5,664,860,000	0.2%		34	South Carolina	18,557,166,000	0.7%
7	Ohio	111,094,276,000	4.4%		35	Utah	15,642,129,000	0.6%
25	Oklahoma	27,087,264,000	1.1%		36	Nevada	13,727,425,000	0.5%
28	Oregon	22,716,602,000	0.9%		37	Rhode Island	10,992,338,000	0.4%
8	Pennsylvania	108,961,515,000	4.3%		38	Mississippi	10,458,549,000	0.4%
37	Rhode Island	10,992,338,000	0.4%		39	New Hampshire	8,807,691,000	0.3%
34	South Carolina	18,557,166,000	0.7%		40	New Mexico	7,866,206,000	0.3%
46	South Dakota	5,136,249,000	0.2%		41	Idaho	7,622,490,000	0.3%
20	Tennessee	47,010,303,000	1.9%		42	Hawaii	6,511,578,000	0.3%
2	Texas	219,459,878,000	8.7%		43	West Virginia	6,498,502,000	0.3%
35	Utah	15,642,129,000	0.6%		44	Maine	6,229,189,000	0.2%
50	Vermont	3,524,887,000	0.1%		45	North Dakota	5,664,860,000	0.2%
12	Virginia	64,297,400,000	2.5%		46	South Dakota	5,136,249,000	0.2%
15	Washington	52,443,862,000	2.1%		47	Alaska	4,898,780,000	0.2%
43	West Virginia	6,498,502,000	0.3%		48	Montana	4,383,727,000	0.2%
21	Wisconsin	41,498,033,000	1.6%		49	Wyoming	3,828,379,000	0.2%
49	Wyoming	3,828,379,000	0.2%		50	Vermont	3,524,887,000	0.1%
						District of Columbia	20,747,652,000	0.8%

Source: U.S. Department of the Treasury, Internal Revenue Service
  "Fiscal Year 2012 IRS Data Book" (http://www.irs.gov/uac/SOI-Tax-Stats-IRS-Data-Book)
*Total includes $12,549,273,000 from U.S. citizens abroad and other miscellaneous returns not shown separately.

Per Capita Internal Revenue Service Gross Collections in 2012

National Per Capita = $8,001*

ALPHA ORDER

RANK	STATE	PER CAPITA
46	Alabama	$4,331
27	Alaska	6,697
40	Arizona	5,318
11	Arkansas	8,579
20	California	7,691
17	Colorado	7,952
3	Connecticut	13,164
1	Delaware	23,809
31	Florida	6,328
30	Georgia	6,603
44	Hawaii	4,677
42	Idaho	4,777
9	Illinois	9,664
19	Indiana	7,838
34	Iowa	6,100
22	Kansas	7,590
37	Kentucky	5,727
23	Louisiana	7,565
43	Maine	4,686
14	Maryland	8,175
5	Massachusetts	12,011
35	Michigan	5,991
2	Minnesota	14,628
49	Mississippi	3,504
16	Missouri	8,039
45	Montana	4,361
6	Nebraska	10,668
41	Nevada	4,976
28	New Hampshire	6,669
4	New Jersey	12,564
48	New Mexico	3,772
8	New York	10,279
32	North Carolina	6,317
15	North Dakota	8,097
10	Ohio	9,623
26	Oklahoma	7,101
36	Oregon	5,826
12	Pennsylvania	8,537
7	Rhode Island	10,466
47	South Carolina	3,929
33	South Dakota	6,163
24	Tennessee	7,281
13	Texas	8,422
39	Utah	5,478
38	Vermont	5,631
18	Virginia	7,855
21	Washington	7,604
50	West Virginia	3,502
25	Wisconsin	7,247
29	Wyoming	6,642

RANK ORDER

RANK	STATE	PER CAPITA
1	Delaware	$23,809
2	Minnesota	14,628
3	Connecticut	13,164
4	New Jersey	12,564
5	Massachusetts	12,011
6	Nebraska	10,668
7	Rhode Island	10,466
8	New York	10,279
9	Illinois	9,664
10	Ohio	9,623
11	Arkansas	8,579
12	Pennsylvania	8,537
13	Texas	8,422
14	Maryland	8,175
15	North Dakota	8,097
16	Missouri	8,039
17	Colorado	7,952
18	Virginia	7,855
19	Indiana	7,838
20	California	7,691
21	Washington	7,604
22	Kansas	7,590
23	Louisiana	7,565
24	Tennessee	7,281
25	Wisconsin	7,247
26	Oklahoma	7,101
27	Alaska	6,697
28	New Hampshire	6,669
29	Wyoming	6,642
30	Georgia	6,603
31	Florida	6,328
32	North Carolina	6,317
33	South Dakota	6,163
34	Iowa	6,100
35	Michigan	5,991
36	Oregon	5,826
37	Kentucky	5,727
38	Vermont	5,631
39	Utah	5,478
40	Arizona	5,318
41	Nevada	4,976
42	Idaho	4,777
43	Maine	4,686
44	Hawaii	4,677
45	Montana	4,361
46	Alabama	4,331
47	South Carolina	3,929
48	New Mexico	3,772
49	Mississippi	3,504
50	West Virginia	3,502

District of Columbia   32,812

Source: CQ Press using data from U.S. Department of the Treasury, Internal Revenue Service
"Fiscal Year 2012 IRS Data Book" (http://www.irs.gov/uac/SOI-Tax-Stats-IRS-Data-Book)
*National per capita does not include collections from U.S. citizens abroad and other miscellaneous returns not shown separately.

Federal Individual Income Tax Collections in 2012

National Total = $2,172,233,368,000*

ALPHA ORDER

RANK	STATE	COLLECTIONS	% of USA
28	Alabama	$19,500,672,000	0.9%
47	Alaska	4,640,174,000	0.2%
24	Arizona	29,968,613,000	1.4%
30	Arkansas	18,266,603,000	0.8%
1	California	249,275,399,000	11.5%
21	Colorado	36,113,422,000	1.7%
20	Connecticut	40,875,490,000	1.9%
33	Delaware	14,602,084,000	0.7%
4	Florida	113,188,889,000	5.2%
13	Georgia	53,987,301,000	2.5%
43	Hawaii	5,922,132,000	0.3%
41	Idaho	7,169,783,000	0.3%
5	Illinois	103,654,375,000	4.8%
16	Indiana	47,141,859,000	2.2%
31	Iowa	17,210,796,000	0.8%
29	Kansas	18,510,512,000	0.9%
25	Kentucky	22,986,776,000	1.1%
23	Louisiana	33,187,181,000	1.5%
44	Maine	5,542,557,000	0.3%
17	Maryland	45,186,159,000	2.1%
9	Massachusetts	73,152,183,000	3.4%
11	Michigan	54,959,506,000	2.5%
10	Minnesota	61,712,466,000	2.8%
37	Mississippi	9,693,914,000	0.4%
19	Missouri	40,997,767,000	1.9%
48	Montana	4,147,270,000	0.2%
34	Nebraska	13,470,845,000	0.6%
36	Nevada	12,737,643,000	0.6%
39	New Hampshire	8,370,452,000	0.4%
8	New Jersey	92,020,482,000	4.2%
40	New Mexico	7,494,229,000	0.3%
2	New York	176,938,759,000	8.1%
12	North Carolina	54,747,979,000	2.5%
45	North Dakota	5,268,271,000	0.2%
6	Ohio	95,611,009,000	4.4%
27	Oklahoma	19,789,170,000	0.9%
26	Oregon	21,131,294,000	1.0%
7	Pennsylvania	94,747,441,000	4.4%
38	Rhode Island	8,607,614,000	0.4%
32	South Carolina	17,064,717,000	0.8%
46	South Dakota	4,840,542,000	0.2%
18	Tennessee	41,867,521,000	1.9%
3	Texas	171,880,172,000	7.9%
35	Utah	13,227,408,000	0.6%
50	Vermont	3,236,379,000	0.1%
14	Virginia	53,807,056,000	2.5%
15	Washington	47,600,345,000	2.2%
42	West Virginia	6,082,100,000	0.3%
22	Wisconsin	35,757,347,000	1.6%
49	Wyoming	3,495,933,000	0.2%

RANK ORDER

RANK	STATE	COLLECTIONS	% of USA
1	California	$249,275,399,000	11.5%
2	New York	176,938,759,000	8.1%
3	Texas	171,880,172,000	7.9%
4	Florida	113,188,889,000	5.2%
5	Illinois	103,654,375,000	4.8%
6	Ohio	95,611,009,000	4.4%
7	Pennsylvania	94,747,441,000	4.4%
8	New Jersey	92,020,482,000	4.2%
9	Massachusetts	73,152,183,000	3.4%
10	Minnesota	61,712,466,000	2.8%
11	Michigan	54,959,506,000	2.5%
12	North Carolina	54,747,979,000	2.5%
13	Georgia	53,987,301,000	2.5%
14	Virginia	53,807,056,000	2.5%
15	Washington	47,600,345,000	2.2%
16	Indiana	47,141,859,000	2.2%
17	Maryland	45,186,159,000	2.1%
18	Tennessee	41,867,521,000	1.9%
19	Missouri	40,997,767,000	1.9%
20	Connecticut	40,875,490,000	1.9%
21	Colorado	36,113,422,000	1.7%
22	Wisconsin	35,757,347,000	1.6%
23	Louisiana	33,187,181,000	1.5%
24	Arizona	29,968,613,000	1.4%
25	Kentucky	22,986,776,000	1.1%
26	Oregon	21,131,294,000	1.0%
27	Oklahoma	19,789,170,000	0.9%
28	Alabama	19,500,672,000	0.9%
29	Kansas	18,510,512,000	0.9%
30	Arkansas	18,266,603,000	0.8%
31	Iowa	17,210,796,000	0.8%
32	South Carolina	17,064,717,000	0.8%
33	Delaware	14,602,084,000	0.7%
34	Nebraska	13,470,845,000	0.6%
35	Utah	13,227,408,000	0.6%
36	Nevada	12,737,643,000	0.6%
37	Mississippi	9,693,914,000	0.4%
38	Rhode Island	8,607,614,000	0.4%
39	New Hampshire	8,370,452,000	0.4%
40	New Mexico	7,494,229,000	0.3%
41	Idaho	7,169,783,000	0.3%
42	West Virginia	6,082,100,000	0.3%
43	Hawaii	5,922,132,000	0.3%
44	Maine	5,542,557,000	0.3%
45	North Dakota	5,268,271,000	0.2%
46	South Dakota	4,840,542,000	0.2%
47	Alaska	4,640,174,000	0.2%
48	Montana	4,147,270,000	0.2%
49	Wyoming	3,495,933,000	0.2%
50	Vermont	3,236,379,000	0.1%
	District of Columbia	20,139,227,000	0.9%

Source: U.S. Department of the Treasury, Internal Revenue Service
  "Fiscal Year 2012 IRS Data Book" (http://www.irs.gov/uac/SOI-Tax-Stats-IRS-Data-Book)
*Total includes $10,705,550,000 from U.S. citizens abroad and other miscellaneous returns not shown separately.

Average Revenue Collection per Federal Individual Income Tax Return in 2012

National Average = $14,853 per Return*

ALPHA ORDER

RANK	STATE	PER RETURN
43	Alabama	$9,310
27	Alaska	12,555
39	Arizona	10,820
20	Arkansas	14,854
21	California	14,719
18	Colorado	15,061
3	Connecticut	23,474
1	Delaware	33,854
37	Florida	11,625
34	Georgia	11,960
44	Hawaii	8,992
40	Idaho	10,762
8	Illinois	16,983
12	Indiana	15,675
31	Iowa	12,173
24	Kansas	13,988
30	Kentucky	12,291
10	Louisiana	16,476
45	Maine	8,808
11	Maryland	16,015
4	Massachusetts	22,628
36	Michigan	11,794
2	Minnesota	23,846
50	Mississippi	7,538
17	Missouri	15,090
46	Montana	8,682
13	Nebraska	15,533
42	Nevada	9,869
28	New Hampshire	12,401
5	New Jersey	21,306
48	New Mexico	8,216
6	New York	18,915
26	North Carolina	12,844
14	North Dakota	15,500
7	Ohio	17,410
29	Oklahoma	12,326
32	Oregon	12,082
15	Pennsylvania	15,349
9	Rhode Island	16,799
47	South Carolina	8,234
35	South Dakota	11,819
22	Tennessee	14,468
16	Texas	15,221
38	Utah	11,479
41	Vermont	10,152
23	Virginia	14,235
19	Washington	14,908
49	West Virginia	7,708
25	Wisconsin	12,921
33	Wyoming	12,000

RANK ORDER

RANK	STATE	PER RETURN
1	Delaware	$33,854
2	Minnesota	23,846
3	Connecticut	23,474
4	Massachusetts	22,628
5	New Jersey	21,306
6	New York	18,915
7	Ohio	17,410
8	Illinois	16,983
9	Rhode Island	16,799
10	Louisiana	16,476
11	Maryland	16,015
12	Indiana	15,675
13	Nebraska	15,533
14	North Dakota	15,500
15	Pennsylvania	15,349
16	Texas	15,221
17	Missouri	15,090
18	Colorado	15,061
19	Washington	14,908
20	Arkansas	14,854
21	California	14,719
22	Tennessee	14,468
23	Virginia	14,235
24	Kansas	13,988
25	Wisconsin	12,921
26	North Carolina	12,844
27	Alaska	12,555
28	New Hampshire	12,401
29	Oklahoma	12,326
30	Kentucky	12,291
31	Iowa	12,173
32	Oregon	12,082
33	Wyoming	12,000
34	Georgia	11,960
35	South Dakota	11,819
36	Michigan	11,794
37	Florida	11,625
38	Utah	11,479
39	Arizona	10,820
40	Idaho	10,762
41	Vermont	10,152
42	Nevada	9,869
43	Alabama	9,310
44	Hawaii	8,992
45	Maine	8,808
46	Montana	8,682
47	South Carolina	8,234
48	New Mexico	8,216
49	West Virginia	7,708
50	Mississippi	7,538

District of Columbia	61,602

Source: CQ Press using data from U.S. Department of the Treasury, Internal Revenue Service
"Fiscal Year 2012 IRS Data Book" (http://www.irs.gov/uac/SOI-Tax-Stats-IRS-Data-Book)
*National Rate includes collections and returns from U.S. citizens abroad and other miscellaneous returns not shown separately.

Adjusted Gross Income in 2011

National Total = $8,378,794,024,000*

ALPHA ORDER

RANK	STATE	A.G.I.	% of USA
24	Alabama	$100,317,597,000	1.2%
46	Alaska	21,706,335,000	0.3%
21	Arizona	141,315,182,000	1.7%
34	Arkansas	57,281,450,000	0.7%
1	California	1,066,049,949,000	12.7%
17	Colorado	150,645,967,000	1.8%
20	Connecticut	146,101,673,000	1.7%
44	Delaware	24,590,469,000	0.3%
4	Florida	485,461,200,000	5.8%
12	Georgia	223,940,849,000	2.7%
40	Hawaii	34,372,459,000	0.4%
41	Idaho	30,728,223,000	0.4%
5	Illinois	371,414,191,000	4.4%
19	Indiana	147,573,636,000	1.8%
30	Iowa	75,359,890,000	0.9%
31	Kansas	73,272,170,000	0.9%
28	Kentucky	88,207,428,000	1.1%
25	Louisiana	99,162,456,000	1.2%
42	Maine	30,652,089,000	0.4%
15	Maryland	194,974,934,000	2.3%
10	Massachusetts	241,984,679,000	2.9%
11	Michigan	234,472,007,000	2.8%
16	Minnesota	157,793,380,000	1.9%
35	Mississippi	52,669,845,000	0.6%
23	Missouri	138,422,030,000	1.7%
45	Montana	22,419,479,000	0.3%
36	Nebraska	46,459,002,000	0.6%
32	Nevada	67,018,285,000	0.8%
37	New Hampshire	42,423,770,000	0.5%
7	New Jersey	316,448,772,000	3.8%
38	New Mexico	41,850,497,000	0.5%
3	New York	646,261,837,000	7.7%
13	North Carolina	215,963,437,000	2.6%
48	North Dakota	20,833,480,000	0.2%
8	Ohio	277,608,472,000	3.3%
29	Oklahoma	84,813,229,000	1.0%
27	Oregon	91,954,276,000	1.1%
6	Pennsylvania	348,612,836,000	4.2%
43	Rhode Island	29,193,327,000	0.3%
26	South Carolina	96,747,846,000	1.2%
47	South Dakota	21,289,609,000	0.3%
22	Tennessee	140,012,114,000	1.7%
2	Texas	665,901,147,000	7.9%
33	Utah	61,131,021,000	0.7%
50	Vermont	16,394,126,000	0.2%
9	Virginia	252,170,828,000	3.0%
14	Washington	200,197,882,000	2.4%
39	West Virginia	37,424,201,000	0.4%
18	Wisconsin	148,183,780,000	1.8%
49	Wyoming	18,086,478,000	0.2%

RANK ORDER

RANK	STATE	A.G.I.	% of USA
1	California	$1,066,049,949,000	12.7%
2	Texas	665,901,147,000	7.9%
3	New York	646,261,837,000	7.7%
4	Florida	485,461,200,000	5.8%
5	Illinois	371,414,191,000	4.4%
6	Pennsylvania	348,612,836,000	4.2%
7	New Jersey	316,448,772,000	3.8%
8	Ohio	277,608,472,000	3.3%
9	Virginia	252,170,828,000	3.0%
10	Massachusetts	241,984,679,000	2.9%
11	Michigan	234,472,007,000	2.8%
12	Georgia	223,940,849,000	2.7%
13	North Carolina	215,963,437,000	2.6%
14	Washington	200,197,882,000	2.4%
15	Maryland	194,974,934,000	2.3%
16	Minnesota	157,793,380,000	1.9%
17	Colorado	150,645,967,000	1.8%
18	Wisconsin	148,183,780,000	1.8%
19	Indiana	147,573,636,000	1.8%
20	Connecticut	146,101,673,000	1.7%
21	Arizona	141,315,182,000	1.7%
22	Tennessee	140,012,114,000	1.7%
23	Missouri	138,422,030,000	1.7%
24	Alabama	100,317,597,000	1.2%
25	Louisiana	99,162,456,000	1.2%
26	South Carolina	96,747,846,000	1.2%
27	Oregon	91,954,276,000	1.1%
28	Kentucky	88,207,428,000	1.1%
29	Oklahoma	84,813,229,000	1.0%
30	Iowa	75,359,890,000	0.9%
31	Kansas	73,272,170,000	0.9%
32	Nevada	67,018,285,000	0.8%
33	Utah	61,131,021,000	0.7%
34	Arkansas	57,281,450,000	0.7%
35	Mississippi	52,669,845,000	0.6%
36	Nebraska	46,459,002,000	0.6%
37	New Hampshire	42,423,770,000	0.5%
38	New Mexico	41,850,497,000	0.5%
39	West Virginia	37,424,201,000	0.4%
40	Hawaii	34,372,459,000	0.4%
41	Idaho	30,728,223,000	0.4%
42	Maine	30,652,089,000	0.4%
43	Rhode Island	29,193,327,000	0.3%
44	Delaware	24,590,469,000	0.3%
45	Montana	22,419,479,000	0.3%
46	Alaska	21,706,335,000	0.3%
47	South Dakota	21,289,609,000	0.3%
48	North Dakota	20,833,480,000	0.2%
49	Wyoming	18,086,478,000	0.2%
50	Vermont	16,394,126,000	0.2%
	District of Columbia	25,217,823,000	0.3%

Source: U.S. Department of the Treasury, Internal Revenue Service
"Individual Tax Statistics, State Income" (http://www.irs.gov/taxstats/index.html)
*Total includes $55,706,382,000 from U.S. citizens abroad and other miscellaneous returns not shown separately.

Per Capita Adjusted Gross Income in 2011

National Per Capita = $26,712*

ALPHA ORDER

RANK	STATE	PER CAPITA
43	Alabama	$20,883
10	Alaska	29,987
40	Arizona	21,851
48	Arkansas	19,493
15	California	28,289
12	Colorado	29,444
1	Connecticut	40,734
18	Delaware	27,078
24	Florida	25,440
34	Georgia	22,822
26	Hawaii	24,941
49	Idaho	19,402
14	Illinois	28,882
35	Indiana	22,647
28	Iowa	24,594
23	Kansas	25,527
45	Kentucky	20,199
42	Louisiana	21,676
32	Maine	23,072
4	Maryland	33,389
2	Massachusetts	36,625
31	Michigan	23,740
11	Minnesota	29,509
50	Mississippi	17,690
33	Missouri	23,036
36	Montana	22,472
25	Nebraska	25,219
27	Nevada	24,639
6	New Hampshire	32,193
3	New Jersey	35,819
47	New Mexico	20,133
5	New York	33,139
38	North Carolina	22,377
9	North Dakota	30,425
29	Ohio	24,054
37	Oklahoma	22,413
30	Oregon	23,772
17	Pennsylvania	27,355
16	Rhode Island	27,786
44	South Carolina	20,702
22	South Dakota	25,850
39	Tennessee	21,878
20	Texas	25,980
41	Utah	21,721
19	Vermont	26,164
8	Virginia	31,115
13	Washington	29,340
46	West Virginia	20,176
21	Wisconsin	25,952
7	Wyoming	31,879

RANK ORDER

RANK	STATE	PER CAPITA
1	Connecticut	$40,734
2	Massachusetts	36,625
3	New Jersey	35,819
4	Maryland	33,389
5	New York	33,139
6	New Hampshire	32,193
7	Wyoming	31,879
8	Virginia	31,115
9	North Dakota	30,425
10	Alaska	29,987
11	Minnesota	29,509
12	Colorado	29,444
13	Washington	29,340
14	Illinois	28,882
15	California	28,289
16	Rhode Island	27,786
17	Pennsylvania	27,355
18	Delaware	27,078
19	Vermont	26,164
20	Texas	25,980
21	Wisconsin	25,952
22	South Dakota	25,850
23	Kansas	25,527
24	Florida	25,440
25	Nebraska	25,219
26	Hawaii	24,941
27	Nevada	24,639
28	Iowa	24,594
29	Ohio	24,054
30	Oregon	23,772
31	Michigan	23,740
32	Maine	23,072
33	Missouri	23,036
34	Georgia	22,822
35	Indiana	22,647
36	Montana	22,472
37	Oklahoma	22,413
38	North Carolina	22,377
39	Tennessee	21,878
40	Arizona	21,851
41	Utah	21,721
42	Louisiana	21,676
43	Alabama	20,883
44	South Carolina	20,702
45	Kentucky	20,199
46	West Virginia	20,176
47	New Mexico	20,133
48	Arkansas	19,493
49	Idaho	19,402
50	Mississippi	17,690

| | District of Columbia | 40,738 |

Source: CQ Press using data from U.S. Department of the Treasury, Internal Revenue Service
"Individual Tax Statistics, State Income" (http://www.irs.gov/taxstats/index.html)
*National per capita does not include income from U.S. citizens abroad and other miscellaneous returns not shown separately.

Federal Business Income Tax Collections in 2012

National Total = $281,461,580,000*

ALPHA ORDER

RANK	STATE	COLLECTIONS	% of USA
35	Alabama	$1,102,865,000	0.4%
47	Alaska	191,060,000	0.1%
25	Arizona	3,408,925,000	1.2%
14	Arkansas	6,304,626,000	2.2%
1	California	37,181,407,000	13.2%
21	Colorado	3,968,517,000	1.4%
17	Connecticut	5,431,458,000	1.9%
11	Delaware	7,087,549,000	2.5%
12	Florida	6,609,351,000	2.3%
10	Georgia	8,417,016,000	3.0%
40	Hawaii	398,720,000	0.1%
41	Idaho	367,921,000	0.1%
5	Illinois	17,337,038,000	6.2%
26	Indiana	3,228,361,000	1.1%
32	Iowa	1,315,070,000	0.5%
29	Kansas	1,980,014,000	0.7%
31	Kentucky	1,764,142,000	0.6%
36	Louisiana	1,102,737,000	0.4%
39	Maine	509,393,000	0.2%
27	Maryland	2,626,431,000	0.9%
18	Massachusetts	5,278,522,000	1.9%
23	Michigan	3,841,440,000	1.4%
6	Minnesota	16,121,685,000	5.7%
38	Mississippi	609,194,000	0.2%
16	Missouri	6,082,671,000	2.2%
49	Montana	156,415,000	0.1%
15	Nebraska	6,149,516,000	2.2%
37	Nevada	757,762,000	0.3%
46	New Hampshire	205,260,000	0.1%
4	New Jersey	17,459,934,000	6.2%
50	New Mexico	150,549,000	0.1%
3	New York	21,269,375,000	7.6%
13	North Carolina	6,411,802,000	2.3%
43	North Dakota	301,698,000	0.1%
7	Ohio	11,604,143,000	4.1%
20	Oklahoma	3,982,694,000	1.4%
33	Oregon	1,229,807,000	0.4%
8	Pennsylvania	11,222,657,000	4.0%
28	Rhode Island	2,327,315,000	0.8%
34	South Carolina	1,211,525,000	0.4%
45	South Dakota	235,097,000	0.1%
22	Tennessee	3,903,991,000	1.4%
2	Texas	27,984,282,000	9.9%
30	Utah	1,809,517,000	0.6%
44	Vermont	255,605,000	0.1%
9	Virginia	9,994,059,000	3.6%
24	Washington	3,793,982,000	1.3%
42	West Virginia	315,740,000	0.1%
19	Wisconsin	4,641,696,000	1.6%
48	Wyoming	175,685,000	0.1%

RANK ORDER

RANK	STATE	COLLECTIONS	% of USA
1	California	$37,181,407,000	13.2%
2	Texas	27,984,282,000	9.9%
3	New York	21,269,375,000	7.6%
4	New Jersey	17,459,934,000	6.2%
5	Illinois	17,337,038,000	6.2%
6	Minnesota	16,121,685,000	5.7%
7	Ohio	11,604,143,000	4.1%
8	Pennsylvania	11,222,657,000	4.0%
9	Virginia	9,994,059,000	3.6%
10	Georgia	8,417,016,000	3.0%
11	Delaware	7,087,549,000	2.5%
12	Florida	6,609,351,000	2.3%
13	North Carolina	6,411,802,000	2.3%
14	Arkansas	6,304,626,000	2.2%
15	Nebraska	6,149,516,000	2.2%
16	Missouri	6,082,671,000	2.2%
17	Connecticut	5,431,458,000	1.9%
18	Massachusetts	5,278,522,000	1.9%
19	Wisconsin	4,641,696,000	1.6%
20	Oklahoma	3,982,694,000	1.4%
21	Colorado	3,968,517,000	1.4%
22	Tennessee	3,903,991,000	1.4%
23	Michigan	3,841,440,000	1.4%
24	Washington	3,793,982,000	1.3%
25	Arizona	3,408,925,000	1.2%
26	Indiana	3,228,361,000	1.1%
27	Maryland	2,626,431,000	0.9%
28	Rhode Island	2,327,315,000	0.8%
29	Kansas	1,980,014,000	0.7%
30	Utah	1,809,517,000	0.6%
31	Kentucky	1,764,142,000	0.6%
32	Iowa	1,315,070,000	0.5%
33	Oregon	1,229,807,000	0.4%
34	South Carolina	1,211,525,000	0.4%
35	Alabama	1,102,865,000	0.4%
36	Louisiana	1,102,737,000	0.4%
37	Nevada	757,762,000	0.3%
38	Mississippi	609,194,000	0.2%
39	Maine	509,393,000	0.2%
40	Hawaii	398,720,000	0.1%
41	Idaho	367,921,000	0.1%
42	West Virginia	315,740,000	0.1%
43	North Dakota	301,698,000	0.1%
44	Vermont	255,605,000	0.1%
45	South Dakota	235,097,000	0.1%
46	New Hampshire	205,260,000	0.1%
47	Alaska	191,060,000	0.1%
48	Wyoming	175,685,000	0.1%
49	Montana	156,415,000	0.1%
50	New Mexico	150,549,000	0.1%
	District of Columbia	392,793,000	0.1%

Source: U.S. Department of the Treasury, Internal Revenue Service
   "Fiscal Year 2012 IRS Data Book" (http://www.irs.gov/uac/SOI-Tax-Stats-IRS-Data-Book)
*Total includes collections and returns from international sources and others not distributed by state. Includes taxes on corporation income (Form 1120 series) and unrelated business income from tax-exempt organizations.

Average Revenue Collection per Federal Business Income Tax Return in 2012

National Average = $41,196 per Return*

<table>
<tr><td colspan="3">ALPHA ORDER</td><td colspan="3">RANK ORDER</td></tr>
<tr><td>RANK</td><td>STATE</td><td>PER RETURN</td><td>RANK</td><td>STATE</td><td>PER RETURN</td></tr>
<tr><td>35</td><td>Alabama</td><td>$15,743</td><td>1</td><td>Delaware</td><td>$289,950</td></tr>
<tr><td>37</td><td>Alaska</td><td>15,483</td><td>2</td><td>Nebraska</td><td>140,892</td></tr>
<tr><td>23</td><td>Arizona</td><td>28,889</td><td>3</td><td>Minnesota</td><td>123,788</td></tr>
<tr><td>4</td><td>Arkansas</td><td>115,465</td><td>4</td><td>Arkansas</td><td>115,465</td></tr>
<tr><td>16</td><td>California</td><td>49,139</td><td>5</td><td>Connecticut</td><td>99,883</td></tr>
<tr><td>27</td><td>Colorado</td><td>25,580</td><td>6</td><td>Rhode Island</td><td>93,253</td></tr>
<tr><td>5</td><td>Connecticut</td><td>99,883</td><td>7</td><td>New Jersey</td><td>87,000</td></tr>
<tr><td>1</td><td>Delaware</td><td>289,950</td><td>8</td><td>Ohio</td><td>64,686</td></tr>
<tr><td>48</td><td>Florida</td><td>8,380</td><td>9</td><td>Texas</td><td>63,997</td></tr>
<tr><td>19</td><td>Georgia</td><td>37,605</td><td>10</td><td>Virginia</td><td>60,480</td></tr>
<tr><td>40</td><td>Hawaii</td><td>14,227</td><td>11</td><td>Missouri</td><td>60,106</td></tr>
<tr><td>45</td><td>Idaho</td><td>10,367</td><td>12</td><td>Tennessee</td><td>57,340</td></tr>
<tr><td>14</td><td>Illinois</td><td>50,966</td><td>13</td><td>Oklahoma</td><td>54,495</td></tr>
<tr><td>24</td><td>Indiana</td><td>28,438</td><td>14</td><td>Illinois</td><td>50,966</td></tr>
<tr><td>29</td><td>Iowa</td><td>21,081</td><td>15</td><td>Pennsylvania</td><td>50,182</td></tr>
<tr><td>18</td><td>Kansas</td><td>38,161</td><td>16</td><td>California</td><td>49,139</td></tr>
<tr><td>26</td><td>Kentucky</td><td>26,104</td><td>17</td><td>Wisconsin</td><td>49,087</td></tr>
<tr><td>42</td><td>Louisiana</td><td>13,276</td><td>18</td><td>Kansas</td><td>38,161</td></tr>
<tr><td>33</td><td>Maine</td><td>16,470</td><td>19</td><td>Georgia</td><td>37,605</td></tr>
<tr><td>30</td><td>Maryland</td><td>20,807</td><td>20</td><td>Massachusetts</td><td>36,563</td></tr>
<tr><td>20</td><td>Massachusetts</td><td>36,563</td><td>21</td><td>North Carolina</td><td>33,115</td></tr>
<tr><td>32</td><td>Michigan</td><td>19,811</td><td>22</td><td>New York</td><td>32,461</td></tr>
<tr><td>3</td><td>Minnesota</td><td>123,788</td><td>23</td><td>Arizona</td><td>28,889</td></tr>
<tr><td>39</td><td>Mississippi</td><td>14,867</td><td>24</td><td>Indiana</td><td>28,438</td></tr>
<tr><td>11</td><td>Missouri</td><td>60,106</td><td>25</td><td>Washington</td><td>27,808</td></tr>
<tr><td>50</td><td>Montana</td><td>4,552</td><td>26</td><td>Kentucky</td><td>26,104</td></tr>
<tr><td>2</td><td>Nebraska</td><td>140,892</td><td>27</td><td>Colorado</td><td>25,580</td></tr>
<tr><td>44</td><td>Nevada</td><td>10,597</td><td>28</td><td>Utah</td><td>25,203</td></tr>
<tr><td>47</td><td>New Hampshire</td><td>9,093</td><td>29</td><td>Iowa</td><td>21,081</td></tr>
<tr><td>7</td><td>New Jersey</td><td>87,000</td><td>30</td><td>Maryland</td><td>20,807</td></tr>
<tr><td>49</td><td>New Mexico</td><td>4,959</td><td>31</td><td>North Dakota</td><td>20,113</td></tr>
<tr><td>22</td><td>New York</td><td>32,461</td><td>32</td><td>Michigan</td><td>19,811</td></tr>
<tr><td>21</td><td>North Carolina</td><td>33,115</td><td>33</td><td>Maine</td><td>16,470</td></tr>
<tr><td>31</td><td>North Dakota</td><td>20,113</td><td>34</td><td>Oregon</td><td>16,030</td></tr>
<tr><td>8</td><td>Ohio</td><td>64,686</td><td>35</td><td>Alabama</td><td>15,743</td></tr>
<tr><td>13</td><td>Oklahoma</td><td>54,495</td><td>36</td><td>Vermont</td><td>15,573</td></tr>
<tr><td>34</td><td>Oregon</td><td>16,030</td><td>37</td><td>Alaska</td><td>15,483</td></tr>
<tr><td>15</td><td>Pennsylvania</td><td>50,182</td><td>38</td><td>West Virginia</td><td>15,471</td></tr>
<tr><td>6</td><td>Rhode Island</td><td>93,253</td><td>39</td><td>Mississippi</td><td>14,867</td></tr>
<tr><td>41</td><td>South Carolina</td><td>14,160</td><td>40</td><td>Hawaii</td><td>14,227</td></tr>
<tr><td>43</td><td>South Dakota</td><td>12,681</td><td>41</td><td>South Carolina</td><td>14,160</td></tr>
<tr><td>12</td><td>Tennessee</td><td>57,340</td><td>42</td><td>Louisiana</td><td>13,276</td></tr>
<tr><td>9</td><td>Texas</td><td>63,997</td><td>43</td><td>South Dakota</td><td>12,681</td></tr>
<tr><td>28</td><td>Utah</td><td>25,203</td><td>44</td><td>Nevada</td><td>10,597</td></tr>
<tr><td>36</td><td>Vermont</td><td>15,573</td><td>45</td><td>Idaho</td><td>10,367</td></tr>
<tr><td>10</td><td>Virginia</td><td>60,480</td><td>46</td><td>Wyoming</td><td>9,857</td></tr>
<tr><td>25</td><td>Washington</td><td>27,808</td><td>47</td><td>New Hampshire</td><td>9,093</td></tr>
<tr><td>38</td><td>West Virginia</td><td>15,471</td><td>48</td><td>Florida</td><td>8,380</td></tr>
<tr><td>17</td><td>Wisconsin</td><td>49,087</td><td>49</td><td>New Mexico</td><td>4,959</td></tr>
<tr><td>46</td><td>Wyoming</td><td>9,857</td><td>50</td><td>Montana</td><td>4,552</td></tr>
<tr><td></td><td></td><td></td><td></td><td>District of Columbia</td><td>23,397</td></tr>
</table>

Source: CQ Press using data from U.S. Department of the Treasury, Internal Revenue Service
"Fiscal Year 2012 IRS Data Book" (http://www.irs.gov/uac/SOI-Tax-Stats-IRS-Data-Book)
*National average does not include income from U.S. citizens abroad and other miscellaneous returns not shown separately.
Includes taxes on corporation income (Form 1120 series) and unrelated business income from tax-exempt organizations.

Federal Tax Returns Filed in 2012

National Total = 237,345,350 Returns*

<table>
<tr><td colspan="4">ALPHA ORDER</td><td colspan="4">RANK ORDER</td></tr>
<tr><td>RANK</td><td>STATE</td><td>RETURNS</td><td>% of USA</td><td>RANK</td><td>STATE</td><td>RETURNS</td><td>% of USA</td></tr>
<tr><td>25</td><td>Alabama</td><td>3,147,518</td><td>1.3%</td><td>1</td><td>California</td><td>28,198,973</td><td>11.9%</td></tr>
<tr><td>48</td><td>Alaska</td><td>596,965</td><td>0.3%</td><td>2</td><td>Texas</td><td>17,834,945</td><td>7.5%</td></tr>
<tr><td>17</td><td>Arizona</td><td>4,427,579</td><td>1.9%</td><td>3</td><td>Florida</td><td>16,473,456</td><td>6.9%</td></tr>
<tr><td>34</td><td>Arkansas</td><td>1,955,546</td><td>0.8%</td><td>4</td><td>New York</td><td>15,713,652</td><td>6.6%</td></tr>
<tr><td>1</td><td>California</td><td>28,198,973</td><td>11.9%</td><td>5</td><td>Illinois</td><td>9,941,483</td><td>4.2%</td></tr>
<tr><td>22</td><td>Colorado</td><td>4,248,818</td><td>1.8%</td><td>6</td><td>Pennsylvania</td><td>9,735,275</td><td>4.1%</td></tr>
<tr><td>27</td><td>Connecticut</td><td>2,937,407</td><td>1.2%</td><td>7</td><td>Ohio</td><td>8,406,967</td><td>3.5%</td></tr>
<tr><td>45</td><td>Delaware</td><td>741,786</td><td>0.3%</td><td>8</td><td>New Jersey</td><td>7,373,699</td><td>3.1%</td></tr>
<tr><td>3</td><td>Florida</td><td>16,473,456</td><td>6.9%</td><td>9</td><td>Michigan</td><td>7,188,168</td><td>3.0%</td></tr>
<tr><td>10</td><td>Georgia</td><td>6,998,715</td><td>2.9%</td><td>10</td><td>Georgia</td><td>6,998,715</td><td>2.9%</td></tr>
<tr><td>41</td><td>Hawaii</td><td>1,082,377</td><td>0.5%</td><td>11</td><td>North Carolina</td><td>6,662,337</td><td>2.8%</td></tr>
<tr><td>39</td><td>Idaho</td><td>1,140,121</td><td>0.5%</td><td>12</td><td>Virginia</td><td>6,076,121</td><td>2.6%</td></tr>
<tr><td>5</td><td>Illinois</td><td>9,941,483</td><td>4.2%</td><td>13</td><td>Massachusetts</td><td>5,435,185</td><td>2.3%</td></tr>
<tr><td>15</td><td>Indiana</td><td>4,573,728</td><td>1.9%</td><td>14</td><td>Washington</td><td>5,338,459</td><td>2.2%</td></tr>
<tr><td>30</td><td>Iowa</td><td>2,373,242</td><td>1.0%</td><td>15</td><td>Indiana</td><td>4,573,728</td><td>1.9%</td></tr>
<tr><td>31</td><td>Kansas</td><td>2,194,379</td><td>0.9%</td><td>16</td><td>Maryland</td><td>4,568,093</td><td>1.9%</td></tr>
<tr><td>28</td><td>Kentucky</td><td>2,848,123</td><td>1.2%</td><td>17</td><td>Arizona</td><td>4,427,579</td><td>1.9%</td></tr>
<tr><td>23</td><td>Louisiana</td><td>3,188,326</td><td>1.3%</td><td>18</td><td>Missouri</td><td>4,400,636</td><td>1.9%</td></tr>
<tr><td>42</td><td>Maine</td><td>1,078,155</td><td>0.5%</td><td>19</td><td>Wisconsin</td><td>4,373,339</td><td>1.8%</td></tr>
<tr><td>16</td><td>Maryland</td><td>4,568,093</td><td>1.9%</td><td>20</td><td>Minnesota</td><td>4,319,712</td><td>1.8%</td></tr>
<tr><td>13</td><td>Massachusetts</td><td>5,435,185</td><td>2.3%</td><td>21</td><td>Tennessee</td><td>4,291,438</td><td>1.8%</td></tr>
<tr><td>9</td><td>Michigan</td><td>7,188,168</td><td>3.0%</td><td>22</td><td>Colorado</td><td>4,248,818</td><td>1.8%</td></tr>
<tr><td>20</td><td>Minnesota</td><td>4,319,712</td><td>1.8%</td><td>23</td><td>Louisiana</td><td>3,188,326</td><td>1.3%</td></tr>
<tr><td>35</td><td>Mississippi</td><td>1,890,372</td><td>0.8%</td><td>24</td><td>South Carolina</td><td>3,176,909</td><td>1.3%</td></tr>
<tr><td>18</td><td>Missouri</td><td>4,400,636</td><td>1.9%</td><td>25</td><td>Alabama</td><td>3,147,518</td><td>1.3%</td></tr>
<tr><td>43</td><td>Montana</td><td>909,370</td><td>0.4%</td><td>26</td><td>Oregon</td><td>3,019,820</td><td>1.3%</td></tr>
<tr><td>36</td><td>Nebraska</td><td>1,465,428</td><td>0.6%</td><td>27</td><td>Connecticut</td><td>2,937,407</td><td>1.2%</td></tr>
<tr><td>32</td><td>Nevada</td><td>2,049,796</td><td>0.9%</td><td>28</td><td>Kentucky</td><td>2,848,123</td><td>1.2%</td></tr>
<tr><td>40</td><td>New Hampshire</td><td>1,099,721</td><td>0.5%</td><td>29</td><td>Oklahoma</td><td>2,669,079</td><td>1.1%</td></tr>
<tr><td>8</td><td>New Jersey</td><td>7,373,699</td><td>3.1%</td><td>30</td><td>Iowa</td><td>2,373,242</td><td>1.0%</td></tr>
<tr><td>37</td><td>New Mexico</td><td>1,423,252</td><td>0.6%</td><td>31</td><td>Kansas</td><td>2,194,379</td><td>0.9%</td></tr>
<tr><td>4</td><td>New York</td><td>15,713,652</td><td>6.6%</td><td>32</td><td>Nevada</td><td>2,049,796</td><td>0.9%</td></tr>
<tr><td>11</td><td>North Carolina</td><td>6,662,337</td><td>2.8%</td><td>33</td><td>Utah</td><td>1,966,432</td><td>0.8%</td></tr>
<tr><td>47</td><td>North Dakota</td><td>626,940</td><td>0.3%</td><td>34</td><td>Arkansas</td><td>1,955,546</td><td>0.8%</td></tr>
<tr><td>7</td><td>Ohio</td><td>8,406,967</td><td>3.5%</td><td>35</td><td>Mississippi</td><td>1,890,372</td><td>0.8%</td></tr>
<tr><td>29</td><td>Oklahoma</td><td>2,669,079</td><td>1.1%</td><td>36</td><td>Nebraska</td><td>1,465,428</td><td>0.6%</td></tr>
<tr><td>26</td><td>Oregon</td><td>3,019,820</td><td>1.3%</td><td>37</td><td>New Mexico</td><td>1,423,252</td><td>0.6%</td></tr>
<tr><td>6</td><td>Pennsylvania</td><td>9,735,275</td><td>4.1%</td><td>38</td><td>West Virginia</td><td>1,173,944</td><td>0.5%</td></tr>
<tr><td>44</td><td>Rhode Island</td><td>851,844</td><td>0.4%</td><td>39</td><td>Idaho</td><td>1,140,121</td><td>0.5%</td></tr>
<tr><td>24</td><td>South Carolina</td><td>3,176,909</td><td>1.3%</td><td>40</td><td>New Hampshire</td><td>1,099,721</td><td>0.5%</td></tr>
<tr><td>46</td><td>South Dakota</td><td>732,691</td><td>0.3%</td><td>41</td><td>Hawaii</td><td>1,082,377</td><td>0.5%</td></tr>
<tr><td>21</td><td>Tennessee</td><td>4,291,438</td><td>1.8%</td><td>42</td><td>Maine</td><td>1,078,155</td><td>0.5%</td></tr>
<tr><td>2</td><td>Texas</td><td>17,834,945</td><td>7.5%</td><td>43</td><td>Montana</td><td>909,370</td><td>0.4%</td></tr>
<tr><td>33</td><td>Utah</td><td>1,966,432</td><td>0.8%</td><td>44</td><td>Rhode Island</td><td>851,844</td><td>0.4%</td></tr>
<tr><td>49</td><td>Vermont</td><td>567,858</td><td>0.2%</td><td>45</td><td>Delaware</td><td>741,786</td><td>0.3%</td></tr>
<tr><td>12</td><td>Virginia</td><td>6,076,121</td><td>2.6%</td><td>46</td><td>South Dakota</td><td>732,691</td><td>0.3%</td></tr>
<tr><td>14</td><td>Washington</td><td>5,338,459</td><td>2.2%</td><td>47</td><td>North Dakota</td><td>626,940</td><td>0.3%</td></tr>
<tr><td>38</td><td>West Virginia</td><td>1,173,944</td><td>0.5%</td><td>48</td><td>Alaska</td><td>596,965</td><td>0.3%</td></tr>
<tr><td>19</td><td>Wisconsin</td><td>4,373,339</td><td>1.8%</td><td>49</td><td>Vermont</td><td>567,858</td><td>0.2%</td></tr>
<tr><td>50</td><td>Wyoming</td><td>530,793</td><td>0.2%</td><td>50</td><td>Wyoming</td><td>530,793</td><td>0.2%</td></tr>
<tr><td></td><td></td><td></td><td></td><td></td><td>District of Columbia</td><td>567,560</td><td>0.2%</td></tr>
</table>

Source: U.S. Department of the Treasury, Internal Revenue Service
"Fiscal Year 2012 IRS Data Book" (http://www.irs.gov/uac/SOI-Tax-Stats-IRS-Data-Book)
*Total includes returns from international sources and other miscellaneous returns not shown separately.

Percent of Federal Returns Filed Electronically in 2012

National Percent = 60.9%*

ALPHA ORDER

RANK ORDER

RANK	STATE	PERCENT		RANK	STATE	PERCENT
7	Alabama	64.2		1	New York	66.0
33	Alaska	59.8		2	Rhode Island	65.5
30	Arizona	60.3		3	Georgia	65.0
18	Arkansas	61.7		4	Massachusetts	64.6
35	California	59.7		5	Michigan	64.4
45	Colorado	57.1		6	Mississippi	64.3
35	Connecticut	59.7		7	Alabama	64.2
32	Delaware	60.0		8	South Carolina	63.9
25	Florida	60.6		9	Ohio	63.6
3	Georgia	65.0		9	Tennessee	63.6
50	Hawaii	52.3		11	Indiana	63.4
38	Idaho	59.5		12	Kentucky	63.3
33	Illinois	59.8		12	Utah	63.3
11	Indiana	63.4		14	Wisconsin	63.2
28	Iowa	60.4		15	Nevada	63.0
16	Kansas	62.3		16	Kansas	62.3
12	Kentucky	63.3		17	Minnesota	62.0
21	Louisiana	61.1		18	Arkansas	61.7
46	Maine	56.7		19	Texas	61.3
44	Maryland	57.8		20	Nebraska	61.2
4	Massachusetts	64.6		21	Louisiana	61.1
5	Michigan	64.4		22	New Jersey	61.0
17	Minnesota	62.0		23	Oklahoma	60.8
6	Mississippi	64.3		24	North Carolina	60.7
28	Missouri	60.4		25	Florida	60.6
47	Montana	55.7		25	Pennsylvania	60.6
20	Nebraska	61.2		27	West Virginia	60.5
15	Nevada	63.0		28	Iowa	60.4
31	New Hampshire	60.2		28	Missouri	60.4
22	New Jersey	61.0		30	Arizona	60.3
37	New Mexico	59.6		31	New Hampshire	60.2
1	New York	66.0		32	Delaware	60.0
24	North Carolina	60.7		33	Alaska	59.8
49	North Dakota	54.5		33	Illinois	59.8
9	Ohio	63.6		35	California	59.7
23	Oklahoma	60.8		35	Connecticut	59.7
41	Oregon	58.9		37	New Mexico	59.6
25	Pennsylvania	60.6		38	Idaho	59.5
2	Rhode Island	65.5		38	Virginia	59.5
8	South Carolina	63.9		40	Washington	59.2
42	South Dakota	58.1		41	Oregon	58.9
9	Tennessee	63.6		42	South Dakota	58.1
19	Texas	61.3		43	Wyoming	58.0
12	Utah	63.3		44	Maryland	57.8
48	Vermont	54.8		45	Colorado	57.1
38	Virginia	59.5		46	Maine	56.7
40	Washington	59.2		47	Montana	55.7
27	West Virginia	60.5		48	Vermont	54.8
14	Wisconsin	63.2		49	North Dakota	54.5
43	Wyoming	58.0		50	Hawaii	52.3

District of Columbia   57.5

Source: CQ Press using data from U.S. Department of the Treasury, Internal Revenue Service
"Fiscal Year 2012 IRS Data Book" (http://www.irs.gov/uac/SOI-Tax-Stats-IRS-Data-Book)
*Total includes returns from international sources and other miscellaneous returns. Includes corporate, individual, partnership, estate, employment and other returns. Excludes returns that cannot be filed electronically including informational returns. Forty-seven percent of individual income tax returns were filed electronically.

Federal Individual Income Tax Returns Filed in 2012

National Total = 146,243,886 Returns*

ALPHA ORDER

RANK	STATE	RETURNS	% of USA
23	Alabama	2,094,553	1.4%
47	Alaska	369,581	0.3%
18	Arizona	2,769,832	1.9%
34	Arkansas	1,229,757	0.8%
1	California	16,935,887	11.6%
22	Colorado	2,397,815	1.6%
28	Connecticut	1,741,293	1.2%
45	Delaware	431,325	0.3%
3	Florida	9,736,734	6.7%
9	Georgia	4,514,150	3.1%
41	Hawaii	658,626	0.5%
40	Idaho	666,204	0.5%
6	Illinois	6,103,373	4.2%
15	Indiana	3,007,521	2.1%
30	Iowa	1,413,882	1.0%
31	Kansas	1,323,293	0.9%
26	Kentucky	1,870,180	1.3%
25	Louisiana	2,014,306	1.4%
42	Maine	629,281	0.4%
17	Maryland	2,821,455	1.9%
13	Massachusetts	3,232,880	2.2%
8	Michigan	4,660,114	3.2%
21	Minnesota	2,587,955	1.8%
33	Mississippi	1,285,923	0.9%
20	Missouri	2,716,941	1.9%
44	Montana	477,712	0.3%
37	Nebraska	867,235	0.6%
32	Nevada	1,290,641	0.9%
39	New Hampshire	674,965	0.5%
10	New Jersey	4,319,000	3.0%
36	New Mexico	912,132	0.6%
4	New York	9,354,490	6.4%
11	North Carolina	4,262,480	2.9%
48	North Dakota	339,892	0.2%
7	Ohio	5,491,871	3.8%
29	Oklahoma	1,605,475	1.1%
27	Oregon	1,748,979	1.2%
5	Pennsylvania	6,172,712	4.2%
43	Rhode Island	512,377	0.4%
24	South Carolina	2,072,346	1.4%
46	South Dakota	409,547	0.3%
16	Tennessee	2,893,799	2.0%
2	Texas	11,292,464	7.7%
35	Utah	1,152,313	0.8%
49	Vermont	318,780	0.2%
12	Virginia	3,779,854	2.6%
14	Washington	3,192,891	2.2%
38	West Virginia	789,106	0.5%
19	Wisconsin	2,767,383	1.9%
50	Wyoming	291,332	0.2%

RANK ORDER

RANK	STATE	RETURNS	% of USA
1	California	16,935,887	11.6%
2	Texas	11,292,464	7.7%
3	Florida	9,736,734	6.7%
4	New York	9,354,490	6.4%
5	Pennsylvania	6,172,712	4.2%
6	Illinois	6,103,373	4.2%
7	Ohio	5,491,871	3.8%
8	Michigan	4,660,114	3.2%
9	Georgia	4,514,150	3.1%
10	New Jersey	4,319,000	3.0%
11	North Carolina	4,262,480	2.9%
12	Virginia	3,779,854	2.6%
13	Massachusetts	3,232,880	2.2%
14	Washington	3,192,891	2.2%
15	Indiana	3,007,521	2.1%
16	Tennessee	2,893,799	2.0%
17	Maryland	2,821,455	1.9%
18	Arizona	2,769,832	1.9%
19	Wisconsin	2,767,383	1.9%
20	Missouri	2,716,941	1.9%
21	Minnesota	2,587,955	1.8%
22	Colorado	2,397,815	1.6%
23	Alabama	2,094,553	1.4%
24	South Carolina	2,072,346	1.4%
25	Louisiana	2,014,306	1.4%
26	Kentucky	1,870,180	1.3%
27	Oregon	1,748,979	1.2%
28	Connecticut	1,741,293	1.2%
29	Oklahoma	1,605,475	1.1%
30	Iowa	1,413,882	1.0%
31	Kansas	1,323,293	0.9%
32	Nevada	1,290,641	0.9%
33	Mississippi	1,285,923	0.9%
34	Arkansas	1,229,757	0.8%
35	Utah	1,152,313	0.8%
36	New Mexico	912,132	0.6%
37	Nebraska	867,235	0.6%
38	West Virginia	789,106	0.5%
39	New Hampshire	674,965	0.5%
40	Idaho	666,204	0.5%
41	Hawaii	658,626	0.5%
42	Maine	629,281	0.4%
43	Rhode Island	512,377	0.4%
44	Montana	477,712	0.3%
45	Delaware	431,325	0.3%
46	South Dakota	409,547	0.3%
47	Alaska	369,581	0.3%
48	North Dakota	339,892	0.2%
49	Vermont	318,780	0.2%
50	Wyoming	291,332	0.2%
	District of Columbia	326,925	0.2%

Source: U.S. Department of the Treasury, Internal Revenue Service
"Fiscal Year 2012 IRS Data Book" (http://www.irs.gov/uac/SOI-Tax-Stats-IRS-Data-Book)
*Total includes returns from international sources and other miscellaneous returns not shown separately.

Federal Business Income Tax Returns Filed in 2012

National Total = 6,842,630 Returns*

ALPHA ORDER					RANK ORDER			
RANK	STATE	RETURNS	% of USA		RANK	STATE	RETURNS	% of USA
28	Alabama	70,056	1.0%		1	Florida	788,677	11.5%
50	Alaska	12,340	0.2%		2	California	756,661	11.1%
18	Arizona	118,001	1.7%		3	New York	655,238	9.6%
32	Arkansas	54,602	0.8%		4	Texas	437,278	6.4%
2	California	756,661	11.1%		5	Illinois	340,166	5.0%
13	Colorado	155,142	2.3%		6	Georgia	223,828	3.3%
33	Connecticut	54,378	0.8%		7	Pennsylvania	223,637	3.3%
43	Delaware	24,444	0.4%		8	New Jersey	200,689	2.9%
1	Florida	788,677	11.5%		9	Michigan	193,909	2.8%
6	Georgia	223,828	3.3%		10	North Carolina	193,621	2.8%
41	Hawaii	28,025	0.4%		11	Ohio	179,393	2.6%
37	Idaho	35,491	0.5%		12	Virginia	165,245	2.4%
5	Illinois	340,166	5.0%		13	Colorado	155,142	2.3%
19	Indiana	113,522	1.7%		14	Massachusetts	144,366	2.1%
31	Iowa	62,383	0.9%		15	Washington	136,437	2.0%
34	Kansas	51,886	0.8%		16	Minnesota	130,236	1.9%
30	Kentucky	67,582	1.0%		17	Maryland	126,230	1.8%
23	Louisiana	83,061	1.2%		18	Arizona	118,001	1.7%
39	Maine	30,929	0.5%		19	Indiana	113,522	1.7%
17	Maryland	126,230	1.8%		20	Missouri	101,199	1.5%
14	Massachusetts	144,366	2.1%		21	Wisconsin	94,561	1.4%
9	Michigan	193,909	2.8%		22	South Carolina	85,557	1.3%
16	Minnesota	130,236	1.9%		23	Louisiana	83,061	1.2%
36	Mississippi	40,975	0.6%		24	Oregon	76,720	1.1%
20	Missouri	101,199	1.5%		25	Oklahoma	73,083	1.1%
38	Montana	34,360	0.5%		26	Utah	71,799	1.0%
35	Nebraska	43,647	0.6%		27	Nevada	71,507	1.0%
27	Nevada	71,507	1.0%		28	Alabama	70,056	1.0%
44	New Hampshire	22,573	0.3%		29	Tennessee	68,085	1.0%
8	New Jersey	200,689	2.9%		30	Kentucky	67,582	1.0%
40	New Mexico	30,360	0.4%		31	Iowa	62,383	0.9%
3	New York	655,238	9.6%		32	Arkansas	54,602	0.8%
10	North Carolina	193,621	2.8%		33	Connecticut	54,378	0.8%
49	North Dakota	15,000	0.2%		34	Kansas	51,886	0.8%
11	Ohio	179,393	2.6%		35	Nebraska	43,647	0.6%
25	Oklahoma	73,083	1.1%		36	Mississippi	40,975	0.6%
24	Oregon	76,720	1.1%		37	Idaho	35,491	0.5%
7	Pennsylvania	223,637	3.3%		38	Montana	34,360	0.5%
42	Rhode Island	24,957	0.4%		39	Maine	30,929	0.5%
22	South Carolina	85,557	1.3%		40	New Mexico	30,360	0.4%
46	South Dakota	18,540	0.3%		41	Hawaii	28,025	0.4%
29	Tennessee	68,085	1.0%		42	Rhode Island	24,957	0.4%
4	Texas	437,278	6.4%		43	Delaware	24,444	0.4%
26	Utah	71,799	1.0%		44	New Hampshire	22,573	0.3%
48	Vermont	16,413	0.2%		45	West Virginia	20,409	0.3%
12	Virginia	165,245	2.4%		46	South Dakota	18,540	0.3%
15	Washington	136,437	2.0%		47	Wyoming	17,823	0.3%
45	West Virginia	20,409	0.3%		48	Vermont	16,413	0.2%
21	Wisconsin	94,561	1.4%		49	North Dakota	15,000	0.2%
47	Wyoming	17,823	0.3%		50	Alaska	12,340	0.2%
						District of Columbia	16,788	0.2%

Source: U.S. Department of the Treasury, Internal Revenue Service
   "Fiscal Year 2012 IRS Data Book" (http://www.irs.gov/uac/SOI-Tax-Stats-IRS-Data-Book)
*Total includes returns from international sources and other miscellaneous returns not shown separately.

Federal Tax Refunds in 2012

National Total = 123,358,811 Refunds*

ALPHA ORDER

RANK	STATE	REFUNDS	% of USA
23	Alabama	1,804,690	1.5%
47	Alaska	308,862	0.3%
20	Arizona	2,283,380	1.9%
34	Arkansas	1,049,181	0.9%
1	California	13,862,370	11.2%
22	Colorado	1,962,632	1.6%
27	Connecticut	1,464,462	1.2%
45	Delaware	374,282	0.3%
3	Florida	8,389,372	6.8%
9	Georgia	3,908,253	3.2%
41	Hawaii	550,994	0.4%
40	Idaho	554,643	0.4%
6	Illinois	5,295,743	4.3%
15	Indiana	2,626,268	2.1%
30	Iowa	1,171,417	0.9%
33	Kansas	1,089,736	0.9%
26	Kentucky	1,634,618	1.3%
24	Louisiana	1,753,536	1.4%
42	Maine	531,900	0.4%
17	Maryland	2,386,855	1.9%
14	Massachusetts	2,693,489	2.2%
8	Michigan	3,925,143	3.2%
21	Minnesota	2,118,566	1.7%
31	Mississippi	1,119,145	0.9%
18	Missouri	2,300,059	1.9%
44	Montana	384,348	0.3%
37	Nebraska	723,006	0.6%
32	Nevada	1,111,970	0.9%
39	New Hampshire	574,120	0.5%
10	New Jersey	3,631,643	2.9%
36	New Mexico	771,191	0.6%
4	New York	7,949,259	6.4%
11	North Carolina	3,589,629	2.9%
48	North Dakota	272,606	0.2%
7	Ohio	4,740,122	3.8%
29	Oklahoma	1,353,063	1.1%
28	Oregon	1,409,483	1.1%
5	Pennsylvania	5,297,935	4.3%
43	Rhode Island	448,757	0.4%
25	South Carolina	1,753,491	1.4%
46	South Dakota	337,431	0.3%
16	Tennessee	2,544,287	2.1%
2	Texas	9,893,591	8.0%
35	Utah	1,005,036	0.8%
49	Vermont	266,367	0.2%
12	Virginia	3,210,945	2.6%
13	Washington	2,706,375	2.2%
38	West Virginia	697,819	0.6%
19	Wisconsin	2,299,788	1.9%
50	Wyoming	247,976	0.2%

RANK ORDER

RANK	STATE	REFUNDS	% of USA
1	California	13,862,370	11.2%
2	Texas	9,893,591	8.0%
3	Florida	8,389,372	6.8%
4	New York	7,949,259	6.4%
5	Pennsylvania	5,297,935	4.3%
6	Illinois	5,295,743	4.3%
7	Ohio	4,740,122	3.8%
8	Michigan	3,925,143	3.2%
9	Georgia	3,908,253	3.2%
10	New Jersey	3,631,643	2.9%
11	North Carolina	3,589,629	2.9%
12	Virginia	3,210,945	2.6%
13	Washington	2,706,375	2.2%
14	Massachusetts	2,693,489	2.2%
15	Indiana	2,626,268	2.1%
16	Tennessee	2,544,287	2.1%
17	Maryland	2,386,855	1.9%
18	Missouri	2,300,059	1.9%
19	Wisconsin	2,299,788	1.9%
20	Arizona	2,283,380	1.9%
21	Minnesota	2,118,566	1.7%
22	Colorado	1,962,632	1.6%
23	Alabama	1,804,690	1.5%
24	Louisiana	1,753,536	1.4%
25	South Carolina	1,753,491	1.4%
26	Kentucky	1,634,618	1.3%
27	Connecticut	1,464,462	1.2%
28	Oregon	1,409,483	1.1%
29	Oklahoma	1,353,063	1.1%
30	Iowa	1,171,417	0.9%
31	Mississippi	1,119,145	0.9%
32	Nevada	1,111,970	0.9%
33	Kansas	1,089,736	0.9%
34	Arkansas	1,049,181	0.9%
35	Utah	1,005,036	0.8%
36	New Mexico	771,191	0.6%
37	Nebraska	723,006	0.6%
38	West Virginia	697,819	0.6%
39	New Hampshire	574,120	0.5%
40	Idaho	554,643	0.4%
41	Hawaii	550,994	0.4%
42	Maine	531,900	0.4%
43	Rhode Island	448,757	0.4%
44	Montana	384,348	0.3%
45	Delaware	374,282	0.3%
46	South Dakota	337,431	0.3%
47	Alaska	308,862	0.3%
48	North Dakota	272,606	0.2%
49	Vermont	266,367	0.2%
50	Wyoming	247,976	0.2%
	District of Columbia	278,935	0.2%

Source: U.S. Department of the Treasury, Internal Revenue Service
   "Fiscal Year 2012 IRS Data Book" (http://www.irs.gov/uac/SOI-Tax-Stats-IRS-Data-Book)
*Total includes refunds to international sources and other miscellaneous refunds not shown separately.

Value of Federal Tax Refunds in 2012

National Total = $373,428,754,000*

ALPHA ORDER

RANK	STATE	REFUNDS	% of USA
24	Alabama	$5,289,399,000	1.4%
47	Alaska	811,368,000	0.2%
21	Arizona	6,290,211,000	1.7%
35	Arkansas	2,931,984,000	0.8%
1	California	41,894,334,000	11.2%
23	Colorado	5,625,018,000	1.5%
18	Connecticut	6,593,434,000	1.8%
29	Delaware	3,888,671,000	1.0%
4	Florida	23,865,014,000	6.4%
9	Georgia	12,022,713,000	3.2%
42	Hawaii	1,433,423,000	0.4%
43	Idaho	1,387,668,000	0.4%
5	Illinois	16,767,195,000	4.5%
17	Indiana	7,087,659,000	1.9%
34	Iowa	2,977,650,000	0.8%
36	Kansas	2,862,001,000	0.8%
28	Kentucky	4,430,116,000	1.2%
25	Louisiana	5,287,798,000	1.4%
44	Maine	1,343,896,000	0.4%
16	Maryland	7,257,470,000	1.9%
13	Massachusetts	8,674,056,000	2.3%
10	Michigan	10,792,947,000	2.9%
19	Minnesota	6,557,810,000	1.8%
31	Mississippi	3,332,747,000	0.9%
20	Missouri	6,442,756,000	1.7%
45	Montana	862,743,000	0.2%
38	Nebraska	1,880,669,000	0.5%
32	Nevada	3,141,754,000	0.8%
41	New Hampshire	1,488,585,000	0.4%
8	New Jersey	12,258,226,000	3.3%
37	New Mexico	1,975,230,000	0.5%
3	New York	28,481,035,000	7.6%
11	North Carolina	10,066,606,000	2.7%
48	North Dakota	700,946,000	0.2%
7	Ohio	13,063,147,000	3.5%
27	Oklahoma	4,444,247,000	1.2%
30	Oregon	3,572,129,000	1.0%
6	Pennsylvania	14,766,611,000	4.0%
40	Rhode Island	1,522,007,000	0.4%
26	South Carolina	4,467,036,000	1.2%
46	South Dakota	836,521,000	0.2%
14	Tennessee	8,081,139,000	2.2%
2	Texas	33,464,687,000	9.0%
33	Utah	3,004,212,000	0.8%
49	Vermont	671,390,000	0.2%
12	Virginia	9,593,063,000	2.6%
15	Washington	7,475,082,000	2.0%
39	West Virginia	1,793,899,000	0.5%
22	Wisconsin	5,947,952,000	1.6%
50	Wyoming	668,210,000	0.2%

RANK ORDER

RANK	STATE	REFUNDS	% of USA
1	California	$41,894,334,000	11.2%
2	Texas	33,464,687,000	9.0%
3	New York	28,481,035,000	7.6%
4	Florida	23,865,014,000	6.4%
5	Illinois	16,767,195,000	4.5%
6	Pennsylvania	14,766,611,000	4.0%
7	Ohio	13,063,147,000	3.5%
8	New Jersey	12,258,226,000	3.3%
9	Georgia	12,022,713,000	3.2%
10	Michigan	10,792,947,000	2.9%
11	North Carolina	10,066,606,000	2.7%
12	Virginia	9,593,063,000	2.6%
13	Massachusetts	8,674,056,000	2.3%
14	Tennessee	8,081,139,000	2.2%
15	Washington	7,475,082,000	2.0%
16	Maryland	7,257,470,000	1.9%
17	Indiana	7,087,659,000	1.9%
18	Connecticut	6,593,434,000	1.8%
19	Minnesota	6,557,810,000	1.8%
20	Missouri	6,442,756,000	1.7%
21	Arizona	6,290,211,000	1.7%
22	Wisconsin	5,947,952,000	1.6%
23	Colorado	5,625,018,000	1.5%
24	Alabama	5,289,399,000	1.4%
25	Louisiana	5,287,798,000	1.4%
26	South Carolina	4,467,036,000	1.2%
27	Oklahoma	4,444,247,000	1.2%
28	Kentucky	4,430,116,000	1.2%
29	Delaware	3,888,671,000	1.0%
30	Oregon	3,572,129,000	1.0%
31	Mississippi	3,332,747,000	0.9%
32	Nevada	3,141,754,000	0.8%
33	Utah	3,004,212,000	0.8%
34	Iowa	2,977,650,000	0.8%
35	Arkansas	2,931,984,000	0.8%
36	Kansas	2,862,001,000	0.8%
37	New Mexico	1,975,230,000	0.5%
38	Nebraska	1,880,669,000	0.5%
39	West Virginia	1,793,899,000	0.5%
40	Rhode Island	1,522,007,000	0.4%
41	New Hampshire	1,488,585,000	0.4%
42	Hawaii	1,433,423,000	0.4%
43	Idaho	1,387,668,000	0.4%
44	Maine	1,343,896,000	0.4%
45	Montana	862,743,000	0.2%
46	South Dakota	836,521,000	0.2%
47	Alaska	811,368,000	0.2%
48	North Dakota	700,946,000	0.2%
49	Vermont	671,390,000	0.2%
50	Wyoming	668,210,000	0.2%
	District of Columbia	833,947,000	0.2%

Source: U.S. Department of the Treasury, Internal Revenue Service
   "Fiscal Year 2012 IRS Data Book" (http://www.irs.gov/uac/SOI-Tax-Stats-IRS-Data-Book)
*Total includes refunds to international sources and other miscellaneous refunds not shown separately.

Average Value of Federal Tax Refunds in 2012

National Average = $3,027*

ALPHA ORDER

RANK	STATE	AVERAGE REFUND
19	Alabama	$2,931
34	Alaska	2,627
29	Arizona	2,755
25	Arkansas	2,795
14	California	3,022
20	Colorado	2,866
2	Connecticut	4,502
1	Delaware	10,390
21	Florida	2,845
12	Georgia	3,076
36	Hawaii	2,602
48	Idaho	2,502
10	Illinois	3,166
32	Indiana	2,699
44	Iowa	2,542
35	Kansas	2,626
31	Kentucky	2,710
15	Louisiana	3,016
46	Maine	2,527
13	Maryland	3,041
8	Massachusetts	3,220
30	Michigan	2,750
11	Minnesota	3,095
18	Mississippi	2,978
24	Missouri	2,801
50	Montana	2,245
37	Nebraska	2,601
22	Nevada	2,825
38	New Hampshire	2,593
6	New Jersey	3,375
42	New Mexico	2,561
3	New York	3,583
23	North Carolina	2,804
40	North Dakota	2,571
28	Ohio	2,756
7	Oklahoma	3,285
45	Oregon	2,534
26	Pennsylvania	2,787
4	Rhode Island	3,392
43	South Carolina	2,548
49	South Dakota	2,479
9	Tennessee	3,176
5	Texas	3,382
16	Utah	2,989
47	Vermont	2,521
17	Virginia	2,988
27	Washington	2,762
40	West Virginia	2,571
39	Wisconsin	2,586
33	Wyoming	2,695

RANK ORDER

RANK	STATE	AVERAGE REFUND
1	Delaware	$10,390
2	Connecticut	4,502
3	New York	3,583
4	Rhode Island	3,392
5	Texas	3,382
6	New Jersey	3,375
7	Oklahoma	3,285
8	Massachusetts	3,220
9	Tennessee	3,176
10	Illinois	3,166
11	Minnesota	3,095
12	Georgia	3,076
13	Maryland	3,041
14	California	3,022
15	Louisiana	3,016
16	Utah	2,989
17	Virginia	2,988
18	Mississippi	2,978
19	Alabama	2,931
20	Colorado	2,866
21	Florida	2,845
22	Nevada	2,825
23	North Carolina	2,804
24	Missouri	2,801
25	Arkansas	2,795
26	Pennsylvania	2,787
27	Washington	2,762
28	Ohio	2,756
29	Arizona	2,755
30	Michigan	2,750
31	Kentucky	2,710
32	Indiana	2,699
33	Wyoming	2,695
34	Alaska	2,627
35	Kansas	2,626
36	Hawaii	2,602
37	Nebraska	2,601
38	New Hampshire	2,593
39	Wisconsin	2,586
40	North Dakota	2,571
40	West Virginia	2,571
42	New Mexico	2,561
43	South Carolina	2,548
44	Iowa	2,542
45	Oregon	2,534
46	Maine	2,527
47	Vermont	2,521
48	Idaho	2,502
49	South Dakota	2,479
50	Montana	2,245

District of Columbia 2,990

Source: CQ Press using data from U.S. Department of the Treasury, Internal Revenue Service
"Fiscal Year 2012 IRS Data Book" (http://www.irs.gov/uac/SOI-Tax-Stats-IRS-Data-Book)
*National average includes refunds to international sources and other miscellaneous refunds not shown separately.

Value of Federal Individual Income Tax Refunds in 2012

National Total = $322,666,998,000*

<table>
<tr><td colspan="4">ALPHA ORDER</td><td colspan="4">RANK ORDER</td></tr>
<tr><td>RANK</td><td>STATE</td><td>REFUNDS</td><td>% of USA</td><td>RANK</td><td>STATE</td><td>REFUNDS</td><td>% of USA</td></tr>
<tr><td>21</td><td>Alabama</td><td>$4,929,830,000</td><td>1.5%</td><td>1</td><td>California</td><td>$37,102,177,000</td><td>11.5%</td></tr>
<tr><td>47</td><td>Alaska</td><td>765,027,000</td><td>0.2%</td><td>2</td><td>Texas</td><td>28,522,439,000</td><td>8.8%</td></tr>
<tr><td>18</td><td>Arizona</td><td>5,784,097,000</td><td>1.8%</td><td>3</td><td>Florida</td><td>22,760,604,000</td><td>7.1%</td></tr>
<tr><td>33</td><td>Arkansas</td><td>2,680,057,000</td><td>0.8%</td><td>4</td><td>New York</td><td>22,683,218,000</td><td>7.0%</td></tr>
<tr><td>1</td><td>California</td><td>37,102,177,000</td><td>11.5%</td><td>5</td><td>Illinois</td><td>14,713,626,000</td><td>4.6%</td></tr>
<tr><td>24</td><td>Colorado</td><td>4,886,442,000</td><td>1.5%</td><td>6</td><td>Pennsylvania</td><td>12,971,622,000</td><td>4.0%</td></tr>
<tr><td>26</td><td>Connecticut</td><td>4,190,561,000</td><td>1.3%</td><td>7</td><td>Ohio</td><td>11,277,078,000</td><td>3.5%</td></tr>
<tr><td>44</td><td>Delaware</td><td>918,221,000</td><td>0.3%</td><td>8</td><td>New Jersey</td><td>10,513,293,000</td><td>3.3%</td></tr>
<tr><td>3</td><td>Florida</td><td>22,760,604,000</td><td>7.1%</td><td>9</td><td>Georgia</td><td>10,472,192,000</td><td>3.2%</td></tr>
<tr><td>9</td><td>Georgia</td><td>10,472,192,000</td><td>3.2%</td><td>10</td><td>Michigan</td><td>9,439,101,000</td><td>2.9%</td></tr>
<tr><td>40</td><td>Hawaii</td><td>1,326,139,000</td><td>0.4%</td><td>11</td><td>North Carolina</td><td>8,975,090,000</td><td>2.8%</td></tr>
<tr><td>41</td><td>Idaho</td><td>1,282,373,000</td><td>0.4%</td><td>12</td><td>Virginia</td><td>8,352,177,000</td><td>2.6%</td></tr>
<tr><td>5</td><td>Illinois</td><td>14,713,626,000</td><td>4.6%</td><td>13</td><td>Massachusetts</td><td>6,993,226,000</td><td>2.2%</td></tr>
<tr><td>16</td><td>Indiana</td><td>6,568,931,000</td><td>2.0%</td><td>14</td><td>Washington</td><td>6,842,995,000</td><td>2.1%</td></tr>
<tr><td>32</td><td>Iowa</td><td>2,763,798,000</td><td>0.9%</td><td>15</td><td>Tennessee</td><td>6,611,272,000</td><td>2.0%</td></tr>
<tr><td>34</td><td>Kansas</td><td>2,623,951,000</td><td>0.8%</td><td>16</td><td>Indiana</td><td>6,568,931,000</td><td>2.0%</td></tr>
<tr><td>27</td><td>Kentucky</td><td>4,149,368,000</td><td>1.3%</td><td>17</td><td>Maryland</td><td>6,392,264,000</td><td>2.0%</td></tr>
<tr><td>22</td><td>Louisiana</td><td>4,912,424,000</td><td>1.5%</td><td>18</td><td>Arizona</td><td>5,784,097,000</td><td>1.8%</td></tr>
<tr><td>42</td><td>Maine</td><td>1,152,149,000</td><td>0.4%</td><td>19</td><td>Missouri</td><td>5,601,452,000</td><td>1.7%</td></tr>
<tr><td>17</td><td>Maryland</td><td>6,392,264,000</td><td>2.0%</td><td>20</td><td>Wisconsin</td><td>5,206,458,000</td><td>1.6%</td></tr>
<tr><td>13</td><td>Massachusetts</td><td>6,993,226,000</td><td>2.2%</td><td>21</td><td>Alabama</td><td>4,929,830,000</td><td>1.5%</td></tr>
<tr><td>10</td><td>Michigan</td><td>9,439,101,000</td><td>2.9%</td><td>22</td><td>Louisiana</td><td>4,912,424,000</td><td>1.5%</td></tr>
<tr><td>23</td><td>Minnesota</td><td>4,896,523,000</td><td>1.5%</td><td>23</td><td>Minnesota</td><td>4,896,523,000</td><td>1.5%</td></tr>
<tr><td>29</td><td>Mississippi</td><td>3,135,297,000</td><td>1.0%</td><td>24</td><td>Colorado</td><td>4,886,442,000</td><td>1.5%</td></tr>
<tr><td>19</td><td>Missouri</td><td>5,601,452,000</td><td>1.7%</td><td>25</td><td>South Carolina</td><td>4,292,094,000</td><td>1.3%</td></tr>
<tr><td>45</td><td>Montana</td><td>820,375,000</td><td>0.3%</td><td>26</td><td>Connecticut</td><td>4,190,561,000</td><td>1.3%</td></tr>
<tr><td>38</td><td>Nebraska</td><td>1,671,329,000</td><td>0.5%</td><td>27</td><td>Kentucky</td><td>4,149,368,000</td><td>1.3%</td></tr>
<tr><td>31</td><td>Nevada</td><td>2,977,230,000</td><td>0.9%</td><td>28</td><td>Oklahoma</td><td>3,476,301,000</td><td>1.1%</td></tr>
<tr><td>39</td><td>New Hampshire</td><td>1,385,507,000</td><td>0.4%</td><td>29</td><td>Mississippi</td><td>3,135,297,000</td><td>1.0%</td></tr>
<tr><td>8</td><td>New Jersey</td><td>10,513,293,000</td><td>3.3%</td><td>30</td><td>Oregon</td><td>3,127,983,000</td><td>1.0%</td></tr>
<tr><td>36</td><td>New Mexico</td><td>1,899,656,000</td><td>0.6%</td><td>31</td><td>Nevada</td><td>2,977,230,000</td><td>0.9%</td></tr>
<tr><td>4</td><td>New York</td><td>22,683,218,000</td><td>7.0%</td><td>32</td><td>Iowa</td><td>2,763,798,000</td><td>0.9%</td></tr>
<tr><td>11</td><td>North Carolina</td><td>8,975,090,000</td><td>2.8%</td><td>33</td><td>Arkansas</td><td>2,680,057,000</td><td>0.8%</td></tr>
<tr><td>49</td><td>North Dakota</td><td>624,362,000</td><td>0.2%</td><td>34</td><td>Kansas</td><td>2,623,951,000</td><td>0.8%</td></tr>
<tr><td>7</td><td>Ohio</td><td>11,277,078,000</td><td>3.5%</td><td>35</td><td>Utah</td><td>2,599,157,000</td><td>0.8%</td></tr>
<tr><td>28</td><td>Oklahoma</td><td>3,476,301,000</td><td>1.1%</td><td>36</td><td>New Mexico</td><td>1,899,656,000</td><td>0.6%</td></tr>
<tr><td>30</td><td>Oregon</td><td>3,127,983,000</td><td>1.0%</td><td>37</td><td>West Virginia</td><td>1,712,175,000</td><td>0.5%</td></tr>
<tr><td>6</td><td>Pennsylvania</td><td>12,971,622,000</td><td>4.0%</td><td>38</td><td>Nebraska</td><td>1,671,329,000</td><td>0.5%</td></tr>
<tr><td>43</td><td>Rhode Island</td><td>1,106,239,000</td><td>0.3%</td><td>39</td><td>New Hampshire</td><td>1,385,507,000</td><td>0.4%</td></tr>
<tr><td>25</td><td>South Carolina</td><td>4,292,094,000</td><td>1.3%</td><td>40</td><td>Hawaii</td><td>1,326,139,000</td><td>0.4%</td></tr>
<tr><td>46</td><td>South Dakota</td><td>775,476,000</td><td>0.2%</td><td>41</td><td>Idaho</td><td>1,282,373,000</td><td>0.4%</td></tr>
<tr><td>15</td><td>Tennessee</td><td>6,611,272,000</td><td>2.0%</td><td>42</td><td>Maine</td><td>1,152,149,000</td><td>0.4%</td></tr>
<tr><td>2</td><td>Texas</td><td>28,522,439,000</td><td>8.8%</td><td>43</td><td>Rhode Island</td><td>1,106,239,000</td><td>0.3%</td></tr>
<tr><td>35</td><td>Utah</td><td>2,599,157,000</td><td>0.8%</td><td>44</td><td>Delaware</td><td>918,221,000</td><td>0.3%</td></tr>
<tr><td>50</td><td>Vermont</td><td>574,037,000</td><td>0.2%</td><td>45</td><td>Montana</td><td>820,375,000</td><td>0.3%</td></tr>
<tr><td>12</td><td>Virginia</td><td>8,352,177,000</td><td>2.6%</td><td>46</td><td>South Dakota</td><td>775,476,000</td><td>0.2%</td></tr>
<tr><td>14</td><td>Washington</td><td>6,842,995,000</td><td>2.1%</td><td>47</td><td>Alaska</td><td>765,027,000</td><td>0.2%</td></tr>
<tr><td>37</td><td>West Virginia</td><td>1,712,175,000</td><td>0.5%</td><td>48</td><td>Wyoming</td><td>626,865,000</td><td>0.2%</td></tr>
<tr><td>20</td><td>Wisconsin</td><td>5,206,458,000</td><td>1.6%</td><td>49</td><td>North Dakota</td><td>624,362,000</td><td>0.2%</td></tr>
<tr><td>48</td><td>Wyoming</td><td>626,865,000</td><td>0.2%</td><td>50</td><td>Vermont</td><td>574,037,000</td><td>0.2%</td></tr>
<tr><td></td><td></td><td></td><td></td><td></td><td>District of Columbia</td><td>726,932,000</td><td>0.2%</td></tr>
</table>

Source: U.S. Department of the Treasury, Internal Revenue Service
    "Fiscal Year 2012 IRS Data Book" (http://www.irs.gov/uac/SOI-Tax-Stats-IRS-Data-Book)
*Total includes refunds to international sources and other miscellaneous refunds not shown separately.

Average Value of Federal Individual Income Tax Refunds in 2012

National Average = $2,674*

ALPHA ORDER

RANK	STATE	AVERAGE REFUND
8	Alabama	$2,788
24	Alaska	2,554
23	Arizona	2,581
20	Arkansas	2,618
10	California	2,733
25	Colorado	2,553
3	Connecticut	2,925
28	Delaware	2,526
9	Florida	2,772
13	Georgia	2,728
37	Hawaii	2,469
42	Idaho	2,384
7	Illinois	2,838
27	Indiana	2,545
39	Iowa	2,421
35	Kansas	2,473
22	Kentucky	2,586
5	Louisiana	2,874
50	Maine	2,216
10	Maryland	2,733
16	Massachusetts	2,652
38	Michigan	2,454
45	Minnesota	2,365
6	Mississippi	2,867
34	Missouri	2,492
48	Montana	2,222
44	Nebraska	2,380
12	Nevada	2,730
36	New Hampshire	2,471
1	New Jersey	2,957
29	New Mexico	2,520
4	New York	2,919
26	North Carolina	2,549
43	North Dakota	2,381
39	Ohio	2,421
18	Oklahoma	2,638
47	Oregon	2,275
33	Pennsylvania	2,494
30	Rhode Island	2,515
32	South Carolina	2,500
41	South Dakota	2,385
15	Tennessee	2,654
2	Texas	2,955
17	Utah	2,649
49	Vermont	2,221
14	Virginia	2,656
21	Washington	2,597
31	West Virginia	2,506
46	Wisconsin	2,313
19	Wyoming	2,633

RANK ORDER

RANK	STATE	AVERAGE REFUND
1	New Jersey	$2,957
2	Texas	2,955
3	Connecticut	2,925
4	New York	2,919
5	Louisiana	2,874
6	Mississippi	2,867
7	Illinois	2,838
8	Alabama	2,788
9	Florida	2,772
10	California	2,733
10	Maryland	2,733
12	Nevada	2,730
13	Georgia	2,728
14	Virginia	2,656
15	Tennessee	2,654
16	Massachusetts	2,652
17	Utah	2,649
18	Oklahoma	2,638
19	Wyoming	2,633
20	Arkansas	2,618
21	Washington	2,597
22	Kentucky	2,586
23	Arizona	2,581
24	Alaska	2,554
25	Colorado	2,553
26	North Carolina	2,549
27	Indiana	2,545
28	Delaware	2,526
29	New Mexico	2,520
30	Rhode Island	2,515
31	West Virginia	2,506
32	South Carolina	2,500
33	Pennsylvania	2,494
34	Missouri	2,492
35	Kansas	2,473
36	New Hampshire	2,471
37	Hawaii	2,469
38	Michigan	2,454
39	Iowa	2,421
39	Ohio	2,421
41	South Dakota	2,385
42	Idaho	2,384
43	North Dakota	2,381
44	Nebraska	2,380
45	Minnesota	2,365
46	Wisconsin	2,313
47	Oregon	2,275
48	Montana	2,222
49	Vermont	2,221
50	Maine	2,216

| | District of Columbia | 2,674 |

Source: CQ Press using data from U.S. Department of the Treasury, Internal Revenue Service
   "Fiscal Year 2012 IRS Data Book" (http://www.irs.gov/uac/SOI-Tax-Stats-IRS-Data-Book)
*National average includes refunds to international sources and other miscellaneous refunds not shown separately.

Value of Federal Business Income Tax Refunds in 2012

National Total = $43,970,393,000*

ALPHA ORDER

RANK ORDER

RANK	STATE	REFUNDS	% of USA		RANK	STATE	REFUNDS	% of USA
28	Alabama	$321,437,000	0.7%		1	New York	$4,994,691,000	11.4%
48	Alaska	31,412,000	0.1%		2	Texas	4,385,589,000	10.0%
25	Arizona	406,589,000	0.9%		3	California	4,124,217,000	9.4%
32	Arkansas	214,902,000	0.5%		4	Delaware	2,788,966,000	6.3%
3	California	4,124,217,000	9.4%		5	Connecticut	2,274,714,000	5.2%
21	Colorado	644,095,000	1.5%		6	Illinois	1,655,613,000	3.8%
5	Connecticut	2,274,714,000	5.2%		7	Pennsylvania	1,591,304,000	3.6%
4	Delaware	2,788,966,000	6.3%		8	Ohio	1,560,233,000	3.5%
18	Florida	773,984,000	1.8%		9	Minnesota	1,523,973,000	3.5%
12	Georgia	1,382,782,000	3.1%		10	New Jersey	1,519,885,000	3.5%
40	Hawaii	91,421,000	0.2%		11	Massachusetts	1,482,065,000	3.4%
41	Idaho	90,762,000	0.2%		12	Georgia	1,382,782,000	3.1%
6	Illinois	1,655,613,000	3.8%		13	Tennessee	1,322,440,000	3.0%
24	Indiana	441,851,000	1.0%		14	Virginia	1,124,912,000	2.6%
34	Iowa	183,375,000	0.4%		15	Michigan	1,090,473,000	2.5%
33	Kansas	189,154,000	0.4%		16	North Carolina	985,125,000	2.2%
31	Kentucky	220,675,000	0.5%		17	Oklahoma	824,731,000	1.9%
29	Louisiana	302,873,000	0.7%		18	Florida	773,984,000	1.8%
35	Maine	179,652,000	0.4%		19	Maryland	764,633,000	1.7%
19	Maryland	764,633,000	1.7%		20	Missouri	709,395,000	1.6%
11	Massachusetts	1,482,065,000	3.4%		21	Colorado	644,095,000	1.5%
15	Michigan	1,090,473,000	2.5%		22	Wisconsin	632,066,000	1.4%
9	Minnesota	1,523,973,000	3.5%		23	Washington	520,547,000	1.2%
36	Mississippi	167,362,000	0.4%		24	Indiana	441,851,000	1.0%
20	Missouri	709,395,000	1.6%		25	Arizona	406,589,000	0.9%
49	Montana	30,137,000	0.1%		26	Oregon	406,585,000	0.9%
37	Nebraska	161,251,000	0.4%		27	Rhode Island	392,497,000	0.9%
39	Nevada	110,656,000	0.3%		28	Alabama	321,437,000	0.7%
43	New Hampshire	79,270,000	0.2%		29	Louisiana	302,873,000	0.7%
10	New Jersey	1,519,885,000	3.5%		30	Utah	291,146,000	0.7%
46	New Mexico	52,379,000	0.1%		31	Kentucky	220,675,000	0.5%
1	New York	4,994,691,000	11.4%		32	Arkansas	214,902,000	0.5%
16	North Carolina	985,125,000	2.2%		33	Kansas	189,154,000	0.4%
44	North Dakota	64,312,000	0.1%		34	Iowa	183,375,000	0.4%
8	Ohio	1,560,233,000	3.5%		35	Maine	179,652,000	0.4%
17	Oklahoma	824,731,000	1.9%		36	Mississippi	167,362,000	0.4%
26	Oregon	406,585,000	0.9%		37	Nebraska	161,251,000	0.4%
7	Pennsylvania	1,591,304,000	3.6%		38	South Carolina	145,403,000	0.3%
27	Rhode Island	392,497,000	0.9%		39	Nevada	110,656,000	0.3%
38	South Carolina	145,403,000	0.3%		40	Hawaii	91,421,000	0.2%
47	South Dakota	37,280,000	0.1%		41	Idaho	90,762,000	0.2%
13	Tennessee	1,322,440,000	3.0%		42	Vermont	90,535,000	0.2%
2	Texas	4,385,589,000	10.0%		43	New Hampshire	79,270,000	0.2%
30	Utah	291,146,000	0.7%		44	North Dakota	64,312,000	0.1%
42	Vermont	90,535,000	0.2%		45	West Virginia	64,244,000	0.1%
14	Virginia	1,124,912,000	2.6%		46	New Mexico	52,379,000	0.1%
23	Washington	520,547,000	1.2%		47	South Dakota	37,280,000	0.1%
45	West Virginia	64,244,000	0.1%		48	Alaska	31,412,000	0.1%
22	Wisconsin	632,066,000	1.4%		49	Montana	30,137,000	0.1%
50	Wyoming	22,176,000	0.1%		50	Wyoming	22,176,000	0.1%
						District of Columbia	72,274,000	0.2%

Source: U.S. Department of the Treasury, Internal Revenue Service
 "Fiscal Year 2012 IRS Data Book" (http://www.irs.gov/uac/SOI-Tax-Stats-IRS-Data-Book)
*Total includes refunds to international sources and other miscellaneous refunds not shown separately. Includes taxes on corporation income (Form 1120 series) and unrelated business income from tax-exempt organizations.

Average Value of Federal Business Income Tax Refunds in 2012

National Average = $98,720*

ALPHA ORDER

RANK	STATE	AVERAGE REFUND
25	Alabama	$69,111
42	Alaska	31,163
30	Arizona	62,475
29	Arkansas	63,244
23	California	71,213
18	Colorado	83,768
2	Connecticut	479,695
1	Delaware	1,536,620
44	Florida	27,230
11	Georgia	120,399
41	Hawaii	32,066
36	Idaho	41,749
17	Illinois	87,962
26	Indiana	64,826
45	Iowa	27,034
40	Kansas	33,850
31	Kentucky	52,818
33	Louisiana	49,240
20	Maine	78,076
15	Maryland	96,740
6	Massachusetts	165,835
22	Michigan	72,722
8	Minnesota	151,368
34	Mississippi	47,438
19	Missouri	79,743
50	Montana	9,023
35	Nebraska	43,370
46	Nevada	25,782
37	New Hampshire	37,216
10	New Jersey	122,938
47	New Mexico	22,176
5	New York	173,012
16	North Carolina	89,794
38	North Dakota	36,940
12	Ohio	105,958
7	Oklahoma	161,112
28	Oregon	63,618
14	Pennsylvania	100,158
3	Rhode Island	301,689
43	South Carolina	30,832
48	South Dakota	16,945
4	Tennessee	206,955
9	Texas	127,019
21	Utah	78,013
24	Vermont	70,730
13	Virginia	101,289
32	Washington	51,074
39	West Virginia	36,774
27	Wisconsin	64,300
49	Wyoming	13,825

RANK ORDER

RANK	STATE	AVERAGE REFUND
1	Delaware	$1,536,620
2	Connecticut	479,695
3	Rhode Island	301,689
4	Tennessee	206,955
5	New York	173,012
6	Massachusetts	165,835
7	Oklahoma	161,112
8	Minnesota	151,368
9	Texas	127,019
10	New Jersey	122,938
11	Georgia	120,399
12	Ohio	105,958
13	Virginia	101,289
14	Pennsylvania	100,158
15	Maryland	96,740
16	North Carolina	89,794
17	Illinois	87,962
18	Colorado	83,768
19	Missouri	79,743
20	Maine	78,076
21	Utah	78,013
22	Michigan	72,722
23	California	71,213
24	Vermont	70,730
25	Alabama	69,111
26	Indiana	64,826
27	Wisconsin	64,300
28	Oregon	63,618
29	Arkansas	63,244
30	Arizona	62,475
31	Kentucky	52,818
32	Washington	51,074
33	Louisiana	49,240
34	Mississippi	47,438
35	Nebraska	43,370
36	Idaho	41,749
37	New Hampshire	37,216
38	North Dakota	36,940
39	West Virginia	36,774
40	Kansas	33,850
41	Hawaii	32,066
42	Alaska	31,163
43	South Carolina	30,832
44	Florida	27,230
45	Iowa	27,034
46	Nevada	25,782
47	New Mexico	22,176
48	South Dakota	16,945
49	Wyoming	13,825
50	Montana	9,023

District of Columbia 57,912

Source: CQ Press using data from U.S. Department of the Treasury, Internal Revenue Service
"Fiscal Year 2012 IRS Data Book" (http://www.irs.gov/uac/SOI-Tax-Stats-IRS-Data-Book)
*National average includes refunds to international sources and other miscellaneous refunds not shown separately.

Per Capita Federal Economic Stimulus Funds as of 2013

National Per Capita = $860*

ALPHA ORDER			RANK ORDER		
RANK	STATE	PER CAPITA	RANK	STATE	PER CAPITA
37	Alabama	$752	1	Alaska	$3,151
1	Alaska	3,151	2	Vermont	1,678
9	Arizona	1,160	3	South Dakota	1,599
32	Arkansas	789	4	North Dakota	1,519
24	California	903	5	Montana	1,504
14	Colorado	1,069	6	New Mexico	1,304
44	Connecticut	706	7	Washington	1,206
18	Delaware	1,019	8	Maryland	1,184
50	Florida	564	9	Arizona	1,160
46	Georgia	701	9	Rhode Island	1,160
17	Hawaii	1,034	11	Wyoming	1,142
15	Idaho	1,056	12	Massachusetts	1,141
21	Illinois	932	13	Maine	1,093
47	Indiana	687	14	Colorado	1,069
40	Iowa	734	15	Idaho	1,056
30	Kansas	803	16	Nevada	1,040
29	Kentucky	814	17	Hawaii	1,034
42	Louisiana	721	18	Delaware	1,019
13	Maine	1,093	19	South Carolina	976
8	Maryland	1,184	20	West Virginia	973
12	Massachusetts	1,141	21	Illinois	932
25	Michigan	875	22	Tennessee	916
38	Minnesota	740	23	Mississippi	909
23	Mississippi	909	24	California	903
28	Missouri	816	25	Michigan	875
5	Montana	1,504	26	New York	874
43	Nebraska	714	27	Oregon	829
16	Nevada	1,040	28	Missouri	816
39	New Hampshire	739	29	Kentucky	814
49	New Jersey	632	30	Kansas	803
6	New Mexico	1,304	31	Oklahoma	794
26	New York	874	32	Arkansas	789
35	North Carolina	774	33	Ohio	787
4	North Dakota	1,519	34	Virginia	780
33	Ohio	787	35	North Carolina	774
31	Oklahoma	794	36	Utah	762
27	Oregon	829	37	Alabama	752
41	Pennsylvania	729	38	Minnesota	740
9	Rhode Island	1,160	39	New Hampshire	739
19	South Carolina	976	40	Iowa	734
3	South Dakota	1,599	41	Pennsylvania	729
22	Tennessee	916	42	Louisiana	721
48	Texas	651	43	Nebraska	714
36	Utah	762	44	Connecticut	706
2	Vermont	1,678	45	Wisconsin	704
34	Virginia	780	46	Georgia	701
7	Washington	1,206	47	Indiana	687
20	West Virginia	973	48	Texas	651
45	Wisconsin	704	49	New Jersey	632
11	Wyoming	1,142	50	Florida	564
				District of Columbia	9,257

Source: CQ Press using data from Recovery Accountability and Transparency Board
"Funding Awarded by State "
(http://www.recovery.gov/arra/Pages/TextView.aspx?data=recipientFundingAwardedByState)
*Funds awarded from February 17, 2009 to December 31, 2013. Updated as of January 30, 2014.

Federal Government Expenditures in 2012

National Total = $3,160,300,000,000*

ALPHA ORDER

RANK ORDER

RANK	STATE	EXPENDITURES	% of USA
21	Alabama	$45,500,000,000	1.4%
46	Alaska	7,000,000,000	0.2%
18	Arizona	51,000,000,000	1.6%
34	Arkansas	19,600,000,000	0.6%
3	California	258,900,000,000	8.2%
24	Colorado	33,600,000,000	1.1%
22	Connecticut	39,300,000,000	1.2%
41	Delaware	10,900,000,000	0.3%
1	Florida	528,400,000,000	16.7%
13	Georgia	68,300,000,000	2.2%
33	Hawaii	20,200,000,000	0.6%
42	Idaho	10,400,000,000	0.3%
12	Illinois	69,500,000,000	2.2%
23	Indiana	34,100,000,000	1.1%
32	Iowa	20,500,000,000	0.6%
36	Kansas	15,500,000,000	0.5%
24	Kentucky	33,600,000,000	1.1%
5	Louisiana	116,000,000,000	3.7%
40	Maine	11,000,000,000	0.3%
14	Maryland	63,600,000,000	2.0%
16	Massachusetts	57,800,000,000	1.8%
15	Michigan	60,500,000,000	1.9%
28	Minnesota	27,600,000,000	0.9%
26	Mississippi	32,100,000,000	1.0%
19	Missouri	48,100,000,000	1.5%
47	Montana	6,700,000,000	0.2%
39	Nebraska	11,300,000,000	0.4%
35	Nevada	15,800,000,000	0.5%
44	New Hampshire	9,400,000,000	0.3%
8	New Jersey	94,200,000,000	3.0%
31	New Mexico	21,600,000,000	0.7%
4	New York	151,700,000,000	4.8%
9	North Carolina	81,900,000,000	2.6%
45	North Dakota	8,000,000,000	0.3%
11	Ohio	70,900,000,000	2.2%
30	Oklahoma	24,000,000,000	0.8%
29	Oregon	26,800,000,000	0.8%
7	Pennsylvania	95,300,000,000	3.0%
43	Rhode Island	10,000,000,000	0.3%
10	South Carolina	74,100,000,000	2.3%
48	South Dakota	6,000,000,000	0.2%
20	Tennessee	47,900,000,000	1.5%
2	Texas	277,000,000,000	8.8%
38	Utah	13,100,000,000	0.4%
49	Vermont	5,000,000,000	0.2%
6	Virginia	112,100,000,000	3.5%
17	Washington	53,100,000,000	1.7%
37	West Virginia	14,400,000,000	0.5%
27	Wisconsin	28,400,000,000	0.9%
50	Wyoming	3,500,000,000	0.1%

RANK	STATE	EXPENDITURES	% of USA
1	Florida	$528,400,000,000	16.7%
2	Texas	277,000,000,000	8.8%
3	California	258,900,000,000	8.2%
4	New York	151,700,000,000	4.8%
5	Louisiana	116,000,000,000	3.7%
6	Virginia	112,100,000,000	3.5%
7	Pennsylvania	95,300,000,000	3.0%
8	New Jersey	94,200,000,000	3.0%
9	North Carolina	81,900,000,000	2.6%
10	South Carolina	74,100,000,000	2.3%
11	Ohio	70,900,000,000	2.2%
12	Illinois	69,500,000,000	2.2%
13	Georgia	68,300,000,000	2.2%
14	Maryland	63,600,000,000	2.0%
15	Michigan	60,500,000,000	1.9%
16	Massachusetts	57,800,000,000	1.8%
17	Washington	53,100,000,000	1.7%
18	Arizona	51,000,000,000	1.6%
19	Missouri	48,100,000,000	1.5%
20	Tennessee	47,900,000,000	1.5%
21	Alabama	45,500,000,000	1.4%
22	Connecticut	39,300,000,000	1.2%
23	Indiana	34,100,000,000	1.1%
24	Colorado	33,600,000,000	1.1%
24	Kentucky	33,600,000,000	1.1%
26	Mississippi	32,100,000,000	1.0%
27	Wisconsin	28,400,000,000	0.9%
28	Minnesota	27,600,000,000	0.9%
29	Oregon	26,800,000,000	0.8%
30	Oklahoma	24,000,000,000	0.8%
31	New Mexico	21,600,000,000	0.7%
32	Iowa	20,500,000,000	0.6%
33	Hawaii	20,200,000,000	0.6%
34	Arkansas	19,600,000,000	0.6%
35	Nevada	15,800,000,000	0.5%
36	Kansas	15,500,000,000	0.5%
37	West Virginia	14,400,000,000	0.5%
38	Utah	13,100,000,000	0.4%
39	Nebraska	11,300,000,000	0.4%
40	Maine	11,000,000,000	0.3%
41	Delaware	10,900,000,000	0.3%
42	Idaho	10,400,000,000	0.3%
43	Rhode Island	10,000,000,000	0.3%
44	New Hampshire	9,400,000,000	0.3%
45	North Dakota	8,000,000,000	0.3%
46	Alaska	7,000,000,000	0.2%
47	Montana	6,700,000,000	0.2%
48	South Dakota	6,000,000,000	0.2%
49	Vermont	5,000,000,000	0.2%
50	Wyoming	3,500,000,000	0.1%
	District of Columbia	23,700,000,000	0.7%

Source: U.S. Office of Management and Budget, USAspending.gov
   "Prime Award Spending Data Summary" (http://www.usaspending.gov/explore, as of January 31, 2014)
*Total includes $28,775,900,000 in U.S. territories and $162,624,100,000 in expenditures not distributed by state. Expenditures allocated based on place of performance of a contract. Includes Contracts, Grants, Direct Payments, Insurance, and "Other."
This source replaces a previous data series by the U.S. Census and definitions differ.

Per Capita Federal Government Expenditures in 2012

National Per Capita = $9,459*

ALPHA ORDER				RANK ORDER		
RANK	STATE	PER CAPITA		RANK	STATE	PER CAPITA
16	Alabama	$9,445		1	Florida	$27,349
14	Alaska	9,585		2	Louisiana	25,206
22	Arizona	7,785		3	South Carolina	15,688
36	Arkansas	6,644		4	Hawaii	14,531
33	California	6,813		5	Virginia	13,693
38	Colorado	6,475		6	Delaware	11,886
8	Connecticut	10,942		7	North Dakota	11,407
6	Delaware	11,886		8	Connecticut	10,942
1	Florida	27,349		9	Maryland	10,807
31	Georgia	6,888		10	Mississippi	10,749
4	Hawaii	14,531		11	Texas	10,629
37	Idaho	6,518		12	New Jersey	10,623
45	Illinois	5,401		13	New Mexico	10,367
47	Indiana	5,216		14	Alaska	9,585
34	Iowa	6,667		15	Rhode Island	9,521
46	Kansas	5,372		16	Alabama	9,445
26	Kentucky	7,672		17	Massachusetts	8,698
2	Louisiana	25,206		18	North Carolina	8,401
19	Maine	8,280		19	Maine	8,280
9	Maryland	10,807		20	Vermont	7,988
17	Massachusetts	8,698		21	Missouri	7,984
41	Michigan	6,122		22	Arizona	7,785
48	Minnesota	5,130		23	West Virginia	7,756
10	Mississippi	10,749		24	New York	7,749
21	Missouri	7,984		25	Washington	7,701
35	Montana	6,663		26	Kentucky	7,672
42	Nebraska	6,090		27	Pennsylvania	7,466
44	Nevada	5,736		28	Tennessee	7,421
30	New Hampshire	7,112		29	South Dakota	7,194
12	New Jersey	10,623		30	New Hampshire	7,112
13	New Mexico	10,367		31	Georgia	6,888
24	New York	7,749		32	Oregon	6,872
18	North Carolina	8,401		33	California	6,813
7	North Dakota	11,407		34	Iowa	6,667
40	Ohio	6,137		35	Montana	6,663
39	Oklahoma	6,290		36	Arkansas	6,644
32	Oregon	6,872		37	Idaho	6,518
27	Pennsylvania	7,466		38	Colorado	6,475
15	Rhode Island	9,521		39	Oklahoma	6,290
3	South Carolina	15,688		40	Ohio	6,137
29	South Dakota	7,194		41	Michigan	6,122
28	Tennessee	7,421		42	Nebraska	6,090
11	Texas	10,629		43	Wyoming	6,070
50	Utah	4,589		44	Nevada	5,736
20	Vermont	7,988		45	Illinois	5,401
5	Virginia	13,693		46	Kansas	5,372
25	Washington	7,701		47	Indiana	5,216
23	West Virginia	7,756		48	Minnesota	5,130
49	Wisconsin	4,961		49	Wisconsin	4,961
43	Wyoming	6,070		50	Utah	4,589
					District of Columbia	37,416

Source: CQ Press using data from U.S. Office of Management and Budget, USAspending.gov
   "Prime Award Spending Data Summary" (http://www.usaspending.gov/explore, as of January 31, 2014)
*National per capita excludes expenditures and population for territories and undistributed amounts. Expenditures allocated based
on place of performance of a contract. Includes Contracts, Grants, Direct Payments, Insurance, and "Other." This source
replaces a previous data series by the U.S. Census and definitions differ.

Federal Government Grants in 2012

National Total = $539,500,000,000*

ALPHA ORDER

RANK	STATE	EXPENDITURES	% of USA
21	Alabama	$7,100,000,000	1.3%
36	Alaska	2,300,000,000	0.4%
14	Arizona	9,500,000,000	1.8%
28	Arkansas	4,900,000,000	0.9%
1	California	51,500,000,000	9.5%
26	Colorado	5,400,000,000	1.0%
23	Connecticut	6,300,000,000	1.2%
47	Delaware	1,500,000,000	0.3%
6	Florida	18,200,000,000	3.4%
11	Georgia	11,400,000,000	2.1%
42	Hawaii	1,700,000,000	0.3%
42	Idaho	1,700,000,000	0.3%
9	Illinois	14,000,000,000	2.6%
32	Indiana	3,800,000,000	0.7%
30	Iowa	4,400,000,000	0.8%
36	Kansas	2,300,000,000	0.4%
18	Kentucky	8,100,000,000	1.5%
16	Louisiana	9,000,000,000	1.7%
35	Maine	2,600,000,000	0.5%
19	Maryland	8,000,000,000	1.5%
10	Massachusetts	12,300,000,000	2.3%
8	Michigan	14,900,000,000	2.8%
24	Minnesota	5,900,000,000	1.1%
40	Mississippi	2,100,000,000	0.4%
16	Missouri	9,000,000,000	1.7%
42	Montana	1,700,000,000	0.3%
39	Nebraska	2,200,000,000	0.4%
36	Nevada	2,300,000,000	0.4%
48	New Hampshire	1,300,000,000	0.2%
13	New Jersey	10,800,000,000	2.0%
27	New Mexico	5,000,000,000	0.9%
2	New York	42,700,000,000	7.9%
7	North Carolina	15,700,000,000	2.9%
45	North Dakota	1,600,000,000	0.3%
4	Ohio	20,000,000,000	3.7%
25	Oklahoma	5,500,000,000	1.0%
29	Oregon	4,600,000,000	0.9%
5	Pennsylvania	19,900,000,000	3.7%
40	Rhode Island	2,100,000,000	0.4%
22	South Carolina	6,800,000,000	1.3%
48	South Dakota	1,300,000,000	0.2%
12	Tennessee	11,200,000,000	2.1%
3	Texas	31,000,000,000	5.7%
34	Utah	2,900,000,000	0.5%
45	Vermont	1,600,000,000	0.3%
20	Virginia	7,600,000,000	1.4%
15	Washington	9,200,000,000	1.7%
33	West Virginia	3,100,000,000	0.6%
31	Wisconsin	4,200,000,000	0.8%
50	Wyoming	964,200,000	0.2%

RANK ORDER

RANK	STATE	EXPENDITURES	% of USA
1	California	$51,500,000,000	9.5%
2	New York	42,700,000,000	7.9%
3	Texas	31,000,000,000	5.7%
4	Ohio	20,000,000,000	3.7%
5	Pennsylvania	19,900,000,000	3.7%
6	Florida	18,200,000,000	3.4%
7	North Carolina	15,700,000,000	2.9%
8	Michigan	14,900,000,000	2.8%
9	Illinois	14,000,000,000	2.6%
10	Massachusetts	12,300,000,000	2.3%
11	Georgia	11,400,000,000	2.1%
12	Tennessee	11,200,000,000	2.1%
13	New Jersey	10,800,000,000	2.0%
14	Arizona	9,500,000,000	1.8%
15	Washington	9,200,000,000	1.7%
16	Louisiana	9,000,000,000	1.7%
16	Missouri	9,000,000,000	1.7%
18	Kentucky	8,100,000,000	1.5%
19	Maryland	8,000,000,000	1.5%
20	Virginia	7,600,000,000	1.4%
21	Alabama	7,100,000,000	1.3%
22	South Carolina	6,800,000,000	1.3%
23	Connecticut	6,300,000,000	1.2%
24	Minnesota	5,900,000,000	1.1%
25	Oklahoma	5,500,000,000	1.0%
26	Colorado	5,400,000,000	1.0%
27	New Mexico	5,000,000,000	0.9%
28	Arkansas	4,900,000,000	0.9%
29	Oregon	4,600,000,000	0.9%
30	Iowa	4,400,000,000	0.8%
31	Wisconsin	4,200,000,000	0.8%
32	Indiana	3,800,000,000	0.7%
33	West Virginia	3,100,000,000	0.6%
34	Utah	2,900,000,000	0.5%
35	Maine	2,600,000,000	0.5%
36	Alaska	2,300,000,000	0.4%
36	Kansas	2,300,000,000	0.4%
36	Nevada	2,300,000,000	0.4%
39	Nebraska	2,200,000,000	0.4%
40	Mississippi	2,100,000,000	0.4%
40	Rhode Island	2,100,000,000	0.4%
42	Hawaii	1,700,000,000	0.3%
42	Idaho	1,700,000,000	0.3%
42	Montana	1,700,000,000	0.3%
45	North Dakota	1,600,000,000	0.3%
45	Vermont	1,600,000,000	0.3%
47	Delaware	1,500,000,000	0.3%
48	New Hampshire	1,300,000,000	0.2%
48	South Dakota	1,300,000,000	0.2%
50	Wyoming	964,200,000	0.2%
	District of Columbia	3,200,000,000	0.6%

Source: U.S. Office of Management and Budget, USAspending.gov
 "Prime Award Spending Data Summary" (http://www.usaspending.gov/explore, as of January 31, 2014)
*Total includes $6,937,500,000 in U.S. territories and $96,198,300,000 in expenditures not distributed by state. Expenditures allocated based on place of performance of a contract. Includes funds awarded to a non-federal entity for a defined public or private purpose in which services are not rendered to the federal government. This source replaces a previous data series by the U.S. Census and definitions differ.

Per Capita Expenditures for Federal Government Grants in 2012

National Per Capita = $1,390*

ALPHA ORDER				RANK ORDER		
RANK	STATE	PER CAPITA		RANK	STATE	PER CAPITA
24	Alabama	$1,474		1	Alaska	$3,149
1	Alaska	3,149		2	Vermont	2,556
25	Arizona	1,450		3	New Mexico	2,400
17	Arkansas	1,661		4	North Dakota	2,281
30	California	1,355		5	New York	2,181
41	Colorado	1,041		6	Rhode Island	1,999
11	Connecticut	1,754		7	Maine	1,957
18	Delaware	1,636		8	Louisiana	1,956
44	Florida	942		9	Massachusetts	1,851
37	Georgia	1,150		10	Kentucky	1,849
32	Hawaii	1,223		11	Connecticut	1,754
40	Idaho	1,065		12	Tennessee	1,735
39	Illinois	1,088		13	Ohio	1,731
50	Indiana	581		14	Montana	1,691
28	Iowa	1,431		15	Wyoming	1,672
47	Kansas	797		16	West Virginia	1,670
10	Kentucky	1,849		17	Arkansas	1,661
8	Louisiana	1,956		18	Delaware	1,636
7	Maine	1,957		19	North Carolina	1,611
29	Maryland	1,359		20	Pennsylvania	1,559
9	Massachusetts	1,851		20	South Dakota	1,559
22	Michigan	1,508		22	Michigan	1,508
38	Minnesota	1,097		23	Missouri	1,494
49	Mississippi	703		24	Alabama	1,474
23	Missouri	1,494		25	Arizona	1,450
14	Montana	1,691		26	Oklahoma	1,441
35	Nebraska	1,186		27	South Carolina	1,440
46	Nevada	835		28	Iowa	1,431
43	New Hampshire	984		29	Maryland	1,359
33	New Jersey	1,218		30	California	1,355
3	New Mexico	2,400		31	Washington	1,334
5	New York	2,181		32	Hawaii	1,223
19	North Carolina	1,611		33	New Jersey	1,218
4	North Dakota	2,281		34	Texas	1,190
13	Ohio	1,731		35	Nebraska	1,186
26	Oklahoma	1,441		36	Oregon	1,180
36	Oregon	1,180		37	Georgia	1,150
20	Pennsylvania	1,559		38	Minnesota	1,097
6	Rhode Island	1,999		39	Illinois	1,088
27	South Carolina	1,440		40	Idaho	1,065
20	South Dakota	1,559		41	Colorado	1,041
12	Tennessee	1,735		42	Utah	1,016
34	Texas	1,190		43	New Hampshire	984
42	Utah	1,016		44	Florida	942
2	Vermont	2,556		45	Virginia	928
45	Virginia	928		46	Nevada	835
31	Washington	1,334		47	Kansas	797
16	West Virginia	1,670		48	Wisconsin	734
48	Wisconsin	734		49	Mississippi	703
15	Wyoming	1,672		50	Indiana	581
					District of Columbia	5,052

Source: CQ Press using data from U.S. Office of Management and Budget, USAspending.gov
"Prime Award Spending Data Summary" (http://www.usaspending.gov/explore, as of January 31, 2014)
*National per capita excludes expenditures and population for territories and undistributed amounts. Expenditures allocated based on place of performance of a contract. Includes funds awarded to a non-federal entity for a defined public or private purpose in which services are not rendered to the federal government. This source replaces a previous data series by the U.S. Census and definitions differ.

Federal Government Procurement Contract Awards in 2012

National Total = $517,500,000,000*

ALPHA ORDER

RANK	STATE	EXPENDITURES	% of USA
14	Alabama	$10,700,000,000	2.1%
34	Alaska	2,400,000,000	0.5%
9	Arizona	14,200,000,000	2.7%
41	Arkansas	1,100,000,000	0.2%
2	California	51,900,000,000	10.0%
12	Colorado	11,100,000,000	2.1%
11	Connecticut	13,000,000,000	2.5%
48	Delaware	527,700,000	0.1%
6	Florida	15,400,000,000	3.0%
17	Georgia	7,900,000,000	1.5%
32	Hawaii	2,800,000,000	0.5%
34	Idaho	2,400,000,000	0.5%
13	Illinois	10,900,000,000	2.1%
27	Indiana	3,700,000,000	0.7%
38	Iowa	1,700,000,000	0.3%
36	Kansas	2,100,000,000	0.4%
22	Kentucky	6,500,000,000	1.3%
26	Louisiana	4,300,000,000	0.8%
38	Maine	1,700,000,000	0.3%
4	Maryland	27,300,000,000	5.3%
7	Massachusetts	15,100,000,000	2.9%
23	Michigan	6,300,000,000	1.2%
33	Minnesota	2,700,000,000	0.5%
21	Mississippi	6,600,000,000	1.3%
7	Missouri	15,100,000,000	2.9%
47	Montana	573,200,000	0.1%
41	Nebraska	1,100,000,000	0.2%
31	Nevada	2,900,000,000	0.6%
37	New Hampshire	1,900,000,000	0.4%
20	New Jersey	6,900,000,000	1.3%
19	New Mexico	7,200,000,000	1.4%
15	New York	10,500,000,000	2.0%
25	North Carolina	5,400,000,000	1.0%
44	North Dakota	866,300,000	0.2%
18	Ohio	7,400,000,000	1.4%
30	Oklahoma	3,100,000,000	0.6%
40	Oregon	1,500,000,000	0.3%
5	Pennsylvania	18,800,000,000	3.6%
45	Rhode Island	713,400,000	0.1%
23	South Carolina	6,300,000,000	1.2%
46	South Dakota	642,300,000	0.1%
16	Tennessee	8,600,000,000	1.7%
3	Texas	38,200,000,000	7.4%
28	Utah	3,400,000,000	0.7%
49	Vermont	408,500,000	0.1%
1	Virginia	55,200,000,000	10.7%
10	Washington	13,200,000,000	2.6%
41	West Virginia	1,100,000,000	0.2%
29	Wisconsin	3,200,000,000	0.6%
50	Wyoming	348,000,000	0.1%

RANK ORDER

RANK	STATE	EXPENDITURES	% of USA
1	Virginia	$55,200,000,000	10.7%
2	California	51,900,000,000	10.0%
3	Texas	38,200,000,000	7.4%
4	Maryland	27,300,000,000	5.3%
5	Pennsylvania	18,800,000,000	3.6%
6	Florida	15,400,000,000	3.0%
7	Massachusetts	15,100,000,000	2.9%
7	Missouri	15,100,000,000	2.9%
9	Arizona	14,200,000,000	2.7%
10	Washington	13,200,000,000	2.6%
11	Connecticut	13,000,000,000	2.5%
12	Colorado	11,100,000,000	2.1%
13	Illinois	10,900,000,000	2.1%
14	Alabama	10,700,000,000	2.1%
15	New York	10,500,000,000	2.0%
16	Tennessee	8,600,000,000	1.7%
17	Georgia	7,900,000,000	1.5%
18	Ohio	7,400,000,000	1.4%
19	New Mexico	7,200,000,000	1.4%
20	New Jersey	6,900,000,000	1.3%
21	Mississippi	6,600,000,000	1.3%
22	Kentucky	6,500,000,000	1.3%
23	Michigan	6,300,000,000	1.2%
23	South Carolina	6,300,000,000	1.2%
25	North Carolina	5,400,000,000	1.0%
26	Louisiana	4,300,000,000	0.8%
27	Indiana	3,700,000,000	0.7%
28	Utah	3,400,000,000	0.7%
29	Wisconsin	3,200,000,000	0.6%
30	Oklahoma	3,100,000,000	0.6%
31	Nevada	2,900,000,000	0.6%
32	Hawaii	2,800,000,000	0.5%
33	Minnesota	2,700,000,000	0.5%
34	Alaska	2,400,000,000	0.5%
34	Idaho	2,400,000,000	0.5%
36	Kansas	2,100,000,000	0.4%
37	New Hampshire	1,900,000,000	0.4%
38	Iowa	1,700,000,000	0.3%
38	Maine	1,700,000,000	0.3%
40	Oregon	1,500,000,000	0.3%
41	Arkansas	1,100,000,000	0.2%
41	Nebraska	1,100,000,000	0.2%
41	West Virginia	1,100,000,000	0.2%
44	North Dakota	866,300,000	0.2%
45	Rhode Island	713,400,000	0.1%
46	South Dakota	642,300,000	0.1%
47	Montana	573,200,000	0.1%
48	Delaware	527,700,000	0.1%
49	Vermont	408,500,000	0.1%
50	Wyoming	348,000,000	0.1%
	District of Columbia	18,700,000,000	3.6%

Source: U.S. Office of Management and Budget, USAspending.gov
   "Prime Award Spending Data Summary" (http://www.usaspending.gov/explore, as of January 31, 2014)
*Total includes $1,318,500,000 in U.S. territories and $60,602,100,000 in expenditures not distributed by state. Expenditures allocated based on place of performance of a contract. Does not include grants, co-operative agreements, or contracts under grants. This source replaces a previous data series by the U.S. Census and definitions differ.

Per Capita Expenditures for Federal Government Procurement Contract Awards in 2012
National Per Capita = $1,451*

ALPHA ORDER

RANK	STATE	PER CAPITA
8	Alabama	$2,221
5	Alaska	3,286
10	Arizona	2,168
50	Arkansas	373
19	California	1,366
11	Colorado	2,139
3	Connecticut	3,619
41	Delaware	575
29	Florida	797
29	Georgia	797
12	Hawaii	2,014
14	Idaho	1,504
27	Illinois	847
43	Indiana	566
46	Iowa	553
33	Kansas	728
15	Kentucky	1,484
26	Louisiana	934
22	Maine	1,280
2	Maryland	4,639
7	Massachusetts	2,272
37	Michigan	637
48	Minnesota	502
9	Mississippi	2,210
6	Missouri	2,506
42	Montana	570
39	Nebraska	593
25	Nevada	1,053
18	New Hampshire	1,438
31	New Jersey	778
4	New Mexico	3,456
47	New York	536
45	North Carolina	554
23	North Dakota	1,235
36	Ohio	641
28	Oklahoma	812
49	Oregon	385
16	Pennsylvania	1,473
34	Rhode Island	679
20	South Carolina	1,334
32	South Dakota	770
21	Tennessee	1,332
17	Texas	1,466
24	Utah	1,191
35	Vermont	653
1	Virginia	6,743
13	Washington	1,914
40	West Virginia	592
44	Wisconsin	559
38	Wyoming	604

RANK ORDER

RANK	STATE	PER CAPITA
1	Virginia	$6,743
2	Maryland	4,639
3	Connecticut	3,619
4	New Mexico	3,456
5	Alaska	3,286
6	Missouri	2,506
7	Massachusetts	2,272
8	Alabama	2,221
9	Mississippi	2,210
10	Arizona	2,168
11	Colorado	2,139
12	Hawaii	2,014
13	Washington	1,914
14	Idaho	1,504
15	Kentucky	1,484
16	Pennsylvania	1,473
17	Texas	1,466
18	New Hampshire	1,438
19	California	1,366
20	South Carolina	1,334
21	Tennessee	1,332
22	Maine	1,280
23	North Dakota	1,235
24	Utah	1,191
25	Nevada	1,053
26	Louisiana	934
27	Illinois	847
28	Oklahoma	812
29	Florida	797
29	Georgia	797
31	New Jersey	778
32	South Dakota	770
33	Kansas	728
34	Rhode Island	679
35	Vermont	653
36	Ohio	641
37	Michigan	637
38	Wyoming	604
39	Nebraska	593
40	West Virginia	592
41	Delaware	575
42	Montana	570
43	Indiana	566
44	Wisconsin	559
45	North Carolina	554
46	Iowa	553
47	New York	536
48	Minnesota	502
49	Oregon	385
50	Arkansas	373

District of Columbia   29,522

Source: CQ Press using data from U.S. Office of Management and Budget, USAspending.gov
"Prime Award Spending Data Summary" (http://www.usaspending.gov/explore, as of January 31, 2014)
*National per capita excludes expenditures and population for territories and undistributed amounts. Expenditures allocated based on place of performance of a contract. Does not include grants, co-operative agreements, or contracts under grants. This source replaces a previous data series by the U.S. Census and definitions differ.

Federal Government Direct Payments to Individuals in 2012

National Total = $959,600,000,000*

RANK	STATE	EXPENDITURES	% of USA
20	Alabama	$17,800,000,000	1.9%
50	Alaska	1,600,000,000	0.2%
15	Arizona	20,600,000,000	2.1%
30	Arkansas	10,900,000,000	1.1%
1	California	90,100,000,000	9.4%
26	Colorado	13,000,000,000	1.4%
29	Connecticut	11,000,000,000	1.1%
45	Delaware	3,100,000,000	0.3%
2	Florida	66,900,000,000	7.0%
10	Georgia	27,300,000,000	2.8%
42	Hawaii	4,000,000,000	0.4%
40	Idaho	4,800,000,000	0.5%
7	Illinois	36,200,000,000	3.8%
14	Indiana	21,300,000,000	2.2%
31	Iowa	10,800,000,000	1.1%
33	Kansas	9,100,000,000	0.9%
23	Kentucky	15,500,000,000	1.6%
25	Louisiana	13,400,000,000	1.4%
39	Maine	5,000,000,000	0.5%
24	Maryland	15,400,000,000	1.6%
18	Massachusetts	19,700,000,000	2.1%
8	Michigan	35,200,000,000	3.7%
22	Minnesota	16,100,000,000	1.7%
32	Mississippi	10,100,000,000	1.1%
17	Missouri	20,100,000,000	2.1%
44	Montana	3,500,000,000	0.4%
37	Nebraska	5,900,000,000	0.6%
35	Nevada	7,300,000,000	0.8%
41	New Hampshire	4,400,000,000	0.5%
11	New Jersey	26,500,000,000	2.8%
36	New Mexico	6,400,000,000	0.7%
4	New York	58,700,000,000	6.1%
9	North Carolina	31,400,000,000	3.3%
47	North Dakota	2,200,000,000	0.2%
6	Ohio	36,500,000,000	3.8%
28	Oklahoma	12,500,000,000	1.3%
26	Oregon	13,000,000,000	1.4%
5	Pennsylvania	44,300,000,000	4.6%
43	Rhode Island	3,600,000,000	0.4%
21	South Carolina	16,600,000,000	1.7%
46	South Dakota	2,800,000,000	0.3%
13	Tennessee	21,700,000,000	2.3%
3	Texas	62,100,000,000	6.5%
37	Utah	5,900,000,000	0.6%
47	Vermont	2,200,000,000	0.2%
12	Virginia	23,700,000,000	2.5%
16	Washington	20,400,000,000	2.1%
34	West Virginia	7,700,000,000	0.8%
19	Wisconsin	18,400,000,000	1.9%
49	Wyoming	1,700,000,000	0.2%

RANK ORDER

RANK	STATE	EXPENDITURES	% of USA
1	California	$90,100,000,000	9.4%
2	Florida	66,900,000,000	7.0%
3	Texas	62,100,000,000	6.5%
4	New York	58,700,000,000	6.1%
5	Pennsylvania	44,300,000,000	4.6%
6	Ohio	36,500,000,000	3.8%
7	Illinois	36,200,000,000	3.8%
8	Michigan	35,200,000,000	3.7%
9	North Carolina	31,400,000,000	3.3%
10	Georgia	27,300,000,000	2.8%
11	New Jersey	26,500,000,000	2.8%
12	Virginia	23,700,000,000	2.5%
13	Tennessee	21,700,000,000	2.3%
14	Indiana	21,300,000,000	2.2%
15	Arizona	20,600,000,000	2.1%
16	Washington	20,400,000,000	2.1%
17	Missouri	20,100,000,000	2.1%
18	Massachusetts	19,700,000,000	2.1%
19	Wisconsin	18,400,000,000	1.9%
20	Alabama	17,800,000,000	1.9%
21	South Carolina	16,600,000,000	1.7%
22	Minnesota	16,100,000,000	1.7%
23	Kentucky	15,500,000,000	1.6%
24	Maryland	15,400,000,000	1.6%
25	Louisiana	13,400,000,000	1.4%
26	Colorado	13,000,000,000	1.4%
26	Oregon	13,000,000,000	1.4%
28	Oklahoma	12,500,000,000	1.3%
29	Connecticut	11,000,000,000	1.1%
30	Arkansas	10,900,000,000	1.1%
31	Iowa	10,800,000,000	1.1%
32	Mississippi	10,100,000,000	1.1%
33	Kansas	9,100,000,000	0.9%
34	West Virginia	7,700,000,000	0.8%
35	Nevada	7,300,000,000	0.8%
36	New Mexico	6,400,000,000	0.7%
37	Nebraska	5,900,000,000	0.6%
37	Utah	5,900,000,000	0.6%
39	Maine	5,000,000,000	0.5%
40	Idaho	4,800,000,000	0.5%
41	New Hampshire	4,400,000,000	0.5%
42	Hawaii	4,000,000,000	0.4%
43	Rhode Island	3,600,000,000	0.4%
44	Montana	3,500,000,000	0.4%
45	Delaware	3,100,000,000	0.3%
46	South Dakota	2,800,000,000	0.3%
47	North Dakota	2,200,000,000	0.2%
47	Vermont	2,200,000,000	0.2%
49	Wyoming	1,700,000,000	0.2%
50	Alaska	1,600,000,000	0.2%
	District of Columbia	1,400,000,000	0.1%

Source: U.S. Office of Management and Budget, USAspending.gov
"Prime Award Spending Data Summary" (http://www.usaspending.gov/explore, as of January 31, 2014)
*Total includes $14,495,491,700 in U.S. territories and $5,304,508,300 in expenditures not distributed by state. Expenditures allocated based on place of performance of a contract. Includes funds paid to individuals who have been assessed as needing services, in lieu of social service provisions, generally for the large entitlement programs such as Social Security, Unemployment Insurance, and Federal Pell Grants. This source replaces a previous data series by the U.S. Census and definitions differ.

Government Finances: Federal   283

Per Capita Federal Government Direct Payments to Individuals in 2012

National Per Capita = $2,994*

<table>
<tr><td colspan="3">ALPHA ORDER</td><td colspan="3">RANK ORDER</td></tr>
<tr><td>RANK</td><td>STATE</td><td>PER CAPITA</td><td>RANK</td><td>STATE</td><td>PER CAPITA</td></tr>
<tr><td>3</td><td>Alabama</td><td>$3,695</td><td>1</td><td>West Virginia</td><td>$4,147</td></tr>
<tr><td>49</td><td>Alaska</td><td>2,191</td><td>2</td><td>Maine</td><td>3,764</td></tr>
<tr><td>28</td><td>Arizona</td><td>3,144</td><td>3</td><td>Alabama</td><td>3,695</td></tr>
<tr><td>3</td><td>Arkansas</td><td>3,695</td><td>3</td><td>Arkansas</td><td>3,695</td></tr>
<tr><td>48</td><td>California</td><td>2,371</td><td>5</td><td>Michigan</td><td>3,562</td></tr>
<tr><td>46</td><td>Colorado</td><td>2,505</td><td>6</td><td>Kentucky</td><td>3,539</td></tr>
<tr><td>31</td><td>Connecticut</td><td>3,063</td><td>7</td><td>Vermont</td><td>3,515</td></tr>
<tr><td>15</td><td>Delaware</td><td>3,380</td><td>8</td><td>South Carolina</td><td>3,514</td></tr>
<tr><td>12</td><td>Florida</td><td>3,463</td><td>9</td><td>Iowa</td><td>3,512</td></tr>
<tr><td>43</td><td>Georgia</td><td>2,753</td><td>10</td><td>Montana</td><td>3,481</td></tr>
<tr><td>41</td><td>Hawaii</td><td>2,878</td><td>11</td><td>Pennsylvania</td><td>3,471</td></tr>
<tr><td>32</td><td>Idaho</td><td>3,008</td><td>12</td><td>Florida</td><td>3,463</td></tr>
<tr><td>42</td><td>Illinois</td><td>2,813</td><td>13</td><td>Rhode Island</td><td>3,428</td></tr>
<tr><td>22</td><td>Indiana</td><td>3,258</td><td>14</td><td>Mississippi</td><td>3,382</td></tr>
<tr><td>9</td><td>Iowa</td><td>3,512</td><td>15</td><td>Delaware</td><td>3,380</td></tr>
<tr><td>27</td><td>Kansas</td><td>3,154</td><td>16</td><td>Tennessee</td><td>3,362</td></tr>
<tr><td>6</td><td>Kentucky</td><td>3,539</td><td>17</td><td>South Dakota</td><td>3,357</td></tr>
<tr><td>39</td><td>Louisiana</td><td>2,912</td><td>18</td><td>Missouri</td><td>3,336</td></tr>
<tr><td>2</td><td>Maine</td><td>3,764</td><td>19</td><td>Oregon</td><td>3,334</td></tr>
<tr><td>45</td><td>Maryland</td><td>2,617</td><td>20</td><td>New Hampshire</td><td>3,329</td></tr>
<tr><td>36</td><td>Massachusetts</td><td>2,964</td><td>21</td><td>Oklahoma</td><td>3,276</td></tr>
<tr><td>5</td><td>Michigan</td><td>3,562</td><td>22</td><td>Indiana</td><td>3,258</td></tr>
<tr><td>34</td><td>Minnesota</td><td>2,993</td><td>23</td><td>North Carolina</td><td>3,221</td></tr>
<tr><td>14</td><td>Mississippi</td><td>3,382</td><td>24</td><td>Wisconsin</td><td>3,214</td></tr>
<tr><td>18</td><td>Missouri</td><td>3,336</td><td>25</td><td>Nebraska</td><td>3,180</td></tr>
<tr><td>10</td><td>Montana</td><td>3,481</td><td>26</td><td>Ohio</td><td>3,159</td></tr>
<tr><td>25</td><td>Nebraska</td><td>3,180</td><td>27</td><td>Kansas</td><td>3,154</td></tr>
<tr><td>44</td><td>Nevada</td><td>2,650</td><td>28</td><td>Arizona</td><td>3,144</td></tr>
<tr><td>20</td><td>New Hampshire</td><td>3,329</td><td>29</td><td>North Dakota</td><td>3,137</td></tr>
<tr><td>35</td><td>New Jersey</td><td>2,988</td><td>30</td><td>New Mexico</td><td>3,072</td></tr>
<tr><td>30</td><td>New Mexico</td><td>3,072</td><td>31</td><td>Connecticut</td><td>3,063</td></tr>
<tr><td>33</td><td>New York</td><td>2,999</td><td>32</td><td>Idaho</td><td>3,008</td></tr>
<tr><td>23</td><td>North Carolina</td><td>3,221</td><td>33</td><td>New York</td><td>2,999</td></tr>
<tr><td>29</td><td>North Dakota</td><td>3,137</td><td>34</td><td>Minnesota</td><td>2,993</td></tr>
<tr><td>26</td><td>Ohio</td><td>3,159</td><td>35</td><td>New Jersey</td><td>2,988</td></tr>
<tr><td>21</td><td>Oklahoma</td><td>3,276</td><td>36</td><td>Massachusetts</td><td>2,964</td></tr>
<tr><td>19</td><td>Oregon</td><td>3,334</td><td>37</td><td>Washington</td><td>2,959</td></tr>
<tr><td>11</td><td>Pennsylvania</td><td>3,471</td><td>38</td><td>Wyoming</td><td>2,948</td></tr>
<tr><td>13</td><td>Rhode Island</td><td>3,428</td><td>39</td><td>Louisiana</td><td>2,912</td></tr>
<tr><td>8</td><td>South Carolina</td><td>3,514</td><td>40</td><td>Virginia</td><td>2,895</td></tr>
<tr><td>17</td><td>South Dakota</td><td>3,357</td><td>41</td><td>Hawaii</td><td>2,878</td></tr>
<tr><td>16</td><td>Tennessee</td><td>3,362</td><td>42</td><td>Illinois</td><td>2,813</td></tr>
<tr><td>47</td><td>Texas</td><td>2,383</td><td>43</td><td>Georgia</td><td>2,753</td></tr>
<tr><td>50</td><td>Utah</td><td>2,067</td><td>44</td><td>Nevada</td><td>2,650</td></tr>
<tr><td>7</td><td>Vermont</td><td>3,515</td><td>45</td><td>Maryland</td><td>2,617</td></tr>
<tr><td>40</td><td>Virginia</td><td>2,895</td><td>46</td><td>Colorado</td><td>2,505</td></tr>
<tr><td>37</td><td>Washington</td><td>2,959</td><td>47</td><td>Texas</td><td>2,383</td></tr>
<tr><td>1</td><td>West Virginia</td><td>4,147</td><td>48</td><td>California</td><td>2,371</td></tr>
<tr><td>24</td><td>Wisconsin</td><td>3,214</td><td>49</td><td>Alaska</td><td>2,191</td></tr>
<tr><td>38</td><td>Wyoming</td><td>2,948</td><td>50</td><td>Utah</td><td>2,067</td></tr>
<tr><td></td><td></td><td></td><td></td><td>District of Columbia</td><td>2,210</td></tr>
</table>

Source: CQ Press using data from U.S. Office of Management and Budget, USAspending.gov
"Prime Award Spending Data Summary" (http://www.usaspending.gov/explore, as of January 31, 2014)
*National per capita excludes expenditures and population for territories and undistributed amounts. Expenditures allocated based on place of performance of a contract. Includes funds paid to individuals who have been assessed as needing services, in lieu of social service provisions, generally for the large entitlement programs such as Social Security, Unemployment Insurance, and Federal Pell Grants. This source replaces a previous data series by the U.S. Census and definitions differ.

Federal Government Insurance Payments in 2012

National Total = $1,138,000,000,000*

ALPHA ORDER					RANK ORDER			
RANK	STATE	EXPENDITURES	% of USA		RANK	STATE	EXPENDITURES	% of USA
17	Alabama	$9,800,000,000	0.9%		1	Florida	$427,500,000,000	37.6%
49	Alaska	622,000,000	0.1%		2	Texas	145,700,000,000	12.8%
22	Arizona	6,600,000,000	0.6%		3	Louisiana	89,200,000,000	7.8%
37	Arkansas	2,700,000,000	0.2%		4	California	65,100,000,000	5.7%
4	California	65,100,000,000	5.7%		5	New Jersey	50,000,000,000	4.4%
26	Colorado	4,100,000,000	0.4%		6	South Carolina	44,300,000,000	3.9%
18	Connecticut	8,900,000,000	0.8%		7	New York	39,700,000,000	3.5%
24	Delaware	5,800,000,000	0.5%		8	North Carolina	29,300,000,000	2.6%
1	Florida	427,500,000,000	37.6%		9	Virginia	25,500,000,000	2.2%
10	Georgia	21,500,000,000	1.9%		10	Georgia	21,500,000,000	1.9%
14	Hawaii	11,600,000,000	1.0%		11	Mississippi	13,200,000,000	1.2%
44	Idaho	1,500,000,000	0.1%		12	Maryland	12,900,000,000	1.1%
19	Illinois	8,200,000,000	0.7%		13	Pennsylvania	12,600,000,000	1.1%
25	Indiana	5,100,000,000	0.4%		14	Hawaii	11,600,000,000	1.0%
30	Iowa	3,400,000,000	0.3%		15	Massachusetts	10,600,000,000	0.9%
41	Kansas	2,000,000,000	0.2%		16	Washington	10,400,000,000	0.9%
31	Kentucky	3,200,000,000	0.3%		17	Alabama	9,800,000,000	0.9%
3	Louisiana	89,200,000,000	7.8%		18	Connecticut	8,900,000,000	0.8%
42	Maine	1,700,000,000	0.1%		19	Illinois	8,200,000,000	0.7%
12	Maryland	12,900,000,000	1.1%		20	Oregon	7,500,000,000	0.7%
15	Massachusetts	10,600,000,000	0.9%		21	Ohio	6,700,000,000	0.6%
27	Michigan	3,900,000,000	0.3%		22	Arizona	6,600,000,000	0.6%
36	Minnesota	2,800,000,000	0.2%		23	Tennessee	6,300,000,000	0.6%
11	Mississippi	13,200,000,000	1.2%		24	Delaware	5,800,000,000	0.5%
28	Missouri	3,800,000,000	0.3%		25	Indiana	5,100,000,000	0.4%
47	Montana	919,200,000	0.1%		26	Colorado	4,100,000,000	0.4%
40	Nebraska	2,100,000,000	0.2%		27	Michigan	3,900,000,000	0.3%
31	Nevada	3,200,000,000	0.3%		28	Missouri	3,800,000,000	0.3%
42	New Hampshire	1,700,000,000	0.1%		29	Rhode Island	3,600,000,000	0.3%
5	New Jersey	50,000,000,000	4.4%		30	Iowa	3,400,000,000	0.3%
34	New Mexico	2,900,000,000	0.3%		31	Kentucky	3,200,000,000	0.3%
7	New York	39,700,000,000	3.5%		31	Nevada	3,200,000,000	0.3%
8	North Carolina	29,300,000,000	2.6%		31	North Dakota	3,200,000,000	0.3%
31	North Dakota	3,200,000,000	0.3%		34	New Mexico	2,900,000,000	0.3%
21	Ohio	6,700,000,000	0.6%		34	Oklahoma	2,900,000,000	0.3%
34	Oklahoma	2,900,000,000	0.3%		36	Minnesota	2,800,000,000	0.2%
20	Oregon	7,500,000,000	0.7%		37	Arkansas	2,700,000,000	0.2%
13	Pennsylvania	12,600,000,000	1.1%		38	Wisconsin	2,500,000,000	0.2%
29	Rhode Island	3,600,000,000	0.3%		39	West Virginia	2,400,000,000	0.2%
6	South Carolina	44,300,000,000	3.9%		40	Nebraska	2,100,000,000	0.2%
45	South Dakota	1,100,000,000	0.1%		41	Kansas	2,000,000,000	0.2%
23	Tennessee	6,300,000,000	0.6%		42	Maine	1,700,000,000	0.1%
2	Texas	145,700,000,000	12.8%		42	New Hampshire	1,700,000,000	0.1%
46	Utah	941,000,000	0.1%		44	Idaho	1,500,000,000	0.1%
48	Vermont	756,800,000	0.1%		45	South Dakota	1,100,000,000	0.1%
9	Virginia	25,500,000,000	2.2%		46	Utah	941,000,000	0.1%
16	Washington	10,400,000,000	0.9%		47	Montana	919,200,000	0.1%
39	West Virginia	2,400,000,000	0.2%		48	Vermont	756,800,000	0.1%
38	Wisconsin	2,500,000,000	0.2%		49	Alaska	622,000,000	0.1%
50	Wyoming	470,700,000	0.0%		50	Wyoming	470,700,000	0.0%
						District of Columbia	344,700,000	0.0%

Source: U.S. Office of Management and Budget, USAspending.gov

"Prime Award Spending Data Summary" (http://www.usaspending.gov/explore, as of January 31, 2014)

*Total includes $5,022,199,100 in U.S. territories in expenditures not distributed by state. Expenditures allocated based on place of performance of a contract. Includes financial assistance provided to assure reimbursement for losses sustained under specified conditions. Coverage may be provided directly by the federal government or through private carriers and may or may not involve the payment of premiums. This source replaces a previous data series by the U.S. Census and definitions differ.

Per Capita Federal Government Insurance Payments in 2012

National Per Capita = $3,609*

ALPHA ORDER				RANK ORDER		
RANK	STATE	PER CAPITA		RANK	STATE	PER CAPITA
16	Alabama	$2,034		1	Florida	$22,126
37	Alaska	852		2	Louisiana	19,382
31	Arizona	1,007		3	South Carolina	9,379
35	Arkansas	915		4	Hawaii	8,345
19	California	1,713		5	Delaware	6,325
39	Colorado	790		6	New Jersey	5,638
13	Connecticut	2,478		7	Texas	5,591
5	Delaware	6,325		8	North Dakota	4,563
1	Florida	22,126		9	Mississippi	4,420
15	Georgia	2,168		10	Rhode Island	3,428
4	Hawaii	8,345		11	Virginia	3,115
34	Idaho	940		12	North Carolina	3,006
44	Illinois	637		13	Connecticut	2,478
40	Indiana	780		14	Maryland	2,192
30	Iowa	1,106		15	Georgia	2,168
43	Kansas	693		16	Alabama	2,034
42	Kentucky	731		17	New York	2,028
2	Louisiana	19,382		18	Oregon	1,923
26	Maine	1,280		19	California	1,713
14	Maryland	2,192		20	Massachusetts	1,595
20	Massachusetts	1,595		21	Washington	1,508
49	Michigan	395		22	New Mexico	1,392
47	Minnesota	520		23	South Dakota	1,319
9	Mississippi	4,420		24	West Virginia	1,293
45	Missouri	631		25	New Hampshire	1,286
36	Montana	914		26	Maine	1,280
29	Nebraska	1,132		27	Vermont	1,209
28	Nevada	1,162		28	Nevada	1,162
25	New Hampshire	1,286		29	Nebraska	1,132
6	New Jersey	5,638		30	Iowa	1,106
22	New Mexico	1,392		31	Arizona	1,007
17	New York	2,028		32	Pennsylvania	987
12	North Carolina	3,006		33	Tennessee	976
8	North Dakota	4,563		34	Idaho	940
46	Ohio	580		35	Arkansas	915
41	Oklahoma	760		36	Montana	914
18	Oregon	1,923		37	Alaska	852
32	Pennsylvania	987		38	Wyoming	816
10	Rhode Island	3,428		39	Colorado	790
3	South Carolina	9,379		40	Indiana	780
23	South Dakota	1,319		41	Oklahoma	760
33	Tennessee	976		42	Kentucky	731
7	Texas	5,591		43	Kansas	693
50	Utah	330		44	Illinois	637
27	Vermont	1,209		45	Missouri	631
11	Virginia	3,115		46	Ohio	580
21	Washington	1,508		47	Minnesota	520
24	West Virginia	1,293		48	Wisconsin	437
48	Wisconsin	437		49	Michigan	395
38	Wyoming	816		50	Utah	330
					District of Columbia	544

Source: CQ Press using data from U.S. Office of Management and Budget, USAspending.gov
"Prime Award Spending Data Summary" (http://www.usaspending.gov/explore, as of January 31, 2014)
*National per capita excludes expenditures and population for territories. Expenditures allocated based on place of performance of a contract. Includes financial assistance provided to assure reimbursement for losses sustained under specified conditions. Coverage may be provided directly by the federal government or through private carriers and may or may not involve the payment of premiums. This source replaces a previous data series by the U.S. Census and definitions differ.

Federal Government Loans, Guarantees, and Other Expenditures in 2012

National Total = $5,700,000,000*

<table>
<tr><td colspan="4">ALPHA ORDER</td><td colspan="4">RANK ORDER</td></tr>
<tr><th>RANK</th><th>STATE</th><th>EXPENDITURES</th><th>% of USA</th><th>RANK</th><th>STATE</th><th>EXPENDITURES</th><th>% of USA</th></tr>
<tr><td>18</td><td>Alabama</td><td>$107,200,000</td><td>1.9%</td><td>1</td><td>Florida</td><td>$396,100,000</td><td>6.9%</td></tr>
<tr><td>44</td><td>Alaska</td><td>19,000,000</td><td>0.3%</td><td>2</td><td>California</td><td>391,300,000</td><td>6.9%</td></tr>
<tr><td>17</td><td>Arizona</td><td>111,400,000</td><td>2.0%</td><td>3</td><td>New York</td><td>268,100,000</td><td>4.7%</td></tr>
<tr><td>22</td><td>Arkansas</td><td>101,200,000</td><td>1.8%</td><td>4</td><td>North Carolina</td><td>249,500,000</td><td>4.4%</td></tr>
<tr><td>2</td><td>California</td><td>391,300,000</td><td>6.9%</td><td>5</td><td>Ohio</td><td>244,000,000</td><td>4.3%</td></tr>
<tr><td>30</td><td>Colorado</td><td>63,600,000</td><td>1.1%</td><td>6</td><td>Illinois</td><td>200,300,000</td><td>3.5%</td></tr>
<tr><td>34</td><td>Connecticut</td><td>46,200,000</td><td>0.8%</td><td>7</td><td>Georgia</td><td>198,800,000</td><td>3.5%</td></tr>
<tr><td>46</td><td>Delaware</td><td>15,100,000</td><td>0.3%</td><td>8</td><td>Oregon</td><td>193,000,000</td><td>3.4%</td></tr>
<tr><td>1</td><td>Florida</td><td>396,100,000</td><td>6.9%</td><td>9</td><td>Michigan</td><td>167,100,000</td><td>2.9%</td></tr>
<tr><td>7</td><td>Georgia</td><td>198,800,000</td><td>3.5%</td><td>10</td><td>Tennessee</td><td>144,600,000</td><td>2.5%</td></tr>
<tr><td>42</td><td>Hawaii</td><td>21,277,700</td><td>0.4%</td><td>11</td><td>Virginia</td><td>143,000,000</td><td>2.5%</td></tr>
<tr><td>37</td><td>Idaho</td><td>43,200,000</td><td>0.8%</td><td>12</td><td>Missouri</td><td>142,100,000</td><td>2.5%</td></tr>
<tr><td>6</td><td>Illinois</td><td>200,300,000</td><td>3.5%</td><td>13</td><td>Indiana</td><td>139,800,000</td><td>2.5%</td></tr>
<tr><td>13</td><td>Indiana</td><td>139,800,000</td><td>2.5%</td><td>14</td><td>Kentucky</td><td>125,200,000</td><td>2.2%</td></tr>
<tr><td>24</td><td>Iowa</td><td>97,700,000</td><td>1.7%</td><td>15</td><td>Wisconsin</td><td>119,700,000</td><td>2.1%</td></tr>
<tr><td>31</td><td>Kansas</td><td>56,700,000</td><td>1.0%</td><td>16</td><td>Minnesota</td><td>113,000,000</td><td>2.0%</td></tr>
<tr><td>14</td><td>Kentucky</td><td>125,200,000</td><td>2.2%</td><td>17</td><td>Arizona</td><td>111,400,000</td><td>2.0%</td></tr>
<tr><td>20</td><td>Louisiana</td><td>105,200,000</td><td>1.8%</td><td>18</td><td>Alabama</td><td>107,200,000</td><td>1.9%</td></tr>
<tr><td>35</td><td>Maine</td><td>44,400,000</td><td>0.8%</td><td>19</td><td>Mississippi</td><td>106,100,000</td><td>1.9%</td></tr>
<tr><td>27</td><td>Maryland</td><td>82,600,000</td><td>1.4%</td><td>20</td><td>Louisiana</td><td>105,200,000</td><td>1.8%</td></tr>
<tr><td>26</td><td>Massachusetts</td><td>88,300,000</td><td>1.5%</td><td>21</td><td>South Carolina</td><td>102,300,000</td><td>1.8%</td></tr>
<tr><td>9</td><td>Michigan</td><td>167,100,000</td><td>2.9%</td><td>22</td><td>Arkansas</td><td>101,200,000</td><td>1.8%</td></tr>
<tr><td>16</td><td>Minnesota</td><td>113,000,000</td><td>2.0%</td><td>23</td><td>Oklahoma</td><td>101,100,000</td><td>1.8%</td></tr>
<tr><td>19</td><td>Mississippi</td><td>106,100,000</td><td>1.9%</td><td>24</td><td>Iowa</td><td>97,700,000</td><td>1.7%</td></tr>
<tr><td>12</td><td>Missouri</td><td>142,100,000</td><td>2.5%</td><td>25</td><td>Nevada</td><td>96,400,000</td><td>1.7%</td></tr>
<tr><td>40</td><td>Montana</td><td>32,400,000</td><td>0.6%</td><td>26</td><td>Massachusetts</td><td>88,300,000</td><td>1.5%</td></tr>
<tr><td>32</td><td>Nebraska</td><td>55,500,000</td><td>1.0%</td><td>27</td><td>Maryland</td><td>82,600,000</td><td>1.4%</td></tr>
<tr><td>25</td><td>Nevada</td><td>96,400,000</td><td>1.7%</td><td>28</td><td>New Jersey</td><td>73,200,000</td><td>1.3%</td></tr>
<tr><td>41</td><td>New Hampshire</td><td>31,300,000</td><td>0.5%</td><td>29</td><td>West Virginia</td><td>66,900,000</td><td>1.2%</td></tr>
<tr><td>28</td><td>New Jersey</td><td>73,200,000</td><td>1.3%</td><td>30</td><td>Colorado</td><td>63,600,000</td><td>1.1%</td></tr>
<tr><td>33</td><td>New Mexico</td><td>51,800,000</td><td>0.9%</td><td>31</td><td>Kansas</td><td>56,700,000</td><td>1.0%</td></tr>
<tr><td>3</td><td>New York</td><td>268,100,000</td><td>4.7%</td><td>32</td><td>Nebraska</td><td>55,500,000</td><td>1.0%</td></tr>
<tr><td>4</td><td>North Carolina</td><td>249,500,000</td><td>4.4%</td><td>33</td><td>New Mexico</td><td>51,800,000</td><td>0.9%</td></tr>
<tr><td>39</td><td>North Dakota</td><td>34,600,000</td><td>0.6%</td><td>34</td><td>Connecticut</td><td>46,200,000</td><td>0.8%</td></tr>
<tr><td>5</td><td>Ohio</td><td>244,000,000</td><td>4.3%</td><td>35</td><td>Maine</td><td>44,400,000</td><td>0.8%</td></tr>
<tr><td>23</td><td>Oklahoma</td><td>101,100,000</td><td>1.8%</td><td>36</td><td>South Dakota</td><td>44,000,000</td><td>0.8%</td></tr>
<tr><td>8</td><td>Oregon</td><td>193,000,000</td><td>3.4%</td><td>37</td><td>Idaho</td><td>43,200,000</td><td>0.8%</td></tr>
<tr><td>50</td><td>Pennsylvania</td><td>(218,800,000)</td><td></td><td>38</td><td>Utah</td><td>38,300,000</td><td>0.7%</td></tr>
<tr><td>43</td><td>Rhode Island</td><td>19,330,300</td><td>0.3%</td><td>39</td><td>North Dakota</td><td>34,600,000</td><td>0.6%</td></tr>
<tr><td>21</td><td>South Carolina</td><td>102,300,000</td><td>1.8%</td><td>40</td><td>Montana</td><td>32,400,000</td><td>0.6%</td></tr>
<tr><td>36</td><td>South Dakota</td><td>44,000,000</td><td>0.8%</td><td>41</td><td>New Hampshire</td><td>31,300,000</td><td>0.5%</td></tr>
<tr><td>10</td><td>Tennessee</td><td>144,600,000</td><td>2.5%</td><td>42</td><td>Hawaii</td><td>21,277,700</td><td>0.4%</td></tr>
<tr><td>48</td><td>Texas</td><td>(10,600,000)</td><td></td><td>43</td><td>Rhode Island</td><td>19,330,300</td><td>0.3%</td></tr>
<tr><td>38</td><td>Utah</td><td>38,300,000</td><td>0.7%</td><td>44</td><td>Alaska</td><td>19,000,000</td><td>0.3%</td></tr>
<tr><td>47</td><td>Vermont</td><td>15,000,000</td><td>0.3%</td><td>45</td><td>Wyoming</td><td>18,300,000</td><td>0.3%</td></tr>
<tr><td>11</td><td>Virginia</td><td>143,000,000</td><td>2.5%</td><td>46</td><td>Delaware</td><td>15,100,000</td><td>0.3%</td></tr>
<tr><td>49</td><td>Washington</td><td>(214,800,000)</td><td></td><td>47</td><td>Vermont</td><td>15,000,000</td><td>0.3%</td></tr>
<tr><td>29</td><td>West Virginia</td><td>66,900,000</td><td>1.2%</td><td>48</td><td>Texas</td><td>(10,600,000)</td><td></td></tr>
<tr><td>15</td><td>Wisconsin</td><td>119,700,000</td><td>2.1%</td><td>49</td><td>Washington</td><td>(214,800,000)</td><td></td></tr>
<tr><td>45</td><td>Wyoming</td><td>18,300,000</td><td>0.3%</td><td>50</td><td>Pennsylvania</td><td>(218,800,000)</td><td></td></tr>
<tr><td></td><td></td><td></td><td></td><td></td><td>District of Columbia</td><td>8,000,000</td><td>0.1%</td></tr>
</table>

Source: U.S. Office of Management and Budget, USAspending.gov

"Prime Award Spending Data Summary" (http://www.usaspending.gov/explore, as of January 31, 2014)

*Total includes $1,066,882,500 in U.S. territories and -$55,890,500 in expenditures not distributed by state. Expenditures allocated based on place of performance of a contract. Loans are awards where a Federal agency provides funds to a non-Federal recipient that require repayment. Includes cost of loan and is net of repayments. "Other" represents all other reimbursable, indirect, contingent, intangible financial assistance. This source replaces a previous data series by the U.S. Census and definitions differ.

Per Capita Federal Government Loans, Guarantees, and Other Expenditures in 2012
National Per Capita = $15*

ALPHA ORDER

RANK	STATE	PER CAPITA
23	Alabama	$22
15	Alaska	26
34	Arizona	17
7	Arkansas	34
46	California	10
45	Colorado	12
42	Connecticut	13
37	Delaware	16
26	Florida	21
31	Georgia	20
39	Hawaii	15
14	Idaho	27
37	Illinois	16
26	Indiana	21
9	Iowa	32
31	Kansas	20
13	Kentucky	29
22	Louisiana	23
8	Maine	33
40	Maryland	14
42	Massachusetts	13
34	Michigan	17
26	Minnesota	21
4	Mississippi	36
19	Missouri	24
9	Montana	32
12	Nebraska	30
6	Nevada	35
19	New Hampshire	24
47	New Jersey	8
18	New Mexico	25
40	New York	14
15	North Carolina	26
2	North Dakota	49
26	Ohio	21
15	Oklahoma	26
2	Oregon	49
49	Pennsylvania	(17)
33	Rhode Island	18
23	South Carolina	22
1	South Dakota	53
23	Tennessee	22
48	Texas	0
42	Utah	13
19	Vermont	24
34	Virginia	17
50	Washington	(31)
4	West Virginia	36
26	Wisconsin	21
9	Wyoming	32

RANK ORDER

RANK	STATE	PER CAPITA
1	South Dakota	$53
2	North Dakota	49
2	Oregon	49
4	Mississippi	36
4	West Virginia	36
6	Nevada	35
7	Arkansas	34
8	Maine	33
9	Iowa	32
9	Montana	32
9	Wyoming	32
12	Nebraska	30
13	Kentucky	29
14	Idaho	27
15	Alaska	26
15	North Carolina	26
15	Oklahoma	26
18	New Mexico	25
19	Missouri	24
19	New Hampshire	24
19	Vermont	24
22	Louisiana	23
23	Alabama	22
23	South Carolina	22
23	Tennessee	22
26	Florida	21
26	Indiana	21
26	Minnesota	21
26	Ohio	21
26	Wisconsin	21
31	Georgia	20
31	Kansas	20
33	Rhode Island	18
34	Arizona	17
34	Michigan	17
34	Virginia	17
37	Delaware	16
37	Illinois	16
39	Hawaii	15
40	Maryland	14
40	New York	14
42	Connecticut	13
42	Massachusetts	13
42	Utah	13
45	Colorado	12
46	California	10
47	New Jersey	8
48	Texas	0
49	Pennsylvania	(17)
50	Washington	(31)
	District of Columbia	13

Source: CQ Press using data from U.S. Office of Management and Budget, USAspending.gov

"Prime Award Spending Data Summary" (http://www.usaspending.gov/explore, as of January 31, 2014)

*National per capita excludes expenditures and population for territories and undistributed amounts. Expenditures allocated based on place of performance of a contract. Loans are awards where a Federal agency provides funds to a non-Federal recipient that require repayment. Includes cost of loan and is net of repayments. "Other" represents all other reimbursable, indirect, contingent, intangible financial assistance. This source replaces a previous data series by the U.S. Census and definitions differ.

Federal Civilian Employees in 2012

National Total = 1,850,311 Employees*

ALPHA ORDER

RANK	STATE	EMPLOYEES	% of USA
13	Alabama	38,986	2.1%
36	Alaska	11,170	0.6%
14	Arizona	37,320	2.0%
35	Arkansas	12,864	0.7%
1	California	150,762	8.1%
16	Colorado	36,282	2.0%
41	Connecticut	7,762	0.4%
50	Delaware	3,031	0.2%
5	Florida	82,915	4.5%
6	Georgia	71,486	3.9%
23	Hawaii	23,446	1.3%
43	Idaho	7,388	0.4%
11	Illinois	45,801	2.5%
26	Indiana	22,007	1.2%
42	Iowa	7,715	0.4%
33	Kansas	15,515	0.8%
24	Kentucky	23,198	1.3%
28	Louisiana	19,307	1.0%
39	Maine	9,873	0.5%
4	Maryland	119,816	6.5%
21	Massachusetts	24,926	1.3%
18	Michigan	27,693	1.5%
32	Minnesota	15,864	0.9%
30	Mississippi	17,088	0.9%
17	Missouri	32,933	1.8%
40	Montana	8,637	0.5%
38	Nebraska	9,979	0.5%
37	Nevada	11,102	0.6%
49	New Hampshire	4,069	0.2%
22	New Jersey	24,806	1.3%
25	New Mexico	23,032	1.2%
8	New York	62,011	3.4%
12	North Carolina	39,886	2.2%
46	North Dakota	5,409	0.3%
10	Ohio	48,422	2.6%
15	Oklahoma	36,382	2.0%
31	Oregon	16,857	0.9%
7	Pennsylvania	63,137	3.4%
45	Rhode Island	6,245	0.3%
27	South Carolina	20,198	1.1%
44	South Dakota	7,261	0.4%
20	Tennessee	25,140	1.4%
3	Texas	131,580	7.1%
19	Utah	25,508	1.4%
48	Vermont	4,234	0.2%
2	Virginia	144,753	7.8%
9	Washington	50,300	2.7%
29	West Virginia	18,093	1.0%
34	Wisconsin	13,455	0.7%
47	Wyoming	4,818	0.3%

RANK ORDER

RANK	STATE	EMPLOYEES	% of USA
1	California	150,762	8.1%
2	Virginia	144,753	7.8%
3	Texas	131,580	7.1%
4	Maryland	119,816	6.5%
5	Florida	82,915	4.5%
6	Georgia	71,486	3.9%
7	Pennsylvania	63,137	3.4%
8	New York	62,011	3.4%
9	Washington	50,300	2.7%
10	Ohio	48,422	2.6%
11	Illinois	45,801	2.5%
12	North Carolina	39,886	2.2%
13	Alabama	38,986	2.1%
14	Arizona	37,320	2.0%
15	Oklahoma	36,382	2.0%
16	Colorado	36,282	2.0%
17	Missouri	32,933	1.8%
18	Michigan	27,693	1.5%
19	Utah	25,508	1.4%
20	Tennessee	25,140	1.4%
21	Massachusetts	24,926	1.3%
22	New Jersey	24,806	1.3%
23	Hawaii	23,446	1.3%
24	Kentucky	23,198	1.3%
25	New Mexico	23,032	1.2%
26	Indiana	22,007	1.2%
27	South Carolina	20,198	1.1%
28	Louisiana	19,307	1.0%
29	West Virginia	18,093	1.0%
30	Mississippi	17,088	0.9%
31	Oregon	16,857	0.9%
32	Minnesota	15,864	0.9%
33	Kansas	15,515	0.8%
34	Wisconsin	13,455	0.7%
35	Arkansas	12,864	0.7%
36	Alaska	11,170	0.6%
37	Nevada	11,102	0.6%
38	Nebraska	9,979	0.5%
39	Maine	9,873	0.5%
40	Montana	8,637	0.5%
41	Connecticut	7,762	0.4%
42	Iowa	7,715	0.4%
43	Idaho	7,388	0.4%
44	South Dakota	7,261	0.4%
45	Rhode Island	6,245	0.3%
46	North Dakota	5,409	0.3%
47	Wyoming	4,818	0.3%
48	Vermont	4,234	0.2%
49	New Hampshire	4,069	0.2%
50	Delaware	3,031	0.2%
	District of Columbia	143,537	7.8%

Source: U.S. Office of Personnel Management
"Common Characteristics of the Government" (http://www.opm.gov/feddata/)
*Head count based on place of employment. There were an average of 2,782,467 federal civilian employees in 2012. Excludes Central Intelligence Agency, Defense Intelligence Agency, and National Security Agency.

Rate of Federal Civilian Employees in 2012

National Rate = 59 Employees per 10,000 Population*

ALPHA ORDER

RANK	STATE	RATE
12	Alabama	81
4	Alaska	153
20	Arizona	57
29	Arkansas	44
36	California	40
17	Colorado	70
50	Connecticut	22
42	Delaware	33
30	Florida	43
16	Georgia	72
3	Hawaii	168
28	Idaho	46
40	Illinois	36
41	Indiana	34
48	Iowa	25
23	Kansas	54
25	Kentucky	53
33	Louisiana	42
14	Maine	74
1	Maryland	204
39	Massachusetts	38
46	Michigan	28
45	Minnesota	29
20	Mississippi	57
22	Missouri	55
10	Montana	86
23	Nebraska	54
36	Nevada	40
44	New Hampshire	31
46	New Jersey	28
5	New Mexico	110
43	New York	32
35	North Carolina	41
13	North Dakota	77
33	Ohio	42
7	Oklahoma	95
30	Oregon	43
27	Pennsylvania	49
19	Rhode Island	59
30	South Carolina	43
9	South Dakota	87
38	Tennessee	39
26	Texas	50
8	Utah	89
18	Vermont	68
2	Virginia	177
15	Washington	73
6	West Virginia	98
49	Wisconsin	23
11	Wyoming	84

RANK ORDER

RANK	STATE	RATE
1	Maryland	204
2	Virginia	177
3	Hawaii	168
4	Alaska	153
5	New Mexico	110
6	West Virginia	98
7	Oklahoma	95
8	Utah	89
9	South Dakota	87
10	Montana	86
11	Wyoming	84
12	Alabama	81
13	North Dakota	77
14	Maine	74
15	Washington	73
16	Georgia	72
17	Colorado	70
18	Vermont	68
19	Rhode Island	59
20	Arizona	57
20	Mississippi	57
22	Missouri	55
23	Kansas	54
23	Nebraska	54
25	Kentucky	53
26	Texas	50
27	Pennsylvania	49
28	Idaho	46
29	Arkansas	44
30	Florida	43
30	Oregon	43
30	South Carolina	43
33	Louisiana	42
33	Ohio	42
35	North Carolina	41
36	California	40
36	Nevada	40
38	Tennessee	39
39	Massachusetts	38
40	Illinois	36
41	Indiana	34
42	Delaware	33
43	New York	32
44	New Hampshire	31
45	Minnesota	29
46	Michigan	28
46	New Jersey	28
48	Iowa	25
49	Wisconsin	23
50	Connecticut	22

District of Columbia	2,270

Source: CQ Press using data from U.S. Office of Personnel Management
    "Common Characteristics of the Government" (http://www.opm.gov/feddata/)
*Head count based on place of employment. There were an average of 2,782,467 federal civilian employees in 2012. Excludes Central Intelligence Agency, Defense Intelligence Agency, and National Security Agency.

X. Government Finances: State and Local

(Continued)

(Continued)

State and Local Government Total Revenue in 2011

National Total = $3,433,535,571,000*

ALPHA ORDER					RANK ORDER			

ALPHA ORDER

RANK	STATE	REVENUE	% of USA
28	Alabama	$40,658,127,000	1.2%
39	Alaska	18,444,157,000	0.5%
19	Arizona	58,722,643,000	1.7%
33	Arkansas	27,841,110,000	0.8%
1	California	519,381,834,000	15.1%
22	Colorado	53,015,083,000	1.5%
26	Connecticut	42,151,373,000	1.2%
45	Delaware	11,200,911,000	0.3%
4	Florida	181,173,802,000	5.3%
11	Georgia	85,077,189,000	2.5%
40	Hawaii	15,958,833,000	0.5%
41	Idaho	14,096,854,000	0.4%
6	Illinois	133,625,891,000	3.9%
21	Indiana	56,855,910,000	1.7%
30	Iowa	34,540,917,000	1.0%
32	Kansas	28,561,910,000	0.8%
27	Kentucky	40,787,680,000	1.2%
23	Louisiana	49,138,661,000	1.4%
42	Maine	13,985,949,000	0.4%
16	Maryland	62,842,897,000	1.8%
12	Massachusetts	82,041,677,000	2.4%
9	Michigan	93,406,207,000	2.7%
15	Minnesota	63,624,439,000	1.9%
31	Mississippi	31,412,414,000	0.9%
20	Missouri	57,095,221,000	1.7%
46	Montana	10,234,859,000	0.3%
37	Nebraska	21,652,714,000	0.6%
34	Nevada	25,913,959,000	0.8%
44	New Hampshire	12,218,517,000	0.4%
8	New Jersey	105,224,674,000	3.1%
36	New Mexico	24,272,770,000	0.7%
2	New York	323,769,304,000	9.4%
10	North Carolina	93,302,012,000	2.7%
48	North Dakota	9,645,315,000	0.3%
7	Ohio	131,659,008,000	3.8%
29	Oklahoma	35,378,005,000	1.0%
24	Oregon	47,046,783,000	1.4%
5	Pennsylvania	134,309,794,000	3.9%
43	Rhode Island	12,742,033,000	0.4%
25	South Carolina	45,778,673,000	1.3%
49	South Dakota	8,463,415,000	0.2%
18	Tennessee	60,326,708,000	1.8%
3	Texas	224,474,606,000	6.5%
35	Utah	25,187,556,000	0.7%
50	Vermont	7,580,598,000	0.2%
14	Virginia	76,354,585,000	2.2%
13	Washington	77,839,836,000	2.3%
38	West Virginia	18,738,643,000	0.5%
17	Wisconsin	62,693,308,000	1.8%
47	Wyoming	10,208,346,000	0.3%

RANK ORDER

RANK	STATE	REVENUE	% of USA
1	California	$519,381,834,000	15.1%
2	New York	323,769,304,000	9.4%
3	Texas	224,474,606,000	6.5%
4	Florida	181,173,802,000	5.3%
5	Pennsylvania	134,309,794,000	3.9%
6	Illinois	133,625,891,000	3.9%
7	Ohio	131,659,008,000	3.8%
8	New Jersey	105,224,674,000	3.1%
9	Michigan	93,406,207,000	2.7%
10	North Carolina	93,302,012,000	2.7%
11	Georgia	85,077,189,000	2.5%
12	Massachusetts	82,041,677,000	2.4%
13	Washington	77,839,836,000	2.3%
14	Virginia	76,354,585,000	2.2%
15	Minnesota	63,624,439,000	1.9%
16	Maryland	62,842,897,000	1.8%
17	Wisconsin	62,693,308,000	1.8%
18	Tennessee	60,326,708,000	1.8%
19	Arizona	58,722,643,000	1.7%
20	Missouri	57,095,221,000	1.7%
21	Indiana	56,855,910,000	1.7%
22	Colorado	53,015,083,000	1.5%
23	Louisiana	49,138,661,000	1.4%
24	Oregon	47,046,783,000	1.4%
25	South Carolina	45,778,673,000	1.3%
26	Connecticut	42,151,373,000	1.2%
27	Kentucky	40,787,680,000	1.2%
28	Alabama	40,658,127,000	1.2%
29	Oklahoma	35,378,005,000	1.0%
30	Iowa	34,540,917,000	1.0%
31	Mississippi	31,412,414,000	0.9%
32	Kansas	28,561,910,000	0.8%
33	Arkansas	27,841,110,000	0.8%
34	Nevada	25,913,959,000	0.8%
35	Utah	25,187,556,000	0.7%
36	New Mexico	24,272,770,000	0.7%
37	Nebraska	21,652,714,000	0.6%
38	West Virginia	18,738,643,000	0.5%
39	Alaska	18,444,157,000	0.5%
40	Hawaii	15,958,833,000	0.5%
41	Idaho	14,096,854,000	0.4%
42	Maine	13,985,949,000	0.4%
43	Rhode Island	12,742,033,000	0.4%
44	New Hampshire	12,218,517,000	0.4%
45	Delaware	11,200,911,000	0.3%
46	Montana	10,234,859,000	0.3%
47	Wyoming	10,208,346,000	0.3%
48	North Dakota	9,645,315,000	0.3%
49	South Dakota	8,463,415,000	0.2%
50	Vermont	7,580,598,000	0.2%
	District of Columbia	12,877,861,000	0.4%

Source: U.S. Bureau of the Census, Governments Division
    "2011 State and Local Government Finances" (http://www.census.gov/govs/local/)
*Total revenue includes all money received from external sources. This includes taxes, intergovernmental transfers and insurance trust revenue, and revenue from government owned utilities and other commercial or auxiliary enterprise.

Per Capita State and Local Government Revenue in 2011

National Per Capita = $11,019*

ALPHA ORDER			RANK ORDER		
RANK	STATE	PER CAPITA	RANK	STATE	PER CAPITA
50	Alabama	$8,464	1	Alaska	$25,480
1	Alaska	25,480	2	Wyoming	17,993
44	Arizona	9,080	3	New York	16,602
37	Arkansas	9,474	4	North Dakota	14,086
5	California	13,783	5	California	13,783
27	Colorado	10,362	6	Massachusetts	12,417
14	Connecticut	11,752	7	Delaware	12,334
7	Delaware	12,334	8	Oregon	12,162
36	Florida	9,494	9	Rhode Island	12,128
49	Georgia	8,670	10	Vermont	12,098
16	Hawaii	11,580	11	New Jersey	11,910
46	Idaho	8,901	12	Minnesota	11,898
26	Illinois	10,391	13	Nebraska	11,754
48	Indiana	8,725	14	Connecticut	11,752
19	Iowa	11,273	15	New Mexico	11,677
31	Kansas	9,951	16	Hawaii	11,580
42	Kentucky	9,340	17	Ohio	11,408
22	Louisiana	10,741	17	Washington	11,408
25	Maine	10,527	19	Iowa	11,273
21	Maryland	10,762	20	Wisconsin	10,980
6	Massachusetts	12,417	21	Maryland	10,762
38	Michigan	9,457	22	Louisiana	10,741
12	Minnesota	11,898	23	Mississippi	10,550
23	Mississippi	10,550	24	Pennsylvania	10,539
35	Missouri	9,502	25	Maine	10,527
29	Montana	10,259	26	Illinois	10,391
13	Nebraska	11,754	27	Colorado	10,362
34	Nevada	9,527	28	South Dakota	10,276
43	New Hampshire	9,272	29	Montana	10,259
11	New Jersey	11,910	30	West Virginia	10,102
15	New Mexico	11,677	31	Kansas	9,951
3	New York	16,602	32	South Carolina	9,796
33	North Carolina	9,667	33	North Carolina	9,667
4	North Dakota	14,086	34	Nevada	9,527
17	Ohio	11,408	35	Missouri	9,502
41	Oklahoma	9,349	36	Florida	9,494
8	Oregon	12,162	37	Arkansas	9,474
24	Pennsylvania	10,539	38	Michigan	9,457
9	Rhode Island	12,128	39	Tennessee	9,426
32	South Carolina	9,796	40	Virginia	9,421
28	South Dakota	10,276	41	Oklahoma	9,349
39	Tennessee	9,426	42	Kentucky	9,340
47	Texas	8,758	43	New Hampshire	9,272
45	Utah	8,950	44	Arizona	9,080
10	Vermont	12,098	45	Utah	8,950
40	Virginia	9,421	46	Idaho	8,901
17	Washington	11,408	47	Texas	8,758
30	West Virginia	10,102	48	Indiana	8,725
20	Wisconsin	10,980	49	Georgia	8,670
2	Wyoming	17,993	50	Alabama	8,464
				District of Columbia	20,804

Source: CQ Press using data from U.S. Bureau of the Census, Governments Division
   "2011 State and Local Government Finances" (http://www.census.gov/govs/local/)
*Total revenue includes all money received from external sources. This includes taxes, intergovernmental transfers and insurance trust revenue, and revenue from government owned utilities and other commercial or auxiliary enterprise.

State and Local Government Revenue from the Federal Government in 2011

National Total = $645,961,684,000

ALPHA ORDER

ALPHA ORDER

RANK	STATE	REVENUE	% of USA
23	Alabama	$9,590,191,000	1.5%
40	Alaska	3,360,673,000	0.5%
14	Arizona	13,025,856,000	2.0%
33	Arkansas	6,723,216,000	1.0%
1	California	75,876,661,000	11.7%
30	Colorado	7,445,767,000	1.2%
31	Connecticut	7,201,164,000	1.1%
50	Delaware	1,899,144,000	0.3%
4	Florida	32,023,819,000	5.0%
10	Georgia	16,552,641,000	2.6%
41	Hawaii	3,180,863,000	0.5%
42	Idaho	2,987,651,000	0.5%
7	Illinois	22,527,224,000	3.5%
19	Indiana	11,538,049,000	1.8%
29	Iowa	7,524,475,000	1.2%
34	Kansas	5,158,672,000	0.8%
24	Kentucky	9,414,784,000	1.5%
13	Louisiana	13,649,946,000	2.1%
38	Maine	3,399,180,000	0.5%
17	Maryland	12,452,869,000	1.9%
11	Massachusetts	15,518,145,000	2.4%
8	Michigan	21,859,003,000	3.4%
22	Minnesota	10,576,654,000	1.6%
25	Mississippi	9,322,736,000	1.4%
16	Missouri	12,526,052,000	1.9%
44	Montana	2,669,071,000	0.4%
37	Nebraska	3,747,101,000	0.6%
39	Nevada	3,367,932,000	0.5%
46	New Hampshire	2,128,172,000	0.3%
12	New Jersey	15,246,954,000	2.4%
32	New Mexico	6,744,161,000	1.0%
2	New York	59,816,881,000	9.3%
9	North Carolina	17,989,311,000	2.8%
49	North Dakota	1,903,346,000	0.3%
6	Ohio	26,041,221,000	4.0%
28	Oklahoma	8,199,932,000	1.3%
26	Oregon	8,748,975,000	1.4%
5	Pennsylvania	27,103,241,000	4.2%
43	Rhode Island	2,889,426,000	0.4%
27	South Carolina	8,725,520,000	1.4%
48	South Dakota	2,054,905,000	0.3%
15	Tennessee	13,013,643,000	2.0%
3	Texas	46,737,257,000	7.2%
35	Utah	5,046,312,000	0.8%
47	Vermont	2,116,754,000	0.3%
20	Virginia	11,511,209,000	1.8%
18	Washington	12,385,327,000	1.9%
36	West Virginia	4,945,437,000	0.8%
21	Wisconsin	11,023,893,000	1.7%
45	Wyoming	2,353,678,000	0.4%

RANK ORDER

RANK	STATE	REVENUE	% of USA
1	California	$75,876,661,000	11.7%
2	New York	59,816,881,000	9.3%
3	Texas	46,737,257,000	7.2%
4	Florida	32,023,819,000	5.0%
5	Pennsylvania	27,103,241,000	4.2%
6	Ohio	26,041,221,000	4.0%
7	Illinois	22,527,224,000	3.5%
8	Michigan	21,859,003,000	3.4%
9	North Carolina	17,989,311,000	2.8%
10	Georgia	16,552,641,000	2.6%
11	Massachusetts	15,518,145,000	2.4%
12	New Jersey	15,246,954,000	2.4%
13	Louisiana	13,649,946,000	2.1%
14	Arizona	13,025,856,000	2.0%
15	Tennessee	13,013,643,000	2.0%
16	Missouri	12,526,052,000	1.9%
17	Maryland	12,452,869,000	1.9%
18	Washington	12,385,327,000	1.9%
19	Indiana	11,538,049,000	1.8%
20	Virginia	11,511,209,000	1.8%
21	Wisconsin	11,023,893,000	1.7%
22	Minnesota	10,576,654,000	1.6%
23	Alabama	9,590,191,000	1.5%
24	Kentucky	9,414,784,000	1.5%
25	Mississippi	9,322,736,000	1.4%
26	Oregon	8,748,975,000	1.4%
27	South Carolina	8,725,520,000	1.4%
28	Oklahoma	8,199,932,000	1.3%
29	Iowa	7,524,475,000	1.2%
30	Colorado	7,445,767,000	1.2%
31	Connecticut	7,201,164,000	1.1%
32	New Mexico	6,744,161,000	1.0%
33	Arkansas	6,723,216,000	1.0%
34	Kansas	5,158,672,000	0.8%
35	Utah	5,046,312,000	0.8%
36	West Virginia	4,945,437,000	0.8%
37	Nebraska	3,747,101,000	0.6%
38	Maine	3,399,180,000	0.5%
39	Nevada	3,367,932,000	0.5%
40	Alaska	3,360,673,000	0.5%
41	Hawaii	3,180,863,000	0.5%
42	Idaho	2,987,651,000	0.5%
43	Rhode Island	2,889,426,000	0.4%
44	Montana	2,669,071,000	0.4%
45	Wyoming	2,353,678,000	0.4%
46	New Hampshire	2,128,172,000	0.3%
47	Vermont	2,116,754,000	0.3%
48	South Dakota	2,054,905,000	0.3%
49	North Dakota	1,903,346,000	0.3%
50	Delaware	1,899,144,000	0.3%
	District of Columbia	4,116,590,000	0.6%

Source: U.S. Bureau of the Census, Governments Division
"2011 State and Local Government Finances" (http://www.census.gov/govs/local/)

Per Capita State and Local Government Revenue
from the Federal Government in 2011
National Per Capita = $2,073

ALPHA ORDER			RANK ORDER		
RANK	STATE	PER CAPITA	RANK	STATE	PER CAPITA
32	Alabama	$1,996	1	Alaska	$4,643
1	Alaska	4,643	2	Wyoming	4,149
29	Arizona	2,014	3	Vermont	3,378
17	Arkansas	2,288	4	New Mexico	3,244
29	California	2,014	5	Mississippi	3,131
48	Colorado	1,455	6	New York	3,067
31	Connecticut	2,008	7	Louisiana	2,984
25	Delaware	2,091	8	North Dakota	2,780
46	Florida	1,678	9	Rhode Island	2,750
45	Georgia	1,687	10	Montana	2,675
16	Hawaii	2,308	11	West Virginia	2,666
35	Idaho	1,886	12	Maine	2,559
43	Illinois	1,752	13	South Dakota	2,495
42	Indiana	1,771	14	Iowa	2,456
14	Iowa	2,456	15	Massachusetts	2,349
40	Kansas	1,797	16	Hawaii	2,308
22	Kentucky	2,156	17	Arkansas	2,288
7	Louisiana	2,984	18	Oregon	2,262
12	Maine	2,559	19	Ohio	2,256
23	Maryland	2,132	20	Michigan	2,213
15	Massachusetts	2,349	21	Oklahoma	2,167
20	Michigan	2,213	22	Kentucky	2,156
33	Minnesota	1,978	23	Maryland	2,132
5	Mississippi	3,131	24	Pennsylvania	2,127
26	Missouri	2,085	25	Delaware	2,091
10	Montana	2,675	26	Missouri	2,085
27	Nebraska	2,034	27	Nebraska	2,034
50	Nevada	1,238	28	Tennessee	2,033
47	New Hampshire	1,615	29	Arizona	2,014
44	New Jersey	1,726	29	California	2,014
4	New Mexico	3,244	31	Connecticut	2,008
6	New York	3,067	32	Alabama	1,996
37	North Carolina	1,864	33	Minnesota	1,978
8	North Dakota	2,780	34	Wisconsin	1,931
19	Ohio	2,256	35	Idaho	1,886
21	Oklahoma	2,167	36	South Carolina	1,867
18	Oregon	2,262	37	North Carolina	1,864
24	Pennsylvania	2,127	38	Texas	1,823
9	Rhode Island	2,750	39	Washington	1,815
36	South Carolina	1,867	40	Kansas	1,797
13	South Dakota	2,495	41	Utah	1,793
28	Tennessee	2,033	42	Indiana	1,771
38	Texas	1,823	43	Illinois	1,752
41	Utah	1,793	44	New Jersey	1,726
3	Vermont	3,378	45	Georgia	1,687
49	Virginia	1,420	46	Florida	1,678
39	Washington	1,815	47	New Hampshire	1,615
11	West Virginia	2,666	48	Colorado	1,455
34	Wisconsin	1,931	49	Virginia	1,420
2	Wyoming	4,149	50	Nevada	1,238
				District of Columbia	6,650

Source: CQ Press using data from U.S. Bureau of the Census, Governments Division
"2011 State and Local Government Finances" (http://www.census.gov/govs/local/)

Percent of State and Local Government Revenue
from the Federal Government in 2011
National Percent = 18.8%*

ALPHA ORDER

RANK	STATE	PERCENT
10	Alabama	23.6
35	Alaska	18.2
16	Arizona	22.2
9	Arkansas	24.1
47	California	14.6
49	Colorado	14.0
41	Connecticut	17.1
42	Delaware	17.0
37	Florida	17.7
29	Georgia	19.5
25	Hawaii	19.9
20	Idaho	21.2
43	Illinois	16.9
22	Indiana	20.3
18	Iowa	21.8
36	Kansas	18.1
13	Kentucky	23.1
3	Louisiana	27.8
7	Maine	24.3
26	Maryland	19.8
32	Massachusetts	18.9
11	Michigan	23.4
44	Minnesota	16.6
1	Mississippi	29.7
17	Missouri	21.9
6	Montana	26.1
40	Nebraska	17.3
50	Nevada	13.0
39	New Hampshire	17.4
48	New Jersey	14.5
3	New Mexico	27.8
34	New York	18.5
30	North Carolina	19.3
28	North Dakota	19.7
26	Ohio	19.8
12	Oklahoma	23.2
33	Oregon	18.6
23	Pennsylvania	20.2
15	Rhode Island	22.7
31	South Carolina	19.1
7	South Dakota	24.3
19	Tennessee	21.6
21	Texas	20.8
24	Utah	20.0
2	Vermont	27.9
46	Virginia	15.1
45	Washington	15.9
5	West Virginia	26.4
38	Wisconsin	17.6
13	Wyoming	23.1

RANK ORDER

RANK	STATE	PERCENT
1	Mississippi	29.7
2	Vermont	27.9
3	Louisiana	27.8
3	New Mexico	27.8
5	West Virginia	26.4
6	Montana	26.1
7	Maine	24.3
7	South Dakota	24.3
9	Arkansas	24.1
10	Alabama	23.6
11	Michigan	23.4
12	Oklahoma	23.2
13	Kentucky	23.1
13	Wyoming	23.1
15	Rhode Island	22.7
16	Arizona	22.2
17	Missouri	21.9
18	Iowa	21.8
19	Tennessee	21.6
20	Idaho	21.2
21	Texas	20.8
22	Indiana	20.3
23	Pennsylvania	20.2
24	Utah	20.0
25	Hawaii	19.9
26	Maryland	19.8
26	Ohio	19.8
28	North Dakota	19.7
29	Georgia	19.5
30	North Carolina	19.3
31	South Carolina	19.1
32	Massachusetts	18.9
33	Oregon	18.6
34	New York	18.5
35	Alaska	18.2
36	Kansas	18.1
37	Florida	17.7
38	Wisconsin	17.6
39	New Hampshire	17.4
40	Nebraska	17.3
41	Connecticut	17.1
42	Delaware	17.0
43	Illinois	16.9
44	Minnesota	16.6
45	Washington	15.9
46	Virginia	15.1
47	California	14.6
48	New Jersey	14.5
49	Colorado	14.0
50	Nevada	13.0

District of Columbia 32.0

Source: CQ Press using data from U.S. Bureau of the Census, Governments Division
"2011 State and Local Government Finances" (http://www.census.gov/govs/local/)
*As a percent of total revenue.

State and Local Government Own Source Revenue in 2011

National Total = $1,966,815,199,000*

ALPHA ORDER

RANK	STATE	REVENUE	% of USA
26	Alabama	$24,983,377,000	1.3%
36	Alaska	12,458,955,000	0.6%
20	Arizona	30,987,666,000	1.6%
34	Arkansas	14,820,451,000	0.8%
1	California	268,224,294,000	13.6%
19	Colorado	34,058,466,000	1.7%
23	Connecticut	27,739,815,000	1.4%
45	Delaware	6,965,208,000	0.4%
4	Florida	106,851,087,000	5.4%
13	Georgia	47,551,004,000	2.4%
40	Hawaii	9,731,812,000	0.5%
42	Idaho	7,772,507,000	0.4%
5	Illinois	79,558,403,000	4.0%
18	Indiana	35,759,783,000	1.8%
29	Iowa	20,042,046,000	1.0%
31	Kansas	18,379,745,000	0.9%
28	Kentucky	22,225,736,000	1.1%
24	Louisiana	26,920,095,000	1.4%
41	Maine	8,079,918,000	0.4%
15	Maryland	38,661,990,000	2.0%
11	Massachusetts	49,379,348,000	2.5%
9	Michigan	56,352,420,000	2.9%
16	Minnesota	38,215,621,000	1.9%
32	Mississippi	15,448,529,000	0.8%
21	Missouri	29,785,399,000	1.5%
48	Montana	5,272,157,000	0.3%
38	Nebraska	11,645,121,000	0.6%
35	Nevada	14,511,065,000	0.7%
43	New Hampshire	7,670,223,000	0.4%
7	New Jersey	69,591,556,000	3.5%
37	New Mexico	12,053,657,000	0.6%
2	New York	190,882,845,000	9.7%
10	North Carolina	53,023,022,000	2.7%
46	North Dakota	6,447,656,000	0.3%
8	Ohio	67,646,836,000	3.4%
30	Oklahoma	19,557,046,000	1.0%
27	Oregon	23,025,353,000	1.2%
6	Pennsylvania	79,525,919,000	4.0%
44	Rhode Island	7,241,946,000	0.4%
25	South Carolina	26,609,197,000	1.4%
50	South Dakota	4,147,634,000	0.2%
22	Tennessee	29,634,638,000	1.5%
3	Texas	135,218,244,000	6.9%
33	Utah	15,069,235,000	0.8%
49	Vermont	4,347,785,000	0.2%
12	Virginia	49,175,882,000	2.5%
14	Washington	43,604,806,000	2.2%
39	West Virginia	10,844,014,000	0.6%
17	Wisconsin	36,232,114,000	1.8%
47	Wyoming	6,226,129,000	0.3%

RANK ORDER

RANK	STATE	REVENUE	% of USA
1	California	$268,224,294,000	13.6%
2	New York	190,882,845,000	9.7%
3	Texas	135,218,244,000	6.9%
4	Florida	106,851,087,000	5.4%
5	Illinois	79,558,403,000	4.0%
6	Pennsylvania	79,525,919,000	4.0%
7	New Jersey	69,591,556,000	3.5%
8	Ohio	67,646,836,000	3.4%
9	Michigan	56,352,420,000	2.9%
10	North Carolina	53,023,022,000	2.7%
11	Massachusetts	49,379,348,000	2.5%
12	Virginia	49,175,882,000	2.5%
13	Georgia	47,551,004,000	2.4%
14	Washington	43,604,806,000	2.2%
15	Maryland	38,661,990,000	2.0%
16	Minnesota	38,215,621,000	1.9%
17	Wisconsin	36,232,114,000	1.8%
18	Indiana	35,759,783,000	1.8%
19	Colorado	34,058,466,000	1.7%
20	Arizona	30,987,666,000	1.6%
21	Missouri	29,785,399,000	1.5%
22	Tennessee	29,634,638,000	1.5%
23	Connecticut	27,739,815,000	1.4%
24	Louisiana	26,920,095,000	1.4%
25	South Carolina	26,609,197,000	1.4%
26	Alabama	24,983,377,000	1.3%
27	Oregon	23,025,353,000	1.2%
28	Kentucky	22,225,736,000	1.1%
29	Iowa	20,042,046,000	1.0%
30	Oklahoma	19,557,046,000	1.0%
31	Kansas	18,379,745,000	0.9%
32	Mississippi	15,448,529,000	0.8%
33	Utah	15,069,235,000	0.8%
34	Arkansas	14,820,451,000	0.8%
35	Nevada	14,511,065,000	0.7%
36	Alaska	12,458,955,000	0.6%
37	New Mexico	12,053,657,000	0.6%
38	Nebraska	11,645,121,000	0.6%
39	West Virginia	10,844,014,000	0.6%
40	Hawaii	9,731,812,000	0.5%
41	Maine	8,079,918,000	0.4%
42	Idaho	7,772,507,000	0.4%
43	New Hampshire	7,670,223,000	0.4%
44	Rhode Island	7,241,946,000	0.4%
45	Delaware	6,965,208,000	0.4%
46	North Dakota	6,447,656,000	0.3%
47	Wyoming	6,226,129,000	0.3%
48	Montana	5,272,157,000	0.3%
49	Vermont	4,347,785,000	0.2%
50	South Dakota	4,147,634,000	0.2%
	District of Columbia	6,657,444,000	0.3%

Source: U.S. Bureau of the Census, Governments Division
   "2011 State and Local Government Finances" (http://www.census.gov/govs/local/)
*Own source revenue includes taxes, current charges, and miscellaneous general revenue. Excluded are intergovernmental transfers, insurance trust revenue, and revenue from government owned utilities and other commercial or auxiliary enterprise.

Per Capita State and Local Government Own Source Revenue in 2011

National Per Capita = $6,312*

ALPHA ORDER

RANK	STATE	PER CAPITA
40	Alabama	$5,201
1	Alaska	17,212
49	Arizona	4,791
44	Arkansas	5,043
10	California	7,118
14	Colorado	6,657
6	Connecticut	7,734
7	Delaware	7,670
33	Florida	5,599
48	Georgia	4,846
11	Hawaii	7,062
47	Idaho	4,908
22	Illinois	6,187
35	Indiana	5,488
16	Iowa	6,541
17	Kansas	6,403
43	Kentucky	5,090
26	Louisiana	5,884
23	Maine	6,082
15	Maryland	6,621
8	Massachusetts	7,474
31	Michigan	5,706
9	Minnesota	7,147
41	Mississippi	5,188
46	Missouri	4,957
38	Montana	5,284
20	Nebraska	6,321
37	Nevada	5,335
29	New Hampshire	5,820
5	New Jersey	7,877
30	New Mexico	5,799
3	New York	9,788
34	North Carolina	5,494
4	North Dakota	9,416
27	Ohio	5,861
42	Oklahoma	5,168
25	Oregon	5,952
21	Pennsylvania	6,240
13	Rhode Island	6,893
32	South Carolina	5,694
45	South Dakota	5,036
50	Tennessee	4,631
39	Texas	5,275
36	Utah	5,354
12	Vermont	6,939
24	Virginia	6,068
18	Washington	6,391
28	West Virginia	5,846
19	Wisconsin	6,346
2	Wyoming	10,974

RANK ORDER

RANK	STATE	PER CAPITA
1	Alaska	$17,212
2	Wyoming	10,974
3	New York	9,788
4	North Dakota	9,416
5	New Jersey	7,877
6	Connecticut	7,734
7	Delaware	7,670
8	Massachusetts	7,474
9	Minnesota	7,147
10	California	7,118
11	Hawaii	7,062
12	Vermont	6,939
13	Rhode Island	6,893
14	Colorado	6,657
15	Maryland	6,621
16	Iowa	6,541
17	Kansas	6,403
18	Washington	6,391
19	Wisconsin	6,346
20	Nebraska	6,321
21	Pennsylvania	6,240
22	Illinois	6,187
23	Maine	6,082
24	Virginia	6,068
25	Oregon	5,952
26	Louisiana	5,884
27	Ohio	5,861
28	West Virginia	5,846
29	New Hampshire	5,820
30	New Mexico	5,799
31	Michigan	5,706
32	South Carolina	5,694
33	Florida	5,599
34	North Carolina	5,494
35	Indiana	5,488
36	Utah	5,354
37	Nevada	5,335
38	Montana	5,284
39	Texas	5,275
40	Alabama	5,201
41	Mississippi	5,188
42	Oklahoma	5,168
43	Kentucky	5,090
44	Arkansas	5,043
45	South Dakota	5,036
46	Missouri	4,957
47	Idaho	4,908
48	Georgia	4,846
49	Arizona	4,791
50	Tennessee	4,631

District of Columbia — 10,755

Source: CQ Press using data from U.S. Bureau of the Census, Governments Division
   "2011 State and Local Government Finances" (http://www.census.gov/govs/local/)
*Own source revenue includes taxes, current charges, and miscellaneous general revenue. Excluded are intergovernmental
transfers, insurance trust revenue, and revenue from government owned utilities and other commercial or auxiliary enterprise.

State and Local Government Tax Revenue in 2011

National Total = $1,338,436,677,000

ALPHA ORDER

RANK	STATE	REVENUE	% of USA
27	Alabama	$13,878,574,000	1.0%
37	Alaska	7,292,155,000	0.5%
21	Arizona	21,655,498,000	1.6%
33	Arkansas	9,949,704,000	0.7%
1	California	185,218,208,000	13.8%
20	Colorado	21,791,868,000	1.6%
19	Connecticut	22,762,680,000	1.7%
46	Delaware	4,072,252,000	0.3%
4	Florida	65,259,273,000	4.9%
13	Georgia	31,132,743,000	2.3%
40	Hawaii	6,572,749,000	0.5%
44	Idaho	4,711,409,000	0.4%
5	Illinois	59,551,953,000	4.4%
18	Indiana	23,152,483,000	1.7%
29	Iowa	12,649,129,000	0.9%
31	Kansas	11,756,882,000	0.9%
25	Kentucky	14,556,418,000	1.1%
24	Louisiana	16,612,385,000	1.2%
41	Maine	6,054,014,000	0.5%
14	Maryland	29,037,074,000	2.2%
10	Massachusetts	35,841,109,000	2.7%
9	Michigan	36,102,277,000	2.7%
16	Minnesota	26,822,750,000	2.0%
34	Mississippi	9,269,168,000	0.7%
22	Missouri	19,641,850,000	1.5%
48	Montana	3,434,612,000	0.3%
36	Nebraska	7,800,549,000	0.6%
32	Nevada	10,214,320,000	0.8%
42	New Hampshire	5,311,294,000	0.4%
7	New Jersey	53,149,940,000	4.0%
38	New Mexico	7,249,589,000	0.5%
2	New York	144,733,996,000	10.8%
11	North Carolina	33,710,615,000	2.5%
45	North Dakota	4,709,350,000	0.4%
8	Ohio	45,123,778,000	3.4%
30	Oklahoma	12,010,585,000	0.9%
26	Oregon	14,110,679,000	1.1%
6	Pennsylvania	55,770,938,000	4.2%
43	Rhode Island	5,080,343,000	0.4%
28	South Carolina	13,743,802,000	1.0%
50	South Dakota	2,699,154,000	0.2%
23	Tennessee	19,077,703,000	1.4%
3	Texas	90,778,181,000	6.8%
35	Utah	9,057,134,000	0.7%
49	Vermont	3,140,119,000	0.2%
12	Virginia	32,152,972,000	2.4%
15	Washington	28,409,657,000	2.1%
39	West Virginia	6,975,261,000	0.5%
17	Wisconsin	25,605,386,000	1.9%
47	Wyoming	3,673,312,000	0.3%

RANK ORDER

RANK	STATE	REVENUE	% of USA
1	California	$185,218,208,000	13.8%
2	New York	144,733,996,000	10.8%
3	Texas	90,778,181,000	6.8%
4	Florida	65,259,273,000	4.9%
5	Illinois	59,551,953,000	4.4%
6	Pennsylvania	55,770,938,000	4.2%
7	New Jersey	53,149,940,000	4.0%
8	Ohio	45,123,778,000	3.4%
9	Michigan	36,102,277,000	2.7%
10	Massachusetts	35,841,109,000	2.7%
11	North Carolina	33,710,615,000	2.5%
12	Virginia	32,152,972,000	2.4%
13	Georgia	31,132,743,000	2.3%
14	Maryland	29,037,074,000	2.2%
15	Washington	28,409,657,000	2.1%
16	Minnesota	26,822,750,000	2.0%
17	Wisconsin	25,605,386,000	1.9%
18	Indiana	23,152,483,000	1.7%
19	Connecticut	22,762,680,000	1.7%
20	Colorado	21,791,868,000	1.6%
21	Arizona	21,655,498,000	1.6%
22	Missouri	19,641,850,000	1.5%
23	Tennessee	19,077,703,000	1.4%
24	Louisiana	16,612,385,000	1.2%
25	Kentucky	14,556,418,000	1.1%
26	Oregon	14,110,679,000	1.1%
27	Alabama	13,878,574,000	1.0%
28	South Carolina	13,743,802,000	1.0%
29	Iowa	12,649,129,000	0.9%
30	Oklahoma	12,010,585,000	0.9%
31	Kansas	11,756,882,000	0.9%
32	Nevada	10,214,320,000	0.8%
33	Arkansas	9,949,704,000	0.7%
34	Mississippi	9,269,168,000	0.7%
35	Utah	9,057,134,000	0.7%
36	Nebraska	7,800,549,000	0.6%
37	Alaska	7,292,155,000	0.5%
38	New Mexico	7,249,589,000	0.5%
39	West Virginia	6,975,261,000	0.5%
40	Hawaii	6,572,749,000	0.5%
41	Maine	6,054,014,000	0.5%
42	New Hampshire	5,311,294,000	0.4%
43	Rhode Island	5,080,343,000	0.4%
44	Idaho	4,711,409,000	0.4%
45	North Dakota	4,709,350,000	0.4%
46	Delaware	4,072,252,000	0.3%
47	Wyoming	3,673,312,000	0.3%
48	Montana	3,434,612,000	0.3%
49	Vermont	3,140,119,000	0.2%
50	South Dakota	2,699,154,000	0.2%
	District of Columbia	5,368,803,000	0.4%

Source: U.S. Bureau of the Census, Governments Division
   "2011 State and Local Government Finances" (http://www.census.gov/govs/local/)

Per Capita State and Local Government Tax Revenue in 2011

National Per Capita = $4,296

ALPHA ORDER				RANK ORDER		
RANK	STATE	PER CAPITA		RANK	STATE	PER CAPITA
50	Alabama	$2,889		1	Alaska	$10,074
1	Alaska	10,074		2	New York	7,422
39	Arizona	3,348		3	North Dakota	6,878
38	Arkansas	3,386		4	Wyoming	6,474
11	California	4,915		5	Connecticut	6,346
19	Colorado	4,259		6	New Jersey	6,016
5	Connecticut	6,346		7	Massachusetts	5,425
16	Delaware	4,484		8	Minnesota	5,016
37	Florida	3,420		9	Vermont	5,011
45	Georgia	3,173		10	Maryland	4,972
13	Hawaii	4,769		11	California	4,915
48	Idaho	2,975		12	Rhode Island	4,835
14	Illinois	4,631		13	Hawaii	4,769
32	Indiana	3,553		14	Illinois	4,631
22	Iowa	4,128		15	Maine	4,557
23	Kansas	4,096		16	Delaware	4,484
40	Kentucky	3,333		16	Wisconsin	4,484
31	Louisiana	3,631		18	Pennsylvania	4,376
15	Maine	4,557		19	Colorado	4,259
10	Maryland	4,972		20	Nebraska	4,234
7	Massachusetts	5,425		21	Washington	4,164
29	Michigan	3,655		22	Iowa	4,128
8	Minnesota	5,016		23	Kansas	4,096
46	Mississippi	3,113		24	New Hampshire	4,030
42	Missouri	3,269		25	Virginia	3,967
36	Montana	3,443		26	Ohio	3,910
20	Nebraska	4,234		27	West Virginia	3,760
28	Nevada	3,755		28	Nevada	3,755
24	New Hampshire	4,030		29	Michigan	3,655
6	New Jersey	6,016		30	Oregon	3,648
35	New Mexico	3,488		31	Louisiana	3,631
2	New York	7,422		32	Indiana	3,553
34	North Carolina	3,493		33	Texas	3,542
3	North Dakota	6,878		34	North Carolina	3,493
26	Ohio	3,910		35	New Mexico	3,488
44	Oklahoma	3,174		36	Montana	3,443
30	Oregon	3,648		37	Florida	3,420
18	Pennsylvania	4,376		38	Arkansas	3,386
12	Rhode Island	4,835		39	Arizona	3,348
49	South Carolina	2,941		40	Kentucky	3,333
41	South Dakota	3,277		41	South Dakota	3,277
47	Tennessee	2,981		42	Missouri	3,269
33	Texas	3,542		43	Utah	3,218
43	Utah	3,218		44	Oklahoma	3,174
9	Vermont	5,011		45	Georgia	3,173
25	Virginia	3,967		46	Mississippi	3,113
21	Washington	4,164		47	Tennessee	2,981
27	West Virginia	3,760		48	Idaho	2,975
16	Wisconsin	4,484		49	South Carolina	2,941
4	Wyoming	6,474		50	Alabama	2,889
					District of Columbia	8,673

Source: CQ Press using data from U.S. Bureau of the Census, Governments Division
"2011 State and Local Government Finances" (http://www.census.gov/govs/local/)

Percent of State and Local Government Revenue from Taxes in 2011

National Percent = 39.0%

<table>
<tr><td colspan="3">ALPHA ORDER</td><td colspan="3">RANK ORDER</td></tr>
<tr><td>RANK</td><td>STATE</td><td>PERCENT</td><td>RANK</td><td>STATE</td><td>PERCENT</td></tr>
<tr><td>40</td><td>Alabama</td><td>34.1</td><td>1</td><td>Connecticut</td><td>54.0</td></tr>
<tr><td>21</td><td>Alaska</td><td>39.5</td><td>2</td><td>New Jersey</td><td>50.5</td></tr>
<tr><td>25</td><td>Arizona</td><td>36.9</td><td>3</td><td>North Dakota</td><td>48.8</td></tr>
<tr><td>35</td><td>Arkansas</td><td>35.7</td><td>4</td><td>Maryland</td><td>46.2</td></tr>
<tr><td>35</td><td>California</td><td>35.7</td><td>5</td><td>New York</td><td>44.7</td></tr>
<tr><td>16</td><td>Colorado</td><td>41.1</td><td>6</td><td>Illinois</td><td>44.6</td></tr>
<tr><td>1</td><td>Connecticut</td><td>54.0</td><td>7</td><td>Massachusetts</td><td>43.7</td></tr>
<tr><td>29</td><td>Delaware</td><td>36.4</td><td>8</td><td>New Hampshire</td><td>43.5</td></tr>
<tr><td>31</td><td>Florida</td><td>36.0</td><td>9</td><td>Maine</td><td>43.3</td></tr>
<tr><td>26</td><td>Georgia</td><td>36.6</td><td>10</td><td>Minnesota</td><td>42.2</td></tr>
<tr><td>14</td><td>Hawaii</td><td>41.2</td><td>11</td><td>Virginia</td><td>42.1</td></tr>
<tr><td>44</td><td>Idaho</td><td>33.4</td><td>12</td><td>Pennsylvania</td><td>41.5</td></tr>
<tr><td>6</td><td>Illinois</td><td>44.6</td><td>13</td><td>Vermont</td><td>41.4</td></tr>
<tr><td>18</td><td>Indiana</td><td>40.7</td><td>14</td><td>Hawaii</td><td>41.2</td></tr>
<tr><td>26</td><td>Iowa</td><td>36.6</td><td>14</td><td>Kansas</td><td>41.2</td></tr>
<tr><td>14</td><td>Kansas</td><td>41.2</td><td>16</td><td>Colorado</td><td>41.1</td></tr>
<tr><td>35</td><td>Kentucky</td><td>35.7</td><td>17</td><td>Wisconsin</td><td>40.8</td></tr>
<tr><td>42</td><td>Louisiana</td><td>33.8</td><td>18</td><td>Indiana</td><td>40.7</td></tr>
<tr><td>9</td><td>Maine</td><td>43.3</td><td>19</td><td>Texas</td><td>40.4</td></tr>
<tr><td>4</td><td>Maryland</td><td>46.2</td><td>20</td><td>Rhode Island</td><td>39.9</td></tr>
<tr><td>7</td><td>Massachusetts</td><td>43.7</td><td>21</td><td>Alaska</td><td>39.5</td></tr>
<tr><td>23</td><td>Michigan</td><td>38.7</td><td>22</td><td>Nevada</td><td>39.4</td></tr>
<tr><td>10</td><td>Minnesota</td><td>42.2</td><td>23</td><td>Michigan</td><td>38.7</td></tr>
<tr><td>50</td><td>Mississippi</td><td>29.5</td><td>24</td><td>West Virginia</td><td>37.2</td></tr>
<tr><td>38</td><td>Missouri</td><td>34.4</td><td>25</td><td>Arizona</td><td>36.9</td></tr>
<tr><td>43</td><td>Montana</td><td>33.6</td><td>26</td><td>Georgia</td><td>36.6</td></tr>
<tr><td>31</td><td>Nebraska</td><td>36.0</td><td>26</td><td>Iowa</td><td>36.6</td></tr>
<tr><td>22</td><td>Nevada</td><td>39.4</td><td>28</td><td>Washington</td><td>36.5</td></tr>
<tr><td>8</td><td>New Hampshire</td><td>43.5</td><td>29</td><td>Delaware</td><td>36.4</td></tr>
<tr><td>2</td><td>New Jersey</td><td>50.5</td><td>30</td><td>North Carolina</td><td>36.1</td></tr>
<tr><td>49</td><td>New Mexico</td><td>29.9</td><td>31</td><td>Florida</td><td>36.0</td></tr>
<tr><td>5</td><td>New York</td><td>44.7</td><td>31</td><td>Nebraska</td><td>36.0</td></tr>
<tr><td>30</td><td>North Carolina</td><td>36.1</td><td>31</td><td>Utah</td><td>36.0</td></tr>
<tr><td>3</td><td>North Dakota</td><td>48.8</td><td>31</td><td>Wyoming</td><td>36.0</td></tr>
<tr><td>39</td><td>Ohio</td><td>34.3</td><td>35</td><td>Arkansas</td><td>35.7</td></tr>
<tr><td>41</td><td>Oklahoma</td><td>33.9</td><td>35</td><td>California</td><td>35.7</td></tr>
<tr><td>47</td><td>Oregon</td><td>30.0</td><td>35</td><td>Kentucky</td><td>35.7</td></tr>
<tr><td>12</td><td>Pennsylvania</td><td>41.5</td><td>38</td><td>Missouri</td><td>34.4</td></tr>
<tr><td>20</td><td>Rhode Island</td><td>39.9</td><td>39</td><td>Ohio</td><td>34.3</td></tr>
<tr><td>47</td><td>South Carolina</td><td>30.0</td><td>40</td><td>Alabama</td><td>34.1</td></tr>
<tr><td>45</td><td>South Dakota</td><td>31.9</td><td>41</td><td>Oklahoma</td><td>33.9</td></tr>
<tr><td>46</td><td>Tennessee</td><td>31.6</td><td>42</td><td>Louisiana</td><td>33.8</td></tr>
<tr><td>19</td><td>Texas</td><td>40.4</td><td>43</td><td>Montana</td><td>33.6</td></tr>
<tr><td>31</td><td>Utah</td><td>36.0</td><td>44</td><td>Idaho</td><td>33.4</td></tr>
<tr><td>13</td><td>Vermont</td><td>41.4</td><td>45</td><td>South Dakota</td><td>31.9</td></tr>
<tr><td>11</td><td>Virginia</td><td>42.1</td><td>46</td><td>Tennessee</td><td>31.6</td></tr>
<tr><td>28</td><td>Washington</td><td>36.5</td><td>47</td><td>Oregon</td><td>30.0</td></tr>
<tr><td>24</td><td>West Virginia</td><td>37.2</td><td>47</td><td>South Carolina</td><td>30.0</td></tr>
<tr><td>17</td><td>Wisconsin</td><td>40.8</td><td>49</td><td>New Mexico</td><td>29.9</td></tr>
<tr><td>31</td><td>Wyoming</td><td>36.0</td><td>50</td><td>Mississippi</td><td>29.5</td></tr>
<tr><td></td><td></td><td></td><td></td><td>District of Columbia</td><td>41.7</td></tr>
</table>

Source: CQ Press using data from U.S. Bureau of the Census, Governments Division
"2011 State and Local Government Finances" (http://www.census.gov/govs/local/)

State and Local Government Tax Revenue
as a Percent of Personal Income in 2011
National Percent = 10.3% of Personal Income*

ALPHA ORDER

RANK	STATE	PERCENT
48	Alabama	8.3
1	Alaska	22.1
36	Arizona	9.5
23	Arkansas	10.0
8	California	11.3
30	Colorado	9.7
13	Connecticut	11.0
15	Delaware	10.8
44	Florida	8.6
40	Georgia	8.8
12	Hawaii	11.1
39	Idaho	9.0
16	Illinois	10.6
23	Indiana	10.0
23	Iowa	10.0
23	Kansas	10.0
28	Kentucky	9.8
38	Louisiana	9.4
6	Maine	11.9
28	Maryland	9.8
19	Massachusetts	10.2
21	Michigan	10.1
8	Minnesota	11.3
30	Mississippi	9.7
44	Missouri	8.6
34	Montana	9.6
23	Nebraska	10.0
21	Nevada	10.1
40	New Hampshire	8.8
7	New Jersey	11.5
19	New Mexico	10.2
3	New York	14.5
30	North Carolina	9.7
2	North Dakota	14.6
17	Ohio	10.3
47	Oklahoma	8.4
30	Oregon	9.7
17	Pennsylvania	10.3
13	Rhode Island	11.0
40	South Carolina	8.8
50	South Dakota	7.4
49	Tennessee	8.1
40	Texas	8.8
34	Utah	9.6
5	Vermont	12.1
44	Virginia	8.6
36	Washington	9.5
8	West Virginia	11.3
8	Wisconsin	11.3
4	Wyoming	13.5

RANK ORDER

RANK	STATE	PERCENT
1	Alaska	22.1
2	North Dakota	14.6
3	New York	14.5
4	Wyoming	13.5
5	Vermont	12.1
6	Maine	11.9
7	New Jersey	11.5
8	California	11.3
8	Minnesota	11.3
8	West Virginia	11.3
8	Wisconsin	11.3
12	Hawaii	11.1
13	Connecticut	11.0
13	Rhode Island	11.0
15	Delaware	10.8
16	Illinois	10.6
17	Ohio	10.3
17	Pennsylvania	10.3
19	Massachusetts	10.2
19	New Mexico	10.2
21	Michigan	10.1
21	Nevada	10.1
23	Arkansas	10.0
23	Indiana	10.0
23	Iowa	10.0
23	Kansas	10.0
23	Nebraska	10.0
28	Kentucky	9.8
28	Maryland	9.8
30	Colorado	9.7
30	Mississippi	9.7
30	North Carolina	9.7
30	Oregon	9.7
34	Montana	9.6
34	Utah	9.6
36	Arizona	9.5
36	Washington	9.5
38	Louisiana	9.4
39	Idaho	9.0
40	Georgia	8.8
40	New Hampshire	8.8
40	South Carolina	8.8
40	Texas	8.8
44	Florida	8.6
44	Missouri	8.6
44	Virginia	8.6
47	Oklahoma	8.4
48	Alabama	8.3
49	Tennessee	8.1
50	South Dakota	7.4

District of Columbia — 11.8

Source: CQ Press using data from Bureau of Economic Analysis and U.S. Census Bureau
"Annual State Personal Income" (http://www.bea.gov/iTable/index_regional.cfm) and
"2011 State and Local Government Finances" (http://www.census.gov/govs/local/)
*The personal income total used for this table is the sum of state estimates. This total differs from the national income and product accounts (NIPA) estimate of personal income because it omits the earnings of federal civilian and military personnel stationed abroad and of U.S. residents employed abroad temporarily by private U.S. firms.

State and Local Government General Sales Tax Revenue in 2011

National Total = $301,370,080,000*

ALPHA ORDER

RANK	STATE	REVENUE	% of USA
23	Alabama	$3,973,861,000	1.3%
46	Alaska	334,183,000	0.1%
12	Arizona	8,219,119,000	2.7%
26	Arkansas	3,650,422,000	1.2%
1	California	40,101,659,000	13.3%
17	Colorado	5,223,887,000	1.7%
28	Connecticut	3,252,123,000	1.1%
47	Delaware	0	0.0%
4	Florida	21,123,834,000	7.0%
10	Georgia	8,543,263,000	2.8%
35	Hawaii	2,495,807,000	0.8%
39	Idaho	1,187,070,000	0.4%
9	Illinois	9,089,870,000	3.0%
16	Indiana	6,269,721,000	2.1%
32	Iowa	2,902,001,000	1.0%
27	Kansas	3,285,008,000	1.1%
33	Kentucky	2,896,252,000	1.0%
15	Louisiana	6,555,162,000	2.2%
42	Maine	1,010,241,000	0.3%
25	Maryland	3,896,700,000	1.3%
19	Massachusetts	4,920,521,000	1.6%
8	Michigan	9,477,156,000	3.1%
20	Minnesota	4,762,431,000	1.6%
31	Mississippi	2,969,375,000	1.0%
18	Missouri	4,953,603,000	1.6%
47	Montana	0	0.0%
37	Nebraska	1,690,657,000	0.6%
29	Nevada	3,237,683,000	1.1%
47	New Hampshire	0	0.0%
13	New Jersey	8,144,397,000	2.7%
34	New Mexico	2,797,554,000	0.9%
3	New York	24,007,985,000	8.0%
11	North Carolina	8,277,295,000	2.7%
43	North Dakota	902,874,000	0.3%
7	Ohio	9,501,144,000	3.2%
24	Oklahoma	3,919,090,000	1.3%
47	Oregon	0	0.0%
6	Pennsylvania	9,586,705,000	3.2%
44	Rhode Island	824,507,000	0.3%
30	South Carolina	3,149,831,000	1.0%
40	South Dakota	1,097,373,000	0.4%
14	Tennessee	8,142,474,000	2.7%
2	Texas	27,251,830,000	9.0%
36	Utah	2,441,482,000	0.8%
45	Vermont	335,012,000	0.1%
21	Virginia	4,477,825,000	1.5%
5	Washington	12,914,466,000	4.3%
38	West Virginia	1,210,255,000	0.4%
22	Wisconsin	4,437,614,000	1.5%
41	Wyoming	1,047,557,000	0.3%

RANK ORDER

RANK	STATE	REVENUE	% of USA
1	California	$40,101,659,000	13.3%
2	Texas	27,251,830,000	9.0%
3	New York	24,007,985,000	8.0%
4	Florida	21,123,834,000	7.0%
5	Washington	12,914,466,000	4.3%
6	Pennsylvania	9,586,705,000	3.2%
7	Ohio	9,501,144,000	3.2%
8	Michigan	9,477,156,000	3.1%
9	Illinois	9,089,870,000	3.0%
10	Georgia	8,543,263,000	2.8%
11	North Carolina	8,277,295,000	2.7%
12	Arizona	8,219,119,000	2.7%
13	New Jersey	8,144,397,000	2.7%
14	Tennessee	8,142,474,000	2.7%
15	Louisiana	6,555,162,000	2.2%
16	Indiana	6,269,721,000	2.1%
17	Colorado	5,223,887,000	1.7%
18	Missouri	4,953,603,000	1.6%
19	Massachusetts	4,920,521,000	1.6%
20	Minnesota	4,762,431,000	1.6%
21	Virginia	4,477,825,000	1.5%
22	Wisconsin	4,437,614,000	1.5%
23	Alabama	3,973,861,000	1.3%
24	Oklahoma	3,919,090,000	1.3%
25	Maryland	3,896,700,000	1.3%
26	Arkansas	3,650,422,000	1.2%
27	Kansas	3,285,008,000	1.1%
28	Connecticut	3,252,123,000	1.1%
29	Nevada	3,237,683,000	1.1%
30	South Carolina	3,149,831,000	1.0%
31	Mississippi	2,969,375,000	1.0%
32	Iowa	2,902,001,000	1.0%
33	Kentucky	2,896,252,000	1.0%
34	New Mexico	2,797,554,000	0.9%
35	Hawaii	2,495,807,000	0.8%
36	Utah	2,441,482,000	0.8%
37	Nebraska	1,690,657,000	0.6%
38	West Virginia	1,210,255,000	0.4%
39	Idaho	1,187,070,000	0.4%
40	South Dakota	1,097,373,000	0.4%
41	Wyoming	1,047,557,000	0.3%
42	Maine	1,010,241,000	0.3%
43	North Dakota	902,874,000	0.3%
44	Rhode Island	824,507,000	0.3%
45	Vermont	335,012,000	0.1%
46	Alaska	334,183,000	0.1%
47	Delaware	0	0.0%
47	Montana	0	0.0%
47	New Hampshire	0	0.0%
47	Oregon	0	0.0%
	District of Columbia	881,201,000	0.3%

Source: U.S. Bureau of the Census, Governments Division
"2011 State and Local Government Finances" (http://www.census.gov/govs/local/)
*Does not include special sales taxes such as those on sale of alcohol, gasoline, or tobacco.

Per Capita State and Local Government General Sales Tax Revenue in 2011

National Per Capita = $967*

ALPHA ORDER

RANK	STATE	PER CAPITA
30	Alabama	$827
46	Alaska	462
9	Arizona	1,271
10	Arkansas	1,242
15	California	1,064
18	Colorado	1,021
25	Connecticut	907
47	Delaware	0
14	Florida	1,107
27	Georgia	871
3	Hawaii	1,811
37	Idaho	750
39	Illinois	707
20	Indiana	962
22	Iowa	947
13	Kansas	1,144
42	Kentucky	663
4	Louisiana	1,433
35	Maine	760
41	Maryland	667
38	Massachusetts	745
21	Michigan	960
26	Minnesota	891
19	Mississippi	997
31	Missouri	824
47	Montana	0
24	Nebraska	918
12	Nevada	1,190
47	New Hampshire	0
23	New Jersey	922
5	New Mexico	1,346
11	New York	1,231
29	North Carolina	858
7	North Dakota	1,319
32	Ohio	823
17	Oklahoma	1,036
47	Oregon	0
36	Pennsylvania	752
33	Rhode Island	785
40	South Carolina	674
6	South Dakota	1,332
8	Tennessee	1,272
16	Texas	1,063
28	Utah	868
45	Vermont	535
44	Virginia	553
1	Washington	1,893
43	West Virginia	652
34	Wisconsin	777
2	Wyoming	1,846

RANK ORDER

RANK	STATE	PER CAPITA
1	Washington	$1,893
2	Wyoming	1,846
3	Hawaii	1,811
4	Louisiana	1,433
5	New Mexico	1,346
6	South Dakota	1,332
7	North Dakota	1,319
8	Tennessee	1,272
9	Arizona	1,271
10	Arkansas	1,242
11	New York	1,231
12	Nevada	1,190
13	Kansas	1,144
14	Florida	1,107
15	California	1,064
16	Texas	1,063
17	Oklahoma	1,036
18	Colorado	1,021
19	Mississippi	997
20	Indiana	962
21	Michigan	960
22	Iowa	947
23	New Jersey	922
24	Nebraska	918
25	Connecticut	907
26	Minnesota	891
27	Georgia	871
28	Utah	868
29	North Carolina	858
30	Alabama	827
31	Missouri	824
32	Ohio	823
33	Rhode Island	785
34	Wisconsin	777
35	Maine	760
36	Pennsylvania	752
37	Idaho	750
38	Massachusetts	745
39	Illinois	707
40	South Carolina	674
41	Maryland	667
42	Kentucky	663
43	West Virginia	652
44	Virginia	553
45	Vermont	535
46	Alaska	462
47	Delaware	0
47	Montana	0
47	New Hampshire	0
47	Oregon	0
	District of Columbia	1,424

Source: CQ Press using data from U.S. Bureau of the Census, Governments Division
"2011 State and Local Government Finances" (http://www.census.gov/govs/local/)
*Does not include special sales taxes such as those on sale of alcohol, gasoline, or tobacco.

State and Local Government Property Tax Revenue in 2011

National Total = $443,259,172,000

<table>
<tr><td colspan="4">ALPHA ORDER</td><td colspan="4">RANK ORDER</td></tr>
<tr><td>RANK</td><td>STATE</td><td>REVENUE</td><td>% of USA</td><td>RANK</td><td>STATE</td><td>REVENUE</td><td>% of USA</td></tr>
<tr><td>33</td><td>Alabama</td><td>$2,588,390,000</td><td>0.6%</td><td>1</td><td>California</td><td>$53,506,490,000</td><td>12.1%</td></tr>
<tr><td>40</td><td>Alaska</td><td>1,492,499,000</td><td>0.3%</td><td>2</td><td>New York</td><td>45,420,289,000</td><td>10.2%</td></tr>
<tr><td>20</td><td>Arizona</td><td>7,104,412,000</td><td>1.6%</td><td>3</td><td>Texas</td><td>39,596,363,000</td><td>8.9%</td></tr>
<tr><td>39</td><td>Arkansas</td><td>1,812,948,000</td><td>0.4%</td><td>4</td><td>Florida</td><td>25,934,924,000</td><td>5.9%</td></tr>
<tr><td>1</td><td>California</td><td>53,506,490,000</td><td>12.1%</td><td>5</td><td>New Jersey</td><td>25,513,862,000</td><td>5.8%</td></tr>
<tr><td>18</td><td>Colorado</td><td>8,320,119,000</td><td>1.9%</td><td>6</td><td>Illinois</td><td>24,172,045,000</td><td>5.5%</td></tr>
<tr><td>14</td><td>Connecticut</td><td>9,229,775,000</td><td>2.1%</td><td>7</td><td>Pennsylvania</td><td>16,610,320,000</td><td>3.7%</td></tr>
<tr><td>50</td><td>Delaware</td><td>666,240,000</td><td>0.2%</td><td>8</td><td>Michigan</td><td>13,568,841,000</td><td>3.1%</td></tr>
<tr><td>4</td><td>Florida</td><td>25,934,924,000</td><td>5.9%</td><td>9</td><td>Massachusetts</td><td>13,286,932,000</td><td>3.0%</td></tr>
<tr><td>12</td><td>Georgia</td><td>10,349,138,000</td><td>2.3%</td><td>10</td><td>Ohio</td><td>13,159,029,000</td><td>3.0%</td></tr>
<tr><td>46</td><td>Hawaii</td><td>1,324,771,000</td><td>0.3%</td><td>11</td><td>Virginia</td><td>11,103,895,000</td><td>2.5%</td></tr>
<tr><td>43</td><td>Idaho</td><td>1,367,956,000</td><td>0.3%</td><td>12</td><td>Georgia</td><td>10,349,138,000</td><td>2.3%</td></tr>
<tr><td>6</td><td>Illinois</td><td>24,172,045,000</td><td>5.5%</td><td>13</td><td>Wisconsin</td><td>9,827,091,000</td><td>2.2%</td></tr>
<tr><td>21</td><td>Indiana</td><td>6,313,350,000</td><td>1.4%</td><td>14</td><td>Connecticut</td><td>9,229,775,000</td><td>2.1%</td></tr>
<tr><td>26</td><td>Iowa</td><td>4,369,466,000</td><td>1.0%</td><td>15</td><td>Washington</td><td>8,674,647,000</td><td>2.0%</td></tr>
<tr><td>27</td><td>Kansas</td><td>3,915,805,000</td><td>0.9%</td><td>16</td><td>North Carolina</td><td>8,640,184,000</td><td>1.9%</td></tr>
<tr><td>31</td><td>Kentucky</td><td>3,003,461,000</td><td>0.7%</td><td>17</td><td>Maryland</td><td>8,425,357,000</td><td>1.9%</td></tr>
<tr><td>28</td><td>Louisiana</td><td>3,536,943,000</td><td>0.8%</td><td>18</td><td>Colorado</td><td>8,320,119,000</td><td>1.9%</td></tr>
<tr><td>36</td><td>Maine</td><td>2,400,881,000</td><td>0.5%</td><td>19</td><td>Minnesota</td><td>8,179,949,000</td><td>1.8%</td></tr>
<tr><td>17</td><td>Maryland</td><td>8,425,357,000</td><td>1.9%</td><td>20</td><td>Arizona</td><td>7,104,412,000</td><td>1.6%</td></tr>
<tr><td>9</td><td>Massachusetts</td><td>13,286,932,000</td><td>3.0%</td><td>21</td><td>Indiana</td><td>6,313,350,000</td><td>1.4%</td></tr>
<tr><td>8</td><td>Michigan</td><td>13,568,841,000</td><td>3.1%</td><td>22</td><td>Missouri</td><td>5,877,847,000</td><td>1.3%</td></tr>
<tr><td>19</td><td>Minnesota</td><td>8,179,949,000</td><td>1.8%</td><td>23</td><td>Tennessee</td><td>5,101,115,000</td><td>1.2%</td></tr>
<tr><td>35</td><td>Mississippi</td><td>2,546,095,000</td><td>0.6%</td><td>24</td><td>Oregon</td><td>5,054,454,000</td><td>1.1%</td></tr>
<tr><td>22</td><td>Missouri</td><td>5,877,847,000</td><td>1.3%</td><td>25</td><td>South Carolina</td><td>4,804,227,000</td><td>1.1%</td></tr>
<tr><td>45</td><td>Montana</td><td>1,339,480,000</td><td>0.3%</td><td>26</td><td>Iowa</td><td>4,369,466,000</td><td>1.0%</td></tr>
<tr><td>32</td><td>Nebraska</td><td>2,874,399,000</td><td>0.6%</td><td>27</td><td>Kansas</td><td>3,915,805,000</td><td>0.9%</td></tr>
<tr><td>30</td><td>Nevada</td><td>3,010,793,000</td><td>0.7%</td><td>28</td><td>Louisiana</td><td>3,536,943,000</td><td>0.8%</td></tr>
<tr><td>29</td><td>New Hampshire</td><td>3,317,013,000</td><td>0.7%</td><td>29</td><td>New Hampshire</td><td>3,317,013,000</td><td>0.7%</td></tr>
<tr><td>5</td><td>New Jersey</td><td>25,513,862,000</td><td>5.8%</td><td>30</td><td>Nevada</td><td>3,010,793,000</td><td>0.7%</td></tr>
<tr><td>44</td><td>New Mexico</td><td>1,365,810,000</td><td>0.3%</td><td>31</td><td>Kentucky</td><td>3,003,461,000</td><td>0.7%</td></tr>
<tr><td>2</td><td>New York</td><td>45,420,289,000</td><td>10.2%</td><td>32</td><td>Nebraska</td><td>2,874,399,000</td><td>0.6%</td></tr>
<tr><td>16</td><td>North Carolina</td><td>8,640,184,000</td><td>1.9%</td><td>33</td><td>Alabama</td><td>2,588,390,000</td><td>0.6%</td></tr>
<tr><td>49</td><td>North Dakota</td><td>730,146,000</td><td>0.2%</td><td>34</td><td>Utah</td><td>2,550,899,000</td><td>0.6%</td></tr>
<tr><td>10</td><td>Ohio</td><td>13,159,029,000</td><td>3.0%</td><td>35</td><td>Mississippi</td><td>2,546,095,000</td><td>0.6%</td></tr>
<tr><td>38</td><td>Oklahoma</td><td>2,223,834,000</td><td>0.5%</td><td>36</td><td>Maine</td><td>2,400,881,000</td><td>0.5%</td></tr>
<tr><td>24</td><td>Oregon</td><td>5,054,454,000</td><td>1.1%</td><td>37</td><td>Rhode Island</td><td>2,273,300,000</td><td>0.5%</td></tr>
<tr><td>7</td><td>Pennsylvania</td><td>16,610,320,000</td><td>3.7%</td><td>38</td><td>Oklahoma</td><td>2,223,834,000</td><td>0.5%</td></tr>
<tr><td>37</td><td>Rhode Island</td><td>2,273,300,000</td><td>0.5%</td><td>39</td><td>Arkansas</td><td>1,812,948,000</td><td>0.4%</td></tr>
<tr><td>25</td><td>South Carolina</td><td>4,804,227,000</td><td>1.1%</td><td>40</td><td>Alaska</td><td>1,492,499,000</td><td>0.3%</td></tr>
<tr><td>48</td><td>South Dakota</td><td>980,962,000</td><td>0.2%</td><td>41</td><td>West Virginia</td><td>1,428,863,000</td><td>0.3%</td></tr>
<tr><td>23</td><td>Tennessee</td><td>5,101,115,000</td><td>1.2%</td><td>42</td><td>Vermont</td><td>1,375,819,000</td><td>0.3%</td></tr>
<tr><td>3</td><td>Texas</td><td>39,596,363,000</td><td>8.9%</td><td>43</td><td>Idaho</td><td>1,367,956,000</td><td>0.3%</td></tr>
<tr><td>34</td><td>Utah</td><td>2,550,899,000</td><td>0.6%</td><td>44</td><td>New Mexico</td><td>1,365,810,000</td><td>0.3%</td></tr>
<tr><td>42</td><td>Vermont</td><td>1,375,819,000</td><td>0.3%</td><td>45</td><td>Montana</td><td>1,339,480,000</td><td>0.3%</td></tr>
<tr><td>11</td><td>Virginia</td><td>11,103,895,000</td><td>2.5%</td><td>46</td><td>Hawaii</td><td>1,324,771,000</td><td>0.3%</td></tr>
<tr><td>15</td><td>Washington</td><td>8,674,647,000</td><td>2.0%</td><td>47</td><td>Wyoming</td><td>1,230,548,000</td><td>0.3%</td></tr>
<tr><td>41</td><td>West Virginia</td><td>1,428,863,000</td><td>0.3%</td><td>48</td><td>South Dakota</td><td>980,962,000</td><td>0.2%</td></tr>
<tr><td>13</td><td>Wisconsin</td><td>9,827,091,000</td><td>2.2%</td><td>49</td><td>North Dakota</td><td>730,146,000</td><td>0.2%</td></tr>
<tr><td>47</td><td>Wyoming</td><td>1,230,548,000</td><td>0.3%</td><td>50</td><td>Delaware</td><td>666,240,000</td><td>0.2%</td></tr>
<tr><td></td><td></td><td></td><td></td><td></td><td>District of Columbia</td><td>1,757,196,000</td><td>0.4%</td></tr>
</table>

Source: U.S. Bureau of the Census, Governments Division
"2011 State and Local Government Finances" (http://www.census.gov/govs/local/)

Per Capita State and Local Government Property Tax Revenue in 2011

National Per Capita = $1,423

ALPHA ORDER

RANK	STATE	PER CAPITA
50	Alabama	$539
8	Alaska	2,062
31	Arizona	1,099
48	Arkansas	617
19	California	1,420
13	Colorado	1,626
2	Connecticut	2,573
45	Delaware	734
23	Florida	1,359
33	Georgia	1,055
37	Hawaii	961
40	Idaho	864
10	Illinois	1,880
36	Indiana	969
18	Iowa	1,426
22	Kansas	1,364
46	Kentucky	688
43	Louisiana	773
11	Maine	1,807
17	Maryland	1,443
9	Massachusetts	2,011
20	Michigan	1,374
16	Minnesota	1,530
41	Mississippi	855
35	Missouri	978
24	Montana	1,343
14	Nebraska	1,560
30	Nevada	1,107
3	New Hampshire	2,517
1	New Jersey	2,888
47	New Mexico	657
4	New York	2,329
39	North Carolina	895
32	North Dakota	1,066
29	Ohio	1,140
49	Oklahoma	588
25	Oregon	1,307
26	Pennsylvania	1,303
7	Rhode Island	2,164
34	South Carolina	1,028
28	South Dakota	1,191
42	Tennessee	797
15	Texas	1,545
38	Utah	906
5	Vermont	2,196
21	Virginia	1,370
27	Washington	1,271
44	West Virginia	770
12	Wisconsin	1,721
6	Wyoming	2,169

RANK ORDER

RANK	STATE	PER CAPITA
1	New Jersey	$2,888
2	Connecticut	2,573
3	New Hampshire	2,517
4	New York	2,329
5	Vermont	2,196
6	Wyoming	2,169
7	Rhode Island	2,164
8	Alaska	2,062
9	Massachusetts	2,011
10	Illinois	1,880
11	Maine	1,807
12	Wisconsin	1,721
13	Colorado	1,626
14	Nebraska	1,560
15	Texas	1,545
16	Minnesota	1,530
17	Maryland	1,443
18	Iowa	1,426
19	California	1,420
20	Michigan	1,374
21	Virginia	1,370
22	Kansas	1,364
23	Florida	1,359
24	Montana	1,343
25	Oregon	1,307
26	Pennsylvania	1,303
27	Washington	1,271
28	South Dakota	1,191
29	Ohio	1,140
30	Nevada	1,107
31	Arizona	1,099
32	North Dakota	1,066
33	Georgia	1,055
34	South Carolina	1,028
35	Missouri	978
36	Indiana	969
37	Hawaii	961
38	Utah	906
39	North Carolina	895
40	Idaho	864
41	Mississippi	855
42	Tennessee	797
43	Louisiana	773
44	West Virginia	770
45	Delaware	734
46	Kentucky	688
47	New Mexico	657
48	Arkansas	617
49	Oklahoma	588
50	Alabama	539
	District of Columbia	2,839

Source: CQ Press using data from U.S. Bureau of the Census, Governments Division
"2011 State and Local Government Finances" (http://www.census.gov/govs/local/)

State and Local Government Property Tax as a Percent of State and Local Government Total Revenue in 2011
National Percent = 12.9%

ALPHA ORDER

RANK	STATE	PERCENT
47	Alabama	6.4
40	Alaska	8.1
24	Arizona	12.1
46	Arkansas	6.5
32	California	10.3
10	Colorado	15.7
3	Connecticut	21.9
49	Delaware	5.9
14	Florida	14.3
23	Georgia	12.2
39	Hawaii	8.3
36	Idaho	9.7
4	Illinois	18.1
28	Indiana	11.1
21	Iowa	12.7
16	Kansas	13.7
44	Kentucky	7.4
45	Louisiana	7.2
8	Maine	17.2
17	Maryland	13.4
9	Massachusetts	16.2
12	Michigan	14.5
20	Minnesota	12.9
40	Mississippi	8.1
32	Missouri	10.3
19	Montana	13.1
18	Nebraska	13.3
26	Nevada	11.6
1	New Hampshire	27.1
2	New Jersey	24.2
50	New Mexico	5.6
15	New York	14.0
37	North Carolina	9.3
42	North Dakota	7.6
35	Ohio	10.0
48	Oklahoma	6.3
30	Oregon	10.7
22	Pennsylvania	12.4
6	Rhode Island	17.8
31	South Carolina	10.5
26	South Dakota	11.6
38	Tennessee	8.5
7	Texas	17.6
34	Utah	10.1
4	Vermont	18.1
12	Virginia	14.5
28	Washington	11.1
42	West Virginia	7.6
10	Wisconsin	15.7
24	Wyoming	12.1

RANK ORDER

RANK	STATE	PERCENT
1	New Hampshire	27.1
2	New Jersey	24.2
3	Connecticut	21.9
4	Illinois	18.1
4	Vermont	18.1
6	Rhode Island	17.8
7	Texas	17.6
8	Maine	17.2
9	Massachusetts	16.2
10	Colorado	15.7
10	Wisconsin	15.7
12	Michigan	14.5
12	Virginia	14.5
14	Florida	14.3
15	New York	14.0
16	Kansas	13.7
17	Maryland	13.4
18	Nebraska	13.3
19	Montana	13.1
20	Minnesota	12.9
21	Iowa	12.7
22	Pennsylvania	12.4
23	Georgia	12.2
24	Arizona	12.1
24	Wyoming	12.1
26	Nevada	11.6
26	South Dakota	11.6
28	Indiana	11.1
28	Washington	11.1
30	Oregon	10.7
31	South Carolina	10.5
32	California	10.3
32	Missouri	10.3
34	Utah	10.1
35	Ohio	10.0
36	Idaho	9.7
37	North Carolina	9.3
38	Tennessee	8.5
39	Hawaii	8.3
40	Alaska	8.1
40	Mississippi	8.1
42	North Dakota	7.6
42	West Virginia	7.6
44	Kentucky	7.4
45	Louisiana	7.2
46	Arkansas	6.5
47	Alabama	6.4
48	Oklahoma	6.3
49	Delaware	5.9
50	New Mexico	5.6

| | District of Columbia | 13.6 |

Source: CQ Press using data from U.S. Bureau of the Census, Governments Division
"2011 State and Local Government Finances" (http://www.census.gov/govs/local/)

State and Local Government Property Tax Revenue as a Percent of State and Local Government Own Source Revenue in 2011
National Percent = 22.5%*

ALPHA ORDER

RANK	STATE	PERCENT
49	Alabama	10.4
45	Alaska	12.0
18	Arizona	22.9
44	Arkansas	12.2
28	California	19.9
13	Colorado	24.4
3	Connecticut	33.3
50	Delaware	9.6
14	Florida	24.3
21	Georgia	21.8
40	Hawaii	13.6
35	Idaho	17.6
6	Illinois	30.4
34	Indiana	17.7
21	Iowa	21.8
25	Kansas	21.3
41	Kentucky	13.5
43	Louisiana	13.1
7	Maine	29.7
21	Maryland	21.8
10	Massachusetts	26.9
15	Michigan	24.1
24	Minnesota	21.4
38	Mississippi	16.5
31	Missouri	19.7
11	Montana	25.4
12	Nebraska	24.7
27	Nevada	20.7
1	New Hampshire	43.2
2	New Jersey	36.7
47	New Mexico	11.3
16	New York	23.8
39	North Carolina	16.3
47	North Dakota	11.3
32	Ohio	19.5
46	Oklahoma	11.4
20	Oregon	22.0
26	Pennsylvania	20.9
5	Rhode Island	31.4
33	South Carolina	18.1
17	South Dakota	23.7
36	Tennessee	17.2
8	Texas	29.3
37	Utah	16.9
4	Vermont	31.6
19	Virginia	22.6
28	Washington	19.9
42	West Virginia	13.2
9	Wisconsin	27.1
30	Wyoming	19.8

RANK ORDER

RANK	STATE	PERCENT
1	New Hampshire	43.2
2	New Jersey	36.7
3	Connecticut	33.3
4	Vermont	31.6
5	Rhode Island	31.4
6	Illinois	30.4
7	Maine	29.7
8	Texas	29.3
9	Wisconsin	27.1
10	Massachusetts	26.9
11	Montana	25.4
12	Nebraska	24.7
13	Colorado	24.4
14	Florida	24.3
15	Michigan	24.1
16	New York	23.8
17	South Dakota	23.7
18	Arizona	22.9
19	Virginia	22.6
20	Oregon	22.0
21	Georgia	21.8
21	Iowa	21.8
21	Maryland	21.8
24	Minnesota	21.4
25	Kansas	21.3
26	Pennsylvania	20.9
27	Nevada	20.7
28	California	19.9
28	Washington	19.9
30	Wyoming	19.8
31	Missouri	19.7
32	Ohio	19.5
33	South Carolina	18.1
34	Indiana	17.7
35	Idaho	17.6
36	Tennessee	17.2
37	Utah	16.9
38	Mississippi	16.5
39	North Carolina	16.3
40	Hawaii	13.6
41	Kentucky	13.5
42	West Virginia	13.2
43	Louisiana	13.1
44	Arkansas	12.2
45	Alaska	12.0
46	Oklahoma	11.4
47	New Mexico	11.3
47	North Dakota	11.3
49	Alabama	10.4
50	Delaware	9.6

| | District of Columbia | 26.4 |

Source: CQ Press using data from U.S. Bureau of the Census, Governments Division
   "2011 State and Local Government Finances" (http://www.census.gov/govs/local/)
*Own source revenue includes taxes, current charges, and miscellaneous general revenue. Excluded are intergovernmental transfers, insurance trust revenue, and revenue from government owned utilities and other commercial or auxiliary enterprise.

State and Local Tax Burden as a Percent of Income in 2010

National Percent = 9.9% of Income*

RANK	STATE	PERCENT
42	Alabama	8.2
50	Alaska	7.0
39	Arizona	8.4
15	Arkansas	10.0
4	California	11.2
32	Colorado	9.1
3	Connecticut	12.3
27	Delaware	9.3
27	Florida	9.3
33	Georgia	9.0
13	Hawaii	10.1
25	Idaho	9.4
10	Illinois	10.2
23	Indiana	9.6
23	Iowa	9.6
19	Kansas	9.7
25	Kentucky	9.4
46	Louisiana	7.8
9	Maine	10.3
10	Maryland	10.2
8	Massachusetts	10.4
18	Michigan	9.8
7	Minnesota	10.8
36	Mississippi	8.7
33	Missouri	9.0
38	Montana	8.6
19	Nebraska	9.7
42	Nevada	8.2
44	New Hampshire	8.1
2	New Jersey	12.4
39	New Mexico	8.4
1	New York	12.8
17	North Carolina	9.9
35	North Dakota	8.9
19	Ohio	9.7
36	Oklahoma	8.7
15	Oregon	10.0
10	Pennsylvania	10.2
6	Rhode Island	10.9
39	South Carolina	8.4
49	South Dakota	7.6
48	Tennessee	7.7
45	Texas	7.9
27	Utah	9.3
13	Vermont	10.1
27	Virginia	9.3
27	Washington	9.3
19	West Virginia	9.7
5	Wisconsin	11.1
46	Wyoming	7.8

RANK	STATE	PERCENT
1	New York	12.8
2	New Jersey	12.4
3	Connecticut	12.3
4	California	11.2
5	Wisconsin	11.1
6	Rhode Island	10.9
7	Minnesota	10.8
8	Massachusetts	10.4
9	Maine	10.3
10	Illinois	10.2
10	Maryland	10.2
10	Pennsylvania	10.2
13	Hawaii	10.1
13	Vermont	10.1
15	Arkansas	10.0
15	Oregon	10.0
17	North Carolina	9.9
18	Michigan	9.8
19	Kansas	9.7
19	Nebraska	9.7
19	Ohio	9.7
19	West Virginia	9.7
23	Indiana	9.6
23	Iowa	9.6
25	Idaho	9.4
25	Kentucky	9.4
27	Delaware	9.3
27	Florida	9.3
27	Utah	9.3
27	Virginia	9.3
27	Washington	9.3
32	Colorado	9.1
33	Georgia	9.0
33	Missouri	9.0
35	North Dakota	8.9
36	Mississippi	8.7
36	Oklahoma	8.7
38	Montana	8.6
39	Arizona	8.4
39	New Mexico	8.4
39	South Carolina	8.4
42	Alabama	8.2
42	Nevada	8.2
44	New Hampshire	8.1
45	Texas	7.9
46	Louisiana	7.8
46	Wyoming	7.8
48	Tennessee	7.7
49	South Dakota	7.6
50	Alaska	7.0

	District of Columbia	9.2

Source: The Tax Foundation
"State and Local Tax Burdens: All States, One Year, 1977-2010" (www.taxfoundation.org/research/show/336.html)
*All state and local taxes.

State and Local Government Total Expenditures in 2011

National Total = $3,162,628,274,000*

ALPHA ORDER

RANK	STATE	EXPENDITURES	% of USA
25	Alabama	$42,161,028,000	1.3%
39	Alaska	14,687,040,000	0.5%
20	Arizona	52,533,819,000	1.7%
34	Arkansas	23,768,782,000	0.8%
1	California	457,591,036,000	14.5%
21	Colorado	51,576,659,000	1.6%
26	Connecticut	40,675,690,000	1.3%
45	Delaware	9,897,809,000	0.3%
4	Florida	164,062,212,000	5.2%
11	Georgia	78,093,549,000	2.5%
40	Hawaii	14,389,261,000	0.5%
42	Idaho	12,065,995,000	0.4%
6	Illinois	130,777,103,000	4.1%
19	Indiana	52,682,140,000	1.7%
30	Iowa	30,324,897,000	1.0%
32	Kansas	26,534,127,000	0.8%
28	Kentucky	39,062,585,000	1.2%
23	Louisiana	48,756,593,000	1.5%
41	Maine	12,615,776,000	0.4%
15	Maryland	57,612,277,000	1.8%
12	Massachusetts	75,734,282,000	2.4%
9	Michigan	89,817,860,000	2.8%
17	Minnesota	55,683,581,000	1.8%
31	Mississippi	27,307,717,000	0.9%
22	Missouri	49,876,922,000	1.6%
46	Montana	9,293,762,000	0.3%
37	Nebraska	19,527,121,000	0.6%
35	Nevada	23,268,683,000	0.7%
43	New Hampshire	11,637,435,000	0.4%
8	New Jersey	101,255,553,000	3.2%
36	New Mexico	22,415,452,000	0.7%
2	New York	300,324,433,000	9.5%
10	North Carolina	80,849,495,000	2.6%
48	North Dakota	7,137,121,000	0.2%
7	Ohio	116,246,959,000	3.7%
29	Oklahoma	30,717,191,000	1.0%
27	Oregon	39,932,203,000	1.3%
5	Pennsylvania	132,879,459,000	4.2%
44	Rhode Island	11,465,758,000	0.4%
24	South Carolina	42,784,130,000	1.4%
49	South Dakota	7,013,644,000	0.2%
18	Tennessee	55,155,159,000	1.7%
3	Texas	221,029,984,000	7.0%
33	Utah	24,927,890,000	0.8%
50	Vermont	6,922,191,000	0.2%
14	Virginia	69,225,717,000	2.2%
13	Washington	74,904,561,000	2.4%
38	West Virginia	16,400,370,000	0.5%
16	Wisconsin	56,696,015,000	1.8%
47	Wyoming	8,687,958,000	0.3%

RANK ORDER

RANK	STATE	EXPENDITURES	% of USA
1	California	$457,591,036,000	14.5%
2	New York	300,324,433,000	9.5%
3	Texas	221,029,984,000	7.0%
4	Florida	164,062,212,000	5.2%
5	Pennsylvania	132,879,459,000	4.2%
6	Illinois	130,777,103,000	4.1%
7	Ohio	116,246,959,000	3.7%
8	New Jersey	101,255,553,000	3.2%
9	Michigan	89,817,860,000	2.8%
10	North Carolina	80,849,495,000	2.6%
11	Georgia	78,093,549,000	2.5%
12	Massachusetts	75,734,282,000	2.4%
13	Washington	74,904,561,000	2.4%
14	Virginia	69,225,717,000	2.2%
15	Maryland	57,612,277,000	1.8%
16	Wisconsin	56,696,015,000	1.8%
17	Minnesota	55,683,581,000	1.8%
18	Tennessee	55,155,159,000	1.7%
19	Indiana	52,682,140,000	1.7%
20	Arizona	52,533,819,000	1.7%
21	Colorado	51,576,659,000	1.6%
22	Missouri	49,876,922,000	1.6%
23	Louisiana	48,756,593,000	1.5%
24	South Carolina	42,784,130,000	1.4%
25	Alabama	42,161,028,000	1.3%
26	Connecticut	40,675,690,000	1.3%
27	Oregon	39,932,203,000	1.3%
28	Kentucky	39,062,585,000	1.2%
29	Oklahoma	30,717,191,000	1.0%
30	Iowa	30,324,897,000	1.0%
31	Mississippi	27,307,717,000	0.9%
32	Kansas	26,534,127,000	0.8%
33	Utah	24,927,890,000	0.8%
34	Arkansas	23,768,782,000	0.8%
35	Nevada	23,268,683,000	0.7%
36	New Mexico	22,415,452,000	0.7%
37	Nebraska	19,527,121,000	0.6%
38	West Virginia	16,400,370,000	0.5%
39	Alaska	14,687,040,000	0.5%
40	Hawaii	14,389,261,000	0.5%
41	Maine	12,615,776,000	0.4%
42	Idaho	12,065,995,000	0.4%
43	New Hampshire	11,637,435,000	0.4%
44	Rhode Island	11,465,758,000	0.4%
45	Delaware	9,897,809,000	0.3%
46	Montana	9,293,762,000	0.3%
47	Wyoming	8,687,958,000	0.3%
48	North Dakota	7,137,121,000	0.2%
49	South Dakota	7,013,644,000	0.2%
50	Vermont	6,922,191,000	0.2%
	District of Columbia	13,641,290,000	0.4%

Source: U.S. Bureau of the Census, Governments Division
   "2011 State and Local Government Finances" (http://www.census.gov/govs/local/)
*Total expenditures includes all money paid other than for retirement of debt and extension of loans. Includes payments from all sources of funds including current revenues and proceeds from borrowing and prior year fund balances. Includes intergovernmental transfers and expenditures for government owned utilities and other commercial or auxiliary enterprise, and insurance trust expenditures.

Per Capita State and Local Government Total Expenditures in 2011

National Per Capita = $10,150*

ALPHA ORDER				RANK ORDER		
RANK	STATE	PER CAPITA		RANK	STATE	PER CAPITA
36	Alabama	$8,777		1	Alaska	$20,290
1	Alaska	20,290		2	New York	15,400
45	Arizona	8,123		3	Wyoming	15,313
47	Arkansas	8,089		4	California	12,143
4	California	12,143		5	Massachusetts	11,463
21	Colorado	10,081		6	New Jersey	11,461
7	Connecticut	11,341		7	Connecticut	11,341
11	Delaware	10,899		8	Vermont	11,047
39	Florida	8,598		9	Washington	10,978
49	Georgia	7,959		10	Rhode Island	10,913
15	Hawaii	10,441		11	Delaware	10,899
50	Idaho	7,619		12	New Mexico	10,784
20	Illinois	10,169		13	Louisiana	10,658
48	Indiana	8,085		14	Nebraska	10,600
24	Iowa	9,897		15	Hawaii	10,441
28	Kansas	9,244		16	Pennsylvania	10,427
32	Kentucky	8,945		17	North Dakota	10,423
13	Louisiana	10,658		18	Minnesota	10,413
26	Maine	9,496		19	Oregon	10,323
25	Maryland	9,866		20	Illinois	10,169
5	Massachusetts	11,463		21	Colorado	10,081
31	Michigan	9,094		22	Ohio	10,073
18	Minnesota	10,413		23	Wisconsin	9,930
29	Mississippi	9,171		24	Iowa	9,897
44	Missouri	8,300		25	Maryland	9,866
27	Montana	9,315		26	Maine	9,496
14	Nebraska	10,600		27	Montana	9,315
40	Nevada	8,555		28	Kansas	9,244
35	New Hampshire	8,831		29	Mississippi	9,171
6	New Jersey	11,461		30	South Carolina	9,155
12	New Mexico	10,784		31	Michigan	9,094
2	New York	15,400		32	Kentucky	8,945
43	North Carolina	8,377		33	Utah	8,857
17	North Dakota	10,423		34	West Virginia	8,842
22	Ohio	10,073		35	New Hampshire	8,831
46	Oklahoma	8,117		36	Alabama	8,777
19	Oregon	10,323		37	Texas	8,623
16	Pennsylvania	10,427		38	Tennessee	8,618
10	Rhode Island	10,913		39	Florida	8,598
30	South Carolina	9,155		40	Nevada	8,555
42	South Dakota	8,516		41	Virginia	8,542
38	Tennessee	8,618		42	South Dakota	8,516
37	Texas	8,623		43	North Carolina	8,377
33	Utah	8,857		44	Missouri	8,300
8	Vermont	11,047		45	Arizona	8,123
41	Virginia	8,542		46	Oklahoma	8,117
9	Washington	10,978		47	Arkansas	8,089
34	West Virginia	8,842		48	Indiana	8,085
23	Wisconsin	9,930		49	Georgia	7,959
3	Wyoming	15,313		50	Idaho	7,619
					District of Columbia	22,037

Source: CQ Press using data from U.S. Bureau of the Census, Governments Division
   "2011 State and Local Government Finances" (http://www.census.gov/govs/local/)
*Total expenditures includes all money paid other than for retirement of debt and extension of loans. Includes payments from all sources of funds including current revenues and proceeds from borrowing and prior year fund balances. Includes intergovernmental transfers and expenditures for government owned utilities and other commercial or auxiliary enterprise, and insurance trust expenditures.

State and Local Government Direct General Expenditures in 2011

National Total = $2,583,100,739,000*

ALPHA ORDER

RANK	STATE	EXPENDITURES	% of USA
25	Alabama	$35,385,191,000	1.4%
39	Alaska	12,790,477,000	0.5%
20	Arizona	42,684,746,000	1.7%
33	Arkansas	20,784,517,000	0.8%
1	California	353,674,626,000	13.7%
23	Colorado	41,285,551,000	1.6%
26	Connecticut	33,366,550,000	1.3%
45	Delaware	8,586,127,000	0.3%
4	Florida	137,974,357,000	5.3%
11	Georgia	64,037,873,000	2.5%
40	Hawaii	12,205,684,000	0.5%
42	Idaho	10,488,457,000	0.4%
6	Illinois	104,305,704,000	4.0%
18	Indiana	45,838,359,000	1.8%
29	Iowa	26,457,162,000	1.0%
32	Kansas	22,966,622,000	0.9%
27	Kentucky	32,329,416,000	1.3%
19	Louisiana	42,827,115,000	1.7%
41	Maine	11,353,942,000	0.4%
15	Maryland	49,842,519,000	1.9%
12	Massachusetts	61,545,455,000	2.4%
9	Michigan	73,705,470,000	2.9%
17	Minnesota	47,241,100,000	1.8%
31	Mississippi	23,831,060,000	0.9%
22	Missouri	41,478,542,000	1.6%
46	Montana	8,112,395,000	0.3%
37	Nebraska	14,523,597,000	0.6%
36	Nevada	18,694,662,000	0.7%
43	New Hampshire	10,237,502,000	0.4%
8	New Jersey	81,559,227,000	3.2%
35	New Mexico	19,440,075,000	0.8%
2	New York	235,261,859,000	9.1%
10	North Carolina	67,309,269,000	2.6%
48	North Dakota	6,426,326,000	0.2%
7	Ohio	94,278,105,000	3.6%
30	Oklahoma	25,758,613,000	1.0%
28	Oregon	31,797,518,000	1.2%
5	Pennsylvania	108,685,034,000	4.2%
44	Rhode Island	9,230,061,000	0.4%
24	South Carolina	35,579,527,000	1.4%
50	South Dakota	6,165,418,000	0.2%
21	Tennessee	42,056,487,000	1.6%
3	Texas	185,643,845,000	7.2%
34	Utah	20,369,821,000	0.8%
49	Vermont	6,173,633,000	0.2%
13	Virginia	60,912,146,000	2.4%
14	Washington	57,776,930,000	2.2%
38	West Virginia	14,466,087,000	0.6%
16	Wisconsin	47,713,578,000	1.8%
47	Wyoming	7,556,910,000	0.3%

RANK ORDER

RANK	STATE	EXPENDITURES	% of USA
1	California	$353,674,626,000	13.7%
2	New York	235,261,859,000	9.1%
3	Texas	185,643,845,000	7.2%
4	Florida	137,974,357,000	5.3%
5	Pennsylvania	108,685,034,000	4.2%
6	Illinois	104,305,704,000	4.0%
7	Ohio	94,278,105,000	3.6%
8	New Jersey	81,559,227,000	3.2%
9	Michigan	73,705,470,000	2.9%
10	North Carolina	67,309,269,000	2.6%
11	Georgia	64,037,873,000	2.5%
12	Massachusetts	61,545,455,000	2.4%
13	Virginia	60,912,146,000	2.4%
14	Washington	57,776,930,000	2.2%
15	Maryland	49,842,519,000	1.9%
16	Wisconsin	47,713,578,000	1.8%
17	Minnesota	47,241,100,000	1.8%
18	Indiana	45,838,359,000	1.8%
19	Louisiana	42,827,115,000	1.7%
20	Arizona	42,684,746,000	1.7%
21	Tennessee	42,056,487,000	1.6%
22	Missouri	41,478,542,000	1.6%
23	Colorado	41,285,551,000	1.6%
24	South Carolina	35,579,527,000	1.4%
25	Alabama	35,385,191,000	1.4%
26	Connecticut	33,366,550,000	1.3%
27	Kentucky	32,329,416,000	1.3%
28	Oregon	31,797,518,000	1.2%
29	Iowa	26,457,162,000	1.0%
30	Oklahoma	25,758,613,000	1.0%
31	Mississippi	23,831,060,000	0.9%
32	Kansas	22,966,622,000	0.9%
33	Arkansas	20,784,517,000	0.8%
34	Utah	20,369,821,000	0.8%
35	New Mexico	19,440,075,000	0.8%
36	Nevada	18,694,662,000	0.7%
37	Nebraska	14,523,597,000	0.6%
38	West Virginia	14,466,087,000	0.6%
39	Alaska	12,790,477,000	0.5%
40	Hawaii	12,205,684,000	0.5%
41	Maine	11,353,942,000	0.4%
42	Idaho	10,488,457,000	0.4%
43	New Hampshire	10,237,502,000	0.4%
44	Rhode Island	9,230,061,000	0.4%
45	Delaware	8,586,127,000	0.3%
46	Montana	8,112,395,000	0.3%
47	Wyoming	7,556,910,000	0.3%
48	North Dakota	6,426,326,000	0.2%
49	Vermont	6,173,633,000	0.2%
50	South Dakota	6,165,418,000	0.2%
	District of Columbia	10,385,492,000	0.4%

Source: U.S. Bureau of the Census, Governments Division
   "2011 State and Local Government Finances" (http://www.census.gov/govs/local/)
*Direct general expenditures include expenditures for current operations, assistance and subsidies, interest on debt, and capital outlay. Excludes intergovernmental transfers, expenditures for government owned utilities and other commercial or auxiliary enterprise, and insurance trust expenditures.

Per Capita State and Local Government Direct General Expenditures in 2011

National Per Capita = $8,290*

ALPHA ORDER				RANK ORDER		
RANK	STATE	PER CAPITA		RANK	STATE	PER CAPITA
37	Alabama	$7,366		1	Alaska	$17,670
1	Alaska	17,670		2	Wyoming	13,320
48	Arizona	6,600		3	New York	12,064
41	Arkansas	7,073		4	Vermont	9,853
6	California	9,385		5	Delaware	9,455
26	Colorado	8,069		6	California	9,385
11	Connecticut	9,303		6	North Dakota	9,385
5	Delaware	9,455		8	Louisiana	9,362
40	Florida	7,231		9	New Mexico	9,352
50	Georgia	6,526		10	Massachusetts	9,315
13	Hawaii	8,857		11	Connecticut	9,303
47	Idaho	6,623		12	New Jersey	9,232
25	Illinois	8,111		13	Hawaii	8,857
42	Indiana	7,034		14	Minnesota	8,835
16	Iowa	8,635		15	Rhode Island	8,785
28	Kansas	8,001		16	Iowa	8,635
36	Kentucky	7,403		17	Maine	8,546
8	Louisiana	9,362		18	Maryland	8,535
17	Maine	8,546		19	Pennsylvania	8,528
18	Maryland	8,535		20	Washington	8,468
10	Massachusetts	9,315		21	Wisconsin	8,356
35	Michigan	7,462		22	Oregon	8,220
14	Minnesota	8,835		23	Ohio	8,169
27	Mississippi	8,004		24	Montana	8,131
44	Missouri	6,903		25	Illinois	8,111
24	Montana	8,131		26	Colorado	8,069
29	Nebraska	7,884		27	Mississippi	8,004
45	Nevada	6,873		28	Kansas	8,001
31	New Hampshire	7,769		29	Nebraska	7,884
12	New Jersey	9,232		30	West Virginia	7,799
9	New Mexico	9,352		31	New Hampshire	7,769
3	New York	12,064		32	South Carolina	7,613
43	North Carolina	6,974		33	Virginia	7,516
6	North Dakota	9,385		34	South Dakota	7,486
23	Ohio	8,169		35	Michigan	7,462
46	Oklahoma	6,807		36	Kentucky	7,403
22	Oregon	8,220		37	Alabama	7,366
19	Pennsylvania	8,528		38	Texas	7,243
15	Rhode Island	8,785		39	Utah	7,238
32	South Carolina	7,613		40	Florida	7,231
34	South Dakota	7,486		41	Arkansas	7,073
49	Tennessee	6,572		42	Indiana	7,034
38	Texas	7,243		43	North Carolina	6,974
39	Utah	7,238		44	Missouri	6,903
4	Vermont	9,853		45	Nevada	6,873
33	Virginia	7,516		46	Oklahoma	6,807
20	Washington	8,468		47	Idaho	6,623
30	West Virginia	7,799		48	Arizona	6,600
21	Wisconsin	8,356		49	Tennessee	6,572
2	Wyoming	13,320		50	Georgia	6,526
					District of Columbia	16,777

Source: CQ Press using data from U.S. Bureau of the Census, Governments Division
   "2011 State and Local Government Finances" (http://www.census.gov/govs/local/)
*Direct general expenditures include expenditures for current operations, assistance and subsidies, interest on debt, and capital outlay. Excludes intergovernmental transfers, expenditures for government owned utilities and other commercial or auxiliary enterprise, and insurance trust expenditures.

State and Local Government Debt Outstanding in 2011

National Total = $2,907,756,031,000*

ALPHA ORDER

RANK	STATE	DEBT	% of USA
28	Alabama	$29,315,372,000	1.0%
42	Alaska	10,197,865,000	0.4%
16	Arizona	50,926,194,000	1.8%
36	Arkansas	13,543,811,000	0.5%
1	California	418,832,878,000	14.4%
14	Colorado	52,186,187,000	1.8%
23	Connecticut	41,490,174,000	1.4%
44	Delaware	8,277,935,000	0.3%
4	Florida	151,903,834,000	5.2%
13	Georgia	54,367,087,000	1.9%
37	Hawaii	13,377,007,000	0.5%
45	Idaho	6,230,994,000	0.2%
5	Illinois	145,485,105,000	5.0%
17	Indiana	49,405,141,000	1.7%
33	Iowa	18,327,971,000	0.6%
30	Kansas	27,124,892,000	0.9%
22	Kentucky	42,167,519,000	1.5%
25	Louisiana	38,621,989,000	1.3%
43	Maine	8,983,385,000	0.3%
20	Maryland	44,603,401,000	1.5%
8	Massachusetts	92,558,199,000	3.2%
11	Michigan	73,842,390,000	2.5%
18	Minnesota	46,761,005,000	1.6%
35	Mississippi	14,186,468,000	0.5%
19	Missouri	46,105,095,000	1.6%
46	Montana	5,976,760,000	0.2%
38	Nebraska	12,941,977,000	0.4%
29	Nevada	27,708,291,000	1.0%
40	New Hampshire	11,237,885,000	0.4%
7	New Jersey	102,259,634,000	3.5%
34	New Mexico	16,648,925,000	0.6%
2	New York	334,622,001,000	11.5%
15	North Carolina	51,187,426,000	1.8%
49	North Dakota	4,425,916,000	0.2%
9	Ohio	77,533,373,000	2.7%
32	Oklahoma	19,202,119,000	0.7%
27	Oregon	34,753,649,000	1.2%
6	Pennsylvania	123,483,715,000	4.2%
39	Rhode Island	11,939,950,000	0.4%
24	South Carolina	41,054,098,000	1.4%
47	South Dakota	5,734,814,000	0.2%
26	Tennessee	38,303,352,000	1.3%
3	Texas	258,240,642,000	8.9%
31	Utah	20,133,390,000	0.7%
48	Vermont	4,729,149,000	0.2%
12	Virginia	63,816,250,000	2.2%
10	Washington	74,091,088,000	2.5%
41	West Virginia	10,991,723,000	0.4%
21	Wisconsin	44,271,580,000	1.5%
50	Wyoming	2,369,891,000	0.1%

RANK ORDER

RANK	STATE	DEBT	% of USA
1	California	$418,832,878,000	14.4%
2	New York	334,622,001,000	11.5%
3	Texas	258,240,642,000	8.9%
4	Florida	151,903,834,000	5.2%
5	Illinois	145,485,105,000	5.0%
6	Pennsylvania	123,483,715,000	4.2%
7	New Jersey	102,259,634,000	3.5%
8	Massachusetts	92,558,199,000	3.2%
9	Ohio	77,533,373,000	2.7%
10	Washington	74,091,088,000	2.5%
11	Michigan	73,842,390,000	2.5%
12	Virginia	63,816,250,000	2.2%
13	Georgia	54,367,087,000	1.9%
14	Colorado	52,186,187,000	1.8%
15	North Carolina	51,187,426,000	1.8%
16	Arizona	50,926,194,000	1.8%
17	Indiana	49,405,141,000	1.7%
18	Minnesota	46,761,005,000	1.6%
19	Missouri	46,105,095,000	1.6%
20	Maryland	44,603,401,000	1.5%
21	Wisconsin	44,271,580,000	1.5%
22	Kentucky	42,167,519,000	1.5%
23	Connecticut	41,490,174,000	1.4%
24	South Carolina	41,054,098,000	1.4%
25	Louisiana	38,621,989,000	1.3%
26	Tennessee	38,303,352,000	1.3%
27	Oregon	34,753,649,000	1.2%
28	Alabama	29,315,372,000	1.0%
29	Nevada	27,708,291,000	1.0%
30	Kansas	27,124,892,000	0.9%
31	Utah	20,133,390,000	0.7%
32	Oklahoma	19,202,119,000	0.7%
33	Iowa	18,327,971,000	0.6%
34	New Mexico	16,648,925,000	0.6%
35	Mississippi	14,186,468,000	0.5%
36	Arkansas	13,543,811,000	0.5%
37	Hawaii	13,377,007,000	0.5%
38	Nebraska	12,941,977,000	0.4%
39	Rhode Island	11,939,950,000	0.4%
40	New Hampshire	11,237,885,000	0.4%
41	West Virginia	10,991,723,000	0.4%
42	Alaska	10,197,865,000	0.4%
43	Maine	8,983,385,000	0.3%
44	Delaware	8,277,935,000	0.3%
45	Idaho	6,230,994,000	0.2%
46	Montana	5,976,760,000	0.2%
47	South Dakota	5,734,814,000	0.2%
48	Vermont	4,729,149,000	0.2%
49	North Dakota	4,425,916,000	0.2%
50	Wyoming	2,369,891,000	0.1%
	District of Columbia	11,276,535,000	0.4%

Source: U.S. Bureau of the Census, Governments Division
  "2011 State and Local Government Finances" (http://www.census.gov/govs/local/)
*Includes short-term, long-term, full faith and credit, nonguaranteed, and public debt for private purposes.

Per Capita State and Local Government Debt Outstanding in 2011

National Per Capita = $9,332*

ALPHA ORDER				RANK ORDER		
RANK	STATE	PER CAPITA		RANK	STATE	PER CAPITA
39	Alabama	$6,103		1	New York	$17,159
2	Alaska	14,088		2	Alaska	14,088
25	Arizona	7,874		3	Massachusetts	14,009
48	Arkansas	4,609		4	New Jersey	11,575
8	California	11,114		5	Connecticut	11,568
10	Colorado	10,200		6	Rhode Island	11,364
5	Connecticut	11,568		7	Illinois	11,313
17	Delaware	9,115		8	California	11,114
24	Florida	7,960		9	Washington	10,859
44	Georgia	5,541		10	Colorado	10,200
13	Hawaii	9,707		11	Nevada	10,187
50	Idaho	3,934		12	Texas	10,075
7	Illinois	11,313		13	Hawaii	9,707
30	Indiana	7,582		14	Pennsylvania	9,690
42	Iowa	5,982		15	Kentucky	9,656
16	Kansas	9,450		16	Kansas	9,450
15	Kentucky	9,656		17	Delaware	9,115
22	Louisiana	8,442		18	Oregon	8,984
36	Maine	6,762		19	South Carolina	8,785
29	Maryland	7,638		20	Minnesota	8,745
3	Massachusetts	14,009		21	New Hampshire	8,528
32	Michigan	7,476		22	Louisiana	8,442
20	Minnesota	8,745		23	New Mexico	8,009
47	Mississippi	4,765		24	Florida	7,960
28	Missouri	7,673		25	Arizona	7,874
40	Montana	5,991		25	Virginia	7,874
34	Nebraska	7,025		27	Wisconsin	7,754
11	Nevada	10,187		28	Missouri	7,673
21	New Hampshire	8,528		29	Maryland	7,638
4	New Jersey	11,575		30	Indiana	7,582
23	New Mexico	8,009		31	Vermont	7,547
1	New York	17,159		32	Michigan	7,476
45	North Carolina	5,304		33	Utah	7,154
38	North Dakota	6,464		34	Nebraska	7,025
37	Ohio	6,718		35	South Dakota	6,963
46	Oklahoma	5,074		36	Maine	6,762
18	Oregon	8,984		37	Ohio	6,718
14	Pennsylvania	9,690		38	North Dakota	6,464
6	Rhode Island	11,364		39	Alabama	6,103
19	South Carolina	8,785		40	Montana	5,991
35	South Dakota	6,963		41	Tennessee	5,985
41	Tennessee	5,985		42	Iowa	5,982
12	Texas	10,075		43	West Virginia	5,926
33	Utah	7,154		44	Georgia	5,541
31	Vermont	7,547		45	North Carolina	5,304
25	Virginia	7,874		46	Oklahoma	5,074
9	Washington	10,859		47	Mississippi	4,765
43	West Virginia	5,926		48	Arkansas	4,609
27	Wisconsin	7,754		49	Wyoming	4,177
49	Wyoming	4,177		50	Idaho	3,934
					District of Columbia	18,217

Source: CQ Press using data from U.S. Bureau of the Census, Governments Division
  "2011 State and Local Government Finances" (http://www.census.gov/govs/local/)
*Includes short-term, long-term, full faith and credit, nonguaranteed, and public debt for private purposes.

State and Local Government Full-Time Equivalent Employees in 2011

National Total = 16,358,439 FTE Employees*

ALPHA ORDER

RANK	STATE	EMPLOYEES	% of USA
19	Alabama	284,778	1.7%
44	Alaska	54,743	0.3%
22	Arizona	280,795	1.7%
31	Arkansas	189,608	1.2%
1	California	1,752,070	10.7%
24	Colorado	270,166	1.7%
32	Connecticut	185,209	1.1%
46	Delaware	49,751	0.3%
4	Florida	888,159	5.4%
9	Georgia	509,276	3.1%
41	Hawaii	73,669	0.5%
39	Idaho	78,569	0.5%
5	Illinois	626,921	3.8%
14	Indiana	329,503	2.0%
33	Iowa	177,268	1.1%
29	Kansas	196,847	1.2%
26	Kentucky	246,859	1.5%
21	Louisiana	281,597	1.7%
40	Maine	75,370	0.5%
18	Maryland	307,031	1.9%
16	Massachusetts	320,738	2.0%
11	Michigan	456,578	2.8%
23	Minnesota	277,179	1.7%
30	Mississippi	191,995	1.2%
17	Missouri	317,310	1.9%
43	Montana	57,874	0.4%
36	Nebraska	120,974	0.7%
37	Nevada	114,307	0.7%
42	New Hampshire	72,273	0.4%
10	New Jersey	488,114	3.0%
35	New Mexico	125,664	0.8%
3	New York	1,175,681	7.2%
8	North Carolina	556,065	3.4%
49	North Dakota	45,047	0.3%
6	Ohio	594,695	3.6%
27	Oklahoma	214,757	1.3%
28	Oregon	197,299	1.2%
7	Pennsylvania	591,926	3.6%
47	Rhode Island	49,746	0.3%
25	South Carolina	253,574	1.6%
48	South Dakota	45,851	0.3%
15	Tennessee	327,457	2.0%
2	Texas	1,450,198	8.9%
34	Utah	147,591	0.9%
50	Vermont	39,649	0.2%
12	Virginia	438,837	2.7%
13	Washington	346,367	2.1%
38	West Virginia	103,701	0.6%
20	Wisconsin	283,568	1.7%
45	Wyoming	52,732	0.3%

RANK ORDER

RANK	STATE	EMPLOYEES	% of USA
1	California	1,752,070	10.7%
2	Texas	1,450,198	8.9%
3	New York	1,175,681	7.2%
4	Florida	888,159	5.4%
5	Illinois	626,921	3.8%
6	Ohio	594,695	3.6%
7	Pennsylvania	591,926	3.6%
8	North Carolina	556,065	3.4%
9	Georgia	509,276	3.1%
10	New Jersey	488,114	3.0%
11	Michigan	456,578	2.8%
12	Virginia	438,837	2.7%
13	Washington	346,367	2.1%
14	Indiana	329,503	2.0%
15	Tennessee	327,457	2.0%
16	Massachusetts	320,738	2.0%
17	Missouri	317,310	1.9%
18	Maryland	307,031	1.9%
19	Alabama	284,778	1.7%
20	Wisconsin	283,568	1.7%
21	Louisiana	281,597	1.7%
22	Arizona	280,795	1.7%
23	Minnesota	277,179	1.7%
24	Colorado	270,166	1.7%
25	South Carolina	253,574	1.6%
26	Kentucky	246,859	1.5%
27	Oklahoma	214,757	1.3%
28	Oregon	197,299	1.2%
29	Kansas	196,847	1.2%
30	Mississippi	191,995	1.2%
31	Arkansas	189,608	1.2%
32	Connecticut	185,209	1.1%
33	Iowa	177,268	1.1%
34	Utah	147,591	0.9%
35	New Mexico	125,664	0.8%
36	Nebraska	120,974	0.7%
37	Nevada	114,307	0.7%
38	West Virginia	103,701	0.6%
39	Idaho	78,569	0.5%
40	Maine	75,370	0.5%
41	Hawaii	73,669	0.5%
42	New Hampshire	72,273	0.4%
43	Montana	57,874	0.4%
44	Alaska	54,743	0.3%
45	Wyoming	52,732	0.3%
46	Delaware	49,751	0.3%
47	Rhode Island	49,746	0.3%
48	South Dakota	45,851	0.3%
49	North Dakota	45,047	0.3%
50	Vermont	39,649	0.2%
	District of Columbia	42,502	0.3%

Source: U.S. Bureau of the Census, Governments Division
"Government Employment and Payroll" (http://www.census.gov/govs/apes/index.html)
*As of March 2011.

Rate of State and Local Government Full-Time Equivalent Employees in 2011

National Rate = 525 State/Local Government Employees per 10,000 Population*

ALPHA ORDER

RANK	STATE	RATE
12	Alabama	593
2	Alaska	756
49	Arizona	434
6	Arkansas	645
45	California	465
28	Colorado	528
34	Connecticut	516
23	Delaware	548
45	Florida	465
32	Georgia	519
27	Hawaii	535
41	Idaho	496
42	Illinois	488
39	Indiana	506
14	Iowa	579
3	Kansas	686
19	Kentucky	565
9	Louisiana	616
17	Maine	567
30	Maryland	526
43	Massachusetts	485
48	Michigan	462
33	Minnesota	518
6	Mississippi	645
28	Missouri	528
13	Montana	580
5	Nebraska	657
50	Nevada	420
23	New Hampshire	548
22	New Jersey	552
10	New Mexico	605
11	New York	603
15	North Carolina	576
4	North Dakota	658
35	Ohio	515
16	Oklahoma	568
37	Oregon	510
47	Pennsylvania	464
44	Rhode Island	473
25	South Carolina	543
21	South Dakota	557
36	Tennessee	512
18	Texas	566
31	Utah	524
8	Vermont	633
26	Virginia	541
38	Washington	508
20	West Virginia	559
40	Wisconsin	497
1	Wyoming	929

RANK ORDER

RANK	STATE	RATE
1	Wyoming	929
2	Alaska	756
3	Kansas	686
4	North Dakota	658
5	Nebraska	657
6	Arkansas	645
6	Mississippi	645
8	Vermont	633
9	Louisiana	616
10	New Mexico	605
11	New York	603
12	Alabama	593
13	Montana	580
14	Iowa	579
15	North Carolina	576
16	Oklahoma	568
17	Maine	567
18	Texas	566
19	Kentucky	565
20	West Virginia	559
21	South Dakota	557
22	New Jersey	552
23	Delaware	548
23	New Hampshire	548
25	South Carolina	543
26	Virginia	541
27	Hawaii	535
28	Colorado	528
28	Missouri	528
30	Maryland	526
31	Utah	524
32	Georgia	519
33	Minnesota	518
34	Connecticut	516
35	Ohio	515
36	Tennessee	512
37	Oregon	510
38	Washington	508
39	Indiana	506
40	Wisconsin	497
41	Idaho	496
42	Illinois	488
43	Massachusetts	485
44	Rhode Island	473
45	California	465
45	Florida	465
47	Pennsylvania	464
48	Michigan	462
49	Arizona	434
50	Nevada	420

	District of Columbia	687

Source: CQ Press using data from U.S. Bureau of the Census, Governments Division
   "Government Employment and Payroll" (http://www.census.gov/govs/apes/index.html)
*As of March 2011.

Average Annual Earnings of Full-Time State and Local Government Employees in 2011
National Average = $53,298*

<table>
<tr><td colspan="3">ALPHA ORDER</td><td colspan="3">RANK ORDER</td></tr>
<tr><td>RANK</td><td>STATE</td><td>SALARY</td><td>RANK</td><td>STATE</td><td>SALARY</td></tr>
<tr><td>42</td><td>Alabama</td><td>$42,444</td><td>1</td><td>California</td><td>$71,155</td></tr>
<tr><td>7</td><td>Alaska</td><td>62,117</td><td>2</td><td>New Jersey</td><td>67,550</td></tr>
<tr><td>22</td><td>Arizona</td><td>50,073</td><td>3</td><td>New York</td><td>65,897</td></tr>
<tr><td>50</td><td>Arkansas</td><td>37,416</td><td>4</td><td>Connecticut</td><td>65,097</td></tr>
<tr><td>1</td><td>California</td><td>71,155</td><td>5</td><td>Washington</td><td>64,986</td></tr>
<tr><td>16</td><td>Colorado</td><td>53,587</td><td>6</td><td>Rhode Island</td><td>62,718</td></tr>
<tr><td>4</td><td>Connecticut</td><td>65,097</td><td>7</td><td>Alaska</td><td>62,117</td></tr>
<tr><td>19</td><td>Delaware</td><td>52,757</td><td>8</td><td>Nevada</td><td>60,683</td></tr>
<tr><td>28</td><td>Florida</td><td>47,694</td><td>9</td><td>Maryland</td><td>60,063</td></tr>
<tr><td>39</td><td>Georgia</td><td>42,793</td><td>10</td><td>Massachusetts</td><td>59,996</td></tr>
<tr><td>21</td><td>Hawaii</td><td>50,681</td><td>11</td><td>Illinois</td><td>59,046</td></tr>
<tr><td>37</td><td>Idaho</td><td>43,392</td><td>12</td><td>Michigan</td><td>58,263</td></tr>
<tr><td>11</td><td>Illinois</td><td>59,046</td><td>13</td><td>Minnesota</td><td>57,451</td></tr>
<tr><td>33</td><td>Indiana</td><td>45,362</td><td>14</td><td>Wisconsin</td><td>54,529</td></tr>
<tr><td>18</td><td>Iowa</td><td>52,832</td><td>15</td><td>Oregon</td><td>54,279</td></tr>
<tr><td>38</td><td>Kansas</td><td>43,077</td><td>16</td><td>Colorado</td><td>53,587</td></tr>
<tr><td>46</td><td>Kentucky</td><td>40,279</td><td>17</td><td>Pennsylvania</td><td>53,512</td></tr>
<tr><td>35</td><td>Louisiana</td><td>43,720</td><td>18</td><td>Iowa</td><td>52,832</td></tr>
<tr><td>48</td><td>Maine</td><td>38,812</td><td>19</td><td>Delaware</td><td>52,757</td></tr>
<tr><td>9</td><td>Maryland</td><td>60,063</td><td>20</td><td>Ohio</td><td>52,280</td></tr>
<tr><td>10</td><td>Massachusetts</td><td>59,996</td><td>21</td><td>Hawaii</td><td>50,681</td></tr>
<tr><td>12</td><td>Michigan</td><td>58,263</td><td>22</td><td>Arizona</td><td>50,073</td></tr>
<tr><td>13</td><td>Minnesota</td><td>57,451</td><td>23</td><td>Wyoming</td><td>49,658</td></tr>
<tr><td>49</td><td>Mississippi</td><td>38,235</td><td>24</td><td>New Hampshire</td><td>48,937</td></tr>
<tr><td>40</td><td>Missouri</td><td>42,624</td><td>25</td><td>Vermont</td><td>48,501</td></tr>
<tr><td>32</td><td>Montana</td><td>45,483</td><td>26</td><td>Virginia</td><td>48,175</td></tr>
<tr><td>27</td><td>Nebraska</td><td>47,996</td><td>27</td><td>Nebraska</td><td>47,996</td></tr>
<tr><td>8</td><td>Nevada</td><td>60,683</td><td>28</td><td>Florida</td><td>47,694</td></tr>
<tr><td>24</td><td>New Hampshire</td><td>48,937</td><td>29</td><td>Utah</td><td>46,521</td></tr>
<tr><td>2</td><td>New Jersey</td><td>67,550</td><td>30</td><td>North Dakota</td><td>46,209</td></tr>
<tr><td>36</td><td>New Mexico</td><td>43,651</td><td>31</td><td>Texas</td><td>45,867</td></tr>
<tr><td>3</td><td>New York</td><td>65,897</td><td>32</td><td>Montana</td><td>45,483</td></tr>
<tr><td>34</td><td>North Carolina</td><td>43,941</td><td>33</td><td>Indiana</td><td>45,362</td></tr>
<tr><td>30</td><td>North Dakota</td><td>46,209</td><td>34</td><td>North Carolina</td><td>43,941</td></tr>
<tr><td>20</td><td>Ohio</td><td>52,280</td><td>35</td><td>Louisiana</td><td>43,720</td></tr>
<tr><td>47</td><td>Oklahoma</td><td>40,046</td><td>36</td><td>New Mexico</td><td>43,651</td></tr>
<tr><td>15</td><td>Oregon</td><td>54,279</td><td>37</td><td>Idaho</td><td>43,392</td></tr>
<tr><td>17</td><td>Pennsylvania</td><td>53,512</td><td>38</td><td>Kansas</td><td>43,077</td></tr>
<tr><td>6</td><td>Rhode Island</td><td>62,718</td><td>39</td><td>Georgia</td><td>42,793</td></tr>
<tr><td>41</td><td>South Carolina</td><td>42,497</td><td>40</td><td>Missouri</td><td>42,624</td></tr>
<tr><td>44</td><td>South Dakota</td><td>40,763</td><td>41</td><td>South Carolina</td><td>42,497</td></tr>
<tr><td>43</td><td>Tennessee</td><td>40,917</td><td>42</td><td>Alabama</td><td>42,444</td></tr>
<tr><td>31</td><td>Texas</td><td>45,867</td><td>43</td><td>Tennessee</td><td>40,917</td></tr>
<tr><td>29</td><td>Utah</td><td>46,521</td><td>44</td><td>South Dakota</td><td>40,763</td></tr>
<tr><td>25</td><td>Vermont</td><td>48,501</td><td>45</td><td>West Virginia</td><td>40,364</td></tr>
<tr><td>26</td><td>Virginia</td><td>48,175</td><td>46</td><td>Kentucky</td><td>40,279</td></tr>
<tr><td>5</td><td>Washington</td><td>64,986</td><td>47</td><td>Oklahoma</td><td>40,046</td></tr>
<tr><td>45</td><td>West Virginia</td><td>40,364</td><td>48</td><td>Maine</td><td>38,812</td></tr>
<tr><td>14</td><td>Wisconsin</td><td>54,529</td><td>49</td><td>Mississippi</td><td>38,235</td></tr>
<tr><td>23</td><td>Wyoming</td><td>49,658</td><td>50</td><td>Arkansas</td><td>37,416</td></tr>
<tr><td></td><td></td><td></td><td></td><td>District of Columbia</td><td>72,821</td></tr>
</table>

Source: CQ Press using data from U.S. Bureau of the Census, Governments Division
"Government Employment and Payroll" (http://www.census.gov/govs/apes/index.html)
*March 2011 full-time payroll (multiplied by 12) divided by full-time employees.

State Government Total Revenue in 2011

National Total = $2,265,212,581,000*

ALPHA ORDER

RANK	STATE	REVENUE	% of USA
28	Alabama	$26,305,162,000	1.2%
38	Alaska	14,920,900,000	0.7%
20	Arizona	38,028,534,000	1.7%
32	Arkansas	22,785,157,000	1.0%
1	California	334,311,421,000	14.8%
26	Colorado	29,488,801,000	1.3%
27	Connecticut	28,904,574,000	1.3%
44	Delaware	9,349,728,000	0.4%
4	Florida	106,166,255,000	4.7%
12	Georgia	52,294,783,000	2.3%
39	Hawaii	12,931,811,000	0.6%
42	Idaho	10,476,454,000	0.5%
7	Illinois	80,685,183,000	3.6%
18	Indiana	38,894,976,000	1.7%
30	Iowa	24,088,747,000	1.1%
34	Kansas	18,582,208,000	0.8%
25	Kentucky	31,051,859,000	1.4%
23	Louisiana	33,974,652,000	1.5%
41	Maine	10,611,116,000	0.5%
17	Maryland	41,737,483,000	1.8%
11	Massachusetts	56,634,466,000	2.5%
9	Michigan	64,429,901,000	2.8%
15	Minnesota	45,684,189,000	2.0%
31	Mississippi	23,441,796,000	1.0%
19	Missouri	38,606,945,000	1.7%
46	Montana	7,950,510,000	0.4%
40	Nebraska	11,523,401,000	0.5%
35	Nevada	17,597,124,000	0.8%
45	New Hampshire	8,542,308,000	0.4%
8	New Jersey	70,798,018,000	3.1%
33	New Mexico	19,771,493,000	0.9%
2	New York	205,546,377,000	9.1%
10	North Carolina	63,194,017,000	2.8%
47	North Dakota	7,805,674,000	0.3%
5	Ohio	96,872,947,000	4.3%
29	Oklahoma	26,234,738,000	1.2%
21	Oregon	34,797,285,000	1.5%
6	Pennsylvania	91,705,305,000	4.0%
43	Rhode Island	9,388,083,000	0.4%
24	South Carolina	31,733,200,000	1.4%
50	South Dakota	6,017,179,000	0.3%
22	Tennessee	34,653,154,000	1.5%
3	Texas	134,302,447,000	5.9%
36	Utah	16,984,797,000	0.7%
49	Vermont	6,506,203,000	0.3%
13	Virginia	50,781,571,000	2.2%
14	Washington	50,420,289,000	2.2%
37	West Virginia	15,397,630,000	0.7%
16	Wisconsin	44,807,389,000	2.0%
48	Wyoming	7,494,341,000	0.3%

RANK ORDER

RANK	STATE	REVENUE	% of USA
1	California	$334,311,421,000	14.8%
2	New York	205,546,377,000	9.1%
3	Texas	134,302,447,000	5.9%
4	Florida	106,166,255,000	4.7%
5	Ohio	96,872,947,000	4.3%
6	Pennsylvania	91,705,305,000	4.0%
7	Illinois	80,685,183,000	3.6%
8	New Jersey	70,798,018,000	3.1%
9	Michigan	64,429,901,000	2.8%
10	North Carolina	63,194,017,000	2.8%
11	Massachusetts	56,634,466,000	2.5%
12	Georgia	52,294,783,000	2.3%
13	Virginia	50,781,571,000	2.2%
14	Washington	50,420,289,000	2.2%
15	Minnesota	45,684,189,000	2.0%
16	Wisconsin	44,807,389,000	2.0%
17	Maryland	41,737,483,000	1.8%
18	Indiana	38,894,976,000	1.7%
19	Missouri	38,606,945,000	1.7%
20	Arizona	38,028,534,000	1.7%
21	Oregon	34,797,285,000	1.5%
22	Tennessee	34,653,154,000	1.5%
23	Louisiana	33,974,652,000	1.5%
24	South Carolina	31,733,200,000	1.4%
25	Kentucky	31,051,859,000	1.4%
26	Colorado	29,488,801,000	1.3%
27	Connecticut	28,904,574,000	1.3%
28	Alabama	26,305,162,000	1.2%
29	Oklahoma	26,234,738,000	1.2%
30	Iowa	24,088,747,000	1.1%
31	Mississippi	23,441,796,000	1.0%
32	Arkansas	22,785,157,000	1.0%
33	New Mexico	19,771,493,000	0.9%
34	Kansas	18,582,208,000	0.8%
35	Nevada	17,597,124,000	0.8%
36	Utah	16,984,797,000	0.7%
37	West Virginia	15,397,630,000	0.7%
38	Alaska	14,920,900,000	0.7%
39	Hawaii	12,931,811,000	0.6%
40	Nebraska	11,523,401,000	0.5%
41	Maine	10,611,116,000	0.5%
42	Idaho	10,476,454,000	0.5%
43	Rhode Island	9,388,083,000	0.4%
44	Delaware	9,349,728,000	0.4%
45	New Hampshire	8,542,308,000	0.4%
46	Montana	7,950,510,000	0.4%
47	North Dakota	7,805,674,000	0.3%
48	Wyoming	7,494,341,000	0.3%
49	Vermont	6,506,203,000	0.3%
50	South Dakota	6,017,179,000	0.3%

District of Columbia**   NA   NA

Source: U.S. Bureau of the Census, Governments Division
    "2011 State and Local Government Finances" (http://www.census.gov/govs/local/)
*Total revenue includes all money received from external sources. This includes taxes, intergovernmental transfers and insurance trust revenue, and revenue from government owned utilities and other commercial or auxiliary enterprise.
**Not applicable.

Per Capita State Government Total Revenue in 2011

National Per Capita = $7,284*

ALPHA ORDER

RANK	STATE	PER CAPITA
47	Alabama	$5,476
1	Alaska	20,613
44	Arizona	5,880
23	Arkansas	7,754
11	California	8,871
45	Colorado	5,764
16	Connecticut	8,059
6	Delaware	10,296
46	Florida	5,564
49	Georgia	5,329
8	Hawaii	9,384
32	Idaho	6,615
39	Illinois	6,274
43	Indiana	5,969
21	Iowa	7,862
36	Kansas	6,474
29	Kentucky	7,111
24	Louisiana	7,427
18	Maine	7,987
28	Maryland	7,147
12	Massachusetts	8,572
34	Michigan	6,523
13	Minnesota	8,543
20	Mississippi	7,873
38	Missouri	6,425
19	Montana	7,969
41	Nebraska	6,255
37	Nevada	6,469
35	New Hampshire	6,482
17	New Jersey	8,014
7	New Mexico	9,512
4	New York	10,540
33	North Carolina	6,548
3	North Dakota	11,399
14	Ohio	8,394
30	Oklahoma	6,933
9	Oregon	8,996
27	Pennsylvania	7,196
10	Rhode Island	8,936
31	South Carolina	6,790
26	South Dakota	7,306
48	Tennessee	5,415
50	Texas	5,240
42	Utah	6,035
5	Vermont	10,383
40	Virginia	6,266
25	Washington	7,389
15	West Virginia	8,301
22	Wisconsin	7,847
2	Wyoming	13,209

RANK ORDER

RANK	STATE	PER CAPITA
1	Alaska	$20,613
2	Wyoming	13,209
3	North Dakota	11,399
4	New York	10,540
5	Vermont	10,383
6	Delaware	10,296
7	New Mexico	9,512
8	Hawaii	9,384
9	Oregon	8,996
10	Rhode Island	8,936
11	California	8,871
12	Massachusetts	8,572
13	Minnesota	8,543
14	Ohio	8,394
15	West Virginia	8,301
16	Connecticut	8,059
17	New Jersey	8,014
18	Maine	7,987
19	Montana	7,969
20	Mississippi	7,873
21	Iowa	7,862
22	Wisconsin	7,847
23	Arkansas	7,754
24	Louisiana	7,427
25	Washington	7,389
26	South Dakota	7,306
27	Pennsylvania	7,196
28	Maryland	7,147
29	Kentucky	7,111
30	Oklahoma	6,933
31	South Carolina	6,790
32	Idaho	6,615
33	North Carolina	6,548
34	Michigan	6,523
35	New Hampshire	6,482
36	Kansas	6,474
37	Nevada	6,469
38	Missouri	6,425
39	Illinois	6,274
40	Virginia	6,266
41	Nebraska	6,255
42	Utah	6,035
43	Indiana	5,969
44	Arizona	5,880
45	Colorado	5,764
46	Florida	5,564
47	Alabama	5,476
48	Tennessee	5,415
49	Georgia	5,329
50	Texas	5,240

District of Columbia**   NA

Source: CQ Press using data from U.S. Bureau of the Census, Governments Division
    "2011 State and Local Government Finances" (http://www.census.gov/govs/local/)
*Total revenue includes all money received from external sources. This includes taxes, intergovernmental transfers and
insurance trust revenue, and revenue from government owned utilities and other commercial or auxiliary enterprise.
**Not applicable.

State Government Intergovernmental Revenue in 2011

National Total = $592,997,583,000*

ALPHA ORDER

RANK	STATE	REVENUE	% of USA
24	Alabama	$8,881,520,000	1.5%
39	Alaska	3,040,677,000	0.5%
14	Arizona	12,360,358,000	2.1%
32	Arkansas	6,313,263,000	1.1%
1	California	68,508,784,000	11.6%
33	Colorado	6,248,609,000	1.1%
30	Connecticut	6,561,366,000	1.1%
48	Delaware	1,890,925,000	0.3%
4	Florida	27,804,346,000	4.7%
10	Georgia	15,266,487,000	2.6%
40	Hawaii	2,918,445,000	0.5%
42	Idaho	2,804,663,000	0.5%
8	Illinois	19,586,991,000	3.3%
19	Indiana	10,858,319,000	1.8%
29	Iowa	7,043,992,000	1.2%
34	Kansas	4,940,903,000	0.8%
23	Kentucky	9,025,194,000	1.5%
13	Louisiana	12,532,918,000	2.1%
38	Maine	3,241,435,000	0.5%
17	Maryland	11,335,533,000	1.9%
12	Massachusetts	14,136,989,000	2.4%
7	Michigan	19,914,367,000	3.4%
22	Minnesota	9,819,493,000	1.7%
25	Mississippi	8,726,548,000	1.5%
16	Missouri	12,015,114,000	2.0%
44	Montana	2,414,552,000	0.4%
37	Nebraska	3,401,587,000	0.6%
41	Nevada	2,826,846,000	0.5%
46	New Hampshire	2,158,531,000	0.4%
11	New Jersey	14,792,596,000	2.5%
31	New Mexico	6,364,080,000	1.1%
2	New York	60,200,009,000	10.2%
9	North Carolina	16,048,794,000	2.7%
50	North Dakota	1,737,078,000	0.3%
5	Ohio	24,133,257,000	4.1%
27	Oklahoma	7,873,706,000	1.3%
28	Oregon	7,608,740,000	1.3%
6	Pennsylvania	23,842,639,000	4.0%
43	Rhode Island	2,731,772,000	0.5%
26	South Carolina	8,689,743,000	1.5%
49	South Dakota	1,878,950,000	0.3%
15	Tennessee	12,116,843,000	2.0%
3	Texas	42,858,907,000	7.2%
36	Utah	4,364,882,000	0.7%
47	Vermont	2,035,378,000	0.3%
21	Virginia	10,512,522,000	1.8%
18	Washington	10,944,017,000	1.8%
35	West Virginia	4,748,528,000	0.8%
20	Wisconsin	10,535,845,000	1.8%
45	Wyoming	2,400,542,000	0.4%

RANK ORDER

RANK	STATE	REVENUE	% of USA
1	California	$68,508,784,000	11.6%
2	New York	60,200,009,000	10.2%
3	Texas	42,858,907,000	7.2%
4	Florida	27,804,346,000	4.7%
5	Ohio	24,133,257,000	4.1%
6	Pennsylvania	23,842,639,000	4.0%
7	Michigan	19,914,367,000	3.4%
8	Illinois	19,586,991,000	3.3%
9	North Carolina	16,048,794,000	2.7%
10	Georgia	15,266,487,000	2.6%
11	New Jersey	14,792,596,000	2.5%
12	Massachusetts	14,136,989,000	2.4%
13	Louisiana	12,532,918,000	2.1%
14	Arizona	12,360,358,000	2.1%
15	Tennessee	12,116,843,000	2.0%
16	Missouri	12,015,114,000	2.0%
17	Maryland	11,335,533,000	1.9%
18	Washington	10,944,017,000	1.8%
19	Indiana	10,858,319,000	1.8%
20	Wisconsin	10,535,845,000	1.8%
21	Virginia	10,512,522,000	1.8%
22	Minnesota	9,819,493,000	1.7%
23	Kentucky	9,025,194,000	1.5%
24	Alabama	8,881,520,000	1.5%
25	Mississippi	8,726,548,000	1.5%
26	South Carolina	8,689,743,000	1.5%
27	Oklahoma	7,873,706,000	1.3%
28	Oregon	7,608,740,000	1.3%
29	Iowa	7,043,992,000	1.2%
30	Connecticut	6,561,366,000	1.1%
31	New Mexico	6,364,080,000	1.1%
32	Arkansas	6,313,263,000	1.1%
33	Colorado	6,248,609,000	1.1%
34	Kansas	4,940,903,000	0.8%
35	West Virginia	4,748,528,000	0.8%
36	Utah	4,364,882,000	0.7%
37	Nebraska	3,401,587,000	0.6%
38	Maine	3,241,435,000	0.5%
39	Alaska	3,040,677,000	0.5%
40	Hawaii	2,918,445,000	0.5%
41	Nevada	2,826,846,000	0.5%
42	Idaho	2,804,663,000	0.5%
43	Rhode Island	2,731,772,000	0.5%
44	Montana	2,414,552,000	0.4%
45	Wyoming	2,400,542,000	0.4%
46	New Hampshire	2,158,531,000	0.4%
47	Vermont	2,035,378,000	0.3%
48	Delaware	1,890,925,000	0.3%
49	South Dakota	1,878,950,000	0.3%
50	North Dakota	1,737,078,000	0.3%
	District of Columbia**	NA	NA

Source: U.S. Bureau of the Census, Governments Division
   "2011 State and Local Government Finances" (http://www.census.gov/govs/local/)
*Includes revenue from federal and local government sources.
**Not applicable.

Per Capita State Government Intergovernmental Revenue in 2011

National Per Capita = $1,907*

ALPHA ORDER			RANK ORDER		
RANK	STATE	PER CAPITA	RANK	STATE	PER CAPITA
30	Alabama	$1,849	1	Wyoming	$4,231
2	Alaska	4,201	2	Alaska	4,201
26	Arizona	1,911	3	Vermont	3,248
15	Arkansas	2,148	4	New York	3,087
35	California	1,818	5	New Mexico	3,062
49	Colorado	1,221	6	Mississippi	2,931
34	Connecticut	1,829	7	Louisiana	2,740
19	Delaware	2,082	8	Rhode Island	2,600
47	Florida	1,457	9	West Virginia	2,560
44	Georgia	1,556	10	North Dakota	2,537
17	Hawaii	2,118	11	Maine	2,440
36	Idaho	1,771	12	Montana	2,420
46	Illinois	1,523	13	Iowa	2,299
40	Indiana	1,666	14	South Dakota	2,281
13	Iowa	2,299	15	Arkansas	2,148
37	Kansas	1,721	16	Massachusetts	2,140
21	Kentucky	2,067	17	Hawaii	2,118
7	Louisiana	2,740	18	Ohio	2,091
11	Maine	2,440	19	Delaware	2,082
25	Maryland	1,941	20	Oklahoma	2,081
16	Massachusetts	2,140	21	Kentucky	2,067
22	Michigan	2,016	22	Michigan	2,016
33	Minnesota	1,836	23	Missouri	2,000
6	Mississippi	2,931	24	Oregon	1,967
23	Missouri	2,000	25	Maryland	1,941
12	Montana	2,420	26	Arizona	1,911
31	Nebraska	1,846	27	Tennessee	1,893
50	Nevada	1,039	28	Pennsylvania	1,871
42	New Hampshire	1,638	29	South Carolina	1,859
38	New Jersey	1,674	30	Alabama	1,849
5	New Mexico	3,062	31	Nebraska	1,846
4	New York	3,087	32	Wisconsin	1,845
41	North Carolina	1,663	33	Minnesota	1,836
10	North Dakota	2,537	34	Connecticut	1,829
18	Ohio	2,091	35	California	1,818
20	Oklahoma	2,081	36	Idaho	1,771
24	Oregon	1,967	37	Kansas	1,721
28	Pennsylvania	1,871	38	New Jersey	1,674
8	Rhode Island	2,600	39	Texas	1,672
29	South Carolina	1,859	40	Indiana	1,666
14	South Dakota	2,281	41	North Carolina	1,663
27	Tennessee	1,893	42	New Hampshire	1,638
39	Texas	1,672	43	Washington	1,604
45	Utah	1,551	44	Georgia	1,556
3	Vermont	3,248	45	Utah	1,551
48	Virginia	1,297	46	Illinois	1,523
43	Washington	1,604	47	Florida	1,457
9	West Virginia	2,560	48	Virginia	1,297
32	Wisconsin	1,845	49	Colorado	1,221
1	Wyoming	4,231	50	Nevada	1,039
				District of Columbia**	NA

Source: CQ Press using data from U.S. Bureau of the Census, Governments Division
   "2011 State and Local Government Finances" (http://www.census.gov/govs/local/)
*Includes revenue from federal and local government sources.
**Not applicable.

State Government Own Source Revenue in 2011

National Total = $1,061,315,859,000*

ALPHA ORDER

RANK	STATE	REVENUE	% of USA
26	Alabama	$14,395,261,000	1.4%
33	Alaska	9,624,998,000	0.9%
20	Arizona	16,105,419,000	1.5%
30	Arkansas	11,117,905,000	1.0%
1	California	142,927,463,000	13.5%
23	Colorado	14,856,336,000	1.4%
19	Connecticut	16,923,583,000	1.6%
41	Delaware	5,662,509,000	0.5%
4	Florida	47,486,660,000	4.5%
15	Georgia	21,901,338,000	2.1%
39	Hawaii	7,285,231,000	0.7%
44	Idaho	4,539,438,000	0.4%
6	Illinois	39,788,077,000	3.7%
18	Indiana	20,591,592,000	1.9%
31	Iowa	11,053,370,000	1.0%
32	Kansas	10,047,317,000	0.9%
24	Kentucky	14,543,181,000	1.4%
25	Louisiana	14,406,106,000	1.4%
42	Maine	5,007,698,000	0.5%
16	Maryland	21,684,192,000	2.0%
10	Massachusetts	30,758,571,000	2.9%
9	Michigan	34,802,577,000	3.3%
14	Minnesota	23,632,196,000	2.2%
35	Mississippi	8,916,360,000	0.8%
22	Missouri	15,067,790,000	1.4%
49	Montana	3,354,033,000	0.3%
40	Nebraska	5,987,566,000	0.6%
38	Nevada	7,617,002,000	0.7%
46	New Hampshire	4,114,855,000	0.4%
8	New Jersey	36,883,804,000	3.5%
36	New Mexico	8,490,181,000	0.8%
2	New York	88,640,813,000	8.4%
11	North Carolina	29,803,864,000	2.8%
43	North Dakota	4,946,010,000	0.5%
7	Ohio	37,707,073,000	3.6%
29	Oklahoma	12,325,729,000	1.2%
28	Oregon	13,214,540,000	1.2%
5	Pennsylvania	45,656,641,000	4.3%
45	Rhode Island	4,425,487,000	0.4%
27	South Carolina	14,101,763,000	1.3%
50	South Dakota	2,245,368,000	0.2%
21	Tennessee	15,375,775,000	1.4%
3	Texas	64,288,789,000	6.1%
34	Utah	9,469,719,000	0.9%
48	Vermont	3,592,519,000	0.3%
12	Virginia	28,681,524,000	2.7%
13	Washington	24,048,996,000	2.3%
37	West Virginia	7,965,706,000	0.8%
17	Wisconsin	21,597,017,000	2.0%
47	Wyoming	3,655,917,000	0.3%

RANK ORDER

RANK	STATE	REVENUE	% of USA
1	California	$142,927,463,000	13.5%
2	New York	88,640,813,000	8.4%
3	Texas	64,288,789,000	6.1%
4	Florida	47,486,660,000	4.5%
5	Pennsylvania	45,656,641,000	4.3%
6	Illinois	39,788,077,000	3.7%
7	Ohio	37,707,073,000	3.6%
8	New Jersey	36,883,804,000	3.5%
9	Michigan	34,802,577,000	3.3%
10	Massachusetts	30,758,571,000	2.9%
11	North Carolina	29,803,864,000	2.8%
12	Virginia	28,681,524,000	2.7%
13	Washington	24,048,996,000	2.3%
14	Minnesota	23,632,196,000	2.2%
15	Georgia	21,901,338,000	2.1%
16	Maryland	21,684,192,000	2.0%
17	Wisconsin	21,597,017,000	2.0%
18	Indiana	20,591,592,000	1.9%
19	Connecticut	16,923,583,000	1.6%
20	Arizona	16,105,419,000	1.5%
21	Tennessee	15,375,775,000	1.4%
22	Missouri	15,067,790,000	1.4%
23	Colorado	14,856,336,000	1.4%
24	Kentucky	14,543,181,000	1.4%
25	Louisiana	14,406,106,000	1.4%
26	Alabama	14,395,261,000	1.4%
27	South Carolina	14,101,763,000	1.3%
28	Oregon	13,214,540,000	1.2%
29	Oklahoma	12,325,729,000	1.2%
30	Arkansas	11,117,905,000	1.0%
31	Iowa	11,053,370,000	1.0%
32	Kansas	10,047,317,000	0.9%
33	Alaska	9,624,998,000	0.9%
34	Utah	9,469,719,000	0.9%
35	Mississippi	8,916,360,000	0.8%
36	New Mexico	8,490,181,000	0.8%
37	West Virginia	7,965,706,000	0.8%
38	Nevada	7,617,002,000	0.7%
39	Hawaii	7,285,231,000	0.7%
40	Nebraska	5,987,566,000	0.6%
41	Delaware	5,662,509,000	0.5%
42	Maine	5,007,698,000	0.5%
43	North Dakota	4,946,010,000	0.5%
44	Idaho	4,539,438,000	0.4%
45	Rhode Island	4,425,487,000	0.4%
46	New Hampshire	4,114,855,000	0.4%
47	Wyoming	3,655,917,000	0.3%
48	Vermont	3,592,519,000	0.3%
49	Montana	3,354,033,000	0.3%
50	South Dakota	2,245,368,000	0.2%
	District of Columbia**	NA	NA

Source: U.S. Bureau of the Census, Governments Division
    "2011 State and Local Government Finances" (http://www.census.gov/govs/local/)
*Own source revenue includes taxes, current charges, and miscellaneous general revenue. Excluded are intergovernmental transfers, insurance trust revenue, and revenue from government owned utilities and other commercial or auxiliary enterprise.
**Not applicable.

Per Capita State Government Own Source Revenue in 2011

National Per Capita = $3,413*

ALPHA ORDER			RANK ORDER		
RANK	STATE	PER CAPITA	RANK	STATE	PER CAPITA
39	Alabama	$2,997	1	Alaska	$13,297
1	Alaska	13,297	2	North Dakota	7,223
47	Arizona	2,490	3	Wyoming	6,444
16	Arkansas	3,783	4	Delaware	6,235
15	California	3,793	5	Vermont	5,733
41	Colorado	2,904	6	Hawaii	5,286
7	Connecticut	4,718	7	Connecticut	4,718
4	Delaware	6,235	8	Massachusetts	4,655
48	Florida	2,489	9	New York	4,545
50	Georgia	2,232	10	Minnesota	4,419
6	Hawaii	5,286	11	West Virginia	4,294
42	Idaho	2,866	12	Rhode Island	4,212
36	Illinois	3,094	13	New Jersey	4,175
33	Indiana	3,160	14	New Mexico	4,084
20	Iowa	3,607	15	California	3,793
25	Kansas	3,500	16	Arkansas	3,783
29	Kentucky	3,330	17	Wisconsin	3,782
34	Louisiana	3,149	18	Maine	3,769
18	Maine	3,769	19	Maryland	3,713
19	Maryland	3,713	20	Iowa	3,607
8	Massachusetts	4,655	21	Pennsylvania	3,583
24	Michigan	3,524	22	Virginia	3,539
10	Minnesota	4,419	23	Washington	3,525
40	Mississippi	2,995	24	Michigan	3,524
45	Missouri	2,508	25	Kansas	3,500
28	Montana	3,362	26	Oregon	3,416
32	Nebraska	3,250	27	Utah	3,365
43	Nevada	2,800	28	Montana	3,362
35	New Hampshire	3,123	29	Kentucky	3,330
13	New Jersey	4,175	30	Ohio	3,267
14	New Mexico	4,084	31	Oklahoma	3,257
9	New York	4,545	32	Nebraska	3,250
37	North Carolina	3,088	33	Indiana	3,160
2	North Dakota	7,223	34	Louisiana	3,149
30	Ohio	3,267	35	New Hampshire	3,123
31	Oklahoma	3,257	36	Illinois	3,094
26	Oregon	3,416	37	North Carolina	3,088
21	Pennsylvania	3,583	38	South Carolina	3,017
12	Rhode Island	4,212	39	Alabama	2,997
38	South Carolina	3,017	40	Mississippi	2,995
44	South Dakota	2,726	41	Colorado	2,904
49	Tennessee	2,403	42	Idaho	2,866
45	Texas	2,508	43	Nevada	2,800
27	Utah	3,365	44	South Dakota	2,726
5	Vermont	5,733	45	Missouri	2,508
22	Virginia	3,539	45	Texas	2,508
23	Washington	3,525	47	Arizona	2,490
11	West Virginia	4,294	48	Florida	2,489
17	Wisconsin	3,782	49	Tennessee	2,403
3	Wyoming	6,444	50	Georgia	2,232
				District of Columbia**	NA

Source: CQ Press using data from U.S. Bureau of the Census, Governments Division
  "2011 State and Local Government Finances" (http://www.census.gov/govs/local/)
*Own source revenue includes taxes, current charges, and miscellaneous general revenue. Excluded are intergovernmental transfers, insurance trust revenue, and revenue from government owned utilities and other commercial or auxiliary enterprise.
**Not applicable.

Profits of State Lotteries in 2012

National Total = $19,409,080,000*

ALPHA ORDER					RANK ORDER			
RANK	STATE	PROFITS	% of USA		RANK	STATE	PROFITS	% of USA
NA	Alabama**	NA	NA		1	New York	$2,887,990,000	14.9%
NA	Alaska**	NA	NA		2	Florida	1,321,600,000	6.8%
25	Arizona	164,700,000	0.8%		3	California	1,320,000,000	6.8%
32	Arkansas	97,500,000	0.5%		4	Texas	1,156,560,000	6.0%
3	California	1,320,000,000	6.8%		5	Pennsylvania	1,060,890,000	5.5%
30	Colorado	123,200,000	0.6%		6	New Jersey	950,000,000	4.9%
19	Connecticut	310,000,000	1.6%		7	Georgia	901,300,000	4.6%
22	Delaware	271,330,000	1.4%		8	Massachusetts	833,900,000	4.3%
2	Florida	1,321,600,000	6.8%		9	Ohio	771,030,000	4.0%
7	Georgia	901,300,000	4.6%		10	Michigan	770,000,000	4.0%
NA	Hawaii**	NA	NA		11	Illinois	708,500,000	3.7%
38	Idaho	41,500,000	0.2%		12	Maryland	683,070,000	3.5%
11	Illinois	708,500,000	3.7%		13	West Virginia	662,980,000	3.4%
24	Indiana	210,840,000	1.1%		14	Oregon	526,600,000	2.7%
33	Iowa	78,730,000	0.4%		15	Virginia	487,060,000	2.5%
34	Kansas	72,000,000	0.4%		16	North Carolina	456,760,000	2.4%
23	Kentucky	216,400,000	1.1%		17	Rhode Island	377,700,000	1.9%
26	Louisiana	156,900,000	0.8%		18	Tennessee	323,400,000	1.7%
37	Maine	54,300,000	0.3%		19	Connecticut	310,000,000	1.6%
12	Maryland	683,070,000	3.5%		20	South Carolina	297,740,000	1.5%
8	Massachusetts	833,900,000	4.3%		21	Missouri	280,000,000	1.4%
10	Michigan	770,000,000	4.0%		22	Delaware	271,330,000	1.4%
29	Minnesota	123,650,000	0.6%		23	Kentucky	216,400,000	1.1%
NA	Mississippi**	NA	NA		24	Indiana	210,840,000	1.1%
21	Missouri	280,000,000	1.4%		25	Arizona	164,700,000	0.8%
42	Montana	13,100,000	0.1%		26	Louisiana	156,900,000	0.8%
40	Nebraska	36,080,000	0.2%		27	Wisconsin	149,900,000	0.8%
NA	Nevada**	NA	NA		28	Washington	138,000,000	0.7%
36	New Hampshire	66,770,000	0.3%		29	Minnesota	123,650,000	0.6%
6	New Jersey	950,000,000	4.9%		30	Colorado	123,200,000	0.6%
39	New Mexico	41,300,000	0.2%		31	South Dakota	100,400,000	0.5%
1	New York	2,887,990,000	14.9%		32	Arkansas	97,500,000	0.5%
16	North Carolina	456,760,000	2.4%		33	Iowa	78,730,000	0.4%
43	North Dakota	7,620,000	0.0%		34	Kansas	72,000,000	0.4%
9	Ohio	771,030,000	4.0%		35	Oklahoma	69,990,000	0.4%
35	Oklahoma	69,990,000	0.4%		36	New Hampshire	66,770,000	0.3%
14	Oregon	526,600,000	2.7%		37	Maine	54,300,000	0.3%
5	Pennsylvania	1,060,890,000	5.5%		38	Idaho	41,500,000	0.2%
17	Rhode Island	377,700,000	1.9%		39	New Mexico	41,300,000	0.2%
20	South Carolina	297,740,000	1.5%		40	Nebraska	36,080,000	0.2%
31	South Dakota	100,400,000	0.5%		41	Vermont	22,300,000	0.1%
18	Tennessee	323,400,000	1.7%		42	Montana	13,100,000	0.1%
4	Texas	1,156,560,000	6.0%		43	North Dakota	7,620,000	0.0%
NA	Utah**	NA	NA		NA	Alabama**	NA	NA
41	Vermont	22,300,000	0.1%		NA	Alaska**	NA	NA
15	Virginia	487,060,000	2.5%		NA	Hawaii**	NA	NA
28	Washington	138,000,000	0.7%		NA	Mississippi**	NA	NA
13	West Virginia	662,980,000	3.4%		NA	Nevada**	NA	NA
27	Wisconsin	149,900,000	0.8%		NA	Utah**	NA	NA
NA	Wyoming**	NA	NA		NA	Wyoming**	NA	NA
						District of Columbia	65,500,000	0.3%

Source: North American Association of State and Provincial Lotteries, Willoughby Hills, OH
   "Lottery Sales and Profits" (http://www.naspl.org/index.cfm?fuseaction=content&menuid=17&pageid=1025)
*Reported profits for fiscal year 2012 on sales of $68,778,740,000. National total does not include profits for Puerto Rico.
**No lottery as of fiscal year 2012.

Per Capita Profits of State Lotteries in 2012

National Per Capita = $65.18*

ALPHA ORDER

RANK	STATE	PER CAPITA
NA	Alabama**	NA
NA	Alaska**	NA
34	Arizona	25.13
29	Arkansas	33.06
27	California	34.70
36	Colorado	23.75
11	Connecticut	86.34
3	Delaware	295.86
14	Florida	68.41
10	Georgia	90.86
NA	Hawaii**	NA
32	Idaho	26.01
18	Illinois	55.03
30	Indiana	32.25
33	Iowa	25.61
35	Kansas	24.95
21	Kentucky	49.40
28	Louisiana	34.09
25	Maine	40.85
8	Maryland	116.08
6	Massachusetts	125.47
13	Michigan	77.91
37	Minnesota	22.99
NA	Mississippi**	NA
23	Missouri	46.50
42	Montana	13.03
40	Nebraska	19.44
NA	Nevada**	NA
19	New Hampshire	50.56
9	New Jersey	107.17
39	New Mexico	19.80
4	New York	147.57
22	North Carolina	46.84
43	North Dakota	10.89
15	Ohio	66.79
41	Oklahoma	18.35
5	Oregon	135.05
12	Pennsylvania	83.12
1	Rhode Island	359.61
16	South Carolina	63.03
7	South Dakota	120.48
20	Tennessee	50.09
24	Texas	44.38
NA	Utah**	NA
26	Vermont	35.62
17	Virginia	59.50
38	Washington	20.01
2	West Virginia	357.32
31	Wisconsin	26.18
NA	Wyoming**	NA

RANK ORDER

RANK	STATE	PER CAPITA
1	Rhode Island	$359.61
2	West Virginia	357.32
3	Delaware	295.86
4	New York	147.57
5	Oregon	135.05
6	Massachusetts	125.47
7	South Dakota	120.48
8	Maryland	116.08
9	New Jersey	107.17
10	Georgia	90.86
11	Connecticut	86.34
12	Pennsylvania	83.12
13	Michigan	77.91
14	Florida	68.41
15	Ohio	66.79
16	South Carolina	63.03
17	Virginia	59.50
18	Illinois	55.03
19	New Hampshire	50.56
20	Tennessee	50.09
21	Kentucky	49.40
22	North Carolina	46.84
23	Missouri	46.50
24	Texas	44.38
25	Maine	40.85
26	Vermont	35.62
27	California	34.70
28	Louisiana	34.09
29	Arkansas	33.06
30	Indiana	32.25
31	Wisconsin	26.18
32	Idaho	26.01
33	Iowa	25.61
34	Arizona	25.13
35	Kansas	24.95
36	Colorado	23.75
37	Minnesota	22.99
38	Washington	20.01
39	New Mexico	19.80
40	Nebraska	19.44
41	Oklahoma	18.35
42	Montana	13.03
43	North Dakota	10.89
NA	Alabama**	NA
NA	Alaska**	NA
NA	Hawaii**	NA
NA	Mississippi**	NA
NA	Nevada**	NA
NA	Utah**	NA
NA	Wyoming**	NA
	District of Columbia	103.59

Source: CQ Press using data from North American Association of State and Provincial Lotteries, Willoughby Hills, OH
"Lottery Sales and Profits" (http://www.naspl.org/index.cfm?fuseaction=content&menuid=17&pageid=1025)
*For fiscal year 2012. National rate is based on population of states with a lottery.
**No lottery as of fiscal year 2012.

Projected vs. Actual State Tax Collections in 2013

National Percent = 103.1% of Projected Taxes*

ALPHA ORDER

RANK	STATE	PERCENT
18	Alabama	103.7
50	Alaska	77.3
24	Arizona	102.7
3	Arkansas	115.9
26	California	102.6
4	Colorado	114.1
45	Connecticut	99.7
14	Delaware	105.2
37	Florida	101.2
22	Georgia	103.0
7	Hawaii	107.7
20	Idaho	103.3
8	Illinois	107.6
34	Indiana	101.6
16	Iowa	105.0
35	Kansas	101.4
30	Kentucky	102.1
40	Louisiana	100.7
38	Maine	101.1
36	Maryland	101.3
43	Massachusetts	99.8
31	Michigan	102.0
6	Minnesota	107.8
12	Mississippi	106.7
13	Missouri	106.3
11	Montana	107.3
10	Nebraska	107.5
8	Nevada	107.6
5	New Hampshire	108.1
47	New Jersey	98.7
48	New Mexico	97.9
41	New York	100.0
28	North Carolina	102.3
1	North Dakota	182.0
24	Ohio	102.7
14	Oklahoma	105.2
39	Oregon	100.9
42	Pennsylvania	99.9
43	Rhode Island	99.8
17	South Carolina	104.7
33	South Dakota	101.7
19	Tennessee	103.5
2	Texas	118.7
22	Utah	103.0
20	Vermont	103.3
27	Virginia	102.4
49	Washington	92.6
46	West Virginia	98.9
29	Wisconsin	102.2
32	Wyoming	101.8

RANK ORDER

RANK	STATE	PERCENT
1	North Dakota	182.0
2	Texas	118.7
3	Arkansas	115.9
4	Colorado	114.1
5	New Hampshire	108.1
6	Minnesota	107.8
7	Hawaii	107.7
8	Illinois	107.6
8	Nevada	107.6
10	Nebraska	107.5
11	Montana	107.3
12	Mississippi	106.7
13	Missouri	106.3
14	Delaware	105.2
14	Oklahoma	105.2
16	Iowa	105.0
17	South Carolina	104.7
18	Alabama	103.7
19	Tennessee	103.5
20	Idaho	103.3
20	Vermont	103.3
22	Georgia	103.0
22	Utah	103.0
24	Arizona	102.7
24	Ohio	102.7
26	California	102.6
27	Virginia	102.4
28	North Carolina	102.3
29	Wisconsin	102.2
30	Kentucky	102.1
31	Michigan	102.0
32	Wyoming	101.8
33	South Dakota	101.7
34	Indiana	101.6
35	Kansas	101.4
36	Maryland	101.3
37	Florida	101.2
38	Maine	101.1
39	Oregon	100.9
40	Louisiana	100.7
41	New York	100.0
42	Pennsylvania	99.9
43	Massachusetts	99.8
43	Rhode Island	99.8
45	Connecticut	99.7
46	West Virginia	98.9
47	New Jersey	98.7
48	New Mexico	97.9
49	Washington	92.6
50	Alaska	77.3

District of Columbia**	NA

Source: CQ Press using data from National Association of State Budget Officers
    "The Fiscal Survey of States" (Fall 2013, http://www.nasbo.org)
*For fiscal year 2013. This table compares sales, personal, and corporate income tax collections projected in adopting budgets with the amount collected.
**Not available.

State Government Tax Revenue in 2012

National Total = $794,570,079,000

RANK	STATE	REVENUE	% of USA
25	Alabama	$9,052,880,000	1.1%
33	Alaska	7,049,398,000	0.9%
20	Arizona	12,973,265,000	1.6%
29	Arkansas	8,287,744,000	1.0%
1	California	112,372,263,000	14.1%
24	Colorado	10,250,628,000	1.3%
18	Connecticut	15,419,556,000	1.9%
44	Delaware	3,360,235,000	0.4%
5	Florida	32,997,012,000	4.2%
16	Georgia	16,576,903,000	2.1%
38	Hawaii	5,516,146,000	0.7%
43	Idaho	3,374,304,000	0.4%
4	Illinois	36,437,803,000	4.6%
17	Indiana	15,704,680,000	2.0%
31	Iowa	7,832,388,000	1.0%
32	Kansas	7,418,341,000	0.9%
23	Kentucky	10,472,861,000	1.3%
26	Louisiana	8,994,053,000	1.1%
42	Maine	3,777,130,000	0.5%
15	Maryland	17,064,468,000	2.1%
10	Massachusetts	22,805,644,000	2.9%
9	Michigan	23,968,760,000	3.0%
12	Minnesota	20,560,540,000	2.6%
34	Mississippi	6,953,362,000	0.9%
22	Missouri	10,800,741,000	1.4%
48	Montana	2,459,324,000	0.3%
41	Nebraska	4,358,328,000	0.5%
35	Nevada	6,775,112,000	0.9%
49	New Hampshire	2,206,329,000	0.3%
7	New Jersey	27,456,175,000	3.5%
40	New Mexico	5,088,335,000	0.6%
2	New York	71,545,745,000	9.0%
11	North Carolina	22,713,357,000	2.9%
37	North Dakota	5,620,036,000	0.7%
8	Ohio	25,924,024,000	3.3%
27	Oklahoma	8,826,132,000	1.1%
28	Oregon	8,699,626,000	1.1%
6	Pennsylvania	32,949,917,000	4.1%
45	Rhode Island	2,805,287,000	0.4%
30	South Carolina	8,036,482,000	1.0%
50	South Dakota	1,521,477,000	0.2%
21	Tennessee	11,982,345,000	1.5%
3	Texas	48,596,548,000	6.1%
36	Utah	5,809,953,000	0.7%
46	Vermont	2,757,370,000	0.3%
13	Virginia	18,137,586,000	2.3%
14	Washington	17,624,715,000	2.2%
39	West Virginia	5,355,809,000	0.7%
19	Wisconsin	14,747,971,000	1.9%
47	Wyoming	2,550,991,000	0.3%

RANK	STATE	REVENUE	% of USA
1	California	$112,372,263,000	14.1%
2	New York	71,545,745,000	9.0%
3	Texas	48,596,548,000	6.1%
4	Illinois	36,437,803,000	4.6%
5	Florida	32,997,012,000	4.2%
6	Pennsylvania	32,949,917,000	4.1%
7	New Jersey	27,456,175,000	3.5%
8	Ohio	25,924,024,000	3.3%
9	Michigan	23,968,760,000	3.0%
10	Massachusetts	22,805,644,000	2.9%
11	North Carolina	22,713,357,000	2.9%
12	Minnesota	20,560,540,000	2.6%
13	Virginia	18,137,586,000	2.3%
14	Washington	17,624,715,000	2.2%
15	Maryland	17,064,468,000	2.1%
16	Georgia	16,576,903,000	2.1%
17	Indiana	15,704,680,000	2.0%
18	Connecticut	15,419,556,000	1.9%
19	Wisconsin	14,747,971,000	1.9%
20	Arizona	12,973,265,000	1.6%
21	Tennessee	11,982,345,000	1.5%
22	Missouri	10,800,741,000	1.4%
23	Kentucky	10,472,861,000	1.3%
24	Colorado	10,250,628,000	1.3%
25	Alabama	9,052,880,000	1.1%
26	Louisiana	8,994,053,000	1.1%
27	Oklahoma	8,826,132,000	1.1%
28	Oregon	8,699,626,000	1.1%
29	Arkansas	8,287,744,000	1.0%
30	South Carolina	8,036,482,000	1.0%
31	Iowa	7,832,388,000	1.0%
32	Kansas	7,418,341,000	0.9%
33	Alaska	7,049,398,000	0.9%
34	Mississippi	6,953,362,000	0.9%
35	Nevada	6,775,112,000	0.9%
36	Utah	5,809,953,000	0.7%
37	North Dakota	5,620,036,000	0.7%
38	Hawaii	5,516,146,000	0.7%
39	West Virginia	5,355,809,000	0.7%
40	New Mexico	5,088,335,000	0.6%
41	Nebraska	4,358,328,000	0.5%
42	Maine	3,777,130,000	0.5%
43	Idaho	3,374,304,000	0.4%
44	Delaware	3,360,235,000	0.4%
45	Rhode Island	2,805,287,000	0.4%
46	Vermont	2,757,370,000	0.3%
47	Wyoming	2,550,991,000	0.3%
48	Montana	2,459,324,000	0.3%
49	New Hampshire	2,206,329,000	0.3%
50	South Dakota	1,521,477,000	0.2%
	District of Columbia*	NA	NA

Source: U.S. Bureau of the Census, Governments Division
    "2012 State Government Tax Collections" (http://www.census.gov/govs/statetax/)
*Not applicable.

Per Capita State Government Tax Revenue in 2012

National Per Capita = $2,536

ALPHA ORDER

RANK	STATE	PER CAPITA
42	Alabama	$1,877
1	Alaska	9,638
39	Arizona	1,980
17	Arkansas	2,810
12	California	2,954
40	Colorado	1,976
5	Connecticut	4,295
8	Delaware	3,664
47	Florida	1,708
49	Georgia	1,671
6	Hawaii	3,962
37	Idaho	2,115
16	Illinois	2,830
28	Indiana	2,402
23	Iowa	2,548
21	Kansas	2,571
29	Kentucky	2,391
41	Louisiana	1,954
15	Maine	2,842
13	Maryland	2,900
10	Massachusetts	3,431
27	Michigan	2,425
7	Minnesota	3,822
31	Mississippi	2,329
46	Missouri	1,794
25	Montana	2,447
30	Nebraska	2,349
24	Nevada	2,456
49	New Hampshire	1,671
11	New Jersey	3,097
26	New Mexico	2,440
9	New York	3,656
31	North Carolina	2,329
2	North Dakota	8,033
34	Ohio	2,246
33	Oklahoma	2,314
35	Oregon	2,231
19	Pennsylvania	2,582
18	Rhode Island	2,671
48	South Carolina	1,701
45	South Dakota	1,826
44	Tennessee	1,856
43	Texas	1,865
38	Utah	2,035
4	Vermont	4,405
36	Virginia	2,216
22	Washington	2,555
14	West Virginia	2,887
20	Wisconsin	2,575
3	Wyoming	4,426

RANK ORDER

RANK	STATE	PER CAPITA
1	Alaska	$9,638
2	North Dakota	8,033
3	Wyoming	4,426
4	Vermont	4,405
5	Connecticut	4,295
6	Hawaii	3,962
7	Minnesota	3,822
8	Delaware	3,664
9	New York	3,656
10	Massachusetts	3,431
11	New Jersey	3,097
12	California	2,954
13	Maryland	2,900
14	West Virginia	2,887
15	Maine	2,842
16	Illinois	2,830
17	Arkansas	2,810
18	Rhode Island	2,671
19	Pennsylvania	2,582
20	Wisconsin	2,575
21	Kansas	2,571
22	Washington	2,555
23	Iowa	2,548
24	Nevada	2,456
25	Montana	2,447
26	New Mexico	2,440
27	Michigan	2,425
28	Indiana	2,402
29	Kentucky	2,391
30	Nebraska	2,349
31	Mississippi	2,329
31	North Carolina	2,329
33	Oklahoma	2,314
34	Ohio	2,246
35	Oregon	2,231
36	Virginia	2,216
37	Idaho	2,115
38	Utah	2,035
39	Arizona	1,980
40	Colorado	1,976
41	Louisiana	1,954
42	Alabama	1,877
43	Texas	1,865
44	Tennessee	1,856
45	South Dakota	1,826
46	Missouri	1,794
47	Florida	1,708
48	South Carolina	1,701
49	Georgia	1,671
49	New Hampshire	1,671
	District of Columbia*	NA

Source: CQ Press using data from U.S. Bureau of the Census, Governments Division
    "2012 State Government Tax Collections" (http://www.census.gov/govs/statetax/)
*Not applicable.

State Government Tax Revenue as a Percent of Personal Income in 2012

National Percent = 5.9% of Personal Income*

ALPHA ORDER

RANK	STATE	PERCENT
39	Alabama	5.3
1	Alaska	20.6
37	Arizona	5.5
9	Arkansas	8.1
16	California	6.6
47	Colorado	4.4
10	Connecticut	7.3
6	Delaware	8.7
48	Florida	4.2
45	Georgia	4.5
5	Hawaii	9.0
22	Idaho	6.3
22	Illinois	6.3
18	Indiana	6.5
27	Iowa	6.0
26	Kansas	6.1
15	Kentucky	6.8
40	Louisiana	5.0
11	Maine	7.2
35	Maryland	5.6
22	Massachusetts	6.3
18	Michigan	6.5
8	Minnesota	8.3
12	Mississippi	7.0
44	Missouri	4.6
18	Montana	6.5
38	Nebraska	5.4
16	Nevada	6.6
50	New Hampshire	3.5
32	New Jersey	5.8
12	New Mexico	7.0
12	New York	7.0
22	North Carolina	6.3
2	North Dakota	15.5
34	Ohio	5.7
28	Oklahoma	5.9
32	Oregon	5.8
28	Pennsylvania	5.9
28	Rhode Island	5.9
40	South Carolina	5.0
48	South Dakota	4.2
42	Tennessee	4.9
45	Texas	4.5
28	Utah	5.9
3	Vermont	10.2
43	Virginia	4.7
35	Washington	5.6
7	West Virginia	8.4
21	Wisconsin	6.4
4	Wyoming	9.1

RANK ORDER

RANK	STATE	PERCENT
1	Alaska	20.6
2	North Dakota	15.5
3	Vermont	10.2
4	Wyoming	9.1
5	Hawaii	9.0
6	Delaware	8.7
7	West Virginia	8.4
8	Minnesota	8.3
9	Arkansas	8.1
10	Connecticut	7.3
11	Maine	7.2
12	Mississippi	7.0
12	New Mexico	7.0
12	New York	7.0
15	Kentucky	6.8
16	California	6.6
16	Nevada	6.6
18	Indiana	6.5
18	Michigan	6.5
18	Montana	6.5
21	Wisconsin	6.4
22	Idaho	6.3
22	Illinois	6.3
22	Massachusetts	6.3
22	North Carolina	6.3
26	Kansas	6.1
27	Iowa	6.0
28	Oklahoma	5.9
28	Pennsylvania	5.9
28	Rhode Island	5.9
28	Utah	5.9
32	New Jersey	5.8
32	Oregon	5.8
34	Ohio	5.7
35	Maryland	5.6
35	Washington	5.6
37	Arizona	5.5
38	Nebraska	5.4
39	Alabama	5.3
40	Louisiana	5.0
40	South Carolina	5.0
42	Tennessee	4.9
43	Virginia	4.7
44	Missouri	4.6
45	Georgia	4.5
45	Texas	4.5
47	Colorado	4.4
48	Florida	4.2
48	South Dakota	4.2
50	New Hampshire	3.5

District of Columbia** — NA

Source: CQ Press using data from U.S. Bureau of the Census, Governments Division
  "2012 State Government Tax Collections" (http://www.census.gov/govs/statetax/) and
  U.S. Department of Commerce, Bureau of Economic Analysis
  "Annual State Personal Income" (http://www.bea.gov/iTable/index.cfm)
*National figure does not include personal income or taxes from the District of Columbia.
**Not applicable.

State Government Individual Income Tax Revenue in 2012

National Total = $280,359,640,000

RANK	STATE	REVENUE	% of USA
24	Alabama	$3,017,437,000	1.1%
44	Alaska	0	0.0%
22	Arizona	3,093,904,000	1.1%
29	Arkansas	2,401,902,000	0.9%
1	California	55,024,435,000	19.6%
18	Colorado	4,875,627,000	1.7%
12	Connecticut	7,371,189,000	2.6%
35	Delaware	1,311,589,000	0.5%
44	Florida	0	0.0%
10	Georgia	8,142,371,000	2.9%
32	Hawaii	1,540,746,000	0.5%
36	Idaho	1,213,335,000	0.4%
3	Illinois	15,692,351,000	5.6%
19	Indiana	4,765,566,000	1.7%
23	Iowa	3,029,709,000	1.1%
25	Kansas	2,891,743,000	1.0%
20	Kentucky	3,512,075,000	1.3%
27	Louisiana	2,474,606,000	0.9%
34	Maine	1,441,926,000	0.5%
13	Maryland	7,116,605,000	2.5%
4	Massachusetts	11,933,452,000	4.3%
14	Michigan	6,827,913,000	2.4%
11	Minnesota	7,988,084,000	2.8%
33	Mississippi	1,501,267,000	0.5%
17	Missouri	5,131,686,000	1.8%
39	Montana	900,180,000	0.3%
30	Nebraska	1,838,344,000	0.7%
44	Nevada	0	0.0%
43	New Hampshire	81,557,000	0.0%
5	New Jersey	11,128,418,000	4.0%
37	New Mexico	1,150,468,000	0.4%
2	New York	38,771,968,000	13.8%
6	North Carolina	10,383,796,000	3.7%
41	North Dakota	432,527,000	0.2%
9	Ohio	9,029,657,000	3.2%
26	Oklahoma	2,774,376,000	1.0%
16	Oregon	5,825,797,000	2.1%
8	Pennsylvania	10,102,113,000	3.6%
38	Rhode Island	1,064,447,000	0.4%
21	South Carolina	3,096,834,000	1.1%
44	South Dakota	0	0.0%
42	Tennessee	182,251,000	0.1%
44	Texas	0	0.0%
28	Utah	2,466,495,000	0.9%
40	Vermont	598,450,000	0.2%
7	Virginia	10,216,148,000	3.6%
44	Washington	0	0.0%
31	West Virginia	1,755,746,000	0.6%
15	Wisconsin	6,260,550,000	2.2%
44	Wyoming	0	0.0%

RANK	STATE	REVENUE	% of USA
1	California	$55,024,435,000	19.6%
2	New York	38,771,968,000	13.8%
3	Illinois	15,692,351,000	5.6%
4	Massachusetts	11,933,452,000	4.3%
5	New Jersey	11,128,418,000	4.0%
6	North Carolina	10,383,796,000	3.7%
7	Virginia	10,216,148,000	3.6%
8	Pennsylvania	10,102,113,000	3.6%
9	Ohio	9,029,657,000	3.2%
10	Georgia	8,142,371,000	2.9%
11	Minnesota	7,988,084,000	2.8%
12	Connecticut	7,371,189,000	2.6%
13	Maryland	7,116,605,000	2.5%
14	Michigan	6,827,913,000	2.4%
15	Wisconsin	6,260,550,000	2.2%
16	Oregon	5,825,797,000	2.1%
17	Missouri	5,131,686,000	1.8%
18	Colorado	4,875,627,000	1.7%
19	Indiana	4,765,566,000	1.7%
20	Kentucky	3,512,075,000	1.3%
21	South Carolina	3,096,834,000	1.1%
22	Arizona	3,093,904,000	1.1%
23	Iowa	3,029,709,000	1.1%
24	Alabama	3,017,437,000	1.1%
25	Kansas	2,891,743,000	1.0%
26	Oklahoma	2,774,376,000	1.0%
27	Louisiana	2,474,606,000	0.9%
28	Utah	2,466,495,000	0.9%
29	Arkansas	2,401,902,000	0.9%
30	Nebraska	1,838,344,000	0.7%
31	West Virginia	1,755,746,000	0.6%
32	Hawaii	1,540,746,000	0.5%
33	Mississippi	1,501,267,000	0.5%
34	Maine	1,441,926,000	0.5%
35	Delaware	1,311,589,000	0.5%
36	Idaho	1,213,335,000	0.4%
37	New Mexico	1,150,468,000	0.4%
38	Rhode Island	1,064,447,000	0.4%
39	Montana	900,180,000	0.3%
40	Vermont	598,450,000	0.2%
41	North Dakota	432,527,000	0.2%
42	Tennessee	182,251,000	0.1%
43	New Hampshire	81,557,000	0.0%
44	Alaska	0	0.0%
44	Florida	0	0.0%
44	Nevada	0	0.0%
44	South Dakota	0	0.0%
44	Texas	0	0.0%
44	Washington	0	0.0%
44	Wyoming	0	0.0%
	District of Columbia*	NA	NA

Source: U.S. Bureau of the Census, Governments Division
"2012 State Government Tax Collections" (http://www.census.gov/govs/statetax/)
*Not applicable.

Per Capita State Government Individual Income Tax Revenue in 2012

National Per Capita = $895

ALPHA ORDER				RANK ORDER		
RANK	STATE	PER CAPITA		RANK	STATE	PER CAPITA
36	Alabama	$626		1	Connecticut	$2,053
44	Alaska	0		2	New York	1,981
41	Arizona	472		3	Massachusetts	1,796
27	Arkansas	814		4	Oregon	1,494
6	California	1,446		5	Minnesota	1,485
22	Colorado	940		6	California	1,446
1	Connecticut	2,053		7	Delaware	1,430
7	Delaware	1,430		8	New Jersey	1,255
44	Florida	0		9	Virginia	1,248
26	Georgia	821		10	Illinois	1,219
12	Hawaii	1,107		11	Maryland	1,209
31	Idaho	760		12	Hawaii	1,107
10	Illinois	1,219		13	Wisconsin	1,093
32	Indiana	729		14	Maine	1,085
19	Iowa	986		15	North Carolina	1,065
17	Kansas	1,002		16	Rhode Island	1,013
28	Kentucky	802		17	Kansas	1,002
39	Louisiana	538		18	Nebraska	991
14	Maine	1,085		19	Iowa	986
11	Maryland	1,209		20	Vermont	956
3	Massachusetts	1,796		21	West Virginia	946
34	Michigan	691		22	Colorado	940
5	Minnesota	1,485		23	Montana	896
40	Mississippi	503		24	Utah	864
25	Missouri	852		25	Missouri	852
23	Montana	896		26	Georgia	821
18	Nebraska	991		27	Arkansas	814
44	Nevada	0		28	Kentucky	802
42	New Hampshire	62		29	Pennsylvania	791
8	New Jersey	1,255		30	Ohio	782
38	New Mexico	552		31	Idaho	760
2	New York	1,981		32	Indiana	729
15	North Carolina	1,065		33	Oklahoma	727
37	North Dakota	618		34	Michigan	691
30	Ohio	782		35	South Carolina	656
33	Oklahoma	727		36	Alabama	626
4	Oregon	1,494		37	North Dakota	618
29	Pennsylvania	791		38	New Mexico	552
16	Rhode Island	1,013		39	Louisiana	538
35	South Carolina	656		40	Mississippi	503
44	South Dakota	0		41	Arizona	472
43	Tennessee	28		42	New Hampshire	62
44	Texas	0		43	Tennessee	28
24	Utah	864		44	Alaska	0
20	Vermont	956		44	Florida	0
9	Virginia	1,248		44	Nevada	0
44	Washington	0		44	South Dakota	0
21	West Virginia	946		44	Texas	0
13	Wisconsin	1,093		44	Washington	0
44	Wyoming	0		44	Wyoming	0
					District of Columbia*	NA

Source: CQ Press using data from U.S. Bureau of the Census, Governments Division
  "2012 State Government Tax Collections" (http://www.census.gov/govs/statetax/)
*Not applicable.

State Government Corporation Net Income Tax Revenue in 2012

National Total = $41,741,281,000

ALPHA ORDER

RANK	STATE	REVENUE	% of USA
26	Alabama	$413,253,000	1.0%
15	Alaska	663,144,000	1.6%
16	Arizona	647,809,000	1.6%
27	Arkansas	404,083,000	1.0%
1	California	7,949,000,000	19.0%
22	Colorado	492,224,000	1.2%
17	Connecticut	625,320,000	1.5%
33	Delaware	262,378,000	0.6%
4	Florida	2,003,490,000	4.8%
19	Georgia	590,676,000	1.4%
45	Hawaii	80,256,000	0.2%
40	Idaho	188,589,000	0.5%
3	Illinois	3,494,539,000	8.4%
11	Indiana	958,800,000	2.3%
25	Iowa	425,776,000	1.0%
29	Kansas	317,578,000	0.8%
20	Kentucky	575,164,000	1.4%
31	Louisiana	290,389,000	0.7%
37	Maine	232,118,000	0.6%
13	Maryland	880,356,000	2.1%
5	Massachusetts	2,001,780,000	4.8%
18	Michigan	608,829,000	1.5%
10	Minnesota	1,066,022,000	2.6%
28	Mississippi	395,678,000	0.9%
30	Missouri	301,681,000	0.7%
41	Montana	132,361,000	0.3%
36	Nebraska	234,296,000	0.6%
47	Nevada	0	0.0%
21	New Hampshire	521,309,000	1.2%
6	New Jersey	1,929,133,000	4.6%
32	New Mexico	281,047,000	0.7%
2	New York	4,567,889,000	10.9%
9	North Carolina	1,220,072,000	2.9%
38	North Dakota	215,622,000	0.5%
43	Ohio	117,446,000	0.3%
23	Oklahoma	446,009,000	1.1%
24	Oregon	433,126,000	1.0%
7	Pennsylvania	1,837,374,000	4.4%
42	Rhode Island	122,197,000	0.3%
35	South Carolina	252,904,000	0.6%
46	South Dakota	59,837,000	0.1%
8	Tennessee	1,225,890,000	2.9%
47	Texas	0	0.0%
34	Utah	258,578,000	0.6%
44	Vermont	96,579,000	0.2%
14	Virginia	838,790,000	2.0%
47	Washington	0	0.0%
39	West Virginia	192,385,000	0.5%
12	Wisconsin	889,505,000	2.1%
47	Wyoming	0	0.0%

RANK ORDER

RANK	STATE	REVENUE	% of USA
1	California	$7,949,000,000	19.0%
2	New York	4,567,889,000	10.9%
3	Illinois	3,494,539,000	8.4%
4	Florida	2,003,490,000	4.8%
5	Massachusetts	2,001,780,000	4.8%
6	New Jersey	1,929,133,000	4.6%
7	Pennsylvania	1,837,374,000	4.4%
8	Tennessee	1,225,890,000	2.9%
9	North Carolina	1,220,072,000	2.9%
10	Minnesota	1,066,022,000	2.6%
11	Indiana	958,800,000	2.3%
12	Wisconsin	889,505,000	2.1%
13	Maryland	880,356,000	2.1%
14	Virginia	838,790,000	2.0%
15	Alaska	663,144,000	1.6%
16	Arizona	647,809,000	1.6%
17	Connecticut	625,320,000	1.5%
18	Michigan	608,829,000	1.5%
19	Georgia	590,676,000	1.4%
20	Kentucky	575,164,000	1.4%
21	New Hampshire	521,309,000	1.2%
22	Colorado	492,224,000	1.2%
23	Oklahoma	446,009,000	1.1%
24	Oregon	433,126,000	1.0%
25	Iowa	425,776,000	1.0%
26	Alabama	413,253,000	1.0%
27	Arkansas	404,083,000	1.0%
28	Mississippi	395,678,000	0.9%
29	Kansas	317,578,000	0.8%
30	Missouri	301,681,000	0.7%
31	Louisiana	290,389,000	0.7%
32	New Mexico	281,047,000	0.7%
33	Delaware	262,378,000	0.6%
34	Utah	258,578,000	0.6%
35	South Carolina	252,904,000	0.6%
36	Nebraska	234,296,000	0.6%
37	Maine	232,118,000	0.6%
38	North Dakota	215,622,000	0.5%
39	West Virginia	192,385,000	0.5%
40	Idaho	188,589,000	0.5%
41	Montana	132,361,000	0.3%
42	Rhode Island	122,197,000	0.3%
43	Ohio	117,446,000	0.3%
44	Vermont	96,579,000	0.2%
45	Hawaii	80,256,000	0.2%
46	South Dakota	59,837,000	0.1%
47	Nevada	0	0.0%
47	Texas	0	0.0%
47	Washington	0	0.0%
47	Wyoming	0	0.0%
	District of Columbia*	NA	NA

Source: U.S. Bureau of the Census, Governments Division
"2012 State Government Tax Collections" (http://www.census.gov/govs/statetax/)
*Not applicable.

Per Capita State Government Corporation Net Income Tax Revenue in 2012

National Per Capita = $133

RANK	STATE	PER CAPITA
38	Alabama	$86
1	Alaska	907
35	Arizona	99
20	Arkansas	137
9	California	209
36	Colorado	95
13	Connecticut	174
5	Delaware	286
32	Florida	104
42	Georgia	60
43	Hawaii	58
27	Idaho	118
6	Illinois	271
17	Indiana	147
19	Iowa	139
31	Kansas	110
24	Kentucky	131
40	Louisiana	63
12	Maine	175
16	Maryland	150
4	Massachusetts	301
41	Michigan	62
10	Minnesota	198
22	Mississippi	133
45	Missouri	50
23	Montana	132
25	Nebraska	126
47	Nevada	0
2	New Hampshire	395
8	New Jersey	218
21	New Mexico	135
7	New York	233
26	North Carolina	125
3	North Dakota	308
46	Ohio	10
28	Oklahoma	117
30	Oregon	111
18	Pennsylvania	144
29	Rhode Island	116
44	South Carolina	54
39	South Dakota	72
11	Tennessee	190
47	Texas	0
37	Utah	91
15	Vermont	154
34	Virginia	102
47	Washington	0
32	West Virginia	104
14	Wisconsin	155
47	Wyoming	0

RANK	STATE	PER CAPITA
1	Alaska	$907
2	New Hampshire	395
3	North Dakota	308
4	Massachusetts	301
5	Delaware	286
6	Illinois	271
7	New York	233
8	New Jersey	218
9	California	209
10	Minnesota	198
11	Tennessee	190
12	Maine	175
13	Connecticut	174
14	Wisconsin	155
15	Vermont	154
16	Maryland	150
17	Indiana	147
18	Pennsylvania	144
19	Iowa	139
20	Arkansas	137
21	New Mexico	135
22	Mississippi	133
23	Montana	132
24	Kentucky	131
25	Nebraska	126
26	North Carolina	125
27	Idaho	118
28	Oklahoma	117
29	Rhode Island	116
30	Oregon	111
31	Kansas	110
32	Florida	104
32	West Virginia	104
34	Virginia	102
35	Arizona	99
36	Colorado	95
37	Utah	91
38	Alabama	86
39	South Dakota	72
40	Louisiana	63
41	Michigan	62
42	Georgia	60
43	Hawaii	58
44	South Carolina	54
45	Missouri	50
46	Ohio	10
47	Nevada	0
47	Texas	0
47	Washington	0
47	Wyoming	0

District of Columbia*	NA

Source: CQ Press using data from U.S. Bureau of the Census, Governments Division
   "2012 State Government Tax Collections" (http://www.census.gov/govs/statetax/)
*Not applicable.

State Government General Sales Tax Revenue in 2012

National Total = $242,697,113,000*

ALPHA ORDER

RANK	STATE	REVENUE	% of USA
34	Alabama	$2,274,658,000	0.9%
46	Alaska	0	0.0%
13	Arizona	6,210,756,000	2.6%
29	Arkansas	2,809,416,000	1.2%
1	California	28,536,238,000	11.8%
33	Colorado	2,302,333,000	0.9%
20	Connecticut	3,758,881,000	1.5%
46	Delaware	0	0.0%
3	Florida	19,403,788,000	8.0%
15	Georgia	5,303,524,000	2.2%
30	Hawaii	2,697,951,000	1.1%
39	Idaho	1,224,656,000	0.5%
10	Illinois	8,034,466,000	3.3%
11	Indiana	6,621,954,000	2.7%
31	Iowa	2,423,160,000	1.0%
27	Kansas	2,825,880,000	1.2%
25	Kentucky	3,052,236,000	1.3%
28	Louisiana	2,815,919,000	1.2%
41	Maine	1,064,342,000	0.4%
18	Maryland	4,076,578,000	1.7%
16	Massachusetts	5,079,105,000	2.1%
6	Michigan	9,565,702,000	3.9%
17	Minnesota	4,942,140,000	2.0%
24	Mississippi	3,072,243,000	1.3%
23	Missouri	3,103,410,000	1.3%
46	Montana	0	0.0%
37	Nebraska	1,456,625,000	0.6%
22	Nevada	3,433,958,000	1.4%
46	New Hampshire	0	0.0%
9	New Jersey	8,099,549,000	3.3%
35	New Mexico	1,990,535,000	0.8%
4	New York	11,904,357,000	4.9%
14	North Carolina	5,573,658,000	2.3%
40	North Dakota	1,122,783,000	0.5%
8	Ohio	8,272,728,000	3.4%
32	Oklahoma	2,415,964,000	1.0%
46	Oregon	0	0.0%
7	Pennsylvania	9,166,842,000	3.8%
43	Rhode Island	839,414,000	0.3%
26	South Carolina	2,926,177,000	1.2%
44	South Dakota	838,240,000	0.3%
12	Tennessee	6,512,362,000	2.7%
2	Texas	24,500,909,000	10.1%
36	Utah	1,857,035,000	0.8%
45	Vermont	342,085,000	0.1%
21	Virginia	3,487,343,000	1.4%
5	Washington	10,614,137,000	4.4%
38	West Virginia	1,277,328,000	0.5%
19	Wisconsin	3,871,581,000	1.6%
42	Wyoming	994,167,000	0.4%

RANK ORDER

RANK	STATE	REVENUE	% of USA
1	California	$28,536,238,000	11.8%
2	Texas	24,500,909,000	10.1%
3	Florida	19,403,788,000	8.0%
4	New York	11,904,357,000	4.9%
5	Washington	10,614,137,000	4.4%
6	Michigan	9,565,702,000	3.9%
7	Pennsylvania	9,166,842,000	3.8%
8	Ohio	8,272,728,000	3.4%
9	New Jersey	8,099,549,000	3.3%
10	Illinois	8,034,466,000	3.3%
11	Indiana	6,621,954,000	2.7%
12	Tennessee	6,512,362,000	2.7%
13	Arizona	6,210,756,000	2.6%
14	North Carolina	5,573,658,000	2.3%
15	Georgia	5,303,524,000	2.2%
16	Massachusetts	5,079,105,000	2.1%
17	Minnesota	4,942,140,000	2.0%
18	Maryland	4,076,578,000	1.7%
19	Wisconsin	3,871,581,000	1.6%
20	Connecticut	3,758,881,000	1.5%
21	Virginia	3,487,343,000	1.4%
22	Nevada	3,433,958,000	1.4%
23	Missouri	3,103,410,000	1.3%
24	Mississippi	3,072,243,000	1.3%
25	Kentucky	3,052,236,000	1.3%
26	South Carolina	2,926,177,000	1.2%
27	Kansas	2,825,880,000	1.2%
28	Louisiana	2,815,919,000	1.2%
29	Arkansas	2,809,416,000	1.2%
30	Hawaii	2,697,951,000	1.1%
31	Iowa	2,423,160,000	1.0%
32	Oklahoma	2,415,964,000	1.0%
33	Colorado	2,302,333,000	0.9%
34	Alabama	2,274,658,000	0.9%
35	New Mexico	1,990,535,000	0.8%
36	Utah	1,857,035,000	0.8%
37	Nebraska	1,456,625,000	0.6%
38	West Virginia	1,277,328,000	0.5%
39	Idaho	1,224,656,000	0.5%
40	North Dakota	1,122,783,000	0.5%
41	Maine	1,064,342,000	0.4%
42	Wyoming	994,167,000	0.4%
43	Rhode Island	839,414,000	0.3%
44	South Dakota	838,240,000	0.3%
45	Vermont	342,085,000	0.1%
46	Alaska	0	0.0%
46	Delaware	0	0.0%
46	Montana	0	0.0%
46	New Hampshire	0	0.0%
46	Oregon	0	0.0%
	District of Columbia**	NA	NA

Source: U.S. Bureau of the Census, Governments Division
   "2012 State Government Tax Collections" (http://www.census.gov/govs/statetax/)
*Does not include special sales taxes such as those on sale of alcohol, gasoline, or tobacco.
**Not applicable.

Per Capita State Government General Sales Tax Revenue in 2012

National Per Capita = $775*

ALPHA ORDER

RANK	STATE	PER CAPITA
43	Alabama	$472
46	Alaska	0
16	Arizona	948
15	Arkansas	953
26	California	750
44	Colorado	444
6	Connecticut	1,047
46	Delaware	0
11	Florida	1,004
41	Georgia	535
1	Hawaii	1,938
24	Idaho	767
35	Illinois	624
8	Indiana	1,013
22	Iowa	788
12	Kansas	979
29	Kentucky	697
37	Louisiana	612
20	Maine	801
30	Maryland	693
25	Massachusetts	764
13	Michigan	968
18	Minnesota	919
7	Mississippi	1,029
42	Missouri	515
46	Montana	0
23	Nebraska	785
5	Nevada	1,245
46	New Hampshire	0
19	New Jersey	914
14	New Mexico	954
38	New York	608
39	North Carolina	572
3	North Dakota	1,605
28	Ohio	717
34	Oklahoma	633
46	Oregon	0
27	Pennsylvania	718
21	Rhode Island	799
36	South Carolina	619
10	South Dakota	1,006
9	Tennessee	1,009
17	Texas	940
33	Utah	650
40	Vermont	546
45	Virginia	426
4	Washington	1,539
31	West Virginia	688
32	Wisconsin	676
2	Wyoming	1,725

RANK ORDER

RANK	STATE	PER CAPITA
1	Hawaii	$1,938
2	Wyoming	1,725
3	North Dakota	1,605
4	Washington	1,539
5	Nevada	1,245
6	Connecticut	1,047
7	Mississippi	1,029
8	Indiana	1,013
9	Tennessee	1,009
10	South Dakota	1,006
11	Florida	1,004
12	Kansas	979
13	Michigan	968
14	New Mexico	954
15	Arkansas	953
16	Arizona	948
17	Texas	940
18	Minnesota	919
19	New Jersey	914
20	Maine	801
21	Rhode Island	799
22	Iowa	788
23	Nebraska	785
24	Idaho	767
25	Massachusetts	764
26	California	750
27	Pennsylvania	718
28	Ohio	717
29	Kentucky	697
30	Maryland	693
31	West Virginia	688
32	Wisconsin	676
33	Utah	650
34	Oklahoma	633
35	Illinois	624
36	South Carolina	619
37	Louisiana	612
38	New York	608
39	North Carolina	572
40	Vermont	546
41	Georgia	535
42	Missouri	515
43	Alabama	472
44	Colorado	444
45	Virginia	426
46	Alaska	0
46	Delaware	0
46	Montana	0
46	New Hampshire	0
46	Oregon	0
	District of Columbia**	NA

Source: CQ Press using data from U.S. Bureau of the Census, Governments Division
"2012 State Government Tax Collections" (http://www.census.gov/govs/statetax/)
*Does not include special sales taxes such as those on sale of alcohol, gasoline, or tobacco.
**Not applicable.

State Government Motor Fuels Sales Tax Revenue in 2012

National Total = $39,914,893,000

ALPHA ORDER

RANK	STATE	REVENUE	% of USA
24	Alabama	$541,499,000	1.4%
50	Alaska	40,980,000	0.1%
11	Arizona	896,983,000	2.2%
29	Arkansas	467,055,000	1.2%
1	California	5,544,530,000	13.9%
22	Colorado	630,573,000	1.6%
28	Connecticut	487,104,000	1.2%
46	Delaware	112,908,000	0.3%
3	Florida	2,273,685,000	5.7%
13	Georgia	880,987,000	2.2%
48	Hawaii	93,349,000	0.2%
39	Idaho	236,769,000	0.6%
8	Illinois	1,290,266,000	3.2%
18	Indiana	783,897,000	2.0%
31	Iowa	440,161,000	1.1%
32	Kansas	435,049,000	1.1%
17	Kentucky	790,229,000	2.0%
23	Louisiana	575,063,000	1.4%
38	Maine	242,124,000	0.6%
19	Maryland	733,410,000	1.8%
21	Massachusetts	668,112,000	1.7%
10	Michigan	973,502,000	2.4%
15	Minnesota	849,218,000	2.1%
33	Mississippi	417,048,000	1.0%
20	Missouri	708,064,000	1.8%
41	Montana	211,992,000	0.5%
36	Nebraska	299,764,000	0.8%
37	Nevada	291,400,000	0.7%
43	New Hampshire	143,794,000	0.4%
25	New Jersey	539,714,000	1.4%
40	New Mexico	234,796,000	0.6%
7	New York	1,604,727,000	4.0%
5	North Carolina	1,861,838,000	4.7%
42	North Dakota	204,573,000	0.5%
6	Ohio	1,684,209,000	4.2%
30	Oklahoma	444,636,000	1.1%
26	Oregon	533,420,000	1.3%
4	Pennsylvania	2,073,677,000	5.2%
45	Rhode Island	117,663,000	0.3%
27	South Carolina	531,615,000	1.3%
44	South Dakota	136,431,000	0.3%
16	Tennessee	837,787,000	2.1%
2	Texas	3,178,419,000	8.0%
35	Utah	372,212,000	0.9%
47	Vermont	108,177,000	0.3%
14	Virginia	866,243,000	2.2%
9	Washington	1,177,987,000	3.0%
34	West Virginia	387,040,000	1.0%
12	Wisconsin	893,771,000	2.2%
49	Wyoming	66,443,000	0.2%

RANK ORDER

RANK	STATE	REVENUE	% of USA
1	California	$5,544,530,000	13.9%
2	Texas	3,178,419,000	8.0%
3	Florida	2,273,685,000	5.7%
4	Pennsylvania	2,073,677,000	5.2%
5	North Carolina	1,861,838,000	4.7%
6	Ohio	1,684,209,000	4.2%
7	New York	1,604,727,000	4.0%
8	Illinois	1,290,266,000	3.2%
9	Washington	1,177,987,000	3.0%
10	Michigan	973,502,000	2.4%
11	Arizona	896,983,000	2.2%
12	Wisconsin	893,771,000	2.2%
13	Georgia	880,987,000	2.2%
14	Virginia	866,243,000	2.2%
15	Minnesota	849,218,000	2.1%
16	Tennessee	837,787,000	2.1%
17	Kentucky	790,229,000	2.0%
18	Indiana	783,897,000	2.0%
19	Maryland	733,410,000	1.8%
20	Missouri	708,064,000	1.8%
21	Massachusetts	668,112,000	1.7%
22	Colorado	630,573,000	1.6%
23	Louisiana	575,063,000	1.4%
24	Alabama	541,499,000	1.4%
25	New Jersey	539,714,000	1.4%
26	Oregon	533,420,000	1.3%
27	South Carolina	531,615,000	1.3%
28	Connecticut	487,104,000	1.2%
29	Arkansas	467,055,000	1.2%
30	Oklahoma	444,636,000	1.1%
31	Iowa	440,161,000	1.1%
32	Kansas	435,049,000	1.1%
33	Mississippi	417,048,000	1.0%
34	West Virginia	387,040,000	1.0%
35	Utah	372,212,000	0.9%
36	Nebraska	299,764,000	0.8%
37	Nevada	291,400,000	0.7%
38	Maine	242,124,000	0.6%
39	Idaho	236,769,000	0.6%
40	New Mexico	234,796,000	0.6%
41	Montana	211,992,000	0.5%
42	North Dakota	204,573,000	0.5%
43	New Hampshire	143,794,000	0.4%
44	South Dakota	136,431,000	0.3%
45	Rhode Island	117,663,000	0.3%
46	Delaware	112,908,000	0.3%
47	Vermont	108,177,000	0.3%
48	Hawaii	93,349,000	0.2%
49	Wyoming	66,443,000	0.2%
50	Alaska	40,980,000	0.1%

District of Columbia*   NA   NA

Source: U.S. Bureau of the Census, Governments Division
   "2012 State Government Tax Collections" (http://www.census.gov/govs/statetax/)
*Not applicable.

Per Capita State Government Motor Fuel Sales Tax Revenue in 2012

National Per Capita = $127

ALPHA ORDER

ALPHA ORDER

RANK	STATE	PER CAPITA
38	Alabama	$112
50	Alaska	56
21	Arizona	137
12	Arkansas	158
17	California	146
29	Colorado	122
23	Connecticut	136
28	Delaware	123
32	Florida	118
46	Georgia	89
48	Hawaii	67
16	Idaho	148
44	Illinois	100
31	Indiana	120
19	Iowa	143
15	Kansas	151
6	Kentucky	180
26	Louisiana	125
5	Maine	182
26	Maryland	125
43	Massachusetts	101
45	Michigan	98
12	Minnesota	158
20	Mississippi	140
32	Missouri	118
2	Montana	211
10	Nebraska	162
41	Nevada	106
40	New Hampshire	109
49	New Jersey	61
36	New Mexico	113
47	New York	82
4	North Carolina	191
1	North Dakota	292
17	Ohio	146
34	Oklahoma	117
21	Oregon	137
10	Pennsylvania	162
38	Rhode Island	112
36	South Carolina	113
9	South Dakota	164
24	Tennessee	130
29	Texas	122
24	Utah	130
7	Vermont	173
41	Virginia	106
8	Washington	171
3	West Virginia	209
14	Wisconsin	156
35	Wyoming	115

RANK ORDER

RANK	STATE	PER CAPITA
1	North Dakota	$292
2	Montana	211
3	West Virginia	209
4	North Carolina	191
5	Maine	182
6	Kentucky	180
7	Vermont	173
8	Washington	171
9	South Dakota	164
10	Nebraska	162
10	Pennsylvania	162
12	Arkansas	158
12	Minnesota	158
14	Wisconsin	156
15	Kansas	151
16	Idaho	148
17	California	146
17	Ohio	146
19	Iowa	143
20	Mississippi	140
21	Arizona	137
21	Oregon	137
23	Connecticut	136
24	Tennessee	130
24	Utah	130
26	Louisiana	125
26	Maryland	125
28	Delaware	123
29	Colorado	122
29	Texas	122
31	Indiana	120
32	Florida	118
32	Missouri	118
34	Oklahoma	117
35	Wyoming	115
36	New Mexico	113
36	South Carolina	113
38	Alabama	112
38	Rhode Island	112
40	New Hampshire	109
41	Nevada	106
41	Virginia	106
43	Massachusetts	101
44	Illinois	100
45	Michigan	98
46	Georgia	89
47	New York	82
48	Hawaii	67
49	New Jersey	61
50	Alaska	56

District of Columbia*	NA

Source: CQ Press using data from U.S. Bureau of the Census, Governments Division
"2012 State Government Tax Collections" (http://www.census.gov/govs/statetax/)
*Not applicable.

State Tax Rates on Gasoline in 2013

National Median = 23.00 Cents per Gallon*

ALPHA ORDER

RANK	STATE	CENTS PER GALLON
40	Alabama	18.00
50	Alaska	8.00
36	Arizona	19.00
28	Arkansas	21.80
1	California	43.00
26	Colorado	22.00
19	Connecticut	25.00
24	Delaware	23.00
46	Florida	16.90
35	Georgia	19.50
44	Hawaii	17.00
16	Idaho	26.00
32	Illinois	20.10
40	Indiana	18.00
26	Iowa	22.00
18	Kansas	25.03
10	Kentucky	29.90
31	Louisiana	20.13
8	Maine	30.00
23	Maryland	23.50
30	Massachusetts	21.00
36	Michigan	19.00
11	Minnesota	28.60
39	Mississippi	18.40
43	Missouri	17.30
13	Montana	27.00
17	Nebraska	25.50
22	Nevada	23.81
34	New Hampshire	19.63
48	New Jersey	14.50
38	New Mexico	18.88
15	New York	26.60
2	North Carolina	37.75
24	North Dakota	23.00
12	Ohio	28.00
44	Oklahoma	17.00
8	Oregon	30.00
7	Pennsylvania	31.20
5	Rhode Island	33.00
47	South Carolina	16.75
21	South Dakota	24.00
29	Tennessee	21.40
33	Texas	20.00
20	Utah	24.50
14	Vermont	26.68
42	Virginia	17.50
3	Washington	37.50
4	West Virginia	34.70
6	Wisconsin	32.90
49	Wyoming	14.00

RANK ORDER

RANK	STATE	CENTS PER GALLON
1	California	43.00
2	North Carolina	37.75
3	Washington	37.50
4	West Virginia	34.70
5	Rhode Island	33.00
6	Wisconsin	32.90
7	Pennsylvania	31.20
8	Maine	30.00
8	Oregon	30.00
10	Kentucky	29.90
11	Minnesota	28.60
12	Ohio	28.00
13	Montana	27.00
14	Vermont	26.68
15	New York	26.60
16	Idaho	26.00
17	Nebraska	25.50
18	Kansas	25.03
19	Connecticut	25.00
20	Utah	24.50
21	South Dakota	24.00
22	Nevada	23.81
23	Maryland	23.50
24	Delaware	23.00
24	North Dakota	23.00
26	Colorado	22.00
26	Iowa	22.00
28	Arkansas	21.80
29	Tennessee	21.40
30	Massachusetts	21.00
31	Louisiana	20.13
32	Illinois	20.10
33	Texas	20.00
34	New Hampshire	19.63
35	Georgia	19.50
36	Arizona	19.00
36	Michigan	19.00
38	New Mexico	18.88
39	Mississippi	18.40
40	Alabama	18.00
40	Indiana	18.00
42	Virginia	17.50
43	Missouri	17.30
44	Hawaii	17.00
44	Oklahoma	17.00
46	Florida	16.90
47	South Carolina	16.75
48	New Jersey	14.50
49	Wyoming	14.00
50	Alaska	8.00
	District of Columbia	23.50

Source: Federation of Tax Administrators
   "Motor Fuel Excise Tax Rates" (http://www.taxadmin.org/fta/rate/tax_stru.html)
*As of January 1, 2013. Federal gasoline tax rate is an additional 18.4 cents per gallon. Many states also allow additional local option taxes on gasoline.

State Government Motor Vehicle and Operators' License Tax Revenue in 2012

National Total = $25,221,629,000

ALPHA ORDER					RANK ORDER			
RANK	STATE	REVENUE	% of USA		RANK	STATE	REVENUE	% of USA
26	Alabama	$223,554,000	0.9%		1	California	$3,836,019,000	15.2%
48	Alaska	58,196,000	0.2%		2	Texas	1,963,629,000	7.8%
32	Arizona	176,112,000	0.7%		3	Illinois	1,725,176,000	6.8%
35	Arkansas	171,699,000	0.7%		4	Florida	1,655,169,000	6.6%
1	California	3,836,019,000	15.2%		5	New York	1,550,829,000	6.1%
19	Colorado	486,730,000	1.9%		6	Michigan	972,814,000	3.9%
25	Connecticut	252,631,000	1.0%		7	Pennsylvania	900,338,000	3.6%
50	Delaware	55,071,000	0.2%		8	Ohio	796,006,000	3.2%
4	Florida	1,655,169,000	6.6%		9	North Carolina	692,597,000	2.7%
22	Georgia	355,328,000	1.4%		10	Oklahoma	680,189,000	2.7%
27	Hawaii	206,651,000	0.8%		11	Minnesota	676,531,000	2.7%
38	Idaho	139,276,000	0.6%		12	New Jersey	658,291,000	2.6%
3	Illinois	1,725,176,000	6.8%		13	Indiana	541,803,000	2.1%
13	Indiana	541,803,000	2.1%		14	Washington	540,761,000	2.1%
15	Iowa	529,008,000	2.1%		15	Iowa	529,008,000	2.1%
28	Kansas	206,015,000	0.8%		16	Oregon	506,605,000	2.0%
29	Kentucky	204,452,000	0.8%		17	Wisconsin	496,592,000	2.0%
37	Louisiana	144,192,000	0.6%		18	Virginia	491,933,000	2.0%
41	Maine	109,795,000	0.4%		19	Colorado	486,730,000	1.9%
21	Maryland	470,200,000	1.9%		20	Massachusetts	475,451,000	1.9%
20	Massachusetts	475,451,000	1.9%		21	Maryland	470,200,000	1.9%
6	Michigan	972,814,000	3.9%		22	Georgia	355,328,000	1.4%
11	Minnesota	676,531,000	2.7%		23	Tennessee	308,737,000	1.2%
33	Mississippi	174,886,000	0.7%		24	Missouri	285,327,000	1.1%
24	Missouri	285,327,000	1.1%		25	Connecticut	252,631,000	1.0%
36	Montana	151,851,000	0.6%		26	Alabama	223,554,000	0.9%
39	Nebraska	128,406,000	0.5%		27	Hawaii	206,651,000	0.8%
30	Nevada	182,876,000	0.7%		28	Kansas	206,015,000	0.8%
43	New Hampshire	106,866,000	0.4%		29	Kentucky	204,452,000	0.8%
12	New Jersey	658,291,000	2.6%		30	Nevada	182,876,000	0.7%
44	New Mexico	96,393,000	0.4%		31	South Carolina	179,150,000	0.7%
5	New York	1,550,829,000	6.1%		32	Arizona	176,112,000	0.7%
9	North Carolina	692,597,000	2.7%		33	Mississippi	174,886,000	0.7%
40	North Dakota	110,521,000	0.4%		34	Utah	173,156,000	0.7%
8	Ohio	796,006,000	3.2%		35	Arkansas	171,699,000	0.7%
10	Oklahoma	680,189,000	2.7%		36	Montana	151,851,000	0.6%
16	Oregon	506,605,000	2.0%		37	Louisiana	144,192,000	0.6%
7	Pennsylvania	900,338,000	3.6%		38	Idaho	139,276,000	0.6%
49	Rhode Island	57,518,000	0.2%		39	Nebraska	128,406,000	0.5%
31	South Carolina	179,150,000	0.7%		40	North Dakota	110,521,000	0.4%
46	South Dakota	68,502,000	0.3%		41	Maine	109,795,000	0.4%
23	Tennessee	308,737,000	1.2%		42	West Virginia	107,649,000	0.4%
2	Texas	1,963,629,000	7.8%		43	New Hampshire	106,866,000	0.4%
34	Utah	173,156,000	0.7%		44	New Mexico	96,393,000	0.4%
45	Vermont	72,257,000	0.3%		45	Vermont	72,257,000	0.3%
18	Virginia	491,933,000	2.0%		46	South Dakota	68,502,000	0.3%
14	Washington	540,761,000	2.1%		47	Wyoming	67,891,000	0.3%
42	West Virginia	107,649,000	0.4%		48	Alaska	58,196,000	0.2%
17	Wisconsin	496,592,000	2.0%		49	Rhode Island	57,518,000	0.2%
47	Wyoming	67,891,000	0.3%		50	Delaware	55,071,000	0.2%
						District of Columbia*	NA	NA

Source: U.S. Bureau of the Census, Governments Division
  "2012 State Government Tax Collections" (http://www.census.gov/govs/statetax/)
*Not applicable.

Per Capita State Government Motor Vehicle and Operators' License Tax Revenue in 2012

National Per Capita = $80.51

ALPHA ORDER

RANK	STATE	PER CAPITA
45	Alabama	$46.36
22	Alaska	79.56
50	Arizona	26.87
39	Arkansas	58.22
11	California	100.84
13	Colorado	93.83
31	Connecticut	70.36
37	Delaware	60.05
16	Florida	85.68
48	Georgia	35.82
5	Hawaii	148.42
14	Idaho	87.28
6	Illinois	133.99
17	Indiana	82.88
2	Iowa	172.08
28	Kansas	71.39
44	Kentucky	46.67
49	Louisiana	31.33
18	Maine	82.60
21	Maryland	79.90
27	Massachusetts	71.54
12	Michigan	98.43
8	Minnesota	125.77
38	Mississippi	58.59
43	Missouri	47.38
4	Montana	151.07
32	Nebraska	69.20
34	Nevada	66.29
20	New Hampshire	80.92
26	New Jersey	74.26
46	New Mexico	46.22
23	New York	79.24
29	North Carolina	71.02
3	North Dakota	157.97
33	Ohio	68.95
1	Oklahoma	178.30
7	Oregon	129.92
30	Pennsylvania	70.54
41	Rhode Island	54.76
47	South Carolina	37.93
19	South Dakota	82.20
42	Tennessee	47.82
25	Texas	75.35
35	Utah	60.64
10	Vermont	115.42
36	Virginia	60.10
24	Washington	78.41
40	West Virginia	58.02
15	Wisconsin	86.72
9	Wyoming	117.78

RANK ORDER

RANK	STATE	PER CAPITA
1	Oklahoma	$178.30
2	Iowa	172.08
3	North Dakota	157.97
4	Montana	151.07
5	Hawaii	148.42
6	Illinois	133.99
7	Oregon	129.92
8	Minnesota	125.77
9	Wyoming	117.78
10	Vermont	115.42
11	California	100.84
12	Michigan	98.43
13	Colorado	93.83
14	Idaho	87.28
15	Wisconsin	86.72
16	Florida	85.68
17	Indiana	82.88
18	Maine	82.60
19	South Dakota	82.20
20	New Hampshire	80.92
21	Maryland	79.90
22	Alaska	79.56
23	New York	79.24
24	Washington	78.41
25	Texas	75.35
26	New Jersey	74.26
27	Massachusetts	71.54
28	Kansas	71.39
29	North Carolina	71.02
30	Pennsylvania	70.54
31	Connecticut	70.36
32	Nebraska	69.20
33	Ohio	68.95
34	Nevada	66.29
35	Utah	60.64
36	Virginia	60.10
37	Delaware	60.05
38	Mississippi	58.59
39	Arkansas	58.22
40	West Virginia	58.02
41	Rhode Island	54.76
42	Tennessee	47.82
43	Missouri	47.38
44	Kentucky	46.67
45	Alabama	46.36
46	New Mexico	46.22
47	South Carolina	37.93
48	Georgia	35.82
49	Louisiana	31.33
50	Arizona	26.87

District of Columbia*   NA

Source: CQ Press using data from U.S. Bureau of the Census, Governments Division
   "2012 State Government Tax Collections" (http://www.census.gov/govs/statetax/)
*Not applicable.

State Government Tobacco Product Sales Tax Revenue in 2012

National Total = $17,086,174,000

ALPHA ORDER

RANK	STATE	REVENUE	% of USA
33	Alabama	$126,151,000	0.7%
44	Alaska	67,382,000	0.4%
17	Arizona	319,467,000	1.9%
23	Arkansas	246,976,000	1.4%
5	California	895,677,000	5.2%
27	Colorado	203,399,000	1.2%
14	Connecticut	418,231,000	2.4%
36	Delaware	120,850,000	0.7%
16	Florida	381,485,000	2.2%
24	Georgia	227,146,000	1.3%
35	Hawaii	121,971,000	0.7%
46	Idaho	48,461,000	0.3%
8	Illinois	606,422,000	3.5%
12	Indiana	465,200,000	2.7%
25	Iowa	225,499,000	1.3%
39	Kansas	103,639,000	0.6%
21	Kentucky	276,544,000	1.6%
31	Louisiana	133,194,000	0.8%
30	Maine	139,729,000	0.8%
15	Maryland	411,427,000	2.4%
10	Massachusetts	573,759,000	3.4%
4	Michigan	951,319,000	5.6%
13	Minnesota	421,545,000	2.5%
29	Mississippi	157,433,000	0.9%
38	Missouri	104,918,000	0.6%
41	Montana	87,148,000	0.5%
47	Nebraska	33,725,000	0.2%
40	Nevada	102,644,000	0.6%
26	New Hampshire	215,161,000	1.3%
7	New Jersey	792,066,000	4.6%
43	New Mexico	74,800,000	0.4%
1	New York	1,631,995,000	9.6%
18	North Carolina	294,754,000	1.7%
48	North Dakota	28,240,000	0.2%
6	Ohio	843,180,000	4.9%
19	Oklahoma	292,973,000	1.7%
22	Oregon	255,652,000	1.5%
3	Pennsylvania	1,118,961,000	6.5%
32	Rhode Island	130,811,000	0.8%
49	South Carolina	26,247,000	0.2%
45	South Dakota	60,372,000	0.4%
20	Tennessee	279,017,000	1.6%
2	Texas	1,469,712,000	8.6%
34	Utah	123,988,000	0.7%
42	Vermont	80,230,000	0.5%
28	Virginia	192,441,000	1.1%
11	Washington	470,765,000	2.8%
37	West Virginia	109,618,000	0.6%
9	Wisconsin	597,866,000	3.5%
50	Wyoming	25,984,000	0.2%

RANK ORDER

RANK	STATE	REVENUE	% of USA
1	New York	$1,631,995,000	9.6%
2	Texas	1,469,712,000	8.6%
3	Pennsylvania	1,118,961,000	6.5%
4	Michigan	951,319,000	5.6%
5	California	895,677,000	5.2%
6	Ohio	843,180,000	4.9%
7	New Jersey	792,066,000	4.6%
8	Illinois	606,422,000	3.5%
9	Wisconsin	597,866,000	3.5%
10	Massachusetts	573,759,000	3.4%
11	Washington	470,765,000	2.8%
12	Indiana	465,200,000	2.7%
13	Minnesota	421,545,000	2.5%
14	Connecticut	418,231,000	2.4%
15	Maryland	411,427,000	2.4%
16	Florida	381,485,000	2.2%
17	Arizona	319,467,000	1.9%
18	North Carolina	294,754,000	1.7%
19	Oklahoma	292,973,000	1.7%
20	Tennessee	279,017,000	1.6%
21	Kentucky	276,544,000	1.6%
22	Oregon	255,652,000	1.5%
23	Arkansas	246,976,000	1.4%
24	Georgia	227,146,000	1.3%
25	Iowa	225,499,000	1.3%
26	New Hampshire	215,161,000	1.3%
27	Colorado	203,399,000	1.2%
28	Virginia	192,441,000	1.1%
29	Mississippi	157,433,000	0.9%
30	Maine	139,729,000	0.8%
31	Louisiana	133,194,000	0.8%
32	Rhode Island	130,811,000	0.8%
33	Alabama	126,151,000	0.7%
34	Utah	123,988,000	0.7%
35	Hawaii	121,971,000	0.7%
36	Delaware	120,850,000	0.7%
37	West Virginia	109,618,000	0.6%
38	Missouri	104,918,000	0.6%
39	Kansas	103,639,000	0.6%
40	Nevada	102,644,000	0.6%
41	Montana	87,148,000	0.5%
42	Vermont	80,230,000	0.5%
43	New Mexico	74,800,000	0.4%
44	Alaska	67,382,000	0.4%
45	South Dakota	60,372,000	0.4%
46	Idaho	48,461,000	0.3%
47	Nebraska	33,725,000	0.2%
48	North Dakota	28,240,000	0.2%
49	South Carolina	26,247,000	0.2%
50	Wyoming	25,984,000	0.2%
	District of Columbia*	NA	NA

Source: U.S. Bureau of the Census, Governments Division
"2012 State Government Tax Collections" (http://www.census.gov/govs/statetax/)
*Not applicable.

Per Capita State Government Tobacco Sales Tax Revenue in 2012

National Per Capita = $54.54

ALPHA ORDER

RANK	STATE	PER CAPITA
43	Alabama	$26.16
9	Alaska	92.12
30	Arizona	48.75
15	Arkansas	83.75
44	California	23.54
36	Colorado	39.21
5	Connecticut	116.49
2	Delaware	131.78
47	Florida	19.75
46	Georgia	22.90
12	Hawaii	87.60
40	Idaho	30.37
31	Illinois	47.10
22	Indiana	71.16
19	Iowa	73.35
38	Kansas	35.91
26	Kentucky	63.13
42	Louisiana	28.94
6	Maine	105.12
23	Maryland	69.92
14	Massachusetts	86.33
8	Michigan	96.25
17	Minnesota	78.37
29	Mississippi	52.74
49	Missouri	17.42
13	Montana	86.70
48	Nebraska	18.18
37	Nevada	37.20
1	New Hampshire	162.91
10	New Jersey	89.35
39	New Mexico	35.87
16	New York	83.39
41	North Carolina	30.22
35	North Dakota	40.36
20	Ohio	73.04
18	Oklahoma	76.80
25	Oregon	65.56
11	Pennsylvania	87.67
4	Rhode Island	124.55
50	South Carolina	5.56
21	South Dakota	72.44
34	Tennessee	43.22
28	Texas	56.40
33	Utah	43.42
3	Vermont	128.16
45	Virginia	23.51
24	Washington	68.26
27	West Virginia	59.08
7	Wisconsin	104.41
32	Wyoming	45.08

RANK ORDER

RANK	STATE	PER CAPITA
1	New Hampshire	$162.91
2	Delaware	131.78
3	Vermont	128.16
4	Rhode Island	124.55
5	Connecticut	116.49
6	Maine	105.12
7	Wisconsin	104.41
8	Michigan	96.25
9	Alaska	92.12
10	New Jersey	89.35
11	Pennsylvania	87.67
12	Hawaii	87.60
13	Montana	86.70
14	Massachusetts	86.33
15	Arkansas	83.75
16	New York	83.39
17	Minnesota	78.37
18	Oklahoma	76.80
19	Iowa	73.35
20	Ohio	73.04
21	South Dakota	72.44
22	Indiana	71.16
23	Maryland	69.92
24	Washington	68.26
25	Oregon	65.56
26	Kentucky	63.13
27	West Virginia	59.08
28	Texas	56.40
29	Mississippi	52.74
30	Arizona	48.75
31	Illinois	47.10
32	Wyoming	45.08
33	Utah	43.42
34	Tennessee	43.22
35	North Dakota	40.36
36	Colorado	39.21
37	Nevada	37.20
38	Kansas	35.91
39	New Mexico	35.87
40	Idaho	30.37
41	North Carolina	30.22
42	Louisiana	28.94
43	Alabama	26.16
44	California	23.54
45	Virginia	23.51
46	Georgia	22.90
47	Florida	19.75
48	Nebraska	18.18
49	Missouri	17.42
50	South Carolina	5.56

District of Columbia*   NA

Source: CQ Press using data from U.S. Bureau of the Census, Governments Division
"2012 State Government Tax Collections" (http://www.census.gov/govs/statetax/)
*Not applicable.

State Tax on a Pack of Cigarettes in 2014

National Median = $1.36 per Pack*

ALPHA ORDER				RANK ORDER		
RANK	STATE	TAX PER PACK		RANK	STATE	TAX PER PACK
46	Alabama	$0.43		1	New York	$4.35
11	Alaska	2.00		2	Massachusetts	3.51
11	Arizona	2.00		3	Rhode Island	3.50
29	Arkansas	1.15		4	Connecticut	3.40
32	California	0.87		5	Hawaii	3.20
33	Colorado	0.84		6	Washington	3.03
4	Connecticut	3.40		7	Minnesota	2.83
21	Delaware	1.60		8	New Jersey	2.70
26	Florida	1.34		9	Vermont	2.62
47	Georgia	0.37		10	Wisconsin	2.52
5	Hawaii	3.20		11	Alaska	2.00
41	Idaho	0.57		11	Arizona	2.00
16	Illinois	1.98		11	Maine	2.00
31	Indiana	1.00		11	Maryland	2.00
25	Iowa	1.36		11	Michigan	2.00
35	Kansas	0.79		16	Illinois	1.98
39	Kentucky	0.60		17	New Hampshire	1.78
48	Louisiana	0.36		18	Montana	1.70
11	Maine	2.00		18	Utah	1.70
11	Maryland	2.00		20	New Mexico	1.66
2	Massachusetts	3.51		21	Delaware	1.60
11	Michigan	2.00		21	Pennsylvania	1.60
7	Minnesota	2.83		23	South Dakota	1.53
36	Mississippi	0.68		24	Texas	1.41
50	Missouri	0.17		25	Iowa	1.36
18	Montana	1.70		26	Florida	1.34
37	Nebraska	0.64		27	Oregon	1.31
34	Nevada	0.80		28	Ohio	1.25
17	New Hampshire	1.78		29	Arkansas	1.15
8	New Jersey	2.70		30	Oklahoma	1.03
20	New Mexico	1.66		31	Indiana	1.00
1	New York	4.35		32	California	0.87
44	North Carolina	0.45		33	Colorado	0.84
45	North Dakota	0.44		34	Nevada	0.80
28	Ohio	1.25		35	Kansas	0.79
30	Oklahoma	1.03		36	Mississippi	0.68
27	Oregon	1.31		37	Nebraska	0.64
21	Pennsylvania	1.60		38	Tennessee	0.62
3	Rhode Island	3.50		39	Kentucky	0.60
41	South Carolina	0.57		39	Wyoming	0.60
23	South Dakota	1.53		41	Idaho	0.57
38	Tennessee	0.62		41	South Carolina	0.57
24	Texas	1.41		43	West Virginia	0.55
18	Utah	1.70		44	North Carolina	0.45
9	Vermont	2.62		45	North Dakota	0.44
49	Virginia	0.30		46	Alabama	0.43
6	Washington	3.03		47	Georgia	0.37
43	West Virginia	0.55		48	Louisiana	0.36
10	Wisconsin	2.52		49	Virginia	0.30
39	Wyoming	0.60		50	Missouri	0.17
				District of Columbia		2.50

Source: Federation of Tax Administrators
   "State Excise Tax Rates on Cigarettes" (http://www.taxadmin.org/FTA/rate/tax_stru.html)
*As of January 1, 2014. Many states also allow additional local option taxes on cigarettes.

State Government Alcoholic Beverage Sales Tax Revenue in 2012

National Total = $6,018,645,000

ALPHA ORDER

RANK	STATE	REVENUE	% of USA
11	Alabama	$173,251,000	2.9%
34	Alaska	40,230,000	0.7%
23	Arizona	68,379,000	1.1%
28	Arkansas	48,803,000	0.8%
4	California	346,000,000	5.7%
35	Colorado	38,817,000	0.6%
24	Connecticut	60,595,000	1.0%
41	Delaware	17,654,000	0.3%
2	Florida	527,016,000	8.8%
10	Georgia	175,051,000	2.9%
27	Hawaii	48,854,000	0.8%
49	Idaho	8,099,000	0.1%
7	Illinois	279,270,000	4.6%
30	Indiana	44,155,000	0.7%
45	Iowa	14,727,000	0.2%
17	Kansas	118,202,000	2.0%
16	Kentucky	118,253,000	2.0%
25	Louisiana	56,869,000	0.9%
42	Maine	17,352,000	0.3%
38	Maryland	31,010,000	0.5%
22	Massachusetts	77,861,000	1.3%
13	Michigan	149,159,000	2.5%
21	Minnesota	79,389,000	1.3%
31	Mississippi	42,183,000	0.7%
36	Missouri	34,341,000	0.6%
37	Montana	34,019,000	0.6%
39	Nebraska	28,472,000	0.5%
32	Nevada	41,695,000	0.7%
47	New Hampshire	9,723,000	0.2%
14	New Jersey	135,304,000	2.2%
33	New Mexico	40,574,000	0.7%
8	New York	238,932,000	4.0%
6	North Carolina	322,970,000	5.4%
48	North Dakota	8,463,000	0.1%
19	Ohio	98,113,000	1.6%
18	Oklahoma	103,831,000	1.7%
43	Oregon	17,322,000	0.3%
5	Pennsylvania	324,024,000	5.4%
46	Rhode Island	12,785,000	0.2%
12	South Carolina	153,951,000	2.6%
44	South Dakota	15,449,000	0.3%
15	Tennessee	133,055,000	2.2%
1	Texas	937,614,000	15.6%
29	Utah	45,823,000	0.8%
40	Vermont	22,403,000	0.4%
9	Virginia	190,796,000	3.2%
3	Washington	349,164,000	5.8%
20	West Virginia	87,240,000	1.4%
26	Wisconsin	49,661,000	0.8%
50	Wyoming	1,742,000	0.0%

RANK ORDER

RANK	STATE	REVENUE	% of USA
1	Texas	$937,614,000	15.6%
2	Florida	527,016,000	8.8%
3	Washington	349,164,000	5.8%
4	California	346,000,000	5.7%
5	Pennsylvania	324,024,000	5.4%
6	North Carolina	322,970,000	5.4%
7	Illinois	279,270,000	4.6%
8	New York	238,932,000	4.0%
9	Virginia	190,796,000	3.2%
10	Georgia	175,051,000	2.9%
11	Alabama	173,251,000	2.9%
12	South Carolina	153,951,000	2.6%
13	Michigan	149,159,000	2.5%
14	New Jersey	135,304,000	2.2%
15	Tennessee	133,055,000	2.2%
16	Kentucky	118,253,000	2.0%
17	Kansas	118,202,000	2.0%
18	Oklahoma	103,831,000	1.7%
19	Ohio	98,113,000	1.6%
20	West Virginia	87,240,000	1.4%
21	Minnesota	79,389,000	1.3%
22	Massachusetts	77,861,000	1.3%
23	Arizona	68,379,000	1.1%
24	Connecticut	60,595,000	1.0%
25	Louisiana	56,869,000	0.9%
26	Wisconsin	49,661,000	0.8%
27	Hawaii	48,854,000	0.8%
28	Arkansas	48,803,000	0.8%
29	Utah	45,823,000	0.8%
30	Indiana	44,155,000	0.7%
31	Mississippi	42,183,000	0.7%
32	Nevada	41,695,000	0.7%
33	New Mexico	40,574,000	0.7%
34	Alaska	40,230,000	0.7%
35	Colorado	38,817,000	0.6%
36	Missouri	34,341,000	0.6%
37	Montana	34,019,000	0.6%
38	Maryland	31,010,000	0.5%
39	Nebraska	28,472,000	0.5%
40	Vermont	22,403,000	0.4%
41	Delaware	17,654,000	0.3%
42	Maine	17,352,000	0.3%
43	Oregon	17,322,000	0.3%
44	South Dakota	15,449,000	0.3%
45	Iowa	14,727,000	0.2%
46	Rhode Island	12,785,000	0.2%
47	New Hampshire	9,723,000	0.2%
48	North Dakota	8,463,000	0.1%
49	Idaho	8,099,000	0.1%
50	Wyoming	1,742,000	0.0%
	District of Columbia*	NA	NA

Source: U.S. Bureau of the Census, Governments Division
  "2012 State Government Tax Collections" (http://www.census.gov/govs/statetax/)
*Not applicable.

Per Capita State Government Alcoholic Beverage Sales Tax Revenue in 2012

National Per Capita = $19.21

ALPHA ORDER

RANK	STATE	PER CAPITA
6	Alabama	$35.93
1	Alaska	55.00
38	Arizona	10.43
24	Arkansas	16.55
39	California	9.10
42	Colorado	7.48
23	Connecticut	16.88
20	Delaware	19.25
12	Florida	27.28
22	Georgia	17.65
8	Hawaii	35.09
47	Idaho	5.08
17	Illinois	21.69
44	Indiana	6.75
48	Iowa	4.79
4	Kansas	40.96
14	Kentucky	27.00
33	Louisiana	12.36
32	Maine	13.05
46	Maryland	5.27
37	Massachusetts	11.72
29	Michigan	15.09
30	Minnesota	14.76
31	Mississippi	14.13
45	Missouri	5.70
9	Montana	33.85
26	Nebraska	15.34
28	Nevada	15.11
43	New Hampshire	7.36
27	New Jersey	15.26
19	New Mexico	19.45
34	New York	12.21
10	North Carolina	33.12
36	North Dakota	12.10
41	Ohio	8.50
13	Oklahoma	27.22
49	Oregon	4.44
15	Pennsylvania	25.39
35	Rhode Island	12.17
11	South Carolina	32.59
21	South Dakota	18.54
18	Tennessee	20.61
5	Texas	35.98
25	Utah	16.05
7	Vermont	35.79
16	Virginia	23.31
2	Washington	50.63
3	West Virginia	47.02
40	Wisconsin	8.67
50	Wyoming	3.02

RANK ORDER

RANK	STATE	PER CAPITA
1	Alaska	$55.00
2	Washington	50.63
3	West Virginia	47.02
4	Kansas	40.96
5	Texas	35.98
6	Alabama	35.93
7	Vermont	35.79
8	Hawaii	35.09
9	Montana	33.85
10	North Carolina	33.12
11	South Carolina	32.59
12	Florida	27.28
13	Oklahoma	27.22
14	Kentucky	27.00
15	Pennsylvania	25.39
16	Virginia	23.31
17	Illinois	21.69
18	Tennessee	20.61
19	New Mexico	19.45
20	Delaware	19.25
21	South Dakota	18.54
22	Georgia	17.65
23	Connecticut	16.88
24	Arkansas	16.55
25	Utah	16.05
26	Nebraska	15.34
27	New Jersey	15.26
28	Nevada	15.11
29	Michigan	15.09
30	Minnesota	14.76
31	Mississippi	14.13
32	Maine	13.05
33	Louisiana	12.36
34	New York	12.21
35	Rhode Island	12.17
36	North Dakota	12.10
37	Massachusetts	11.72
38	Arizona	10.43
39	California	9.10
40	Wisconsin	8.67
41	Ohio	8.50
42	Colorado	7.48
43	New Hampshire	7.36
44	Indiana	6.75
45	Missouri	5.70
46	Maryland	5.27
47	Idaho	5.08
48	Iowa	4.79
49	Oregon	4.44
50	Wyoming	3.02
	District of Columbia*	NA

Source: CQ Press using data from U.S. Bureau of the Census, Governments Division
"2012 State Government Tax Collections" (http://www.census.gov/govs/statetax/)
*Not applicable.

State Government Total Expenditures in 2011

National Total = $2,004,325,002,000*

ALPHA ORDER

RANK	STATE	EXPENDITURES	% of USA
27	Alabama	$28,061,237,000	1.4%
39	Alaska	11,320,127,000	0.6%
20	Arizona	32,875,412,000	1.6%
32	Arkansas	18,861,507,000	0.9%
1	California	282,524,665,000	14.1%
25	Colorado	28,413,134,000	1.4%
26	Connecticut	28,094,106,000	1.4%
44	Delaware	7,936,467,000	0.4%
5	Florida	84,633,065,000	4.2%
14	Georgia	44,750,297,000	2.2%
38	Hawaii	11,475,771,000	0.6%
42	Idaho	8,733,485,000	0.4%
7	Illinois	74,655,351,000	3.7%
18	Indiana	35,261,522,000	1.8%
31	Iowa	19,937,080,000	1.0%
34	Kansas	16,686,643,000	0.8%
23	Kentucky	29,369,940,000	1.5%
19	Louisiana	33,396,449,000	1.7%
41	Maine	9,099,085,000	0.5%
17	Maryland	37,672,576,000	1.9%
11	Massachusetts	52,550,586,000	2.6%
9	Michigan	63,108,508,000	3.1%
16	Minnesota	38,488,350,000	1.9%
30	Mississippi	20,157,417,000	1.0%
22	Missouri	30,646,880,000	1.5%
46	Montana	7,105,366,000	0.4%
40	Nebraska	9,356,473,000	0.5%
36	Nevada	13,203,265,000	0.7%
45	New Hampshire	7,638,166,000	0.4%
8	New Jersey	67,114,331,000	3.3%
33	New Mexico	17,865,171,000	0.9%
2	New York	184,009,243,000	9.2%
10	North Carolina	53,088,745,000	2.6%
49	North Dakota	5,515,725,000	0.3%
6	Ohio	79,201,570,000	4.0%
29	Oklahoma	22,377,598,000	1.1%
28	Oregon	27,336,568,000	1.4%
4	Pennsylvania	90,791,525,000	4.5%
43	Rhode Island	8,270,898,000	0.4%
24	South Carolina	29,352,302,000	1.5%
50	South Dakota	4,498,447,000	0.2%
21	Tennessee	30,841,226,000	1.5%
3	Texas	125,939,778,000	6.3%
35	Utah	16,682,581,000	0.8%
47	Vermont	5,853,842,000	0.3%
13	Virginia	45,549,347,000	2.3%
12	Washington	45,999,749,000	2.3%
37	West Virginia	13,000,033,000	0.6%
15	Wisconsin	39,349,832,000	2.0%
48	Wyoming	5,673,561,000	0.3%

RANK ORDER

RANK	STATE	EXPENDITURES	% of USA
1	California	$282,524,665,000	14.1%
2	New York	184,009,243,000	9.2%
3	Texas	125,939,778,000	6.3%
4	Pennsylvania	90,791,525,000	4.5%
5	Florida	84,633,065,000	4.2%
6	Ohio	79,201,570,000	4.0%
7	Illinois	74,655,351,000	3.7%
8	New Jersey	67,114,331,000	3.3%
9	Michigan	63,108,508,000	3.1%
10	North Carolina	53,088,745,000	2.6%
11	Massachusetts	52,550,586,000	2.6%
12	Washington	45,999,749,000	2.3%
13	Virginia	45,549,347,000	2.3%
14	Georgia	44,750,297,000	2.2%
15	Wisconsin	39,349,832,000	2.0%
16	Minnesota	38,488,350,000	1.9%
17	Maryland	37,672,576,000	1.9%
18	Indiana	35,261,522,000	1.8%
19	Louisiana	33,396,449,000	1.7%
20	Arizona	32,875,412,000	1.6%
21	Tennessee	30,841,226,000	1.5%
22	Missouri	30,646,880,000	1.5%
23	Kentucky	29,369,940,000	1.5%
24	South Carolina	29,352,302,000	1.5%
25	Colorado	28,413,134,000	1.4%
26	Connecticut	28,094,106,000	1.4%
27	Alabama	28,061,237,000	1.4%
28	Oregon	27,336,568,000	1.4%
29	Oklahoma	22,377,598,000	1.1%
30	Mississippi	20,157,417,000	1.0%
31	Iowa	19,937,080,000	1.0%
32	Arkansas	18,861,507,000	0.9%
33	New Mexico	17,865,171,000	0.9%
34	Kansas	16,686,643,000	0.8%
35	Utah	16,682,581,000	0.8%
36	Nevada	13,203,265,000	0.7%
37	West Virginia	13,000,033,000	0.6%
38	Hawaii	11,475,771,000	0.6%
39	Alaska	11,320,127,000	0.6%
40	Nebraska	9,356,473,000	0.5%
41	Maine	9,099,085,000	0.5%
42	Idaho	8,733,485,000	0.4%
43	Rhode Island	8,270,898,000	0.4%
44	Delaware	7,936,467,000	0.4%
45	New Hampshire	7,638,166,000	0.4%
46	Montana	7,105,366,000	0.4%
47	Vermont	5,853,842,000	0.3%
48	Wyoming	5,673,561,000	0.3%
49	North Dakota	5,515,725,000	0.3%
50	South Dakota	4,498,447,000	0.2%
	District of Columbia**	NA	NA

Source: U.S. Bureau of the Census, Governments Division

"2011 State and Local Government Finances" (http://www.census.gov/govs/local/)

*Total expenditures includes all money paid other than for retirement of debt and extension of loans. Includes payments from all sources of funds including current revenues and proceeds from borrowing and prior year fund balances. Includes intergovernmental transfers and expenditures for government owned utilities and other commercial or auxiliary enterprise, and insurance trust expenditures. **Not applicable.

Per Capita State Government Total Expenditures in 2011

National Per Capita = $6,445*

ALPHA ORDER

RANK	STATE	PER CAPITA
33	Alabama	$5,842
1	Alaska	15,639
44	Arizona	5,083
28	Arkansas	6,419
13	California	7,497
38	Colorado	5,553
11	Connecticut	7,833
5	Delaware	8,739
50	Florida	4,435
49	Georgia	4,561
7	Hawaii	8,327
39	Idaho	5,514
35	Illinois	5,805
42	Indiana	5,411
26	Iowa	6,507
34	Kansas	5,813
25	Kentucky	6,726
14	Louisiana	7,300
22	Maine	6,849
27	Maryland	6,451
9	Massachusetts	7,954
29	Michigan	6,390
15	Minnesota	7,198
23	Mississippi	6,770
43	Missouri	5,100
17	Montana	7,122
45	Nebraska	5,079
47	Nevada	4,854
36	New Hampshire	5,796
12	New Jersey	7,597
6	New Mexico	8,595
3	New York	9,436
40	North Carolina	5,501
8	North Dakota	8,055
21	Ohio	6,863
32	Oklahoma	5,913
18	Oregon	7,067
16	Pennsylvania	7,124
10	Rhode Island	7,872
30	South Carolina	6,281
41	South Dakota	5,462
48	Tennessee	4,819
46	Texas	4,913
31	Utah	5,928
4	Vermont	9,342
37	Virginia	5,620
24	Washington	6,742
19	West Virginia	7,008
20	Wisconsin	6,892
2	Wyoming	10,000

RANK ORDER

RANK	STATE	PER CAPITA
1	Alaska	$15,639
2	Wyoming	10,000
3	New York	9,436
4	Vermont	9,342
5	Delaware	8,739
6	New Mexico	8,595
7	Hawaii	8,327
8	North Dakota	8,055
9	Massachusetts	7,954
10	Rhode Island	7,872
11	Connecticut	7,833
12	New Jersey	7,597
13	California	7,497
14	Louisiana	7,300
15	Minnesota	7,198
16	Pennsylvania	7,124
17	Montana	7,122
18	Oregon	7,067
19	West Virginia	7,008
20	Wisconsin	6,892
21	Ohio	6,863
22	Maine	6,849
23	Mississippi	6,770
24	Washington	6,742
25	Kentucky	6,726
26	Iowa	6,507
27	Maryland	6,451
28	Arkansas	6,419
29	Michigan	6,390
30	South Carolina	6,281
31	Utah	5,928
32	Oklahoma	5,913
33	Alabama	5,842
34	Kansas	5,813
35	Illinois	5,805
36	New Hampshire	5,796
37	Virginia	5,620
38	Colorado	5,553
39	Idaho	5,514
40	North Carolina	5,501
41	South Dakota	5,462
42	Indiana	5,411
43	Missouri	5,100
44	Arizona	5,083
45	Nebraska	5,079
46	Texas	4,913
47	Nevada	4,854
48	Tennessee	4,819
49	Georgia	4,561
50	Florida	4,435

District of Columbia**   NA

Source: CQ Press using data from U.S. Bureau of the Census, Governments Division
    "2011 State and Local Government Finances" (http://www.census.gov/govs/local/)
*Total expenditures includes all money paid other than for retirement of debt and extension of loans. Includes payments from all sources of funds including current revenues and proceeds from borrowing and prior year fund balances. Includes intergovernmental transfers and expenditures for government owned utilities and other commercial or auxiliary enterprise, and insurance trust expenditures. **Not applicable.

State Government Direct General Expenditures in 2011

National Total = $1,158,125,621,000*

ALPHA ORDER

RANK	STATE	EXPENDITURES	% of USA
26	Alabama	$17,489,681,000	1.5%
38	Alaska	8,233,111,000	0.7%
23	Arizona	19,454,708,000	1.7%
32	Arkansas	11,707,930,000	1.0%
1	California	135,802,688,000	11.7%
27	Colorado	15,939,368,000	1.4%
25	Connecticut	17,763,271,000	1.5%
42	Delaware	5,764,611,000	0.5%
5	Florida	52,259,669,000	4.5%
14	Georgia	26,810,367,000	2.3%
36	Hawaii	9,755,259,000	0.8%
43	Idaho	5,368,437,000	0.5%
6	Illinois	43,793,443,000	3.8%
18	Indiana	21,637,009,000	1.9%
31	Iowa	12,067,286,000	1.0%
35	Kansas	10,318,064,000	0.9%
22	Kentucky	19,607,046,000	1.7%
17	Louisiana	22,554,788,000	1.9%
39	Maine	6,703,456,000	0.6%
15	Maryland	24,181,403,000	2.1%
9	Massachusetts	34,354,818,000	3.0%
10	Michigan	32,323,402,000	2.8%
19	Minnesota	21,568,056,000	1.9%
30	Mississippi	12,293,075,000	1.1%
21	Missouri	19,824,240,000	1.7%
46	Montana	4,729,095,000	0.4%
40	Nebraska	6,310,373,000	0.5%
41	Nevada	6,085,569,000	0.5%
45	New Hampshire	5,184,468,000	0.4%
8	New Jersey	37,565,232,000	3.2%
34	New Mexico	11,268,727,000	1.0%
2	New York	86,379,987,000	7.5%
11	North Carolina	30,701,730,000	2.7%
48	North Dakota	3,731,468,000	0.3%
7	Ohio	42,501,306,000	3.7%
29	Oklahoma	14,533,770,000	1.3%
28	Oregon	15,336,841,000	1.3%
4	Pennsylvania	53,513,356,000	4.6%
44	Rhode Island	5,333,920,000	0.5%
24	South Carolina	18,073,794,000	1.6%
49	South Dakota	3,287,711,000	0.3%
20	Tennessee	20,460,980,000	1.8%
3	Texas	78,933,692,000	6.8%
33	Utah	11,602,054,000	1.0%
47	Vermont	3,837,768,000	0.3%
12	Virginia	28,861,034,000	2.5%
13	Washington	27,541,976,000	2.4%
37	West Virginia	8,912,094,000	0.8%
16	Wisconsin	22,611,704,000	2.0%
50	Wyoming	3,251,786,000	0.3%

RANK ORDER

RANK	STATE	EXPENDITURES	% of USA
1	California	$135,802,688,000	11.7%
2	New York	86,379,987,000	7.5%
3	Texas	78,933,692,000	6.8%
4	Pennsylvania	53,513,356,000	4.6%
5	Florida	52,259,669,000	4.5%
6	Illinois	43,793,443,000	3.8%
7	Ohio	42,501,306,000	3.7%
8	New Jersey	37,565,232,000	3.2%
9	Massachusetts	34,354,818,000	3.0%
10	Michigan	32,323,402,000	2.8%
11	North Carolina	30,701,730,000	2.7%
12	Virginia	28,861,034,000	2.5%
13	Washington	27,541,976,000	2.4%
14	Georgia	26,810,367,000	2.3%
15	Maryland	24,181,403,000	2.1%
16	Wisconsin	22,611,704,000	2.0%
17	Louisiana	22,554,788,000	1.9%
18	Indiana	21,637,009,000	1.9%
19	Minnesota	21,568,056,000	1.9%
20	Tennessee	20,460,980,000	1.8%
21	Missouri	19,824,240,000	1.7%
22	Kentucky	19,607,046,000	1.7%
23	Arizona	19,454,708,000	1.7%
24	South Carolina	18,073,794,000	1.6%
25	Connecticut	17,763,271,000	1.5%
26	Alabama	17,489,681,000	1.5%
27	Colorado	15,939,368,000	1.4%
28	Oregon	15,336,841,000	1.3%
29	Oklahoma	14,533,770,000	1.3%
30	Mississippi	12,293,075,000	1.1%
31	Iowa	12,067,286,000	1.0%
32	Arkansas	11,707,930,000	1.0%
33	Utah	11,602,054,000	1.0%
34	New Mexico	11,268,727,000	1.0%
35	Kansas	10,318,064,000	0.9%
36	Hawaii	9,755,259,000	0.8%
37	West Virginia	8,912,094,000	0.8%
38	Alaska	8,233,111,000	0.7%
39	Maine	6,703,456,000	0.6%
40	Nebraska	6,310,373,000	0.5%
41	Nevada	6,085,569,000	0.5%
42	Delaware	5,764,611,000	0.5%
43	Idaho	5,368,437,000	0.5%
44	Rhode Island	5,333,920,000	0.5%
45	New Hampshire	5,184,468,000	0.4%
46	Montana	4,729,095,000	0.4%
47	Vermont	3,837,768,000	0.3%
48	North Dakota	3,731,468,000	0.3%
49	South Dakota	3,287,711,000	0.3%
50	Wyoming	3,251,786,000	0.3%
	District of Columbia**	NA	NA

Source: U.S. Bureau of the Census, Governments Division
     "2011 State and Local Government Finances" (http://www.census.gov/govs/local/)
*Direct general expenditures include expenditures for current operations, assistance and subsidies, interest on debt, and capital outlay. Excludes intergovernmental transfers, expenditures for government owned utilities and other commercial or auxiliary enterprise, and insurance trust expenditures.
**Not applicable.

Per Capita State Government Direct General Expenditures in 2011

National Per Capita = $3,724*

ALPHA ORDER

ALPHA ORDER

RANK	STATE	PER CAPITA
33	Alabama	$3,641
1	Alaska	11,374
47	Arizona	3,008
25	Arkansas	3,984
34	California	3,604
45	Colorado	3,115
11	Connecticut	4,953
3	Delaware	6,348
48	Florida	2,739
49	Georgia	2,732
2	Hawaii	7,079
39	Idaho	3,390
38	Illinois	3,405
40	Indiana	3,320
28	Iowa	3,938
35	Kansas	3,595
15	Kentucky	4,490
12	Louisiana	4,930
10	Maine	5,046
19	Maryland	4,141
8	Massachusetts	5,200
42	Michigan	3,273
23	Minnesota	4,033
20	Mississippi	4,129
41	Missouri	3,299
14	Montana	4,740
37	Nebraska	3,425
50	Nevada	2,237
29	New Hampshire	3,934
17	New Jersey	4,252
7	New Mexico	5,421
16	New York	4,429
44	North Carolina	3,181
6	North Dakota	5,449
32	Ohio	3,683
31	Oklahoma	3,841
26	Oregon	3,965
18	Pennsylvania	4,199
9	Rhode Island	5,077
30	South Carolina	3,867
24	South Dakota	3,992
43	Tennessee	3,197
46	Texas	3,080
21	Utah	4,122
4	Vermont	6,125
36	Virginia	3,561
22	Washington	4,036
13	West Virginia	4,805
27	Wisconsin	3,960
5	Wyoming	5,731

RANK ORDER

RANK	STATE	PER CAPITA
1	Alaska	$11,374
2	Hawaii	7,079
3	Delaware	6,348
4	Vermont	6,125
5	Wyoming	5,731
6	North Dakota	5,449
7	New Mexico	5,421
8	Massachusetts	5,200
9	Rhode Island	5,077
10	Maine	5,046
11	Connecticut	4,953
12	Louisiana	4,930
13	West Virginia	4,805
14	Montana	4,740
15	Kentucky	4,490
16	New York	4,429
17	New Jersey	4,252
18	Pennsylvania	4,199
19	Maryland	4,141
20	Mississippi	4,129
21	Utah	4,122
22	Washington	4,036
23	Minnesota	4,033
24	South Dakota	3,992
25	Arkansas	3,984
26	Oregon	3,965
27	Wisconsin	3,960
28	Iowa	3,938
29	New Hampshire	3,934
30	South Carolina	3,867
31	Oklahoma	3,841
32	Ohio	3,683
33	Alabama	3,641
34	California	3,604
35	Kansas	3,595
36	Virginia	3,561
37	Nebraska	3,425
38	Illinois	3,405
39	Idaho	3,390
40	Indiana	3,320
41	Missouri	3,299
42	Michigan	3,273
43	Tennessee	3,197
44	North Carolina	3,181
45	Colorado	3,115
46	Texas	3,080
47	Arizona	3,008
48	Florida	2,739
49	Georgia	2,732
50	Nevada	2,237

District of Columbia**   NA

Source: CQ Press using data from U.S. Bureau of the Census, Governments Division
  "2011 State and Local Government Finances" (http://www.census.gov/govs/local/)
*Direct general expenditures include expenditures for current operations, assistance and subsidies, interest on debt, and capital outlay. Excludes intergovernmental transfers, expenditures for government owned utilities and other commercial or auxiliary enterprise, and insurance trust expenditures.
**Not applicable.

State Government Debt Outstanding in 2011

National Total = $1,132,814,566,000*

ALPHA ORDER

RANK	STATE	DEBT	% of USA
29	Alabama	$9,067,280,000	0.8%
38	Alaska	6,417,682,000	0.6%
23	Arizona	14,163,076,000	1.3%
45	Arkansas	3,748,749,000	0.3%
1	California	149,670,954,000	13.2%
20	Colorado	16,335,260,000	1.4%
11	Connecticut	30,523,708,000	2.7%
41	Delaware	5,807,957,000	0.5%
7	Florida	43,471,755,000	3.8%
25	Georgia	13,402,568,000	1.2%
32	Hawaii	7,912,833,000	0.7%
44	Idaho	3,928,080,000	0.3%
4	Illinois	64,801,423,000	5.7%
16	Indiana	22,144,251,000	2.0%
33	Iowa	7,573,811,000	0.7%
36	Kansas	6,893,030,000	0.6%
22	Kentucky	14,751,471,000	1.3%
19	Louisiana	18,447,200,000	1.6%
39	Maine	5,904,221,000	0.5%
14	Maryland	25,250,138,000	2.2%
3	Massachusetts	74,315,823,000	6.6%
9	Michigan	30,975,273,000	2.7%
26	Minnesota	12,896,921,000	1.1%
37	Mississippi	6,768,371,000	0.6%
17	Missouri	20,682,303,000	1.8%
42	Montana	4,266,731,000	0.4%
48	Nebraska	2,345,750,000	0.2%
43	Nevada	4,201,115,000	0.4%
30	New Hampshire	8,450,218,000	0.7%
5	New Jersey	64,004,651,000	5.7%
31	New Mexico	8,118,832,000	0.7%
2	New York	134,928,505,000	11.9%
18	North Carolina	18,556,175,000	1.6%
49	North Dakota	2,060,516,000	0.2%
10	Ohio	30,974,275,000	2.7%
27	Oklahoma	10,254,716,000	0.9%
24	Oregon	14,069,253,000	1.2%
6	Pennsylvania	45,267,281,000	4.0%
28	Rhode Island	9,173,572,000	0.8%
21	South Carolina	15,341,040,000	1.4%
46	South Dakota	3,544,772,000	0.3%
40	Tennessee	5,899,369,000	0.5%
8	Texas	38,530,338,000	3.4%
35	Utah	7,205,779,000	0.6%
47	Vermont	3,485,346,000	0.3%
13	Virginia	26,479,450,000	2.3%
12	Washington	28,153,562,000	2.5%
34	West Virginia	7,406,254,000	0.7%
15	Wisconsin	22,878,524,000	2.0%
50	Wyoming	1,364,404,000	0.1%

RANK ORDER

RANK	STATE	DEBT	% of USA
1	California	$149,670,954,000	13.2%
2	New York	134,928,505,000	11.9%
3	Massachusetts	74,315,823,000	6.6%
4	Illinois	64,801,423,000	5.7%
5	New Jersey	64,004,651,000	5.7%
6	Pennsylvania	45,267,281,000	4.0%
7	Florida	43,471,755,000	3.8%
8	Texas	38,530,338,000	3.4%
9	Michigan	30,975,273,000	2.7%
10	Ohio	30,974,275,000	2.7%
11	Connecticut	30,523,708,000	2.7%
12	Washington	28,153,562,000	2.5%
13	Virginia	26,479,450,000	2.3%
14	Maryland	25,250,138,000	2.2%
15	Wisconsin	22,878,524,000	2.0%
16	Indiana	22,144,251,000	2.0%
17	Missouri	20,682,303,000	1.8%
18	North Carolina	18,556,175,000	1.6%
19	Louisiana	18,447,200,000	1.6%
20	Colorado	16,335,260,000	1.4%
21	South Carolina	15,341,040,000	1.4%
22	Kentucky	14,751,471,000	1.3%
23	Arizona	14,163,076,000	1.3%
24	Oregon	14,069,253,000	1.2%
25	Georgia	13,402,568,000	1.2%
26	Minnesota	12,896,921,000	1.1%
27	Oklahoma	10,254,716,000	0.9%
28	Rhode Island	9,173,572,000	0.8%
29	Alabama	9,067,280,000	0.8%
30	New Hampshire	8,450,218,000	0.7%
31	New Mexico	8,118,832,000	0.7%
32	Hawaii	7,912,833,000	0.7%
33	Iowa	7,573,811,000	0.7%
34	West Virginia	7,406,254,000	0.7%
35	Utah	7,205,779,000	0.6%
36	Kansas	6,893,030,000	0.6%
37	Mississippi	6,768,371,000	0.6%
38	Alaska	6,417,682,000	0.6%
39	Maine	5,904,221,000	0.5%
40	Tennessee	5,899,369,000	0.5%
41	Delaware	5,807,957,000	0.5%
42	Montana	4,266,731,000	0.4%
43	Nevada	4,201,115,000	0.4%
44	Idaho	3,928,080,000	0.3%
45	Arkansas	3,748,749,000	0.3%
46	South Dakota	3,544,772,000	0.3%
47	Vermont	3,485,346,000	0.3%
48	Nebraska	2,345,750,000	0.2%
49	North Dakota	2,060,516,000	0.2%
50	Wyoming	1,364,404,000	0.1%
	District of Columbia**	NA	NA

Source: U.S. Bureau of the Census, Governments Division
   "2011 State and Local Government Finances" (http://www.census.gov/govs/local/)
*Includes short-term, long-term, full faith and credit, nonguaranteed, and public debt for private purposes.
**Not applicable.

Per Capita State Government Debt Outstanding in 2011

National Per Capita = $3,643*

<table>
<tr><td colspan="3">ALPHA ORDER</td><td colspan="3">RANK ORDER</td></tr>
<tr><td>RANK</td><td>STATE</td><td>PER CAPITA</td><td>RANK</td><td>STATE</td><td>PER CAPITA</td></tr>
<tr><td>44</td><td>Alabama</td><td>$1,888</td><td>1</td><td>Massachusetts</td><td>$11,248</td></tr>
<tr><td>2</td><td>Alaska</td><td>8,866</td><td>2</td><td>Alaska</td><td>8,866</td></tr>
<tr><td>42</td><td>Arizona</td><td>2,190</td><td>3</td><td>Rhode Island</td><td>8,731</td></tr>
<tr><td>48</td><td>Arkansas</td><td>1,276</td><td>4</td><td>Connecticut</td><td>8,510</td></tr>
<tr><td>20</td><td>California</td><td>3,972</td><td>5</td><td>New Jersey</td><td>7,245</td></tr>
<tr><td>29</td><td>Colorado</td><td>3,193</td><td>6</td><td>New York</td><td>6,919</td></tr>
<tr><td>4</td><td>Connecticut</td><td>8,510</td><td>7</td><td>New Hampshire</td><td>6,412</td></tr>
<tr><td>8</td><td>Delaware</td><td>6,395</td><td>8</td><td>Delaware</td><td>6,395</td></tr>
<tr><td>40</td><td>Florida</td><td>2,278</td><td>9</td><td>Hawaii</td><td>5,742</td></tr>
<tr><td>47</td><td>Georgia</td><td>1,366</td><td>10</td><td>Vermont</td><td>5,562</td></tr>
<tr><td>9</td><td>Hawaii</td><td>5,742</td><td>11</td><td>Illinois</td><td>5,039</td></tr>
<tr><td>35</td><td>Idaho</td><td>2,480</td><td>12</td><td>Maine</td><td>4,444</td></tr>
<tr><td>11</td><td>Illinois</td><td>5,039</td><td>13</td><td>Maryland</td><td>4,324</td></tr>
<tr><td>25</td><td>Indiana</td><td>3,398</td><td>14</td><td>South Dakota</td><td>4,304</td></tr>
<tr><td>36</td><td>Iowa</td><td>2,472</td><td>15</td><td>Montana</td><td>4,277</td></tr>
<tr><td>39</td><td>Kansas</td><td>2,401</td><td>16</td><td>Washington</td><td>4,126</td></tr>
<tr><td>26</td><td>Kentucky</td><td>3,378</td><td>17</td><td>Louisiana</td><td>4,032</td></tr>
<tr><td>17</td><td>Louisiana</td><td>4,032</td><td>18</td><td>Wisconsin</td><td>4,007</td></tr>
<tr><td>12</td><td>Maine</td><td>4,444</td><td>19</td><td>West Virginia</td><td>3,993</td></tr>
<tr><td>13</td><td>Maryland</td><td>4,324</td><td>20</td><td>California</td><td>3,972</td></tr>
<tr><td>1</td><td>Massachusetts</td><td>11,248</td><td>21</td><td>New Mexico</td><td>3,906</td></tr>
<tr><td>30</td><td>Michigan</td><td>3,136</td><td>22</td><td>Oregon</td><td>3,637</td></tr>
<tr><td>37</td><td>Minnesota</td><td>2,412</td><td>23</td><td>Pennsylvania</td><td>3,552</td></tr>
<tr><td>41</td><td>Mississippi</td><td>2,273</td><td>24</td><td>Missouri</td><td>3,442</td></tr>
<tr><td>24</td><td>Missouri</td><td>3,442</td><td>25</td><td>Indiana</td><td>3,398</td></tr>
<tr><td>15</td><td>Montana</td><td>4,277</td><td>26</td><td>Kentucky</td><td>3,378</td></tr>
<tr><td>49</td><td>Nebraska</td><td>1,273</td><td>27</td><td>South Carolina</td><td>3,283</td></tr>
<tr><td>45</td><td>Nevada</td><td>1,545</td><td>28</td><td>Virginia</td><td>3,267</td></tr>
<tr><td>7</td><td>New Hampshire</td><td>6,412</td><td>29</td><td>Colorado</td><td>3,193</td></tr>
<tr><td>5</td><td>New Jersey</td><td>7,245</td><td>30</td><td>Michigan</td><td>3,136</td></tr>
<tr><td>21</td><td>New Mexico</td><td>3,906</td><td>31</td><td>North Dakota</td><td>3,009</td></tr>
<tr><td>6</td><td>New York</td><td>6,919</td><td>32</td><td>Oklahoma</td><td>2,710</td></tr>
<tr><td>43</td><td>North Carolina</td><td>1,923</td><td>33</td><td>Ohio</td><td>2,684</td></tr>
<tr><td>31</td><td>North Dakota</td><td>3,009</td><td>34</td><td>Utah</td><td>2,560</td></tr>
<tr><td>33</td><td>Ohio</td><td>2,684</td><td>35</td><td>Idaho</td><td>2,480</td></tr>
<tr><td>32</td><td>Oklahoma</td><td>2,710</td><td>36</td><td>Iowa</td><td>2,472</td></tr>
<tr><td>22</td><td>Oregon</td><td>3,637</td><td>37</td><td>Minnesota</td><td>2,412</td></tr>
<tr><td>23</td><td>Pennsylvania</td><td>3,552</td><td>38</td><td>Wyoming</td><td>2,405</td></tr>
<tr><td>3</td><td>Rhode Island</td><td>8,731</td><td>39</td><td>Kansas</td><td>2,401</td></tr>
<tr><td>27</td><td>South Carolina</td><td>3,283</td><td>40</td><td>Florida</td><td>2,278</td></tr>
<tr><td>14</td><td>South Dakota</td><td>4,304</td><td>41</td><td>Mississippi</td><td>2,273</td></tr>
<tr><td>50</td><td>Tennessee</td><td>922</td><td>42</td><td>Arizona</td><td>2,190</td></tr>
<tr><td>46</td><td>Texas</td><td>1,503</td><td>43</td><td>North Carolina</td><td>1,923</td></tr>
<tr><td>34</td><td>Utah</td><td>2,560</td><td>44</td><td>Alabama</td><td>1,888</td></tr>
<tr><td>10</td><td>Vermont</td><td>5,562</td><td>45</td><td>Nevada</td><td>1,545</td></tr>
<tr><td>28</td><td>Virginia</td><td>3,267</td><td>46</td><td>Texas</td><td>1,503</td></tr>
<tr><td>16</td><td>Washington</td><td>4,126</td><td>47</td><td>Georgia</td><td>1,366</td></tr>
<tr><td>19</td><td>West Virginia</td><td>3,993</td><td>48</td><td>Arkansas</td><td>1,276</td></tr>
<tr><td>18</td><td>Wisconsin</td><td>4,007</td><td>49</td><td>Nebraska</td><td>1,273</td></tr>
<tr><td>38</td><td>Wyoming</td><td>2,405</td><td>50</td><td>Tennessee</td><td>922</td></tr>
<tr><td></td><td></td><td></td><td></td><td>District of Columbia**</td><td>NA</td></tr>
</table>

Source: CQ Press using data from U.S. Bureau of the Census, Governments Division
   "2011 State and Local Government Finances" (http://www.census.gov/govs/local/)
*Includes short-term, long-term, full faith and credit, nonguaranteed, and public debt for private purposes.
**Not applicable.

State Government Full-Time Equivalent Employees in 2011

National Total = 4,359,380 FTE Employees*

ALPHA ORDER

RANK	STATE	EMPLOYEES	% of USA
16	Alabama	89,768	2.1%
40	Alaska	26,747	0.6%
26	Arizona	68,786	1.6%
29	Arkansas	62,562	1.4%
1	California	407,321	9.3%
24	Colorado	72,113	1.7%
30	Connecticut	62,090	1.4%
41	Delaware	26,215	0.6%
4	Florida	184,237	4.2%
12	Georgia	123,627	2.8%
31	Hawaii	58,142	1.3%
42	Idaho	21,773	0.5%
10	Illinois	131,153	3.0%
15	Indiana	89,796	2.1%
34	Iowa	50,378	1.2%
36	Kansas	43,555	1.0%
21	Kentucky	81,493	1.9%
20	Louisiana	84,402	1.9%
43	Maine	21,354	0.5%
18	Maryland	86,714	2.0%
14	Massachusetts	92,033	2.1%
8	Michigan	144,921	3.3%
22	Minnesota	79,672	1.8%
32	Mississippi	57,656	1.3%
17	Missouri	87,361	2.0%
44	Montana	20,795	0.5%
38	Nebraska	32,065	0.7%
39	Nevada	28,121	0.6%
45	New Hampshire	19,394	0.4%
7	New Jersey	146,801	3.4%
35	New Mexico	46,794	1.1%
3	New York	243,647	5.6%
6	North Carolina	154,364	3.5%
47	North Dakota	18,592	0.4%
9	Ohio	139,049	3.2%
27	Oklahoma	68,339	1.6%
28	Oregon	65,542	1.5%
5	Pennsylvania	168,548	3.9%
46	Rhode Island	18,900	0.4%
23	South Carolina	77,342	1.8%
48	South Dakota	14,458	0.3%
19	Tennessee	86,215	2.0%
2	Texas	318,370	7.3%
33	Utah	53,501	1.2%
49	Vermont	14,419	0.3%
11	Virginia	124,930	2.9%
13	Washington	121,136	2.8%
37	West Virginia	39,882	0.9%
25	Wisconsin	70,891	1.6%
50	Wyoming	13,416	0.3%

RANK ORDER

RANK	STATE	EMPLOYEES	% of USA
1	California	407,321	9.3%
2	Texas	318,370	7.3%
3	New York	243,647	5.6%
4	Florida	184,237	4.2%
5	Pennsylvania	168,548	3.9%
6	North Carolina	154,364	3.5%
7	New Jersey	146,801	3.4%
8	Michigan	144,921	3.3%
9	Ohio	139,049	3.2%
10	Illinois	131,153	3.0%
11	Virginia	124,930	2.9%
12	Georgia	123,627	2.8%
13	Washington	121,136	2.8%
14	Massachusetts	92,033	2.1%
15	Indiana	89,796	2.1%
16	Alabama	89,768	2.1%
17	Missouri	87,361	2.0%
18	Maryland	86,714	2.0%
19	Tennessee	86,215	2.0%
20	Louisiana	84,402	1.9%
21	Kentucky	81,493	1.9%
22	Minnesota	79,672	1.8%
23	South Carolina	77,342	1.8%
24	Colorado	72,113	1.7%
25	Wisconsin	70,891	1.6%
26	Arizona	68,786	1.6%
27	Oklahoma	68,339	1.6%
28	Oregon	65,542	1.5%
29	Arkansas	62,562	1.4%
30	Connecticut	62,090	1.4%
31	Hawaii	58,142	1.3%
32	Mississippi	57,656	1.3%
33	Utah	53,501	1.2%
34	Iowa	50,378	1.2%
35	New Mexico	46,794	1.1%
36	Kansas	43,555	1.0%
37	West Virginia	39,882	0.9%
38	Nebraska	32,065	0.7%
39	Nevada	28,121	0.6%
40	Alaska	26,747	0.6%
41	Delaware	26,215	0.6%
42	Idaho	21,773	0.5%
43	Maine	21,354	0.5%
44	Montana	20,795	0.5%
45	New Hampshire	19,394	0.4%
46	Rhode Island	18,900	0.4%
47	North Dakota	18,592	0.4%
48	South Dakota	14,458	0.3%
49	Vermont	14,419	0.3%
50	Wyoming	13,416	0.3%
	District of Columbia**	NA	NA

Source: U.S. Bureau of the Census, Governments Division
"Government Employment and Payroll" (http://www.census.gov/govs/apes/index.html)
*As of March 2011.
**Not applicable.

Rate of State Government Full-Time Equivalent Employees in 2011

National Rate = 140 State Government Employees per 10,000 Population*

ALPHA ORDER			RANK ORDER		
RANK	STATE	RATE	RANK	STATE	RATE
13	Alabama	187	1	Hawaii	422
2	Alaska	370	2	Alaska	370
47	Arizona	106	3	Delaware	289
9	Arkansas	213	4	North Dakota	272
46	California	108	5	Wyoming	236
35	Colorado	141	6	Vermont	230
21	Connecticut	173	7	New Mexico	225
3	Delaware	289	8	West Virginia	215
50	Florida	97	9	Arkansas	213
41	Georgia	126	10	Montana	208
1	Hawaii	422	11	Mississippi	194
38	Idaho	137	12	Utah	190
49	Illinois	102	13	Alabama	187
37	Indiana	138	13	Kentucky	187
25	Iowa	164	15	Louisiana	184
29	Kansas	152	16	Oklahoma	181
13	Kentucky	187	17	Rhode Island	180
15	Louisiana	184	18	Washington	178
26	Maine	161	19	South Dakota	176
31	Maryland	148	20	Nebraska	174
36	Massachusetts	139	21	Connecticut	173
32	Michigan	147	22	Oregon	169
30	Minnesota	149	23	New Jersey	166
11	Mississippi	194	24	South Carolina	165
34	Missouri	145	25	Iowa	164
10	Montana	208	26	Maine	161
20	Nebraska	174	27	North Carolina	160
48	Nevada	103	28	Virginia	154
32	New Hampshire	147	29	Kansas	152
23	New Jersey	166	30	Minnesota	149
7	New Mexico	225	31	Maryland	148
42	New York	125	32	Michigan	147
27	North Carolina	160	32	New Hampshire	147
4	North Dakota	272	34	Missouri	145
45	Ohio	120	35	Colorado	141
16	Oklahoma	181	36	Massachusetts	139
22	Oregon	169	37	Indiana	138
40	Pennsylvania	132	38	Idaho	137
17	Rhode Island	180	39	Tennessee	135
24	South Carolina	165	40	Pennsylvania	132
19	South Dakota	176	41	Georgia	126
39	Tennessee	135	42	New York	125
43	Texas	124	43	Texas	124
12	Utah	190	43	Wisconsin	124
6	Vermont	230	45	Ohio	120
28	Virginia	154	46	California	108
18	Washington	178	47	Arizona	106
8	West Virginia	215	48	Nevada	103
43	Wisconsin	124	49	Illinois	102
5	Wyoming	236	50	Florida	97
			District of Columbia**		NA

Source: CQ Press using data from U.S. Bureau of the Census, Governments Division
  "Government Employment and Payroll" (http://www.census.gov/govs/apes/index.html)
*Full-time equivalent as of March 2011.
**Not applicable.

Average Annual Earnings of Full-Time State Government Employees in 2011

National Average = $56,825*

ALPHA ORDER

RANK	STATE	SALARY
32	Alabama	$50,063
9	Alaska	63,739
24	Arizona	53,211
41	Arkansas	47,277
1	California	73,928
14	Colorado	60,525
3	Connecticut	70,388
30	Delaware	50,887
44	Florida	46,595
43	Georgia	46,883
37	Hawaii	48,286
22	Idaho	54,121
8	Illinois	65,179
33	Indiana	49,893
5	Iowa	67,310
31	Kansas	50,741
45	Kentucky	46,401
27	Louisiana	51,754
34	Maine	49,875
17	Maryland	56,434
11	Massachusetts	61,316
10	Michigan	63,650
7	Minnesota	65,246
48	Mississippi	44,281
50	Missouri	42,588
35	Montana	49,516
36	Nebraska	49,505
16	Nevada	58,272
19	New Hampshire	55,803
2	New Jersey	71,159
40	New Mexico	47,527
4	New York	68,145
39	North Carolina	47,560
28	North Dakota	51,063
13	Ohio	60,583
42	Oklahoma	46,962
20	Oregon	55,469
18	Pennsylvania	56,240
6	Rhode Island	65,796
46	South Carolina	45,592
38	South Dakota	47,650
47	Tennessee	44,620
25	Texas	52,705
23	Utah	53,250
21	Vermont	55,304
26	Virginia	52,481
12	Washington	61,028
49	West Virginia	43,421
15	Wisconsin	60,039
29	Wyoming	50,973

RANK ORDER

RANK	STATE	SALARY
1	California	$73,928
2	New Jersey	71,159
3	Connecticut	70,388
4	New York	68,145
5	Iowa	67,310
6	Rhode Island	65,796
7	Minnesota	65,246
8	Illinois	65,179
9	Alaska	63,739
10	Michigan	63,650
11	Massachusetts	61,316
12	Washington	61,028
13	Ohio	60,583
14	Colorado	60,525
15	Wisconsin	60,039
16	Nevada	58,272
17	Maryland	56,434
18	Pennsylvania	56,240
19	New Hampshire	55,803
20	Oregon	55,469
21	Vermont	55,304
22	Idaho	54,121
23	Utah	53,250
24	Arizona	53,211
25	Texas	52,705
26	Virginia	52,481
27	Louisiana	51,754
28	North Dakota	51,063
29	Wyoming	50,973
30	Delaware	50,887
31	Kansas	50,741
32	Alabama	50,063
33	Indiana	49,893
34	Maine	49,875
35	Montana	49,516
36	Nebraska	49,505
37	Hawaii	48,286
38	South Dakota	47,650
39	North Carolina	47,560
40	New Mexico	47,527
41	Arkansas	47,277
42	Oklahoma	46,962
43	Georgia	46,883
44	Florida	46,595
45	Kentucky	46,401
46	South Carolina	45,592
47	Tennessee	44,620
48	Mississippi	44,281
49	West Virginia	43,421
50	Missouri	42,588
	District of Columbia**	NA

Source: CQ Press using data from U.S. Bureau of the Census, Governments Division
    "Government Employment and Payroll" (http://www.census.gov/govs/apes/index.html)
*March 2011 full-time payroll (multiplied by 12) divided by full-time employees.
**Not applicable.

Local Government Total Revenue in 2011

National Total = $1,669,420,996,000*

ALPHA ORDER

ALPHA ORDER

RANK	STATE	REVENUE	% of USA
24	Alabama	$20,705,515,000	1.2%
41	Alaska	5,246,497,000	0.3%
17	Arizona	28,806,773,000	1.7%
36	Arkansas	9,832,080,000	0.6%
1	California	278,013,471,000	16.7%
16	Colorado	29,736,610,000	1.8%
27	Connecticut	17,624,161,000	1.1%
48	Delaware	3,221,109,000	0.2%
4	Florida	95,465,342,000	5.7%
10	Georgia	44,066,127,000	2.6%
46	Hawaii	3,271,098,000	0.2%
38	Idaho	5,666,197,000	0.3%
5	Illinois	71,336,467,000	4.3%
21	Indiana	27,354,430,000	1.6%
28	Iowa	15,240,763,000	0.9%
30	Kansas	13,972,569,000	0.8%
29	Kentucky	14,563,516,000	0.9%
23	Louisiana	21,949,574,000	1.3%
42	Maine	4,775,680,000	0.3%
19	Maryland	28,584,801,000	1.7%
14	Massachusetts	34,068,076,000	2.0%
8	Michigan	47,631,914,000	2.9%
18	Minnesota	28,652,509,000	1.7%
33	Mississippi	12,712,805,000	0.8%
22	Missouri	25,149,616,000	1.5%
45	Montana	3,512,643,000	0.2%
34	Nebraska	12,467,736,000	0.7%
32	Nevada	12,892,864,000	0.8%
40	New Hampshire	5,399,050,000	0.3%
9	New Jersey	46,411,965,000	2.8%
37	New Mexico	8,542,927,000	0.5%
2	New York	176,178,833,000	10.6%
11	North Carolina	42,852,468,000	2.6%
49	North Dakota	2,850,102,000	0.2%
7	Ohio	55,419,558,000	3.3%
31	Oklahoma	13,295,347,000	0.8%
26	Oregon	17,945,906,000	1.1%
6	Pennsylvania	63,998,283,000	3.8%
44	Rhode Island	4,426,503,000	0.3%
25	South Carolina	19,352,896,000	1.2%
47	South Dakota	3,261,447,000	0.2%
15	Tennessee	32,412,749,000	1.9%
3	Texas	121,552,443,000	7.3%
35	Utah	11,026,526,000	0.7%
50	Vermont	2,577,674,000	0.2%
13	Virginia	36,459,561,000	2.2%
12	Washington	38,165,146,000	2.3%
39	West Virginia	5,465,978,000	0.3%
20	Wisconsin	27,805,037,000	1.7%
43	Wyoming	4,621,793,000	0.3%

RANK ORDER

RANK	STATE	REVENUE	% of USA
1	California	$278,013,471,000	16.7%
2	New York	176,178,833,000	10.6%
3	Texas	121,552,443,000	7.3%
4	Florida	95,465,342,000	5.7%
5	Illinois	71,336,467,000	4.3%
6	Pennsylvania	63,998,283,000	3.8%
7	Ohio	55,419,558,000	3.3%
8	Michigan	47,631,914,000	2.9%
9	New Jersey	46,411,965,000	2.8%
10	Georgia	44,066,127,000	2.6%
11	North Carolina	42,852,468,000	2.6%
12	Washington	38,165,146,000	2.3%
13	Virginia	36,459,561,000	2.2%
14	Massachusetts	34,068,076,000	2.0%
15	Tennessee	32,412,749,000	1.9%
16	Colorado	29,736,610,000	1.8%
17	Arizona	28,806,773,000	1.7%
18	Minnesota	28,652,509,000	1.7%
19	Maryland	28,584,801,000	1.7%
20	Wisconsin	27,805,037,000	1.7%
21	Indiana	27,354,430,000	1.6%
22	Missouri	25,149,616,000	1.5%
23	Louisiana	21,949,574,000	1.3%
24	Alabama	20,705,515,000	1.2%
25	South Carolina	19,352,896,000	1.2%
26	Oregon	17,945,906,000	1.1%
27	Connecticut	17,624,161,000	1.1%
28	Iowa	15,240,763,000	0.9%
29	Kentucky	14,563,516,000	0.9%
30	Kansas	13,972,569,000	0.8%
31	Oklahoma	13,295,347,000	0.8%
32	Nevada	12,892,864,000	0.8%
33	Mississippi	12,712,805,000	0.8%
34	Nebraska	12,467,736,000	0.7%
35	Utah	11,026,526,000	0.7%
36	Arkansas	9,832,080,000	0.6%
37	New Mexico	8,542,927,000	0.5%
38	Idaho	5,666,197,000	0.3%
39	West Virginia	5,465,978,000	0.3%
40	New Hampshire	5,399,050,000	0.3%
41	Alaska	5,246,497,000	0.3%
42	Maine	4,775,680,000	0.3%
43	Wyoming	4,621,793,000	0.3%
44	Rhode Island	4,426,503,000	0.3%
45	Montana	3,512,643,000	0.2%
46	Hawaii	3,271,098,000	0.2%
47	South Dakota	3,261,447,000	0.2%
48	Delaware	3,221,109,000	0.2%
49	North Dakota	2,850,102,000	0.2%
50	Vermont	2,577,674,000	0.2%
	District of Columbia	12,877,861,000	0.8%

Source: U.S. Bureau of the Census, Governments Division
    "2011 State and Local Government Finances" (http://www.census.gov/govs/local/)
*Total revenue includes all money received from external sources. This includes taxes, intergovernmental transfers and
insurance trust revenue, and revenue from government owned utilities and other commercial or auxiliary enterprise.

Per Capita Local Government Total Revenue in 2011

National Per Capita = $5,358*

ALPHA ORDER			RANK ORDER		
RANK	STATE	PER CAPITA	RANK	STATE	PER CAPITA
30	Alabama	$4,310	1	New York	$9,034
4	Alaska	7,248	2	Wyoming	8,146
28	Arizona	4,454	3	California	7,378
47	Arkansas	3,346	4	Alaska	7,248
3	California	7,378	5	Nebraska	6,768
6	Colorado	5,812	6	Colorado	5,812
16	Connecticut	4,914	7	Washington	5,593
44	Delaware	3,547	8	Illinois	5,547
14	Florida	5,003	9	Minnesota	5,358
27	Georgia	4,491	10	New Jersey	5,253
50	Hawaii	2,374	11	Massachusetts	5,156
43	Idaho	3,578	12	Tennessee	5,065
8	Illinois	5,547	13	Pennsylvania	5,022
33	Indiana	4,198	14	Florida	5,003
15	Iowa	4,974	15	Iowa	4,974
19	Kansas	4,868	16	Connecticut	4,914
48	Kentucky	3,335	17	Maryland	4,895
22	Louisiana	4,798	18	Wisconsin	4,870
42	Maine	3,595	19	Kansas	4,868
17	Maryland	4,895	20	Michigan	4,823
11	Massachusetts	5,156	21	Ohio	4,802
20	Michigan	4,823	22	Louisiana	4,798
9	Minnesota	5,358	23	Texas	4,742
31	Mississippi	4,270	24	Nevada	4,740
34	Missouri	4,185	25	Oregon	4,639
45	Montana	3,521	26	Virginia	4,499
5	Nebraska	6,768	27	Georgia	4,491
24	Nevada	4,740	28	Arizona	4,454
39	New Hampshire	4,097	29	North Carolina	4,440
10	New Jersey	5,253	30	Alabama	4,310
38	New Mexico	4,110	31	Mississippi	4,270
1	New York	9,034	32	Rhode Island	4,213
29	North Carolina	4,440	33	Indiana	4,198
35	North Dakota	4,162	34	Missouri	4,185
21	Ohio	4,802	35	North Dakota	4,162
46	Oklahoma	3,513	36	South Carolina	4,141
25	Oregon	4,639	37	Vermont	4,114
13	Pennsylvania	5,022	38	New Mexico	4,110
32	Rhode Island	4,213	39	New Hampshire	4,097
36	South Carolina	4,141	40	South Dakota	3,960
40	South Dakota	3,960	41	Utah	3,918
12	Tennessee	5,065	42	Maine	3,595
23	Texas	4,742	43	Idaho	3,578
41	Utah	3,918	44	Delaware	3,547
37	Vermont	4,114	45	Montana	3,521
26	Virginia	4,499	46	Oklahoma	3,513
7	Washington	5,593	47	Arkansas	3,346
49	West Virginia	2,947	48	Kentucky	3,335
18	Wisconsin	4,870	49	West Virginia	2,947
2	Wyoming	8,146	50	Hawaii	2,374
				District of Columbia	20,804

Source: CQ Press using data from U.S. Bureau of the Census, Governments Division
"2011 State and Local Government Finances" (http://www.census.gov/govs/local/)
*Total revenue includes all money received from external sources. This includes taxes, intergovernmental transfers and insurance trust revenue, and revenue from government owned utilities and other commercial or auxiliary enterprise.

Local Government Revenue from the Federal Government in 2011

National Total = $72,558,179,000

RANK	STATE	REVENUE	% of USA
18	Alabama	$1,092,738,000	1.5%
37	Alaska	325,774,000	0.4%
20	Arizona	966,667,000	1.3%
35	Arkansas	418,010,000	0.6%
1	California	11,294,779,000	15.6%
15	Colorado	1,273,529,000	1.8%
30	Connecticut	649,087,000	0.9%
50	Delaware	72,859,000	0.1%
3	Florida	4,668,556,000	6.4%
12	Georgia	1,564,413,000	2.2%
40	Hawaii	269,656,000	0.4%
45	Idaho	192,896,000	0.3%
6	Illinois	3,308,226,000	4.6%
24	Indiana	746,230,000	1.0%
28	Iowa	702,499,000	1.0%
38	Kansas	287,588,000	0.4%
32	Kentucky	553,167,000	0.8%
16	Louisiana	1,212,434,000	1.7%
47	Maine	170,877,000	0.2%
14	Maryland	1,475,705,000	2.0%
11	Massachusetts	1,675,224,000	2.3%
9	Michigan	2,146,529,000	3.0%
22	Minnesota	920,989,000	1.3%
25	Mississippi	715,484,000	1.0%
23	Missouri	822,576,000	1.1%
41	Montana	262,117,000	0.4%
36	Nebraska	394,065,000	0.5%
26	Nevada	711,502,000	1.0%
46	New Hampshire	185,191,000	0.3%
19	New Jersey	1,091,886,000	1.5%
31	New Mexico	568,921,000	0.8%
2	New York	6,103,031,000	8.4%
8	North Carolina	2,278,463,000	3.1%
43	North Dakota	202,381,000	0.3%
7	Ohio	2,471,660,000	3.4%
34	Oklahoma	444,374,000	0.6%
17	Oregon	1,159,929,000	1.6%
5	Pennsylvania	3,489,115,000	4.8%
44	Rhode Island	201,554,000	0.3%
33	South Carolina	490,917,000	0.7%
42	South Dakota	204,469,000	0.3%
21	Tennessee	964,360,000	1.3%
4	Texas	4,518,628,000	6.2%
29	Utah	686,826,000	0.9%
49	Vermont	91,220,000	0.1%
13	Virginia	1,513,802,000	2.1%
10	Washington	1,748,567,000	2.4%
39	West Virginia	277,153,000	0.4%
27	Wisconsin	705,359,000	1.0%
48	Wyoming	149,607,000	0.2%

RANK	STATE	REVENUE	% of USA
1	California	$11,294,779,000	15.6%
2	New York	6,103,031,000	8.4%
3	Florida	4,668,556,000	6.4%
4	Texas	4,518,628,000	6.2%
5	Pennsylvania	3,489,115,000	4.8%
6	Illinois	3,308,226,000	4.6%
7	Ohio	2,471,660,000	3.4%
8	North Carolina	2,278,463,000	3.1%
9	Michigan	2,146,529,000	3.0%
10	Washington	1,748,567,000	2.4%
11	Massachusetts	1,675,224,000	2.3%
12	Georgia	1,564,413,000	2.2%
13	Virginia	1,513,802,000	2.1%
14	Maryland	1,475,705,000	2.0%
15	Colorado	1,273,529,000	1.8%
16	Louisiana	1,212,434,000	1.7%
17	Oregon	1,159,929,000	1.6%
18	Alabama	1,092,738,000	1.5%
19	New Jersey	1,091,886,000	1.5%
20	Arizona	966,667,000	1.3%
21	Tennessee	964,360,000	1.3%
22	Minnesota	920,989,000	1.3%
23	Missouri	822,576,000	1.1%
24	Indiana	746,230,000	1.0%
25	Mississippi	715,484,000	1.0%
26	Nevada	711,502,000	1.0%
27	Wisconsin	705,359,000	1.0%
28	Iowa	702,499,000	1.0%
29	Utah	686,826,000	0.9%
30	Connecticut	649,087,000	0.9%
31	New Mexico	568,921,000	0.8%
32	Kentucky	553,167,000	0.8%
33	South Carolina	490,917,000	0.7%
34	Oklahoma	444,374,000	0.6%
35	Arkansas	418,010,000	0.6%
36	Nebraska	394,065,000	0.5%
37	Alaska	325,774,000	0.4%
38	Kansas	287,588,000	0.4%
39	West Virginia	277,153,000	0.4%
40	Hawaii	269,656,000	0.4%
41	Montana	262,117,000	0.4%
42	South Dakota	204,469,000	0.3%
43	North Dakota	202,381,000	0.3%
44	Rhode Island	201,554,000	0.3%
45	Idaho	192,896,000	0.3%
46	New Hampshire	185,191,000	0.3%
47	Maine	170,877,000	0.2%
48	Wyoming	149,607,000	0.2%
49	Vermont	91,220,000	0.1%
50	Delaware	72,859,000	0.1%
	District of Columbia	4,116,590,000	5.7%

Source: U.S. Bureau of the Census, Governments Division
"2011 State and Local Government Finances" (http://www.census.gov/govs/local/)

Per Capita Local Government Revenue from the Federal Government in 2011

National Per Capita = $233

ALPHA ORDER

RANK	STATE	PER CAPITA
23	Alabama	$227
1	Alaska	450
35	Arizona	149
38	Arkansas	142
3	California	300
16	Colorado	249
30	Connecticut	181
50	Delaware	80
18	Florida	245
33	Georgia	159
27	Hawaii	196
45	Idaho	122
12	Illinois	257
47	Indiana	115
22	Iowa	229
49	Kansas	100
42	Kentucky	127
8	Louisiana	265
41	Maine	129
15	Maryland	253
14	Massachusetts	254
24	Michigan	217
32	Minnesota	172
20	Mississippi	240
40	Missouri	137
10	Montana	263
25	Nebraska	214
11	Nevada	262
39	New Hampshire	141
43	New Jersey	124
6	New Mexico	274
2	New York	313
21	North Carolina	236
5	North Dakota	296
25	Ohio	214
46	Oklahoma	117
3	Oregon	300
6	Pennsylvania	274
28	Rhode Island	192
48	South Carolina	105
17	South Dakota	248
34	Tennessee	151
31	Texas	176
19	Utah	244
37	Vermont	146
29	Virginia	187
13	Washington	256
35	West Virginia	149
43	Wisconsin	124
9	Wyoming	264

RANK ORDER

RANK	STATE	PER CAPITA
1	Alaska	$450
2	New York	313
3	California	300
3	Oregon	300
5	North Dakota	296
6	New Mexico	274
6	Pennsylvania	274
8	Louisiana	265
9	Wyoming	264
10	Montana	263
11	Nevada	262
12	Illinois	257
13	Washington	256
14	Massachusetts	254
15	Maryland	253
16	Colorado	249
17	South Dakota	248
18	Florida	245
19	Utah	244
20	Mississippi	240
21	North Carolina	236
22	Iowa	229
23	Alabama	227
24	Michigan	217
25	Nebraska	214
25	Ohio	214
27	Hawaii	196
28	Rhode Island	192
29	Virginia	187
30	Connecticut	181
31	Texas	176
32	Minnesota	172
33	Georgia	159
34	Tennessee	151
35	Arizona	149
35	West Virginia	149
37	Vermont	146
38	Arkansas	142
39	New Hampshire	141
40	Missouri	137
41	Maine	129
42	Kentucky	127
43	New Jersey	124
43	Wisconsin	124
45	Idaho	122
46	Oklahoma	117
47	Indiana	115
48	South Carolina	105
49	Kansas	100
50	Delaware	80

District of Columbia	6,650

Source: CQ Press using data from U.S. Bureau of the Census, Governments Division
"2011 State and Local Government Finances" (http://www.census.gov/govs/local/)

Local Government Own Source Revenue in 2011

National Total = $905,499,340,000*

ALPHA ORDER

RANK	STATE	REVENUE	% of USA
26	Alabama	$10,588,116,000	1.2%
42	Alaska	2,833,957,000	0.3%
18	Arizona	14,882,247,000	1.6%
36	Arkansas	3,702,546,000	0.4%
1	California	125,296,831,000	13.8%
14	Colorado	19,202,130,000	2.1%
25	Connecticut	10,816,232,000	1.2%
49	Delaware	1,302,699,000	0.1%
4	Florida	59,364,427,000	6.6%
9	Georgia	25,649,666,000	2.8%
45	Hawaii	2,446,581,000	0.3%
39	Idaho	3,233,069,000	0.4%
5	Illinois	39,770,326,000	4.4%
17	Indiana	15,168,191,000	1.7%
28	Iowa	8,988,676,000	1.0%
29	Kansas	8,332,428,000	0.9%
30	Kentucky	7,682,555,000	0.8%
23	Louisiana	12,513,989,000	1.4%
40	Maine	3,072,220,000	0.3%
16	Maryland	16,977,798,000	1.9%
15	Massachusetts	18,620,777,000	2.1%
11	Michigan	21,549,843,000	2.4%
21	Minnesota	14,583,425,000	1.6%
33	Mississippi	6,532,169,000	0.7%
19	Missouri	14,717,609,000	1.6%
46	Montana	1,918,124,000	0.2%
34	Nebraska	5,657,555,000	0.6%
32	Nevada	6,894,063,000	0.8%
38	New Hampshire	3,555,368,000	0.4%
7	New Jersey	32,707,752,000	3.6%
37	New Mexico	3,563,476,000	0.4%
2	New York	102,242,032,000	11.3%
10	North Carolina	23,219,158,000	2.6%
48	North Dakota	1,501,646,000	0.2%
8	Ohio	29,939,763,000	3.3%
31	Oklahoma	7,231,317,000	0.8%
27	Oregon	9,810,813,000	1.1%
6	Pennsylvania	33,869,278,000	3.7%
43	Rhode Island	2,816,459,000	0.3%
24	South Carolina	12,507,434,000	1.4%
47	South Dakota	1,902,266,000	0.2%
22	Tennessee	14,258,863,000	1.6%
3	Texas	70,929,455,000	7.8%
35	Utah	5,599,516,000	0.6%
50	Vermont	755,266,000	0.1%
12	Virginia	20,494,358,000	2.3%
13	Washington	19,555,810,000	2.2%
41	West Virginia	2,878,308,000	0.3%
20	Wisconsin	14,635,097,000	1.6%
44	Wyoming	2,570,212,000	0.3%

RANK ORDER

RANK	STATE	REVENUE	% of USA
1	California	$125,296,831,000	13.8%
2	New York	102,242,032,000	11.3%
3	Texas	70,929,455,000	7.8%
4	Florida	59,364,427,000	6.6%
5	Illinois	39,770,326,000	4.4%
6	Pennsylvania	33,869,278,000	3.7%
7	New Jersey	32,707,752,000	3.6%
8	Ohio	29,939,763,000	3.3%
9	Georgia	25,649,666,000	2.8%
10	North Carolina	23,219,158,000	2.6%
11	Michigan	21,549,843,000	2.4%
12	Virginia	20,494,358,000	2.3%
13	Washington	19,555,810,000	2.2%
14	Colorado	19,202,130,000	2.1%
15	Massachusetts	18,620,777,000	2.1%
16	Maryland	16,977,798,000	1.9%
17	Indiana	15,168,191,000	1.7%
18	Arizona	14,882,247,000	1.6%
19	Missouri	14,717,609,000	1.6%
20	Wisconsin	14,635,097,000	1.6%
21	Minnesota	14,583,425,000	1.6%
22	Tennessee	14,258,863,000	1.6%
23	Louisiana	12,513,989,000	1.4%
24	South Carolina	12,507,434,000	1.4%
25	Connecticut	10,816,232,000	1.2%
26	Alabama	10,588,116,000	1.2%
27	Oregon	9,810,813,000	1.1%
28	Iowa	8,988,676,000	1.0%
29	Kansas	8,332,428,000	0.9%
30	Kentucky	7,682,555,000	0.8%
31	Oklahoma	7,231,317,000	0.8%
32	Nevada	6,894,063,000	0.8%
33	Mississippi	6,532,169,000	0.7%
34	Nebraska	5,657,555,000	0.6%
35	Utah	5,599,516,000	0.6%
36	Arkansas	3,702,546,000	0.4%
37	New Mexico	3,563,476,000	0.4%
38	New Hampshire	3,555,368,000	0.4%
39	Idaho	3,233,069,000	0.4%
40	Maine	3,072,220,000	0.3%
41	West Virginia	2,878,308,000	0.3%
42	Alaska	2,833,957,000	0.3%
43	Rhode Island	2,816,459,000	0.3%
44	Wyoming	2,570,212,000	0.3%
45	Hawaii	2,446,581,000	0.3%
46	Montana	1,918,124,000	0.2%
47	South Dakota	1,902,266,000	0.2%
48	North Dakota	1,501,646,000	0.2%
49	Delaware	1,302,699,000	0.1%
50	Vermont	755,266,000	0.1%
	District of Columbia	6,657,444,000	0.7%

Source: U.S. Bureau of the Census, Governments Division
"2011 State and Local Government Finances" (http://www.census.gov/govs/local/)
*Own source revenue includes taxes, current charges, and miscellaneous general revenue. Excluded are intergovernmental transfers, insurance trust revenue, and revenue from government owned utilities and other commercial or auxiliary enterprise.

Per Capita Local Government Own Source Revenue in 2011

National Per Capita = $2,906*

ALPHA ORDER

RANK	STATE	PER CAPITA	RANK	STATE	PER CAPITA
36	Alabama	$2,204	1	New York	$5,243
3	Alaska	3,915	2	Wyoming	4,530
34	Arizona	2,301	3	Alaska	3,915
49	Arkansas	1,260	4	Colorado	3,753
6	California	3,325	5	New Jersey	3,702
4	Colorado	3,753	6	California	3,325
10	Connecticut	3,016	7	Florida	3,111
48	Delaware	1,434	8	Illinois	3,093
7	Florida	3,111	9	Nebraska	3,071
23	Georgia	2,614	10	Connecticut	3,016
44	Hawaii	1,775	11	Iowa	2,934
40	Idaho	2,041	12	Maryland	2,907
8	Illinois	3,093	13	Kansas	2,903
31	Indiana	2,328	14	Washington	2,866
11	Iowa	2,934	15	Massachusetts	2,818
13	Kansas	2,903	16	Texas	2,767
45	Kentucky	1,759	17	Louisiana	2,735
17	Louisiana	2,735	18	Minnesota	2,727
32	Maine	2,312	19	New Hampshire	2,698
12	Maryland	2,907	20	Rhode Island	2,681
15	Massachusetts	2,818	21	South Carolina	2,676
39	Michigan	2,182	22	Pennsylvania	2,658
18	Minnesota	2,727	23	Georgia	2,614
37	Mississippi	2,194	24	Ohio	2,594
29	Missouri	2,449	25	Wisconsin	2,563
42	Montana	1,923	26	Oregon	2,536
9	Nebraska	3,071	27	Nevada	2,535
27	Nevada	2,535	28	Virginia	2,529
19	New Hampshire	2,698	29	Missouri	2,449
5	New Jersey	3,702	30	North Carolina	2,406
46	New Mexico	1,714	31	Indiana	2,328
1	New York	5,243	32	Maine	2,312
30	North Carolina	2,406	33	South Dakota	2,310
38	North Dakota	2,193	34	Arizona	2,301
24	Ohio	2,594	35	Tennessee	2,228
43	Oklahoma	1,911	36	Alabama	2,204
26	Oregon	2,536	37	Mississippi	2,194
22	Pennsylvania	2,658	38	North Dakota	2,193
20	Rhode Island	2,681	39	Michigan	2,182
21	South Carolina	2,676	40	Idaho	2,041
33	South Dakota	2,310	41	Utah	1,990
35	Tennessee	2,228	42	Montana	1,923
16	Texas	2,767	43	Oklahoma	1,911
41	Utah	1,990	44	Hawaii	1,775
50	Vermont	1,205	45	Kentucky	1,759
28	Virginia	2,529	46	New Mexico	1,714
14	Washington	2,866	47	West Virginia	1,552
47	West Virginia	1,552	48	Delaware	1,434
25	Wisconsin	2,563	49	Arkansas	1,260
2	Wyoming	4,530	50	Vermont	1,205
				District of Columbia	10,755

Source: CQ Press using data from U.S. Bureau of the Census, Governments Division
   "2011 State and Local Government Finances" (http://www.census.gov/govs/local/)
*Own source revenue includes taxes, current charges, and miscellaneous general revenue. Excluded are intergovernmental transfers, insurance trust revenue, and revenue from government owned utilities and other commercial or auxiliary enterprise.

Local Government Tax Revenue in 2011

National Total = $578,177,391,000

ALPHA ORDER

ALPHA ORDER

RANK	STATE	REVENUE	% of USA
28	Alabama	$5,243,047,000	0.9%
42	Alaska	1,754,476,000	0.3%
19	Arizona	9,390,279,000	1.6%
40	Arkansas	1,996,880,000	0.3%
2	California	68,522,924,000	11.9%
14	Colorado	12,324,184,000	2.1%
20	Connecticut	9,353,756,000	1.6%
49	Delaware	810,658,000	0.1%
4	Florida	32,700,603,000	5.7%
9	Georgia	15,129,493,000	2.6%
43	Hawaii	1,715,020,000	0.3%
44	Idaho	1,449,687,000	0.3%
5	Illinois	28,945,752,000	5.0%
21	Indiana	8,243,067,000	1.4%
27	Iowa	5,412,653,000	0.9%
29	Kansas	4,959,381,000	0.9%
30	Kentucky	4,357,618,000	0.8%
24	Louisiana	7,746,964,000	1.3%
37	Maine	2,378,204,000	0.4%
12	Maryland	13,013,566,000	2.3%
11	Massachusetts	13,753,911,000	2.4%
13	Michigan	12,572,577,000	2.2%
23	Minnesota	7,869,831,000	1.4%
36	Mississippi	2,719,389,000	0.5%
18	Missouri	9,531,932,000	1.6%
47	Montana	1,131,096,000	0.2%
33	Nebraska	3,647,436,000	0.6%
32	Nevada	3,882,192,000	0.7%
35	New Hampshire	2,970,133,000	0.5%
6	New Jersey	25,967,187,000	4.5%
38	New Mexico	2,364,663,000	0.4%
1	New York	76,788,844,000	13.3%
15	North Carolina	11,310,041,000	2.0%
48	North Dakota	887,003,000	0.2%
8	Ohio	20,105,645,000	3.5%
31	Oklahoma	4,234,439,000	0.7%
26	Oregon	5,991,950,000	1.0%
7	Pennsylvania	23,418,652,000	4.1%
39	Rhode Island	2,325,842,000	0.4%
25	South Carolina	6,056,306,000	1.0%
45	South Dakota	1,319,547,000	0.2%
22	Tennessee	7,869,998,000	1.4%
3	Texas	47,632,085,000	8.2%
34	Utah	3,581,230,000	0.6%
50	Vermont	452,193,000	0.1%
10	Virginia	14,743,900,000	2.6%
16	Washington	10,998,624,000	1.9%
41	West Virginia	1,764,336,000	0.3%
17	Wisconsin	10,258,059,000	1.8%
46	Wyoming	1,211,335,000	0.2%

RANK ORDER

RANK	STATE	REVENUE	% of USA
1	New York	$76,788,844,000	13.3%
2	California	68,522,924,000	11.9%
3	Texas	47,632,085,000	8.2%
4	Florida	32,700,603,000	5.7%
5	Illinois	28,945,752,000	5.0%
6	New Jersey	25,967,187,000	4.5%
7	Pennsylvania	23,418,652,000	4.1%
8	Ohio	20,105,645,000	3.5%
9	Georgia	15,129,493,000	2.6%
10	Virginia	14,743,900,000	2.6%
11	Massachusetts	13,753,911,000	2.4%
12	Maryland	13,013,566,000	2.3%
13	Michigan	12,572,577,000	2.2%
14	Colorado	12,324,184,000	2.1%
15	North Carolina	11,310,041,000	2.0%
16	Washington	10,998,624,000	1.9%
17	Wisconsin	10,258,059,000	1.8%
18	Missouri	9,531,932,000	1.6%
19	Arizona	9,390,279,000	1.6%
20	Connecticut	9,353,756,000	1.6%
21	Indiana	8,243,067,000	1.4%
22	Tennessee	7,869,998,000	1.4%
23	Minnesota	7,869,831,000	1.4%
24	Louisiana	7,746,964,000	1.3%
25	South Carolina	6,056,306,000	1.0%
26	Oregon	5,991,950,000	1.0%
27	Iowa	5,412,653,000	0.9%
28	Alabama	5,243,047,000	0.9%
29	Kansas	4,959,381,000	0.9%
30	Kentucky	4,357,618,000	0.8%
31	Oklahoma	4,234,439,000	0.7%
32	Nevada	3,882,192,000	0.7%
33	Nebraska	3,647,436,000	0.6%
34	Utah	3,581,230,000	0.6%
35	New Hampshire	2,970,133,000	0.5%
36	Mississippi	2,719,389,000	0.5%
37	Maine	2,378,204,000	0.4%
38	New Mexico	2,364,663,000	0.4%
39	Rhode Island	2,325,842,000	0.4%
40	Arkansas	1,996,880,000	0.3%
41	West Virginia	1,764,336,000	0.3%
42	Alaska	1,754,476,000	0.3%
43	Hawaii	1,715,020,000	0.3%
44	Idaho	1,449,687,000	0.3%
45	South Dakota	1,319,547,000	0.2%
46	Wyoming	1,211,335,000	0.2%
47	Montana	1,131,096,000	0.2%
48	North Dakota	887,003,000	0.2%
49	Delaware	810,658,000	0.1%
50	Vermont	452,193,000	0.1%
	District of Columbia	5,368,803,000	0.9%

Source: U.S. Bureau of the Census, Governments Division
"2011 State and Local Government Finances" (http://www.census.gov/govs/local/)

Per Capita Local Government Tax Revenue in 2011

National Per Capita = $1,856

ALPHA ORDER

RANK	STATE	PER CAPITA
43	Alabama	$1,091
4	Alaska	2,424
30	Arizona	1,452
50	Arkansas	680
16	California	1,818
5	Colorado	2,409
3	Connecticut	2,608
48	Delaware	893
22	Florida	1,714
28	Georgia	1,542
37	Hawaii	1,244
46	Idaho	915
7	Illinois	2,251
36	Indiana	1,265
19	Iowa	1,766
21	Kansas	1,728
44	Kentucky	998
23	Louisiana	1,693
18	Maine	1,790
8	Maryland	2,229
11	Massachusetts	2,082
34	Michigan	1,273
29	Minnesota	1,472
47	Mississippi	913
26	Missouri	1,586
41	Montana	1,134
12	Nebraska	1,980
31	Nevada	1,427
6	New Hampshire	2,254
2	New Jersey	2,939
40	New Mexico	1,138
1	New York	3,938
39	North Carolina	1,172
33	North Dakota	1,295
20	Ohio	1,742
42	Oklahoma	1,119
27	Oregon	1,549
14	Pennsylvania	1,838
9	Rhode Island	2,214
32	South Carolina	1,296
25	South Dakota	1,602
38	Tennessee	1,230
13	Texas	1,858
35	Utah	1,272
49	Vermont	722
15	Virginia	1,819
24	Washington	1,612
45	West Virginia	951
17	Wisconsin	1,797
10	Wyoming	2,135

RANK ORDER

RANK	STATE	PER CAPITA
1	New York	$3,938
2	New Jersey	2,939
3	Connecticut	2,608
4	Alaska	2,424
5	Colorado	2,409
6	New Hampshire	2,254
7	Illinois	2,251
8	Maryland	2,229
9	Rhode Island	2,214
10	Wyoming	2,135
11	Massachusetts	2,082
12	Nebraska	1,980
13	Texas	1,858
14	Pennsylvania	1,838
15	Virginia	1,819
16	California	1,818
17	Wisconsin	1,797
18	Maine	1,790
19	Iowa	1,766
20	Ohio	1,742
21	Kansas	1,728
22	Florida	1,714
23	Louisiana	1,693
24	Washington	1,612
25	South Dakota	1,602
26	Missouri	1,586
27	Oregon	1,549
28	Georgia	1,542
29	Minnesota	1,472
30	Arizona	1,452
31	Nevada	1,427
32	South Carolina	1,296
33	North Dakota	1,295
34	Michigan	1,273
35	Utah	1,272
36	Indiana	1,265
37	Hawaii	1,244
38	Tennessee	1,230
39	North Carolina	1,172
40	New Mexico	1,138
41	Montana	1,134
42	Oklahoma	1,119
43	Alabama	1,091
44	Kentucky	998
45	West Virginia	951
46	Idaho	915
47	Mississippi	913
48	Delaware	893
49	Vermont	722
50	Arkansas	680

District of Columbia   8,673

Source: CQ Press using data from U.S. Bureau of the Census, Governments Division
"2011 State and Local Government Finances" (http://www.census.gov/govs/local/)

Local Government Total Expenditures in 2011

National Total = $1,664,493,675,000*

ALPHA ORDER

RANK	STATE	EXPENDITURES	% of USA
24	Alabama	$20,930,846,000	1.3%
41	Alaska	5,089,936,000	0.3%
17	Arizona	28,490,919,000	1.7%
36	Arkansas	10,068,451,000	0.6%
1	California	264,385,783,000	15.9%
16	Colorado	29,540,236,000	1.8%
27	Connecticut	17,072,375,000	1.0%
47	Delaware	3,255,320,000	0.2%
4	Florida	99,516,831,000	6.0%
10	Georgia	43,986,680,000	2.6%
48	Hawaii	3,121,124,000	0.2%
39	Idaho	5,370,342,000	0.3%
5	Illinois	71,832,853,000	4.3%
21	Indiana	26,666,866,000	1.6%
28	Iowa	15,638,247,000	0.9%
30	Kansas	14,054,702,000	0.8%
29	Kentucky	14,773,793,000	0.9%
23	Louisiana	21,950,803,000	1.3%
42	Maine	4,815,473,000	0.3%
19	Maryland	28,162,561,000	1.7%
14	Massachusetts	32,680,752,000	2.0%
8	Michigan	46,803,227,000	2.8%
18	Minnesota	28,396,919,000	1.7%
34	Mississippi	12,404,929,000	0.7%
22	Missouri	25,095,876,000	1.5%
45	Montana	3,541,586,000	0.2%
33	Nebraska	12,433,533,000	0.7%
31	Nevada	13,997,084,000	0.8%
40	New Hampshire	5,249,410,000	0.3%
9	New Jersey	45,696,118,000	2.7%
37	New Mexico	8,909,817,000	0.5%
2	New York	183,668,748,000	11.0%
11	North Carolina	41,540,149,000	2.5%
49	North Dakota	2,927,586,000	0.2%
7	Ohio	55,973,542,000	3.4%
32	Oklahoma	12,760,087,000	0.8%
26	Oregon	18,374,983,000	1.1%
6	Pennsylvania	61,901,587,000	3.7%
44	Rhode Island	4,248,226,000	0.3%
25	South Carolina	19,048,447,000	1.1%
46	South Dakota	3,290,451,000	0.2%
15	Tennessee	31,413,686,000	1.9%
3	Texas	125,844,891,000	7.6%
35	Utah	11,386,104,000	0.7%
50	Vermont	2,621,864,000	0.2%
13	Virginia	35,200,193,000	2.1%
12	Washington	38,311,888,000	2.3%
38	West Virginia	5,937,445,000	0.4%
20	Wisconsin	27,807,304,000	1.7%
43	Wyoming	4,661,812,000	0.3%

RANK ORDER

RANK	STATE	EXPENDITURES	% of USA
1	California	$264,385,783,000	15.9%
2	New York	183,668,748,000	11.0%
3	Texas	125,844,891,000	7.6%
4	Florida	99,516,831,000	6.0%
5	Illinois	71,832,853,000	4.3%
6	Pennsylvania	61,901,587,000	3.7%
7	Ohio	55,973,542,000	3.4%
8	Michigan	46,803,227,000	2.8%
9	New Jersey	45,696,118,000	2.7%
10	Georgia	43,986,680,000	2.6%
11	North Carolina	41,540,149,000	2.5%
12	Washington	38,311,888,000	2.3%
13	Virginia	35,200,193,000	2.1%
14	Massachusetts	32,680,752,000	2.0%
15	Tennessee	31,413,686,000	1.9%
16	Colorado	29,540,236,000	1.8%
17	Arizona	28,490,919,000	1.7%
18	Minnesota	28,396,919,000	1.7%
19	Maryland	28,162,561,000	1.7%
20	Wisconsin	27,807,304,000	1.7%
21	Indiana	26,666,866,000	1.6%
22	Missouri	25,095,876,000	1.5%
23	Louisiana	21,950,803,000	1.3%
24	Alabama	20,930,846,000	1.3%
25	South Carolina	19,048,447,000	1.1%
26	Oregon	18,374,983,000	1.1%
27	Connecticut	17,072,375,000	1.0%
28	Iowa	15,638,247,000	0.9%
29	Kentucky	14,773,793,000	0.9%
30	Kansas	14,054,702,000	0.8%
31	Nevada	13,997,084,000	0.8%
32	Oklahoma	12,760,087,000	0.8%
33	Nebraska	12,433,533,000	0.7%
34	Mississippi	12,404,929,000	0.7%
35	Utah	11,386,104,000	0.7%
36	Arkansas	10,068,451,000	0.6%
37	New Mexico	8,909,817,000	0.5%
38	West Virginia	5,937,445,000	0.4%
39	Idaho	5,370,342,000	0.3%
40	New Hampshire	5,249,410,000	0.3%
41	Alaska	5,089,936,000	0.3%
42	Maine	4,815,473,000	0.3%
43	Wyoming	4,661,812,000	0.3%
44	Rhode Island	4,248,226,000	0.3%
45	Montana	3,541,586,000	0.2%
46	South Dakota	3,290,451,000	0.2%
47	Delaware	3,255,320,000	0.2%
48	Hawaii	3,121,124,000	0.2%
49	North Dakota	2,927,586,000	0.2%
50	Vermont	2,621,864,000	0.2%
	District of Columbia	13,641,290,000	0.8%

Source: U.S. Bureau of the Census, Governments Division
"2011 State and Local Government Finances" (http://www.census.gov/govs/local/)
*Total expenditures includes all money paid other than for retirement of debt and extension of loans. Includes payments from all sources of funds including current revenues and proceeds from borrowing and prior year fund balances. Includes intergovernmental transfers and expenditures for government owned utilities and other commercial or auxiliary enterprise and insurance trust expenditures.

Per Capita Local Government Total Expenditures in 2011

National Per Capita = $5,342*

<table>
<tr><td colspan="3">ALPHA ORDER</td><td colspan="3">RANK ORDER</td></tr>
<tr><td>RANK</td><td>STATE</td><td>PER CAPITA</td><td>RANK</td><td>STATE</td><td>PER CAPITA</td></tr>
<tr><td>28</td><td>Alabama</td><td>$4,357</td><td>1</td><td>New York</td><td>$9,418</td></tr>
<tr><td>3</td><td>Alaska</td><td>7,032</td><td>2</td><td>Wyoming</td><td>8,217</td></tr>
<tr><td>27</td><td>Arizona</td><td>4,405</td><td>3</td><td>Alaska</td><td>7,032</td></tr>
<tr><td>45</td><td>Arkansas</td><td>3,426</td><td>4</td><td>California</td><td>7,016</td></tr>
<tr><td>4</td><td>California</td><td>7,016</td><td>5</td><td>Nebraska</td><td>6,749</td></tr>
<tr><td>6</td><td>Colorado</td><td>5,774</td><td>6</td><td>Colorado</td><td>5,774</td></tr>
<tr><td>23</td><td>Connecticut</td><td>4,760</td><td>7</td><td>Washington</td><td>5,615</td></tr>
<tr><td>43</td><td>Delaware</td><td>3,585</td><td>8</td><td>Illinois</td><td>5,586</td></tr>
<tr><td>10</td><td>Florida</td><td>5,215</td><td>9</td><td>Minnesota</td><td>5,311</td></tr>
<tr><td>26</td><td>Georgia</td><td>4,483</td><td>10</td><td>Florida</td><td>5,215</td></tr>
<tr><td>50</td><td>Hawaii</td><td>2,265</td><td>11</td><td>New Jersey</td><td>5,172</td></tr>
<tr><td>46</td><td>Idaho</td><td>3,391</td><td>12</td><td>Nevada</td><td>5,146</td></tr>
<tr><td>8</td><td>Illinois</td><td>5,586</td><td>13</td><td>Iowa</td><td>5,104</td></tr>
<tr><td>36</td><td>Indiana</td><td>4,092</td><td>14</td><td>Massachusetts</td><td>4,946</td></tr>
<tr><td>13</td><td>Iowa</td><td>5,104</td><td>15</td><td>Texas</td><td>4,910</td></tr>
<tr><td>17</td><td>Kansas</td><td>4,896</td><td>16</td><td>Tennessee</td><td>4,909</td></tr>
<tr><td>47</td><td>Kentucky</td><td>3,383</td><td>17</td><td>Kansas</td><td>4,896</td></tr>
<tr><td>22</td><td>Louisiana</td><td>4,798</td><td>18</td><td>Wisconsin</td><td>4,870</td></tr>
<tr><td>42</td><td>Maine</td><td>3,625</td><td>19</td><td>Pennsylvania</td><td>4,857</td></tr>
<tr><td>21</td><td>Maryland</td><td>4,823</td><td>20</td><td>Ohio</td><td>4,850</td></tr>
<tr><td>14</td><td>Massachusetts</td><td>4,946</td><td>21</td><td>Maryland</td><td>4,823</td></tr>
<tr><td>25</td><td>Michigan</td><td>4,739</td><td>22</td><td>Louisiana</td><td>4,798</td></tr>
<tr><td>9</td><td>Minnesota</td><td>5,311</td><td>23</td><td>Connecticut</td><td>4,760</td></tr>
<tr><td>35</td><td>Mississippi</td><td>4,166</td><td>24</td><td>Oregon</td><td>4,750</td></tr>
<tr><td>34</td><td>Missouri</td><td>4,176</td><td>25</td><td>Michigan</td><td>4,739</td></tr>
<tr><td>44</td><td>Montana</td><td>3,550</td><td>26</td><td>Georgia</td><td>4,483</td></tr>
<tr><td>5</td><td>Nebraska</td><td>6,749</td><td>27</td><td>Arizona</td><td>4,405</td></tr>
<tr><td>12</td><td>Nevada</td><td>5,146</td><td>28</td><td>Alabama</td><td>4,357</td></tr>
<tr><td>41</td><td>New Hampshire</td><td>3,983</td><td>29</td><td>Virginia</td><td>4,343</td></tr>
<tr><td>11</td><td>New Jersey</td><td>5,172</td><td>30</td><td>North Carolina</td><td>4,304</td></tr>
<tr><td>31</td><td>New Mexico</td><td>4,286</td><td>31</td><td>New Mexico</td><td>4,286</td></tr>
<tr><td>1</td><td>New York</td><td>9,418</td><td>32</td><td>North Dakota</td><td>4,275</td></tr>
<tr><td>30</td><td>North Carolina</td><td>4,304</td><td>33</td><td>Vermont</td><td>4,184</td></tr>
<tr><td>32</td><td>North Dakota</td><td>4,275</td><td>34</td><td>Missouri</td><td>4,176</td></tr>
<tr><td>20</td><td>Ohio</td><td>4,850</td><td>35</td><td>Mississippi</td><td>4,166</td></tr>
<tr><td>48</td><td>Oklahoma</td><td>3,372</td><td>36</td><td>Indiana</td><td>4,092</td></tr>
<tr><td>24</td><td>Oregon</td><td>4,750</td><td>37</td><td>South Carolina</td><td>4,076</td></tr>
<tr><td>19</td><td>Pennsylvania</td><td>4,857</td><td>38</td><td>Utah</td><td>4,046</td></tr>
<tr><td>39</td><td>Rhode Island</td><td>4,043</td><td>39</td><td>Rhode Island</td><td>4,043</td></tr>
<tr><td>37</td><td>South Carolina</td><td>4,076</td><td>40</td><td>South Dakota</td><td>3,995</td></tr>
<tr><td>40</td><td>South Dakota</td><td>3,995</td><td>41</td><td>New Hampshire</td><td>3,983</td></tr>
<tr><td>16</td><td>Tennessee</td><td>4,909</td><td>42</td><td>Maine</td><td>3,625</td></tr>
<tr><td>15</td><td>Texas</td><td>4,910</td><td>43</td><td>Delaware</td><td>3,585</td></tr>
<tr><td>38</td><td>Utah</td><td>4,046</td><td>44</td><td>Montana</td><td>3,550</td></tr>
<tr><td>33</td><td>Vermont</td><td>4,184</td><td>45</td><td>Arkansas</td><td>3,426</td></tr>
<tr><td>29</td><td>Virginia</td><td>4,343</td><td>46</td><td>Idaho</td><td>3,391</td></tr>
<tr><td>7</td><td>Washington</td><td>5,615</td><td>47</td><td>Kentucky</td><td>3,383</td></tr>
<tr><td>49</td><td>West Virginia</td><td>3,201</td><td>48</td><td>Oklahoma</td><td>3,372</td></tr>
<tr><td>18</td><td>Wisconsin</td><td>4,870</td><td>49</td><td>West Virginia</td><td>3,201</td></tr>
<tr><td>2</td><td>Wyoming</td><td>8,217</td><td>50</td><td>Hawaii</td><td>2,265</td></tr>
<tr><td></td><td></td><td></td><td></td><td>District of Columbia</td><td>22,037</td></tr>
</table>

Source: CQ Press using data from U.S. Bureau of the Census, Governments Division
"2011 State and Local Government Finances" (http://www.census.gov/govs/local/)
*Total expenditures includes all money paid other than for retirement of debt and extension of loans. Includes payments from all sources of funds including current revenues and proceeds from borrowing and prior year fund balances. Includes intergovernmental transfers and expenditures for government owned utilities and other commercial or auxiliary enterprise and insurance trust expenditures.

Local Government Direct General Expenditures in 2011

National Total = $1,424,975,118,000*

ALPHA ORDER

RANK	STATE	EXPENDITURES	% of USA
24	Alabama	$17,895,510,000	1.3%
42	Alaska	4,557,366,000	0.3%
20	Arizona	23,230,038,000	1.6%
34	Arkansas	9,076,587,000	0.6%
1	California	217,871,938,000	15.3%
17	Colorado	25,346,183,000	1.8%
27	Connecticut	15,603,279,000	1.1%
47	Delaware	2,821,516,000	0.2%
4	Florida	85,714,688,000	6.0%
10	Georgia	37,227,506,000	2.6%
49	Hawaii	2,450,425,000	0.2%
39	Idaho	5,120,020,000	0.4%
5	Illinois	60,512,261,000	4.2%
19	Indiana	24,201,350,000	1.7%
28	Iowa	14,389,876,000	1.0%
30	Kansas	12,648,558,000	0.9%
29	Kentucky	12,722,370,000	0.9%
23	Louisiana	20,272,327,000	1.4%
41	Maine	4,650,486,000	0.3%
16	Maryland	25,661,116,000	1.8%
14	Massachusetts	27,190,637,000	1.9%
9	Michigan	41,382,068,000	2.9%
15	Minnesota	25,673,044,000	1.8%
32	Mississippi	11,537,985,000	0.8%
21	Missouri	21,654,302,000	1.5%
45	Montana	3,383,300,000	0.2%
36	Nebraska	8,213,224,000	0.6%
31	Nevada	12,609,093,000	0.9%
40	New Hampshire	5,053,034,000	0.4%
8	New Jersey	43,993,995,000	3.1%
37	New Mexico	8,171,348,000	0.6%
2	New York	148,881,872,000	10.4%
11	North Carolina	36,607,539,000	2.6%
48	North Dakota	2,694,858,000	0.2%
7	Ohio	51,776,799,000	3.6%
33	Oklahoma	11,224,843,000	0.8%
26	Oregon	16,460,677,000	1.2%
6	Pennsylvania	55,171,678,000	3.9%
44	Rhode Island	3,896,141,000	0.3%
25	South Carolina	17,505,733,000	1.2%
46	South Dakota	2,877,707,000	0.2%
22	Tennessee	21,595,507,000	1.5%
3	Texas	106,710,153,000	7.5%
35	Utah	8,767,767,000	0.6%
50	Vermont	2,335,865,000	0.2%
12	Virginia	32,051,112,000	2.2%
13	Washington	30,234,954,000	2.1%
38	West Virginia	5,553,993,000	0.4%
18	Wisconsin	25,101,874,000	1.8%
43	Wyoming	4,305,124,000	0.3%

RANK ORDER

RANK	STATE	EXPENDITURES	% of USA
1	California	$217,871,938,000	15.3%
2	New York	148,881,872,000	10.4%
3	Texas	106,710,153,000	7.5%
4	Florida	85,714,688,000	6.0%
5	Illinois	60,512,261,000	4.2%
6	Pennsylvania	55,171,678,000	3.9%
7	Ohio	51,776,799,000	3.6%
8	New Jersey	43,993,995,000	3.1%
9	Michigan	41,382,068,000	2.9%
10	Georgia	37,227,506,000	2.6%
11	North Carolina	36,607,539,000	2.6%
12	Virginia	32,051,112,000	2.2%
13	Washington	30,234,954,000	2.1%
14	Massachusetts	27,190,637,000	1.9%
15	Minnesota	25,673,044,000	1.8%
16	Maryland	25,661,116,000	1.8%
17	Colorado	25,346,183,000	1.8%
18	Wisconsin	25,101,874,000	1.8%
19	Indiana	24,201,350,000	1.7%
20	Arizona	23,230,038,000	1.6%
21	Missouri	21,654,302,000	1.5%
22	Tennessee	21,595,507,000	1.5%
23	Louisiana	20,272,327,000	1.4%
24	Alabama	17,895,510,000	1.3%
25	South Carolina	17,505,733,000	1.2%
26	Oregon	16,460,677,000	1.2%
27	Connecticut	15,603,279,000	1.1%
28	Iowa	14,389,876,000	1.0%
29	Kentucky	12,722,370,000	0.9%
30	Kansas	12,648,558,000	0.9%
31	Nevada	12,609,093,000	0.9%
32	Mississippi	11,537,985,000	0.8%
33	Oklahoma	11,224,843,000	0.8%
34	Arkansas	9,076,587,000	0.6%
35	Utah	8,767,767,000	0.6%
36	Nebraska	8,213,224,000	0.6%
37	New Mexico	8,171,348,000	0.6%
38	West Virginia	5,553,993,000	0.4%
39	Idaho	5,120,020,000	0.4%
40	New Hampshire	5,053,034,000	0.4%
41	Maine	4,650,486,000	0.3%
42	Alaska	4,557,366,000	0.3%
43	Wyoming	4,305,124,000	0.3%
44	Rhode Island	3,896,141,000	0.3%
45	Montana	3,383,300,000	0.2%
46	South Dakota	2,877,707,000	0.2%
47	Delaware	2,821,516,000	0.2%
48	North Dakota	2,694,858,000	0.2%
49	Hawaii	2,450,425,000	0.2%
50	Vermont	2,335,865,000	0.2%
	District of Columbia	10,385,492,000	0.7%

Source: U.S. Bureau of the Census, Governments Division
"2011 State and Local Government Finances" (http://www.census.gov/govs/local/)
*Direct general expenditures include expenditures for current operations, assistance and subsidies, interest on debt, and capital outlay. Excludes intergovernmental transfers, expenditures for government owned utilities and other commercial or auxiliary enterprise, and insurance trust expenditures.

Per Capita Local Government Direct General Expenditures in 2011

National Per Capita = $4,573*

ALPHA ORDER

RANK	STATE	PER CAPITA
34	Alabama	$3,725
3	Alaska	6,296
38	Arizona	3,592
46	Arkansas	3,089
4	California	5,782
6	Colorado	4,954
19	Connecticut	4,350
45	Delaware	3,107
11	Florida	4,492
30	Georgia	3,794
50	Hawaii	1,778
43	Idaho	3,233
8	Illinois	4,706
35	Indiana	3,714
9	Iowa	4,696
16	Kansas	4,407
49	Kentucky	2,913
14	Louisiana	4,431
39	Maine	3,500
18	Maryland	4,394
24	Massachusetts	4,115
22	Michigan	4,190
7	Minnesota	4,801
28	Mississippi	3,875
37	Missouri	3,604
41	Montana	3,391
13	Nebraska	4,458
10	Nevada	4,636
29	New Hampshire	3,834
5	New Jersey	4,980
27	New Mexico	3,931
1	New York	7,634
31	North Carolina	3,793
26	North Dakota	3,936
12	Ohio	4,486
48	Oklahoma	2,966
21	Oregon	4,255
20	Pennsylvania	4,329
36	Rhode Island	3,708
32	South Carolina	3,746
40	South Dakota	3,494
42	Tennessee	3,374
23	Texas	4,163
44	Utah	3,115
33	Vermont	3,728
25	Virginia	3,955
14	Washington	4,431
47	West Virginia	2,994
17	Wisconsin	4,396
2	Wyoming	7,588

RANK ORDER

RANK	STATE	PER CAPITA
1	New York	$7,634
2	Wyoming	7,588
3	Alaska	6,296
4	California	5,782
5	New Jersey	4,980
6	Colorado	4,954
7	Minnesota	4,801
8	Illinois	4,706
9	Iowa	4,696
10	Nevada	4,636
11	Florida	4,492
12	Ohio	4,486
13	Nebraska	4,458
14	Louisiana	4,431
14	Washington	4,431
16	Kansas	4,407
17	Wisconsin	4,396
18	Maryland	4,394
19	Connecticut	4,350
20	Pennsylvania	4,329
21	Oregon	4,255
22	Michigan	4,190
23	Texas	4,163
24	Massachusetts	4,115
25	Virginia	3,955
26	North Dakota	3,936
27	New Mexico	3,931
28	Mississippi	3,875
29	New Hampshire	3,834
30	Georgia	3,794
31	North Carolina	3,793
32	South Carolina	3,746
33	Vermont	3,728
34	Alabama	3,725
35	Indiana	3,714
36	Rhode Island	3,708
37	Missouri	3,604
38	Arizona	3,592
39	Maine	3,500
40	South Dakota	3,494
41	Montana	3,391
42	Tennessee	3,374
43	Idaho	3,233
44	Utah	3,115
45	Delaware	3,107
46	Arkansas	3,089
47	West Virginia	2,994
48	Oklahoma	2,966
49	Kentucky	2,913
50	Hawaii	1,778

District of Columbia 16,777

Source: CQ Press using data from U.S. Bureau of the Census, Governments Division
"2011 State and Local Government Finances" (http://www.census.gov/govs/local/)
*Direct general expenditures include expenditures for current operations, assistance and subsidies, interest on debt, and capital outlay. Excludes intergovernmental transfers, expenditures for government owned utilities and other commercial or auxiliary enterprise, and insurance trust expenditures.

Local Government Debt Outstanding in 2011

National Total = $1,774,941,465,000*

ALPHA ORDER

RANK	STATE	DEBT	% of USA
25	Alabama	$20,248,092,000	1.1%
39	Alaska	3,780,183,000	0.2%
13	Arizona	36,763,118,000	2.1%
34	Arkansas	9,795,062,000	0.6%
1	California	269,161,924,000	15.2%
14	Colorado	35,850,927,000	2.0%
31	Connecticut	10,966,466,000	0.6%
44	Delaware	2,469,978,000	0.1%
4	Florida	108,432,079,000	6.1%
10	Georgia	40,964,519,000	2.3%
38	Hawaii	5,464,174,000	0.3%
46	Idaho	2,302,914,000	0.1%
5	Illinois	80,683,682,000	4.5%
19	Indiana	27,260,890,000	1.5%
32	Iowa	10,754,160,000	0.6%
26	Kansas	20,231,862,000	1.1%
18	Kentucky	27,416,048,000	1.5%
27	Louisiana	20,174,789,000	1.1%
41	Maine	3,079,164,000	0.2%
28	Maryland	19,353,263,000	1.1%
29	Massachusetts	18,242,376,000	1.0%
9	Michigan	42,867,117,000	2.4%
15	Minnesota	33,864,084,000	1.9%
37	Mississippi	7,418,097,000	0.4%
21	Missouri	25,422,792,000	1.4%
48	Montana	1,710,029,000	0.1%
33	Nebraska	10,596,227,000	0.6%
22	Nevada	23,507,176,000	1.3%
42	New Hampshire	2,787,667,000	0.2%
11	New Jersey	38,254,983,000	2.2%
36	New Mexico	8,530,093,000	0.5%
3	New York	199,693,496,000	11.3%
16	North Carolina	32,631,251,000	1.8%
45	North Dakota	2,365,400,000	0.1%
7	Ohio	46,559,098,000	2.6%
35	Oklahoma	8,947,403,000	0.5%
24	Oregon	20,684,396,000	1.2%
6	Pennsylvania	78,216,434,000	4.4%
43	Rhode Island	2,766,378,000	0.2%
20	South Carolina	25,713,058,000	1.4%
47	South Dakota	2,190,042,000	0.1%
17	Tennessee	32,403,983,000	1.8%
2	Texas	219,710,304,000	12.4%
30	Utah	12,927,611,000	0.7%
49	Vermont	1,243,803,000	0.1%
12	Virginia	37,336,800,000	2.1%
8	Washington	45,937,526,000	2.6%
40	West Virginia	3,585,469,000	0.2%
23	Wisconsin	21,393,056,000	1.2%
50	Wyoming	1,005,487,000	0.1%

RANK ORDER

RANK	STATE	DEBT	% of USA
1	California	$269,161,924,000	15.2%
2	Texas	219,710,304,000	12.4%
3	New York	199,693,496,000	11.3%
4	Florida	108,432,079,000	6.1%
5	Illinois	80,683,682,000	4.5%
6	Pennsylvania	78,216,434,000	4.4%
7	Ohio	46,559,098,000	2.6%
8	Washington	45,937,526,000	2.6%
9	Michigan	42,867,117,000	2.4%
10	Georgia	40,964,519,000	2.3%
11	New Jersey	38,254,983,000	2.2%
12	Virginia	37,336,800,000	2.1%
13	Arizona	36,763,118,000	2.1%
14	Colorado	35,850,927,000	2.0%
15	Minnesota	33,864,084,000	1.9%
16	North Carolina	32,631,251,000	1.8%
17	Tennessee	32,403,983,000	1.8%
18	Kentucky	27,416,048,000	1.5%
19	Indiana	27,260,890,000	1.5%
20	South Carolina	25,713,058,000	1.4%
21	Missouri	25,422,792,000	1.4%
22	Nevada	23,507,176,000	1.3%
23	Wisconsin	21,393,056,000	1.2%
24	Oregon	20,684,396,000	1.2%
25	Alabama	20,248,092,000	1.1%
26	Kansas	20,231,862,000	1.1%
27	Louisiana	20,174,789,000	1.1%
28	Maryland	19,353,263,000	1.1%
29	Massachusetts	18,242,376,000	1.0%
30	Utah	12,927,611,000	0.7%
31	Connecticut	10,966,466,000	0.6%
32	Iowa	10,754,160,000	0.6%
33	Nebraska	10,596,227,000	0.6%
34	Arkansas	9,795,062,000	0.6%
35	Oklahoma	8,947,403,000	0.5%
36	New Mexico	8,530,093,000	0.5%
37	Mississippi	7,418,097,000	0.4%
38	Hawaii	5,464,174,000	0.3%
39	Alaska	3,780,183,000	0.2%
40	West Virginia	3,585,469,000	0.2%
41	Maine	3,079,164,000	0.2%
42	New Hampshire	2,787,667,000	0.2%
43	Rhode Island	2,766,378,000	0.2%
44	Delaware	2,469,978,000	0.1%
45	North Dakota	2,365,400,000	0.1%
46	Idaho	2,302,914,000	0.1%
47	South Dakota	2,190,042,000	0.1%
48	Montana	1,710,029,000	0.1%
49	Vermont	1,243,803,000	0.1%
50	Wyoming	1,005,487,000	0.1%
	District of Columbia	11,276,535,000	0.6%

Source: U.S. Bureau of the Census, Governments Division
"2011 State and Local Government Finances" (http://www.census.gov/govs/local/)
*Includes short-term, long-term, full faith and credit, nonguaranteed, and public debt for private purposes.

Per Capita Local Government Debt Outstanding in 2011

National Per Capita = $5,696*

ALPHA ORDER

RANK ORDER

RANK	STATE	PER CAPITA	RANK	STATE	PER CAPITA
25	Alabama	$4,215	1	New York	$10,240
17	Alaska	5,222	2	Nevada	8,642
13	Arizona	5,684	3	Texas	8,572
35	Arkansas	3,333	4	California	7,143
4	California	7,143	5	Kansas	7,048
6	Colorado	7,007	6	Colorado	7,007
37	Connecticut	3,058	7	Washington	6,732
39	Delaware	2,720	8	Minnesota	6,333
14	Florida	5,682	9	Kentucky	6,278
27	Georgia	4,175	10	Illinois	6,274
30	Hawaii	3,965	11	Pennsylvania	6,138
50	Idaho	1,454	12	Nebraska	5,752
10	Illinois	6,274	13	Arizona	5,684
26	Indiana	4,183	14	Florida	5,682
32	Iowa	3,510	15	South Carolina	5,502
5	Kansas	7,048	16	Oregon	5,347
9	Kentucky	6,278	17	Alaska	5,222
21	Louisiana	4,410	18	Tennessee	5,063
44	Maine	2,318	19	Virginia	4,607
36	Maryland	3,314	20	Utah	4,593
38	Massachusetts	2,761	21	Louisiana	4,410
22	Michigan	4,340	22	Michigan	4,340
8	Minnesota	6,333	23	New Jersey	4,330
42	Mississippi	2,491	24	Missouri	4,231
24	Missouri	4,231	25	Alabama	4,215
49	Montana	1,714	26	Indiana	4,183
12	Nebraska	5,752	27	Georgia	4,175
2	Nevada	8,642	28	New Mexico	4,104
45	New Hampshire	2,115	29	Ohio	4,034
23	New Jersey	4,330	30	Hawaii	3,965
28	New Mexico	4,104	31	Wisconsin	3,747
1	New York	10,240	32	Iowa	3,510
34	North Carolina	3,381	33	North Dakota	3,454
33	North Dakota	3,454	34	North Carolina	3,381
29	Ohio	4,034	35	Arkansas	3,333
43	Oklahoma	2,364	36	Maryland	3,314
16	Oregon	5,347	37	Connecticut	3,058
11	Pennsylvania	6,138	38	Massachusetts	2,761
41	Rhode Island	2,633	39	Delaware	2,720
15	South Carolina	5,502	40	South Dakota	2,659
40	South Dakota	2,659	41	Rhode Island	2,633
18	Tennessee	5,063	42	Mississippi	2,491
3	Texas	8,572	43	Oklahoma	2,364
20	Utah	4,593	44	Maine	2,318
46	Vermont	1,985	45	New Hampshire	2,115
19	Virginia	4,607	46	Vermont	1,985
7	Washington	6,732	47	West Virginia	1,933
47	West Virginia	1,933	48	Wyoming	1,772
31	Wisconsin	3,747	49	Montana	1,714
48	Wyoming	1,772	50	Idaho	1,454
				District of Columbia	18,217

Source: CQ Press using data from U.S. Bureau of the Census, Governments Division
   "2011 State and Local Government Finances" (http://www.census.gov/govs/local/)
*Includes short-term, long-term, full faith and credit, nonguaranteed, and public debt for private purposes.

Local Government Full-Time Equivalent Employees in 2011

National Total = 11,999,059 FTE Employees*

ALPHA ORDER

RANK	STATE	EMPLOYEES	% of USA
24	Alabama	195,010	1.6%
46	Alaska	27,996	0.2%
20	Arizona	212,009	1.8%
31	Arkansas	127,046	1.1%
1	California	1,344,749	11.2%
21	Colorado	198,053	1.7%
33	Connecticut	123,119	1.0%
49	Delaware	23,536	0.2%
4	Florida	703,922	5.9%
9	Georgia	385,649	3.2%
50	Hawaii	15,527	0.1%
39	Idaho	56,796	0.5%
5	Illinois	495,768	4.1%
14	Indiana	239,707	2.0%
32	Iowa	126,890	1.1%
27	Kansas	153,292	1.3%
26	Kentucky	165,366	1.4%
23	Louisiana	197,195	1.6%
40	Maine	54,016	0.5%
18	Maryland	220,317	1.8%
16	Massachusetts	228,705	1.9%
12	Michigan	311,657	2.6%
22	Minnesota	197,507	1.6%
29	Mississippi	134,339	1.1%
15	Missouri	229,949	1.9%
43	Montana	37,079	0.3%
35	Nebraska	88,909	0.7%
36	Nevada	86,186	0.7%
41	New Hampshire	52,879	0.4%
10	New Jersey	341,313	2.8%
37	New Mexico	78,870	0.7%
3	New York	932,034	7.8%
8	North Carolina	401,701	3.3%
47	North Dakota	26,455	0.2%
6	Ohio	455,646	3.8%
28	Oklahoma	146,418	1.2%
30	Oregon	131,757	1.1%
7	Pennsylvania	423,378	3.5%
45	Rhode Island	30,846	0.3%
25	South Carolina	176,232	1.5%
44	South Dakota	31,393	0.3%
13	Tennessee	241,242	2.0%
2	Texas	1,131,828	9.4%
34	Utah	94,090	0.8%
48	Vermont	25,230	0.2%
11	Virginia	313,907	2.6%
17	Washington	225,231	1.9%
38	West Virginia	63,819	0.5%
19	Wisconsin	212,677	1.8%
42	Wyoming	39,316	0.3%

RANK ORDER

RANK	STATE	EMPLOYEES	% of USA
1	California	1,344,749	11.2%
2	Texas	1,131,828	9.4%
3	New York	932,034	7.8%
4	Florida	703,922	5.9%
5	Illinois	495,768	4.1%
6	Ohio	455,646	3.8%
7	Pennsylvania	423,378	3.5%
8	North Carolina	401,701	3.3%
9	Georgia	385,649	3.2%
10	New Jersey	341,313	2.8%
11	Virginia	313,907	2.6%
12	Michigan	311,657	2.6%
13	Tennessee	241,242	2.0%
14	Indiana	239,707	2.0%
15	Missouri	229,949	1.9%
16	Massachusetts	228,705	1.9%
17	Washington	225,231	1.9%
18	Maryland	220,317	1.8%
19	Wisconsin	212,677	1.8%
20	Arizona	212,009	1.8%
21	Colorado	198,053	1.7%
22	Minnesota	197,507	1.6%
23	Louisiana	197,195	1.6%
24	Alabama	195,010	1.6%
25	South Carolina	176,232	1.5%
26	Kentucky	165,366	1.4%
27	Kansas	153,292	1.3%
28	Oklahoma	146,418	1.2%
29	Mississippi	134,339	1.1%
30	Oregon	131,757	1.1%
31	Arkansas	127,046	1.1%
32	Iowa	126,890	1.1%
33	Connecticut	123,119	1.0%
34	Utah	94,090	0.8%
35	Nebraska	88,909	0.7%
36	Nevada	86,186	0.7%
37	New Mexico	78,870	0.7%
38	West Virginia	63,819	0.5%
39	Idaho	56,796	0.5%
40	Maine	54,016	0.5%
41	New Hampshire	52,879	0.4%
42	Wyoming	39,316	0.3%
43	Montana	37,079	0.3%
44	South Dakota	31,393	0.3%
45	Rhode Island	30,846	0.3%
46	Alaska	27,996	0.2%
47	North Dakota	26,455	0.2%
48	Vermont	25,230	0.2%
49	Delaware	23,536	0.2%
50	Hawaii	15,527	0.1%
	District of Columbia	42,502	0.4%

Source: U.S. Bureau of the Census, Governments Division
   "Government Employment and Payroll" (http://www.census.gov/govs/apes/index.html)
*As of March 2011.

Rate of Local Government Full-Time Equivalent Employees in 2011

National Rate = 385 Local Government Employees per 10,000 Population*

ALPHA ORDER

RANK	STATE	RATE
12	Alabama	406
17	Alaska	387
45	Arizona	328
7	Arkansas	432
37	California	357
17	Colorado	387
40	Connecticut	343
49	Delaware	259
33	Florida	369
16	Georgia	393
50	Hawaii	113
36	Idaho	359
21	Illinois	386
35	Indiana	368
10	Iowa	414
2	Kansas	534
26	Kentucky	379
8	Louisiana	431
11	Maine	407
28	Maryland	377
38	Massachusetts	346
47	Michigan	316
33	Minnesota	369
5	Mississippi	451
24	Missouri	383
31	Montana	372
3	Nebraska	483
46	Nevada	317
14	New Hampshire	401
21	New Jersey	386
26	New Mexico	379
4	New York	478
9	North Carolina	416
21	North Dakota	386
15	Ohio	395
17	Oklahoma	387
41	Oregon	341
43	Pennsylvania	332
48	Rhode Island	294
28	South Carolina	377
25	South Dakota	381
28	Tennessee	377
6	Texas	442
42	Utah	334
13	Vermont	403
17	Virginia	387
44	Washington	330
39	West Virginia	344
31	Wisconsin	372
1	Wyoming	693

RANK ORDER

RANK	STATE	RATE
1	Wyoming	693
2	Kansas	534
3	Nebraska	483
4	New York	478
5	Mississippi	451
6	Texas	442
7	Arkansas	432
8	Louisiana	431
9	North Carolina	416
10	Iowa	414
11	Maine	407
12	Alabama	406
13	Vermont	403
14	New Hampshire	401
15	Ohio	395
16	Georgia	393
17	Alaska	387
17	Colorado	387
17	Oklahoma	387
17	Virginia	387
21	Illinois	386
21	New Jersey	386
21	North Dakota	386
24	Missouri	383
25	South Dakota	381
26	Kentucky	379
26	New Mexico	379
28	Maryland	377
28	South Carolina	377
28	Tennessee	377
31	Montana	372
31	Wisconsin	372
33	Florida	369
33	Minnesota	369
35	Indiana	368
36	Idaho	359
37	California	357
38	Massachusetts	346
39	West Virginia	344
40	Connecticut	343
41	Oregon	341
42	Utah	334
43	Pennsylvania	332
44	Washington	330
45	Arizona	328
46	Nevada	317
47	Michigan	316
48	Rhode Island	294
49	Delaware	259
50	Hawaii	113
	District of Columbia	687

Source: CQ Press using data from U.S. Bureau of the Census, Governments Division
"Government Employment and Payroll" (http://www.census.gov/govs/apes/index.html)
*Full-time equivalent as of March 2011.

Average Annual Earnings of Full-Time Local Government Employees in 2011

National Average = $52,061*

<table>
<tr><td colspan="3">ALPHA ORDER</td><td colspan="3">RANK ORDER</td></tr>
<tr><td>RANK</td><td>STATE</td><td>SALARY</td><td>RANK</td><td>STATE</td><td>SALARY</td></tr>
<tr><td>43</td><td>Alabama</td><td>$39,132</td><td>1</td><td>California</td><td>$70,351</td></tr>
<tr><td>9</td><td>Alaska</td><td>60,536</td><td>2</td><td>Washington</td><td>67,134</td></tr>
<tr><td>22</td><td>Arizona</td><td>49,116</td><td>3</td><td>New Jersey</td><td>65,985</td></tr>
<tr><td>50</td><td>Arkansas</td><td>32,755</td><td>4</td><td>New York</td><td>65,304</td></tr>
<tr><td>1</td><td>California</td><td>70,351</td><td>5</td><td>Connecticut</td><td>62,529</td></tr>
<tr><td>19</td><td>Colorado</td><td>51,357</td><td>6</td><td>Maryland</td><td>61,506</td></tr>
<tr><td>5</td><td>Connecticut</td><td>62,529</td><td>7</td><td>Nevada</td><td>61,497</td></tr>
<tr><td>14</td><td>Delaware</td><td>54,878</td><td>8</td><td>Rhode Island</td><td>60,863</td></tr>
<tr><td>23</td><td>Florida</td><td>47,978</td><td>9</td><td>Alaska</td><td>60,536</td></tr>
<tr><td>36</td><td>Georgia</td><td>41,540</td><td>10</td><td>Massachusetts</td><td>59,479</td></tr>
<tr><td>11</td><td>Hawaii</td><td>59,163</td><td>11</td><td>Hawaii</td><td>59,163</td></tr>
<tr><td>42</td><td>Idaho</td><td>39,464</td><td>12</td><td>Illinois</td><td>57,569</td></tr>
<tr><td>12</td><td>Illinois</td><td>57,569</td><td>13</td><td>Michigan</td><td>55,824</td></tr>
<tr><td>30</td><td>Indiana</td><td>43,781</td><td>14</td><td>Delaware</td><td>54,878</td></tr>
<tr><td>25</td><td>Iowa</td><td>47,307</td><td>15</td><td>Minnesota</td><td>54,296</td></tr>
<tr><td>39</td><td>Kansas</td><td>40,918</td><td>16</td><td>Oregon</td><td>53,655</td></tr>
<tr><td>46</td><td>Kentucky</td><td>37,420</td><td>17</td><td>Wisconsin</td><td>52,783</td></tr>
<tr><td>40</td><td>Louisiana</td><td>40,364</td><td>18</td><td>Pennsylvania</td><td>52,495</td></tr>
<tr><td>49</td><td>Maine</td><td>34,636</td><td>19</td><td>Colorado</td><td>51,357</td></tr>
<tr><td>6</td><td>Maryland</td><td>61,506</td><td>20</td><td>Ohio</td><td>49,910</td></tr>
<tr><td>10</td><td>Massachusetts</td><td>59,479</td><td>21</td><td>Wyoming</td><td>49,167</td></tr>
<tr><td>13</td><td>Michigan</td><td>55,824</td><td>22</td><td>Arizona</td><td>49,116</td></tr>
<tr><td>15</td><td>Minnesota</td><td>54,296</td><td>23</td><td>Florida</td><td>47,978</td></tr>
<tr><td>48</td><td>Mississippi</td><td>35,679</td><td>24</td><td>Nebraska</td><td>47,493</td></tr>
<tr><td>34</td><td>Missouri</td><td>42,638</td><td>25</td><td>Iowa</td><td>47,307</td></tr>
<tr><td>31</td><td>Montana</td><td>43,346</td><td>26</td><td>Virginia</td><td>46,588</td></tr>
<tr><td>24</td><td>Nebraska</td><td>47,493</td><td>27</td><td>New Hampshire</td><td>46,563</td></tr>
<tr><td>7</td><td>Nevada</td><td>61,497</td><td>28</td><td>Vermont</td><td>44,367</td></tr>
<tr><td>27</td><td>New Hampshire</td><td>46,563</td><td>29</td><td>Texas</td><td>44,031</td></tr>
<tr><td>3</td><td>New Jersey</td><td>65,985</td><td>30</td><td>Indiana</td><td>43,781</td></tr>
<tr><td>37</td><td>New Mexico</td><td>41,456</td><td>31</td><td>Montana</td><td>43,346</td></tr>
<tr><td>4</td><td>New York</td><td>65,304</td><td>32</td><td>North Dakota</td><td>42,750</td></tr>
<tr><td>35</td><td>North Carolina</td><td>42,608</td><td>33</td><td>Utah</td><td>42,663</td></tr>
<tr><td>32</td><td>North Dakota</td><td>42,750</td><td>34</td><td>Missouri</td><td>42,638</td></tr>
<tr><td>20</td><td>Ohio</td><td>49,910</td><td>35</td><td>North Carolina</td><td>42,608</td></tr>
<tr><td>47</td><td>Oklahoma</td><td>37,044</td><td>36</td><td>Georgia</td><td>41,540</td></tr>
<tr><td>16</td><td>Oregon</td><td>53,655</td><td>37</td><td>New Mexico</td><td>41,456</td></tr>
<tr><td>18</td><td>Pennsylvania</td><td>52,495</td><td>38</td><td>South Carolina</td><td>41,176</td></tr>
<tr><td>8</td><td>Rhode Island</td><td>60,863</td><td>39</td><td>Kansas</td><td>40,918</td></tr>
<tr><td>38</td><td>South Carolina</td><td>41,176</td><td>40</td><td>Louisiana</td><td>40,364</td></tr>
<tr><td>45</td><td>South Dakota</td><td>37,595</td><td>41</td><td>Tennessee</td><td>39,660</td></tr>
<tr><td>41</td><td>Tennessee</td><td>39,660</td><td>42</td><td>Idaho</td><td>39,464</td></tr>
<tr><td>29</td><td>Texas</td><td>44,031</td><td>43</td><td>Alabama</td><td>39,132</td></tr>
<tr><td>33</td><td>Utah</td><td>42,663</td><td>44</td><td>West Virginia</td><td>38,486</td></tr>
<tr><td>28</td><td>Vermont</td><td>44,367</td><td>45</td><td>South Dakota</td><td>37,595</td></tr>
<tr><td>26</td><td>Virginia</td><td>46,588</td><td>46</td><td>Kentucky</td><td>37,420</td></tr>
<tr><td>2</td><td>Washington</td><td>67,134</td><td>47</td><td>Oklahoma</td><td>37,044</td></tr>
<tr><td>44</td><td>West Virginia</td><td>38,486</td><td>48</td><td>Mississippi</td><td>35,679</td></tr>
<tr><td>17</td><td>Wisconsin</td><td>52,783</td><td>49</td><td>Maine</td><td>34,636</td></tr>
<tr><td>21</td><td>Wyoming</td><td>49,167</td><td>50</td><td>Arkansas</td><td>32,755</td></tr>
<tr><td></td><td></td><td></td><td></td><td>District of Columbia</td><td>72,821</td></tr>
</table>

Source: CQ Press using data from U.S. Bureau of the Census, Governments Division
"Government Employment and Payroll" (http://www.census.gov/govs/apes/index.html)
*March 2011 full-time payroll (multiplied by 12) divided by full-time employees.

XI. Health

Average Annual Single Coverage Health Insurance Premium per Enrolled Employee in 2012
National Average = $5,384*

ALPHA ORDER

RANK	STATE	PREMIUM
45	Alabama	$4,961
1	Alaska	7,420
31	Arizona	5,196
49	Arkansas	4,459
18	California	5,422
30	Colorado	5,275
4	Connecticut	5,934
14	Delaware	5,583
32	Florida	5,179
34	Georgia	5,159
41	Hawaii	5,076
50	Idaho	4,439
20	Illinois	5,404
16	Indiana	5,504
36	Iowa	5,141
44	Kansas	4,968
21	Kentucky	5,397
23	Louisiana	5,381
10	Maine	5,692
29	Maryland	5,302
2	Massachusetts	6,121
26	Michigan	5,365
27	Minnesota	5,338
48	Mississippi	4,713
35	Missouri	5,150
13	Montana	5,585
38	Nebraska	5,101
46	Nevada	4,949
11	New Hampshire	5,688
8	New Jersey	5,837
43	New Mexico	5,035
3	New York	6,033
12	North Carolina	5,632
24	North Dakota	5,377
40	Ohio	5,081
47	Oklahoma	4,851
17	Oregon	5,460
22	Pennsylvania	5,385
6	Rhode Island	5,870
39	South Carolina	5,098
19	South Dakota	5,409
42	Tennessee	5,067
37	Texas	5,124
33	Utah	5,162
15	Vermont	5,580
28	Virginia	5,309
25	Washington	5,368
5	West Virginia	5,884
9	Wisconsin	5,737
7	Wyoming	5,861

RANK ORDER

RANK	STATE	PREMIUM
1	Alaska	$7,420
2	Massachusetts	6,121
3	New York	6,033
4	Connecticut	5,934
5	West Virginia	5,884
6	Rhode Island	5,870
7	Wyoming	5,861
8	New Jersey	5,837
9	Wisconsin	5,737
10	Maine	5,692
11	New Hampshire	5,688
12	North Carolina	5,632
13	Montana	5,585
14	Delaware	5,583
15	Vermont	5,580
16	Indiana	5,504
17	Oregon	5,460
18	California	5,422
19	South Dakota	5,409
20	Illinois	5,404
21	Kentucky	5,397
22	Pennsylvania	5,385
23	Louisiana	5,381
24	North Dakota	5,377
25	Washington	5,368
26	Michigan	5,365
27	Minnesota	5,338
28	Virginia	5,309
29	Maryland	5,302
30	Colorado	5,275
31	Arizona	5,196
32	Florida	5,179
33	Utah	5,162
34	Georgia	5,159
35	Missouri	5,150
36	Iowa	5,141
37	Texas	5,124
38	Nebraska	5,101
39	South Carolina	5,098
40	Ohio	5,081
41	Hawaii	5,076
42	Tennessee	5,067
43	New Mexico	5,035
44	Kansas	4,968
45	Alabama	4,961
46	Nevada	4,949
47	Oklahoma	4,851
48	Mississippi	4,713
49	Arkansas	4,459
50	Idaho	4,439

	District of Columbia	5,581

Source: U.S. Department of Health and Human Services, Agency for Healthcare Research and Quality
"Private-Sector Data by Firm Size and State" (Table II Series, Medical Expenditures Panel Survey)
(http://www.meps.ahrq.gov/mepsweb/survey_comp/Insurance.jsp)
*Enrolled employees at private-sector establishments that offer health insurance coverage.

Average Annual Family Coverage Health Insurance Premium per Enrolled Employee in 2012
National Average = $15,473*

RANK	STATE	PREMIUM
50	Alabama	$12,764
1	Alaska	17,902
27	Arizona	15,250
48	Arkansas	13,295
11	California	15,898
10	Colorado	16,037
5	Connecticut	16,891
18	Delaware	15,599
21	Florida	15,471
36	Georgia	14,646
34	Hawaii	14,722
45	Idaho	14,057
14	Illinois	15,753
22	Indiana	15,461
42	Iowa	14,310
46	Kansas	13,750
15	Kentucky	15,734
30	Louisiana	15,091
9	Maine	16,203
28	Maryland	15,239
2	Massachusetts	17,129
40	Michigan	14,397
24	Minnesota	15,408
44	Mississippi	14,172
32	Missouri	14,986
35	Montana	14,704
39	Nebraska	14,472
49	Nevada	12,904
6	New Hampshire	16,372
3	New Jersey	16,947
12	New Mexico	15,880
4	New York	16,924
17	North Carolina	15,606
41	North Dakota	14,348
23	Ohio	15,455
47	Oklahoma	13,554
20	Oregon	15,487
26	Pennsylvania	15,369
13	Rhode Island	15,863
43	South Carolina	14,285
31	South Dakota	14,999
33	Tennessee	14,888
37	Texas	14,616
38	Utah	14,558
29	Vermont	15,093
25	Virginia	15,376
7	Washington	16,291
16	West Virginia	15,640
8	Wisconsin	16,248
19	Wyoming	15,598

RANK	STATE	PREMIUM
1	Alaska	$17,902
2	Massachusetts	17,129
3	New Jersey	16,947
4	New York	16,924
5	Connecticut	16,891
6	New Hampshire	16,372
7	Washington	16,291
8	Wisconsin	16,248
9	Maine	16,203
10	Colorado	16,037
11	California	15,898
12	New Mexico	15,880
13	Rhode Island	15,863
14	Illinois	15,753
15	Kentucky	15,734
16	West Virginia	15,640
17	North Carolina	15,606
18	Delaware	15,599
19	Wyoming	15,598
20	Oregon	15,487
21	Florida	15,471
22	Indiana	15,461
23	Ohio	15,455
24	Minnesota	15,408
25	Virginia	15,376
26	Pennsylvania	15,369
27	Arizona	15,250
28	Maryland	15,239
29	Vermont	15,093
30	Louisiana	15,091
31	South Dakota	14,999
32	Missouri	14,986
33	Tennessee	14,888
34	Hawaii	14,722
35	Montana	14,704
36	Georgia	14,646
37	Texas	14,616
38	Utah	14,558
39	Nebraska	14,472
40	Michigan	14,397
41	North Dakota	14,348
42	Iowa	14,310
43	South Carolina	14,285
44	Mississippi	14,172
45	Idaho	14,057
46	Kansas	13,750
47	Oklahoma	13,554
48	Arkansas	13,295
49	Nevada	12,904
50	Alabama	12,764
	District of Columbia	17,206

Source: U.S. Department of Health and Human Services, Agency for Healthcare Research and Quality
"Private-Sector Data by Firm Size and State" (Table II Series, Medical Expenditures Panel Survey)
(http://www.meps.ahrq.gov/mepsweb/survey_comp/Insurance.jsp)
*Enrolled employees at private-sector establishments that offer health insurance coverage.

Percent of Private-Sector Establishments That Offer Health Insurance: 2012

National Percent = 50.1%

RANK	STATE	PERCENT
16	Alabama	52.4
47	Alaska	40.3
38	Arizona	46.0
31	Arkansas	47.5
17	California	51.3
33	Colorado	47.2
8	Connecticut	55.8
9	Delaware	54.5
43	Florida	44.7
30	Georgia	47.7
1	Hawaii	84.1
48	Idaho	39.1
39	Illinois	45.8
41	Indiana	44.9
19	Iowa	50.7
15	Kansas	52.6
10	Kentucky	54.4
44	Louisiana	44.2
32	Maine	47.4
5	Maryland	56.8
2	Massachusetts	58.6
29	Michigan	48.2
21	Minnesota	50.1
28	Mississippi	48.3
14	Missouri	52.7
49	Montana	39.0
50	Nebraska	36.9
7	Nevada	56.2
11	New Hampshire	54.1
3	New Jersey	57.9
37	New Mexico	46.2
13	New York	53.0
34	North Carolina	46.5
42	North Dakota	44.8
6	Ohio	56.4
19	Oklahoma	50.7
23	Oregon	49.9
4	Pennsylvania	57.7
12	Rhode Island	53.4
34	South Carolina	46.5
40	South Dakota	45.0
24	Tennessee	49.8
34	Texas	46.5
45	Utah	43.3
18	Vermont	50.8
27	Virginia	48.7
26	Washington	49.3
22	West Virginia	50.0
25	Wisconsin	49.6
46	Wyoming	41.2

RANK	STATE	PERCENT
1	Hawaii	84.1
2	Massachusetts	58.6
3	New Jersey	57.9
4	Pennsylvania	57.7
5	Maryland	56.8
6	Ohio	56.4
7	Nevada	56.2
8	Connecticut	55.8
9	Delaware	54.5
10	Kentucky	54.4
11	New Hampshire	54.1
12	Rhode Island	53.4
13	New York	53.0
14	Missouri	52.7
15	Kansas	52.6
16	Alabama	52.4
17	California	51.3
18	Vermont	50.8
19	Iowa	50.7
19	Oklahoma	50.7
21	Minnesota	50.1
22	West Virginia	50.0
23	Oregon	49.9
24	Tennessee	49.8
25	Wisconsin	49.6
26	Washington	49.3
27	Virginia	48.7
28	Mississippi	48.3
29	Michigan	48.2
30	Georgia	47.7
31	Arkansas	47.5
32	Maine	47.4
33	Colorado	47.2
34	North Carolina	46.5
34	South Carolina	46.5
34	Texas	46.5
37	New Mexico	46.2
38	Arizona	46.0
39	Illinois	45.8
40	South Dakota	45.0
41	Indiana	44.9
42	North Dakota	44.8
43	Florida	44.7
44	Louisiana	44.2
45	Utah	43.3
46	Wyoming	41.2
47	Alaska	40.3
48	Idaho	39.1
49	Montana	39.0
50	Nebraska	36.9

	District of Columbia	66.0

Source: U.S. Department of Health and Human Services, Agency for Healthcare Research and Quality
"Private-Sector Data by Firm Size and State" (Table II Series, Medical Expenditures Panel Survey)
(http://www.meps.ahrq.gov/mepsweb/survey_comp/Insurance.jsp)

Persons Not Covered by Health Insurance in 2012

National Total = 47,951,000 Uninsured

ALPHA ORDER

RANK	STATE	UNINSURED	% of USA
20	Alabama	711,000	1.5%
42	Alaska	134,000	0.3%
11	Arizona	1,198,000	2.5%
28	Arkansas	535,000	1.1%
1	California	6,787,000	14.2%
21	Colorado	705,000	1.5%
35	Connecticut	284,000	0.6%
47	Delaware	97,000	0.2%
3	Florida	4,116,000	8.6%
5	Georgia	1,856,000	3.9%
46	Hawaii	105,000	0.2%
38	Idaho	253,000	0.5%
6	Illinois	1,732,000	3.6%
16	Indiana	849,000	1.8%
34	Iowa	306,000	0.6%
33	Kansas	358,000	0.7%
22	Kentucky	682,000	1.4%
17	Louisiana	819,000	1.7%
44	Maine	126,000	0.3%
19	Maryland	733,000	1.5%
36	Massachusetts	272,000	0.6%
12	Michigan	1,060,000	2.2%
31	Minnesota	443,000	0.9%
30	Mississippi	444,000	0.9%
18	Missouri	794,000	1.7%
40	Montana	181,000	0.4%
39	Nebraska	245,000	0.5%
24	Nevada	642,000	1.3%
41	New Hampshire	157,000	0.3%
10	New Jersey	1,223,000	2.6%
29	New Mexico	453,000	0.9%
4	New York	2,185,000	4.6%
7	North Carolina	1,658,000	3.5%
49	North Dakota	80,000	0.2%
9	Ohio	1,402,000	2.9%
25	Oklahoma	640,000	1.3%
26	Oregon	597,000	1.2%
8	Pennsylvania	1,521,000	3.2%
43	Rhode Island	128,000	0.3%
23	South Carolina	665,000	1.4%
45	South Dakota	119,000	0.2%
15	Tennessee	892,000	1.9%
2	Texas	6,426,000	13.4%
32	Utah	411,000	0.9%
50	Vermont	43,000	0.1%
13	Virginia	998,000	2.1%
14	Washington	933,000	1.9%
37	West Virginia	264,000	0.6%
27	Wisconsin	550,000	1.1%
48	Wyoming	89,000	0.2%

RANK ORDER

RANK	STATE	UNINSURED	% of USA
1	California	6,787,000	14.2%
2	Texas	6,426,000	13.4%
3	Florida	4,116,000	8.6%
4	New York	2,185,000	4.6%
5	Georgia	1,856,000	3.9%
6	Illinois	1,732,000	3.6%
7	North Carolina	1,658,000	3.5%
8	Pennsylvania	1,521,000	3.2%
9	Ohio	1,402,000	2.9%
10	New Jersey	1,223,000	2.6%
11	Arizona	1,198,000	2.5%
12	Michigan	1,060,000	2.2%
13	Virginia	998,000	2.1%
14	Washington	933,000	1.9%
15	Tennessee	892,000	1.9%
16	Indiana	849,000	1.8%
17	Louisiana	819,000	1.7%
18	Missouri	794,000	1.7%
19	Maryland	733,000	1.5%
20	Alabama	711,000	1.5%
21	Colorado	705,000	1.5%
22	Kentucky	682,000	1.4%
23	South Carolina	665,000	1.4%
24	Nevada	642,000	1.3%
25	Oklahoma	640,000	1.3%
26	Oregon	597,000	1.2%
27	Wisconsin	550,000	1.1%
28	Arkansas	535,000	1.1%
29	New Mexico	453,000	0.9%
30	Mississippi	444,000	0.9%
31	Minnesota	443,000	0.9%
32	Utah	411,000	0.9%
33	Kansas	358,000	0.7%
34	Iowa	306,000	0.6%
35	Connecticut	284,000	0.6%
36	Massachusetts	272,000	0.6%
37	West Virginia	264,000	0.6%
38	Idaho	253,000	0.5%
39	Nebraska	245,000	0.5%
40	Montana	181,000	0.4%
41	New Hampshire	157,000	0.3%
42	Alaska	134,000	0.3%
43	Rhode Island	128,000	0.3%
44	Maine	126,000	0.3%
45	South Dakota	119,000	0.2%
46	Hawaii	105,000	0.2%
47	Delaware	97,000	0.2%
48	Wyoming	89,000	0.2%
49	North Dakota	80,000	0.2%
50	Vermont	43,000	0.1%
	District of Columbia	50,000	0.1%

Source: U.S. Bureau of the Census
  "Income, Poverty, and Health Insurance Coverage: 2012"
  (http://www.census.gov/hhes/www/hlthins/data/incpovhlth/index.html)

Percent of Population Not Covered by Health Insurance in 2012

National Percent = 15.8% of Population*

ALPHA ORDER

RANK	STATE	PERCENT
21	Alabama	14.4
8	Alaska	18.4
9	Arizona	18.2
11	Arkansas	18.1
7	California	19.0
25	Colorado	14.1
46	Connecticut	9.3
43	Delaware	10.7
4	Florida	20.7
6	Georgia	19.3
49	Hawaii	7.8
14	Idaho	17.3
21	Illinois	14.4
34	Indiana	12.9
42	Iowa	10.8
34	Kansas	12.9
19	Kentucky	15.0
5	Louisiana	19.7
45	Maine	9.6
32	Maryland	13.0
50	Massachusetts	4.3
37	Michigan	12.1
47	Minnesota	9.1
13	Mississippi	17.5
26	Missouri	14.0
9	Montana	18.2
32	Nebraska	13.0
2	Nevada	22.5
39	New Hampshire	11.6
19	New Jersey	15.0
3	New Mexico	21.0
34	New York	12.9
16	North Carolina	16.9
40	North Dakota	11.3
31	Ohio	13.2
15	Oklahoma	17.1
18	Oregon	15.1
41	Pennsylvania	11.2
38	Rhode Island	12.0
12	South Carolina	17.9
29	South Dakota	13.5
28	Tennessee	13.9
1	Texas	24.3
23	Utah	14.3
48	Vermont	8.3
30	Virginia	13.3
26	Washington	14.0
23	West Virginia	14.3
44	Wisconsin	9.8
17	Wyoming	16.8

RANK ORDER

RANK	STATE	PERCENT
1	Texas	24.3
2	Nevada	22.5
3	New Mexico	21.0
4	Florida	20.7
5	Louisiana	19.7
6	Georgia	19.3
7	California	19.0
8	Alaska	18.4
9	Arizona	18.2
9	Montana	18.2
11	Arkansas	18.1
12	South Carolina	17.9
13	Mississippi	17.5
14	Idaho	17.3
15	Oklahoma	17.1
16	North Carolina	16.9
17	Wyoming	16.8
18	Oregon	15.1
19	Kentucky	15.0
19	New Jersey	15.0
21	Alabama	14.4
21	Illinois	14.4
23	Utah	14.3
23	West Virginia	14.3
25	Colorado	14.1
26	Missouri	14.0
26	Washington	14.0
28	Tennessee	13.9
29	South Dakota	13.5
30	Virginia	13.3
31	Ohio	13.2
32	Maryland	13.0
32	Nebraska	13.0
34	Indiana	12.9
34	Kansas	12.9
34	New York	12.9
37	Michigan	12.1
38	Rhode Island	12.0
39	New Hampshire	11.6
40	North Dakota	11.3
41	Pennsylvania	11.2
42	Iowa	10.8
43	Delaware	10.7
44	Wisconsin	9.8
45	Maine	9.6
46	Connecticut	9.3
47	Minnesota	9.1
48	Vermont	8.3
49	Hawaii	7.8
50	Massachusetts	4.3

| | District of Columbia | 9.7 |

Source: U.S. Bureau of the Census
    "Income, Poverty, and Health Insurance Coverage: 2012"
    (http://www.census.gov/hhes/www/hlthins/data/incpovhlth/index.html)
*Three-year average for 2010 through 2012.

Percent of Population Lacking Access to Primary Care in 2013

National Percent = 10.9% of Population*

ALPHA ORDER				RANK ORDER		
RANK	STATE	PERCENT		RANK	STATE	PERCENT
9	Alabama	19.5		1	Mississippi	34.3
11	Alaska	17.7		2	New Mexico	30.8
10	Arizona	18.6		3	Louisiana	24.4
31	Arkansas	8.7		4	Missouri	23.4
34	California	8.3		5	Oklahoma	23.2
25	Colorado	10.8		6	North Dakota	20.3
29	Connecticut	9.5		7	South Dakota	20.2
27	Delaware	9.7		7	Wyoming	20.2
13	Florida	16.4		9	Alabama	19.5
23	Georgia	11.8		10	Arizona	18.6
45	Hawaii	2.5		11	Alaska	17.7
12	Idaho	17.4		12	Idaho	17.4
14	Illinois	16.2		13	Florida	16.4
32	Indiana	8.6		14	Illinois	16.2
19	Iowa	12.3		15	Montana	15.9
17	Kansas	13.0		16	South Carolina	13.7
30	Kentucky	9.0		17	Kansas	13.0
3	Louisiana	24.4		18	Washington	12.7
43	Maine	3.2		19	Iowa	12.3
28	Maryland	9.6		20	Texas	12.0
42	Massachusetts	3.4		21	Nevada	11.9
26	Michigan	9.9		21	Oregon	11.9
41	Minnesota	4.6		23	Georgia	11.8
1	Mississippi	34.3		24	New York	11.4
4	Missouri	23.4		25	Colorado	10.8
15	Montana	15.9		26	Michigan	9.9
47	Nebraska	1.2		27	Delaware	9.7
21	Nevada	11.9		28	Maryland	9.6
46	New Hampshire	2.3		29	Connecticut	9.5
49	New Jersey	0.1		30	Kentucky	9.0
2	New Mexico	30.8		31	Arkansas	8.7
24	New York	11.4		32	Indiana	8.6
39	North Carolina	6.7		32	Wisconsin	8.6
6	North Dakota	20.3		34	California	8.3
40	Ohio	4.9		35	West Virginia	8.1
5	Oklahoma	23.2		36	Utah	7.6
21	Oregon	11.9		37	Virginia	7.4
43	Pennsylvania	3.2		38	Tennessee	7.0
50	Rhode Island	0.0		39	North Carolina	6.7
16	South Carolina	13.7		40	Ohio	4.9
7	South Dakota	20.2		41	Minnesota	4.6
38	Tennessee	7.0		42	Massachusetts	3.4
20	Texas	12.0		43	Maine	3.2
36	Utah	7.6		43	Pennsylvania	3.2
48	Vermont	1.0		45	Hawaii	2.5
37	Virginia	7.4		46	New Hampshire	2.3
18	Washington	12.7		47	Nebraska	1.2
35	West Virginia	8.1		48	Vermont	1.0
32	Wisconsin	8.6		49	New Jersey	0.1
7	Wyoming	20.2		50	Rhode Island	0.0
					District of Columbia	24.9

Source: CQ Press using data from U.S. Department of Health and Human Services, Division of Shortage Designation
   "State Population and HPSA Designation Population Statistics" (as of January 9, 2013)
      (http://datawarehouse.hrsa.gov/hpsadetail.aspx)
*Percent of population considered under-served by primary medical practitioners (Family and General Practice doctors, Internists, Ob/Gyns, and Pediatricians). An under-served population does not have primary medical care within reasonable economic and geographic bounds.

Physicians in 2012

National Total = 1,012,546 Physicians*

ALPHA ORDER

RANK	STATE	PHYSICIANS	% of USA
27	Alabama	12,051	1.2%
49	Alaska	1,913	0.2%
18	Arizona	17,867	1.8%
32	Arkansas	7,050	0.7%
1	California	123,474	12.2%
21	Colorado	16,632	1.6%
23	Connecticut	15,987	1.6%
46	Delaware	2,706	0.3%
4	Florida	60,644	6.0%
14	Georgia	25,784	2.5%
38	Hawaii	5,099	0.5%
43	Idaho	3,262	0.3%
6	Illinois	43,179	4.3%
22	Indiana	16,498	1.6%
33	Iowa	6,943	0.7%
30	Kansas	7,821	0.8%
28	Kentucky	11,747	1.2%
24	Louisiana	14,326	1.4%
42	Maine	4,567	0.5%
12	Maryland	28,478	2.8%
8	Massachusetts	36,578	3.6%
10	Michigan	30,430	3.0%
17	Minnesota	19,003	1.9%
34	Mississippi	6,341	0.6%
20	Missouri	17,424	1.7%
45	Montana	2,760	0.3%
37	Nebraska	5,326	0.5%
35	Nevada	6,153	0.6%
41	New Hampshire	4,724	0.5%
9	New Jersey	32,097	3.2%
36	New Mexico	6,036	0.6%
2	New York	89,947	8.9%
11	North Carolina	29,122	2.9%
48	North Dakota	1,987	0.2%
7	Ohio	37,406	3.7%
29	Oklahoma	7,930	0.8%
25	Oregon	13,665	1.3%
5	Pennsylvania	46,186	4.6%
40	Rhode Island	4,741	0.5%
26	South Carolina	12,780	1.3%
47	South Dakota	2,226	0.2%
16	Tennessee	19,823	2.0%
3	Texas	64,708	6.4%
31	Utah	7,103	0.7%
44	Vermont	2,856	0.3%
13	Virginia	26,549	2.6%
15	Washington	22,661	2.2%
39	West Virginia	5,049	0.5%
19	Wisconsin	17,787	1.8%
50	Wyoming	1,285	0.1%

RANK ORDER

RANK	STATE	PHYSICIANS	% of USA
1	California	123,474	12.2%
2	New York	89,947	8.9%
3	Texas	64,708	6.4%
4	Florida	60,644	6.0%
5	Pennsylvania	46,186	4.6%
6	Illinois	43,179	4.3%
7	Ohio	37,406	3.7%
8	Massachusetts	36,578	3.6%
9	New Jersey	32,097	3.2%
10	Michigan	30,430	3.0%
11	North Carolina	29,122	2.9%
12	Maryland	28,478	2.8%
13	Virginia	26,549	2.6%
14	Georgia	25,784	2.5%
15	Washington	22,661	2.2%
16	Tennessee	19,823	2.0%
17	Minnesota	19,003	1.9%
18	Arizona	17,867	1.8%
19	Wisconsin	17,787	1.8%
20	Missouri	17,424	1.7%
21	Colorado	16,632	1.6%
22	Indiana	16,498	1.6%
23	Connecticut	15,987	1.6%
24	Louisiana	14,326	1.4%
25	Oregon	13,665	1.3%
26	South Carolina	12,780	1.3%
27	Alabama	12,051	1.2%
28	Kentucky	11,747	1.2%
29	Oklahoma	7,930	0.8%
30	Kansas	7,821	0.8%
31	Utah	7,103	0.7%
32	Arkansas	7,050	0.7%
33	Iowa	6,943	0.7%
34	Mississippi	6,341	0.6%
35	Nevada	6,153	0.6%
36	New Mexico	6,036	0.6%
37	Nebraska	5,326	0.5%
38	Hawaii	5,099	0.5%
39	West Virginia	5,049	0.5%
40	Rhode Island	4,741	0.5%
41	New Hampshire	4,724	0.5%
42	Maine	4,567	0.5%
43	Idaho	3,262	0.3%
44	Vermont	2,856	0.3%
45	Montana	2,760	0.3%
46	Delaware	2,706	0.3%
47	South Dakota	2,226	0.2%
48	North Dakota	1,987	0.2%
49	Alaska	1,913	0.2%
50	Wyoming	1,285	0.1%
	District of Columbia	5,835	0.6%

Source: American Medical Association (Chicago, Illinois)
    "Physician Characteristics and Distribution in the U.S." (2014 Edition)
*As of December 31, 2012. Total does not include 14,242 physicians in the U.S. territories and possessions, at APOs and FPOs, or whose addresses are unknown.

Rate of Physicians in 2012

National Rate = 323 Physicians per 100,000 Population*

ALPHA ORDER

RANK	STATE	RATE
41	Alabama	250
38	Alaska	262
32	Arizona	273
44	Arkansas	239
16	California	325
19	Colorado	320
6	Connecticut	445
26	Delaware	295
20	Florida	314
39	Georgia	260
7	Hawaii	367
50	Idaho	204
14	Illinois	336
40	Indiana	252
45	Iowa	226
34	Kansas	271
36	Kentucky	268
21	Louisiana	311
13	Maine	344
2	Maryland	484
1	Massachusetts	550
23	Michigan	308
11	Minnesota	353
48	Mississippi	212
28	Missouri	289
31	Montana	274
29	Nebraska	287
46	Nevada	223
10	New Hampshire	357
8	New Jersey	362
27	New Mexico	290
3	New York	459
25	North Carolina	299
30	North Dakota	283
17	Ohio	324
49	Oklahoma	208
12	Oregon	350
8	Pennsylvania	362
5	Rhode Island	451
34	South Carolina	271
37	South Dakota	267
24	Tennessee	307
43	Texas	248
42	Utah	249
4	Vermont	456
17	Virginia	324
15	Washington	329
33	West Virginia	272
21	Wisconsin	311
46	Wyoming	223

RANK ORDER

RANK	STATE	RATE
1	Massachusetts	550
2	Maryland	484
3	New York	459
4	Vermont	456
5	Rhode Island	451
6	Connecticut	445
7	Hawaii	367
8	New Jersey	362
8	Pennsylvania	362
10	New Hampshire	357
11	Minnesota	353
12	Oregon	350
13	Maine	344
14	Illinois	336
15	Washington	329
16	California	325
17	Ohio	324
17	Virginia	324
19	Colorado	320
20	Florida	314
21	Louisiana	311
21	Wisconsin	311
23	Michigan	308
24	Tennessee	307
25	North Carolina	299
26	Delaware	295
27	New Mexico	290
28	Missouri	289
29	Nebraska	287
30	North Dakota	283
31	Montana	274
32	Arizona	273
33	West Virginia	272
34	Kansas	271
34	South Carolina	271
36	Kentucky	268
37	South Dakota	267
38	Alaska	262
39	Georgia	260
40	Indiana	252
41	Alabama	250
42	Utah	249
43	Texas	248
44	Arkansas	239
45	Iowa	226
46	Nevada	223
46	Wyoming	223
48	Mississippi	212
49	Oklahoma	208
50	Idaho	204

District of Columbia   921

Source: CQ Press using data from American Medical Association (Chicago, Illinois)
   "Physician Characteristics and Distribution in the U.S." (2014 Edition)
*As of December 31, 2012. National rate does not include physicians in the U.S. territories and possessions, at APOs and FPOs, or whose addresses are unknown.

Rate of Registered Nurses in 2012

National Rate = 839 Nurses per 100,000 Population*

RANK	STATE	RATE
22	Alabama	908
39	Alaska	733
46	Arizona	696
34	Arkansas	796
47	California	658
33	Colorado	797
15	Connecticut	969
7	Delaware	1,053
30	Florida	847
48	Georgia	647
40	Hawaii	724
42	Idaho	716
24	Illinois	892
23	Indiana	894
8	Iowa	1,046
21	Kansas	914
14	Kentucky	980
27	Louisiana	873
6	Maine	1,073
35	Maryland	775
2	Massachusetts	1,197
20	Michigan	916
10	Minnesota	1,021
18	Mississippi	944
4	Missouri	1,083
32	Montana	835
12	Nebraska	1,002
50	Nevada	610
17	New Hampshire	948
31	New Jersey	842
44	New Mexico	709
29	New York	853
26	North Carolina	885
5	North Dakota	1,081
9	Ohio	1,043
45	Oklahoma	704
38	Oregon	740
13	Pennsylvania	981
3	Rhode Island	1,127
25	South Carolina	886
1	South Dakota	1,322
28	Tennessee	861
41	Texas	719
49	Utah	628
11	Vermont	1,008
42	Virginia	716
37	Washington	741
19	West Virginia	939
16	Wisconsin	954
36	Wyoming	773

RANK	STATE	RATE
1	South Dakota	1,322
2	Massachusetts	1,197
3	Rhode Island	1,127
4	Missouri	1,083
5	North Dakota	1,081
6	Maine	1,073
7	Delaware	1,053
8	Iowa	1,046
9	Ohio	1,043
10	Minnesota	1,021
11	Vermont	1,008
12	Nebraska	1,002
13	Pennsylvania	981
14	Kentucky	980
15	Connecticut	969
16	Wisconsin	954
17	New Hampshire	948
18	Mississippi	944
19	West Virginia	939
20	Michigan	916
21	Kansas	914
22	Alabama	908
23	Indiana	894
24	Illinois	892
25	South Carolina	886
26	North Carolina	885
27	Louisiana	873
28	Tennessee	861
29	New York	853
30	Florida	847
31	New Jersey	842
32	Montana	835
33	Colorado	797
34	Arkansas	796
35	Maryland	775
36	Wyoming	773
37	Washington	741
38	Oregon	740
39	Alaska	733
40	Hawaii	724
41	Texas	719
42	Idaho	716
42	Virginia	716
44	New Mexico	709
45	Oklahoma	704
46	Arizona	696
47	California	658
48	Georgia	647
49	Utah	628
50	Nevada	610

District of Columbia	1,786

Source: CQ Press using data from U.S. Department of Labor, Bureau of Labor Statistics
"Occupational Employment and Wages, 2012" (http://www.bls.gov/oes/)
*Does not include self-employed.

Rate of Dentists in 2011

National Rate = 62 Dentists per 100,000 Population*

RANK	STATE	RATE
48	Alabama	44
3	Alaska	81
28	Arizona	55
49	Arkansas	42
7	California	78
11	Colorado	69
5	Connecticut	79
43	Delaware	48
28	Florida	55
45	Georgia	47
5	Hawaii	79
22	Idaho	59
12	Illinois	68
40	Indiana	49
25	Iowa	56
33	Kansas	52
25	Kentucky	56
37	Louisiana	50
35	Maine	51
8	Maryland	75
1	Massachusetts	86
17	Michigan	62
17	Minnesota	62
49	Mississippi	42
37	Missouri	50
17	Montana	62
16	Nebraska	63
30	Nevada	54
14	New Hampshire	65
2	New Jersey	83
40	New Mexico	49
4	New York	80
45	North Carolina	47
25	North Dakota	56
30	Ohio	54
37	Oklahoma	50
10	Oregon	71
15	Pennsylvania	64
22	Rhode Island	59
43	South Carolina	48
30	South Dakota	54
35	Tennessee	51
40	Texas	49
13	Utah	67
21	Vermont	60
17	Virginia	62
9	Washington	72
45	West Virginia	47
24	Wisconsin	58
33	Wyoming	52

RANK	STATE	RATE
1	Massachusetts	86
2	New Jersey	83
3	Alaska	81
4	New York	80
5	Connecticut	79
5	Hawaii	79
7	California	78
8	Maryland	75
9	Washington	72
10	Oregon	71
11	Colorado	69
12	Illinois	68
13	Utah	67
14	New Hampshire	65
15	Pennsylvania	64
16	Nebraska	63
17	Michigan	62
17	Minnesota	62
17	Montana	62
17	Virginia	62
21	Vermont	60
22	Idaho	59
22	Rhode Island	59
24	Wisconsin	58
25	Iowa	56
25	Kentucky	56
25	North Dakota	56
28	Arizona	55
28	Florida	55
30	Nevada	54
30	Ohio	54
30	South Dakota	54
33	Kansas	52
33	Wyoming	52
35	Maine	51
35	Tennessee	51
37	Louisiana	50
37	Missouri	50
37	Oklahoma	50
40	Indiana	49
40	New Mexico	49
40	Texas	49
43	Delaware	48
43	South Carolina	48
45	Georgia	47
45	North Carolina	47
45	West Virginia	47
48	Alabama	44
49	Arkansas	42
49	Mississippi	42
	District of Columbia	108

Source: American Dental Association
    "Dentist Supply in the US: 1993 - 2011" (http://www.ada.org/1443.aspx)
*Professionally active dentists. National figure includes 36 dentists for whom state is not known.

Community Hospitals in 2012

National Total = 4,999 Hospitals*

RANK	STATE	HOSPITALS	% of USA
22	Alabama	97	1.9%
47	Alaska	23	0.5%
30	Arizona	72	1.4%
26	Arkansas	83	1.7%
2	California	349	7.0%
28	Colorado	82	1.6%
43	Connecticut	34	0.7%
50	Delaware	7	0.1%
3	Florida	216	4.3%
9	Georgia	148	3.0%
45	Hawaii	24	0.5%
39	Idaho	40	0.8%
5	Illinois	188	3.8%
14	Indiana	124	2.5%
17	Iowa	118	2.4%
12	Kansas	131	2.6%
20	Kentucky	106	2.1%
14	Louisiana	124	2.5%
41	Maine	37	0.7%
35	Maryland	50	1.0%
26	Massachusetts	83	1.7%
8	Michigan	151	3.0%
10	Minnesota	133	2.7%
21	Mississippi	98	2.0%
16	Missouri	123	2.5%
36	Montana	48	1.0%
24	Nebraska	89	1.8%
40	Nevada	38	0.8%
44	New Hampshire	28	0.6%
29	New Jersey	77	1.5%
41	New Mexico	37	0.7%
7	New York	178	3.6%
17	North Carolina	118	2.4%
38	North Dakota	44	0.9%
6	Ohio	185	3.7%
19	Oklahoma	117	2.3%
32	Oregon	58	1.2%
4	Pennsylvania	192	3.8%
49	Rhode Island	11	0.2%
31	South Carolina	67	1.3%
34	South Dakota	54	1.1%
11	Tennessee	132	2.6%
1	Texas	425	8.5%
37	Utah	47	0.9%
48	Vermont	14	0.3%
23	Virginia	94	1.9%
25	Washington	87	1.7%
33	West Virginia	55	1.1%
13	Wisconsin	128	2.6%
45	Wyoming	24	0.5%

RANK	STATE	HOSPITALS	% of USA
1	Texas	425	8.5%
2	California	349	7.0%
3	Florida	216	4.3%
4	Pennsylvania	192	3.8%
5	Illinois	188	3.8%
6	Ohio	185	3.7%
7	New York	178	3.6%
8	Michigan	151	3.0%
9	Georgia	148	3.0%
10	Minnesota	133	2.7%
11	Tennessee	132	2.6%
12	Kansas	131	2.6%
13	Wisconsin	128	2.6%
14	Indiana	124	2.5%
14	Louisiana	124	2.5%
16	Missouri	123	2.5%
17	Iowa	118	2.4%
17	North Carolina	118	2.4%
19	Oklahoma	117	2.3%
20	Kentucky	106	2.1%
21	Mississippi	98	2.0%
22	Alabama	97	1.9%
23	Virginia	94	1.9%
24	Nebraska	89	1.8%
25	Washington	87	1.7%
26	Arkansas	83	1.7%
26	Massachusetts	83	1.7%
28	Colorado	82	1.6%
29	New Jersey	77	1.5%
30	Arizona	72	1.4%
31	South Carolina	67	1.3%
32	Oregon	58	1.2%
33	West Virginia	55	1.1%
34	South Dakota	54	1.1%
35	Maryland	50	1.0%
36	Montana	48	1.0%
37	Utah	47	0.9%
38	North Dakota	44	0.9%
39	Idaho	40	0.8%
40	Nevada	38	0.8%
41	Maine	37	0.7%
41	New Mexico	37	0.7%
43	Connecticut	34	0.7%
44	New Hampshire	28	0.6%
45	Hawaii	24	0.5%
45	Wyoming	24	0.5%
47	Alaska	23	0.5%
48	Vermont	14	0.3%
49	Rhode Island	11	0.2%
50	Delaware	7	0.1%
	District of Columbia	11	0.2%

Source: American Hospital Association (Chicago, IL)
      "Hospital Statistics" (2014 edition)
*Community hospitals are all nonfederal, short-term general, and special hospitals whose facilities and services are available to the public.

Rate of Community Hospitals in 2012

National Rate = 1.6 Community Hospitals per 100,000 Population*

ALPHA ORDER

RANK	STATE	RATE
21	Alabama	2.0
9	Alaska	3.1
41	Arizona	1.1
12	Arkansas	2.8
45	California	0.9
27	Colorado	1.6
45	Connecticut	0.9
49	Delaware	0.8
41	Florida	1.1
31	Georgia	1.5
26	Hawaii	1.7
15	Idaho	2.5
31	Illinois	1.5
24	Indiana	1.9
7	Iowa	3.8
5	Kansas	4.5
17	Kentucky	2.4
14	Louisiana	2.7
12	Maine	2.8
49	Maryland	0.8
39	Massachusetts	1.2
31	Michigan	1.5
15	Minnesota	2.5
8	Mississippi	3.3
21	Missouri	2.0
3	Montana	4.8
3	Nebraska	4.8
36	Nevada	1.4
20	New Hampshire	2.1
45	New Jersey	0.9
25	New Mexico	1.8
45	New York	0.9
39	North Carolina	1.2
2	North Dakota	6.3
27	Ohio	1.6
9	Oklahoma	3.1
31	Oregon	1.5
31	Pennsylvania	1.5
44	Rhode Island	1.0
36	South Carolina	1.4
1	South Dakota	6.5
21	Tennessee	2.0
27	Texas	1.6
27	Utah	1.6
18	Vermont	2.2
41	Virginia	1.1
38	Washington	1.3
11	West Virginia	3.0
18	Wisconsin	2.2
6	Wyoming	4.2

RANK ORDER

RANK	STATE	RATE
1	South Dakota	6.5
2	North Dakota	6.3
3	Montana	4.8
3	Nebraska	4.8
5	Kansas	4.5
6	Wyoming	4.2
7	Iowa	3.8
8	Mississippi	3.3
9	Alaska	3.1
9	Oklahoma	3.1
11	West Virginia	3.0
12	Arkansas	2.8
12	Maine	2.8
14	Louisiana	2.7
15	Idaho	2.5
15	Minnesota	2.5
17	Kentucky	2.4
18	Vermont	2.2
18	Wisconsin	2.2
20	New Hampshire	2.1
21	Alabama	2.0
21	Missouri	2.0
21	Tennessee	2.0
24	Indiana	1.9
25	New Mexico	1.8
26	Hawaii	1.7
27	Colorado	1.6
27	Ohio	1.6
27	Texas	1.6
27	Utah	1.6
31	Georgia	1.5
31	Illinois	1.5
31	Michigan	1.5
31	Oregon	1.5
31	Pennsylvania	1.5
36	Nevada	1.4
36	South Carolina	1.4
38	Washington	1.3
39	Massachusetts	1.2
39	North Carolina	1.2
41	Arizona	1.1
41	Florida	1.1
41	Virginia	1.1
44	Rhode Island	1.0
45	California	0.9
45	Connecticut	0.9
45	New Jersey	0.9
45	New York	0.9
49	Delaware	0.8
49	Maryland	0.8

District of Columbia   1.7

Source: CQ Press using data from American Hospital Association (Chicago, IL)
     "Hospital Statistics" (2014 edition)
*Community hospitals are all nonfederal, short-term general, and special hospitals whose facilities and services are available to the public.

Births in 2012

National Total = 3,952,841 Live Births*

ALPHA ORDER

RANK	STATE	BIRTHS	% of USA
24	Alabama	58,448	1.5%
45	Alaska	11,187	0.3%
14	Arizona	86,441	2.2%
33	Arkansas	38,347	1.0%
1	California	503,755	12.7%
22	Colorado	65,187	1.6%
34	Connecticut	36,539	0.9%
46	Delaware	11,023	0.3%
4	Florida	213,148	5.4%
8	Georgia	130,280	3.3%
40	Hawaii	18,980	0.5%
38	Idaho	22,963	0.6%
5	Illinois	159,160	4.0%
15	Indiana	83,227	2.1%
31	Iowa	38,702	1.0%
30	Kansas	40,341	1.0%
26	Kentucky	55,758	1.4%
23	Louisiana	62,642	1.6%
41	Maine	12,798	0.3%
18	Maryland	72,883	1.8%
19	Massachusetts	72,439	1.8%
10	Michigan	113,091	2.9%
20	Minnesota	68,772	1.7%
32	Mississippi	38,669	1.0%
17	Missouri	75,446	1.9%
43	Montana	12,118	0.3%
37	Nebraska	25,942	0.7%
35	Nevada	34,911	0.9%
42	New Hampshire	12,352	0.3%
11	New Jersey	104,230	2.6%
36	New Mexico	27,068	0.7%
3	New York	240,916	6.1%
9	North Carolina	119,831	3.0%
48	North Dakota	10,106	0.3%
7	Ohio	138,483	3.5%
27	Oklahoma	52,751	1.3%
29	Oregon	45,067	1.1%
6	Pennsylvania	142,514	3.6%
47	Rhode Island	10,926	0.3%
25	South Carolina	57,155	1.4%
44	South Dakota	12,104	0.3%
16	Tennessee	80,371	2.0%
2	Texas	382,727	9.7%
28	Utah	51,465	1.3%
50	Vermont	6,009	0.2%
12	Virginia	103,013	2.6%
13	Washington	87,463	2.2%
39	West Virginia	20,827	0.5%
21	Wisconsin	67,295	1.7%
49	Wyoming	7,572	0.2%

RANK ORDER

RANK	STATE	BIRTHS	% of USA
1	California	503,755	12.7%
2	Texas	382,727	9.7%
3	New York	240,916	6.1%
4	Florida	213,148	5.4%
5	Illinois	159,160	4.0%
6	Pennsylvania	142,514	3.6%
7	Ohio	138,483	3.5%
8	Georgia	130,280	3.3%
9	North Carolina	119,831	3.0%
10	Michigan	113,091	2.9%
11	New Jersey	104,230	2.6%
12	Virginia	103,013	2.6%
13	Washington	87,463	2.2%
14	Arizona	86,441	2.2%
15	Indiana	83,227	2.1%
16	Tennessee	80,371	2.0%
17	Missouri	75,446	1.9%
18	Maryland	72,883	1.8%
19	Massachusetts	72,439	1.8%
20	Minnesota	68,772	1.7%
21	Wisconsin	67,295	1.7%
22	Colorado	65,187	1.6%
23	Louisiana	62,642	1.6%
24	Alabama	58,448	1.5%
25	South Carolina	57,155	1.4%
26	Kentucky	55,758	1.4%
27	Oklahoma	52,751	1.3%
28	Utah	51,465	1.3%
29	Oregon	45,067	1.1%
30	Kansas	40,341	1.0%
31	Iowa	38,702	1.0%
32	Mississippi	38,669	1.0%
33	Arkansas	38,347	1.0%
34	Connecticut	36,539	0.9%
35	Nevada	34,911	0.9%
36	New Mexico	27,068	0.7%
37	Nebraska	25,942	0.7%
38	Idaho	22,963	0.6%
39	West Virginia	20,827	0.5%
40	Hawaii	18,980	0.5%
41	Maine	12,798	0.3%
42	New Hampshire	12,352	0.3%
43	Montana	12,118	0.3%
44	South Dakota	12,104	0.3%
45	Alaska	11,187	0.3%
46	Delaware	11,023	0.3%
47	Rhode Island	10,926	0.3%
48	North Dakota	10,106	0.3%
49	Wyoming	7,572	0.2%
50	Vermont	6,009	0.2%
	District of Columbia	9,399	0.2%

Source: U.S. Department of Health and Human Services, National Center for Health Statistics
    "National Vital Statistics Reports" (Vol. 62, No. 9, December 30, 2013, http://www.cdc.gov/nchs/births.htm)
*Final data by state of residence.

Birth Rate in 2012

National Rate = 12.6 Live Births per 1,000 Population*

ALPHA ORDER				RANK ORDER		
RANK	STATE	RATE		RANK	STATE	RATE
33	Alabama	12.1		1	Utah	18.0
2	Alaska	15.3		2	Alaska	15.3
12	Arizona	13.2		3	Texas	14.7
16	Arkansas	13.0		4	South Dakota	14.5
12	California	13.2		5	Idaho	14.4
24	Colorado	12.6		5	North Dakota	14.4
47	Connecticut	10.2		7	Kansas	14.0
36	Delaware	12.0		7	Nebraska	14.0
44	Florida	11.0		9	Oklahoma	13.8
14	Georgia	13.1		10	Hawaii	13.6
10	Hawaii	13.6		10	Louisiana	13.6
5	Idaho	14.4		12	Arizona	13.2
28	Illinois	12.4		12	California	13.2
20	Indiana	12.7		14	Georgia	13.1
24	Iowa	12.6		14	Wyoming	13.1
7	Kansas	14.0		16	Arkansas	13.0
20	Kentucky	12.7		16	Mississippi	13.0
10	Louisiana	13.6		16	New Mexico	13.0
48	Maine	9.6		19	Minnesota	12.8
28	Maryland	12.4		20	Indiana	12.7
45	Massachusetts	10.9		20	Kentucky	12.7
41	Michigan	11.4		20	Nevada	12.7
19	Minnesota	12.8		20	Washington	12.7
16	Mississippi	13.0		24	Colorado	12.6
27	Missouri	12.5		24	Iowa	12.6
33	Montana	12.1		24	Virginia	12.6
7	Nebraska	14.0		27	Missouri	12.5
20	Nevada	12.7		28	Illinois	12.4
50	New Hampshire	9.4		28	Maryland	12.4
38	New Jersey	11.8		28	Tennessee	12.4
16	New Mexico	13.0		31	New York	12.3
31	New York	12.3		31	North Carolina	12.3
31	North Carolina	12.3		33	Alabama	12.1
5	North Dakota	14.4		33	Montana	12.1
36	Ohio	12.0		33	South Carolina	12.1
9	Oklahoma	13.8		36	Delaware	12.0
40	Oregon	11.6		36	Ohio	12.0
42	Pennsylvania	11.2		38	New Jersey	11.8
46	Rhode Island	10.4		38	Wisconsin	11.8
33	South Carolina	12.1		40	Oregon	11.6
4	South Dakota	14.5		41	Michigan	11.4
28	Tennessee	12.4		42	Pennsylvania	11.2
3	Texas	14.7		42	West Virginia	11.2
1	Utah	18.0		44	Florida	11.0
48	Vermont	9.6		45	Massachusetts	10.9
24	Virginia	12.6		46	Rhode Island	10.4
20	Washington	12.7		47	Connecticut	10.2
42	West Virginia	11.2		48	Maine	9.6
38	Wisconsin	11.8		48	Vermont	9.6
14	Wyoming	13.1		50	New Hampshire	9.4
					District of Columbia	14.9

Source: U.S. Department of Health and Human Services, National Center for Health Statistics
  "National Vital Statistics Reports" (Vol. 62, No. 9, December 30, 2013, http://www.cdc.gov/nchs/births.htm)
*Final data by state of residence.

Births of Low Birthweight as a Percent of All Births in 2011

National Percent = 8.1% of Live Births*

ALPHA ORDER				RANK ORDER		
RANK	STATE	PERCENT		RANK	STATE	PERCENT
3	Alabama	9.9		1	Mississippi	11.8
50	Alaska	6.0		2	Louisiana	10.9
37	Arizona	7.0		3	Alabama	9.9
7	Arkansas	9.1		3	South Carolina	9.9
39	California	6.8		5	West Virginia	9.6
13	Colorado	8.7		6	Georgia	9.4
30	Connecticut	7.7		7	Arkansas	9.1
19	Delaware	8.4		7	Kentucky	9.1
13	Florida	8.7		9	North Carolina	9.0
6	Georgia	9.4		9	Tennessee	9.0
21	Hawaii	8.2		11	Maryland	8.9
47	Idaho	6.1		12	New Mexico	8.8
21	Illinois	8.2		13	Colorado	8.7
25	Indiana	8.1		13	Florida	8.7
44	Iowa	6.5		15	Ohio	8.6
33	Kansas	7.2		16	New Jersey	8.5
7	Kentucky	9.1		16	Oklahoma	8.5
2	Louisiana	10.9		16	Texas	8.5
40	Maine	6.7		19	Delaware	8.4
11	Maryland	8.9		20	Michigan	8.3
31	Massachusetts	7.6		21	Hawaii	8.2
20	Michigan	8.3		21	Illinois	8.2
45	Minnesota	6.4		21	Nevada	8.2
1	Mississippi	11.8		21	Pennsylvania	8.2
29	Missouri	7.9		25	Indiana	8.1
33	Montana	7.2		25	New York	8.1
43	Nebraska	6.6		25	Wyoming	8.1
21	Nevada	8.2		28	Virginia	8.0
36	New Hampshire	7.1		29	Missouri	7.9
16	New Jersey	8.5		30	Connecticut	7.7
12	New Mexico	8.8		31	Massachusetts	7.6
25	New York	8.1		32	Rhode Island	7.4
9	North Carolina	9.0		33	Kansas	7.2
40	North Dakota	6.7		33	Montana	7.2
15	Ohio	8.6		33	Wisconsin	7.2
16	Oklahoma	8.5		36	New Hampshire	7.1
47	Oregon	6.1		37	Arizona	7.0
21	Pennsylvania	8.2		38	Utah	6.9
32	Rhode Island	7.4		39	California	6.8
3	South Carolina	9.9		40	Maine	6.7
46	South Dakota	6.3		40	North Dakota	6.7
9	Tennessee	9.0		40	Vermont	6.7
16	Texas	8.5		43	Nebraska	6.6
38	Utah	6.9		44	Iowa	6.5
40	Vermont	6.7		45	Minnesota	6.4
28	Virginia	8.0		46	South Dakota	6.3
47	Washington	6.1		47	Idaho	6.1
5	West Virginia	9.6		47	Oregon	6.1
33	Wisconsin	7.2		47	Washington	6.1
25	Wyoming	8.1		50	Alaska	6.0
					District of Columbia	10.4

Source: U.S. Department of Health and Human Services, National Center for Health Statistics
   "National Vital Statistics Reports" (Vol. 62, No. 1, June 2013, http://www.cdc.gov/nchs/births.htm)
*Final data by state of residence. Births of less than 2,500 grams (5 pounds 8 ounces).

Births to Teenage Mothers as a Percent of All Births in 2011

National Percent = 8.3% of Live Births*

<table>
<tr><td colspan="3">ALPHA ORDER</td><td colspan="3">RANK ORDER</td></tr>
<tr><td>RANK</td><td>STATE</td><td>PERCENT</td><td>RANK</td><td>STATE</td><td>PERCENT</td></tr>
<tr><td>8</td><td>Alabama</td><td>11.1</td><td>1</td><td>Mississippi</td><td>13.5</td></tr>
<tr><td>26</td><td>Alaska</td><td>7.7</td><td>2</td><td>New Mexico</td><td>12.6</td></tr>
<tr><td>12</td><td>Arizona</td><td>9.8</td><td>3</td><td>Arkansas</td><td>12.5</td></tr>
<tr><td>3</td><td>Arkansas</td><td>12.5</td><td>4</td><td>West Virginia</td><td>11.9</td></tr>
<tr><td>28</td><td>California</td><td>7.6</td><td>5</td><td>Oklahoma</td><td>11.5</td></tr>
<tr><td>31</td><td>Colorado</td><td>7.3</td><td>6</td><td>Louisiana</td><td>11.3</td></tr>
<tr><td>45</td><td>Connecticut</td><td>5.4</td><td>6</td><td>Texas</td><td>11.3</td></tr>
<tr><td>24</td><td>Delaware</td><td>8.0</td><td>8</td><td>Alabama</td><td>11.1</td></tr>
<tr><td>24</td><td>Florida</td><td>8.0</td><td>9</td><td>Kentucky</td><td>11.0</td></tr>
<tr><td>12</td><td>Georgia</td><td>9.8</td><td>10</td><td>Tennessee</td><td>10.7</td></tr>
<tr><td>42</td><td>Hawaii</td><td>6.3</td><td>11</td><td>South Carolina</td><td>10.5</td></tr>
<tr><td>32</td><td>Idaho</td><td>7.1</td><td>12</td><td>Arizona</td><td>9.8</td></tr>
<tr><td>22</td><td>Illinois</td><td>8.1</td><td>12</td><td>Georgia</td><td>9.8</td></tr>
<tr><td>14</td><td>Indiana</td><td>9.5</td><td>14</td><td>Indiana</td><td>9.5</td></tr>
<tr><td>33</td><td>Iowa</td><td>7.0</td><td>15</td><td>North Carolina</td><td>9.2</td></tr>
<tr><td>18</td><td>Kansas</td><td>8.8</td><td>16</td><td>Missouri</td><td>9.1</td></tr>
<tr><td>9</td><td>Kentucky</td><td>11.0</td><td>17</td><td>Ohio</td><td>8.9</td></tr>
<tr><td>6</td><td>Louisiana</td><td>11.3</td><td>18</td><td>Kansas</td><td>8.8</td></tr>
<tr><td>35</td><td>Maine</td><td>6.8</td><td>19</td><td>Nevada</td><td>8.7</td></tr>
<tr><td>38</td><td>Maryland</td><td>6.6</td><td>20</td><td>Michigan</td><td>8.5</td></tr>
<tr><td>50</td><td>Massachusetts</td><td>4.8</td><td>21</td><td>Wyoming</td><td>8.4</td></tr>
<tr><td>20</td><td>Michigan</td><td>8.5</td><td>22</td><td>Illinois</td><td>8.1</td></tr>
<tr><td>46</td><td>Minnesota</td><td>5.1</td><td>22</td><td>South Dakota</td><td>8.1</td></tr>
<tr><td>1</td><td>Mississippi</td><td>13.5</td><td>24</td><td>Delaware</td><td>8.0</td></tr>
<tr><td>16</td><td>Missouri</td><td>9.1</td><td>24</td><td>Florida</td><td>8.0</td></tr>
<tr><td>26</td><td>Montana</td><td>7.7</td><td>26</td><td>Alaska</td><td>7.7</td></tr>
<tr><td>37</td><td>Nebraska</td><td>6.7</td><td>26</td><td>Montana</td><td>7.7</td></tr>
<tr><td>19</td><td>Nevada</td><td>8.7</td><td>28</td><td>California</td><td>7.6</td></tr>
<tr><td>49</td><td>New Hampshire</td><td>4.9</td><td>28</td><td>Pennsylvania</td><td>7.6</td></tr>
<tr><td>46</td><td>New Jersey</td><td>5.1</td><td>28</td><td>Rhode Island</td><td>7.6</td></tr>
<tr><td>2</td><td>New Mexico</td><td>12.6</td><td>31</td><td>Colorado</td><td>7.3</td></tr>
<tr><td>44</td><td>New York</td><td>5.7</td><td>32</td><td>Idaho</td><td>7.1</td></tr>
<tr><td>15</td><td>North Carolina</td><td>9.2</td><td>33</td><td>Iowa</td><td>7.0</td></tr>
<tr><td>35</td><td>North Dakota</td><td>6.8</td><td>34</td><td>Oregon</td><td>6.9</td></tr>
<tr><td>17</td><td>Ohio</td><td>8.9</td><td>35</td><td>Maine</td><td>6.8</td></tr>
<tr><td>5</td><td>Oklahoma</td><td>11.5</td><td>35</td><td>North Dakota</td><td>6.8</td></tr>
<tr><td>34</td><td>Oregon</td><td>6.9</td><td>37</td><td>Nebraska</td><td>6.7</td></tr>
<tr><td>28</td><td>Pennsylvania</td><td>7.6</td><td>38</td><td>Maryland</td><td>6.6</td></tr>
<tr><td>28</td><td>Rhode Island</td><td>7.6</td><td>38</td><td>Wisconsin</td><td>6.6</td></tr>
<tr><td>11</td><td>South Carolina</td><td>10.5</td><td>40</td><td>Virginia</td><td>6.4</td></tr>
<tr><td>22</td><td>South Dakota</td><td>8.1</td><td>40</td><td>Washington</td><td>6.4</td></tr>
<tr><td>10</td><td>Tennessee</td><td>10.7</td><td>42</td><td>Hawaii</td><td>6.3</td></tr>
<tr><td>6</td><td>Texas</td><td>11.3</td><td>43</td><td>Vermont</td><td>6.2</td></tr>
<tr><td>48</td><td>Utah</td><td>5.0</td><td>44</td><td>New York</td><td>5.7</td></tr>
<tr><td>43</td><td>Vermont</td><td>6.2</td><td>45</td><td>Connecticut</td><td>5.4</td></tr>
<tr><td>40</td><td>Virginia</td><td>6.4</td><td>46</td><td>Minnesota</td><td>5.1</td></tr>
<tr><td>40</td><td>Washington</td><td>6.4</td><td>46</td><td>New Jersey</td><td>5.1</td></tr>
<tr><td>4</td><td>West Virginia</td><td>11.9</td><td>48</td><td>Utah</td><td>5.0</td></tr>
<tr><td>38</td><td>Wisconsin</td><td>6.6</td><td>49</td><td>New Hampshire</td><td>4.9</td></tr>
<tr><td>21</td><td>Wyoming</td><td>8.4</td><td>50</td><td>Massachusetts</td><td>4.8</td></tr>
<tr><td></td><td></td><td></td><td></td><td>District of Columbia</td><td>9.5</td></tr>
</table>

Source: CQ Press using data from U.S. Department of Health and Human Services, Centers for Disease Control and Prevention
"National Vital Statistics Reports" (Vol. 61, No. 1, August 2012, http://www.cdc.gov/nchs/births.htm) and
"CDC Wonder" (http://wonder.cdc.gov)
*Final data. Live births to women 15 to 19 years old by state of residence.

Births to Unmarried Women as a Percent of All Births in 2011

National Percent = 40.7% of Live Births*

ALPHA ORDER			RANK ORDER		
RANK	STATE	PERCENT	RANK	STATE	PERCENT
17	Alabama	42.1	1	Mississippi	54.4
35	Alaska	36.8	2	Louisiana	52.9
9	Arizona	44.7	3	New Mexico	51.3
8	Arkansas	44.9	4	Delaware	48.6
26	California	40.4	5	Florida	47.6
49	Colorado	23.7	6	South Carolina	47.1
31	Connecticut	38.0	7	Georgia	45.4
4	Delaware	48.6	8	Arkansas	44.9
5	Florida	47.6	9	Arizona	44.7
7	Georgia	45.4	10	Rhode Island	44.5
32	Hawaii	37.5	11	Nevada	44.2
48	Idaho	26.8	12	Tennessee	44.1
28	Illinois	40.0	13	West Virginia	43.9
15	Indiana	42.7	14	Ohio	43.4
43	Iowa	33.8	15	Indiana	42.7
33	Kansas	37.3	16	Michigan	42.3
22	Kentucky	41.5	17	Alabama	42.1
2	Louisiana	52.9	18	Texas	42.0
19	Maine	41.8	19	Maine	41.8
23	Maryland	41.2	19	Oklahoma	41.8
40	Massachusetts	34.7	21	Pennsylvania	41.7
16	Michigan	42.3	22	Kentucky	41.5
47	Minnesota	32.7	23	Maryland	41.2
1	Mississippi	54.4	24	New York	41.1
27	Missouri	40.1	25	North Carolina	40.9
36	Montana	36.5	26	California	40.4
45	Nebraska	33.2	27	Missouri	40.1
11	Nevada	44.2	28	Illinois	40.0
41	New Hampshire	34.5	29	Vermont	39.5
37	New Jersey	35.9	30	South Dakota	38.9
3	New Mexico	51.3	31	Connecticut	38.0
24	New York	41.1	32	Hawaii	37.5
25	North Carolina	40.9	33	Kansas	37.3
44	North Dakota	33.4	34	Wisconsin	36.9
14	Ohio	43.4	35	Alaska	36.8
19	Oklahoma	41.8	36	Montana	36.5
38	Oregon	35.7	37	New Jersey	35.9
21	Pennsylvania	41.7	38	Oregon	35.7
10	Rhode Island	44.5	39	Virginia	35.5
6	South Carolina	47.1	40	Massachusetts	34.7
30	South Dakota	38.9	41	New Hampshire	34.5
12	Tennessee	44.1	41	Wyoming	34.5
18	Texas	42.0	43	Iowa	33.8
50	Utah	18.7	44	North Dakota	33.4
29	Vermont	39.5	45	Nebraska	33.2
39	Virginia	35.5	46	Washington	32.8
46	Washington	32.8	47	Minnesota	32.7
13	West Virginia	43.9	48	Idaho	26.8
34	Wisconsin	36.9	49	Colorado	23.7
41	Wyoming	34.5	50	Utah	18.7
				District of Columbia	53.6

Source: U.S. Department of Health and Human Services, National Center for Health Statistics
"National Vital Statistics Reports" (Vol. 62, No. 1, June 2013, http://www.cdc.gov/nchs/births.htm)
*Final data by state of residence.

Percent of Women Receiving Late or No Prenatal Care in 2011

National Percent = 6.0% of Women*

ALPHA ORDER

RANK	STATE	PERCENT
NA	Alabama**	NA
NA	Alaska**	NA
NA	Arizona**	NA
NA	Arkansas**	NA
35	California	3.4
11	Colorado	6.7
NA	Connecticut**	NA
6	Delaware	7.4
19	Florida	5.5
7	Georgia	7.3
NA	Hawaii**	NA
24	Idaho	4.8
24	Illinois	4.8
13	Indiana	6.4
34	Iowa	3.7
26	Kansas	4.6
20	Kentucky	5.4
17	Louisiana	6.0
NA	Maine**	NA
3	Maryland	8.4
NA	Massachusetts**	NA
28	Michigan	4.5
NA	Minnesota**	NA
NA	Mississippi**	NA
26	Missouri	4.6
20	Montana	5.4
28	Nebraska	4.5
1	Nevada	11.5
33	New Hampshire	3.8
NA	New Jersey**	NA
4	New Mexico	8.3
20	New York	5.4
20	North Carolina	5.4
8	North Dakota	7.2
18	Ohio	5.6
5	Oklahoma	8.2
30	Oregon	4.4
12	Pennsylvania	6.6
NA	Rhode Island**	NA
8	South Carolina	7.2
15	South Dakota	6.1
10	Tennessee	6.9
2	Texas	10.4
31	Utah	4.0
36	Vermont	2.4
NA	Virginia**	NA
13	Washington	6.4
NA	West Virginia**	NA
32	Wisconsin	3.9
15	Wyoming	6.1

RANK ORDER

RANK	STATE	PERCENT
1	Nevada	11.5
2	Texas	10.4
3	Maryland	8.4
4	New Mexico	8.3
5	Oklahoma	8.2
6	Delaware	7.4
7	Georgia	7.3
8	North Dakota	7.2
8	South Carolina	7.2
10	Tennessee	6.9
11	Colorado	6.7
12	Pennsylvania	6.6
13	Indiana	6.4
13	Washington	6.4
15	South Dakota	6.1
15	Wyoming	6.1
17	Louisiana	6.0
18	Ohio	5.6
19	Florida	5.5
20	Kentucky	5.4
20	Montana	5.4
20	New York	5.4
20	North Carolina	5.4
24	Idaho	4.8
24	Illinois	4.8
26	Kansas	4.6
26	Missouri	4.6
28	Michigan	4.5
28	Nebraska	4.5
30	Oregon	4.4
31	Utah	4.0
32	Wisconsin	3.9
33	New Hampshire	3.8
34	Iowa	3.7
35	California	3.4
36	Vermont	2.4
NA	Alabama**	NA
NA	Alaska**	NA
NA	Arizona**	NA
NA	Arkansas**	NA
NA	Connecticut**	NA
NA	Hawaii**	NA
NA	Maine**	NA
NA	Massachusetts**	NA
NA	Minnesota**	NA
NA	Mississippi**	NA
NA	New Jersey**	NA
NA	Rhode Island**	NA
NA	Virginia**	NA
NA	West Virginia**	NA

District of Columbia   9.2

Source: CQ Press using data from U.S. Department of Health and Human Services, Centers for Disease Control and Prevention
   "CDC Wonder" (http://wonder.cdc.gov)
*Final data by state of residence. "Late" means care begun in third trimester. National figure is for reporting states only.
**Not available.

Reported Legal Abortions in 2010

Reporting States' Total = 765,651 Abortions*

	ALPHA ORDER					RANK ORDER		
RANK	STATE	ABORTIONS	% of USA		RANK	STATE	ABORTIONS	% of USA
19	Alabama	10,280	1.3%		1	New York	115,724	15.1%
42	Alaska	1,715	0.2%		2	Florida	79,908	10.4%
17	Arizona	11,438	1.5%		3	Texas	77,463	10.1%
32	Arkansas	4,532	0.6%		4	Illinois	41,859	5.5%
NA	California**	NA	NA		5	Pennsylvania	36,778	4.8%
18	Colorado	11,210	1.5%		6	Georgia	34,585	4.5%
15	Connecticut	13,438	1.8%		7	North Carolina	30,952	4.0%
31	Delaware	4,666	0.6%		8	New Jersey	28,217	3.7%
2	Florida	79,908	10.4%		9	Ohio	28,123	3.7%
6	Georgia	34,585	4.5%		10	Virginia	25,943	3.4%
36	Hawaii	3,064	0.4%		11	Michigan	23,307	3.0%
43	Idaho	1,510	0.2%		12	Washington	21,124	2.8%
4	Illinois	41,859	5.5%		13	Massachusetts	20,802	2.7%
20	Indiana	10,048	1.3%		14	Tennessee	16,373	2.1%
29	Iowa	5,399	0.7%		15	Connecticut	13,438	1.8%
23	Kansas	8,333	1.1%		16	Minnesota	11,505	1.5%
34	Kentucky	3,929	0.5%		17	Arizona	11,438	1.5%
22	Louisiana	8,872	1.2%		18	Colorado	11,210	1.5%
38	Maine	2,311	0.3%		19	Alabama	10,280	1.3%
NA	Maryland**	NA	NA		20	Indiana	10,048	1.3%
13	Massachusetts	20,802	2.7%		21	Oregon	9,990	1.3%
11	Michigan	23,307	3.0%		22	Louisiana	8,872	1.2%
16	Minnesota	11,505	1.5%		23	Kansas	8,333	1.1%
39	Mississippi	2,297	0.3%		24	Wisconsin	7,825	1.0%
27	Missouri	6,163	0.8%		25	Nevada	7,787	1.0%
40	Montana	2,160	0.3%		26	South Carolina	6,464	0.8%
37	Nebraska	2,464	0.3%		27	Missouri	6,163	0.8%
25	Nevada	7,787	1.0%		28	Oklahoma	6,097	0.8%
NA	New Hampshire**	NA	NA		29	Iowa	5,399	0.7%
8	New Jersey	28,217	3.7%		30	New Mexico	4,779	0.6%
30	New Mexico	4,779	0.6%		31	Delaware	4,666	0.6%
1	New York	115,724	15.1%		32	Arkansas	4,532	0.6%
7	North Carolina	30,952	4.0%		33	Rhode Island	4,181	0.5%
45	North Dakota	1,291	0.2%		34	Kentucky	3,929	0.5%
9	Ohio	28,123	3.7%		35	Utah	3,780	0.5%
28	Oklahoma	6,097	0.8%		36	Hawaii	3,064	0.4%
21	Oregon	9,990	1.3%		37	Nebraska	2,464	0.3%
5	Pennsylvania	36,778	4.8%		38	Maine	2,311	0.3%
33	Rhode Island	4,181	0.5%		39	Mississippi	2,297	0.3%
26	South Carolina	6,464	0.8%		40	Montana	2,160	0.3%
46	South Dakota	737	0.1%		41	West Virginia	1,999	0.3%
14	Tennessee	16,373	2.1%		42	Alaska	1,715	0.2%
3	Texas	77,463	10.1%		43	Idaho	1,510	0.2%
35	Utah	3,780	0.5%		44	Vermont	1,333	0.2%
44	Vermont	1,333	0.2%		45	North Dakota	1,291	0.2%
10	Virginia	25,943	3.4%		46	South Dakota	737	0.1%
12	Washington	21,124	2.8%		NA	California**	NA	NA
41	West Virginia	1,999	0.3%		NA	Maryland**	NA	NA
24	Wisconsin	7,825	1.0%		NA	New Hampshire**	NA	NA
NA	Wyoming**	NA	NA		NA	Wyoming**	NA	NA
						District of Columbia	2,896	0.4%

Source: U.S. Department of Health and Human Services, Centers for Disease Control and Prevention
"Abortion Surveillance-United States, 2010" (MMWR, Vol. 62, No. SS-8, 11/29/13, www.cdc.gov/mmwr/mmwr_ss/ss_pvol.html)
*By state of occurrence. Total is for reporting states only.
**Not reported.

Reported Legal Abortions per 1,000 Live Births in 2010

Reporting States' Ratio = 228 Abortions per 1,000 Live Births*

ALPHA ORDER			RANK ORDER		
RANK	STATE	RATIO	RANK	STATE	RATIO
25	Alabama	171	1	New York	474
29	Alaska	150	2	Delaware	411
33	Arizona	131	3	Rhode Island	374
35	Arkansas	118	4	Florida	372
NA	California**	NA	5	Connecticut	356
26	Colorado	169	6	Massachusetts	285
5	Connecticut	356	7	New Jersey	264
2	Delaware	411	8	Georgia	258
4	Florida	372	9	Pennsylvania	257
8	Georgia	258	10	Illinois	253
28	Hawaii	161	10	North Carolina	253
44	Idaho	65	12	Virginia	252
10	Illinois	253	13	Washington	244
34	Indiana	120	14	Oregon	219
32	Iowa	139	15	Nevada	217
18	Kansas	205	16	Vermont	214
43	Kentucky	70	17	Tennessee	206
30	Louisiana	142	18	Kansas	205
23	Maine	178	19	Michigan	203
NA	Maryland**	NA	20	Ohio	202
6	Massachusetts	285	21	Texas	201
19	Michigan	203	22	Montana	179
27	Minnesota	168	23	Maine	178
46	Mississippi	57	24	New Mexico	172
41	Missouri	80	25	Alabama	171
22	Montana	179	26	Colorado	169
40	Nebraska	95	27	Minnesota	168
15	Nevada	217	28	Hawaii	161
NA	New Hampshire**	NA	29	Alaska	150
7	New Jersey	264	30	Louisiana	142
24	New Mexico	172	30	North Dakota	142
1	New York	474	32	Iowa	139
10	North Carolina	253	33	Arizona	131
30	North Dakota	142	34	Indiana	120
20	Ohio	202	35	Arkansas	118
36	Oklahoma	115	36	Oklahoma	115
14	Oregon	219	37	Wisconsin	114
9	Pennsylvania	257	38	South Carolina	111
3	Rhode Island	374	39	West Virginia	98
38	South Carolina	111	40	Nebraska	95
45	South Dakota	62	41	Missouri	80
17	Tennessee	206	42	Utah	72
21	Texas	201	43	Kentucky	70
42	Utah	72	44	Idaho	65
16	Vermont	214	45	South Dakota	62
12	Virginia	252	46	Mississippi	57
13	Washington	244	NA	California**	NA
39	West Virginia	98	NA	Maryland**	NA
37	Wisconsin	114	NA	New Hampshire**	NA
NA	Wyoming**	NA	NA	Wyoming**	NA
				District of Columbia	316

Source: U.S. Department of Health and Human Services, Centers for Disease Control and Prevention
"Abortion Surveillance-United States, 2010" (MMWR, Vol. 62, No. SS-8, 11/29/13, www.cdc.gov/mmwr/mmwr_ss/ss_pvol.html)
*By state of occurrence. National figure is for reporting states only.
**Not reported.

Infant Deaths in 2010

National Total = 24,586 Infant Deaths*

RANK	STATE	DEATHS	% of USA
14	Alabama	523	2.1%
49	Alaska	43	0.2%
15	Arizona	522	2.1%
29	Arkansas	282	1.1%
1	California	2,420	9.8%
23	Colorado	392	1.6%
34	Connecticut	199	0.8%
41	Delaware	87	0.4%
3	Florida	1,403	5.7%
8	Georgia	860	3.5%
39	Hawaii	117	0.5%
40	Idaho	112	0.5%
5	Illinois	1,118	4.5%
12	Indiana	640	2.6%
35	Iowa	189	0.8%
31	Kansas	253	1.0%
26	Kentucky	379	1.5%
19	Louisiana	474	1.9%
45	Maine	70	0.3%
18	Maryland	498	2.0%
27	Massachusetts	323	1.3%
10	Michigan	817	3.3%
28	Minnesota	308	1.3%
25	Mississippi	387	1.6%
17	Missouri	507	2.1%
44	Montana	71	0.3%
38	Nebraska	136	0.6%
33	Nevada	201	0.8%
47	New Hampshire	51	0.2%
16	New Jersey	514	2.1%
36	New Mexico	157	0.6%
4	New York	1,243	5.1%
9	North Carolina	858	3.5%
46	North Dakota	62	0.3%
6	Ohio	1,072	4.4%
21	Oklahoma	404	1.6%
32	Oregon	225	0.9%
7	Pennsylvania	1,039	4.2%
43	Rhode Island	79	0.3%
20	South Carolina	430	1.7%
42	South Dakota	82	0.3%
13	Tennessee	630	2.6%
2	Texas	2,368	9.6%
30	Utah	254	1.0%
50	Vermont	26	0.1%
11	Virginia	700	2.8%
24	Washington	389	1.6%
37	West Virginia	149	0.6%
22	Wisconsin	400	1.6%
47	Wyoming	51	0.2%

RANK	STATE	DEATHS	% of USA
1	California	2,420	9.8%
2	Texas	2,368	9.6%
3	Florida	1,403	5.7%
4	New York	1,243	5.1%
5	Illinois	1,118	4.5%
6	Ohio	1,072	4.4%
7	Pennsylvania	1,039	4.2%
8	Georgia	860	3.5%
9	North Carolina	858	3.5%
10	Michigan	817	3.3%
11	Virginia	700	2.8%
12	Indiana	640	2.6%
13	Tennessee	630	2.6%
14	Alabama	523	2.1%
15	Arizona	522	2.1%
16	New Jersey	514	2.1%
17	Missouri	507	2.1%
18	Maryland	498	2.0%
19	Louisiana	474	1.9%
20	South Carolina	430	1.7%
21	Oklahoma	404	1.6%
22	Wisconsin	400	1.6%
23	Colorado	392	1.6%
24	Washington	389	1.6%
25	Mississippi	387	1.6%
26	Kentucky	379	1.5%
27	Massachusetts	323	1.3%
28	Minnesota	308	1.3%
29	Arkansas	282	1.1%
30	Utah	254	1.0%
31	Kansas	253	1.0%
32	Oregon	225	0.9%
33	Nevada	201	0.8%
34	Connecticut	199	0.8%
35	Iowa	189	0.8%
36	New Mexico	157	0.6%
37	West Virginia	149	0.6%
38	Nebraska	136	0.6%
39	Hawaii	117	0.5%
40	Idaho	112	0.5%
41	Delaware	87	0.4%
42	South Dakota	82	0.3%
43	Rhode Island	79	0.3%
44	Montana	71	0.3%
45	Maine	70	0.3%
46	North Dakota	62	0.3%
47	New Hampshire	51	0.2%
47	Wyoming	51	0.2%
49	Alaska	43	0.2%
50	Vermont	26	0.1%
	District of Columbia	72	0.3%

Source: U.S. Department of Health and Human Services, National Center for Health Statistics
   "National Vital Statistics Reports" (Vol. 61, No. 4, May 8, 2013, http://www.cdc.gov/nchs/deaths.htm)
*Final data. Deaths of infants under 1 year old by state of residence.

Infant Mortality Rate in 2010

National Rate = 6.2 Infant Deaths per 1,000 Live Births*

ALPHA ORDER				RANK ORDER		
RANK	STATE	RATE		RANK	STATE	RATE
2	Alabama	8.7		1	Mississippi	9.7
50	Alaska	3.8		2	Alabama	8.7
29	Arizona	6.0		3	Tennessee	7.9
10	Arkansas	7.3		4	Ohio	7.7
44	California	4.7		5	Delaware	7.7
30	Colorado	5.9		6	Indiana	7.6
36	Connecticut	5.3		7	Louisiana	7.6
5	Delaware	7.7		8	Oklahoma	7.6
24	Florida	6.5		9	South Carolina	7.4
25	Georgia	6.4		10	Arkansas	7.3
27	Hawaii	6.2		11	West Virginia	7.3
42	Idaho	4.8		12	Pennsylvania	7.3
20	Illinois	6.8		13	Michigan	7.1
6	Indiana	7.6		14	Rhode Island	7.1
40	Iowa	4.9		15	North Carolina	7.0
26	Kansas	6.2		16	South Dakota	6.9
19	Kentucky	6.8		17	North Dakota	6.8
7	Louisiana	7.6		18	Virginia	6.8
35	Maine	5.4		19	Kentucky	6.8
21	Maryland	6.8		20	Illinois	6.8
47	Massachusetts	4.4		21	Maryland	6.8
13	Michigan	7.1		21	Wyoming	6.8
46	Minnesota	4.5		23	Missouri	6.6
1	Mississippi	9.7		24	Florida	6.5
23	Missouri	6.6		25	Georgia	6.4
31	Montana	5.9		26	Kansas	6.2
37	Nebraska	5.3		27	Hawaii	6.2
34	Nevada	5.6		28	Texas	6.1
49	New Hampshire	4.0		29	Arizona	6.0
43	New Jersey	4.8		30	Colorado	5.9
33	New Mexico	5.6		31	Montana	5.9
38	New York	5.1		32	Wisconsin	5.8
15	North Carolina	7.0		33	New Mexico	5.6
17	North Dakota	6.8		34	Nevada	5.6
4	Ohio	7.7		35	Maine	5.4
8	Oklahoma	7.6		36	Connecticut	5.3
39	Oregon	4.9		37	Nebraska	5.3
12	Pennsylvania	7.3		38	New York	5.1
14	Rhode Island	7.1		39	Oregon	4.9
9	South Carolina	7.4		40	Iowa	4.9
16	South Dakota	6.9		41	Utah	4.9
3	Tennessee	7.9		42	Idaho	4.8
28	Texas	6.1		43	New Jersey	4.8
41	Utah	4.9		44	California	4.7
48	Vermont	4.2		45	Washington	4.5
18	Virginia	6.8		46	Minnesota	4.5
45	Washington	4.5		47	Massachusetts	4.4
11	West Virginia	7.3		48	Vermont	4.2
32	Wisconsin	5.8		49	New Hampshire	4.0
21	Wyoming	6.8		50	Alaska	3.8
					District of Columbia	7.9

Source: U.S. Department of Health and Human Services, National Center for Health Statistics
  "National Vital Statistics Reports" (Vol. 61, No. 4, May 8, 2013, http://www.cdc.gov/nchs/deaths.htm)
*Final data. Deaths of infants under 1 year old by state of residence.

Deaths in 2011

National Total = 2,513,171 Deaths*

ALPHA ORDER

RANK	STATE	DEATHS	% of USA
18	Alabama	48,683	1.9%
50	Alaska	3,849	0.2%
20	Arizona	48,381	1.9%
29	Arkansas	29,632	1.2%
1	California	238,993	9.5%
28	Colorado	32,563	1.3%
30	Connecticut	29,548	1.2%
45	Delaware	7,840	0.3%
2	Florida	173,961	6.9%
11	Georgia	70,401	2.8%
42	Hawaii	9,921	0.4%
40	Idaho	12,026	0.5%
7	Illinois	101,898	4.1%
14	Indiana	58,195	2.3%
32	Iowa	28,184	1.1%
33	Kansas	25,119	1.0%
22	Kentucky	42,624	1.7%
24	Louisiana	40,680	1.6%
39	Maine	13,031	0.5%
21	Maryland	43,750	1.7%
16	Massachusetts	53,699	2.1%
8	Michigan	89,496	3.6%
25	Minnesota	39,822	1.6%
31	Mississippi	29,278	1.2%
15	Missouri	55,813	2.2%
44	Montana	9,117	0.4%
37	Nebraska	15,477	0.6%
35	Nevada	20,340	0.8%
41	New Hampshire	10,821	0.4%
10	New Jersey	70,553	2.8%
36	New Mexico	16,434	0.7%
4	New York	148,903	5.9%
9	North Carolina	79,875	3.2%
47	North Dakota	5,964	0.2%
6	Ohio	111,444	4.4%
26	Oklahoma	37,142	1.5%
27	Oregon	32,786	1.3%
5	Pennsylvania	128,290	5.1%
43	Rhode Island	9,585	0.4%
23	South Carolina	42,093	1.7%
46	South Dakota	7,313	0.3%
13	Tennessee	60,544	2.4%
3	Texas	168,643	6.7%
38	Utah	15,265	0.6%
48	Vermont	5,434	0.2%
12	Virginia	60,807	2.4%
17	Washington	49,692	2.0%
34	West Virginia	21,868	0.9%
19	Wisconsin	48,419	1.9%
49	Wyoming	4,387	0.2%

RANK ORDER

RANK	STATE	DEATHS	% of USA
1	California	238,993	9.5%
2	Florida	173,961	6.9%
3	Texas	168,643	6.7%
4	New York	148,903	5.9%
5	Pennsylvania	128,290	5.1%
6	Ohio	111,444	4.4%
7	Illinois	101,898	4.1%
8	Michigan	89,496	3.6%
9	North Carolina	79,875	3.2%
10	New Jersey	70,553	2.8%
11	Georgia	70,401	2.8%
12	Virginia	60,807	2.4%
13	Tennessee	60,544	2.4%
14	Indiana	58,195	2.3%
15	Missouri	55,813	2.2%
16	Massachusetts	53,699	2.1%
17	Washington	49,692	2.0%
18	Alabama	48,683	1.9%
19	Wisconsin	48,419	1.9%
20	Arizona	48,381	1.9%
21	Maryland	43,750	1.7%
22	Kentucky	42,624	1.7%
23	South Carolina	42,093	1.7%
24	Louisiana	40,680	1.6%
25	Minnesota	39,822	1.6%
26	Oklahoma	37,142	1.5%
27	Oregon	32,786	1.3%
28	Colorado	32,563	1.3%
29	Arkansas	29,632	1.2%
30	Connecticut	29,548	1.2%
31	Mississippi	29,278	1.2%
32	Iowa	28,184	1.1%
33	Kansas	25,119	1.0%
34	West Virginia	21,868	0.9%
35	Nevada	20,340	0.8%
36	New Mexico	16,434	0.7%
37	Nebraska	15,477	0.6%
38	Utah	15,265	0.6%
39	Maine	13,031	0.5%
40	Idaho	12,026	0.5%
41	New Hampshire	10,821	0.4%
42	Hawaii	9,921	0.4%
43	Rhode Island	9,585	0.4%
44	Montana	9,117	0.4%
45	Delaware	7,840	0.3%
46	South Dakota	7,313	0.3%
47	North Dakota	5,964	0.2%
48	Vermont	5,434	0.2%
49	Wyoming	4,387	0.2%
50	Alaska	3,849	0.2%
	District of Columbia	4,589	0.2%

Source: U.S. Department of Health and Human Services, National Center for Health Statistics
"National Vital Statistics Reports" (Vol. 61, No. 6, October 10, 2012, http://www.cdc.gov/nchs/deaths.htm)
*Preliminary data by state of residence.

Age-Adjusted Death Rate in 2011

National Rate = 740.6 Deaths per 100,000 Population*

ALPHA ORDER

RANK	STATE	RATE
3	Alabama	933.7
25	Alaska	747.9
42	Arizona	688.9
6	Arkansas	894.6
49	California	638.8
43	Colorado	677.8
47	Connecticut	660.9
19	Delaware	763.4
44	Florida	677.1
13	Georgia	806.2
50	Hawaii	584.8
26	Idaho	744.9
28	Illinois	737.3
10	Indiana	825.0
30	Iowa	722.7
18	Kansas	767.2
4	Kentucky	910.3
7	Louisiana	882.1
23	Maine	749.5
34	Maryland	715.9
45	Massachusetts	676.1
16	Michigan	784.2
48	Minnesota	659.2
1	Mississippi	956.2
12	Missouri	811.4
20	Montana	760.7
33	Nebraska	719.8
15	Nevada	789.6
36	New Hampshire	710.0
40	New Jersey	690.6
24	New Mexico	748.0
46	New York	664.2
14	North Carolina	790.8
39	North Dakota	697.3
11	Ohio	822.0
5	Oklahoma	910.1
29	Oregon	724.1
17	Pennsylvania	776.1
37	Rhode Island	707.6
9	South Carolina	839.9
32	South Dakota	720.4
8	Tennessee	879.1
22	Texas	751.6
38	Utah	699.0
35	Vermont	711.0
27	Virginia	741.6
41	Washington	690.4
2	West Virginia	953.3
31	Wisconsin	721.3
21	Wyoming	754.6

RANK ORDER

RANK	STATE	RATE
1	Mississippi	956.2
2	West Virginia	953.3
3	Alabama	933.7
4	Kentucky	910.3
5	Oklahoma	910.1
6	Arkansas	894.6
7	Louisiana	882.1
8	Tennessee	879.1
9	South Carolina	839.9
10	Indiana	825.0
11	Ohio	822.0
12	Missouri	811.4
13	Georgia	806.2
14	North Carolina	790.8
15	Nevada	789.6
16	Michigan	784.2
17	Pennsylvania	776.1
18	Kansas	767.2
19	Delaware	763.4
20	Montana	760.7
21	Wyoming	754.6
22	Texas	751.6
23	Maine	749.5
24	New Mexico	748.0
25	Alaska	747.9
26	Idaho	744.9
27	Virginia	741.6
28	Illinois	737.3
29	Oregon	724.1
30	Iowa	722.7
31	Wisconsin	721.3
32	South Dakota	720.4
33	Nebraska	719.8
34	Maryland	715.9
35	Vermont	711.0
36	New Hampshire	710.0
37	Rhode Island	707.6
38	Utah	699.0
39	North Dakota	697.3
40	New Jersey	690.6
41	Washington	690.4
42	Arizona	688.9
43	Colorado	677.8
44	Florida	677.1
45	Massachusetts	676.1
46	New York	664.2
47	Connecticut	660.9
48	Minnesota	659.2
49	California	638.8
50	Hawaii	584.8

	District of Columbia	756.0

Source: U.S. Department of Health and Human Services, National Center for Health Statistics
   "National Vital Statistics Reports" (Vol. 61, No. 6, October 10, 2012, http://www.cdc.gov/nchs/deaths.htm)
*Preliminary data by state of residence. Age-adjusted rates eliminate the distorting effects of the aging of the population. Rates
based on the year 2000 standard population.

Estimated Deaths by Cancer in 2013

National Estimated Total = 580,350 Deaths

ALPHA ORDER

RANK	STATE	DEATHS	% of USA
21	Alabama	10,430	1.8%
49	Alaska	980	0.2%
19	Arizona	11,210	1.9%
30	Arkansas	6,650	1.1%
1	California	57,290	9.9%
28	Colorado	7,350	1.3%
29	Connecticut	6,890	1.2%
45	Delaware	1,940	0.3%
2	Florida	42,370	7.3%
11	Georgia	16,010	2.8%
42	Hawaii	2,400	0.4%
41	Idaho	2,660	0.5%
7	Illinois	24,000	4.1%
14	Indiana	13,250	2.3%
31	Iowa	6,420	1.1%
33	Kansas	5,430	0.9%
22	Kentucky	9,970	1.7%
25	Louisiana	9,040	1.6%
38	Maine	3,240	0.6%
20	Maryland	10,480	1.8%
15	Massachusetts	12,840	2.2%
8	Michigan	20,570	3.5%
24	Minnesota	9,610	1.7%
32	Mississippi	6,300	1.1%
16	Missouri	12,730	2.2%
44	Montana	2,000	0.3%
37	Nebraska	3,440	0.6%
34	Nevada	4,760	0.8%
40	New Hampshire	2,680	0.5%
10	New Jersey	16,410	2.8%
36	New Mexico	3,540	0.6%
4	New York	34,240	5.9%
9	North Carolina	18,620	3.2%
48	North Dakota	1,280	0.2%
6	Ohio	25,130	4.3%
26	Oklahoma	7,850	1.4%
27	Oregon	7,820	1.3%
5	Pennsylvania	28,680	4.9%
43	Rhode Island	2,140	0.4%
23	South Carolina	9,800	1.7%
46	South Dakota	1,590	0.3%
13	Tennessee	14,080	2.4%
3	Texas	37,180	6.4%
39	Utah	2,790	0.5%
47	Vermont	1,300	0.2%
12	Virginia	14,720	2.5%
17	Washington	12,390	2.1%
35	West Virginia	4,660	0.8%
18	Wisconsin	11,220	1.9%
50	Wyoming	950	0.2%

RANK ORDER

RANK	STATE	DEATHS	% of USA
1	California	57,290	9.9%
2	Florida	42,370	7.3%
3	Texas	37,180	6.4%
4	New York	34,240	5.9%
5	Pennsylvania	28,680	4.9%
6	Ohio	25,130	4.3%
7	Illinois	24,000	4.1%
8	Michigan	20,570	3.5%
9	North Carolina	18,620	3.2%
10	New Jersey	16,410	2.8%
11	Georgia	16,010	2.8%
12	Virginia	14,720	2.5%
13	Tennessee	14,080	2.4%
14	Indiana	13,250	2.3%
15	Massachusetts	12,840	2.2%
16	Missouri	12,730	2.2%
17	Washington	12,390	2.1%
18	Wisconsin	11,220	1.9%
19	Arizona	11,210	1.9%
20	Maryland	10,480	1.8%
21	Alabama	10,430	1.8%
22	Kentucky	9,970	1.7%
23	South Carolina	9,800	1.7%
24	Minnesota	9,610	1.7%
25	Louisiana	9,040	1.6%
26	Oklahoma	7,850	1.4%
27	Oregon	7,820	1.3%
28	Colorado	7,350	1.3%
29	Connecticut	6,890	1.2%
30	Arkansas	6,650	1.1%
31	Iowa	6,420	1.1%
32	Mississippi	6,300	1.1%
33	Kansas	5,430	0.9%
34	Nevada	4,760	0.8%
35	West Virginia	4,660	0.8%
36	New Mexico	3,540	0.6%
37	Nebraska	3,440	0.6%
38	Maine	3,240	0.6%
39	Utah	2,790	0.5%
40	New Hampshire	2,680	0.5%
41	Idaho	2,660	0.5%
42	Hawaii	2,400	0.4%
43	Rhode Island	2,140	0.4%
44	Montana	2,000	0.3%
45	Delaware	1,940	0.3%
46	South Dakota	1,590	0.3%
47	Vermont	1,300	0.2%
48	North Dakota	1,280	0.2%
49	Alaska	980	0.2%
50	Wyoming	950	0.2%
	District of Columbia	1,030	0.2%

Source: American Cancer Society
"Cancer Facts & Figures 2013" (Copyright 2013, American Cancer Society, www.cancer.org/Research/CancerFactsFigures/)

Estimated Death Rate by Cancer in 2013

National Estimated Rate = 184.9 Deaths per 100,000 Population*

ALPHA ORDER

RANK	STATE	RATE
9	Alabama	216.3
49	Alaska	134.0
41	Arizona	171.1
4	Arkansas	225.5
46	California	150.6
48	Colorado	141.7
26	Connecticut	191.9
10	Delaware	211.5
6	Florida	219.3
45	Georgia	161.4
40	Hawaii	172.4
43	Idaho	166.7
30	Illinois	186.4
20	Indiana	202.7
13	Iowa	208.8
29	Kansas	188.2
3	Kentucky	227.6
23	Louisiana	196.4
2	Maine	243.8
37	Maryland	178.1
25	Massachusetts	193.2
14	Michigan	208.1
36	Minnesota	178.7
12	Mississippi	211.1
11	Missouri	211.4
22	Montana	199.0
31	Nebraska	185.4
39	Nevada	172.5
19	New Hampshire	202.9
32	New Jersey	185.1
42	New Mexico	169.7
38	New York	175.0
27	North Carolina	190.9
33	North Dakota	183.0
8	Ohio	217.7
17	Oklahoma	205.8
21	Oregon	200.5
5	Pennsylvania	224.7
18	Rhode Island	203.8
16	South Carolina	207.5
28	South Dakota	190.8
7	Tennessee	218.1
47	Texas	142.7
50	Utah	97.7
15	Vermont	207.7
34	Virginia	179.8
35	Washington	179.6
1	West Virginia	251.2
24	Wisconsin	195.9
44	Wyoming	164.8

RANK ORDER

RANK	STATE	RATE
1	West Virginia	251.2
2	Maine	243.8
3	Kentucky	227.6
4	Arkansas	225.5
5	Pennsylvania	224.7
6	Florida	219.3
7	Tennessee	218.1
8	Ohio	217.7
9	Alabama	216.3
10	Delaware	211.5
11	Missouri	211.4
12	Mississippi	211.1
13	Iowa	208.8
14	Michigan	208.1
15	Vermont	207.7
16	South Carolina	207.5
17	Oklahoma	205.8
18	Rhode Island	203.8
19	New Hampshire	202.9
20	Indiana	202.7
21	Oregon	200.5
22	Montana	199.0
23	Louisiana	196.4
24	Wisconsin	195.9
25	Massachusetts	193.2
26	Connecticut	191.9
27	North Carolina	190.9
28	South Dakota	190.8
29	Kansas	188.2
30	Illinois	186.4
31	Nebraska	185.4
32	New Jersey	185.1
33	North Dakota	183.0
34	Virginia	179.8
35	Washington	179.6
36	Minnesota	178.7
37	Maryland	178.1
38	New York	175.0
39	Nevada	172.5
40	Hawaii	172.4
41	Arizona	171.1
42	New Mexico	169.7
43	Idaho	166.7
44	Wyoming	164.8
45	Georgia	161.4
46	California	150.6
47	Texas	142.7
48	Colorado	141.7
49	Alaska	134.0
50	Utah	97.7
	District of Columbia	162.9

Source: CQ Press using data from American Cancer Society
"Cancer Facts & Figures 2013" (Copyright 2013, American Cancer Society, www.cancer.org/Research/CancerFactsFigures/)
*Rates calculated using 2012 Census resident population estimates. Not age-adjusted.

Estimated New Cancer Cases in 2013

National Estimated Total = 1,660,290 New Cases*

RANK	STATE	CASES	% of USA	RANK	STATE	CASES	% of USA
23	Alabama	27,080	1.6%	1	California	171,330	10.3%
49	Alaska	3,290	0.2%	2	Florida	118,320	7.1%
17	Arizona	34,010	2.0%	3	Texas	112,230	6.8%
31	Arkansas	16,330	1.0%	4	New York	108,760	6.6%
1	California	171,330	10.3%	5	Pennsylvania	79,560	4.8%
26	Colorado	23,410	1.4%	6	Ohio	66,610	4.0%
28	Connecticut	21,180	1.3%	7	Illinois	66,090	4.0%
45	Delaware	5,370	0.3%	8	Michigan	57,560	3.5%
2	Florida	118,320	7.1%	9	North Carolina	53,200	3.2%
11	Georgia	49,280	3.0%	10	New Jersey	49,440	3.0%
42	Hawaii	6,650	0.4%	11	Georgia	49,280	3.0%
41	Idaho	7,670	0.5%	12	Virginia	40,870	2.5%
7	Illinois	66,090	4.0%	13	Massachusetts	38,250	2.3%
16	Indiana	35,550	2.1%	14	Washington	37,290	2.2%
30	Iowa	17,480	1.1%	15	Tennessee	36,580	2.2%
33	Kansas	14,370	0.9%	16	Indiana	35,550	2.1%
24	Kentucky	25,100	1.5%	17	Arizona	34,010	2.0%
25	Louisiana	24,930	1.5%	18	Missouri	33,950	2.0%
38	Maine	9,190	0.6%	19	Wisconsin	31,590	1.9%
20	Maryland	30,680	1.8%	20	Maryland	30,680	1.8%
13	Massachusetts	38,250	2.3%	21	Minnesota	28,410	1.7%
8	Michigan	57,560	3.5%	22	South Carolina	27,620	1.7%
21	Minnesota	28,410	1.7%	23	Alabama	27,080	1.6%
32	Mississippi	15,830	1.0%	24	Kentucky	25,100	1.5%
18	Missouri	33,950	2.0%	25	Louisiana	24,930	1.5%
44	Montana	5,450	0.3%	26	Colorado	23,410	1.4%
39	Nebraska	9,060	0.5%	27	Oregon	21,720	1.3%
34	Nevada	13,830	0.8%	28	Connecticut	21,180	1.3%
40	New Hampshire	8,470	0.5%	29	Oklahoma	20,160	1.2%
10	New Jersey	49,440	3.0%	30	Iowa	17,480	1.1%
37	New Mexico	10,090	0.6%	31	Arkansas	16,330	1.0%
4	New York	108,760	6.6%	32	Mississippi	15,830	1.0%
9	North Carolina	53,200	3.2%	33	Kansas	14,370	0.9%
48	North Dakota	3,510	0.2%	34	Nevada	13,830	0.8%
6	Ohio	66,610	4.0%	35	West Virginia	11,450	0.7%
29	Oklahoma	20,160	1.2%	36	Utah	10,810	0.7%
27	Oregon	21,720	1.3%	37	New Mexico	10,090	0.6%
5	Pennsylvania	79,560	4.8%	38	Maine	9,190	0.6%
43	Rhode Island	6,280	0.4%	39	Nebraska	9,060	0.5%
22	South Carolina	27,620	1.7%	40	New Hampshire	8,470	0.5%
46	South Dakota	4,570	0.3%	41	Idaho	7,670	0.5%
15	Tennessee	36,580	2.2%	42	Hawaii	6,650	0.4%
3	Texas	112,230	6.8%	43	Rhode Island	6,280	0.4%
36	Utah	10,810	0.7%	44	Montana	5,450	0.3%
47	Vermont	4,200	0.3%	45	Delaware	5,370	0.3%
12	Virginia	40,870	2.5%	46	South Dakota	4,570	0.3%
14	Washington	37,290	2.2%	47	Vermont	4,200	0.3%
35	West Virginia	11,450	0.7%	48	North Dakota	3,510	0.2%
19	Wisconsin	31,590	1.9%	49	Alaska	3,290	0.2%
50	Wyoming	2,700	0.2%	50	Wyoming	2,700	0.2%
					District of Columbia	2,920	0.2%

ALPHA ORDER — RANK ORDER

Source: American Cancer Society
    "Cancer Facts & Figures 2013" (Copyright 2013, American Cancer Society, www.cancer.org/Research/CancerFactsFigures/)
*These estimates are offered as a rough guide and should not be regarded as definitive. They are calculated by the American Cancer Society using a model based on 1995-2009 incidence data. Totals do not include basal and squamous cell skin cancers or in situ carcinomas except urinary bladder.

Estimated Rate of New Cancer Cases in 2013

National Estimated Rate = 528.9 New Cases per 100,000 Population*

ALPHA ORDER				RANK ORDER		
RANK	STATE	RATE		RANK	STATE	RATE
18	Alabama	561.6		1	Maine	691.4
48	Alaska	449.8		2	Vermont	670.9
34	Arizona	519.0		3	New Hampshire	641.3
22	Arkansas	553.7		4	Pennsylvania	623.3
47	California	450.4		5	West Virginia	617.1
46	Colorado	451.3		6	Florida	612.5
8	Connecticut	589.9		7	Rhode Island	597.9
9	Delaware	585.5		8	Connecticut	589.9
6	Florida	612.5		9	Delaware	585.5
40	Georgia	496.8		10	South Carolina	584.7
44	Hawaii	477.6		11	Michigan	582.4
43	Idaho	480.7		12	Ohio	577.0
35	Illinois	513.3		13	Massachusetts	575.5
26	Indiana	543.8		14	Kentucky	573.0
15	Iowa	568.6		15	Iowa	568.6
39	Kansas	497.9		16	Tennessee	566.6
14	Kentucky	573.0		17	Missouri	563.8
28	Louisiana	541.7		18	Alabama	561.6
1	Maine	691.4		19	New Jersey	557.7
33	Maryland	521.4		20	Oregon	557.0
13	Massachusetts	575.5		21	New York	555.7
11	Michigan	582.4		22	Arkansas	553.7
32	Minnesota	528.2		23	Wisconsin	551.7
30	Mississippi	530.3		24	South Dakota	548.4
17	Missouri	563.8		25	North Carolina	545.5
27	Montana	542.2		26	Indiana	543.8
41	Nebraska	488.3		27	Montana	542.2
37	Nevada	501.3		28	Louisiana	541.7
3	New Hampshire	641.3		29	Washington	540.7
19	New Jersey	557.7		30	Mississippi	530.3
42	New Mexico	483.8		31	Oklahoma	528.5
21	New York	555.7		32	Minnesota	528.2
25	North Carolina	545.5		33	Maryland	521.4
36	North Dakota	501.7		34	Arizona	519.0
12	Ohio	577.0		35	Illinois	513.3
31	Oklahoma	528.5		36	North Dakota	501.7
20	Oregon	557.0		37	Nevada	501.3
4	Pennsylvania	623.3		38	Virginia	499.3
7	Rhode Island	597.9		39	Kansas	497.9
10	South Carolina	584.7		40	Georgia	496.8
24	South Dakota	548.4		41	Nebraska	488.3
16	Tennessee	566.6		42	New Mexico	483.8
49	Texas	430.7		43	Idaho	480.7
50	Utah	378.6		44	Hawaii	477.6
2	Vermont	670.9		45	Wyoming	468.4
38	Virginia	499.3		46	Colorado	451.3
29	Washington	540.7		47	California	450.4
5	West Virginia	617.1		48	Alaska	449.8
23	Wisconsin	551.7		49	Texas	430.7
45	Wyoming	468.4		50	Utah	378.6
					District of Columbia	461.8

Source: CQ Press using data from American Cancer Society
"Cancer Facts & Figures 2013" (Copyright 2013, American Cancer Society, www.cancer.org/Research/CancerFactsFigures/)
*These estimates are offered as a rough guide and should not be regarded as definitive. They are calculated by the American Cancer Society using a model based on 1995-2009 incidence data. Totals do not include basal and squamous cell skin cancers or in situ carcinomas except urinary bladder. Rates calculated using 2012 Census resident population estimates.

Deaths by Accidents in 2010

National Total = 120,859 Deaths*

ALPHA ORDER

RANK	STATE	DEATHS	% of USA
20	Alabama	2,394	2.0%
46	Alaska	366	0.3%
12	Arizona	3,018	2.5%
29	Arkansas	1,461	1.2%
1	California	10,435	8.6%
23	Colorado	2,106	1.7%
31	Connecticut	1,337	1.1%
47	Delaware	357	0.3%
3	Florida	8,875	7.3%
10	Georgia	3,745	3.1%
44	Hawaii	432	0.4%
39	Idaho	654	0.5%
8	Illinois	3,997	3.3%
16	Indiana	2,534	2.1%
33	Iowa	1,273	1.1%
32	Kansas	1,317	1.1%
14	Kentucky	2,632	2.2%
26	Louisiana	1,999	1.7%
41	Maine	540	0.4%
30	Maryland	1,446	1.2%
25	Massachusetts	2,060	1.7%
9	Michigan	3,770	3.1%
24	Minnesota	2,103	1.7%
27	Mississippi	1,685	1.4%
13	Missouri	2,975	2.5%
40	Montana	548	0.5%
38	Nebraska	700	0.6%
36	Nevada	1,088	0.9%
42	New Hampshire	517	0.4%
19	New Jersey	2,486	2.1%
35	New Mexico	1,233	1.0%
6	New York	5,004	4.1%
7	North Carolina	4,144	3.4%
50	North Dakota	285	0.2%
5	Ohio	5,124	4.2%
21	Oklahoma	2,288	1.9%
28	Oregon	1,566	1.3%
4	Pennsylvania	5,751	4.8%
43	Rhode Island	475	0.4%
22	South Carolina	2,274	1.9%
45	South Dakota	393	0.3%
11	Tennessee	3,539	2.9%
2	Texas	9,212	7.6%
37	Utah	970	0.8%
49	Vermont	298	0.2%
17	Virginia	2,527	2.1%
15	Washington	2,609	2.2%
34	West Virginia	1,234	1.0%
18	Wisconsin	2,525	2.1%
48	Wyoming	346	0.3%

RANK ORDER

RANK	STATE	DEATHS	% of USA
1	California	10,435	8.6%
2	Texas	9,212	7.6%
3	Florida	8,875	7.3%
4	Pennsylvania	5,751	4.8%
5	Ohio	5,124	4.2%
6	New York	5,004	4.1%
7	North Carolina	4,144	3.4%
8	Illinois	3,997	3.3%
9	Michigan	3,770	3.1%
10	Georgia	3,745	3.1%
11	Tennessee	3,539	2.9%
12	Arizona	3,018	2.5%
13	Missouri	2,975	2.5%
14	Kentucky	2,632	2.2%
15	Washington	2,609	2.2%
16	Indiana	2,534	2.1%
17	Virginia	2,527	2.1%
18	Wisconsin	2,525	2.1%
19	New Jersey	2,486	2.1%
20	Alabama	2,394	2.0%
21	Oklahoma	2,288	1.9%
22	South Carolina	2,274	1.9%
23	Colorado	2,106	1.7%
24	Minnesota	2,103	1.7%
25	Massachusetts	2,060	1.7%
26	Louisiana	1,999	1.7%
27	Mississippi	1,685	1.4%
28	Oregon	1,566	1.3%
29	Arkansas	1,461	1.2%
30	Maryland	1,446	1.2%
31	Connecticut	1,337	1.1%
32	Kansas	1,317	1.1%
33	Iowa	1,273	1.1%
34	West Virginia	1,234	1.0%
35	New Mexico	1,233	1.0%
36	Nevada	1,088	0.9%
37	Utah	970	0.8%
38	Nebraska	700	0.6%
39	Idaho	654	0.5%
40	Montana	548	0.5%
41	Maine	540	0.4%
42	New Hampshire	517	0.4%
43	Rhode Island	475	0.4%
44	Hawaii	432	0.4%
45	South Dakota	393	0.3%
46	Alaska	366	0.3%
47	Delaware	357	0.3%
48	Wyoming	346	0.3%
49	Vermont	298	0.2%
50	North Dakota	285	0.2%
	District of Columbia	212	0.2%

Source: U.S. Department of Health and Human Services, National Center for Health Statistics
"National Vital Statistics Reports" (Vol. 61, No. 4, May 8, 2013, http://www.cdc.gov/nchs/deaths.htm)
*Final data by state of residence. Includes motor vehicle deaths, poisoning, falls, drowning, and other accidents.

Age-Adjusted Death Rate by Accidents in 2010

National Rate = 38.0 Deaths per 100,000 Population*

ALPHA ORDER

RANK	STATE	RATE
10	Alabama	49.6
6	Alaska	58.7
14	Arizona	46.7
11	Arkansas	49.4
47	California	27.8
18	Colorado	43.5
42	Connecticut	33.6
30	Delaware	39.2
20	Florida	43.1
27	Georgia	40.7
45	Hawaii	29.6
23	Idaho	42.1
44	Illinois	30.4
33	Indiana	38.5
36	Iowa	37.2
17	Kansas	44.0
3	Kentucky	60.5
16	Louisiana	44.4
39	Maine	36.5
49	Maryland	24.7
46	Massachusetts	28.5
40	Michigan	36.2
38	Minnesota	36.7
7	Mississippi	56.8
13	Missouri	47.9
9	Montana	53.2
41	Nebraska	35.8
24	Nevada	41.3
36	New Hampshire	37.2
48	New Jersey	26.7
2	New Mexico	60.7
50	New York	24.2
19	North Carolina	43.2
32	North Dakota	38.8
22	Ohio	42.4
4	Oklahoma	60.3
34	Oregon	37.8
25	Pennsylvania	41.1
29	Rhode Island	40.0
12	South Carolina	48.9
15	South Dakota	44.5
8	Tennessee	54.9
31	Texas	39.0
28	Utah	40.6
21	Vermont	42.7
43	Virginia	31.6
35	Washington	37.6
1	West Virginia	63.7
26	Wisconsin	40.8
5	Wyoming	59.8

RANK ORDER

RANK	STATE	RATE
1	West Virginia	63.7
2	New Mexico	60.7
3	Kentucky	60.5
4	Oklahoma	60.3
5	Wyoming	59.8
6	Alaska	58.7
7	Mississippi	56.8
8	Tennessee	54.9
9	Montana	53.2
10	Alabama	49.6
11	Arkansas	49.4
12	South Carolina	48.9
13	Missouri	47.9
14	Arizona	46.7
15	South Dakota	44.5
16	Louisiana	44.4
17	Kansas	44.0
18	Colorado	43.5
19	North Carolina	43.2
20	Florida	43.1
21	Vermont	42.7
22	Ohio	42.4
23	Idaho	42.1
24	Nevada	41.3
25	Pennsylvania	41.1
26	Wisconsin	40.8
27	Georgia	40.7
28	Utah	40.6
29	Rhode Island	40.0
30	Delaware	39.2
31	Texas	39.0
32	North Dakota	38.8
33	Indiana	38.5
34	Oregon	37.8
35	Washington	37.6
36	Iowa	37.2
36	New Hampshire	37.2
38	Minnesota	36.7
39	Maine	36.5
40	Michigan	36.2
41	Nebraska	35.8
42	Connecticut	33.6
43	Virginia	31.6
44	Illinois	30.4
45	Hawaii	29.6
46	Massachusetts	28.5
47	California	27.8
48	New Jersey	26.7
49	Maryland	24.7
50	New York	24.2
	District of Columbia	35.1

Source: U.S. Department of Health and Human Services, National Center for Health Statistics
"National Vital Statistics Reports" (Vol. 61, No. 4, May 8, 2013, http://www.cdc.gov/nchs/deaths.htm)
*Final data by state of residence. Includes motor vehicle deaths, poisoning, falls, drowning, and other accidents. Age-adjusted rates based on the year 2000 standard population.

Deaths by Cerebrovascular Diseases in 2010

National Total = 129,476 Deaths*

ALPHA ORDER

RANK	STATE	DEATHS	% of USA
16	Alabama	2,619	2.0%
50	Alaska	167	0.1%
23	Arizona	2,138	1.7%
28	Arkansas	1,741	1.3%
1	California	13,662	10.6%
29	Colorado	1,607	1.2%
33	Connecticut	1,349	1.0%
46	Delaware	407	0.3%
3	Florida	8,432	6.5%
10	Georgia	3,762	2.9%
40	Hawaii	605	0.5%
39	Idaho	642	0.5%
7	Illinois	5,349	4.1%
14	Indiana	3,082	2.4%
30	Iowa	1,537	1.2%
32	Kansas	1,370	1.1%
24	Kentucky	1,992	1.5%
26	Louisiana	1,977	1.5%
41	Maine	602	0.5%
21	Maryland	2,279	1.8%
19	Massachusetts	2,516	1.9%
8	Michigan	4,474	3.5%
22	Minnesota	2,167	1.7%
31	Mississippi	1,520	1.2%
15	Missouri	3,001	2.3%
43	Montana	494	0.4%
35	Nebraska	876	0.7%
37	Nevada	796	0.6%
42	New Hampshire	500	0.4%
11	New Jersey	3,402	2.6%
36	New Mexico	806	0.6%
5	New York	6,213	4.8%
9	North Carolina	4,298	3.3%
47	North Dakota	382	0.3%
6	Ohio	5,755	4.4%
25	Oklahoma	1,980	1.5%
27	Oregon	1,793	1.4%
4	Pennsylvania	6,701	5.2%
44	Rhode Island	431	0.3%
20	South Carolina	2,293	1.8%
45	South Dakota	416	0.3%
13	Tennessee	3,205	2.5%
2	Texas	9,180	7.1%
38	Utah	739	0.6%
48	Vermont	265	0.2%
12	Virginia	3,293	2.5%
18	Washington	2,548	2.0%
34	West Virginia	1,104	0.9%
17	Wisconsin	2,609	2.0%
49	Wyoming	204	0.2%

RANK ORDER

RANK	STATE	DEATHS	% of USA
1	California	13,662	10.6%
2	Texas	9,180	7.1%
3	Florida	8,432	6.5%
4	Pennsylvania	6,701	5.2%
5	New York	6,213	4.8%
6	Ohio	5,755	4.4%
7	Illinois	5,349	4.1%
8	Michigan	4,474	3.5%
9	North Carolina	4,298	3.3%
10	Georgia	3,762	2.9%
11	New Jersey	3,402	2.6%
12	Virginia	3,293	2.5%
13	Tennessee	3,205	2.5%
14	Indiana	3,082	2.4%
15	Missouri	3,001	2.3%
16	Alabama	2,619	2.0%
17	Wisconsin	2,609	2.0%
18	Washington	2,548	2.0%
19	Massachusetts	2,516	1.9%
20	South Carolina	2,293	1.8%
21	Maryland	2,279	1.8%
22	Minnesota	2,167	1.7%
23	Arizona	2,138	1.7%
24	Kentucky	1,992	1.5%
25	Oklahoma	1,980	1.5%
26	Louisiana	1,977	1.5%
27	Oregon	1,793	1.4%
28	Arkansas	1,741	1.3%
29	Colorado	1,607	1.2%
30	Iowa	1,537	1.2%
31	Mississippi	1,520	1.2%
32	Kansas	1,370	1.1%
33	Connecticut	1,349	1.0%
34	West Virginia	1,104	0.9%
35	Nebraska	876	0.7%
36	New Mexico	806	0.6%
37	Nevada	796	0.6%
38	Utah	739	0.6%
39	Idaho	642	0.5%
40	Hawaii	605	0.5%
41	Maine	602	0.5%
42	New Hampshire	500	0.4%
43	Montana	494	0.4%
44	Rhode Island	431	0.3%
45	South Dakota	416	0.3%
46	Delaware	407	0.3%
47	North Dakota	382	0.3%
48	Vermont	265	0.2%
49	Wyoming	204	0.2%
50	Alaska	167	0.1%
	District of Columbia	196	0.2%

Source: U.S. Department of Health and Human Services, National Center for Health Statistics
"National Vital Statistics Reports" (Vol. 61, No. 4, May 8, 2013, http://www.cdc.gov/nchs/deaths.htm)
*Final data by state of residence. Cerebrovascular diseases include stroke and other disorders of the blood vessels of the brain.

Age-Adjusted Death Rate by Cerebrovascular Diseases in 2010

National Rate = 39.1 Deaths per 100,000 Population*

ALPHA ORDER

RANK	STATE	RATE
2	Alabama	51.6
21	Alaska	40.9
46	Arizona	31.9
1	Arkansas	53.8
32	California	38.1
37	Colorado	36.1
49	Connecticut	29.4
22	Delaware	40.7
45	Florida	32.8
8	Georgia	46.3
39	Hawaii	35.8
18	Idaho	42.0
28	Illinois	39.2
11	Indiana	44.5
33	Iowa	38.0
20	Kansas	41.2
13	Kentucky	44.1
9	Louisiana	44.9
41	Maine	34.5
29	Maryland	38.8
48	Massachusetts	31.3
26	Michigan	39.5
37	Minnesota	36.1
3	Mississippi	51.2
14	Missouri	44.0
19	Montana	41.8
23	Nebraska	40.5
43	Nevada	33.3
42	New Hampshire	33.5
43	New Jersey	33.3
31	New Mexico	38.4
50	New York	27.9
10	North Carolina	44.7
15	North Dakota	42.9
16	Ohio	42.6
4	Oklahoma	50.0
24	Oregon	40.1
27	Pennsylvania	39.3
47	Rhode Island	31.4
6	South Carolina	47.9
25	South Dakota	39.9
5	Tennessee	48.7
12	Texas	44.4
35	Utah	37.1
40	Vermont	35.3
17	Virginia	42.1
36	Washington	37.0
7	West Virginia	47.8
30	Wisconsin	38.7
34	Wyoming	37.2

RANK ORDER

RANK	STATE	RATE
1	Arkansas	53.8
2	Alabama	51.6
3	Mississippi	51.2
4	Oklahoma	50.0
5	Tennessee	48.7
6	South Carolina	47.9
7	West Virginia	47.8
8	Georgia	46.3
9	Louisiana	44.9
10	North Carolina	44.7
11	Indiana	44.5
12	Texas	44.4
13	Kentucky	44.1
14	Missouri	44.0
15	North Dakota	42.9
16	Ohio	42.6
17	Virginia	42.1
18	Idaho	42.0
19	Montana	41.8
20	Kansas	41.2
21	Alaska	40.9
22	Delaware	40.7
23	Nebraska	40.5
24	Oregon	40.1
25	South Dakota	39.9
26	Michigan	39.5
27	Pennsylvania	39.3
28	Illinois	39.2
29	Maryland	38.8
30	Wisconsin	38.7
31	New Mexico	38.4
32	California	38.1
33	Iowa	38.0
34	Wyoming	37.2
35	Utah	37.1
36	Washington	37.0
37	Colorado	36.1
37	Minnesota	36.1
39	Hawaii	35.8
40	Vermont	35.3
41	Maine	34.5
42	New Hampshire	33.5
43	Nevada	33.3
43	New Jersey	33.3
45	Florida	32.8
46	Arizona	31.9
47	Rhode Island	31.4
48	Massachusetts	31.3
49	Connecticut	29.4
50	New York	27.9
	District of Columbia	32.7

Source: U.S. Department of Health and Human Services, National Center for Health Statistics
"National Vital Statistics Reports" (Vol. 61, No. 4, May 8, 2013, http://www.cdc.gov/nchs/deaths.htm)
*Final data by state of residence. Cerebrovascular diseases include stroke and other disorders of the blood vessels of the brain. Age-adjusted rates based on the year 2000 standard population.

Deaths by Diseases of the Heart in 2010

National Total = 597,689 Deaths*

RANK	STATE	DEATHS	% of USA
16	Alabama	12,083	2.0%
50	Alaska	707	0.1%
22	Arizona	9,954	1.7%
27	Arkansas	7,274	1.2%
1	California	58,641	9.8%
32	Colorado	6,038	1.0%
29	Connecticut	7,127	1.2%
45	Delaware	1,776	0.3%
3	Florida	41,737	7.0%
11	Georgia	15,987	2.7%
43	Hawaii	2,239	0.4%
40	Idaho	2,495	0.4%
7	Illinois	24,959	4.2%
15	Indiana	13,388	2.2%
30	Iowa	6,880	1.2%
33	Kansas	5,433	0.9%
23	Kentucky	9,662	1.6%
21	Louisiana	10,282	1.7%
39	Maine	2,628	0.4%
19	Maryland	10,915	1.8%
17	Massachusetts	12,043	2.0%
8	Michigan	23,326	3.9%
28	Minnesota	7,185	1.2%
26	Mississippi	7,542	1.3%
13	Missouri	13,840	2.3%
44	Montana	1,849	0.3%
36	Nebraska	3,355	0.6%
35	Nevada	4,811	0.8%
42	New Hampshire	2,290	0.4%
9	New Jersey	18,730	3.1%
37	New Mexico	3,224	0.5%
2	New York	44,981	7.5%
10	North Carolina	17,154	2.9%
47	North Dakota	1,395	0.2%
6	Ohio	26,164	4.4%
24	Oklahoma	9,426	1.6%
31	Oregon	6,198	1.0%
5	Pennsylvania	31,556	5.3%
41	Rhode Island	2,322	0.4%
25	South Carolina	9,295	1.6%
46	South Dakota	1,616	0.3%
12	Tennessee	14,582	2.4%
4	Texas	38,253	6.4%
38	Utah	2,889	0.5%
48	Vermont	1,172	0.2%
14	Virginia	13,404	2.2%
20	Washington	10,602	1.8%
34	West Virginia	4,897	0.8%
18	Wisconsin	11,115	1.9%
49	Wyoming	962	0.2%

RANK	STATE	DEATHS	% of USA
1	California	58,641	9.8%
2	New York	44,981	7.5%
3	Florida	41,737	7.0%
4	Texas	38,253	6.4%
5	Pennsylvania	31,556	5.3%
6	Ohio	26,164	4.4%
7	Illinois	24,959	4.2%
8	Michigan	23,326	3.9%
9	New Jersey	18,730	3.1%
10	North Carolina	17,154	2.9%
11	Georgia	15,987	2.7%
12	Tennessee	14,582	2.4%
13	Missouri	13,840	2.3%
14	Virginia	13,404	2.2%
15	Indiana	13,388	2.2%
16	Alabama	12,083	2.0%
17	Massachusetts	12,043	2.0%
18	Wisconsin	11,115	1.9%
19	Maryland	10,915	1.8%
20	Washington	10,602	1.8%
21	Louisiana	10,282	1.7%
22	Arizona	9,954	1.7%
23	Kentucky	9,662	1.6%
24	Oklahoma	9,426	1.6%
25	South Carolina	9,295	1.6%
26	Mississippi	7,542	1.3%
27	Arkansas	7,274	1.2%
28	Minnesota	7,185	1.2%
29	Connecticut	7,127	1.2%
30	Iowa	6,880	1.2%
31	Oregon	6,198	1.0%
32	Colorado	6,038	1.0%
33	Kansas	5,433	0.9%
34	West Virginia	4,897	0.8%
35	Nevada	4,811	0.8%
36	Nebraska	3,355	0.6%
37	New Mexico	3,224	0.5%
38	Utah	2,889	0.5%
39	Maine	2,628	0.4%
40	Idaho	2,495	0.4%
41	Rhode Island	2,322	0.4%
42	New Hampshire	2,290	0.4%
43	Hawaii	2,239	0.4%
44	Montana	1,849	0.3%
45	Delaware	1,776	0.3%
46	South Dakota	1,616	0.3%
47	North Dakota	1,395	0.2%
48	Vermont	1,172	0.2%
49	Wyoming	962	0.2%
50	Alaska	707	0.1%
	District of Columbia	1,306	0.2%

Source: U.S. Department of Health and Human Services, National Center for Health Statistics
"National Vital Statistics Reports" (Vol. 61, No. 4, May 8, 2013, http://www.cdc.gov/nchs/deaths.htm)
*Final data by state of residence.

Age-Adjusted Death Rate by Diseases of the Heart in 2010

National Rate = 179.1 Deaths per 100,000 Population*

ALPHA ORDER

RANK	STATE	RATE
2	Alabama	236.0
40	Alaska	151.5
45	Arizona	146.7
5	Arkansas	222.5
31	California	161.9
49	Colorado	132.8
34	Connecticut	155.7
22	Delaware	175.7
30	Florida	162.3
13	Georgia	192.6
48	Hawaii	134.7
32	Idaho	159.3
20	Illinois	181.7
15	Indiana	191.8
24	Iowa	173.3
29	Kansas	164.9
8	Kentucky	210.1
4	Louisiana	229.4
43	Maine	151.1
18	Maryland	182.2
44	Massachusetts	150.0
9	Michigan	204.2
50	Minnesota	119.4
1	Mississippi	251.1
10	Missouri	201.8
36	Montana	154.2
36	Nebraska	154.2
12	Nevada	197.3
39	New Hampshire	152.7
19	New Jersey	182.0
42	New Mexico	151.2
11	New York	199.9
23	North Carolina	174.9
33	North Dakota	158.0
14	Ohio	192.4
3	Oklahoma	235.2
47	Oregon	137.9
17	Pennsylvania	187.0
27	Rhode Island	167.1
16	South Carolina	189.9
35	South Dakota	155.2
6	Tennessee	217.4
21	Texas	181.1
46	Utah	143.2
38	Vermont	153.6
26	Virginia	168.5
40	Washington	151.5
7	West Virginia	211.2
28	Wisconsin	165.1
25	Wyoming	169.8

RANK ORDER

RANK	STATE	RATE
1	Mississippi	251.1
2	Alabama	236.0
3	Oklahoma	235.2
4	Louisiana	229.4
5	Arkansas	222.5
6	Tennessee	217.4
7	West Virginia	211.2
8	Kentucky	210.1
9	Michigan	204.2
10	Missouri	201.8
11	New York	199.9
12	Nevada	197.3
13	Georgia	192.6
14	Ohio	192.4
15	Indiana	191.8
16	South Carolina	189.9
17	Pennsylvania	187.0
18	Maryland	182.2
19	New Jersey	182.0
20	Illinois	181.7
21	Texas	181.1
22	Delaware	175.7
23	North Carolina	174.9
24	Iowa	173.3
25	Wyoming	169.8
26	Virginia	168.5
27	Rhode Island	167.1
28	Wisconsin	165.1
29	Kansas	164.9
30	Florida	162.3
31	California	161.9
32	Idaho	159.3
33	North Dakota	158.0
34	Connecticut	155.7
35	South Dakota	155.2
36	Montana	154.2
36	Nebraska	154.2
38	Vermont	153.6
39	New Hampshire	152.7
40	Alaska	151.5
40	Washington	151.5
42	New Mexico	151.2
43	Maine	151.1
44	Massachusetts	150.0
45	Arizona	146.7
46	Utah	143.2
47	Oregon	137.9
48	Hawaii	134.7
49	Colorado	132.8
50	Minnesota	119.4

| | District of Columbia | 222.4 |

Source: U.S. Department of Health and Human Services, National Center for Health Statistics
"National Vital Statistics Reports" (Vol. 61, No. 4, May 8, 2013, http://www.cdc.gov/nchs/deaths.htm)
*Final data by state of residence. Age-adjusted rates based on the year 2000 standard population.

Deaths by Suicide in 2010

National Total = 38,364 Suicides*

ALPHA ORDER

RANK	STATE	DEATHS	% of USA
21	Alabama	679	1.8%
44	Alaska	164	0.4%
11	Arizona	1,093	2.8%
31	Arkansas	447	1.2%
1	California	3,913	10.2%
15	Colorado	865	2.3%
36	Connecticut	353	0.9%
48	Delaware	106	0.3%
3	Florida	2,789	7.3%
10	Georgia	1,133	3.0%
40	Hawaii	207	0.5%
37	Idaho	290	0.8%
8	Illinois	1,178	3.1%
16	Indiana	864	2.3%
35	Iowa	372	1.0%
33	Kansas	401	1.0%
23	Kentucky	631	1.6%
27	Louisiana	557	1.5%
43	Maine	186	0.5%
29	Maryland	502	1.3%
26	Massachusetts	598	1.6%
7	Michigan	1,263	3.3%
25	Minnesota	606	1.6%
34	Mississippi	388	1.0%
17	Missouri	856	2.2%
39	Montana	227	0.6%
42	Nebraska	193	0.5%
28	Nevada	547	1.4%
41	New Hampshire	196	0.5%
19	New Jersey	719	1.9%
32	New Mexico	413	1.1%
5	New York	1,547	4.0%
9	North Carolina	1,174	3.1%
48	North Dakota	106	0.3%
6	Ohio	1,439	3.8%
24	Oklahoma	618	1.6%
20	Oregon	685	1.8%
4	Pennsylvania	1,576	4.1%
47	Rhode Island	129	0.3%
22	South Carolina	637	1.7%
45	South Dakota	140	0.4%
14	Tennessee	943	2.5%
2	Texas	2,891	7.5%
30	Utah	473	1.2%
48	Vermont	106	0.3%
12	Virginia	963	2.5%
13	Washington	957	2.5%
38	West Virginia	279	0.7%
18	Wisconsin	793	2.1%
46	Wyoming	131	0.3%

RANK ORDER

RANK	STATE	DEATHS	% of USA
1	California	3,913	10.2%
2	Texas	2,891	7.5%
3	Florida	2,789	7.3%
4	Pennsylvania	1,576	4.1%
5	New York	1,547	4.0%
6	Ohio	1,439	3.8%
7	Michigan	1,263	3.3%
8	Illinois	1,178	3.1%
9	North Carolina	1,174	3.1%
10	Georgia	1,133	3.0%
11	Arizona	1,093	2.8%
12	Virginia	963	2.5%
13	Washington	957	2.5%
14	Tennessee	943	2.5%
15	Colorado	865	2.3%
16	Indiana	864	2.3%
17	Missouri	856	2.2%
18	Wisconsin	793	2.1%
19	New Jersey	719	1.9%
20	Oregon	685	1.8%
21	Alabama	679	1.8%
22	South Carolina	637	1.7%
23	Kentucky	631	1.6%
24	Oklahoma	618	1.6%
25	Minnesota	606	1.6%
26	Massachusetts	598	1.6%
27	Louisiana	557	1.5%
28	Nevada	547	1.4%
29	Maryland	502	1.3%
30	Utah	473	1.2%
31	Arkansas	447	1.2%
32	New Mexico	413	1.1%
33	Kansas	401	1.0%
34	Mississippi	388	1.0%
35	Iowa	372	1.0%
36	Connecticut	353	0.9%
37	Idaho	290	0.8%
38	West Virginia	279	0.7%
39	Montana	227	0.6%
40	Hawaii	207	0.5%
41	New Hampshire	196	0.5%
42	Nebraska	193	0.5%
43	Maine	186	0.5%
44	Alaska	164	0.4%
45	South Dakota	140	0.4%
46	Wyoming	131	0.3%
47	Rhode Island	129	0.3%
48	Delaware	106	0.3%
48	North Dakota	106	0.3%
48	Vermont	106	0.3%
	District of Columbia	41	0.1%

Source: U.S. Department of Health and Human Services, National Center for Health Statistics
 "National Vital Statistics Reports" (Vol. 61, No. 4, May 8, 2013, http://www.cdc.gov/nchs/deaths.htm)
*Final data by state of residence. Also referred to as "Intentional self-harm."

Age-Adjusted Death Rate by Suicide in 2010

National Rate = 12.1 Deaths per 100,000 Population*

RANK	STATE	RATE
21	Alabama	14.0
1	Alaska	22.8
10	Arizona	17.0
15	Arkansas	15.5
44	California	10.3
11	Colorado	16.8
45	Connecticut	9.4
41	Delaware	11.3
25	Florida	13.7
38	Georgia	11.7
16	Hawaii	15.0
6	Idaho	18.8
46	Illinois	9.0
29	Indiana	13.1
35	Iowa	12.1
23	Kansas	13.9
18	Kentucky	14.2
32	Louisiana	12.3
28	Maine	13.2
48	Maryland	8.3
47	Massachusetts	8.8
31	Michigan	12.5
42	Minnesota	11.2
30	Mississippi	13.0
21	Missouri	14.0
3	Montana	21.8
43	Nebraska	10.4
5	Nevada	19.8
19	New Hampshire	14.1
49	New Jersey	7.7
4	New Mexico	20.1
49	New York	7.7
36	North Carolina	12.0
14	North Dakota	15.6
34	Ohio	12.2
12	Oklahoma	16.5
9	Oregon	17.1
37	Pennsylvania	11.9
32	Rhode Island	12.3
26	South Carolina	13.5
8	South Dakota	17.5
17	Tennessee	14.6
38	Texas	11.7
7	Utah	18.3
13	Vermont	15.7
38	Virginia	11.7
23	Washington	13.9
19	West Virginia	14.1
27	Wisconsin	13.4
2	Wyoming	22.4

RANK	STATE	RATE
1	Alaska	22.8
2	Wyoming	22.4
3	Montana	21.8
4	New Mexico	20.1
5	Nevada	19.8
6	Idaho	18.8
7	Utah	18.3
8	South Dakota	17.5
9	Oregon	17.1
10	Arizona	17.0
11	Colorado	16.8
12	Oklahoma	16.5
13	Vermont	15.7
14	North Dakota	15.6
15	Arkansas	15.5
16	Hawaii	15.0
17	Tennessee	14.6
18	Kentucky	14.2
19	New Hampshire	14.1
19	West Virginia	14.1
21	Alabama	14.0
21	Missouri	14.0
23	Kansas	13.9
23	Washington	13.9
25	Florida	13.7
26	South Carolina	13.5
27	Wisconsin	13.4
28	Maine	13.2
29	Indiana	13.1
30	Mississippi	13.0
31	Michigan	12.5
32	Louisiana	12.3
32	Rhode Island	12.3
34	Ohio	12.2
35	Iowa	12.1
36	North Carolina	12.0
37	Pennsylvania	11.9
38	Georgia	11.7
38	Texas	11.7
38	Virginia	11.7
41	Delaware	11.3
42	Minnesota	11.2
43	Nebraska	10.4
44	California	10.3
45	Connecticut	9.4
46	Illinois	9.0
47	Massachusetts	8.8
48	Maryland	8.3
49	New Jersey	7.7
49	New York	7.7
	District of Columbia	6.9

Source: U.S. Department of Health and Human Services, National Center for Health Statistics
"National Vital Statistics Reports" (Vol. 61, No. 4, May 8, 2013, http://www.cdc.gov/nchs/deaths.htm)
*Final data by state of residence. Also referred to as "Intentional self-harm." Age-adjusted rates based on the year 2000 standard population.

Deaths by AIDS in 2010

National Total = 8,369 Deaths*

ALPHA ORDER

RANK	STATE	DEATHS	% of USA
14	Alabama	153	1.8%
48	Alaska	6	0.1%
21	Arizona	102	1.2%
26	Arkansas	64	0.8%
4	California	742	8.9%
25	Colorado	67	0.8%
23	Connecticut	83	1.0%
33	Delaware	46	0.5%
1	Florida	1,068	12.8%
5	Georgia	495	5.9%
39	Hawaii	13	0.2%
43	Idaho	9	0.1%
9	Illinois	300	3.6%
22	Indiana	91	1.1%
37	Iowa	15	0.2%
35	Kansas	27	0.3%
28	Kentucky	53	0.6%
11	Louisiana	225	2.7%
43	Maine	9	0.1%
8	Maryland	316	3.8%
18	Massachusetts	120	1.4%
15	Michigan	150	1.8%
31	Minnesota	48	0.6%
19	Mississippi	118	1.4%
20	Missouri	105	1.3%
46	Montana	7	0.1%
41	Nebraska	12	0.1%
27	Nevada	60	0.7%
43	New Hampshire	9	0.1%
6	New Jersey	378	4.5%
34	New Mexico	33	0.4%
2	New York	990	11.8%
7	North Carolina	328	3.9%
50	North Dakota	2	0.0%
17	Ohio	138	1.6%
30	Oklahoma	50	0.6%
32	Oregon	47	0.6%
10	Pennsylvania	266	3.2%
36	Rhode Island	20	0.2%
13	South Carolina	184	2.2%
42	South Dakota	10	0.1%
12	Tennessee	207	2.5%
3	Texas	773	9.2%
39	Utah	13	0.2%
46	Vermont	7	0.1%
16	Virginia	142	1.7%
24	Washington	76	0.9%
38	West Virginia	14	0.2%
29	Wisconsin	51	0.6%
48	Wyoming	6	0.1%

RANK ORDER

RANK	STATE	DEATHS	% of USA
1	Florida	1,068	12.8%
2	New York	990	11.8%
3	Texas	773	9.2%
4	California	742	8.9%
5	Georgia	495	5.9%
6	New Jersey	378	4.5%
7	North Carolina	328	3.9%
8	Maryland	316	3.8%
9	Illinois	300	3.6%
10	Pennsylvania	266	3.2%
11	Louisiana	225	2.7%
12	Tennessee	207	2.5%
13	South Carolina	184	2.2%
14	Alabama	153	1.8%
15	Michigan	150	1.8%
16	Virginia	142	1.7%
17	Ohio	138	1.6%
18	Massachusetts	120	1.4%
19	Mississippi	118	1.4%
20	Missouri	105	1.3%
21	Arizona	102	1.2%
22	Indiana	91	1.1%
23	Connecticut	83	1.0%
24	Washington	76	0.9%
25	Colorado	67	0.8%
26	Arkansas	64	0.8%
27	Nevada	60	0.7%
28	Kentucky	53	0.6%
29	Wisconsin	51	0.6%
30	Oklahoma	50	0.6%
31	Minnesota	48	0.6%
32	Oregon	47	0.6%
33	Delaware	46	0.5%
34	New Mexico	33	0.4%
35	Kansas	27	0.3%
36	Rhode Island	20	0.2%
37	Iowa	15	0.2%
38	West Virginia	14	0.2%
39	Hawaii	13	0.2%
39	Utah	13	0.2%
41	Nebraska	12	0.1%
42	South Dakota	10	0.1%
43	Idaho	9	0.1%
43	Maine	9	0.1%
43	New Hampshire	9	0.1%
46	Montana	7	0.1%
46	Vermont	7	0.1%
48	Alaska	6	0.1%
48	Wyoming	6	0.1%
50	North Dakota	2	0.0%

District of Columbia	121	1.4%

Source: U.S. Department of Health and Human Services, National Center for Health Statistics
"National Vital Statistics Reports" (Vol. 61, No. 4, May 8, 2013, http://www.cdc.gov/nchs/deaths.htm)
*Final data by state of residence. AIDS is Acquired Immunodeficiency Syndrome. It is a specific group of diseases or conditions which are indicative of severe immunosuppression related to infection with the Human Immunodeficiency Virus (HIV).

Age-Adjusted Death Rate by AIDS in 2010

National Rate = 2.6 Deaths per 100,000 Population*

ALPHA ORDER			RANK ORDER		
RANK	STATE	RATE	RANK	STATE	RATE
11	Alabama	3.2	1	Florida	5.4
NA	Alaska**	NA	2	Georgia	5.0
23	Arizona	1.6	2	Louisiana	5.0
15	Arkansas	2.2	2	Maryland	5.0
18	California	1.9	5	Delaware	4.9
29	Colorado	1.2	6	New York	4.7
17	Connecticut	2.0	7	Mississippi	4.2
5	Delaware	4.9	8	New Jersey	3.9
1	Florida	5.4	8	South Carolina	3.9
2	Georgia	5.0	10	North Carolina	3.3
NA	Hawaii**	NA	11	Alabama	3.2
NA	Idaho**	NA	11	Tennessee	3.2
14	Illinois	2.3	11	Texas	3.2
26	Indiana	1.5	14	Illinois	2.3
NA	Iowa**	NA	15	Arkansas	2.2
34	Kansas	0.9	15	Nevada	2.2
29	Kentucky	1.2	17	Connecticut	2.0
2	Louisiana	5.0	18	California	1.9
NA	Maine**	NA	18	Pennsylvania	1.9
2	Maryland	5.0	20	Missouri	1.8
23	Massachusetts	1.6	20	Rhode Island	1.8
26	Michigan	1.5	22	Virginia	1.7
34	Minnesota	0.9	23	Arizona	1.6
7	Mississippi	4.2	23	Massachusetts	1.6
20	Missouri	1.8	23	New Mexico	1.6
NA	Montana**	NA	26	Indiana	1.5
NA	Nebraska**	NA	26	Michigan	1.5
15	Nevada	2.2	28	Oklahoma	1.4
NA	New Hampshire**	NA	29	Colorado	1.2
8	New Jersey	3.9	29	Kentucky	1.2
23	New Mexico	1.6	29	Oregon	1.2
6	New York	4.7	32	Ohio	1.1
10	North Carolina	3.3	33	Washington	1.0
NA	North Dakota**	NA	34	Kansas	0.9
32	Ohio	1.1	34	Minnesota	0.9
28	Oklahoma	1.4	36	Wisconsin	0.8
29	Oregon	1.2	NA	Alaska**	NA
18	Pennsylvania	1.9	NA	Hawaii**	NA
20	Rhode Island	1.8	NA	Idaho**	NA
8	South Carolina	3.9	NA	Iowa**	NA
NA	South Dakota**	NA	NA	Maine**	NA
11	Tennessee	3.2	NA	Montana**	NA
11	Texas	3.2	NA	Nebraska**	NA
NA	Utah**	NA	NA	New Hampshire**	NA
NA	Vermont**	NA	NA	North Dakota**	NA
22	Virginia	1.7	NA	South Dakota**	NA
33	Washington	1.0	NA	Utah**	NA
NA	West Virginia**	NA	NA	Vermont**	NA
36	Wisconsin	0.8	NA	West Virginia**	NA
NA	Wyoming**	NA	NA	Wyoming**	NA
				District of Columbia	20.4

Source: U.S. Department of Health and Human Services, National Center for Health Statistics
"National Vital Statistics Reports" (Vol. 61, No. 4, May 8, 2013, http://www.cdc.gov/nchs/deaths.htm)
*Final data by state of residence. AIDS is Acquired Immunodeficiency Syndrome. It is a specific group of diseases or
conditions which are indicative of severe immunosuppression related to infection with the Human Immunodeficiency Virus (HIV).
Age-adjusted rates based on the year 2000 standard population.
**Insufficient data to determine a reliable rate.

Adult Per Capita Alcohol Consumption in 2011

National Per Capita = 2.6 Gallons Consumed per Adult 21 Years and Older*

ALPHA ORDER

RANK	STATE	PER CAPITA
42	Alabama	2.2
6	Alaska	3.3
22	Arizona	2.7
49	Arkansas	1.9
27	California	2.6
9	Colorado	3.1
22	Connecticut	2.7
2	Delaware	4.0
16	Florida	2.8
42	Georgia	2.2
16	Hawaii	2.8
11	Idaho	3.0
22	Illinois	2.7
39	Indiana	2.3
27	Iowa	2.6
42	Kansas	2.2
48	Kentucky	2.0
13	Louisiana	2.9
16	Maine	2.8
33	Maryland	2.5
13	Massachusetts	2.9
27	Michigan	2.6
16	Minnesota	2.8
33	Mississippi	2.5
16	Missouri	2.8
7	Montana	3.2
27	Nebraska	2.6
3	Nevada	3.8
1	New Hampshire	5.3
22	New Jersey	2.7
22	New Mexico	2.7
37	New York	2.4
39	North Carolina	2.3
4	North Dakota	3.6
42	Ohio	2.2
42	Oklahoma	2.2
16	Oregon	2.8
33	Pennsylvania	2.5
11	Rhode Island	3.0
27	South Carolina	2.6
9	South Dakota	3.1
39	Tennessee	2.3
27	Texas	2.6
50	Utah	1.6
7	Vermont	3.2
37	Virginia	2.4
33	Washington	2.5
47	West Virginia	2.1
5	Wisconsin	3.4
13	Wyoming	2.9

RANK ORDER

RANK	STATE	PER CAPITA
1	New Hampshire	5.3
2	Delaware	4.0
3	Nevada	3.8
4	North Dakota	3.6
5	Wisconsin	3.4
6	Alaska	3.3
7	Montana	3.2
7	Vermont	3.2
9	Colorado	3.1
9	South Dakota	3.1
11	Idaho	3.0
11	Rhode Island	3.0
13	Louisiana	2.9
13	Massachusetts	2.9
13	Wyoming	2.9
16	Florida	2.8
16	Hawaii	2.8
16	Maine	2.8
16	Minnesota	2.8
16	Missouri	2.8
16	Oregon	2.8
22	Arizona	2.7
22	Connecticut	2.7
22	Illinois	2.7
22	New Jersey	2.7
22	New Mexico	2.7
27	California	2.6
27	Iowa	2.6
27	Michigan	2.6
27	Nebraska	2.6
27	South Carolina	2.6
27	Texas	2.6
33	Maryland	2.5
33	Mississippi	2.5
33	Pennsylvania	2.5
33	Washington	2.5
37	New York	2.4
37	Virginia	2.4
39	Indiana	2.3
39	North Carolina	2.3
39	Tennessee	2.3
42	Alabama	2.2
42	Georgia	2.2
42	Kansas	2.2
42	Ohio	2.2
42	Oklahoma	2.2
47	West Virginia	2.1
48	Kentucky	2.0
49	Arkansas	1.9
50	Utah	1.6
	District of Columbia	4.3

Source: CQ Press using data from U.S. Dept of Health and Human Services, National Institute on Alcohol Abuse and Alcoholism "Apparent Per Capita Alcohol Consumption, 1977-2011" (http://pubs.niaaa.nih.gov/publications/surveillance97/CONS11.htm)
*This is apparent consumption of actual alcohol, not entire volume of an alcoholic beverage (for example, wine is roughly 11% absolute alcohol content). Apparent consumption is based on several sources which together approximate sales but do not actually measure consumption. Accordingly, figures for some states may be skewed by purchases by nonresidents.

Percent of Adults Who Smoke: 2012

National Median = 19.6% of Adults*

ALPHA ORDER

RANK	STATE	PERCENT
9	Alabama	23.8
19	Alaska	20.5
41	Arizona	17.1
3	Arkansas	25.0
49	California	12.6
35	Colorado	17.7
47	Connecticut	16.0
23	Delaware	19.7
35	Florida	17.7
20	Georgia	20.4
48	Hawaii	14.6
43	Idaho	16.4
30	Illinois	18.6
6	Indiana	24.0
32	Iowa	18.1
26	Kansas	19.4
1	Kentucky	28.3
5	Louisiana	24.8
22	Maine	20.3
45	Maryland	16.2
43	Massachusetts	16.4
10	Michigan	23.3
29	Minnesota	18.8
6	Mississippi	24.0
8	Missouri	23.9
23	Montana	19.7
23	Nebraska	19.7
32	Nevada	18.1
39	New Hampshire	17.2
38	New Jersey	17.3
27	New Mexico	19.3
45	New York	16.2
18	North Carolina	20.9
17	North Dakota	21.2
10	Ohio	23.3
10	Oklahoma	23.3
34	Oregon	17.9
16	Pennsylvania	21.4
37	Rhode Island	17.4
13	South Carolina	22.5
14	South Dakota	22.0
4	Tennessee	24.9
31	Texas	18.2
50	Utah	10.6
42	Vermont	16.5
28	Virginia	19.0
39	Washington	17.2
2	West Virginia	28.2
20	Wisconsin	20.4
15	Wyoming	21.8

RANK ORDER

RANK	STATE	PERCENT
1	Kentucky	28.3
2	West Virginia	28.2
3	Arkansas	25.0
4	Tennessee	24.9
5	Louisiana	24.8
6	Indiana	24.0
6	Mississippi	24.0
8	Missouri	23.9
9	Alabama	23.8
10	Michigan	23.3
10	Ohio	23.3
10	Oklahoma	23.3
13	South Carolina	22.5
14	South Dakota	22.0
15	Wyoming	21.8
16	Pennsylvania	21.4
17	North Dakota	21.2
18	North Carolina	20.9
19	Alaska	20.5
20	Georgia	20.4
20	Wisconsin	20.4
22	Maine	20.3
23	Delaware	19.7
23	Montana	19.7
23	Nebraska	19.7
26	Kansas	19.4
27	New Mexico	19.3
28	Virginia	19.0
29	Minnesota	18.8
30	Illinois	18.6
31	Texas	18.2
32	Iowa	18.1
32	Nevada	18.1
34	Oregon	17.9
35	Colorado	17.7
35	Florida	17.7
37	Rhode Island	17.4
38	New Jersey	17.3
39	New Hampshire	17.2
39	Washington	17.2
41	Arizona	17.1
42	Vermont	16.5
43	Idaho	16.4
43	Massachusetts	16.4
45	Maryland	16.2
45	New York	16.2
47	Connecticut	16.0
48	Hawaii	14.6
49	California	12.6
50	Utah	10.6

| | District of Columbia | 19.6 |

Source: U.S. Department of Health and Human Services, Centers for Disease Control and Prevention
   "2012 Behavioral Risk Factor Surveillance Summary Prevalence Data" (http://apps.nccd.cdc.gov/brfss/)
*Persons 18 and older who have smoked more than 100 cigarettes during their lifetime and who currently smoke every day or some days.

Percent of Adults Overweight or Obese: 2012

National Median = 63.4% of Adults*

ALPHA ORDER				RANK ORDER		
RANK	STATE	PERCENT		RANK	STATE	PERCENT
5	Alabama	67.8		1	Louisiana	69.5
23	Alaska	64.8		2	Mississippi	68.9
40	Arizona	62.0		3	Arkansas	68.7
3	Arkansas	68.7		4	West Virginia	68.3
45	California	60.3		5	Alabama	67.8
50	Colorado	55.7		5	Oklahoma	67.8
36	Connecticut	62.3		7	Kentucky	66.9
11	Delaware	66.0		8	Wisconsin	66.5
38	Florida	62.1		9	North Dakota	66.3
25	Georgia	64.6		10	South Carolina	66.1
49	Hawaii	56.1		11	Delaware	66.0
34	Idaho	62.6		11	South Dakota	66.0
27	Illinois	63.9		13	North Carolina	65.9
17	Indiana	65.5		14	Missouri	65.8
24	Iowa	64.7		15	Michigan	65.7
16	Kansas	65.6		16	Kansas	65.6
7	Kentucky	66.9		17	Indiana	65.5
1	Louisiana	69.5		18	Ohio	65.3
26	Maine	64.2		18	Tennessee	65.3
28	Maryland	63.8		20	Texas	65.1
47	Massachusetts	58.8		21	Nebraska	65.0
15	Michigan	65.7		21	Pennsylvania	65.0
31	Minnesota	63.0		23	Alaska	64.8
2	Mississippi	68.9		24	Iowa	64.7
14	Missouri	65.8		25	Georgia	64.6
42	Montana	61.3		26	Maine	64.2
21	Nebraska	65.0		27	Illinois	63.9
35	Nevada	62.5		28	Maryland	63.8
38	New Hampshire	62.1		29	Virginia	63.6
41	New Jersey	61.6		30	Wyoming	63.3
33	New Mexico	62.8		31	Minnesota	63.0
44	New York	60.6		32	Rhode Island	62.9
13	North Carolina	65.9		33	New Mexico	62.8
9	North Dakota	66.3		34	Idaho	62.6
18	Ohio	65.3		35	Nevada	62.5
5	Oklahoma	67.8		36	Connecticut	62.3
43	Oregon	61.1		37	Washington	62.2
21	Pennsylvania	65.0		38	Florida	62.1
32	Rhode Island	62.9		38	New Hampshire	62.1
10	South Carolina	66.1		40	Arizona	62.0
11	South Dakota	66.0		41	New Jersey	61.6
18	Tennessee	65.3		42	Montana	61.3
20	Texas	65.1		43	Oregon	61.1
48	Utah	57.8		44	New York	60.6
45	Vermont	60.3		45	California	60.3
29	Virginia	63.6		45	Vermont	60.3
37	Washington	62.2		47	Massachusetts	58.8
4	West Virginia	68.3		48	Utah	57.8
8	Wisconsin	66.5		49	Hawaii	56.1
30	Wyoming	63.3		50	Colorado	55.7

District of Columbia	51.9

Source: CQ Press using data from U.S. Department of Health and Human Services, Centers for Disease Control and Prevention
"2012 Behavioral Risk Factor Surveillance Summary Prevalence Data" (http://apps.nccd.cdc.gov/brfss/)
*Persons 18 and older. Overweight is defined as a Body Mass Index (BMI) of 25.0 to 29.9 regardless of sex. Obese is a BMI of
30.0 or greater. BMI is a ratio of height to weight. As an example, a person 5' 8" and weighing 165 pounds has a BMI of 25. The
same height at 197 pounds has a BMI of 30. See http://www.cdc.gov/healthyweight/assessing/bmi/index.html.

Percent of Children Aged 19 to 35 Months Fully Immunized in 2012

National Percent = 68.4%*

ALPHA ORDER

RANK	STATE	PERCENT
21	Alabama	71.3
50	Alaska	59.5
29	Arizona	67.5
36	Arkansas	66.4
32	California	66.8
18	Colorado	71.7
4	Connecticut	77.1
12	Delaware	72.6
24	Florida	68.6
8	Georgia	74.7
1	Hawaii	80.2
46	Idaho	63.0
25	Illinois	68.5
47	Indiana	61.4
7	Iowa	74.8
40	Kansas	65.0
28	Kentucky	68.2
25	Louisiana	68.5
12	Maine	72.6
31	Maryland	67.1
9	Massachusetts	73.5
22	Michigan	70.5
37	Minnesota	66.2
3	Mississippi	77.5
42	Missouri	63.9
35	Montana	66.5
12	Nebraska	72.6
38	Nevada	65.3
2	New Hampshire	80.1
20	New Jersey	71.5
19	New Mexico	71.6
43	New York	63.7
5	North Carolina	75.4
16	North Dakota	72.2
32	Ohio	66.8
48	Oklahoma	61.0
34	Oregon	66.7
27	Pennsylvania	68.3
15	Rhode Island	72.5
17	South Carolina	71.8
44	South Dakota	63.6
10	Tennessee	73.1
41	Texas	64.8
11	Utah	73.0
45	Vermont	63.2
23	Virginia	69.8
39	Washington	65.2
49	West Virginia	60.8
6	Wisconsin	75.2
30	Wyoming	67.2

RANK ORDER

RANK	STATE	PERCENT
1	Hawaii	80.2
2	New Hampshire	80.1
3	Mississippi	77.5
4	Connecticut	77.1
5	North Carolina	75.4
6	Wisconsin	75.2
7	Iowa	74.8
8	Georgia	74.7
9	Massachusetts	73.5
10	Tennessee	73.1
11	Utah	73.0
12	Delaware	72.6
12	Maine	72.6
12	Nebraska	72.6
15	Rhode Island	72.5
16	North Dakota	72.2
17	South Carolina	71.8
18	Colorado	71.7
19	New Mexico	71.6
20	New Jersey	71.5
21	Alabama	71.3
22	Michigan	70.5
23	Virginia	69.8
24	Florida	68.6
25	Illinois	68.5
25	Louisiana	68.5
27	Pennsylvania	68.3
28	Kentucky	68.2
29	Arizona	67.5
30	Wyoming	67.2
31	Maryland	67.1
32	California	66.8
32	Ohio	66.8
34	Oregon	66.7
35	Montana	66.5
36	Arkansas	66.4
37	Minnesota	66.2
38	Nevada	65.3
39	Washington	65.2
40	Kansas	65.0
41	Texas	64.8
42	Missouri	63.9
43	New York	63.7
44	South Dakota	63.6
45	Vermont	63.2
46	Idaho	63.0
47	Indiana	61.4
48	Oklahoma	61.0
49	West Virginia	60.8
50	Alaska	59.5

District of Columbia	73.4

Source: U.S. Department of Health and Human Services, Centers for Disease Control and Prevention
"State Vaccination Coverage Levels" (MMWR, Vol. 62, No. 36, September 13, 2013, http://www.cdc.gov/mmwr/)
*Fully immunized (4:3:1:3:3:1:4 series) children received four doses of DTP/DT/DTaP (Diphtheria, Tetanus, Pertussis [Whooping Cough], Acellular Pertussis), three doses of OPV (Oral Poliovirus Vaccine), one dose of MCV (Measles-Containing Vaccine), three doses of Hib (Haemophilus influenzae type b), three doses of Hepatitis B vaccine, one dose of Varicella (chickenpox) vaccine, and four doses of PCV (pneumococcal conjugate vaccine). This differs from previous "fully" immunized tables.

XII. Households and Housing

Households in 2012

National Total = 115,969,540 Households*

ALPHA ORDER

RANK	STATE	HOUSEHOLDS	% of USA
23	Alabama	1,845,169	1.6%
49	Alaska	251,651	0.2%
17	Arizona	2,392,168	2.1%
31	Arkansas	1,143,859	1.0%
1	California	12,552,658	10.8%
22	Colorado	1,996,088	1.7%
29	Connecticut	1,357,812	1.2%
45	Delaware	340,308	0.3%
4	Florida	7,197,943	6.2%
10	Georgia	3,532,908	3.0%
42	Hawaii	447,748	0.4%
39	Idaho	583,106	0.5%
6	Illinois	4,770,194	4.1%
16	Indiana	2,480,077	2.1%
30	Iowa	1,227,048	1.1%
32	Kansas	1,113,911	1.0%
26	Kentucky	1,707,004	1.5%
25	Louisiana	1,719,473	1.5%
40	Maine	554,543	0.5%
20	Maryland	2,157,717	1.9%
14	Massachusetts	2,522,394	2.2%
8	Michigan	3,819,068	3.3%
21	Minnesota	2,111,943	1.8%
33	Mississippi	1,090,521	0.9%
18	Missouri	2,359,135	2.0%
44	Montana	408,938	0.4%
38	Nebraska	733,570	0.6%
34	Nevada	1,006,605	0.9%
41	New Hampshire	519,137	0.4%
11	New Jersey	3,198,799	2.8%
36	New Mexico	764,996	0.7%
3	New York	7,238,922	6.2%
9	North Carolina	3,731,325	3.2%
47	North Dakota	290,944	0.3%
7	Ohio	4,554,672	3.9%
28	Oklahoma	1,446,667	1.2%
27	Oregon	1,516,957	1.3%
5	Pennsylvania	4,958,249	4.3%
43	Rhode Island	413,083	0.4%
24	South Carolina	1,787,340	1.5%
46	South Dakota	323,765	0.3%
15	Tennessee	2,480,090	2.1%
2	Texas	8,970,959	7.7%
35	Utah	895,691	0.8%
48	Vermont	258,520	0.2%
12	Virginia	3,038,967	2.6%
13	Washington	2,636,817	2.3%
37	West Virginia	741,544	0.6%
19	Wisconsin	2,288,362	2.0%
50	Wyoming	223,513	0.2%

RANK ORDER

RANK	STATE	HOUSEHOLDS	% of USA
1	California	12,552,658	10.8%
2	Texas	8,970,959	7.7%
3	New York	7,238,922	6.2%
4	Florida	7,197,943	6.2%
5	Pennsylvania	4,958,249	4.3%
6	Illinois	4,770,194	4.1%
7	Ohio	4,554,672	3.9%
8	Michigan	3,819,068	3.3%
9	North Carolina	3,731,325	3.2%
10	Georgia	3,532,908	3.0%
11	New Jersey	3,198,799	2.8%
12	Virginia	3,038,967	2.6%
13	Washington	2,636,817	2.3%
14	Massachusetts	2,522,394	2.2%
15	Tennessee	2,480,090	2.1%
16	Indiana	2,480,077	2.1%
17	Arizona	2,392,168	2.1%
18	Missouri	2,359,135	2.0%
19	Wisconsin	2,288,362	2.0%
20	Maryland	2,157,717	1.9%
21	Minnesota	2,111,943	1.8%
22	Colorado	1,996,088	1.7%
23	Alabama	1,845,169	1.6%
24	South Carolina	1,787,340	1.5%
25	Louisiana	1,719,473	1.5%
26	Kentucky	1,707,004	1.5%
27	Oregon	1,516,957	1.3%
28	Oklahoma	1,446,667	1.2%
29	Connecticut	1,357,812	1.2%
30	Iowa	1,227,048	1.1%
31	Arkansas	1,143,859	1.0%
32	Kansas	1,113,911	1.0%
33	Mississippi	1,090,521	0.9%
34	Nevada	1,006,605	0.9%
35	Utah	895,691	0.8%
36	New Mexico	764,996	0.7%
37	West Virginia	741,544	0.6%
38	Nebraska	733,570	0.6%
39	Idaho	583,106	0.5%
40	Maine	554,543	0.5%
41	New Hampshire	519,137	0.4%
42	Hawaii	447,748	0.4%
43	Rhode Island	413,083	0.4%
44	Montana	408,938	0.4%
45	Delaware	340,308	0.3%
46	South Dakota	323,765	0.3%
47	North Dakota	290,944	0.3%
48	Vermont	258,520	0.2%
49	Alaska	251,651	0.2%
50	Wyoming	223,513	0.2%
	District of Columbia	266,662	0.2%

Source: U.S. Bureau of the Census
    "2012 American Community Survey-Table S2501" (http://www.census.gov/acs/www/index.html)
*A household includes all persons who occupy a housing unit. A household consists of a single family, one person living alone,
two or more families living together, or any other group of related or unrelated persons who share living arrangements.

Persons per Household in 2012

National Rate = 2.64 Persons per Household*

ALPHA ORDER				RANK ORDER		
RANK	STATE	PERSONS		RANK	STATE	PERSONS
25	Alabama	2.55		1	Utah	3.14
5	Alaska	2.80		2	Hawaii	3.01
10	Arizona	2.68		3	California	2.97
33	Arkansas	2.51		4	Texas	2.84
3	California	2.97		5	Alaska	2.80
27	Colorado	2.54		6	Georgia	2.73
21	Connecticut	2.56		7	New Jersey	2.71
15	Delaware	2.62		8	Nevada	2.70
15	Florida	2.62		9	Idaho	2.69
6	Georgia	2.73		10	Arizona	2.68
2	Hawaii	3.01		11	New Mexico	2.67
9	Idaho	2.69		12	Maryland	2.66
14	Illinois	2.64		13	Mississippi	2.65
21	Indiana	2.56		14	Illinois	2.64
46	Iowa	2.42		15	Delaware	2.62
31	Kansas	2.52		15	Florida	2.62
35	Kentucky	2.49		15	New York	2.62
19	Louisiana	2.60		18	Virginia	2.61
48	Maine	2.33		19	Louisiana	2.60
12	Maryland	2.66		20	South Carolina	2.57
27	Massachusetts	2.54		21	Connecticut	2.56
30	Michigan	2.53		21	Indiana	2.56
37	Minnesota	2.48		21	Oklahoma	2.56
13	Mississippi	2.65		21	Washington	2.56
37	Missouri	2.48		25	Alabama	2.55
47	Montana	2.39		25	North Carolina	2.55
42	Nebraska	2.46		27	Colorado	2.54
8	Nevada	2.70		27	Massachusetts	2.54
39	New Hampshire	2.47		27	Tennessee	2.54
7	New Jersey	2.71		30	Michigan	2.53
11	New Mexico	2.67		31	Kansas	2.52
15	New York	2.62		31	Wyoming	2.52
25	North Carolina	2.55		33	Arkansas	2.51
49	North Dakota	2.32		33	Oregon	2.51
39	Ohio	2.47		35	Kentucky	2.49
21	Oklahoma	2.56		35	Pennsylvania	2.49
33	Oregon	2.51		37	Minnesota	2.48
35	Pennsylvania	2.49		37	Missouri	2.48
43	Rhode Island	2.44		39	New Hampshire	2.47
20	South Carolina	2.57		39	Ohio	2.47
39	South Dakota	2.47		39	South Dakota	2.47
27	Tennessee	2.54		42	Nebraska	2.46
4	Texas	2.84		43	Rhode Island	2.44
1	Utah	3.14		43	West Virginia	2.44
49	Vermont	2.32		43	Wisconsin	2.44
18	Virginia	2.61		46	Iowa	2.42
21	Washington	2.56		47	Montana	2.39
43	West Virginia	2.44		48	Maine	2.33
43	Wisconsin	2.44		49	North Dakota	2.32
31	Wyoming	2.52		49	Vermont	2.32
					District of Columbia	2.22

Source: U.S. Bureau of the Census
"2012 American Community Survey-Table R1105" (http://www.census.gov/acs/www/index.html)
*A household includes all persons who occupy a housing unit. A household consists of a single family, one person living alone, two or more families living together, or any other group of related or unrelated persons who share living arrangements.

Percent of Households with One Person in 2012

National Percent = 27.8% of Households*

ALPHA ORDER

RANK	STATE	PERCENT
17	Alabama	28.9
42	Alaska	26.7
36	Arizona	27.5
16	Arkansas	29.0
47	California	24.4
24	Colorado	28.2
33	Connecticut	27.8
40	Delaware	27.1
8	Florida	29.6
41	Georgia	26.8
48	Hawaii	24.0
48	Idaho	24.0
20	Illinois	28.8
29	Indiana	27.9
21	Iowa	28.6
17	Kansas	28.9
29	Kentucky	27.9
12	Louisiana	29.3
10	Maine	29.5
36	Maryland	27.5
17	Massachusetts	28.9
14	Michigan	29.2
28	Minnesota	28.0
36	Mississippi	27.5
10	Missouri	29.5
7	Montana	29.7
12	Nebraska	29.3
39	Nevada	27.4
44	New Hampshire	26.1
45	New Jersey	25.8
21	New Mexico	28.6
5	New York	30.0
29	North Carolina	27.9
1	North Dakota	32.3
3	Ohio	30.3
24	Oklahoma	28.2
34	Oregon	27.7
8	Pennsylvania	29.6
5	Rhode Island	30.0
35	South Carolina	27.6
3	South Dakota	30.3
23	Tennessee	28.5
46	Texas	25.2
50	Utah	19.8
29	Vermont	27.9
43	Virginia	26.6
24	Washington	28.2
2	West Virginia	31.1
14	Wisconsin	29.2
27	Wyoming	28.1

RANK ORDER

RANK	STATE	PERCENT
1	North Dakota	32.3
2	West Virginia	31.1
3	Ohio	30.3
3	South Dakota	30.3
5	New York	30.0
5	Rhode Island	30.0
7	Montana	29.7
8	Florida	29.6
8	Pennsylvania	29.6
10	Maine	29.5
10	Missouri	29.5
12	Louisiana	29.3
12	Nebraska	29.3
14	Michigan	29.2
14	Wisconsin	29.2
16	Arkansas	29.0
17	Alabama	28.9
17	Kansas	28.9
17	Massachusetts	28.9
20	Illinois	28.8
21	Iowa	28.6
21	New Mexico	28.6
23	Tennessee	28.5
24	Colorado	28.2
24	Oklahoma	28.2
24	Washington	28.2
27	Wyoming	28.1
28	Minnesota	28.0
29	Indiana	27.9
29	Kentucky	27.9
29	North Carolina	27.9
29	Vermont	27.9
33	Connecticut	27.8
34	Oregon	27.7
35	South Carolina	27.6
36	Arizona	27.5
36	Maryland	27.5
36	Mississippi	27.5
39	Nevada	27.4
40	Delaware	27.1
41	Georgia	26.8
42	Alaska	26.7
43	Virginia	26.6
44	New Hampshire	26.1
45	New Jersey	25.8
46	Texas	25.2
47	California	24.4
48	Hawaii	24.0
48	Idaho	24.0
50	Utah	19.8

	District of Columbia	45.8

Source: U.S. Bureau of the Census
    "2012 American Community Survey-Table S2501" (http://www.census.gov/acs/www/index.html)
*A household includes all persons who occupy a housing unit. A household consists of a single family, one person living alone,
two or more families living together, or any other group of related or unrelated persons who share living arrangements.

Percent of Households Headed by Married Couples in 2012

National Percent = 48.1% of Households*

ALPHA ORDER

RANK	STATE	PERCENT
35	Alabama	47.9
18	Alaska	49.0
41	Arizona	46.9
21	Arkansas	48.8
25	California	48.6
21	Colorado	48.8
24	Connecticut	48.7
33	Delaware	48.0
44	Florida	46.1
35	Georgia	47.9
5	Hawaii	51.2
2	Idaho	55.3
33	Illinois	48.0
14	Indiana	49.6
7	Iowa	51.0
10	Kansas	50.6
19	Kentucky	48.9
50	Louisiana	43.3
21	Maine	48.8
39	Maryland	47.2
43	Massachusetts	46.5
37	Michigan	47.7
6	Minnesota	51.1
47	Mississippi	44.1
37	Missouri	47.7
11	Montana	50.3
11	Nebraska	50.3
46	Nevada	44.2
3	New Hampshire	51.8
8	New Jersey	50.8
45	New Mexico	45.4
49	New York	43.5
29	North Carolina	48.1
29	North Dakota	48.1
42	Ohio	46.8
26	Oklahoma	48.5
29	Oregon	48.1
29	Pennsylvania	48.1
48	Rhode Island	43.7
40	South Carolina	47.0
16	South Dakota	49.3
27	Tennessee	48.4
13	Texas	50.1
1	Utah	60.6
19	Vermont	48.9
9	Virginia	50.7
15	Washington	49.4
27	West Virginia	48.4
17	Wisconsin	49.2
4	Wyoming	51.6

RANK ORDER

RANK	STATE	PERCENT
1	Utah	60.6
2	Idaho	55.3
3	New Hampshire	51.8
4	Wyoming	51.6
5	Hawaii	51.2
6	Minnesota	51.1
7	Iowa	51.0
8	New Jersey	50.8
9	Virginia	50.7
10	Kansas	50.6
11	Montana	50.3
11	Nebraska	50.3
13	Texas	50.1
14	Indiana	49.6
15	Washington	49.4
16	South Dakota	49.3
17	Wisconsin	49.2
18	Alaska	49.0
19	Kentucky	48.9
19	Vermont	48.9
21	Arkansas	48.8
21	Colorado	48.8
21	Maine	48.8
24	Connecticut	48.7
25	California	48.6
26	Oklahoma	48.5
27	Tennessee	48.4
27	West Virginia	48.4
29	North Carolina	48.1
29	North Dakota	48.1
29	Oregon	48.1
29	Pennsylvania	48.1
33	Delaware	48.0
33	Illinois	48.0
35	Alabama	47.9
35	Georgia	47.9
37	Michigan	47.7
37	Missouri	47.7
39	Maryland	47.2
40	South Carolina	47.0
41	Arizona	46.9
42	Ohio	46.8
43	Massachusetts	46.5
44	Florida	46.1
45	New Mexico	45.4
46	Nevada	44.2
47	Mississippi	44.1
48	Rhode Island	43.7
49	New York	43.5
50	Louisiana	43.3

| District of Columbia | 23.3 |

Source: U.S. Bureau of the Census
   "2012 American Community Survey-Table R1101" (http://www.census.gov/acs/www/index.html)
*A household includes all persons who occupy a housing unit. A household consists of a single family, one person living alone, two or more families living together, or any other group of related or unrelated persons who share living arrangements.

Percent of Households Headed by Single Mothers in 2012

National Percent = 7.3% of Households*

ALPHA ORDER				RANK ORDER		
RANK	STATE	PERCENT		RANK	STATE	PERCENT
8	Alabama	8.1		1	Mississippi	10.6
8	Alaska	8.1		2	Louisiana	9.6
17	Arizona	7.3		3	Georgia	8.8
17	Arkansas	7.3		4	South Carolina	8.7
22	California	7.2		5	New Mexico	8.4
33	Colorado	6.4		5	Texas	8.4
15	Connecticut	7.4		7	Nevada	8.3
22	Delaware	7.2		8	Alabama	8.1
26	Florida	7.1		8	Alaska	8.1
3	Georgia	8.8		10	Rhode Island	7.9
49	Hawaii	5.4		11	North Carolina	7.8
40	Idaho	6.2		12	New York	7.6
26	Illinois	7.1		13	Kentucky	7.5
17	Indiana	7.3		13	Maryland	7.5
39	Iowa	6.3		15	Connecticut	7.4
33	Kansas	6.4		15	Ohio	7.4
13	Kentucky	7.5		17	Arizona	7.3
2	Louisiana	9.6		17	Arkansas	7.3
41	Maine	6.0		17	Indiana	7.3
13	Maryland	7.5		17	Michigan	7.3
29	Massachusetts	7.0		17	Oklahoma	7.3
17	Michigan	7.3		22	California	7.2
33	Minnesota	6.4		22	Delaware	7.2
1	Mississippi	10.6		22	Missouri	7.2
22	Missouri	7.2		22	Tennessee	7.2
50	Montana	5.1		26	Florida	7.1
32	Nebraska	6.5		26	Illinois	7.1
7	Nevada	8.3		26	New Jersey	7.1
45	New Hampshire	5.8		29	Massachusetts	7.0
26	New Jersey	7.1		30	South Dakota	6.9
5	New Mexico	8.4		31	Virginia	6.6
12	New York	7.6		32	Nebraska	6.5
11	North Carolina	7.8		33	Colorado	6.4
48	North Dakota	5.5		33	Kansas	6.4
15	Ohio	7.4		33	Minnesota	6.4
17	Oklahoma	7.3		33	Oregon	6.4
33	Oregon	6.4		33	Pennsylvania	6.4
33	Pennsylvania	6.4		33	Wisconsin	6.4
10	Rhode Island	7.9		39	Iowa	6.3
4	South Carolina	8.7		40	Idaho	6.2
30	South Dakota	6.9		41	Maine	6.0
22	Tennessee	7.2		41	Washington	6.0
5	Texas	8.4		43	West Virginia	5.9
47	Utah	5.7		43	Wyoming	5.9
45	Vermont	5.8		45	New Hampshire	5.8
31	Virginia	6.6		45	Vermont	5.8
41	Washington	6.0		47	Utah	5.7
43	West Virginia	5.9		48	North Dakota	5.5
33	Wisconsin	6.4		49	Hawaii	5.4
43	Wyoming	5.9		50	Montana	5.1
					District of Columbia	7.5

Source: U.S. Bureau of the Census
"2012 American Community Survey-Table CP02" (http://www.census.gov/acs/www/index.html)
*No spouse present in household with children under 18 years old. A household includes all persons who occupy a housing unit.
A household consists of a single family, one person living alone, two or more families living together, or any other group of
related or unrelated persons who share living arrangements.

Percent of Households Headed by Single Fathers in 2012

National Percent = 2.3% of Households*

<table>
<tr><td colspan="3">ALPHA ORDER</td><td colspan="3">RANK ORDER</td></tr>
<tr><td>RANK</td><td>STATE</td><td>PERCENT</td><td>RANK</td><td>STATE</td><td>PERCENT</td></tr>
<tr><td>50</td><td>Alabama</td><td>1.6</td><td>1</td><td>Nevada</td><td>3.2</td></tr>
<tr><td>4</td><td>Alaska</td><td>2.9</td><td>2</td><td>New Mexico</td><td>3.1</td></tr>
<tr><td>4</td><td>Arizona</td><td>2.9</td><td>3</td><td>Wyoming</td><td>3.0</td></tr>
<tr><td>34</td><td>Arkansas</td><td>2.2</td><td>4</td><td>Alaska</td><td>2.9</td></tr>
<tr><td>6</td><td>California</td><td>2.8</td><td>4</td><td>Arizona</td><td>2.9</td></tr>
<tr><td>19</td><td>Colorado</td><td>2.4</td><td>6</td><td>California</td><td>2.8</td></tr>
<tr><td>37</td><td>Connecticut</td><td>2.1</td><td>7</td><td>Montana</td><td>2.7</td></tr>
<tr><td>13</td><td>Delaware</td><td>2.5</td><td>8</td><td>Idaho</td><td>2.6</td></tr>
<tr><td>37</td><td>Florida</td><td>2.1</td><td>8</td><td>Kansas</td><td>2.6</td></tr>
<tr><td>34</td><td>Georgia</td><td>2.2</td><td>8</td><td>Louisiana</td><td>2.6</td></tr>
<tr><td>48</td><td>Hawaii</td><td>1.7</td><td>8</td><td>Nebraska</td><td>2.6</td></tr>
<tr><td>8</td><td>Idaho</td><td>2.6</td><td>8</td><td>Oklahoma</td><td>2.6</td></tr>
<tr><td>37</td><td>Illinois</td><td>2.1</td><td>13</td><td>Delaware</td><td>2.5</td></tr>
<tr><td>13</td><td>Indiana</td><td>2.5</td><td>13</td><td>Indiana</td><td>2.5</td></tr>
<tr><td>13</td><td>Iowa</td><td>2.5</td><td>13</td><td>Iowa</td><td>2.5</td></tr>
<tr><td>8</td><td>Kansas</td><td>2.6</td><td>13</td><td>Oregon</td><td>2.5</td></tr>
<tr><td>19</td><td>Kentucky</td><td>2.4</td><td>13</td><td>Texas</td><td>2.5</td></tr>
<tr><td>8</td><td>Louisiana</td><td>2.6</td><td>13</td><td>Wisconsin</td><td>2.5</td></tr>
<tr><td>19</td><td>Maine</td><td>2.4</td><td>19</td><td>Colorado</td><td>2.4</td></tr>
<tr><td>25</td><td>Maryland</td><td>2.3</td><td>19</td><td>Kentucky</td><td>2.4</td></tr>
<tr><td>48</td><td>Massachusetts</td><td>1.7</td><td>19</td><td>Maine</td><td>2.4</td></tr>
<tr><td>37</td><td>Michigan</td><td>2.1</td><td>19</td><td>Mississippi</td><td>2.4</td></tr>
<tr><td>25</td><td>Minnesota</td><td>2.3</td><td>19</td><td>South Dakota</td><td>2.4</td></tr>
<tr><td>19</td><td>Mississippi</td><td>2.4</td><td>19</td><td>Washington</td><td>2.4</td></tr>
<tr><td>25</td><td>Missouri</td><td>2.3</td><td>25</td><td>Maryland</td><td>2.3</td></tr>
<tr><td>7</td><td>Montana</td><td>2.7</td><td>25</td><td>Minnesota</td><td>2.3</td></tr>
<tr><td>8</td><td>Nebraska</td><td>2.6</td><td>25</td><td>Missouri</td><td>2.3</td></tr>
<tr><td>1</td><td>Nevada</td><td>3.2</td><td>25</td><td>New Hampshire</td><td>2.3</td></tr>
<tr><td>25</td><td>New Hampshire</td><td>2.3</td><td>25</td><td>North Carolina</td><td>2.3</td></tr>
<tr><td>45</td><td>New Jersey</td><td>2.0</td><td>25</td><td>North Dakota</td><td>2.3</td></tr>
<tr><td>2</td><td>New Mexico</td><td>3.1</td><td>25</td><td>Ohio</td><td>2.3</td></tr>
<tr><td>37</td><td>New York</td><td>2.1</td><td>25</td><td>Tennessee</td><td>2.3</td></tr>
<tr><td>25</td><td>North Carolina</td><td>2.3</td><td>25</td><td>Utah</td><td>2.3</td></tr>
<tr><td>25</td><td>North Dakota</td><td>2.3</td><td>34</td><td>Arkansas</td><td>2.2</td></tr>
<tr><td>25</td><td>Ohio</td><td>2.3</td><td>34</td><td>Georgia</td><td>2.2</td></tr>
<tr><td>8</td><td>Oklahoma</td><td>2.6</td><td>34</td><td>Vermont</td><td>2.2</td></tr>
<tr><td>13</td><td>Oregon</td><td>2.5</td><td>37</td><td>Connecticut</td><td>2.1</td></tr>
<tr><td>37</td><td>Pennsylvania</td><td>2.1</td><td>37</td><td>Florida</td><td>2.1</td></tr>
<tr><td>45</td><td>Rhode Island</td><td>2.0</td><td>37</td><td>Illinois</td><td>2.1</td></tr>
<tr><td>37</td><td>South Carolina</td><td>2.1</td><td>37</td><td>Michigan</td><td>2.1</td></tr>
<tr><td>19</td><td>South Dakota</td><td>2.4</td><td>37</td><td>New York</td><td>2.1</td></tr>
<tr><td>25</td><td>Tennessee</td><td>2.3</td><td>37</td><td>Pennsylvania</td><td>2.1</td></tr>
<tr><td>13</td><td>Texas</td><td>2.5</td><td>37</td><td>South Carolina</td><td>2.1</td></tr>
<tr><td>25</td><td>Utah</td><td>2.3</td><td>37</td><td>Virginia</td><td>2.1</td></tr>
<tr><td>34</td><td>Vermont</td><td>2.2</td><td>45</td><td>New Jersey</td><td>2.0</td></tr>
<tr><td>37</td><td>Virginia</td><td>2.1</td><td>45</td><td>Rhode Island</td><td>2.0</td></tr>
<tr><td>19</td><td>Washington</td><td>2.4</td><td>45</td><td>West Virginia</td><td>2.0</td></tr>
<tr><td>45</td><td>West Virginia</td><td>2.0</td><td>48</td><td>Hawaii</td><td>1.7</td></tr>
<tr><td>13</td><td>Wisconsin</td><td>2.5</td><td>48</td><td>Massachusetts</td><td>1.7</td></tr>
<tr><td>3</td><td>Wyoming</td><td>3.0</td><td>50</td><td>Alabama</td><td>1.6</td></tr>
<tr><td></td><td></td><td></td><td></td><td>District of Columbia</td><td>1.2</td></tr>
</table>

Source: U.S. Bureau of the Census
   "2012 American Community Survey-Table CP02" (http://www.census.gov/acs/www/index.html)
*No spouse present in household with children under 18 years old. A household includes all persons who occupy a housing unit.
A household consists of a single family, one person living alone, two or more families living together, or any other group of
related or unrelated persons who share living arrangements.

Housing Units in 2012

National Total = 132,452,249 Housing Units*

ALPHA ORDER

RANK	STATE	HOUSING UNITS	% of USA
23	Alabama	2,189,567	1.7%
49	Alaska	307,628	0.2%
14	Arizona	2,871,486	2.2%
31	Arkansas	1,328,225	1.0%
1	California	13,708,197	10.3%
22	Colorado	2,230,536	1.7%
29	Connecticut	1,488,002	1.1%
45	Delaware	410,308	0.3%
3	Florida	9,031,530	6.8%
10	Georgia	4,107,554	3.1%
42	Hawaii	524,387	0.4%
40	Idaho	673,048	0.5%
6	Illinois	5,290,149	4.0%
17	Indiana	2,808,430	2.1%
30	Iowa	1,345,711	1.0%
33	Kansas	1,238,703	0.9%
26	Kentucky	1,937,321	1.5%
25	Louisiana	1,987,059	1.5%
39	Maine	724,187	0.5%
20	Maryland	2,395,635	1.8%
16	Massachusetts	2,810,394	2.1%
8	Michigan	4,525,081	3.4%
21	Minnesota	2,361,074	1.8%
32	Mississippi	1,283,897	1.0%
18	Missouri	2,720,087	2.1%
43	Montana	486,161	0.4%
38	Nebraska	804,274	0.6%
34	Nevada	1,182,842	0.9%
41	New Hampshire	617,005	0.5%
11	New Jersey	3,574,763	2.7%
36	New Mexico	906,838	0.7%
4	New York	8,123,585	6.1%
9	North Carolina	4,375,400	3.3%
47	North Dakota	329,249	0.2%
7	Ohio	5,128,846	3.9%
28	Oklahoma	1,677,646	1.3%
27	Oregon	1,682,531	1.3%
5	Pennsylvania	5,572,765	4.2%
44	Rhode Island	462,618	0.3%
24	South Carolina	2,156,768	1.6%
46	South Dakota	368,247	0.3%
15	Tennessee	2,834,808	2.1%
2	Texas	10,154,835	7.7%
35	Utah	996,777	0.8%
48	Vermont	324,052	0.2%
12	Virginia	3,398,389	2.6%
13	Washington	2,914,775	2.2%
37	West Virginia	882,800	0.7%
19	Wisconsin	2,632,625	2.0%
50	Wyoming	265,207	0.2%

RANK ORDER

RANK	STATE	HOUSING UNITS	% of USA
1	California	13,708,197	10.3%
2	Texas	10,154,835	7.7%
3	Florida	9,031,530	6.8%
4	New York	8,123,585	6.1%
5	Pennsylvania	5,572,765	4.2%
6	Illinois	5,290,149	4.0%
7	Ohio	5,128,846	3.9%
8	Michigan	4,525,081	3.4%
9	North Carolina	4,375,400	3.3%
10	Georgia	4,107,554	3.1%
11	New Jersey	3,574,763	2.7%
12	Virginia	3,398,389	2.6%
13	Washington	2,914,775	2.2%
14	Arizona	2,871,486	2.2%
15	Tennessee	2,834,808	2.1%
16	Massachusetts	2,810,394	2.1%
17	Indiana	2,808,430	2.1%
18	Missouri	2,720,087	2.1%
19	Wisconsin	2,632,625	2.0%
20	Maryland	2,395,635	1.8%
21	Minnesota	2,361,074	1.8%
22	Colorado	2,230,536	1.7%
23	Alabama	2,189,567	1.7%
24	South Carolina	2,156,768	1.6%
25	Louisiana	1,987,059	1.5%
26	Kentucky	1,937,321	1.5%
27	Oregon	1,682,531	1.3%
28	Oklahoma	1,677,646	1.3%
29	Connecticut	1,488,002	1.1%
30	Iowa	1,345,711	1.0%
31	Arkansas	1,328,225	1.0%
32	Mississippi	1,283,897	1.0%
33	Kansas	1,238,703	0.9%
34	Nevada	1,182,842	0.9%
35	Utah	996,777	0.8%
36	New Mexico	906,838	0.7%
37	West Virginia	882,800	0.7%
38	Nebraska	804,274	0.6%
39	Maine	724,187	0.5%
40	Idaho	673,048	0.5%
41	New Hampshire	617,005	0.5%
42	Hawaii	524,387	0.4%
43	Montana	486,161	0.4%
44	Rhode Island	462,618	0.3%
45	Delaware	410,308	0.3%
46	South Dakota	368,247	0.3%
47	North Dakota	329,249	0.2%
48	Vermont	324,052	0.2%
49	Alaska	307,628	0.2%
50	Wyoming	265,207	0.2%
	District of Columbia	300,247	0.2%

Source: U.S. Bureau of the Census
   "2012 American Community Survey-Table B25001" (http://www.census.gov/acs/www/index.html)
*A housing unit is a house, an apartment, a mobile home, a group of rooms, or a single room that is occupied (or if vacant, is intended for occupancy) as separate living quarters. Separate living quarters are those in which the occupants live and eat separately from any other persons in the building and which have direct access from the outside of the building or through a common hall.

Housing Units per Square Mile in 2012

National Average = 37.4 Housing Units*

RANK	STATE	RATE
26	Alabama	43.1
50	Alaska	0.5
34	Arizona	25.3
33	Arkansas	25.5
13	California	87.9
38	Colorado	21.5
4	Connecticut	307.1
6	Delaware	210.0
8	Florida	167.5
19	Georgia	70.9
15	Hawaii	81.6
44	Idaho	8.1
11	Illinois	95.2
17	Indiana	78.3
36	Iowa	24.1
40	Kansas	15.1
22	Kentucky	48.8
24	Louisiana	45.6
37	Maine	23.5
5	Maryland	245.1
3	Massachusetts	358.5
16	Michigan	79.7
31	Minnesota	29.7
32	Mississippi	27.4
27	Missouri	39.5
48	Montana	3.3
43	Nebraska	10.5
42	Nevada	10.8
20	New Hampshire	68.8
1	New Jersey	482.0
45	New Mexico	7.5
7	New York	172.1
12	North Carolina	89.8
47	North Dakota	4.8
9	Ohio	125.3
35	Oklahoma	24.4
39	Oregon	17.5
10	Pennsylvania	124.3
2	Rhode Island	442.7
18	South Carolina	71.6
46	South Dakota	4.9
20	Tennessee	68.8
28	Texas	38.8
41	Utah	12.1
30	Vermont	35.0
14	Virginia	85.8
25	Washington	43.8
29	West Virginia	36.7
23	Wisconsin	48.5
49	Wyoming	2.7

RANK	STATE	RATE
1	New Jersey	482.0
2	Rhode Island	442.7
3	Massachusetts	358.5
4	Connecticut	307.1
5	Maryland	245.1
6	Delaware	210.0
7	New York	172.1
8	Florida	167.5
9	Ohio	125.3
10	Pennsylvania	124.3
11	Illinois	95.2
12	North Carolina	89.8
13	California	87.9
14	Virginia	85.8
15	Hawaii	81.6
16	Michigan	79.7
17	Indiana	78.3
18	South Carolina	71.6
19	Georgia	70.9
20	New Hampshire	68.8
20	Tennessee	68.8
22	Kentucky	48.8
23	Wisconsin	48.5
24	Louisiana	45.6
25	Washington	43.8
26	Alabama	43.1
27	Missouri	39.5
28	Texas	38.8
29	West Virginia	36.7
30	Vermont	35.0
31	Minnesota	29.7
32	Mississippi	27.4
33	Arkansas	25.5
34	Arizona	25.3
35	Oklahoma	24.4
36	Iowa	24.1
37	Maine	23.5
38	Colorado	21.5
39	Oregon	17.5
40	Kansas	15.1
41	Utah	12.1
42	Nevada	10.8
43	Nebraska	10.5
44	Idaho	8.1
45	New Mexico	7.5
46	South Dakota	4.9
47	North Dakota	4.8
48	Montana	3.3
49	Wyoming	2.7
50	Alaska	0.5

District of Columbia 4,922.1

Source: CQ Press using data from U.S. Bureau of the Census
  "2012 American Community Survey-Table B25001" (http://www.census.gov/acs/www/index.html)
*Based on land area. A housing unit is a house, an apartment, a mobile home, a group of rooms, or a single room that is occupied (or if vacant, is intended for occupancy) as separate living quarters. Separate living quarters are those in which the occupants live and eat separately from any other persons in the building and which have direct access from the outside of the building or through a common hall.

Percent of Housing Units That Are Owner-Occupied in 2012

National Percent = 63.9% of Housing Units*

ALPHA ORDER

RANK	STATE	PERCENT
13	Alabama	68.8
40	Alaska	63.4
41	Arizona	62.6
31	Arkansas	66.2
49	California	54.0
38	Colorado	64.0
23	Connecticut	66.9
8	Delaware	70.8
34	Florida	65.6
39	Georgia	63.7
47	Hawaii	56.9
14	Idaho	68.4
25	Illinois	66.6
10	Indiana	69.4
2	Iowa	71.9
27	Kansas	66.4
22	Kentucky	67.0
33	Louisiana	65.7
3	Maine	71.4
26	Maryland	66.5
44	Massachusetts	62.2
5	Michigan	71.1
3	Minnesota	71.4
15	Mississippi	68.2
18	Missouri	67.5
20	Montana	67.1
29	Nebraska	66.3
48	Nevada	54.9
7	New Hampshire	70.9
36	New Jersey	65.1
17	New Mexico	67.7
50	New York	53.7
35	North Carolina	65.4
37	North Dakota	65.0
29	Ohio	66.3
27	Oklahoma	66.4
45	Oregon	61.6
12	Pennsylvania	68.9
46	Rhode Island	60.0
16	South Carolina	68.1
20	South Dakota	67.1
24	Tennessee	66.7
42	Texas	62.3
9	Utah	69.6
6	Vermont	71.0
31	Virginia	66.2
42	Washington	62.3
1	West Virginia	72.0
19	Wisconsin	67.3
11	Wyoming	69.0

RANK ORDER

RANK	STATE	PERCENT
1	West Virginia	72.0
2	Iowa	71.9
3	Maine	71.4
3	Minnesota	71.4
5	Michigan	71.1
6	Vermont	71.0
7	New Hampshire	70.9
8	Delaware	70.8
9	Utah	69.6
10	Indiana	69.4
11	Wyoming	69.0
12	Pennsylvania	68.9
13	Alabama	68.8
14	Idaho	68.4
15	Mississippi	68.2
16	South Carolina	68.1
17	New Mexico	67.7
18	Missouri	67.5
19	Wisconsin	67.3
20	Montana	67.1
20	South Dakota	67.1
22	Kentucky	67.0
23	Connecticut	66.9
24	Tennessee	66.7
25	Illinois	66.6
26	Maryland	66.5
27	Kansas	66.4
27	Oklahoma	66.4
29	Nebraska	66.3
29	Ohio	66.3
31	Arkansas	66.2
31	Virginia	66.2
33	Louisiana	65.7
34	Florida	65.6
35	North Carolina	65.4
36	New Jersey	65.1
37	North Dakota	65.0
38	Colorado	64.0
39	Georgia	63.7
40	Alaska	63.4
41	Arizona	62.6
42	Texas	62.3
42	Washington	62.3
44	Massachusetts	62.2
45	Oregon	61.6
46	Rhode Island	60.0
47	Hawaii	56.9
48	Nevada	54.9
49	California	54.0
50	New York	53.7
	District of Columbia	41.5

Source: U.S. Bureau of the Census
   "2012 American Community Survey-Table R2512" (http://www.census.gov/acs/www/index.html)
*For occupied housing units.

New Housing Units Authorized in 2013

National Total = 976,369 Units*

<table>
<tr><td colspan="4">ALPHA ORDER</td><td colspan="4">RANK ORDER</td></tr>
<tr><th>RANK</th><th>STATE</th><th>UNITS</th><th>% of USA</th><th>RANK</th><th>STATE</th><th>UNITS</th><th>% of USA</th></tr>
<tr><td>29</td><td>Alabama</td><td>10,954</td><td>1.1%</td><td>1</td><td>Texas</td><td>146,372</td><td>15.0%</td></tr>
<tr><td>49</td><td>Alaska</td><td>1,081</td><td>0.1%</td><td>2</td><td>Florida</td><td>87,432</td><td>9.0%</td></tr>
<tr><td>11</td><td>Arizona</td><td>23,765</td><td>2.4%</td><td>3</td><td>California</td><td>79,028</td><td>8.1%</td></tr>
<tr><td>36</td><td>Arkansas</td><td>6,548</td><td>0.7%</td><td>4</td><td>North Carolina</td><td>50,787</td><td>5.2%</td></tr>
<tr><td>3</td><td>California</td><td>79,028</td><td>8.1%</td><td>5</td><td>Georgia</td><td>34,721</td><td>3.6%</td></tr>
<tr><td>9</td><td>Colorado</td><td>27,296</td><td>2.8%</td><td>6</td><td>New York</td><td>32,938</td><td>3.4%</td></tr>
<tr><td>37</td><td>Connecticut</td><td>5,762</td><td>0.6%</td><td>7</td><td>Washington</td><td>31,664</td><td>3.2%</td></tr>
<tr><td>41</td><td>Delaware</td><td>4,875</td><td>0.5%</td><td>8</td><td>Virginia</td><td>31,367</td><td>3.2%</td></tr>
<tr><td>2</td><td>Florida</td><td>87,432</td><td>9.0%</td><td>9</td><td>Colorado</td><td>27,296</td><td>2.8%</td></tr>
<tr><td>5</td><td>Georgia</td><td>34,721</td><td>3.6%</td><td>10</td><td>New Jersey</td><td>24,270</td><td>2.5%</td></tr>
<tr><td>43</td><td>Hawaii</td><td>3,866</td><td>0.4%</td><td>11</td><td>Arizona</td><td>23,765</td><td>2.4%</td></tr>
<tr><td>33</td><td>Idaho</td><td>8,847</td><td>0.9%</td><td>12</td><td>South Carolina</td><td>23,637</td><td>2.4%</td></tr>
<tr><td>21</td><td>Illinois</td><td>15,348</td><td>1.6%</td><td>13</td><td>Tennessee</td><td>23,036</td><td>2.4%</td></tr>
<tr><td>17</td><td>Indiana</td><td>18,029</td><td>1.8%</td><td>14</td><td>Pennsylvania</td><td>22,116</td><td>2.3%</td></tr>
<tr><td>30</td><td>Iowa</td><td>10,826</td><td>1.1%</td><td>15</td><td>Ohio</td><td>21,310</td><td>2.2%</td></tr>
<tr><td>34</td><td>Kansas</td><td>7,985</td><td>0.8%</td><td>16</td><td>Maryland</td><td>18,138</td><td>1.9%</td></tr>
<tr><td>31</td><td>Kentucky</td><td>8,885</td><td>0.9%</td><td>17</td><td>Indiana</td><td>18,029</td><td>1.8%</td></tr>
<tr><td>25</td><td>Louisiana</td><td>13,964</td><td>1.4%</td><td>18</td><td>Minnesota</td><td>16,524</td><td>1.7%</td></tr>
<tr><td>44</td><td>Maine</td><td>3,212</td><td>0.3%</td><td>19</td><td>Michigan</td><td>15,934</td><td>1.6%</td></tr>
<tr><td>16</td><td>Maryland</td><td>18,138</td><td>1.9%</td><td>20</td><td>Utah</td><td>15,602</td><td>1.6%</td></tr>
<tr><td>23</td><td>Massachusetts</td><td>14,538</td><td>1.5%</td><td>21</td><td>Illinois</td><td>15,348</td><td>1.6%</td></tr>
<tr><td>19</td><td>Michigan</td><td>15,934</td><td>1.6%</td><td>22</td><td>Oregon</td><td>14,969</td><td>1.5%</td></tr>
<tr><td>18</td><td>Minnesota</td><td>16,524</td><td>1.7%</td><td>23</td><td>Massachusetts</td><td>14,538</td><td>1.5%</td></tr>
<tr><td>39</td><td>Mississippi</td><td>5,298</td><td>0.5%</td><td>24</td><td>Wisconsin</td><td>13,984</td><td>1.4%</td></tr>
<tr><td>27</td><td>Missouri</td><td>12,799</td><td>1.3%</td><td>25</td><td>Louisiana</td><td>13,964</td><td>1.4%</td></tr>
<tr><td>42</td><td>Montana</td><td>4,103</td><td>0.4%</td><td>26</td><td>Oklahoma</td><td>13,417</td><td>1.4%</td></tr>
<tr><td>35</td><td>Nebraska</td><td>7,863</td><td>0.8%</td><td>27</td><td>Missouri</td><td>12,799</td><td>1.3%</td></tr>
<tr><td>28</td><td>Nevada</td><td>11,232</td><td>1.2%</td><td>28</td><td>Nevada</td><td>11,232</td><td>1.2%</td></tr>
<tr><td>45</td><td>New Hampshire</td><td>2,662</td><td>0.3%</td><td>29</td><td>Alabama</td><td>10,954</td><td>1.1%</td></tr>
<tr><td>10</td><td>New Jersey</td><td>24,270</td><td>2.5%</td><td>30</td><td>Iowa</td><td>10,826</td><td>1.1%</td></tr>
<tr><td>40</td><td>New Mexico</td><td>4,987</td><td>0.5%</td><td>31</td><td>Kentucky</td><td>8,885</td><td>0.9%</td></tr>
<tr><td>6</td><td>New York</td><td>32,938</td><td>3.4%</td><td>32</td><td>North Dakota</td><td>8,855</td><td>0.9%</td></tr>
<tr><td>4</td><td>North Carolina</td><td>50,787</td><td>5.2%</td><td>33</td><td>Idaho</td><td>8,847</td><td>0.9%</td></tr>
<tr><td>32</td><td>North Dakota</td><td>8,855</td><td>0.9%</td><td>34</td><td>Kansas</td><td>7,985</td><td>0.8%</td></tr>
<tr><td>15</td><td>Ohio</td><td>21,310</td><td>2.2%</td><td>35</td><td>Nebraska</td><td>7,863</td><td>0.8%</td></tr>
<tr><td>26</td><td>Oklahoma</td><td>13,417</td><td>1.4%</td><td>36</td><td>Arkansas</td><td>6,548</td><td>0.7%</td></tr>
<tr><td>22</td><td>Oregon</td><td>14,969</td><td>1.5%</td><td>37</td><td>Connecticut</td><td>5,762</td><td>0.6%</td></tr>
<tr><td>14</td><td>Pennsylvania</td><td>22,116</td><td>2.3%</td><td>38</td><td>South Dakota</td><td>5,390</td><td>0.6%</td></tr>
<tr><td>50</td><td>Rhode Island</td><td>915</td><td>0.1%</td><td>39</td><td>Mississippi</td><td>5,298</td><td>0.5%</td></tr>
<tr><td>12</td><td>South Carolina</td><td>23,637</td><td>2.4%</td><td>40</td><td>New Mexico</td><td>4,987</td><td>0.5%</td></tr>
<tr><td>38</td><td>South Dakota</td><td>5,390</td><td>0.6%</td><td>41</td><td>Delaware</td><td>4,875</td><td>0.5%</td></tr>
<tr><td>13</td><td>Tennessee</td><td>23,036</td><td>2.4%</td><td>42</td><td>Montana</td><td>4,103</td><td>0.4%</td></tr>
<tr><td>1</td><td>Texas</td><td>146,372</td><td>15.0%</td><td>43</td><td>Hawaii</td><td>3,866</td><td>0.4%</td></tr>
<tr><td>20</td><td>Utah</td><td>15,602</td><td>1.6%</td><td>44</td><td>Maine</td><td>3,212</td><td>0.3%</td></tr>
<tr><td>48</td><td>Vermont</td><td>1,455</td><td>0.1%</td><td>45</td><td>New Hampshire</td><td>2,662</td><td>0.3%</td></tr>
<tr><td>8</td><td>Virginia</td><td>31,367</td><td>3.2%</td><td>46</td><td>West Virginia</td><td>2,335</td><td>0.2%</td></tr>
<tr><td>7</td><td>Washington</td><td>31,664</td><td>3.2%</td><td>47</td><td>Wyoming</td><td>2,193</td><td>0.2%</td></tr>
<tr><td>46</td><td>West Virginia</td><td>2,335</td><td>0.2%</td><td>48</td><td>Vermont</td><td>1,455</td><td>0.1%</td></tr>
<tr><td>24</td><td>Wisconsin</td><td>13,984</td><td>1.4%</td><td>49</td><td>Alaska</td><td>1,081</td><td>0.1%</td></tr>
<tr><td>47</td><td>Wyoming</td><td>2,193</td><td>0.2%</td><td>50</td><td>Rhode Island</td><td>915</td><td>0.1%</td></tr>
<tr><td></td><td></td><td></td><td></td><td></td><td>District of Columbia</td><td>3,255</td><td>0.3%</td></tr>
</table>

Source: U.S. Bureau of the Census
"Building Permits Survey" (http://www.census.gov/construction/bps/statemonthly.html)
*Preliminary and unadjusted year-to-date monthly data as of December 2013. Includes single and multifamily privately owned units. All places issuing building permits for privately-owned residential structures. More than 98 percent of all privately-owned residential buildings constructed are in permit-issuing places.

Value of New Housing Units Authorized in 2013

National Total = $175,155,053,000*

RANK	STATE	VALUE	% of USA
29	Alabama	$1,952,195,000	1.1%
48	Alaska	258,950,000	0.1%
8	Arizona	5,149,389,000	2.9%
37	Arkansas	1,086,972,000	0.6%
3	California	17,976,515,000	10.3%
6	Colorado	5,897,200,000	3.4%
36	Connecticut	1,126,179,000	0.6%
43	Delaware	592,117,000	0.3%
2	Florida	18,319,434,000	10.5%
7	Georgia	5,444,945,000	3.1%
38	Hawaii	1,018,149,000	0.6%
31	Idaho	1,640,654,000	0.9%
20	Illinois	3,127,597,000	1.8%
21	Indiana	3,110,635,000	1.8%
28	Iowa	1,965,720,000	1.1%
32	Kansas	1,399,345,000	0.8%
34	Kentucky	1,164,228,000	0.7%
24	Louisiana	2,516,033,000	1.4%
45	Maine	568,327,000	0.3%
22	Maryland	2,852,125,000	1.6%
14	Massachusetts	3,698,244,000	2.1%
17	Michigan	3,240,632,000	1.9%
15	Minnesota	3,548,356,000	2.0%
40	Mississippi	798,400,000	0.5%
27	Missouri	2,104,251,000	1.2%
42	Montana	633,425,000	0.4%
33	Nebraska	1,268,495,000	0.7%
30	Nevada	1,758,328,000	1.0%
44	New Hampshire	586,185,000	0.3%
18	New Jersey	3,233,931,000	1.8%
39	New Mexico	819,180,000	0.5%
10	New York	4,665,631,000	2.7%
4	North Carolina	8,089,818,000	4.6%
35	North Dakota	1,146,830,000	0.7%
16	Ohio	3,508,940,000	2.0%
26	Oklahoma	2,272,276,000	1.3%
23	Oregon	2,763,563,000	1.6%
12	Pennsylvania	3,873,436,000	2.2%
50	Rhode Island	173,522,000	0.1%
11	South Carolina	4,618,515,000	2.6%
41	South Dakota	726,924,000	0.4%
13	Tennessee	3,699,763,000	2.1%
1	Texas	22,263,422,000	12.7%
19	Utah	3,198,777,000	1.8%
49	Vermont	256,873,000	0.1%
9	Virginia	4,818,065,000	2.8%
5	Washington	6,612,131,000	3.8%
47	West Virginia	363,585,000	0.2%
25	Wisconsin	2,458,079,000	1.4%
46	Wyoming	508,876,000	0.3%

RANK	STATE	VALUE	% of USA
1	Texas	$22,263,422,000	12.7%
2	Florida	18,319,434,000	10.5%
3	California	17,976,515,000	10.3%
4	North Carolina	8,089,818,000	4.6%
5	Washington	6,612,131,000	3.8%
6	Colorado	5,897,200,000	3.4%
7	Georgia	5,444,945,000	3.1%
8	Arizona	5,149,389,000	2.9%
9	Virginia	4,818,065,000	2.8%
10	New York	4,665,631,000	2.7%
11	South Carolina	4,618,515,000	2.6%
12	Pennsylvania	3,873,436,000	2.2%
13	Tennessee	3,699,763,000	2.1%
14	Massachusetts	3,698,244,000	2.1%
15	Minnesota	3,548,356,000	2.0%
16	Ohio	3,508,940,000	2.0%
17	Michigan	3,240,632,000	1.9%
18	New Jersey	3,233,931,000	1.8%
19	Utah	3,198,777,000	1.8%
20	Illinois	3,127,597,000	1.8%
21	Indiana	3,110,635,000	1.8%
22	Maryland	2,852,125,000	1.6%
23	Oregon	2,763,563,000	1.6%
24	Louisiana	2,516,033,000	1.4%
25	Wisconsin	2,458,079,000	1.4%
26	Oklahoma	2,272,276,000	1.3%
27	Missouri	2,104,251,000	1.2%
28	Iowa	1,965,720,000	1.1%
29	Alabama	1,952,195,000	1.1%
30	Nevada	1,758,328,000	1.0%
31	Idaho	1,640,654,000	0.9%
32	Kansas	1,399,345,000	0.8%
33	Nebraska	1,268,495,000	0.7%
34	Kentucky	1,164,228,000	0.7%
35	North Dakota	1,146,830,000	0.7%
36	Connecticut	1,126,179,000	0.6%
37	Arkansas	1,086,972,000	0.6%
38	Hawaii	1,018,149,000	0.6%
39	New Mexico	819,180,000	0.5%
40	Mississippi	798,400,000	0.5%
41	South Dakota	726,924,000	0.4%
42	Montana	633,425,000	0.4%
43	Delaware	592,117,000	0.3%
44	New Hampshire	586,185,000	0.3%
45	Maine	568,327,000	0.3%
46	Wyoming	508,876,000	0.3%
47	West Virginia	363,585,000	0.2%
48	Alaska	258,950,000	0.1%
49	Vermont	256,873,000	0.1%
50	Rhode Island	173,522,000	0.1%
	District of Columbia	279,888,000	0.2%

Source: U.S. Bureau of the Census
"Building Permits Survey" (http://www.census.gov/construction/bps/statemonthly.html)
*Preliminary and unadjusted year-to-date monthly data as of December 2013. Includes single and multifamily privately owned units. All places issuing building permits for privately-owned residential structures. More than 98 percent of all privately-owned residential buildings constructed are in permit-issuing places.

Average Value of New Housing Units in 2013

National Average = $179,394 per Unit*

ALPHA ORDER

RANK	STATE	VALUE
22	Alabama	$178,218
3	Alaska	239,547
7	Arizona	216,680
30	Arkansas	166,001
5	California	227,470
8	Colorado	216,046
15	Connecticut	195,449
50	Delaware	121,460
10	Florida	209,528
38	Georgia	156,820
1	Hawaii	263,360
18	Idaho	185,447
13	Illinois	203,779
28	Indiana	172,535
20	Iowa	181,574
26	Kansas	175,247
48	Kentucky	131,033
21	Louisiana	180,180
23	Maine	176,939
37	Maryland	157,246
2	Massachusetts	254,385
14	Michigan	203,378
9	Minnesota	214,740
44	Mississippi	150,698
32	Missouri	164,407
41	Montana	154,381
34	Nebraska	161,325
39	Nevada	156,546
6	New Hampshire	220,205
47	New Jersey	133,248
33	New Mexico	164,263
45	New York	141,649
36	North Carolina	159,289
49	North Dakota	129,512
31	Ohio	164,662
29	Oklahoma	169,358
19	Oregon	184,619
27	Pennsylvania	175,142
17	Rhode Island	189,642
16	South Carolina	195,393
46	South Dakota	134,865
35	Tennessee	160,608
43	Texas	152,102
12	Utah	205,024
24	Vermont	176,545
42	Virginia	153,603
11	Washington	208,822
40	West Virginia	155,711
25	Wisconsin	175,778
4	Wyoming	232,046

RANK ORDER

RANK	STATE	VALUE
1	Hawaii	$263,360
2	Massachusetts	254,385
3	Alaska	239,547
4	Wyoming	232,046
5	California	227,470
6	New Hampshire	220,205
7	Arizona	216,680
8	Colorado	216,046
9	Minnesota	214,740
10	Florida	209,528
11	Washington	208,822
12	Utah	205,024
13	Illinois	203,779
14	Michigan	203,378
15	Connecticut	195,449
16	South Carolina	195,393
17	Rhode Island	189,642
18	Idaho	185,447
19	Oregon	184,619
20	Iowa	181,574
21	Louisiana	180,180
22	Alabama	178,218
23	Maine	176,939
24	Vermont	176,545
25	Wisconsin	175,778
26	Kansas	175,247
27	Pennsylvania	175,142
28	Indiana	172,535
29	Oklahoma	169,358
30	Arkansas	166,001
31	Ohio	164,662
32	Missouri	164,407
33	New Mexico	164,263
34	Nebraska	161,325
35	Tennessee	160,608
36	North Carolina	159,289
37	Maryland	157,246
38	Georgia	156,820
39	Nevada	156,546
40	West Virginia	155,711
41	Montana	154,381
42	Virginia	153,603
43	Texas	152,102
44	Mississippi	150,698
45	New York	141,649
46	South Dakota	134,865
47	New Jersey	133,248
48	Kentucky	131,033
49	North Dakota	129,512
50	Delaware	121,460
	District of Columbia	85,987

Source: CQ Press using data from U.S. Bureau of the Census
"Building Permits Survey" (http://www.census.gov/construction/bps/statemonthly.html)
*Preliminary and unadjusted year-to-date monthly data as of December 2013. Includes single and multifamily privately owned units. All places issuing building permits for privately-owned residential structures. More than 98 percent of all privately-owned residential buildings constructed are in permit-issuing places.

Median Value of Owner-Occupied Housing in 2012

National Median = $171,900*

RANK	STATE	MEDIAN
43	Alabama	$123,200
8	Alaska	245,100
27	Arizona	151,500
48	Arkansas	107,600
2	California	349,400
12	Colorado	234,900
7	Connecticut	267,800
14	Delaware	226,900
30	Florida	148,200
32	Georgia	142,300
1	Hawaii	496,600
26	Idaho	154,500
22	Illinois	170,600
44	Indiana	122,700
42	Iowa	126,300
38	Kansas	130,100
45	Kentucky	120,800
33	Louisiana	139,500
21	Maine	172,300
6	Maryland	279,900
3	Massachusetts	323,800
46	Michigan	115,700
20	Minnesota	178,400
50	Mississippi	99,800
36	Missouri	135,000
19	Montana	184,800
40	Nebraska	128,300
28	Nevada	150,700
11	New Hampshire	236,000
4	New Jersey	311,600
25	New Mexico	157,500
5	New York	280,900
29	North Carolina	150,100
31	North Dakota	142,500
41	Ohio	127,600
47	Oklahoma	114,300
15	Oregon	223,900
24	Pennsylvania	163,800
13	Rhode Island	234,600
35	South Carolina	135,500
37	South Dakota	134,300
34	Tennessee	137,800
39	Texas	129,200
17	Utah	199,700
16	Vermont	216,900
10	Virginia	237,800
9	Washington	243,000
49	West Virginia	100,400
23	Wisconsin	165,200
18	Wyoming	187,400

RANK	STATE	MEDIAN
1	Hawaii	$496,600
2	California	349,400
3	Massachusetts	323,800
4	New Jersey	311,600
5	New York	280,900
6	Maryland	279,900
7	Connecticut	267,800
8	Alaska	245,100
9	Washington	243,000
10	Virginia	237,800
11	New Hampshire	236,000
12	Colorado	234,900
13	Rhode Island	234,600
14	Delaware	226,900
15	Oregon	223,900
16	Vermont	216,900
17	Utah	199,700
18	Wyoming	187,400
19	Montana	184,800
20	Minnesota	178,400
21	Maine	172,300
22	Illinois	170,600
23	Wisconsin	165,200
24	Pennsylvania	163,800
25	New Mexico	157,500
26	Idaho	154,500
27	Arizona	151,500
28	Nevada	150,700
29	North Carolina	150,100
30	Florida	148,200
31	North Dakota	142,500
32	Georgia	142,300
33	Louisiana	139,500
34	Tennessee	137,800
35	South Carolina	135,500
36	Missouri	135,000
37	South Dakota	134,300
38	Kansas	130,100
39	Texas	129,200
40	Nebraska	128,300
41	Ohio	127,600
42	Iowa	126,300
43	Alabama	123,200
44	Indiana	122,700
45	Kentucky	120,800
46	Michigan	115,700
47	Oklahoma	114,300
48	Arkansas	107,600
49	West Virginia	100,400
50	Mississippi	99,800
	District of Columbia	460,700

Source: U.S. Bureau of the Census
"2012 American Community Survey-Table R2510" (http://www.census.gov/acs/www/index.html)
*Housing units with a mortgage.

Percent Change in House Prices: 2012 to 2013

National Percent Change = 8.4% Increase*

ALPHA ORDER				RANK ORDER		
RANK	STATE	PERCENT CHANGE		RANK	STATE	PERCENT CHANGE
29	Alabama	5.0		1	Nevada	25.2
43	Alaska	3.1		2	California	22.8
3	Arizona	15.2		3	Arizona	15.2
41	Arkansas	3.8		4	Florida	12.0
2	California	22.8		5	Washington	11.9
11	Colorado	10.3		6	Utah	11.8
47	Connecticut	2.3		7	Oregon	11.5
46	Delaware	2.4		8	Michigan	11.4
4	Florida	12.0		9	Georgia	11.2
9	Georgia	11.2		10	Hawaii	10.7
10	Hawaii	10.7		11	Colorado	10.3
12	Idaho	9.6		12	Idaho	9.6
35	Illinois	4.3		13	Minnesota	8.9
27	Indiana	5.3		14	Maryland	7.2
37	Iowa	4.1		15	Texas	7.1
40	Kansas	3.9		16	Montana	6.8
34	Kentucky	4.5		16	North Dakota	6.8
39	Louisiana	4.0		18	Tennessee	6.7
32	Maine	4.7		19	North Carolina	6.6
14	Maryland	7.2		19	Rhode Island	6.6
22	Massachusetts	6.2		21	South Carolina	6.3
8	Michigan	11.4		22	Massachusetts	6.2
13	Minnesota	8.9		23	New Hampshire	5.9
50	Mississippi	1.3		23	West Virginia	5.9
25	Missouri	5.8		25	Missouri	5.8
16	Montana	6.8		26	South Dakota	5.7
28	Nebraska	5.2		27	Indiana	5.3
1	Nevada	25.2		28	Nebraska	5.2
23	New Hampshire	5.9		29	Alabama	5.0
42	New Jersey	3.3		30	Pennsylvania	4.8
48	New Mexico	2.1		30	Virginia	4.8
44	New York	3.0		32	Maine	4.7
19	North Carolina	6.6		33	Wisconsin	4.6
16	North Dakota	6.8		34	Kentucky	4.5
35	Ohio	4.3		35	Illinois	4.3
37	Oklahoma	4.1		35	Ohio	4.3
7	Oregon	11.5		37	Iowa	4.1
30	Pennsylvania	4.8		37	Oklahoma	4.1
19	Rhode Island	6.6		39	Louisiana	4.0
21	South Carolina	6.3		40	Kansas	3.9
26	South Dakota	5.7		41	Arkansas	3.8
18	Tennessee	6.7		42	New Jersey	3.3
15	Texas	7.1		43	Alaska	3.1
6	Utah	11.8		44	New York	3.0
45	Vermont	2.7		45	Vermont	2.7
30	Virginia	4.8		46	Delaware	2.4
5	Washington	11.9		47	Connecticut	2.3
23	West Virginia	5.9		48	New Mexico	2.1
33	Wisconsin	4.6		49	Wyoming	2.0
49	Wyoming	2.0		50	Mississippi	1.3
				District of Columbia		11.8

Source: Federal Housing Finance Agency
   "State HPI Summary" (http://www.fhfa.gov/Default.aspx?Page=215&Type=summary)
*Single-family house prices. As of September 30, 2013.

Percent Change in House Prices: 2009 to 2013

National Percent Change = 0.2% Increase*

ALPHA ORDER

ALPHA ORDER

RANK ORDER

RANK	STATE	PERCENT CHANGE		RANK	STATE	PERCENT CHANGE
34	Alabama	(4.3)		1	North Dakota	27.1
9	Alaska	5.6		2	Colorado	13.5
42	Arizona	(7.9)		3	Texas	11.2
19	Arkansas	1.2		4	California	10.3
4	California	10.3		5	South Dakota	8.6
2	Colorado	13.5		6	Nebraska	8.2
44	Connecticut	(8.8)		7	Oklahoma	6.2
45	Delaware	(9.1)		8	West Virginia	5.8
39	Florida	(6.3)		9	Alaska	5.6
38	Georgia	(5.9)		9	Michigan	5.6
18	Hawaii	1.5		11	Iowa	5.0
46	Idaho	(9.9)		12	Louisiana	4.9
49	Illinois	(10.5)		13	Massachusetts	3.0
14	Indiana	2.8		14	Indiana	2.8
11	Iowa	5.0		15	Kentucky	2.7
17	Kansas	1.8		16	Vermont	2.1
15	Kentucky	2.7		17	Kansas	1.8
12	Louisiana	4.9		18	Hawaii	1.5
33	Maine	(4.0)		19	Arkansas	1.2
37	Maryland	(5.2)		20	Montana	0.8
13	Massachusetts	3.0		20	Tennessee	0.8
9	Michigan	5.6		22	Virginia	0.0
24	Minnesota	(0.5)		22	Wyoming	0.0
30	Mississippi	(3.5)		24	Minnesota	(0.5)
26	Missouri	(1.1)		25	Pennsylvania	(0.7)
20	Montana	0.8		26	Missouri	(1.1)
6	Nebraska	8.2		26	Ohio	(1.1)
50	Nevada	(15.4)		28	Utah	(3.1)
36	New Hampshire	(4.8)		29	New York	(3.3)
47	New Jersey	(10.1)		30	Mississippi	(3.5)
48	New Mexico	(10.4)		31	North Carolina	(3.9)
29	New York	(3.3)		31	South Carolina	(3.9)
31	North Carolina	(3.9)		33	Maine	(4.0)
1	North Dakota	27.1		34	Alabama	(4.3)
26	Ohio	(1.1)		35	Wisconsin	(4.7)
7	Oklahoma	6.2		36	New Hampshire	(4.8)
40	Oregon	(7.1)		37	Maryland	(5.2)
25	Pennsylvania	(0.7)		38	Georgia	(5.9)
41	Rhode Island	(7.3)		39	Florida	(6.3)
31	South Carolina	(3.9)		40	Oregon	(7.1)
5	South Dakota	8.6		41	Rhode Island	(7.3)
20	Tennessee	0.8		42	Arizona	(7.9)
3	Texas	11.2		43	Washington	(8.2)
28	Utah	(3.1)		44	Connecticut	(8.8)
16	Vermont	2.1		45	Delaware	(9.1)
22	Virginia	0.0		46	Idaho	(9.9)
43	Washington	(8.2)		47	New Jersey	(10.1)
8	West Virginia	5.8		48	New Mexico	(10.4)
35	Wisconsin	(4.7)		49	Illinois	(10.5)
22	Wyoming	0.0		50	Nevada	(15.4)
					District of Columbia	28.1

Source: Federal Housing Finance Agency
"State HPI Summary" (http://www.fhfa.gov/Default.aspx?Page=215&Type=summary)
*Single-family house prices. As of September 30, 2013.

Existing Home Sales in 2011

National Total = 4,880,000 Homes*

ALPHA ORDER					RANK ORDER			
RANK	STATE		HOMES	% of USA	RANK	STATE	HOMES	% of USA
24	Alabama		72,000	1.5%	1	California	475,600	9.7%
43	Alaska		19,600	0.4%	2	Texas	426,400	8.7%
8	Arizona		163,600	3.4%	3	Florida	385,600	7.9%
28	Arkansas		63,200	1.3%	4	Ohio	232,000	4.8%
1	California		475,600	9.7%	5	New York	226,800	4.6%
18	Colorado		88,000	1.8%	6	Georgia	182,400	3.7%
34	Connecticut		40,800	0.8%	7	Illinois	169,200	3.5%
48	Delaware		10,800	0.2%	8	Arizona	163,600	3.4%
3	Florida		385,600	7.9%	9	Pennsylvania	155,200	3.2%
6	Georgia		182,400	3.7%	10	Michigan	144,000	3.0%
42	Hawaii		20,000	0.4%	11	North Carolina	129,200	2.6%
35	Idaho		38,000	0.8%	12	Nevada	106,000	2.2%
7	Illinois		169,200	3.5%	12	Virginia	106,000	2.2%
17	Indiana		94,400	1.9%	14	New Jersey	101,400	2.1%
30	Iowa		53,200	1.1%	15	Tennessee	99,600	2.0%
32	Kansas		50,000	1.0%	16	Massachusetts	96,400	2.0%
27	Kentucky		68,000	1.4%	17	Indiana	94,400	1.9%
29	Louisiana		58,000	1.2%	18	Colorado	88,000	1.8%
40	Maine		21,200	0.4%	19	Missouri	87,600	1.8%
25	Maryland		70,400	1.4%	20	Washington	82,300	1.7%
16	Massachusetts		96,400	2.0%	21	Wisconsin	77,200	1.6%
10	Michigan		144,000	3.0%	22	Minnesota	76,400	1.6%
22	Minnesota		76,400	1.6%	23	Oklahoma	74,800	1.5%
33	Mississippi		44,000	0.9%	24	Alabama	72,000	1.5%
19	Missouri		87,600	1.8%	25	Maryland	70,400	1.4%
41	Montana		20,800	0.4%	26	South Carolina	69,600	1.4%
36	Nebraska		33,200	0.7%	27	Kentucky	68,000	1.4%
12	Nevada		106,000	2.2%	28	Arkansas	63,200	1.3%
43	New Hampshire		19,600	0.4%	29	Louisiana	58,000	1.2%
14	New Jersey		101,400	2.1%	30	Iowa	53,200	1.1%
38	New Mexico		28,400	0.6%	30	Oregon	53,200	1.1%
5	New York		226,800	4.6%	32	Kansas	50,000	1.0%
11	North Carolina		129,200	2.6%	33	Mississippi	44,000	0.9%
47	North Dakota		12,800	0.3%	34	Connecticut	40,800	0.8%
4	Ohio		232,000	4.8%	35	Idaho	38,000	0.8%
23	Oklahoma		74,800	1.5%	36	Nebraska	33,200	0.7%
30	Oregon		53,200	1.1%	37	Utah	30,400	0.6%
9	Pennsylvania		155,200	3.2%	38	New Mexico	28,400	0.6%
46	Rhode Island		13,200	0.3%	39	West Virginia	27,200	0.6%
26	South Carolina		69,600	1.4%	40	Maine	21,200	0.4%
45	South Dakota		15,200	0.3%	41	Montana	20,800	0.4%
15	Tennessee		99,600	2.0%	42	Hawaii	20,000	0.4%
2	Texas		426,400	8.7%	43	Alaska	19,600	0.4%
37	Utah		30,400	0.6%	43	New Hampshire	19,600	0.4%
48	Vermont		10,800	0.2%	45	South Dakota	15,200	0.3%
12	Virginia		106,000	2.2%	46	Rhode Island	13,200	0.3%
20	Washington		82,300	1.7%	47	North Dakota	12,800	0.3%
39	West Virginia		27,200	0.6%	48	Delaware	10,800	0.2%
21	Wisconsin		77,200	1.6%	48	Vermont	10,800	0.2%
50	Wyoming		8,000	0.2%	50	Wyoming	8,000	0.2%
						District of Columbia	8,400	0.2%

Source: National Association of Realtors®, Economics and Research Division
"Existing Home Sales" (http://www.realtor.org/research/research/metroprice)
*Seasonally adjusted preliminary data as of September 2011. Includes existing houses, apartment condos, and co-ops. Excludes new construction. National Association of Realtors has ceased publication of this data.

Percent Change in Existing Home Sales: 2010 to 2011

National Percent Change = 17.0% Increase*

ALPHA ORDER				RANK ORDER		
RANK	STATE	PERCENT CHANGE		RANK	STATE	PERCENT CHANGE
41	Alabama	12.5		1	North Dakota	39.1
30	Alaska	16.7		2	Utah	38.2
14	Arizona	22.5		3	Nebraska	36.1
34	Arkansas	16.2		4	Idaho	33.8
47	California	7.4		5	Iowa	33.0
22	Colorado	20.2		6	Wisconsin	29.5
47	Connecticut	7.4		7	Delaware	28.6
7	Delaware	28.6		7	Vermont	28.6
44	Florida	10.6		9	Oklahoma	27.2
16	Georgia	22.3		10	South Dakota	26.7
49	Hawaii	6.4		11	Minnesota	23.2
4	Idaho	33.8		12	Oregon	23.1
23	Illinois	19.8		13	Ohio	22.6
26	Indiana	18.6		14	Arizona	22.5
5	Iowa	33.0		14	Kansas	22.5
14	Kansas	22.5		16	Georgia	22.3
32	Kentucky	16.4		17	Washington	21.7
21	Louisiana	20.8		18	Tennessee	21.5
40	Maine	12.8		19	Missouri	21.0
45	Maryland	10.0		20	Montana	20.9
42	Massachusetts	12.1		21	Louisiana	20.8
29	Michigan	17.3		22	Colorado	20.2
11	Minnesota	23.2		23	Illinois	19.8
38	Mississippi	13.4		24	Nevada	19.4
19	Missouri	21.0		25	South Carolina	19.2
20	Montana	20.9		26	Indiana	18.6
3	Nebraska	36.1		27	Texas	18.4
24	Nevada	19.4		28	North Carolina	18.3
30	New Hampshire	16.7		29	Michigan	17.3
39	New Jersey	13.0		30	Alaska	16.7
32	New Mexico	16.4		30	New Hampshire	16.7
36	New York	14.5		32	Kentucky	16.4
28	North Carolina	18.3		32	New Mexico	16.4
1	North Dakota	39.1		34	Arkansas	16.2
13	Ohio	22.6		35	Pennsylvania	15.1
9	Oklahoma	27.2		36	New York	14.5
12	Oregon	23.1		37	Rhode Island	13.8
35	Pennsylvania	15.1		38	Mississippi	13.4
37	Rhode Island	13.8		39	New Jersey	13.0
25	South Carolina	19.2		40	Maine	12.8
10	South Dakota	26.7		41	Alabama	12.5
18	Tennessee	21.5		42	Massachusetts	12.1
27	Texas	18.4		43	Wyoming	11.1
2	Utah	38.2		44	Florida	10.6
7	Vermont	28.6		45	Maryland	10.0
50	Virginia	3.5		46	West Virginia	9.7
17	Washington	21.7		47	California	7.4
46	West Virginia	9.7		47	Connecticut	7.4
6	Wisconsin	29.5		49	Hawaii	6.4
43	Wyoming	11.1		50	Virginia	3.5
					District of Columbia	5.0

Source: National Association of Realtors®, Economics and Research Division
   "Existing Home Sales" (http://www.realtor.org/research/research/metroprice)
*Seasonally adjusted preliminary data as of September 2011. Includes existing houses, apartment condos, and co-ops. Excludes new construction. National Association of Realtors has ceased publication of this data.

Percent of Owner-Occupied Housing Units with a Mortgage in 2012

National Percent = 65.7% with Mortgages

ALPHA ORDER				RANK ORDER		
RANK	STATE	PERCENT		RANK	STATE	PERCENT
41	Alabama	58.3		1	Maryland	75.2
26	Alaska	65.2		2	California	73.9
22	Arizona	66.2		2	Colorado	73.9
44	Arkansas	57.6		4	Utah	72.9
2	California	73.9		5	Nevada	71.7
2	Colorado	73.9		6	Massachusetts	71.5
10	Connecticut	70.7		6	Rhode Island	71.5
12	Delaware	69.7		8	Virginia	71.4
36	Florida	61.1		9	Washington	70.8
13	Georgia	69.4		10	Connecticut	70.7
18	Hawaii	67.8		11	New Jersey	70.1
18	Idaho	67.8		12	Delaware	69.7
18	Illinois	67.8		13	Georgia	69.4
17	Indiana	68.0		14	Minnesota	68.7
35	Iowa	61.8		15	New Hampshire	68.5
32	Kansas	62.5		16	Oregon	68.3
39	Kentucky	60.8		17	Indiana	68.0
47	Louisiana	55.5		18	Hawaii	67.8
29	Maine	63.9		18	Idaho	67.8
1	Maryland	75.2		18	Illinois	67.8
6	Massachusetts	71.5		21	Wisconsin	66.4
30	Michigan	63.6		22	Arizona	66.2
14	Minnesota	68.7		23	North Carolina	66.0
49	Mississippi	52.9		24	Ohio	65.9
28	Missouri	64.1		25	Vermont	65.6
42	Montana	57.9		26	Alaska	65.2
31	Nebraska	63.1		27	New York	64.4
5	Nevada	71.7		28	Missouri	64.1
15	New Hampshire	68.5		29	Maine	63.9
11	New Jersey	70.1		30	Michigan	63.6
40	New Mexico	58.4		31	Nebraska	63.1
27	New York	64.4		32	Kansas	62.5
23	North Carolina	66.0		33	Pennsylvania	62.1
48	North Dakota	53.5		34	Tennessee	61.9
24	Ohio	65.9		35	Iowa	61.8
43	Oklahoma	57.8		36	Florida	61.1
16	Oregon	68.3		36	South Carolina	61.1
33	Pennsylvania	62.1		36	Texas	61.1
6	Rhode Island	71.5		39	Kentucky	60.8
36	South Carolina	61.1		40	New Mexico	58.4
46	South Dakota	57.4		41	Alabama	58.3
34	Tennessee	61.9		42	Montana	57.9
36	Texas	61.1		43	Oklahoma	57.8
4	Utah	72.9		44	Arkansas	57.6
25	Vermont	65.6		45	Wyoming	57.5
8	Virginia	71.4		46	South Dakota	57.4
9	Washington	70.8		47	Louisiana	55.5
50	West Virginia	48.3		48	North Dakota	53.5
21	Wisconsin	66.4		49	Mississippi	52.9
45	Wyoming	57.5		50	West Virginia	48.3
					District of Columbia	78.7

Source: CQ Press using data from U.S. Bureau of the Census
"2012 American Community Survey-Table B25027" (http://www.census.gov/acs/www/index.html)

Median Monthly Mortgage Payment in 2012

National Median = $1,460*

ALPHA ORDER

RANK	STATE	MEDIAN
45	Alabama	$1,104
8	Alaska	1,831
26	Arizona	1,320
49	Arkansas	975
3	California	2,119
14	Colorado	1,551
4	Connecticut	2,027
16	Delaware	1,517
20	Florida	1,425
25	Georgia	1,331
2	Hawaii	2,244
38	Idaho	1,174
13	Illinois	1,618
47	Indiana	1,069
43	Iowa	1,140
29	Kansas	1,250
46	Kentucky	1,084
41	Louisiana	1,148
27	Maine	1,300
7	Maryland	1,918
5	Massachusetts	2,010
30	Michigan	1,233
18	Minnesota	1,465
48	Mississippi	1,031
37	Missouri	1,176
30	Montana	1,233
32	Nebraska	1,229
19	Nevada	1,433
9	New Hampshire	1,828
1	New Jersey	2,342
36	New Mexico	1,193
6	New York	1,967
34	North Carolina	1,209
35	North Dakota	1,205
33	Ohio	1,215
44	Oklahoma	1,111
15	Oregon	1,544
22	Pennsylvania	1,382
10	Rhode Island	1,774
40	South Carolina	1,155
38	South Dakota	1,174
42	Tennessee	1,143
24	Texas	1,374
21	Utah	1,396
17	Vermont	1,478
12	Virginia	1,670
11	Washington	1,715
50	West Virginia	931
23	Wisconsin	1,376
28	Wyoming	1,297

RANK ORDER

RANK	STATE	MEDIAN
1	New Jersey	$2,342
2	Hawaii	2,244
3	California	2,119
4	Connecticut	2,027
5	Massachusetts	2,010
6	New York	1,967
7	Maryland	1,918
8	Alaska	1,831
9	New Hampshire	1,828
10	Rhode Island	1,774
11	Washington	1,715
12	Virginia	1,670
13	Illinois	1,618
14	Colorado	1,551
15	Oregon	1,544
16	Delaware	1,517
17	Vermont	1,478
18	Minnesota	1,465
19	Nevada	1,433
20	Florida	1,425
21	Utah	1,396
22	Pennsylvania	1,382
23	Wisconsin	1,376
24	Texas	1,374
25	Georgia	1,331
26	Arizona	1,320
27	Maine	1,300
28	Wyoming	1,297
29	Kansas	1,250
30	Michigan	1,233
30	Montana	1,233
32	Nebraska	1,229
33	Ohio	1,215
34	North Carolina	1,209
35	North Dakota	1,205
36	New Mexico	1,193
37	Missouri	1,176
38	Idaho	1,174
38	South Dakota	1,174
40	South Carolina	1,155
41	Louisiana	1,148
42	Tennessee	1,143
43	Iowa	1,140
44	Oklahoma	1,111
45	Alabama	1,104
46	Kentucky	1,084
47	Indiana	1,069
48	Mississippi	1,031
49	Arkansas	975
50	West Virginia	931
	District of Columbia	2,262

Source: U.S. Bureau of the Census
   "2012 American Community Survey-Table R2511" (http://www.census.gov/acs/www/index.html)
*Monthly housing costs for owner-occupied housing.

Percent of Home Owners Spending 30% or More of Household Income on Housing Costs in 2012
National Percent = 33.7% of Home Owners*

ALPHA ORDER

ALPHA ORDER

RANK	STATE	PERCENT
36	Alabama	28.1
26	Alaska	31.5
16	Arizona	33.4
42	Arkansas	25.3
2	California	45.5
22	Colorado	32.1
7	Connecticut	38.7
19	Delaware	33.1
4	Florida	42.9
20	Georgia	32.5
1	Hawaii	47.9
20	Idaho	32.5
13	Illinois	35.1
46	Indiana	23.7
49	Iowa	22.3
43	Kansas	25.0
40	Kentucky	26.1
35	Louisiana	28.5
15	Maine	34.4
18	Maryland	33.2
13	Massachusetts	35.1
29	Michigan	30.4
39	Minnesota	26.9
23	Mississippi	31.7
37	Missouri	27.7
23	Montana	31.7
45	Nebraska	24.2
6	Nevada	39.1
9	New Hampshire	37.8
3	New Jersey	43.7
16	New Mexico	33.4
5	New York	39.3
29	North Carolina	30.4
50	North Dakota	17.3
38	Ohio	27.2
41	Oklahoma	26.0
8	Oregon	37.9
31	Pennsylvania	30.1
9	Rhode Island	37.8
32	South Carolina	30.0
47	South Dakota	23.2
28	Tennessee	30.5
34	Texas	29.0
23	Utah	31.7
12	Vermont	35.8
27	Virginia	31.3
11	Washington	36.6
48	West Virginia	22.4
33	Wisconsin	29.8
44	Wyoming	24.4

RANK ORDER

RANK	STATE	PERCENT
1	Hawaii	47.9
2	California	45.5
3	New Jersey	43.7
4	Florida	42.9
5	New York	39.3
6	Nevada	39.1
7	Connecticut	38.7
8	Oregon	37.9
9	New Hampshire	37.8
9	Rhode Island	37.8
11	Washington	36.6
12	Vermont	35.8
13	Illinois	35.1
13	Massachusetts	35.1
15	Maine	34.4
16	Arizona	33.4
16	New Mexico	33.4
18	Maryland	33.2
19	Delaware	33.1
20	Georgia	32.5
20	Idaho	32.5
22	Colorado	32.1
23	Mississippi	31.7
23	Montana	31.7
23	Utah	31.7
26	Alaska	31.5
27	Virginia	31.3
28	Tennessee	30.5
29	Michigan	30.4
29	North Carolina	30.4
31	Pennsylvania	30.1
32	South Carolina	30.0
33	Wisconsin	29.8
34	Texas	29.0
35	Louisiana	28.5
36	Alabama	28.1
37	Missouri	27.7
38	Ohio	27.2
39	Minnesota	26.9
40	Kentucky	26.1
41	Oklahoma	26.0
42	Arkansas	25.3
43	Kansas	25.0
44	Wyoming	24.4
45	Nebraska	24.2
46	Indiana	23.7
47	South Dakota	23.2
48	West Virginia	22.4
49	Iowa	22.3
50	North Dakota	17.3
	District of Columbia	31.9

Source: U.S. Bureau of the Census
   "2012 American Community Survey-Table R2513" (http://www.census.gov/acs/www/index.html)
*For owner-occupied housing units with a mortgage.

Median Annual Real Estate Taxes in 2012

National Median = $2,075*

RANK ORDER

ALPHA ORDER

RANK	STATE	MEDIAN	RANK	STATE	MEDIAN
50	Alabama	$535	1	New Jersey	$7,183
12	Alaska	2,904	2	Connecticut	5,075
35	Arizona	1,327	3	New Hampshire	4,987
47	Arkansas	671	4	New York	4,402
11	California	2,945	5	Illinois	3,939
29	Colorado	1,478	6	Rhode Island	3,842
2	Connecticut	5,075	7	Massachusetts	3,821
38	Delaware	1,191	8	Vermont	3,652
27	Florida	1,643	9	Wisconsin	3,223
32	Georgia	1,390	10	Maryland	3,066
33	Hawaii	1,377	11	California	2,945
37	Idaho	1,194	12	Alaska	2,904
5	Illinois	3,939	13	Washington	2,759
41	Indiana	1,053	14	Oregon	2,474
23	Iowa	1,834	15	Texas	2,473
24	Kansas	1,805	16	Pennsylvania	2,448
43	Kentucky	1,015	17	Nebraska	2,399
48	Louisiana	653	18	Minnesota	2,186
19	Maine	2,127	19	Maine	2,127
10	Maryland	3,066	20	Michigan	2,114
7	Massachusetts	3,821	21	Ohio	1,979
20	Michigan	2,114	22	Virginia	1,884
18	Minnesota	2,186	23	Iowa	1,834
45	Mississippi	771	24	Kansas	1,805
34	Missouri	1,359	25	South Dakota	1,797
28	Montana	1,609	26	North Dakota	1,737
17	Nebraska	2,399	27	Florida	1,643
30	Nevada	1,460	28	Montana	1,609
3	New Hampshire	4,987	29	Colorado	1,478
1	New Jersey	7,183	30	Nevada	1,460
39	New Mexico	1,163	31	Utah	1,431
4	New York	4,402	32	Georgia	1,390
36	North Carolina	1,286	33	Hawaii	1,377
26	North Dakota	1,737	34	Missouri	1,359
21	Ohio	1,979	35	Arizona	1,327
44	Oklahoma	982	36	North Carolina	1,286
14	Oregon	2,474	37	Idaho	1,194
16	Pennsylvania	2,448	38	Delaware	1,191
6	Rhode Island	3,842	39	New Mexico	1,163
46	South Carolina	765	40	Wyoming	1,149
25	South Dakota	1,797	41	Indiana	1,053
42	Tennessee	1,018	42	Tennessee	1,018
15	Texas	2,473	43	Kentucky	1,015
31	Utah	1,431	44	Oklahoma	982
8	Vermont	3,652	45	Mississippi	771
22	Virginia	1,884	46	South Carolina	765
13	Washington	2,759	47	Arkansas	671
49	West Virginia	587	48	Louisiana	653
9	Wisconsin	3,223	49	West Virginia	587
40	Wyoming	1,149	50	Alabama	535
				District of Columbia	2,635

Source: U.S. Bureau of the Census
  "2012 American Community Survey-Table B25103" (http://www.census.gov/acs/www/index.html)
*For owner-occupied housing units with or without mortgages.

Homeownership Rate in 2012

National Rate = 65.4%*

RANK	STATE	RATE
11	Alabama	71.9
43	Alaska	63.7
39	Arizona	65.3
37	Arkansas	66.0
49	California	54.5
39	Colorado	65.3
20	Connecticut	68.8
6	Delaware	73.4
31	Florida	67.0
41	Georgia	64.3
47	Hawaii	57.2
8	Idaho	73.0
32	Illinois	66.8
9	Indiana	72.1
17	Iowa	70.2
45	Kansas	63.2
22	Kentucky	68.7
22	Louisiana	68.7
5	Maine	74.1
24	Maryland	68.5
38	Massachusetts	65.8
2	Michigan	74.8
10	Minnesota	72.0
4	Mississippi	74.2
15	Missouri	70.8
27	Montana	67.8
18	Nebraska	69.3
48	Nevada	55.7
2	New Hampshire	74.8
34	New Jersey	66.6
32	New Mexico	66.8
50	New York	53.6
30	North Carolina	67.2
35	North Dakota	66.2
25	Ohio	67.9
20	Oklahoma	68.8
36	Oregon	66.1
14	Pennsylvania	71.0
46	Rhode Island	62.1
12	South Carolina	71.5
19	South Dakota	69.2
25	Tennessee	67.9
41	Texas	64.3
13	Utah	71.1
6	Vermont	73.4
27	Virginia	67.8
44	Washington	63.5
1	West Virginia	75.8
29	Wisconsin	67.5
16	Wyoming	70.3

RANK	STATE	RATE
1	West Virginia	75.8
2	Michigan	74.8
2	New Hampshire	74.8
4	Mississippi	74.2
5	Maine	74.1
6	Delaware	73.4
6	Vermont	73.4
8	Idaho	73.0
9	Indiana	72.1
10	Minnesota	72.0
11	Alabama	71.9
12	South Carolina	71.5
13	Utah	71.1
14	Pennsylvania	71.0
15	Missouri	70.8
16	Wyoming	70.3
17	Iowa	70.2
18	Nebraska	69.3
19	South Dakota	69.2
20	Connecticut	68.8
20	Oklahoma	68.8
22	Kentucky	68.7
22	Louisiana	68.7
24	Maryland	68.5
25	Ohio	67.9
25	Tennessee	67.9
27	Montana	67.8
27	Virginia	67.8
29	Wisconsin	67.5
30	North Carolina	67.2
31	Florida	67.0
32	Illinois	66.8
32	New Mexico	66.8
34	New Jersey	66.6
35	North Dakota	66.2
36	Oregon	66.1
37	Arkansas	66.0
38	Massachusetts	65.8
39	Arizona	65.3
39	Colorado	65.3
41	Georgia	64.3
41	Texas	64.3
43	Alaska	63.7
44	Washington	63.5
45	Kansas	63.2
46	Rhode Island	62.1
47	Hawaii	57.2
48	Nevada	55.7
49	California	54.5
50	New York	53.6
	District of Columbia	45.0

Source: U.S. Bureau of the Census
"Housing Vacancies and Homeownership, Annual Statistics: 2012"
(http://www.census.gov/housing/hvs/data/ann12ind.html)
*Percent of households occupied by the owner.

Percent of Housing Units That Are Renter-Occupied in 2012

National Percent = 36.1% of Housing Units*

ALPHA ORDER

RANK	STATE	PERCENT
38	Alabama	31.2
11	Alaska	36.6
10	Arizona	37.4
19	Arkansas	33.8
2	California	46.0
13	Colorado	36.0
28	Connecticut	33.1
43	Delaware	29.2
17	Florida	34.4
12	Georgia	36.3
4	Hawaii	43.1
37	Idaho	31.6
26	Illinois	33.4
41	Indiana	30.6
49	Iowa	28.1
23	Kansas	33.6
29	Kentucky	33.0
18	Louisiana	34.3
47	Maine	28.6
25	Maryland	33.5
7	Massachusetts	37.8
46	Michigan	28.9
47	Minnesota	28.6
36	Mississippi	31.8
33	Missouri	32.5
30	Montana	32.9
21	Nebraska	33.7
3	Nevada	45.1
44	New Hampshire	29.1
15	New Jersey	34.9
34	New Mexico	32.3
1	New York	46.3
16	North Carolina	34.6
14	North Dakota	35.0
21	Ohio	33.7
23	Oklahoma	33.6
6	Oregon	38.4
39	Pennsylvania	31.1
5	Rhode Island	40.0
35	South Carolina	31.9
30	South Dakota	32.9
27	Tennessee	33.3
8	Texas	37.7
42	Utah	30.4
45	Vermont	29.0
19	Virginia	33.8
8	Washington	37.7
50	West Virginia	28.0
32	Wisconsin	32.7
40	Wyoming	31.0

RANK ORDER

RANK	STATE	PERCENT
1	New York	46.3
2	California	46.0
3	Nevada	45.1
4	Hawaii	43.1
5	Rhode Island	40.0
6	Oregon	38.4
7	Massachusetts	37.8
8	Texas	37.7
8	Washington	37.7
10	Arizona	37.4
11	Alaska	36.6
12	Georgia	36.3
13	Colorado	36.0
14	North Dakota	35.0
15	New Jersey	34.9
16	North Carolina	34.6
17	Florida	34.4
18	Louisiana	34.3
19	Arkansas	33.8
19	Virginia	33.8
21	Nebraska	33.7
21	Ohio	33.7
23	Kansas	33.6
23	Oklahoma	33.6
25	Maryland	33.5
26	Illinois	33.4
27	Tennessee	33.3
28	Connecticut	33.1
29	Kentucky	33.0
30	Montana	32.9
30	South Dakota	32.9
32	Wisconsin	32.7
33	Missouri	32.5
34	New Mexico	32.3
35	South Carolina	31.9
36	Mississippi	31.8
37	Idaho	31.6
38	Alabama	31.2
39	Pennsylvania	31.1
40	Wyoming	31.0
41	Indiana	30.6
42	Utah	30.4
43	Delaware	29.2
44	New Hampshire	29.1
45	Vermont	29.0
46	Michigan	28.9
47	Maine	28.6
47	Minnesota	28.6
49	Iowa	28.1
50	West Virginia	28.0
	District of Columbia	58.5

Source: U.S. Bureau of the Census
   "2012 American Community Survey-Table R2512" (http://www.census.gov/acs/www/index.html)
*For occupied housing units.

Median Monthly Rental Payment in 2012

National Median = $884*

ALPHA ORDER

RANK	STATE	MEDIAN
41	Alabama	$689
5	Alaska	1,120
16	Arizona	888
48	Arkansas	640
2	California	1,200
15	Colorado	934
9	Connecticut	1,019
11	Delaware	960
12	Florida	954
22	Georgia	837
1	Hawaii	1,379
38	Idaho	702
18	Illinois	868
35	Indiana	715
45	Iowa	661
36	Kansas	711
49	Kentucky	636
30	Louisiana	747
31	Maine	744
3	Maryland	1,170
8	Massachusetts	1,036
29	Michigan	748
24	Minnesota	813
44	Mississippi	666
37	Missouri	706
43	Montana	681
40	Nebraska	692
14	Nevada	944
10	New Hampshire	967
4	New Jersey	1,148
28	New Mexico	753
6	New York	1,079
26	North Carolina	756
47	North Dakota	644
39	Ohio	700
42	Oklahoma	686
19	Oregon	862
25	Pennsylvania	798
17	Rhode Island	878
27	South Carolina	754
46	South Dakota	651
34	Tennessee	730
23	Texas	831
21	Utah	851
20	Vermont	860
7	Virginia	1,068
12	Washington	954
50	West Virginia	607
32	Wisconsin	743
33	Wyoming	742

RANK ORDER

RANK	STATE	MEDIAN
1	Hawaii	$1,379
2	California	1,200
3	Maryland	1,170
4	New Jersey	1,148
5	Alaska	1,120
6	New York	1,079
7	Virginia	1,068
8	Massachusetts	1,036
9	Connecticut	1,019
10	New Hampshire	967
11	Delaware	960
12	Florida	954
12	Washington	954
14	Nevada	944
15	Colorado	934
16	Arizona	888
17	Rhode Island	878
18	Illinois	868
19	Oregon	862
20	Vermont	860
21	Utah	851
22	Georgia	837
23	Texas	831
24	Minnesota	813
25	Pennsylvania	798
26	North Carolina	756
27	South Carolina	754
28	New Mexico	753
29	Michigan	748
30	Louisiana	747
31	Maine	744
32	Wisconsin	743
33	Wyoming	742
34	Tennessee	730
35	Indiana	715
36	Kansas	711
37	Missouri	706
38	Idaho	702
39	Ohio	700
40	Nebraska	692
41	Alabama	689
42	Oklahoma	686
43	Montana	681
44	Mississippi	666
45	Iowa	661
46	South Dakota	651
47	North Dakota	644
48	Arkansas	640
49	Kentucky	636
50	West Virginia	607
	District of Columbia	1,235

Source: U.S. Bureau of the Census
  "2012 American Community Survey-Table R2514" (http://www.census.gov/acs/www/index.html)
*Monthly housing costs for renter-occupied housing.

Percent of Renters Spending 30% or More of Household Income on Rent and Utilities in 2012
National Percent = 48.1% of Renters

RANK	STATE	PERCENT
40	Alabama	42.6
38	Alaska	44.3
13	Arizona	47.7
41	Arkansas	42.5
1	California	54.6
9	Colorado	48.6
8	Connecticut	49.6
30	Delaware	45.6
2	Florida	54.2
13	Georgia	47.7
5	Hawaii	50.3
28	Idaho	45.8
17	Illinois	47.0
31	Indiana	45.4
44	Iowa	41.5
45	Kansas	40.9
39	Kentucky	42.7
29	Louisiana	45.7
16	Maine	47.2
11	Maryland	48.0
19	Massachusetts	46.8
7	Michigan	49.8
33	Minnesota	45.3
35	Mississippi	45.2
20	Missouri	46.4
43	Montana	42.3
46	Nebraska	39.4
9	Nevada	48.6
24	New Hampshire	46.1
3	New Jersey	51.3
25	New Mexico	46.0
4	New York	50.4
36	North Carolina	44.8
50	North Dakota	31.7
31	Ohio	45.4
42	Oklahoma	42.4
6	Oregon	50.0
26	Pennsylvania	45.9
12	Rhode Island	47.8
23	South Carolina	46.3
49	South Dakota	36.7
33	Tennessee	45.3
37	Texas	44.5
20	Utah	46.4
18	Vermont	46.9
20	Virginia	46.4
13	Washington	47.7
47	West Virginia	38.9
26	Wisconsin	45.9
48	Wyoming	38.8

RANK	STATE	PERCENT
1	California	54.6
2	Florida	54.2
3	New Jersey	51.3
4	New York	50.4
5	Hawaii	50.3
6	Oregon	50.0
7	Michigan	49.8
8	Connecticut	49.6
9	Colorado	48.6
9	Nevada	48.6
11	Maryland	48.0
12	Rhode Island	47.8
13	Arizona	47.7
13	Georgia	47.7
13	Washington	47.7
16	Maine	47.2
17	Illinois	47.0
18	Vermont	46.9
19	Massachusetts	46.8
20	Missouri	46.4
20	Utah	46.4
20	Virginia	46.4
23	South Carolina	46.3
24	New Hampshire	46.1
25	New Mexico	46.0
26	Pennsylvania	45.9
26	Wisconsin	45.9
28	Idaho	45.8
29	Louisiana	45.7
30	Delaware	45.6
31	Indiana	45.4
31	Ohio	45.4
33	Minnesota	45.3
33	Tennessee	45.3
35	Mississippi	45.2
36	North Carolina	44.8
37	Texas	44.5
38	Alaska	44.3
39	Kentucky	42.7
40	Alabama	42.6
41	Arkansas	42.5
42	Oklahoma	42.4
43	Montana	42.3
44	Iowa	41.5
45	Kansas	40.9
46	Nebraska	39.4
47	West Virginia	38.9
48	Wyoming	38.8
49	South Dakota	36.7
50	North Dakota	31.7
	District of Columbia	45.8

Source: U.S. Bureau of the Census

"2012 American Community Survey-Table R2515" (http://www.census.gov/acs/www/index.html)

State and Local Government Expenditures
for Housing and Community Development in 2011
National Total = $56,121,299,000*

ALPHA ORDER

RANK	STATE	EXPENDITURES	% of USA
25	Alabama	$603,227,000	1.1%
28	Alaska	383,675,000	0.7%
23	Arizona	634,630,000	1.1%
36	Arkansas	257,379,000	0.5%
1	California	10,189,560,000	18.2%
22	Colorado	719,777,000	1.3%
20	Connecticut	876,813,000	1.6%
43	Delaware	165,953,000	0.3%
3	Florida	3,329,648,000	5.9%
12	Georgia	1,363,359,000	2.4%
38	Hawaii	231,268,000	0.4%
45	Idaho	147,308,000	0.3%
7	Illinois	2,328,735,000	4.1%
15	Indiana	1,209,742,000	2.2%
34	Iowa	301,554,000	0.5%
35	Kansas	290,710,000	0.5%
27	Kentucky	448,476,000	0.8%
9	Louisiana	1,650,521,000	2.9%
33	Maine	319,752,000	0.6%
14	Maryland	1,305,031,000	2.3%
8	Massachusetts	2,151,517,000	3.8%
13	Michigan	1,348,458,000	2.4%
19	Minnesota	948,748,000	1.7%
31	Mississippi	349,881,000	0.6%
21	Missouri	742,371,000	1.3%
46	Montana	147,243,000	0.3%
42	Nebraska	175,634,000	0.3%
37	Nevada	251,414,000	0.4%
39	New Hampshire	230,916,000	0.4%
10	New Jersey	1,558,752,000	2.8%
41	New Mexico	215,746,000	0.4%
2	New York	5,533,718,000	9.9%
17	North Carolina	1,111,134,000	2.0%
49	North Dakota	91,863,000	0.2%
4	Ohio	2,458,002,000	4.4%
30	Oklahoma	358,501,000	0.6%
24	Oregon	622,443,000	1.1%
6	Pennsylvania	2,331,851,000	4.2%
40	Rhode Island	225,342,000	0.4%
26	South Carolina	569,312,000	1.0%
48	South Dakota	111,662,000	0.2%
16	Tennessee	1,175,533,000	2.1%
5	Texas	2,447,832,000	4.4%
29	Utah	364,834,000	0.7%
47	Vermont	141,596,000	0.3%
18	Virginia	978,208,000	1.7%
11	Washington	1,546,020,000	2.8%
44	West Virginia	150,252,000	0.3%
32	Wisconsin	338,518,000	0.6%
50	Wyoming	27,464,000	0.0%

RANK ORDER

RANK	STATE	EXPENDITURES	% of USA
1	California	$10,189,560,000	18.2%
2	New York	5,533,718,000	9.9%
3	Florida	3,329,648,000	5.9%
4	Ohio	2,458,002,000	4.4%
5	Texas	2,447,832,000	4.4%
6	Pennsylvania	2,331,851,000	4.2%
7	Illinois	2,328,735,000	4.1%
8	Massachusetts	2,151,517,000	3.8%
9	Louisiana	1,650,521,000	2.9%
10	New Jersey	1,558,752,000	2.8%
11	Washington	1,546,020,000	2.8%
12	Georgia	1,363,359,000	2.4%
13	Michigan	1,348,458,000	2.4%
14	Maryland	1,305,031,000	2.3%
15	Indiana	1,209,742,000	2.2%
16	Tennessee	1,175,533,000	2.1%
17	North Carolina	1,111,134,000	2.0%
18	Virginia	978,208,000	1.7%
19	Minnesota	948,748,000	1.7%
20	Connecticut	876,813,000	1.6%
21	Missouri	742,371,000	1.3%
22	Colorado	719,777,000	1.3%
23	Arizona	634,630,000	1.1%
24	Oregon	622,443,000	1.1%
25	Alabama	603,227,000	1.1%
26	South Carolina	569,312,000	1.0%
27	Kentucky	448,476,000	0.8%
28	Alaska	383,675,000	0.7%
29	Utah	364,834,000	0.7%
30	Oklahoma	358,501,000	0.6%
31	Mississippi	349,881,000	0.6%
32	Wisconsin	338,518,000	0.6%
33	Maine	319,752,000	0.6%
34	Iowa	301,554,000	0.5%
35	Kansas	290,710,000	0.5%
36	Arkansas	257,379,000	0.5%
37	Nevada	251,414,000	0.4%
38	Hawaii	231,268,000	0.4%
39	New Hampshire	230,916,000	0.4%
40	Rhode Island	225,342,000	0.4%
41	New Mexico	215,746,000	0.4%
42	Nebraska	175,634,000	0.3%
43	Delaware	165,953,000	0.3%
44	West Virginia	150,252,000	0.3%
45	Idaho	147,308,000	0.3%
46	Montana	147,243,000	0.3%
47	Vermont	141,596,000	0.3%
48	South Dakota	111,662,000	0.2%
49	North Dakota	91,863,000	0.2%
50	Wyoming	27,464,000	0.0%
	District of Columbia	659,416,000	1.2%

Source: U.S. Bureau of the Census, Governments Division
  "2011 State and Local Government Finances" (http://www.census.gov/govs/local/)
*Direct general expenditures.

Per Capita State and Local Government Expenditures for Housing and Community Development in 2011
National Per Capita = $180*

ALPHA ORDER

RANK	STATE	PER CAPITA
31	Alabama	$126
1	Alaska	530
40	Arizona	98
47	Arkansas	88
5	California	270
25	Colorado	141
6	Connecticut	244
15	Delaware	183
21	Florida	174
26	Georgia	139
22	Hawaii	168
45	Idaho	93
17	Illinois	181
13	Indiana	186
40	Iowa	98
39	Kansas	101
38	Kentucky	103
2	Louisiana	361
7	Maine	241
10	Maryland	223
3	Massachusetts	326
27	Michigan	137
18	Minnesota	177
35	Mississippi	118
32	Missouri	124
24	Montana	148
42	Nebraska	95
46	Nevada	92
20	New Hampshire	175
19	New Jersey	176
37	New Mexico	104
4	New York	284
36	North Carolina	115
29	North Dakota	134
12	Ohio	213
42	Oklahoma	95
23	Oregon	161
15	Pennsylvania	183
11	Rhode Island	214
33	South Carolina	122
28	South Dakota	136
14	Tennessee	184
42	Texas	95
30	Utah	130
9	Vermont	226
34	Virginia	121
8	Washington	227
48	West Virginia	81
49	Wisconsin	59
50	Wyoming	48

RANK ORDER

RANK	STATE	PER CAPITA
1	Alaska	$530
2	Louisiana	361
3	Massachusetts	326
4	New York	284
5	California	270
6	Connecticut	244
7	Maine	241
8	Washington	227
9	Vermont	226
10	Maryland	223
11	Rhode Island	214
12	Ohio	213
13	Indiana	186
14	Tennessee	184
15	Delaware	183
15	Pennsylvania	183
17	Illinois	181
18	Minnesota	177
19	New Jersey	176
20	New Hampshire	175
21	Florida	174
22	Hawaii	168
23	Oregon	161
24	Montana	148
25	Colorado	141
26	Georgia	139
27	Michigan	137
28	South Dakota	136
29	North Dakota	134
30	Utah	130
31	Alabama	126
32	Missouri	124
33	South Carolina	122
34	Virginia	121
35	Mississippi	118
36	North Carolina	115
37	New Mexico	104
38	Kentucky	103
39	Kansas	101
40	Arizona	98
40	Iowa	98
42	Nebraska	95
42	Oklahoma	95
42	Texas	95
45	Idaho	93
46	Nevada	92
47	Arkansas	88
48	West Virginia	81
49	Wisconsin	59
50	Wyoming	48
	District of Columbia	1,065

Source: CQ Press using data from U.S. Bureau of the Census, Governments Division
"2011 State and Local Government Finances" (http://www.census.gov/govs/local/)
*Direct general expenditures.

State & Local Government Spending for Housing and Community Development as a Percent of All State and Local Government Expenditures in 2011
National Percent = 2.2%*

ALPHA ORDER

RANK	STATE	PERCENT
30	Alabama	1.7
3	Alaska	3.0
35	Arizona	1.5
44	Arkansas	1.2
4	California	2.9
30	Colorado	1.7
8	Connecticut	2.6
22	Delaware	1.9
12	Florida	2.4
18	Georgia	2.1
22	Hawaii	1.9
37	Idaho	1.4
17	Illinois	2.2
8	Indiana	2.6
46	Iowa	1.1
41	Kansas	1.3
37	Kentucky	1.4
1	Louisiana	3.9
5	Maine	2.8
8	Maryland	2.6
2	Massachusetts	3.5
25	Michigan	1.8
20	Minnesota	2.0
35	Mississippi	1.5
25	Missouri	1.8
25	Montana	1.8
44	Nebraska	1.2
41	Nevada	1.3
15	New Hampshire	2.3
22	New Jersey	1.9
46	New Mexico	1.1
12	New York	2.4
30	North Carolina	1.7
37	North Dakota	1.4
8	Ohio	2.6
37	Oklahoma	1.4
20	Oregon	2.0
18	Pennsylvania	2.1
12	Rhode Island	2.4
33	South Carolina	1.6
25	South Dakota	1.8
5	Tennessee	2.8
41	Texas	1.3
25	Utah	1.8
15	Vermont	2.3
33	Virginia	1.6
7	Washington	2.7
48	West Virginia	1.0
49	Wisconsin	0.7
50	Wyoming	0.4

RANK ORDER

RANK	STATE	PERCENT
1	Louisiana	3.9
2	Massachusetts	3.5
3	Alaska	3.0
4	California	2.9
5	Maine	2.8
5	Tennessee	2.8
7	Washington	2.7
8	Connecticut	2.6
8	Indiana	2.6
8	Maryland	2.6
8	Ohio	2.6
12	Florida	2.4
12	New York	2.4
12	Rhode Island	2.4
15	New Hampshire	2.3
15	Vermont	2.3
17	Illinois	2.2
18	Georgia	2.1
18	Pennsylvania	2.1
20	Minnesota	2.0
20	Oregon	2.0
22	Delaware	1.9
22	Hawaii	1.9
22	New Jersey	1.9
25	Michigan	1.8
25	Missouri	1.8
25	Montana	1.8
25	South Dakota	1.8
25	Utah	1.8
30	Alabama	1.7
30	Colorado	1.7
30	North Carolina	1.7
33	South Carolina	1.6
33	Virginia	1.6
35	Arizona	1.5
35	Mississippi	1.5
37	Idaho	1.4
37	Kentucky	1.4
37	North Dakota	1.4
37	Oklahoma	1.4
41	Kansas	1.3
41	Nevada	1.3
41	Texas	1.3
44	Arkansas	1.2
44	Nebraska	1.2
46	Iowa	1.1
46	New Mexico	1.1
48	West Virginia	1.0
49	Wisconsin	0.7
50	Wyoming	0.4
	District of Columbia	6.3

Source: CQ Press using data from U.S. Bureau of the Census, Governments Division
"2011 State and Local Government Finances" (http://www.census.gov/govs/local/)
*As a percent of direct general expenditures.

XIII. Population

Apportionment Population in 2010

National Total = 309,183,463*

ALPHA ORDER

RANK	STATE	POPULATION	% of USA
23	Alabama	4,802,982	1.6%
47	Alaska	721,523	0.2%
16	Arizona	6,412,700	2.1%
32	Arkansas	2,926,229	0.9%
1	California	37,341,989	12.1%
22	Colorado	5,044,930	1.6%
29	Connecticut	3,581,628	1.2%
45	Delaware	900,877	0.3%
4	Florida	18,900,773	6.1%
9	Georgia	9,727,566	3.1%
40	Hawaii	1,366,862	0.4%
39	Idaho	1,573,499	0.5%
5	Illinois	12,864,380	4.2%
15	Indiana	6,501,582	2.1%
30	Iowa	3,053,787	1.0%
33	Kansas	2,863,813	0.9%
26	Kentucky	4,350,606	1.4%
25	Louisiana	4,553,962	1.5%
41	Maine	1,333,074	0.4%
19	Maryland	5,789,929	1.9%
14	Massachusetts	6,559,644	2.1%
8	Michigan	9,911,626	3.2%
21	Minnesota	5,314,879	1.7%
31	Mississippi	2,978,240	1.0%
18	Missouri	6,011,478	1.9%
44	Montana	994,416	0.3%
38	Nebraska	1,831,825	0.6%
35	Nevada	2,709,432	0.9%
42	New Hampshire	1,321,445	0.4%
11	New Jersey	8,807,501	2.8%
36	New Mexico	2,067,273	0.7%
3	New York	19,421,055	6.3%
10	North Carolina	9,565,781	3.1%
48	North Dakota	675,905	0.2%
7	Ohio	11,568,495	3.7%
28	Oklahoma	3,764,882	1.2%
27	Oregon	3,848,606	1.2%
6	Pennsylvania	12,734,905	4.1%
43	Rhode Island	1,055,247	0.3%
24	South Carolina	4,645,975	1.5%
46	South Dakota	819,761	0.3%
17	Tennessee	6,375,431	2.1%
2	Texas	25,268,418	8.2%
34	Utah	2,770,765	0.9%
49	Vermont	630,337	0.2%
12	Virginia	8,037,736	2.6%
13	Washington	6,753,369	2.2%
37	West Virginia	1,859,815	0.6%
20	Wisconsin	5,698,230	1.8%
50	Wyoming	568,300	0.2%

RANK ORDER

RANK	STATE	POPULATION	% of USA
1	California	37,341,989	12.1%
2	Texas	25,268,418	8.2%
3	New York	19,421,055	6.3%
4	Florida	18,900,773	6.1%
5	Illinois	12,864,380	4.2%
6	Pennsylvania	12,734,905	4.1%
7	Ohio	11,568,495	3.7%
8	Michigan	9,911,626	3.2%
9	Georgia	9,727,566	3.1%
10	North Carolina	9,565,781	3.1%
11	New Jersey	8,807,501	2.8%
12	Virginia	8,037,736	2.6%
13	Washington	6,753,369	2.2%
14	Massachusetts	6,559,644	2.1%
15	Indiana	6,501,582	2.1%
16	Arizona	6,412,700	2.1%
17	Tennessee	6,375,431	2.1%
18	Missouri	6,011,478	1.9%
19	Maryland	5,789,929	1.9%
20	Wisconsin	5,698,230	1.8%
21	Minnesota	5,314,879	1.7%
22	Colorado	5,044,930	1.6%
23	Alabama	4,802,982	1.6%
24	South Carolina	4,645,975	1.5%
25	Louisiana	4,553,962	1.5%
26	Kentucky	4,350,606	1.4%
27	Oregon	3,848,606	1.2%
28	Oklahoma	3,764,882	1.2%
29	Connecticut	3,581,628	1.2%
30	Iowa	3,053,787	1.0%
31	Mississippi	2,978,240	1.0%
32	Arkansas	2,926,229	0.9%
33	Kansas	2,863,813	0.9%
34	Utah	2,770,765	0.9%
35	Nevada	2,709,432	0.9%
36	New Mexico	2,067,273	0.7%
37	West Virginia	1,859,815	0.6%
38	Nebraska	1,831,825	0.6%
39	Idaho	1,573,499	0.5%
40	Hawaii	1,366,862	0.4%
41	Maine	1,333,074	0.4%
42	New Hampshire	1,321,445	0.4%
43	Rhode Island	1,055,247	0.3%
44	Montana	994,416	0.3%
45	Delaware	900,877	0.3%
46	South Dakota	819,761	0.3%
47	Alaska	721,523	0.2%
48	North Dakota	675,905	0.2%
49	Vermont	630,337	0.2%
50	Wyoming	568,300	0.2%
	District of Columbia**	NA	NA

Source: U.S. Bureau of the Census

"Congressional Apportionment" (http://www.census.gov/population/apportionment/)

*Apportionment population includes the resident population for the 50 states, as ascertained by the Twenty-Third Decennial Census under Title 13, United States Code, and counts of overseas U.S. military and federal civilian employees (and their dependents living with them) allocated to their home state, as reported by the employing federal agencies. The apportionment population excludes the population of the District of Columbia. **Not applicable.

Population in 2013

National Total = 316,128,839*

ALPHA ORDER

ALPHA ORDER

RANK	STATE	POPULATION	% of USA
23	Alabama	4,833,722	1.5%
47	Alaska	735,132	0.2%
15	Arizona	6,626,624	2.1%
32	Arkansas	2,959,373	0.9%
1	California	38,332,521	12.1%
22	Colorado	5,268,367	1.7%
29	Connecticut	3,596,080	1.1%
45	Delaware	925,749	0.3%
4	Florida	19,552,860	6.2%
8	Georgia	9,992,167	3.2%
40	Hawaii	1,404,054	0.4%
39	Idaho	1,612,136	0.5%
5	Illinois	12,882,135	4.1%
16	Indiana	6,570,902	2.1%
30	Iowa	3,090,416	1.0%
34	Kansas	2,893,957	0.9%
26	Kentucky	4,395,295	1.4%
25	Louisiana	4,625,470	1.5%
41	Maine	1,328,302	0.4%
19	Maryland	5,928,814	1.9%
14	Massachusetts	6,692,824	2.1%
9	Michigan	9,895,622	3.1%
21	Minnesota	5,420,380	1.7%
31	Mississippi	2,991,207	0.9%
18	Missouri	6,044,171	1.9%
44	Montana	1,015,165	0.3%
37	Nebraska	1,868,516	0.6%
35	Nevada	2,790,136	0.9%
42	New Hampshire	1,323,459	0.4%
11	New Jersey	8,899,339	2.8%
36	New Mexico	2,085,287	0.7%
3	New York	19,651,127	6.2%
10	North Carolina	9,848,060	3.1%
48	North Dakota	723,393	0.2%
7	Ohio	11,570,808	3.7%
28	Oklahoma	3,850,568	1.2%
27	Oregon	3,930,065	1.2%
6	Pennsylvania	12,773,801	4.0%
43	Rhode Island	1,051,511	0.3%
24	South Carolina	4,774,839	1.5%
46	South Dakota	844,877	0.3%
17	Tennessee	6,495,978	2.1%
2	Texas	26,448,193	8.4%
33	Utah	2,900,872	0.9%
49	Vermont	626,630	0.2%
12	Virginia	8,260,405	2.6%
13	Washington	6,971,406	2.2%
38	West Virginia	1,854,304	0.6%
20	Wisconsin	5,742,713	1.8%
50	Wyoming	582,658	0.2%

RANK ORDER

RANK	STATE	POPULATION	% of USA
1	California	38,332,521	12.1%
2	Texas	26,448,193	8.4%
3	New York	19,651,127	6.2%
4	Florida	19,552,860	6.2%
5	Illinois	12,882,135	4.1%
6	Pennsylvania	12,773,801	4.0%
7	Ohio	11,570,808	3.7%
8	Georgia	9,992,167	3.2%
9	Michigan	9,895,622	3.1%
10	North Carolina	9,848,060	3.1%
11	New Jersey	8,899,339	2.8%
12	Virginia	8,260,405	2.6%
13	Washington	6,971,406	2.2%
14	Massachusetts	6,692,824	2.1%
15	Arizona	6,626,624	2.1%
16	Indiana	6,570,902	2.1%
17	Tennessee	6,495,978	2.1%
18	Missouri	6,044,171	1.9%
19	Maryland	5,928,814	1.9%
20	Wisconsin	5,742,713	1.8%
21	Minnesota	5,420,380	1.7%
22	Colorado	5,268,367	1.7%
23	Alabama	4,833,722	1.5%
24	South Carolina	4,774,839	1.5%
25	Louisiana	4,625,470	1.5%
26	Kentucky	4,395,295	1.4%
27	Oregon	3,930,065	1.2%
28	Oklahoma	3,850,568	1.2%
29	Connecticut	3,596,080	1.1%
30	Iowa	3,090,416	1.0%
31	Mississippi	2,991,207	0.9%
32	Arkansas	2,959,373	0.9%
33	Utah	2,900,872	0.9%
34	Kansas	2,893,957	0.9%
35	Nevada	2,790,136	0.9%
36	New Mexico	2,085,287	0.7%
37	Nebraska	1,868,516	0.6%
38	West Virginia	1,854,304	0.6%
39	Idaho	1,612,136	0.5%
40	Hawaii	1,404,054	0.4%
41	Maine	1,328,302	0.4%
42	New Hampshire	1,323,459	0.4%
43	Rhode Island	1,051,511	0.3%
44	Montana	1,015,165	0.3%
45	Delaware	925,749	0.3%
46	South Dakota	844,877	0.3%
47	Alaska	735,132	0.2%
48	North Dakota	723,393	0.2%
49	Vermont	626,630	0.2%
50	Wyoming	582,658	0.2%
	District of Columbia	646,449	0.2%

Source: U.S. Bureau of the Census
"Population Estimates" (December 2013, http://www.census.gov/popest/data/index.html)
*Resident population estimate as of July 1, 2013.

Population in 2012

National Total = 313,873,685*

ALPHA ORDER

RANK	STATE	POPULATION	% of USA
23	Alabama	4,817,528	1.5%
47	Alaska	730,307	0.2%
15	Arizona	6,551,149	2.1%
32	Arkansas	2,949,828	0.9%
1	California	37,999,878	12.1%
22	Colorado	5,189,458	1.7%
29	Connecticut	3,591,765	1.1%
45	Delaware	917,053	0.3%
4	Florida	19,320,749	6.2%
8	Georgia	9,915,646	3.2%
40	Hawaii	1,390,090	0.4%
39	Idaho	1,595,590	0.5%
5	Illinois	12,868,192	4.1%
16	Indiana	6,537,782	2.1%
30	Iowa	3,075,039	1.0%
33	Kansas	2,885,398	0.9%
26	Kentucky	4,379,730	1.4%
25	Louisiana	4,602,134	1.5%
41	Maine	1,328,501	0.4%
19	Maryland	5,884,868	1.9%
14	Massachusetts	6,645,303	2.1%
9	Michigan	9,882,519	3.1%
21	Minnesota	5,379,646	1.7%
31	Mississippi	2,986,450	1.0%
18	Missouri	6,024,522	1.9%
44	Montana	1,005,494	0.3%
38	Nebraska	1,855,350	0.6%
35	Nevada	2,754,354	0.9%
42	New Hampshire	1,321,617	0.4%
11	New Jersey	8,867,749	2.8%
36	New Mexico	2,083,540	0.7%
3	New York	19,576,125	6.2%
10	North Carolina	9,748,364	3.1%
48	North Dakota	701,345	0.2%
7	Ohio	11,553,031	3.7%
28	Oklahoma	3,815,780	1.2%
27	Oregon	3,899,801	1.2%
6	Pennsylvania	12,764,475	4.1%
43	Rhode Island	1,050,304	0.3%
24	South Carolina	4,723,417	1.5%
46	South Dakota	834,047	0.3%
17	Tennessee	6,454,914	2.1%
2	Texas	26,060,796	8.3%
34	Utah	2,854,871	0.9%
49	Vermont	625,953	0.2%
12	Virginia	8,186,628	2.6%
13	Washington	6,895,318	2.2%
37	West Virginia	1,856,680	0.6%
20	Wisconsin	5,724,554	1.8%
50	Wyoming	576,626	0.2%

RANK ORDER

RANK	STATE	POPULATION	% of USA
1	California	37,999,878	12.1%
2	Texas	26,060,796	8.3%
3	New York	19,576,125	6.2%
4	Florida	19,320,749	6.2%
5	Illinois	12,868,192	4.1%
6	Pennsylvania	12,764,475	4.1%
7	Ohio	11,553,031	3.7%
8	Georgia	9,915,646	3.2%
9	Michigan	9,882,519	3.1%
10	North Carolina	9,748,364	3.1%
11	New Jersey	8,867,749	2.8%
12	Virginia	8,186,628	2.6%
13	Washington	6,895,318	2.2%
14	Massachusetts	6,645,303	2.1%
15	Arizona	6,551,149	2.1%
16	Indiana	6,537,782	2.1%
17	Tennessee	6,454,914	2.1%
18	Missouri	6,024,522	1.9%
19	Maryland	5,884,868	1.9%
20	Wisconsin	5,724,554	1.8%
21	Minnesota	5,379,646	1.7%
22	Colorado	5,189,458	1.7%
23	Alabama	4,817,528	1.5%
24	South Carolina	4,723,417	1.5%
25	Louisiana	4,602,134	1.5%
26	Kentucky	4,379,730	1.4%
27	Oregon	3,899,801	1.2%
28	Oklahoma	3,815,780	1.2%
29	Connecticut	3,591,765	1.1%
30	Iowa	3,075,039	1.0%
31	Mississippi	2,986,450	1.0%
32	Arkansas	2,949,828	0.9%
33	Kansas	2,885,398	0.9%
34	Utah	2,854,871	0.9%
35	Nevada	2,754,354	0.9%
36	New Mexico	2,083,540	0.7%
37	West Virginia	1,856,680	0.6%
38	Nebraska	1,855,350	0.6%
39	Idaho	1,595,590	0.5%
40	Hawaii	1,390,090	0.4%
41	Maine	1,328,501	0.4%
42	New Hampshire	1,321,617	0.4%
43	Rhode Island	1,050,304	0.3%
44	Montana	1,005,494	0.3%
45	Delaware	917,053	0.3%
46	South Dakota	834,047	0.3%
47	Alaska	730,307	0.2%
48	North Dakota	701,345	0.2%
49	Vermont	625,953	0.2%
50	Wyoming	576,626	0.2%
	District of Columbia	633,427	0.2%

Source: U.S. Bureau of the Census
  "Population Estimates" (December 2013, http://www.census.gov/popest/data/index.html)
*Resident population. Revised estimates of July 1, 2013.

Numerical Population Change: 2012 to 2013

National Total = 2,255,154 Increase*

ALPHA ORDER

RANK	STATE	GAIN/LOSS	% of USA
28	Alabama	16,194	0.7%
42	Alaska	4,825	0.2%
8	Arizona	75,475	3.3%
37	Arkansas	9,545	0.4%
2	California	332,643	14.8%
5	Colorado	78,909	3.5%
44	Connecticut	4,315	0.2%
39	Delaware	8,696	0.4%
3	Florida	232,111	10.3%
6	Georgia	76,521	3.4%
31	Hawaii	13,964	0.6%
27	Idaho	16,546	0.7%
32	Illinois	13,943	0.6%
19	Indiana	33,120	1.5%
30	Iowa	15,377	0.7%
40	Kansas	8,559	0.4%
29	Kentucky	15,565	0.7%
22	Louisiana	23,336	1.0%
49	Maine	(199)	
14	Maryland	43,946	1.9%
12	Massachusetts	47,521	2.1%
34	Michigan	13,103	0.6%
16	Minnesota	40,734	1.8%
43	Mississippi	4,757	0.2%
24	Missouri	19,649	0.9%
36	Montana	9,671	0.4%
33	Nebraska	13,166	0.6%
17	Nevada	35,782	1.6%
45	New Hampshire	1,842	0.1%
20	New Jersey	31,590	1.4%
46	New Mexico	1,747	0.1%
9	New York	75,002	3.3%
4	North Carolina	99,696	4.4%
23	North Dakota	22,048	1.0%
26	Ohio	17,777	0.8%
18	Oklahoma	34,788	1.5%
21	Oregon	30,264	1.3%
38	Pennsylvania	9,326	0.4%
47	Rhode Island	1,207	0.1%
11	South Carolina	51,422	2.3%
35	South Dakota	10,830	0.5%
15	Tennessee	41,064	1.8%
1	Texas	387,397	17.2%
13	Utah	46,001	2.0%
48	Vermont	677	0.0%
10	Virginia	73,777	3.3%
7	Washington	76,088	3.4%
50	West Virginia	(2,376)	
25	Wisconsin	18,159	0.8%
41	Wyoming	6,032	0.3%

RANK ORDER

RANK	STATE	GAIN/LOSS	% of USA
1	Texas	387,397	17.2%
2	California	332,643	14.8%
3	Florida	232,111	10.3%
4	North Carolina	99,696	4.4%
5	Colorado	78,909	3.5%
6	Georgia	76,521	3.4%
7	Washington	76,088	3.4%
8	Arizona	75,475	3.3%
9	New York	75,002	3.3%
10	Virginia	73,777	3.3%
11	South Carolina	51,422	2.3%
12	Massachusetts	47,521	2.1%
13	Utah	46,001	2.0%
14	Maryland	43,946	1.9%
15	Tennessee	41,064	1.8%
16	Minnesota	40,734	1.8%
17	Nevada	35,782	1.6%
18	Oklahoma	34,788	1.5%
19	Indiana	33,120	1.5%
20	New Jersey	31,590	1.4%
21	Oregon	30,264	1.3%
22	Louisiana	23,336	1.0%
23	North Dakota	22,048	1.0%
24	Missouri	19,649	0.9%
25	Wisconsin	18,159	0.8%
26	Ohio	17,777	0.8%
27	Idaho	16,546	0.7%
28	Alabama	16,194	0.7%
29	Kentucky	15,565	0.7%
30	Iowa	15,377	0.7%
31	Hawaii	13,964	0.6%
32	Illinois	13,943	0.6%
33	Nebraska	13,166	0.6%
34	Michigan	13,103	0.6%
35	South Dakota	10,830	0.5%
36	Montana	9,671	0.4%
37	Arkansas	9,545	0.4%
38	Pennsylvania	9,326	0.4%
39	Delaware	8,696	0.4%
40	Kansas	8,559	0.4%
41	Wyoming	6,032	0.3%
42	Alaska	4,825	0.2%
43	Mississippi	4,757	0.2%
44	Connecticut	4,315	0.2%
45	New Hampshire	1,842	0.1%
46	New Mexico	1,747	0.1%
47	Rhode Island	1,207	0.1%
48	Vermont	677	0.0%
49	Maine	(199)	
50	West Virginia	(2,376)	
	District of Columbia	13,022	0.6%

Source: CQ Press using data from U.S. Bureau of the Census
"Population Estimates" (December 2013, http://www.census.gov/popest/data/index.html)
*Resident population from July 1, 2012 to July 1, 2013.

Percent Change in Population: 2012 to 2013

National Percent Change = 0.7% Increase*

RANK	STATE	PERCENT CHANGE
34	Alabama	0.3
23	Alaska	0.7
7	Arizona	1.2
34	Arkansas	0.3
16	California	0.9
3	Colorado	1.5
41	Connecticut	0.1
16	Delaware	0.9
7	Florida	1.2
20	Georgia	0.8
11	Hawaii	1.0
11	Idaho	1.0
41	Illinois	0.1
28	Indiana	0.5
28	Iowa	0.5
34	Kansas	0.3
31	Kentucky	0.4
28	Louisiana	0.5
49	Maine	0.0
23	Maryland	0.7
23	Massachusetts	0.7
41	Michigan	0.1
20	Minnesota	0.8
39	Mississippi	0.2
34	Missouri	0.3
11	Montana	1.0
23	Nebraska	0.7
5	Nevada	1.3
41	New Hampshire	0.1
31	New Jersey	0.4
41	New Mexico	0.1
31	New York	0.4
11	North Carolina	1.0
1	North Dakota	3.1
39	Ohio	0.2
16	Oklahoma	0.9
20	Oregon	0.8
41	Pennsylvania	0.1
41	Rhode Island	0.1
9	South Carolina	1.1
5	South Dakota	1.3
27	Tennessee	0.6
3	Texas	1.5
2	Utah	1.6
41	Vermont	0.1
16	Virginia	0.9
9	Washington	1.1
50	West Virginia	(0.1)
34	Wisconsin	0.3
11	Wyoming	1.0

RANK	STATE	PERCENT CHANGE
1	North Dakota	3.1
2	Utah	1.6
3	Colorado	1.5
3	Texas	1.5
5	Nevada	1.3
5	South Dakota	1.3
7	Arizona	1.2
7	Florida	1.2
9	South Carolina	1.1
9	Washington	1.1
11	Hawaii	1.0
11	Idaho	1.0
11	Montana	1.0
11	North Carolina	1.0
11	Wyoming	1.0
16	California	0.9
16	Delaware	0.9
16	Oklahoma	0.9
16	Virginia	0.9
20	Georgia	0.8
20	Minnesota	0.8
20	Oregon	0.8
23	Alaska	0.7
23	Maryland	0.7
23	Massachusetts	0.7
23	Nebraska	0.7
27	Tennessee	0.6
28	Indiana	0.5
28	Iowa	0.5
28	Louisiana	0.5
31	Kentucky	0.4
31	New Jersey	0.4
31	New York	0.4
34	Alabama	0.3
34	Arkansas	0.3
34	Kansas	0.3
34	Missouri	0.3
34	Wisconsin	0.3
39	Mississippi	0.2
39	Ohio	0.2
41	Connecticut	0.1
41	Illinois	0.1
41	Michigan	0.1
41	New Hampshire	0.1
41	New Mexico	0.1
41	Pennsylvania	0.1
41	Rhode Island	0.1
41	Vermont	0.1
49	Maine	0.0
50	West Virginia	(0.1)

District of Columbia   2.1

Source: CQ Press using data from U.S. Bureau of the Census
   "Population Estimates" (December 2013, http://www.census.gov/popest/data/index.html)
*Resident population from July 1, 2012 to July 1, 2013.

Population in 2010 Census

National Total = 308,745,538*

<table>
<tr><td colspan="4">ALPHA ORDER</td><td colspan="4">RANK ORDER</td></tr>
<tr><th>RANK</th><th>STATE</th><th>POPULATION</th><th>% of USA</th><th>RANK</th><th>STATE</th><th>POPULATION</th><th>% of USA</th></tr>
<tr><td>23</td><td>Alabama</td><td>4,779,736</td><td>1.5%</td><td>1</td><td>California</td><td>37,253,956</td><td>12.1%</td></tr>
<tr><td>47</td><td>Alaska</td><td>710,231</td><td>0.2%</td><td>2</td><td>Texas</td><td>25,145,561</td><td>8.1%</td></tr>
<tr><td>16</td><td>Arizona</td><td>6,392,017</td><td>2.1%</td><td>3</td><td>New York</td><td>19,378,102</td><td>6.3%</td></tr>
<tr><td>32</td><td>Arkansas</td><td>2,915,918</td><td>0.9%</td><td>4</td><td>Florida</td><td>18,801,310</td><td>6.1%</td></tr>
<tr><td>1</td><td>California</td><td>37,253,956</td><td>12.1%</td><td>5</td><td>Illinois</td><td>12,830,632</td><td>4.2%</td></tr>
<tr><td>22</td><td>Colorado</td><td>5,029,196</td><td>1.6%</td><td>6</td><td>Pennsylvania</td><td>12,702,379</td><td>4.1%</td></tr>
<tr><td>29</td><td>Connecticut</td><td>3,574,097</td><td>1.2%</td><td>7</td><td>Ohio</td><td>11,536,504</td><td>3.7%</td></tr>
<tr><td>45</td><td>Delaware</td><td>897,934</td><td>0.3%</td><td>8</td><td>Michigan</td><td>9,883,640</td><td>3.2%</td></tr>
<tr><td>4</td><td>Florida</td><td>18,801,310</td><td>6.1%</td><td>9</td><td>Georgia</td><td>9,687,653</td><td>3.1%</td></tr>
<tr><td>9</td><td>Georgia</td><td>9,687,653</td><td>3.1%</td><td>10</td><td>North Carolina</td><td>9,535,483</td><td>3.1%</td></tr>
<tr><td>40</td><td>Hawaii</td><td>1,360,301</td><td>0.4%</td><td>11</td><td>New Jersey</td><td>8,791,894</td><td>2.8%</td></tr>
<tr><td>39</td><td>Idaho</td><td>1,567,582</td><td>0.5%</td><td>12</td><td>Virginia</td><td>8,001,024</td><td>2.6%</td></tr>
<tr><td>5</td><td>Illinois</td><td>12,830,632</td><td>4.2%</td><td>13</td><td>Washington</td><td>6,724,540</td><td>2.2%</td></tr>
<tr><td>15</td><td>Indiana</td><td>6,483,802</td><td>2.1%</td><td>14</td><td>Massachusetts</td><td>6,547,629</td><td>2.1%</td></tr>
<tr><td>30</td><td>Iowa</td><td>3,046,355</td><td>1.0%</td><td>15</td><td>Indiana</td><td>6,483,802</td><td>2.1%</td></tr>
<tr><td>33</td><td>Kansas</td><td>2,853,118</td><td>0.9%</td><td>16</td><td>Arizona</td><td>6,392,017</td><td>2.1%</td></tr>
<tr><td>26</td><td>Kentucky</td><td>4,339,367</td><td>1.4%</td><td>17</td><td>Tennessee</td><td>6,346,105</td><td>2.1%</td></tr>
<tr><td>25</td><td>Louisiana</td><td>4,533,372</td><td>1.5%</td><td>18</td><td>Missouri</td><td>5,988,927</td><td>1.9%</td></tr>
<tr><td>41</td><td>Maine</td><td>1,328,361</td><td>0.4%</td><td>19</td><td>Maryland</td><td>5,773,552</td><td>1.9%</td></tr>
<tr><td>19</td><td>Maryland</td><td>5,773,552</td><td>1.9%</td><td>20</td><td>Wisconsin</td><td>5,686,986</td><td>1.8%</td></tr>
<tr><td>14</td><td>Massachusetts</td><td>6,547,629</td><td>2.1%</td><td>21</td><td>Minnesota</td><td>5,303,925</td><td>1.7%</td></tr>
<tr><td>8</td><td>Michigan</td><td>9,883,640</td><td>3.2%</td><td>22</td><td>Colorado</td><td>5,029,196</td><td>1.6%</td></tr>
<tr><td>21</td><td>Minnesota</td><td>5,303,925</td><td>1.7%</td><td>23</td><td>Alabama</td><td>4,779,736</td><td>1.5%</td></tr>
<tr><td>31</td><td>Mississippi</td><td>2,967,297</td><td>1.0%</td><td>24</td><td>South Carolina</td><td>4,625,364</td><td>1.5%</td></tr>
<tr><td>18</td><td>Missouri</td><td>5,988,927</td><td>1.9%</td><td>25</td><td>Louisiana</td><td>4,533,372</td><td>1.5%</td></tr>
<tr><td>44</td><td>Montana</td><td>989,415</td><td>0.3%</td><td>26</td><td>Kentucky</td><td>4,339,367</td><td>1.4%</td></tr>
<tr><td>38</td><td>Nebraska</td><td>1,826,341</td><td>0.6%</td><td>27</td><td>Oregon</td><td>3,831,074</td><td>1.2%</td></tr>
<tr><td>35</td><td>Nevada</td><td>2,700,551</td><td>0.9%</td><td>28</td><td>Oklahoma</td><td>3,751,351</td><td>1.2%</td></tr>
<tr><td>42</td><td>New Hampshire</td><td>1,316,470</td><td>0.4%</td><td>29</td><td>Connecticut</td><td>3,574,097</td><td>1.2%</td></tr>
<tr><td>11</td><td>New Jersey</td><td>8,791,894</td><td>2.8%</td><td>30</td><td>Iowa</td><td>3,046,355</td><td>1.0%</td></tr>
<tr><td>36</td><td>New Mexico</td><td>2,059,179</td><td>0.7%</td><td>31</td><td>Mississippi</td><td>2,967,297</td><td>1.0%</td></tr>
<tr><td>3</td><td>New York</td><td>19,378,102</td><td>6.3%</td><td>32</td><td>Arkansas</td><td>2,915,918</td><td>0.9%</td></tr>
<tr><td>10</td><td>North Carolina</td><td>9,535,483</td><td>3.1%</td><td>33</td><td>Kansas</td><td>2,853,118</td><td>0.9%</td></tr>
<tr><td>48</td><td>North Dakota</td><td>672,591</td><td>0.2%</td><td>34</td><td>Utah</td><td>2,763,885</td><td>0.9%</td></tr>
<tr><td>7</td><td>Ohio</td><td>11,536,504</td><td>3.7%</td><td>35</td><td>Nevada</td><td>2,700,551</td><td>0.9%</td></tr>
<tr><td>28</td><td>Oklahoma</td><td>3,751,351</td><td>1.2%</td><td>36</td><td>New Mexico</td><td>2,059,179</td><td>0.7%</td></tr>
<tr><td>27</td><td>Oregon</td><td>3,831,074</td><td>1.2%</td><td>37</td><td>West Virginia</td><td>1,852,994</td><td>0.6%</td></tr>
<tr><td>6</td><td>Pennsylvania</td><td>12,702,379</td><td>4.1%</td><td>38</td><td>Nebraska</td><td>1,826,341</td><td>0.6%</td></tr>
<tr><td>43</td><td>Rhode Island</td><td>1,052,567</td><td>0.3%</td><td>39</td><td>Idaho</td><td>1,567,582</td><td>0.5%</td></tr>
<tr><td>24</td><td>South Carolina</td><td>4,625,364</td><td>1.5%</td><td>40</td><td>Hawaii</td><td>1,360,301</td><td>0.4%</td></tr>
<tr><td>46</td><td>South Dakota</td><td>814,180</td><td>0.3%</td><td>41</td><td>Maine</td><td>1,328,361</td><td>0.4%</td></tr>
<tr><td>17</td><td>Tennessee</td><td>6,346,105</td><td>2.1%</td><td>42</td><td>New Hampshire</td><td>1,316,470</td><td>0.4%</td></tr>
<tr><td>2</td><td>Texas</td><td>25,145,561</td><td>8.1%</td><td>43</td><td>Rhode Island</td><td>1,052,567</td><td>0.3%</td></tr>
<tr><td>34</td><td>Utah</td><td>2,763,885</td><td>0.9%</td><td>44</td><td>Montana</td><td>989,415</td><td>0.3%</td></tr>
<tr><td>49</td><td>Vermont</td><td>625,741</td><td>0.2%</td><td>45</td><td>Delaware</td><td>897,934</td><td>0.3%</td></tr>
<tr><td>12</td><td>Virginia</td><td>8,001,024</td><td>2.6%</td><td>46</td><td>South Dakota</td><td>814,180</td><td>0.3%</td></tr>
<tr><td>13</td><td>Washington</td><td>6,724,540</td><td>2.2%</td><td>47</td><td>Alaska</td><td>710,231</td><td>0.2%</td></tr>
<tr><td>37</td><td>West Virginia</td><td>1,852,994</td><td>0.6%</td><td>48</td><td>North Dakota</td><td>672,591</td><td>0.2%</td></tr>
<tr><td>20</td><td>Wisconsin</td><td>5,686,986</td><td>1.8%</td><td>49</td><td>Vermont</td><td>625,741</td><td>0.2%</td></tr>
<tr><td>50</td><td>Wyoming</td><td>563,626</td><td>0.2%</td><td>50</td><td>Wyoming</td><td>563,626</td><td>0.2%</td></tr>
<tr><td></td><td></td><td></td><td></td><td></td><td>District of Columbia</td><td>601,723</td><td>0.2%</td></tr>
</table>

Source: U.S. Bureau of the Census
"First 2010 Census Results" (http://www.census.gov/2010census/news/press-kits/apportionment/apport.html)
*Resident population as of April 2010 Census.

Projected State Population in 2030

National Total = 363,584,435*

ALPHA ORDER

RANK	STATE	POPULATION	% of USA
24	Alabama	4,874,243	1.3%
46	Alaska	867,674	0.2%
10	Arizona	10,712,397	2.9%
32	Arkansas	3,240,208	0.9%
1	California	46,444,861	12.8%
22	Colorado	5,792,357	1.6%
30	Connecticut	3,688,630	1.0%
45	Delaware	1,012,658	0.3%
3	Florida	28,685,769	7.9%
8	Georgia	12,017,838	3.3%
41	Hawaii	1,466,046	0.4%
37	Idaho	1,969,624	0.5%
5	Illinois	13,432,892	3.7%
18	Indiana	6,810,108	1.9%
34	Iowa	2,955,172	0.8%
35	Kansas	2,940,084	0.8%
27	Kentucky	4,554,998	1.3%
26	Louisiana	4,802,633	1.3%
42	Maine	1,411,097	0.4%
16	Maryland	7,022,251	1.9%
17	Massachusetts	7,012,009	1.9%
11	Michigan	10,694,172	2.9%
20	Minnesota	6,306,130	1.7%
33	Mississippi	3,092,410	0.9%
19	Missouri	6,430,173	1.8%
44	Montana	1,044,898	0.3%
38	Nebraska	1,820,247	0.5%
28	Nevada	4,282,102	1.2%
40	New Hampshire	1,646,471	0.5%
13	New Jersey	9,802,440	2.7%
36	New Mexico	2,099,708	0.6%
4	New York	19,477,429	5.4%
7	North Carolina	12,227,739	3.4%
49	North Dakota	606,566	0.2%
9	Ohio	11,550,528	3.2%
29	Oklahoma	3,913,251	1.1%
25	Oregon	4,833,918	1.3%
6	Pennsylvania	12,768,184	3.5%
43	Rhode Island	1,152,941	0.3%
23	South Carolina	5,148,569	1.4%
47	South Dakota	800,462	0.2%
15	Tennessee	7,380,634	2.0%
2	Texas	33,317,744	9.2%
31	Utah	3,485,367	1.0%
48	Vermont	711,867	0.2%
12	Virginia	9,825,019	2.7%
14	Washington	8,624,801	2.4%
39	West Virginia	1,719,959	0.5%
21	Wisconsin	6,150,764	1.7%
50	Wyoming	522,979	0.1%

RANK ORDER

RANK	STATE	POPULATION	% of USA
1	California	46,444,861	12.8%
2	Texas	33,317,744	9.2%
3	Florida	28,685,769	7.9%
4	New York	19,477,429	5.4%
5	Illinois	13,432,892	3.7%
6	Pennsylvania	12,768,184	3.5%
7	North Carolina	12,227,739	3.4%
8	Georgia	12,017,838	3.3%
9	Ohio	11,550,528	3.2%
10	Arizona	10,712,397	2.9%
11	Michigan	10,694,172	2.9%
12	Virginia	9,825,019	2.7%
13	New Jersey	9,802,440	2.7%
14	Washington	8,624,801	2.4%
15	Tennessee	7,380,634	2.0%
16	Maryland	7,022,251	1.9%
17	Massachusetts	7,012,009	1.9%
18	Indiana	6,810,108	1.9%
19	Missouri	6,430,173	1.8%
20	Minnesota	6,306,130	1.7%
21	Wisconsin	6,150,764	1.7%
22	Colorado	5,792,357	1.6%
23	South Carolina	5,148,569	1.4%
24	Alabama	4,874,243	1.3%
25	Oregon	4,833,918	1.3%
26	Louisiana	4,802,633	1.3%
27	Kentucky	4,554,998	1.3%
28	Nevada	4,282,102	1.2%
29	Oklahoma	3,913,251	1.1%
30	Connecticut	3,688,630	1.0%
31	Utah	3,485,367	1.0%
32	Arkansas	3,240,208	0.9%
33	Mississippi	3,092,410	0.9%
34	Iowa	2,955,172	0.8%
35	Kansas	2,940,084	0.8%
36	New Mexico	2,099,708	0.6%
37	Idaho	1,969,624	0.5%
38	Nebraska	1,820,247	0.5%
39	West Virginia	1,719,959	0.5%
40	New Hampshire	1,646,471	0.5%
41	Hawaii	1,466,046	0.4%
42	Maine	1,411,097	0.4%
43	Rhode Island	1,152,941	0.3%
44	Montana	1,044,898	0.3%
45	Delaware	1,012,658	0.3%
46	Alaska	867,674	0.2%
47	South Dakota	800,462	0.2%
48	Vermont	711,867	0.2%
49	North Dakota	606,566	0.2%
50	Wyoming	522,979	0.1%
	District of Columbia	433,414	0.1%

Source: U.S. Bureau of the Census
   "State Interim Population Projections: 2004-2030"
      (http://www.census.gov/population/www/projections/projectionsagesex.html)
*Based on 2000 Census.

Population per Square Mile in 2013

National Rate = 89.5 Persons per Square Mile*

ALPHA ORDER

RANK	STATE	RATE
27	Alabama	95.4
50	Alaska	1.3
33	Arizona	58.3
34	Arkansas	56.9
11	California	246.1
37	Colorado	50.8
4	Connecticut	743.0
6	Delaware	475.0
8	Florida	364.8
18	Georgia	173.8
13	Hawaii	218.4
44	Idaho	19.5
12	Illinois	232.0
16	Indiana	183.4
36	Iowa	55.3
40	Kansas	35.4
22	Kentucky	111.3
23	Louisiana	107.1
38	Maine	43.1
5	Maryland	610.9
3	Massachusetts	857.9
17	Michigan	175.1
30	Minnesota	68.1
32	Mississippi	63.8
28	Missouri	88.0
48	Montana	7.0
43	Nebraska	24.3
42	Nevada	25.4
21	New Hampshire	147.8
1	New Jersey	1,210.1
45	New Mexico	17.2
7	New York	417.0
15	North Carolina	202.6
47	North Dakota	10.5
10	Ohio	283.2
35	Oklahoma	56.1
39	Oregon	40.9
9	Pennsylvania	285.5
2	Rhode Island	1,016.9
19	South Carolina	158.8
46	South Dakota	11.1
20	Tennessee	157.5
26	Texas	101.2
41	Utah	35.3
31	Vermont	68.0
14	Virginia	209.2
25	Washington	104.9
29	West Virginia	77.1
24	Wisconsin	106.0
49	Wyoming	6.0

RANK ORDER

RANK	STATE	RATE
1	New Jersey	1,210.1
2	Rhode Island	1,016.9
3	Massachusetts	857.9
4	Connecticut	743.0
5	Maryland	610.9
6	Delaware	475.0
7	New York	417.0
8	Florida	364.8
9	Pennsylvania	285.5
10	Ohio	283.2
11	California	246.1
12	Illinois	232.0
13	Hawaii	218.4
14	Virginia	209.2
15	North Carolina	202.6
16	Indiana	183.4
17	Michigan	175.1
18	Georgia	173.8
19	South Carolina	158.8
20	Tennessee	157.5
21	New Hampshire	147.8
22	Kentucky	111.3
23	Louisiana	107.1
24	Wisconsin	106.0
25	Washington	104.9
26	Texas	101.2
27	Alabama	95.4
28	Missouri	88.0
29	West Virginia	77.1
30	Minnesota	68.1
31	Vermont	68.0
32	Mississippi	63.8
33	Arizona	58.3
34	Arkansas	56.9
35	Oklahoma	56.1
36	Iowa	55.3
37	Colorado	50.8
38	Maine	43.1
39	Oregon	40.9
40	Kansas	35.4
41	Utah	35.3
42	Nevada	25.4
43	Nebraska	24.3
44	Idaho	19.5
45	New Mexico	17.2
46	South Dakota	11.1
47	North Dakota	10.5
48	Montana	7.0
49	Wyoming	6.0
50	Alaska	1.3
	District of Columbia	10,597.5

Source: CQ Press using data from U.S. Bureau of the Census
  "Population Estimates" (December 2013, http://www.census.gov/popest/data/index.html)
*Resident population. Based on land area of states.

Male Population in 2012

National Total = 154,492,067 Males

ALPHA ORDER

RANK	STATE	MALES	% of USA
23	Alabama	2,338,557	1.5%
47	Alaska	381,238	0.2%
14	Arizona	3,258,483	2.1%
32	Arkansas	1,448,490	0.9%
1	California	18,918,564	12.2%
22	Colorado	2,603,705	1.7%
29	Connecticut	1,749,916	1.1%
45	Delaware	444,358	0.3%
4	Florida	9,447,827	6.1%
8	Georgia	4,851,024	3.1%
40	Hawaii	701,965	0.5%
39	Idaho	798,612	0.5%
5	Illinois	6,319,455	4.1%
16	Indiana	3,218,190	2.1%
30	Iowa	1,524,488	1.0%
34	Kansas	1,435,281	0.9%
26	Kentucky	2,157,711	1.4%
25	Louisiana	2,252,050	1.5%
42	Maine	650,278	0.4%
19	Maryland	2,850,403	1.8%
15	Massachusetts	3,220,373	2.1%
9	Michigan	4,850,511	3.1%
21	Minnesota	2,672,169	1.7%
31	Mississippi	1,449,291	0.9%
18	Missouri	2,951,036	1.9%
44	Montana	504,949	0.3%
37	Nebraska	922,302	0.6%
35	Nevada	1,391,207	0.9%
41	New Hampshire	652,237	0.4%
11	New Jersey	4,323,685	2.8%
36	New Mexico	1,032,707	0.7%
3	New York	9,489,217	6.1%
10	North Carolina	4,752,898	3.1%
48	North Dakota	355,742	0.2%
7	Ohio	5,642,620	3.7%
28	Oklahoma	1,889,825	1.2%
27	Oregon	1,930,712	1.2%
6	Pennsylvania	6,230,177	4.0%
43	Rhode Island	508,276	0.3%
24	South Carolina	2,297,213	1.5%
46	South Dakota	418,316	0.3%
17	Tennessee	3,148,763	2.0%
2	Texas	12,947,734	8.4%
33	Utah	1,435,860	0.9%
49	Vermont	308,778	0.2%
12	Virginia	4,021,525	2.6%
13	Washington	3,441,550	2.2%
38	West Virginia	915,405	0.6%
20	Wisconsin	2,843,072	1.8%
50	Wyoming	294,281	0.2%

RANK ORDER

RANK	STATE	MALES	% of USA
1	California	18,918,564	12.2%
2	Texas	12,947,734	8.4%
3	New York	9,489,217	6.1%
4	Florida	9,447,827	6.1%
5	Illinois	6,319,455	4.1%
6	Pennsylvania	6,230,177	4.0%
7	Ohio	5,642,620	3.7%
8	Georgia	4,851,024	3.1%
9	Michigan	4,850,511	3.1%
10	North Carolina	4,752,898	3.1%
11	New Jersey	4,323,685	2.8%
12	Virginia	4,021,525	2.6%
13	Washington	3,441,550	2.2%
14	Arizona	3,258,483	2.1%
15	Massachusetts	3,220,373	2.1%
16	Indiana	3,218,190	2.1%
17	Tennessee	3,148,763	2.0%
18	Missouri	2,951,036	1.9%
19	Maryland	2,850,403	1.8%
20	Wisconsin	2,843,072	1.8%
21	Minnesota	2,672,169	1.7%
22	Colorado	2,603,705	1.7%
23	Alabama	2,338,557	1.5%
24	South Carolina	2,297,213	1.5%
25	Louisiana	2,252,050	1.5%
26	Kentucky	2,157,711	1.4%
27	Oregon	1,930,712	1.2%
28	Oklahoma	1,889,825	1.2%
29	Connecticut	1,749,916	1.1%
30	Iowa	1,524,488	1.0%
31	Mississippi	1,449,291	0.9%
32	Arkansas	1,448,490	0.9%
33	Utah	1,435,860	0.9%
34	Kansas	1,435,281	0.9%
35	Nevada	1,391,207	0.9%
36	New Mexico	1,032,707	0.7%
37	Nebraska	922,302	0.6%
38	West Virginia	915,405	0.6%
39	Idaho	798,612	0.5%
40	Hawaii	701,965	0.5%
41	New Hampshire	652,237	0.4%
42	Maine	650,278	0.4%
43	Rhode Island	508,276	0.3%
44	Montana	504,949	0.3%
45	Delaware	444,358	0.3%
46	South Dakota	418,316	0.3%
47	Alaska	381,238	0.2%
48	North Dakota	355,742	0.2%
49	Vermont	308,778	0.2%
50	Wyoming	294,281	0.2%
	District of Columbia	299,041	0.2%

Source: U.S. Bureau of the Census
    "State Characteristics: Vintage 2012" (http://www.census.gov/popest/data/state/asrh/2012/index.html)

Female Population in 2012

National Total = 159,421,973 Females

ALPHA ORDER					RANK ORDER			
RANK	STATE	FEMALES	% of USA		RANK	STATE	FEMALES	% of USA
23	Alabama	2,483,466	1.6%		1	California	19,122,866	12.0%
47	Alaska	350,211	0.2%		2	Texas	13,111,469	8.2%
17	Arizona	3,294,772	2.1%		3	New York	10,081,044	6.3%
32	Arkansas	1,500,641	0.9%		4	Florida	9,869,741	6.2%
1	California	19,122,866	12.0%		5	Illinois	6,555,800	4.1%
22	Colorado	2,583,877	1.6%		6	Pennsylvania	6,533,359	4.1%
29	Connecticut	1,840,431	1.2%		7	Ohio	5,901,605	3.7%
45	Delaware	472,734	0.3%		8	Georgia	5,068,921	3.2%
4	Florida	9,869,741	6.2%		9	Michigan	5,032,849	3.2%
8	Georgia	5,068,921	3.2%		10	North Carolina	4,999,175	3.1%
40	Hawaii	690,348	0.4%		11	New Jersey	4,540,905	2.8%
39	Idaho	797,116	0.5%		12	Virginia	4,164,342	2.6%
5	Illinois	6,555,800	4.1%		13	Washington	3,455,462	2.2%
15	Indiana	3,319,144	2.1%		14	Massachusetts	3,425,771	2.1%
30	Iowa	1,549,698	1.0%		15	Indiana	3,319,144	2.1%
33	Kansas	1,450,624	0.9%		16	Tennessee	3,307,480	2.1%
26	Kentucky	2,222,704	1.4%		17	Arizona	3,294,772	2.1%
25	Louisiana	2,349,843	1.5%		18	Missouri	3,070,952	1.9%
41	Maine	678,914	0.4%		19	Maryland	3,034,160	1.9%
19	Maryland	3,034,160	1.9%		20	Wisconsin	2,883,326	1.8%
14	Massachusetts	3,425,771	2.1%		21	Minnesota	2,706,970	1.7%
9	Michigan	5,032,849	3.2%		22	Colorado	2,583,877	1.6%
21	Minnesota	2,706,970	1.7%		23	Alabama	2,483,466	1.6%
31	Mississippi	1,535,635	1.0%		24	South Carolina	2,426,510	1.5%
18	Missouri	3,070,952	1.9%		25	Louisiana	2,349,843	1.5%
44	Montana	500,192	0.3%		26	Kentucky	2,222,704	1.4%
38	Nebraska	933,223	0.6%		27	Oregon	1,968,641	1.2%
35	Nevada	1,367,724	0.9%		28	Oklahoma	1,924,995	1.2%
42	New Hampshire	668,481	0.4%		29	Connecticut	1,840,431	1.2%
11	New Jersey	4,540,905	2.8%		30	Iowa	1,549,698	1.0%
36	New Mexico	1,052,831	0.7%		31	Mississippi	1,535,635	1.0%
3	New York	10,081,044	6.3%		32	Arkansas	1,500,641	0.9%
10	North Carolina	4,999,175	3.1%		33	Kansas	1,450,624	0.9%
48	North Dakota	343,886	0.2%		34	Utah	1,419,427	0.9%
7	Ohio	5,901,605	3.7%		35	Nevada	1,367,724	0.9%
28	Oklahoma	1,924,995	1.2%		36	New Mexico	1,052,831	0.7%
27	Oregon	1,968,641	1.2%		37	West Virginia	940,008	0.6%
6	Pennsylvania	6,533,359	4.1%		38	Nebraska	933,223	0.6%
43	Rhode Island	542,016	0.3%		39	Idaho	797,116	0.5%
24	South Carolina	2,426,510	1.5%		40	Hawaii	690,348	0.4%
46	South Dakota	415,038	0.3%		41	Maine	678,914	0.4%
16	Tennessee	3,307,480	2.1%		42	New Hampshire	668,481	0.4%
2	Texas	13,111,469	8.2%		43	Rhode Island	542,016	0.3%
34	Utah	1,419,427	0.9%		44	Montana	500,192	0.3%
49	Vermont	317,233	0.2%		45	Delaware	472,734	0.3%
12	Virginia	4,164,342	2.6%		46	South Dakota	415,038	0.3%
13	Washington	3,455,462	2.2%		47	Alaska	350,211	0.2%
37	West Virginia	940,008	0.6%		48	North Dakota	343,886	0.2%
20	Wisconsin	2,883,326	1.8%		49	Vermont	317,233	0.2%
50	Wyoming	282,131	0.2%		50	Wyoming	282,131	0.2%
						District of Columbia	333,282	0.2%

Source: U.S. Bureau of the Census
"State Characteristics: Vintage 2012" (http://www.census.gov/popest/data/state/asrh/2012/index.html)

Male to Female Ratio in 2012

National Ratio = 96.9 Males per 100 Females

ALPHA ORDER

RANK	STATE	RATIO
45	Alabama	94.2
1	Alaska	108.9
12	Arizona	98.9
29	Arkansas	96.5
12	California	98.9
8	Colorado	100.8
41	Connecticut	95.1
47	Delaware	94.0
35	Florida	95.7
35	Georgia	95.7
4	Hawaii	101.7
10	Idaho	100.2
30	Illinois	96.4
27	Indiana	97.0
19	Iowa	98.4
12	Kansas	98.9
26	Kentucky	97.1
33	Louisiana	95.8
33	Maine	95.8
49	Maryland	93.9
47	Massachusetts	94.0
30	Michigan	96.4
17	Minnesota	98.7
44	Mississippi	94.4
32	Missouri	96.1
7	Montana	101.0
15	Nebraska	98.8
4	Nevada	101.7
23	New Hampshire	97.6
39	New Jersey	95.2
21	New Mexico	98.1
46	New York	94.1
41	North Carolina	95.1
3	North Dakota	103.4
37	Ohio	95.6
20	Oklahoma	98.2
21	Oregon	98.1
38	Pennsylvania	95.4
50	Rhode Island	93.8
43	South Carolina	94.7
8	South Dakota	100.8
39	Tennessee	95.2
15	Texas	98.8
6	Utah	101.2
25	Vermont	97.3
28	Virginia	96.6
11	Washington	99.6
24	West Virginia	97.4
18	Wisconsin	98.6
2	Wyoming	104.3

RANK ORDER

RANK	STATE	RATIO
1	Alaska	108.9
2	Wyoming	104.3
3	North Dakota	103.4
4	Hawaii	101.7
4	Nevada	101.7
6	Utah	101.2
7	Montana	101.0
8	Colorado	100.8
8	South Dakota	100.8
10	Idaho	100.2
11	Washington	99.6
12	Arizona	98.9
12	California	98.9
12	Kansas	98.9
15	Nebraska	98.8
15	Texas	98.8
17	Minnesota	98.7
18	Wisconsin	98.6
19	Iowa	98.4
20	Oklahoma	98.2
21	New Mexico	98.1
21	Oregon	98.1
23	New Hampshire	97.6
24	West Virginia	97.4
25	Vermont	97.3
26	Kentucky	97.1
27	Indiana	97.0
28	Virginia	96.6
29	Arkansas	96.5
30	Illinois	96.4
30	Michigan	96.4
32	Missouri	96.1
33	Louisiana	95.8
33	Maine	95.8
35	Florida	95.7
35	Georgia	95.7
37	Ohio	95.6
38	Pennsylvania	95.4
39	New Jersey	95.2
39	Tennessee	95.2
41	Connecticut	95.1
41	North Carolina	95.1
43	South Carolina	94.7
44	Mississippi	94.4
45	Alabama	94.2
46	New York	94.1
47	Delaware	94.0
47	Massachusetts	94.0
49	Maryland	93.9
50	Rhode Island	93.8
	District of Columbia	89.7

Source: CQ Press using data from U.S. Bureau of the Census
"State Characteristics: Vintage 2012" (http://www.census.gov/popest/data/state/asrh/2012/index.html)

White Population in 2012

National Total = 244,495,567*

RANK	STATE	POPULATION	% of USA
25	Alabama	3,373,844	1.4%
49	Alaska	493,430	0.2%
16	Arizona	5,522,144	2.3%
33	Arkansas	2,359,569	1.0%
1	California	28,033,826	11.5%
21	Colorado	4,572,022	1.9%
27	Connecticut	2,942,335	1.2%
45	Delaware	654,352	0.3%
3	Florida	15,120,082	6.2%
11	Georgia	6,231,978	2.5%
50	Hawaii	363,544	0.1%
39	Idaho	1,497,404	0.6%
6	Illinois	10,028,832	4.1%
13	Indiana	5,659,668	2.3%
30	Iowa	2,851,533	1.2%
32	Kansas	2,517,663	1.0%
22	Kentucky	3,882,987	1.6%
28	Louisiana	2,930,137	1.2%
40	Maine	1,266,849	0.5%
23	Maryland	3,579,276	1.5%
15	Massachusetts	5,560,222	2.3%
8	Michigan	7,920,263	3.2%
20	Minnesota	4,654,134	1.9%
35	Mississippi	1,788,664	0.7%
19	Missouri	5,049,604	2.1%
43	Montana	901,340	0.4%
38	Nebraska	1,668,779	0.7%
34	Nevada	2,128,047	0.9%
41	New Hampshire	1,247,076	0.5%
10	New Jersey	6,538,430	2.7%
37	New Mexico	1,735,255	0.7%
4	New York	13,930,819	5.7%
9	North Carolina	7,013,116	2.9%
46	North Dakota	630,215	0.3%
7	Ohio	9,630,901	3.9%
29	Oklahoma	2,881,880	1.2%
24	Oregon	3,444,767	1.4%
5	Pennsylvania	10,655,948	4.4%
42	Rhode Island	902,439	0.4%
26	South Carolina	3,229,346	1.3%
44	South Dakota	718,352	0.3%
17	Tennessee	5,117,456	2.1%
2	Texas	21,001,450	8.6%
31	Utah	2,620,788	1.1%
47	Vermont	597,050	0.2%
12	Virginia	5,818,810	2.4%
14	Washington	5,625,335	2.3%
36	West Virginia	1,743,721	0.7%
18	Wisconsin	5,052,112	2.1%
48	Wyoming	536,450	0.2%

RANK	STATE	POPULATION	% of USA
1	California	28,033,826	11.5%
2	Texas	21,001,450	8.6%
3	Florida	15,120,082	6.2%
4	New York	13,930,819	5.7%
5	Pennsylvania	10,655,948	4.4%
6	Illinois	10,028,832	4.1%
7	Ohio	9,630,901	3.9%
8	Michigan	7,920,263	3.2%
9	North Carolina	7,013,116	2.9%
10	New Jersey	6,538,430	2.7%
11	Georgia	6,231,978	2.5%
12	Virginia	5,818,810	2.4%
13	Indiana	5,659,668	2.3%
14	Washington	5,625,335	2.3%
15	Massachusetts	5,560,222	2.3%
16	Arizona	5,522,144	2.3%
17	Tennessee	5,117,456	2.1%
18	Wisconsin	5,052,112	2.1%
19	Missouri	5,049,604	2.1%
20	Minnesota	4,654,134	1.9%
21	Colorado	4,572,022	1.9%
22	Kentucky	3,882,987	1.6%
23	Maryland	3,579,276	1.5%
24	Oregon	3,444,767	1.4%
25	Alabama	3,373,844	1.4%
26	South Carolina	3,229,346	1.3%
27	Connecticut	2,942,335	1.2%
28	Louisiana	2,930,137	1.2%
29	Oklahoma	2,881,880	1.2%
30	Iowa	2,851,533	1.2%
31	Utah	2,620,788	1.1%
32	Kansas	2,517,663	1.0%
33	Arkansas	2,359,569	1.0%
34	Nevada	2,128,047	0.9%
35	Mississippi	1,788,664	0.7%
36	West Virginia	1,743,721	0.7%
37	New Mexico	1,735,255	0.7%
38	Nebraska	1,668,779	0.7%
39	Idaho	1,497,404	0.6%
40	Maine	1,266,849	0.5%
41	New Hampshire	1,247,076	0.5%
42	Rhode Island	902,439	0.4%
43	Montana	901,340	0.4%
44	South Dakota	718,352	0.3%
45	Delaware	654,352	0.3%
46	North Dakota	630,215	0.3%
47	Vermont	597,050	0.2%
48	Wyoming	536,450	0.2%
49	Alaska	493,430	0.2%
50	Hawaii	363,544	0.1%
	District of Columbia	271,323	0.1%

Source: U.S. Bureau of the Census

"State Characteristics: Vintage 2012" (http://www.census.gov/popest/data/state/asrh/2012/index.html)

*Those who identified themselves as one race. "White" is defined by Census as a person having origins in any of the original peoples of Europe, North Africa, or the Middle East. There are 197,705,655 non-Hispanic whites. Census states "Race is a self-identification data item in which respondents choose the race or races with which they most closely identify."

Percent of Population White in 2012

National Percent = 77.9%*

ALPHA ORDER

RANK	STATE	PERCENT
43	Alabama	70.0
45	Alaska	67.5
21	Arizona	84.3
31	Arkansas	80.0
38	California	73.7
15	Colorado	88.1
27	Connecticut	82.0
40	Delaware	71.4
33	Florida	78.3
47	Georgia	62.8
50	Hawaii	26.1
5	Idaho	93.8
34	Illinois	77.9
17	Indiana	86.6
7	Iowa	92.8
16	Kansas	87.2
12	Kentucky	88.6
46	Louisiana	63.7
2	Maine	95.3
48	Maryland	60.8
23	Massachusetts	83.7
30	Michigan	80.1
18	Minnesota	86.5
49	Mississippi	59.9
22	Missouri	83.9
11	Montana	89.7
10	Nebraska	89.9
35	Nevada	77.1
3	New Hampshire	94.4
37	New Jersey	73.8
26	New Mexico	83.2
41	New York	71.2
39	North Carolina	71.9
9	North Dakota	90.1
25	Ohio	83.4
36	Oklahoma	75.5
13	Oregon	88.3
24	Pennsylvania	83.5
20	Rhode Island	85.9
44	South Carolina	68.4
19	South Dakota	86.2
32	Tennessee	79.3
29	Texas	80.6
8	Utah	91.8
1	Vermont	95.4
42	Virginia	71.1
28	Washington	81.6
4	West Virginia	94.0
14	Wisconsin	88.2
6	Wyoming	93.1

RANK ORDER

RANK	STATE	PERCENT
1	Vermont	95.4
2	Maine	95.3
3	New Hampshire	94.4
4	West Virginia	94.0
5	Idaho	93.8
6	Wyoming	93.1
7	Iowa	92.8
8	Utah	91.8
9	North Dakota	90.1
10	Nebraska	89.9
11	Montana	89.7
12	Kentucky	88.6
13	Oregon	88.3
14	Wisconsin	88.2
15	Colorado	88.1
16	Kansas	87.2
17	Indiana	86.6
18	Minnesota	86.5
19	South Dakota	86.2
20	Rhode Island	85.9
21	Arizona	84.3
22	Missouri	83.9
23	Massachusetts	83.7
24	Pennsylvania	83.5
25	Ohio	83.4
26	New Mexico	83.2
27	Connecticut	82.0
28	Washington	81.6
29	Texas	80.6
30	Michigan	80.1
31	Arkansas	80.0
32	Tennessee	79.3
33	Florida	78.3
34	Illinois	77.9
35	Nevada	77.1
36	Oklahoma	75.5
37	New Jersey	73.8
38	California	73.7
39	North Carolina	71.9
40	Delaware	71.4
41	New York	71.2
42	Virginia	71.1
43	Alabama	70.0
44	South Carolina	68.4
45	Alaska	67.5
46	Louisiana	63.7
47	Georgia	62.8
48	Maryland	60.8
49	Mississippi	59.9
50	Hawaii	26.1

	District of Columbia	42.9

Source: CQ Press using data from U.S. Bureau of the Census
    "State Characteristics: Vintage 2012" (http://www.census.gov/popest/data/state/asrh/2012/index.html)
*Those who identified themselves as one race. "White" is defined by Census as a person having origins in any of the original peoples of Europe, North Africa, or the Middle East. Non-Hispanic whites comprise 63.0% of the total population. Census states "Race is a self-identification data item in which respondents choose the race or races with which they most closely identify."

Black Population in 2012

National Total = 41,204,793*

ALPHA ORDER

RANK	STATE	POPULATION	% of USA
16	Alabama	1,279,805	3.1%
42	Alaska	27,373	0.1%
26	Arizona	297,985	0.7%
22	Arkansas	459,739	1.1%
5	California	2,515,716	6.1%
31	Colorado	225,390	0.5%
23	Connecticut	401,496	1.0%
32	Delaware	202,090	0.5%
3	Florida	3,206,350	7.8%
4	Georgia	3,091,904	7.5%
41	Hawaii	29,905	0.1%
46	Idaho	12,037	0.0%
7	Illinois	1,900,578	4.6%
20	Indiana	616,199	1.5%
34	Iowa	97,080	0.2%
33	Kansas	178,820	0.4%
25	Kentucky	354,119	0.9%
10	Louisiana	1,491,433	3.6%
44	Maine	17,603	0.0%
8	Maryland	1,766,990	4.3%
21	Massachusetts	525,799	1.3%
13	Michigan	1,415,107	3.4%
27	Minnesota	297,962	0.7%
17	Mississippi	1,116,367	2.7%
19	Missouri	706,079	1.7%
50	Montana	5,679	0.0%
35	Nebraska	88,758	0.2%
30	Nevada	244,462	0.6%
43	New Hampshire	18,374	0.0%
15	New Jersey	1,298,879	3.2%
39	New Mexico	51,087	0.1%
1	New York	3,422,914	8.3%
6	North Carolina	2,147,599	5.2%
47	North Dakota	10,547	0.0%
12	Ohio	1,439,598	3.5%
28	Oklahoma	291,551	0.7%
36	Oregon	77,564	0.2%
11	Pennsylvania	1,456,977	3.5%
37	Rhode Island	77,123	0.2%
14	South Carolina	1,322,528	3.2%
45	South Dakota	13,939	0.0%
18	Tennessee	1,097,978	2.7%
2	Texas	3,216,242	7.8%
40	Utah	36,717	0.1%
49	Vermont	6,879	0.0%
9	Virginia	1,612,713	3.9%
29	Washington	268,660	0.7%
38	West Virginia	65,787	0.2%
24	Wisconsin	373,275	0.9%
48	Wyoming	8,555	0.0%

RANK ORDER

RANK	STATE	POPULATION	% of USA
1	New York	3,422,914	8.3%
2	Texas	3,216,242	7.8%
3	Florida	3,206,350	7.8%
4	Georgia	3,091,904	7.5%
5	California	2,515,716	6.1%
6	North Carolina	2,147,599	5.2%
7	Illinois	1,900,578	4.6%
8	Maryland	1,766,990	4.3%
9	Virginia	1,612,713	3.9%
10	Louisiana	1,491,433	3.6%
11	Pennsylvania	1,456,977	3.5%
12	Ohio	1,439,598	3.5%
13	Michigan	1,415,107	3.4%
14	South Carolina	1,322,528	3.2%
15	New Jersey	1,298,879	3.2%
16	Alabama	1,279,805	3.1%
17	Mississippi	1,116,367	2.7%
18	Tennessee	1,097,978	2.7%
19	Missouri	706,079	1.7%
20	Indiana	616,199	1.5%
21	Massachusetts	525,799	1.3%
22	Arkansas	459,739	1.1%
23	Connecticut	401,496	1.0%
24	Wisconsin	373,275	0.9%
25	Kentucky	354,119	0.9%
26	Arizona	297,985	0.7%
27	Minnesota	297,962	0.7%
28	Oklahoma	291,551	0.7%
29	Washington	268,660	0.7%
30	Nevada	244,462	0.6%
31	Colorado	225,390	0.5%
32	Delaware	202,090	0.5%
33	Kansas	178,820	0.4%
34	Iowa	97,080	0.2%
35	Nebraska	88,758	0.2%
36	Oregon	77,564	0.2%
37	Rhode Island	77,123	0.2%
38	West Virginia	65,787	0.2%
39	New Mexico	51,087	0.1%
40	Utah	36,717	0.1%
41	Hawaii	29,905	0.1%
42	Alaska	27,373	0.1%
43	New Hampshire	18,374	0.0%
44	Maine	17,603	0.0%
45	South Dakota	13,939	0.0%
46	Idaho	12,037	0.0%
47	North Dakota	10,547	0.0%
48	Wyoming	8,555	0.0%
49	Vermont	6,879	0.0%
50	Montana	5,679	0.0%
	District of Columbia	316,482	0.8%

Source: U.S. Bureau of the Census
"State Characteristics: Vintage 2012" (http://www.census.gov/popest/data/state/asrh/2012/index.html)
*Those who identified themselves as one race. "Black" is defined by Census as a person having origins in any of the Black racial groups of Africa. Census states "Race is a self-identification data item in which respondents choose the race or races with which they most closely identify."

Percent of Population Black in 2012

National Percent = 13.1%*

ALPHA ORDER

RANK	STATE	PERCENT
6	Alabama	26.5
36	Alaska	3.7
33	Arizona	4.5
13	Arkansas	15.6
28	California	6.6
34	Colorado	4.3
21	Connecticut	11.2
7	Delaware	22.0
12	Florida	16.6
3	Georgia	31.2
40	Hawaii	2.1
49	Idaho	0.8
14	Illinois	14.8
22	Indiana	9.4
38	Iowa	3.2
30	Kansas	6.2
24	Kentucky	8.1
2	Louisiana	32.4
46	Maine	1.3
4	Maryland	30.0
25	Massachusetts	7.9
16	Michigan	14.3
31	Minnesota	5.5
1	Mississippi	37.4
19	Missouri	11.7
50	Montana	0.6
32	Nebraska	4.8
23	Nevada	8.9
45	New Hampshire	1.4
15	New Jersey	14.7
39	New Mexico	2.4
10	New York	17.5
7	North Carolina	22.0
43	North Dakota	1.5
17	Ohio	12.5
26	Oklahoma	7.6
41	Oregon	2.0
20	Pennsylvania	11.4
27	Rhode Island	7.3
5	South Carolina	28.0
42	South Dakota	1.7
11	Tennessee	17.0
18	Texas	12.3
46	Utah	1.3
48	Vermont	1.1
9	Virginia	19.7
35	Washington	3.9
37	West Virginia	3.5
29	Wisconsin	6.5
43	Wyoming	1.5

RANK ORDER

RANK	STATE	PERCENT
1	Mississippi	37.4
2	Louisiana	32.4
3	Georgia	31.2
4	Maryland	30.0
5	South Carolina	28.0
6	Alabama	26.5
7	Delaware	22.0
7	North Carolina	22.0
9	Virginia	19.7
10	New York	17.5
11	Tennessee	17.0
12	Florida	16.6
13	Arkansas	15.6
14	Illinois	14.8
15	New Jersey	14.7
16	Michigan	14.3
17	Ohio	12.5
18	Texas	12.3
19	Missouri	11.7
20	Pennsylvania	11.4
21	Connecticut	11.2
22	Indiana	9.4
23	Nevada	8.9
24	Kentucky	8.1
25	Massachusetts	7.9
26	Oklahoma	7.6
27	Rhode Island	7.3
28	California	6.6
29	Wisconsin	6.5
30	Kansas	6.2
31	Minnesota	5.5
32	Nebraska	4.8
33	Arizona	4.5
34	Colorado	4.3
35	Washington	3.9
36	Alaska	3.7
37	West Virginia	3.5
38	Iowa	3.2
39	New Mexico	2.4
40	Hawaii	2.1
41	Oregon	2.0
42	South Dakota	1.7
43	North Dakota	1.5
43	Wyoming	1.5
45	New Hampshire	1.4
46	Maine	1.3
46	Utah	1.3
48	Vermont	1.1
49	Idaho	0.8
50	Montana	0.6

District of Columbia — 50.1

Source: CQ Press using data from U.S. Bureau of the Census
"State Characteristics: Vintage 2012" (http://www.census.gov/popest/data/state/asrh/2012/index.html)
*Those who identified themselves as one race. "Black" is defined by Census as a person having origins in any of the Black racial groups of Africa. Census states "Race is a self-identification data item in which respondents choose the race or races with which they most closely identify."

Hispanic Population in 2012

National Total = 53,027,708*

ALPHA ORDER

RANK	STATE	POPULATION	% of USA
33	Alabama	196,032	0.4%
43	Alaska	44,869	0.1%
6	Arizona	1,976,106	3.7%
32	Arkansas	199,693	0.4%
1	California	14,537,666	27.4%
8	Colorado	1,088,744	2.1%
18	Connecticut	510,645	1.0%
41	Delaware	78,813	0.1%
3	Florida	4,484,199	8.5%
10	Georgia	909,902	1.7%
39	Hawaii	131,744	0.2%
34	Idaho	185,160	0.3%
5	Illinois	2,101,208	4.0%
21	Indiana	412,609	0.8%
36	Iowa	162,894	0.3%
26	Kansas	317,061	0.6%
37	Kentucky	142,028	0.3%
31	Louisiana	208,325	0.4%
48	Maine	18,599	0.0%
17	Maryland	512,010	1.0%
16	Massachusetts	674,073	1.3%
20	Michigan	456,330	0.9%
28	Minnesota	264,359	0.5%
40	Mississippi	85,260	0.2%
30	Missouri	225,314	0.4%
45	Montana	31,552	0.1%
35	Nebraska	179,970	0.3%
14	Nevada	752,049	1.4%
44	New Hampshire	40,042	0.1%
7	New Jersey	1,641,398	3.1%
9	New Mexico	979,722	1.8%
4	New York	3,552,781	6.7%
11	North Carolina	850,853	1.6%
49	North Dakota	17,230	0.0%
23	Ohio	377,119	0.7%
24	Oklahoma	356,300	0.7%
19	Oregon	474,157	0.9%
13	Pennsylvania	781,202	1.5%
38	Rhode Island	138,549	0.3%
29	South Carolina	249,712	0.5%
46	South Dakota	25,715	0.0%
27	Tennessee	312,732	0.6%
2	Texas	9,960,900	18.8%
22	Utah	379,436	0.7%
50	Vermont	10,057	0.0%
15	Virginia	687,496	1.3%
12	Washington	807,599	1.5%
47	West Virginia	24,530	0.0%
25	Wisconsin	355,468	0.7%
42	Wyoming	54,770	0.1%

RANK ORDER

RANK	STATE	POPULATION	% of USA
1	California	14,537,666	27.4%
2	Texas	9,960,900	18.8%
3	Florida	4,484,199	8.5%
4	New York	3,552,781	6.7%
5	Illinois	2,101,208	4.0%
6	Arizona	1,976,106	3.7%
7	New Jersey	1,641,398	3.1%
8	Colorado	1,088,744	2.1%
9	New Mexico	979,722	1.8%
10	Georgia	909,902	1.7%
11	North Carolina	850,853	1.6%
12	Washington	807,599	1.5%
13	Pennsylvania	781,202	1.5%
14	Nevada	752,049	1.4%
15	Virginia	687,496	1.3%
16	Massachusetts	674,073	1.3%
17	Maryland	512,010	1.0%
18	Connecticut	510,645	1.0%
19	Oregon	474,157	0.9%
20	Michigan	456,330	0.9%
21	Indiana	412,609	0.8%
22	Utah	379,436	0.7%
23	Ohio	377,119	0.7%
24	Oklahoma	356,300	0.7%
25	Wisconsin	355,468	0.7%
26	Kansas	317,061	0.6%
27	Tennessee	312,732	0.6%
28	Minnesota	264,359	0.5%
29	South Carolina	249,712	0.5%
30	Missouri	225,314	0.4%
31	Louisiana	208,325	0.4%
32	Arkansas	199,693	0.4%
33	Alabama	196,032	0.4%
34	Idaho	185,160	0.3%
35	Nebraska	179,970	0.3%
36	Iowa	162,894	0.3%
37	Kentucky	142,028	0.3%
38	Rhode Island	138,549	0.3%
39	Hawaii	131,744	0.2%
40	Mississippi	85,260	0.2%
41	Delaware	78,813	0.1%
42	Wyoming	54,770	0.1%
43	Alaska	44,869	0.1%
44	New Hampshire	40,042	0.1%
45	Montana	31,552	0.1%
46	South Dakota	25,715	0.0%
47	West Virginia	24,530	0.0%
48	Maine	18,599	0.0%
49	North Dakota	17,230	0.0%
50	Vermont	10,057	0.0%
	District of Columbia	62,726	0.1%

Source: U.S. Bureau of the Census
   "State Characteristics: Vintage 2012" (http://www.census.gov/popest/data/state/asrh/2012/index.html)
*Persons of Hispanic origin may be of any race. Census states "Race is a self-identification data item in which respondents choose the race or races with which they most closely identify."

Percent of Population Hispanic in 2012

National Percent = 16.9%*

ALPHA ORDER

RANK	STATE	PERCENT
39	Alabama	4.1
31	Alaska	6.1
4	Arizona	30.2
28	Arkansas	6.8
2	California	38.2
7	Colorado	21.0
11	Connecticut	14.2
26	Delaware	8.6
6	Florida	23.2
23	Georgia	9.2
20	Hawaii	9.5
16	Idaho	11.6
10	Illinois	16.3
29	Indiana	6.3
33	Iowa	5.3
17	Kansas	11.0
42	Kentucky	3.2
38	Louisiana	4.5
49	Maine	1.4
24	Maryland	8.7
18	Massachusetts	10.1
37	Michigan	4.6
35	Minnesota	4.9
46	Mississippi	2.9
40	Missouri	3.7
43	Montana	3.1
19	Nebraska	9.7
5	Nevada	27.3
45	New Hampshire	3.0
8	New Jersey	18.5
1	New Mexico	47.0
9	New York	18.2
24	North Carolina	8.7
47	North Dakota	2.5
41	Ohio	3.3
22	Oklahoma	9.3
14	Oregon	12.2
31	Pennsylvania	6.1
13	Rhode Island	13.2
33	South Carolina	5.3
43	South Dakota	3.1
36	Tennessee	4.8
2	Texas	38.2
12	Utah	13.3
48	Vermont	1.6
27	Virginia	8.4
15	Washington	11.7
50	West Virginia	1.3
30	Wisconsin	6.2
20	Wyoming	9.5

RANK ORDER

RANK	STATE	PERCENT
1	New Mexico	47.0
2	California	38.2
2	Texas	38.2
4	Arizona	30.2
5	Nevada	27.3
6	Florida	23.2
7	Colorado	21.0
8	New Jersey	18.5
9	New York	18.2
10	Illinois	16.3
11	Connecticut	14.2
12	Utah	13.3
13	Rhode Island	13.2
14	Oregon	12.2
15	Washington	11.7
16	Idaho	11.6
17	Kansas	11.0
18	Massachusetts	10.1
19	Nebraska	9.7
20	Hawaii	9.5
20	Wyoming	9.5
22	Oklahoma	9.3
23	Georgia	9.2
24	Maryland	8.7
24	North Carolina	8.7
26	Delaware	8.6
27	Virginia	8.4
28	Arkansas	6.8
29	Indiana	6.3
30	Wisconsin	6.2
31	Alaska	6.1
31	Pennsylvania	6.1
33	Iowa	5.3
33	South Carolina	5.3
35	Minnesota	4.9
36	Tennessee	4.8
37	Michigan	4.6
38	Louisiana	4.5
39	Alabama	4.1
40	Missouri	3.7
41	Ohio	3.3
42	Kentucky	3.2
43	Montana	3.1
43	South Dakota	3.1
45	New Hampshire	3.0
46	Mississippi	2.9
47	North Dakota	2.5
48	Vermont	1.6
49	Maine	1.4
50	West Virginia	1.3
	District of Columbia	9.9

Source: CQ Press using data from U.S. Bureau of the Census

"State Characteristics: Vintage 2012" (http://www.census.gov/popest/data/state/asrh/2012/index.html)

*Persons of Hispanic origin may be of any race. Census states "Race is a self-identification data item in which respondents choose the race or races with which they most closely identify."

Asian Population in 2012

National Total = 16,145,821*

ALPHA ORDER

RANK	STATE	POPULATION	% of USA
33	Alabama	59,602	0.4%
35	Alaska	41,986	0.3%
19	Arizona	204,840	1.3%
36	Arkansas	41,338	0.3%
1	California	5,294,255	32.8%
21	Colorado	155,031	1.0%
22	Connecticut	150,529	0.9%
40	Delaware	32,141	0.2%
8	Florida	511,960	3.2%
13	Georgia	351,734	2.2%
6	Hawaii	532,599	3.3%
43	Idaho	21,899	0.1%
5	Illinois	638,108	4.0%
24	Indiana	116,029	0.7%
32	Iowa	60,004	0.4%
28	Kansas	74,598	0.5%
34	Kentucky	55,336	0.3%
27	Louisiana	77,252	0.5%
44	Maine	14,810	0.1%
12	Maryland	352,347	2.2%
10	Massachusetts	387,770	2.4%
14	Michigan	259,806	1.6%
16	Minnesota	235,120	1.5%
42	Mississippi	28,255	0.2%
25	Missouri	107,092	0.7%
49	Montana	7,315	0.0%
37	Nebraska	36,467	0.2%
17	Nevada	217,264	1.3%
41	New Hampshire	31,126	0.2%
4	New Jersey	794,923	4.9%
39	New Mexico	33,665	0.2%
2	New York	1,566,191	9.7%
15	North Carolina	238,933	1.5%
48	North Dakota	7,840	0.0%
18	Ohio	210,865	1.3%
29	Oklahoma	72,539	0.4%
20	Oregon	156,077	1.0%
11	Pennsylvania	383,917	2.4%
38	Rhode Island	33,852	0.2%
30	South Carolina	67,529	0.4%
46	South Dakota	9,005	0.1%
26	Tennessee	102,862	0.6%
3	Texas	1,095,443	6.8%
31	Utah	63,857	0.4%
47	Vermont	8,912	0.1%
9	Virginia	487,505	3.0%
7	Washington	531,395	3.3%
45	West Virginia	13,796	0.1%
23	Wisconsin	140,885	0.9%
50	Wyoming	5,183	0.0%

RANK ORDER

RANK	STATE	POPULATION	% of USA
1	California	5,294,255	32.8%
2	New York	1,566,191	9.7%
3	Texas	1,095,443	6.8%
4	New Jersey	794,923	4.9%
5	Illinois	638,108	4.0%
6	Hawaii	532,599	3.3%
7	Washington	531,395	3.3%
8	Florida	511,960	3.2%
9	Virginia	487,505	3.0%
10	Massachusetts	387,770	2.4%
11	Pennsylvania	383,917	2.4%
12	Maryland	352,347	2.2%
13	Georgia	351,734	2.2%
14	Michigan	259,806	1.6%
15	North Carolina	238,933	1.5%
16	Minnesota	235,120	1.5%
17	Nevada	217,264	1.3%
18	Ohio	210,865	1.3%
19	Arizona	204,840	1.3%
20	Oregon	156,077	1.0%
21	Colorado	155,031	1.0%
22	Connecticut	150,529	0.9%
23	Wisconsin	140,885	0.9%
24	Indiana	116,029	0.7%
25	Missouri	107,092	0.7%
26	Tennessee	102,862	0.6%
27	Louisiana	77,252	0.5%
28	Kansas	74,598	0.5%
29	Oklahoma	72,539	0.4%
30	South Carolina	67,529	0.4%
31	Utah	63,857	0.4%
32	Iowa	60,004	0.4%
33	Alabama	59,602	0.4%
34	Kentucky	55,336	0.3%
35	Alaska	41,986	0.3%
36	Arkansas	41,338	0.3%
37	Nebraska	36,467	0.2%
38	Rhode Island	33,852	0.2%
39	New Mexico	33,665	0.2%
40	Delaware	32,141	0.2%
41	New Hampshire	31,126	0.2%
42	Mississippi	28,255	0.2%
43	Idaho	21,899	0.1%
44	Maine	14,810	0.1%
45	West Virginia	13,796	0.1%
46	South Dakota	9,005	0.1%
47	Vermont	8,912	0.1%
48	North Dakota	7,840	0.0%
49	Montana	7,315	0.0%
50	Wyoming	5,183	0.0%
	District of Columbia	24,034	0.1%

Source: U.S. Bureau of the Census
    "State Characteristics: Vintage 2012" (http://www.census.gov/popest/data/state/asrh/2012/index.html)
*Those who identified themselves as one race. Census states "Race is a self-identification data item in which respondents choose the race or races with which they most closely identify."

Percent of Population Asian in 2012

National Percent = 5.1%*

<table>
<tr><td colspan="3">ALPHA ORDER</td><td colspan="3">RANK ORDER</td></tr>
<tr><td>RANK</td><td>STATE</td><td>PERCENT</td><td>RANK</td><td>STATE</td><td>PERCENT</td></tr>
<tr><td>43</td><td>Alabama</td><td>1.2</td><td>1</td><td>Hawaii</td><td>38.3</td></tr>
<tr><td>10</td><td>Alaska</td><td>5.7</td><td>2</td><td>California</td><td>13.9</td></tr>
<tr><td>19</td><td>Arizona</td><td>3.1</td><td>3</td><td>New Jersey</td><td>9.0</td></tr>
<tr><td>38</td><td>Arkansas</td><td>1.4</td><td>4</td><td>New York</td><td>8.0</td></tr>
<tr><td>2</td><td>California</td><td>13.9</td><td>5</td><td>Nevada</td><td>7.9</td></tr>
<tr><td>20</td><td>Colorado</td><td>3.0</td><td>6</td><td>Washington</td><td>7.7</td></tr>
<tr><td>13</td><td>Connecticut</td><td>4.2</td><td>7</td><td>Maryland</td><td>6.0</td></tr>
<tr><td>16</td><td>Delaware</td><td>3.5</td><td>7</td><td>Virginia</td><td>6.0</td></tr>
<tr><td>22</td><td>Florida</td><td>2.7</td><td>9</td><td>Massachusetts</td><td>5.8</td></tr>
<tr><td>16</td><td>Georgia</td><td>3.5</td><td>10</td><td>Alaska</td><td>5.7</td></tr>
<tr><td>1</td><td>Hawaii</td><td>38.3</td><td>11</td><td>Illinois</td><td>5.0</td></tr>
<tr><td>38</td><td>Idaho</td><td>1.4</td><td>12</td><td>Minnesota</td><td>4.4</td></tr>
<tr><td>11</td><td>Illinois</td><td>5.0</td><td>13</td><td>Connecticut</td><td>4.2</td></tr>
<tr><td>32</td><td>Indiana</td><td>1.8</td><td>13</td><td>Texas</td><td>4.2</td></tr>
<tr><td>29</td><td>Iowa</td><td>2.0</td><td>15</td><td>Oregon</td><td>4.0</td></tr>
<tr><td>23</td><td>Kansas</td><td>2.6</td><td>16</td><td>Delaware</td><td>3.5</td></tr>
<tr><td>42</td><td>Kentucky</td><td>1.3</td><td>16</td><td>Georgia</td><td>3.5</td></tr>
<tr><td>35</td><td>Louisiana</td><td>1.7</td><td>18</td><td>Rhode Island</td><td>3.2</td></tr>
<tr><td>44</td><td>Maine</td><td>1.1</td><td>19</td><td>Arizona</td><td>3.1</td></tr>
<tr><td>7</td><td>Maryland</td><td>6.0</td><td>20</td><td>Colorado</td><td>3.0</td></tr>
<tr><td>9</td><td>Massachusetts</td><td>5.8</td><td>20</td><td>Pennsylvania</td><td>3.0</td></tr>
<tr><td>23</td><td>Michigan</td><td>2.6</td><td>22</td><td>Florida</td><td>2.7</td></tr>
<tr><td>12</td><td>Minnesota</td><td>4.4</td><td>23</td><td>Kansas</td><td>2.6</td></tr>
<tr><td>47</td><td>Mississippi</td><td>0.9</td><td>23</td><td>Michigan</td><td>2.6</td></tr>
<tr><td>32</td><td>Missouri</td><td>1.8</td><td>25</td><td>North Carolina</td><td>2.5</td></tr>
<tr><td>49</td><td>Montana</td><td>0.7</td><td>25</td><td>Wisconsin</td><td>2.5</td></tr>
<tr><td>29</td><td>Nebraska</td><td>2.0</td><td>27</td><td>New Hampshire</td><td>2.4</td></tr>
<tr><td>5</td><td>Nevada</td><td>7.9</td><td>28</td><td>Utah</td><td>2.2</td></tr>
<tr><td>27</td><td>New Hampshire</td><td>2.4</td><td>29</td><td>Iowa</td><td>2.0</td></tr>
<tr><td>3</td><td>New Jersey</td><td>9.0</td><td>29</td><td>Nebraska</td><td>2.0</td></tr>
<tr><td>36</td><td>New Mexico</td><td>1.6</td><td>31</td><td>Oklahoma</td><td>1.9</td></tr>
<tr><td>4</td><td>New York</td><td>8.0</td><td>32</td><td>Indiana</td><td>1.8</td></tr>
<tr><td>25</td><td>North Carolina</td><td>2.5</td><td>32</td><td>Missouri</td><td>1.8</td></tr>
<tr><td>44</td><td>North Dakota</td><td>1.1</td><td>32</td><td>Ohio</td><td>1.8</td></tr>
<tr><td>32</td><td>Ohio</td><td>1.8</td><td>35</td><td>Louisiana</td><td>1.7</td></tr>
<tr><td>31</td><td>Oklahoma</td><td>1.9</td><td>36</td><td>New Mexico</td><td>1.6</td></tr>
<tr><td>15</td><td>Oregon</td><td>4.0</td><td>36</td><td>Tennessee</td><td>1.6</td></tr>
<tr><td>20</td><td>Pennsylvania</td><td>3.0</td><td>38</td><td>Arkansas</td><td>1.4</td></tr>
<tr><td>18</td><td>Rhode Island</td><td>3.2</td><td>38</td><td>Idaho</td><td>1.4</td></tr>
<tr><td>38</td><td>South Carolina</td><td>1.4</td><td>38</td><td>South Carolina</td><td>1.4</td></tr>
<tr><td>44</td><td>South Dakota</td><td>1.1</td><td>38</td><td>Vermont</td><td>1.4</td></tr>
<tr><td>36</td><td>Tennessee</td><td>1.6</td><td>42</td><td>Kentucky</td><td>1.3</td></tr>
<tr><td>13</td><td>Texas</td><td>4.2</td><td>43</td><td>Alabama</td><td>1.2</td></tr>
<tr><td>28</td><td>Utah</td><td>2.2</td><td>44</td><td>Maine</td><td>1.1</td></tr>
<tr><td>38</td><td>Vermont</td><td>1.4</td><td>44</td><td>North Dakota</td><td>1.1</td></tr>
<tr><td>7</td><td>Virginia</td><td>6.0</td><td>44</td><td>South Dakota</td><td>1.1</td></tr>
<tr><td>6</td><td>Washington</td><td>7.7</td><td>47</td><td>Mississippi</td><td>0.9</td></tr>
<tr><td>49</td><td>West Virginia</td><td>0.7</td><td>47</td><td>Wyoming</td><td>0.9</td></tr>
<tr><td>25</td><td>Wisconsin</td><td>2.5</td><td>49</td><td>Montana</td><td>0.7</td></tr>
<tr><td>47</td><td>Wyoming</td><td>0.9</td><td>49</td><td>West Virginia</td><td>0.7</td></tr>
<tr><td></td><td></td><td></td><td></td><td>District of Columbia</td><td>3.8</td></tr>
</table>

Source: CQ Press using data from U.S. Bureau of the Census
"State Characteristics: Vintage 2012" (http://www.census.gov/popest/data/state/asrh/2012/index.html)
*Those who identified themselves as one race. Census states "Race is a self-identification data item in which respondents choose the race or races with which they most closely identify."

American Indian Population in 2012

National Total = 3,857,495*

RANK	STATE	POPULATION	% of USA
28	Alabama	33,579	0.9%
9	Alaska	108,249	2.8%
2	Arizona	345,622	9.0%
33	Arkansas	27,647	0.7%
1	California	639,740	16.6%
11	Colorado	81,688	2.1%
39	Connecticut	17,688	0.5%
46	Delaware	6,161	0.2%
10	Florida	95,218	2.5%
20	Georgia	50,539	1.3%
47	Hawaii	5,507	0.1%
35	Idaho	26,684	0.7%
12	Illinois	75,948	2.0%
36	Indiana	25,494	0.7%
42	Iowa	14,179	0.4%
27	Kansas	33,909	0.9%
43	Kentucky	12,429	0.3%
26	Louisiana	34,249	0.9%
45	Maine	8,859	0.2%
29	Maryland	32,275	0.8%
31	Massachusetts	31,172	0.8%
14	Michigan	69,751	1.8%
15	Minnesota	68,961	1.8%
40	Mississippi	17,501	0.5%
30	Missouri	31,631	0.8%
17	Montana	65,164	1.7%
38	Nebraska	24,281	0.6%
21	Nevada	44,571	1.2%
49	New Hampshire	3,633	0.1%
19	New Jersey	52,255	1.4%
5	New Mexico	213,081	5.5%
6	New York	186,613	4.8%
7	North Carolina	150,965	3.9%
25	North Dakota	38,283	1.0%
32	Ohio	30,606	0.8%
3	Oklahoma	341,844	8.9%
16	Oregon	68,955	1.8%
24	Pennsylvania	41,680	1.1%
44	Rhode Island	9,358	0.2%
37	South Carolina	25,254	0.7%
13	South Dakota	74,223	1.9%
34	Tennessee	27,247	0.7%
4	Texas	265,563	6.9%
23	Utah	42,049	1.1%
50	Vermont	2,280	0.1%
22	Virginia	43,768	1.1%
8	Washington	126,526	3.3%
48	West Virginia	4,104	0.1%
18	Wisconsin	62,021	1.6%
41	Wyoming	15,003	0.4%

RANK	STATE	POPULATION	% of USA
1	California	639,740	16.6%
2	Arizona	345,622	9.0%
3	Oklahoma	341,844	8.9%
4	Texas	265,563	6.9%
5	New Mexico	213,081	5.5%
6	New York	186,613	4.8%
7	North Carolina	150,965	3.9%
8	Washington	126,526	3.3%
9	Alaska	108,249	2.8%
10	Florida	95,218	2.5%
11	Colorado	81,688	2.1%
12	Illinois	75,948	2.0%
13	South Dakota	74,223	1.9%
14	Michigan	69,751	1.8%
15	Minnesota	68,961	1.8%
16	Oregon	68,955	1.8%
17	Montana	65,164	1.7%
18	Wisconsin	62,021	1.6%
19	New Jersey	52,255	1.4%
20	Georgia	50,539	1.3%
21	Nevada	44,571	1.2%
22	Virginia	43,768	1.1%
23	Utah	42,049	1.1%
24	Pennsylvania	41,680	1.1%
25	North Dakota	38,283	1.0%
26	Louisiana	34,249	0.9%
27	Kansas	33,909	0.9%
28	Alabama	33,579	0.9%
29	Maryland	32,275	0.8%
30	Missouri	31,631	0.8%
31	Massachusetts	31,172	0.8%
32	Ohio	30,606	0.8%
33	Arkansas	27,647	0.7%
34	Tennessee	27,247	0.7%
35	Idaho	26,684	0.7%
36	Indiana	25,494	0.7%
37	South Carolina	25,254	0.7%
38	Nebraska	24,281	0.6%
39	Connecticut	17,688	0.5%
40	Mississippi	17,501	0.5%
41	Wyoming	15,003	0.4%
42	Iowa	14,179	0.4%
43	Kentucky	12,429	0.3%
44	Rhode Island	9,358	0.2%
45	Maine	8,859	0.2%
46	Delaware	6,161	0.2%
47	Hawaii	5,507	0.1%
48	West Virginia	4,104	0.1%
49	New Hampshire	3,633	0.1%
50	Vermont	2,280	0.1%
	District of Columbia	3,488	0.1%

Source: U.S. Bureau of the Census
   "State Characteristics: Vintage 2012" (http://www.census.gov/popest/data/state/asrh/2012/index.html)
*Those who identified themselves as one race. Includes Alaska Native populations. Census states "Race is a self-identification data item in which respondents choose the race or races with which they most closely identify."

Percent of Population American Indian in 2012

National Percent = 1.2%*

ALPHA ORDER

RANK	STATE	PERCENT
25	Alabama	0.7
1	Alaska	14.8
7	Arizona	5.3
23	Arkansas	0.9
11	California	1.7
13	Colorado	1.6
33	Connecticut	0.5
25	Delaware	0.7
33	Florida	0.5
33	Georgia	0.5
42	Hawaii	0.4
11	Idaho	1.7
30	Illinois	0.6
42	Indiana	0.4
33	Iowa	0.5
19	Kansas	1.2
46	Kentucky	0.3
25	Louisiana	0.7
25	Maine	0.7
33	Maryland	0.5
33	Massachusetts	0.5
25	Michigan	0.7
17	Minnesota	1.3
30	Mississippi	0.6
33	Missouri	0.5
5	Montana	6.5
17	Nebraska	1.3
13	Nevada	1.6
46	New Hampshire	0.3
30	New Jersey	0.6
2	New Mexico	10.2
21	New York	1.0
15	North Carolina	1.5
6	North Dakota	5.5
46	Ohio	0.3
3	Oklahoma	9.0
9	Oregon	1.8
46	Pennsylvania	0.3
23	Rhode Island	0.9
33	South Carolina	0.5
4	South Dakota	8.9
42	Tennessee	0.4
21	Texas	1.0
15	Utah	1.5
42	Vermont	0.4
33	Virginia	0.5
9	Washington	1.8
50	West Virginia	0.2
20	Wisconsin	1.1
8	Wyoming	2.6

RANK ORDER

RANK	STATE	PERCENT
1	Alaska	14.8
2	New Mexico	10.2
3	Oklahoma	9.0
4	South Dakota	8.9
5	Montana	6.5
6	North Dakota	5.5
7	Arizona	5.3
8	Wyoming	2.6
9	Oregon	1.8
9	Washington	1.8
11	California	1.7
11	Idaho	1.7
13	Colorado	1.6
13	Nevada	1.6
15	North Carolina	1.5
15	Utah	1.5
17	Minnesota	1.3
17	Nebraska	1.3
19	Kansas	1.2
20	Wisconsin	1.1
21	New York	1.0
21	Texas	1.0
23	Arkansas	0.9
23	Rhode Island	0.9
25	Alabama	0.7
25	Delaware	0.7
25	Louisiana	0.7
25	Maine	0.7
25	Michigan	0.7
30	Illinois	0.6
30	Mississippi	0.6
30	New Jersey	0.6
33	Connecticut	0.5
33	Florida	0.5
33	Georgia	0.5
33	Iowa	0.5
33	Maryland	0.5
33	Massachusetts	0.5
33	Missouri	0.5
33	South Carolina	0.5
33	Virginia	0.5
42	Hawaii	0.4
42	Indiana	0.4
42	Tennessee	0.4
42	Vermont	0.4
46	Kentucky	0.3
46	New Hampshire	0.3
46	Ohio	0.3
46	Pennsylvania	0.3
50	West Virginia	0.2

District of Columbia — 0.6

Source: CQ Press using data from U.S. Bureau of the Census
"State Characteristics: Vintage 2012" (http://www.census.gov/popest/data/state/asrh/2012/index.html)
*Those who identified themselves as one race. Includes Alaska Native populations. Census states "Race is a self-identification data item in which respondents choose the race or races with which they most closely identify."

Native Hawaiian or Other Pacific Islander Population in 2012

National Total = 707,228*

ALPHA ORDER				RANK ORDER			
RANK	STATE	POPULATION	% of USA	RANK	STATE	POPULATION	% of USA
26	Alabama	5,270	0.7%	1	California	187,855	26.6%
15	Alaska	8,558	1.2%	2	Hawaii	140,112	19.8%
9	Arizona	16,922	2.4%	3	Washington	46,143	6.5%
20	Arkansas	7,495	1.1%	4	Texas	33,980	4.8%
1	California	187,855	26.6%	5	Utah	27,563	3.9%
13	Colorado	9,231	1.3%	6	New York	25,101	3.5%
30	Connecticut	3,641	0.5%	7	Florida	20,454	2.9%
43	Delaware	766	0.1%	8	Nevada	20,121	2.8%
7	Florida	20,454	2.9%	9	Arizona	16,922	2.4%
11	Georgia	11,061	1.6%	10	Oregon	15,848	2.2%
2	Hawaii	140,112	19.8%	11	Georgia	11,061	1.6%
35	Idaho	2,916	0.4%	12	North Carolina	10,834	1.5%
17	Illinois	7,877	1.1%	13	Colorado	9,231	1.3%
28	Indiana	3,769	0.5%	14	Virginia	8,830	1.2%
38	Iowa	2,634	0.4%	15	Alaska	8,558	1.2%
34	Kansas	2,953	0.4%	16	New Jersey	8,228	1.2%
31	Kentucky	3,441	0.5%	17	Illinois	7,877	1.1%
36	Louisiana	2,781	0.4%	18	Missouri	7,821	1.1%
48	Maine	513	0.1%	19	Pennsylvania	7,723	1.1%
24	Maryland	5,674	0.8%	20	Arkansas	7,495	1.1%
21	Massachusetts	6,304	0.9%	21	Massachusetts	6,304	0.9%
29	Michigan	3,720	0.5%	22	Oklahoma	5,976	0.8%
33	Minnesota	3,206	0.5%	23	Tennessee	5,788	0.8%
40	Mississippi	1,715	0.2%	24	Maryland	5,674	0.8%
18	Missouri	7,821	1.1%	25	Ohio	5,597	0.8%
42	Montana	774	0.1%	26	Alabama	5,270	0.7%
39	Nebraska	2,163	0.3%	27	South Carolina	4,104	0.6%
8	Nevada	20,121	2.8%	28	Indiana	3,769	0.5%
45	New Hampshire	596	0.1%	29	Michigan	3,720	0.5%
16	New Jersey	8,228	1.2%	30	Connecticut	3,641	0.5%
32	New Mexico	3,327	0.5%	31	Kentucky	3,441	0.5%
6	New York	25,101	3.5%	32	New Mexico	3,327	0.5%
12	North Carolina	10,834	1.5%	33	Minnesota	3,206	0.5%
49	North Dakota	475	0.1%	34	Kansas	2,953	0.4%
25	Ohio	5,597	0.8%	35	Idaho	2,916	0.4%
22	Oklahoma	5,976	0.8%	36	Louisiana	2,781	0.4%
10	Oregon	15,848	2.2%	37	Wisconsin	2,640	0.4%
19	Pennsylvania	7,723	1.1%	38	Iowa	2,634	0.4%
41	Rhode Island	1,648	0.2%	39	Nebraska	2,163	0.3%
27	South Carolina	4,104	0.6%	40	Mississippi	1,715	0.2%
44	South Dakota	608	0.1%	41	Rhode Island	1,648	0.2%
23	Tennessee	5,788	0.8%	42	Montana	774	0.1%
4	Texas	33,980	4.8%	43	Delaware	766	0.1%
5	Utah	27,563	3.9%	44	South Dakota	608	0.1%
50	Vermont	203	0.0%	45	New Hampshire	596	0.1%
14	Virginia	8,830	1.2%	46	Wyoming	575	0.1%
3	Washington	46,143	6.5%	47	West Virginia	563	0.1%
47	West Virginia	563	0.1%	48	Maine	513	0.1%
37	Wisconsin	2,640	0.4%	49	North Dakota	475	0.1%
46	Wyoming	575	0.1%	50	Vermont	203	0.0%
					District of Columbia	1,131	0.2%

Source: U.S. Bureau of the Census

"State Characteristics: Vintage 2012" (http://www.census.gov/popest/data/state/asrh/2012/index.html)

*Those who identified themselves as one race. Census states "Race is a self-identification data item in which respondents choose the race or races with which they most closely identify."

Percent of Population Native Hawaiian or Other Pacific Islander in 2012

National Percent = 0.2%*

<table>
<tr><td colspan="3">ALPHA ORDER</td><td colspan="3">RANK ORDER</td></tr>
<tr><td>RANK</td><td>STATE</td><td>PERCENT</td><td>RANK</td><td>STATE</td><td>PERCENT</td></tr>
<tr><td>15</td><td>Alabama</td><td>0.1</td><td>1</td><td>Hawaii</td><td>10.1</td></tr>
<tr><td>2</td><td>Alaska</td><td>1.2</td><td>2</td><td>Alaska</td><td>1.2</td></tr>
<tr><td>8</td><td>Arizona</td><td>0.3</td><td>3</td><td>Utah</td><td>1.0</td></tr>
<tr><td>8</td><td>Arkansas</td><td>0.3</td><td>4</td><td>Nevada</td><td>0.7</td></tr>
<tr><td>6</td><td>California</td><td>0.5</td><td>4</td><td>Washington</td><td>0.7</td></tr>
<tr><td>10</td><td>Colorado</td><td>0.2</td><td>6</td><td>California</td><td>0.5</td></tr>
<tr><td>15</td><td>Connecticut</td><td>0.1</td><td>7</td><td>Oregon</td><td>0.4</td></tr>
<tr><td>15</td><td>Delaware</td><td>0.1</td><td>8</td><td>Arizona</td><td>0.3</td></tr>
<tr><td>15</td><td>Florida</td><td>0.1</td><td>8</td><td>Arkansas</td><td>0.3</td></tr>
<tr><td>15</td><td>Georgia</td><td>0.1</td><td>10</td><td>Colorado</td><td>0.2</td></tr>
<tr><td>1</td><td>Hawaii</td><td>10.1</td><td>10</td><td>Idaho</td><td>0.2</td></tr>
<tr><td>10</td><td>Idaho</td><td>0.2</td><td>10</td><td>New Mexico</td><td>0.2</td></tr>
<tr><td>15</td><td>Illinois</td><td>0.1</td><td>10</td><td>Oklahoma</td><td>0.2</td></tr>
<tr><td>15</td><td>Indiana</td><td>0.1</td><td>10</td><td>Rhode Island</td><td>0.2</td></tr>
<tr><td>15</td><td>Iowa</td><td>0.1</td><td>15</td><td>Alabama</td><td>0.1</td></tr>
<tr><td>15</td><td>Kansas</td><td>0.1</td><td>15</td><td>Connecticut</td><td>0.1</td></tr>
<tr><td>15</td><td>Kentucky</td><td>0.1</td><td>15</td><td>Delaware</td><td>0.1</td></tr>
<tr><td>15</td><td>Louisiana</td><td>0.1</td><td>15</td><td>Florida</td><td>0.1</td></tr>
<tr><td>44</td><td>Maine</td><td>0.0</td><td>15</td><td>Georgia</td><td>0.1</td></tr>
<tr><td>15</td><td>Maryland</td><td>0.1</td><td>15</td><td>Illinois</td><td>0.1</td></tr>
<tr><td>15</td><td>Massachusetts</td><td>0.1</td><td>15</td><td>Indiana</td><td>0.1</td></tr>
<tr><td>44</td><td>Michigan</td><td>0.0</td><td>15</td><td>Iowa</td><td>0.1</td></tr>
<tr><td>15</td><td>Minnesota</td><td>0.1</td><td>15</td><td>Kansas</td><td>0.1</td></tr>
<tr><td>15</td><td>Mississippi</td><td>0.1</td><td>15</td><td>Kentucky</td><td>0.1</td></tr>
<tr><td>15</td><td>Missouri</td><td>0.1</td><td>15</td><td>Louisiana</td><td>0.1</td></tr>
<tr><td>15</td><td>Montana</td><td>0.1</td><td>15</td><td>Maryland</td><td>0.1</td></tr>
<tr><td>15</td><td>Nebraska</td><td>0.1</td><td>15</td><td>Massachusetts</td><td>0.1</td></tr>
<tr><td>4</td><td>Nevada</td><td>0.7</td><td>15</td><td>Minnesota</td><td>0.1</td></tr>
<tr><td>44</td><td>New Hampshire</td><td>0.0</td><td>15</td><td>Mississippi</td><td>0.1</td></tr>
<tr><td>15</td><td>New Jersey</td><td>0.1</td><td>15</td><td>Missouri</td><td>0.1</td></tr>
<tr><td>10</td><td>New Mexico</td><td>0.2</td><td>15</td><td>Montana</td><td>0.1</td></tr>
<tr><td>15</td><td>New York</td><td>0.1</td><td>15</td><td>Nebraska</td><td>0.1</td></tr>
<tr><td>15</td><td>North Carolina</td><td>0.1</td><td>15</td><td>New Jersey</td><td>0.1</td></tr>
<tr><td>15</td><td>North Dakota</td><td>0.1</td><td>15</td><td>New York</td><td>0.1</td></tr>
<tr><td>44</td><td>Ohio</td><td>0.0</td><td>15</td><td>North Carolina</td><td>0.1</td></tr>
<tr><td>10</td><td>Oklahoma</td><td>0.2</td><td>15</td><td>North Dakota</td><td>0.1</td></tr>
<tr><td>7</td><td>Oregon</td><td>0.4</td><td>15</td><td>Pennsylvania</td><td>0.1</td></tr>
<tr><td>15</td><td>Pennsylvania</td><td>0.1</td><td>15</td><td>South Carolina</td><td>0.1</td></tr>
<tr><td>10</td><td>Rhode Island</td><td>0.2</td><td>15</td><td>South Dakota</td><td>0.1</td></tr>
<tr><td>15</td><td>South Carolina</td><td>0.1</td><td>15</td><td>Tennessee</td><td>0.1</td></tr>
<tr><td>15</td><td>South Dakota</td><td>0.1</td><td>15</td><td>Texas</td><td>0.1</td></tr>
<tr><td>15</td><td>Tennessee</td><td>0.1</td><td>15</td><td>Virginia</td><td>0.1</td></tr>
<tr><td>15</td><td>Texas</td><td>0.1</td><td>15</td><td>Wyoming</td><td>0.1</td></tr>
<tr><td>3</td><td>Utah</td><td>1.0</td><td>44</td><td>Maine</td><td>0.0</td></tr>
<tr><td>44</td><td>Vermont</td><td>0.0</td><td>44</td><td>Michigan</td><td>0.0</td></tr>
<tr><td>15</td><td>Virginia</td><td>0.1</td><td>44</td><td>New Hampshire</td><td>0.0</td></tr>
<tr><td>4</td><td>Washington</td><td>0.7</td><td>44</td><td>Ohio</td><td>0.0</td></tr>
<tr><td>44</td><td>West Virginia</td><td>0.0</td><td>44</td><td>Vermont</td><td>0.0</td></tr>
<tr><td>44</td><td>Wisconsin</td><td>0.0</td><td>44</td><td>West Virginia</td><td>0.0</td></tr>
<tr><td>15</td><td>Wyoming</td><td>0.1</td><td>44</td><td>Wisconsin</td><td>0.0</td></tr>
<tr><td></td><td></td><td></td><td></td><td>District of Columbia</td><td>0.2</td></tr>
</table>

Source: CQ Press using data from U.S. Bureau of the Census
   "State Characteristics: Vintage 2012" (http://www.census.gov/popest/data/state/asrh/2012/index.html)
*Those who identified themselves as one race. Census states "Race is a self-identification data item in which respondents choose the race or races with which they most closely identify."

Non-Hispanic White Population in 2012

National Total = 197,705,655*

ALPHA ORDER

ALPHA ORDER

RANK	STATE	POPULATION	% of USA
23	Alabama	3,210,178	1.6%
49	Alaska	461,208	0.2%
21	Arizona	3,739,038	1.9%
33	Arkansas	2,180,732	1.1%
1	California	14,971,342	7.6%
22	Colorado	3,608,087	1.8%
30	Connecticut	2,522,870	1.3%
46	Delaware	592,014	0.3%
4	Florida	11,008,396	5.6%
10	Georgia	5,469,942	2.8%
50	Hawaii	318,118	0.2%
38	Idaho	1,331,650	0.7%
7	Illinois	8,114,559	4.1%
11	Indiana	5,295,511	2.7%
28	Iowa	2,705,594	1.4%
32	Kansas	2,235,436	1.1%
20	Kentucky	3,761,002	1.9%
27	Louisiana	2,755,571	1.4%
39	Maine	1,251,365	0.6%
24	Maryland	3,170,288	1.6%
14	Massachusetts	5,037,923	2.5%
8	Michigan	7,533,928	3.8%
19	Minnesota	4,429,871	2.2%
35	Mississippi	1,720,045	0.9%
16	Missouri	4,856,485	2.5%
41	Montana	876,823	0.4%
36	Nebraska	1,510,296	0.8%
37	Nevada	1,458,379	0.7%
40	New Hampshire	1,213,106	0.6%
13	New Jersey	5,161,886	2.6%
42	New Mexico	830,454	0.4%
3	New York	11,272,085	5.7%
9	North Carolina	6,309,775	3.2%
45	North Dakota	616,336	0.3%
6	Ohio	9,321,104	4.7%
29	Oklahoma	2,588,845	1.3%
25	Oregon	3,033,807	1.5%
5	Pennsylvania	10,054,425	5.1%
43	Rhode Island	797,099	0.4%
26	South Carolina	3,021,140	1.5%
44	South Dakota	698,668	0.4%
17	Tennessee	4,848,546	2.5%
2	Texas	11,583,831	5.9%
31	Utah	2,281,568	1.2%
47	Vermont	588,677	0.3%
12	Virginia	5,245,511	2.7%
15	Washington	4,935,687	2.5%
34	West Virginia	1,722,801	0.9%
18	Wisconsin	4,741,504	2.4%
48	Wyoming	487,822	0.2%

RANK ORDER

RANK	STATE	POPULATION	% of USA
1	California	14,971,342	7.6%
2	Texas	11,583,831	5.9%
3	New York	11,272,085	5.7%
4	Florida	11,008,396	5.6%
5	Pennsylvania	10,054,425	5.1%
6	Ohio	9,321,104	4.7%
7	Illinois	8,114,559	4.1%
8	Michigan	7,533,928	3.8%
9	North Carolina	6,309,775	3.2%
10	Georgia	5,469,942	2.8%
11	Indiana	5,295,511	2.7%
12	Virginia	5,245,511	2.7%
13	New Jersey	5,161,886	2.6%
14	Massachusetts	5,037,923	2.5%
15	Washington	4,935,687	2.5%
16	Missouri	4,856,485	2.5%
17	Tennessee	4,848,546	2.5%
18	Wisconsin	4,741,504	2.4%
19	Minnesota	4,429,871	2.2%
20	Kentucky	3,761,002	1.9%
21	Arizona	3,739,038	1.9%
22	Colorado	3,608,087	1.8%
23	Alabama	3,210,178	1.6%
24	Maryland	3,170,288	1.6%
25	Oregon	3,033,807	1.5%
26	South Carolina	3,021,140	1.5%
27	Louisiana	2,755,571	1.4%
28	Iowa	2,705,594	1.4%
29	Oklahoma	2,588,845	1.3%
30	Connecticut	2,522,870	1.3%
31	Utah	2,281,568	1.2%
32	Kansas	2,235,436	1.1%
33	Arkansas	2,180,732	1.1%
34	West Virginia	1,722,801	0.9%
35	Mississippi	1,720,045	0.9%
36	Nebraska	1,510,296	0.8%
37	Nevada	1,458,379	0.7%
38	Idaho	1,331,650	0.7%
39	Maine	1,251,365	0.6%
40	New Hampshire	1,213,106	0.6%
41	Montana	876,823	0.4%
42	New Mexico	830,454	0.4%
43	Rhode Island	797,099	0.4%
44	South Dakota	698,668	0.4%
45	North Dakota	616,336	0.3%
46	Delaware	592,014	0.3%
47	Vermont	588,677	0.3%
48	Wyoming	487,822	0.2%
49	Alaska	461,208	0.2%
50	Hawaii	318,118	0.2%
	District of Columbia	224,327	0.1%

Source: U.S. Bureau of the Census
   "State Characteristics: Vintage 2012" (http://www.census.gov/popest/data/state/asrh/2012/index.html)
*Those who identified themselves as one race. "White" is defined by Census as a person having origins in any of the original peoples of Europe, North Africa, or the Middle East. This is a subset of the 244,495,567 white population. There are 6,237,796 non-Hispanics identified as one of the other five race categories. Persons of Hispanic origin may be of any race. Census states "Race is a self-identification data item in which respondents choose the race or races with which they most closely identify."

Percent of Population Non-Hispanic White in 2012

National Percent = 63.0%*

ALPHA ORDER

RANK	STATE	PERCENT
31	Alabama	66.6
36	Alaska	63.1
42	Arizona	57.1
26	Arkansas	73.9
49	California	39.4
29	Colorado	69.6
28	Connecticut	70.3
33	Delaware	64.6
43	Florida	57.0
44	Georgia	55.1
50	Hawaii	22.8
11	Idaho	83.5
37	Illinois	63.0
15	Indiana	81.0
6	Iowa	88.0
21	Kansas	77.5
8	Kentucky	85.9
38	Louisiana	59.9
1	Maine	94.1
45	Maryland	53.9
24	Massachusetts	75.8
22	Michigan	76.2
13	Minnesota	82.4
40	Mississippi	57.6
17	Missouri	80.6
7	Montana	87.2
14	Nebraska	81.4
46	Nevada	52.9
4	New Hampshire	91.9
39	New Jersey	58.2
48	New Mexico	39.8
40	New York	57.6
32	North Carolina	64.7
5	North Dakota	88.1
16	Ohio	80.7
30	Oklahoma	67.9
20	Oregon	77.8
19	Pennsylvania	78.8
23	Rhode Island	75.9
35	South Carolina	64.0
10	South Dakota	83.8
25	Tennessee	75.1
47	Texas	44.5
18	Utah	79.9
2	Vermont	94.0
34	Virginia	64.1
27	Washington	71.6
3	West Virginia	92.9
12	Wisconsin	82.8
9	Wyoming	84.6

RANK ORDER

RANK	STATE	PERCENT
1	Maine	94.1
2	Vermont	94.0
3	West Virginia	92.9
4	New Hampshire	91.9
5	North Dakota	88.1
6	Iowa	88.0
7	Montana	87.2
8	Kentucky	85.9
9	Wyoming	84.6
10	South Dakota	83.8
11	Idaho	83.5
12	Wisconsin	82.8
13	Minnesota	82.4
14	Nebraska	81.4
15	Indiana	81.0
16	Ohio	80.7
17	Missouri	80.6
18	Utah	79.9
19	Pennsylvania	78.8
20	Oregon	77.8
21	Kansas	77.5
22	Michigan	76.2
23	Rhode Island	75.9
24	Massachusetts	75.8
25	Tennessee	75.1
26	Arkansas	73.9
27	Washington	71.6
28	Connecticut	70.3
29	Colorado	69.6
30	Oklahoma	67.9
31	Alabama	66.6
32	North Carolina	64.7
33	Delaware	64.6
34	Virginia	64.1
35	South Carolina	64.0
36	Alaska	63.1
37	Illinois	63.0
38	Louisiana	59.9
39	New Jersey	58.2
40	Mississippi	57.6
40	New York	57.6
42	Arizona	57.1
43	Florida	57.0
44	Georgia	55.1
45	Maryland	53.9
46	Nevada	52.9
47	Texas	44.5
48	New Mexico	39.8
49	California	39.4
50	Hawaii	22.8

	District of Columbia	35.5

Source: CQ Press using data from U.S. Bureau of the Census
    "State Characteristics: Vintage 2012" (http://www.census.gov/popest/data/state/asrh/2012/index.html)
*Those who identified themselves as one race. "White" is defined by Census as a person having origins in any of the original peoples of Europe, North Africa, or the Middle East. This non-Hispanic white subset is 80.1% of the total white population. Persons of Hispanic origin may be of any race. Census states "Race is a self-identification data item in which respondents choose the race or races with which they most closely identify."

Multiple Race Population in 2012

National Total = 7,503,136*

<table>
<tr><th colspan="4">ALPHA ORDER</th><th colspan="4">RANK ORDER</th></tr>
<tr><th>RANK</th><th>STATE</th><th>POPULATION</th><th>% of USA</th><th>RANK</th><th>STATE</th><th>POPULATION</th><th>% of USA</th></tr>
<tr><td>31</td><td>Alabama</td><td>69,923</td><td>0.9%</td><td>1</td><td>California</td><td>1,370,038</td><td>18.3%</td></tr>
<tr><td>35</td><td>Alaska</td><td>51,853</td><td>0.7%</td><td>2</td><td>Texas</td><td>446,525</td><td>6.0%</td></tr>
<tr><td>16</td><td>Arizona</td><td>165,742</td><td>2.2%</td><td>3</td><td>New York</td><td>438,623</td><td>5.8%</td></tr>
<tr><td>34</td><td>Arkansas</td><td>53,343</td><td>0.7%</td><td>4</td><td>Florida</td><td>363,504</td><td>4.8%</td></tr>
<tr><td>1</td><td>California</td><td>1,370,038</td><td>18.3%</td><td>5</td><td>Hawaii</td><td>320,646</td><td>4.3%</td></tr>
<tr><td>18</td><td>Colorado</td><td>144,220</td><td>1.9%</td><td>6</td><td>Washington</td><td>298,953</td><td>4.0%</td></tr>
<tr><td>29</td><td>Connecticut</td><td>74,658</td><td>1.0%</td><td>7</td><td>Ohio</td><td>226,658</td><td>3.0%</td></tr>
<tr><td>44</td><td>Delaware</td><td>21,582</td><td>0.3%</td><td>8</td><td>Illinois</td><td>223,912</td><td>3.0%</td></tr>
<tr><td>4</td><td>Florida</td><td>363,504</td><td>4.8%</td><td>9</td><td>Oklahoma</td><td>221,030</td><td>2.9%</td></tr>
<tr><td>14</td><td>Georgia</td><td>182,729</td><td>2.4%</td><td>10</td><td>Pennsylvania</td><td>217,291</td><td>2.9%</td></tr>
<tr><td>5</td><td>Hawaii</td><td>320,646</td><td>4.3%</td><td>11</td><td>Michigan</td><td>214,713</td><td>2.9%</td></tr>
<tr><td>39</td><td>Idaho</td><td>34,788</td><td>0.5%</td><td>12</td><td>Virginia</td><td>214,241</td><td>2.9%</td></tr>
<tr><td>8</td><td>Illinois</td><td>223,912</td><td>3.0%</td><td>13</td><td>North Carolina</td><td>190,626</td><td>2.5%</td></tr>
<tr><td>23</td><td>Indiana</td><td>116,175</td><td>1.5%</td><td>14</td><td>Georgia</td><td>182,729</td><td>2.4%</td></tr>
<tr><td>37</td><td>Iowa</td><td>48,756</td><td>0.6%</td><td>15</td><td>New Jersey</td><td>171,875</td><td>2.3%</td></tr>
<tr><td>27</td><td>Kansas</td><td>77,962</td><td>1.0%</td><td>16</td><td>Arizona</td><td>165,742</td><td>2.2%</td></tr>
<tr><td>30</td><td>Kentucky</td><td>72,103</td><td>1.0%</td><td>17</td><td>Maryland</td><td>148,001</td><td>2.0%</td></tr>
<tr><td>32</td><td>Louisiana</td><td>66,041</td><td>0.9%</td><td>18</td><td>Colorado</td><td>144,220</td><td>1.9%</td></tr>
<tr><td>45</td><td>Maine</td><td>20,558</td><td>0.3%</td><td>19</td><td>Oregon</td><td>136,142</td><td>1.8%</td></tr>
<tr><td>17</td><td>Maryland</td><td>148,001</td><td>2.0%</td><td>20</td><td>Massachusetts</td><td>134,877</td><td>1.8%</td></tr>
<tr><td>20</td><td>Massachusetts</td><td>134,877</td><td>1.8%</td><td>21</td><td>Missouri</td><td>119,761</td><td>1.6%</td></tr>
<tr><td>11</td><td>Michigan</td><td>214,713</td><td>2.9%</td><td>22</td><td>Minnesota</td><td>119,756</td><td>1.6%</td></tr>
<tr><td>22</td><td>Minnesota</td><td>119,756</td><td>1.6%</td><td>23</td><td>Indiana</td><td>116,175</td><td>1.5%</td></tr>
<tr><td>40</td><td>Mississippi</td><td>32,424</td><td>0.4%</td><td>24</td><td>Tennessee</td><td>104,912</td><td>1.4%</td></tr>
<tr><td>21</td><td>Missouri</td><td>119,761</td><td>1.6%</td><td>25</td><td>Nevada</td><td>104,466</td><td>1.4%</td></tr>
<tr><td>43</td><td>Montana</td><td>24,869</td><td>0.3%</td><td>26</td><td>Wisconsin</td><td>95,465</td><td>1.3%</td></tr>
<tr><td>38</td><td>Nebraska</td><td>35,077</td><td>0.5%</td><td>27</td><td>Kansas</td><td>77,962</td><td>1.0%</td></tr>
<tr><td>25</td><td>Nevada</td><td>104,466</td><td>1.4%</td><td>28</td><td>South Carolina</td><td>74,962</td><td>1.0%</td></tr>
<tr><td>46</td><td>New Hampshire</td><td>19,913</td><td>0.3%</td><td>29</td><td>Connecticut</td><td>74,658</td><td>1.0%</td></tr>
<tr><td>15</td><td>New Jersey</td><td>171,875</td><td>2.3%</td><td>30</td><td>Kentucky</td><td>72,103</td><td>1.0%</td></tr>
<tr><td>36</td><td>New Mexico</td><td>49,123</td><td>0.7%</td><td>31</td><td>Alabama</td><td>69,923</td><td>0.9%</td></tr>
<tr><td>3</td><td>New York</td><td>438,623</td><td>5.8%</td><td>32</td><td>Louisiana</td><td>66,041</td><td>0.9%</td></tr>
<tr><td>13</td><td>North Carolina</td><td>190,626</td><td>2.5%</td><td>33</td><td>Utah</td><td>64,313</td><td>0.9%</td></tr>
<tr><td>48</td><td>North Dakota</td><td>12,268</td><td>0.2%</td><td>34</td><td>Arkansas</td><td>53,343</td><td>0.7%</td></tr>
<tr><td>7</td><td>Ohio</td><td>226,658</td><td>3.0%</td><td>35</td><td>Alaska</td><td>51,853</td><td>0.7%</td></tr>
<tr><td>9</td><td>Oklahoma</td><td>221,030</td><td>2.9%</td><td>36</td><td>New Mexico</td><td>49,123</td><td>0.7%</td></tr>
<tr><td>19</td><td>Oregon</td><td>136,142</td><td>1.8%</td><td>37</td><td>Iowa</td><td>48,756</td><td>0.6%</td></tr>
<tr><td>10</td><td>Pennsylvania</td><td>217,291</td><td>2.9%</td><td>38</td><td>Nebraska</td><td>35,077</td><td>0.5%</td></tr>
<tr><td>42</td><td>Rhode Island</td><td>25,872</td><td>0.3%</td><td>39</td><td>Idaho</td><td>34,788</td><td>0.5%</td></tr>
<tr><td>28</td><td>South Carolina</td><td>74,962</td><td>1.0%</td><td>40</td><td>Mississippi</td><td>32,424</td><td>0.4%</td></tr>
<tr><td>47</td><td>South Dakota</td><td>17,227</td><td>0.2%</td><td>41</td><td>West Virginia</td><td>27,442</td><td>0.4%</td></tr>
<tr><td>24</td><td>Tennessee</td><td>104,912</td><td>1.4%</td><td>42</td><td>Rhode Island</td><td>25,872</td><td>0.3%</td></tr>
<tr><td>2</td><td>Texas</td><td>446,525</td><td>6.0%</td><td>43</td><td>Montana</td><td>24,869</td><td>0.3%</td></tr>
<tr><td>33</td><td>Utah</td><td>64,313</td><td>0.9%</td><td>44</td><td>Delaware</td><td>21,582</td><td>0.3%</td></tr>
<tr><td>49</td><td>Vermont</td><td>10,687</td><td>0.1%</td><td>45</td><td>Maine</td><td>20,558</td><td>0.3%</td></tr>
<tr><td>12</td><td>Virginia</td><td>214,241</td><td>2.9%</td><td>46</td><td>New Hampshire</td><td>19,913</td><td>0.3%</td></tr>
<tr><td>6</td><td>Washington</td><td>298,953</td><td>4.0%</td><td>47</td><td>South Dakota</td><td>17,227</td><td>0.2%</td></tr>
<tr><td>41</td><td>West Virginia</td><td>27,442</td><td>0.4%</td><td>48</td><td>North Dakota</td><td>12,268</td><td>0.2%</td></tr>
<tr><td>26</td><td>Wisconsin</td><td>95,465</td><td>1.3%</td><td>49</td><td>Vermont</td><td>10,687</td><td>0.1%</td></tr>
<tr><td>50</td><td>Wyoming</td><td>10,646</td><td>0.1%</td><td>50</td><td>Wyoming</td><td>10,646</td><td>0.1%</td></tr>
<tr><td></td><td></td><td></td><td></td><td></td><td>District of Columbia</td><td>15,865</td><td>0.2%</td></tr>
</table>

Source: U.S. Bureau of the Census

"State Characteristics: Vintage 2012" (http://www.census.gov/popest/data/state/asrh/2012/index.html)

*This includes those who identified themselves as two or more races. This is the population who did not identify themselves as one race (White, Black, American Indian/Native Alaska Native, Asian, or Native Hawaiian or Other Pacific Islander) but as a member of multiple racial groups. Census states "Race is a self-identification data item in which respondents choose the race or races with which they most closely identify."

Percent of Population Multiple Races in 2012

National Percent = 2.4%*

ALPHA ORDER

RANK	STATE	PERCENT
45	Alabama	1.5
2	Alaska	7.1
11	Arizona	2.5
31	Arkansas	1.8
6	California	3.6
8	Colorado	2.8
22	Connecticut	2.1
15	Delaware	2.4
28	Florida	1.9
31	Georgia	1.8
1	Hawaii	23.0
18	Idaho	2.2
36	Illinois	1.7
31	Indiana	1.8
41	Iowa	1.6
9	Kansas	2.7
41	Kentucky	1.6
49	Louisiana	1.4
45	Maine	1.5
11	Maryland	2.5
24	Massachusetts	2.0
18	Michigan	2.2
18	Minnesota	2.2
50	Mississippi	1.1
24	Missouri	2.0
11	Montana	2.5
28	Nebraska	1.9
5	Nevada	3.8
45	New Hampshire	1.5
28	New Jersey	1.9
15	New Mexico	2.4
18	New York	2.2
24	North Carolina	2.0
31	North Dakota	1.8
24	Ohio	2.0
3	Oklahoma	5.8
7	Oregon	3.5
36	Pennsylvania	1.7
11	Rhode Island	2.5
41	South Carolina	1.6
22	South Dakota	2.1
41	Tennessee	1.6
36	Texas	1.7
17	Utah	2.3
36	Vermont	1.7
10	Virginia	2.6
4	Washington	4.3
45	West Virginia	1.5
36	Wisconsin	1.7
31	Wyoming	1.8

RANK ORDER

RANK	STATE	PERCENT
1	Hawaii	23.0
2	Alaska	7.1
3	Oklahoma	5.8
4	Washington	4.3
5	Nevada	3.8
6	California	3.6
7	Oregon	3.5
8	Colorado	2.8
9	Kansas	2.7
10	Virginia	2.6
11	Arizona	2.5
11	Maryland	2.5
11	Montana	2.5
11	Rhode Island	2.5
15	Delaware	2.4
15	New Mexico	2.4
17	Utah	2.3
18	Idaho	2.2
18	Michigan	2.2
18	Minnesota	2.2
18	New York	2.2
22	Connecticut	2.1
22	South Dakota	2.1
24	Massachusetts	2.0
24	Missouri	2.0
24	North Carolina	2.0
24	Ohio	2.0
28	Florida	1.9
28	Nebraska	1.9
28	New Jersey	1.9
31	Arkansas	1.8
31	Georgia	1.8
31	Indiana	1.8
31	North Dakota	1.8
31	Wyoming	1.8
36	Illinois	1.7
36	Pennsylvania	1.7
36	Texas	1.7
36	Vermont	1.7
36	Wisconsin	1.7
41	Iowa	1.6
41	Kentucky	1.6
41	South Carolina	1.6
41	Tennessee	1.6
45	Alabama	1.5
45	Maine	1.5
45	New Hampshire	1.5
45	West Virginia	1.5
49	Louisiana	1.4
50	Mississippi	1.1
	District of Columbia	2.5

Source: CQ Press using data from U.S. Bureau of the Census
   "State Characteristics: Vintage 2012" (http://www.census.gov/popest/data/state/asrh/2012/index.html)
*This includes those who identified themselves as two or more races. This is the population who did not identify themselves as one race (White, Black, American Indian/Native Alaska Native, Asian, or Native Hawaiian or Other Pacific Islander) but as a member of multiple racial groups. Census states "Race is a self-identification data item in which respondents choose the race or races with which they most closely identify."

Median Age in 2012

National Median = 37.4 Years Old

RANK	STATE	MEDIAN AGE
21	Alabama	38.2
49	Alaska	33.7
37	Arizona	36.5
27	Arkansas	37.6
46	California	35.5
38	Colorado	36.3
6	Connecticut	40.5
13	Delaware	39.2
5	Florida	41.3
45	Georgia	35.7
18	Hawaii	38.3
47	Idaho	35.2
32	Illinois	37.0
31	Indiana	37.2
22	Iowa	38.1
43	Kansas	36.0
18	Kentucky	38.3
44	Louisiana	35.9
1	Maine	43.5
22	Maryland	38.1
11	Massachusetts	39.3
10	Michigan	39.4
27	Minnesota	37.6
38	Mississippi	36.3
22	Missouri	38.1
8	Montana	40.1
40	Nebraska	36.2
33	Nevada	36.9
3	New Hampshire	42.0
11	New Jersey	39.3
36	New Mexico	36.8
22	New York	38.1
26	North Carolina	37.8
42	North Dakota	36.1
13	Ohio	39.2
40	Oklahoma	36.2
16	Oregon	38.8
6	Pennsylvania	40.5
9	Rhode Island	39.8
17	South Carolina	38.4
33	South Dakota	36.9
18	Tennessee	38.3
48	Texas	33.9
50	Utah	29.9
2	Vermont	42.3
27	Virginia	37.6
30	Washington	37.5
4	West Virginia	41.7
15	Wisconsin	38.9
33	Wyoming	36.9

RANK	STATE	MEDIAN AGE
1	Maine	43.5
2	Vermont	42.3
3	New Hampshire	42.0
4	West Virginia	41.7
5	Florida	41.3
6	Connecticut	40.5
6	Pennsylvania	40.5
8	Montana	40.1
9	Rhode Island	39.8
10	Michigan	39.4
11	Massachusetts	39.3
11	New Jersey	39.3
13	Delaware	39.2
13	Ohio	39.2
15	Wisconsin	38.9
16	Oregon	38.8
17	South Carolina	38.4
18	Hawaii	38.3
18	Kentucky	38.3
18	Tennessee	38.3
21	Alabama	38.2
22	Iowa	38.1
22	Maryland	38.1
22	Missouri	38.1
22	New York	38.1
26	North Carolina	37.8
27	Arkansas	37.6
27	Minnesota	37.6
27	Virginia	37.6
30	Washington	37.5
31	Indiana	37.2
32	Illinois	37.0
33	Nevada	36.9
33	South Dakota	36.9
33	Wyoming	36.9
36	New Mexico	36.8
37	Arizona	36.5
38	Colorado	36.3
38	Mississippi	36.3
40	Nebraska	36.2
40	Oklahoma	36.2
42	North Dakota	36.1
43	Kansas	36.0
44	Louisiana	35.9
45	Georgia	35.7
46	California	35.5
47	Idaho	35.2
48	Texas	33.9
49	Alaska	33.7
50	Utah	29.9
	District of Columbia	33.6

Source: U.S. Bureau of the Census
   "State Characteristics: Vintage 2012" (http://www.census.gov/popest/data/state/asrh/2012/index.html)

Population under 5 Years Old in 2012

National Total = 19,999,344

ALPHA ORDER

RANK ORDER

RANK	STATE	POPULATION	% of USA	RANK	STATE	POPULATION	% of USA
24	Alabama	305,267	1.5%	1	California	2,541,497	12.7%
47	Alaska	54,791	0.3%	2	Texas	1,941,845	9.7%
14	Arizona	439,633	2.2%	3	New York	1,167,185	5.8%
33	Arkansas	194,019	1.0%	4	Florida	1,071,463	5.4%
1	California	2,541,497	12.7%	5	Illinois	816,278	4.1%
22	Colorado	337,568	1.7%	6	Pennsylvania	719,703	3.6%
34	Connecticut	193,456	1.0%	7	Ohio	694,870	3.5%
45	Delaware	56,279	0.3%	8	Georgia	675,032	3.4%
4	Florida	1,071,463	5.4%	9	North Carolina	619,940	3.1%
8	Georgia	675,032	3.4%	10	Michigan	575,714	2.9%
40	Hawaii	89,149	0.4%	11	New Jersey	527,649	2.6%
38	Idaho	115,972	0.6%	12	Virginia	509,602	2.5%
5	Illinois	816,278	4.1%	13	Washington	443,157	2.2%
15	Indiana	425,503	2.1%	14	Arizona	439,633	2.2%
32	Iowa	196,366	1.0%	15	Indiana	425,503	2.1%
31	Kansas	203,267	1.0%	16	Tennessee	403,976	2.0%
26	Kentucky	279,535	1.4%	17	Missouri	379,246	1.9%
23	Louisiana	314,766	1.6%	18	Massachusetts	365,557	1.8%
41	Maine	66,904	0.3%	19	Maryland	365,224	1.8%
19	Maryland	365,224	1.8%	20	Wisconsin	350,581	1.8%
18	Massachusetts	365,557	1.8%	21	Minnesota	348,338	1.7%
10	Michigan	575,714	2.9%	22	Colorado	337,568	1.7%
21	Minnesota	348,338	1.7%	23	Louisiana	314,766	1.6%
30	Mississippi	203,828	1.0%	24	Alabama	305,267	1.5%
17	Missouri	379,246	1.9%	25	South Carolina	296,401	1.5%
43	Montana	60,964	0.3%	26	Kentucky	279,535	1.4%
37	Nebraska	132,268	0.7%	27	Oklahoma	261,958	1.3%
35	Nevada	183,301	0.9%	28	Utah	257,848	1.3%
42	New Hampshire	65,953	0.3%	29	Oregon	232,516	1.2%
11	New Jersey	527,649	2.6%	30	Mississippi	203,828	1.0%
36	New Mexico	143,536	0.7%	31	Kansas	203,267	1.0%
3	New York	1,167,185	5.8%	32	Iowa	196,366	1.0%
9	North Carolina	619,940	3.1%	33	Arkansas	194,019	1.0%
48	North Dakota	46,109	0.2%	34	Connecticut	193,456	1.0%
7	Ohio	694,870	3.5%	35	Nevada	183,301	0.9%
27	Oklahoma	261,958	1.3%	36	New Mexico	143,536	0.7%
29	Oregon	232,516	1.2%	37	Nebraska	132,268	0.7%
6	Pennsylvania	719,703	3.6%	38	Idaho	115,972	0.6%
46	Rhode Island	55,068	0.3%	39	West Virginia	103,071	0.5%
25	South Carolina	296,401	1.5%	40	Hawaii	89,149	0.4%
44	South Dakota	59,202	0.3%	41	Maine	66,904	0.3%
16	Tennessee	403,976	2.0%	42	New Hampshire	65,953	0.3%
2	Texas	1,941,845	9.7%	43	Montana	60,964	0.3%
28	Utah	257,848	1.3%	44	South Dakota	59,202	0.3%
50	Vermont	30,521	0.2%	45	Delaware	56,279	0.3%
12	Virginia	509,602	2.5%	46	Rhode Island	55,068	0.3%
13	Washington	443,157	2.2%	47	Alaska	54,791	0.3%
39	West Virginia	103,071	0.5%	48	North Dakota	46,109	0.2%
20	Wisconsin	350,581	1.8%	49	Wyoming	38,592	0.2%
49	Wyoming	38,592	0.2%	50	Vermont	30,521	0.2%
					District of Columbia	38,876	0.2%

Source: U.S. Bureau of the Census
"State Characteristics: Vintage 2012" (http://www.census.gov/popest/data/state/asrh/2012/index.html)

Percent of Population under 5 Years Old in 2012

National Percent = 6.4% of Population

ALPHA ORDER			RANK ORDER		
RANK	STATE	PERCENT	RANK	STATE	PERCENT
27	Alabama	6.3	1	Utah	9.0
2	Alaska	7.5	2	Alaska	7.5
13	Arizona	6.7	2	Texas	7.5
16	Arkansas	6.6	4	Idaho	7.3
13	California	6.7	5	Nebraska	7.1
19	Colorado	6.5	5	South Dakota	7.1
46	Connecticut	5.4	7	Kansas	7.0
34	Delaware	6.1	8	New Mexico	6.9
44	Florida	5.5	8	Oklahoma	6.9
10	Georgia	6.8	10	Georgia	6.8
22	Hawaii	6.4	10	Louisiana	6.8
4	Idaho	7.3	10	Mississippi	6.8
27	Illinois	6.3	13	Arizona	6.7
19	Indiana	6.5	13	California	6.7
22	Iowa	6.4	13	Wyoming	6.7
7	Kansas	7.0	16	Arkansas	6.6
22	Kentucky	6.4	16	Nevada	6.6
10	Louisiana	6.8	16	North Dakota	6.6
48	Maine	5.0	19	Colorado	6.5
32	Maryland	6.2	19	Indiana	6.5
44	Massachusetts	5.5	19	Minnesota	6.5
41	Michigan	5.8	22	Hawaii	6.4
19	Minnesota	6.5	22	Iowa	6.4
10	Mississippi	6.8	22	Kentucky	6.4
27	Missouri	6.3	22	North Carolina	6.4
34	Montana	6.1	22	Washington	6.4
5	Nebraska	7.1	27	Alabama	6.3
16	Nevada	6.6	27	Illinois	6.3
48	New Hampshire	5.0	27	Missouri	6.3
37	New Jersey	6.0	27	South Carolina	6.3
8	New Mexico	6.9	27	Tennessee	6.3
37	New York	6.0	32	Maryland	6.2
22	North Carolina	6.4	32	Virginia	6.2
16	North Dakota	6.6	34	Delaware	6.1
37	Ohio	6.0	34	Montana	6.1
8	Oklahoma	6.9	34	Wisconsin	6.1
37	Oregon	6.0	37	New Jersey	6.0
42	Pennsylvania	5.6	37	New York	6.0
47	Rhode Island	5.2	37	Ohio	6.0
27	South Carolina	6.3	37	Oregon	6.0
5	South Dakota	7.1	41	Michigan	5.8
27	Tennessee	6.3	42	Pennsylvania	5.6
2	Texas	7.5	42	West Virginia	5.6
1	Utah	9.0	44	Florida	5.5
50	Vermont	4.9	44	Massachusetts	5.5
32	Virginia	6.2	46	Connecticut	5.4
22	Washington	6.4	47	Rhode Island	5.2
42	West Virginia	5.6	48	Maine	5.0
34	Wisconsin	6.1	48	New Hampshire	5.0
13	Wyoming	6.7	50	Vermont	4.9
				District of Columbia	6.1

Source: CQ Press using data from U.S. Bureau of the Census
"State Characteristics: Vintage 2012" (http://www.census.gov/popest/data/state/asrh/2012/index.html)

Population 5 to 17 Years Old in 2012

National Total = 53,728,744

ALPHA ORDER

ALPHA ORDER

RANK	STATE	POPULATION	% of USA
23	Alabama	819,139	1.5%
47	Alaska	132,309	0.2%
13	Arizona	1,181,261	2.2%
34	Arkansas	516,862	1.0%
1	California	6,698,722	12.5%
22	Colorado	893,790	1.7%
30	Connecticut	600,102	1.1%
45	Delaware	148,771	0.3%
4	Florida	2,931,017	5.5%
8	Georgia	1,815,093	3.4%
40	Hawaii	213,862	0.4%
38	Idaho	310,681	0.6%
5	Illinois	2,247,787	4.2%
14	Indiana	1,165,974	2.2%
32	Iowa	526,587	1.0%
33	Kansas	521,037	1.0%
26	Kentucky	738,703	1.4%
24	Louisiana	803,037	1.5%
42	Maine	199,014	0.4%
19	Maryland	978,576	1.8%
17	Massachusetts	1,035,858	1.9%
9	Michigan	1,691,156	3.1%
21	Minnesota	927,810	1.7%
31	Mississippi	541,505	1.0%
18	Missouri	1,024,229	1.9%
44	Montana	161,016	0.3%
37	Nebraska	331,137	0.6%
35	Nevada	480,282	0.9%
41	New Hampshire	208,887	0.4%
11	New Jersey	1,498,735	2.8%
36	New Mexico	370,906	0.7%
3	New York	3,095,969	5.8%
10	North Carolina	1,666,588	3.1%
48	North Dakota	108,499	0.2%
7	Ohio	1,968,804	3.7%
27	Oklahoma	675,405	1.3%
29	Oregon	628,108	1.2%
6	Pennsylvania	2,019,683	3.8%
43	Rhode Island	161,406	0.3%
25	South Carolina	783,689	1.5%
46	South Dakota	144,967	0.3%
16	Tennessee	1,090,040	2.0%
2	Texas	5,043,794	9.4%
28	Utah	630,124	1.2%
50	Vermont	93,430	0.2%
12	Virginia	1,347,135	2.5%
15	Washington	1,141,810	2.1%
39	West Virginia	280,970	0.5%
20	Wisconsin	966,976	1.8%
49	Wyoming	96,898	0.2%

RANK ORDER

RANK	STATE	POPULATION	% of USA
1	California	6,698,722	12.5%
2	Texas	5,043,794	9.4%
3	New York	3,095,969	5.8%
4	Florida	2,931,017	5.5%
5	Illinois	2,247,787	4.2%
6	Pennsylvania	2,019,683	3.8%
7	Ohio	1,968,804	3.7%
8	Georgia	1,815,093	3.4%
9	Michigan	1,691,156	3.1%
10	North Carolina	1,666,588	3.1%
11	New Jersey	1,498,735	2.8%
12	Virginia	1,347,135	2.5%
13	Arizona	1,181,261	2.2%
14	Indiana	1,165,974	2.2%
15	Washington	1,141,810	2.1%
16	Tennessee	1,090,040	2.0%
17	Massachusetts	1,035,858	1.9%
18	Missouri	1,024,229	1.9%
19	Maryland	978,576	1.8%
20	Wisconsin	966,976	1.8%
21	Minnesota	927,810	1.7%
22	Colorado	893,790	1.7%
23	Alabama	819,139	1.5%
24	Louisiana	803,037	1.5%
25	South Carolina	783,689	1.5%
26	Kentucky	738,703	1.4%
27	Oklahoma	675,405	1.3%
28	Utah	630,124	1.2%
29	Oregon	628,108	1.2%
30	Connecticut	600,102	1.1%
31	Mississippi	541,505	1.0%
32	Iowa	526,587	1.0%
33	Kansas	521,037	1.0%
34	Arkansas	516,862	1.0%
35	Nevada	480,282	0.9%
36	New Mexico	370,906	0.7%
37	Nebraska	331,137	0.6%
38	Idaho	310,681	0.6%
39	West Virginia	280,970	0.5%
40	Hawaii	213,862	0.4%
41	New Hampshire	208,887	0.4%
42	Maine	199,014	0.4%
43	Rhode Island	161,406	0.3%
44	Montana	161,016	0.3%
45	Delaware	148,771	0.3%
46	South Dakota	144,967	0.3%
47	Alaska	132,309	0.2%
48	North Dakota	108,499	0.2%
49	Wyoming	96,898	0.2%
50	Vermont	93,430	0.2%
	District of Columbia	70,604	0.1%

Source: CQ Press using data from U.S. Bureau of the Census
"State Characteristics: Vintage 2012" (http://www.census.gov/popest/data/state/asrh/2012/index.html)

Percent of Population 5 to 17 Years Old in 2012

National Percent = 17.1% of Population

ALPHA ORDER

ALPHA ORDER

RANK ORDER

RANK	STATE	PERCENT	RANK	STATE	PERCENT
25	Alabama	17.0	1	Utah	22.1
5	Alaska	18.1	2	Idaho	19.5
8	Arizona	18.0	3	Texas	19.4
14	Arkansas	17.5	4	Georgia	18.3
13	California	17.6	5	Alaska	18.1
19	Colorado	17.2	5	Kansas	18.1
32	Connecticut	16.7	5	Mississippi	18.1
37	Delaware	16.2	8	Arizona	18.0
47	Florida	15.2	9	Indiana	17.8
4	Georgia	18.3	9	Nebraska	17.8
45	Hawaii	15.4	9	New Mexico	17.8
2	Idaho	19.5	12	Oklahoma	17.7
14	Illinois	17.5	13	California	17.6
9	Indiana	17.8	14	Arkansas	17.5
21	Iowa	17.1	14	Illinois	17.5
5	Kansas	18.1	14	Louisiana	17.5
27	Kentucky	16.9	17	Nevada	17.4
14	Louisiana	17.5	17	South Dakota	17.4
49	Maine	15.0	19	Colorado	17.2
33	Maryland	16.6	19	Minnesota	17.2
43	Massachusetts	15.6	21	Iowa	17.1
21	Michigan	17.1	21	Michigan	17.1
19	Minnesota	17.2	21	North Carolina	17.1
5	Mississippi	18.1	21	Ohio	17.1
25	Missouri	17.0	25	Alabama	17.0
39	Montana	16.0	25	Missouri	17.0
9	Nebraska	17.8	27	Kentucky	16.9
17	Nevada	17.4	27	New Jersey	16.9
40	New Hampshire	15.8	27	Tennessee	16.9
27	New Jersey	16.9	27	Wisconsin	16.9
9	New Mexico	17.8	31	Wyoming	16.8
40	New York	15.8	32	Connecticut	16.7
21	North Carolina	17.1	33	Maryland	16.6
44	North Dakota	15.5	33	South Carolina	16.6
21	Ohio	17.1	33	Washington	16.6
12	Oklahoma	17.7	36	Virginia	16.5
38	Oregon	16.1	37	Delaware	16.2
40	Pennsylvania	15.8	38	Oregon	16.1
45	Rhode Island	15.4	39	Montana	16.0
33	South Carolina	16.6	40	New Hampshire	15.8
17	South Dakota	17.4	40	New York	15.8
27	Tennessee	16.9	40	Pennsylvania	15.8
3	Texas	19.4	43	Massachusetts	15.6
1	Utah	22.1	44	North Dakota	15.5
50	Vermont	14.9	45	Hawaii	15.4
36	Virginia	16.5	45	Rhode Island	15.4
33	Washington	16.6	47	Florida	15.2
48	West Virginia	15.1	48	West Virginia	15.1
27	Wisconsin	16.9	49	Maine	15.0
31	Wyoming	16.8	50	Vermont	14.9
				District of Columbia	11.2

Source: CQ Press using data from U.S. Bureau of the Census
"State Characteristics: Vintage 2012" (http://www.census.gov/popest/data/state/asrh/2012/index.html)

Population 18 Years Old and Older in 2012

National Total = 240,185,952

ALPHA ORDER

RANK	STATE	POPULATION	% of USA
23	Alabama	3,697,617	1.5%
48	Alaska	544,349	0.2%
17	Arizona	4,932,361	2.1%
32	Arkansas	2,238,250	0.9%
1	California	28,801,211	12.0%
22	Colorado	3,956,224	1.6%
29	Connecticut	2,796,789	1.2%
45	Delaware	712,042	0.3%
3	Florida	15,315,088	6.4%
10	Georgia	7,429,820	3.1%
40	Hawaii	1,089,302	0.5%
39	Idaho	1,169,075	0.5%
6	Illinois	9,811,190	4.1%
16	Indiana	4,945,857	2.1%
30	Iowa	2,351,233	1.0%
33	Kansas	2,161,601	0.9%
26	Kentucky	3,362,177	1.4%
25	Louisiana	3,484,090	1.5%
41	Maine	1,063,274	0.4%
19	Maryland	4,540,763	1.9%
14	Massachusetts	5,244,729	2.2%
8	Michigan	7,616,490	3.2%
21	Minnesota	4,102,991	1.7%
31	Mississippi	2,239,593	0.9%
18	Missouri	4,618,513	1.9%
44	Montana	783,161	0.3%
38	Nebraska	1,392,120	0.6%
34	Nevada	2,095,348	0.9%
42	New Hampshire	1,045,878	0.4%
11	New Jersey	6,838,206	2.8%
36	New Mexico	1,571,096	0.7%
4	New York	15,307,107	6.4%
9	North Carolina	7,465,545	3.1%
47	North Dakota	545,020	0.2%
7	Ohio	8,880,551	3.7%
28	Oklahoma	2,877,457	1.2%
27	Oregon	3,038,729	1.3%
5	Pennsylvania	10,024,150	4.2%
43	Rhode Island	833,818	0.3%
24	South Carolina	3,643,633	1.5%
46	South Dakota	629,185	0.3%
15	Tennessee	4,962,227	2.1%
2	Texas	19,073,564	7.9%
35	Utah	1,967,315	0.8%
49	Vermont	502,060	0.2%
12	Virginia	6,329,130	2.6%
13	Washington	5,312,045	2.2%
37	West Virginia	1,471,372	0.6%
20	Wisconsin	4,408,841	1.8%
50	Wyoming	440,922	0.2%

RANK ORDER

RANK	STATE	POPULATION	% of USA
1	California	28,801,211	12.0%
2	Texas	19,073,564	7.9%
3	Florida	15,315,088	6.4%
4	New York	15,307,107	6.4%
5	Pennsylvania	10,024,150	4.2%
6	Illinois	9,811,190	4.1%
7	Ohio	8,880,551	3.7%
8	Michigan	7,616,490	3.2%
9	North Carolina	7,465,545	3.1%
10	Georgia	7,429,820	3.1%
11	New Jersey	6,838,206	2.8%
12	Virginia	6,329,130	2.6%
13	Washington	5,312,045	2.2%
14	Massachusetts	5,244,729	2.2%
15	Tennessee	4,962,227	2.1%
16	Indiana	4,945,857	2.1%
17	Arizona	4,932,361	2.1%
18	Missouri	4,618,513	1.9%
19	Maryland	4,540,763	1.9%
20	Wisconsin	4,408,841	1.8%
21	Minnesota	4,102,991	1.7%
22	Colorado	3,956,224	1.6%
23	Alabama	3,697,617	1.5%
24	South Carolina	3,643,633	1.5%
25	Louisiana	3,484,090	1.5%
26	Kentucky	3,362,177	1.4%
27	Oregon	3,038,729	1.3%
28	Oklahoma	2,877,457	1.2%
29	Connecticut	2,796,789	1.2%
30	Iowa	2,351,233	1.0%
31	Mississippi	2,239,593	0.9%
32	Arkansas	2,238,250	0.9%
33	Kansas	2,161,601	0.9%
34	Nevada	2,095,348	0.9%
35	Utah	1,967,315	0.8%
36	New Mexico	1,571,096	0.7%
37	West Virginia	1,471,372	0.6%
38	Nebraska	1,392,120	0.6%
39	Idaho	1,169,075	0.5%
40	Hawaii	1,089,302	0.5%
41	Maine	1,063,274	0.4%
42	New Hampshire	1,045,878	0.4%
43	Rhode Island	833,818	0.3%
44	Montana	783,161	0.3%
45	Delaware	712,042	0.3%
46	South Dakota	629,185	0.3%
47	North Dakota	545,020	0.2%
48	Alaska	544,349	0.2%
49	Vermont	502,060	0.2%
50	Wyoming	440,922	0.2%
	District of Columbia	522,843	0.2%

Source: U.S. Bureau of the Census

"State Characteristics: Vintage 2012" (http://www.census.gov/popest/data/state/asrh/2012/index.html)

Percent of Population 18 Years Old and Older in 2012

National Percent = 76.5% of Population

ALPHA ORDER

RANK	STATE	PERCENT
26	Alabama	76.7
47	Alaska	74.4
41	Arizona	75.3
34	Arkansas	75.9
36	California	75.7
31	Colorado	76.3
11	Connecticut	77.9
15	Delaware	77.6
4	Florida	79.3
45	Georgia	74.9
9	Hawaii	78.2
48	Idaho	73.3
33	Illinois	76.2
36	Indiana	75.7
29	Iowa	76.5
45	Kansas	74.9
25	Kentucky	76.8
36	Louisiana	75.7
2	Maine	80.0
17	Maryland	77.2
7	Massachusetts	78.9
18	Michigan	77.1
31	Minnesota	76.3
43	Mississippi	75.0
26	Missouri	76.7
11	Montana	77.9
43	Nebraska	75.0
34	Nevada	75.9
6	New Hampshire	79.2
18	New Jersey	77.1
41	New Mexico	75.3
9	New York	78.2
28	North Carolina	76.6
11	North Dakota	77.9
23	Ohio	76.9
40	Oklahoma	75.4
11	Oregon	77.9
8	Pennsylvania	78.5
3	Rhode Island	79.4
18	South Carolina	77.1
39	South Dakota	75.5
23	Tennessee	76.9
49	Texas	73.2
50	Utah	68.9
1	Vermont	80.2
16	Virginia	77.3
21	Washington	77.0
4	West Virginia	79.3
21	Wisconsin	77.0
29	Wyoming	76.5

RANK ORDER

RANK	STATE	PERCENT
1	Vermont	80.2
2	Maine	80.0
3	Rhode Island	79.4
4	Florida	79.3
4	West Virginia	79.3
6	New Hampshire	79.2
7	Massachusetts	78.9
8	Pennsylvania	78.5
9	Hawaii	78.2
9	New York	78.2
11	Connecticut	77.9
11	Montana	77.9
11	North Dakota	77.9
11	Oregon	77.9
15	Delaware	77.6
16	Virginia	77.3
17	Maryland	77.2
18	Michigan	77.1
18	New Jersey	77.1
18	South Carolina	77.1
21	Washington	77.0
21	Wisconsin	77.0
23	Ohio	76.9
23	Tennessee	76.9
25	Kentucky	76.8
26	Alabama	76.7
26	Missouri	76.7
28	North Carolina	76.6
29	Iowa	76.5
29	Wyoming	76.5
31	Colorado	76.3
31	Minnesota	76.3
33	Illinois	76.2
34	Arkansas	75.9
34	Nevada	75.9
36	California	75.7
36	Indiana	75.7
36	Louisiana	75.7
39	South Dakota	75.5
40	Oklahoma	75.4
41	Arizona	75.3
41	New Mexico	75.3
43	Mississippi	75.0
43	Nebraska	75.0
45	Georgia	74.9
45	Kansas	74.9
47	Alaska	74.4
48	Idaho	73.3
49	Texas	73.2
50	Utah	68.9

| | District of Columbia | 82.7 |

Source: CQ Press using data from U.S. Bureau of the Census
"State Characteristics: Vintage 2012" (http://www.census.gov/popest/data/state/asrh/2012/index.html)

Population 18 to 24 Years Old in 2012

National Total = 31,359,915

ALPHA ORDER

RANK	STATE	POPULATION	% of USA
23	Alabama	484,941	1.5%
48	Alaska	79,667	0.3%
16	Arizona	652,951	2.1%
34	Arkansas	286,692	0.9%
1	California	4,021,243	12.8%
21	Colorado	506,670	1.6%
29	Connecticut	337,068	1.1%
45	Delaware	93,661	0.3%
4	Florida	1,790,985	5.7%
8	Georgia	1,016,282	3.2%
40	Hawaii	136,870	0.4%
39	Idaho	156,847	0.5%
6	Illinois	1,254,647	4.0%
15	Indiana	662,480	2.1%
31	Iowa	314,290	1.0%
33	Kansas	296,942	0.9%
26	Kentucky	423,887	1.4%
25	Louisiana	475,856	1.5%
43	Maine	115,693	0.4%
19	Maryland	567,740	1.8%
13	Massachusetts	685,561	2.2%
9	Michigan	998,675	3.2%
22	Minnesota	506,376	1.6%
32	Mississippi	311,121	1.0%
18	Missouri	593,526	1.9%
44	Montana	98,514	0.3%
37	Nebraska	185,681	0.6%
35	Nevada	254,747	0.8%
41	New Hampshire	125,753	0.4%
12	New Jersey	785,211	2.5%
36	New Mexico	207,225	0.7%
3	New York	1,997,646	6.4%
10	North Carolina	972,162	3.1%
46	North Dakota	87,393	0.3%
7	Ohio	1,108,674	3.5%
27	Oklahoma	391,504	1.2%
28	Oregon	365,004	1.2%
5	Pennsylvania	1,263,768	4.0%
42	Rhode Island	120,461	0.4%
24	South Carolina	484,411	1.5%
47	South Dakota	83,612	0.3%
17	Tennessee	624,228	2.0%
2	Texas	2,683,024	8.6%
30	Utah	326,987	1.0%
49	Vermont	66,323	0.2%
11	Virginia	823,193	2.6%
14	Washington	667,879	2.1%
38	West Virginia	171,139	0.5%
20	Wisconsin	554,069	1.8%
50	Wyoming	58,144	0.2%

RANK ORDER

RANK	STATE	POPULATION	% of USA
1	California	4,021,243	12.8%
2	Texas	2,683,024	8.6%
3	New York	1,997,646	6.4%
4	Florida	1,790,985	5.7%
5	Pennsylvania	1,263,768	4.0%
6	Illinois	1,254,647	4.0%
7	Ohio	1,108,674	3.5%
8	Georgia	1,016,282	3.2%
9	Michigan	998,675	3.2%
10	North Carolina	972,162	3.1%
11	Virginia	823,193	2.6%
12	New Jersey	785,211	2.5%
13	Massachusetts	685,561	2.2%
14	Washington	667,879	2.1%
15	Indiana	662,480	2.1%
16	Arizona	652,951	2.1%
17	Tennessee	624,228	2.0%
18	Missouri	593,526	1.9%
19	Maryland	567,740	1.8%
20	Wisconsin	554,069	1.8%
21	Colorado	506,670	1.6%
22	Minnesota	506,376	1.6%
23	Alabama	484,941	1.5%
24	South Carolina	484,411	1.5%
25	Louisiana	475,856	1.5%
26	Kentucky	423,887	1.4%
27	Oklahoma	391,504	1.2%
28	Oregon	365,004	1.2%
29	Connecticut	337,068	1.1%
30	Utah	326,987	1.0%
31	Iowa	314,290	1.0%
32	Mississippi	311,121	1.0%
33	Kansas	296,942	0.9%
34	Arkansas	286,692	0.9%
35	Nevada	254,747	0.8%
36	New Mexico	207,225	0.7%
37	Nebraska	185,681	0.6%
38	West Virginia	171,139	0.5%
39	Idaho	156,847	0.5%
40	Hawaii	136,870	0.4%
41	New Hampshire	125,753	0.4%
42	Rhode Island	120,461	0.4%
43	Maine	115,693	0.4%
44	Montana	98,514	0.3%
45	Delaware	93,661	0.3%
46	North Dakota	87,393	0.3%
47	South Dakota	83,612	0.3%
48	Alaska	79,667	0.3%
49	Vermont	66,323	0.2%
50	Wyoming	58,144	0.2%
	District of Columbia	82,492	0.3%

Source: CQ Press using data from U.S. Bureau of the Census
  "State Characteristics: Vintage 2012" (http://www.census.gov/popest/data/state/asrh/2012/index.html)

Percent of Population 18 to 24 Years Old in 2012

National Percent = 10.0% of Population

ALPHA ORDER

RANK	STATE	PERCENT
18	Alabama	10.1
4	Alaska	10.9
23	Arizona	10.0
34	Arkansas	9.7
5	California	10.6
30	Colorado	9.8
43	Connecticut	9.4
14	Delaware	10.2
46	Florida	9.3
14	Georgia	10.2
30	Hawaii	9.8
30	Idaho	9.8
34	Illinois	9.7
18	Indiana	10.1
14	Iowa	10.2
8	Kansas	10.3
34	Kentucky	9.7
8	Louisiana	10.3
50	Maine	8.7
40	Maryland	9.6
8	Massachusetts	10.3
18	Michigan	10.1
43	Minnesota	9.4
7	Mississippi	10.4
27	Missouri	9.9
30	Montana	9.8
23	Nebraska	10.0
47	Nevada	9.2
42	New Hampshire	9.5
49	New Jersey	8.9
27	New Mexico	9.9
14	New York	10.2
23	North Carolina	10.0
1	North Dakota	12.5
40	Ohio	9.6
8	Oklahoma	10.3
43	Oregon	9.4
27	Pennsylvania	9.9
2	Rhode Island	11.5
8	South Carolina	10.3
23	South Dakota	10.0
34	Tennessee	9.7
8	Texas	10.3
2	Utah	11.5
5	Vermont	10.6
18	Virginia	10.1
34	Washington	9.7
47	West Virginia	9.2
34	Wisconsin	9.7
18	Wyoming	10.1

RANK ORDER

RANK	STATE	PERCENT
1	North Dakota	12.5
2	Rhode Island	11.5
2	Utah	11.5
4	Alaska	10.9
5	California	10.6
5	Vermont	10.6
7	Mississippi	10.4
8	Kansas	10.3
8	Louisiana	10.3
8	Massachusetts	10.3
8	Oklahoma	10.3
8	South Carolina	10.3
8	Texas	10.3
14	Delaware	10.2
14	Georgia	10.2
14	Iowa	10.2
14	New York	10.2
18	Alabama	10.1
18	Indiana	10.1
18	Michigan	10.1
18	Virginia	10.1
18	Wyoming	10.1
23	Arizona	10.0
23	Nebraska	10.0
23	North Carolina	10.0
23	South Dakota	10.0
27	Missouri	9.9
27	New Mexico	9.9
27	Pennsylvania	9.9
30	Colorado	9.8
30	Hawaii	9.8
30	Idaho	9.8
30	Montana	9.8
34	Arkansas	9.7
34	Illinois	9.7
34	Kentucky	9.7
34	Tennessee	9.7
34	Washington	9.7
34	Wisconsin	9.7
40	Maryland	9.6
40	Ohio	9.6
42	New Hampshire	9.5
43	Connecticut	9.4
43	Minnesota	9.4
43	Oregon	9.4
46	Florida	9.3
47	Nevada	9.2
47	West Virginia	9.2
49	New Jersey	8.9
50	Maine	8.7
	District of Columbia	13.0

Source: CQ Press using data from U.S. Bureau of the Census
"State Characteristics: Vintage 2012" (http://www.census.gov/popest/data/state/asrh/2012/index.html)

Population 25 to 44 Years Old in 2012

National Total = 82,825,741

ALPHA ORDER

RANK	STATE	POPULATION	% of USA
23	Alabama	1,224,424	1.5%
47	Alaska	203,103	0.2%
15	Arizona	1,704,005	2.1%
34	Arkansas	747,881	0.9%
1	California	10,644,074	12.9%
20	Colorado	1,469,016	1.8%
29	Connecticut	892,999	1.1%
45	Delaware	227,779	0.3%
4	Florida	4,804,301	5.8%
8	Georgia	2,744,780	3.3%
40	Hawaii	374,049	0.5%
39	Idaho	404,451	0.5%
5	Illinois	3,480,142	4.2%
17	Indiana	1,661,297	2.0%
33	Iowa	749,469	0.9%
35	Kansas	730,489	0.9%
26	Kentucky	1,133,798	1.4%
24	Louisiana	1,212,463	1.5%
42	Maine	309,665	0.4%
18	Maryland	1,577,257	1.9%
14	Massachusetts	1,745,608	2.1%
10	Michigan	2,399,581	2.9%
22	Minnesota	1,404,314	1.7%
32	Mississippi	758,556	0.9%
19	Missouri	1,522,521	1.8%
44	Montana	239,194	0.3%
37	Nebraska	472,662	0.6%
31	Nevada	771,724	0.9%
41	New Hampshire	316,659	0.4%
11	New Jersey	2,332,643	2.8%
36	New Mexico	522,485	0.6%
3	New York	5,296,680	6.4%
9	North Carolina	2,579,838	3.1%
48	North Dakota	175,862	0.2%
7	Ohio	2,862,615	3.5%
28	Oklahoma	983,633	1.2%
27	Oregon	1,038,829	1.3%
6	Pennsylvania	3,126,423	3.8%
43	Rhode Island	260,131	0.3%
25	South Carolina	1,200,302	1.4%
46	South Dakota	204,168	0.2%
16	Tennessee	1,685,981	2.0%
2	Texas	7,300,015	8.8%
30	Utah	801,747	1.0%
50	Vermont	145,199	0.2%
12	Virginia	2,235,331	2.7%
13	Washington	1,886,869	2.3%
38	West Virginia	452,561	0.5%
21	Wisconsin	1,433,567	1.7%
49	Wyoming	149,367	0.2%

RANK ORDER

RANK	STATE	POPULATION	% of USA
1	California	10,644,074	12.9%
2	Texas	7,300,015	8.8%
3	New York	5,296,680	6.4%
4	Florida	4,804,301	5.8%
5	Illinois	3,480,142	4.2%
6	Pennsylvania	3,126,423	3.8%
7	Ohio	2,862,615	3.5%
8	Georgia	2,744,780	3.3%
9	North Carolina	2,579,838	3.1%
10	Michigan	2,399,581	2.9%
11	New Jersey	2,332,643	2.8%
12	Virginia	2,235,331	2.7%
13	Washington	1,886,869	2.3%
14	Massachusetts	1,745,608	2.1%
15	Arizona	1,704,005	2.1%
16	Tennessee	1,685,981	2.0%
17	Indiana	1,661,297	2.0%
18	Maryland	1,577,257	1.9%
19	Missouri	1,522,521	1.8%
20	Colorado	1,469,016	1.8%
21	Wisconsin	1,433,567	1.7%
22	Minnesota	1,404,314	1.7%
23	Alabama	1,224,424	1.5%
24	Louisiana	1,212,463	1.5%
25	South Carolina	1,200,302	1.4%
26	Kentucky	1,133,798	1.4%
27	Oregon	1,038,829	1.3%
28	Oklahoma	983,633	1.2%
29	Connecticut	892,999	1.1%
30	Utah	801,747	1.0%
31	Nevada	771,724	0.9%
32	Mississippi	758,556	0.9%
33	Iowa	749,469	0.9%
34	Arkansas	747,881	0.9%
35	Kansas	730,489	0.9%
36	New Mexico	522,485	0.6%
37	Nebraska	472,662	0.6%
38	West Virginia	452,561	0.5%
39	Idaho	404,451	0.5%
40	Hawaii	374,049	0.5%
41	New Hampshire	316,659	0.4%
42	Maine	309,665	0.4%
43	Rhode Island	260,131	0.3%
44	Montana	239,194	0.3%
45	Delaware	227,779	0.3%
46	South Dakota	204,168	0.2%
47	Alaska	203,103	0.2%
48	North Dakota	175,862	0.2%
49	Wyoming	149,367	0.2%
50	Vermont	145,199	0.2%
	District of Columbia	225,234	0.3%

Source: CQ Press using data from U.S. Bureau of the Census
"State Characteristics: Vintage 2012" (http://www.census.gov/popest/data/state/asrh/2012/index.html)

Percent of Population 25 to 44 Years Old in 2012

National Percent = 26.4% of Population

<table>
<tr><td colspan="3">ALPHA ORDER</td><td colspan="3">RANK ORDER</td></tr>
<tr><th>RANK</th><th>STATE</th><th>PERCENT</th><th>RANK</th><th>STATE</th><th>PERCENT</th></tr>
<tr><td>26</td><td>Alabama</td><td>25.4</td><td>1</td><td>Colorado</td><td>28.3</td></tr>
<tr><td>6</td><td>Alaska</td><td>27.8</td><td>2</td><td>Utah</td><td>28.1</td></tr>
<tr><td>21</td><td>Arizona</td><td>26.0</td><td>3</td><td>California</td><td>28.0</td></tr>
<tr><td>26</td><td>Arkansas</td><td>25.4</td><td>3</td><td>Nevada</td><td>28.0</td></tr>
<tr><td>3</td><td>California</td><td>28.0</td><td>3</td><td>Texas</td><td>28.0</td></tr>
<tr><td>1</td><td>Colorado</td><td>28.3</td><td>6</td><td>Alaska</td><td>27.8</td></tr>
<tr><td>37</td><td>Connecticut</td><td>24.9</td><td>7</td><td>Georgia</td><td>27.7</td></tr>
<tr><td>39</td><td>Delaware</td><td>24.8</td><td>8</td><td>Washington</td><td>27.4</td></tr>
<tr><td>37</td><td>Florida</td><td>24.9</td><td>9</td><td>Virginia</td><td>27.3</td></tr>
<tr><td>7</td><td>Georgia</td><td>27.7</td><td>10</td><td>New York</td><td>27.1</td></tr>
<tr><td>12</td><td>Hawaii</td><td>26.9</td><td>11</td><td>Illinois</td><td>27.0</td></tr>
<tr><td>31</td><td>Idaho</td><td>25.3</td><td>12</td><td>Hawaii</td><td>26.9</td></tr>
<tr><td>11</td><td>Illinois</td><td>27.0</td><td>13</td><td>Maryland</td><td>26.8</td></tr>
<tr><td>26</td><td>Indiana</td><td>25.4</td><td>14</td><td>Oregon</td><td>26.6</td></tr>
<tr><td>44</td><td>Iowa</td><td>24.4</td><td>15</td><td>North Carolina</td><td>26.5</td></tr>
<tr><td>31</td><td>Kansas</td><td>25.3</td><td>16</td><td>Louisiana</td><td>26.3</td></tr>
<tr><td>22</td><td>Kentucky</td><td>25.9</td><td>16</td><td>Massachusetts</td><td>26.3</td></tr>
<tr><td>16</td><td>Louisiana</td><td>26.3</td><td>16</td><td>New Jersey</td><td>26.3</td></tr>
<tr><td>49</td><td>Maine</td><td>23.3</td><td>19</td><td>Minnesota</td><td>26.1</td></tr>
<tr><td>13</td><td>Maryland</td><td>26.8</td><td>19</td><td>Tennessee</td><td>26.1</td></tr>
<tr><td>16</td><td>Massachusetts</td><td>26.3</td><td>21</td><td>Arizona</td><td>26.0</td></tr>
<tr><td>46</td><td>Michigan</td><td>24.3</td><td>22</td><td>Kentucky</td><td>25.9</td></tr>
<tr><td>19</td><td>Minnesota</td><td>26.1</td><td>22</td><td>Wyoming</td><td>25.9</td></tr>
<tr><td>26</td><td>Mississippi</td><td>25.4</td><td>24</td><td>Oklahoma</td><td>25.8</td></tr>
<tr><td>31</td><td>Missouri</td><td>25.3</td><td>25</td><td>Nebraska</td><td>25.5</td></tr>
<tr><td>48</td><td>Montana</td><td>23.8</td><td>26</td><td>Alabama</td><td>25.4</td></tr>
<tr><td>25</td><td>Nebraska</td><td>25.5</td><td>26</td><td>Arkansas</td><td>25.4</td></tr>
<tr><td>3</td><td>Nevada</td><td>28.0</td><td>26</td><td>Indiana</td><td>25.4</td></tr>
<tr><td>47</td><td>New Hampshire</td><td>24.0</td><td>26</td><td>Mississippi</td><td>25.4</td></tr>
<tr><td>16</td><td>New Jersey</td><td>26.3</td><td>26</td><td>South Carolina</td><td>25.4</td></tr>
<tr><td>34</td><td>New Mexico</td><td>25.1</td><td>31</td><td>Idaho</td><td>25.3</td></tr>
<tr><td>10</td><td>New York</td><td>27.1</td><td>31</td><td>Kansas</td><td>25.3</td></tr>
<tr><td>15</td><td>North Carolina</td><td>26.5</td><td>31</td><td>Missouri</td><td>25.3</td></tr>
<tr><td>34</td><td>North Dakota</td><td>25.1</td><td>34</td><td>New Mexico</td><td>25.1</td></tr>
<tr><td>39</td><td>Ohio</td><td>24.8</td><td>34</td><td>North Dakota</td><td>25.1</td></tr>
<tr><td>24</td><td>Oklahoma</td><td>25.8</td><td>36</td><td>Wisconsin</td><td>25.0</td></tr>
<tr><td>14</td><td>Oregon</td><td>26.6</td><td>37</td><td>Connecticut</td><td>24.9</td></tr>
<tr><td>42</td><td>Pennsylvania</td><td>24.5</td><td>37</td><td>Florida</td><td>24.9</td></tr>
<tr><td>39</td><td>Rhode Island</td><td>24.8</td><td>39</td><td>Delaware</td><td>24.8</td></tr>
<tr><td>26</td><td>South Carolina</td><td>25.4</td><td>39</td><td>Ohio</td><td>24.8</td></tr>
<tr><td>42</td><td>South Dakota</td><td>24.5</td><td>39</td><td>Rhode Island</td><td>24.8</td></tr>
<tr><td>19</td><td>Tennessee</td><td>26.1</td><td>42</td><td>Pennsylvania</td><td>24.5</td></tr>
<tr><td>3</td><td>Texas</td><td>28.0</td><td>42</td><td>South Dakota</td><td>24.5</td></tr>
<tr><td>2</td><td>Utah</td><td>28.1</td><td>44</td><td>Iowa</td><td>24.4</td></tr>
<tr><td>50</td><td>Vermont</td><td>23.2</td><td>44</td><td>West Virginia</td><td>24.4</td></tr>
<tr><td>9</td><td>Virginia</td><td>27.3</td><td>46</td><td>Michigan</td><td>24.3</td></tr>
<tr><td>8</td><td>Washington</td><td>27.4</td><td>47</td><td>New Hampshire</td><td>24.0</td></tr>
<tr><td>44</td><td>West Virginia</td><td>24.4</td><td>48</td><td>Montana</td><td>23.8</td></tr>
<tr><td>36</td><td>Wisconsin</td><td>25.0</td><td>49</td><td>Maine</td><td>23.3</td></tr>
<tr><td>22</td><td>Wyoming</td><td>25.9</td><td>50</td><td>Vermont</td><td>23.2</td></tr>
<tr><td></td><td></td><td></td><td></td><td>District of Columbia</td><td>35.6</td></tr>
</table>

Source: CQ Press using data from U.S. Bureau of the Census
"State Characteristics: Vintage 2012" (http://www.census.gov/popest/data/state/asrh/2012/index.html)

Population 45 to 64 Years Old in 2012

National Total = 82,854,940

ALPHA ORDER

RANK	STATE	POPULATION	% of USA
23	Alabama	1,288,872	1.6%
47	Alaska	199,082	0.2%
19	Arizona	1,603,872	1.9%
32	Arkansas	761,087	0.9%
1	California	9,535,809	11.5%
22	Colorado	1,367,297	1.7%
28	Connecticut	1,034,010	1.2%
45	Delaware	250,128	0.3%
4	Florida	5,210,087	6.3%
10	Georgia	2,529,059	3.1%
42	Hawaii	367,582	0.4%
41	Idaho	395,199	0.5%
6	Illinois	3,381,964	4.1%
16	Indiana	1,732,932	2.1%
30	Iowa	817,169	1.0%
33	Kansas	739,901	0.9%
26	Kentucky	1,189,839	1.4%
25	Louisiana	1,200,566	1.4%
39	Maine	411,540	0.5%
17	Maryland	1,632,747	2.0%
13	Massachusetts	1,855,066	2.2%
8	Michigan	2,775,520	3.3%
21	Minnesota	1,462,534	1.8%
31	Mississippi	765,841	0.9%
18	Missouri	1,619,285	2.0%
44	Montana	287,164	0.3%
38	Nebraska	476,423	0.6%
34	Nevada	707,963	0.9%
40	New Hampshire	409,663	0.5%
11	New Jersey	2,469,797	3.0%
36	New Mexico	546,553	0.7%
3	New York	5,255,209	6.3%
9	North Carolina	2,565,676	3.1%
49	North Dakota	181,099	0.2%
7	Ohio	3,204,140	3.9%
29	Oklahoma	968,073	1.2%
27	Oregon	1,053,277	1.3%
5	Pennsylvania	3,591,098	4.3%
43	Rhode Island	294,597	0.4%
24	South Carolina	1,263,461	1.5%
46	South Dakota	219,222	0.3%
15	Tennessee	1,733,511	2.1%
2	Texas	6,251,230	7.5%
35	Utah	567,162	0.7%
48	Vermont	192,094	0.2%
12	Virginia	2,208,101	2.7%
14	Washington	1,848,880	2.2%
37	West Virginia	535,723	0.6%
20	Wisconsin	1,596,705	1.9%
50	Wyoming	157,903	0.2%

RANK ORDER

RANK	STATE	POPULATION	% of USA
1	California	9,535,809	11.5%
2	Texas	6,251,230	7.5%
3	New York	5,255,209	6.3%
4	Florida	5,210,087	6.3%
5	Pennsylvania	3,591,098	4.3%
6	Illinois	3,381,964	4.1%
7	Ohio	3,204,140	3.9%
8	Michigan	2,775,520	3.3%
9	North Carolina	2,565,676	3.1%
10	Georgia	2,529,059	3.1%
11	New Jersey	2,469,797	3.0%
12	Virginia	2,208,101	2.7%
13	Massachusetts	1,855,066	2.2%
14	Washington	1,848,880	2.2%
15	Tennessee	1,733,511	2.1%
16	Indiana	1,732,932	2.1%
17	Maryland	1,632,747	2.0%
18	Missouri	1,619,285	2.0%
19	Arizona	1,603,872	1.9%
20	Wisconsin	1,596,705	1.9%
21	Minnesota	1,462,534	1.8%
22	Colorado	1,367,297	1.7%
23	Alabama	1,288,872	1.6%
24	South Carolina	1,263,461	1.5%
25	Louisiana	1,200,566	1.4%
26	Kentucky	1,189,839	1.4%
27	Oregon	1,053,277	1.3%
28	Connecticut	1,034,010	1.2%
29	Oklahoma	968,073	1.2%
30	Iowa	817,169	1.0%
31	Mississippi	765,841	0.9%
32	Arkansas	761,087	0.9%
33	Kansas	739,901	0.9%
34	Nevada	707,963	0.9%
35	Utah	567,162	0.7%
36	New Mexico	546,553	0.7%
37	West Virginia	535,723	0.6%
38	Nebraska	476,423	0.6%
39	Maine	411,540	0.5%
40	New Hampshire	409,663	0.5%
41	Idaho	395,199	0.5%
42	Hawaii	367,582	0.4%
43	Rhode Island	294,597	0.4%
44	Montana	287,164	0.3%
45	Delaware	250,128	0.3%
46	South Dakota	219,222	0.3%
47	Alaska	199,082	0.2%
48	Vermont	192,094	0.2%
49	North Dakota	181,099	0.2%
50	Wyoming	157,903	0.2%
	District of Columbia	143,228	0.2%

Source: U.S. Bureau of the Census
   "State Characteristics: Vintage 2012" (http://www.census.gov/popest/data/state/asrh/2012/index.html)

Percent of Population 45 to 64 Years Old in 2012

National Percent = 26.4% of Population

ALPHA ORDER

RANK	STATE	PERCENT
27	Alabama	26.7
17	Alaska	27.2
48	Arizona	24.5
39	Arkansas	25.8
46	California	25.1
31	Colorado	26.4
5	Connecticut	28.8
16	Delaware	27.3
20	Florida	27.0
44	Georgia	25.5
31	Hawaii	26.4
47	Idaho	24.8
33	Illinois	26.3
30	Indiana	26.5
29	Iowa	26.6
43	Kansas	25.6
17	Kentucky	27.2
37	Louisiana	26.1
1	Maine	31.0
14	Maryland	27.7
10	Massachusetts	27.9
7	Michigan	28.1
17	Minnesota	27.2
40	Mississippi	25.7
23	Missouri	26.9
6	Montana	28.6
40	Nebraska	25.7
40	Nevada	25.7
1	New Hampshire	31.0
10	New Jersey	27.9
36	New Mexico	26.2
23	New York	26.9
33	North Carolina	26.3
38	North Dakota	25.9
13	Ohio	27.8
45	Oklahoma	25.4
20	Oregon	27.0
7	Pennsylvania	28.1
9	Rhode Island	28.0
27	South Carolina	26.7
33	South Dakota	26.3
23	Tennessee	26.9
49	Texas	24.0
50	Utah	19.9
3	Vermont	30.7
20	Virginia	27.0
26	Washington	26.8
4	West Virginia	28.9
10	Wisconsin	27.9
15	Wyoming	27.4

RANK ORDER

RANK	STATE	PERCENT
1	Maine	31.0
1	New Hampshire	31.0
3	Vermont	30.7
4	West Virginia	28.9
5	Connecticut	28.8
6	Montana	28.6
7	Michigan	28.1
7	Pennsylvania	28.1
9	Rhode Island	28.0
10	Massachusetts	27.9
10	New Jersey	27.9
10	Wisconsin	27.9
13	Ohio	27.8
14	Maryland	27.7
15	Wyoming	27.4
16	Delaware	27.3
17	Alaska	27.2
17	Kentucky	27.2
17	Minnesota	27.2
20	Florida	27.0
20	Oregon	27.0
20	Virginia	27.0
23	Missouri	26.9
23	New York	26.9
23	Tennessee	26.9
26	Washington	26.8
27	Alabama	26.7
27	South Carolina	26.7
29	Iowa	26.6
30	Indiana	26.5
31	Colorado	26.4
31	Hawaii	26.4
33	Illinois	26.3
33	North Carolina	26.3
33	South Dakota	26.3
36	New Mexico	26.2
37	Louisiana	26.1
38	North Dakota	25.9
39	Arkansas	25.8
40	Mississippi	25.7
40	Nebraska	25.7
40	Nevada	25.7
43	Kansas	25.6
44	Georgia	25.5
45	Oklahoma	25.4
46	California	25.1
47	Idaho	24.8
48	Arizona	24.5
49	Texas	24.0
50	Utah	19.9

District of Columbia 22.7

Source: CQ Press using data from U.S. Bureau of the Census
"State Characteristics: Vintage 2012" (http://www.census.gov/popest/data/state/asrh/2012/index.html)

Population 65 Years Old and Older in 2012

National Total = 43,145,356

ALPHA ORDER

RANK	STATE	POPULATION	% of USA
22	Alabama	699,380	1.6%
50	Alaska	62,497	0.1%
13	Arizona	971,533	2.3%
31	Arkansas	442,590	1.0%
1	California	4,600,085	10.7%
25	Colorado	613,241	1.4%
29	Connecticut	532,712	1.2%
45	Delaware	140,474	0.3%
2	Florida	3,509,715	8.1%
11	Georgia	1,139,699	2.6%
41	Hawaii	210,801	0.5%
40	Idaho	212,578	0.5%
7	Illinois	1,694,437	3.9%
17	Indiana	889,148	2.1%
30	Iowa	470,305	1.1%
33	Kansas	394,269	0.9%
24	Kentucky	614,653	1.4%
26	Louisiana	595,205	1.4%
39	Maine	226,376	0.5%
20	Maryland	763,019	1.8%
14	Massachusetts	958,494	2.2%
8	Michigan	1,442,714	3.3%
21	Minnesota	729,767	1.7%
32	Mississippi	404,075	0.9%
18	Missouri	883,181	2.0%
44	Montana	158,289	0.4%
38	Nebraska	257,354	0.6%
34	Nevada	360,914	0.8%
42	New Hampshire	193,803	0.4%
10	New Jersey	1,250,555	2.9%
36	New Mexico	294,833	0.7%
4	New York	2,757,572	6.4%
9	North Carolina	1,347,869	3.1%
47	North Dakota	100,666	0.2%
6	Ohio	1,705,122	4.0%
28	Oklahoma	534,247	1.2%
27	Oregon	581,619	1.3%
5	Pennsylvania	2,042,861	4.7%
43	Rhode Island	158,629	0.4%
23	South Carolina	695,459	1.6%
46	South Dakota	122,183	0.3%
15	Tennessee	918,507	2.1%
3	Texas	2,839,295	6.6%
37	Utah	271,419	0.6%
48	Vermont	98,444	0.2%
12	Virginia	1,062,505	2.5%
16	Washington	908,417	2.1%
35	West Virginia	311,949	0.7%
19	Wisconsin	824,500	1.9%
49	Wyoming	75,508	0.2%

RANK ORDER

RANK	STATE	POPULATION	% of USA
1	California	4,600,085	10.7%
2	Florida	3,509,715	8.1%
3	Texas	2,839,295	6.6%
4	New York	2,757,572	6.4%
5	Pennsylvania	2,042,861	4.7%
6	Ohio	1,705,122	4.0%
7	Illinois	1,694,437	3.9%
8	Michigan	1,442,714	3.3%
9	North Carolina	1,347,869	3.1%
10	New Jersey	1,250,555	2.9%
11	Georgia	1,139,699	2.6%
12	Virginia	1,062,505	2.5%
13	Arizona	971,533	2.3%
14	Massachusetts	958,494	2.2%
15	Tennessee	918,507	2.1%
16	Washington	908,417	2.1%
17	Indiana	889,148	2.1%
18	Missouri	883,181	2.0%
19	Wisconsin	824,500	1.9%
20	Maryland	763,019	1.8%
21	Minnesota	729,767	1.7%
22	Alabama	699,380	1.6%
23	South Carolina	695,459	1.6%
24	Kentucky	614,653	1.4%
25	Colorado	613,241	1.4%
26	Louisiana	595,205	1.4%
27	Oregon	581,619	1.3%
28	Oklahoma	534,247	1.2%
29	Connecticut	532,712	1.2%
30	Iowa	470,305	1.1%
31	Arkansas	442,590	1.0%
32	Mississippi	404,075	0.9%
33	Kansas	394,269	0.9%
34	Nevada	360,914	0.8%
35	West Virginia	311,949	0.7%
36	New Mexico	294,833	0.7%
37	Utah	271,419	0.6%
38	Nebraska	257,354	0.6%
39	Maine	226,376	0.5%
40	Idaho	212,578	0.5%
41	Hawaii	210,801	0.5%
42	New Hampshire	193,803	0.4%
43	Rhode Island	158,629	0.4%
44	Montana	158,289	0.4%
45	Delaware	140,474	0.3%
46	South Dakota	122,183	0.3%
47	North Dakota	100,666	0.2%
48	Vermont	98,444	0.2%
49	Wyoming	75,508	0.2%
50	Alaska	62,497	0.1%
	District of Columbia	71,889	0.2%

Source: U.S. Bureau of the Census
"State Characteristics: Vintage 2012" (http://www.census.gov/popest/data/state/asrh/2012/index.html)

Percent of Population 65 Years Old and Older in 2012

National Percent = 13.7% of Population

ALPHA ORDER			RANK ORDER		
RANK	STATE	PERCENT	RANK	STATE	PERCENT
21	Alabama	14.5	1	Florida	18.2
50	Alaska	8.5	2	Maine	17.0
13	Arizona	14.8	3	West Virginia	16.8
11	Arkansas	15.0	4	Pennsylvania	16.0
45	California	12.1	5	Montana	15.7
46	Colorado	11.8	5	Vermont	15.7
13	Connecticut	14.8	7	Delaware	15.3
7	Delaware	15.3	7	Iowa	15.3
1	Florida	18.2	9	Hawaii	15.1
47	Georgia	11.5	9	Rhode Island	15.1
9	Hawaii	15.1	11	Arkansas	15.0
37	Idaho	13.3	12	Oregon	14.9
38	Illinois	13.2	13	Arizona	14.8
34	Indiana	13.6	13	Connecticut	14.8
7	Iowa	15.3	13	Ohio	14.8
33	Kansas	13.7	16	Missouri	14.7
29	Kentucky	14.0	16	New Hampshire	14.7
44	Louisiana	12.9	16	South Carolina	14.7
2	Maine	17.0	16	South Dakota	14.7
42	Maryland	13.0	20	Michigan	14.6
22	Massachusetts	14.4	21	Alabama	14.5
20	Michigan	14.6	22	Massachusetts	14.4
34	Minnesota	13.6	22	North Dakota	14.4
36	Mississippi	13.5	22	Wisconsin	14.4
16	Missouri	14.7	25	Tennessee	14.2
5	Montana	15.7	26	New Jersey	14.1
31	Nebraska	13.9	26	New Mexico	14.1
40	Nevada	13.1	26	New York	14.1
16	New Hampshire	14.7	29	Kentucky	14.0
26	New Jersey	14.1	29	Oklahoma	14.0
26	New Mexico	14.1	31	Nebraska	13.9
26	New York	14.1	32	North Carolina	13.8
32	North Carolina	13.8	33	Kansas	13.7
22	North Dakota	14.4	34	Indiana	13.6
13	Ohio	14.8	34	Minnesota	13.6
29	Oklahoma	14.0	36	Mississippi	13.5
12	Oregon	14.9	37	Idaho	13.3
4	Pennsylvania	16.0	38	Illinois	13.2
9	Rhode Island	15.1	38	Washington	13.2
16	South Carolina	14.7	40	Nevada	13.1
16	South Dakota	14.7	40	Wyoming	13.1
25	Tennessee	14.2	42	Maryland	13.0
48	Texas	10.9	42	Virginia	13.0
49	Utah	9.5	44	Louisiana	12.9
5	Vermont	15.7	45	California	12.1
42	Virginia	13.0	46	Colorado	11.8
38	Washington	13.2	47	Georgia	11.5
3	West Virginia	16.8	48	Texas	10.9
22	Wisconsin	14.4	49	Utah	9.5
40	Wyoming	13.1	50	Alaska	8.5
				District of Columbia	11.4

Source: CQ Press using data from U.S. Bureau of the Census
"State Characteristics: Vintage 2012" (http://www.census.gov/popest/data/state/asrh/2012/index.html)

Population 85 Years Old and Older in 2012

National Total = 5,887,300

ALPHA ORDER

RANK	STATE	POPULATION	% of USA
24	Alabama	80,104	1.4%
50	Alaska	5,373	0.1%
18	Arizona	114,425	1.9%
32	Arkansas	53,920	0.9%
1	California	654,281	11.1%
26	Colorado	76,510	1.3%
22	Connecticut	88,168	1.5%
47	Delaware	16,820	0.3%
2	Florida	482,753	8.2%
15	Georgia	123,483	2.1%
38	Hawaii	34,623	0.6%
42	Idaho	26,610	0.5%
6	Illinois	247,838	4.2%
16	Indiana	121,927	2.1%
25	Iowa	77,372	1.3%
31	Kansas	62,168	1.1%
28	Kentucky	72,971	1.2%
29	Louisiana	70,740	1.2%
40	Maine	30,473	0.5%
21	Maryland	105,808	1.8%
11	Massachusetts	153,113	2.6%
8	Michigan	203,914	3.5%
19	Minnesota	112,619	1.9%
33	Mississippi	47,229	0.8%
17	Missouri	120,285	2.0%
44	Montana	21,081	0.4%
34	Nebraska	40,950	0.7%
37	Nevada	34,744	0.6%
43	New Hampshire	26,414	0.4%
9	New Jersey	189,119	3.2%
36	New Mexico	34,877	0.6%
3	New York	414,385	7.0%
10	North Carolina	159,872	2.7%
46	North Dakota	17,330	0.3%
7	Ohio	243,513	4.1%
30	Oklahoma	65,560	1.1%
23	Oregon	82,133	1.4%
5	Pennsylvania	322,052	5.5%
41	Rhode Island	27,564	0.5%
27	South Carolina	76,103	1.3%
45	South Dakota	20,171	0.3%
20	Tennessee	106,389	1.8%
4	Texas	335,632	5.7%
39	Utah	33,457	0.6%
48	Vermont	13,502	0.2%
12	Virginia	132,220	2.2%
13	Washington	124,598	2.1%
35	West Virginia	37,733	0.6%
14	Wisconsin	124,180	2.1%
49	Wyoming	9,221	0.2%

RANK ORDER

RANK	STATE	POPULATION	% of USA
1	California	654,281	11.1%
2	Florida	482,753	8.2%
3	New York	414,385	7.0%
4	Texas	335,632	5.7%
5	Pennsylvania	322,052	5.5%
6	Illinois	247,838	4.2%
7	Ohio	243,513	4.1%
8	Michigan	203,914	3.5%
9	New Jersey	189,119	3.2%
10	North Carolina	159,872	2.7%
11	Massachusetts	153,113	2.6%
12	Virginia	132,220	2.2%
13	Washington	124,598	2.1%
14	Wisconsin	124,180	2.1%
15	Georgia	123,483	2.1%
16	Indiana	121,927	2.1%
17	Missouri	120,285	2.0%
18	Arizona	114,425	1.9%
19	Minnesota	112,619	1.9%
20	Tennessee	106,389	1.8%
21	Maryland	105,808	1.8%
22	Connecticut	88,168	1.5%
23	Oregon	82,133	1.4%
24	Alabama	80,104	1.4%
25	Iowa	77,372	1.3%
26	Colorado	76,510	1.3%
27	South Carolina	76,103	1.3%
28	Kentucky	72,971	1.2%
29	Louisiana	70,740	1.2%
30	Oklahoma	65,560	1.1%
31	Kansas	62,168	1.1%
32	Arkansas	53,920	0.9%
33	Mississippi	47,229	0.8%
34	Nebraska	40,950	0.7%
35	West Virginia	37,733	0.6%
36	New Mexico	34,877	0.6%
37	Nevada	34,744	0.6%
38	Hawaii	34,623	0.6%
39	Utah	33,457	0.6%
40	Maine	30,473	0.5%
41	Rhode Island	27,564	0.5%
42	Idaho	26,610	0.5%
43	New Hampshire	26,414	0.4%
44	Montana	21,081	0.4%
45	South Dakota	20,171	0.3%
46	North Dakota	17,330	0.3%
47	Delaware	16,820	0.3%
48	Vermont	13,502	0.2%
49	Wyoming	9,221	0.2%
50	Alaska	5,373	0.1%
	District of Columbia	11,003	0.2%

Source: U.S. Bureau of the Census
   "State Characteristics: Vintage 2012" (http://www.census.gov/popest/data/state/asrh/2012/index.html)

Percent of Population 85 Years Old and Older in 2012

National Percent = 1.9% of Population

<table>
<tr><td colspan="3">ALPHA ORDER</td><td colspan="3">RANK ORDER</td></tr>
<tr><td>RANK</td><td>STATE</td><td>PERCENT</td><td>RANK</td><td>STATE</td><td>PERCENT</td></tr>
<tr><td>31</td><td>Alabama</td><td>1.7</td><td>1</td><td>Rhode Island</td><td>2.6</td></tr>
<tr><td>50</td><td>Alaska</td><td>0.7</td><td>2</td><td>Connecticut</td><td>2.5</td></tr>
<tr><td>31</td><td>Arizona</td><td>1.7</td><td>2</td><td>Florida</td><td>2.5</td></tr>
<tr><td>27</td><td>Arkansas</td><td>1.8</td><td>2</td><td>Hawaii</td><td>2.5</td></tr>
<tr><td>31</td><td>California</td><td>1.7</td><td>2</td><td>Iowa</td><td>2.5</td></tr>
<tr><td>44</td><td>Colorado</td><td>1.5</td><td>2</td><td>North Dakota</td><td>2.5</td></tr>
<tr><td>2</td><td>Connecticut</td><td>2.5</td><td>2</td><td>Pennsylvania</td><td>2.5</td></tr>
<tr><td>27</td><td>Delaware</td><td>1.8</td><td>8</td><td>South Dakota</td><td>2.4</td></tr>
<tr><td>2</td><td>Florida</td><td>2.5</td><td>9</td><td>Maine</td><td>2.3</td></tr>
<tr><td>48</td><td>Georgia</td><td>1.2</td><td>9</td><td>Massachusetts</td><td>2.3</td></tr>
<tr><td>2</td><td>Hawaii</td><td>2.5</td><td>11</td><td>Kansas</td><td>2.2</td></tr>
<tr><td>31</td><td>Idaho</td><td>1.7</td><td>11</td><td>Nebraska</td><td>2.2</td></tr>
<tr><td>25</td><td>Illinois</td><td>1.9</td><td>11</td><td>Vermont</td><td>2.2</td></tr>
<tr><td>25</td><td>Indiana</td><td>1.9</td><td>11</td><td>Wisconsin</td><td>2.2</td></tr>
<tr><td>2</td><td>Iowa</td><td>2.5</td><td>15</td><td>Michigan</td><td>2.1</td></tr>
<tr><td>11</td><td>Kansas</td><td>2.2</td><td>15</td><td>Minnesota</td><td>2.1</td></tr>
<tr><td>31</td><td>Kentucky</td><td>1.7</td><td>15</td><td>Montana</td><td>2.1</td></tr>
<tr><td>44</td><td>Louisiana</td><td>1.5</td><td>15</td><td>New Jersey</td><td>2.1</td></tr>
<tr><td>9</td><td>Maine</td><td>2.3</td><td>15</td><td>New York</td><td>2.1</td></tr>
<tr><td>27</td><td>Maryland</td><td>1.8</td><td>15</td><td>Ohio</td><td>2.1</td></tr>
<tr><td>9</td><td>Massachusetts</td><td>2.3</td><td>15</td><td>Oregon</td><td>2.1</td></tr>
<tr><td>15</td><td>Michigan</td><td>2.1</td><td>22</td><td>Missouri</td><td>2.0</td></tr>
<tr><td>15</td><td>Minnesota</td><td>2.1</td><td>22</td><td>New Hampshire</td><td>2.0</td></tr>
<tr><td>38</td><td>Mississippi</td><td>1.6</td><td>22</td><td>West Virginia</td><td>2.0</td></tr>
<tr><td>22</td><td>Missouri</td><td>2.0</td><td>25</td><td>Illinois</td><td>1.9</td></tr>
<tr><td>15</td><td>Montana</td><td>2.1</td><td>25</td><td>Indiana</td><td>1.9</td></tr>
<tr><td>11</td><td>Nebraska</td><td>2.2</td><td>27</td><td>Arkansas</td><td>1.8</td></tr>
<tr><td>46</td><td>Nevada</td><td>1.3</td><td>27</td><td>Delaware</td><td>1.8</td></tr>
<tr><td>22</td><td>New Hampshire</td><td>2.0</td><td>27</td><td>Maryland</td><td>1.8</td></tr>
<tr><td>15</td><td>New Jersey</td><td>2.1</td><td>27</td><td>Washington</td><td>1.8</td></tr>
<tr><td>31</td><td>New Mexico</td><td>1.7</td><td>31</td><td>Alabama</td><td>1.7</td></tr>
<tr><td>15</td><td>New York</td><td>2.1</td><td>31</td><td>Arizona</td><td>1.7</td></tr>
<tr><td>38</td><td>North Carolina</td><td>1.6</td><td>31</td><td>California</td><td>1.7</td></tr>
<tr><td>2</td><td>North Dakota</td><td>2.5</td><td>31</td><td>Idaho</td><td>1.7</td></tr>
<tr><td>15</td><td>Ohio</td><td>2.1</td><td>31</td><td>Kentucky</td><td>1.7</td></tr>
<tr><td>31</td><td>Oklahoma</td><td>1.7</td><td>31</td><td>New Mexico</td><td>1.7</td></tr>
<tr><td>15</td><td>Oregon</td><td>2.1</td><td>31</td><td>Oklahoma</td><td>1.7</td></tr>
<tr><td>2</td><td>Pennsylvania</td><td>2.5</td><td>38</td><td>Mississippi</td><td>1.6</td></tr>
<tr><td>1</td><td>Rhode Island</td><td>2.6</td><td>38</td><td>North Carolina</td><td>1.6</td></tr>
<tr><td>38</td><td>South Carolina</td><td>1.6</td><td>38</td><td>South Carolina</td><td>1.6</td></tr>
<tr><td>8</td><td>South Dakota</td><td>2.4</td><td>38</td><td>Tennessee</td><td>1.6</td></tr>
<tr><td>38</td><td>Tennessee</td><td>1.6</td><td>38</td><td>Virginia</td><td>1.6</td></tr>
<tr><td>46</td><td>Texas</td><td>1.3</td><td>38</td><td>Wyoming</td><td>1.6</td></tr>
<tr><td>48</td><td>Utah</td><td>1.2</td><td>44</td><td>Colorado</td><td>1.5</td></tr>
<tr><td>11</td><td>Vermont</td><td>2.2</td><td>44</td><td>Louisiana</td><td>1.5</td></tr>
<tr><td>38</td><td>Virginia</td><td>1.6</td><td>46</td><td>Nevada</td><td>1.3</td></tr>
<tr><td>27</td><td>Washington</td><td>1.8</td><td>46</td><td>Texas</td><td>1.3</td></tr>
<tr><td>22</td><td>West Virginia</td><td>2.0</td><td>48</td><td>Georgia</td><td>1.2</td></tr>
<tr><td>11</td><td>Wisconsin</td><td>2.2</td><td>48</td><td>Utah</td><td>1.2</td></tr>
<tr><td>38</td><td>Wyoming</td><td>1.6</td><td>50</td><td>Alaska</td><td>0.7</td></tr>
<tr><td></td><td></td><td></td><td></td><td>District of Columbia</td><td>1.7</td></tr>
</table>

Source: CQ Press using data from U.S. Bureau of the Census
"State Characteristics: Vintage 2012" (http://www.census.gov/popest/data/state/asrh/2012/index.html)

Percent of Native Population Born in Their State of Residence in 2012

National Percent = 67.6%

<table>
<tr><td colspan="3">ALPHA ORDER</td><td colspan="3">RANK ORDER</td></tr>
<tr><td>RANK</td><td>STATE</td><td>PERCENT</td><td>RANK</td><td>STATE</td><td>PERCENT</td></tr>
<tr><td>13</td><td>Alabama</td><td>72.7</td><td>1</td><td>New York</td><td>82.1</td></tr>
<tr><td>48</td><td>Alaska</td><td>43.5</td><td>2</td><td>Michigan</td><td>81.7</td></tr>
<tr><td>45</td><td>Arizona</td><td>44.4</td><td>3</td><td>Louisiana</td><td>81.6</td></tr>
<tr><td>28</td><td>Arkansas</td><td>64.3</td><td>4</td><td>Pennsylvania</td><td>78.5</td></tr>
<tr><td>9</td><td>California</td><td>74.6</td><td>5</td><td>Ohio</td><td>78.1</td></tr>
<tr><td>44</td><td>Colorado</td><td>46.6</td><td>6</td><td>Illinois</td><td>77.8</td></tr>
<tr><td>30</td><td>Connecticut</td><td>64.0</td><td>7</td><td>Wisconsin</td><td>75.0</td></tr>
<tr><td>43</td><td>Delaware</td><td>49.1</td><td>8</td><td>Iowa</td><td>74.9</td></tr>
<tr><td>47</td><td>Florida</td><td>44.3</td><td>9</td><td>California</td><td>74.6</td></tr>
<tr><td>33</td><td>Georgia</td><td>61.1</td><td>10</td><td>Minnesota</td><td>74.2</td></tr>
<tr><td>25</td><td>Hawaii</td><td>66.2</td><td>11</td><td>Massachusetts</td><td>74.1</td></tr>
<tr><td>42</td><td>Idaho</td><td>50.3</td><td>12</td><td>Mississippi</td><td>73.5</td></tr>
<tr><td>6</td><td>Illinois</td><td>77.8</td><td>13</td><td>Alabama</td><td>72.7</td></tr>
<tr><td>16</td><td>Indiana</td><td>71.7</td><td>14</td><td>Texas</td><td>72.4</td></tr>
<tr><td>8</td><td>Iowa</td><td>74.9</td><td>15</td><td>Kentucky</td><td>72.1</td></tr>
<tr><td>31</td><td>Kansas</td><td>63.5</td><td>16</td><td>Indiana</td><td>71.7</td></tr>
<tr><td>15</td><td>Kentucky</td><td>72.1</td><td>17</td><td>West Virginia</td><td>70.6</td></tr>
<tr><td>3</td><td>Louisiana</td><td>81.6</td><td>18</td><td>Nebraska</td><td>69.6</td></tr>
<tr><td>21</td><td>Maine</td><td>67.6</td><td>19</td><td>Missouri</td><td>69.2</td></tr>
<tr><td>37</td><td>Maryland</td><td>55.2</td><td>20</td><td>North Dakota</td><td>68.8</td></tr>
<tr><td>11</td><td>Massachusetts</td><td>74.1</td><td>21</td><td>Maine</td><td>67.6</td></tr>
<tr><td>2</td><td>Michigan</td><td>81.7</td><td>22</td><td>Utah</td><td>67.5</td></tr>
<tr><td>10</td><td>Minnesota</td><td>74.2</td><td>23</td><td>Rhode Island</td><td>67.1</td></tr>
<tr><td>12</td><td>Mississippi</td><td>73.5</td><td>24</td><td>New Jersey</td><td>66.8</td></tr>
<tr><td>19</td><td>Missouri</td><td>69.2</td><td>25</td><td>Hawaii</td><td>66.2</td></tr>
<tr><td>39</td><td>Montana</td><td>54.2</td><td>25</td><td>South Dakota</td><td>66.2</td></tr>
<tr><td>18</td><td>Nebraska</td><td>69.6</td><td>27</td><td>Oklahoma</td><td>64.5</td></tr>
<tr><td>50</td><td>Nevada</td><td>30.9</td><td>28</td><td>Arkansas</td><td>64.3</td></tr>
<tr><td>45</td><td>New Hampshire</td><td>44.4</td><td>28</td><td>Tennessee</td><td>64.3</td></tr>
<tr><td>24</td><td>New Jersey</td><td>66.8</td><td>30</td><td>Connecticut</td><td>64.0</td></tr>
<tr><td>35</td><td>New Mexico</td><td>58.8</td><td>31</td><td>Kansas</td><td>63.5</td></tr>
<tr><td>1</td><td>New York</td><td>82.1</td><td>32</td><td>North Carolina</td><td>62.8</td></tr>
<tr><td>32</td><td>North Carolina</td><td>62.8</td><td>33</td><td>Georgia</td><td>61.1</td></tr>
<tr><td>20</td><td>North Dakota</td><td>68.8</td><td>33</td><td>South Carolina</td><td>61.1</td></tr>
<tr><td>5</td><td>Ohio</td><td>78.1</td><td>35</td><td>New Mexico</td><td>58.8</td></tr>
<tr><td>27</td><td>Oklahoma</td><td>64.5</td><td>36</td><td>Virginia</td><td>55.8</td></tr>
<tr><td>41</td><td>Oregon</td><td>50.7</td><td>37</td><td>Maryland</td><td>55.2</td></tr>
<tr><td>4</td><td>Pennsylvania</td><td>78.5</td><td>38</td><td>Washington</td><td>54.7</td></tr>
<tr><td>23</td><td>Rhode Island</td><td>67.1</td><td>39</td><td>Montana</td><td>54.2</td></tr>
<tr><td>33</td><td>South Carolina</td><td>61.1</td><td>40</td><td>Vermont</td><td>53.7</td></tr>
<tr><td>25</td><td>South Dakota</td><td>66.2</td><td>41</td><td>Oregon</td><td>50.7</td></tr>
<tr><td>28</td><td>Tennessee</td><td>64.3</td><td>42</td><td>Idaho</td><td>50.3</td></tr>
<tr><td>14</td><td>Texas</td><td>72.4</td><td>43</td><td>Delaware</td><td>49.1</td></tr>
<tr><td>22</td><td>Utah</td><td>67.5</td><td>44</td><td>Colorado</td><td>46.6</td></tr>
<tr><td>40</td><td>Vermont</td><td>53.7</td><td>45</td><td>Arizona</td><td>44.4</td></tr>
<tr><td>36</td><td>Virginia</td><td>55.8</td><td>45</td><td>New Hampshire</td><td>44.4</td></tr>
<tr><td>38</td><td>Washington</td><td>54.7</td><td>47</td><td>Florida</td><td>44.3</td></tr>
<tr><td>17</td><td>West Virginia</td><td>70.6</td><td>48</td><td>Alaska</td><td>43.5</td></tr>
<tr><td>7</td><td>Wisconsin</td><td>75.0</td><td>49</td><td>Wyoming</td><td>42.0</td></tr>
<tr><td>49</td><td>Wyoming</td><td>42.0</td><td>50</td><td>Nevada</td><td>30.9</td></tr>
<tr><td></td><td></td><td></td><td></td><td>District of Columbia</td><td>43.3</td></tr>
</table>

Source: U.S. Bureau of the Census
"2012 American Community Survey-Table R0601" (http://www.census.gov/acs/www/index.html)

Domestic Migration of Population: 2012 to 2013

National Net Migration = 0 People*

ALPHA ORDER				RANK ORDER		
RANK	STATE	NET MIGRATION		RANK	STATE	NET MIGRATION
21	Alabama	451		1	Texas	113,528
35	Alaska	(4,006)		2	Florida	91,484
6	Arizona	26,417		3	North Carolina	37,240
29	Arkansas	(2,031)		4	Colorado	36,284
48	California	(49,259)		5	South Carolina	29,324
4	Colorado	36,284		6	Arizona	26,417
43	Connecticut	(17,224)		7	Washington	17,027
18	Delaware	3,010		8	North Dakota	16,961
2	Florida	91,484		9	Oklahoma	14,268
36	Georgia	(6,347)		10	Nevada	12,854
27	Hawaii	(1,457)		11	Tennessee	12,649
16	Idaho	4,579		12	Oregon	10,215
49	Illinois	(67,313)		13	Utah	5,567
25	Indiana	(1,179)		14	Montana	5,467
20	Iowa	671		15	South Dakota	4,762
42	Kansas	(12,557)		16	Idaho	4,579
30	Kentucky	(2,290)		17	Virginia	3,099
32	Louisiana	(2,492)		18	Delaware	3,010
26	Maine	(1,423)		19	Wyoming	2,616
40	Maryland	(8,525)		20	Iowa	671
33	Massachusetts	(2,833)		21	Alabama	451
45	Michigan	(28,539)		22	Vermont	(653)
24	Minnesota	(1,147)		23	Nebraska	(695)
37	Mississippi	(7,038)		24	Minnesota	(1,147)
38	Missouri	(7,612)		25	Indiana	(1,179)
14	Montana	5,467		26	Maine	(1,423)
23	Nebraska	(695)		27	Hawaii	(1,457)
10	Nevada	12,854		28	West Virginia	(1,894)
31	New Hampshire	(2,355)		29	Arkansas	(2,031)
47	New Jersey	(45,035)		30	Kentucky	(2,290)
41	New Mexico	(10,526)		31	New Hampshire	(2,355)
50	New York	(104,470)		32	Louisiana	(2,492)
3	North Carolina	37,240		33	Massachusetts	(2,833)
8	North Dakota	16,961		34	Rhode Island	(3,922)
44	Ohio	(23,094)		35	Alaska	(4,006)
9	Oklahoma	14,268		36	Georgia	(6,347)
12	Oregon	10,215		37	Mississippi	(7,038)
46	Pennsylvania	(30,718)		38	Missouri	(7,612)
34	Rhode Island	(3,922)		39	Wisconsin	(8,158)
5	South Carolina	29,324		40	Maryland	(8,525)
15	South Dakota	4,762		41	New Mexico	(10,526)
11	Tennessee	12,649		42	Kansas	(12,557)
1	Texas	113,528		43	Connecticut	(17,224)
13	Utah	5,567		44	Ohio	(23,094)
22	Vermont	(653)		45	Michigan	(28,539)
17	Virginia	3,099		46	Pennsylvania	(30,718)
7	Washington	17,027		47	New Jersey	(45,035)
28	West Virginia	(1,894)		48	California	(49,259)
39	Wisconsin	(8,158)		49	Illinois	(67,313)
19	Wyoming	2,616		50	New York	(104,470)
					District of Columbia	6,319

Source: U.S. Bureau of the Census

"Components of Population Change" (http://www.census.gov/popest/data/datasets.html)

*From July 1, 2012 to June 30, 2013. Includes armed forces residing in each state. Net Domestic Migration is the difference between domestic inmigration to an area and domestic outmigration from it during the period. Domestic inmigration and outmigration consist of moves where both the origins and destinations are within the United States (excluding Puerto Rico).

Net International Migration: 2012 to 2013

National Net = 843,145 Immigrants*

ALPHA ORDER

RANK	STATE	IMMIGRANTS	% of USA
30	Alabama	5,256	0.6%
40	Alaska	1,828	0.2%
18	Arizona	10,864	1.3%
37	Arkansas	2,965	0.4%
1	California	123,217	14.6%
20	Colorado	8,573	1.0%
16	Connecticut	15,702	1.9%
38	Delaware	2,422	0.3%
3	Florida	99,454	11.8%
11	Georgia	22,343	2.6%
24	Hawaii	7,459	0.9%
43	Idaho	1,563	0.2%
8	Illinois	27,751	3.3%
19	Indiana	9,404	1.1%
34	Iowa	4,143	0.5%
31	Kansas	5,105	0.6%
29	Kentucky	5,569	0.7%
25	Louisiana	6,695	0.8%
45	Maine	1,042	0.1%
10	Maryland	24,944	3.0%
6	Massachusetts	31,349	3.7%
14	Michigan	17,488	2.1%
17	Minnesota	12,208	1.4%
39	Mississippi	2,232	0.3%
23	Missouri	7,462	0.9%
48	Montana	725	0.1%
36	Nebraska	3,214	0.4%
22	Nevada	7,463	0.9%
41	New Hampshire	1,781	0.2%
5	New Jersey	46,373	5.5%
42	New Mexico	1,717	0.2%
2	New York	101,778	12.1%
13	North Carolina	20,545	2.4%
44	North Dakota	1,090	0.1%
15	Ohio	15,708	1.9%
32	Oklahoma	4,756	0.6%
27	Oregon	6,375	0.8%
9	Pennsylvania	24,996	3.0%
35	Rhode Island	3,688	0.4%
26	South Carolina	6,513	0.8%
46	South Dakota	1,040	0.1%
21	Tennessee	8,155	1.0%
4	Texas	64,187	7.6%
33	Utah	4,353	0.5%
49	Vermont	464	0.1%
7	Virginia	29,762	3.5%
12	Washington	21,384	2.5%
47	West Virginia	981	0.1%
28	Wisconsin	5,876	0.7%
50	Wyoming	325	0.0%

RANK ORDER

RANK	STATE	IMMIGRANTS	% of USA
1	California	123,217	14.6%
2	New York	101,778	12.1%
3	Florida	99,454	11.8%
4	Texas	64,187	7.6%
5	New Jersey	46,373	5.5%
6	Massachusetts	31,349	3.7%
7	Virginia	29,762	3.5%
8	Illinois	27,751	3.3%
9	Pennsylvania	24,996	3.0%
10	Maryland	24,944	3.0%
11	Georgia	22,343	2.6%
12	Washington	21,384	2.5%
13	North Carolina	20,545	2.4%
14	Michigan	17,488	2.1%
15	Ohio	15,708	1.9%
16	Connecticut	15,702	1.9%
17	Minnesota	12,208	1.4%
18	Arizona	10,864	1.3%
19	Indiana	9,404	1.1%
20	Colorado	8,573	1.0%
21	Tennessee	8,155	1.0%
22	Nevada	7,463	0.9%
23	Missouri	7,462	0.9%
24	Hawaii	7,459	0.9%
25	Louisiana	6,695	0.8%
26	South Carolina	6,513	0.8%
27	Oregon	6,375	0.8%
28	Wisconsin	5,876	0.7%
29	Kentucky	5,569	0.7%
30	Alabama	5,256	0.6%
31	Kansas	5,105	0.6%
32	Oklahoma	4,756	0.6%
33	Utah	4,353	0.5%
34	Iowa	4,143	0.5%
35	Rhode Island	3,688	0.4%
36	Nebraska	3,214	0.4%
37	Arkansas	2,965	0.4%
38	Delaware	2,422	0.3%
39	Mississippi	2,232	0.3%
40	Alaska	1,828	0.2%
41	New Hampshire	1,781	0.2%
42	New Mexico	1,717	0.2%
43	Idaho	1,563	0.2%
44	North Dakota	1,090	0.1%
45	Maine	1,042	0.1%
46	South Dakota	1,040	0.1%
47	West Virginia	981	0.1%
48	Montana	725	0.1%
49	Vermont	464	0.1%
50	Wyoming	325	0.0%
	District of Columbia	2,858	0.3%

Source: U.S. Bureau of the Census
"Components of Population Change" (http://www.census.gov/popest/data/datasets.html)
*From July 1, 2012 to June 30, 2013. Net International Migration is the difference between migration to an area from outside the United States (immigration) and migration from the area to outside the United States (emigration) during the period. Includes legal immigration and estimates of undocumented immigration.

Percent of Population Foreign Born in 2012

National Percent = 13.0% of Population*

ALPHA ORDER

RANK	STATE	PERCENT
43	Alabama	3.4
23	Alaska	7.2
12	Arizona	13.4
37	Arkansas	4.4
1	California	27.1
16	Colorado	9.8
11	Connecticut	13.8
20	Delaware	8.5
4	Florida	19.4
18	Georgia	9.5
6	Hawaii	18.1
27	Idaho	6.1
10	Illinois	13.9
34	Indiana	4.6
35	Iowa	4.5
25	Kansas	6.5
45	Kentucky	3.1
41	Louisiana	3.7
42	Maine	3.5
9	Maryland	14.3
8	Massachusetts	15.0
27	Michigan	6.1
23	Minnesota	7.2
48	Mississippi	2.0
40	Missouri	3.8
49	Montana	1.8
26	Nebraska	6.4
5	Nevada	19.2
31	New Hampshire	5.4
3	New Jersey	21.2
19	New Mexico	9.2
2	New York	22.6
22	North Carolina	7.7
46	North Dakota	2.8
39	Ohio	3.9
30	Oklahoma	5.6
17	Oregon	9.6
29	Pennsylvania	6.0
13	Rhode Island	13.3
33	South Carolina	4.7
47	South Dakota	2.7
35	Tennessee	4.5
7	Texas	16.4
21	Utah	8.4
38	Vermont	4.1
15	Virginia	11.6
13	Washington	13.3
50	West Virginia	1.4
32	Wisconsin	4.8
43	Wyoming	3.4

RANK ORDER

RANK	STATE	PERCENT
1	California	27.1
2	New York	22.6
3	New Jersey	21.2
4	Florida	19.4
5	Nevada	19.2
6	Hawaii	18.1
7	Texas	16.4
8	Massachusetts	15.0
9	Maryland	14.3
10	Illinois	13.9
11	Connecticut	13.8
12	Arizona	13.4
13	Rhode Island	13.3
13	Washington	13.3
15	Virginia	11.6
16	Colorado	9.8
17	Oregon	9.6
18	Georgia	9.5
19	New Mexico	9.2
20	Delaware	8.5
21	Utah	8.4
22	North Carolina	7.7
23	Alaska	7.2
23	Minnesota	7.2
25	Kansas	6.5
26	Nebraska	6.4
27	Idaho	6.1
27	Michigan	6.1
29	Pennsylvania	6.0
30	Oklahoma	5.6
31	New Hampshire	5.4
32	Wisconsin	4.8
33	South Carolina	4.7
34	Indiana	4.6
35	Iowa	4.5
35	Tennessee	4.5
37	Arkansas	4.4
38	Vermont	4.1
39	Ohio	3.9
40	Missouri	3.8
41	Louisiana	3.7
42	Maine	3.5
43	Alabama	3.4
43	Wyoming	3.4
45	Kentucky	3.1
46	North Dakota	2.8
47	South Dakota	2.7
48	Mississippi	2.0
49	Montana	1.8
50	West Virginia	1.4

District of Columbia   14.3

Source: U.S. Bureau of the Census
   "2012 American Community Survey-Table R0501" (http://www.census.gov/acs/www/index.html)
*"Foreign born" are persons not born in the United States, Puerto Rico, a U.S. Island Area, or abroad of American parent or parents.

Percent of Population Speaking a Language Other than English at Home in 2012
National Percent = 21.0%*

ALPHA ORDER

RANK	STATE	PERCENT
46	Alabama	5.1
17	Alaska	16.6
8	Arizona	27.1
39	Arkansas	6.9
1	California	44.3
16	Colorado	17.0
12	Connecticut	22.2
22	Delaware	12.9
7	Florida	27.9
21	Georgia	13.4
9	Hawaii	25.1
28	Idaho	10.4
10	Illinois	22.6
32	Indiana	8.5
36	Iowa	7.2
23	Kansas	11.2
47	Kentucky	4.9
33	Louisiana	8.4
37	Maine	7.1
15	Maryland	17.2
11	Massachusetts	22.3
30	Michigan	9.4
26	Minnesota	10.9
49	Mississippi	3.6
43	Missouri	6.0
48	Montana	4.3
23	Nebraska	11.2
6	Nevada	30.2
34	New Hampshire	7.9
4	New Jersey	30.4
2	New Mexico	35.4
4	New York	30.4
25	North Carolina	11.1
44	North Dakota	5.8
40	Ohio	6.7
29	Oklahoma	9.7
19	Oregon	14.7
27	Pennsylvania	10.6
13	Rhode Island	20.9
38	South Carolina	7.0
42	South Dakota	6.3
40	Tennessee	6.7
3	Texas	35.2
19	Utah	14.7
45	Vermont	5.4
18	Virginia	15.5
14	Washington	19.3
50	West Virginia	2.4
31	Wisconsin	8.8
35	Wyoming	7.6

RANK ORDER

RANK	STATE	PERCENT
1	California	44.3
2	New Mexico	35.4
3	Texas	35.2
4	New Jersey	30.4
4	New York	30.4
6	Nevada	30.2
7	Florida	27.9
8	Arizona	27.1
9	Hawaii	25.1
10	Illinois	22.6
11	Massachusetts	22.3
12	Connecticut	22.2
13	Rhode Island	20.9
14	Washington	19.3
15	Maryland	17.2
16	Colorado	17.0
17	Alaska	16.6
18	Virginia	15.5
19	Oregon	14.7
19	Utah	14.7
21	Georgia	13.4
22	Delaware	12.9
23	Kansas	11.2
23	Nebraska	11.2
25	North Carolina	11.1
26	Minnesota	10.9
27	Pennsylvania	10.6
28	Idaho	10.4
29	Oklahoma	9.7
30	Michigan	9.4
31	Wisconsin	8.8
32	Indiana	8.5
33	Louisiana	8.4
34	New Hampshire	7.9
35	Wyoming	7.6
36	Iowa	7.2
37	Maine	7.1
38	South Carolina	7.0
39	Arkansas	6.9
40	Ohio	6.7
40	Tennessee	6.7
42	South Dakota	6.3
43	Missouri	6.0
44	North Dakota	5.8
45	Vermont	5.4
46	Alabama	5.1
47	Kentucky	4.9
48	Montana	4.3
49	Mississippi	3.6
50	West Virginia	2.4
	District of Columbia	16.6

Source: U.S. Bureau of the Census
    "2012 American Community Survey-Table R1601" (http://www.census.gov/acs/www/index.html)
*Population five years old and older.

Percent of Population Speaking Spanish at Home in 2012

National Percent = 13.0%*

ALPHA ORDER

RANK	STATE	PERCENT
37	Alabama	3.2
36	Alaska	3.5
5	Arizona	20.8
27	Arkansas	5.0
2	California	29.0
10	Colorado	11.9
11	Connecticut	11.2
22	Delaware	7.1
6	Florida	20.5
17	Georgia	7.9
45	Hawaii	1.8
18	Idaho	7.7
9	Illinois	13.1
29	Indiana	4.6
32	Iowa	3.9
19	Kansas	7.5
39	Kentucky	2.5
35	Louisiana	3.6
50	Maine	1.0
22	Maryland	7.1
16	Massachusetts	8.4
38	Michigan	3.1
32	Minnesota	3.9
42	Mississippi	2.2
39	Missouri	2.5
47	Montana	1.5
20	Nebraska	7.4
4	Nevada	21.1
43	New Hampshire	2.0
7	New Jersey	15.7
3	New Mexico	27.8
8	New York	15.0
20	North Carolina	7.4
46	North Dakota	1.6
41	Ohio	2.3
25	Oklahoma	6.6
14	Oregon	8.6
29	Pennsylvania	4.6
12	Rhode Island	11.1
31	South Carolina	4.5
44	South Dakota	1.9
32	Tennessee	3.9
1	Texas	29.8
13	Utah	10.0
48	Vermont	1.1
24	Virginia	6.7
15	Washington	8.5
48	West Virginia	1.1
28	Wisconsin	4.7
26	Wyoming	5.4

RANK ORDER

RANK	STATE	PERCENT
1	Texas	29.8
2	California	29.0
3	New Mexico	27.8
4	Nevada	21.1
5	Arizona	20.8
6	Florida	20.5
7	New Jersey	15.7
8	New York	15.0
9	Illinois	13.1
10	Colorado	11.9
11	Connecticut	11.2
12	Rhode Island	11.1
13	Utah	10.0
14	Oregon	8.6
15	Washington	8.5
16	Massachusetts	8.4
17	Georgia	7.9
18	Idaho	7.7
19	Kansas	7.5
20	Nebraska	7.4
20	North Carolina	7.4
22	Delaware	7.1
22	Maryland	7.1
24	Virginia	6.7
25	Oklahoma	6.6
26	Wyoming	5.4
27	Arkansas	5.0
28	Wisconsin	4.7
29	Indiana	4.6
29	Pennsylvania	4.6
31	South Carolina	4.5
32	Iowa	3.9
32	Minnesota	3.9
32	Tennessee	3.9
35	Louisiana	3.6
36	Alaska	3.5
37	Alabama	3.2
38	Michigan	3.1
39	Kentucky	2.5
39	Missouri	2.5
41	Ohio	2.3
42	Mississippi	2.2
43	New Hampshire	2.0
44	South Dakota	1.9
45	Hawaii	1.8
46	North Dakota	1.6
47	Montana	1.5
48	Vermont	1.1
48	West Virginia	1.1
50	Maine	1.0
	District of Columbia	8.0

Source: U.S. Bureau of the Census
   "2012 American Community Survey-Table R1602" (http://www.census.gov/acs/www/index.html)
*Population five years old and older.

Marriages in 2011

National Total = 2,118,000 Marriages*

ALPHA ORDER

RANK	STATE	MARRIAGES	% of USA
17	Alabama	40,300	1.9%
46	Alaska	5,600	0.3%
19	Arizona	37,000	1.7%
25	Arkansas	30,600	1.4%
1	California	218,600	10.3%
21	Colorado	35,800	1.7%
34	Connecticut	19,700	0.9%
48	Delaware	4,700	0.2%
3	Florida	141,000	6.7%
9	Georgia	64,800	3.1%
31	Hawaii	24,200	1.1%
38	Idaho	13,600	0.6%
6	Illinois	72,100	3.4%
14	Indiana	44,300	2.1%
33	Iowa	20,500	1.0%
35	Kansas	18,100	0.9%
24	Kentucky	32,800	1.5%
28	Louisiana	29,300	1.4%
41	Maine	9,600	0.5%
22	Maryland	33,800	1.6%
20	Massachusetts	36,200	1.7%
12	Michigan	56,300	2.7%
27	Minnesota	29,900	1.4%
37	Mississippi	14,600	0.7%
18	Missouri	39,700	1.9%
43	Montana	7,800	0.4%
40	Nebraska	12,200	0.6%
5	Nevada	100,500	4.7%
42	New Hampshire	9,400	0.4%
15	New Jersey	42,300	2.0%
36	New Mexico	16,700	0.8%
4	New York	134,300	6.3%
10	North Carolina	64,700	3.1%
49	North Dakota	4,600	0.2%
7	Ohio	68,100	3.2%
29	Oklahoma	26,200	1.2%
30	Oregon	25,600	1.2%
8	Pennsylvania	67,500	3.2%
44	Rhode Island	6,300	0.3%
23	South Carolina	33,700	1.6%
45	South Dakota	6,200	0.3%
11	Tennessee	57,600	2.7%
2	Texas	182,300	8.6%
31	Utah	24,200	1.1%
47	Vermont	5,200	0.2%
13	Virginia	55,100	2.6%
16	Washington	41,700	2.0%
39	West Virginia	13,400	0.6%
26	Wisconsin	30,300	1.4%
50	Wyoming	4,400	0.2%

RANK ORDER

RANK	STATE	MARRIAGES	% of USA
1	California	218,600	10.3%
2	Texas	182,300	8.6%
3	Florida	141,000	6.7%
4	New York	134,300	6.3%
5	Nevada	100,500	4.7%
6	Illinois	72,100	3.4%
7	Ohio	68,100	3.2%
8	Pennsylvania	67,500	3.2%
9	Georgia	64,800	3.1%
10	North Carolina	64,700	3.1%
11	Tennessee	57,600	2.7%
12	Michigan	56,300	2.7%
13	Virginia	55,100	2.6%
14	Indiana	44,300	2.1%
15	New Jersey	42,300	2.0%
16	Washington	41,700	2.0%
17	Alabama	40,300	1.9%
18	Missouri	39,700	1.9%
19	Arizona	37,000	1.7%
20	Massachusetts	36,200	1.7%
21	Colorado	35,800	1.7%
22	Maryland	33,800	1.6%
23	South Carolina	33,700	1.6%
24	Kentucky	32,800	1.5%
25	Arkansas	30,600	1.4%
26	Wisconsin	30,300	1.4%
27	Minnesota	29,900	1.4%
28	Louisiana	29,300	1.4%
29	Oklahoma	26,200	1.2%
30	Oregon	25,600	1.2%
31	Hawaii	24,200	1.1%
31	Utah	24,200	1.1%
33	Iowa	20,500	1.0%
34	Connecticut	19,700	0.9%
35	Kansas	18,100	0.9%
36	New Mexico	16,700	0.8%
37	Mississippi	14,600	0.7%
38	Idaho	13,600	0.6%
39	West Virginia	13,400	0.6%
40	Nebraska	12,200	0.6%
41	Maine	9,600	0.5%
42	New Hampshire	9,400	0.4%
43	Montana	7,800	0.4%
44	Rhode Island	6,300	0.3%
45	South Dakota	6,200	0.3%
46	Alaska	5,600	0.3%
47	Vermont	5,200	0.2%
48	Delaware	4,700	0.2%
49	North Dakota	4,600	0.2%
50	Wyoming	4,400	0.2%
	District of Columbia	5,400	0.3%

Source: CQ Press using data from U.S. Department of Health and Human Services, National Center for Health Statistics
"National Vital Statistics System, Marriages and Divorces" (http://www.cdc.gov/nchs/mardiv.htm)
*Provisional estimates by state of occurrence.

Marriage Rate in 2011

National Rate = 6.8 Marriages per 1,000 Population*

ALPHA ORDER				RANK ORDER		
RANK	STATE	RATE		RANK	STATE	RATE
7	Alabama	8.4		1	Nevada	36.9
10	Alaska	7.8		2	Hawaii	17.6
40	Arizona	5.7		3	Arkansas	10.4
3	Arkansas	10.4		4	Tennessee	9.0
38	California	5.8		5	Idaho	8.6
21	Colorado	7.0		5	Utah	8.6
44	Connecticut	5.5		7	Alabama	8.4
48	Delaware	5.2		8	Vermont	8.3
15	Florida	7.4		9	New Mexico	8.0
29	Georgia	6.6		10	Alaska	7.8
2	Hawaii	17.6		10	Montana	7.8
5	Idaho	8.6		10	Wyoming	7.8
42	Illinois	5.6		13	Kentucky	7.5
24	Indiana	6.8		13	South Dakota	7.5
26	Iowa	6.7		15	Florida	7.4
34	Kansas	6.3		16	Maine	7.2
13	Kentucky	7.5		16	South Carolina	7.2
33	Louisiana	6.4		16	West Virginia	7.2
16	Maine	7.2		19	New Hampshire	7.1
38	Maryland	5.8		19	Texas	7.1
44	Massachusetts	5.5		21	Colorado	7.0
40	Michigan	5.7		22	New York	6.9
42	Minnesota	5.6		22	Oklahoma	6.9
49	Mississippi	4.9		24	Indiana	6.8
29	Missouri	6.6		24	Virginia	6.8
10	Montana	7.8		26	Iowa	6.7
29	Nebraska	6.6		26	North Carolina	6.7
1	Nevada	36.9		26	North Dakota	6.7
19	New Hampshire	7.1		29	Georgia	6.6
50	New Jersey	4.8		29	Missouri	6.6
9	New Mexico	8.0		29	Nebraska	6.6
22	New York	6.9		29	Oregon	6.6
26	North Carolina	6.7		33	Louisiana	6.4
26	North Dakota	6.7		34	Kansas	6.3
37	Ohio	5.9		35	Washington	6.1
22	Oklahoma	6.9		36	Rhode Island	6.0
29	Oregon	6.6		37	Ohio	5.9
46	Pennsylvania	5.3		38	California	5.8
36	Rhode Island	6.0		38	Maryland	5.8
16	South Carolina	7.2		40	Arizona	5.7
13	South Dakota	7.5		40	Michigan	5.7
4	Tennessee	9.0		42	Illinois	5.6
19	Texas	7.1		42	Minnesota	5.6
5	Utah	8.6		44	Connecticut	5.5
8	Vermont	8.3		44	Massachusetts	5.5
24	Virginia	6.8		46	Pennsylvania	5.3
35	Washington	6.1		46	Wisconsin	5.3
16	West Virginia	7.2		48	Delaware	5.2
46	Wisconsin	5.3		49	Mississippi	4.9
10	Wyoming	7.8		50	New Jersey	4.8
					District of Columbia	8.7

Source: U.S. Department of Health and Human Services, National Center for Health Statistics
   "National Vital Statistics System, Marriages and Divorces" (http://www.cdc.gov/nchs/mardiv.htm)
*Provisional data by state of occurrence.

Estimated Median Age of Men at First Marriage in 2012

National Median = 29.1 Years*

ALPHA ORDER

RANK	STATE	AGE
38	Alabama	27.7
21	Alaska	28.7
19	Arizona	28.8
45	Arkansas	26.9
7	California	30.0
32	Colorado	28.1
6	Connecticut	30.3
10	Delaware	29.7
8	Florida	29.9
16	Georgia	29.0
26	Hawaii	28.4
49	Idaho	26.3
10	Illinois	29.7
35	Indiana	27.8
39	Iowa	27.6
44	Kansas	27.0
40	Kentucky	27.3
18	Louisiana	28.9
21	Maine	28.7
10	Maryland	29.7
3	Massachusetts	30.7
14	Michigan	29.5
19	Minnesota	28.8
26	Mississippi	28.4
35	Missouri	27.8
25	Montana	28.5
40	Nebraska	27.3
26	Nevada	28.4
10	New Hampshire	29.7
4	New Jersey	30.6
45	New Mexico	26.9
2	New York	30.9
29	North Carolina	28.3
40	North Dakota	27.3
16	Ohio	29.0
48	Oklahoma	26.6
15	Oregon	29.1
9	Pennsylvania	29.8
1	Rhode Island	31.6
29	South Carolina	28.3
29	South Dakota	28.3
34	Tennessee	27.9
35	Texas	27.8
50	Utah	26.2
4	Vermont	30.6
21	Virginia	28.7
32	Washington	28.1
43	West Virginia	27.1
24	Wisconsin	28.6
45	Wyoming	26.9

RANK ORDER

RANK	STATE	AGE
1	Rhode Island	31.6
2	New York	30.9
3	Massachusetts	30.7
4	New Jersey	30.6
4	Vermont	30.6
6	Connecticut	30.3
7	California	30.0
8	Florida	29.9
9	Pennsylvania	29.8
10	Delaware	29.7
10	Illinois	29.7
10	Maryland	29.7
10	New Hampshire	29.7
14	Michigan	29.5
15	Oregon	29.1
16	Georgia	29.0
16	Ohio	29.0
18	Louisiana	28.9
19	Arizona	28.8
19	Minnesota	28.8
21	Alaska	28.7
21	Maine	28.7
21	Virginia	28.7
24	Wisconsin	28.6
25	Montana	28.5
26	Hawaii	28.4
26	Mississippi	28.4
26	Nevada	28.4
29	North Carolina	28.3
29	South Carolina	28.3
29	South Dakota	28.3
32	Colorado	28.1
32	Washington	28.1
34	Tennessee	27.9
35	Indiana	27.8
35	Missouri	27.8
35	Texas	27.8
38	Alabama	27.7
39	Iowa	27.6
40	Kentucky	27.3
40	Nebraska	27.3
40	North Dakota	27.3
43	West Virginia	27.1
44	Kansas	27.0
45	Arkansas	26.9
45	New Mexico	26.9
45	Wyoming	26.9
48	Oklahoma	26.6
49	Idaho	26.3
50	Utah	26.2

	District of Columbia	30.2

Source: U.S. Bureau of the Census
    "2012 American Community Survey-Table R1204" (http://www.census.gov/acs/www/index.html)
*The median age at first marriage is calculated indirectly by estimating the proportion of young people who will marry during their lifetime, calculating one-half of this proportion, and determining the age (at the time of the survey) of people at this half-way mark. It does not represent the actual median age of the population who married during the calendar year.

Estimated Median Age of Women at First Marriage in 2012

National Median = 27.1 Years*

<table>
<tr><td colspan="3">ALPHA ORDER</td><td colspan="3">RANK ORDER</td></tr>
<tr><td>RANK</td><td>STATE</td><td>AGE</td><td>RANK</td><td>STATE</td><td>AGE</td></tr>
<tr><td>38</td><td>Alabama</td><td>26.0</td><td>1</td><td>Rhode Island</td><td>29.5</td></tr>
<tr><td>45</td><td>Alaska</td><td>25.5</td><td>2</td><td>New York</td><td>29.3</td></tr>
<tr><td>15</td><td>Arizona</td><td>27.3</td><td>3</td><td>Massachusetts</td><td>29.2</td></tr>
<tr><td>47</td><td>Arkansas</td><td>25.2</td><td>4</td><td>Vermont</td><td>28.8</td></tr>
<tr><td>9</td><td>California</td><td>27.9</td><td>5</td><td>Connecticut</td><td>28.7</td></tr>
<tr><td>27</td><td>Colorado</td><td>26.5</td><td>6</td><td>New Jersey</td><td>28.4</td></tr>
<tr><td>5</td><td>Connecticut</td><td>28.7</td><td>7</td><td>Illinois</td><td>28.2</td></tr>
<tr><td>12</td><td>Delaware</td><td>27.6</td><td>8</td><td>Maryland</td><td>28.1</td></tr>
<tr><td>10</td><td>Florida</td><td>27.8</td><td>9</td><td>California</td><td>27.9</td></tr>
<tr><td>21</td><td>Georgia</td><td>26.8</td><td>10</td><td>Florida</td><td>27.8</td></tr>
<tr><td>20</td><td>Hawaii</td><td>26.9</td><td>11</td><td>Pennsylvania</td><td>27.7</td></tr>
<tr><td>49</td><td>Idaho</td><td>24.4</td><td>12</td><td>Delaware</td><td>27.6</td></tr>
<tr><td>7</td><td>Illinois</td><td>28.2</td><td>12</td><td>Oregon</td><td>27.6</td></tr>
<tr><td>31</td><td>Indiana</td><td>26.3</td><td>14</td><td>Michigan</td><td>27.5</td></tr>
<tr><td>34</td><td>Iowa</td><td>26.1</td><td>15</td><td>Arizona</td><td>27.3</td></tr>
<tr><td>41</td><td>Kansas</td><td>25.7</td><td>16</td><td>Louisiana</td><td>27.1</td></tr>
<tr><td>44</td><td>Kentucky</td><td>25.6</td><td>16</td><td>New Hampshire</td><td>27.1</td></tr>
<tr><td>16</td><td>Louisiana</td><td>27.1</td><td>16</td><td>Ohio</td><td>27.1</td></tr>
<tr><td>29</td><td>Maine</td><td>26.4</td><td>19</td><td>Wisconsin</td><td>27.0</td></tr>
<tr><td>8</td><td>Maryland</td><td>28.1</td><td>20</td><td>Hawaii</td><td>26.9</td></tr>
<tr><td>3</td><td>Massachusetts</td><td>29.2</td><td>21</td><td>Georgia</td><td>26.8</td></tr>
<tr><td>14</td><td>Michigan</td><td>27.5</td><td>21</td><td>Nevada</td><td>26.8</td></tr>
<tr><td>25</td><td>Minnesota</td><td>26.6</td><td>21</td><td>South Carolina</td><td>26.8</td></tr>
<tr><td>29</td><td>Mississippi</td><td>26.4</td><td>21</td><td>Virginia</td><td>26.8</td></tr>
<tr><td>27</td><td>Missouri</td><td>26.5</td><td>25</td><td>Minnesota</td><td>26.6</td></tr>
<tr><td>34</td><td>Montana</td><td>26.1</td><td>25</td><td>North Carolina</td><td>26.6</td></tr>
<tr><td>39</td><td>Nebraska</td><td>25.8</td><td>27</td><td>Colorado</td><td>26.5</td></tr>
<tr><td>21</td><td>Nevada</td><td>26.8</td><td>27</td><td>Missouri</td><td>26.5</td></tr>
<tr><td>16</td><td>New Hampshire</td><td>27.1</td><td>29</td><td>Maine</td><td>26.4</td></tr>
<tr><td>6</td><td>New Jersey</td><td>28.4</td><td>29</td><td>Mississippi</td><td>26.4</td></tr>
<tr><td>31</td><td>New Mexico</td><td>26.3</td><td>31</td><td>Indiana</td><td>26.3</td></tr>
<tr><td>2</td><td>New York</td><td>29.3</td><td>31</td><td>New Mexico</td><td>26.3</td></tr>
<tr><td>25</td><td>North Carolina</td><td>26.6</td><td>31</td><td>Washington</td><td>26.3</td></tr>
<tr><td>39</td><td>North Dakota</td><td>25.8</td><td>34</td><td>Iowa</td><td>26.1</td></tr>
<tr><td>16</td><td>Ohio</td><td>27.1</td><td>34</td><td>Montana</td><td>26.1</td></tr>
<tr><td>46</td><td>Oklahoma</td><td>25.3</td><td>34</td><td>Tennessee</td><td>26.1</td></tr>
<tr><td>12</td><td>Oregon</td><td>27.6</td><td>34</td><td>Texas</td><td>26.1</td></tr>
<tr><td>11</td><td>Pennsylvania</td><td>27.7</td><td>38</td><td>Alabama</td><td>26.0</td></tr>
<tr><td>1</td><td>Rhode Island</td><td>29.5</td><td>39</td><td>Nebraska</td><td>25.8</td></tr>
<tr><td>21</td><td>South Carolina</td><td>26.8</td><td>39</td><td>North Dakota</td><td>25.8</td></tr>
<tr><td>41</td><td>South Dakota</td><td>25.7</td><td>41</td><td>Kansas</td><td>25.7</td></tr>
<tr><td>34</td><td>Tennessee</td><td>26.1</td><td>41</td><td>South Dakota</td><td>25.7</td></tr>
<tr><td>34</td><td>Texas</td><td>26.1</td><td>41</td><td>West Virginia</td><td>25.7</td></tr>
<tr><td>50</td><td>Utah</td><td>24.1</td><td>44</td><td>Kentucky</td><td>25.6</td></tr>
<tr><td>4</td><td>Vermont</td><td>28.8</td><td>45</td><td>Alaska</td><td>25.5</td></tr>
<tr><td>21</td><td>Virginia</td><td>26.8</td><td>46</td><td>Oklahoma</td><td>25.3</td></tr>
<tr><td>31</td><td>Washington</td><td>26.3</td><td>47</td><td>Arkansas</td><td>25.2</td></tr>
<tr><td>41</td><td>West Virginia</td><td>25.7</td><td>48</td><td>Wyoming</td><td>25.0</td></tr>
<tr><td>19</td><td>Wisconsin</td><td>27.0</td><td>49</td><td>Idaho</td><td>24.4</td></tr>
<tr><td>48</td><td>Wyoming</td><td>25.0</td><td>50</td><td>Utah</td><td>24.1</td></tr>
<tr><td></td><td></td><td></td><td></td><td>District of Columbia</td><td>29.8</td></tr>
</table>

Source: U.S. Bureau of the Census

"2012 American Community Survey-Table R1205" (http://www.census.gov/acs/www/index.html)

*The median age at first marriage is calculated indirectly by estimating the proportion of young people who will marry during their lifetime, calculating one-half of this proportion, and determining the age (at the time of the survey) of people at this half-way mark. It does not represent the actual median age of the population who married during the calendar year.

Ratio of Unmarried Men to Unmarried Women in 2012

National Ratio = 110.9 Unmarried Men for Every 100 Unmarried Women*

RANK	STATE	RATIO
43	Alabama	106.8
1	Alaska	138.1
15	Arizona	114.1
25	Arkansas	111.6
13	California	114.7
7	Colorado	119.0
41	Connecticut	107.4
47	Delaware	105.0
28	Florida	110.7
40	Georgia	107.5
3	Hawaii	124.9
13	Idaho	114.7
35	Illinois	108.8
32	Indiana	109.7
18	Iowa	113.7
9	Kansas	116.9
23	Kentucky	112.1
39	Louisiana	108.0
42	Maine	107.2
48	Maryland	104.3
48	Massachusetts	104.3
31	Michigan	110.1
20	Minnesota	112.9
50	Mississippi	103.1
37	Missouri	108.5
5	Montana	120.3
10	Nebraska	116.1
8	Nevada	117.2
24	New Hampshire	111.9
26	New Jersey	111.5
29	New Mexico	110.5
43	New York	106.8
34	North Carolina	109.2
2	North Dakota	125.9
35	Ohio	108.8
12	Oklahoma	114.9
22	Oregon	112.6
33	Pennsylvania	109.4
45	Rhode Island	106.3
46	South Carolina	105.2
6	South Dakota	119.4
38	Tennessee	108.4
20	Texas	112.9
15	Utah	114.1
30	Vermont	110.3
27	Virginia	111.4
11	Washington	115.1
17	West Virginia	113.8
19	Wisconsin	113.0
4	Wyoming	122.2

RANK	STATE	RATIO
1	Alaska	138.1
2	North Dakota	125.9
3	Hawaii	124.9
4	Wyoming	122.2
5	Montana	120.3
6	South Dakota	119.4
7	Colorado	119.0
8	Nevada	117.2
9	Kansas	116.9
10	Nebraska	116.1
11	Washington	115.1
12	Oklahoma	114.9
13	California	114.7
13	Idaho	114.7
15	Arizona	114.1
15	Utah	114.1
17	West Virginia	113.8
18	Iowa	113.7
19	Wisconsin	113.0
20	Minnesota	112.9
20	Texas	112.9
22	Oregon	112.6
23	Kentucky	112.1
24	New Hampshire	111.9
25	Arkansas	111.6
26	New Jersey	111.5
27	Virginia	111.4
28	Florida	110.7
29	New Mexico	110.5
30	Vermont	110.3
31	Michigan	110.1
32	Indiana	109.7
33	Pennsylvania	109.4
34	North Carolina	109.2
35	Illinois	108.8
35	Ohio	108.8
37	Missouri	108.5
38	Tennessee	108.4
39	Louisiana	108.0
40	Georgia	107.5
41	Connecticut	107.4
42	Maine	107.2
43	Alabama	106.8
43	New York	106.8
45	Rhode Island	106.3
46	South Carolina	105.2
47	Delaware	105.0
48	Maryland	104.3
48	Massachusetts	104.3
50	Mississippi	103.1
	District of Columbia	90.2

Source: U.S. Bureau of the Census
   "2012 American Community Survey-Table R1203" (http://www.census.gov/acs/www/index.html)
*Population 15 to 44 years old.

Divorces in 2011

Reporting States' Total = 877,000 Divorces*

ALPHA ORDER

RANK	STATE	DIVORCES	% of USA
16	Alabama	20,700	2.4%
38	Alaska	3,500	0.4%
13	Arizona	25,300	2.9%
22	Arkansas	15,600	1.8%
NA	California**	NA	NA
15	Colorado	22,500	2.6%
28	Connecticut	11,100	1.3%
40	Delaware	3,300	0.4%
1	Florida	85,800	9.8%
NA	Georgia**	NA	NA
NA	Hawaii**	NA	NA
31	Idaho	7,800	0.9%
8	Illinois	33,500	3.8%
NA	Indiana**	NA	NA
32	Iowa	7,400	0.8%
27	Kansas	11,200	1.3%
18	Kentucky	19,200	2.2%
NA	Louisiana**	NA	NA
35	Maine	5,600	0.6%
20	Maryland	16,900	1.9%
19	Massachusetts	17,800	2.0%
7	Michigan	33,600	3.8%
NA	Minnesota**	NA	NA
26	Mississippi	11,900	1.4%
14	Missouri	23,400	2.7%
37	Montana	4,000	0.5%
34	Nebraska	6,400	0.7%
23	Nevada	15,300	1.7%
36	New Hampshire	5,000	0.6%
12	New Jersey	25,600	2.9%
33	New Mexico	6,900	0.8%
3	New York	56,400	6.4%
5	North Carolina	35,700	4.1%
44	North Dakota	1,800	0.2%
4	Ohio	39,300	4.5%
17	Oklahoma	19,700	2.2%
25	Oregon	14,700	1.7%
5	Pennsylvania	35,700	4.1%
39	Rhode Island	3,400	0.4%
24	South Carolina	15,000	1.7%
41	South Dakota	2,700	0.3%
11	Tennessee	27,500	3.1%
2	Texas	82,200	9.4%
29	Utah	10,400	1.2%
43	Vermont	2,300	0.3%
9	Virginia	30,800	3.5%
10	Washington	28,000	3.2%
30	West Virginia	9,600	1.1%
21	Wisconsin	16,600	1.9%
41	Wyoming	2,700	0.3%

RANK ORDER

RANK	STATE	DIVORCES	% of USA
1	Florida	85,800	9.8%
2	Texas	82,200	9.4%
3	New York	56,400	6.4%
4	Ohio	39,300	4.5%
5	North Carolina	35,700	4.1%
5	Pennsylvania	35,700	4.1%
7	Michigan	33,600	3.8%
8	Illinois	33,500	3.8%
9	Virginia	30,800	3.5%
10	Washington	28,000	3.2%
11	Tennessee	27,500	3.1%
12	New Jersey	25,600	2.9%
13	Arizona	25,300	2.9%
14	Missouri	23,400	2.7%
15	Colorado	22,500	2.6%
16	Alabama	20,700	2.4%
17	Oklahoma	19,700	2.2%
18	Kentucky	19,200	2.2%
19	Massachusetts	17,800	2.0%
20	Maryland	16,900	1.9%
21	Wisconsin	16,600	1.9%
22	Arkansas	15,600	1.8%
23	Nevada	15,300	1.7%
24	South Carolina	15,000	1.7%
25	Oregon	14,700	1.7%
26	Mississippi	11,900	1.4%
27	Kansas	11,200	1.3%
28	Connecticut	11,100	1.3%
29	Utah	10,400	1.2%
30	West Virginia	9,600	1.1%
31	Idaho	7,800	0.9%
32	Iowa	7,400	0.8%
33	New Mexico	6,900	0.8%
34	Nebraska	6,400	0.7%
35	Maine	5,600	0.6%
36	New Hampshire	5,000	0.6%
37	Montana	4,000	0.5%
38	Alaska	3,500	0.4%
39	Rhode Island	3,400	0.4%
40	Delaware	3,300	0.4%
41	South Dakota	2,700	0.3%
41	Wyoming	2,700	0.3%
43	Vermont	2,300	0.3%
44	North Dakota	1,800	0.2%
NA	California**	NA	NA
NA	Georgia**	NA	NA
NA	Hawaii**	NA	NA
NA	Indiana**	NA	NA
NA	Louisiana**	NA	NA
NA	Minnesota**	NA	NA
	District of Columbia	1,800	0.2%

Source: CQ Press using data from U.S. Department of Health and Human Services, National Center for Health Statistics
   "National Vital Statistics System, Marriages and Divorces" (http://www.cdc.gov/nchs/mardiv.htm)
*Provisional estimates by state of occurrence. National total is only for reporting states.
**Not available.

Divorce Rate in 2011

Reporting States' Rate = 3.6 Divorces per 1,000 Population*

ALPHA ORDER

RANK	STATE	RATE
11	Alabama	4.3
6	Alaska	4.8
17	Arizona	3.9
2	Arkansas	5.3
NA	California**	NA
9	Colorado	4.4
35	Connecticut	3.1
25	Delaware	3.6
8	Florida	4.5
NA	Georgia**	NA
NA	Hawaii**	NA
5	Idaho	4.9
43	Illinois	2.6
NA	Indiana**	NA
44	Iowa	2.4
17	Kansas	3.9
9	Kentucky	4.4
NA	Louisiana**	NA
13	Maine	4.2
36	Maryland	2.9
41	Massachusetts	2.7
28	Michigan	3.4
NA	Minnesota**	NA
15	Mississippi	4.0
17	Missouri	3.9
15	Montana	4.0
27	Nebraska	3.5
1	Nevada	5.6
20	New Hampshire	3.8
36	New Jersey	2.9
30	New Mexico	3.3
36	New York	2.9
23	North Carolina	3.7
41	North Dakota	2.7
28	Ohio	3.4
3	Oklahoma	5.2
20	Oregon	3.8
40	Pennsylvania	2.8
32	Rhode Island	3.2
32	South Carolina	3.2
30	South Dakota	3.3
11	Tennessee	4.3
32	Texas	3.2
23	Utah	3.7
25	Vermont	3.6
20	Virginia	3.8
14	Washington	4.1
3	West Virginia	5.2
36	Wisconsin	2.9
6	Wyoming	4.8

RANK ORDER

RANK	STATE	RATE
1	Nevada	5.6
2	Arkansas	5.3
3	Oklahoma	5.2
3	West Virginia	5.2
5	Idaho	4.9
6	Alaska	4.8
6	Wyoming	4.8
8	Florida	4.5
9	Colorado	4.4
9	Kentucky	4.4
11	Alabama	4.3
11	Tennessee	4.3
13	Maine	4.2
14	Washington	4.1
15	Mississippi	4.0
15	Montana	4.0
17	Arizona	3.9
17	Kansas	3.9
17	Missouri	3.9
20	New Hampshire	3.8
20	Oregon	3.8
20	Virginia	3.8
23	North Carolina	3.7
23	Utah	3.7
25	Delaware	3.6
25	Vermont	3.6
27	Nebraska	3.5
28	Michigan	3.4
28	Ohio	3.4
30	New Mexico	3.3
30	South Dakota	3.3
32	Rhode Island	3.2
32	South Carolina	3.2
32	Texas	3.2
35	Connecticut	3.1
36	Maryland	2.9
36	New Jersey	2.9
36	New York	2.9
36	Wisconsin	2.9
40	Pennsylvania	2.8
41	Massachusetts	2.7
41	North Dakota	2.7
43	Illinois	2.6
44	Iowa	2.4
NA	California**	NA
NA	Georgia**	NA
NA	Hawaii**	NA
NA	Indiana**	NA
NA	Louisiana**	NA
NA	Minnesota**	NA

	District of Columbia	2.9

Source: U.S. Department of Health and Human Services, National Center for Health Statistics
"National Vital Statistics System, Marriages and Divorces" (http://www.cdc.gov/nchs/mardiv.htm)
*Provisional data by state of occurrence. National rate is only for reporting states.
**Not available.

Average Family Size in 2012

National Average = 3.25 Persons per Family

ALPHA ORDER

RANK	STATE	PERSONS
19	Alabama	3.17
4	Alaska	3.44
10	Arizona	3.29
32	Arkansas	3.10
3	California	3.57
24	Colorado	3.14
23	Connecticut	3.15
18	Delaware	3.19
13	Florida	3.27
6	Georgia	3.34
2	Hawaii	3.61
17	Idaho	3.21
10	Illinois	3.29
24	Indiana	3.14
45	Iowa	2.98
30	Kansas	3.12
41	Kentucky	3.04
15	Louisiana	3.24
49	Maine	2.86
14	Maryland	3.26
21	Massachusetts	3.16
24	Michigan	3.14
39	Minnesota	3.05
15	Mississippi	3.24
34	Missouri	3.08
47	Montana	2.96
41	Nebraska	3.04
7	Nevada	3.32
45	New Hampshire	2.98
10	New Jersey	3.29
7	New Mexico	3.32
9	New York	3.31
30	North Carolina	3.12
48	North Dakota	2.95
34	Ohio	3.08
24	Oklahoma	3.14
37	Oregon	3.06
32	Pennsylvania	3.10
37	Rhode Island	3.06
28	South Carolina	3.13
34	South Dakota	3.08
28	Tennessee	3.13
4	Texas	3.44
1	Utah	3.64
50	Vermont	2.84
19	Virginia	3.17
21	Washington	3.16
39	West Virginia	3.05
44	Wisconsin	3.02
41	Wyoming	3.04

RANK ORDER

RANK	STATE	PERSONS
1	Utah	3.64
2	Hawaii	3.61
3	California	3.57
4	Alaska	3.44
4	Texas	3.44
6	Georgia	3.34
7	Nevada	3.32
7	New Mexico	3.32
9	New York	3.31
10	Arizona	3.29
10	Illinois	3.29
10	New Jersey	3.29
13	Florida	3.27
14	Maryland	3.26
15	Louisiana	3.24
15	Mississippi	3.24
17	Idaho	3.21
18	Delaware	3.19
19	Alabama	3.17
19	Virginia	3.17
21	Massachusetts	3.16
21	Washington	3.16
23	Connecticut	3.15
24	Colorado	3.14
24	Indiana	3.14
24	Michigan	3.14
24	Oklahoma	3.14
28	South Carolina	3.13
28	Tennessee	3.13
30	Kansas	3.12
30	North Carolina	3.12
32	Arkansas	3.10
32	Pennsylvania	3.10
34	Missouri	3.08
34	Ohio	3.08
34	South Dakota	3.08
37	Oregon	3.06
37	Rhode Island	3.06
39	Minnesota	3.05
39	West Virginia	3.05
41	Kentucky	3.04
41	Nebraska	3.04
41	Wyoming	3.04
44	Wisconsin	3.02
45	Iowa	2.98
45	New Hampshire	2.98
47	Montana	2.96
48	North Dakota	2.95
49	Maine	2.86
50	Vermont	2.84

	District of Columbia	3.25

Source: U.S. Bureau of the Census
"2012 American Community Survey-Table DP02" (http://www.census.gov/acs/www/index.html)

Seats in the U.S. House of Representatives in 2014

National Total = 435 Seats*

ALPHA ORDER

RANK	STATE	SEATS	% of USA
22	Alabama	7	1.6%
44	Alaska	1	0.2%
14	Arizona	9	2.1%
30	Arkansas	4	0.9%
1	California	53	12.2%
22	Colorado	7	1.6%
27	Connecticut	5	1.1%
44	Delaware	1	0.2%
3	Florida	27	6.2%
8	Georgia	14	3.2%
39	Hawaii	2	0.5%
39	Idaho	2	0.5%
5	Illinois	18	4.1%
14	Indiana	9	2.1%
30	Iowa	4	0.9%
30	Kansas	4	0.9%
25	Kentucky	6	1.4%
25	Louisiana	6	1.4%
39	Maine	2	0.5%
18	Maryland	8	1.8%
14	Massachusetts	9	2.1%
8	Michigan	14	3.2%
18	Minnesota	8	1.8%
30	Mississippi	4	0.9%
18	Missouri	8	1.8%
44	Montana	1	0.2%
36	Nebraska	3	0.7%
30	Nevada	4	0.9%
39	New Hampshire	2	0.5%
11	New Jersey	12	2.8%
36	New Mexico	3	0.7%
3	New York	27	6.2%
10	North Carolina	13	3.0%
44	North Dakota	1	0.2%
7	Ohio	16	3.7%
27	Oklahoma	5	1.1%
27	Oregon	5	1.1%
5	Pennsylvania	18	4.1%
39	Rhode Island	2	0.5%
22	South Carolina	7	1.6%
44	South Dakota	1	0.2%
14	Tennessee	9	2.1%
2	Texas	36	8.3%
30	Utah	4	0.9%
44	Vermont	1	0.2%
12	Virginia	11	2.5%
13	Washington	10	2.3%
36	West Virginia	3	0.7%
18	Wisconsin	8	1.8%
44	Wyoming	1	0.2%

RANK ORDER

RANK	STATE	SEATS	% of USA
1	California	53	12.2%
2	Texas	36	8.3%
3	Florida	27	6.2%
3	New York	27	6.2%
5	Illinois	18	4.1%
5	Pennsylvania	18	4.1%
7	Ohio	16	3.7%
8	Georgia	14	3.2%
8	Michigan	14	3.2%
10	North Carolina	13	3.0%
11	New Jersey	12	2.8%
12	Virginia	11	2.5%
13	Washington	10	2.3%
14	Arizona	9	2.1%
14	Indiana	9	2.1%
14	Massachusetts	9	2.1%
14	Tennessee	9	2.1%
18	Maryland	8	1.8%
18	Minnesota	8	1.8%
18	Missouri	8	1.8%
18	Wisconsin	8	1.8%
22	Alabama	7	1.6%
22	Colorado	7	1.6%
22	South Carolina	7	1.6%
25	Kentucky	6	1.4%
25	Louisiana	6	1.4%
27	Connecticut	5	1.1%
27	Oklahoma	5	1.1%
27	Oregon	5	1.1%
30	Arkansas	4	0.9%
30	Iowa	4	0.9%
30	Kansas	4	0.9%
30	Mississippi	4	0.9%
30	Nevada	4	0.9%
30	Utah	4	0.9%
36	Nebraska	3	0.7%
36	New Mexico	3	0.7%
36	West Virginia	3	0.7%
39	Hawaii	2	0.5%
39	Idaho	2	0.5%
39	Maine	2	0.5%
39	New Hampshire	2	0.5%
39	Rhode Island	2	0.5%
44	Alaska	1	0.2%
44	Delaware	1	0.2%
44	Montana	1	0.2%
44	North Dakota	1	0.2%
44	South Dakota	1	0.2%
44	Vermont	1	0.2%
44	Wyoming	1	0.2%
	District of Columbia	0	0.0%

Source: U.S. Bureau of the Census
"Congressional Apportionment" (http://www.census.gov/population/apportionment/)
*This table shows the number of seats after reapportionment of the 2010 Census. This apportionment became effective with the Congress elected in November 2012 and that took office in January 2013.
**The District of Columbia has one non-voting delegate. Each state has two members in the U.S. Senate.

Estimated Population per U.S. House Seat in 2014

National Rate = 725,247 Persons per House Member*

ALPHA ORDER

RANK	STATE	RATE
41	Alabama	690,532
19	Alaska	735,132
18	Arizona	736,292
17	Arkansas	739,843
28	California	723,255
11	Colorado	752,624
31	Connecticut	719,216
2	Delaware	925,749
25	Florida	724,180
34	Georgia	713,726
37	Hawaii	702,027
4	Idaho	806,068
33	Illinois	715,674
22	Indiana	730,100
6	Iowa	772,604
26	Kansas	723,489
21	Kentucky	732,549
7	Louisiana	770,912
44	Maine	664,151
16	Maryland	741,102
14	Massachusetts	743,647
36	Michigan	706,830
43	Minnesota	677,548
13	Mississippi	747,802
10	Missouri	755,521
1	Montana	1,015,165
47	Nebraska	622,839
38	Nevada	697,534
45	New Hampshire	661,730
15	New Jersey	741,612
40	New Mexico	695,096
23	New York	727,820
9	North Carolina	757,543
27	North Dakota	723,393
29	Ohio	723,176
8	Oklahoma	770,114
5	Oregon	786,013
35	Pennsylvania	709,656
50	Rhode Island	525,756
42	South Carolina	682,120
3	South Dakota	844,877
30	Tennessee	721,775
20	Texas	734,672
24	Utah	725,218
46	Vermont	626,630
12	Virginia	750,946
39	Washington	697,141
48	West Virginia	618,101
32	Wisconsin	717,839
49	Wyoming	582,658

RANK ORDER

RANK	STATE	RATE
1	Montana	1,015,165
2	Delaware	925,749
3	South Dakota	844,877
4	Idaho	806,068
5	Oregon	786,013
6	Iowa	772,604
7	Louisiana	770,912
8	Oklahoma	770,114
9	North Carolina	757,543
10	Missouri	755,521
11	Colorado	752,624
12	Virginia	750,946
13	Mississippi	747,802
14	Massachusetts	743,647
15	New Jersey	741,612
16	Maryland	741,102
17	Arkansas	739,843
18	Arizona	736,292
19	Alaska	735,132
20	Texas	734,672
21	Kentucky	732,549
22	Indiana	730,100
23	New York	727,820
24	Utah	725,218
25	Florida	724,180
26	Kansas	723,489
27	North Dakota	723,393
28	California	723,255
29	Ohio	723,176
30	Tennessee	721,775
31	Connecticut	719,216
32	Wisconsin	717,839
33	Illinois	715,674
34	Georgia	713,726
35	Pennsylvania	709,656
36	Michigan	706,830
37	Hawaii	702,027
38	Nevada	697,534
39	Washington	697,141
40	New Mexico	695,096
41	Alabama	690,532
42	South Carolina	682,120
43	Minnesota	677,548
44	Maine	664,151
45	New Hampshire	661,730
46	Vermont	626,630
47	Nebraska	622,839
48	West Virginia	618,101
49	Wyoming	582,658
50	Rhode Island	525,756

District of Columbia**   NA

Source: CQ Press using data from U.S. Bureau of the Census

"Congressional Apportionment" (http://www.census.gov/population/apportionment/)

*Rates calculated using 2013 population estimates and do not include population of the District of Columbia. The District has one non-voting delegate. Each state has two members in the U.S. Senate. This table is based only on U.S. Representatives and not U.S. Senate members. This table reflects reapportionment resulting from the 2010 census and taking effect after the 2012 election. **Not applicable.

State Legislators in 2013

National Total = 7,383 Legislators*

ALPHA ORDER

RANK	STATE	LEGISLATORS	% of USA
27	Alabama	140	1.9%
49	Alaska	60	0.8%
43	Arizona	90	1.2%
30	Arkansas	135	1.8%
35	California	120	1.6%
42	Colorado	100	1.4%
9	Connecticut	187	2.5%
48	Delaware	62	0.8%
18	Florida	160	2.2%
3	Georgia	236	3.2%
46	Hawaii	76	1.0%
39	Idaho	105	1.4%
13	Illinois	177	2.4%
19	Indiana	150	2.0%
19	Iowa	150	2.0%
17	Kansas	165	2.2%
29	Kentucky	138	1.9%
25	Louisiana	144	2.0%
10	Maine	186	2.5%
8	Maryland	188	2.5%
6	Massachusetts	200	2.7%
23	Michigan	148	2.0%
5	Minnesota	201	2.7%
14	Mississippi	174	2.4%
7	Missouri	197	2.7%
19	Montana	150	2.0%
50	Nebraska	49	0.7%
47	Nevada	63	0.9%
1	New Hampshire	424	5.7%
35	New Jersey	120	1.6%
38	New Mexico	112	1.5%
4	New York	213	2.9%
15	North Carolina	170	2.3%
26	North Dakota	141	1.9%
32	Ohio	132	1.8%
22	Oklahoma	149	2.0%
43	Oregon	90	1.2%
2	Pennsylvania	253	3.4%
37	Rhode Island	113	1.5%
15	South Carolina	170	2.3%
39	South Dakota	105	1.4%
32	Tennessee	132	1.8%
11	Texas	181	2.5%
41	Utah	104	1.4%
12	Vermont	180	2.4%
27	Virginia	140	1.9%
24	Washington	147	2.0%
31	West Virginia	134	1.8%
32	Wisconsin	132	1.8%
43	Wyoming	90	1.2%

RANK ORDER

RANK	STATE	LEGISLATORS	% of USA
1	New Hampshire	424	5.7%
2	Pennsylvania	253	3.4%
3	Georgia	236	3.2%
4	New York	213	2.9%
5	Minnesota	201	2.7%
6	Massachusetts	200	2.7%
7	Missouri	197	2.7%
8	Maryland	188	2.5%
9	Connecticut	187	2.5%
10	Maine	186	2.5%
11	Texas	181	2.5%
12	Vermont	180	2.4%
13	Illinois	177	2.4%
14	Mississippi	174	2.4%
15	North Carolina	170	2.3%
15	South Carolina	170	2.3%
17	Kansas	165	2.2%
18	Florida	160	2.2%
19	Indiana	150	2.0%
19	Iowa	150	2.0%
19	Montana	150	2.0%
22	Oklahoma	149	2.0%
23	Michigan	148	2.0%
24	Washington	147	2.0%
25	Louisiana	144	2.0%
26	North Dakota	141	1.9%
27	Alabama	140	1.9%
27	Virginia	140	1.9%
29	Kentucky	138	1.9%
30	Arkansas	135	1.8%
31	West Virginia	134	1.8%
32	Ohio	132	1.8%
32	Tennessee	132	1.8%
32	Wisconsin	132	1.8%
35	California	120	1.6%
35	New Jersey	120	1.6%
37	Rhode Island	113	1.5%
38	New Mexico	112	1.5%
39	Idaho	105	1.4%
39	South Dakota	105	1.4%
41	Utah	104	1.4%
42	Colorado	100	1.4%
43	Arizona	90	1.2%
43	Oregon	90	1.2%
43	Wyoming	90	1.2%
46	Hawaii	76	1.0%
47	Nevada	63	0.9%
48	Delaware	62	0.8%
49	Alaska	60	0.8%
50	Nebraska	49	0.7%

	District of Columbia**	NA	NA

Source: National Conference of State Legislatures (Denver, CO)

"2013 Partisan Composition" (http://www.ncsl.org/research/about-state-legislatures/partisan-composition.aspx)

*There are 1,972 state senators (including Nebraska's 49 unicameral seats) and 5,411 state house members.

**Not applicable.

Population per State Legislator in 2013

National Rate = 42,731 Population per Legislator*

ALPHA ORDER

RANK	STATE	RATE
22	Alabama	34,527
42	Alaska	12,252
7	Arizona	73,629
32	Arkansas	21,921
1	California	319,438
12	Colorado	52,684
34	Connecticut	19,230
40	Delaware	14,931
3	Florida	122,205
20	Georgia	42,340
36	Hawaii	18,474
39	Idaho	15,354
8	Illinois	72,780
17	Indiana	43,806
33	Iowa	20,603
37	Kansas	17,539
25	Kentucky	31,850
24	Louisiana	32,121
45	Maine	7,141
26	Maryland	31,536
23	Massachusetts	33,464
9	Michigan	66,862
30	Minnesota	26,967
38	Mississippi	17,191
27	Missouri	30,681
46	Montana	6,768
21	Nebraska	38,133
16	Nevada	44,288
50	New Hampshire	3,121
6	New Jersey	74,161
35	New Mexico	18,619
4	New York	92,259
11	North Carolina	57,930
48	North Dakota	5,130
5	Ohio	87,658
31	Oklahoma	25,843
18	Oregon	43,667
13	Pennsylvania	50,489
43	Rhode Island	9,305
28	South Carolina	28,087
44	South Dakota	8,046
14	Tennessee	49,212
2	Texas	146,123
29	Utah	27,893
49	Vermont	3,481
10	Virginia	59,003
15	Washington	47,425
41	West Virginia	13,838
19	Wisconsin	43,505
47	Wyoming	6,474

RANK ORDER

RANK	STATE	RATE
1	California	319,438
2	Texas	146,123
3	Florida	122,205
4	New York	92,259
5	Ohio	87,658
6	New Jersey	74,161
7	Arizona	73,629
8	Illinois	72,780
9	Michigan	66,862
10	Virginia	59,003
11	North Carolina	57,930
12	Colorado	52,684
13	Pennsylvania	50,489
14	Tennessee	49,212
15	Washington	47,425
16	Nevada	44,288
17	Indiana	43,806
18	Oregon	43,667
19	Wisconsin	43,505
20	Georgia	42,340
21	Nebraska	38,133
22	Alabama	34,527
23	Massachusetts	33,464
24	Louisiana	32,121
25	Kentucky	31,850
26	Maryland	31,536
27	Missouri	30,681
28	South Carolina	28,087
29	Utah	27,893
30	Minnesota	26,967
31	Oklahoma	25,843
32	Arkansas	21,921
33	Iowa	20,603
34	Connecticut	19,230
35	New Mexico	18,619
36	Hawaii	18,474
37	Kansas	17,539
38	Mississippi	17,191
39	Idaho	15,354
40	Delaware	14,931
41	West Virginia	13,838
42	Alaska	12,252
43	Rhode Island	9,305
44	South Dakota	8,046
45	Maine	7,141
46	Montana	6,768
47	Wyoming	6,474
48	North Dakota	5,130
49	Vermont	3,481
50	New Hampshire	3,121

District of Columbia**   NA

Source: CQ Press using data from National Conference of State Legislatures (Denver, CO)
  "2013 Partisan Composition" (http://www.ncsl.org/research/about-state-legislatures/partisan-composition.aspx)
*There are 1,972 state senators (including Nebraska's 49 unicameral seats) and 5,411 state house members. National rate does not include population for the District of Columbia. Calculated using 2013 population estimates.
**Not applicable.

Registered Voters in 2012

National Total = 153,157,000

ALPHA ORDER

RANK	STATE	REGISTERED	% of USA
23	Alabama	2,556,000	1.7%
48	Alaska	361,000	0.2%
21	Arizona	2,812,000	1.8%
33	Arkansas	1,376,000	0.9%
1	California	15,356,000	10.0%
22	Colorado	2,635,000	1.7%
30	Connecticut	1,760,000	1.1%
45	Delaware	470,000	0.3%
3	Florida	9,102,000	5.9%
10	Georgia	4,767,000	3.1%
44	Hawaii	547,000	0.4%
41	Idaho	745,000	0.5%
6	Illinois	6,425,000	4.2%
17	Indiana	3,270,000	2.1%
31	Iowa	1,745,000	1.1%
32	Kansas	1,467,000	1.0%
26	Kentucky	2,303,000	1.5%
24	Louisiana	2,498,000	1.6%
39	Maine	787,000	0.5%
20	Maryland	2,888,000	1.9%
13	Massachusetts	3,759,000	2.5%
8	Michigan	5,620,000	3.7%
19	Minnesota	3,085,000	2.0%
29	Mississippi	1,794,000	1.2%
15	Missouri	3,384,000	2.2%
42	Montana	553,000	0.4%
38	Nebraska	901,000	0.6%
34	Nevada	1,176,000	0.8%
40	New Hampshire	752,000	0.5%
11	New Jersey	4,326,000	2.8%
37	New Mexico	978,000	0.6%
4	New York	8,887,000	5.8%
9	North Carolina	5,295,000	3.5%
47	North Dakota	383,000	0.3%
7	Ohio	6,076,000	4.0%
28	Oklahoma	1,806,000	1.2%
27	Oregon	2,086,000	1.4%
5	Pennsylvania	6,795,000	4.4%
43	Rhode Island	552,000	0.4%
25	South Carolina	2,479,000	1.6%
46	South Dakota	454,000	0.3%
18	Tennessee	3,210,000	2.1%
2	Texas	10,749,000	7.0%
35	Utah	1,138,000	0.7%
49	Vermont	357,000	0.2%
12	Virginia	4,210,000	2.7%
14	Washington	3,533,000	2.3%
36	West Virginia	982,000	0.6%
16	Wisconsin	3,318,000	2.2%
50	Wyoming	268,000	0.2%

RANK ORDER

RANK	STATE	REGISTERED	% of USA
1	California	15,356,000	10.0%
2	Texas	10,749,000	7.0%
3	Florida	9,102,000	5.9%
4	New York	8,887,000	5.8%
5	Pennsylvania	6,795,000	4.4%
6	Illinois	6,425,000	4.2%
7	Ohio	6,076,000	4.0%
8	Michigan	5,620,000	3.7%
9	North Carolina	5,295,000	3.5%
10	Georgia	4,767,000	3.1%
11	New Jersey	4,326,000	2.8%
12	Virginia	4,210,000	2.7%
13	Massachusetts	3,759,000	2.5%
14	Washington	3,533,000	2.3%
15	Missouri	3,384,000	2.2%
16	Wisconsin	3,318,000	2.2%
17	Indiana	3,270,000	2.1%
18	Tennessee	3,210,000	2.1%
19	Minnesota	3,085,000	2.0%
20	Maryland	2,888,000	1.9%
21	Arizona	2,812,000	1.8%
22	Colorado	2,635,000	1.7%
23	Alabama	2,556,000	1.7%
24	Louisiana	2,498,000	1.6%
25	South Carolina	2,479,000	1.6%
26	Kentucky	2,303,000	1.5%
27	Oregon	2,086,000	1.4%
28	Oklahoma	1,806,000	1.2%
29	Mississippi	1,794,000	1.2%
30	Connecticut	1,760,000	1.1%
31	Iowa	1,745,000	1.1%
32	Kansas	1,467,000	1.0%
33	Arkansas	1,376,000	0.9%
34	Nevada	1,176,000	0.8%
35	Utah	1,138,000	0.7%
36	West Virginia	982,000	0.6%
37	New Mexico	978,000	0.6%
38	Nebraska	901,000	0.6%
39	Maine	787,000	0.5%
40	New Hampshire	752,000	0.5%
41	Idaho	745,000	0.5%
42	Montana	553,000	0.4%
43	Rhode Island	552,000	0.4%
44	Hawaii	547,000	0.4%
45	Delaware	470,000	0.3%
46	South Dakota	454,000	0.3%
47	North Dakota	383,000	0.3%
48	Alaska	361,000	0.2%
49	Vermont	357,000	0.2%
50	Wyoming	268,000	0.2%
	District of Columbia	385,000	0.3%

Source: U.S. Bureau of the Census
  "Voting and Registration" (Table 4a, http://www.census.gov/hhes/www/socdemo/voting/index.html)

Percent of Eligible Voters Reported Registered in 2012

National Percent = 71.2%*

ALPHA ORDER			RANK ORDER		
RANK	STATE	PERCENT	RANK	STATE	PERCENT
18	Alabama	73.5	1	Mississippi	84.2
26	Alaska	72.8	2	Minnesota	79.0
46	Arizona	65.2	3	North Carolina	78.9
45	Arkansas	65.3	4	Massachusetts	78.7
44	California	65.6	5	Iowa	78.2
15	Colorado	74.4	6	Wisconsin	78.1
33	Connecticut	70.4	7	Michigan	77.8
21	Delaware	73.3	8	Louisiana	77.1
39	Florida	68.3	8	Maine	77.1
32	Georgia	70.7	10	Missouri	76.7
50	Hawaii	58.9	11	New Hampshire	75.9
34	Idaho	70.0	12	South Dakota	74.8
27	Illinois	72.7	13	Virginia	74.6
36	Indiana	69.2	14	North Dakota	74.5
5	Iowa	78.2	15	Colorado	74.4
15	Kansas	74.4	15	Kansas	74.4
28	Kentucky	72.1	17	Oregon	74.3
8	Louisiana	77.1	18	Alabama	73.5
8	Maine	77.1	18	Rhode Island	73.5
28	Maryland	72.1	20	Vermont	73.4
4	Massachusetts	78.7	21	Delaware	73.3
7	Michigan	77.8	21	Montana	73.3
2	Minnesota	79.0	21	South Carolina	73.3
1	Mississippi	84.2	24	Washington	73.1
10	Missouri	76.7	25	New Jersey	73.0
21	Montana	73.3	26	Alaska	72.8
35	Nebraska	69.5	27	Illinois	72.7
47	Nevada	65.0	28	Kentucky	72.1
11	New Hampshire	75.9	28	Maryland	72.1
25	New Jersey	73.0	30	Pennsylvania	71.9
37	New Mexico	68.6	31	Ohio	71.1
41	New York	67.9	32	Georgia	70.7
3	North Carolina	78.9	33	Connecticut	70.4
14	North Dakota	74.5	34	Idaho	70.0
31	Ohio	71.1	35	Nebraska	69.5
43	Oklahoma	66.1	36	Indiana	69.2
17	Oregon	74.3	37	New Mexico	68.6
30	Pennsylvania	71.9	37	Tennessee	68.6
18	Rhode Island	73.5	39	Florida	68.3
21	South Carolina	73.3	40	West Virginia	68.1
12	South Dakota	74.8	41	New York	67.9
37	Tennessee	68.6	42	Texas	66.9
42	Texas	66.9	43	Oklahoma	66.1
49	Utah	63.5	44	California	65.6
20	Vermont	73.4	45	Arkansas	65.3
13	Virginia	74.6	46	Arizona	65.2
24	Washington	73.1	47	Nevada	65.0
40	West Virginia	68.1	48	Wyoming	63.9
6	Wisconsin	78.1	49	Utah	63.5
48	Wyoming	63.9	50	Hawaii	58.9
				District of Columbia	83.4

Source: U.S. Bureau of the Census
"Voting and Registration" (Table 4a, http://www.census.gov/hhes/www/socdemo/voting/index.html)
*As a percent of citizen population 18 and older.

Persons Voting in 2012

National Total = 132,948,000

ALPHA ORDER

RANK	STATE	VOTERS	% of USA
24	Alabama	2,154,000	1.6%
49	Alaska	289,000	0.2%
22	Arizona	2,412,000	1.8%
33	Arkansas	1,124,000	0.8%
1	California	13,462,000	10.1%
21	Colorado	2,495,000	1.9%
29	Connecticut	1,568,000	1.2%
45	Delaware	431,000	0.3%
3	Florida	8,107,000	6.1%
10	Georgia	4,168,000	3.1%
43	Hawaii	480,000	0.4%
41	Idaho	679,000	0.5%
6	Illinois	5,428,000	4.1%
18	Indiana	2,801,000	2.1%
30	Iowa	1,548,000	1.2%
32	Kansas	1,249,000	0.9%
27	Kentucky	1,895,000	1.4%
25	Louisiana	2,148,000	1.6%
38	Maine	700,000	0.5%
19	Maryland	2,609,000	2.0%
13	Massachusetts	3,382,000	2.5%
8	Michigan	4,832,000	3.6%
16	Minnesota	2,859,000	2.2%
28	Mississippi	1,588,000	1.2%
17	Missouri	2,818,000	2.1%
42	Montana	495,000	0.4%
37	Nebraska	798,000	0.6%
34	Nevada	1,048,000	0.8%
40	New Hampshire	688,000	0.5%
12	New Jersey	3,670,000	2.8%
36	New Mexico	878,000	0.7%
4	New York	7,675,000	5.8%
9	North Carolina	4,624,000	3.5%
47	North Dakota	328,000	0.2%
7	Ohio	5,395,000	4.1%
31	Oklahoma	1,431,000	1.1%
26	Oregon	1,897,000	1.4%
5	Pennsylvania	5,824,000	4.4%
44	Rhode Island	469,000	0.4%
23	South Carolina	2,187,000	1.6%
46	South Dakota	370,000	0.3%
20	Tennessee	2,606,000	2.0%
2	Texas	8,643,000	6.5%
35	Utah	1,022,000	0.8%
48	Vermont	308,000	0.2%
11	Virginia	3,778,000	2.8%
14	Washington	3,172,000	2.4%
39	West Virginia	690,000	0.5%
15	Wisconsin	3,127,000	2.4%
50	Wyoming	247,000	0.2%

RANK ORDER

RANK	STATE	VOTERS	% of USA
1	California	13,462,000	10.1%
2	Texas	8,643,000	6.5%
3	Florida	8,107,000	6.1%
4	New York	7,675,000	5.8%
5	Pennsylvania	5,824,000	4.4%
6	Illinois	5,428,000	4.1%
7	Ohio	5,395,000	4.1%
8	Michigan	4,832,000	3.6%
9	North Carolina	4,624,000	3.5%
10	Georgia	4,168,000	3.1%
11	Virginia	3,778,000	2.8%
12	New Jersey	3,670,000	2.8%
13	Massachusetts	3,382,000	2.5%
14	Washington	3,172,000	2.4%
15	Wisconsin	3,127,000	2.4%
16	Minnesota	2,859,000	2.2%
17	Missouri	2,818,000	2.1%
18	Indiana	2,801,000	2.1%
19	Maryland	2,609,000	2.0%
20	Tennessee	2,606,000	2.0%
21	Colorado	2,495,000	1.9%
22	Arizona	2,412,000	1.8%
23	South Carolina	2,187,000	1.6%
24	Alabama	2,154,000	1.6%
25	Louisiana	2,148,000	1.6%
26	Oregon	1,897,000	1.4%
27	Kentucky	1,895,000	1.4%
28	Mississippi	1,588,000	1.2%
29	Connecticut	1,568,000	1.2%
30	Iowa	1,548,000	1.2%
31	Oklahoma	1,431,000	1.1%
32	Kansas	1,249,000	0.9%
33	Arkansas	1,124,000	0.8%
34	Nevada	1,048,000	0.8%
35	Utah	1,022,000	0.8%
36	New Mexico	878,000	0.7%
37	Nebraska	798,000	0.6%
38	Maine	700,000	0.5%
39	West Virginia	690,000	0.5%
40	New Hampshire	688,000	0.5%
41	Idaho	679,000	0.5%
42	Montana	495,000	0.4%
43	Hawaii	480,000	0.4%
44	Rhode Island	469,000	0.4%
45	Delaware	431,000	0.3%
46	South Dakota	370,000	0.3%
47	North Dakota	328,000	0.2%
48	Vermont	308,000	0.2%
49	Alaska	289,000	0.2%
50	Wyoming	247,000	0.2%
	District of Columbia	350,000	0.3%

Source: U.S. Bureau of the Census
"Voting and Registration" (Table 4a, http://www.census.gov/hhes/www/socdemo/voting/index.html)

Percent of Eligible Population Reported Voting in 2012

National Percent = 61.8%*

ALPHA ORDER

RANK	STATE	PERCENT
27	Alabama	61.9
40	Alaska	58.4
44	Arizona	55.9
47	Arkansas	53.3
42	California	57.5
5	Colorado	70.4
25	Connecticut	62.7
11	Delaware	67.3
35	Florida	60.8
27	Georgia	61.9
49	Hawaii	51.6
19	Idaho	63.9
33	Illinois	61.5
36	Indiana	59.3
6	Iowa	69.4
22	Kansas	63.3
36	Kentucky	59.3
14	Louisiana	66.3
9	Maine	68.6
17	Maryland	65.1
4	Massachusetts	70.8
13	Michigan	66.8
3	Minnesota	73.2
1	Mississippi	74.5
19	Missouri	63.9
15	Montana	65.7
30	Nebraska	61.6
41	Nevada	57.9
6	New Hampshire	69.4
27	New Jersey	61.9
30	New Mexico	61.6
39	New York	58.7
8	North Carolina	68.9
19	North Dakota	63.9
24	Ohio	63.1
48	Oklahoma	52.4
10	Oregon	67.6
30	Pennsylvania	61.6
26	Rhode Island	62.5
18	South Carolina	64.7
34	South Dakota	61.0
45	Tennessee	55.7
46	Texas	53.8
43	Utah	57.0
22	Vermont	63.3
12	Virginia	66.9
16	Washington	65.6
50	West Virginia	47.8
2	Wisconsin	73.6
38	Wyoming	58.9

RANK ORDER

RANK	STATE	PERCENT
1	Mississippi	74.5
2	Wisconsin	73.6
3	Minnesota	73.2
4	Massachusetts	70.8
5	Colorado	70.4
6	Iowa	69.4
6	New Hampshire	69.4
8	North Carolina	68.9
9	Maine	68.6
10	Oregon	67.6
11	Delaware	67.3
12	Virginia	66.9
13	Michigan	66.8
14	Louisiana	66.3
15	Montana	65.7
16	Washington	65.6
17	Maryland	65.1
18	South Carolina	64.7
19	Idaho	63.9
19	Missouri	63.9
19	North Dakota	63.9
22	Kansas	63.3
22	Vermont	63.3
24	Ohio	63.1
25	Connecticut	62.7
26	Rhode Island	62.5
27	Alabama	61.9
27	Georgia	61.9
27	New Jersey	61.9
30	Nebraska	61.6
30	New Mexico	61.6
30	Pennsylvania	61.6
33	Illinois	61.5
34	South Dakota	61.0
35	Florida	60.8
36	Indiana	59.3
36	Kentucky	59.3
38	Wyoming	58.9
39	New York	58.7
40	Alaska	58.4
41	Nevada	57.9
42	California	57.5
43	Utah	57.0
44	Arizona	55.9
45	Tennessee	55.7
46	Texas	53.8
47	Arkansas	53.3
48	Oklahoma	52.4
49	Hawaii	51.6
50	West Virginia	47.8

District of Columbia	75.9

Source: U.S. Bureau of the Census
   "Voting and Registration" (Table 4a, http://www.census.gov/hhes/www/socdemo/voting/index.html)
*As a percent of citizen population 18 and older.

Percent of Registered Population Reported Voting in 2012

National Percent = 86.8%*

ALPHA ORDER

RANK	STATE	PERCENT
41	Alabama	84.3
48	Alaska	80.1
33	Arizona	85.8
44	Arkansas	81.7
26	California	87.7
1	Colorado	94.7
16	Connecticut	89.1
5	Delaware	91.7
16	Florida	89.1
27	Georgia	87.4
25	Hawaii	87.8
7	Idaho	91.1
40	Illinois	84.5
34	Indiana	85.7
21	Iowa	88.7
37	Kansas	85.1
43	Kentucky	82.3
31	Louisiana	86.0
19	Maine	88.9
9	Maryland	90.3
10	Massachusetts	90.0
31	Michigan	86.0
3	Minnesota	92.7
23	Mississippi	88.5
42	Missouri	83.3
15	Montana	89.5
22	Nebraska	88.6
16	Nevada	89.1
6	New Hampshire	91.5
39	New Jersey	84.8
11	New Mexico	89.8
29	New York	86.4
28	North Carolina	87.3
36	North Dakota	85.6
20	Ohio	88.8
49	Oklahoma	79.2
8	Oregon	90.9
34	Pennsylvania	85.7
38	Rhode Island	85.0
24	South Carolina	88.2
45	South Dakota	81.5
46	Tennessee	81.2
47	Texas	80.4
11	Utah	89.8
30	Vermont	86.3
14	Virginia	89.7
11	Washington	89.8
50	West Virginia	70.3
2	Wisconsin	94.2
4	Wyoming	92.2

RANK ORDER

RANK	STATE	PERCENT
1	Colorado	94.7
2	Wisconsin	94.2
3	Minnesota	92.7
4	Wyoming	92.2
5	Delaware	91.7
6	New Hampshire	91.5
7	Idaho	91.1
8	Oregon	90.9
9	Maryland	90.3
10	Massachusetts	90.0
11	New Mexico	89.8
11	Utah	89.8
11	Washington	89.8
14	Virginia	89.7
15	Montana	89.5
16	Connecticut	89.1
16	Florida	89.1
16	Nevada	89.1
19	Maine	88.9
20	Ohio	88.8
21	Iowa	88.7
22	Nebraska	88.6
23	Mississippi	88.5
24	South Carolina	88.2
25	Hawaii	87.8
26	California	87.7
27	Georgia	87.4
28	North Carolina	87.3
29	New York	86.4
30	Vermont	86.3
31	Louisiana	86.0
31	Michigan	86.0
33	Arizona	85.8
34	Indiana	85.7
34	Pennsylvania	85.7
36	North Dakota	85.6
37	Kansas	85.1
38	Rhode Island	85.0
39	New Jersey	84.8
40	Illinois	84.5
41	Alabama	84.3
42	Missouri	83.3
43	Kentucky	82.3
44	Arkansas	81.7
45	South Dakota	81.5
46	Tennessee	81.2
47	Texas	80.4
48	Alaska	80.1
49	Oklahoma	79.2
50	West Virginia	70.3

District of Columbia   90.9

Source: CQ Press using data from U.S. Bureau of the Census
"Voting and Registration" (Table 4a, http://www.census.gov/hhes/www/socdemo/voting/index.html)
*As a percent of citizen population 18 and older registered to vote.

XIV. Social Welfare

Poverty Rate in 2012

National Rate = 15.7% of Population in Poverty*

ALPHA ORDER			RANK ORDER		
RANK	STATE	PERCENT	RANK	STATE	PERCENT
6	Alabama	19.0	1	Mississippi	23.0
48	Alaska	10.2	2	New Mexico	21.0
9	Arizona	18.3	3	Louisiana	19.6
4	Arkansas	19.3	4	Arkansas	19.3
18	California	16.4	5	Kentucky	19.2
33	Colorado	13.5	6	Alabama	19.0
46	Connecticut	10.5	7	Georgia	18.7
40	Delaware	11.9	8	South Carolina	18.5
16	Florida	16.8	9	Arizona	18.3
7	Georgia	18.7	10	Texas	18.1
44	Hawaii	11.5	10	West Virginia	18.1
19	Idaho	16.1	12	Tennessee	17.9
26	Illinois	14.5	13	North Carolina	17.8
23	Indiana	15.6	14	Michigan	17.3
37	Iowa	12.7	15	Oklahoma	17.1
30	Kansas	13.8	16	Florida	16.8
5	Kentucky	19.2	16	Oregon	16.8
3	Louisiana	19.6	18	California	16.4
28	Maine	14.0	19	Idaho	16.1
49	Maryland	10.1	19	Ohio	16.1
43	Massachusetts	11.6	21	Nevada	15.8
14	Michigan	17.3	22	Missouri	15.7
42	Minnesota	11.7	23	Indiana	15.6
1	Mississippi	23.0	23	New York	15.6
22	Missouri	15.7	25	Montana	15.2
25	Montana	15.2	26	Illinois	14.5
36	Nebraska	13.0	27	Rhode Island	14.2
21	Nevada	15.8	28	Maine	14.0
50	New Hampshire	8.9	29	South Dakota	13.9
46	New Jersey	10.5	30	Kansas	13.8
2	New Mexico	21.0	31	Washington	13.7
23	New York	15.6	32	Pennsylvania	13.6
13	North Carolina	17.8	33	Colorado	13.5
38	North Dakota	12.2	34	Utah	13.2
19	Ohio	16.1	34	Wisconsin	13.2
15	Oklahoma	17.1	36	Nebraska	13.0
16	Oregon	16.8	37	Iowa	12.7
32	Pennsylvania	13.6	38	North Dakota	12.2
27	Rhode Island	14.2	39	Vermont	12.0
8	South Carolina	18.5	40	Delaware	11.9
29	South Dakota	13.9	40	Wyoming	11.9
12	Tennessee	17.9	42	Minnesota	11.7
10	Texas	18.1	43	Massachusetts	11.6
34	Utah	13.2	44	Hawaii	11.5
39	Vermont	12.0	44	Virginia	11.5
44	Virginia	11.5	46	Connecticut	10.5
31	Washington	13.7	46	New Jersey	10.5
10	West Virginia	18.1	48	Alaska	10.2
34	Wisconsin	13.2	49	Maryland	10.1
40	Wyoming	11.9	50	New Hampshire	8.9
				District of Columbia	18.8

Source: U.S. Bureau of the Census
   "2012 American Community Survey-Table GCT1701" (http://www.census.gov/acs/www/index.html)
*Three-year average: 2010-2012. The poverty threshold for a family of four (two children) in 2012 was $23,283.

Percent of Senior Citizens Living in Poverty in 2012

National Percent = 9.5%*

ALPHA ORDER

RANK	STATE	PERCENT
8	Alabama	11.1
50	Alaska	4.4
25	Arizona	8.3
9	Arkansas	10.9
11	California	10.4
34	Colorado	7.8
44	Connecticut	6.9
41	Delaware	7.4
12	Florida	10.2
7	Georgia	11.2
44	Hawaii	6.9
18	Idaho	9.7
22	Illinois	8.8
43	Indiana	7.2
34	Iowa	7.8
47	Kansas	6.7
3	Kentucky	12.3
2	Louisiana	12.6
28	Maine	8.2
37	Maryland	7.6
20	Massachusetts	9.3
25	Michigan	8.3
31	Minnesota	7.9
1	Mississippi	15.1
21	Missouri	9.0
24	Montana	8.6
41	Nebraska	7.4
29	Nevada	8.1
48	New Hampshire	6.6
31	New Jersey	7.9
4	New Mexico	11.9
6	New York	11.4
14	North Carolina	10.0
10	North Dakota	10.6
30	Ohio	8.0
17	Oklahoma	9.9
38	Oregon	7.5
25	Pennsylvania	8.3
18	Rhode Island	9.7
13	South Carolina	10.1
14	South Dakota	10.0
14	Tennessee	10.0
5	Texas	11.6
46	Utah	6.8
38	Vermont	7.5
31	Virginia	7.9
34	Washington	7.8
22	West Virginia	8.8
38	Wisconsin	7.5
49	Wyoming	4.8

RANK ORDER

RANK	STATE	PERCENT
1	Mississippi	15.1
2	Louisiana	12.6
3	Kentucky	12.3
4	New Mexico	11.9
5	Texas	11.6
6	New York	11.4
7	Georgia	11.2
8	Alabama	11.1
9	Arkansas	10.9
10	North Dakota	10.6
11	California	10.4
12	Florida	10.2
13	South Carolina	10.1
14	North Carolina	10.0
14	South Dakota	10.0
14	Tennessee	10.0
17	Oklahoma	9.9
18	Idaho	9.7
18	Rhode Island	9.7
20	Massachusetts	9.3
21	Missouri	9.0
22	Illinois	8.8
22	West Virginia	8.8
24	Montana	8.6
25	Arizona	8.3
25	Michigan	8.3
25	Pennsylvania	8.3
28	Maine	8.2
29	Nevada	8.1
30	Ohio	8.0
31	Minnesota	7.9
31	New Jersey	7.9
31	Virginia	7.9
34	Colorado	7.8
34	Iowa	7.8
34	Washington	7.8
37	Maryland	7.6
38	Oregon	7.5
38	Vermont	7.5
38	Wisconsin	7.5
41	Delaware	7.4
41	Nebraska	7.4
43	Indiana	7.2
44	Connecticut	6.9
44	Hawaii	6.9
46	Utah	6.8
47	Kansas	6.7
48	New Hampshire	6.6
49	Wyoming	4.8
50	Alaska	4.4
	District of Columbia	11.9

Source: U.S. Bureau of the Census
   "2012 American Community Survey-Table GCT1703" (http://www.census.gov/acs/www/index.html)
*People 65 years and older living with incomes below the poverty level.

Percent of Children Living in Poverty in 2012

National Percent = 22.3%*

ALPHA ORDER

RANK	STATE	PERCENT
5	Alabama	27.3
48	Alaska	13.5
8	Arizona	26.6
3	Arkansas	28.1
18	California	23.5
31	Colorado	18.1
46	Connecticut	14.6
35	Delaware	17.1
13	Florida	25.1
6	Georgia	27.0
37	Hawaii	16.6
24	Idaho	20.4
24	Illinois	20.4
23	Indiana	22.0
39	Iowa	15.6
30	Kansas	18.7
9	Kentucky	26.2
4	Louisiana	28.0
24	Maine	20.4
48	Maryland	13.5
42	Massachusetts	15.0
14	Michigan	24.5
47	Minnesota	14.2
1	Mississippi	34.6
22	Missouri	22.2
27	Montana	19.8
34	Nebraska	17.5
17	Nevada	23.6
41	New Hampshire	15.1
40	New Jersey	15.2
2	New Mexico	29.2
20	New York	22.6
10	North Carolina	25.7
50	North Dakota	12.9
19	Ohio	23.4
16	Oklahoma	23.8
20	Oregon	22.6
28	Pennsylvania	19.4
29	Rhode Island	19.0
7	South Carolina	26.7
36	South Dakota	17.0
11	Tennessee	25.5
11	Texas	25.5
45	Utah	14.8
44	Vermont	14.9
42	Virginia	15.0
31	Washington	18.1
15	West Virginia	24.2
33	Wisconsin	17.9
37	Wyoming	16.6

RANK ORDER

RANK	STATE	PERCENT
1	Mississippi	34.6
2	New Mexico	29.2
3	Arkansas	28.1
4	Louisiana	28.0
5	Alabama	27.3
6	Georgia	27.0
7	South Carolina	26.7
8	Arizona	26.6
9	Kentucky	26.2
10	North Carolina	25.7
11	Tennessee	25.5
11	Texas	25.5
13	Florida	25.1
14	Michigan	24.5
15	West Virginia	24.2
16	Oklahoma	23.8
17	Nevada	23.6
18	California	23.5
19	Ohio	23.4
20	New York	22.6
20	Oregon	22.6
22	Missouri	22.2
23	Indiana	22.0
24	Idaho	20.4
24	Illinois	20.4
24	Maine	20.4
27	Montana	19.8
28	Pennsylvania	19.4
29	Rhode Island	19.0
30	Kansas	18.7
31	Colorado	18.1
31	Washington	18.1
33	Wisconsin	17.9
34	Nebraska	17.5
35	Delaware	17.1
36	South Dakota	17.0
37	Hawaii	16.6
37	Wyoming	16.6
39	Iowa	15.6
40	New Jersey	15.2
41	New Hampshire	15.1
42	Massachusetts	15.0
42	Virginia	15.0
44	Vermont	14.9
45	Utah	14.8
46	Connecticut	14.6
47	Minnesota	14.2
48	Alaska	13.5
48	Maryland	13.5
50	North Dakota	12.9

District of Columbia 26.4

Source: U.S. Bureau of the Census
   "2012 American Community Survey-Table GCT1702" (http://www.census.gov/acs/www/index.html)
*Children 17 and under living in families with incomes below the poverty level.

Percent of Families Living in Poverty in 2012

National Percent = 11.6%*

ALPHA ORDER				RANK ORDER		
RANK	**STATE**	**PERCENT**		**RANK**	**STATE**	**PERCENT**
4	Alabama	14.8		1	Mississippi	18.2
48	Alaska	7.2		2	New Mexico	16.4
11	Arizona	13.4		3	Louisiana	15.3
6	Arkansas	14.5		4	Alabama	14.8
16	California	12.3		5	Kentucky	14.6
33	Colorado	9.2		6	Arkansas	14.5
44	Connecticut	7.7		7	Georgia	14.4
41	Delaware	8.0		8	South Carolina	14.1
16	Florida	12.3		8	Texas	14.1
7	Georgia	14.4		10	Tennessee	13.6
40	Hawaii	8.1		11	Arizona	13.4
21	Idaho	11.7		12	North Carolina	13.3
25	Illinois	10.6		13	West Virginia	13.1
23	Indiana	11.2		14	Oklahoma	12.8
37	Iowa	8.4		15	Michigan	12.4
30	Kansas	9.4		16	California	12.3
5	Kentucky	14.6		16	Florida	12.3
3	Louisiana	15.3		18	New York	12.0
31	Maine	9.3		19	Nevada	11.9
49	Maryland	7.0		20	Ohio	11.8
38	Massachusetts	8.3		21	Idaho	11.7
15	Michigan	12.4		21	Oregon	11.7
45	Minnesota	7.6		23	Indiana	11.2
1	Mississippi	18.2		23	Missouri	11.2
23	Missouri	11.2		25	Illinois	10.6
26	Montana	10.0		26	Montana	10.0
36	Nebraska	8.9		27	Utah	9.9
19	Nevada	11.9		28	Rhode Island	9.7
50	New Hampshire	5.9		29	Pennsylvania	9.5
43	New Jersey	7.9		30	Kansas	9.4
2	New Mexico	16.4		31	Maine	9.3
18	New York	12.0		31	Washington	9.3
12	North Carolina	13.3		33	Colorado	9.2
45	North Dakota	7.6		34	South Dakota	9.1
20	Ohio	11.8		35	Wisconsin	9.0
14	Oklahoma	12.8		36	Nebraska	8.9
21	Oregon	11.7		37	Iowa	8.4
29	Pennsylvania	9.5		38	Massachusetts	8.3
28	Rhode Island	9.7		39	Virginia	8.2
8	South Carolina	14.1		40	Hawaii	8.1
34	South Dakota	9.1		41	Delaware	8.0
10	Tennessee	13.6		41	Wyoming	8.0
8	Texas	14.1		43	New Jersey	7.9
27	Utah	9.9		44	Connecticut	7.7
45	Vermont	7.6		45	Minnesota	7.6
39	Virginia	8.2		45	North Dakota	7.6
31	Washington	9.3		45	Vermont	7.6
13	West Virginia	13.1		48	Alaska	7.2
35	Wisconsin	9.0		49	Maryland	7.0
41	Wyoming	8.0		50	New Hampshire	5.9
					District of Columbia	14.6

Source: U.S. Bureau of the Census
   "2012 American Community Survey-Table DP03" (http://www.census.gov/acs/www/index.html)
*Families living with incomes below the poverty level.

Percent of Female-Headed Families with Children Living in Poverty in 2012

National Percent = 40.6%*

ALPHA ORDER

RANK	STATE	PERCENT
2	Alabama	49.8
49	Alaska	27.3
24	Arizona	40.1
5	Arkansas	48.4
34	California	37.4
40	Colorado	35.8
47	Connecticut	31.7
48	Delaware	30.7
32	Florida	38.4
15	Georgia	43.9
46	Hawaii	31.8
13	Idaho	44.6
22	Illinois	40.3
17	Indiana	43.0
29	Iowa	39.3
24	Kansas	40.1
4	Kentucky	49.7
5	Louisiana	48.4
27	Maine	39.5
50	Maryland	26.5
41	Massachusetts	35.7
8	Michigan	45.9
39	Minnesota	36.4
1	Mississippi	52.4
19	Missouri	41.9
19	Montana	41.9
30	Nebraska	38.8
42	Nevada	34.4
45	New Hampshire	32.1
44	New Jersey	33.2
10	New Mexico	45.4
33	New York	38.3
13	North Carolina	44.6
21	North Dakota	40.9
9	Ohio	45.7
12	Oklahoma	44.7
16	Oregon	43.7
23	Pennsylvania	40.2
36	Rhode Island	37.0
7	South Carolina	46.3
31	South Dakota	38.5
10	Tennessee	45.4
18	Texas	42.3
35	Utah	37.2
37	Vermont	36.9
43	Virginia	34.0
37	Washington	36.9
2	West Virginia	49.8
26	Wisconsin	39.7
28	Wyoming	39.4

RANK ORDER

RANK	STATE	PERCENT
1	Mississippi	52.4
2	Alabama	49.8
2	West Virginia	49.8
4	Kentucky	49.7
5	Arkansas	48.4
5	Louisiana	48.4
7	South Carolina	46.3
8	Michigan	45.9
9	Ohio	45.7
10	New Mexico	45.4
10	Tennessee	45.4
12	Oklahoma	44.7
13	Idaho	44.6
13	North Carolina	44.6
15	Georgia	43.9
16	Oregon	43.7
17	Indiana	43.0
18	Texas	42.3
19	Missouri	41.9
19	Montana	41.9
21	North Dakota	40.9
22	Illinois	40.3
23	Pennsylvania	40.2
24	Arizona	40.1
24	Kansas	40.1
26	Wisconsin	39.7
27	Maine	39.5
28	Wyoming	39.4
29	Iowa	39.3
30	Nebraska	38.8
31	South Dakota	38.5
32	Florida	38.4
33	New York	38.3
34	California	37.4
35	Utah	37.2
36	Rhode Island	37.0
37	Vermont	36.9
37	Washington	36.9
39	Minnesota	36.4
40	Colorado	35.8
41	Massachusetts	35.7
42	Nevada	34.4
43	Virginia	34.0
44	New Jersey	33.2
45	New Hampshire	32.1
46	Hawaii	31.8
47	Connecticut	31.7
48	Delaware	30.7
49	Alaska	27.3
50	Maryland	26.5

	District of Columbia	38.6

Source: U.S. Bureau of the Census

"2012 American Community Survey-Table DP03" (http://www.census.gov/acs/www/index.html)

*Households headed by females with own children under 18 years living with them with incomes below the poverty level as a percent of all such female-headed households.

State and Local Government Expenditures for Public Welfare Programs in 2011

National Total = $492,007,114,000*

ALPHA ORDER

ALPHA ORDER

RANK	STATE	EXPENDITURES	% of USA
26	Alabama	$5,940,027,000	1.2%
44	Alaska	1,857,227,000	0.4%
18	Arizona	9,205,490,000	1.9%
32	Arkansas	4,501,060,000	0.9%
1	California	67,669,710,000	13.8%
30	Colorado	4,944,789,000	1.0%
25	Connecticut	6,157,405,000	1.3%
45	Delaware	1,755,102,000	0.4%
5	Florida	23,542,869,000	4.8%
14	Georgia	10,119,428,000	2.1%
42	Hawaii	2,147,032,000	0.4%
40	Idaho	2,210,201,000	0.4%
7	Illinois	18,488,172,000	3.8%
20	Indiana	8,495,515,000	1.7%
31	Iowa	4,830,388,000	1.0%
34	Kansas	3,566,432,000	0.7%
22	Kentucky	7,235,398,000	1.5%
24	Louisiana	6,417,506,000	1.3%
36	Maine	2,926,188,000	0.6%
17	Maryland	9,502,330,000	1.9%
8	Massachusetts	14,508,196,000	2.9%
10	Michigan	13,293,251,000	2.7%
11	Minnesota	11,889,794,000	2.4%
29	Mississippi	5,180,726,000	1.1%
21	Missouri	7,740,656,000	1.6%
47	Montana	1,411,016,000	0.3%
41	Nebraska	2,178,328,000	0.4%
38	Nevada	2,346,121,000	0.5%
43	New Hampshire	2,092,820,000	0.4%
9	New Jersey	14,372,123,000	2.9%
33	New Mexico	4,429,189,000	0.9%
2	New York	50,390,083,000	10.2%
12	North Carolina	11,388,371,000	2.3%
49	North Dakota	961,866,000	0.2%
6	Ohio	20,287,667,000	4.1%
28	Oklahoma	5,433,864,000	1.1%
27	Oregon	5,672,523,000	1.2%
4	Pennsylvania	25,676,334,000	5.2%
39	Rhode Island	2,332,616,000	0.5%
23	South Carolina	6,812,062,000	1.4%
48	South Dakota	973,120,000	0.2%
15	Tennessee	10,059,567,000	2.0%
3	Texas	30,825,703,000	6.3%
37	Utah	2,863,288,000	0.6%
46	Vermont	1,464,380,000	0.3%
13	Virginia	10,188,489,000	2.1%
19	Washington	8,851,696,000	1.8%
35	West Virginia	3,237,674,000	0.7%
16	Wisconsin	10,035,317,000	2.0%
50	Wyoming	764,252,000	0.2%

RANK ORDER

RANK	STATE	EXPENDITURES	% of USA
1	California	$67,669,710,000	13.8%
2	New York	50,390,083,000	10.2%
3	Texas	30,825,703,000	6.3%
4	Pennsylvania	25,676,334,000	5.2%
5	Florida	23,542,869,000	4.8%
6	Ohio	20,287,667,000	4.1%
7	Illinois	18,488,172,000	3.8%
8	Massachusetts	14,508,196,000	2.9%
9	New Jersey	14,372,123,000	2.9%
10	Michigan	13,293,251,000	2.7%
11	Minnesota	11,889,794,000	2.4%
12	North Carolina	11,388,371,000	2.3%
13	Virginia	10,188,489,000	2.1%
14	Georgia	10,119,428,000	2.1%
15	Tennessee	10,059,567,000	2.0%
16	Wisconsin	10,035,317,000	2.0%
17	Maryland	9,502,330,000	1.9%
18	Arizona	9,205,490,000	1.9%
19	Washington	8,851,696,000	1.8%
20	Indiana	8,495,515,000	1.7%
21	Missouri	7,740,656,000	1.6%
22	Kentucky	7,235,398,000	1.5%
23	South Carolina	6,812,062,000	1.4%
24	Louisiana	6,417,506,000	1.3%
25	Connecticut	6,157,405,000	1.3%
26	Alabama	5,940,027,000	1.2%
27	Oregon	5,672,523,000	1.2%
28	Oklahoma	5,433,864,000	1.1%
29	Mississippi	5,180,726,000	1.1%
30	Colorado	4,944,789,000	1.0%
31	Iowa	4,830,388,000	1.0%
32	Arkansas	4,501,060,000	0.9%
33	New Mexico	4,429,189,000	0.9%
34	Kansas	3,566,432,000	0.7%
35	West Virginia	3,237,674,000	0.7%
36	Maine	2,926,188,000	0.6%
37	Utah	2,863,288,000	0.6%
38	Nevada	2,346,121,000	0.5%
39	Rhode Island	2,332,616,000	0.5%
40	Idaho	2,210,201,000	0.4%
41	Nebraska	2,178,328,000	0.4%
42	Hawaii	2,147,032,000	0.4%
43	New Hampshire	2,092,820,000	0.4%
44	Alaska	1,857,227,000	0.4%
45	Delaware	1,755,102,000	0.4%
46	Vermont	1,464,380,000	0.3%
47	Montana	1,411,016,000	0.3%
48	South Dakota	973,120,000	0.2%
49	North Dakota	961,866,000	0.2%
50	Wyoming	764,252,000	0.2%
	District of Columbia	2,833,753,000	0.6%

Source: U.S. Bureau of the Census, Governments Division
   "2011 State and Local Government Finances" (http://www.census.gov/govs/local/)
*Direct general expenditures. Includes funds for cash assistance programs, medical and other vendor payments, welfare institutions, and other public welfare programs.

Per Capita State and Local Government Expenditures
for Public Welfare Programs in 2011
National Per Capita = $1,579*

ALPHA ORDER

RANK ORDER

RANK	STATE	PER CAPITA		RANK	STATE	PER CAPITA
41	Alabama	$1,237		1	New York	$2,584
2	Alaska	2,566		2	Alaska	2,566
29	Arizona	1,423		3	Vermont	2,337
24	Arkansas	1,532		4	Minnesota	2,224
11	California	1,796		5	Rhode Island	2,220
49	Colorado	966		6	Maine	2,203
16	Connecticut	1,717		7	Massachusetts	2,196
10	Delaware	1,933		8	New Mexico	2,131
42	Florida	1,234		9	Pennsylvania	2,015
47	Georgia	1,031		10	Delaware	1,933
23	Hawaii	1,558		11	California	1,796
33	Idaho	1,396		12	Ohio	1,758
27	Illinois	1,438		12	Wisconsin	1,758
36	Indiana	1,304		14	West Virginia	1,745
21	Iowa	1,576		15	Mississippi	1,740
40	Kansas	1,242		16	Connecticut	1,717
17	Kentucky	1,657		17	Kentucky	1,657
32	Louisiana	1,403		18	Maryland	1,627
6	Maine	2,203		18	New Jersey	1,627
18	Maryland	1,627		20	New Hampshire	1,588
7	Massachusetts	2,196		21	Iowa	1,576
35	Michigan	1,346		22	Tennessee	1,572
4	Minnesota	2,224		23	Hawaii	1,558
15	Mississippi	1,740		24	Arkansas	1,532
38	Missouri	1,288		25	Oregon	1,466
30	Montana	1,414		26	South Carolina	1,458
44	Nebraska	1,182		27	Illinois	1,438
50	Nevada	863		28	Oklahoma	1,436
20	New Hampshire	1,588		29	Arizona	1,423
18	New Jersey	1,627		30	Montana	1,414
8	New Mexico	2,131		31	North Dakota	1,405
1	New York	2,584		32	Louisiana	1,403
46	North Carolina	1,180		33	Idaho	1,396
31	North Dakota	1,405		34	Wyoming	1,347
12	Ohio	1,758		35	Michigan	1,346
28	Oklahoma	1,436		36	Indiana	1,304
25	Oregon	1,466		37	Washington	1,297
9	Pennsylvania	2,015		38	Missouri	1,288
5	Rhode Island	2,220		39	Virginia	1,257
26	South Carolina	1,458		40	Kansas	1,242
44	South Dakota	1,182		41	Alabama	1,237
22	Tennessee	1,572		42	Florida	1,234
43	Texas	1,203		43	Texas	1,203
48	Utah	1,017		44	Nebraska	1,182
3	Vermont	2,337		44	South Dakota	1,182
39	Virginia	1,257		46	North Carolina	1,180
37	Washington	1,297		47	Georgia	1,031
14	West Virginia	1,745		48	Utah	1,017
12	Wisconsin	1,758		49	Colorado	966
34	Wyoming	1,347		50	Nevada	863

District of Columbia   4,578

Source: CQ Press using data from U.S. Bureau of the Census, Governments Division
    "2011 State and Local Government Finances" (http://www.census.gov/govs/local/)
*Direct general expenditures. Includes funds for cash assistance programs, medical and other vendor payments, welfare institutions, and other public welfare programs.

State and Local Government Spending for Public Welfare Programs as a Percent of All State and Local Government Expenditures in 2011
National Percent = 19.0%*

ALPHA ORDER

RANK	STATE	PERCENT
36	Alabama	16.8
46	Alaska	14.5
13	Arizona	21.6
11	Arkansas	21.7
21	California	19.1
49	Colorado	12.0
25	Connecticut	18.5
19	Delaware	20.4
34	Florida	17.1
39	Georgia	15.8
31	Hawaii	17.6
16	Idaho	21.1
30	Illinois	17.7
25	Indiana	18.5
27	Iowa	18.3
41	Kansas	15.5
9	Kentucky	22.4
43	Louisiana	15.0
1	Maine	25.8
21	Maryland	19.1
6	Massachusetts	23.6
28	Michigan	18.0
3	Minnesota	25.2
11	Mississippi	21.7
24	Missouri	18.7
33	Montana	17.4
43	Nebraska	15.0
48	Nevada	12.5
19	New Hampshire	20.4
31	New Jersey	17.6
8	New Mexico	22.8
15	New York	21.4
35	North Carolina	16.9
43	North Dakota	15.0
14	Ohio	21.5
16	Oklahoma	21.1
29	Oregon	17.8
6	Pennsylvania	23.6
2	Rhode Island	25.3
21	South Carolina	19.1
39	South Dakota	15.8
4	Tennessee	23.9
38	Texas	16.6
47	Utah	14.1
5	Vermont	23.7
37	Virginia	16.7
42	Washington	15.3
9	West Virginia	22.4
18	Wisconsin	21.0
50	Wyoming	10.1

RANK ORDER

RANK	STATE	PERCENT
1	Maine	25.8
2	Rhode Island	25.3
3	Minnesota	25.2
4	Tennessee	23.9
5	Vermont	23.7
6	Massachusetts	23.6
6	Pennsylvania	23.6
8	New Mexico	22.8
9	Kentucky	22.4
9	West Virginia	22.4
11	Arkansas	21.7
11	Mississippi	21.7
13	Arizona	21.6
14	Ohio	21.5
15	New York	21.4
16	Idaho	21.1
16	Oklahoma	21.1
18	Wisconsin	21.0
19	Delaware	20.4
19	New Hampshire	20.4
21	California	19.1
21	Maryland	19.1
21	South Carolina	19.1
24	Missouri	18.7
25	Connecticut	18.5
25	Indiana	18.5
27	Iowa	18.3
28	Michigan	18.0
29	Oregon	17.8
30	Illinois	17.7
31	Hawaii	17.6
31	New Jersey	17.6
33	Montana	17.4
34	Florida	17.1
35	North Carolina	16.9
36	Alabama	16.8
37	Virginia	16.7
38	Texas	16.6
39	Georgia	15.8
39	South Dakota	15.8
41	Kansas	15.5
42	Washington	15.3
43	Louisiana	15.0
43	Nebraska	15.0
43	North Dakota	15.0
46	Alaska	14.5
47	Utah	14.1
48	Nevada	12.5
49	Colorado	12.0
50	Wyoming	10.1

District of Columbia   27.3

Source: CQ Press using data from U.S. Bureau of the Census, Governments Division
"2011 State and Local Government Finances" (http://www.census.gov/govs/local/)
*As a percent of direct general expenditures. Includes funds for cash assistance programs, medical and other vendor payments, welfare institutions, and other public welfare programs.

Social Security (OASDI) Payments in 2011

National Total = $724,943,000,000*

ALPHA ORDER

RANK	STATE	PAYMENTS	% of USA
20	Alabama	$13,156,000,000	1.8%
50	Alaska	1,010,000,000	0.1%
18	Arizona	14,744,000,000	2.0%
30	Arkansas	7,964,000,000	1.1%
1	California	66,661,000,000	9.2%
27	Colorado	9,382,000,000	1.3%
29	Connecticut	9,111,000,000	1.3%
45	Delaware	2,482,000,000	0.3%
2	Florida	50,986,000,000	7.0%
11	Georgia	19,578,000,000	2.7%
42	Hawaii	3,056,000,000	0.4%
41	Idaho	3,549,000,000	0.5%
8	Illinois	28,189,000,000	3.9%
13	Indiana	16,709,000,000	2.3%
31	Iowa	7,840,000,000	1.1%
33	Kansas	6,705,000,000	0.9%
24	Kentucky	11,379,000,000	1.6%
25	Louisiana	9,941,000,000	1.4%
39	Maine	3,740,000,000	0.5%
23	Maryland	11,879,000,000	1.6%
15	Massachusetts	15,439,000,000	2.1%
7	Michigan	28,270,000,000	3.9%
22	Minnesota	12,123,000,000	1.7%
32	Mississippi	7,415,000,000	1.0%
16	Missouri	15,416,000,000	2.1%
44	Montana	2,485,000,000	0.3%
38	Nebraska	4,093,000,000	0.6%
35	Nevada	5,607,000,000	0.8%
40	New Hampshire	3,554,000,000	0.5%
10	New Jersey	21,865,000,000	3.0%
36	New Mexico	4,524,000,000	0.6%
3	New York	45,819,000,000	6.3%
9	North Carolina	23,505,000,000	3.2%
48	North Dakota	1,519,000,000	0.2%
6	Ohio	28,618,000,000	3.9%
28	Oklahoma	9,136,000,000	1.3%
26	Oregon	9,743,000,000	1.3%
5	Pennsylvania	35,656,000,000	4.9%
43	Rhode Island	2,739,000,000	0.4%
21	South Carolina	12,453,000,000	1.7%
46	South Dakota	1,934,000,000	0.3%
14	Tennessee	16,512,000,000	2.3%
4	Texas	44,966,000,000	6.2%
37	Utah	4,385,000,000	0.6%
47	Vermont	1,710,000,000	0.2%
12	Virginia	17,400,000,000	2.4%
17	Washington	15,317,000,000	2.1%
34	West Virginia	5,867,000,000	0.8%
19	Wisconsin	14,657,000,000	2.0%
49	Wyoming	1,240,000,000	0.2%

RANK ORDER

RANK	STATE	PAYMENTS	% of USA
1	California	$66,661,000,000	9.2%
2	Florida	50,986,000,000	7.0%
3	New York	45,819,000,000	6.3%
4	Texas	44,966,000,000	6.2%
5	Pennsylvania	35,656,000,000	4.9%
6	Ohio	28,618,000,000	3.9%
7	Michigan	28,270,000,000	3.9%
8	Illinois	28,189,000,000	3.9%
9	North Carolina	23,505,000,000	3.2%
10	New Jersey	21,865,000,000	3.0%
11	Georgia	19,578,000,000	2.7%
12	Virginia	17,400,000,000	2.4%
13	Indiana	16,709,000,000	2.3%
14	Tennessee	16,512,000,000	2.3%
15	Massachusetts	15,439,000,000	2.1%
16	Missouri	15,416,000,000	2.1%
17	Washington	15,317,000,000	2.1%
18	Arizona	14,744,000,000	2.0%
19	Wisconsin	14,657,000,000	2.0%
20	Alabama	13,156,000,000	1.8%
21	South Carolina	12,453,000,000	1.7%
22	Minnesota	12,123,000,000	1.7%
23	Maryland	11,879,000,000	1.6%
24	Kentucky	11,379,000,000	1.6%
25	Louisiana	9,941,000,000	1.4%
26	Oregon	9,743,000,000	1.3%
27	Colorado	9,382,000,000	1.3%
28	Oklahoma	9,136,000,000	1.3%
29	Connecticut	9,111,000,000	1.3%
30	Arkansas	7,964,000,000	1.1%
31	Iowa	7,840,000,000	1.1%
32	Mississippi	7,415,000,000	1.0%
33	Kansas	6,705,000,000	0.9%
34	West Virginia	5,867,000,000	0.8%
35	Nevada	5,607,000,000	0.8%
36	New Mexico	4,524,000,000	0.6%
37	Utah	4,385,000,000	0.6%
38	Nebraska	4,093,000,000	0.6%
39	Maine	3,740,000,000	0.5%
40	New Hampshire	3,554,000,000	0.5%
41	Idaho	3,549,000,000	0.5%
42	Hawaii	3,056,000,000	0.4%
43	Rhode Island	2,739,000,000	0.4%
44	Montana	2,485,000,000	0.3%
45	Delaware	2,482,000,000	0.3%
46	South Dakota	1,934,000,000	0.3%
47	Vermont	1,710,000,000	0.2%
48	North Dakota	1,519,000,000	0.2%
49	Wyoming	1,240,000,000	0.2%
50	Alaska	1,010,000,000	0.1%
	District of Columbia	904,000,000	0.1%

Source: Social Security Administration
"Social Security Bulletin, Annual Statistical Supplement 2012" (http://www.ssa.gov/policy/docs/statcomps/supplement/2012/)
*"OASDI" is Old Age, Survivors and Disability Insurance. National total includes $12,016,000,000 in payments to recipients in U.S. territories and foreign countries.

Per Capita Social Security (OASDI) Payments in 2011

National Per Capita = $2,288*

ALPHA ORDER

RANK	STATE	PER CAPITA
5	Alabama	$2,740
50	Alaska	1,396
31	Arizona	2,279
8	Arkansas	2,710
47	California	1,770
46	Colorado	1,833
19	Connecticut	2,539
6	Delaware	2,734
10	Florida	2,672
45	Georgia	1,996
36	Hawaii	2,219
34	Idaho	2,241
38	Illinois	2,193
17	Indiana	2,564
18	Iowa	2,559
29	Kansas	2,337
13	Kentucky	2,606
41	Louisiana	2,173
3	Maine	2,817
44	Maryland	2,034
29	Massachusetts	2,337
2	Michigan	2,863
32	Minnesota	2,267
22	Mississippi	2,490
16	Missouri	2,565
21	Montana	2,491
35	Nebraska	2,222
43	Nevada	2,063
9	New Hampshire	2,696
24	New Jersey	2,474
40	New Mexico	2,177
27	New York	2,349
25	North Carolina	2,435
37	North Dakota	2,218
23	Ohio	2,478
26	Oklahoma	2,413
20	Oregon	2,519
4	Pennsylvania	2,798
12	Rhode Island	2,608
11	South Carolina	2,665
28	South Dakota	2,348
14	Tennessee	2,581
48	Texas	1,754
49	Utah	1,558
7	Vermont	2,730
42	Virginia	2,147
33	Washington	2,245
1	West Virginia	3,162
15	Wisconsin	2,567
39	Wyoming	2,186

RANK ORDER

RANK	STATE	PER CAPITA
1	West Virginia	$3,162
2	Michigan	2,863
3	Maine	2,817
4	Pennsylvania	2,798
5	Alabama	2,740
6	Delaware	2,734
7	Vermont	2,730
8	Arkansas	2,710
9	New Hampshire	2,696
10	Florida	2,672
11	South Carolina	2,665
12	Rhode Island	2,608
13	Kentucky	2,606
14	Tennessee	2,581
15	Wisconsin	2,567
16	Missouri	2,565
17	Indiana	2,564
18	Iowa	2,559
19	Connecticut	2,539
20	Oregon	2,519
21	Montana	2,491
22	Mississippi	2,490
23	Ohio	2,478
24	New Jersey	2,474
25	North Carolina	2,435
26	Oklahoma	2,413
27	New York	2,349
28	South Dakota	2,348
29	Kansas	2,337
29	Massachusetts	2,337
31	Arizona	2,279
32	Minnesota	2,267
33	Washington	2,245
34	Idaho	2,241
35	Nebraska	2,222
36	Hawaii	2,219
37	North Dakota	2,218
38	Illinois	2,193
39	Wyoming	2,186
40	New Mexico	2,177
41	Louisiana	2,173
42	Virginia	2,147
43	Nevada	2,063
44	Maryland	2,034
45	Georgia	1,996
46	Colorado	1,833
47	California	1,770
48	Texas	1,754
49	Utah	1,558
50	Alaska	1,396

| | District of Columbia | 1,459 |

Source: CQ Press using data from Social Security Administration
"Social Security Bulletin, Annual Statistical Supplement 2012" (http://www.ssa.gov/policy/docs/statcomps/supplement/2012/)
*"OASDI" is Old Age, Survivors and Disability Insurance. National per capita does not include payments or population in U.S. territories and foreign countries.

Social Security (OASDI) Monthly Payments in 2011

National Total = $62,213,382,000*

ALPHA ORDER

RANK	STATE	PAYMENTS	% of USA
20	Alabama	$1,111,578,000	1.8%
50	Alaska	87,416,000	0.1%
18	Arizona	1,282,882,000	2.1%
30	Arkansas	673,482,000	1.1%
1	California	5,760,530,000	9.3%
27	Colorado	815,841,000	1.3%
28	Connecticut	787,707,000	1.3%
44	Delaware	214,792,000	0.3%
2	Florida	4,429,118,000	7.1%
11	Georgia	1,684,659,000	2.7%
42	Hawaii	267,756,000	0.4%
41	Idaho	307,240,000	0.5%
8	Illinois	2,407,184,000	3.9%
13	Indiana	1,428,630,000	2.3%
31	Iowa	671,839,000	1.1%
33	Kansas	575,137,000	0.9%
24	Kentucky	954,128,000	1.5%
26	Louisiana	826,634,000	1.3%
39	Maine	319,869,000	0.5%
23	Maryland	1,026,641,000	1.7%
16	Massachusetts	1,324,894,000	2.1%
7	Michigan	2,419,079,000	3.9%
22	Minnesota	1,051,199,000	1.7%
32	Mississippi	624,863,000	1.0%
17	Missouri	1,313,771,000	2.1%
45	Montana	214,245,000	0.3%
38	Nebraska	350,845,000	0.6%
34	Nevada	489,418,000	0.8%
40	New Hampshire	308,497,000	0.5%
10	New Jersey	1,889,187,000	3.0%
36	New Mexico	388,287,000	0.6%
3	New York	3,934,524,000	6.3%
9	North Carolina	2,028,201,000	3.3%
48	North Dakota	128,944,000	0.2%
6	Ohio	2,425,438,000	3.9%
29	Oklahoma	774,739,000	1.2%
25	Oregon	845,343,000	1.4%
5	Pennsylvania	3,044,365,000	4.9%
43	Rhode Island	235,870,000	0.4%
21	South Carolina	1,073,608,000	1.7%
46	South Dakota	166,328,000	0.3%
14	Tennessee	1,411,408,000	2.3%
4	Texas	3,838,870,000	6.2%
37	Utah	379,672,000	0.6%
47	Vermont	147,883,000	0.2%
12	Virginia	1,498,922,000	2.4%
15	Washington	1,330,257,000	2.1%
35	West Virginia	487,983,000	0.8%
19	Wisconsin	1,265,027,000	2.0%
49	Wyoming	107,270,000	0.2%

RANK ORDER

RANK	STATE	PAYMENTS	% of USA
1	California	$5,760,530,000	9.3%
2	Florida	4,429,118,000	7.1%
3	New York	3,934,524,000	6.3%
4	Texas	3,838,870,000	6.2%
5	Pennsylvania	3,044,365,000	4.9%
6	Ohio	2,425,438,000	3.9%
7	Michigan	2,419,079,000	3.9%
8	Illinois	2,407,184,000	3.9%
9	North Carolina	2,028,201,000	3.3%
10	New Jersey	1,889,187,000	3.0%
11	Georgia	1,684,659,000	2.7%
12	Virginia	1,498,922,000	2.4%
13	Indiana	1,428,630,000	2.3%
14	Tennessee	1,411,408,000	2.3%
15	Washington	1,330,257,000	2.1%
16	Massachusetts	1,324,894,000	2.1%
17	Missouri	1,313,771,000	2.1%
18	Arizona	1,282,882,000	2.1%
19	Wisconsin	1,265,027,000	2.0%
20	Alabama	1,111,578,000	1.8%
21	South Carolina	1,073,608,000	1.7%
22	Minnesota	1,051,199,000	1.7%
23	Maryland	1,026,641,000	1.7%
24	Kentucky	954,128,000	1.5%
25	Oregon	845,343,000	1.4%
26	Louisiana	826,634,000	1.3%
27	Colorado	815,841,000	1.3%
28	Connecticut	787,707,000	1.3%
29	Oklahoma	774,739,000	1.2%
30	Arkansas	673,482,000	1.1%
31	Iowa	671,839,000	1.1%
32	Mississippi	624,863,000	1.0%
33	Kansas	575,137,000	0.9%
34	Nevada	489,418,000	0.8%
35	West Virginia	487,983,000	0.8%
36	New Mexico	388,287,000	0.6%
37	Utah	379,672,000	0.6%
38	Nebraska	350,845,000	0.6%
39	Maine	319,869,000	0.5%
40	New Hampshire	308,497,000	0.5%
41	Idaho	307,240,000	0.5%
42	Hawaii	267,756,000	0.4%
43	Rhode Island	235,870,000	0.4%
44	Delaware	214,792,000	0.3%
45	Montana	214,245,000	0.3%
46	South Dakota	166,328,000	0.3%
47	Vermont	147,883,000	0.2%
48	North Dakota	128,944,000	0.2%
49	Wyoming	107,270,000	0.2%
50	Alaska	87,416,000	0.1%
	District of Columbia	77,584,000	0.1%

Source: Social Security Administration
     "Social Security Bulletin, Annual Statistical Supplement 2012" (http://www.ssa.gov/policy/docs/statcomps/supplement/2012/)
*For December 2011. "OASDI" is Old Age, Survivors and Disability Insurance. National total includes $1,003,799,000 in payments to recipients in U.S. territories and foreign countries.

Social Security (OASDI) Beneficiaries in 2011

National Total = 55,404,480*

ALPHA ORDER

RANK	STATE	BENEFICIARIES	% of USA
20	Alabama	1,037,438	1.9%
50	Alaska	82,109	0.1%
18	Arizona	1,104,545	2.0%
29	Arkansas	647,077	1.2%
1	California	5,129,529	9.3%
27	Colorado	721,274	1.3%
30	Connecticut	630,447	1.1%
45	Delaware	176,885	0.3%
2	Florida	3,894,179	7.0%
10	Georgia	1,524,263	2.8%
42	Hawaii	234,314	0.4%
40	Idaho	278,563	0.5%
7	Illinois	2,065,432	3.7%
14	Indiana	1,219,879	2.2%
32	Iowa	592,000	1.1%
33	Kansas	498,707	0.9%
22	Kentucky	913,548	1.6%
25	Louisiana	809,450	1.5%
39	Maine	306,600	0.6%
24	Maryland	872,919	1.6%
16	Massachusetts	1,161,122	2.1%
8	Michigan	2,016,684	3.6%
23	Minnesota	904,803	1.6%
31	Mississippi	609,651	1.1%
15	Missouri	1,188,437	2.1%
44	Montana	198,230	0.4%
38	Nebraska	313,087	0.6%
35	Nevada	424,836	0.8%
41	New Hampshire	262,952	0.5%
11	New Jersey	1,500,403	2.7%
36	New Mexico	370,911	0.7%
4	New York	3,337,276	6.0%
9	North Carolina	1,808,331	3.3%
48	North Dakota	121,335	0.2%
6	Ohio	2,166,271	3.9%
28	Oklahoma	717,398	1.3%
26	Oregon	734,841	1.3%
5	Pennsylvania	2,617,879	4.7%
43	Rhode Island	207,122	0.4%
21	South Carolina	956,097	1.7%
46	South Dakota	156,102	0.3%
13	Tennessee	1,287,683	2.3%
3	Texas	3,551,961	6.4%
37	Utah	335,444	0.6%
47	Vermont	132,268	0.2%
12	Virginia	1,318,580	2.4%
17	Washington	1,127,126	2.0%
34	West Virginia	451,039	0.8%
19	Wisconsin	1,085,632	2.0%
49	Wyoming	93,748	0.2%

RANK ORDER

RANK	STATE	BENEFICIARIES	% of USA
1	California	5,129,529	9.3%
2	Florida	3,894,179	7.0%
3	Texas	3,551,961	6.4%
4	New York	3,337,276	6.0%
5	Pennsylvania	2,617,879	4.7%
6	Ohio	2,166,271	3.9%
7	Illinois	2,065,432	3.7%
8	Michigan	2,016,684	3.6%
9	North Carolina	1,808,331	3.3%
10	Georgia	1,524,263	2.8%
11	New Jersey	1,500,403	2.7%
12	Virginia	1,318,580	2.4%
13	Tennessee	1,287,683	2.3%
14	Indiana	1,219,879	2.2%
15	Missouri	1,188,437	2.1%
16	Massachusetts	1,161,122	2.1%
17	Washington	1,127,126	2.0%
18	Arizona	1,104,545	2.0%
19	Wisconsin	1,085,632	2.0%
20	Alabama	1,037,438	1.9%
21	South Carolina	956,097	1.7%
22	Kentucky	913,548	1.6%
23	Minnesota	904,803	1.6%
24	Maryland	872,919	1.6%
25	Louisiana	809,450	1.5%
26	Oregon	734,841	1.3%
27	Colorado	721,274	1.3%
28	Oklahoma	717,398	1.3%
29	Arkansas	647,077	1.2%
30	Connecticut	630,447	1.1%
31	Mississippi	609,651	1.1%
32	Iowa	592,000	1.1%
33	Kansas	498,707	0.9%
34	West Virginia	451,039	0.8%
35	Nevada	424,836	0.8%
36	New Mexico	370,911	0.7%
37	Utah	335,444	0.6%
38	Nebraska	313,087	0.6%
39	Maine	306,600	0.6%
40	Idaho	278,563	0.5%
41	New Hampshire	262,952	0.5%
42	Hawaii	234,314	0.4%
43	Rhode Island	207,122	0.4%
44	Montana	198,230	0.4%
45	Delaware	176,885	0.3%
46	South Dakota	156,102	0.3%
47	Vermont	132,268	0.2%
48	North Dakota	121,335	0.2%
49	Wyoming	93,748	0.2%
50	Alaska	82,109	0.1%
	District of Columbia	75,755	0.1%

Source: Social Security Administration
"Social Security Bulletin, Annual Statistical Supplement 2012" (http://www.ssa.gov/policy/docs/statcomps/supplement/2012/)
*For December 2011. "OASDI" is Old Age, Survivors and Disability Insurance. National total includes 1,432,318 beneficiaries in U.S. territories and foreign countries.

Average Monthly Social Security (OASDI) Payment in 2011

National Average = $1,134 Each Month per Beneficiary*

ALPHA ORDER

RANK	STATE	PER BENEFICIARY
41	Alabama	$1,071
43	Alaska	1,065
14	Arizona	1,161
48	Arkansas	1,041
27	California	1,123
26	Colorado	1,131
2	Connecticut	1,249
3	Delaware	1,214
22	Florida	1,137
33	Georgia	1,105
19	Hawaii	1,143
35	Idaho	1,103
10	Illinois	1,165
9	Indiana	1,171
24	Iowa	1,135
15	Kansas	1,153
46	Kentucky	1,044
50	Louisiana	1,021
47	Maine	1,043
7	Maryland	1,176
20	Massachusetts	1,141
4	Michigan	1,200
13	Minnesota	1,162
49	Mississippi	1,025
33	Missouri	1,105
38	Montana	1,081
30	Nebraska	1,121
16	Nevada	1,152
8	New Hampshire	1,173
1	New Jersey	1,259
45	New Mexico	1,047
6	New York	1,179
29	North Carolina	1,122
44	North Dakota	1,063
31	Ohio	1,120
40	Oklahoma	1,080
17	Oregon	1,150
12	Pennsylvania	1,163
21	Rhode Island	1,139
27	South Carolina	1,123
42	South Dakota	1,066
36	Tennessee	1,096
38	Texas	1,081
25	Utah	1,132
32	Vermont	1,118
22	Virginia	1,137
5	Washington	1,180
37	West Virginia	1,082
10	Wisconsin	1,165
18	Wyoming	1,144

RANK ORDER

RANK	STATE	PER BENEFICIARY
1	New Jersey	$1,259
2	Connecticut	1,249
3	Delaware	1,214
4	Michigan	1,200
5	Washington	1,180
6	New York	1,179
7	Maryland	1,176
8	New Hampshire	1,173
9	Indiana	1,171
10	Illinois	1,165
10	Wisconsin	1,165
12	Pennsylvania	1,163
13	Minnesota	1,162
14	Arizona	1,161
15	Kansas	1,153
16	Nevada	1,152
17	Oregon	1,150
18	Wyoming	1,144
19	Hawaii	1,143
20	Massachusetts	1,141
21	Rhode Island	1,139
22	Florida	1,137
22	Virginia	1,137
24	Iowa	1,135
25	Utah	1,132
26	Colorado	1,131
27	California	1,123
27	South Carolina	1,123
29	North Carolina	1,122
30	Nebraska	1,121
31	Ohio	1,120
32	Vermont	1,118
33	Georgia	1,105
33	Missouri	1,105
35	Idaho	1,103
36	Tennessee	1,096
37	West Virginia	1,082
38	Montana	1,081
38	Texas	1,081
40	Oklahoma	1,080
41	Alabama	1,071
42	South Dakota	1,066
43	Alaska	1,065
44	North Dakota	1,063
45	New Mexico	1,047
46	Kentucky	1,044
47	Maine	1,043
48	Arkansas	1,041
49	Mississippi	1,025
50	Louisiana	1,021
	District of Columbia	1,024

Source: CQ Press using data from Social Security Administration
   "Social Security Bulletin, Annual Statistical Supplement 2012" (http://www.ssa.gov/policy/docs/statcomps/supplement/2012/)
*As of December 2011. "OASDI" is Old Age, Survivors and Disability Insurance. National average does not include
beneficiaries or payments in U.S. territories or foreign countries.

Social Security Supplemental Security Income Beneficiaries in 2011

National Total = 8,112,773 Beneficiaries*

ALPHA ORDER

RANK	STATE	BENEFICIARIES	% of USA
15	Alabama	174,917	2.2%
48	Alaska	12,675	0.2%
23	Arizona	112,757	1.4%
26	Arkansas	109,881	1.4%
1	California	1,286,271	15.9%
31	Colorado	68,725	0.8%
33	Connecticut	59,731	0.7%
45	Delaware	16,155	0.2%
4	Florida	505,807	6.2%
9	Georgia	238,751	2.9%
42	Hawaii	25,330	0.3%
40	Idaho	28,202	0.3%
7	Illinois	276,332	3.4%
21	Indiana	122,084	1.5%
34	Iowa	48,903	0.6%
35	Kansas	47,372	0.6%
12	Kentucky	193,023	2.4%
14	Louisiana	178,727	2.2%
37	Maine	36,316	0.4%
24	Maryland	111,275	1.4%
11	Massachusetts	197,503	2.4%
8	Michigan	264,699	3.3%
28	Minnesota	88,731	1.1%
20	Mississippi	126,307	1.6%
19	Missouri	137,169	1.7%
44	Montana	18,167	0.2%
41	Nebraska	26,530	0.3%
36	Nevada	43,713	0.5%
43	New Hampshire	18,693	0.2%
16	New Jersey	173,143	2.1%
32	New Mexico	61,838	0.8%
2	New York	690,258	8.5%
10	North Carolina	224,780	2.8%
49	North Dakota	8,361	0.1%
6	Ohio	294,920	3.6%
27	Oklahoma	95,510	1.2%
30	Oregon	77,980	1.0%
5	Pennsylvania	367,274	4.5%
38	Rhode Island	32,114	0.4%
22	South Carolina	114,819	1.4%
47	South Dakota	14,154	0.2%
13	Tennessee	179,350	2.2%
3	Texas	639,869	7.9%
39	Utah	29,412	0.4%
46	Vermont	15,684	0.2%
17	Virginia	150,804	1.9%
18	Washington	142,848	1.8%
29	West Virginia	80,734	1.0%
25	Wisconsin	110,881	1.4%
50	Wyoming	6,534	0.1%

RANK ORDER

RANK	STATE	BENEFICIARIES	% of USA
1	California	1,286,271	15.9%
2	New York	690,258	8.5%
3	Texas	639,869	7.9%
4	Florida	505,807	6.2%
5	Pennsylvania	367,274	4.5%
6	Ohio	294,920	3.6%
7	Illinois	276,332	3.4%
8	Michigan	264,699	3.3%
9	Georgia	238,751	2.9%
10	North Carolina	224,780	2.8%
11	Massachusetts	197,503	2.4%
12	Kentucky	193,023	2.4%
13	Tennessee	179,350	2.2%
14	Louisiana	178,727	2.2%
15	Alabama	174,917	2.2%
16	New Jersey	173,143	2.1%
17	Virginia	150,804	1.9%
18	Washington	142,848	1.8%
19	Missouri	137,169	1.7%
20	Mississippi	126,307	1.6%
21	Indiana	122,084	1.5%
22	South Carolina	114,819	1.4%
23	Arizona	112,757	1.4%
24	Maryland	111,275	1.4%
25	Wisconsin	110,881	1.4%
26	Arkansas	109,881	1.4%
27	Oklahoma	95,510	1.2%
28	Minnesota	88,731	1.1%
29	West Virginia	80,734	1.0%
30	Oregon	77,980	1.0%
31	Colorado	68,725	0.8%
32	New Mexico	61,838	0.8%
33	Connecticut	59,731	0.7%
34	Iowa	48,903	0.6%
35	Kansas	47,372	0.6%
36	Nevada	43,713	0.5%
37	Maine	36,316	0.4%
38	Rhode Island	32,114	0.4%
39	Utah	29,412	0.4%
40	Idaho	28,202	0.3%
41	Nebraska	26,530	0.3%
42	Hawaii	25,330	0.3%
43	New Hampshire	18,693	0.2%
44	Montana	18,167	0.2%
45	Delaware	16,155	0.2%
46	Vermont	15,684	0.2%
47	South Dakota	14,154	0.2%
48	Alaska	12,675	0.2%
49	North Dakota	8,361	0.1%
50	Wyoming	6,534	0.1%
	District of Columbia	25,748	0.3%

Source: Social Security Administration
    "Social Security Bulletin, Annual Statistical Supplement 2012" (http://www.ssa.gov/policy/docs/statcomps/supplement/2012/)
*For December 2011. National total includes1,012 beneficiaries in U.S. territories or otherwise not distributed by state. The SSI program provides income support to persons age 65 and older and blind or disabled adults and children.

Average Monthly Social Security
Supplemental Security Income Payment in 2011
National Average = $481.31 Each Month per Beneficiary*

ALPHA ORDER

RANK	STATE	AVERAGE BENEFIT
34	Alabama	$466.61
37	Alaska	464.25
8	Arizona	492.17
28	Arkansas	472.96
22	California	479.76
30	Colorado	471.78
12	Connecticut	486.07
19	Delaware	482.70
21	Florida	480.15
31	Georgia	469.97
11	Hawaii	487.08
29	Idaho	472.14
4	Illinois	504.95
10	Indiana	490.90
43	Iowa	457.67
26	Kansas	473.15
23	Kentucky	478.10
15	Louisiana	483.88
47	Maine	451.97
6	Maryland	499.95
20	Massachusetts	481.48
3	Michigan	505.66
9	Minnesota	491.30
41	Mississippi	460.41
27	Missouri	473.08
42	Montana	458.21
44	Nebraska	457.61
14	Nevada	484.05
36	New Hampshire	464.94
33	New Jersey	467.36
40	New Mexico	461.06
7	New York	494.00
45	North Carolina	456.40
50	North Dakota	430.55
5	Ohio	501.33
24	Oklahoma	477.78
18	Oregon	482.85
1	Pennsylvania	507.50
13	Rhode Island	484.35
38	South Carolina	462.93
49	South Dakota	447.16
35	Tennessee	466.57
39	Texas	461.75
25	Utah	475.97
46	Vermont	452.13
32	Virginia	468.93
2	Washington	507.04
16	West Virginia	483.45
17	Wisconsin	483.21
48	Wyoming	449.87

RANK ORDER

RANK	STATE	AVERAGE BENEFIT
1	Pennsylvania	$507.50
2	Washington	507.04
3	Michigan	505.66
4	Illinois	504.95
5	Ohio	501.33
6	Maryland	499.95
7	New York	494.00
8	Arizona	492.17
9	Minnesota	491.30
10	Indiana	490.90
11	Hawaii	487.08
12	Connecticut	486.07
13	Rhode Island	484.35
14	Nevada	484.05
15	Louisiana	483.88
16	West Virginia	483.45
17	Wisconsin	483.21
18	Oregon	482.85
19	Delaware	482.70
20	Massachusetts	481.48
21	Florida	480.15
22	California	479.76
23	Kentucky	478.10
24	Oklahoma	477.78
25	Utah	475.97
26	Kansas	473.15
27	Missouri	473.08
28	Arkansas	472.96
29	Idaho	472.14
30	Colorado	471.78
31	Georgia	469.97
32	Virginia	468.93
33	New Jersey	467.36
34	Alabama	466.61
35	Tennessee	466.57
36	New Hampshire	464.94
37	Alaska	464.25
38	South Carolina	462.93
39	Texas	461.75
40	New Mexico	461.06
41	Mississippi	460.41
42	Montana	458.21
43	Iowa	457.67
44	Nebraska	457.61
45	North Carolina	456.40
46	Vermont	452.13
47	Maine	451.97
48	Wyoming	449.87
49	South Dakota	447.16
50	North Dakota	430.55

District of Columbia   521.39

Source: Social Security Administration
    "Social Security Bulletin, Annual Statistical Supplement 2012" (http://www.ssa.gov/policy/docs/statcomps/supplement/2012/)
*As of December 2011. National average includes payments to beneficiaries in U.S. territories and foreign countries. The SSI program provides income support to persons age 65 and older and blind or disabled adults and children.

Medicare Enrollees in 2012

National Total = 49,682,146 Enrollees*

ALPHA ORDER

RANK	STATE	ENROLLEES	% of USA
20	Alabama	896,274	1.8%
50	Alaska	72,898	0.1%
18	Arizona	1,009,292	2.0%
30	Arkansas	558,620	1.1%
1	California	5,111,208	10.3%
26	Colorado	688,283	1.4%
29	Connecticut	595,294	1.2%
45	Delaware	161,422	0.3%
2	Florida	3,621,057	7.3%
11	Georgia	1,350,944	2.7%
42	Hawaii	221,514	0.4%
40	Idaho	249,626	0.5%
7	Illinois	1,934,703	3.9%
15	Indiana	1,064,511	2.1%
31	Iowa	537,430	1.1%
33	Kansas	453,927	0.9%
24	Kentucky	804,245	1.6%
25	Louisiana	729,271	1.5%
39	Maine	281,968	0.6%
21	Maryland	844,862	1.7%
14	Massachusetts	1,125,661	2.3%
8	Michigan	1,754,367	3.5%
23	Minnesota	836,205	1.7%
32	Mississippi	523,625	1.1%
16	Missouri	1,058,418	2.1%
44	Montana	181,710	0.4%
38	Nebraska	291,333	0.6%
35	Nevada	394,066	0.8%
41	New Hampshire	240,551	0.5%
10	New Jersey	1,397,532	2.8%
36	New Mexico	336,413	0.7%
4	New York	3,138,042	6.3%
9	North Carolina	1,604,085	3.2%
48	North Dakota	112,330	0.2%
6	Ohio	2,003,455	4.0%
28	Oklahoma	635,525	1.3%
27	Oregon	671,822	1.4%
5	Pennsylvania	2,385,084	4.8%
43	Rhode Island	191,420	0.4%
22	South Carolina	839,989	1.7%
46	South Dakota	143,014	0.3%
13	Tennessee	1,132,942	2.3%
3	Texas	3,256,477	6.6%
37	Utah	307,361	0.6%
47	Vermont	119,759	0.2%
12	Virginia	1,226,577	2.5%
17	Washington	1,055,977	2.1%
34	West Virginia	396,705	0.8%
19	Wisconsin	966,151	1.9%
49	Wyoming	85,708	0.2%

RANK ORDER

RANK	STATE	ENROLLEES	% of USA
1	California	5,111,208	10.3%
2	Florida	3,621,057	7.3%
3	Texas	3,256,477	6.6%
4	New York	3,138,042	6.3%
5	Pennsylvania	2,385,084	4.8%
6	Ohio	2,003,455	4.0%
7	Illinois	1,934,703	3.9%
8	Michigan	1,754,367	3.5%
9	North Carolina	1,604,085	3.2%
10	New Jersey	1,397,532	2.8%
11	Georgia	1,350,944	2.7%
12	Virginia	1,226,577	2.5%
13	Tennessee	1,132,942	2.3%
14	Massachusetts	1,125,661	2.3%
15	Indiana	1,064,511	2.1%
16	Missouri	1,058,418	2.1%
17	Washington	1,055,977	2.1%
18	Arizona	1,009,292	2.0%
19	Wisconsin	966,151	1.9%
20	Alabama	896,274	1.8%
21	Maryland	844,862	1.7%
22	South Carolina	839,989	1.7%
23	Minnesota	836,205	1.7%
24	Kentucky	804,245	1.6%
25	Louisiana	729,271	1.5%
26	Colorado	688,283	1.4%
27	Oregon	671,822	1.4%
28	Oklahoma	635,525	1.3%
29	Connecticut	595,294	1.2%
30	Arkansas	558,620	1.1%
31	Iowa	537,430	1.1%
32	Mississippi	523,625	1.1%
33	Kansas	453,927	0.9%
34	West Virginia	396,705	0.8%
35	Nevada	394,066	0.8%
36	New Mexico	336,413	0.7%
37	Utah	307,361	0.6%
38	Nebraska	291,333	0.6%
39	Maine	281,968	0.6%
40	Idaho	249,626	0.5%
41	New Hampshire	240,551	0.5%
42	Hawaii	221,514	0.4%
43	Rhode Island	191,420	0.4%
44	Montana	181,710	0.4%
45	Delaware	161,422	0.3%
46	South Dakota	143,014	0.3%
47	Vermont	119,759	0.2%
48	North Dakota	112,330	0.2%
49	Wyoming	85,708	0.2%
50	Alaska	72,898	0.1%
	District of Columbia	82,493	0.2%

Source: U.S. Department of Health and Human Services, Centers for Medicare and Medicaid Services
"2013 Medicare and Medicaid Statistical Supplement" (Table 2.8)
(www.cms.gov/Research-Statistics-Data-and-Systems/Statistics-Trends-and-Reports/MedicareMedicaidStatSupp/index.html)
*Includes aged and disabled enrollees. Total does not include enrollees in Puerto Rico and other outlying areas, foreign countries, or whose address is unknown.

Percent of Population Enrolled in Medicare in 2012

National Percent = 15.8% of Population*

ALPHA ORDER

RANK	STATE	PERCENT
7	Alabama	18.6
50	Alaska	10.0
38	Arizona	15.4
4	Arkansas	18.9
46	California	13.4
47	Colorado	13.3
25	Connecticut	16.6
14	Delaware	17.6
5	Florida	18.7
45	Georgia	13.6
31	Hawaii	15.9
36	Idaho	15.6
40	Illinois	15.0
27	Indiana	16.3
16	Iowa	17.5
34	Kansas	15.7
8	Kentucky	18.4
32	Louisiana	15.8
2	Maine	21.2
43	Maryland	14.4
22	Massachusetts	16.9
12	Michigan	17.8
37	Minnesota	15.5
16	Mississippi	17.5
14	Missouri	17.6
11	Montana	18.1
34	Nebraska	15.7
44	Nevada	14.3
9	New Hampshire	18.2
32	New Jersey	15.8
28	New Mexico	16.1
30	New York	16.0
26	North Carolina	16.4
28	North Dakota	16.1
19	Ohio	17.4
24	Oklahoma	16.7
20	Oregon	17.2
5	Pennsylvania	18.7
9	Rhode Island	18.2
12	South Carolina	17.8
20	South Dakota	17.2
16	Tennessee	17.5
48	Texas	12.5
49	Utah	10.8
3	Vermont	19.1
40	Virginia	15.0
39	Washington	15.3
1	West Virginia	21.4
22	Wisconsin	16.9
42	Wyoming	14.9

RANK ORDER

RANK	STATE	PERCENT
1	West Virginia	21.4
2	Maine	21.2
3	Vermont	19.1
4	Arkansas	18.9
5	Florida	18.7
5	Pennsylvania	18.7
7	Alabama	18.6
8	Kentucky	18.4
9	New Hampshire	18.2
9	Rhode Island	18.2
11	Montana	18.1
12	Michigan	17.8
12	South Carolina	17.8
14	Delaware	17.6
14	Missouri	17.6
16	Iowa	17.5
16	Mississippi	17.5
16	Tennessee	17.5
19	Ohio	17.4
20	Oregon	17.2
20	South Dakota	17.2
22	Massachusetts	16.9
22	Wisconsin	16.9
24	Oklahoma	16.7
25	Connecticut	16.6
26	North Carolina	16.4
27	Indiana	16.3
28	New Mexico	16.1
28	North Dakota	16.1
30	New York	16.0
31	Hawaii	15.9
32	Louisiana	15.8
32	New Jersey	15.8
34	Kansas	15.7
34	Nebraska	15.7
36	Idaho	15.6
37	Minnesota	15.5
38	Arizona	15.4
39	Washington	15.3
40	Illinois	15.0
40	Virginia	15.0
42	Wyoming	14.9
43	Maryland	14.4
44	Nevada	14.3
45	Georgia	13.6
46	California	13.4
47	Colorado	13.3
48	Texas	12.5
49	Utah	10.8
50	Alaska	10.0

	District of Columbia	13.0

Source: U.S. Department of Health and Human Services, Centers for Medicare and Medicaid Services
  "2013 Medicare and Medicaid Statistical Supplement" (Table 2.8)
    (www.cms.gov/Research-Statistics-Data-and-Systems/Statistics-Trends-and-Reports/MedicareMedicaidStatSupp/index.html)
*Includes aged and disabled enrollees. National rate includes only residents of the 50 states and the District of Columbia.

Medicare Program Payments in 2011

National Total = $339,587,000,000*

ALPHA ORDER

RANK	STATE	PAYMENTS	% of USA
18	Alabama	$5,949,000,000	1.8%
50	Alaska	525,000,000	0.2%
24	Arizona	5,277,000,000	1.6%
30	Arkansas	3,580,000,000	1.1%
1	California	31,038,000,000	9.1%
31	Colorado	3,456,000,000	1.0%
25	Connecticut	4,882,000,000	1.4%
41	Delaware	1,400,000,000	0.4%
3	Florida	25,495,000,000	7.5%
12	Georgia	8,856,000,000	2.6%
47	Hawaii	780,000,000	0.2%
42	Idaho	1,287,000,000	0.4%
5	Illinois	16,702,000,000	4.9%
15	Indiana	7,556,000,000	2.2%
29	Iowa	3,599,000,000	1.1%
32	Kansas	3,226,000,000	0.9%
20	Kentucky	5,783,000,000	1.7%
21	Louisiana	5,739,000,000	1.7%
37	Maine	1,768,000,000	0.5%
14	Maryland	8,111,000,000	2.4%
11	Massachusetts	9,222,000,000	2.7%
7	Michigan	13,243,000,000	3.9%
27	Minnesota	4,479,000,000	1.3%
28	Mississippi	4,444,000,000	1.3%
17	Missouri	7,011,000,000	2.1%
44	Montana	1,014,000,000	0.3%
36	Nebraska	2,162,000,000	0.6%
35	Nevada	2,474,000,000	0.7%
38	New Hampshire	1,736,000,000	0.5%
9	New Jersey	12,473,000,000	3.7%
39	New Mexico	1,712,000,000	0.5%
4	New York	21,568,000,000	6.4%
10	North Carolina	10,949,000,000	3.2%
48	North Dakota	765,000,000	0.2%
8	Ohio	12,760,000,000	3.8%
26	Oklahoma	4,693,000,000	1.4%
33	Oregon	2,732,000,000	0.8%
6	Pennsylvania	14,091,000,000	4.1%
43	Rhode Island	1,090,000,000	0.3%
19	South Carolina	5,935,000,000	1.7%
45	South Dakota	985,000,000	0.3%
16	Tennessee	7,227,000,000	2.1%
2	Texas	26,255,000,000	7.7%
40	Utah	1,534,000,000	0.5%
46	Vermont	852,000,000	0.3%
13	Virginia	8,127,000,000	2.4%
22	Washington	5,598,000,000	1.6%
34	West Virginia	2,644,000,000	0.8%
23	Wisconsin	5,406,000,000	1.6%
49	Wyoming	617,000,000	0.2%

RANK ORDER

RANK	STATE	PAYMENTS	% of USA
1	California	$31,038,000,000	9.1%
2	Texas	26,255,000,000	7.7%
3	Florida	25,495,000,000	7.5%
4	New York	21,568,000,000	6.4%
5	Illinois	16,702,000,000	4.9%
6	Pennsylvania	14,091,000,000	4.1%
7	Michigan	13,243,000,000	3.9%
8	Ohio	12,760,000,000	3.8%
9	New Jersey	12,473,000,000	3.7%
10	North Carolina	10,949,000,000	3.2%
11	Massachusetts	9,222,000,000	2.7%
12	Georgia	8,856,000,000	2.6%
13	Virginia	8,127,000,000	2.4%
14	Maryland	8,111,000,000	2.4%
15	Indiana	7,556,000,000	2.2%
16	Tennessee	7,227,000,000	2.1%
17	Missouri	7,011,000,000	2.1%
18	Alabama	5,949,000,000	1.8%
19	South Carolina	5,935,000,000	1.7%
20	Kentucky	5,783,000,000	1.7%
21	Louisiana	5,739,000,000	1.7%
22	Washington	5,598,000,000	1.6%
23	Wisconsin	5,406,000,000	1.6%
24	Arizona	5,277,000,000	1.6%
25	Connecticut	4,882,000,000	1.4%
26	Oklahoma	4,693,000,000	1.4%
27	Minnesota	4,479,000,000	1.3%
28	Mississippi	4,444,000,000	1.3%
29	Iowa	3,599,000,000	1.1%
30	Arkansas	3,580,000,000	1.1%
31	Colorado	3,456,000,000	1.0%
32	Kansas	3,226,000,000	0.9%
33	Oregon	2,732,000,000	0.8%
34	West Virginia	2,644,000,000	0.8%
35	Nevada	2,474,000,000	0.7%
36	Nebraska	2,162,000,000	0.6%
37	Maine	1,768,000,000	0.5%
38	New Hampshire	1,736,000,000	0.5%
39	New Mexico	1,712,000,000	0.5%
40	Utah	1,534,000,000	0.5%
41	Delaware	1,400,000,000	0.4%
42	Idaho	1,287,000,000	0.4%
43	Rhode Island	1,090,000,000	0.3%
44	Montana	1,014,000,000	0.3%
45	South Dakota	985,000,000	0.3%
46	Vermont	852,000,000	0.3%
47	Hawaii	780,000,000	0.2%
48	North Dakota	765,000,000	0.2%
49	Wyoming	617,000,000	0.2%
50	Alaska	525,000,000	0.2%
	District of Columbia	783,000,000	0.2%

Source: U.S. Department of Health and Human Services, Centers for Medicare and Medicaid Services
"2012 Medicare and Medicaid Statistical Supplement" (Table 3.5)
(www.cms.gov/Research-Statistics-Data-and-Systems/Statistics-Trends-and-Reports/MedicareMedicaidStatSupp/index.html)
*Figures for calendar year 2011. Includes payments to aged and disabled enrollees. Total does not include payments to beneficiaries in Puerto Rico and other outlying areas.

Medicare Program Payments per Enrollee in 2011

National Rate = $9,468*

ALPHA ORDER				RANK ORDER		
RANK	**STATE**	**PER ENROLLEE**		**RANK**	**STATE**	**PER ENROLLEE**
29	Alabama	$8,623		1	Maryland	$10,852
42	Alaska	7,740		2	Florida	10,823
28	Arizona	8,663		3	Louisiana	10,778
37	Arkansas	7,911		4	Texas	10,596
11	California	9,903		5	New Jersey	10,553
36	Colorado	7,939		6	Connecticut	10,406
6	Connecticut	10,406		7	Michigan	10,320
17	Delaware	9,369		8	Massachusetts	10,264
2	Florida	10,823		9	New York	10,255
24	Georgia	8,836		10	Minnesota	10,000
50	Hawaii	6,368		11	California	9,903
45	Idaho	7,531		12	Ohio	9,882
15	Illinois	9,758		13	Pennsylvania	9,769
20	Indiana	8,957		14	Mississippi	9,767
39	Iowa	7,869		15	Illinois	9,758
32	Kansas	8,336		16	Nevada	9,539
21	Kentucky	8,936		17	Delaware	9,369
3	Louisiana	10,778		18	Rhode Island	9,046
44	Maine	7,538		19	Oklahoma	8,987
1	Maryland	10,852		20	Indiana	8,957
8	Massachusetts	10,264		21	Kentucky	8,936
7	Michigan	10,320		22	South Carolina	8,900
10	Minnesota	10,000		23	Tennessee	8,859
14	Mississippi	9,767		24	Georgia	8,836
27	Missouri	8,679		25	North Carolina	8,725
49	Montana	6,759		26	West Virginia	8,720
30	Nebraska	8,466		27	Missouri	8,679
16	Nevada	9,539		28	Arizona	8,663
33	New Hampshire	8,193		29	Alabama	8,623
5	New Jersey	10,553		30	Nebraska	8,466
47	New Mexico	7,266		31	Wisconsin	8,352
9	New York	10,255		32	Kansas	8,336
25	North Carolina	8,725		33	New Hampshire	8,193
43	North Dakota	7,570		34	Virginia	8,061
12	Ohio	9,882		35	Utah	8,057
19	Oklahoma	8,987		36	Colorado	7,939
48	Oregon	7,087		37	Arkansas	7,911
13	Pennsylvania	9,769		38	South Dakota	7,889
18	Rhode Island	9,046		39	Iowa	7,869
22	South Carolina	8,900		40	Vermont	7,812
38	South Dakota	7,889		41	Wyoming	7,795
23	Tennessee	8,859		42	Alaska	7,740
4	Texas	10,596		43	North Dakota	7,570
35	Utah	8,057		44	Maine	7,538
40	Vermont	7,812		45	Idaho	7,531
34	Virginia	8,061		46	Washington	7,510
46	Washington	7,510		47	New Mexico	7,266
26	West Virginia	8,720		48	Oregon	7,087
31	Wisconsin	8,352		49	Montana	6,759
41	Wyoming	7,795		50	Hawaii	6,368

District of Columbia   10,953

Source: U.S. Department of Health and Human Services, Centers for Medicare and Medicaid Services
    "2012 Medicare and Medicaid Statistical Supplement" (Table 3.5)
        (www.cms.gov/Research-Statistics-Data-and-Systems/Statistics-Trends-and-Reports/MedicareMedicaidStatSupp/index.html)
*Figures for calendar year 2011. Includes payments to aged and disabled enrollees. National figure does not include enrollees in managed care plans in the denominator used to calculate average payments. National rate also does not include payments or enrollees in Puerto Rico and other outlying areas.

Medicaid Enrollment in 2011

National Total = 57,106,941 Enrollees*

ALPHA ORDER

RANK	STATE	ENROLLEES	% of USA
20	Alabama	930,736	1.6%
46	Alaska	120,611	0.2%
12	Arizona	1,351,988	2.4%
29	Arkansas	608,332	1.1%
1	California	7,580,978	13.3%
30	Colorado	583,618	1.0%
31	Connecticut	578,620	1.0%
42	Delaware	200,810	0.4%
4	Florida	3,069,456	5.4%
10	Georgia	1,548,090	2.7%
38	Hawaii	272,218	0.5%
41	Idaho	230,725	0.4%
5	Illinois	2,787,200	4.9%
18	Indiana	1,055,779	1.8%
33	Iowa	440,993	0.8%
35	Kansas	354,664	0.6%
25	Kentucky	823,133	1.4%
14	Louisiana	1,208,859	2.1%
34	Maine	357,706	0.6%
19	Maryland	986,304	1.7%
9	Massachusetts	1,566,222	2.7%
8	Michigan	1,818,312	3.2%
24	Minnesota	847,638	1.5%
28	Mississippi	621,607	1.1%
22	Missouri	895,998	1.6%
48	Montana	106,493	0.2%
40	Nebraska	237,484	0.4%
37	Nevada	297,640	0.5%
45	New Hampshire	135,092	0.2%
17	New Jersey	1,098,608	1.9%
32	New Mexico	551,017	1.0%
2	New York	4,925,236	8.6%
11	North Carolina	1,488,263	2.6%
50	North Dakota	66,698	0.1%
7	Ohio	2,129,706	3.7%
26	Oklahoma	684,387	1.2%
27	Oregon	652,846	1.1%
6	Pennsylvania	2,134,956	3.7%
43	Rhode Island	197,248	0.3%
23	South Carolina	862,145	1.5%
47	South Dakota	120,474	0.2%
13	Tennessee	1,218,676	2.1%
3	Texas	3,943,189	6.9%
39	Utah	269,643	0.5%
44	Vermont	177,108	0.3%
21	Virginia	915,038	1.6%
15	Washington	1,182,587	2.1%
36	West Virginia	326,749	0.6%
16	Wisconsin	1,173,355	2.1%
49	Wyoming	69,947	0.1%

RANK ORDER

RANK	STATE	ENROLLEES	% of USA
1	California	7,580,978	13.3%
2	New York	4,925,236	8.6%
3	Texas	3,943,189	6.9%
4	Florida	3,069,456	5.4%
5	Illinois	2,787,200	4.9%
6	Pennsylvania	2,134,956	3.7%
7	Ohio	2,129,706	3.7%
8	Michigan	1,818,312	3.2%
9	Massachusetts	1,566,222	2.7%
10	Georgia	1,548,090	2.7%
11	North Carolina	1,488,263	2.6%
12	Arizona	1,351,988	2.4%
13	Tennessee	1,218,676	2.1%
14	Louisiana	1,208,859	2.1%
15	Washington	1,182,587	2.1%
16	Wisconsin	1,173,355	2.1%
17	New Jersey	1,098,608	1.9%
18	Indiana	1,055,779	1.8%
19	Maryland	986,304	1.7%
20	Alabama	930,736	1.6%
21	Virginia	915,038	1.6%
22	Missouri	895,998	1.6%
23	South Carolina	862,145	1.5%
24	Minnesota	847,638	1.5%
25	Kentucky	823,133	1.4%
26	Oklahoma	684,387	1.2%
27	Oregon	652,846	1.1%
28	Mississippi	621,607	1.1%
29	Arkansas	608,332	1.1%
30	Colorado	583,618	1.0%
31	Connecticut	578,620	1.0%
32	New Mexico	551,017	1.0%
33	Iowa	440,993	0.8%
34	Maine	357,706	0.6%
35	Kansas	354,664	0.6%
36	West Virginia	326,749	0.6%
37	Nevada	297,640	0.5%
38	Hawaii	272,218	0.5%
39	Utah	269,643	0.5%
40	Nebraska	237,484	0.4%
41	Idaho	230,725	0.4%
42	Delaware	200,810	0.4%
43	Rhode Island	197,248	0.3%
44	Vermont	177,108	0.3%
45	New Hampshire	135,092	0.2%
46	Alaska	120,611	0.2%
47	South Dakota	120,474	0.2%
48	Montana	106,493	0.2%
49	Wyoming	69,947	0.1%
50	North Dakota	66,698	0.1%
	District of Columbia	201,777	0.4%

Source: U.S. Department of Health and Human Services, Centers for Medicare and Medicaid Services
    "2011 Medicaid Managed Care Enrollment Report" (http://www.cms.gov/MedicaidDataSourcesGenInfo/)
*Unduplicated enrollment as of December 31, 2011. National total includes 1,099,982 Medicaid enrollees in Puerto Rico and the Virgin Islands.

Percent of Population Enrolled in Medicaid in 2011

National Percent = 18.0% of Population*

RANK	STATE	PERCENT
15	Alabama	19.4
28	Alaska	16.7
9	Arizona	20.9
11	Arkansas	20.7
13	California	20.1
44	Colorado	11.4
30	Connecticut	16.1
7	Delaware	22.1
30	Florida	16.1
33	Georgia	15.8
14	Hawaii	19.8
37	Idaho	14.6
8	Illinois	21.7
29	Indiana	16.2
39	Iowa	14.4
41	Kansas	12.4
17	Kentucky	18.8
4	Louisiana	26.4
2	Maine	26.9
25	Maryland	16.9
6	Massachusetts	23.7
19	Michigan	18.4
32	Minnesota	15.9
9	Mississippi	20.9
36	Missouri	14.9
47	Montana	10.7
40	Nebraska	12.9
46	Nevada	11.0
48	New Hampshire	10.2
41	New Jersey	12.4
3	New Mexico	26.5
5	New York	25.3
34	North Carolina	15.4
49	North Dakota	9.7
19	Ohio	18.4
22	Oklahoma	18.1
25	Oregon	16.9
27	Pennsylvania	16.8
17	Rhode Island	18.8
19	South Carolina	18.4
37	South Dakota	14.6
16	Tennessee	19.0
34	Texas	15.4
50	Utah	9.6
1	Vermont	28.3
45	Virginia	11.3
24	Washington	17.3
23	West Virginia	17.6
12	Wisconsin	20.6
43	Wyoming	12.3

RANK ORDER

RANK	STATE	PERCENT
1	Vermont	28.3
2	Maine	26.9
3	New Mexico	26.5
4	Louisiana	26.4
5	New York	25.3
6	Massachusetts	23.7
7	Delaware	22.1
8	Illinois	21.7
9	Arizona	20.9
9	Mississippi	20.9
11	Arkansas	20.7
12	Wisconsin	20.6
13	California	20.1
14	Hawaii	19.8
15	Alabama	19.4
16	Tennessee	19.0
17	Kentucky	18.8
17	Rhode Island	18.8
19	Michigan	18.4
19	Ohio	18.4
19	South Carolina	18.4
22	Oklahoma	18.1
23	West Virginia	17.6
24	Washington	17.3
25	Maryland	16.9
25	Oregon	16.9
27	Pennsylvania	16.8
28	Alaska	16.7
29	Indiana	16.2
30	Connecticut	16.1
30	Florida	16.1
32	Minnesota	15.9
33	Georgia	15.8
34	North Carolina	15.4
34	Texas	15.4
36	Missouri	14.9
37	Idaho	14.6
37	South Dakota	14.6
39	Iowa	14.4
40	Nebraska	12.9
41	Kansas	12.4
41	New Jersey	12.4
43	Wyoming	12.3
44	Colorado	11.4
45	Virginia	11.3
46	Nevada	11.0
47	Montana	10.7
48	New Hampshire	10.2
49	North Dakota	9.7
50	Utah	9.6

District of Columbia	32.6

Source: CQ Press using data from U.S. Department of Health and Human Services, Centers for Medicare and Medicaid Services
"2011 Medicaid Managed Care Enrollment Report" (http://www.cms.gov/MedicaidDataSourcesGenInfo/)
*Unduplicated enrollment as of December 31, 2011. National percent does not include recipients or population in U.S. territories.

Estimated Medicaid Expenditures in 2013

National Total = $419,337,000,000*

ALPHA ORDER

ALPHA ORDER

RANK	STATE	EXPENDITURES	% of USA	RANK	STATE	EXPENDITURES	% of USA
24	Alabama	$5,835,000,000	1.4%	1	California	$55,885,000,000	13.3%
42	Alaska	1,646,000,000	0.4%	2	New York	38,792,000,000	9.3%
12	Arizona	9,333,000,000	2.2%	3	Texas	28,707,000,000	6.8%
30	Arkansas	4,617,000,000	1.1%	4	Pennsylvania	23,102,000,000	5.5%
1	California	55,885,000,000	13.3%	5	Florida	21,176,000,000	5.0%
22	Colorado	6,377,000,000	1.5%	6	Illinois	16,784,000,000	4.0%
23	Connecticut	6,202,000,000	1.5%	7	Ohio	14,419,000,000	3.4%
44	Delaware	1,577,000,000	0.4%	8	Massachusetts	12,830,000,000	3.1%
5	Florida	21,176,000,000	5.0%	9	Michigan	12,728,000,000	3.0%
15	Georgia	8,289,000,000	2.0%	10	North Carolina	12,137,000,000	2.9%
43	Hawaii	1,627,000,000	0.4%	11	New Jersey	10,442,000,000	2.5%
40	Idaho	1,916,000,000	0.5%	12	Arizona	9,333,000,000	2.2%
6	Illinois	16,784,000,000	4.0%	13	Tennessee	9,274,000,000	2.2%
14	Indiana	8,789,000,000	2.1%	14	Indiana	8,789,000,000	2.1%
32	Iowa	3,665,000,000	0.9%	15	Georgia	8,289,000,000	2.0%
35	Kansas	2,823,000,000	0.7%	16	Missouri	8,210,000,000	2.0%
25	Kentucky	5,626,000,000	1.3%	17	Minnesota	8,201,000,000	2.0%
20	Louisiana	7,373,000,000	1.8%	18	Maryland	7,718,000,000	1.8%
36	Maine	2,509,000,000	0.6%	19	Virginia	7,634,000,000	1.8%
18	Maryland	7,718,000,000	1.8%	20	Louisiana	7,373,000,000	1.8%
8	Massachusetts	12,830,000,000	3.1%	21	Wisconsin	7,341,000,000	1.8%
9	Michigan	12,728,000,000	3.0%	22	Colorado	6,377,000,000	1.5%
17	Minnesota	8,201,000,000	2.0%	23	Connecticut	6,202,000,000	1.5%
28	Mississippi	5,050,000,000	1.2%	24	Alabama	5,835,000,000	1.4%
16	Missouri	8,210,000,000	2.0%	25	Kentucky	5,626,000,000	1.3%
47	Montana	1,081,000,000	0.3%	26	Oregon	5,499,000,000	1.3%
41	Nebraska	1,822,000,000	0.4%	27	Oklahoma	5,225,000,000	1.2%
38	Nevada	1,994,000,000	0.5%	28	Mississippi	5,050,000,000	1.2%
46	New Hampshire	1,285,000,000	0.3%	29	South Carolina	4,890,000,000	1.2%
11	New Jersey	10,442,000,000	2.5%	30	Arkansas	4,617,000,000	1.1%
33	New Mexico	3,599,000,000	0.9%	31	Washington	4,524,000,000	1.1%
2	New York	38,792,000,000	9.3%	32	Iowa	3,665,000,000	0.9%
10	North Carolina	12,137,000,000	2.9%	33	New Mexico	3,599,000,000	0.9%
49	North Dakota	774,000,000	0.2%	34	West Virginia	3,093,000,000	0.7%
7	Ohio	14,419,000,000	3.4%	35	Kansas	2,823,000,000	0.7%
27	Oklahoma	5,225,000,000	1.2%	36	Maine	2,509,000,000	0.6%
26	Oregon	5,499,000,000	1.3%	37	Utah	2,124,000,000	0.5%
4	Pennsylvania	23,102,000,000	5.5%	38	Nevada	1,994,000,000	0.5%
39	Rhode Island	1,986,000,000	0.5%	39	Rhode Island	1,986,000,000	0.5%
29	South Carolina	4,890,000,000	1.2%	40	Idaho	1,916,000,000	0.5%
48	South Dakota	816,000,000	0.2%	41	Nebraska	1,822,000,000	0.4%
13	Tennessee	9,274,000,000	2.2%	42	Alaska	1,646,000,000	0.4%
3	Texas	28,707,000,000	6.8%	43	Hawaii	1,627,000,000	0.4%
37	Utah	2,124,000,000	0.5%	44	Delaware	1,577,000,000	0.4%
45	Vermont	1,387,000,000	0.3%	45	Vermont	1,387,000,000	0.3%
19	Virginia	7,634,000,000	1.8%	46	New Hampshire	1,285,000,000	0.3%
31	Washington	4,524,000,000	1.1%	47	Montana	1,081,000,000	0.3%
34	West Virginia	3,093,000,000	0.7%	48	South Dakota	816,000,000	0.2%
21	Wisconsin	7,341,000,000	1.8%	49	North Dakota	774,000,000	0.2%
50	Wyoming	604,000,000	0.1%	50	Wyoming	604,000,000	0.1%
					District of Columbia**	NA	NA

Source: National Association of State Budget Officers
    "State Expenditure Report" (http://www.nasbo.org)
*Estimates for fiscal year 2013.
**Not available.

Percent Change in Medicaid Expenditures: 2012 to 2013

National Percent Change = 7.6% Increase*

ALPHA ORDER				RANK ORDER		
RANK	STATE	PERCENT CHANGE		RANK	STATE	PERCENT CHANGE
31	Alabama	3.7		1	California	29.8
4	Alaska	20.2		2	Illinois	29.6
38	Arizona	2.2		3	Indiana	22.4
28	Arkansas	4.4		4	Alaska	20.2
1	California	29.8		5	Mississippi	17.3
20	Colorado	6.8		6	Hawaii	15.1
23	Connecticut	5.4		7	Idaho	12.4
10	Delaware	11.0		8	Oregon	12.0
12	Florida	9.9		9	West Virginia	11.9
44	Georgia	(0.6)		10	Delaware	11.0
6	Hawaii	15.1		11	Nebraska	10.5
7	Idaho	12.4		12	Florida	9.9
2	Illinois	29.6		13	Vermont	9.5
3	Indiana	22.4		14	Montana	8.5
47	Iowa	(1.1)		14	Virginia	8.5
26	Kansas	5.2		16	New Hampshire	8.3
49	Kentucky	(2.7)		17	Wisconsin	7.6
41	Louisiana	2.0		18	Maine	7.5
18	Maine	7.5		19	Washington	7.1
32	Maryland	3.1		20	Colorado	6.8
27	Massachusetts	4.7		21	North Dakota	6.0
33	Michigan	3.0		22	Wyoming	5.6
50	Minnesota	(5.0)		23	Connecticut	5.4
5	Mississippi	17.3		23	North Carolina	5.4
43	Missouri	0.3		23	South Dakota	5.4
14	Montana	8.5		26	Kansas	5.2
11	Nebraska	10.5		27	Massachusetts	4.7
33	Nevada	3.0		28	Arkansas	4.4
16	New Hampshire	8.3		28	Oklahoma	4.4
46	New Jersey	(0.7)		30	Pennsylvania	3.9
33	New Mexico	3.0		31	Alabama	3.7
48	New York	(1.2)		32	Maryland	3.1
23	North Carolina	5.4		33	Michigan	3.0
21	North Dakota	6.0		33	Nevada	3.0
40	Ohio	2.1		33	New Mexico	3.0
28	Oklahoma	4.4		36	Utah	2.9
8	Oregon	12.0		37	Texas	2.8
30	Pennsylvania	3.9		38	Arizona	2.2
42	Rhode Island	0.5		38	South Carolina	2.2
38	South Carolina	2.2		40	Ohio	2.1
23	South Dakota	5.4		41	Louisiana	2.0
44	Tennessee	(0.6)		42	Rhode Island	0.5
37	Texas	2.8		43	Missouri	0.3
36	Utah	2.9		44	Georgia	(0.6)
13	Vermont	9.5		44	Tennessee	(0.6)
14	Virginia	8.5		46	New Jersey	(0.7)
19	Washington	7.1		47	Iowa	(1.1)
9	West Virginia	11.9		48	New York	(1.2)
17	Wisconsin	7.6		49	Kentucky	(2.7)
22	Wyoming	5.6		50	Minnesota	(5.0)
				District of Columbia**		NA

Source: National Association of State Budget Officers
"State Expenditure Report" (http://www.nasbo.org)
*Estimates for fiscal year 2013.
**Not available.

Percent of Population Receiving Public Aid in 2011

National Percent = 4.0% of Population*

ALPHA ORDER

RANK	STATE	PERCENT
8	Alabama	4.8
24	Alaska	3.2
43	Arizona	2.3
13	Arkansas	4.4
1	California	7.2
46	Colorado	2.0
41	Connecticut	2.5
21	Delaware	3.5
25	Florida	3.1
33	Georgia	2.8
17	Hawaii	3.9
46	Idaho	2.0
30	Illinois	2.9
41	Indiana	2.5
28	Iowa	3.0
33	Kansas	2.8
2	Kentucky	5.9
13	Louisiana	4.4
9	Maine	4.6
28	Maryland	3.0
11	Massachusetts	4.5
17	Michigan	3.9
38	Minnesota	2.6
5	Mississippi	5.1
20	Missouri	3.7
36	Montana	2.7
44	Nebraska	2.2
38	Nevada	2.6
44	New Hampshire	2.2
30	New Jersey	2.9
4	New Mexico	5.4
7	New York	5.0
33	North Carolina	2.8
48	North Dakota	1.9
15	Ohio	4.2
25	Oklahoma	3.1
17	Oregon	3.9
11	Pennsylvania	4.5
9	Rhode Island	4.6
23	South Carolina	3.3
38	South Dakota	2.6
5	Tennessee	5.1
30	Texas	2.9
49	Utah	1.5
21	Vermont	3.5
36	Virginia	2.7
16	Washington	4.0
3	West Virginia	5.5
25	Wisconsin	3.1
50	Wyoming	1.3

RANK ORDER

RANK	STATE	PERCENT
1	California	7.2
2	Kentucky	5.9
3	West Virginia	5.5
4	New Mexico	5.4
5	Mississippi	5.1
5	Tennessee	5.1
7	New York	5.0
8	Alabama	4.8
9	Maine	4.6
9	Rhode Island	4.6
11	Massachusetts	4.5
11	Pennsylvania	4.5
13	Arkansas	4.4
13	Louisiana	4.4
15	Ohio	4.2
16	Washington	4.0
17	Hawaii	3.9
17	Michigan	3.9
17	Oregon	3.9
20	Missouri	3.7
21	Delaware	3.5
21	Vermont	3.5
23	South Carolina	3.3
24	Alaska	3.2
25	Florida	3.1
25	Oklahoma	3.1
25	Wisconsin	3.1
28	Iowa	3.0
28	Maryland	3.0
30	Illinois	2.9
30	New Jersey	2.9
30	Texas	2.9
33	Georgia	2.8
33	Kansas	2.8
33	North Carolina	2.8
36	Montana	2.7
36	Virginia	2.7
38	Minnesota	2.6
38	Nevada	2.6
38	South Dakota	2.6
41	Connecticut	2.5
41	Indiana	2.5
43	Arizona	2.3
44	Nebraska	2.2
44	New Hampshire	2.2
46	Colorado	2.0
46	Idaho	2.0
48	North Dakota	1.9
49	Utah	1.5
50	Wyoming	1.3

District of Columbia   7.3

Source: CQ Press using data from U.S. Social Security Administration and
U.S. Department of Health and Human Services
*As of December 2011. Includes recipients of Temporary Assistance to Needy Families (TANF) and/or Supplemental Security Income payments.

Recipients of Temporary Assistance to
Needy Families (TANF) Payments in 2013
National Total = 3,683,855 Monthly Recipients*

ALPHA ORDER

RANK	STATE	RECIPIENTS	% of USA
19	Alabama	44,933	1.2%
43	Alaska	9,436	0.3%
24	Arizona	35,211	1.0%
36	Arkansas	15,135	0.4%
1	California	1,337,981	36.3%
21	Colorado	38,973	1.1%
27	Connecticut	28,849	0.8%
40	Delaware	13,864	0.4%
7	Florida	92,547	2.5%
26	Georgia	33,569	0.9%
30	Hawaii	25,765	0.7%
49	Idaho	2,790	0.1%
20	Illinois	43,892	1.2%
31	Indiana	23,657	0.6%
23	Iowa	36,188	1.0%
34	Kansas	18,560	0.5%
15	Kentucky	60,958	1.7%
37	Louisiana	15,032	0.4%
38	Maine	14,022	0.4%
17	Maryland	51,563	1.4%
8	Massachusetts	89,355	2.4%
10	Michigan	76,014	2.1%
18	Minnesota	46,568	1.3%
32	Mississippi	19,780	0.5%
12	Missouri	74,029	2.0%
45	Montana	7,080	0.2%
41	Nebraska	12,364	0.3%
29	Nevada	26,238	0.7%
44	New Hampshire	7,330	0.2%
11	New Jersey	75,902	2.1%
25	New Mexico	34,828	0.9%
2	New York	274,228	7.4%
22	North Carolina	36,712	1.0%
48	North Dakota	3,546	0.1%
4	Ohio	131,340	3.6%
35	Oklahoma	16,117	0.4%
16	Oregon	59,319	1.6%
3	Pennsylvania	174,695	4.7%
39	Rhode Island	13,931	0.4%
28	South Carolina	27,745	0.8%
47	South Dakota	6,199	0.2%
5	Tennessee	118,084	3.2%
9	Texas	86,148	2.3%
42	Utah	9,761	0.3%
46	Vermont	6,706	0.2%
14	Virginia	61,908	1.7%
6	Washington	104,720	2.8%
33	West Virginia	19,094	0.5%
13	Wisconsin	64,289	1.7%
50	Wyoming	1,216	0.0%

RANK ORDER

RANK	STATE	RECIPIENTS	% of USA
1	California	1,337,981	36.3%
2	New York	274,228	7.4%
3	Pennsylvania	174,695	4.7%
4	Ohio	131,340	3.6%
5	Tennessee	118,084	3.2%
6	Washington	104,720	2.8%
7	Florida	92,547	2.5%
8	Massachusetts	89,355	2.4%
9	Texas	86,148	2.3%
10	Michigan	76,014	2.1%
11	New Jersey	75,902	2.1%
12	Missouri	74,029	2.0%
13	Wisconsin	64,289	1.7%
14	Virginia	61,908	1.7%
15	Kentucky	60,958	1.7%
16	Oregon	59,319	1.6%
17	Maryland	51,563	1.4%
18	Minnesota	46,568	1.3%
19	Alabama	44,933	1.2%
20	Illinois	43,892	1.2%
21	Colorado	38,973	1.1%
22	North Carolina	36,712	1.0%
23	Iowa	36,188	1.0%
24	Arizona	35,211	1.0%
25	New Mexico	34,828	0.9%
26	Georgia	33,569	0.9%
27	Connecticut	28,849	0.8%
28	South Carolina	27,745	0.8%
29	Nevada	26,238	0.7%
30	Hawaii	25,765	0.7%
31	Indiana	23,657	0.6%
32	Mississippi	19,780	0.5%
33	West Virginia	19,094	0.5%
34	Kansas	18,560	0.5%
35	Oklahoma	16,117	0.4%
36	Arkansas	15,135	0.4%
37	Louisiana	15,032	0.4%
38	Maine	14,022	0.4%
39	Rhode Island	13,931	0.4%
40	Delaware	13,864	0.4%
41	Nebraska	12,364	0.3%
42	Utah	9,761	0.3%
43	Alaska	9,436	0.3%
44	New Hampshire	7,330	0.2%
45	Montana	7,080	0.2%
46	Vermont	6,706	0.2%
47	South Dakota	6,199	0.2%
48	North Dakota	3,546	0.1%
49	Idaho	2,790	0.1%
50	Wyoming	1,216	0.0%
	District of Columbia	15,664	0.4%

Source: U.S. Department of Health and Human Services, Administration for Children and Families
  "TANF Caseload Data" (http://www.acf.hhs.gov/programs/ofa/programs/tanf/data-reports)
*As of June 2013. National total includes 40,020 recipients in U.S. territories (35,585 in Puerto Rico).

Percent Change in TANF Recipients: 2012 to 2013

National Percent Change = 8.0% Decrease*

ALPHA ORDER

RANK	STATE	PERCENT CHANGE		RANK	STATE	PERCENT CHANGE
28	Alabama	(9.5)		1	Wyoming	110.4
23	Alaska	(8.4)		2	Wisconsin	7.4
35	Arizona	(12.2)		3	Colorado	5.9
21	Arkansas	(7.2)		4	Kentucky	1.2
10	California	(2.9)		5	Florida	1.0
3	Colorado	5.9		6	Vermont	0.5
9	Connecticut	(1.9)		7	New York	(0.1)
16	Delaware	(5.8)		8	Nevada	(0.9)
5	Florida	1.0		9	Connecticut	(1.9)
15	Georgia	(5.1)		10	California	(2.9)
20	Hawaii	(6.9)		11	Idaho	(3.2)
11	Idaho	(3.2)		12	Minnesota	(4.2)
50	Illinois	(56.1)		13	Nebraska	(4.4)
46	Indiana	(22.7)		14	New Hampshire	(4.8)
30	Iowa	(10.0)		15	Georgia	(5.1)
48	Kansas	(25.3)		16	Delaware	(5.8)
4	Kentucky	1.2		17	West Virginia	(6.0)
45	Louisiana	(22.4)		18	South Dakota	(6.7)
47	Maine	(22.8)		19	New Jersey	(6.8)
32	Maryland	(10.7)		20	Hawaii	(6.9)
23	Massachusetts	(8.4)		21	Arkansas	(7.2)
49	Michigan	(25.5)		22	Virginia	(7.3)
12	Minnesota	(4.2)		23	Alaska	(8.4)
36	Mississippi	(12.4)		23	Massachusetts	(8.4)
27	Missouri	(9.2)		25	North Carolina	(8.6)
30	Montana	(10.0)		26	Pennsylvania	(9.1)
13	Nebraska	(4.4)		27	Missouri	(9.2)
8	Nevada	(0.9)		28	Alabama	(9.5)
14	New Hampshire	(4.8)		29	South Carolina	(9.7)
19	New Jersey	(6.8)		30	Iowa	(10.0)
44	New Mexico	(18.6)		30	Montana	(10.0)
7	New York	(0.1)		32	Maryland	(10.7)
25	North Carolina	(8.6)		33	Rhode Island	(11.0)
34	North Dakota	(11.4)		34	North Dakota	(11.4)
43	Ohio	(17.0)		35	Arizona	(12.2)
37	Oklahoma	(12.6)		36	Mississippi	(12.4)
42	Oregon	(13.8)		37	Oklahoma	(12.6)
26	Pennsylvania	(9.1)		37	Texas	(12.6)
33	Rhode Island	(11.0)		39	Tennessee	(12.8)
29	South Carolina	(9.7)		39	Utah	(12.8)
18	South Dakota	(6.7)		41	Washington	(13.2)
39	Tennessee	(12.8)		42	Oregon	(13.8)
37	Texas	(12.6)		43	Ohio	(17.0)
39	Utah	(12.8)		44	New Mexico	(18.6)
6	Vermont	0.5		45	Louisiana	(22.4)
22	Virginia	(7.3)		46	Indiana	(22.7)
41	Washington	(13.2)		47	Maine	(22.8)
17	West Virginia	(6.0)		48	Kansas	(25.3)
2	Wisconsin	7.4		49	Michigan	(25.5)
1	Wyoming	110.4		50	Illinois	(56.1)

District of Columbia   13.5

Source: CQ Press using data from U.S. Department of Health and Human Services, Administration for Children and Families
"TANF Caseload Data" (http://www.acf.hhs.gov/programs/ofa/programs/tanf/data-reports)
*June 2012 to June 2013. National percent includes recipients in U.S. territories.

TANF Work Participation Rates in 2011

National Rate = 43.6%*

ALPHA ORDER			RANK ORDER		
RANK	STATE	PERCENT	RANK	STATE	PERCENT
24	Alabama	47.5	1	Idaho	91.6
30	Alaska	44.2	2	Nebraska	76.7
38	Arizona	41.1	3	Wisconsin	73.4
29	Arkansas	44.5	4	Wyoming	64.4
27	California	46.6	5	South Dakota	62.9
28	Colorado	44.9	6	Mississippi	61.9
11	Connecticut	58.3	7	North Carolina	61.7
42	Delaware	37.3	8	Montana	61.1
18	Florida	50.8	9	Georgia	60.3
9	Georgia	60.3	10	Iowa	58.4
19	Hawaii	50.0	11	Connecticut	58.3
1	Idaho	91.6	12	Oklahoma	56.4
14	Illinois	53.9	13	Minnesota	55.1
45	Indiana	32.2	14	Illinois	53.9
10	Iowa	58.4	15	North Dakota	52.6
30	Kansas	44.2	16	Pennsylvania	52.2
17	Kentucky	51.8	17	Kentucky	51.8
35	Louisiana	42.0	18	Florida	50.8
44	Maine	32.7	19	Hawaii	50.0
25	Maryland	46.9	19	New Hampshire	50.0
49	Massachusetts	15.6	21	Nevada	48.6
33	Michigan	43.6	22	Texas	48.2
13	Minnesota	55.1	23	West Virginia	47.6
6	Mississippi	61.9	24	Alabama	47.5
50	Missouri	13.5	25	Maryland	46.9
8	Montana	61.1	25	Tennessee	46.9
2	Nebraska	76.7	27	California	46.6
21	Nevada	48.6	28	Colorado	44.9
19	New Hampshire	50.0	29	Arkansas	44.5
46	New Jersey	30.7	30	Alaska	44.2
37	New Mexico	41.5	30	Kansas	44.2
32	New York	44.0	32	New York	44.0
7	North Carolina	61.7	33	Michigan	43.6
15	North Dakota	52.6	34	Utah	43.1
39	Ohio	40.1	35	Louisiana	42.0
12	Oklahoma	56.4	36	South Carolina	41.9
40	Oregon	39.8	37	New Mexico	41.5
16	Pennsylvania	52.2	38	Arizona	41.1
48	Rhode Island	28.1	39	Ohio	40.1
36	South Carolina	41.9	40	Oregon	39.8
5	South Dakota	62.9	41	Virginia	37.6
25	Tennessee	46.9	42	Delaware	37.3
22	Texas	48.2	43	Washington	36.6
34	Utah	43.1	44	Maine	32.7
47	Vermont	30.4	45	Indiana	32.2
41	Virginia	37.6	46	New Jersey	30.7
43	Washington	36.6	47	Vermont	30.4
23	West Virginia	47.6	48	Rhode Island	28.1
3	Wisconsin	73.4	49	Massachusetts	15.6
4	Wyoming	64.4	50	Missouri	13.5
				District of Columbia	22.7

Source: U.S. Department of Health and Human Services, Administration for Children and Families
"Characteristics and Financial Circumstances of TANF Recipients, Fiscal Year 2011 " (Table 28)
(http://www.acf.hhs.gov/programs/ofa/resource/characteristics-financial-circumstances-appendix-fy2011)
*For fiscal year 2011. Percent of parents in TANF families who work for at least 30 hours per week, or 20 hours per week if they have children under age six. National average includes recipients in U.S. territories.

Average Monthly TANF Assistance per Family in 2011

National Average = $386.90*

ALPHA ORDER				RANK ORDER		
RANK	STATE	PER FAMILY		RANK	STATE	PER FAMILY
46	Alabama	$195.70		1	Alaska	$598.40
1	Alaska	598.40		2	Hawaii	555.20
41	Arizona	219.40		3	New York	538.50
49	Arkansas	155.00		4	Utah	511.30
5	California	499.50		5	California	499.50
19	Colorado	366.70		6	New Hampshire	487.90
10	Connecticut	441.90		7	Massachusetts	472.80
36	Delaware	255.60		8	Vermont	465.30
38	Florida	235.40		9	Maryland	455.20
44	Georgia	211.20		10	Connecticut	441.90
2	Hawaii	555.20		11	Wisconsin	441.20
30	Idaho	299.30		12	Oregon	436.10
35	Illinois	255.90		13	Rhode Island	423.50
42	Indiana	216.10		14	Montana	420.30
24	Iowa	318.00		15	Washington	396.40
32	Kansas	284.80		16	Maine	391.60
34	Kentucky	279.10		17	Michigan	387.40
27	Louisiana	304.90		18	South Dakota	385.90
16	Maine	391.60		19	Colorado	366.70
9	Maryland	455.20		20	Wyoming	362.10
7	Massachusetts	472.80		21	Ohio	356.10
17	Michigan	387.40		22	Minnesota	343.20
22	Minnesota	343.20		23	Nevada	342.80
50	Mississippi	148.40		24	Iowa	318.00
39	Missouri	230.20		25	New Jersey	315.50
14	Montana	420.30		26	North Dakota	313.80
31	Nebraska	291.60		27	Louisiana	304.90
23	Nevada	342.80		28	New Mexico	304.80
6	New Hampshire	487.90		29	Pennsylvania	300.20
25	New Jersey	315.50		30	Idaho	299.30
28	New Mexico	304.80		31	Nebraska	291.60
3	New York	538.50		32	Kansas	284.80
43	North Carolina	211.60		33	West Virginia	284.20
26	North Dakota	313.80		34	Kentucky	279.10
21	Ohio	356.10		35	Illinois	255.90
45	Oklahoma	196.40		36	Delaware	255.60
12	Oregon	436.10		37	Virginia	254.50
29	Pennsylvania	300.20		38	Florida	235.40
13	Rhode Island	423.50		39	Missouri	230.20
47	South Carolina	178.90		40	Texas	219.80
18	South Dakota	385.90		41	Arizona	219.40
48	Tennessee	164.90		42	Indiana	216.10
40	Texas	219.80		43	North Carolina	211.60
4	Utah	511.30		44	Georgia	211.20
8	Vermont	465.30		45	Oklahoma	196.40
37	Virginia	254.50		46	Alabama	195.70
15	Washington	396.40		47	South Carolina	178.90
33	West Virginia	284.20		48	Tennessee	164.90
11	Wisconsin	441.20		49	Arkansas	155.00
20	Wyoming	362.10		50	Mississippi	148.40
					District of Columbia	378.80

Source: U.S. Department of Health and Human Services, Administration for Children and Families
"Characteristics and Financial Circumstances of TANF Recipients, Fiscal Year 2011 " (Table 41)
(http://www.acf.hhs.gov/programs/ofa/resource/characteristics-financial-circumstances-appendix-fy2011)
*For fiscal year 2011. National average includes families in U.S. territories.

Percent of Households with Food Insecurity in 2012

National Percent = 14.7% of Households*

ALPHA ORDER				RANK ORDER		
RANK	STATE	PERCENT		RANK	STATE	PERCENT
4	Alabama	17.9		1	Mississippi	20.9
42	Alaska	12.1		2	Arkansas	19.7
18	Arizona	14.9		3	Texas	18.4
2	Arkansas	19.7		4	Alabama	17.9
12	California	15.6		5	North Carolina	17.0
26	Colorado	14.1		6	Georgia	16.9
32	Connecticut	13.4		7	Missouri	16.7
44	Delaware	11.6		8	Nevada	16.6
20	Florida	14.8		9	Tennessee	16.2
6	Georgia	16.9		10	Ohio	16.1
28	Hawaii	14.0		11	Louisiana	15.7
24	Idaho	14.3		12	California	15.6
36	Illinois	13.0		12	Kentucky	15.6
31	Indiana	13.5		14	Rhode Island	15.4
40	Iowa	12.6		14	South Carolina	15.4
23	Kansas	14.4		16	Oklahoma	15.3
12	Kentucky	15.6		17	New Mexico	15.2
11	Louisiana	15.7		18	Arizona	14.9
18	Maine	14.9		18	Maine	14.9
36	Maryland	13.0		20	Florida	14.8
45	Massachusetts	11.4		20	Utah	14.8
32	Michigan	13.4		22	Washington	14.6
47	Minnesota	10.6		23	Kansas	14.4
1	Mississippi	20.9		24	Idaho	14.3
7	Missouri	16.7		25	West Virginia	14.2
26	Montana	14.1		26	Colorado	14.1
32	Nebraska	13.4		26	Montana	14.1
8	Nevada	16.6		28	Hawaii	14.0
48	New Hampshire	9.9		29	Wyoming	13.8
42	New Jersey	12.1		30	Oregon	13.6
17	New Mexico	15.2		31	Indiana	13.5
35	New York	13.2		32	Connecticut	13.4
5	North Carolina	17.0		32	Michigan	13.4
50	North Dakota	8.7		32	Nebraska	13.4
10	Ohio	16.1		35	New York	13.2
16	Oklahoma	15.3		36	Illinois	13.0
30	Oregon	13.6		36	Maryland	13.0
41	Pennsylvania	12.3		38	South Dakota	12.9
14	Rhode Island	15.4		39	Vermont	12.7
14	South Carolina	15.4		40	Iowa	12.6
38	South Dakota	12.9		41	Pennsylvania	12.3
9	Tennessee	16.2		42	Alaska	12.1
3	Texas	18.4		42	New Jersey	12.1
20	Utah	14.8		44	Delaware	11.6
39	Vermont	12.7		45	Massachusetts	11.4
49	Virginia	9.2		46	Wisconsin	11.2
22	Washington	14.6		47	Minnesota	10.6
25	West Virginia	14.2		48	New Hampshire	9.9
46	Wisconsin	11.2		49	Virginia	9.2
29	Wyoming	13.8		50	North Dakota	8.7
					District of Columbia	12.0

Source: U.S. Department of Agriculture, Economic Research Service
"Household Food Security in the United States, 2012" (www.ers.usda.gov/publications/err-economic-research-report/err155.aspx)
*Three-year average for 2010-2012. Refers to households for which access to enough food is limited by a lack of money and other resources. About one-third of food-insecure households have very low food security, meaning that at times the food intake of some household members is reduced and their normal eating patterns are disrupted.

Supplemental Nutrition Assistance Program Benefits in 2013

National Total = $76,067,237,586*

ALPHA ORDER

RANK	STATE	BENEFITS	% of USA
19	Alabama	$1,414,951,864	1.9%
45	Alaska	189,565,646	0.2%
13	Arizona	1,648,236,258	2.2%
30	Arkansas	731,845,896	1.0%
1	California	7,558,333,190	9.9%
28	Colorado	823,529,608	1.1%
31	Connecticut	707,654,612	0.9%
43	Delaware	235,028,481	0.3%
3	Florida	5,906,158,957	7.8%
6	Georgia	3,188,743,586	4.2%
36	Hawaii	494,182,027	0.6%
40	Idaho	346,782,947	0.5%
5	Illinois	3,378,095,657	4.4%
15	Indiana	1,461,136,176	1.9%
33	Iowa	586,542,123	0.8%
37	Kansas	474,255,829	0.6%
22	Kentucky	1,332,998,664	1.8%
14	Louisiana	1,479,828,133	1.9%
39	Maine	367,069,888	0.5%
25	Maryland	1,178,661,930	1.5%
20	Massachusetts	1,394,535,579	1.8%
8	Michigan	2,911,624,110	3.8%
29	Minnesota	771,699,773	1.0%
26	Mississippi	993,077,956	1.3%
17	Missouri	1,428,882,352	1.9%
44	Montana	192,259,685	0.3%
42	Nebraska	264,636,314	0.3%
34	Nevada	535,230,693	0.7%
47	New Hampshire	162,970,800	0.2%
18	New Jersey	1,419,226,622	1.9%
32	New Mexico	679,481,811	0.9%
4	New York	5,621,405,246	7.4%
10	North Carolina	2,491,197,794	3.3%
49	North Dakota	85,530,266	0.1%
7	Ohio	2,923,160,707	3.8%
27	Oklahoma	958,684,325	1.3%
23	Oregon	1,250,684,645	1.6%
9	Pennsylvania	2,748,346,529	3.6%
41	Rhode Island	302,979,333	0.4%
21	South Carolina	1,381,782,118	1.8%
46	South Dakota	165,040,184	0.2%
11	Tennessee	2,127,681,953	2.8%
2	Texas	5,934,441,831	7.8%
38	Utah	377,903,214	0.5%
48	Vermont	150,054,164	0.2%
16	Virginia	1,442,442,319	1.9%
12	Washington	1,678,737,077	2.2%
35	West Virginia	504,485,785	0.7%
24	Wisconsin	1,198,302,422	1.6%
50	Wyoming	56,980,056	0.1%

RANK ORDER

RANK	STATE	BENEFITS	% of USA
1	California	$7,558,333,190	9.9%
2	Texas	5,934,441,831	7.8%
3	Florida	5,906,158,957	7.8%
4	New York	5,621,405,246	7.4%
5	Illinois	3,378,095,657	4.4%
6	Georgia	3,188,743,586	4.2%
7	Ohio	2,923,160,707	3.8%
8	Michigan	2,911,624,110	3.8%
9	Pennsylvania	2,748,346,529	3.6%
10	North Carolina	2,491,197,794	3.3%
11	Tennessee	2,127,681,953	2.8%
12	Washington	1,678,737,077	2.2%
13	Arizona	1,648,236,258	2.2%
14	Louisiana	1,479,828,133	1.9%
15	Indiana	1,461,136,176	1.9%
16	Virginia	1,442,442,319	1.9%
17	Missouri	1,428,882,352	1.9%
18	New Jersey	1,419,226,622	1.9%
19	Alabama	1,414,951,864	1.9%
20	Massachusetts	1,394,535,579	1.8%
21	South Carolina	1,381,782,118	1.8%
22	Kentucky	1,332,998,664	1.8%
23	Oregon	1,250,684,645	1.6%
24	Wisconsin	1,198,302,422	1.6%
25	Maryland	1,178,661,930	1.5%
26	Mississippi	993,077,956	1.3%
27	Oklahoma	958,684,325	1.3%
28	Colorado	823,529,608	1.1%
29	Minnesota	771,699,773	1.0%
30	Arkansas	731,845,896	1.0%
31	Connecticut	707,654,612	0.9%
32	New Mexico	679,481,811	0.9%
33	Iowa	586,542,123	0.8%
34	Nevada	535,230,693	0.7%
35	West Virginia	504,485,785	0.7%
36	Hawaii	494,182,027	0.6%
37	Kansas	474,255,829	0.6%
38	Utah	377,903,214	0.5%
39	Maine	367,069,888	0.5%
40	Idaho	346,782,947	0.5%
41	Rhode Island	302,979,333	0.4%
42	Nebraska	264,636,314	0.3%
43	Delaware	235,028,481	0.3%
44	Montana	192,259,685	0.3%
45	Alaska	189,565,646	0.2%
46	South Dakota	165,040,184	0.2%
47	New Hampshire	162,970,800	0.2%
48	Vermont	150,054,164	0.2%
49	North Dakota	85,530,266	0.1%
50	Wyoming	56,980,056	0.1%
	District of Columbia	235,020,570	0.3%

Source: U.S. Department of Agriculture, Food, Nutrition and Consumer Services
  "Supplemental Nutrition Assistance Program" (http://www.fns.usda.gov/pd/snapmain.htm)
*Preliminary data for fiscal year 2013. National total includes $175,149,881 to U.S. territories. Costs are for benefits only and exclude administrative expenditures. Program formerly called the Food Stamp Program.

Monthly Supplemental Nutrition Assistance Program Recipients in 2013

National Total = 47,636,084 Recipients*

ALPHA ORDER

ALPHA ORDER

RANK	STATE	RECIPIENTS	% of USA
18	Alabama	915,322	1.9%
48	Alaska	91,364	0.2%
13	Arizona	1,111,105	2.3%
30	Arkansas	504,621	1.1%
1	California	4,159,031	8.7%
29	Colorado	507,934	1.1%
32	Connecticut	425,320	0.9%
43	Delaware	153,137	0.3%
3	Florida	3,556,473	7.5%
6	Georgia	1,948,189	4.1%
40	Hawaii	189,350	0.4%
39	Idaho	227,006	0.5%
5	Illinois	2,040,053	4.3%
17	Indiana	926,011	1.9%
33	Iowa	420,344	0.9%
36	Kansas	316,983	0.7%
22	Kentucky	872,439	1.8%
15	Louisiana	940,100	2.0%
38	Maine	249,119	0.5%
25	Maryland	771,021	1.6%
19	Massachusetts	887,619	1.9%
9	Michigan	1,775,646	3.7%
28	Minnesota	552,928	1.2%
26	Mississippi	668,624	1.4%
16	Missouri	929,943	2.0%
44	Montana	128,531	0.3%
42	Nebraska	179,711	0.4%
34	Nevada	360,953	0.8%
45	New Hampshire	117,315	0.2%
20	New Jersey	876,266	1.8%
31	New Mexico	440,362	0.9%
4	New York	3,170,465	6.7%
10	North Carolina	1,703,700	3.6%
49	North Dakota	56,523	0.1%
7	Ohio	1,824,675	3.8%
27	Oklahoma	621,831	1.3%
24	Oregon	817,575	1.7%
8	Pennsylvania	1,784,790	3.7%
41	Rhode Island	179,925	0.4%
21	South Carolina	875,866	1.8%
46	South Dakota	104,052	0.2%
11	Tennessee	1,342,089	2.8%
2	Texas	4,041,891	8.5%
37	Utah	251,626	0.5%
47	Vermont	100,536	0.2%
14	Virginia	940,932	2.0%
12	Washington	1,113,441	2.3%
35	West Virginia	350,695	0.7%
23	Wisconsin	856,730	1.8%
50	Wyoming	38,046	0.1%

RANK ORDER

RANK	STATE	RECIPIENTS	% of USA
1	California	4,159,031	8.7%
2	Texas	4,041,891	8.5%
3	Florida	3,556,473	7.5%
4	New York	3,170,465	6.7%
5	Illinois	2,040,053	4.3%
6	Georgia	1,948,189	4.1%
7	Ohio	1,824,675	3.8%
8	Pennsylvania	1,784,790	3.7%
9	Michigan	1,775,646	3.7%
10	North Carolina	1,703,700	3.6%
11	Tennessee	1,342,089	2.8%
12	Washington	1,113,441	2.3%
13	Arizona	1,111,105	2.3%
14	Virginia	940,932	2.0%
15	Louisiana	940,100	2.0%
16	Missouri	929,943	2.0%
17	Indiana	926,011	1.9%
18	Alabama	915,322	1.9%
19	Massachusetts	887,619	1.9%
20	New Jersey	876,266	1.8%
21	South Carolina	875,866	1.8%
22	Kentucky	872,439	1.8%
23	Wisconsin	856,730	1.8%
24	Oregon	817,575	1.7%
25	Maryland	771,021	1.6%
26	Mississippi	668,624	1.4%
27	Oklahoma	621,831	1.3%
28	Minnesota	552,928	1.2%
29	Colorado	507,934	1.1%
30	Arkansas	504,621	1.1%
31	New Mexico	440,362	0.9%
32	Connecticut	425,320	0.9%
33	Iowa	420,344	0.9%
34	Nevada	360,953	0.8%
35	West Virginia	350,695	0.7%
36	Kansas	316,983	0.7%
37	Utah	251,626	0.5%
38	Maine	249,119	0.5%
39	Idaho	227,006	0.5%
40	Hawaii	189,350	0.4%
41	Rhode Island	179,925	0.4%
42	Nebraska	179,711	0.4%
43	Delaware	153,137	0.3%
44	Montana	128,531	0.3%
45	New Hampshire	117,315	0.2%
46	South Dakota	104,052	0.2%
47	Vermont	100,536	0.2%
48	Alaska	91,364	0.2%
49	North Dakota	56,523	0.1%
50	Wyoming	38,046	0.1%
	District of Columbia	144,889	0.3%

Source: U.S. Department of Agriculture, Food, Nutrition and Consumer Services
    "Supplemental Nutrition Assistance Program" (http://www.fns.usda.gov/pd/snapmain.htm)
*Preliminary for fiscal year 2013. National total includes 72,990 recipients in U.S. territories. Program was formerly called the
Food Stamp Program.

Average Monthly Supplemental Nutrition Assistance Program Benefit per Recipient in 2013
National Average = $133.07 per Recipient*

<u>ALPHA ORDER</u>

RANK	STATE	PER RECIPIENT
20	Alabama	$128.82
2	Alaska	172.90
39	Arizona	123.62
45	Arkansas	120.86
3	California	151.44
11	Colorado	135.11
6	Connecticut	138.65
25	Delaware	127.90
7	Florida	138.39
10	Georgia	136.40
1	Hawaii	217.49
30	Idaho	127.30
8	Illinois	137.99
16	Indiana	131.49
49	Iowa	116.28
35	Kansas	124.68
29	Kentucky	127.33
18	Louisiana	131.18
41	Maine	122.79
28	Maryland	127.39
19	Massachusetts	130.92
9	Michigan	136.65
48	Minnesota	116.31
38	Mississippi	123.77
24	Missouri	128.04
36	Montana	124.65
42	Nebraska	122.71
40	Nevada	123.57
50	New Hampshire	115.76
12	New Jersey	134.97
21	New Mexico	128.58
4	New York	147.75
44	North Carolina	121.85
31	North Dakota	126.10
13	Ohio	133.50
22	Oklahoma	128.48
27	Oregon	127.48
23	Pennsylvania	128.32
5	Rhode Island	140.33
17	South Carolina	131.47
14	South Dakota	132.18
15	Tennessee	132.11
43	Texas	122.35
33	Utah	125.15
37	Vermont	124.38
26	Virginia	127.75
32	Washington	125.64
46	West Virginia	119.88
47	Wisconsin	116.56
34	Wyoming	124.80

<u>RANK ORDER</u>

RANK	STATE	PER RECIPIENT
1	Hawaii	$217.49
2	Alaska	172.90
3	California	151.44
4	New York	147.75
5	Rhode Island	140.33
6	Connecticut	138.65
7	Florida	138.39
8	Illinois	137.99
9	Michigan	136.65
10	Georgia	136.40
11	Colorado	135.11
12	New Jersey	134.97
13	Ohio	133.50
14	South Dakota	132.18
15	Tennessee	132.11
16	Indiana	131.49
17	South Carolina	131.47
18	Louisiana	131.18
19	Massachusetts	130.92
20	Alabama	128.82
21	New Mexico	128.58
22	Oklahoma	128.48
23	Pennsylvania	128.32
24	Missouri	128.04
25	Delaware	127.90
26	Virginia	127.75
27	Oregon	127.48
28	Maryland	127.39
29	Kentucky	127.33
30	Idaho	127.30
31	North Dakota	126.10
32	Washington	125.64
33	Utah	125.15
34	Wyoming	124.80
35	Kansas	124.68
36	Montana	124.65
37	Vermont	124.38
38	Mississippi	123.77
39	Arizona	123.62
40	Nevada	123.57
41	Maine	122.79
42	Nebraska	122.71
43	Texas	122.35
44	North Carolina	121.85
45	Arkansas	120.86
46	West Virginia	119.88
47	Wisconsin	116.56
48	Minnesota	116.31
49	Iowa	116.28
50	New Hampshire	115.76
	District of Columbia	135.17

Source: U.S. Department of Agriculture, Food, Nutrition and Consumer Services
    "Supplemental Nutrition Assistance Program" (http://www.fns.usda.gov/pd/snapmain.htm)
*Preliminary for fiscal year 2013. National average includes recipients in U.S. territories. Program formerly called the Food Stamp Program.

Percent of Population Receiving
Supplemental Nutrition Assistance Program Benefits in 2013
National Percent = 15.0%*

RANK	STATE	PERCENT
8	Alabama	18.9
37	Alaska	12.4
17	Arizona	16.8
15	Arkansas	17.1
42	California	10.8
45	Colorado	9.6
39	Connecticut	11.8
18	Delaware	16.5
12	Florida	18.2
7	Georgia	19.5
32	Hawaii	13.5
28	Idaho	14.1
23	Illinois	15.8
28	Indiana	14.1
31	Iowa	13.6
41	Kansas	11.0
6	Kentucky	19.8
5	Louisiana	20.3
10	Maine	18.8
34	Maryland	13.0
33	Massachusetts	13.3
13	Michigan	17.9
43	Minnesota	10.2
1	Mississippi	22.4
25	Missouri	15.4
36	Montana	12.7
45	Nebraska	9.6
35	Nevada	12.9
47	New Hampshire	8.9
44	New Jersey	9.8
2	New Mexico	21.1
19	New York	16.1
14	North Carolina	17.3
49	North Dakota	7.8
23	Ohio	15.8
19	Oklahoma	16.1
3	Oregon	20.8
30	Pennsylvania	14.0
15	Rhode Island	17.1
11	South Carolina	18.3
38	South Dakota	12.3
4	Tennessee	20.7
26	Texas	15.3
48	Utah	8.7
21	Vermont	16.0
40	Virginia	11.4
21	Washington	16.0
8	West Virginia	18.9
27	Wisconsin	14.9
50	Wyoming	6.5

RANK	STATE	PERCENT
1	Mississippi	22.4
2	New Mexico	21.1
3	Oregon	20.8
4	Tennessee	20.7
5	Louisiana	20.3
6	Kentucky	19.8
7	Georgia	19.5
8	Alabama	18.9
8	West Virginia	18.9
10	Maine	18.8
11	South Carolina	18.3
12	Florida	18.2
13	Michigan	17.9
14	North Carolina	17.3
15	Arkansas	17.1
15	Rhode Island	17.1
17	Arizona	16.8
18	Delaware	16.5
19	New York	16.1
19	Oklahoma	16.1
21	Vermont	16.0
21	Washington	16.0
23	Illinois	15.8
23	Ohio	15.8
25	Missouri	15.4
26	Texas	15.3
27	Wisconsin	14.9
28	Idaho	14.1
28	Indiana	14.1
30	Pennsylvania	14.0
31	Iowa	13.6
32	Hawaii	13.5
33	Massachusetts	13.3
34	Maryland	13.0
35	Nevada	12.9
36	Montana	12.7
37	Alaska	12.4
38	South Dakota	12.3
39	Connecticut	11.8
40	Virginia	11.4
41	Kansas	11.0
42	California	10.8
43	Minnesota	10.2
44	New Jersey	9.8
45	Colorado	9.6
45	Nebraska	9.6
47	New Hampshire	8.9
48	Utah	8.7
49	North Dakota	7.8
50	Wyoming	6.5
	District of Columbia	22.4

Source: CQ Press using data from U.S. Department of Agriculture, Food, Nutrition and Consumer Services
  "Supplemental Nutrition Assistance Program" (http://www.fns.usda.gov/pd/snapmain.htm)
*Preliminary data for fiscal year 2013. National rate does not include recipients in U.S. territories. Program formerly called the
Food Stamp Program.

Percent of Households Receiving
Supplemental Nutrition Assistance Program Benefits in 2013
National Percent = 19.9% of Households*

ALPHA ORDER

RANK	STATE	PERCENT
14	Alabama	22.8
37	Alaska	15.2
22	Arizona	19.9
25	Arkansas	19.6
37	California	15.2
45	Colorado	11.6
33	Connecticut	17.2
19	Delaware	21.2
3	Florida	27.0
6	Georgia	25.7
17	Hawaii	21.4
34	Idaho	16.8
18	Illinois	21.3
34	Indiana	16.8
36	Iowa	16.2
43	Kansas	13.4
8	Kentucky	24.6
7	Louisiana	24.8
12	Maine	23.5
29	Maryland	18.2
24	Massachusetts	19.8
10	Michigan	23.8
44	Minnesota	13.0
2	Mississippi	28.0
28	Missouri	18.5
40	Montana	14.5
47	Nebraska	10.8
32	Nevada	17.3
47	New Hampshire	10.8
42	New Jersey	13.5
5	New Mexico	25.8
11	New York	23.6
20	North Carolina	21.1
49	North Dakota	9.0
26	Ohio	19.5
22	Oklahoma	19.9
1	Oregon	29.8
31	Pennsylvania	17.5
9	Rhode Island	24.3
13	South Carolina	23.3
41	South Dakota	14.0
4	Tennessee	26.7
27	Texas	18.7
46	Utah	11.3
21	Vermont	20.2
39	Virginia	15.0
16	Washington	22.4
15	West Virginia	22.5
29	Wisconsin	18.2
50	Wyoming	7.3

RANK ORDER

RANK	STATE	PERCENT
1	Oregon	29.8
2	Mississippi	28.0
3	Florida	27.0
4	Tennessee	26.7
5	New Mexico	25.8
6	Georgia	25.7
7	Louisiana	24.8
8	Kentucky	24.6
9	Rhode Island	24.3
10	Michigan	23.8
11	New York	23.6
12	Maine	23.5
13	South Carolina	23.3
14	Alabama	22.8
15	West Virginia	22.5
16	Washington	22.4
17	Hawaii	21.4
18	Illinois	21.3
19	Delaware	21.2
20	North Carolina	21.1
21	Vermont	20.2
22	Arizona	19.9
22	Oklahoma	19.9
24	Massachusetts	19.8
25	Arkansas	19.6
26	Ohio	19.5
27	Texas	18.7
28	Missouri	18.5
29	Maryland	18.2
29	Wisconsin	18.2
31	Pennsylvania	17.5
32	Nevada	17.3
33	Connecticut	17.2
34	Idaho	16.8
34	Indiana	16.8
36	Iowa	16.2
37	Alaska	15.2
37	California	15.2
39	Virginia	15.0
40	Montana	14.5
41	South Dakota	14.0
42	New Jersey	13.5
43	Kansas	13.4
44	Minnesota	13.0
45	Colorado	11.6
46	Utah	11.3
47	Nebraska	10.8
47	New Hampshire	10.8
49	North Dakota	9.0
50	Wyoming	7.3

District of Columbia	30.7

Source: CQ Press using data from U.S. Department of Agriculture, Food, Nutrition and Consumer Services
"Supplemental Nutrition Assistance Program" (http://www.fns.usda.gov/pd/snapmain.htm)
*Preliminary data for fiscal year 2013. Percent calculated using 2012 estimated total households. National percent excludes
households in U.S. territories. Program formerly called the Food Stamp Program.

Average Monthly Participants in Women, Infants, and Children (WIC) Special Nutrition Program in 2013
National Total = 8,662,538 Participants*

ALPHA ORDER

RANK	STATE	PARTICIPANTS	% of USA
20	Alabama	139,001	1.6%
43	Alaska	23,253	0.3%
12	Arizona	182,501	2.1%
30	Arkansas	89,777	1.0%
1	California	1,431,778	16.5%
28	Colorado	96,874	1.1%
36	Connecticut	54,250	0.6%
44	Delaware	20,787	0.2%
4	Florida	483,566	5.6%
5	Georgia	289,512	3.3%
40	Hawaii	36,370	0.4%
38	Idaho	43,292	0.5%
6	Illinois	280,463	3.2%
14	Indiana	159,525	1.8%
34	Iowa	65,876	0.8%
32	Kansas	70,615	0.8%
21	Kentucky	129,710	1.5%
19	Louisiana	139,856	1.6%
41	Maine	24,369	0.3%
17	Maryland	144,628	1.7%
24	Massachusetts	119,954	1.4%
9	Michigan	254,126	2.9%
22	Minnesota	124,744	1.4%
29	Mississippi	91,652	1.1%
18	Missouri	140,821	1.6%
46	Montana	19,848	0.2%
39	Nebraska	40,151	0.5%
31	Nevada	75,011	0.9%
47	New Hampshire	15,679	0.2%
13	New Jersey	167,872	1.9%
35	New Mexico	61,405	0.7%
3	New York	513,299	5.9%
7	North Carolina	264,750	3.1%
49	North Dakota	13,273	0.2%
8	Ohio	263,570	3.0%
25	Oklahoma	118,552	1.4%
27	Oregon	107,859	1.2%
10	Pennsylvania	253,258	2.9%
42	Rhode Island	23,416	0.3%
23	South Carolina	124,287	1.4%
45	South Dakota	20,430	0.2%
15	Tennessee	159,426	1.8%
2	Texas	955,072	11.0%
33	Utah	66,726	0.8%
48	Vermont	14,836	0.2%
16	Virginia	155,935	1.8%
11	Washington	191,753	2.2%
37	West Virginia	46,402	0.5%
26	Wisconsin	113,763	1.3%
50	Wyoming	11,980	0.1%

RANK ORDER

RANK	STATE	PARTICIPANTS	% of USA
1	California	1,431,778	16.5%
2	Texas	955,072	11.0%
3	New York	513,299	5.9%
4	Florida	483,566	5.6%
5	Georgia	289,512	3.3%
6	Illinois	280,463	3.2%
7	North Carolina	264,750	3.1%
8	Ohio	263,570	3.0%
9	Michigan	254,126	2.9%
10	Pennsylvania	253,258	2.9%
11	Washington	191,753	2.2%
12	Arizona	182,501	2.1%
13	New Jersey	167,872	1.9%
14	Indiana	159,525	1.8%
15	Tennessee	159,426	1.8%
16	Virginia	155,935	1.8%
17	Maryland	144,628	1.7%
18	Missouri	140,821	1.6%
19	Louisiana	139,856	1.6%
20	Alabama	139,001	1.6%
21	Kentucky	129,710	1.5%
22	Minnesota	124,744	1.4%
23	South Carolina	124,287	1.4%
24	Massachusetts	119,954	1.4%
25	Oklahoma	118,552	1.4%
26	Wisconsin	113,763	1.3%
27	Oregon	107,859	1.2%
28	Colorado	96,874	1.1%
29	Mississippi	91,652	1.1%
30	Arkansas	89,777	1.0%
31	Nevada	75,011	0.9%
32	Kansas	70,615	0.8%
33	Utah	66,726	0.8%
34	Iowa	65,876	0.8%
35	New Mexico	61,405	0.7%
36	Connecticut	54,250	0.6%
37	West Virginia	46,402	0.5%
38	Idaho	43,292	0.5%
39	Nebraska	40,151	0.5%
40	Hawaii	36,370	0.4%
41	Maine	24,369	0.3%
42	Rhode Island	23,416	0.3%
43	Alaska	23,253	0.3%
44	Delaware	20,787	0.2%
45	South Dakota	20,430	0.2%
46	Montana	19,848	0.2%
47	New Hampshire	15,679	0.2%
48	Vermont	14,836	0.2%
49	North Dakota	13,273	0.2%
50	Wyoming	11,980	0.1%
	District of Columbia	15,674	0.2%

Source: U.S. Department of Agriculture, Food, Nutrition and Consumer Services
"WIC Program (http://www.fns.usda.gov/pd/wicmain.htm)
*Preliminary data for fiscal year 2013. National total includes 211,014 participants in outlying areas not shown separately (Puerto Rico has 187,850 participants).

Average Monthly Benefit per Participant in Women, Infants, and Children (WIC) Special Nutrition Program in 2013
National Average = $43.46*

ALPHA ORDER

RANK	STATE	AVERAGE BENEFIT
11	Alabama	$46.58
5	Alaska	50.43
25	Arizona	42.88
13	Arkansas	46.47
15	California	46.05
32	Colorado	40.61
28	Connecticut	41.80
29	Delaware	41.77
20	Florida	44.39
17	Georgia	45.50
4	Hawaii	51.97
43	Idaho	36.90
9	Illinois	48.13
41	Indiana	37.26
47	Iowa	33.03
38	Kansas	37.78
36	Kentucky	40.02
6	Louisiana	50.20
31	Maine	41.02
23	Maryland	43.10
36	Massachusetts	40.02
33	Michigan	40.46
18	Minnesota	45.37
2	Mississippi	53.88
40	Missouri	37.60
26	Montana	42.79
19	Nebraska	44.79
39	Nevada	37.62
48	New Hampshire	32.95
3	New Jersey	53.50
42	New Mexico	36.98
1	New York	56.89
24	North Carolina	42.93
8	North Dakota	49.67
45	Ohio	35.39
34	Oklahoma	40.38
35	Oregon	40.12
16	Pennsylvania	45.55
12	Rhode Island	46.51
14	South Carolina	46.38
10	South Dakota	47.47
27	Tennessee	41.98
50	Texas	26.47
44	Utah	36.10
7	Vermont	49.87
46	Virginia	33.28
30	Washington	41.16
21	West Virginia	43.94
22	Wisconsin	43.33
49	Wyoming	31.67

RANK ORDER

RANK	STATE	AVERAGE BENEFIT
1	New York	$56.89
2	Mississippi	53.88
3	New Jersey	53.50
4	Hawaii	51.97
5	Alaska	50.43
6	Louisiana	50.20
7	Vermont	49.87
8	North Dakota	49.67
9	Illinois	48.13
10	South Dakota	47.47
11	Alabama	46.58
12	Rhode Island	46.51
13	Arkansas	46.47
14	South Carolina	46.38
15	California	46.05
16	Pennsylvania	45.55
17	Georgia	45.50
18	Minnesota	45.37
19	Nebraska	44.79
20	Florida	44.39
21	West Virginia	43.94
22	Wisconsin	43.33
23	Maryland	43.10
24	North Carolina	42.93
25	Arizona	42.88
26	Montana	42.79
27	Tennessee	41.98
28	Connecticut	41.80
29	Delaware	41.77
30	Washington	41.16
31	Maine	41.02
32	Colorado	40.61
33	Michigan	40.46
34	Oklahoma	40.38
35	Oregon	40.12
36	Kentucky	40.02
36	Massachusetts	40.02
38	Kansas	37.78
39	Nevada	37.62
40	Missouri	37.60
41	Indiana	37.26
42	New Mexico	36.98
43	Idaho	36.90
44	Utah	36.10
45	Ohio	35.39
46	Virginia	33.28
47	Iowa	33.03
48	New Hampshire	32.95
49	Wyoming	31.67
50	Texas	26.47
	District of Columbia	43.58

Source: U.S. Department of Agriculture, Food, Nutrition and Consumer Services
"WIC Program (http://www.fns.usda.gov/pd/wicmain.htm)
*Preliminary data for fiscal year 2013. National average includes outlying areas and Indian reservations not shown separately.

Percent of Public Elementary and Secondary School Students Eligible for Free or Reduced-Price Meals in 2011
National Percent = 47.9%*

ALPHA ORDER

RANK	STATE	PERCENT
10	Alabama	54.9
39	Alaska	38.4
24	Arizona	45.1
4	Arkansas	60.5
12	California	53.7
35	Colorado	39.9
47	Connecticut	34.0
19	Delaware	47.7
8	Florida	56.0
6	Georgia	57.4
21	Hawaii	46.8
25	Idaho	45.0
26	Illinois	44.3
22	Indiana	46.6
37	Iowa	38.9
19	Kansas	47.7
7	Kentucky	56.6
3	Louisiana	66.2
28	Maine	43.0
33	Maryland	40.1
46	Massachusetts	34.2
23	Michigan	46.3
45	Minnesota	36.5
1	Mississippi	70.6
26	Missouri	44.3
32	Montana	40.8
30	Nebraska	42.6
15	Nevada	50.3
50	New Hampshire	25.2
48	New Jersey	32.8
2	New Mexico	67.6
18	New York	48.1
15	North Carolina	50.3
49	North Dakota	31.7
30	Ohio	42.6
4	Oklahoma	60.5
14	Oregon	50.6
37	Pennsylvania	38.9
29	Rhode Island	42.9
11	South Carolina	54.5
41	South Dakota	37.1
9	Tennessee	55.0
17	Texas	50.1
40	Utah	38.2
43	Vermont	36.8
44	Virginia	36.7
33	Washington	40.1
13	West Virginia	51.5
36	Wisconsin	39.3
41	Wyoming	37.1

RANK ORDER

RANK	STATE	PERCENT
1	Mississippi	70.6
2	New Mexico	67.6
3	Louisiana	66.2
4	Arkansas	60.5
4	Oklahoma	60.5
6	Georgia	57.4
7	Kentucky	56.6
8	Florida	56.0
9	Tennessee	55.0
10	Alabama	54.9
11	South Carolina	54.5
12	California	53.7
13	West Virginia	51.5
14	Oregon	50.6
15	Nevada	50.3
15	North Carolina	50.3
17	Texas	50.1
18	New York	48.1
19	Delaware	47.7
19	Kansas	47.7
21	Hawaii	46.8
22	Indiana	46.6
23	Michigan	46.3
24	Arizona	45.1
25	Idaho	45.0
26	Illinois	44.3
26	Missouri	44.3
28	Maine	43.0
29	Rhode Island	42.9
30	Nebraska	42.6
30	Ohio	42.6
32	Montana	40.8
33	Maryland	40.1
33	Washington	40.1
35	Colorado	39.9
36	Wisconsin	39.3
37	Iowa	38.9
37	Pennsylvania	38.9
39	Alaska	38.4
40	Utah	38.2
41	South Dakota	37.1
41	Wyoming	37.1
43	Vermont	36.8
44	Virginia	36.7
45	Minnesota	36.5
46	Massachusetts	34.2
47	Connecticut	34.0
48	New Jersey	32.8
49	North Dakota	31.7
50	New Hampshire	25.2

District of Columbia	73.0

Source: CQ Press using data from U.S. Department of Education, National Center for Education Statistics
"Common Core of Data (CCD) Database" (http://nces.ed.gov/ccd/)
*For school year 2010-2011.

Child Support Collections in 2012

National Total = $27,360,483,997*

ALPHA ORDER

RANK	STATE	COLLECTIONS	% of USA
29	Alabama	$290,572,812	1.1%
41	Alaska	99,583,102	0.4%
24	Arizona	323,093,647	1.2%
32	Arkansas	219,645,476	0.8%
2	California	2,208,751,449	8.1%
28	Colorado	293,245,061	1.1%
31	Connecticut	245,369,851	0.9%
46	Delaware	74,451,056	0.3%
5	Florida	1,466,273,345	5.4%
11	Georgia	647,282,139	2.4%
42	Hawaii	96,191,283	0.4%
38	Idaho	151,981,715	0.6%
9	Illinois	802,971,010	2.9%
17	Indiana	580,545,272	2.1%
26	Iowa	313,319,066	1.1%
36	Kansas	189,363,684	0.7%
21	Kentucky	389,349,338	1.4%
22	Louisiana	380,063,605	1.4%
40	Maine	99,657,835	0.4%
20	Maryland	514,934,157	1.9%
15	Massachusetts	604,380,725	2.2%
6	Michigan	1,320,275,023	4.8%
16	Minnesota	582,324,840	2.1%
27	Mississippi	299,798,756	1.1%
18	Missouri	573,548,550	2.1%
49	Montana	59,935,863	0.2%
33	Nebraska	200,318,373	0.7%
37	Nevada	171,931,117	0.6%
45	New Hampshire	83,176,973	0.3%
8	New Jersey	1,131,352,192	4.1%
39	New Mexico	112,170,094	0.4%
3	New York	1,703,265,881	6.2%
10	North Carolina	662,096,486	2.4%
43	North Dakota	89,592,169	0.3%
4	Ohio	1,697,143,384	6.2%
25	Oklahoma	315,117,057	1.2%
23	Oregon	349,474,272	1.3%
7	Pennsylvania	1,320,237,119	4.8%
47	Rhode Island	66,339,200	0.2%
30	South Carolina	255,318,273	0.9%
44	South Dakota	86,280,610	0.3%
19	Tennessee	555,988,101	2.0%
1	Texas	3,320,420,591	12.1%
35	Utah	194,717,309	0.7%
50	Vermont	45,987,161	0.2%
14	Virginia	606,627,426	2.2%
12	Washington	644,113,060	2.4%
34	West Virginia	195,410,794	0.7%
13	Wisconsin	611,876,491	2.2%
48	Wyoming	64,255,732	0.2%

RANK ORDER

RANK	STATE	COLLECTIONS	% of USA
1	Texas	$3,320,420,591	12.1%
2	California	2,208,751,449	8.1%
3	New York	1,703,265,881	6.2%
4	Ohio	1,697,143,384	6.2%
5	Florida	1,466,273,345	5.4%
6	Michigan	1,320,275,023	4.8%
7	Pennsylvania	1,320,237,119	4.8%
8	New Jersey	1,131,352,192	4.1%
9	Illinois	802,971,010	2.9%
10	North Carolina	662,096,486	2.4%
11	Georgia	647,282,139	2.4%
12	Washington	644,113,060	2.4%
13	Wisconsin	611,876,491	2.2%
14	Virginia	606,627,426	2.2%
15	Massachusetts	604,380,725	2.2%
16	Minnesota	582,324,840	2.1%
17	Indiana	580,545,272	2.1%
18	Missouri	573,548,550	2.1%
19	Tennessee	555,988,101	2.0%
20	Maryland	514,934,157	1.9%
21	Kentucky	389,349,338	1.4%
22	Louisiana	380,063,605	1.4%
23	Oregon	349,474,272	1.3%
24	Arizona	323,093,647	1.2%
25	Oklahoma	315,117,057	1.2%
26	Iowa	313,319,066	1.1%
27	Mississippi	299,798,756	1.1%
28	Colorado	293,245,061	1.1%
29	Alabama	290,572,812	1.1%
30	South Carolina	255,318,273	0.9%
31	Connecticut	245,369,851	0.9%
32	Arkansas	219,645,476	0.8%
33	Nebraska	200,318,373	0.7%
34	West Virginia	195,410,794	0.7%
35	Utah	194,717,309	0.7%
36	Kansas	189,363,684	0.7%
37	Nevada	171,931,117	0.6%
38	Idaho	151,981,715	0.6%
39	New Mexico	112,170,094	0.4%
40	Maine	99,657,835	0.4%
41	Alaska	99,583,102	0.4%
42	Hawaii	96,191,283	0.4%
43	North Dakota	89,592,169	0.3%
44	South Dakota	86,280,610	0.3%
45	New Hampshire	83,176,973	0.3%
46	Delaware	74,451,056	0.3%
47	Rhode Island	66,339,200	0.2%
48	Wyoming	64,255,732	0.2%
49	Montana	59,935,863	0.2%
50	Vermont	45,987,161	0.2%
	District of Columbia	50,365,472	0.2%

Source: U.S. Department of Health and Human Services, Office of Child Support Enforcement
"Child Support Enforcement Preliminary Data Report" (www.acf.hhs.gov/programs/css/resource/fy2012-preliminary-report)
*Fiscal year 2012. Total does not include $358,561,790 collected in U.S. territories.

XV. Transportation

Federal Highway Funding in 2011

National Total = $40,248,003,000*

ALPHA ORDER

RANK	STATE	FUNDS	% of USA
16	Alabama	$787,303,000	2.0%
30	Alaska	520,331,000	1.3%
18	Arizona	759,261,000	1.9%
28	Arkansas	537,275,000	1.3%
1	California	3,808,734,000	9.5%
27	Colorado	554,906,000	1.4%
29	Connecticut	521,208,000	1.3%
48	Delaware	175,540,000	0.4%
3	Florida	1,966,140,000	4.9%
8	Georgia	1,339,911,000	3.3%
49	Hawaii	175,514,000	0.4%
41	Idaho	296,811,000	0.7%
6	Illinois	1,475,374,000	3.7%
13	Indiana	988,795,000	2.5%
33	Iowa	499,338,000	1.2%
36	Kansas	392,153,000	1.0%
21	Kentucky	689,494,000	1.7%
19	Louisiana	728,330,000	1.8%
47	Maine	191,557,000	0.5%
26	Maryland	621,866,000	1.5%
25	Massachusetts	630,252,000	1.6%
9	Michigan	1,092,590,000	2.7%
22	Minnesota	676,679,000	1.7%
32	Mississippi	501,891,000	1.2%
14	Missouri	982,398,000	2.4%
35	Montana	425,773,000	1.1%
40	Nebraska	299,946,000	0.7%
38	Nevada	376,815,000	0.9%
50	New Hampshire	171,456,000	0.4%
12	New Jersey	1,036,117,000	2.6%
37	New Mexico	381,081,000	0.9%
4	New York	1,741,861,000	4.3%
10	North Carolina	1,080,286,000	2.7%
44	North Dakota	257,633,000	0.6%
7	Ohio	1,390,981,000	3.5%
23	Oklahoma	658,138,000	1.6%
31	Oregon	518,684,000	1.3%
5	Pennsylvania	1,702,633,000	4.2%
45	Rhode Island	226,948,000	0.6%
24	South Carolina	651,506,000	1.6%
42	South Dakota	292,650,000	0.7%
15	Tennessee	876,909,000	2.2%
2	Texas	3,274,769,000	8.1%
39	Utah	334,327,000	0.8%
46	Vermont	210,610,000	0.5%
11	Virginia	1,056,004,000	2.6%
20	Washington	703,485,000	1.7%
34	West Virginia	453,501,000	1.1%
17	Wisconsin	780,813,000	1.9%
43	Wyoming	265,848,000	0.7%

RANK ORDER

RANK	STATE	FUNDS	% of USA
1	California	$3,808,734,000	9.5%
2	Texas	3,274,769,000	8.1%
3	Florida	1,966,140,000	4.9%
4	New York	1,741,861,000	4.3%
5	Pennsylvania	1,702,633,000	4.2%
6	Illinois	1,475,374,000	3.7%
7	Ohio	1,390,981,000	3.5%
8	Georgia	1,339,911,000	3.3%
9	Michigan	1,092,590,000	2.7%
10	North Carolina	1,080,286,000	2.7%
11	Virginia	1,056,004,000	2.6%
12	New Jersey	1,036,117,000	2.6%
13	Indiana	988,795,000	2.5%
14	Missouri	982,398,000	2.4%
15	Tennessee	876,909,000	2.2%
16	Alabama	787,303,000	2.0%
17	Wisconsin	780,813,000	1.9%
18	Arizona	759,261,000	1.9%
19	Louisiana	728,330,000	1.8%
20	Washington	703,485,000	1.7%
21	Kentucky	689,494,000	1.7%
22	Minnesota	676,679,000	1.7%
23	Oklahoma	658,138,000	1.6%
24	South Carolina	651,506,000	1.6%
25	Massachusetts	630,252,000	1.6%
26	Maryland	621,866,000	1.5%
27	Colorado	554,906,000	1.4%
28	Arkansas	537,275,000	1.3%
29	Connecticut	521,208,000	1.3%
30	Alaska	520,331,000	1.3%
31	Oregon	518,684,000	1.3%
32	Mississippi	501,891,000	1.2%
33	Iowa	499,338,000	1.2%
34	West Virginia	453,501,000	1.1%
35	Montana	425,773,000	1.1%
36	Kansas	392,153,000	1.0%
37	New Mexico	381,081,000	0.9%
38	Nevada	376,815,000	0.9%
39	Utah	334,327,000	0.8%
40	Nebraska	299,946,000	0.7%
41	Idaho	296,811,000	0.7%
42	South Dakota	292,650,000	0.7%
43	Wyoming	265,848,000	0.7%
44	North Dakota	257,633,000	0.6%
45	Rhode Island	226,948,000	0.6%
46	Vermont	210,610,000	0.5%
47	Maine	191,557,000	0.5%
48	Delaware	175,540,000	0.4%
49	Hawaii	175,514,000	0.4%
50	New Hampshire	171,456,000	0.4%
	District of Columbia	165,578,000	0.4%

Source: U.S. Department of Transportation, Federal Highway Administration
   "Federal-aid Highway Fund Apportionments" (http://www.fhwa.dot.gov/policyinformation/statistics/2011/)
*Fiscal Year 2011. National total does not include $185,153,000 in federal funds for U.S. territories.

Per Capita Federal Highway Funding in 2011

National Per Capita = $129*

RANK	STATE	PER CAPITA
15	Alabama	$164
1	Alaska	719
39	Arizona	117
11	Arkansas	183
48	California	101
44	Colorado	108
22	Connecticut	145
9	Delaware	193
46	Florida	103
26	Georgia	137
35	Hawaii	127
10	Idaho	187
41	Illinois	115
21	Indiana	152
16	Iowa	163
26	Kansas	137
20	Kentucky	158
19	Louisiana	159
23	Maine	144
45	Maryland	106
49	Massachusetts	95
43	Michigan	111
35	Minnesota	127
14	Mississippi	169
16	Missouri	163
3	Montana	427
16	Nebraska	163
24	Nevada	139
32	New Hampshire	130
39	New Jersey	117
11	New Mexico	183
50	New York	89
42	North Carolina	112
4	North Dakota	376
37	Ohio	120
13	Oklahoma	174
30	Oregon	134
30	Pennsylvania	134
8	Rhode Island	216
24	South Carolina	139
5	South Dakota	355
26	Tennessee	137
34	Texas	128
38	Utah	119
6	Vermont	336
32	Virginia	130
46	Washington	103
7	West Virginia	244
26	Wisconsin	137
2	Wyoming	469

RANK	STATE	PER CAPITA
1	Alaska	$719
2	Wyoming	469
3	Montana	427
4	North Dakota	376
5	South Dakota	355
6	Vermont	336
7	West Virginia	244
8	Rhode Island	216
9	Delaware	193
10	Idaho	187
11	Arkansas	183
11	New Mexico	183
13	Oklahoma	174
14	Mississippi	169
15	Alabama	164
16	Iowa	163
16	Missouri	163
16	Nebraska	163
19	Louisiana	159
20	Kentucky	158
21	Indiana	152
22	Connecticut	145
23	Maine	144
24	Nevada	139
24	South Carolina	139
26	Georgia	137
26	Kansas	137
26	Tennessee	137
26	Wisconsin	137
30	Oregon	134
30	Pennsylvania	134
32	New Hampshire	130
32	Virginia	130
34	Texas	128
35	Hawaii	127
35	Minnesota	127
37	Ohio	120
38	Utah	119
39	Arizona	117
39	New Jersey	117
41	Illinois	115
42	North Carolina	112
43	Michigan	111
44	Colorado	108
45	Maryland	106
46	Florida	103
46	Washington	103
48	California	101
49	Massachusetts	95
50	New York	89
	District of Columbia	267

Source: CQ Press using data from U.S. Department of Transportation, Federal Highway Administration
"Federal-aid Highway Fund Apportionments" (http://www.fhwa.dot.gov/policyinformation/statistics/2011/)
*Fiscal Year 2011. National per capita does not include population or federal funds for U.S. territories.

Public Road and Street Mileage in 2011

National Total = 4,077,756 Miles*

ALPHA ORDER

RANK	STATE	MILES	% of USA
17	Alabama	101,668	2.5%
45	Alaska	16,675	0.4%
32	Arizona	65,092	1.6%
18	Arkansas	100,082	2.5%
2	California	172,202	4.2%
22	Colorado	88,415	2.2%
44	Connecticut	21,445	0.5%
49	Delaware	6,358	0.2%
10	Florida	121,759	3.0%
7	Georgia	123,546	3.0%
50	Hawaii	4,405	0.1%
35	Idaho	48,553	1.2%
4	Illinois	139,498	3.4%
19	Indiana	97,066	2.4%
14	Iowa	114,387	2.8%
3	Kansas	140,513	3.4%
26	Kentucky	79,220	1.9%
33	Louisiana	61,635	1.5%
43	Maine	22,874	0.6%
41	Maryland	32,321	0.8%
40	Massachusetts	36,303	0.9%
9	Michigan	122,086	3.0%
5	Minnesota	138,702	3.4%
27	Mississippi	75,119	1.8%
6	Missouri	131,667	3.2%
28	Montana	74,880	1.8%
21	Nebraska	93,600	2.3%
39	Nevada	36,839	0.9%
46	New Hampshire	16,076	0.4%
37	New Jersey	39,213	1.0%
30	New Mexico	68,384	1.7%
13	New York	114,592	2.8%
16	North Carolina	105,869	2.6%
23	North Dakota	86,851	2.1%
8	Ohio	123,247	3.0%
15	Oklahoma	112,808	2.8%
34	Oregon	59,148	1.5%
11	Pennsylvania	119,771	2.9%
48	Rhode Island	6,485	0.2%
31	South Carolina	65,997	1.6%
25	South Dakota	82,459	2.0%
20	Tennessee	95,492	2.3%
1	Texas	312,911	7.7%
36	Utah	45,635	1.1%
47	Vermont	14,290	0.4%
29	Virginia	74,461	1.8%
24	Washington	83,743	2.1%
38	West Virginia	38,646	0.9%
12	Wisconsin	115,018	2.8%
42	Wyoming	28,253	0.7%

RANK ORDER

RANK	STATE	MILES	% of USA
1	Texas	312,911	7.7%
2	California	172,202	4.2%
3	Kansas	140,513	3.4%
4	Illinois	139,498	3.4%
5	Minnesota	138,702	3.4%
6	Missouri	131,667	3.2%
7	Georgia	123,546	3.0%
8	Ohio	123,247	3.0%
9	Michigan	122,086	3.0%
10	Florida	121,759	3.0%
11	Pennsylvania	119,771	2.9%
12	Wisconsin	115,018	2.8%
13	New York	114,592	2.8%
14	Iowa	114,387	2.8%
15	Oklahoma	112,808	2.8%
16	North Carolina	105,869	2.6%
17	Alabama	101,668	2.5%
18	Arkansas	100,082	2.5%
19	Indiana	97,066	2.4%
20	Tennessee	95,492	2.3%
21	Nebraska	93,600	2.3%
22	Colorado	88,415	2.2%
23	North Dakota	86,851	2.1%
24	Washington	83,743	2.1%
25	South Dakota	82,459	2.0%
26	Kentucky	79,220	1.9%
27	Mississippi	75,119	1.8%
28	Montana	74,880	1.8%
29	Virginia	74,461	1.8%
30	New Mexico	68,384	1.7%
31	South Carolina	65,997	1.6%
32	Arizona	65,092	1.6%
33	Louisiana	61,635	1.5%
34	Oregon	59,148	1.5%
35	Idaho	48,553	1.2%
36	Utah	45,635	1.1%
37	New Jersey	39,213	1.0%
38	West Virginia	38,646	0.9%
39	Nevada	36,839	0.9%
40	Massachusetts	36,303	0.9%
41	Maryland	32,321	0.8%
42	Wyoming	28,253	0.7%
43	Maine	22,874	0.6%
44	Connecticut	21,445	0.5%
45	Alaska	16,675	0.4%
46	New Hampshire	16,076	0.4%
47	Vermont	14,290	0.4%
48	Rhode Island	6,485	0.2%
49	Delaware	6,358	0.2%
50	Hawaii	4,405	0.1%
	District of Columbia	1,501	0.0%

Source: U.S. Department of Transportation, Federal Highway Administration
   "Highway Statistics 2011" (Table HM-20, http://www.fhwa.dot.gov/policyinformation/statistics/2011/)
*Does not include 16,691 miles of roads and streets in Puerto Rico.

Percent of Public Road and Street Mileage Federally Funded in 2011

National Percent = 24.5% of Public Road and Street Mileage*

<table>
<tr><td colspan="3">ALPHA ORDER</td><td colspan="3">RANK ORDER</td></tr>
<tr><td>RANK</td><td>STATE</td><td>PERCENT</td><td>RANK</td><td>STATE</td><td>PERCENT</td></tr>
<tr><td>20</td><td>Alabama</td><td>25.4</td><td>1</td><td>Hawaii</td><td>35.5</td></tr>
<tr><td>10</td><td>Alaska</td><td>28.3</td><td>2</td><td>California</td><td>32.3</td></tr>
<tr><td>43</td><td>Arizona</td><td>20.4</td><td>3</td><td>South Carolina</td><td>31.8</td></tr>
<tr><td>37</td><td>Arkansas</td><td>21.9</td><td>4</td><td>Oregon</td><td>30.7</td></tr>
<tr><td>2</td><td>California</td><td>32.3</td><td>5</td><td>Massachusetts</td><td>30.6</td></tr>
<tr><td>44</td><td>Colorado</td><td>19.8</td><td>6</td><td>Michigan</td><td>29.8</td></tr>
<tr><td>8</td><td>Connecticut</td><td>28.7</td><td>7</td><td>Virginia</td><td>29.3</td></tr>
<tr><td>25</td><td>Delaware</td><td>24.2</td><td>8</td><td>Connecticut</td><td>28.7</td></tr>
<tr><td>39</td><td>Florida</td><td>21.6</td><td>8</td><td>Mississippi</td><td>28.7</td></tr>
<tr><td>21</td><td>Georgia</td><td>25.2</td><td>10</td><td>Alaska</td><td>28.3</td></tr>
<tr><td>1</td><td>Hawaii</td><td>35.5</td><td>11</td><td>Oklahoma</td><td>28.1</td></tr>
<tr><td>33</td><td>Idaho</td><td>23.4</td><td>12</td><td>Maine</td><td>27.6</td></tr>
<tr><td>19</td><td>Illinois</td><td>25.5</td><td>12</td><td>Wyoming</td><td>27.6</td></tr>
<tr><td>26</td><td>Indiana</td><td>24.0</td><td>14</td><td>Rhode Island</td><td>27.0</td></tr>
<tr><td>35</td><td>Iowa</td><td>22.7</td><td>14</td><td>Vermont</td><td>27.0</td></tr>
<tr><td>22</td><td>Kansas</td><td>24.9</td><td>14</td><td>West Virginia</td><td>27.0</td></tr>
<tr><td>49</td><td>Kentucky</td><td>17.7</td><td>17</td><td>Texas</td><td>26.8</td></tr>
<tr><td>38</td><td>Louisiana</td><td>21.7</td><td>18</td><td>New Jersey</td><td>26.3</td></tr>
<tr><td>12</td><td>Maine</td><td>27.6</td><td>19</td><td>Illinois</td><td>25.5</td></tr>
<tr><td>24</td><td>Maryland</td><td>24.4</td><td>20</td><td>Alabama</td><td>25.4</td></tr>
<tr><td>5</td><td>Massachusetts</td><td>30.6</td><td>21</td><td>Georgia</td><td>25.2</td></tr>
<tr><td>6</td><td>Michigan</td><td>29.8</td><td>22</td><td>Kansas</td><td>24.9</td></tr>
<tr><td>29</td><td>Minnesota</td><td>23.8</td><td>23</td><td>Wisconsin</td><td>24.6</td></tr>
<tr><td>8</td><td>Mississippi</td><td>28.7</td><td>24</td><td>Maryland</td><td>24.4</td></tr>
<tr><td>34</td><td>Missouri</td><td>23.3</td><td>25</td><td>Delaware</td><td>24.2</td></tr>
<tr><td>46</td><td>Montana</td><td>19.5</td><td>26</td><td>Indiana</td><td>24.0</td></tr>
<tr><td>36</td><td>Nebraska</td><td>22.0</td><td>26</td><td>New York</td><td>24.0</td></tr>
<tr><td>47</td><td>Nevada</td><td>19.4</td><td>26</td><td>South Dakota</td><td>24.0</td></tr>
<tr><td>40</td><td>New Hampshire</td><td>21.2</td><td>29</td><td>Minnesota</td><td>23.8</td></tr>
<tr><td>18</td><td>New Jersey</td><td>26.3</td><td>29</td><td>Washington</td><td>23.8</td></tr>
<tr><td>50</td><td>New Mexico</td><td>16.9</td><td>31</td><td>Ohio</td><td>23.6</td></tr>
<tr><td>26</td><td>New York</td><td>24.0</td><td>31</td><td>Pennsylvania</td><td>23.6</td></tr>
<tr><td>42</td><td>North Carolina</td><td>20.8</td><td>33</td><td>Idaho</td><td>23.4</td></tr>
<tr><td>40</td><td>North Dakota</td><td>21.2</td><td>34</td><td>Missouri</td><td>23.3</td></tr>
<tr><td>31</td><td>Ohio</td><td>23.6</td><td>35</td><td>Iowa</td><td>22.7</td></tr>
<tr><td>11</td><td>Oklahoma</td><td>28.1</td><td>36</td><td>Nebraska</td><td>22.0</td></tr>
<tr><td>4</td><td>Oregon</td><td>30.7</td><td>37</td><td>Arkansas</td><td>21.9</td></tr>
<tr><td>31</td><td>Pennsylvania</td><td>23.6</td><td>38</td><td>Louisiana</td><td>21.7</td></tr>
<tr><td>14</td><td>Rhode Island</td><td>27.0</td><td>39</td><td>Florida</td><td>21.6</td></tr>
<tr><td>3</td><td>South Carolina</td><td>31.8</td><td>40</td><td>New Hampshire</td><td>21.2</td></tr>
<tr><td>26</td><td>South Dakota</td><td>24.0</td><td>40</td><td>North Dakota</td><td>21.2</td></tr>
<tr><td>48</td><td>Tennessee</td><td>18.7</td><td>42</td><td>North Carolina</td><td>20.8</td></tr>
<tr><td>17</td><td>Texas</td><td>26.8</td><td>43</td><td>Arizona</td><td>20.4</td></tr>
<tr><td>45</td><td>Utah</td><td>19.7</td><td>44</td><td>Colorado</td><td>19.8</td></tr>
<tr><td>14</td><td>Vermont</td><td>27.0</td><td>45</td><td>Utah</td><td>19.7</td></tr>
<tr><td>7</td><td>Virginia</td><td>29.3</td><td>46</td><td>Montana</td><td>19.5</td></tr>
<tr><td>29</td><td>Washington</td><td>23.8</td><td>47</td><td>Nevada</td><td>19.4</td></tr>
<tr><td>14</td><td>West Virginia</td><td>27.0</td><td>48</td><td>Tennessee</td><td>18.7</td></tr>
<tr><td>23</td><td>Wisconsin</td><td>24.6</td><td>49</td><td>Kentucky</td><td>17.7</td></tr>
<tr><td>12</td><td>Wyoming</td><td>27.6</td><td>50</td><td>New Mexico</td><td>16.9</td></tr>
<tr><td></td><td></td><td></td><td></td><td>District of Columbia</td><td>30.2</td></tr>
</table>

Source: CQ Press using data from U.S. Department of Transportation, Federal Highway Administration
"Highway Statistics 2011" (Table HM-15, http://www.fhwa.dot.gov/policyinformation/statistics/2011/)
*National percent does not include federally-funded highway miles in Puerto Rico.

Interstate Highway Mileage in 2011

National Total = 46,960 Miles*

RANK	STATE	MILES	% of USA
24	Alabama	906	1.9%
17	Alaska	1,084	2.3%
14	Arizona	1,168	2.5%
35	Arkansas	656	1.4%
2	California	2,453	5.2%
19	Colorado	953	2.0%
45	Connecticut	346	0.7%
50	Delaware	41	0.1%
7	Florida	1,495	3.2%
8	Georgia	1,248	2.7%
49	Hawaii	55	0.1%
36	Idaho	612	1.3%
3	Illinois	2,182	4.6%
13	Indiana	1,172	2.5%
29	Iowa	782	1.7%
26	Kansas	874	1.9%
28	Kentucky	801	1.7%
25	Louisiana	898	1.9%
44	Maine	369	0.8%
42	Maryland	481	1.0%
37	Massachusetts	574	1.2%
9	Michigan	1,244	2.6%
22	Minnesota	914	1.9%
33	Mississippi	702	1.5%
10	Missouri	1,206	2.6%
11	Montana	1,192	2.5%
41	Nebraska	482	1.0%
38	Nevada	571	1.2%
47	New Hampshire	225	0.5%
43	New Jersey	431	0.9%
18	New Mexico	1,000	2.1%
5	New York	1,704	3.6%
12	North Carolina	1,174	2.5%
38	North Dakota	571	1.2%
6	Ohio	1,574	3.4%
21	Oklahoma	933	2.0%
32	Oregon	730	1.6%
4	Pennsylvania	1,855	4.0%
48	Rhode Island	71	0.2%
27	South Carolina	851	1.8%
34	South Dakota	679	1.4%
16	Tennessee	1,104	2.4%
1	Texas	3,237	6.9%
20	Utah	937	2.0%
46	Vermont	320	0.7%
15	Virginia	1,119	2.4%
30	Washington	764	1.6%
40	West Virginia	555	1.2%
31	Wisconsin	742	1.6%
22	Wyoming	914	1.9%

RANK	STATE	MILES	% of USA
1	Texas	3,237	6.9%
2	California	2,453	5.2%
3	Illinois	2,182	4.6%
4	Pennsylvania	1,855	4.0%
5	New York	1,704	3.6%
6	Ohio	1,574	3.4%
7	Florida	1,495	3.2%
8	Georgia	1,248	2.7%
9	Michigan	1,244	2.6%
10	Missouri	1,206	2.6%
11	Montana	1,192	2.5%
12	North Carolina	1,174	2.5%
13	Indiana	1,172	2.5%
14	Arizona	1,168	2.5%
15	Virginia	1,119	2.4%
16	Tennessee	1,104	2.4%
17	Alaska	1,084	2.3%
18	New Mexico	1,000	2.1%
19	Colorado	953	2.0%
20	Utah	937	2.0%
21	Oklahoma	933	2.0%
22	Minnesota	914	1.9%
22	Wyoming	914	1.9%
24	Alabama	906	1.9%
25	Louisiana	898	1.9%
26	Kansas	874	1.9%
27	South Carolina	851	1.8%
28	Kentucky	801	1.7%
29	Iowa	782	1.7%
30	Washington	764	1.6%
31	Wisconsin	742	1.6%
32	Oregon	730	1.6%
33	Mississippi	702	1.5%
34	South Dakota	679	1.4%
35	Arkansas	656	1.4%
36	Idaho	612	1.3%
37	Massachusetts	574	1.2%
38	Nevada	571	1.2%
38	North Dakota	571	1.2%
40	West Virginia	555	1.2%
41	Nebraska	482	1.0%
42	Maryland	481	1.0%
43	New Jersey	431	0.9%
44	Maine	369	0.8%
45	Connecticut	346	0.7%
46	Vermont	320	0.7%
47	New Hampshire	225	0.5%
48	Rhode Island	71	0.2%
49	Hawaii	55	0.1%
50	Delaware	41	0.1%
	District of Columbia	13	0.0%

Source: CQ Press using data from U.S. Department of Transportation, Federal Highway Administration
"Highway Statistics 2011" (Table HM-15, http://www.fhwa.dot.gov/policyinformation/statistics/2011/)
*Does not include 282 miles of highway in Puerto Rico that are part of the interstate system.

Toll Road Mileage in 2010

National Total = 4,841 Miles

ALPHA ORDER

RANK	STATE	MILES	% of USA
27	Alabama	3	0.1%
27	Alaska	3	0.1%
21	Arizona	20	0.4%
33	Arkansas	0	0.0%
11	California	135	2.8%
33	Colorado	0	0.0%
33	Connecticut	0	0.0%
17	Delaware	51	1.1%
1	Florida	741	15.3%
25	Georgia	6	0.1%
33	Hawaii	0	0.0%
33	Idaho	0	0.0%
7	Illinois	288	5.9%
9	Indiana	157	3.2%
33	Iowa	0	0.0%
8	Kansas	236	4.9%
33	Kentucky	0	0.0%
18	Louisiana	28	0.6%
13	Maine	106	2.2%
16	Maryland	64	1.3%
10	Massachusetts	142	2.9%
23	Michigan	9	0.2%
19	Minnesota	27	0.6%
33	Mississippi	0	0.0%
33	Missouri	0	0.0%
33	Montana	0	0.0%
31	Nebraska	1	0.0%
25	Nevada	6	0.1%
12	New Hampshire	131	2.7%
5	New Jersey	387	8.0%
33	New Mexico	0	0.0%
4	New York	549	11.3%
23	North Carolina	9	0.2%
33	North Dakota	0	0.0%
33	Ohio	0	0.0%
2	Oklahoma	596	12.3%
29	Oregon	2	0.0%
3	Pennsylvania	574	11.9%
29	Rhode Island	2	0.0%
20	South Carolina	24	0.5%
33	South Dakota	0	0.0%
33	Tennessee	0	0.0%
6	Texas	362	7.5%
31	Utah	1	0.0%
33	Vermont	0	0.0%
15	Virginia	78	1.6%
22	Washington	15	0.3%
14	West Virginia	88	1.8%
33	Wisconsin	0	0.0%
33	Wyoming	0	0.0%

RANK ORDER

RANK	STATE	MILES	% of USA
1	Florida	741	15.3%
2	Oklahoma	596	12.3%
3	Pennsylvania	574	11.9%
4	New York	549	11.3%
5	New Jersey	387	8.0%
6	Texas	362	7.5%
7	Illinois	288	5.9%
8	Kansas	236	4.9%
9	Indiana	157	3.2%
10	Massachusetts	142	2.9%
11	California	135	2.8%
12	New Hampshire	131	2.7%
13	Maine	106	2.2%
14	West Virginia	88	1.8%
15	Virginia	78	1.6%
16	Maryland	64	1.3%
17	Delaware	51	1.1%
18	Louisiana	28	0.6%
19	Minnesota	27	0.6%
20	South Carolina	24	0.5%
21	Arizona	20	0.4%
22	Washington	15	0.3%
23	Michigan	9	0.2%
23	North Carolina	9	0.2%
25	Georgia	6	0.1%
25	Nevada	6	0.1%
27	Alabama	3	0.1%
27	Alaska	3	0.1%
29	Oregon	2	0.0%
29	Rhode Island	2	0.0%
31	Nebraska	1	0.0%
31	Utah	1	0.0%
33	Arkansas	0	0.0%
33	Colorado	0	0.0%
33	Connecticut	0	0.0%
33	Hawaii	0	0.0%
33	Idaho	0	0.0%
33	Iowa	0	0.0%
33	Kentucky	0	0.0%
33	Mississippi	0	0.0%
33	Missouri	0	0.0%
33	Montana	0	0.0%
33	New Mexico	0	0.0%
33	North Dakota	0	0.0%
33	Ohio	0	0.0%
33	South Dakota	0	0.0%
33	Tennessee	0	0.0%
33	Vermont	0	0.0%
33	Wisconsin	0	0.0%
33	Wyoming	0	0.0%
	District of Columbia	0	0.0%

Source: U.S. Department of Transportation, Federal Highway Administration
"Highway Statistics 2010" (Table HM-25, http://www.fhwa.dot.gov/policyinformation/statistics/2010/index.cfm)

Rural Road and Street Mileage in 2011

National Total = 2,982,383 Rural Miles*

RANK	STATE	MILES	% of USA
17	Alabama	76,416	2.6%
42	Alaska	13,987	0.5%
34	Arizona	41,594	1.4%
10	Arkansas	87,069	2.9%
14	California	81,877	2.7%
23	Colorado	68,883	2.3%
47	Connecticut	6,252	0.2%
48	Delaware	3,361	0.1%
35	Florida	40,288	1.4%
13	Georgia	83,548	2.8%
49	Hawaii	2,050	0.1%
33	Idaho	43,000	1.4%
6	Illinois	98,226	3.3%
21	Indiana	70,171	2.4%
5	Iowa	102,986	3.5%
2	Kansas	127,532	4.3%
24	Kentucky	66,588	2.2%
32	Louisiana	44,466	1.5%
40	Maine	19,867	0.7%
41	Maryland	14,323	0.5%
45	Massachusetts	7,988	0.3%
11	Michigan	86,596	2.9%
3	Minnesota	117,885	4.0%
26	Mississippi	64,107	2.1%
4	Missouri	107,827	3.6%
19	Montana	71,698	2.4%
9	Nebraska	87,170	2.9%
38	Nevada	28,622	1.0%
44	New Hampshire	11,147	0.4%
46	New Jersey	7,296	0.2%
27	New Mexico	60,480	2.0%
25	New York	66,157	2.2%
20	North Carolina	70,197	2.4%
12	North Dakota	84,932	2.8%
16	Ohio	78,209	2.6%
7	Oklahoma	96,673	3.2%
31	Oregon	46,237	1.6%
18	Pennsylvania	73,620	2.5%
50	Rhode Island	1,225	0.0%
30	South Carolina	49,623	1.7%
15	South Dakota	79,492	2.7%
22	Tennessee	69,975	2.3%
1	Texas	213,725	7.2%
36	Utah	34,463	1.2%
43	Vermont	12,824	0.4%
29	Virginia	50,391	1.7%
28	Washington	60,059	2.0%
37	West Virginia	33,275	1.1%
8	Wisconsin	92,537	3.1%
39	Wyoming	25,468	0.9%

RANK	STATE	MILES	% of USA
1	Texas	213,725	7.2%
2	Kansas	127,532	4.3%
3	Minnesota	117,885	4.0%
4	Missouri	107,827	3.6%
5	Iowa	102,986	3.5%
6	Illinois	98,226	3.3%
7	Oklahoma	96,673	3.2%
8	Wisconsin	92,537	3.1%
9	Nebraska	87,170	2.9%
10	Arkansas	87,069	2.9%
11	Michigan	86,596	2.9%
12	North Dakota	84,932	2.8%
13	Georgia	83,548	2.8%
14	California	81,877	2.7%
15	South Dakota	79,492	2.7%
16	Ohio	78,209	2.6%
17	Alabama	76,416	2.6%
18	Pennsylvania	73,620	2.5%
19	Montana	71,698	2.4%
20	North Carolina	70,197	2.4%
21	Indiana	70,171	2.4%
22	Tennessee	69,975	2.3%
23	Colorado	68,883	2.3%
24	Kentucky	66,588	2.2%
25	New York	66,157	2.2%
26	Mississippi	64,107	2.1%
27	New Mexico	60,480	2.0%
28	Washington	60,059	2.0%
29	Virginia	50,391	1.7%
30	South Carolina	49,623	1.7%
31	Oregon	46,237	1.6%
32	Louisiana	44,466	1.5%
33	Idaho	43,000	1.4%
34	Arizona	41,594	1.4%
35	Florida	40,288	1.4%
36	Utah	34,463	1.2%
37	West Virginia	33,275	1.1%
38	Nevada	28,622	1.0%
39	Wyoming	25,468	0.9%
40	Maine	19,867	0.7%
41	Maryland	14,323	0.5%
42	Alaska	13,987	0.5%
43	Vermont	12,824	0.4%
44	New Hampshire	11,147	0.4%
45	Massachusetts	7,988	0.3%
46	New Jersey	7,296	0.2%
47	Connecticut	6,252	0.2%
48	Delaware	3,361	0.1%
49	Hawaii	2,050	0.1%
50	Rhode Island	1,225	0.0%
	District of Columbia	0	0.0%

Source: U.S. Department of Transportation, Federal Highway Administration
   "Highway Statistics 2011" (Table HM-20, http://www.fhwa.dot.gov/policyinformation/statistics/2011/)
*Does not include 3,104 miles of rural roads and streets in Puerto Rico.

Urban Road and Street Mileage in 2011

National Total = 1,095,373 Urban Miles*

RANK	STATE	MILES	% of USA
15	Alabama	25,252	2.3%
47	Alaska	2,688	0.2%
19	Arizona	23,498	2.1%
28	Arkansas	13,013	1.2%
2	California	90,324	8.2%
22	Colorado	19,531	1.8%
27	Connecticut	15,193	1.4%
44	Delaware	2,997	0.3%
3	Florida	81,471	7.4%
8	Georgia	39,998	3.7%
48	Hawaii	2,355	0.2%
38	Idaho	5,553	0.5%
7	Illinois	41,273	3.8%
13	Indiana	26,895	2.5%
32	Iowa	11,401	1.0%
29	Kansas	12,980	1.2%
31	Kentucky	12,632	1.2%
24	Louisiana	17,169	1.6%
43	Maine	3,007	0.3%
23	Maryland	17,998	1.6%
12	Massachusetts	28,315	2.6%
10	Michigan	35,490	3.2%
21	Minnesota	20,817	1.9%
34	Mississippi	11,011	1.0%
17	Missouri	23,839	2.2%
42	Montana	3,182	0.3%
37	Nebraska	6,430	0.6%
35	Nevada	8,217	0.8%
41	New Hampshire	4,929	0.4%
11	New Jersey	31,917	2.9%
36	New Mexico	7,904	0.7%
4	New York	48,435	4.4%
9	North Carolina	35,673	3.3%
49	North Dakota	1,919	0.2%
6	Ohio	45,038	4.1%
26	Oklahoma	16,135	1.5%
30	Oregon	12,911	1.2%
5	Pennsylvania	46,151	4.2%
40	Rhode Island	5,260	0.5%
25	South Carolina	16,374	1.5%
45	South Dakota	2,968	0.3%
14	Tennessee	25,517	2.3%
1	Texas	99,185	9.1%
33	Utah	11,172	1.0%
50	Vermont	1,465	0.1%
16	Virginia	24,070	2.2%
18	Washington	23,683	2.2%
39	West Virginia	5,371	0.5%
20	Wisconsin	22,481	2.1%
46	Wyoming	2,785	0.3%

RANK	STATE	MILES	% of USA
1	Texas	99,185	9.1%
2	California	90,324	8.2%
3	Florida	81,471	7.4%
4	New York	48,435	4.4%
5	Pennsylvania	46,151	4.2%
6	Ohio	45,038	4.1%
7	Illinois	41,273	3.8%
8	Georgia	39,998	3.7%
9	North Carolina	35,673	3.3%
10	Michigan	35,490	3.2%
11	New Jersey	31,917	2.9%
12	Massachusetts	28,315	2.6%
13	Indiana	26,895	2.5%
14	Tennessee	25,517	2.3%
15	Alabama	25,252	2.3%
16	Virginia	24,070	2.2%
17	Missouri	23,839	2.2%
18	Washington	23,683	2.2%
19	Arizona	23,498	2.1%
20	Wisconsin	22,481	2.1%
21	Minnesota	20,817	1.9%
22	Colorado	19,531	1.8%
23	Maryland	17,998	1.6%
24	Louisiana	17,169	1.6%
25	South Carolina	16,374	1.5%
26	Oklahoma	16,135	1.5%
27	Connecticut	15,193	1.4%
28	Arkansas	13,013	1.2%
29	Kansas	12,980	1.2%
30	Oregon	12,911	1.2%
31	Kentucky	12,632	1.2%
32	Iowa	11,401	1.0%
33	Utah	11,172	1.0%
34	Mississippi	11,011	1.0%
35	Nevada	8,217	0.8%
36	New Mexico	7,904	0.7%
37	Nebraska	6,430	0.6%
38	Idaho	5,553	0.5%
39	West Virginia	5,371	0.5%
40	Rhode Island	5,260	0.5%
41	New Hampshire	4,929	0.4%
42	Montana	3,182	0.3%
43	Maine	3,007	0.3%
44	Delaware	2,997	0.3%
45	South Dakota	2,968	0.3%
46	Wyoming	2,785	0.3%
47	Alaska	2,688	0.2%
48	Hawaii	2,355	0.2%
49	North Dakota	1,919	0.2%
50	Vermont	1,465	0.1%
	District of Columbia	1,501	0.1%

Source: U.S. Department of Transportation, Federal Highway Administration
"Highway Statistics 2011" (Table HM-20, http://www.fhwa.dot.gov/policyinformation/statistics/2011/)
*Does not include 13,587 miles of urban roads and streets in Puerto Rico.

Percent of Roadways in Mediocre or Poor Condition in 2011

National Percent = 21.5%*

<table>
<tr><td colspan="4">ALPHA ORDER</td><td colspan="4">RANK ORDER</td></tr>
<tr><th>RANK</th><th>STATE</th><th>PERCENT</th><th></th><th>RANK</th><th>STATE</th><th>PERCENT</th></tr>
<tr><td>41</td><td>Alabama</td><td>8.5</td><td></td><td>1</td><td>Kansas</td><td>52.1</td></tr>
<tr><td>18</td><td>Alaska</td><td>24.0</td><td></td><td>2</td><td>Connecticut</td><td>47.9</td></tr>
<tr><td>32</td><td>Arizona</td><td>14.1</td><td></td><td>3</td><td>New Jersey</td><td>44.6</td></tr>
<tr><td>10</td><td>Arkansas</td><td>30.8</td><td></td><td>4</td><td>Hawaii</td><td>38.8</td></tr>
<tr><td>5</td><td>California</td><td>36.6</td><td></td><td>5</td><td>California</td><td>36.6</td></tr>
<tr><td>28</td><td>Colorado</td><td>19.3</td><td></td><td>6</td><td>Oklahoma</td><td>36.0</td></tr>
<tr><td>2</td><td>Connecticut</td><td>47.9</td><td></td><td>7</td><td>West Virginia</td><td>33.3</td></tr>
<tr><td>26</td><td>Delaware</td><td>20.2</td><td></td><td>8</td><td>Rhode Island</td><td>32.6</td></tr>
<tr><td>37</td><td>Florida</td><td>11.0</td><td></td><td>9</td><td>Michigan</td><td>31.5</td></tr>
<tr><td>42</td><td>Georgia</td><td>8.3</td><td></td><td>10</td><td>Arkansas</td><td>30.8</td></tr>
<tr><td>4</td><td>Hawaii</td><td>38.8</td><td></td><td>11</td><td>Maine</td><td>30.0</td></tr>
<tr><td>30</td><td>Idaho</td><td>17.7</td><td></td><td>12</td><td>Mississippi</td><td>29.9</td></tr>
<tr><td>21</td><td>Illinois</td><td>22.6</td><td></td><td>13</td><td>Washington</td><td>27.1</td></tr>
<tr><td>22</td><td>Indiana</td><td>22.5</td><td></td><td>14</td><td>Pennsylvania</td><td>26.8</td></tr>
<tr><td>19</td><td>Iowa</td><td>23.5</td><td></td><td>15</td><td>New York</td><td>26.0</td></tr>
<tr><td>1</td><td>Kansas</td><td>52.1</td><td></td><td>16</td><td>New Mexico</td><td>25.3</td></tr>
<tr><td>43</td><td>Kentucky</td><td>7.9</td><td></td><td>17</td><td>New Hampshire</td><td>25.0</td></tr>
<tr><td>25</td><td>Louisiana</td><td>21.2</td><td></td><td>18</td><td>Alaska</td><td>24.0</td></tr>
<tr><td>11</td><td>Maine</td><td>30.0</td><td></td><td>19</td><td>Iowa</td><td>23.5</td></tr>
<tr><td>24</td><td>Maryland</td><td>22.1</td><td></td><td>20</td><td>Vermont</td><td>23.3</td></tr>
<tr><td>34</td><td>Massachusetts</td><td>13.4</td><td></td><td>21</td><td>Illinois</td><td>22.6</td></tr>
<tr><td>9</td><td>Michigan</td><td>31.5</td><td></td><td>22</td><td>Indiana</td><td>22.5</td></tr>
<tr><td>31</td><td>Minnesota</td><td>15.3</td><td></td><td>23</td><td>Wisconsin</td><td>22.3</td></tr>
<tr><td>12</td><td>Mississippi</td><td>29.9</td><td></td><td>24</td><td>Maryland</td><td>22.1</td></tr>
<tr><td>48</td><td>Missouri</td><td>6.3</td><td></td><td>25</td><td>Louisiana</td><td>21.2</td></tr>
<tr><td>45</td><td>Montana</td><td>7.1</td><td></td><td>26</td><td>Delaware</td><td>20.2</td></tr>
<tr><td>38</td><td>Nebraska</td><td>10.6</td><td></td><td>27</td><td>Ohio</td><td>19.9</td></tr>
<tr><td>47</td><td>Nevada</td><td>6.4</td><td></td><td>28</td><td>Colorado</td><td>19.3</td></tr>
<tr><td>17</td><td>New Hampshire</td><td>25.0</td><td></td><td>29</td><td>Virginia</td><td>17.9</td></tr>
<tr><td>3</td><td>New Jersey</td><td>44.6</td><td></td><td>30</td><td>Idaho</td><td>17.7</td></tr>
<tr><td>16</td><td>New Mexico</td><td>25.3</td><td></td><td>31</td><td>Minnesota</td><td>15.3</td></tr>
<tr><td>15</td><td>New York</td><td>26.0</td><td></td><td>32</td><td>Arizona</td><td>14.1</td></tr>
<tr><td>40</td><td>North Carolina</td><td>10.1</td><td></td><td>33</td><td>South Dakota</td><td>14.0</td></tr>
<tr><td>50</td><td>North Dakota</td><td>5.9</td><td></td><td>34</td><td>Massachusetts</td><td>13.4</td></tr>
<tr><td>27</td><td>Ohio</td><td>19.9</td><td></td><td>35</td><td>Texas</td><td>12.1</td></tr>
<tr><td>6</td><td>Oklahoma</td><td>36.0</td><td></td><td>36</td><td>Utah</td><td>11.4</td></tr>
<tr><td>46</td><td>Oregon</td><td>6.8</td><td></td><td>37</td><td>Florida</td><td>11.0</td></tr>
<tr><td>14</td><td>Pennsylvania</td><td>26.8</td><td></td><td>38</td><td>Nebraska</td><td>10.6</td></tr>
<tr><td>8</td><td>Rhode Island</td><td>32.6</td><td></td><td>39</td><td>South Carolina</td><td>10.4</td></tr>
<tr><td>39</td><td>South Carolina</td><td>10.4</td><td></td><td>40</td><td>North Carolina</td><td>10.1</td></tr>
<tr><td>33</td><td>South Dakota</td><td>14.0</td><td></td><td>41</td><td>Alabama</td><td>8.5</td></tr>
<tr><td>44</td><td>Tennessee</td><td>7.7</td><td></td><td>42</td><td>Georgia</td><td>8.3</td></tr>
<tr><td>35</td><td>Texas</td><td>12.1</td><td></td><td>43</td><td>Kentucky</td><td>7.9</td></tr>
<tr><td>36</td><td>Utah</td><td>11.4</td><td></td><td>44</td><td>Tennessee</td><td>7.7</td></tr>
<tr><td>20</td><td>Vermont</td><td>23.3</td><td></td><td>45</td><td>Montana</td><td>7.1</td></tr>
<tr><td>29</td><td>Virginia</td><td>17.9</td><td></td><td>46</td><td>Oregon</td><td>6.8</td></tr>
<tr><td>13</td><td>Washington</td><td>27.1</td><td></td><td>47</td><td>Nevada</td><td>6.4</td></tr>
<tr><td>7</td><td>West Virginia</td><td>33.3</td><td></td><td>48</td><td>Missouri</td><td>6.3</td></tr>
<tr><td>23</td><td>Wisconsin</td><td>22.3</td><td></td><td>49</td><td>Wyoming</td><td>6.1</td></tr>
<tr><td>49</td><td>Wyoming</td><td>6.1</td><td></td><td>50</td><td>North Dakota</td><td>5.9</td></tr>
<tr><td colspan="4"></td><td></td><td>District of Columbia</td><td>96.8</td></tr>
</table>

Source: CQ Press using data from U.S. Department of Transportation, Bureau of Transportation Statistics
    "State Transportation Statistics 2012" (http://www.bts.gov/publications/state_transportation_statistics/)
*Does not include 24,875 miles for which the condition is not reported.   Road condition ratings are derived from the International Roughness Index (IRI) and the Present Serviceability Rating (PSR). States are required to report to the Federal Highway Administration (FHWA) IRI data for the Interstate system, other principal arterials, rural minor arterials, and the National Highway System regardless of functional system.

Bridges in 2012

National Total = 605,132 Bridges*

ALPHA ORDER

RANK	STATE	BRIDGES	% of USA
15	Alabama	16,070	2.7%
47	Alaska	1,173	0.2%
29	Arizona	7,835	1.3%
23	Arkansas	12,696	2.1%
5	California	24,812	4.1%
27	Colorado	8,591	1.4%
39	Connecticut	4,208	0.7%
49	Delaware	862	0.1%
24	Florida	11,982	2.0%
17	Georgia	14,739	2.4%
48	Hawaii	1,131	0.2%
38	Idaho	4,214	0.7%
3	Illinois	26,514	4.4%
11	Indiana	18,789	3.1%
6	Iowa	24,496	4.0%
4	Kansas	25,176	4.2%
19	Kentucky	14,031	2.3%
21	Louisiana	13,175	2.2%
45	Maine	2,408	0.4%
34	Maryland	5,294	0.9%
35	Massachusetts	5,120	0.8%
25	Michigan	11,000	1.8%
22	Minnesota	13,121	2.2%
14	Mississippi	17,061	2.8%
7	Missouri	24,334	4.0%
35	Montana	5,120	0.8%
16	Nebraska	15,393	2.5%
46	Nevada	1,798	0.3%
44	New Hampshire	2,429	0.4%
32	New Jersey	6,554	1.1%
40	New Mexico	3,924	0.6%
13	New York	17,420	2.9%
12	North Carolina	18,165	3.0%
37	North Dakota	4,453	0.7%
2	Ohio	27,045	4.5%
8	Oklahoma	23,781	3.9%
30	Oregon	7,633	1.3%
9	Pennsylvania	22,669	3.7%
50	Rhode Island	757	0.1%
26	South Carolina	9,271	1.5%
33	South Dakota	5,870	1.0%
10	Tennessee	19,985	3.3%
1	Texas	52,260	8.6%
42	Utah	2,947	0.5%
43	Vermont	2,727	0.5%
20	Virginia	13,769	2.3%
28	Washington	7,840	1.3%
31	West Virginia	7,093	1.2%
18	Wisconsin	14,057	2.3%
41	Wyoming	3,101	0.5%

RANK ORDER

RANK	STATE	BRIDGES	% of USA
1	Texas	52,260	8.6%
2	Ohio	27,045	4.5%
3	Illinois	26,514	4.4%
4	Kansas	25,176	4.2%
5	California	24,812	4.1%
6	Iowa	24,496	4.0%
7	Missouri	24,334	4.0%
8	Oklahoma	23,781	3.9%
9	Pennsylvania	22,669	3.7%
10	Tennessee	19,985	3.3%
11	Indiana	18,789	3.1%
12	North Carolina	18,165	3.0%
13	New York	17,420	2.9%
14	Mississippi	17,061	2.8%
15	Alabama	16,070	2.7%
16	Nebraska	15,393	2.5%
17	Georgia	14,739	2.4%
18	Wisconsin	14,057	2.3%
19	Kentucky	14,031	2.3%
20	Virginia	13,769	2.3%
21	Louisiana	13,175	2.2%
22	Minnesota	13,121	2.2%
23	Arkansas	12,696	2.1%
24	Florida	11,982	2.0%
25	Michigan	11,000	1.8%
26	South Carolina	9,271	1.5%
27	Colorado	8,591	1.4%
28	Washington	7,840	1.3%
29	Arizona	7,835	1.3%
30	Oregon	7,633	1.3%
31	West Virginia	7,093	1.2%
32	New Jersey	6,554	1.1%
33	South Dakota	5,870	1.0%
34	Maryland	5,294	0.9%
35	Massachusetts	5,120	0.8%
35	Montana	5,120	0.8%
37	North Dakota	4,453	0.7%
38	Idaho	4,214	0.7%
39	Connecticut	4,208	0.7%
40	New Mexico	3,924	0.6%
41	Wyoming	3,101	0.5%
42	Utah	2,947	0.5%
43	Vermont	2,727	0.5%
44	New Hampshire	2,429	0.4%
45	Maine	2,408	0.4%
46	Nevada	1,798	0.3%
47	Alaska	1,173	0.2%
48	Hawaii	1,131	0.2%
49	Delaware	862	0.1%
50	Rhode Island	757	0.1%
	District of Columbia	239	0.0%

Source: U.S. Department of Transportation, Federal Highway Administration
"Deficient Bridges by State and Highway System, 2012" (http://www.fhwa.dot.gov/bridge/deficient.htm)
*As of December 2012. Includes federal-aid and nonfederal-aid system bridges. National total does not include 2,248 bridges in Puerto Rico.

Deficient Bridges in 2012

National Total = 150,283 Deficient Bridges*

ALPHA ORDER					RANK ORDER			
RANK	STATE	BRIDGES	% of USA		RANK	STATE	BRIDGES	% of USA
19	Alabama	3,653	2.4%		1	Texas	10,052	6.7%
48	Alaska	275	0.2%		2	Pennsylvania	9,910	6.6%
37	Arizona	968	0.6%		3	California	7,156	4.8%
21	Arkansas	2,929	1.9%		4	Oklahoma	6,986	4.6%
3	California	7,156	4.8%		5	Missouri	6,893	4.6%
33	Colorado	1,473	1.0%		6	New York	6,887	4.6%
32	Connecticut	1,476	1.0%		7	Ohio	6,773	4.5%
50	Delaware	175	0.1%		8	Iowa	6,475	4.3%
27	Florida	2,026	1.3%		9	North Carolina	5,488	3.7%
22	Georgia	2,749	1.8%		10	Kansas	4,617	3.1%
45	Hawaii	505	0.3%		11	Kentucky	4,463	3.0%
40	Idaho	837	0.6%		12	Illinois	4,287	2.9%
12	Illinois	4,287	2.9%		13	Indiana	4,224	2.8%
13	Indiana	4,224	2.8%		14	Tennessee	3,864	2.6%
8	Iowa	6,475	4.3%		15	Nebraska	3,837	2.6%
10	Kansas	4,617	3.1%		16	Louisiana	3,815	2.5%
11	Kentucky	4,463	3.0%		17	Mississippi	3,774	2.5%
16	Louisiana	3,815	2.5%		18	Virginia	3,671	2.4%
42	Maine	792	0.5%		19	Alabama	3,653	2.4%
34	Maryland	1,467	1.0%		20	Michigan	3,026	2.0%
23	Massachusetts	2,707	1.8%		21	Arkansas	2,929	1.9%
20	Michigan	3,026	2.0%		22	Georgia	2,749	1.8%
31	Minnesota	1,613	1.1%		23	Massachusetts	2,707	1.8%
17	Mississippi	3,774	2.5%		24	West Virginia	2,547	1.7%
5	Missouri	6,893	4.6%		25	New Jersey	2,368	1.6%
39	Montana	908	0.6%		26	Washington	2,059	1.4%
15	Nebraska	3,837	2.6%		27	Florida	2,026	1.3%
49	Nevada	256	0.2%		28	South Carolina	1,981	1.3%
41	New Hampshire	807	0.5%		29	Wisconsin	1,936	1.3%
25	New Jersey	2,368	1.6%		30	Oregon	1,774	1.2%
44	New Mexico	657	0.4%		31	Minnesota	1,613	1.1%
6	New York	6,887	4.6%		32	Connecticut	1,476	1.0%
9	North Carolina	5,488	3.7%		33	Colorado	1,473	1.0%
36	North Dakota	993	0.7%		34	Maryland	1,467	1.0%
7	Ohio	6,773	4.5%		35	South Dakota	1,445	1.0%
4	Oklahoma	6,986	4.6%		36	North Dakota	993	0.7%
30	Oregon	1,774	1.2%		37	Arizona	968	0.6%
2	Pennsylvania	9,910	6.6%		38	Vermont	931	0.6%
47	Rhode Island	411	0.3%		39	Montana	908	0.6%
28	South Carolina	1,981	1.3%		40	Idaho	837	0.6%
35	South Dakota	1,445	1.0%		41	New Hampshire	807	0.5%
14	Tennessee	3,864	2.6%		42	Maine	792	0.5%
1	Texas	10,052	6.7%		43	Wyoming	713	0.5%
46	Utah	469	0.3%		44	New Mexico	657	0.4%
38	Vermont	931	0.6%		45	Hawaii	505	0.3%
18	Virginia	3,671	2.4%		46	Utah	469	0.3%
26	Washington	2,059	1.4%		47	Rhode Island	411	0.3%
24	West Virginia	2,547	1.7%		48	Alaska	275	0.2%
29	Wisconsin	1,936	1.3%		49	Nevada	256	0.2%
43	Wyoming	713	0.5%		50	Delaware	175	0.1%
						District of Columbia	185	0.1%

Source: U.S. Department of Transportation, Federal Highway Administration
"Deficient Bridges by State and Highway System, 2012" (http://www.fhwa.dot.gov/bridge/deficient.htm)
*As of December 2012. Includes federal-aid and nonfederal-aid system bridges. National total does not include 1,214 deficient bridges in Puerto Rico. Bridges classified as deficient are either functionally obsolete or structurally deficient and are not necessarily unsafe.

Deficient Bridges as a Percent of Total Bridges in 2012

National Percent = 24.8% of Bridges are Deficient*

ALPHA ORDER

RANK	STATE	PERCENT
30	Alabama	22.7
26	Alaska	23.4
49	Arizona	12.4
28	Arkansas	23.1
16	California	28.8
42	Colorado	17.1
8	Connecticut	35.1
35	Delaware	20.3
43	Florida	16.9
39	Georgia	18.7
3	Hawaii	44.7
36	Idaho	19.9
45	Illinois	16.2
31	Indiana	22.5
21	Iowa	26.4
40	Kansas	18.3
12	Kentucky	31.8
15	Louisiana	29.0
11	Maine	32.9
18	Maryland	27.7
2	Massachusetts	52.9
19	Michigan	27.5
50	Minnesota	12.3
33	Mississippi	22.1
17	Missouri	28.3
41	Montana	17.7
24	Nebraska	24.9
47	Nevada	14.2
10	New Hampshire	33.2
6	New Jersey	36.1
44	New Mexico	16.7
5	New York	39.5
13	North Carolina	30.2
32	North Dakota	22.3
23	Ohio	25.0
14	Oklahoma	29.4
27	Oregon	23.2
4	Pennsylvania	43.7
1	Rhode Island	54.3
34	South Carolina	21.4
25	South Dakota	24.6
37	Tennessee	19.3
38	Texas	19.2
46	Utah	15.9
9	Vermont	34.1
20	Virginia	26.7
22	Washington	26.3
7	West Virginia	35.9
48	Wisconsin	13.8
29	Wyoming	23.0

RANK ORDER

RANK	STATE	PERCENT
1	Rhode Island	54.3
2	Massachusetts	52.9
3	Hawaii	44.7
4	Pennsylvania	43.7
5	New York	39.5
6	New Jersey	36.1
7	West Virginia	35.9
8	Connecticut	35.1
9	Vermont	34.1
10	New Hampshire	33.2
11	Maine	32.9
12	Kentucky	31.8
13	North Carolina	30.2
14	Oklahoma	29.4
15	Louisiana	29.0
16	California	28.8
17	Missouri	28.3
18	Maryland	27.7
19	Michigan	27.5
20	Virginia	26.7
21	Iowa	26.4
22	Washington	26.3
23	Ohio	25.0
24	Nebraska	24.9
25	South Dakota	24.6
26	Alaska	23.4
27	Oregon	23.2
28	Arkansas	23.1
29	Wyoming	23.0
30	Alabama	22.7
31	Indiana	22.5
32	North Dakota	22.3
33	Mississippi	22.1
34	South Carolina	21.4
35	Delaware	20.3
36	Idaho	19.9
37	Tennessee	19.3
38	Texas	19.2
39	Georgia	18.7
40	Kansas	18.3
41	Montana	17.7
42	Colorado	17.1
43	Florida	16.9
44	New Mexico	16.7
45	Illinois	16.2
46	Utah	15.9
47	Nevada	14.2
48	Wisconsin	13.8
49	Arizona	12.4
50	Minnesota	12.3

| | District of Columbia | 77.4 |

Source: CQ Press using data from U.S. Department of Transportation, Federal Highway Administration
  "Deficient Bridges by State and Highway System, 2012" (http://www.fhwa.dot.gov/bridge/deficient.htm)
*As of December 2012. Includes federal-aid and nonfederal-aid system bridges. National percent does not include bridges in Puerto Rico. Bridges classified as deficient are either functionally obsolete or structurally deficient and are not necessarily unsafe.

Vehicle-Miles of Travel in 2011

National Total = 2,946,131,000,000 Miles

<table>
<tr><td colspan="4">ALPHA ORDER</td><td colspan="4">RANK ORDER</td></tr>
<tr><td>RANK</td><td>STATE</td><td>MILES</td><td>% of USA</td><td>RANK</td><td>STATE</td><td>MILES</td><td>% of USA</td></tr>
<tr><td>16</td><td>Alabama</td><td>64,914,000,000</td><td>2.2%</td><td>1</td><td>California</td><td>320,784,000,000</td><td>10.9%</td></tr>
<tr><td>50</td><td>Alaska</td><td>4,593,000,000</td><td>0.2%</td><td>2</td><td>Texas</td><td>237,440,000,000</td><td>8.1%</td></tr>
<tr><td>17</td><td>Arizona</td><td>59,574,000,000</td><td>2.0%</td><td>3</td><td>Florida</td><td>191,855,000,000</td><td>6.5%</td></tr>
<tr><td>30</td><td>Arkansas</td><td>32,953,000,000</td><td>1.1%</td><td>4</td><td>New York</td><td>127,726,000,000</td><td>4.3%</td></tr>
<tr><td>1</td><td>California</td><td>320,784,000,000</td><td>10.9%</td><td>5</td><td>Ohio</td><td>111,990,000,000</td><td>3.8%</td></tr>
<tr><td>26</td><td>Colorado</td><td>46,606,000,000</td><td>1.6%</td><td>6</td><td>Georgia</td><td>108,454,000,000</td><td>3.7%</td></tr>
<tr><td>32</td><td>Connecticut</td><td>31,197,000,000</td><td>1.1%</td><td>7</td><td>North Carolina</td><td>103,772,000,000</td><td>3.5%</td></tr>
<tr><td>46</td><td>Delaware</td><td>9,028,000,000</td><td>0.3%</td><td>8</td><td>Illinois</td><td>103,234,000,000</td><td>3.5%</td></tr>
<tr><td>3</td><td>Florida</td><td>191,855,000,000</td><td>6.5%</td><td>9</td><td>Pennsylvania</td><td>99,204,000,000</td><td>3.4%</td></tr>
<tr><td>6</td><td>Georgia</td><td>108,454,000,000</td><td>3.7%</td><td>10</td><td>Michigan</td><td>94,754,000,000</td><td>3.2%</td></tr>
<tr><td>43</td><td>Hawaii</td><td>10,066,000,000</td><td>0.3%</td><td>11</td><td>Virginia</td><td>80,974,000,000</td><td>2.7%</td></tr>
<tr><td>39</td><td>Idaho</td><td>15,937,000,000</td><td>0.5%</td><td>12</td><td>Indiana</td><td>76,485,000,000</td><td>2.6%</td></tr>
<tr><td>8</td><td>Illinois</td><td>103,234,000,000</td><td>3.5%</td><td>13</td><td>New Jersey</td><td>73,094,000,000</td><td>2.5%</td></tr>
<tr><td>12</td><td>Indiana</td><td>76,485,000,000</td><td>2.6%</td><td>14</td><td>Tennessee</td><td>70,751,000,000</td><td>2.4%</td></tr>
<tr><td>31</td><td>Iowa</td><td>31,274,000,000</td><td>1.1%</td><td>15</td><td>Missouri</td><td>68,789,000,000</td><td>2.3%</td></tr>
<tr><td>33</td><td>Kansas</td><td>30,021,000,000</td><td>1.0%</td><td>16</td><td>Alabama</td><td>64,914,000,000</td><td>2.2%</td></tr>
<tr><td>24</td><td>Kentucky</td><td>48,061,000,000</td><td>1.6%</td><td>17</td><td>Arizona</td><td>59,574,000,000</td><td>2.0%</td></tr>
<tr><td>27</td><td>Louisiana</td><td>46,513,000,000</td><td>1.6%</td><td>18</td><td>Washington</td><td>56,955,000,000</td><td>1.9%</td></tr>
<tr><td>40</td><td>Maine</td><td>14,248,000,000</td><td>0.5%</td><td>19</td><td>Minnesota</td><td>56,685,000,000</td><td>1.9%</td></tr>
<tr><td>20</td><td>Maryland</td><td>56,221,000,000</td><td>1.9%</td><td>20</td><td>Maryland</td><td>56,221,000,000</td><td>1.9%</td></tr>
<tr><td>21</td><td>Massachusetts</td><td>54,792,000,000</td><td>1.9%</td><td>21</td><td>Massachusetts</td><td>54,792,000,000</td><td>1.9%</td></tr>
<tr><td>10</td><td>Michigan</td><td>94,754,000,000</td><td>3.2%</td><td>22</td><td>Wisconsin</td><td>54,402,000,000</td><td>1.8%</td></tr>
<tr><td>19</td><td>Minnesota</td><td>56,685,000,000</td><td>1.9%</td><td>23</td><td>South Carolina</td><td>48,730,000,000</td><td>1.7%</td></tr>
<tr><td>28</td><td>Mississippi</td><td>38,851,000,000</td><td>1.3%</td><td>24</td><td>Kentucky</td><td>48,061,000,000</td><td>1.6%</td></tr>
<tr><td>15</td><td>Missouri</td><td>68,789,000,000</td><td>2.3%</td><td>25</td><td>Oklahoma</td><td>47,464,000,000</td><td>1.6%</td></tr>
<tr><td>42</td><td>Montana</td><td>11,660,000,000</td><td>0.4%</td><td>26</td><td>Colorado</td><td>46,606,000,000</td><td>1.6%</td></tr>
<tr><td>37</td><td>Nebraska</td><td>19,093,000,000</td><td>0.6%</td><td>27</td><td>Louisiana</td><td>46,513,000,000</td><td>1.6%</td></tr>
<tr><td>36</td><td>Nevada</td><td>24,189,000,000</td><td>0.8%</td><td>28</td><td>Mississippi</td><td>38,851,000,000</td><td>1.3%</td></tr>
<tr><td>41</td><td>New Hampshire</td><td>12,720,000,000</td><td>0.4%</td><td>29</td><td>Oregon</td><td>33,373,000,000</td><td>1.1%</td></tr>
<tr><td>13</td><td>New Jersey</td><td>73,094,000,000</td><td>2.5%</td><td>30</td><td>Arkansas</td><td>32,953,000,000</td><td>1.1%</td></tr>
<tr><td>35</td><td>New Mexico</td><td>25,533,000,000</td><td>0.9%</td><td>31</td><td>Iowa</td><td>31,274,000,000</td><td>1.1%</td></tr>
<tr><td>4</td><td>New York</td><td>127,726,000,000</td><td>4.3%</td><td>32</td><td>Connecticut</td><td>31,197,000,000</td><td>1.1%</td></tr>
<tr><td>7</td><td>North Carolina</td><td>103,772,000,000</td><td>3.5%</td><td>33</td><td>Kansas</td><td>30,021,000,000</td><td>1.0%</td></tr>
<tr><td>45</td><td>North Dakota</td><td>9,131,000,000</td><td>0.3%</td><td>34</td><td>Utah</td><td>26,222,000,000</td><td>0.9%</td></tr>
<tr><td>5</td><td>Ohio</td><td>111,990,000,000</td><td>3.8%</td><td>35</td><td>New Mexico</td><td>25,533,000,000</td><td>0.9%</td></tr>
<tr><td>25</td><td>Oklahoma</td><td>47,464,000,000</td><td>1.6%</td><td>36</td><td>Nevada</td><td>24,189,000,000</td><td>0.8%</td></tr>
<tr><td>29</td><td>Oregon</td><td>33,373,000,000</td><td>1.1%</td><td>37</td><td>Nebraska</td><td>19,093,000,000</td><td>0.6%</td></tr>
<tr><td>9</td><td>Pennsylvania</td><td>99,204,000,000</td><td>3.4%</td><td>38</td><td>West Virginia</td><td>18,963,000,000</td><td>0.6%</td></tr>
<tr><td>48</td><td>Rhode Island</td><td>7,901,000,000</td><td>0.3%</td><td>39</td><td>Idaho</td><td>15,937,000,000</td><td>0.5%</td></tr>
<tr><td>23</td><td>South Carolina</td><td>48,730,000,000</td><td>1.7%</td><td>40</td><td>Maine</td><td>14,248,000,000</td><td>0.5%</td></tr>
<tr><td>47</td><td>South Dakota</td><td>9,002,000,000</td><td>0.3%</td><td>41</td><td>New Hampshire</td><td>12,720,000,000</td><td>0.4%</td></tr>
<tr><td>14</td><td>Tennessee</td><td>70,751,000,000</td><td>2.4%</td><td>42</td><td>Montana</td><td>11,660,000,000</td><td>0.4%</td></tr>
<tr><td>2</td><td>Texas</td><td>237,440,000,000</td><td>8.1%</td><td>43</td><td>Hawaii</td><td>10,066,000,000</td><td>0.3%</td></tr>
<tr><td>34</td><td>Utah</td><td>26,222,000,000</td><td>0.9%</td><td>44</td><td>Wyoming</td><td>9,245,000,000</td><td>0.3%</td></tr>
<tr><td>49</td><td>Vermont</td><td>7,141,000,000</td><td>0.2%</td><td>45</td><td>North Dakota</td><td>9,131,000,000</td><td>0.3%</td></tr>
<tr><td>11</td><td>Virginia</td><td>80,974,000,000</td><td>2.7%</td><td>46</td><td>Delaware</td><td>9,028,000,000</td><td>0.3%</td></tr>
<tr><td>18</td><td>Washington</td><td>56,955,000,000</td><td>1.9%</td><td>47</td><td>South Dakota</td><td>9,002,000,000</td><td>0.3%</td></tr>
<tr><td>38</td><td>West Virginia</td><td>18,963,000,000</td><td>0.6%</td><td>48</td><td>Rhode Island</td><td>7,901,000,000</td><td>0.3%</td></tr>
<tr><td>22</td><td>Wisconsin</td><td>54,402,000,000</td><td>1.8%</td><td>49</td><td>Vermont</td><td>7,141,000,000</td><td>0.2%</td></tr>
<tr><td>44</td><td>Wyoming</td><td>9,245,000,000</td><td>0.3%</td><td>50</td><td>Alaska</td><td>4,593,000,000</td><td>0.2%</td></tr>
<tr><td></td><td></td><td></td><td></td><td></td><td>District of Columbia</td><td>3,568,000,000</td><td>0.1%</td></tr>
</table>

Source: U.S. Department of Transportation, Federal Highway Administration
"Highway Statistics 2011" (Table VM-2, http://www.fhwa.dot.gov/policyinformation/statistics/2011/)

Highway Fatalities in 2011

National Total = 32,367 Fatalities

RANK	STATE	FATALITIES	% of USA
11	Alabama	894	2.8%
48	Alaska	72	0.2%
14	Arizona	825	2.5%
24	Arkansas	549	1.7%
2	California	2,791	8.6%
27	Colorado	447	1.4%
37	Connecticut	220	0.7%
46	Delaware	99	0.3%
3	Florida	2,398	7.4%
6	Georgia	1,223	3.8%
45	Hawaii	100	0.3%
40	Idaho	167	0.5%
10	Illinois	918	2.8%
17	Indiana	750	2.3%
30	Iowa	360	1.1%
28	Kansas	386	1.2%
18	Kentucky	721	2.2%
20	Louisiana	675	2.1%
42	Maine	136	0.4%
25	Maryland	485	1.5%
32	Massachusetts	337	1.0%
12	Michigan	889	2.7%
29	Minnesota	368	1.1%
21	Mississippi	630	1.9%
15	Missouri	784	2.4%
38	Montana	209	0.6%
39	Nebraska	181	0.6%
35	Nevada	246	0.8%
47	New Hampshire	90	0.3%
22	New Jersey	627	1.9%
31	New Mexico	353	1.1%
7	New York	1,169	3.6%
5	North Carolina	1,227	3.8%
41	North Dakota	148	0.5%
8	Ohio	1,016	3.1%
19	Oklahoma	696	2.2%
34	Oregon	331	1.0%
4	Pennsylvania	1,286	4.0%
49	Rhode Island	66	0.2%
13	South Carolina	828	2.6%
44	South Dakota	111	0.3%
9	Tennessee	946	2.9%
1	Texas	3,016	9.3%
36	Utah	240	0.7%
50	Vermont	55	0.2%
16	Virginia	764	2.4%
26	Washington	457	1.4%
32	West Virginia	337	1.0%
23	Wisconsin	582	1.8%
43	Wyoming	135	0.4%

RANK	STATE	FATALITIES	% of USA
1	Texas	3,016	9.3%
2	California	2,791	8.6%
3	Florida	2,398	7.4%
4	Pennsylvania	1,286	4.0%
5	North Carolina	1,227	3.8%
6	Georgia	1,223	3.8%
7	New York	1,169	3.6%
8	Ohio	1,016	3.1%
9	Tennessee	946	2.9%
10	Illinois	918	2.8%
11	Alabama	894	2.8%
12	Michigan	889	2.7%
13	South Carolina	828	2.6%
14	Arizona	825	2.5%
15	Missouri	784	2.4%
16	Virginia	764	2.4%
17	Indiana	750	2.3%
18	Kentucky	721	2.2%
19	Oklahoma	696	2.2%
20	Louisiana	675	2.1%
21	Mississippi	630	1.9%
22	New Jersey	627	1.9%
23	Wisconsin	582	1.8%
24	Arkansas	549	1.7%
25	Maryland	485	1.5%
26	Washington	457	1.4%
27	Colorado	447	1.4%
28	Kansas	386	1.2%
29	Minnesota	368	1.1%
30	Iowa	360	1.1%
31	New Mexico	353	1.1%
32	Massachusetts	337	1.0%
32	West Virginia	337	1.0%
34	Oregon	331	1.0%
35	Nevada	246	0.8%
36	Utah	240	0.7%
37	Connecticut	220	0.7%
38	Montana	209	0.6%
39	Nebraska	181	0.6%
40	Idaho	167	0.5%
41	North Dakota	148	0.5%
42	Maine	136	0.4%
43	Wyoming	135	0.4%
44	South Dakota	111	0.3%
45	Hawaii	100	0.3%
46	Delaware	99	0.3%
47	New Hampshire	90	0.3%
48	Alaska	72	0.2%
49	Rhode Island	66	0.2%
50	Vermont	55	0.2%
	District of Columbia	27	0.1%

Source: U.S. Department of Transportation, National Highway Traffic Safety Administration
"Traffic Safety Facts 2011" (http://www-nrd.nhtsa.dot.gov/cats/index.aspx)

Highway Fatality Rate in 2011

National Rate = 1.10 Fatalities per 100 Million Vehicle-Miles of Travel

ALPHA ORDER

RANK	STATE	RATE
12	Alabama	1.38
7	Alaska	1.57
12	Arizona	1.38
4	Arkansas	1.67
41	California	0.87
32	Colorado	0.96
47	Connecticut	0.71
25	Delaware	1.10
19	Florida	1.25
24	Georgia	1.13
29	Hawaii	0.99
27	Idaho	1.05
40	Illinois	0.89
31	Indiana	0.98
22	Iowa	1.15
17	Kansas	1.29
8	Kentucky	1.50
11	Louisiana	1.45
33	Maine	0.95
42	Maryland	0.86
50	Massachusetts	0.62
35	Michigan	0.94
49	Minnesota	0.65
5	Mississippi	1.62
23	Missouri	1.14
1	Montana	1.79
33	Nebraska	0.95
28	Nevada	1.02
47	New Hampshire	0.71
42	New Jersey	0.86
12	New Mexico	1.38
37	New York	0.92
21	North Carolina	1.18
5	North Dakota	1.62
39	Ohio	0.91
9	Oklahoma	1.47
29	Oregon	0.99
16	Pennsylvania	1.30
44	Rhode Island	0.84
3	South Carolina	1.70
20	South Dakota	1.23
15	Tennessee	1.34
18	Texas	1.27
37	Utah	0.92
46	Vermont	0.77
35	Virginia	0.94
45	Washington	0.80
2	West Virginia	1.78
26	Wisconsin	1.07
10	Wyoming	1.46

RANK ORDER

RANK	STATE	RATE
1	Montana	1.79
2	West Virginia	1.78
3	South Carolina	1.70
4	Arkansas	1.67
5	Mississippi	1.62
5	North Dakota	1.62
7	Alaska	1.57
8	Kentucky	1.50
9	Oklahoma	1.47
10	Wyoming	1.46
11	Louisiana	1.45
12	Alabama	1.38
12	Arizona	1.38
12	New Mexico	1.38
15	Tennessee	1.34
16	Pennsylvania	1.30
17	Kansas	1.29
18	Texas	1.27
19	Florida	1.25
20	South Dakota	1.23
21	North Carolina	1.18
22	Iowa	1.15
23	Missouri	1.14
24	Georgia	1.13
25	Delaware	1.10
26	Wisconsin	1.07
27	Idaho	1.05
28	Nevada	1.02
29	Hawaii	0.99
29	Oregon	0.99
31	Indiana	0.98
32	Colorado	0.96
33	Maine	0.95
33	Nebraska	0.95
35	Michigan	0.94
35	Virginia	0.94
37	New York	0.92
37	Utah	0.92
39	Ohio	0.91
40	Illinois	0.89
41	California	0.87
42	Maryland	0.86
42	New Jersey	0.86
44	Rhode Island	0.84
45	Washington	0.80
46	Vermont	0.77
47	Connecticut	0.71
47	New Hampshire	0.71
49	Minnesota	0.65
50	Massachusetts	0.62
	District of Columbia	0.76

Source: U.S. Department of Transportation, National Highway Traffic Safety Administration
"Traffic Safety Facts 2011" (http://www-nrd.nhtsa.dot.gov/cats/index.aspx)

Percent of Traffic Fatalities That Were Speeding-Related in 2011

National Percent = 30.7%*

<table>
<tr><td colspan="3">ALPHA ORDER</td><td colspan="3">RANK ORDER</td></tr>
<tr><td>RANK</td><td>STATE</td><td>PERCENT</td><td>RANK</td><td>STATE</td><td>PERCENT</td></tr>
<tr><td>23</td><td>Alabama</td><td>33.3</td><td>1</td><td>Maine</td><td>50.7</td></tr>
<tr><td>16</td><td>Alaska</td><td>36.1</td><td>2</td><td>Illinois</td><td>47.8</td></tr>
<tr><td>18</td><td>Arizona</td><td>35.6</td><td>2</td><td>Pennsylvania</td><td>47.8</td></tr>
<tr><td>49</td><td>Arkansas</td><td>15.7</td><td>4</td><td>Hawaii</td><td>45.0</td></tr>
<tr><td>27</td><td>California</td><td>31.9</td><td>5</td><td>New Hampshire</td><td>43.3</td></tr>
<tr><td>7</td><td>Colorado</td><td>40.9</td><td>6</td><td>New Mexico</td><td>41.6</td></tr>
<tr><td>26</td><td>Connecticut</td><td>33.2</td><td>7</td><td>Colorado</td><td>40.9</td></tr>
<tr><td>20</td><td>Delaware</td><td>34.3</td><td>8</td><td>Missouri</td><td>39.5</td></tr>
<tr><td>50</td><td>Florida</td><td>12.3</td><td>9</td><td>North Carolina</td><td>38.6</td></tr>
<tr><td>46</td><td>Georgia</td><td>18.0</td><td>9</td><td>Texas</td><td>38.6</td></tr>
<tr><td>4</td><td>Hawaii</td><td>45.0</td><td>11</td><td>Wyoming</td><td>37.8</td></tr>
<tr><td>39</td><td>Idaho</td><td>26.9</td><td>12</td><td>Virginia</td><td>37.6</td></tr>
<tr><td>2</td><td>Illinois</td><td>47.8</td><td>13</td><td>Utah</td><td>37.5</td></tr>
<tr><td>43</td><td>Indiana</td><td>20.4</td><td>14</td><td>Montana</td><td>36.4</td></tr>
<tr><td>47</td><td>Iowa</td><td>17.8</td><td>14</td><td>Vermont</td><td>36.4</td></tr>
<tr><td>37</td><td>Kansas</td><td>28.2</td><td>16</td><td>Alaska</td><td>36.1</td></tr>
<tr><td>44</td><td>Kentucky</td><td>19.6</td><td>16</td><td>Washington</td><td>36.1</td></tr>
<tr><td>28</td><td>Louisiana</td><td>31.7</td><td>18</td><td>Arizona</td><td>35.6</td></tr>
<tr><td>1</td><td>Maine</td><td>50.7</td><td>19</td><td>North Dakota</td><td>34.5</td></tr>
<tr><td>34</td><td>Maryland</td><td>29.3</td><td>20</td><td>Delaware</td><td>34.3</td></tr>
<tr><td>31</td><td>Massachusetts</td><td>30.6</td><td>21</td><td>West Virginia</td><td>33.8</td></tr>
<tr><td>40</td><td>Michigan</td><td>26.8</td><td>22</td><td>Wisconsin</td><td>33.5</td></tr>
<tr><td>41</td><td>Minnesota</td><td>23.4</td><td>23</td><td>Alabama</td><td>33.3</td></tr>
<tr><td>48</td><td>Mississippi</td><td>16.5</td><td>23</td><td>South Carolina</td><td>33.3</td></tr>
<tr><td>8</td><td>Missouri</td><td>39.5</td><td>23</td><td>South Dakota</td><td>33.3</td></tr>
<tr><td>14</td><td>Montana</td><td>36.4</td><td>26</td><td>Connecticut</td><td>33.2</td></tr>
<tr><td>45</td><td>Nebraska</td><td>18.2</td><td>27</td><td>California</td><td>31.9</td></tr>
<tr><td>30</td><td>Nevada</td><td>30.9</td><td>28</td><td>Louisiana</td><td>31.7</td></tr>
<tr><td>5</td><td>New Hampshire</td><td>43.3</td><td>29</td><td>Oregon</td><td>31.1</td></tr>
<tr><td>38</td><td>New Jersey</td><td>27.8</td><td>30</td><td>Nevada</td><td>30.9</td></tr>
<tr><td>6</td><td>New Mexico</td><td>41.6</td><td>31</td><td>Massachusetts</td><td>30.6</td></tr>
<tr><td>35</td><td>New York</td><td>28.9</td><td>31</td><td>Oklahoma</td><td>30.6</td></tr>
<tr><td>9</td><td>North Carolina</td><td>38.6</td><td>33</td><td>Ohio</td><td>29.4</td></tr>
<tr><td>19</td><td>North Dakota</td><td>34.5</td><td>34</td><td>Maryland</td><td>29.3</td></tr>
<tr><td>33</td><td>Ohio</td><td>29.4</td><td>35</td><td>New York</td><td>28.9</td></tr>
<tr><td>31</td><td>Oklahoma</td><td>30.6</td><td>36</td><td>Rhode Island</td><td>28.8</td></tr>
<tr><td>29</td><td>Oregon</td><td>31.1</td><td>37</td><td>Kansas</td><td>28.2</td></tr>
<tr><td>2</td><td>Pennsylvania</td><td>47.8</td><td>38</td><td>New Jersey</td><td>27.8</td></tr>
<tr><td>36</td><td>Rhode Island</td><td>28.8</td><td>39</td><td>Idaho</td><td>26.9</td></tr>
<tr><td>23</td><td>South Carolina</td><td>33.3</td><td>40</td><td>Michigan</td><td>26.8</td></tr>
<tr><td>23</td><td>South Dakota</td><td>33.3</td><td>41</td><td>Minnesota</td><td>23.4</td></tr>
<tr><td>42</td><td>Tennessee</td><td>22.7</td><td>42</td><td>Tennessee</td><td>22.7</td></tr>
<tr><td>9</td><td>Texas</td><td>38.6</td><td>43</td><td>Indiana</td><td>20.4</td></tr>
<tr><td>13</td><td>Utah</td><td>37.5</td><td>44</td><td>Kentucky</td><td>19.6</td></tr>
<tr><td>14</td><td>Vermont</td><td>36.4</td><td>45</td><td>Nebraska</td><td>18.2</td></tr>
<tr><td>12</td><td>Virginia</td><td>37.6</td><td>46</td><td>Georgia</td><td>18.0</td></tr>
<tr><td>16</td><td>Washington</td><td>36.1</td><td>47</td><td>Iowa</td><td>17.8</td></tr>
<tr><td>21</td><td>West Virginia</td><td>33.8</td><td>48</td><td>Mississippi</td><td>16.5</td></tr>
<tr><td>22</td><td>Wisconsin</td><td>33.5</td><td>49</td><td>Arkansas</td><td>15.7</td></tr>
<tr><td>11</td><td>Wyoming</td><td>37.8</td><td>50</td><td>Florida</td><td>12.3</td></tr>
<tr><td></td><td></td><td></td><td></td><td>District of Columbia</td><td>37.0</td></tr>
</table>

Source: CQ Press using data from U.S. Department of Transportation, National Highway Traffic Safety Administration
"Traffic Safety Facts 2011" (http://www-nrd.nhtsa.dot.gov/cats/index.aspx)
*A speeding-related crash is if the driver was charged with a speeding-related offense or if an officer indicated that racing, driving too fast for conditions, or exceeding the posted speed limit was a contributing factor in the crash.

Percent of Vehicles Involved in Fatal Crashes That Were Large Trucks in 2011

National Percent = 8.2%*

ALPHA ORDER

RANK	STATE	PERCENT
26	Alabama	7.8
50	Alaska	0.0
43	Arizona	5.8
3	Arkansas	13.7
35	California	7.0
26	Colorado	7.8
47	Connecticut	4.8
33	Delaware	7.1
41	Florida	6.1
13	Georgia	9.9
48	Hawaii	2.1
24	Idaho	8.3
16	Illinois	9.6
4	Indiana	12.5
10	Iowa	10.4
9	Kansas	10.8
21	Kentucky	8.8
22	Louisiana	8.7
12	Maine	10.1
44	Maryland	5.5
41	Massachusetts	6.1
46	Michigan	4.9
10	Minnesota	10.4
28	Mississippi	7.7
17	Missouri	9.5
17	Montana	9.5
5	Nebraska	11.3
23	Nevada	8.5
39	New Hampshire	6.7
40	New Jersey	6.5
7	New Mexico	11.0
30	New York	7.3
35	North Carolina	7.0
1	North Dakota	17.0
25	Ohio	7.9
6	Oklahoma	11.1
7	Oregon	11.0
19	Pennsylvania	9.1
49	Rhode Island	1.2
32	South Carolina	7.2
29	South Dakota	7.4
38	Tennessee	6.8
14	Texas	9.8
33	Utah	7.1
20	Vermont	9.0
30	Virginia	7.3
44	Washington	5.5
37	West Virginia	6.9
15	Wisconsin	9.7
2	Wyoming	16.6

RANK ORDER

RANK	STATE	PERCENT
1	North Dakota	17.0
2	Wyoming	16.6
3	Arkansas	13.7
4	Indiana	12.5
5	Nebraska	11.3
6	Oklahoma	11.1
7	New Mexico	11.0
7	Oregon	11.0
9	Kansas	10.8
10	Iowa	10.4
10	Minnesota	10.4
12	Maine	10.1
13	Georgia	9.9
14	Texas	9.8
15	Wisconsin	9.7
16	Illinois	9.6
17	Missouri	9.5
17	Montana	9.5
19	Pennsylvania	9.1
20	Vermont	9.0
21	Kentucky	8.8
22	Louisiana	8.7
23	Nevada	8.5
24	Idaho	8.3
25	Ohio	7.9
26	Alabama	7.8
26	Colorado	7.8
28	Mississippi	7.7
29	South Dakota	7.4
30	New York	7.3
30	Virginia	7.3
32	South Carolina	7.2
33	Delaware	7.1
33	Utah	7.1
35	California	7.0
35	North Carolina	7.0
37	West Virginia	6.9
38	Tennessee	6.8
39	New Hampshire	6.7
40	New Jersey	6.5
41	Florida	6.1
41	Massachusetts	6.1
43	Arizona	5.8
44	Maryland	5.5
44	Washington	5.5
46	Michigan	4.9
47	Connecticut	4.8
48	Hawaii	2.1
49	Rhode Island	1.2
50	Alaska	0.0

District of Columbia	6.9

Source: U.S. Department of Transportation, National Highway Traffic Safety Administration
    "Traffic Safety Facts: Large Trucks" (http://www-nrd.nhtsa.dot.gov/cats/Index.aspx)
*Large trucks are those with gross vehicle weight greater than 10,000 pounds. In 2011, 3,608 large trucks were involved in fatal crashes.

Lives Saved by Child Restraints, Seat Belts, Air Bags, and Motorcycle Helmets in 2011
National Total = 16,033 Lives

RANK	STATE	LIVES	% of USA
10	Alabama	454	2.8%
47	Alaska	32	0.2%
20	Arizona	320	2.0%
25	Arkansas	266	1.7%
2	California	1,506	9.4%
30	Colorado	192	1.2%
37	Connecticut	105	0.7%
44	Delaware	39	0.2%
3	Florida	939	5.9%
5	Georgia	678	4.2%
47	Hawaii	32	0.2%
40	Idaho	69	0.4%
12	Illinois	422	2.6%
13	Indiana	415	2.6%
32	Iowa	187	1.2%
29	Kansas	200	1.2%
16	Kentucky	364	2.3%
19	Louisiana	322	2.0%
41	Maine	66	0.4%
26	Maryland	227	1.4%
34	Massachusetts	148	0.9%
7	Michigan	541	3.4%
28	Minnesota	207	1.3%
18	Mississippi	326	2.0%
17	Missouri	338	2.1%
39	Montana	86	0.5%
38	Nebraska	87	0.5%
36	Nevada	111	0.7%
49	New Hampshire	23	0.1%
22	New Jersey	317	2.0%
31	New Mexico	190	1.2%
6	New York	603	3.8%
4	North Carolina	692	4.3%
42	North Dakota	59	0.4%
11	Ohio	447	2.8%
21	Oklahoma	318	2.0%
27	Oregon	209	1.3%
8	Pennsylvania	505	3.1%
49	Rhode Island	23	0.1%
15	South Carolina	390	2.4%
46	South Dakota	38	0.2%
9	Tennessee	489	3.0%
1	Texas	1,690	10.5%
35	Utah	125	0.8%
44	Vermont	39	0.2%
14	Virginia	403	2.5%
23	Washington	279	1.7%
33	West Virginia	166	1.0%
24	Wisconsin	275	1.7%
43	Wyoming	57	0.4%

RANK	STATE	LIVES	% of USA
1	Texas	1,690	10.5%
2	California	1,506	9.4%
3	Florida	939	5.9%
4	North Carolina	692	4.3%
5	Georgia	678	4.2%
6	New York	603	3.8%
7	Michigan	541	3.4%
8	Pennsylvania	505	3.1%
9	Tennessee	489	3.0%
10	Alabama	454	2.8%
11	Ohio	447	2.8%
12	Illinois	422	2.6%
13	Indiana	415	2.6%
14	Virginia	403	2.5%
15	South Carolina	390	2.4%
16	Kentucky	364	2.3%
17	Missouri	338	2.1%
18	Mississippi	326	2.0%
19	Louisiana	322	2.0%
20	Arizona	320	2.0%
21	Oklahoma	318	2.0%
22	New Jersey	317	2.0%
23	Washington	279	1.7%
24	Wisconsin	275	1.7%
25	Arkansas	266	1.7%
26	Maryland	227	1.4%
27	Oregon	209	1.3%
28	Minnesota	207	1.3%
29	Kansas	200	1.2%
30	Colorado	192	1.2%
31	New Mexico	190	1.2%
32	Iowa	187	1.2%
33	West Virginia	166	1.0%
34	Massachusetts	148	0.9%
35	Utah	125	0.8%
36	Nevada	111	0.7%
37	Connecticut	105	0.7%
38	Nebraska	87	0.5%
39	Montana	86	0.5%
40	Idaho	69	0.4%
41	Maine	66	0.4%
42	North Dakota	59	0.4%
43	Wyoming	57	0.4%
44	Delaware	39	0.2%
44	Vermont	39	0.2%
46	South Dakota	38	0.2%
47	Alaska	32	0.2%
47	Hawaii	32	0.2%
49	New Hampshire	23	0.1%
49	Rhode Island	23	0.1%
	District of Columbia	8	0.0%

Source: CQ Press using data from U.S. Department of Transportation, National Highway Traffic Safety Administration
"Traffic Safety Facts: Lives Saved in 2011" (http://www-nrd.nhtsa.dot.gov/cats/Index.aspx)

Safety Belt Usage Rate in 2012

National Rate = 86.0% Use Safety Belts

RANK	STATE	PERCENT
17	Alabama	89.5
19	Alaska	88.1
32	Arizona	82.2
48	Arkansas	71.9
3	California	95.5
36	Colorado	80.7
23	Connecticut	86.8
20	Delaware	87.9
22	Florida	87.4
11	Georgia	92.0
9	Hawaii	93.4
41	Idaho	79.0
5	Illinois	93.6
5	Indiana	93.6
10	Iowa	92.4
38	Kansas	79.5
28	Kentucky	83.7
40	Louisiana	79.3
24	Maine	84.4
13	Maryland	91.1
47	Massachusetts	72.7
5	Michigan	93.6
5	Minnesota	93.6
31	Mississippi	83.2
39	Missouri	79.4
46	Montana	76.3
42	Nebraska	78.6
14	Nevada	90.5
49	New Hampshire	68.6
18	New Jersey	88.3
12	New Mexico	91.4
16	New York	90.4
21	North Carolina	87.5
35	North Dakota	80.9
33	Ohio	82.0
27	Oklahoma	83.8
2	Oregon	96.8
30	Pennsylvania	83.5
44	Rhode Island	77.5
14	South Carolina	90.5
50	South Dakota	66.5
28	Tennessee	83.7
4	Texas	94.0
34	Utah	81.9
25	Vermont	84.2
43	Virginia	78.4
1	Washington	96.9
26	West Virginia	84.0
37	Wisconsin	79.9
45	Wyoming	77.0

RANK	STATE	PERCENT
1	Washington	96.9
2	Oregon	96.8
3	California	95.5
4	Texas	94.0
5	Illinois	93.6
5	Indiana	93.6
5	Michigan	93.6
5	Minnesota	93.6
9	Hawaii	93.4
10	Iowa	92.4
11	Georgia	92.0
12	New Mexico	91.4
13	Maryland	91.1
14	Nevada	90.5
14	South Carolina	90.5
16	New York	90.4
17	Alabama	89.5
18	New Jersey	88.3
19	Alaska	88.1
20	Delaware	87.9
21	North Carolina	87.5
22	Florida	87.4
23	Connecticut	86.8
24	Maine	84.4
25	Vermont	84.2
26	West Virginia	84.0
27	Oklahoma	83.8
28	Kentucky	83.7
28	Tennessee	83.7
30	Pennsylvania	83.5
31	Mississippi	83.2
32	Arizona	82.2
33	Ohio	82.0
34	Utah	81.9
35	North Dakota	80.9
36	Colorado	80.7
37	Wisconsin	79.9
38	Kansas	79.5
39	Missouri	79.4
40	Louisiana	79.3
41	Idaho	79.0
42	Nebraska	78.6
43	Virginia	78.4
44	Rhode Island	77.5
45	Wyoming	77.0
46	Montana	76.3
47	Massachusetts	72.7
48	Arkansas	71.9
49	New Hampshire	68.6
50	South Dakota	66.5
	District of Columbia	92.4

Source: U.S. Department of Transportation, National Highway Traffic Safety Administration
"Traffic Safety Facts: Seat Belt Use in 2012" (http://www-nrd.nhtsa.dot.gov/cats/Index.aspx)

Percent of Passenger Car Occupant Fatalities
Where Victim Used a Seat Belt in 2011
National Percent = 44% of Passenger Car Occupant Fatalities*

ALPHA ORDER

RANK	STATE	PERCENT
28	Alabama	39
44	Alaska	30
28	Arizona	39
35	Arkansas	37
1	California	60
35	Colorado	37
26	Connecticut	40
19	Delaware	44
14	Florida	46
19	Georgia	44
33	Hawaii	38
35	Idaho	37
14	Illinois	46
10	Indiana	49
22	Iowa	43
25	Kansas	41
22	Kentucky	43
38	Louisiana	36
14	Maine	46
13	Maryland	47
42	Massachusetts	31
6	Michigan	55
12	Minnesota	48
33	Mississippi	38
44	Missouri	30
42	Montana	31
44	Nebraska	30
28	Nevada	39
50	New Hampshire	20
5	New Jersey	56
7	New Mexico	54
3	New York	57
9	North Carolina	50
48	North Dakota	26
28	Ohio	39
28	Oklahoma	39
2	Oregon	59
44	Pennsylvania	30
39	Rhode Island	35
17	South Carolina	45
49	South Dakota	25
26	Tennessee	40
10	Texas	49
19	Utah	44
3	Vermont	57
17	Virginia	45
7	Washington	54
41	West Virginia	32
22	Wisconsin	43
39	Wyoming	35

RANK ORDER

RANK	STATE	PERCENT
1	California	60
2	Oregon	59
3	New York	57
3	Vermont	57
5	New Jersey	56
6	Michigan	55
7	New Mexico	54
7	Washington	54
9	North Carolina	50
10	Indiana	49
10	Texas	49
12	Minnesota	48
13	Maryland	47
14	Florida	46
14	Illinois	46
14	Maine	46
17	South Carolina	45
17	Virginia	45
19	Delaware	44
19	Georgia	44
19	Utah	44
22	Iowa	43
22	Kentucky	43
22	Wisconsin	43
25	Kansas	41
26	Connecticut	40
26	Tennessee	40
28	Alabama	39
28	Arizona	39
28	Nevada	39
28	Ohio	39
28	Oklahoma	39
33	Hawaii	38
33	Mississippi	38
35	Arkansas	37
35	Colorado	37
35	Idaho	37
38	Louisiana	36
39	Rhode Island	35
39	Wyoming	35
41	West Virginia	32
42	Massachusetts	31
42	Montana	31
44	Alaska	30
44	Missouri	30
44	Nebraska	30
44	Pennsylvania	30
48	North Dakota	26
49	South Dakota	25
50	New Hampshire	20

| | District of Columbia | 31 |

Source: U.S. Department of Transportation, National Highway Traffic Safety Administration
   "Traffic Safety Facts: Occupant Protection" (http://www-nrd.nhtsa.dot.gov/cats/Index.aspx)
*Only those fatalities where seat belts are known to have been used are counted.

Fatalities in Alcohol-Related Crashes in 2011

National Total = 11,510 Fatalities*

ALPHA ORDER					RANK ORDER			
RANK	STATE	FATALITIES	% of USA		RANK	STATE	FATALITIES	% of USA
11	Alabama	309	2.7%		1	Texas	1,397	12.1%
49	Alaska	24	0.2%		2	California	886	7.7%
16	Arizona	263	2.3%		3	Florida	854	7.4%
23	Arkansas	194	1.7%		4	Pennsylvania	464	4.0%
2	California	886	7.7%		5	North Carolina	417	3.6%
26	Colorado	173	1.5%		6	New York	387	3.4%
34	Connecticut	99	0.9%		7	South Carolina	379	3.3%
43	Delaware	43	0.4%		8	Ohio	358	3.1%
3	Florida	854	7.4%		9	Georgia	323	2.8%
9	Georgia	323	2.8%		9	Illinois	323	2.8%
42	Hawaii	50	0.4%		11	Alabama	309	2.7%
40	Idaho	55	0.5%		12	Tennessee	307	2.7%
9	Illinois	323	2.8%		13	Missouri	299	2.6%
19	Indiana	243	2.1%		14	Michigan	294	2.6%
35	Iowa	96	0.8%		15	Virginia	274	2.4%
28	Kansas	131	1.1%		16	Arizona	263	2.3%
22	Kentucky	201	1.7%		17	Louisiana	255	2.2%
17	Louisiana	255	2.2%		18	Oklahoma	249	2.2%
45	Maine	39	0.3%		19	Indiana	243	2.1%
24	Maryland	192	1.7%		20	New Jersey	227	2.0%
30	Massachusetts	130	1.1%		20	Wisconsin	227	2.0%
14	Michigan	294	2.6%		22	Kentucky	201	1.7%
28	Minnesota	131	1.1%		23	Arkansas	194	1.7%
27	Mississippi	163	1.4%		24	Maryland	192	1.7%
13	Missouri	299	2.6%		25	Washington	182	1.6%
37	Montana	88	0.8%		26	Colorado	173	1.5%
41	Nebraska	54	0.5%		27	Mississippi	163	1.4%
36	Nevada	91	0.8%		28	Kansas	131	1.1%
47	New Hampshire	29	0.3%		28	Minnesota	131	1.1%
20	New Jersey	227	2.0%		30	Massachusetts	130	1.1%
31	New Mexico	119	1.0%		31	New Mexico	119	1.0%
6	New York	387	3.4%		32	Oregon	116	1.0%
5	North Carolina	417	3.6%		33	West Virginia	106	0.9%
38	North Dakota	67	0.6%		34	Connecticut	99	0.9%
8	Ohio	358	3.1%		35	Iowa	96	0.8%
18	Oklahoma	249	2.2%		36	Nevada	91	0.8%
32	Oregon	116	1.0%		37	Montana	88	0.8%
4	Pennsylvania	464	4.0%		38	North Dakota	67	0.6%
48	Rhode Island	27	0.2%		39	Utah	63	0.5%
7	South Carolina	379	3.3%		40	Idaho	55	0.5%
46	South Dakota	37	0.3%		41	Nebraska	54	0.5%
12	Tennessee	307	2.7%		42	Hawaii	50	0.4%
1	Texas	1,397	12.1%		43	Delaware	43	0.4%
39	Utah	63	0.5%		44	Wyoming	41	0.4%
50	Vermont	23	0.2%		45	Maine	39	0.3%
15	Virginia	274	2.4%		46	South Dakota	37	0.3%
25	Washington	182	1.6%		47	New Hampshire	29	0.3%
33	West Virginia	106	0.9%		48	Rhode Island	27	0.2%
20	Wisconsin	227	2.0%		49	Alaska	24	0.2%
44	Wyoming	41	0.4%		50	Vermont	23	0.2%
						District of Columbia	13	0.1%

Source: U.S. Department of Transportation, National Highway Traffic Safety Administration
    "Traffic Safety Facts: Alcohol-Impaired Driving" (http://www-nrd.nhtsa.dot.gov/cats/Index.aspx)
*Drivers with Blood Alcohol Content (BAC) of .01 or more. "Legally Drunk" BAC differs from state to state but is often .08 or higher.

Fatalities in Alcohol-Related Crashes
as a Percent of All Highway Fatalities in 2011
National Percent = 36% of Highway Fatalities*

ALPHA ORDER

RANK	STATE	PERCENT
24	Alabama	35
33	Alaska	33
37	Arizona	32
24	Arkansas	35
37	California	32
12	Colorado	39
4	Connecticut	45
6	Delaware	44
18	Florida	36
48	Georgia	26
1	Hawaii	50
33	Idaho	33
24	Illinois	35
37	Indiana	32
47	Iowa	27
29	Kansas	34
46	Kentucky	28
15	Louisiana	38
45	Maine	29
10	Maryland	40
12	Massachusetts	39
33	Michigan	33
18	Minnesota	36
48	Mississippi	26
15	Missouri	38
7	Montana	42
44	Nebraska	30
17	Nevada	37
37	New Hampshire	32
18	New Jersey	36
29	New Mexico	34
33	New York	33
29	North Carolina	34
4	North Dakota	45
24	Ohio	35
18	Oklahoma	36
24	Oregon	35
18	Pennsylvania	36
9	Rhode Island	41
2	South Carolina	46
29	South Dakota	34
37	Tennessee	32
2	Texas	46
48	Utah	26
7	Vermont	42
18	Virginia	36
10	Washington	40
37	West Virginia	32
12	Wisconsin	39
43	Wyoming	31

RANK ORDER

RANK	STATE	PERCENT
1	Hawaii	50
2	South Carolina	46
2	Texas	46
4	Connecticut	45
4	North Dakota	45
6	Delaware	44
7	Montana	42
7	Vermont	42
9	Rhode Island	41
10	Maryland	40
10	Washington	40
12	Colorado	39
12	Massachusetts	39
12	Wisconsin	39
15	Louisiana	38
15	Missouri	38
17	Nevada	37
18	Florida	36
18	Minnesota	36
18	New Jersey	36
18	Oklahoma	36
18	Pennsylvania	36
18	Virginia	36
24	Alabama	35
24	Arkansas	35
24	Illinois	35
24	Ohio	35
24	Oregon	35
29	Kansas	34
29	New Mexico	34
29	North Carolina	34
29	South Dakota	34
33	Alaska	33
33	Idaho	33
33	Michigan	33
33	New York	33
37	Arizona	32
37	California	32
37	Indiana	32
37	New Hampshire	32
37	Tennessee	32
37	West Virginia	32
43	Wyoming	31
44	Nebraska	30
45	Maine	29
46	Kentucky	28
47	Iowa	27
48	Georgia	26
48	Mississippi	26
48	Utah	26
	District of Columbia	50

Source: U.S. Department of Transportation, National Highway Traffic Safety Administration
 "Traffic Safety Facts: Alcohol-Impaired Driving" (http://www-nrd.nhtsa.dot.gov/cats/Index.aspx)
*Drivers with Blood Alcohol Content (BAC) of .01 or more. "Legally Drunk" BAC differs from state to state but is often .08 or higher.

Percent of Fatal Traffic Accidents Involving Older Drivers in 2011

National Percent = 12.5%*

ALPHA ORDER

RANK	STATE	PERCENT
37	Alabama	11.7
46	Alaska	9.9
25	Arizona	13.5
35	Arkansas	11.9
44	California	10.3
45	Colorado	10.1
31	Connecticut	13.1
9	Delaware	14.9
27	Florida	13.4
10	Georgia	14.7
40	Hawaii	11.4
13	Idaho	14.5
34	Illinois	12.2
21	Indiana	13.7
1	Iowa	19.0
16	Kansas	14.0
39	Kentucky	11.6
49	Louisiana	8.8
7	Maine	15.4
37	Maryland	11.7
27	Massachusetts	13.4
15	Michigan	14.3
4	Minnesota	17.3
47	Mississippi	9.8
35	Missouri	11.9
21	Montana	13.7
30	Nebraska	13.2
16	Nevada	14.0
2	New Hampshire	18.3
14	New Jersey	14.4
43	New Mexico	10.7
32	New York	12.9
33	North Carolina	12.5
18	North Dakota	13.9
23	Ohio	13.6
20	Oklahoma	13.8
5	Oregon	17.1
23	Pennsylvania	13.6
5	Rhode Island	17.1
42	South Carolina	11.2
10	South Dakota	14.7
25	Tennessee	13.5
48	Texas	9.3
41	Utah	11.3
3	Vermont	18.2
27	Virginia	13.4
18	Washington	13.9
10	West Virginia	14.7
8	Wisconsin	15.0
50	Wyoming	8.6

RANK ORDER

RANK	STATE	PERCENT
1	Iowa	19.0
2	New Hampshire	18.3
3	Vermont	18.2
4	Minnesota	17.3
5	Oregon	17.1
5	Rhode Island	17.1
7	Maine	15.4
8	Wisconsin	15.0
9	Delaware	14.9
10	Georgia	14.7
10	South Dakota	14.7
10	West Virginia	14.7
13	Idaho	14.5
14	New Jersey	14.4
15	Michigan	14.3
16	Kansas	14.0
16	Nevada	14.0
18	North Dakota	13.9
18	Washington	13.9
20	Oklahoma	13.8
21	Indiana	13.7
21	Montana	13.7
23	Ohio	13.6
23	Pennsylvania	13.6
25	Arizona	13.5
25	Tennessee	13.5
27	Florida	13.4
27	Massachusetts	13.4
27	Virginia	13.4
30	Nebraska	13.2
31	Connecticut	13.1
32	New York	12.9
33	North Carolina	12.5
34	Illinois	12.2
35	Arkansas	11.9
35	Missouri	11.9
37	Alabama	11.7
37	Maryland	11.7
39	Kentucky	11.6
40	Hawaii	11.4
41	Utah	11.3
42	South Carolina	11.2
43	New Mexico	10.7
44	California	10.3
45	Colorado	10.1
46	Alaska	9.9
47	Mississippi	9.8
48	Texas	9.3
49	Louisiana	8.8
50	Wyoming	8.6
	District of Columbia	3.4

Source: U.S. Department of Transportation, National Highway Traffic Safety Administration
"Traffic Safety Facts: Older Population" (http://www-nrd.nhtsa.dot.gov/cats/Index.aspx)
*Drivers 65 years old and older. People 65 or older make up 13 percent of the total U.S. population.

Percent of Highway Fatalities Who Were Young Drivers in 2011

National Percent = 6.1% of Fatalities*

<table>
<thead>
<tr><th colspan="3">ALPHA ORDER</th><th colspan="3">RANK ORDER</th></tr>
<tr><th>RANK</th><th>STATE</th><th>PERCENT</th><th>RANK</th><th>STATE</th><th>PERCENT</th></tr>
</thead>
<tbody>
<tr><td>13</td><td>Alabama</td><td>7.2</td><td>1</td><td>Idaho</td><td>13.2</td></tr>
<tr><td>47</td><td>Alaska</td><td>4.2</td><td>2</td><td>Vermont</td><td>10.9</td></tr>
<tr><td>39</td><td>Arizona</td><td>5.0</td><td>3</td><td>Maine</td><td>10.3</td></tr>
<tr><td>32</td><td>Arkansas</td><td>5.8</td><td>4</td><td>West Virginia</td><td>9.5</td></tr>
<tr><td>46</td><td>California</td><td>4.3</td><td>5</td><td>Missouri</td><td>8.8</td></tr>
<tr><td>23</td><td>Colorado</td><td>6.7</td><td>6</td><td>Iowa</td><td>8.3</td></tr>
<tr><td>34</td><td>Connecticut</td><td>5.5</td><td>6</td><td>Nebraska</td><td>8.3</td></tr>
<tr><td>38</td><td>Delaware</td><td>5.1</td><td>8</td><td>Kansas</td><td>8.0</td></tr>
<tr><td>42</td><td>Florida</td><td>4.9</td><td>9</td><td>Louisiana</td><td>7.6</td></tr>
<tr><td>34</td><td>Georgia</td><td>5.5</td><td>9</td><td>Pennsylvania</td><td>7.6</td></tr>
<tr><td>39</td><td>Hawaii</td><td>5.0</td><td>11</td><td>Wyoming</td><td>7.4</td></tr>
<tr><td>1</td><td>Idaho</td><td>13.2</td><td>12</td><td>Minnesota</td><td>7.3</td></tr>
<tr><td>30</td><td>Illinois</td><td>6.1</td><td>13</td><td>Alabama</td><td>7.2</td></tr>
<tr><td>13</td><td>Indiana</td><td>7.2</td><td>13</td><td>Indiana</td><td>7.2</td></tr>
<tr><td>6</td><td>Iowa</td><td>8.3</td><td>13</td><td>Montana</td><td>7.2</td></tr>
<tr><td>8</td><td>Kansas</td><td>8.0</td><td>13</td><td>Ohio</td><td>7.2</td></tr>
<tr><td>37</td><td>Kentucky</td><td>5.4</td><td>17</td><td>Michigan</td><td>7.1</td></tr>
<tr><td>9</td><td>Louisiana</td><td>7.6</td><td>18</td><td>Maryland</td><td>7.0</td></tr>
<tr><td>3</td><td>Maine</td><td>10.3</td><td>18</td><td>Tennessee</td><td>7.0</td></tr>
<tr><td>18</td><td>Maryland</td><td>7.0</td><td>20</td><td>Massachusetts</td><td>6.8</td></tr>
<tr><td>20</td><td>Massachusetts</td><td>6.8</td><td>20</td><td>North Dakota</td><td>6.8</td></tr>
<tr><td>17</td><td>Michigan</td><td>7.1</td><td>20</td><td>South Carolina</td><td>6.8</td></tr>
<tr><td>12</td><td>Minnesota</td><td>7.3</td><td>23</td><td>Colorado</td><td>6.7</td></tr>
<tr><td>23</td><td>Mississippi</td><td>6.7</td><td>23</td><td>Mississippi</td><td>6.7</td></tr>
<tr><td>5</td><td>Missouri</td><td>8.8</td><td>23</td><td>New Hampshire</td><td>6.7</td></tr>
<tr><td>13</td><td>Montana</td><td>7.2</td><td>26</td><td>North Carolina</td><td>6.5</td></tr>
<tr><td>6</td><td>Nebraska</td><td>8.3</td><td>27</td><td>South Dakota</td><td>6.3</td></tr>
<tr><td>50</td><td>Nevada</td><td>2.8</td><td>27</td><td>Texas</td><td>6.3</td></tr>
<tr><td>23</td><td>New Hampshire</td><td>6.7</td><td>29</td><td>Virginia</td><td>6.2</td></tr>
<tr><td>43</td><td>New Jersey</td><td>4.8</td><td>30</td><td>Illinois</td><td>6.1</td></tr>
<tr><td>45</td><td>New Mexico</td><td>4.5</td><td>31</td><td>Oklahoma</td><td>6.0</td></tr>
<tr><td>48</td><td>New York</td><td>3.4</td><td>32</td><td>Arkansas</td><td>5.8</td></tr>
<tr><td>26</td><td>North Carolina</td><td>6.5</td><td>33</td><td>Wisconsin</td><td>5.7</td></tr>
<tr><td>20</td><td>North Dakota</td><td>6.8</td><td>34</td><td>Connecticut</td><td>5.5</td></tr>
<tr><td>13</td><td>Ohio</td><td>7.2</td><td>34</td><td>Georgia</td><td>5.5</td></tr>
<tr><td>31</td><td>Oklahoma</td><td>6.0</td><td>34</td><td>Washington</td><td>5.5</td></tr>
<tr><td>43</td><td>Oregon</td><td>4.8</td><td>37</td><td>Kentucky</td><td>5.4</td></tr>
<tr><td>9</td><td>Pennsylvania</td><td>7.6</td><td>38</td><td>Delaware</td><td>5.1</td></tr>
<tr><td>49</td><td>Rhode Island</td><td>3.0</td><td>39</td><td>Arizona</td><td>5.0</td></tr>
<tr><td>20</td><td>South Carolina</td><td>6.8</td><td>39</td><td>Hawaii</td><td>5.0</td></tr>
<tr><td>27</td><td>South Dakota</td><td>6.3</td><td>39</td><td>Utah</td><td>5.0</td></tr>
<tr><td>18</td><td>Tennessee</td><td>7.0</td><td>42</td><td>Florida</td><td>4.9</td></tr>
<tr><td>27</td><td>Texas</td><td>6.3</td><td>43</td><td>New Jersey</td><td>4.8</td></tr>
<tr><td>39</td><td>Utah</td><td>5.0</td><td>43</td><td>Oregon</td><td>4.8</td></tr>
<tr><td>2</td><td>Vermont</td><td>10.9</td><td>45</td><td>New Mexico</td><td>4.5</td></tr>
<tr><td>29</td><td>Virginia</td><td>6.2</td><td>46</td><td>California</td><td>4.3</td></tr>
<tr><td>34</td><td>Washington</td><td>5.5</td><td>47</td><td>Alaska</td><td>4.2</td></tr>
<tr><td>4</td><td>West Virginia</td><td>9.5</td><td>48</td><td>New York</td><td>3.4</td></tr>
<tr><td>33</td><td>Wisconsin</td><td>5.7</td><td>49</td><td>Rhode Island</td><td>3.0</td></tr>
<tr><td>11</td><td>Wyoming</td><td>7.4</td><td>50</td><td>Nevada</td><td>2.8</td></tr>
<tr><td></td><td></td><td></td><td></td><td>District of Columbia</td><td>7.4</td></tr>
</tbody>
</table>

Source: CQ Press using data from U.S. Department of Transportation, National Highway Traffic Safety Administration
"Traffic Safety Facts: Young Drivers" (http://www-nrd.nhtsa.dot.gov/cats/Index.aspx)
*Drivers 15 to 20 years old. Based on 1,987 fatalities of young drivers. An additional 2,780 passengers and nonoccupants were killed in crashes involving young drivers. Young drivers accounted for 6.4 percent of all drivers.

Licensed Drivers in 2011

National Total = 211,874,649 Licensed Drivers

ALPHA ORDER

RANK	STATE	DRIVERS	% of USA
21	Alabama	3,798,552	1.8%
48	Alaska	521,280	0.2%
16	Arizona	4,592,398	2.2%
32	Arkansas	1,956,091	0.9%
1	California	23,856,600	11.3%
22	Colorado	3,669,816	1.7%
26	Connecticut	2,986,267	1.4%
45	Delaware	716,109	0.3%
3	Florida	13,882,423	6.6%
11	Georgia	6,505,690	3.1%
42	Hawaii	911,660	0.4%
39	Idaho	1,083,992	0.5%
6	Illinois	8,373,969	4.0%
9	Indiana	6,569,665	3.1%
30	Iowa	2,191,715	1.0%
31	Kansas	2,025,581	1.0%
27	Kentucky	2,959,881	1.4%
25	Louisiana	3,186,227	1.5%
41	Maine	1,014,826	0.5%
20	Maryland	3,856,604	1.8%
15	Massachusetts	4,683,323	2.2%
8	Michigan	7,059,509	3.3%
24	Minnesota	3,306,139	1.6%
33	Mississippi	1,926,603	0.9%
18	Missouri	4,277,037	2.0%
43	Montana	752,483	0.4%
37	Nebraska	1,356,377	0.6%
35	Nevada	1,700,829	0.8%
40	New Hampshire	1,056,889	0.5%
12	New Jersey	5,977,458	2.8%
36	New Mexico	1,418,641	0.7%
4	New York	11,210,783	5.3%
10	North Carolina	6,569,341	3.1%
49	North Dakota	490,146	0.2%
7	Ohio	7,982,149	3.8%
29	Oklahoma	2,370,643	1.1%
28	Oregon	2,773,956	1.3%
5	Pennsylvania	8,796,774	4.2%
44	Rhode Island	749,706	0.4%
23	South Carolina	3,408,318	1.6%
46	South Dakota	603,258	0.3%
17	Tennessee	4,543,759	2.1%
2	Texas	15,122,518	7.1%
34	Utah	1,747,487	0.8%
47	Vermont	521,666	0.2%
13	Virginia	5,467,045	2.6%
14	Washington	5,178,789	2.4%
38	West Virginia	1,198,837	0.6%
19	Wisconsin	4,147,470	2.0%
50	Wyoming	421,928	0.2%

RANK ORDER

RANK	STATE	DRIVERS	% of USA
1	California	23,856,600	11.3%
2	Texas	15,122,518	7.1%
3	Florida	13,882,423	6.6%
4	New York	11,210,783	5.3%
5	Pennsylvania	8,796,774	4.2%
6	Illinois	8,373,969	4.0%
7	Ohio	7,982,149	3.8%
8	Michigan	7,059,509	3.3%
9	Indiana	6,569,665	3.1%
10	North Carolina	6,569,341	3.1%
11	Georgia	6,505,690	3.1%
12	New Jersey	5,977,458	2.8%
13	Virginia	5,467,045	2.6%
14	Washington	5,178,789	2.4%
15	Massachusetts	4,683,323	2.2%
16	Arizona	4,592,398	2.2%
17	Tennessee	4,543,759	2.1%
18	Missouri	4,277,037	2.0%
19	Wisconsin	4,147,470	2.0%
20	Maryland	3,856,604	1.8%
21	Alabama	3,798,552	1.8%
22	Colorado	3,669,816	1.7%
23	South Carolina	3,408,318	1.6%
24	Minnesota	3,306,139	1.6%
25	Louisiana	3,186,227	1.5%
26	Connecticut	2,986,267	1.4%
27	Kentucky	2,959,881	1.4%
28	Oregon	2,773,956	1.3%
29	Oklahoma	2,370,643	1.1%
30	Iowa	2,191,715	1.0%
31	Kansas	2,025,581	1.0%
32	Arkansas	1,956,091	0.9%
33	Mississippi	1,926,603	0.9%
34	Utah	1,747,487	0.8%
35	Nevada	1,700,829	0.8%
36	New Mexico	1,418,641	0.7%
37	Nebraska	1,356,377	0.6%
38	West Virginia	1,198,837	0.6%
39	Idaho	1,083,992	0.5%
40	New Hampshire	1,056,889	0.5%
41	Maine	1,014,826	0.5%
42	Hawaii	911,660	0.4%
43	Montana	752,483	0.4%
44	Rhode Island	749,706	0.4%
45	Delaware	716,109	0.3%
46	South Dakota	603,258	0.3%
47	Vermont	521,666	0.2%
48	Alaska	521,280	0.2%
49	North Dakota	490,146	0.2%
50	Wyoming	421,928	0.2%
	District of Columbia	395,442	0.2%

Source: U.S. Department of Transportation, Federal Highway Administration
"Highway Statistics 2011" (Table DL-22, http://www.fhwa.dot.gov/policyinformation/statistics/2011/)

Licensed Drivers per 1,000 Driving Age Population in 2011

National Ratio = 860 Licensed Drivers

ALPHA ORDER

RANK	STATE	RATIO
4	Alabama	997
10	Alaska	939
17	Arizona	911
38	Arkansas	848
44	California	808
15	Colorado	913
2	Connecticut	1,038
5	Delaware	986
24	Florida	893
34	Georgia	856
42	Hawaii	826
20	Idaho	901
42	Illinois	826
1	Indiana	1,287
19	Iowa	906
18	Kansas	910
35	Kentucky	854
27	Louisiana	890
13	Maine	928
41	Maryland	831
28	Massachusetts	875
21	Michigan	898
48	Minnesota	785
40	Mississippi	833
21	Missouri	898
11	Montana	938
8	Nebraska	947
46	Nevada	797
6	New Hampshire	984
37	New Jersey	851
28	New Mexico	875
50	New York	714
33	North Carolina	862
26	North Dakota	892
31	Ohio	870
45	Oklahoma	802
24	Oregon	893
36	Pennsylvania	852
30	Rhode Island	872
14	South Carolina	916
11	South Dakota	938
23	Tennessee	894
49	Texas	777
32	Utah	863
3	Vermont	1,009
39	Virginia	847
7	Washington	954
47	West Virginia	791
15	Wisconsin	913
9	Wyoming	942

RANK ORDER

RANK	STATE	RATIO
1	Indiana	1,287
2	Connecticut	1,038
3	Vermont	1,009
4	Alabama	997
5	Delaware	986
6	New Hampshire	984
7	Washington	954
8	Nebraska	947
9	Wyoming	942
10	Alaska	939
11	Montana	938
11	South Dakota	938
13	Maine	928
14	South Carolina	916
15	Colorado	913
15	Wisconsin	913
17	Arizona	911
18	Kansas	910
19	Iowa	906
20	Idaho	901
21	Michigan	898
21	Missouri	898
23	Tennessee	894
24	Florida	893
24	Oregon	893
26	North Dakota	892
27	Louisiana	890
28	Massachusetts	875
28	New Mexico	875
30	Rhode Island	872
31	Ohio	870
32	Utah	863
33	North Carolina	862
34	Georgia	856
35	Kentucky	854
36	Pennsylvania	852
37	New Jersey	851
38	Arkansas	848
39	Virginia	847
40	Mississippi	833
41	Maryland	831
42	Hawaii	826
42	Illinois	826
44	California	808
45	Oklahoma	802
46	Nevada	797
47	West Virginia	791
48	Minnesota	785
49	Texas	777
50	New York	714
	District of Columbia	755

Source: U.S. Department of Transportation, Federal Highway Administration
"Highway Statistics 2011" (Table DL-1C, http://www.fhwa.dot.gov/policyinformation/statistics/2011/)

Transportation

Motor Vehicle Registrations in 2011

National Total = 253,215,681 Motor Vehicles*

RANK	STATE	VEHICLES	% of USA
21	Alabama	4,811,943	1.9%
49	Alaska	757,954	0.3%
19	Arizona	5,109,254	2.0%
31	Arkansas	2,448,310	1.0%
1	California	29,176,697	11.5%
22	Colorado	4,332,251	1.7%
30	Connecticut	2,828,794	1.1%
45	Delaware	929,415	0.4%
3	Florida	15,469,189	6.1%
10	Georgia	7,533,735	3.0%
43	Hawaii	1,148,041	0.5%
38	Idaho	1,625,204	0.6%
4	Illinois	10,445,208	4.1%
13	Indiana	6,132,772	2.4%
27	Iowa	3,496,576	1.4%
32	Kansas	2,445,966	1.0%
26	Kentucky	3,763,027	1.5%
23	Louisiana	4,052,596	1.6%
42	Maine	1,171,280	0.5%
24	Maryland	3,905,629	1.5%
15	Massachusetts	5,695,327	2.2%
8	Michigan	9,182,847	3.6%
20	Minnesota	4,909,634	1.9%
34	Mississippi	2,036,524	0.8%
18	Missouri	5,169,994	2.0%
41	Montana	1,219,158	0.5%
35	Nebraska	1,886,956	0.7%
33	Nevada	2,152,407	0.9%
40	New Hampshire	1,278,484	0.5%
9	New Jersey	7,939,956	3.1%
37	New Mexico	1,772,040	0.7%
5	New York	10,430,559	4.1%
12	North Carolina	6,249,592	2.5%
48	North Dakota	785,866	0.3%
7	Ohio	10,217,277	4.0%
28	Oklahoma	3,428,689	1.4%
29	Oregon	3,128,120	1.2%
6	Pennsylvania	10,302,980	4.1%
46	Rhode Island	918,823	0.4%
25	South Carolina	3,827,208	1.5%
44	South Dakota	995,423	0.4%
16	Tennessee	5,302,335	2.1%
2	Texas	19,617,055	7.7%
36	Utah	1,883,410	0.7%
50	Vermont	605,054	0.2%
11	Virginia	6,998,385	2.8%
14	Washington	5,880,793	2.3%
39	West Virginia	1,458,222	0.6%
17	Wisconsin	5,244,195	2.1%
47	Wyoming	798,296	0.3%

RANK	STATE	VEHICLES	% of USA
1	California	29,176,697	11.5%
2	Texas	19,617,055	7.7%
3	Florida	15,469,189	6.1%
4	Illinois	10,445,208	4.1%
5	New York	10,430,559	4.1%
6	Pennsylvania	10,302,980	4.1%
7	Ohio	10,217,277	4.0%
8	Michigan	9,182,847	3.6%
9	New Jersey	7,939,956	3.1%
10	Georgia	7,533,735	3.0%
11	Virginia	6,998,385	2.8%
12	North Carolina	6,249,592	2.5%
13	Indiana	6,132,772	2.4%
14	Washington	5,880,793	2.3%
15	Massachusetts	5,695,327	2.2%
16	Tennessee	5,302,335	2.1%
17	Wisconsin	5,244,195	2.1%
18	Missouri	5,169,994	2.0%
19	Arizona	5,109,254	2.0%
20	Minnesota	4,909,634	1.9%
21	Alabama	4,811,943	1.9%
22	Colorado	4,332,251	1.7%
23	Louisiana	4,052,596	1.6%
24	Maryland	3,905,629	1.5%
25	South Carolina	3,827,208	1.5%
26	Kentucky	3,763,027	1.5%
27	Iowa	3,496,576	1.4%
28	Oklahoma	3,428,689	1.4%
29	Oregon	3,128,120	1.2%
30	Connecticut	2,828,794	1.1%
31	Arkansas	2,448,310	1.0%
32	Kansas	2,445,966	1.0%
33	Nevada	2,152,407	0.9%
34	Mississippi	2,036,524	0.8%
35	Nebraska	1,886,956	0.7%
36	Utah	1,883,410	0.7%
37	New Mexico	1,772,040	0.7%
38	Idaho	1,625,204	0.6%
39	West Virginia	1,458,222	0.6%
40	New Hampshire	1,278,484	0.5%
41	Montana	1,219,158	0.5%
42	Maine	1,171,280	0.5%
43	Hawaii	1,148,041	0.5%
44	South Dakota	995,423	0.4%
45	Delaware	929,415	0.4%
46	Rhode Island	918,823	0.4%
47	Wyoming	798,296	0.3%
48	North Dakota	785,866	0.3%
49	Alaska	757,954	0.3%
50	Vermont	605,054	0.2%
	District of Columbia	316,231	0.1%

Source: U.S. Department of Transportation, Federal Highway Administration
   "Highway Statistics 2011" (Table MV-1, http://www.fhwa.dot.gov/policyinformation/statistics/2011/)
*Includes automobiles, trucks and buses. Does not include motorcycles.

Motor Vehicles per Driving Age Population in 2011

National Rate = 1.03 Motor Vehicles*

ALPHA ORDER

RANK	STATE	RATE
10	Alabama	1.26
6	Alaska	1.36
36	Arizona	1.01
30	Arkansas	1.06
42	California	0.99
25	Colorado	1.08
44	Connecticut	0.98
9	Delaware	1.28
40	Florida	1.00
42	Georgia	0.99
32	Hawaii	1.04
7	Idaho	1.35
34	Illinois	1.03
11	Indiana	1.20
4	Iowa	1.44
21	Kansas	1.10
22	Kentucky	1.09
18	Louisiana	1.13
28	Maine	1.07
48	Maryland	0.84
30	Massachusetts	1.06
13	Michigan	1.17
13	Minnesota	1.17
47	Mississippi	0.88
22	Missouri	1.09
3	Montana	1.52
8	Nebraska	1.32
36	Nevada	1.01
12	New Hampshire	1.19
18	New Jersey	1.13
22	New Mexico	1.09
50	New York	0.66
49	North Carolina	0.82
5	North Dakota	1.43
20	Ohio	1.11
16	Oklahoma	1.16
36	Oregon	1.01
40	Pennsylvania	1.00
28	Rhode Island	1.07
34	South Carolina	1.03
2	South Dakota	1.55
32	Tennessee	1.04
36	Texas	1.01
46	Utah	0.93
13	Vermont	1.17
25	Virginia	1.08
25	Washington	1.08
45	West Virginia	0.96
17	Wisconsin	1.15
1	Wyoming	1.78

RANK ORDER

RANK	STATE	RATE
1	Wyoming	1.78
2	South Dakota	1.55
3	Montana	1.52
4	Iowa	1.44
5	North Dakota	1.43
6	Alaska	1.36
7	Idaho	1.35
8	Nebraska	1.32
9	Delaware	1.28
10	Alabama	1.26
11	Indiana	1.20
12	New Hampshire	1.19
13	Michigan	1.17
13	Minnesota	1.17
13	Vermont	1.17
16	Oklahoma	1.16
17	Wisconsin	1.15
18	Louisiana	1.13
18	New Jersey	1.13
20	Ohio	1.11
21	Kansas	1.10
22	Kentucky	1.09
22	Missouri	1.09
22	New Mexico	1.09
25	Colorado	1.08
25	Virginia	1.08
25	Washington	1.08
28	Maine	1.07
28	Rhode Island	1.07
30	Arkansas	1.06
30	Massachusetts	1.06
32	Hawaii	1.04
32	Tennessee	1.04
34	Illinois	1.03
34	South Carolina	1.03
36	Arizona	1.01
36	Nevada	1.01
36	Oregon	1.01
36	Texas	1.01
40	Florida	1.00
40	Pennsylvania	1.00
42	California	0.99
42	Georgia	0.99
44	Connecticut	0.98
45	West Virginia	0.96
46	Utah	0.93
47	Mississippi	0.88
48	Maryland	0.84
49	North Carolina	0.82
50	New York	0.66
	District of Columbia	0.60

Source: CQ Press using data from U.S. Department of Transportation, Federal Highway Administration
   "Highway Statistics 2011" (Table MV-1, http://www.fhwa.dot.gov/policyinformation/statistics/2011/)
*Persons age 16 and older. Motor Vehicles include automobiles, trucks and buses. Motorcycles are not included.

Average Travel Time to Work in 2012

National Average = 25.7 Minutes*

ALPHA ORDER				RANK ORDER		
RANK	STATE	MINUTES		RANK	STATE	MINUTES
20	Alabama	24.5		1	Maryland	31.9
43	Alaska	19.6		2	New York	31.8
19	Arizona	24.6		3	New Jersey	30.7
39	Arkansas	21.4		4	Massachusetts	28.3
7	California	27.5		5	Illinois	28.0
20	Colorado	24.5		6	Virginia	27.9
18	Connecticut	24.8		7	California	27.5
14	Delaware	25.8		8	Georgia	26.9
10	Florida	26.2		9	New Hampshire	26.3
8	Georgia	26.9		10	Florida	26.2
12	Hawaii	26.0		11	Pennsylvania	26.1
42	Idaho	20.2		12	Hawaii	26.0
5	Illinois	28.0		12	Washington	26.0
28	Indiana	23.5		14	Delaware	25.8
45	Iowa	18.8		15	Texas	25.3
44	Kansas	19.0		16	Louisiana	25.2
34	Kentucky	22.9		16	West Virginia	25.2
16	Louisiana	25.2		18	Connecticut	24.8
28	Maine	23.5		19	Arizona	24.6
1	Maryland	31.9		20	Alabama	24.5
4	Massachusetts	28.3		20	Colorado	24.5
24	Michigan	24.0		22	Rhode Island	24.4
34	Minnesota	22.9		22	Tennessee	24.4
24	Mississippi	24.0		24	Michigan	24.0
32	Missouri	23.1		24	Mississippi	24.0
46	Montana	18.4		24	Nevada	24.0
47	Nebraska	18.2		27	North Carolina	23.7
24	Nevada	24.0		28	Indiana	23.5
9	New Hampshire	26.3		28	Maine	23.5
3	New Jersey	30.7		28	South Carolina	23.5
39	New Mexico	21.4		31	Ohio	23.2
2	New York	31.8		32	Missouri	23.1
27	North Carolina	23.7		32	Vermont	23.1
49	North Dakota	17.4		34	Kentucky	22.9
31	Ohio	23.2		34	Minnesota	22.9
41	Oklahoma	21.1		36	Oregon	22.7
36	Oregon	22.7		37	Utah	22.0
11	Pennsylvania	26.1		38	Wisconsin	21.8
22	Rhode Island	24.4		39	Arkansas	21.4
28	South Carolina	23.5		39	New Mexico	21.4
50	South Dakota	16.7		41	Oklahoma	21.1
22	Tennessee	24.4		42	Idaho	20.2
15	Texas	25.3		43	Alaska	19.6
37	Utah	22.0		44	Kansas	19.0
32	Vermont	23.1		45	Iowa	18.8
6	Virginia	27.9		46	Montana	18.4
12	Washington	26.0		47	Nebraska	18.2
16	West Virginia	25.2		48	Wyoming	18.1
38	Wisconsin	21.8		49	North Dakota	17.4
48	Wyoming	18.1		50	South Dakota	16.7
					District of Columbia	29.9

Source: U.S. Bureau of the Census
"2012 American Community Survey-Table R0801" (http://www.census.gov/acs/www/index.html)
*Workers 16 and older not working at home.

Percent of Commuters Who Drive to Work Alone in 2012

National Percent = 76.3%*

RANK STATE

ALPHA ORDER

RANK	STATE	PERCENT
1	Alabama	85.3
48	Alaska	66.2
34	Arizona	76.7
11	Arkansas	82.2
42	California	73.4
38	Colorado	74.4
28	Connecticut	78.6
15	Delaware	81.5
24	Florida	79.3
22	Georgia	79.6
49	Hawaii	65.2
31	Idaho	77.8
40	Illinois	73.6
9	Indiana	82.4
21	Iowa	79.9
11	Kansas	82.2
6	Kentucky	82.7
7	Louisiana	82.5
33	Maine	76.9
42	Maryland	73.4
46	Massachusetts	71.9
7	Michigan	82.5
29	Minnesota	78.0
3	Mississippi	83.5
16	Missouri	81.3
38	Montana	74.4
18	Nebraska	80.2
29	Nevada	78.0
13	New Hampshire	81.9
45	New Jersey	72.0
25	New Mexico	78.9
50	New York	53.7
17	North Carolina	80.6
23	North Dakota	79.5
4	Ohio	83.3
10	Oklahoma	82.3
47	Oregon	71.2
35	Pennsylvania	76.5
26	Rhode Island	78.8
5	South Carolina	82.9
27	South Dakota	78.7
2	Tennessee	83.6
20	Texas	80.1
36	Utah	75.7
41	Vermont	73.5
32	Virginia	77.3
44	Washington	72.2
14	West Virginia	81.7
18	Wisconsin	80.2
36	Wyoming	75.7

RANK ORDER

RANK	STATE	PERCENT
1	Alabama	85.3
2	Tennessee	83.6
3	Mississippi	83.5
4	Ohio	83.3
5	South Carolina	82.9
6	Kentucky	82.7
7	Louisiana	82.5
7	Michigan	82.5
9	Indiana	82.4
10	Oklahoma	82.3
11	Arkansas	82.2
11	Kansas	82.2
13	New Hampshire	81.9
14	West Virginia	81.7
15	Delaware	81.5
16	Missouri	81.3
17	North Carolina	80.6
18	Nebraska	80.2
18	Wisconsin	80.2
20	Texas	80.1
21	Iowa	79.9
22	Georgia	79.6
23	North Dakota	79.5
24	Florida	79.3
25	New Mexico	78.9
26	Rhode Island	78.8
27	South Dakota	78.7
28	Connecticut	78.6
29	Minnesota	78.0
29	Nevada	78.0
31	Idaho	77.8
32	Virginia	77.3
33	Maine	76.9
34	Arizona	76.7
35	Pennsylvania	76.5
36	Utah	75.7
36	Wyoming	75.7
38	Colorado	74.4
38	Montana	74.4
40	Illinois	73.6
41	Vermont	73.5
42	California	73.4
42	Maryland	73.4
44	Washington	72.2
45	New Jersey	72.0
46	Massachusetts	71.9
47	Oregon	71.2
48	Alaska	66.2
49	Hawaii	65.2
50	New York	53.7
	District of Columbia	34.1

Source: U.S. Bureau of the Census
   "2012 American Community Survey-Table R0802" (http://www.census.gov/acs/www/index.html)
*Workers 16 and older who traveled to work by car, truck or van.

Percent of Commuters Who Drive to Work in Carpools in 2012

National Percent = 9.7%*

ALPHA ORDER

RANK	STATE	PERCENT
32	Alabama	9.5
2	Alaska	13.3
8	Arizona	11.0
6	Arkansas	11.2
7	California	11.1
27	Colorado	9.7
45	Connecticut	8.2
46	Delaware	8.1
27	Florida	9.7
17	Georgia	10.4
1	Hawaii	15.3
21	Idaho	10.1
39	Illinois	8.9
33	Indiana	9.4
37	Iowa	9.0
27	Kansas	9.7
25	Kentucky	9.8
23	Louisiana	9.9
8	Maine	11.0
25	Maryland	9.8
48	Massachusetts	7.8
37	Michigan	9.0
39	Minnesota	8.9
12	Mississippi	10.7
27	Missouri	9.7
12	Montana	10.7
22	Nebraska	10.0
11	Nevada	10.9
49	New Hampshire	7.2
44	New Jersey	8.3
5	New Mexico	11.3
50	New York	6.9
16	North Carolina	10.5
27	North Dakota	9.7
46	Ohio	8.1
17	Oklahoma	10.4
17	Oregon	10.4
39	Pennsylvania	8.9
39	Rhode Island	8.9
35	South Carolina	9.3
36	South Dakota	9.1
33	Tennessee	9.4
8	Texas	11.0
3	Utah	12.2
20	Vermont	10.2
23	Virginia	9.9
12	Washington	10.7
15	West Virginia	10.6
39	Wisconsin	8.9
4	Wyoming	11.6

RANK ORDER

RANK	STATE	PERCENT
1	Hawaii	15.3
2	Alaska	13.3
3	Utah	12.2
4	Wyoming	11.6
5	New Mexico	11.3
6	Arkansas	11.2
7	California	11.1
8	Arizona	11.0
8	Maine	11.0
8	Texas	11.0
11	Nevada	10.9
12	Mississippi	10.7
12	Montana	10.7
12	Washington	10.7
15	West Virginia	10.6
16	North Carolina	10.5
17	Georgia	10.4
17	Oklahoma	10.4
17	Oregon	10.4
20	Vermont	10.2
21	Idaho	10.1
22	Nebraska	10.0
23	Louisiana	9.9
23	Virginia	9.9
25	Kentucky	9.8
25	Maryland	9.8
27	Colorado	9.7
27	Florida	9.7
27	Kansas	9.7
27	Missouri	9.7
27	North Dakota	9.7
32	Alabama	9.5
33	Indiana	9.4
33	Tennessee	9.4
35	South Carolina	9.3
36	South Dakota	9.1
37	Iowa	9.0
37	Michigan	9.0
39	Illinois	8.9
39	Minnesota	8.9
39	Pennsylvania	8.9
39	Rhode Island	8.9
39	Wisconsin	8.9
44	New Jersey	8.3
45	Connecticut	8.2
46	Delaware	8.1
46	Ohio	8.1
48	Massachusetts	7.8
49	New Hampshire	7.2
50	New York	6.9
	District of Columbia	5.6

Source: U.S. Bureau of the Census
   "2012 American Community Survey-Table R0803" (http://www.census.gov/acs/www/index.html)
*Workers 16 and older who traveled to work by car, truck or van.

Percent of Commuters Who Travel to Work by Public Transportation in 2012

National Percent = 5.0%*

<table>
<tr><td colspan="3">ALPHA ORDER</td><td colspan="3">RANK ORDER</td></tr>
<tr><td>RANK</td><td>STATE</td><td>PERCENT</td><td>RANK</td><td>STATE</td><td>PERCENT</td></tr>
<tr><td>47</td><td>Alabama</td><td>0.4</td><td>1</td><td>New York</td><td>27.3</td></tr>
<tr><td>23</td><td>Alaska</td><td>1.6</td><td>2</td><td>New Jersey</td><td>10.6</td></tr>
<tr><td>20</td><td>Arizona</td><td>2.0</td><td>3</td><td>Massachusetts</td><td>9.4</td></tr>
<tr><td>44</td><td>Arkansas</td><td>0.5</td><td>4</td><td>Maryland</td><td>8.9</td></tr>
<tr><td>9</td><td>California</td><td>5.2</td><td>5</td><td>Illinois</td><td>8.5</td></tr>
<tr><td>15</td><td>Colorado</td><td>3.2</td><td>6</td><td>Hawaii</td><td>6.7</td></tr>
<tr><td>10</td><td>Connecticut</td><td>4.8</td><td>7</td><td>Washington</td><td>5.8</td></tr>
<tr><td>17</td><td>Delaware</td><td>2.5</td><td>8</td><td>Pennsylvania</td><td>5.4</td></tr>
<tr><td>19</td><td>Florida</td><td>2.2</td><td>9</td><td>California</td><td>5.2</td></tr>
<tr><td>20</td><td>Georgia</td><td>2.0</td><td>10</td><td>Connecticut</td><td>4.8</td></tr>
<tr><td>6</td><td>Hawaii</td><td>6.7</td><td>11</td><td>Virginia</td><td>4.4</td></tr>
<tr><td>37</td><td>Idaho</td><td>0.8</td><td>12</td><td>Oregon</td><td>4.1</td></tr>
<tr><td>5</td><td>Illinois</td><td>8.5</td><td>13</td><td>Nevada</td><td>3.6</td></tr>
<tr><td>31</td><td>Indiana</td><td>1.1</td><td>14</td><td>Minnesota</td><td>3.3</td></tr>
<tr><td>31</td><td>Iowa</td><td>1.1</td><td>15</td><td>Colorado</td><td>3.2</td></tr>
<tr><td>41</td><td>Kansas</td><td>0.6</td><td>16</td><td>Rhode Island</td><td>3.1</td></tr>
<tr><td>35</td><td>Kentucky</td><td>1.0</td><td>17</td><td>Delaware</td><td>2.5</td></tr>
<tr><td>29</td><td>Louisiana</td><td>1.2</td><td>17</td><td>Utah</td><td>2.5</td></tr>
<tr><td>41</td><td>Maine</td><td>0.6</td><td>19</td><td>Florida</td><td>2.2</td></tr>
<tr><td>4</td><td>Maryland</td><td>8.9</td><td>20</td><td>Arizona</td><td>2.0</td></tr>
<tr><td>3</td><td>Massachusetts</td><td>9.4</td><td>20</td><td>Georgia</td><td>2.0</td></tr>
<tr><td>27</td><td>Michigan</td><td>1.3</td><td>22</td><td>Wisconsin</td><td>1.8</td></tr>
<tr><td>14</td><td>Minnesota</td><td>3.3</td><td>23</td><td>Alaska</td><td>1.6</td></tr>
<tr><td>47</td><td>Mississippi</td><td>0.4</td><td>23</td><td>Ohio</td><td>1.6</td></tr>
<tr><td>27</td><td>Missouri</td><td>1.3</td><td>23</td><td>Texas</td><td>1.6</td></tr>
<tr><td>35</td><td>Montana</td><td>1.0</td><td>26</td><td>Wyoming</td><td>1.5</td></tr>
<tr><td>41</td><td>Nebraska</td><td>0.6</td><td>27</td><td>Michigan</td><td>1.3</td></tr>
<tr><td>13</td><td>Nevada</td><td>3.6</td><td>27</td><td>Missouri</td><td>1.3</td></tr>
<tr><td>39</td><td>New Hampshire</td><td>0.7</td><td>29</td><td>Louisiana</td><td>1.2</td></tr>
<tr><td>2</td><td>New Jersey</td><td>10.6</td><td>29</td><td>Vermont</td><td>1.2</td></tr>
<tr><td>31</td><td>New Mexico</td><td>1.1</td><td>31</td><td>Indiana</td><td>1.1</td></tr>
<tr><td>1</td><td>New York</td><td>27.3</td><td>31</td><td>Iowa</td><td>1.1</td></tr>
<tr><td>31</td><td>North Carolina</td><td>1.1</td><td>31</td><td>New Mexico</td><td>1.1</td></tr>
<tr><td>47</td><td>North Dakota</td><td>0.4</td><td>31</td><td>North Carolina</td><td>1.1</td></tr>
<tr><td>23</td><td>Ohio</td><td>1.6</td><td>35</td><td>Kentucky</td><td>1.0</td></tr>
<tr><td>47</td><td>Oklahoma</td><td>0.4</td><td>35</td><td>Montana</td><td>1.0</td></tr>
<tr><td>12</td><td>Oregon</td><td>4.1</td><td>37</td><td>Idaho</td><td>0.8</td></tr>
<tr><td>8</td><td>Pennsylvania</td><td>5.4</td><td>37</td><td>Tennessee</td><td>0.8</td></tr>
<tr><td>16</td><td>Rhode Island</td><td>3.1</td><td>39</td><td>New Hampshire</td><td>0.7</td></tr>
<tr><td>44</td><td>South Carolina</td><td>0.5</td><td>39</td><td>West Virginia</td><td>0.7</td></tr>
<tr><td>44</td><td>South Dakota</td><td>0.5</td><td>41</td><td>Kansas</td><td>0.6</td></tr>
<tr><td>37</td><td>Tennessee</td><td>0.8</td><td>41</td><td>Maine</td><td>0.6</td></tr>
<tr><td>23</td><td>Texas</td><td>1.6</td><td>41</td><td>Nebraska</td><td>0.6</td></tr>
<tr><td>17</td><td>Utah</td><td>2.5</td><td>44</td><td>Arkansas</td><td>0.5</td></tr>
<tr><td>29</td><td>Vermont</td><td>1.2</td><td>44</td><td>South Carolina</td><td>0.5</td></tr>
<tr><td>11</td><td>Virginia</td><td>4.4</td><td>44</td><td>South Dakota</td><td>0.5</td></tr>
<tr><td>7</td><td>Washington</td><td>5.8</td><td>47</td><td>Alabama</td><td>0.4</td></tr>
<tr><td>39</td><td>West Virginia</td><td>0.7</td><td>47</td><td>Mississippi</td><td>0.4</td></tr>
<tr><td>22</td><td>Wisconsin</td><td>1.8</td><td>47</td><td>North Dakota</td><td>0.4</td></tr>
<tr><td>26</td><td>Wyoming</td><td>1.5</td><td>47</td><td>Oklahoma</td><td>0.4</td></tr>
<tr><td></td><td></td><td></td><td colspan="2">District of Columbia</td><td>38.6</td></tr>
</table>

Source: U.S. Bureau of the Census
   "2012 American Community Survey-Table R0804" (http://www.census.gov/acs/www/index.html)
*Workers 16 and older.

Annual Miles per Vehicle in 2011

National Annual Average = 11,635 Miles*

ALPHA ORDER

RANK	STATE	MILES
8	Alabama	13,490
50	Alaska	6,060
22	Arizona	11,660
9	Arkansas	13,459
30	California	10,995
32	Colorado	10,758
29	Connecticut	11,028
40	Delaware	9,714
16	Florida	12,402
4	Georgia	14,396
48	Hawaii	8,768
39	Idaho	9,806
38	Illinois	9,883
15	Indiana	12,472
47	Iowa	8,944
17	Kansas	12,274
13	Kentucky	12,772
27	Louisiana	11,477
19	Maine	12,164
5	Maryland	14,395
43	Massachusetts	9,621
35	Michigan	10,319
26	Minnesota	11,546
1	Mississippi	19,077
11	Missouri	13,305
44	Montana	9,564
36	Nebraska	10,118
28	Nevada	11,238
37	New Hampshire	9,949
45	New Jersey	9,206
3	New Mexico	14,409
18	New York	12,245
2	North Carolina	16,605
23	North Dakota	11,619
31	Ohio	10,961
7	Oklahoma	13,843
33	Oregon	10,669
42	Pennsylvania	9,629
49	Rhode Island	8,599
14	South Carolina	12,733
46	South Dakota	9,043
10	Tennessee	13,343
20	Texas	12,104
6	Utah	13,923
21	Vermont	11,802
25	Virginia	11,570
41	Washington	9,685
12	West Virginia	13,004
34	Wisconsin	10,374
24	Wyoming	11,581

RANK ORDER

RANK	STATE	MILES
1	Mississippi	19,077
2	North Carolina	16,605
3	New Mexico	14,409
4	Georgia	14,396
5	Maryland	14,395
6	Utah	13,923
7	Oklahoma	13,843
8	Alabama	13,490
9	Arkansas	13,459
10	Tennessee	13,343
11	Missouri	13,305
12	West Virginia	13,004
13	Kentucky	12,772
14	South Carolina	12,733
15	Indiana	12,472
16	Florida	12,402
17	Kansas	12,274
18	New York	12,245
19	Maine	12,164
20	Texas	12,104
21	Vermont	11,802
22	Arizona	11,660
23	North Dakota	11,619
24	Wyoming	11,581
25	Virginia	11,570
26	Minnesota	11,546
27	Louisiana	11,477
28	Nevada	11,238
29	Connecticut	11,028
30	California	10,995
31	Ohio	10,961
32	Colorado	10,758
33	Oregon	10,669
34	Wisconsin	10,374
35	Michigan	10,319
36	Nebraska	10,118
37	New Hampshire	9,949
38	Illinois	9,883
39	Idaho	9,806
40	Delaware	9,714
41	Washington	9,685
42	Pennsylvania	9,629
43	Massachusetts	9,621
44	Montana	9,564
45	New Jersey	9,206
46	South Dakota	9,043
47	Iowa	8,944
48	Hawaii	8,768
49	Rhode Island	8,599
50	Alaska	6,060

District of Columbia — 11,283

Source: CQ Press using data from U.S. Department of Transportation, Federal Highway Administration
"Highway Statistics 2011" (Tables MV-1 and VM-2, http://www.fhwa.dot.gov/policyinformation/statistics/2011/)
*Includes automobiles, trucks, buses and motorcycles.

Average Miles per Gallon in 2011

National Average = 17.5 Miles per Gallon*

ALPHA ORDER

ALPHA ORDER

RANK	STATE	MILES PER GALLON
3	Alabama	19.7
50	Alaska	11.4
18	Arizona	17.8
36	Arkansas	16.7
8	California	18.8
18	Colorado	17.8
14	Connecticut	18.3
5	Delaware	19.2
1	Florida	20.9
10	Georgia	18.6
3	Hawaii	19.7
21	Idaho	17.7
33	Illinois	17.0
14	Indiana	18.3
47	Iowa	14.1
29	Kansas	17.3
37	Kentucky	16.6
40	Louisiana	15.6
35	Maine	16.9
17	Maryland	18.1
26	Massachusetts	17.5
14	Michigan	18.3
8	Minnesota	18.8
13	Mississippi	18.4
31	Missouri	17.1
39	Montana	15.9
40	Nebraska	15.6
18	Nevada	17.8
38	New Hampshire	16.3
43	New Jersey	15.0
21	New Mexico	17.7
7	New York	19.0
2	North Carolina	19.8
49	North Dakota	12.8
21	Ohio	17.7
10	Oklahoma	18.6
31	Oregon	17.1
42	Pennsylvania	15.2
12	Rhode Island	18.5
43	South Carolina	15.0
47	South Dakota	14.1
25	Tennessee	17.6
45	Texas	14.7
33	Utah	17.0
5	Vermont	19.2
29	Virginia	17.3
21	Washington	17.7
27	West Virginia	17.4
27	Wisconsin	17.4
46	Wyoming	14.5

RANK ORDER

RANK	STATE	MILES PER GALLON
1	Florida	20.9
2	North Carolina	19.8
3	Alabama	19.7
3	Hawaii	19.7
5	Delaware	19.2
5	Vermont	19.2
7	New York	19.0
8	California	18.8
8	Minnesota	18.8
10	Georgia	18.6
10	Oklahoma	18.6
12	Rhode Island	18.5
13	Mississippi	18.4
14	Connecticut	18.3
14	Indiana	18.3
14	Michigan	18.3
17	Maryland	18.1
18	Arizona	17.8
18	Colorado	17.8
18	Nevada	17.8
21	Idaho	17.7
21	New Mexico	17.7
21	Ohio	17.7
21	Washington	17.7
25	Tennessee	17.6
26	Massachusetts	17.5
27	West Virginia	17.4
27	Wisconsin	17.4
29	Kansas	17.3
29	Virginia	17.3
31	Missouri	17.1
31	Oregon	17.1
33	Illinois	17.0
33	Utah	17.0
35	Maine	16.9
36	Arkansas	16.7
37	Kentucky	16.6
38	New Hampshire	16.3
39	Montana	15.9
40	Louisiana	15.6
40	Nebraska	15.6
42	Pennsylvania	15.2
43	New Jersey	15.0
43	South Carolina	15.0
45	Texas	14.7
46	Wyoming	14.5
47	Iowa	14.1
47	South Dakota	14.1
49	North Dakota	12.8
50	Alaska	11.4

District of Columbia   29.0

Source: CQ Press using data from U.S. Department of Transportation, Federal Highway Administration
    "Highway Statistics 2011" (Table VM-2, http://www.fhwa.dot.gov/policyinformation/statistics/2011/)
*Total vehicle-miles for 2011 divided by total highway motor-fuel use. Includes gasoline, gasohol, diesel, and other "special fuels."

Airports in 2011

National Total = 13,205 Airports*

ALPHA ORDER					RANK ORDER			

RANK	STATE	AIRPORTS	% of USA		RANK	STATE	AIRPORTS	% of USA
32	Alabama	182	1.4%		1	Texas	1,450	11.0%
2	Alaska	549	4.2%		2	Alaska	549	4.2%
30	Arizona	188	1.4%		3	California	522	4.0%
26	Arkansas	213	1.6%		4	Florida	497	3.8%
3	California	522	4.0%		5	Ohio	490	3.7%
22	Colorado	259	2.0%		6	Illinois	479	3.6%
47	Connecticut	51	0.4%		7	Wisconsin	439	3.3%
49	Delaware	30	0.2%		8	Pennsylvania	433	3.3%
4	Florida	497	3.8%		9	Indiana	404	3.1%
14	Georgia	335	2.5%		10	New York	395	3.0%
48	Hawaii	32	0.2%		11	Washington	366	2.8%
24	Idaho	224	1.7%		12	Michigan	362	2.7%
6	Illinois	479	3.6%		13	Missouri	359	2.7%
9	Indiana	404	3.1%		14	Georgia	335	2.5%
29	Iowa	196	1.5%		14	North Carolina	335	2.5%
16	Kansas	329	2.5%		16	Kansas	329	2.5%
34	Kentucky	153	1.2%		16	Minnesota	329	2.5%
25	Louisiana	223	1.7%		18	Oregon	322	2.4%
38	Maine	114	0.9%		19	Oklahoma	302	2.3%
35	Maryland	148	1.1%		20	Virginia	290	2.2%
43	Massachusetts	77	0.6%		21	North Dakota	265	2.0%
12	Michigan	362	2.7%		22	Colorado	259	2.0%
16	Minnesota	329	2.5%		23	Montana	232	1.8%
31	Mississippi	186	1.4%		24	Idaho	224	1.7%
13	Missouri	359	2.7%		25	Louisiana	223	1.7%
23	Montana	232	1.8%		26	Arkansas	213	1.6%
28	Nebraska	207	1.6%		27	Tennessee	209	1.6%
40	Nevada	98	0.7%		28	Nebraska	207	1.6%
46	New Hampshire	52	0.4%		29	Iowa	196	1.5%
39	New Jersey	101	0.8%		30	Arizona	188	1.4%
37	New Mexico	143	1.1%		31	Mississippi	186	1.4%
10	New York	395	3.0%		32	Alabama	182	1.4%
14	North Carolina	335	2.5%		33	South Carolina	158	1.2%
21	North Dakota	265	2.0%		34	Kentucky	153	1.2%
5	Ohio	490	3.7%		35	Maryland	148	1.1%
19	Oklahoma	302	2.3%		36	South Dakota	144	1.1%
18	Oregon	322	2.4%		37	New Mexico	143	1.1%
8	Pennsylvania	433	3.3%		38	Maine	114	0.9%
50	Rhode Island	9	0.1%		39	New Jersey	101	0.8%
33	South Carolina	158	1.2%		40	Nevada	98	0.7%
36	South Dakota	144	1.1%		41	Wyoming	93	0.7%
27	Tennessee	209	1.6%		42	Utah	90	0.7%
1	Texas	1,450	11.0%		43	Massachusetts	77	0.6%
42	Utah	90	0.7%		44	West Virginia	76	0.6%
45	Vermont	62	0.5%		45	Vermont	62	0.5%
20	Virginia	290	2.2%		46	New Hampshire	52	0.4%
11	Washington	366	2.8%		47	Connecticut	51	0.4%
44	West Virginia	76	0.6%		48	Hawaii	32	0.2%
7	Wisconsin	439	3.3%		49	Delaware	30	0.2%
41	Wyoming	93	0.7%		50	Rhode Island	9	0.1%
						District of Columbia	3	0.0%

Source: U.S. Department of Transportation, Bureau of Transportation Statistics
 "State Transportation Statistics 2012" (http://www.bts.gov/publications/state_transportation_statistics/)
*This table comprises all U.S. public use and private use airports. Public use facilities are open to the public with no prior authorization or permission required. Private use facilities are not open to the general public and include medical, law enforcement, corporate, and other such facilities.

Inland Waterway Mileage in 2011

National Total = 29,620 Miles*

RANK	STATE	MILES	% of USA	RANK	STATE	MILES	% of USA
6	Alabama	1,270	4.3%	1	Alaska	5,500	18.6%
1	Alaska	5,500	18.6%	2	Louisiana	2,820	9.5%
40	Arizona	0	0.0%	3	Arkansas	1,860	6.3%
3	Arkansas	1,860	6.3%	4	Kentucky	1,590	5.4%
26	California	290	1.0%	5	Florida	1,540	5.2%
40	Colorado	0	0.0%	6	Alabama	1,270	4.3%
31	Connecticut	120	0.4%	7	North Carolina	1,150	3.9%
34	Delaware	100	0.3%	8	Illinois	1,100	3.7%
5	Florida	1,540	5.2%	9	Washington	1,060	3.6%
14	Georgia	720	2.4%	10	Missouri	1,030	3.5%
40	Hawaii	0	0.0%	11	Tennessee	950	3.2%
33	Idaho	110	0.4%	12	Mississippi	870	2.9%
8	Illinois	1,100	3.7%	13	Texas	830	2.8%
24	Indiana	350	1.2%	14	Georgia	720	2.4%
19	Iowa	490	1.7%	15	Oregon	680	2.3%
31	Kansas	120	0.4%	15	West Virginia	680	2.3%
4	Kentucky	1,590	5.4%	17	Virginia	670	2.3%
2	Louisiana	2,820	9.5%	18	Maryland	530	1.8%
37	Maine	70	0.2%	19	Iowa	490	1.7%
18	Maryland	530	1.8%	20	South Carolina	480	1.6%
35	Massachusetts	90	0.3%	21	Ohio	440	1.5%
40	Michigan	0	0.0%	22	New York	390	1.3%
27	Minnesota	260	0.9%	23	New Jersey	360	1.2%
12	Mississippi	870	2.9%	24	Indiana	350	1.2%
10	Missouri	1,030	3.5%	25	Nebraska	320	1.1%
40	Montana	0	0.0%	26	California	290	1.0%
25	Nebraska	320	1.1%	27	Minnesota	260	0.9%
40	Nevada	0	0.0%	27	Pennsylvania	260	0.9%
39	New Hampshire	10	0.0%	29	Wisconsin	230	0.8%
23	New Jersey	360	1.2%	30	Oklahoma	150	0.5%
40	New Mexico	0	0.0%	31	Connecticut	120	0.4%
22	New York	390	1.3%	31	Kansas	120	0.4%
7	North Carolina	1,150	3.9%	33	Idaho	110	0.4%
40	North Dakota	0	0.0%	34	Delaware	100	0.3%
21	Ohio	440	1.5%	35	Massachusetts	90	0.3%
30	Oklahoma	150	0.5%	36	South Dakota	80	0.3%
15	Oregon	680	2.3%	37	Maine	70	0.2%
27	Pennsylvania	260	0.9%	38	Rhode Island	40	0.1%
38	Rhode Island	40	0.1%	39	New Hampshire	10	0.0%
20	South Carolina	480	1.6%	40	Arizona	0	0.0%
36	South Dakota	80	0.3%	40	Colorado	0	0.0%
11	Tennessee	950	3.2%	40	Hawaii	0	0.0%
13	Texas	830	2.8%	40	Michigan	0	0.0%
40	Utah	0	0.0%	40	Montana	0	0.0%
40	Vermont	0	0.0%	40	Nevada	0	0.0%
17	Virginia	670	2.3%	40	New Mexico	0	0.0%
9	Washington	1,060	3.6%	40	North Dakota	0	0.0%
15	West Virginia	680	2.3%	40	Utah	0	0.0%
29	Wisconsin	230	0.8%	40	Vermont	0	0.0%
40	Wyoming	0	0.0%	40	Wyoming	0	0.0%
					District of Columbia	10	0.0%

Source: U.S. Department of Transportation, Bureau of Transportation Statistics
"State Transportation Statistics 2012" (http://www.bts.gov/publications/state_transportation_statistics/)
*Waterway mileage was determined by including the length of channels 1) with a controlling draft of nine feet or greater, 2) with commercial cargo traffic reported for 1998 and 1999, but 3) were not offshore. Channels within major bays are included (e.g., Chesapeake Bay, San Francisco Bay, Puget Sound, Long Island Sound, and major sounds and straits in southeastern Alaska). Channels in the Great Lakes are not included. Approximately 4,300 miles are counted twice as several are state boundaries.

Percent of Recreational Boating Accidents Involving Alcohol in 2012

National Percent = 8.2% of Accidents*

ALPHA ORDER

ALPHA ORDER

RANK	STATE	PERCENT
6	Alabama	15.5
25	Alaska	8.7
34	Arizona	7.1
19	Arkansas	11.8
43	California	3.8
2	Colorado	21.7
18	Connecticut	12.2
7	Delaware	15.4
41	Florida	4.5
33	Georgia	7.2
48	Hawaii	0.0
9	Idaho	15.2
15	Illinois	12.9
23	Indiana	9.3
3	Iowa	21.2
21	Kansas	11.1
16	Kentucky	12.8
11	Louisiana	13.8
36	Maine	6.3
29	Maryland	7.6
10	Massachusetts	14.7
28	Michigan	7.8
22	Minnesota	10.7
35	Mississippi	7.0
26	Missouri	8.5
48	Montana	0.0
24	Nebraska	8.9
38	Nevada	5.3
31	New Hampshire	7.5
40	New Jersey	5.2
5	New Mexico	16.7
27	New York	8.1
29	North Carolina	7.6
4	North Dakota	20.0
32	Ohio	7.4
20	Oklahoma	11.3
46	Oregon	1.4
8	Pennsylvania	15.3
45	Rhode Island	3.2
13	South Carolina	13.0
37	South Dakota	5.6
42	Tennessee	4.1
13	Texas	13.0
47	Utah	1.0
48	Vermont	0.0
44	Virginia	3.4
12	Washington	13.3
38	West Virginia	5.3
17	Wisconsin	12.7
1	Wyoming	22.2

RANK ORDER

RANK	STATE	PERCENT
1	Wyoming	22.2
2	Colorado	21.7
3	Iowa	21.2
4	North Dakota	20.0
5	New Mexico	16.7
6	Alabama	15.5
7	Delaware	15.4
8	Pennsylvania	15.3
9	Idaho	15.2
10	Massachusetts	14.7
11	Louisiana	13.8
12	Washington	13.3
13	South Carolina	13.0
13	Texas	13.0
15	Illinois	12.9
16	Kentucky	12.8
17	Wisconsin	12.7
18	Connecticut	12.2
19	Arkansas	11.8
20	Oklahoma	11.3
21	Kansas	11.1
22	Minnesota	10.7
23	Indiana	9.3
24	Nebraska	8.9
25	Alaska	8.7
26	Missouri	8.5
27	New York	8.1
28	Michigan	7.8
29	Maryland	7.6
29	North Carolina	7.6
31	New Hampshire	7.5
32	Ohio	7.4
33	Georgia	7.2
34	Arizona	7.1
35	Mississippi	7.0
36	Maine	6.3
37	South Dakota	5.6
38	Nevada	5.3
38	West Virginia	5.3
40	New Jersey	5.2
41	Florida	4.5
42	Tennessee	4.1
43	California	3.8
44	Virginia	3.4
45	Rhode Island	3.2
46	Oregon	1.4
47	Utah	1.0
48	Hawaii	0.0
48	Montana	0.0
48	Vermont	0.0
	District of Columbia	0.0

Source: CQ Press using data from United States Coast Guard
"Boating Statistics 2012" (http://www.uscgboating.org/statistics/accident_statistics.aspx)
*Alcohol involvement in a boating accident includes any accident in which alcoholic beverages are consumed in the boat and the investigating official has determined that the operator was impaired or affected while operating the boat.

Railroad Accidents and Incidents in 2012

National Total = 10,926*

<u>ALPHA ORDER</u>

<u>RANK ORDER</u>

RANK	STATE	ACCIDENTS	% of USA
14	Alabama	200	1.8%
39	Alaska	74	0.7%
37	Arizona	94	0.9%
20	Arkansas	169	1.5%
3	California	817	7.5%
26	Colorado	141	1.3%
33	Connecticut	115	1.1%
40	Delaware	60	0.5%
9	Florida	259	2.4%
11	Georgia	254	2.3%
50	Hawaii	0	0.0%
43	Idaho	49	0.4%
2	Illinois	867	7.9%
7	Indiana	289	2.6%
21	Iowa	166	1.5%
17	Kansas	196	1.8%
25	Kentucky	150	1.4%
10	Louisiana	256	2.3%
48	Maine	16	0.1%
27	Maryland	134	1.2%
16	Massachusetts	198	1.8%
27	Michigan	134	1.2%
13	Minnesota	210	1.9%
34	Mississippi	111	1.0%
14	Missouri	200	1.8%
35	Montana	106	1.0%
12	Nebraska	224	2.1%
44	Nevada	37	0.3%
49	New Hampshire	3	0.0%
5	New Jersey	672	6.2%
38	New Mexico	78	0.7%
1	New York	1,178	10.8%
23	North Carolina	164	1.5%
29	North Dakota	131	1.2%
8	Ohio	273	2.5%
24	Oklahoma	162	1.5%
31	Oregon	121	1.1%
6	Pennsylvania	623	5.7%
46	Rhode Island	21	0.2%
31	South Carolina	121	1.1%
45	South Dakota	32	0.3%
21	Tennessee	166	1.5%
4	Texas	799	7.3%
42	Utah	54	0.5%
47	Vermont	20	0.2%
19	Virginia	184	1.7%
18	Washington	194	1.8%
35	West Virginia	106	1.0%
29	Wisconsin	131	1.2%
41	Wyoming	58	0.5%

RANK	STATE	ACCIDENTS	% of USA
1	New York	1,178	10.8%
2	Illinois	867	7.9%
3	California	817	7.5%
4	Texas	799	7.3%
5	New Jersey	672	6.2%
6	Pennsylvania	623	5.7%
7	Indiana	289	2.6%
8	Ohio	273	2.5%
9	Florida	259	2.4%
10	Louisiana	256	2.3%
11	Georgia	254	2.3%
12	Nebraska	224	2.1%
13	Minnesota	210	1.9%
14	Alabama	200	1.8%
14	Missouri	200	1.8%
16	Massachusetts	198	1.8%
17	Kansas	196	1.8%
18	Washington	194	1.8%
19	Virginia	184	1.7%
20	Arkansas	169	1.5%
21	Iowa	166	1.5%
21	Tennessee	166	1.5%
23	North Carolina	164	1.5%
24	Oklahoma	162	1.5%
25	Kentucky	150	1.4%
26	Colorado	141	1.3%
27	Maryland	134	1.2%
27	Michigan	134	1.2%
29	North Dakota	131	1.2%
29	Wisconsin	131	1.2%
31	Oregon	121	1.1%
31	South Carolina	121	1.1%
33	Connecticut	115	1.1%
34	Mississippi	111	1.0%
35	Montana	106	1.0%
35	West Virginia	106	1.0%
37	Arizona	94	0.9%
38	New Mexico	78	0.7%
39	Alaska	74	0.7%
40	Delaware	60	0.5%
41	Wyoming	58	0.5%
42	Utah	54	0.5%
43	Idaho	49	0.4%
44	Nevada	37	0.3%
45	South Dakota	32	0.3%
46	Rhode Island	21	0.2%
47	Vermont	20	0.2%
48	Maine	16	0.1%
49	New Hampshire	3	0.0%
50	Hawaii	0	0.0%
	District of Columbia	109	1.0%

Source: U.S. Department of Transportation, Federal Railroad Administration, Office of Safety Analysis
"Railroad Accidents and Incidents" (http://safetydata.fra.dot.gov/OfficeofSafety/publicsite/Query/stateoverview.aspx)
*Accidents or incidents include all events reportable to the U.S. Department of Transportation. These include train accidents causing damage above an established threshold; highway-rail grade crossing incidents involving impact between railroad equipment and highway users at crossings; and all other reportable incidents that cause a fatality or injury to any person or an occupational illness to a railroad employee. There were 694 fatalities involving railroads.

Railroad Mileage Operated in 2011

National Total = 138,565 Miles of Railroad*

ALPHA ORDER

ALPHA ORDER

RANK	STATE	MILES	% of USA
17	Alabama	3,255	2.3%
45	Alaska	506	0.4%
36	Arizona	1,645	1.2%
25	Arkansas	2,698	1.9%
4	California	5,327	3.8%
26	Colorado	2,667	1.9%
46	Connecticut	364	0.3%
48	Delaware	250	0.2%
24	Florida	2,902	2.1%
7	Georgia	4,666	3.4%
50	Hawaii	0	0.0%
37	Idaho	1,622	1.2%
2	Illinois	7,027	5.1%
9	Indiana	4,273	3.1%
11	Iowa	3,855	2.8%
6	Kansas	4,855	3.5%
28	Kentucky	2,562	1.8%
23	Louisiana	2,912	2.1%
40	Maine	1,116	0.8%
43	Maryland	762	0.5%
42	Massachusetts	892	0.6%
12	Michigan	3,632	2.6%
8	Minnesota	4,449	3.2%
29	Mississippi	2,432	1.8%
10	Missouri	3,958	2.9%
21	Montana	3,172	2.3%
18	Nebraska	3,247	2.3%
39	Nevada	1,192	0.9%
47	New Hampshire	344	0.2%
41	New Jersey	983	0.7%
34	New Mexico	1,835	1.3%
13	New York	3,532	2.5%
19	North Carolina	3,245	2.3%
15	North Dakota	3,328	2.4%
3	Ohio	5,338	3.9%
16	Oklahoma	3,273	2.4%
30	Oregon	2,396	1.7%
5	Pennsylvania	5,127	3.7%
49	Rhode Island	19	0.0%
31	South Carolina	2,292	1.7%
35	South Dakota	1,754	1.3%
27	Tennessee	2,651	1.9%
1	Texas	10,425	7.5%
38	Utah	1,343	1.0%
44	Vermont	590	0.4%
20	Virginia	3,214	2.3%
22	Washington	3,157	2.3%
32	West Virginia	2,213	1.6%
14	Wisconsin	3,385	2.4%
33	Wyoming	1,860	1.3%

RANK ORDER

RANK	STATE	MILES	% of USA
1	Texas	10,425	7.5%
2	Illinois	7,027	5.1%
3	Ohio	5,338	3.9%
4	California	5,327	3.8%
5	Pennsylvania	5,127	3.7%
6	Kansas	4,855	3.5%
7	Georgia	4,666	3.4%
8	Minnesota	4,449	3.2%
9	Indiana	4,273	3.1%
10	Missouri	3,958	2.9%
11	Iowa	3,855	2.8%
12	Michigan	3,632	2.6%
13	New York	3,532	2.5%
14	Wisconsin	3,385	2.4%
15	North Dakota	3,328	2.4%
16	Oklahoma	3,273	2.4%
17	Alabama	3,255	2.3%
18	Nebraska	3,247	2.3%
19	North Carolina	3,245	2.3%
20	Virginia	3,214	2.3%
21	Montana	3,172	2.3%
22	Washington	3,157	2.3%
23	Louisiana	2,912	2.1%
24	Florida	2,902	2.1%
25	Arkansas	2,698	1.9%
26	Colorado	2,667	1.9%
27	Tennessee	2,651	1.9%
28	Kentucky	2,562	1.8%
29	Mississippi	2,432	1.8%
30	Oregon	2,396	1.7%
31	South Carolina	2,292	1.7%
32	West Virginia	2,213	1.6%
33	Wyoming	1,860	1.3%
34	New Mexico	1,835	1.3%
35	South Dakota	1,754	1.3%
36	Arizona	1,645	1.2%
37	Idaho	1,622	1.2%
38	Utah	1,343	1.0%
39	Nevada	1,192	0.9%
40	Maine	1,116	0.8%
41	New Jersey	983	0.7%
42	Massachusetts	892	0.6%
43	Maryland	762	0.5%
44	Vermont	590	0.4%
45	Alaska	506	0.4%
46	Connecticut	364	0.3%
47	New Hampshire	344	0.2%
48	Delaware	250	0.2%
49	Rhode Island	19	0.0%
50	Hawaii	0	0.0%
	District of Columbia	23	0.0%

Source: Association of American Railroads
"Railroads and States" (http://www.aar.org/KeyIssues/Railroads-States.aspx)
*Includes Class I and non-Class I miles. Excludes trackage rights. Synonymous with route-miles, so that a mile of single track is counted the same as a mile of double track.

Sources

ACT, Inc.
500 ACT Drive, P.O. Box 168
Iowa City, IA 52243-0168
319-337-1000
www.act.org

Administration for Children and Families
U.S. Department of Health and Human Services
370 L'Enfant Promenade, SW
Washington, DC 20447
202-401-9215
www.acf.hhs.gov

American Cancer Society, Inc.
250 Williams Street, NW
Atlanta, GA 30303
800-227-2345
www.cancer.org

American Dental Association
211 E. Chicago Avenue
Chicago, IL 60611-2678
800-621-8335
www.ada.org

American Hospital Association
155 N. Wacker Drive
Chicago, IL 60611-5885
312-422-3000
www.aha.org

American Medical Association
330 N. Wabash Avenue
Chicago, IL 60654
800-621-8335
www.ama-assn.org

Association of American Railroads
425 Third Street, SW. Suite 1000
Washington, DC 20024
202-639-2100
www.aar.org

Bureau of the Census
4600 Silver Hill Road
Washington, DC 20233-0001
800-923-8282
www.census.gov

Bureau of Economic Analysis
U.S. Department of Commerce
1441 L Street, NW
Washington, DC 20230
202-606-9900
www.bea.gov

Bureau of Justice Statistics
U.S. Department of Justice
810 Seventh Street, NW
Washington, DC 20531
202-307-0765
www.bjs.gov

Bureau of Labor Statistics
U.S. Department of Labor
2 Massachusetts Avenue, NE
Washington, DC 20212-0001
202-691-5200
www.bls.gov

Bureau of Transportation Statistics
US Department of Transportation
1200 New Jersey Avenue, SE
Washington, DC 20590
800-853-1351
www.bts.gov

Centers for Disease Control and Prevention
1600 Clifton Road
Atlanta, GA 30333
800-232-4636
www.cdc.gov

Centers for Medicare and Medicaid Services
7500 Security Boulevard
Baltimore, MD 21244-1850
877-267-2323
www.cms.hhs.gov

College Board
45 Columbus Avenue
New York, NY 10023-6992
212-713-8000
www.collegeboard.com

Economic Research Service
U.S. Department of Agriculture
1400 Independence Avenue, SW
Mail Stop 1800
Washington, DC 20250-0002
202-694-5050
www.ers.usda.gov

Energy Information Administration
US Department of Energy
1000 Independence Avenue, SW
Washington, DC 20585
202-586-8800
www.eia.doe.gov

Environmental Protection Agency
Ariel Rios Building
1200 Pennsylvania Avenue, NW
Washington, DC 20460
202-272-0167
www.epa.gov

Federal Bureau of Investigation
J Edgar Hoover Building
935 Pennsylvania Avenue, NW
Washington, DC 20535-0001
202-324-3000
www.fbi.gov

Federal Highway Administration
US Department of Transportation
1200 New Jersey Avenue, SE
Washington, DC 20590
202-366-4000
www.fhwa.dot.gov

Federation of Tax Administrators
444 North Capitol Street, NW. Suite 348
Washington, DC 20001
202-624-5890
www.taxadmin.org

Food and Nutrition Service
U.S. Department of Agriculture
3101 Park Center Drive
Alexandria, VA 22302
703-305-2062
www.fns.usda.gov/fns

General Services Administration
One Constitution Square
1800 F Street NW
Washington, DC 20540
800-488-3111
www.gsa.gov

Health Resources and Services Administration
Division of Practitioner Data Banks
5600 Fishers Lane
Rockville, MD 20857
800-275-4772
www.hrsa.gov

Institute of Museum and Library Services
1800 M Street, NW, 9th Floor
Washington, DC 20036-5802
202-653-4657
www.imls.gov

Internal Revenue Service
U.S. Department of the Treasury
10th Street and Pennsylvania Avenue, NW
Washington, DC 20004
800-829-1040
www.irs.gov

Medical Expenditure Panel Survey
Agency for Healthcare Research and Quality
540 Gaither Road
Rockville, MD 20850
301-427-1364
www.meps.ahrq.gov

National Agricultural Statistics Service
1400 Independence Avenue, SW
Washington, DC 20250
800-727-9540
www.nass.usda.gov

National Assembly of State Arts Agencies
1029 Vermont Avenue, NW. 2nd Floor
Washington, DC 20005
202-347-6352
www.nasaa-arts.org

National Association of Realtors
430 N. Michigan Avenue
Chicago, IL 60611
800-874-6500
www.realtor.org

National Association of State Park Directors
8829 Woodyhill Road
Raleigh, NC 27613
919-676-8365
www.naspd1.org

National Center for Education Statistics
U.S. Department of Education
1990 K Street, NW
Washington, DC 20006
202-502-7300
www.nces.ed.gov

National Center for Health Statistics
U.S. Department of Health and Human Services
3311 Toledo Road
Hyattsville, MD 20782
800-232-4636
www.cdc.gov/nchs

National Conference of State Legislatures
7700 E. First Place
Denver, CO 80230
303-364-7700
www.ncsl.org

National Education Association
1201 16th Street, NW
Washington, DC 20036-3290
202-833-4000
www.nea.org

National Highway Traffic Safety Administration
1200 New Jersey Avenue, SE
Washington, DC 20590
888-327-4236
www.nhtsa.dot.gov

National Institute on Alcohol Abuse and Alcoholism
5635 Fishers Lane, MSC 9304
Bethesda, MD 20892-9304
301-443-3860
www.niaaa.nih.gov

National Oceanic & Atmospheric Administration
U.S. Department of Commerce
1401 Constitution Avenue, NW. Room 5128
Washington, DC 20230
202-482-6090
www.noaa.gov

Office of Management and Budget
USAspending.gov
725 17th Street, NW
Washington, DC 20503
202-395-3080
www.USAspending.gov

Social Security Administration
Windsor Park Building
6401 Security Boulevard
Baltimore, MD 21235
800-772-1213 (information)
www.ssa.gov

Storm Prediction Center
National Weather Service
120 David Boren Boulevard
Norman, OK 73072
405-579-0771
www.spc.noaa.gov

Tax Foundation
529 14th Street, NW. Suite 420
Washington, DC 20045-1000
202-464-6200
www.taxfoundation.org

U.S. Department of Defense
Directorate for Public Inquiry and Analysis
Room 2E565 The Pentagon
1400 Defense Pentagon
Washington, DC 20301-1400
703-571-3343
www.defense.gov

U.S. Department of Veterans Affairs
810 Vermont Avenue, NW
Washington, DC 20420
202-273-5400
www.va.gov

U.S. Geological Survey
12201 Sunrise Valley Drive
Reston, VA 20192
703-648-5953
www.usgs.gov

Index